How to Achieve Inclusive Growth

How to Achieve Inclusive Growth

edited by

VALERIE CERRA, BARRY EICHENGREEN,
ASMAA EL-GANAINY, AND
MARTIN SCHINDLER

OXFORD
UNIVERSITY PRESS

OXFORD
UNIVERSITY PRESS

Great Clarendon Street, Oxford, OX2 6DP,
United Kingdom

Oxford University Press is a department of the University of Oxford.
It furthers the University's objective of excellence in research, scholarship,
and education by publishing worldwide. Oxford is a registered trade mark of
Oxford University Press in the UK and in certain other countries

Published in the United States of America by Oxford University Press
198 Madison Avenue, New York, NY 10016, United States of America

British Library Cataloguing in Publication Data
Data available

Library of Congress Control Number: 2021942707

ISBN 978-0-19-284693-8

DOI: 10.1093/oso/9780192846938.001.0001

Printed and bound in Great Britain by
Clays Ltd, Elcograf S.p.A.

Links to third party websites are provided by Oxford in good faith and
for information only. Oxford disclaims any responsibility for the materials
contained in any third party website referenced in this work.

Foreword

Each of us has a perspective on inequality—people sense it from a young age. Growing up under communism, we knew we had less than people in the West. But our nations' political leaders said that we were more equal within our societies. For some people, for a while, that gave some measure of satisfaction.

The privileges those leaders took for themselves eventually became apparent and were an important factor in their undoing. But the larger story in the fall of communism was that market economies created more wealth and were better for everyone—because they provided more opportunities for entrepreneurship, innovation, and growth.

But markets are not perfect. In the first decades after the Second World War, in many places, the trends towards equality were positive. But then they shifted. Even as pro-market reforms in China and other places lifted a billion people out of poverty, the distribution of income and wealth started to become polarized.

As a result, many societies have become more and more unequal over the last five decades. The pandemic is both accelerating dangerous trends in inequality and pushing people back into poverty. And the climate crisis stands to make these trends worse—if we don't act.

How to Achieve Inclusive Growth expertly breaks down the causes of inequality, identifies those most harmed by it, and provides detailed solutions for policymakers. As the fault lines of gender, age, region, race, and ethnicity become wider around the world, this book could not be more important.

History shows that increasing inequality reaches a tipping point and spirals into various forms of social crises. But such developments, and the misery they cause, can be avoided—if countries act to create opportunities for all. At the IMF, we work with a broad range of stakeholders in our member countries on policies that will achieve these goals.

Together with academics and experts from other international organizations, IMF economists have outlined in this book the structural reforms, policies, and business practices from around the world that create inclusive growth. These include fair and efficient product and labor markets, international trade and financial systems, and tax designs; social programs that meet immediate needs and give a hand up; gender budgeting tools that increase women's ability to work and support their families; policies that close digital divides; and climate mitigation and adaptation strategies that create jobs and make communities more resilient.

As the book makes clear, there is no single solution to fostering inclusion. Each country approaches the inclusive growth challenge differently, based on its unique circumstances. And every country's experience provides lessons for others. Learning and working together, I am confident we can build a strong foundation on which everyone can prosper.

Kristalina Georgieva, Managing Director
International Monetary Fund

Foreword

By Jeffrey D. Sachs, University Professor
at Columbia University

The challenge of inclusive growth took on increased urgency during the Covid-19 pandemic, which exacerbated almost every division in the world economy. Stock markets soared while the poor lost their livelihoods. The digital haves went online—for work, schooling, healthcare, and personal connections—while the digital have-nots suffered isolation and the loss of access to crucial services. Jobs for skilled workers rebounded quickly from the 2020 Covid-19 contraction, while jobs for lower-skilled workers remained depressed, or disappeared altogether, even with the post-2020 rebound. Rich countries and individuals were able to borrow at exceptionally low interest rates, while poor countries and individuals had to tighten their belts, if they had belts at all.

In short, economic inequality that was already achingly high before the pandemic became a global emergency in the course of the pandemic. For that reason alone, this important collection of chapters is remarkably timely for policy makers, scholars, and the interested public. Yet the importance of these chapters goes beyond their undoubted timeliness. The chapters are extremely well written, cogent, and comprehensive in the important and varied topics that they cover, and presented in a manner that is accessible to specialists and non-specialists alike.

The world has been grappling for decades—alas, with limited success—with the challenge of economic and social inclusion. In 1948, the member states of the newly-formed United Nations adopted a moral charter of social inclusion: the Universal Declaration of Human Rights (UDHR). The Universal Declaration boldly and powerfully recognized that all people are "born free in dignity and rights" (Article I), including:

> the right to a standard of living adequate for the health and well-being of himself and of his family, including food, clothing, housing and medical care and necessary social services, and the right to security in the event of unemployment, sickness, disability, widowhood, old age or other lack of livelihood in circumstances beyond his control.   (Article 25)

Yet these economic rights have not yet been realized. The world economy today is obviously rich enough to ensure such basic economic rights. The Gross World Product is roughly $100 trillion in 2021, or roughly $12,500 per person. Yet despite this great income, billions of people worldwide still lack access to one or more of their basic economic needs.

In 2015, the 193 UN member states unanimously adopted the 17 Sustainable Development Goals, which can be considered our generation's attempt to make good on the economic rights recognized long ago by the Universal Declaration. Of course, the 17 SDGs also added a crucial new dimension of need that was not recognized in 1948: the need to combine economic wellbeing and social inclusion with environmental sustainability.

The chapters in this important book deal with many of the key policy challenges in achieving the SDGs. There are important chapters on combining the climate-change imperatives with economic inclusion; on promoting gender equality in the economy (as called for by SDG 5); and on constructing a fiscal framework of taxes, outlays, and overall budget management, to underpin inclusive growth. These are vital topics for achieving the 17 SDGs.

In order to ensure a world of inclusive growth and sustainable development, the national budget will play an essential role, or more accurately perhaps, the leading role. As one excellent chapter in this volume states succinctly: "Public expenditure is the most powerful instrument at hands of governments to achieve their objectives of economic development and social welfare" (Chapter 13). The importance of bold and inclusive fiscal outlays is echoed throughout the volume. Governments need to invest boldly and amply to ensure universal access to healthcare, quality education, and vital infrastructure such as digital connectivity. Government investments will play an indispensable role in the transition to zero-carbon energy systems. And government outlays are vital for R&D and for regional development policies to help laggard regions within the country.

Of course, inclusive development requires not only more public outlays in most countries, but also properly directed outlays, meaning public investments and services that aim for gender equality (SDG 6) and that aim to end long-standing patterns of social, ethnic, and racial discrimination. As noted in several chapters, such far-sighted public policies are best promoted through policy transparency, rule of law, citizens' participation, public ethics, a well-trained public administration, and the recognition of the norms of fairness. In my view, the Universal Declaration and the SDGs provide a powerful framework to promote such good governance.

The IMF is to be highly commended for its powerful focus on inclusive growth, and for mobilizing the best evidence and best practices. The chapters in this volume complement another set of important IMF studies in recent years, which have examined the fiscal framework to achieve the SDGs.[1] That complementary work has emphasized the need for low-income developing countries (LIDCs) to increase

---

[1] For the most recent overview, see "A Post-Pandemic Assessment of the Sustainable Development Goals," Dora Benedekt, et al., IMF Discussion Note, SDN/2021/003, April 2021.

markedly the overall level of public outlays and to finance those increased outlays with higher taxes as a share of GDP and with greatly increased development financing from the world community, for example to help finance the energy transition. In fact, the IMF has shown that there is a global SDG financing gap of several hundred billion dollars a year facing the LIDCs. If those countries are to achieve inclusive development, they will need much greater financial flows from the rich countries, for example through the expanded financing by the multilateral development banks.

In the end, this may be the main practical conclusion of the IMF's pathbreaking work: social inclusion requires fiscal solidarity both within and between countries. We need a global fiscal system that raises and directs sufficient revenues to enable all governments, both rich and poor alike, to provide the public outlays needed for inclusive and sustainable development for all.

Jeffrey D. Sachs
University Professor at Columbia University

Preface

Achieving inclusive growth—that is, strong and sustainable economic growth whose benefits are widely shared—is the paramount policy challenge of our day. Inequality has been rising in many countries, and large income disparities persist across regions, genders, ethnicities, and generations. The Covid-19 pandemic has been raging, and inequality, poverty, and exclusion are all but certain to intensify in its wake. Climate change, economic and financial crises, and job-displacing technological change all pose challenges to equitably sharing the fruits of economic growth.

The four of us are educators committed to disseminating practical knowledge, distilled from technical research, to policy makers, practitioners, students, and the public. Collectively, we have been providing practical training to government officials through the IMF's capacity development activities in Washington and around the world, as well as through academic teaching and research. Our interest in editing this volume grew out of our experiences, including delivering courses on inclusive growth, out of our devotion to these educational goals, and out of our desire to contribute to practical approaches to achieving inclusive growth.

How to Achieve Inclusive Growth is designed to fill three gaps in the literature:

- First, while there are an increasing number of works describing rising inequality, especially in the United States, less attention has been paid to the design of practical policies to reverse the trend. This book provides policy-makers and practitioners with information on the state of inclusive growth, both in the United States and globally. But it goes beyond this description of trends. It focuses on the "how to." The book provides guidance for designing policies that foster inclusiveness, taking a comprehensive view of the issues, and considering the full range of policies on each topic. Thus, each chapter succinctly summarizes key issues, debates and questions around a specific issue area, and describes the policy tools available for addressing it. It synthesizes the relevant academic literature, as well as drawing on examples and case studies from country experiences.
- Second, the book takes a global perspective, while also carefully distinguishing the policy options that are most appropriate for advanced versus developing countries.
- Third, inclusive growth has often been considered in piecemeal fashion, with most earlier work focusing on a single theme or issue, and only rarely

bringing together the various strands. In reality, of course, the different dimensions of inclusive growth are interlinked. Climate change affects growth and poverty while also prompting migration, all of which affect the extent to which growth is shared. Technological advancement and globalization generate regional disparities within countries as well as across countries at different stages of economic development. Trade can empower women and reduce informality, although it doesn't always have these effects. Regional disparities can impact intergenerational equity. Likewise, the policies needed to achieve inclusive, sustained, and green growth are multidimensional. They range from the regulation of labor markets, technology, and market concentration to the design and operation of government institutions, services, and redistributive instruments. Understanding, much less achieving, inclusive growth thus requires a comprehensive approach to both problems and policies.

How to Achieve Inclusive Growth draws on the knowledge of a diverse group of experts, including academic economists, IMF economists with experience in building capacity and providing advice on economic and financial policies, and experts from other institutions, such as the World Bank, the World Trade Organization, the European Bank for Reconstruction and Development, and the International Labor Organization, which collectively possess expertise on the entire range of labor, social, and economic issues related to inclusive growth.

We hope the book provides you with at least some useful answers to the question of *How to Achieve Inclusive Growth.*

Valerie, Barry, Asmaa, and Martin
Washington, DC, and Berkeley, California

Contents

List of Figures and Diagrams

Figures

Diagrams

List of Tables

List of Contributors

Editors

Valerie Cerra is an Assistant Director and the Division Chief of the Inclusive Growth and Structural Policies Division at the International Monetary Fund. She has been involved in policy advice, lending, and capacity development in the IMF's Western Hemisphere, African, European, and Asia and Pacific departments, and the IMF Institute. She obtained undergraduate degrees in finance and engineering from the University of Pennsylvania, a PhD in Economics from the University of Washington, and is a CFA. She has published widely in leading economics journals on topics related to international macroeconomics, financial crises, economic scarring, and inclusive growth.

Barry Eichengreen is George C. Pardee and Helen N. Pardee Professor of Economics and Political Science, University of California, Berkeley; Research Associate of the National Bureau of Economic Research; and Research Fellow of the Centre for Economic Policy Research.

Asmaa El-Ganainy is a Deputy Division Chief at the IMF. Previously, she worked in the European and Fiscal Affairs Departments, contributing to IMF's surveillance, lending, research, and capacity development work across a range of countries. Her research interests are in the fields of public finance, sovereign debt, inequality, labor economics, and capital flows.

Martin Schindler is a Deputy Division Chief at the IMF. He has contributed to the IMF's surveillance, lending, and analytical work, covering low-income, emerging and advanced economies on four continents, as well as to capacity development, including as deputy director of the Joint Vienna Institute. He is the lead editor of the IMF book *Jobs and Growth: Supporting the European Recovery* and has published in leading economic journals, including the *Journal of Monetary Economics*, the *Journal of International Economics,* and the *European Economic Review,* among others. He holds a PhD in Economics from the University of Pennsylvania.

Authors

Khaled Abdel-Kader is a staff member of the IMF. He is currently serving as the Deputy Director of the IMF-Middle East Center for Economics and Finance. Most recently, he was a Senior Economist in the IMF's Institute for Capacity Development. Previously, he worked in the IMF's European Department, Communications Department, and, briefly, the Asia and Pacific Department and the Research Department. Before joining the IMF, he was an Economist at the Arab Monetary Fund in the United Arab Emirates, an advisor to the Minister of Planning in Egypt, and an Assistant Professor at the University of Minnesota-Duluth.

Philippe Aghion is a Professor at the College de France and at the London School of Economics, and a fellow of the Econometric Society and of the American Academy of Arts and Sciences. His research focuses on the economics of growth. With Peter Howitt, he pioneered the so-called Schumpeterian Growth paradigm. His books include *The Power of Creative Destruction* (2021, with C. Antonin and S. Bunel), *The Economics of Growth* (2009, with P. Howitt), and *Competition and Growth* (2006, with R. Griffith). He is a recipient of numerous honors and awards. Philippe holds a PhD in Economics from Harvard University.

Marc Bacchetta is Chief of Section in the Economic Research and Statistics Division of the World Trade Organization. He holds a PhD from the University of Geneva where he taught economics for six years before joining the WTO in 1996. Between 2002 and 2004, he worked on trade-related issues at the World Bank. He has contributed to a number of publications on trade and labor including the chapter on "Trade, Value Chains and Labor Markets in Advanced Economies" in the *Global Value Chain Development Report 2019* and has recently co-edited two volumes on *Making Globalization More Inclusive* (World Trade Organization (WTO), 2019) and *Trade Adjustment in Asia* (WTO and the Asian Development Bank Institute, 2020).

Bénédicte Baduel is a Senior Economist at the World Bank in the South Africa Country Office. She is on leave from the International Monetary Fund where she was a Senior Economist in the Middle East and Central Asia Department. She has worked on several emerging and developing economies in Africa, Latin America, and the Middle East. Her analytical work focuses on the connection between macroeconomic and structural policies, especially inclusive growth and governance. Bénédicte holds a PhD in Economics from Sorbonne Nouvelle University.

Sriram Balasubramanian is a Senior Research Officer at the Independent Evaluation Office of the International Monetary Fund. He is an Economist who is an alumnus of both Columbia University and the University of Southern California. Besides prior experience in the private sector and the WBG, his keen interests include macroeconomic policy research, inequality, new growth models, and capital flows management, among others. He is also an author of two published books and is working on a forthcoming third book on economic history.

Adolfo Barajas is a Senior Economist in the IMF's Monetary and Capital Markets Department, leading analytical work for the Fund's Global Financial Stability Report since 2017. He has worked in other departments of the Fund: Institute for Capacity Development, Research Department, and regional area departments. His early career was as a researcher in Colombia's central bank and at Fedesarrollo in Bogotá. He conducts research on financial stability, development and inclusion, macroeconomic effects of remittances, exchange rate policy, and dollarization. He received his Doctorate in Economics from Stanford University, and his undergraduate degree in Economics from the Universidad de los Andes.

Thorsten Beck is currently Professor of Banking and Finance at The Business School (formerly Cass) in London. He is also Director of the Florence School of Banking and Finance and will take up a Chair of Financial Stability at the European University Institute in September 2021. He worked at Tilburg University from 2008 to 2014 and previously worked in the research department of the World Bank from 1997 to 2008. He holds a PhD from the University of Virginia and an MA from the University of Tübingen in Germany.

Mohamed Belhaj is Senior Economist at the IMF Center for Economics and Finance in Kuwait. He was previously Professor of Economics at Ecole Centrale Marseille. He graduated from Tunisia Polytechnic School and holds a PhD in Economics from Toulouse School of Economics. His research interests are finance and network theory. His work has been published in several prestigious academic journals, including *Mathematical Finance, American Economic Journal, Theoretical Economics*, and *Journal of Development Economics*.

Amar Bhattacharya is a Senior Fellow in the Center for Sustainable Development at Brookings. His focus areas are the global economy, development finance, global governance, and the links between climate and development. From 2007–2014 he was Director of the Group of 24, an intergovernmental group of developing country Finance Ministers and Central Bank Governors. Before that, he had a long-standing career in the World Bank, most recently as Senior Advisor and Head of the International Policy and Partnership Group. He completed his undergraduate studies at the University of Delhi and Brandeis University and his graduate education at Princeton University.

Jana Bricco is currently working on structural, fiscal, and external sector issues as the desk Economist for Sweden and Denmark in the European Department of the IMF. Before that she worked on macrofinancial risk assessments, stress testing, and financial stability frameworks in the Financial Sector Assessments and Policy (FSAP) Division. Before joining the IMF eight years ago, she worked at the European Central Bank, Deutsche Bundesbank, and BaFin. Jana holds a Master's and PhD in Economics from the Goethe University in Frankfurt where her research focused on bank supervision, unconventional monetary policies, and contagion in global asset markets.

Sami Ben Naceur earned a PhD in Finance from the University of Paris Sorbonne. He has published extensively on finance and macroeconomics. He is currently the Acting Division Chief of the African Division at the IMF's Institute for Capacity Development (ICD), leading a team of Economists in delivering technical assistance and training in Sub-Saharan Africa. He was Deputy Director of the IMF-Middle East Center for Economics and Finance, and the Chief of the Internal Economic Training Unit in ICD. He was also Senior Economist in the IMF's Middle East and Central Asia Department where he contributed to the Regional Economic Outlook.

Lahcen Bounader is an Economist at the International Monetary Fund. He received his engineering degree from National Institute of Statistics and Applied Economics and obtained his PhD in Economics from Mohamed V University (Rabat). His research focuses on macroeconomics, behavioral and monetary economics.

Reda Cherif is a Senior Economist at the International Monetary Fund. He joined the IMF in 2008. His research covers development economics, natural resources, industrial policy, and growth and innovation. His recent book co-edited with Fuad Hasanov and Min Zhu, *Breaking the Oil Spell* (IMF, 2016), explores economic diversification in oil exporters. Reda holds a PhD in Economics from the University of Chicago.

Balazs Csonto is an Economist in the IMF's African Department. Previously. He worked in the Strategy, Policy, and Review, and Western Hemisphere departments. He has covered a number of countries, such as Dominica, the Kyrgyz Republic, Mexico, Somalia, Uganda, and Yemen, as well as having worked on several policy issues related to monetary policy, IMF surveillance, and the design of post-GFC IMF programs. His research includes work on monetary policy, capital flows and the international monetary system. Prior to joining the IMF, he was an Economist at the European Investment Bank and ING Bank.

Hamid R. Davoodi is a Senior Economist at the IMF. He has published on a variety of topics in economics. He has been with the IMF since 1997, worked on many countries in Europe, Middle East, Central Asia, and Africa and delivered training to government officials worldwide. Prior to joining the IMF, he worked at the World Bank, taught at Georgetown University and was a research associate at Federal Reserve Bank of San Francisco. He holds degrees in Economics from London School of Economics (BSC), University of California (MS), and University of Wisconsin at Madison (PhD).

Ruud De Mooij is an Advisor in the International Monetary Fund's Fiscal Affairs Department, where he previously headed the Tax Policy Division. Before joining the International Monetary Fund, De Mooij was a Professor of Public Economics at Erasmus University in Rotterdam. He has published extensively on tax issues, including in the *American Economic Review* and the *Journal of Public Economics*. De Mooij is also a research fellow at the University of Oxford, the University of Bergen, ZEW in Mannheim, and member of the CESifo network in Munich.

Barbara Dutzler has worked as a Senior Economist at the Joint Vienna Institute since February 2019. For the last ten years, she was a Team Leader at GIZ, the Gesellschaft für Internationale Zusammenarbeit, for Good Financial Governance, in Montenegro, Malawi, South Africa, and Frankfurt. Previously, she worked in the Economic Policy Department, Austrian Ministry of Finance and as lecturer at the Europe Institute, Economic University of Vienna. Barbara holds a PhD in Commerce from the Economic University of Vienna and a Master of Public Administration from Kennedy School of Government, Harvard. Her research interests are fiscal policy, PFM, and development economics.

Drilona Emrullahu is a Research Analyst with the Institute for Capacity Development at the International Monetary Fund. Prior to joining the Fund, she consulted for the International Finance Corporation (IFC) where she supported the Europe and Central Asia team on country strategies and economic research and analysis. Before joining the IFC, she worked alongside faculty at the Duke Center for International Development (DCID) in researching and developing curriculum for international development executive education programs. Drilona holds a Master's in International Development Policy from Duke University and a BA Degree in International Business from Richmond University in London.

Ekkehard Ernst is Chief of the Macroeconomic Policies and Jobs Unit at the International Labour Organization. Currently, his research focuses on the implications of artificial intelligence, robots, and blockchain applications for the future of work and a transition to a sustainable society. Previously, he worked at the Organization for Economic Cooperation and Development and the European Central Bank. He has studied in Germany and France where he received his PhD. He is guest editor of *Frontiers in AI* and serves on the advisory board of various institutions, including the European Parliament's Panel for the Future of Science and Technology.

Raquel Fernández is Silver Professor in the Department of Economics at NYU and a member of the NBER, CEPR, amd BREAD. She has served as the Director of the Public Policy Program of the CEPR, Vice President of the American Economic Association, and currently is President of the Latin American and Caribbean Economic Association and co-chair of the NBER's Inequality and the Macroeconomy group. She is the recipient of numerous NSF grants and is a fellow of the Econometric Society. Fernández has wide research interests that span sovereign debt, culture and economics, development, gender, macroeconomics and inequality, and political economy.

Deon Filmer is Director of the Research Group at the World Bank. He has previously served as Co-Director of the World Development Report 2018: Learning to Realize Education's Promise, and lead Economist in the Human Development department of the Africa Region. He works on issues of human capital and skills, service delivery, and the impact of policies and programs to improve human development outcomes—with research spanning the areas of education, health, social protection, and poverty and inequality. He holds a PhD and MA in Economics from Brown University and a BA from Tufts University.

Holger Floerkemeier is currently Deputy Director of the Joint Vienna Institute. Since joining the IMF in 2002, he has worked on IMF-supported programs, surveillance, and capacity development projects in close to 20 member countries. Previously, he was an assistant Professor for empirical economic research in Freiburg, Germany, and worked in several roles in the market research field. Holger has a Doctorate in Economics from the University of Freiburg and is a Chartered Financial Analyst (CFA).

Roberta Gatti is currently the Chief Economist of the Middle East and North Africa region of the World Bank. In her previous capacity of chief Economist for Human Development, Roberta co-led the conceptualization and release of the Human Capital Index and oversaw the Service Delivery Indicators data initiative. Roberta is the author of numerous flagship reports and her research, spanning topics in health, labor markets, and growth, is published in top field journals. Roberta holds a BA from Università Bocconi and a PhD in Economics from Harvard University. She has taught at Georgetown and Johns Hopkins universities.

Fuad Hasanov is a Senior Economist at the International Monetary Fund and an Adjunct Professor of Economics at Georgetown University. Before joining the IMF in 2007, Fuad was an Assistant Professor of Economics at Oakland University in Rochester, Michigan. His recent research focuses on natural resources, growth and innovation, and industrial policy. He is the co-editor, with Reda Cherif and Min Zhu, of *Breaking the Oil Spell* (IMF, 2016) that examines economic diversification in oil-exporting countries. Fuad received a PhD in Economics from the University of Texas at Austin.

Asel Isakova is an Economist at the African Department of the International Monetary Fund. Prior to joining the IMF, Asel worked at the Joint Vienna Institute in Vienna and at the Office of the chief Economist of the European Bank for Reconstruction and Development in London. She holds a PhD degree in Economics from Charles University in Prague. She has authored and co-authored a number of research papers on various issues, including gender equality, management of natural resources, and international trade. Asel is a Kyrgyz national.

Maksym Ivanyna is a Senior Economist at the IMF, which he joined in 2018. Prior to the IMF he spent seven years at the Joint Vienna Institute, and held several consultancy positions at the World Bank, European Commission, and German Institute for Development. He holds Doctor's degrees in Economics from Regensburg University (Germany) and Michigan State University (United States). His research portfolio includes publications and working papers in the fields of fiscal policy, economic development, environment and sustainability, climate change, governance, fiscal federalism, and structural reform.

Jon Jellema is former Deputy Director for the Commitment to Equity (CEQ) Project (at GDN). He has been applying and teaching CEQ Assessment methodologies and providing advice to governments and multilateral organizations in Africa, East Asia, South Asia, and Eastern Europe since 2013. At the CEQ Institute, he developed applied methodologies for more precise estimation of the burdens created by indirect tax instruments and for a "Child Centric" CEQ Assessment. Jon has also worked for the World Bank as a poverty economist and social development specialist in Indonesia. Jon received his PhD in Economics from the University of California, Berkeley.

Simon Johnson is the Ronald A. Kurtz Professor of Entrepreneurship and head of the Global Economics and Management group at the MIT Sloan School of Management. He has held a wide variety of academic and policy-related positions, including chief Economist of the International Monetary Fund and member of the Congressional Budget Office's Panel of Economic Advisors. He has authored several books and over 300 high-impact articles in leading news media. His research on economic development, corporate finance, and political economy is widely cited.

Zsoka Koczan is Associate Director and Senior Economist in the Office of the Chief Economist at the European Bank for Reconstruction and Development. She holds a PhD in Economics from the University of Cambridge. Prior to joining the EBRD, Zsoka worked as an Economist at the International Monetary Fund in the European Department (on Belarus and the Western Balkans) and in the Research Department (on the World Economic Outlook). Her current research focuses on within-country income disparities, migration, and inequality.

Anton Korinek is a Professor at the Department of Economics and at the Darden School of Business of the University of Virginia, as well as a Research Associate at the NBER, a Research Fellow at the CEPR, a Research Affiliate at the Oxford Future of Humanity Institute's Centre for the Governance of AI, and a Senior Advisor at the Partnership on

AI. He earned his PhD from Columbia University in 2007. His research focuses on the implications of rapid progress in Artificial Intelligence for our economy, our society, and for the future of work as well as on policies to counteract increases in inequality.

Ruy Lama is a Senior Economist at the IMF institute of Capacity Development. Previously, he has worked as a Senior Economist in the Research Department and in the European Department, where he participated on missions to the United Kingdom and Spain. He has published papers on monetary and exchange rate policies in small open economies and on business cycles in emerging economies. He received his PhD in Economics from the University of California in Los Angeles.

Norman Loayza is Director of the Global Indicators Group in the Development Economics Vicepresidency of the World Bank. From 2015 to 2020, he led the Asia hub of the Development Research Group. He was director of the World Development Report 2014: Risk and Opportunity—Managing Risk for Development. He joined the World Bank in 1994 and served most of his career in the Development Research Group. His research covers various areas of economic and social development, including economic growth, macroeconomics, and the business environment. He holds a PhD in Economics from Harvard University.

Francesco Luna is a Senior Economist in the Institute for Capacity Development at the International Monetary Fund. He has worked on "transition" low-income economies, emerging markets, and EU accession countries. Before joining the IMF, Luna held a tenured position at the University of Venice Ca' Foscari, was a visiting Professor at Oberlin College, and a Consultant for the World Bank. His research interests and publications focus on computable economics, agent-based economics, and the history of economic thought.

Nora Lustig is Samuel Z. Stone Professor of Latin American Economics and the founding Director of the Commitment to Equity Institute (CEQ) at Tulane University. She is a Nonresident Senior Fellow at the Brookings Institution, the Center for Global Development and the Inter-American Dialogue. Her research is on economic development, inequality and social policies with emphasis on Latin America. She is President Emeritus of the Latin American and Caribbean Economic Association (LACEA). She serves on the editorial board of the *Journal of Economic Inequality* and is a member of the Society for the Study of Economic Inequality's Executive Council. She received her doctorate in Economics from the University of California, Berkeley.

Rossana Merola is an Economist at the Research Department of the International Labour Organization (ILO) since 2014. Before joining the ILO, she worked at the ESRI and the Trinity College in Dublin, the Organization of Economic Co-operation and Development (OECD) and the European Central Bank. She holds a PhD in Economics from the Université Catholique de Louvain and the University of Rome Tor Vergata. Her research interests cover labour markets, inequality, fiscal policy, DSGE models and artificial intelligence.

Peter Montiel is the Farleigh S. Dickinson Jr. '41 Professor of Economics at Williams College. He has also worked at the International Monetary Fund and at the World Bank, and has served as a consultant for the African Development Bank, the Asian Development Bank and the InterAmerican Development Bank, as well as for several central banks. His research is on macroeconomic issues in developing countries. He has written several books and a number of papers in professional journals.

Priscilla Muthoora is a Senior Economist in the Middle East and Central Asia Department of the IMF. She joined the IMF in 2009 and has worked in the Fiscal Affairs and Western Hemisphere Departments and the Institute for Capacity Development. She holds a PhD in Economics from the University of Oxford.

William Oman is an Economist at the International Monetary Fund. He has held positions in the IMF's European and Monetary and Capital Markets Departments, as well as in the IMF's European Offices. His research interests include climate change, macro-finance, and monetary policy, with a focus on macroeconomic policy coordination and monetary policy frameworks for climate risks. His research has been published in academic journals such as the *International Journal of Central Banking*, and has appeared in the *Financial Times*, *FT Aphaville*, and *Central Banking Magazine*.

Roberta Piermartini is Chief of Trade Costs Analysis at the World Trade Organization. She has 20 years of experience in trade and trade policy, both theory and empirical application. Her research has been published in top economics journals. She is one of the lead authors and coordinator of World Trade Report (WTR) and joint WTO-WB publications on trade and poverty, and trade and women. She has served the WTO Dispute Settlement in several Panel and Arbitration cases. Her work has been covered by *The Economist* and *Le Monde*. She holds a PhD in Economics from the University of Southampton.

Magali Pinat is an Economist in the European Department of the International Monetary Fund. Magali joined the IMF in 2016 and worked for the Asian and Middle East departments, as well as for the Institute for Capacity Development. She previously worked at the World Bank in the office of the Chief Economist of Latin America and in the Research department. Her recent work at the Fund involved macroeconomic forecasting and labor market analysis. Her primary expertise is in the area of international trade and network analysis. Magali holds a PhD in Economics from the University Paris I Sorbonne.

Giovanni Peri is Professor of Economics at UC Davis and Director of the Global Migration Center, a multi-disciplinary research center focused on migrations. He is Research Associate of the National Bureau of Economic Research in Cambridge, Massachusetts. His research focuses on the economic determinants and consequences of international migrations. He has published extensively in academic journals and has received grants from the MacArthur Foundation, the Russell Sage Foundation, the World Bank, and the National Science Foundation. His research is often featured in media outlets such as *The Economist*, the *New York Times*, the *Wall Street Journal*, and NPR news.

Nathalie Pouokam is a Senior Economist at the International Monetary Fund's Institute for Capacity Development (ICD). Prior to joining ICD, she worked at the IMF's African Department. She has also previously worked as Research Analyst at the Federal Reserve Bank of Minneapolis and has taught undergraduate Microeconomics and Macroeconomics at the University of Minnesota. Her research interests include growth and inequality, climate change, political economy, public finance, risk sharing, and financial stability. She holds a PhD degree in Economics and an MS degree in Mathematics from the University of Minnesota.

Barbara Rambousek is the EBRD's Director for Gender and Economic Inclusion. She established the Bank's approach to promoting economic inclusion and gender equality through private sector investments and policy engagement. She has 20 years senior level experience ranging from economic development and refugee programs in the Western Balkans, the Middle East and Asia to urban regeneration programs in London and the UK. Ms Rambousek holds an MBA (London City Business School), an MSc (London School of Economics), and an MA (University of Vienna).

Halsey Rogers is a Lead Economist with the World Bank's Education Global Practice and served as Co-Director of the World Development Report 2018: Learning to Realize Education's Promise. Before that, he co-authored the Bank's Education Strategy 2020 and served in the Bank's research department. His recent research and policy work focuses on learning and the quality of education service delivery, outcome and process metrics, teacher effectiveness, and Covid-19 response. Halsey has published widely in peer-reviewed journals, including the *Quarterly Journal of Economics* and the *Journal of Economic Perspectives*, and has advised governments in every region. He received his PhD from UC Berkeley.

Richard Rogerson joined the faculty of Princeton University in spring of 2011, where he is the Charles and Marie Robertson Professor of Economics and Public Affairs. He is also the Director of the Louis A. Simpson Center for the Study of Macroeconomics. He obtained his PhD in Economics from the University of Minnesota in 1984. Dr. Rogerson's teaching and research interests are in the fields of Macroeconomics and Labor Economics. He has held several editorial positions at leading journals, is a Research Associate at the National Bureau of Economic Research and a fellow of the Econometric Society.

Dmitriy Rozhkov is a Senior Economist in the Fiscal Affairs Department of the International Monetary Fund. He has been working in the IMF since 2000. During his IMF career, he has worked on many developing and emerging market countries in Africa, Asia and Pacific, Middle East, and Central Asia. His research in the IMF focused on financial sector policies and regulation, financial sector development, fiscal frameworks in resource-rich countries, and inclusive growth. He holds a PhD in Economics from Harvard University, MSc in Economics from the London School of Economics, and BSc from Moscow University.

Andrea Salerno, an Italian national, joined the IMF in 2015, where he has since held different roles with growing responsibilities. Previous professional experience with the Inter-American Development Bank (IDB) and the International Financial Corporation (IFC) in Egypt offered opportunities to learn more in depth about Latin America, Middle East, and North Africa. His academic background and research interests focus on governance, corruption, and institutional development.

Maarten Smeets holds a PhD in law and a Master's in Economics and Trade. He managed the WTO Chairs Program (WCP) at the World Trade Organization. He is an Associate

Professor at St Petersburg State University and Shanghai University of International Business and Economics, a senior associate at the Clingendael Academy (Den Haag) and a non-resident fellow at the World Trade Institute (Bern). He has published many articles and edited several books (on digital trade). He was on the board of the IMF-led Joint Vienna Institute (JVI). He worked for 12 years at the OECD and with the Dutch Government.

Nikola Spatafora is a Senior Economist in the IMF Institute for Capacity Development. Previously, he was Lead Economist for East Asia and the Pacific at the World Bank. His research focuses on economic growth, inequality, structural transformation, and natural resources. He has published widely, including in the *Journal of International Economics*, *Journal of Development Economics*, *IMF World Economic Outlook*, and *World Bank Global Economic Prospects*. His research has been featured in *The Economist*, *Financial Times*, and *Wall Street Journal*. He holds a PhD in Economics from Yale, and a BA (First Class) in Politics, Philosophy, and Economics from Oxford.

Nicholas Stern is IG Patel Professor of Economics and Government and Chair of the Grantham Research Institute on Climate Change and the Environment at the London School of Economics. He was Chief Economist at the European Bank for Reconstruction and Development and the World Bank and has held posts at other UK and overseas universities. He was Second Permanent Secretary to Her Majesty's Treasury, Head of the UK Government Economic Service, and led the Stern Review on the economics of climate change. He was knighted for services to economics (2004), made a life peer (2007), and appointed Companion of Honour for services to economics, international relations, and tackling climate change in 2017.

Joseph E. Stiglitz is University Professor at Columbia University. He is co-chair of the High-Level Expert Group on the Measurement of Economic Performance and Social Progress at the OECD, and the Chief Economist of the Roosevelt Institute. A 2001 recipient of the Nobel Memorial Prize in Economic Sciences, he is a former senior vice president and chief Economist of the World Bank and a former chairman of the Council of Economic Advisers. In 2011, Stiglitz was named by *Time Magazine* as one of the 100 most influential people in the world. Known for his pioneering work on asymmetric information, Stiglitz's research focuses on income distribution, risk, corporate governance, public policy, macroeconomics, and globalization. His latest book is *People, Power, and Profits* (W.W. Norton & Company, 2019).

Anna Ter-Martirosyan is a Senior Economist in the International Monetary Fund's Institute for Capacity Development. Previously, she has worked at the IMF's Strategy Policy and Review Department and Middle East and Central Asia Department on the various policy and surveillance issues. At the IMF, she worked with a number of emerging economies including Brazil, Jordan, Kazakhstan, and the Caribbean islands. She holds a graduate degree in Electrical Engineering from the National Polytechnic University of Armenia and a PhD in Economics from George Washington University.

Mohamed Trabelsi is a Senior Economist at the International Monetary Fund's Middle East Center for Economics and Finance (CEF) in Kuwait. Before joining the CEF, he worked as Senior Economist for the Government of Dubai in United Arab Emirates. Also, he was a

Professor of Economics at Carthage University in Tunisia and at United Arab Emirates University (UAEU). He holds a PhD in International Economics from University of Reims (France) and a PhD in Macroeconomics from University of Tunis (Tunisia).

Dmitry Vasilyev is an Economist in the Western Hemisphere Department at the International Monetary Fund whose work has centered on Belize, Barbados, and Honduras. For these countries he has contributed to stabilization programs and policy analysis in the areas of growth diagnostics, climate change, financial stress, and debt restructuring. He concurrently works in the IMF Inter-Departmental Tail Risk Group. His research interests focus on development macroeconomics, the role of risk, and technology. He holds a MSc in Economics from Higher School of Economics in Moscow.

Anthony Venables is Professor of Economics and Research Director of The Productivity Institute University of Manchester, and Senior Research Fellow at the University of Oxford. He is a fellow of the Econometric Society, the Regional Science Association and the British Academy. Former positions include Professor of Economics at Oxford University, Chief Economist at the UK Department for International Development, and Professor at the London School of Economics. He has published in international trade, economic geography, and natural resources. Publications include *The Spatial Economy; Cities, Regions and International Trade*, with M. Fujita and P. Krugman (MIT Press, 1999).

Younes Zouhar is currently the IMF Resident Representative to Benin. He worked previously at the IMF Institute for Capacity Development where he was involved in the design and the delivery of training to officials. Before that, he was in the IMF Middle East Department where he participated in program negotiations in low-income countries and emerging market economies. Prior to joining the Fund, he held senior positions in the Ministry of Finance in Morocco. He is a graduate of the National Institute of Statistics and Applied Economics in Rabat, Morocco, and earned a bachelor's degree in applied mathematics.

1

An Inclusive Growth Framework

Valerie Cerra

"A rising tide lifts every boat,"[1] ...
but while some sip champagne in a yacht,
others struggle to keep their raft afloat.

I. Issues and Perceptions of Inclusive Growth

A. Key Facts and Issues

For the *average* human, this may be the best time to live in the history of the world.[2] Against the backdrop of the long sweep of human history, global growth has been extraordinary over last two millennia, especially in the past 200 years (Figure 1.1). Advances in technology and productivity have thwarted dire Malthusian predictions that the population would outgrow food supplies. Income per person, adjusting for prices, has risen from $2,000 to more than $50,000 in the United States over the two centuries and by a similar rate of expansion for the world on average, albeit from a lower average level (Figure 1.2).

Economic growth has powered improvements in average living standards. Two centuries of growth have reduced the percentage of people living in extreme poverty—from 19 out of 20 people in 1820 to 2 out of 20 people in 2015. Since 1990 alone, extreme poverty declined by more than a billion people, mainly due to strong growth in China, India, and other populous Asian countries. Likewise, economic growth is correlated with other outcomes: it has contributed to a dramatic rise in educational attainment and literacy, vast improvements in health, and a strong increase in the share of the world living in a democracy (Figure 1.3).

That said, vast income differences across countries leave millions still languishing in poverty. Growth has been distributed unevenly, creating large income differences between countries. GDP per capita ranges from more than $100,000

---

[1] Attributed to a 1963 speech by President John F. Kennedy. The quote was also in usage in earlier decades.
[2] I thank Jaime Sarmiento for research assistance and participants in the Inclusive Growth book seminar series organized by the IMF Institute for Capacity Development for their comments.

Valerie Cerra, *An Inclusive Growth Framework* In: *How to Achieve Inclusive Growth*. Edited by: Valerie Cerra, Barry Eichengreen, Asmaa El-Ganainy, and Martin Schindler, Oxford University Press. © Valerie Cerra 2022.
DOI: 10.1093/oso/9780192846938.003.0001

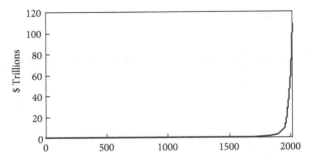

Figure 1.1 World GDP over the Last Two Millennia (Adjusted for inflation and expressed in international-$ in 2011 prices)

Source: Our World in Data based on World Bank & Maddison (2018)

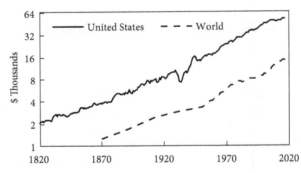

Figure 1.2 GDP per capita, 1820 to 2016 (Adjusted for inflation and expressed in international-$ in 2011 prices and logs)

Source: Maddison Project Database (2018)

annually in Luxembourg to less than $800 per person in Burundi, expressed in comparable international prices (Figure 1.4). About 689 million people were still in extreme poverty in 2017 (World Bank 2020). A person's living conditions are partly shaped by the country in which they live, with sharp differences across countries in indicators of health and education and access to basic services like electricity and water. For example, the mortality rate for children under 5 years of age is nearly 13 percent in Somalia versus 0.2 percent in Iceland; life expectancy is only 52 years in Sierra Leone versus 84 years in Japan; less than 10 percent of the population in South Sudan, Chad, and Burundi have access to electricity versus 100 percent in several rich countries; people older than 24 attained an average of 14 years of schooling in Germany versus 1.5 years in Burkina Faso; and for a child entering school age, the expected schooling is 23 years in Australia versus 5 years in South Sudan.

Increasingly, the income of an individual depends on their economic status within their country. National growth is not enough to ensure the improvement of individual welfare. Recent research finds that within-country inequality has risen from about one-half of total global interpersonal income inequality in 1980

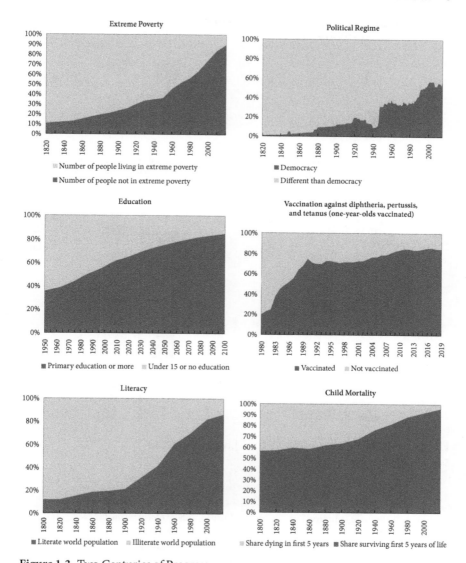

Figure 1.3 Two Centuries of Progress
Source: Max Roser, OurWorldInData.org, https://ourworldindata.org/a-history-of-global-living-conditions-in-5-charts

to about three-quarters in 2018 (Figure 1.5), although data weaknesses and meas-urement issues stir debates on the precise quantification (see Section III.E). Income inequality across countries has declined slightly in recent decades and global interpersonal inequality has also likely fallen, mainly due to strong growth in China and India. However, within-country inequality has risen in many advanced economies (AEs) and several large emerging market economics

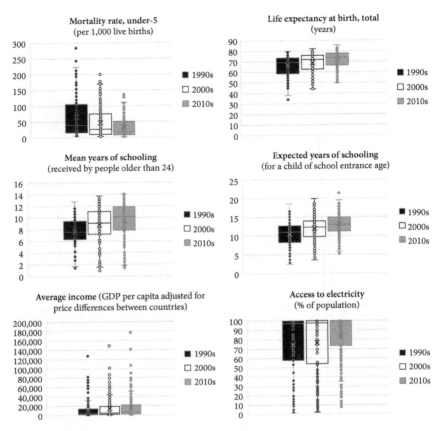

Figure 1.4 Inequality across Countries in Living Conditions
Sources: WB and author's calculations.

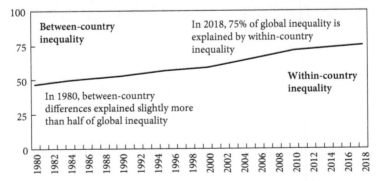

Figure 1.5 Global Income Inequality: Between vs within Country, 1980–2018
Note: Distribution of per adult pretax income measured at PPP
Source: Chancel in World Inequality Report 2018

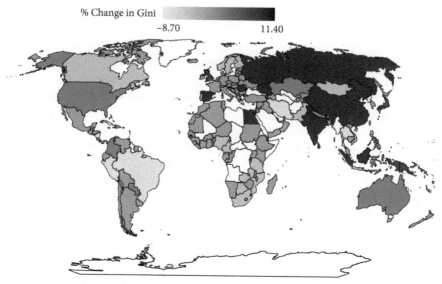

Figure 1.6 Change in Net Gini, 1990s–2010s
Note: White stands for no data
Sources: SWID and author's calculations

(notably China, India, Indonesia, Russia, and South Africa) between the 1990s and 2010s, whether measured by the market Gini, net Gini, or ratio of top 10 to bottom 10 percent (see Section III for definitions). The share of total income accruing to the richest 1 percent of people has been rising rapidly since 1970 in countries like the United States, Canada, Australia, and the United Kingdom (Figure 1.6). In the US and many EMEs, the top 1 percent receives about one-fifth of all income (Alvaredo et al. 2013 and 2018).

Disparities in wealth are also immense: the richest 8 men hold as much wealth as the entire poorest half of the world (Oxfam 2017). Wealth inequality is considerably higher than income inequality in both advanced and emerging market economies. In fact, for advanced economies, the Gini coefficient for wealth is twice as large as the Gini coefficient for income (Davies et al. 2008). Globally, the richest 1 percent of the world holds approximately as much wealth as the remaining 99 percent (Credit Suisse 2019). Top personal income tax rates have declined over time (Chapter 12) and yet a considerable amount of wealth is hidden offshore to evade taxes, undermining government revenues needed for investment and public services. For example, Zucman (2015) estimates that $7.6 trillion of wealth (8 percent of the global financial wealth of households) is concealed in offshore tax havens. Research suggests that the wealthy may exert undue influence over politics and public policy in advanced countries like the US (Bartels 2008; Gilens 2005 and 2012) and developing countries like India (Anderson, Francois, and Kotwal 2015).

Inequality and poverty drive other social ills. An estimated 690 million people worldwide were undernourished in 2019 and 2 billion people did not have access to safe, nutritious and sufficient food, which also contributed to stunting in 21 percent of children under 5 years of age (FAO et al. 2020).

Inequality of opportunity perpetuates inequality of outcomes. Income and wealth inequality are aspects of inequality of outcomes. They are both associated with inequality of opportunity, including disparities in access to health, education, and financial services (Dabla-Norris et al. 2015). Health outcomes are worse for the poor, such as significantly higher infant and female mortality rates in emerging and developing countries and far lower access to health professionals. Access to education is also unequal. For example, in Sub-Saharan Africa, more than half of the youth (ages 20–24) in the poorest income quintile have less than four years of education, compared with 15 percent of the richest quintile. The poor also have lower access to financial services than higher earners for all country income groups. Income inequality and inequality of opportunity leads to lower social mobility between generations (Corak 2013; Chapter 18).

The Global Financial Crisis (GFC) and the COVID-19 pandemic have amplified inequality, poverty, unemployment, and health risks. Studies found that the GFC led to disproportionately larger income losses for lower-income groups (Almeida 2020) and thwarted 64 million people from escaping extreme poverty (Ravalion and Chen 2009). COVID-19 also impacted low-income people more than those at the upper end of the distribution, as they were more vulnerable to losing their jobs and had less access to high-quality medical care. In addition, because their jobs required more person-to-person contact, low-income people were more exposed to obtaining the virus.[3] The COVID pandemic was expected to push between 88 and 115 million people into extreme poverty (World Bank 2020) and increase the number of undernourished by 83–132 million people in 2020 (FAO et al. 2020). In addition, employment losses were larger for women and were expected to widen gender wage gaps (Alon et al. 2020).

Looking to the future, climate change poses an existential danger. Higher global temperatures have already led to unprecedented losses from the more frequent and more severe natural disasters stemming from it. If left unchecked, climate change has the potential to disrupt lives far worse than even financial crises or pandemics, with estimates that up to 132 million could fall into poverty due to climate change (World Bank 2020).

Inclusive growth is multidimensional, with complex interlinkages. The global poor are exposed to a wide range of risks. Most of the global poor have informal jobs and are not easily reached by social safety nets; 132 million live in areas vulnerable to floods and 40 percent of them live in danger of violence and conflict (World Bank 2020). Women face an array of gaps in labor market participation

---

[3] In the United States, COVID-19 also has had a disproportionate impact on racial and ethnic minorities (Tai et al. 2021).

and earnings, political power, and access to health, education, and finance. Structural changes arising from technological change or globalization often adversely impact those with lower educations and less geographic mobility and leave lagging regions behind. Labor market and fiscal policies, including provision of public services, and improvements in governance, among others, are typically all part of the policy package to respond to the various gaps and inequities. The book will explore these and other linkages in more detail.

B. Public Perceptions and Concerns

In line with the facts described in Section I.A., people in advanced, emerging, and developing countries consider inequality to be a major problem. According to surveys conducted by the Pew Research Center, more than 70 percent of respondents think that the system favors the wealthy (Pew 2013). More than half of respondents also reported that the gap between the rich and poor has widened in recent years and this trend toward greater inequality is a very big problem (Pew 2014), and 65 percent in AEs thought the next generation would be worse off than their parents. Across 34 surveyed countries, 65 percent felt pessimistic about reducing inequality (Pew 2019). A Gallup poll in 2018 found 2/3 of US respondents dissatisfied with the distribution of income and wealth. Studies also find that interpersonal trust declines with higher inequality (World Values Survey 2014) and in some countries rising inequality has eroded trust in the economic and political system and in public institutions.

Economic vulnerability remains a big concern. A Gallup World Poll found that 35 percent and 30 percent of people around the world reported not having enough money for food and shelter, respectively (Gallup 2020), with migrants significantly more vulnerable to meeting basic needs than native born. Even in European OECD countries, 1 in 5 people reported having difficulty making ends meet in 2018 (OECD 2020). These surveys were all taken before the outbreak of COVID-19, which is expected to magnify poverty and vulnerability.

In addition to economic disparities, there is an increasing awareness of persisting disparities in social treatment among groups. A 2020 Ipsos survey of 27 countries found only one-third of women agreed that workplaces treat men and women equality (Ipsos Global Advisors 2020). A Gallup 2020 poll found perceptions of racial equality in the US at the lowest level in three decades, with only about one-third of black Americans believing they have equal chances as whites in the job market, education, and affordable housing. This is spawning a rising desire for social justice for all, including for people of different races and genders.

Climate change is seen as a looming threat. A Lloyd's Register Foundation World Risk Poll conducted in 2019 in 142 countries found that at least 60 percent of people in every region consider climate change as a threat to their country in the next 20 years, and billions worry about consuming unsafe food and water, especially in countries with developmental and climate-related issues. Pew Research Center finds climate change tops the list of global threats across 14 polled countries (Pew 2020).

C. Public Preferences for Fairness

These public perceptions can be connected to concepts of justice and fairness. John Rawls, a moral and political philosopher, aimed to resolve seeming conflicts of freedom and equality in his influential treatise, *A Theory of Justice* (1971). He posed a thought experiment, called the "original position," in which people agree to the structure and social contract for a society behind a hypothetical "veil of ignorance" in which they would be unaware of their abilities, characteristics, or social status. He reasoned that under such ignorance of one's status, the social contract would rule out discriminatory solutions and would permit inequality only so far as it improves the position of the worst off ("the difference principle").

People underestimate actual wealth inequality (knowledge gap) and would prefer a society with much less inequality than actually occurs (policy gap). In a nationally representative sample from the US, Norton and Ariely (2011) found that respondents vastly underestimated the share of wealth held by the wealthiest quintile. Then, when asked to construct an ideal distribution from a Rawlsian perspective of entering a random position in the country, respondents chose a far more equal distribution than either the actual distribution or their (incorrectly optimistic) estimate of it.

Why does this book address inclusive growth and not just growth? Because, as just discussed, while growth helps lift people out of poverty over the longer run, it does not uniformly improve equality and other aspects of well-being. This book addresses both the knowledge gap (by providing information on the actual status of inclusive growth) and the policy gap (by providing policy guidance on how to improve inclusive growth). We turn next to our definition of inclusive growth (Section II) and then connect it to concepts and measurement of wellbeing and inclusion (Section III). As inclusive growth is multi-dimensional and interlinked, we present a framework relating its components (Section IV) and draw on this framework in setting out the road map for the rest of the book (Section V).

II. Dimensions of Inclusive Growth

A. What is Inclusive Growth?

Our definition of inclusive growth has three components: (1) strong economic growth that is (2) inclusive and (3) sustainable.

Economic growth refers to increases in the production of goods and services that are valued by people, providing the means for a better standard of living. Growth also has other benefits. It creates job opportunities and helps pull people out of poverty (Chapter 2). It also increases the resources that the government can tap through taxation in order to finance the provision of public services.

Inclusion refers to broadly sharing these improvements in living standards among all groups in society. Inclusion can be summarized by four general objectives: (1) benefit-sharing; (2) opportunity; (3) participation; and (4) empowerment:

- Benefit sharing involves reducing poverty and increasing incomes across the income distribution and across all groups, including different genders, age groups, races and ethnicities, regions, and other aspects of individual characteristics and circumstances. But income is not the only measure of economic resources. Wealth is usually more unequally distributed and may have greater impact on some facets of economic, social, and political life. And there are other dimensions of social well-being that matter too, beyond the growth in income and wealth. Benefit sharing also involves ensuring social mobility from one generation to the next, so that an individual is not trapped into poverty or low income by the circumstance of their birth. Benefit sharing does not necessarily mean complete equality, as most societies prefer some degree of inequality in order to incentivize hard work and other socially beneficial behaviors.

- Opportunity to access basic services such as health, education, and other public services is fundamental to inclusion. It allows each person to cultivate their talents and acquire skills to enable a productive life. Equality of opportunity can be distinguished from equality of outcome. A sports analogy can explain this difference. Equality of opportunity means leveling the playing field so everyone can compete fairly with the same equipment and same rules of the game. Equality of outcomes means that regardless of how well each person plays, the final score is equalized. If a society has equality of opportunities, a person's income tends to be determined mostly by their effort and ability. This provides incentives for hard work and investment in improving skills. Promoting equality of outcomes through a lot of redistribution may entail a tradeoff between equality and growth if it discourages people from working and investing. But promoting equality of opportunities tends to improve both equality and growth at the same time.

- Participation in economic life, especially finding productive employment, is the third aspect of inclusion. The economy needs to be dynamic enough to generate a sufficient level and quality of jobs, which facilitates the adaption of the workforce to new conditions. Referring again to the sports analogy, this principle is associated with being allowed to participate in the game.

- Empowerment in social and political life is another aspect beyond economic wellbeing, ensuring a strong system of governance, public sector accountability and enabling citizens to voice their preferences.

To be inclusive, growth must also be sustainable. Sustainability means that the current path of consumption and social welfare can be sustained into the future of both current and future generations. This means that the current economic growth should not be generated by unsustainable boom-bust policies, such as those that could lead to debt or other financial crises. It also requires maintaining environmental sustainability, ensuring that future generations have the same opportunity to benefit from the natural bounty of the Earth.

How do other institutions define inclusive growth? While there may not be an exact common definition, the definitions and concepts overlap and a key theme is that inclusive growth is multi-dimensional.[4] For example, the European Commission defines inclusive growth as "a high-employment economy delivering economic, social and territorial cohesion." This "means empowering people through high levels of employment, investing in skills, fighting poverty and modernizing labor markets, training and social protection systems so as to help people anticipate and manage change, and build a cohesive society" (EC 2020).

There are several concepts used by other institutions and scholars that are related. For example, the World Bank uses a concept of "shared prosperity" which refers to increasing the incomes and welfare of the bottom 40 percent of society. Some researchers analyze "pro-poor" growth, measured in terms of the mean growth rate of those below the poverty line (Ravallion and Chen 2003).

B. Concepts of Well-being and Economic Welfare

Policy attention often focuses on what is measured. Measurement allows us to assess the status and progress of well-being and a country's health and to evaluate the effectiveness of policies. Lack of appropriate metrics may lead to neglect or the wrong focus (Stiglitz 2018).

GDP is the most commonly used indicator of the state of the economy. GDP measures the value of economic production that takes place and receives market payments. Simon Kuznets pioneered its development during the Great Depression to monitor the state of economic output and that of different sectors and it was augmented by John Maynard Keynes to include government spending. Richard Stone further developed the System of National Accounts (SNA) in the 1950s as conditionality for post-war aid under the Marshall Plan. The system of national

---

[4] Other chapters in the book emphasize the multi-dimensionality of inclusive growth in other contexts (see for example Chapter 3 on labor markets).

accounts was adopted internationally by national statistical agencies of countries, providing conceptually consistent measures across countries. The SNA includes additional indicators of economic welfare, such as household real disposable income and consumption, wealth, and prices (IMF 2020).

GDP has well-known shortcomings, even as a measurement of economic activity and welfare. Since GDP focuses on observable market transactions, it excludes aspects of economic production such as household nonmarket production, informal sector work (for some countries), unpaid and volunteer work, the value of leisure, and social goods (such as "the beauty of our poetry or the strength of our marriages," Robert Kennedy 1968). Conversely, it includes spending on services that reflect the need to overcome societal bads, such as incarceration facilities, security for protection against crime, and military weapons to protect against foreign aggression. GDP fails to deduct items that reduce economic welfare, such as pollution and environmental degradation and the depreciation of assets. National accounts statisticians also face challenges in estimating quality changes of some goods and services, incorporating new products, and in measuring the value of intangible activities such as finance. As a recent example related to this, the welfare growth from free digital services and associated nonmarket production by households and volunteers is not well captured in GDP. Valuation may rely on subsidiary activities such as advertising revenue, but alternative valuation approaches may be needed, such as time spent on the internet or internet traffic (IMF 2020).

Analysis of economic welfare goes beyond GDP and SNA indicators. Complementary indicators could include the value of household nonmarket production and impact of digitization, and deductions for the depletion of natural resources and degradation of the environment. Economic welfare also needs to account for the distribution of income and wealth, for access to financial services and to basic public services such as health and education, and for the creation of enough high-quality jobs. Kuznets warned against applying GDP (or GNP) too generally as a measure of economic health:

> the desirability of as high and sustained a growth rate as is compatible with the costs that society is willing to bear is valid; but when using it to judge economic problems and policies, distinctions must be kept in mind between quantity and quality of growth, between its costs and returns, and between the short and long run.   (Kuznets 1962)

The distribution of economic welfare is not reflected in simple totals and averages. In some cases, a rise in GDP may reflect income growth for only a small minority of the population at the top end of the distribution. Meanwhile, living standards of the majority may be stagnant or declining. Indeed, the majority of OECD countries experienced a rise in inequality of income before taxes and transfers in the three decades since the mid-1990s (OECD 2015). Poverty is particularly pernicious, so its eradication would be a critical component of any framework of economic and social wellbeing. In fact, reducing poverty was a critical objective of the United Nations' Millennium Development Goals (MDGs) and is Goal 1 of the Sustainable Development Goals (SDGs). In short, to understand the economic welfare of a population, it is necessary to go beyond an aggregate and to measure the distribution of income and of other aspects of well-being. Section III below focuses on measuring inequality and poverty, as well as non-income components of inclusion.

Sustainability is not well captured. GDP is a measure of the *current flow* of economic production. It does not measure the stock of economic and natural resources or mounting vulnerabilities that threaten future well-being. For example, it neglects the depletion of natural resources, the loss of physical wealth associated with natural disasters, and the detrimental impacts of human activity on the environment. Likewise, it ignores balance sheet vulnerabilities, such as the excessive buildup of debt, which could lead to economic crises that damage future welfare. Thus, alternative measures and analysis are required to assess economic vulnerabilities and the rising hazard of climate change.

Well-being is a broader concept than economic welfare. Beyond economic welfare, there are also many indicators or measures that would be useful for a broader measure of social well-being. This would include factors such as safety and the lack of crime, life expectancy and educational outcomes, bio-diversity, civic engagement and governance, community, social trust, cultural achievements, and other aspects of happiness and life satisfaction.

Some countries, institutions, and economists have developed other measures of the health of an economy and the wellbeing of its people. For example, Bhutan introduced the "Gross Happiness Index" and its four pillars of (1) environmental conservation, (2) suitable and equitable socio-economic development, (3) preservation and promotion of culture, and (4) good governance. The United Nations Development Program publishes its "Human Development Index" in annual Human Development Reports. The index combines life expectancy, education, and income into a composite measure. For the time being, GDP remains the most widely used indicator, in part due to the frequency, continuity, and cross-country comparability of its measurement. But alternative indicators are likely to increase in usage if their components become standard features of measurement of country statistical agencies.

Some countries have embedded well-being indicators into their policymaking processes. A number of national governments have developed sets of well-being indicators to inform the public and political debate and to guide policy decisions (Exton and Shinwell 2018). Indicators draw from household surveys and objective measures of material living conditions, supplemented by surveys of subjective well-being, often following consultations with a range of stakeholders. These initiatives have been commissioned by different agencies (e.g., the cabinet, finance or planning ministries, or national statistical agencies). Countries use the indicators at different policy stages, including setting their agenda and formulating and evaluating policy, and in some cases established a council to inform parliament as part of the policy formulation and budget cycle.

III. Measuring Inclusion

Measurement of inclusion can focus on the wellbeing of the poorest group within a society or the overall society and can include both monetary and non-monetary indicators. Poverty is typically an absolute measure of inclusion, focusing on the bottom of the distribution. In contrast, inequality is a relative measure of wellbeing in a society and covers the population more broadly. Non-monetary measures may include access to basic goods and services, including those such as education, health, and infrastructure that are at least partly provided by the government.

A. Poverty

Poverty is a level of resources so low that a minimum standard of living cannot be met. Measuring poverty entails selecting an indicator and a threshold.

The "poverty line" identifies the threshold level of welfare required to meet basic needs. Definitions of basic needs vary across countries, but usually emphasize having adequate food to meet nutritional standards, and adequate housing and utilities. The World Bank (WB) and International Monetary Fund (IMF) focus on a global standard, calculated as the average of national poverty lines across all developing countries (currently $3.20 per day, measured in 2011 prices) as well as a global extreme poverty line, calculated as the average of national poverty lines in 15 of the very poorest developing countries (currently $1.90 per day). Countries also have their own national poverty lines, which are highly correlated with countries' average income levels. As an alternative approach to an absolute poverty line, many advanced countries define a relative poverty line as some fraction of their median income. However, a relative measure has the disadvantage of being conflated with a measure of inequality rather than a threshold of basic needs.

The poverty headcount and poverty gap are the two most common indicators. The poverty headcount ratio is the proportion of the population below the poverty line. While a good measure of the scope of poverty, it does not capture the magnitude of it. The poverty gap is the depth or intensity of poverty, taking into account how far below the poverty threshold each poor household lies. It is measured as the average percentage deviation from the poverty line for all who are poor and can also be interpreted as the monetary amount required to bring every poor person up to the poverty line, thus eliminating poverty (assuming no transaction costs).

Poverty severity puts greater weight on the poorest of households. Poverty severity, also called the squared depth of poverty, is calculated as the square of the deviation of each poor household's welfare from the poverty line. The headcount ratio, the poverty gap, and the severity of poverty are special cases of a general set of poverty measures, called the Foster-Greer-Thorbecke (FGT) class of poverty measures, which differ in the weights each measure places on the poorest households among all the poor.

Poverty vulnerability broadens the measure to households currently above the poverty line, but at risk of falling into poverty. Measurement of vulnerability entails modeling the historical probability that households with particular characteristics will suffer a shock—such as from unemployment, illness, or natural disaster—that pushes them below the poverty line during any given time period.

B. Inequality

The simplest measures of inequality consider income shares of various percentiles of the population or production factors. For example, in a society of perfect income equality, the "top 1 percent" of the population would have 1 percent of the income.[5] Likewise, the population can be ordered by income and divided into five groups of 20 percent each (quintiles) to compare the income shares of each quintile. The decile dispersion ratio (DDR), also called the inter-decile ratio (P90/ P10), measures the ratio of the income of the 10 percent highest earners (top decile) to the income of the 10 percent lowest earners (bottom decile). The Palma ratio is the top 10 percent relative to the bottom 40 percent. The labor and capital shares of income from production are also used in measuring inequality, reflecting that capital owners tend to be from the upper end of the income distribution and hold most of the wealth in an industrialized country. That said, chief executive officers (CEOs) and other managers ("agents") operating a firm may be distinct from the owners ("principals") and have different interests. In addition, land ownership in an agrarian society or real estate ownership more generally is another form of non-human wealth. Likewise, labor income combines payments to pure labor services with payment for the embodied skills and knowledge associated with human capital.

The Lorenz Curve and Gini coefficient measure inequality for the entire population. To construct the Lorenz curve, the population is ordered from lowest to

---

[5] In the case of perfect equality, the top 1 percent is not defined since everyone has the same income.

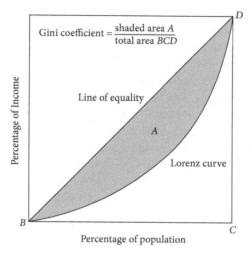

$$\text{Gini coefficient} = \frac{\text{shaded area } A}{\text{total area } BCD}$$

Figure 1.7 Lorenz Curve and Gini Coefficient
Source: Author's illustration.

highest income. The Lorenz curve traces out the relationship between the *cumulative* population on the horizontal axis and the *cumulative* income share on the vertical axis. In a perfectly equal society, the Lorenz curve would be the 45-degree line from B to D in Figure 1.7. In a society in which one person earned all the income, the curve would trace out the path B–C–D. The Gini coefficient is the ratio of the area created by the deviation of the Lorenz curve from the line of equality (area A), relative to the area of perfect inequality (area B-C-D, equal to ½). A Gini coefficient of zero denotes perfect equality, whereas a Gini coefficient of unity denotes perfect inequality. The Gini index is the Gini coefficient expressed as a percentage, thus ranging from 0 to 100. Although the Gini has the advantage of being a single measure for the entire population, it can be sensitive to the demographic structure and cannot distinguish whether the inequality is concentrated at the top, middle, or bottom of the distribution. The Robin Hood index (or Hoover index/Schutz index) is the share of income that would need to be redistributed to achieve perfect equality.

Some measures can be broken down by subgroups of the population. The Gini cannot be decomposed into additive subgroups. In contrast, Atkinson's index and the Theil index (or General Entropy) can be decomposed into subgroups, such as measuring within and between group inequality. Atkinson's index measures the percent of income that would be required for a society to achieve the same welfare as a more equal society. It can be parameterized to social aversion to inequality and used to evaluate the welfare implications of policies. The Theil index ranges from zero (equality) to infinity and can be parameterized (α) to weight differences in income at different parts of the distribution, with lower values more sensitive to changes in the lower tail (Theil L or mean log deviation when $\alpha = 0$; Theil T when $\alpha = 1$; coefficient of variation when $\alpha = 2$).

The growth incidence curve (GIC) measures the dynamics of the distribution. In contrast to the DDR and Gini, which are static measures of inequality, the GIC plots the growth rate of income for every segment of the population to show how the distribution is changing over time. The horizontal axis orders the population from lowest to highest income (similar to the Gini, except not cumulative) and the growth of income of that segment (percentile, quintile, decile, etc) is presented on the vertical axis. A downward sloping line would indicate faster income growth of the poor than the rich, and vice versa. The GIC can be constructed from two or more comparable household surveys. An *anonymous GIC* is indifferent to the composition of individuals in each percentile, so does not track mobility through the distribution over time. A *non-anonymous GIC* plots changes in income for specific individuals at given percentiles of the initial income distribution. A *quasi-non-anonymous* GIC holds the country composition of each global decile constant across time (vs the anonymous GIC where the country composition of each global decile changes over time).

Inequality is composed of intragenerational (within the same age group) and intergenerational (between the young and old) inequality. Over a normal lifecycle, people tend to move from lower- to higher-paying jobs as they gain experience, so intergenerational inequality may be larger than intragenerational inequality. *Absolute* intergenerational social mobility compares living standards across generations, while *relative* intergenerational social mobility measures the probability that a child will attain a different economic status than that of their parents (see Chapter 18). These inclusion indicators measure the opportunity of individuals to achieve income or social status based on merit or other paths beyond the random social assignment conferred at birth. The intergenerational income elasticity (IGE) is a measure of relative intergenerational mobility, calculated as the regression coefficient of log child income on log parent income. The joint distribution of parent and child incomes is composed of the joint distribution of parent and child percentile ranks (the "copula") and the marginal distributions of parent and child income. The "rank-rank slope" measures the relationship between a child's and her/his parents' position in the income distribution (Chetty et al. 2014), drawing on the copula, while the IGE combines the copula and marginal distributions.

C. Measurement Choices

Distributional indicators, such as poverty and inequality, need to choose the unit of observation, particularly whether the focus is the individual or household.

Some data is collected at the household level. Given that children typically consume less than adults and there are economies of scale in household size, matching the income level of individuals with households of different sizes requires "equivalence scales." Relatedly, household indicators may not be comparable over time or across countries given family compositional differences.

Poverty and inequality are commonly measured using either consumption or income. Market income is relatively easy to calculate given most people have few sources, but it is more likely to be underreported to avoid taxation. Consumption is less variable than income, so may provide a better measure of the long-run welfare. However, people responding to surveys may have imperfect recollection of expenditures. In addition, adjustments are required for investment expenditures such as housing to calculate the imputed consumption and price indices are needed to take account of the local variations in the cost of goods.

Distributional information may be drawn from different data sources. Common sources include household surveys and administrative data, such as from tax records and property registers. Some low-income countries may only collect household expenditure data. Tax data may be more accurate, but tax codes vary, complicating comparative analysis. Lower income populations may underreport income due to high informality, and top incomes consistently conceal income through tax avoidance facilitated by loopholes and complex tax systems, as well as through outright tax evasion facilitated by tax haven jurisdictions.

Other choices include measurement before or after taxes and measurement of flows versus stocks. Governments tax market income earned from employment and returns on capital and also provide subsidies and transfers. Taxes and transfers are typically progressive in most countries (Chapter 12), so market income is more unequally distributed than income after taxes and transfers. In addition, the income of a large share of the population is based almost entirely on labor income (Chapter 3), whereas the top of the income distribution also derives a significant component of income from capital income on their wealth. Wealth is more unequally distributed in most countries and also tends to reflect life-cycle dynamics, such as savings accumulated during peak earning years.

D. Non-monetary Measures

Inclusion is about more than income or wealth for purchasing private goods and services. As defined above, inclusion also involves access to public goods and services. It also includes having access to jobs that provide productive and meaningful ways of providing income and having political empowerment.

Access to education, health, finance, and infrastructure are important aspects of inclusion. They are often provided by the government. Education allows individuals to increase human capital and is an important means of obtaining intergenerational social and income mobility. Likewise, health services and infrastructure (such as electricity, water, sanitation, roads, public transport) are aspects of basic needs and serve as critical inputs for a productive life. Common education indicators include the adult literacy rate, the gross primary enrollment ratio, and the educational attainment of the labor force. Health indicators include the maternal mortality ratio, the share of pregnant women receiving prenatal care, the share of births attended by skilled health staff, and the child nutrition indicators such as stunting and wasting. Indicators of access to finance include the share of the population with a bank account or loan. Some indicators of infrastructure include access to electricity, water, and sanitation. A multi-dimensional poverty index combines indicators of poverty based on health, education, and standard of living.

Broader aspects of inclusion account for inclusion in labor markets, governance and political empowerment, and sustainability. Labor market indicators measure opportunities for finding suitable employment. Common indicators are the unemployment rate, youth unemployment rate, labor force participation rate, vulnerable employment and the share of informal sector workers (Chapters 3 and 18). Inclusion in the political process and transparency and accountability of public officials is also important for a fair and just society that represents the welfare of all. Several institutions provide governance indicators that can be based on surveys of perceptions or on observed outcomes (Chapter 10). The World Bank provides indicators such as the world governance indicators and the country policy and institutional assessment (CPIA). The IMF has the fiscal transparency index and the public investment management index. Sustainability includes economic sustainability, which can be measured using various indicators of vulnerability, as well as certain aspects such as the IMF's debt sustainability analysis. Sustainability also includes the sustainability of natural resources (Chapter 19) and environmental sustainability (Chapter 20), with the latter analyzed in the IMF/WB climate change policy assessments.

E. Debates on Trends in Inclusive Growth

Measurement issues underpin several debates on facts and trends in inequality. Anand and Segal (2008) survey research on global income inequality (a pooled global distribution that ignores country of residence) and report numerous measurement and methodological differences between studies including the choice of inequality indicator (e.g., Gini, Theil T, and Theil L—see description in measurement section above), price data for PPP estimation, use of income versus expenditure, source of data (e.g., household survey, national accounts; Penn World Tables, Maddison, World Bank). They conclude that it is difficult to quantify global interpersonal inequality and its changes. Even so, they find agreement among all studies that the level of global inequality is high, with nearly all estimates of the Gini lying above 0.63, and most studies find rising within-country inequality. Bourguignon (2016) and Milanovic (2016) discuss the decline in global income inequality since 1990 and give their views on its causes. Ravallion (2018) critically reviews these two books, arguing that the change in global inequality depends on the measure of relative inequality used. He also points to rising *absolute* global inequality.

More provocatively, debates rage on the extent of within-country inequality. Piketty, Saez, and Zucman (2018) pioneered using tax data to measure inequality and report soaring incomes for the top 1 percent and stagnating incomes for the middle class, especially in the US. These findings have come under scrutiny by researchers. A number of studies find lower inequality after adjusting for self-employment (including firm pass through of earnings of professionals), residential real estate income and wealth, changes in household size, and the starting point of the time series (Auten and Splinter 2018; Zidar and Zwick 2020; Matthew Rognlie 2016; Smith et al. 2019 and 2020). Researchers differ on how to allocate corporate profits across individuals, how to deal with tax evasion, and how to estimate wealth by scaling up capital income flows (Auten and Splinter 2018; Smith, Zidar, and Zwick 2020). Studies tracking incomes of individuals find turnover in their location in the distribution and regression to the mean (Auten, Gee, and Turner 2013; Rank and Hirschl 2015). Researchers also find lower income inequality after taxes and transfers, largely owing to means-tested transfers, mainly for health insurance (Auten and Splinter 2018). Although these adjustments reveal lower inequality, studies nonetheless show that income inequality in the US after taxes and transfers has risen (CBO 2018). More generally, estimates of within-country inequality based on household surveys are typically underestimated since the rich are less likely to participate in household surveys and are more likely to underreport their income (Ravallion 2018), as shown for the US by Burkhauser et al. (2009).

Growth incidence curves are also sensitive to data sources and methodologies. Milanovich (2016) presents a growth incidence curve for the world, where the shape resembles the outline of an elephant, with high cumulative growth in the middle of the distribution (the "torso") from populous emerging markets like China and India, high cumulative growth for the very rich (the "trunk"), and low cumulative growth for the lowest decile and at the 8–9th decile. Kharas and Seidel (2018) revisit the "elephant chart," showing major differences in the GIC due to measurement and methodological choices, including the sample that is used in terms of countries or those with only one survey, the PPP or price adjustment method employed, the sample period and country coverage, the type of data—whether from household surveys, national accounts, or administrative data—and whether the GIC is anonymous or non-anonymous. For example, using a

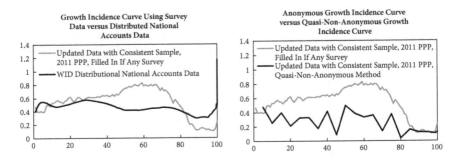

Figure 1.8 Global Growth Incidence Curves
Source: Homi Kharas and Brida Seidel, "What's happening to the world income distribution? The elephant chart revisited," Brookings.

quasi-non-anonymous GIC, the stellar growth at the top of the distribution disappears (Figure 1.8). All of these debates underscore the importance of improving data on distributional issues.

IV. Adopting an Inclusive Growth Framework

A. The Inclusive Growth Framework

Inclusive growth is multidimensional, so a framework is needed to describe the elements and outline how they are connected (Figure 1.9). Promoting strong, sustained and broad-based growth requires inputs from both the private sector and the government. They combine to generate economic activity and to determine its distribution.

In most economies, private individuals and firms generate a substantial share of economic activity. They produce goods and services and earn income on their inputs of labor, capital, and innovation. These inputs can be derived from domestic sources or through globalization, which contributes to the supply of labor, capital, and technology through migration, capital flows, and technology transfers across borders. In addition, the private sector responds to price signals and incentives to ensure that goods and services are produced and sold in markets. So inclusive growth also requires fair and competitive marketplaces with level playing fields—domestically and through international trade—to ensure appropriate prices and opportunities for all to contribute and to reap the output of production.

The government contributes inputs and establishes the right conditions for growth and for inclusion. This starts with an overall governance framework to establish the "rules of the game," direct how the country is managed, and hold political leaders accountable for making decisions in the best interests of the

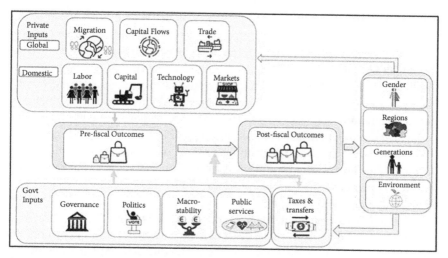

Figure 1.9 The Inclusive Growth Framework
Source: Author's illustration.

country. The political system of the country establishes opportunities for citizens to voice their views on social goals and advocate for reforms to promote higher and more inclusive growth. Among government inputs, macroeconomic stability is critical for inclusive growth. The government uses its macroeconomic tools such as fiscal and monetary stabilization to smooth economic fluctuations and avoid disruptive recessions and crises. Policies to promote stable growth are important because excessive volatility is detrimental to both growth and equity. The government raises taxes and uses these resources to provide an array of public services. Government policies and provision of public services that increase access to health, education, and finance affect the "pre-distribution" phase, affecting the stocks of human and physical capital that feed into the production process. At the stage of production, governments shape the functioning of the market and the incentives firms and individuals face in their employment, investment, and innovation decisions. After production and the distribution of market income, the government also uses its tax and spending instruments to redistribute income to increase the welfare of the very poorest and reduce income disparities according to the weights that the society places on equality. Usually, the market or pre-fiscal outcomes tend to be more unequally distributed than outcomes after government redistribution through taxes and transfers.

The sharing of economic benefits can be analyzed along several dimensions beyond just an aggregate measure of inequality. At a given moment in time, we can examine whether economic benefits are fairly shared across genders and other personal attributes including ethnicity and race. Different regions of a country may grow at different rates with some regions racing forward and others being left behind. Comparing the outcomes of the young and the old is also important, as in some countries these groups tend to be more vulnerable to poverty. We also have to consider the intertemporal aspect of inclusion: namely, the sharing of economic benefits, including from resource wealth, across current and future generations. Therefore, inclusive growth must be sustainable, and sustainability requires addressing the potential detrimental impact of climate change on future generations.

Finally, there is a feedback loop from the distribution of outcomes to private and public sector inputs. The distribution of outcomes affects future production through labor supply, savings, and entrepreneurship, including through its impact on the next generation. Outcomes feed into future government inputs and policies through the political system.

Ultimately, each element of the framework is linked to the rest. The framework illustrates each component and its main function and channels of interaction. But inclusive growth is macroeconomic in nature, and thus all components of the system are fully interdependent. The system is also dynamic. Outcomes create endowments of wealth and capital that affect subsequent inputs to production. Outcomes and factor payments create differential opportunities and rewards that translate into political action for policy reform. Changes in governance or in policies affect outcomes, but also incentives in private production. Thus, in establishing an agenda for reform, it is important to start from a holistic view of the framework. The next section describes the steps for policy action to implement a strategy for enhancing inclusive growth.

B. Integrating Inclusive Growth into Policy Making

Drawing on the inclusive growth framework, policy makers must first *diagnose* the status of growth, inclusion, and sustainability. This entails establishing the current facts as well as factors driving the outlook over the medium and long run. Indicators include aggregate measures on poverty and inequality discussed in Section III, and also specific "gaps" in outcomes or opportunities, such as average incomes of different socio-economic groups and regions; and measures of access to healthcare, education, and other public services. Several organizations and international fora (e.g., United Nations, World Bank, IMF, World Economic Forum, OECD) provide comprehensive sets of country-level indicators that can be used to benchmark performance relative to peer countries and leading countries, or to use as aspirational targets. For example, the United Nations provides granular targets and indicators for its 17 Sustainable Development Goals, which can be mapped into the inclusive growth analytical framework.

Policymakers need to prioritize the goals of the overall strategy. Few countries are likely to do well on all aspects of inclusive growth. Most countries will have scope to improve in many areas. Based on the diagnosis, policy makers need to identify the most pressing concerns on growth, sustainability, and distributional issues, and the driving forces behind these concerns in order to prioritize the goals and targets of the inclusive growth strategy. For example, in some countries, poverty reduction may be the principal issue and may require focused efforts to raise aggregate growth and develop targeted social safety nets. Other countries may already benefit from strong growth, but face highly unequal outcomes or specific groups that have been left behind. Still other countries may be particularly vulnerable to climate shocks. In developing the overarching objectives and strategy of the reform, it is critical to consider the societies' main concerns, as well as stakeholders' interests and their capacity to support or block reform.

Implementation involves devising specific policies and targets for outcomes. After prioritizing the objectives of the IG strategy, an array of policies may still be required to promote strong, sustained, and broad-based growth because of the interdependence of private and government inputs and inclusive growth outcomes. A range of government ministries and agencies have authority over different policy elements. Choosing the specific policies needed to achieve the strategy requires an analysis of the driving forces behind growth, stability, and inclusion; and an analysis of the expected impact of the policy reform as well as its political feasibility. Insights can be gained from the economic literature and comparable country experiences, but inevitably some judgment of the country's specific circumstances will be required in designing the right policy mix.

As the strategy is implemented, it must be monitored and evaluated. First, at the micro level, progress on implementation of each policy action should be monitored and evaluated as to whether it is achieving the milestones on the path toward its targets. At the broader macro level, the full set of policy actions relating to the inclusive growth strategy should be assessed to ensure that the overall strategy is achieving the broad objective of inclusive growth. The process is iterative. There is a feedback between evaluation of the IG policy strategy back into diagnosis for adjusting the strategy over time as experience develops.

V. Road Map to Inclusive Growth

This section sets out the road map for how the book will flow. The structure draws on the inclusive growth framework established above. As noted earlier, inclusive growth is multi-dimensional and elements of the framework interact via complex linkages. The book chapters synthesize the extensive literature on each topic, but more importantly the book brings all the elements together, explores their linkages, and provides an assessment of the issues and policies.

Is there a tradeoff between raising growth and reducing inequality and poverty? Chapter 2 argues that there are complex linkages between growth and inclusion, with causation going in both directions and several channels mediating the relationship. Policy makers have been focused for decades on providing incentives for achieving the highest possible growth. But as discussed in Section I, high national growth has not necessarily been evenly shared. Redistribution can reduce inequality but may undermine incentives for the private sector to save and invest. On the other hand, redistribution may improve equality of opportunity that raises growth. Chapter 2 explores the various interrelationships between growth and inclusion and examines whether there are tradeoffs or synergies.

Private sector production drives growth but also determines the distribution of market incomes to factors of production. Trends in poverty and inequality often depend more on changes in the market or pre-tax distribution than in the post-tax distribution. For example, the lower level of inequality in France than in the US is attributed entirely to pretax inequality (Bozio, Garbinti, Goupille-Lebret, Guillot, and Piketty 2020). Chapters 3–5 consider the contributions to growth and inclusion associated with each of the main factors of production: labor (Chapter 3); capital/finance (Chapter 4); and technology (Chapter 5). Even though this section of the book focuses on the private sector, public policies and regulation can shape outcomes in the markets. Each chapter examines the operation of the private sector and the government policies that influence it.

Labor income absorbs the largest share of the economic pie, and for most people constitutes most if not all of their income. In fact, even in a capital-rich country like the US, relatively affluent people in the 90–95th percentile of the income distribution receive about 85 percent of their income from their labor services (Piketty, 2014). For most people, then, income inequality is directly tied to wage inequality. In many developing countries, informal work constitutes the bulk of employment, carrying little or no pension or welfare benefits, security against shocks, or protection against exploitation. Chapter 3 discusses the drivers of labor market outcomes and the key labor market policies used to influence inclusion.

Financial inclusion complements financial development by ensuring that a wide swath of society has access to vehicles for saving and for borrowing to invest in human capital and business opportunities. The conversion of savings into investment adds to capital and spurs economic growth, while also determining the dynamics of wealth. Chapter 4 identifies how gaps in financial access are related to structural and policy factors, and recommends that policymakers focus on identifying and reducing frictions.

Technological progress is the principal force behind rising global prosperity, but also risks major disruption. Technological progress has contributed to a widening of wage differences between skilled and unskilled labor. Looking ahead, there is fear that technology, including automation and artificial intelligence, will take away human jobs. Chapter 5 analyzes the economic forces behind these developments and delineates economic policies to mitigate adverse effects.

Factors of production do not operate in isolation; they are organized into firms that compete in markets for goods and services. Since 2000, there has been a rise in market concentration and corporate market power. Moreover, while some types of technology may be non-rival in use (so theoretically can facilitate broad-based growth), in practice technology is generated by innovation activity that is excludable and may permit supernormal returns for some time. Chapter 6 considers the debate on the interaction of innovation and competition with inclusive growth.

Countries are becoming increasingly connected, with flows of goods, people, capital, and technology across borders. While Chapters 3–6 consider how factors of production and markets in general impact inclusive growth, Chapters 7–9 examine integration of factor and goods markets across national boundaries. A sizeable part of the income of any individual is determined by her/his country of residence, with wide disparities in income levels across countries. The rise in globalization reflects a strong incentive to share in the global economic pie through trade (Chapter 7), financial integration (Chapter 8), and migration (Chapter 9).

Some have attributed the rise in inequality to the concurrent rise in trade competition, especially from EMEs like China, spurring trade tensions and calls for protection. Chapter 7 investigates the conflicting literature on aggregate benefits of trade versus the adverse and persistent impact of trade, especially import competition, on specific industries and local communities. The chapter then considers the evidence for using trade policies and other complementary policies for adjustment and compensation to those adversely affected.

Capital account liberalization has been both lauded and condemned for its impact on growth, instability, and inequality. Chapter 8 considers the evidence for how capital flows impact inclusive growth. The chapter argues that the impact of financial globalization varies by type of capital flow. It traces the impact through different channels and the implications for policies.

Migration has been another source of globalization triggering backlash in some countries. Chapter 9 reviews the literature on how migrants impact growth and inequality in both the destination and source country. Migration also generates large flows of remittances that have macroeconomic consequences, especially in the country of origin.

The next section of the book explicitly considers the role of the government in fostering inclusive growth. This includes establishing the institutions and governing conditions of the economy (Chapter 10), using its policy instruments to promote economic stability (Chapter 11), and directly impacting the distribution of income through tax policies (Chapter 12) and spending and transfers (Chapter 13), especially in key public services such as health and education (Chapter 14). Understanding the appropriate tools for improving inclusive growth is not enough. Public policies must be implemented within a given national or local system of unequal political power. Chapter 15 considers the political processes that mold policy implementation and reform.

Strong governance is an important aspect of ensuring inclusive prosperity. Governance includes the institutional frameworks and practices of the public sector, mechanisms and quality of oversight of key institutions like the central bank, oversight of the financial system, regulation of the private sector to address market failures, and the rule of law including protection of property rights. Chapter 10 considers options for strengthening governance through enhancing capacity and efficiency of public sector operations and reducing opportunities for corruption.

Macroeconomic volatility and crises can hinder economic growth and elevate poverty and inequality. Macroeconomic stabilization is therefore a critical foundation for improving inclusive growth. Chapter 11 reviews the evidence on how volatility imparts economic damages, and discusses the macroeconomic tools that can be used to avoid crises and to stabilize the economic cycle.

Taxation serves to raise revenue to finance government spending priorities, but can also be a tool for redistribution. Chapter 12 discusses the principles to achieve an efficient and equitable outcome. It then provides guidance on practical tax design and political economy considerations for choosing an appropriate tax structure.

Government expenditure promotes inclusive growth through the provision of public services and infrastructure and typically achieves more redistribution than does taxation. Chapter 13 reviews the evidence for the impact of public spending on inclusive growth and discusses different spending policy instruments and the role of initial conditions and institutions.

Education and health are among the most critical components of public expenditure for eliminating poverty and improving inclusive growth. Chapter 14 delves in depth into how to deliver improvements in learning and well-being, while ensuring that countries are spending most effectively to provide access and quality in education and health care services.

The political economy defines the relationship between the state and its citizens, molding the pre-distribution economic structure and also affecting inequality by redistribution through the tax and spending. Chapter 15 investigates what determines a society's preferences for redistribution and how institutional and legal conditions shape the state's capacity to deliver redistribution.

The next section considers inequalities in outcomes, focusing on key types of disparities (gender, regional, generational). These relate to distributional outcomes and opportunities for subgroups of a population other than the broad categories of factors of production, and they partly reflect historical or cultural influences.

Despite progress in narrowing the gaps, gender disparities persist. Chapter 16 outlines the status of gender gaps in labor market inclusion, as well as other legal, political, and cultural obstacles to women's participation in economic life. Given the pervasive nature of gender disparities, the chapter outlines a panoply of policies to break barriers and foster gender equity.

Different regions within countries face significant disparities in economic performance and living standards, contributing to overall inequality. Chapter 17 debates options for reducing regional disparities through policies focused on raising growth and business opportunities in lagging regions; integrating or better connecting leading and lagging regions; or improving the ability of people in lagging regions to relocate to leading regions.

Poverty is typically concentrated among the young and elderly; increasingly social mobility across generations is declining. Chapter 18 reviews the evidence on the heightened vulnerability among the youth and the elderly. It presents options for improving labor market prospects of the youth and protecting the elderly through public pension and medical programs. It also addresses the declining social mobility and how to improve intergenerational equity.

Many of the poorest people in the world live in resource-based economies that face conflict, corruption, and impending exhaustion of the resource wealth. Chapter 19 considers how to share resource wealth across generations including through adoption of the right fiscal frameworks, as well as by investing in education, health, and improving governance to reduce conflict and fragility.

Climate change is arguably the most significant threat to the wellbeing of future generations. Chapter 20 summarizes the scientific evidence on the impact of climate change. It then elaborates the economic instruments that can be used to mitigate climate change and discusses policy options for the most vulnerable countries to adapt to the coming hazards.

Chapter 21 considers case studies of countries or regions that improved inclusive growth through a holistic set of policies. This complements the examples of country policies on specific topics that are discussed in individual book chapters. The Nordic countries epitomize some of the best practices in inclusive growth policies, serving as an aspirational target. But even while emerging and developing economies face enormous challenges, they can still make progress in improving growth and inclusion. The chapter discusses a few such cases.

Chapter 22 concludes with a recap of some main issues, but also provides a way forward for policy-makers and practitioners interested in taking additional steps to improve inclusive growth. These include identifying areas where additional analysis is most needed and providing resources for further information on the dimensions of inclusive growth. The chapter also includes the role of civil society and international community in supporting countries' IG efforts (e.g., IMF programs, surveillance, and capacity building; UN's SDGs; and aid partners).

References

Almeida, V. 2020. "Income Inequality and Redistribution in the Aftermath of the 2007–2008 Crisis: The U.S. Case." *National Tax Journal* 73(1): 77–114, 77.

Alon, T., M. Doepke, J. Olmstead-Rumsey, and M. Tertilt. 2020. "This Time It's Different: The Role of Women's Employment in a Pandemic Recession," CEPR Discussion Paper 15149.

Alvaredo, Facundo, Lucas Chancel, Thomas Piketty, Emmanuel Saez, and Gabriel Zucman (Eds.). 2018. World Inequality Report.

Alvaredo, Facundo, Anthony B. Atkinson, Thomas Piketty, Emmanuel Saez, and Gabriel Zucman (Eds.). 2013. September 1. The World Wealth and Income Database (WID).

Anand, Sudhir and Paul Segal. 2008. "What Do We Know about Global Income Inequality?" *Journal of Economic Literature*, 46(1), March 2008 (pp. 57–94).

Anderson, S., P. Francois, and A. Kotwal. 2015. "Clientelism in Indian Villages." *American Economic Review 2015*, 105(6): 1780–816.

Atkinson, Anthony. 1970. "On the Measurement of Inequality." *Journal of Economic Theory* 2(3): 244–63. doi:10.1016/0022–0531(70)90039–6

Auten, Gerald, and David Splinter. 2018. "Using Tax Data to Measure Long-Term Trends in US Income Inequality," Treasury Office of Tax Analysis Working Paper.

Auten, Gerald, Geoffrey Gee, and Nicholas Turner. 2013. "Income Inequality, Mobility, and Turnover at the Top in the US, 1987–2010." *American Economic Review: Papers and Proceedings* 103(3): 168–72.

Bartels, Larry. 2008. *Unequal Democracy: The Political Economy of the New Gilded Age*. Princeton, NJ: Princeton University Press.

Bourguignon, François. 2016. *The Globalization of Inequality*. Princeton and Oxford: Princeton University Press.

Bozio, Antoine, Bertrand Garbinti, Malka Guillot, Jonathan Goupille-Lebret, and Thomas Piketty. 2020. "Predistribution vs. Redistribution: Evidence from France and the U.S," Working Papers 2020–24, Center for Research in Economics and Statistics.

Burkhauser, Richard V., Shuaizhang Feng, Stephen P. Jenkins, and Jeff Larrimore. 2009. "Recent Trends in Top Income Shares in the USA: Reconciling Estimates from March CPS and IRS Tax Return Data." National Bureau of Economic Research Working Paper 15320.

Chancel, Lucas. 2019. "Ten facts about Inequality in Advanced Economies." WID. world Working Paper 2019/15.

Chetty, Raj, Nathaniel Hendren, Patrick Kline, and Emmanuel Saez. 2014. "Where is the Land of Opportunity? The Geography of Intergenerational Mobility in the United States." *The Quarterly Journal of Economics* 129(4): 1553–623.

Congressional Budget Office. November 2018. The Distribution of Household Income, 2015.

Corak, M. 2013. "Income Inequality, Equality of Opportunity, and Intergenerational Mobility." *Journal of Economic Perspectives* 27(3): 79–102.

Credit Suisse. 2019. "Global Wealth Report," Research Institute.

Dabla-Norris, Era, Kalpana Kochhar, Nujin Suphaphiphat, Franto Ricka, and Evridiki Tsounta. 2015. *Causes and Consequences of Income Inequality: A Global Perspective*, Staff Discussion Notes No. 15/13.

Davies, J. B., S. Sandström, A. Shorrocks, and E.N. Wolff. 2008. "The World Distribution of Household Wealth," Discussion Paper 2008/03, UNI-WIDER, Helsinki.

European Commission. 2020. "Europe 2020: A Strategy for Smart, Sustainable, and Inclusive Growth," Brussels.

Exton, Carrie, and Michal Shinwell. 2018. "Policy Use of Well-being Metrics: Describing Countries' Experiences," OECD SDD Working Paper No. 94.

FAO, IFAD, UNICEF, WFP, and WHO. 2020. "The State of Food Security and Nutrition in the World 2020. Transforming food systems for affordable healthy diets." Rome, FAO. https://doi.org/10.4060/ca9692en

Foster, James, Joel Greer, and Erik Thorbecke. 1984. "A class of Decomposable Poverty Measures." *Econometrica* 52(3): 761–6. doi:10.2307/1913475

Gallup blog. 2020. "Economics Alone Don't Tell the Full Story of Poverty," https://news.gallup.com/opinion/gallup/320912/economics-alone-don-tell-full-story-poverty.aspx

Gallup blog. 2020. "Optimism About Black Americans' Opportunities in U.S. Falls," https://news.gallup.com/poll/320114/optimism-black-americans-opportunities-falls.aspx

Gilens, Martin. 2005. "Inequality and Democratic Responsiveness." *Public Opinion Quarterly* 69: 778–96.

Gilens, Martin. 2012. *Affluence and Influence: Economic Inequality and Political Power in America*. Russell Sage Foundation and Princeton University Press.

Hoover Jr, Edgar Malone. 1936. "The Measurement of Industrial Localization." *Review of Economics and Statistics* 18: 162–71.

International Monetary Fund. 2020. "Measuring Economic Welfare: What and How?," Washington.

Ipsos Global Advisors. March 2020. "Global Views on Acceptable Behavior and Equality in the Workplace," International Women's Day 2020, https://www.ipsos.com/sites/default/files/ct/news/documents/2020%9603/international-womens-day-global-views-on-gender-equality-and-acceptable-behavior-in-the-workplace-us.pdf

Kennedy, John F. October 3, 1963. "Remarks in Heber Springs, Arkansas, at the Dedication of Grers Ferry Dam." The American Presidency Project.

Kennedy, Robert. 1968. Speech at the University of Kansas on March 18, 1968.

Kharas, Homi, and Brina Seidel. April 2018. "What's Happening to The World Income Distribution? The Elephant Chart Revisited." *Brookings Global Economy & Development Working Paper* 114.

Kuznets, Simon. 1962. "How to Judge Quality." *The New Republic* 147: 29–32.

Lloyd's Register Foundation. 2019. "The Lloyd's Register Foundation World Risk Poll: Full Report and Analysis of the 2019 Poll," London.

Maddison Project Database. 2018. Bolt, Jutta, Robert Inklaar, Herman de Jong, and Jan Luiten van Zanden, "Rebasing 'Maddison': new income comparisons and the shape of long-run economic development," Maddison Project Working paper 10.

Rognlie, Matthew. 2016. "Deciphering the Fall and Rise in the Net Capital Share: Accumulation or Scarcity?" *Brookings Papers on Economic Activity* 2016(1): 1–69.

Milanovich. 2016. *Global Inequality: A New Approach for the Age of Globalization.* Cambridge, MA: Harvard University Press.

Norton, Michael I., and Dan Ariely. 2011. "Building a Better America—One Wealth Quintile at a Time." *Perspectives on Psychological Science* 6(1) (January): 9–12.

OECD. 2015. *In It Together: Why Less Inequality Benefits All.* Paris: OECD Publishing, http://dx.doi.org/10.1787/9789264235120-en.

OECD. 2020. "How's Life? 2020: Measuring Well-being." Paris: OECD Publishing, https://doi.org/10.1787/9870c393-en.

Oxfam. 2017. "An Economy for the 99%," Oxfam Briefing Paper.

Palma, José Gabriel. 2011. "Homogeneous middles vs. heterogeneous tails, and the end of the 'Inverted-U': the share of the rich is what it's all about," Cambridge Working Papers in Economics (CWPE) 1111. Cambridge University.

Pew Research Center. 2013. Global Attitudes Project Spring 2013, Washington, D.C.

Pew Research Center. 2014. Global Attitudes Project Spring 2014, Washington, D.C.

Pew Research Center. 2019. Global Attitudes Project Spring 2019, Washington, D.C.

Pew Research Center. 2020. Global Attitudes Project Spring 2020, Washington, D.C.

Piketty, Thomas. 2014. Capital in the Twenty-First Century. Cambridge, MA: Harvard University Press.

Piketty, Thomas, Emmanuel Saez, and Gabriel Zucman. 2018. "Distributional National Accounts: Methods and Estimates for the United States." *Quarterly Journal of Economics*, forthcoming.

Rank, Mark, and Thomas Hirschl. 2015. "The Likelihood of Experiencing Relative Poverty over the Life Course," *PLOS ONE*.

Ravallion, Martin, and Shaohua Chen, 2009. "The Impact of the Global Financial Crisis on the World's Poorest." VoxEU.

Ravallion, Martin, and Shaohua Chen. 2003. "Measuring Pro-Poor Growth," *Economics Letters* 78: 93–9.

Ravallion, Martin. 2018. "Inequality and Globalization: A Review Essay." *Journal of Economic Literature* 56(2): 620–42.

Rawls, John. 1971. *A Theory of Justice.* Cambridge, MA: Harvard University Press.

Roser, Max. OurWorldInData.org, https://ourworldindata.org/a-history-of-global-living-conditions-in-5-charts.

Smith, Matthew, Danny Yagan, Owen Zidar, and Eric Zwick. 2019. "Capitalists in the Twenty-First Century." *The Quarterly Journal of Economics* 134(4): 1675–745.

Smith, Matthew, Danny Yagan, Owen Zidar, and Eric Zwick. 2020. "The Rise of Pass-Throughs and the Decline of the Labor Share," Manuscript.

Smith, Matthew, Owen Zidar, and Eric Zwick. 2020. "Top Wealth in America: New Estimates and Implications for Taxing the Rich," Working Papers 264, Princeton University, Department of Economics, Center for Economic Policy Studies.

Solt, Frederick. 2020. "Measuring Income Inequality Across Countries and Over Time: The Standardized World Income Inequality Database." *Social Science Quarterly* 101(3): 1183–99. SWIID Version 9.0, October 2020.

Stiglitz, Joseph, Jean-Paul Fitoussi, and Martine Durand. 2018. *Beyond GDP Measuring What Counts for Economic and Social Performance*. Paris: OECD Publishing.

Tai, Don Bambino Geno, Aditya Shah, Chyke A. Doubeni, Irene G. Sia, and Mark L. Wieland. 2021. "The Disproportionate Impact of COVID-19 on Racial and Ethnic Minorities in the United States." *Clinical Infectious Diseases* 72(4), 15 February 2021: 703–6.

Theil, Henri. 1967. *Economics and Information Theory*. Amsterdam: North Holland.

World Bank. 2020. *Poverty and Shared Prosperity: Reversals of Fortune*.

World Values Survey. 2014. https://www.worldvaluessurvey.org/WVSDocumentation WVLjsp

Zidar, Owen, and Eric Zwick. 2020. "A modest tax reform proposal to roll back federal tax policy to 1997," Working Paper.

Zucman, Gabriel. 2015. *The Hidden Wealth of Nations: The Scourge of Tax Havens*. Chicago, IL: University of Chicago Press.

2

Links Between Growth, Inequality, and Poverty

Valerie Cerra, Ruy Lama, and Norman Loayza

I. Introduction

The most commonly used measure of a country's economic activity and the overall well-being is gross domestic product (GDP).[1] It gauges the magnitude of economic production, which in turn affects the payments to factors of production such as capital and labor. GDP *growth* is therefore an estimate of how the aggregate income of a country increases over time. A country's aggregate income, in turn, provides resources that can increase the incomes of families and individuals.[2] Given these relationships, economists have long been concerned about explaining the determinants of economic growth and formulating policies to elevate it.

But whether economic growth is sufficient to improve the welfare of every individual depends on *how* the benefits of growth are spread across the society. If all individuals benefit proportionately, then studying growth through the device of a "representative agent" would be sufficient to determine the economic forces at work and the policy options needed to improve the welfare of each individual. However, if growth does not raise everyone's incomes proportionately, then an analysis of the economic welfare of an individual requires studying aggregate economic growth in conjunction with the distribution of income within the economy.[3]

[1] We thank Izzati Ab Razak and Jaime Sarmiento for their superb research assistance. We also thank Barry Eichengreen, Andrew Berg, Piergiorgio Carapella, Reda Cherif, Fuad Hasanov, Maksym Ivanyna, Futoshi Narita, Marco Pani, Martin Schindler, Nikola Spatafora, Xin Tang, Junjie Wei, Younes Zouhar, and participants in the Inclusive Growth book seminar series organized by the IMF Institute for Capacity Development for their comments.
[2] GDP omits some components of economic production, such as housework and home production, because it measures goods and services traded in market transactions. It also fails to deduct economic "bads" such as environmental degradation or to fully account for other aspects of well-being and happiness. For a full discussion, see the 2020 IMF report, *Measuring Economic Welfare: What and How?*.
[3] While there are multiple ways of measuring inclusiveness, this chapter focuses the analysis on two metrics: the poverty rate and the Gini coefficient of income distribution. The first measure captures the percentage of the population that is unable to meets its needs, based on an estimated threshold defining the cost of consumption basket for satisfying basic needs. To expand the coverage of data, this chapter uses the World Bank's threshold of $3.20 per day in purchasing power parity (PPP) terms, rather than the $1.90 PPP indicator of extreme poverty. The second measure of inclusiveness, the Gini coefficient, captures the degree of dispersion or inequality in the distribution of income, where a value

Valerie Cerra, Ruy Lama, and Norman Loayza, *Links Between Growth, Inequality, and Poverty* In: *How to Achieve Inclusive Growth*. Edited by: Valerie Cerra, Barry Eichengreen, Asmaa El-Ganainy, and Martin Schindler, Oxford University Press.
© Valerie Cerra, Ruy Lama, and Norman Loayza 2022. DOI: 10.1093/oso/9780192846938.003.0002

So, what is the relationship between growth and measures of the inclusion of individuals in the economy and society, such as inequality and poverty? Does growth help pull people out of poverty? And how does growth affect inequality, if at all? What about the reverse relationship: that is, how do poverty and inequality affect growth?

This chapter studies the nexus of growth, poverty, and inequality, seeking answers to these questions. The relationship between inequality and economic activity has been a subject of interest throughout the history of economic thought. In the *Wealth of Nations*, Adam Smith (1776) noted that wealth inequality could lead to social unrest and that the government had a role in protecting property rights and preventing the poor from seizing the property of the rich. From a different perspective, in the mid-nineteenth century, Karl Marx saw capitalism as exacerbating inequality, making capital owners richer and workers poorer over time. He thought that this polarization of income could lead to a revolution, where a communist system eventually would replace capitalism (Marx 1867). The complex relationship between income distribution and growth has continued to receive attention from many other economists, including the seminal works of Simon Kuznets (1955) and Nicholas Kaldor (1957). Furthermore, the study of inequality and growth has been facilitated by developments in data collection on poverty, wealth, and labor market conditions. For instance, Charles Booth (1891), in *Life and Labour of the People in London*, published maps describing wealth and poverty levels street by street in the city of London. About the same time in the United States, Carroll Wright, the first US Commissioner of Labor, was a pioneer in the collection of labor market statistics. He initiated the collection of data on wages and labor conditions of women and also published studies describing how the adoption of new machinery affected wages and employment. These advances in data collection continued over the twentieth century and made it possible to conduct a systematic analysis on the links between growth and inclusiveness.

Multiple channels link growth to inclusion and inclusion to growth, making it difficult to determine causation. Moreover, many factors affect growth and inclusion simultaneously. Compounding these issues, data on poverty and inequality have been difficult to compile, are collected and measured infrequently, and are often unreliable. Estimates are sensitive to assumptions on factors such as capital gains and untaxed income (Chapter 1) and alternative measures may show different trends (Blotevogel et al. 2020). Empirical studies, especially those exploring the link between growth and inequality, sometimes find inconsistent results, no doubt due to these multiple channels, endogenous relationships, and poor data

---

of 1 indicates maximum inequality (whereby one person accrues all income) and 0 indicates perfect equality (whereby everyone in the entire population receives the same income). Additional indicators that might capture different dimensions of inequality, living standards, and inclusiveness are discussed in more detail in Chapter 1, along with their limitations.

quality. As a starting point, the next section presents key stylized facts and trends of inequality, poverty, and economic growth across different world regions and over time. Sections III and IV then discuss the channels linking the variables on this nexus, drawing on the theoretical and empirical literature. Section V concludes with the key takeaways and policy implications.

II. Trends in Inequality, Poverty, and Growth

Market-based income inequality has risen steadily in advanced economies and some large emerging market economies. Figure 2.1 shows the evolution across country groups of income inequality, measured by the Gini coefficients for market-based income (before taxes and transfers) and disposable income (after taxes and transfers). The key distinctive feature of the evolution of income inequality has been the large and sustained increase in the market-based Gini coefficient in advanced economies in each decade from the 1980s through the

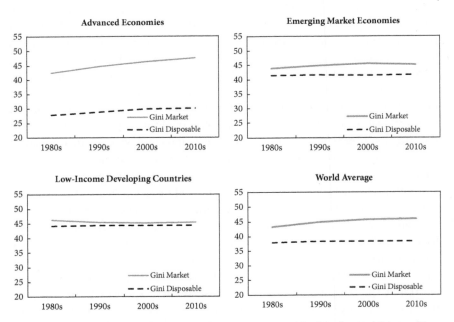

Figure 2.1 Inequality across Country Groups, 1980s–2010s *(Market and Disposable Income Gini Coefficients)*

Note: Gini market indicates the Gini coefficient before taxes and transfers. Gini disposable indicates the Gini coefficient after taxes and transfers. A higher/lower Gini coefficient indicates greater/less inequality. The average index for the 2010s is up to 2019. Country groups are defined according to WEO Methodology. For details see https://www.imf.org/external/pubs/ft/weo/faq.htm#q4b2.

Sources: Standardized World Income Inequality Database (SWIID); and authors' calculations.

2010s.[4] In contrast, income inequality for emerging market and developing economies (EMDEs) as a group has been broadly unchanged since the 1980s.[5] As a result of these contrasting trends, market inequality in advanced economies has surpassed that of EMDEs, on average, in recent decades, from a lower relative level in the 1980s (Table 2.1). Despite the relatively stable trend for EMDEs, some of the largest emerging market countries—notably China, Russia, India, South Africa, and Indonesia—have experienced increasing market inequality (Table 2.1). In addition, inequality varies considerably more across emerging markets and low-income countries—especially the former, where outliers range from a low Gini coefficient (index) in the range 20 to 30 to nearly 70 (Figure 2.2, left panel). The variation in inequality across countries is especially pronounced when comparing the ratio of income of the top decile relative to the bottom decile of each country's income distribution (right panel). For emerging markets and low-income countries, the ratio exceeds 20 for several countries.

Fiscal redistribution through taxes and transfers reduces income inequality, especially in advanced economies. The disposable income (or net) Gini coefficient (after taxes and transfers) drops to an average of 30 points from nearly 50 points for advanced economies, bringing net inequality much below that of other income groups. In contrast, redistribution is very limited in emerging markets and low-income countries, where the tax base and resources available for redistribution tend to be much smaller than in advanced economies.

Poverty rates are low in advanced economies and have been declining in developing countries from a high level. Figure 2.3 illustrates the dynamics of the poverty rate, measured as the fraction of the population that earns less than $3.20 a day in purchasing power parity (PPP) terms. Not surprisingly, the poverty rate in advanced economies has been low and stable during the sample period (top left panel), given that most people in those countries have an income level substantially higher than the poverty threshold (Table 2.1). Most of the dynamics in poverty reduction since the 1970s has been concentrated in emerging markets and low-income countries (top right and bottom left panels of Figure 2.3), with emerging markets experiencing the largest reduction in poverty rates.

While GDP per capita growth in advanced economies has been slowing down every decade since the 1980s, growth has accelerated in emerging markets and low-income countries, particularly since the 2000s (Duttagupta and Narita 2017).[6]

---

[4] This section analyzes trends in poverty and inequality starting in 1980s. Longer time series on wealth and income inequality have been collected by Piketty (2014) and are restricted mostly to advanced economies. Piketty and Saez (2014) report sustained improvements in wealth and income distribution across Europe and the United States from the 1930s to 1970s, followed by a worsening of inequality starting in the 1970s to 1980s. This section captures the rise in inequality in advanced economies starting in the 1980s. Later sections examine several channels that might account for this more recent trend.

[5] Fabrizio et al. (2017) and Tang (2021) provide an overview of income inequality trends and issues in low-income countries.

[6] Johnson and Papageorgiou (2020) present a literature survey on growth convergence.

Table 2.1 Inequality and Poverty in the 2010s Compared to the 1980s, Selected Countries and Country Groups

Country	Initial Gini (1980s)	Final Gini (2010s)	Change in Gini	Initial Poverty (1980s)	Final Poverty (2010s)	Change in Poverty
Brazil	60.9	55.2	−5.8	37.5	8.6	−28.9
Canada	40.7	45.5	4.7	0.4	0.4	0.0
China	30.2	41.4	11.2	...	15.2	...
France	48.2	49.0	0.8	1.6	0.1	−1.5
Germany	42.5	51.9	9.4	...	0.1	...
India	42.1	49.0	6.9	84.9	61.7	−23.2
Indonesia	39.6	42.6	3.1	91.1	33.9	−57.2
Italy	43.9	49.3	5.4	0.8	1.9	1.1
Japan	37.8	45.6	7.8	...	0.6	...
Mexico	46.8	47.2	0.4	19.0	10.2	−8.8
Russia	35.3	45.6	10.4	...	0.5	...
South Africa	65.7	68.5	2.8	...	36.4	...
Turkey	44.4	43.1	−1.3	13.2	2.6	−10.6
United Kingdom	46.4	52.9	6.5	1.2	0.3	−0.9
United States	44.7	50.8	6.1	0.7	1.2	0.5
Country classification						
Advanced economies	42.6	46.9	4.3	0.8	0.5	−0.3
Emerging markets	44.9	45.1	0.2	34.7	9.0	−25.7
Low-income developing countries	46.2	44.9	−1.2	62.3	46.4	−16.0
World average	44.3	45.5	1.2	29.1	12.1	−16.9

Note: A negative/positive change in the Gini market coefficient indicates less/more inequality. Initial Gini market (1980s): average index for the 1980s. Final Gini market (2010s): average index for the 2010s up to 2019. Initial poverty ratio (1980s) at $3.20 a day: average index for the 1980s. Final poverty ratio (2010s) at $3.20 a day: average index for the 2010s up to 2019. The data points given for advanced economies, emerging market economies, and low-income developing countries use the IMF classifications and data for all countries in those categories.

Sources: *Standardized World Income Inequality Database* (SWIID); World Bank; and authors' calculations.

Figure 2.4 shows recent trends in GDP per capita growth across different groups of countries. Globalization allowed a large pool of the workforce in emerging markets and low-income countries to participate in the global markets through international trade, which arguably increased growth and reduced poverty rates (top right and bottom left panels) (Dollar and Kraay 2004). During the same period, advanced economies experienced a slowdown in GDP per capita growth rates, which worsened in the 2010s as a consequence of the global financial crisis (top left panel). Some of the long-term structural factors that might be behind the

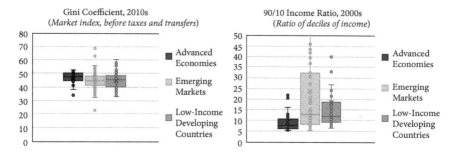

Figure 2.2 Indicators of Inequality across Country Groups, 2000s and 2010s

Note: For each decade, the box in the whisker plot depicts the spread between the 25th and 75th percentiles of the Gini market coefficient (Panel 1) or the income ratio between the bottom 90 percent and top 10 percent of the population (Panel 2) across countries in each country group.

Sources: *Standardized World Income Inequality Database* (SWIID); and authors' calculations.

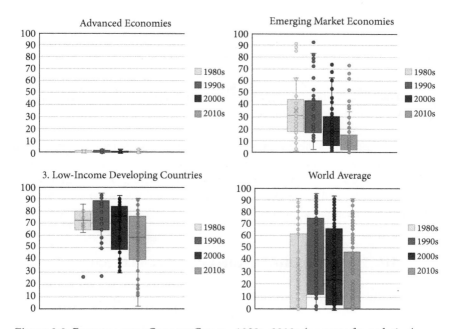

Figure 2.3 Poverty across Country Groups, 1980s–2010s *(percent of population)*

Note: For each decade, the box in the whisker plot depicts the spread in the poverty ratio between the 25th and 75th percentiles of the population across countries in each country group. The poverty ratio is in terms of 2011 purchasing power parity (PPP). The poverty ratio uses the poverty measure of $3.20 per day.

Sources: *Standardized World Income Inequality Database* (SWIID); and authors' calculations.

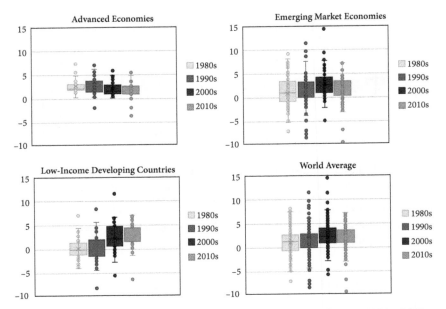

Figure 2.4 Average Growth in GDP per capita across Country Groups, 1980s–2010s
(percent)

Note: For each decade, the box in the whisker plot depicts the spread of the average growth in real GDP
per capita between the 25th and 75th percentiles of the population across countries in each country group.

Sources: World Bank; and authors' calculations.

slowdown in per capita income growth are related to aging (Bloom, Canning, and
Fink 2010) and a generalized slowdown in productivity growth (Gordon 2018).

With these facts and trends on inequality, poverty, and growth examined, the
rest of the chapter will comprehensively review the multiple dimensions through
which inclusiveness and growth are related.

III. How Does Growth Affect Poverty and Inequality?

A. Empirical Estimates of the Impact of Growth on Poverty and Inequality

The impact of growth on poverty and inequality depends on how income growth
at each percentile of the distribution compares with average income (GDP)
growth. Figure 2.5 shows that the income of the poor is strongly correlated with
GDP per capita, both in levels (top left panel) and in growth rates (middle left
panel). This clearly illustrates the adage that a "rising tide lifts all boats," in the
sense that when average GDP per capita rises, income in the lowest decile also
increases and poverty falls.

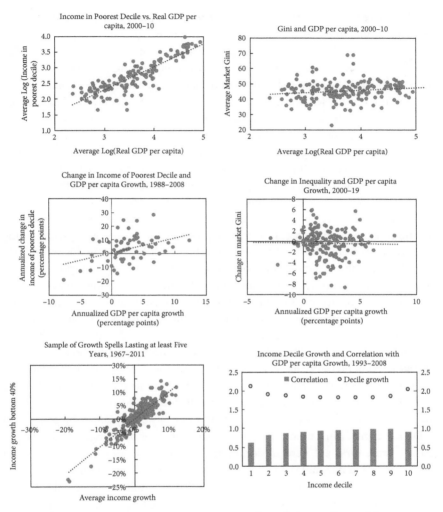

Figure 2.5 Relationships among GDP per capita, Growth, Inequality, and Poverty

Note: In Panel 2, market Gini is before taxes and transfers. All data on GDP per capita, income of the poorest decile, and their growth rates are in real terms.

Sources: Dollar, Kleineberg, and Kraay 2016; World Bank Open Knowledge repository CC By-NC-ND 3.0; *Standardized World Income Inequality Database* (SWIID); IMF staff; and authors' calculations.

The poverty-reducing effect of growth has been corroborated in several studies. Dollar and Kraay (2002) investigate the systematic relationship between economic growth and poverty reduction for a sample of 92 countries from 1950 to 1999. These authors find a robust pattern across countries where the share of income of the first quintile of the population varies proportionally to average incomes. They uncover a strong and positive relationship between these two variables, with a correlation coefficient that is not statistically different from one.

Dollar and Kraay also evaluate the extent to which policies and institutions that have been identified in the literature as promoting growth can play a role in reducing poverty by increasing the share of income of the poorest quantile. The main conclusion of this analysis is that growth-enhancing policies and institutions do benefit the poor and the rest of the society in equal proportions.

Building on this work, using data from a panel of 80 countries, Kraay (2006) decomposes the changes in absolute poverty into three potential sources: the growth rate of average income; the sensitivity of poverty to growth; and a poverty-reducing pattern of growth (changes in relative income). In the short term, growth in average income accounts for 70 percent of the variation in poverty changes, while in the long term, it accounts for 97 percent. This study reemphasizes that growth-enhancing policies and institutions are central to alleviating poverty.

Dollar, Kleineberg, and Kraay (2016) update their analysis on the systematic relationship between average growth and growth of the poorest groups, examining 151 countries from 1967 to 2011. Similar to the result in Dollar and Kraay (2002), they find that the income in the poorest deciles varies in equal proportions with average incomes (Figure 2.5, bottom left panel). They also find that on average, the shares of income accruing to the poorest 20th percentile and 40th percentile are fairly stable over time. These results emphasize the idea that policies aimed directly at increasing economic growth rates are indeed "pro-poor," in the sense that they lift the average income in the lowest deciles of the income distribution.

More recent literature has corroborated the importance of economic growth in reducing poverty. Analyzing the dynamics of the extreme poverty rate (PPP $1.90 per day poverty line) in 135 countries from 1974 to 2018, Bergstrom (2020) finds that 90 percent of the variation of poverty rates can be explained by changes in GDP per capita, while much of the rest is accounted for by changes in inequality.[7] At the same time, a 1 percent decline in inequality (measured as the standard deviation of log income) reduces poverty more than a 1 percent increase in GDP per capita for most countries in the sample. These results are reconciled by the fact that changes in mean growth have been substantially larger than observed changes in inequality. The study confirms that although growth has been the dominant force in poverty reduction, reductions in inequality have great potential in reducing poverty rates.

While both economic growth and inequality have an impact on social welfare, growth has been the dominant force. Dollar, Kleineberg, and Kraay (2015) construct social welfare functions that are sensitive to the bottom deciles, where welfare depends positively on income growth and negatively on inequality. Focusing on five decades of data for 151 countries, they find that most of the variation in welfare across countries is driven by the average growth of income. The role

---

[7] Additional studies such as Bluhm, de Crombrugghe, and Szirmai (2018) and Fosu (2017) also find that poverty reduction has been driven primarily by economic growth, with changes in income distribution playing a secondary, albeit important, role.

played by inequality is relatively minor—again because changes in inequality have been small and generally uncorrelated with growth. These results imply that policies aimed at reducing inequality will improve welfare as long as they are not detrimental to growth but may reduce social welfare if they reduce growth. Complementary results from Jones and Klenow (2016) show that GDP per capita is a good indicator of welfare for most countries, as these two variables have a correlation of 0.98. Moreover, they find that welfare inequality is greater than income inequality across countries. The mortality rate is the most important factor driving the dispersion in welfare.

In contrast to poverty, there is no significant systematic relationship between a country's income level and its market inequality (Figure 2.5, top right panel). The simple cross-country evidence is not consistent with the Kuznets curve model that postulates an inverse U-shaped relationship between development and inequality.[8] Likewise, per capita GDP growth is uncorrelated with contemporaneous changes in inequality, measured in the middle right panel of Figure 2.5 by the market Gini coefficient. The same lack of correlation is observed if inequality is measured by the change in the income ratio of the top to bottom deciles (not shown). Part of the explanation for the weak correlation between growth and inequality lies in the strong correlation between per capita GDP growth and *each* of the income deciles. As shown in the bottom right panel of Figure 2.5, the correlation coefficient ranges between 0.6 to nearly 1.0. In addition, the change in inequality depends on the relative growth in incomes in each decile across the distribution, called the "growth incidence curve" (as discussed in Chapter 1). For the sample of all countries, the income of the bottom and top deciles grew slightly faster than middle deciles over 1993–2008. Fast growth of the bottom would decrease inequality, while fast growth at the top would increase it, for an ambiguous overall impact.

In short, the impact of growth on poverty and inequality depends on how growth is distributed across the rich and poor. The discussion that follows describes the various channels by which growth can result in differential income growth rates for different socioeconomic groups.

B. Channels from Growth to Poverty and Inequality

The Neoclassical Growth Model

What does growth theory predict for the impact of growth on inclusion? The standard workhorse theory is the neoclassical growth model (Solow 1956), in which output is a function $Y=F(A,K,L)$ of factors of production, including capital (K), labor (L), and total factor productivity or TFP (A). Investment leads to

---

[8] Note, however, that the original Kuznets formulation is for structural transformation for a country over time, as discussed in section III.B, and does not necessarily apply to the cross-section of countries.

capital accumulation, which increases the marginal product of labor and the wage paid to workers. In addition, growth arising from increases in TFP raises the marginal products of both capital and labor and therefore the income payments that they receive. Higher investment and/or higher technological progress imply higher production and higher incomes for everyone in the economy. In addition, because of diminishing returns to capital, capital-poor countries are expected to grow faster and eventually converge to capital-rich countries.

This simple model has been the cornerstone of much of growth theory. Given its one-sector structure in which both capital owners and workers benefit from growth, the policy implication is to focus on improving incentives for investment for economies to grow and converge more quickly to the (higher-than-initial) steady state capital stock. The model does not account for any heterogeneity in capital ownership and labor supply within a country but predicts a decline in global poverty and inequality as poor countries catch up. Implicitly, this analytical framework is centered on aggregate growth, rather than on distributional issues.

Drawing on the neoclassical framework, Hausmann, Rodrik, and Velasco (2005) develop a general framework, "growth diagnostics," designed to inform policymakers on how to prioritize growth policies in a context of multiple distortions by targeting the most binding constraints. As in the neoclassical framework, with its emphasis on investment, economic growth depends on three elements: the returns to capital accumulation; their private appropriability; and the cost of financing capital investment. Distortions that can lower the return on capital include high taxes or expropriation risk, large negative externalities, low productivity, or insufficient investment in infrastructure or human capital. Distortions that increase the cost of financing investment include underdeveloped domestic financial markets due to lack of banking competition or a poor regulatory framework, and impediments to international financing due to high country-risk premium, excessive regulation of the capital account, or external debt vulnerabilities. However, the growth diagnostics analysis relies on a representative agent approach, which, like the Solow model, does not illuminate the distributional impacts of growth policies.

The basic neoclassical paradigm features a number of assumptions including: no government sector activities and redistribution; fully employed factors; a fixed and undifferentiated supply of labor; a competitive market structure; and balanced growth (no differential growth across sectors/industries/regions/firms, and so on). Relaxing each of these assumptions creates channels through which growth can have distributional effects, including for inequality and poverty. Each channel is considered in turn next.

The Government: Public Goods and Redistribution
Public Goods and Services
Growth increases aggregate resources, including the tax base and the public sector's capacity to collect taxes. A higher tax ratio facilitates the provision of public

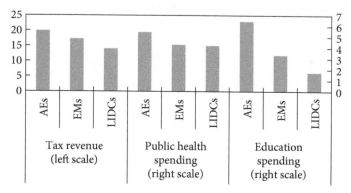

Figure 2.6 Tax Revenues and Spending on Health and Education, by Country Group *(percent of GDP, 2010–19 average)*

Note: AEs = advanced economies; EMs = emerging market economies; LIDCs = low-income developing countries.

Sources: World Bank; and authors' calculations.

goods such as health and education that can be pro-poor. The extent to which growth leads to an expansion of pro-poor public services depends on the society's preferences for private versus public goods and the composition of public goods. As shown in Figure 2.6, it is an empirical regularity that as countries become richer, the government is capable of raising more fiscal revenue and increasing the capacity of providing public goods. This stylized fact is better known as Wagner's Law (Wagner 1893) and captures a channel through which growth leads to an increase in the size of the government, which can reduce poverty and improve the income distribution provided spending is efficient and its composition benefits the poor.

Redistribution

As with public goods, the impact of growth on poverty and inequality through redistribution depends on social preferences. If poverty and inequality are considered social ills, people may be willing to "purchase" reductions in poverty and inequality through redistribution policies as overall incomes rise (that is, poverty and inequality reduction function as "normal goods," in which demand increases with income). Indeed, cross-country evidence shows that higher-income countries engage in more redistribution than developing countries (Figure 2.7), where redistribution is measured as the difference between the Gini before and after taxes and transfers. But the composition and incidence of taxes and transfers is important. For example, developing countries have high energy subsidies. This policy may be intended to support the poor, but instead largely benefits the rich who spend more on energy products (see Chapters 12 and 13 for elaboration on taxation and spending policies).

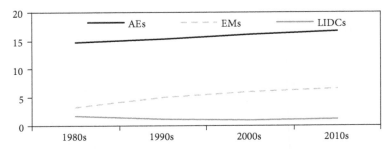

Figure 2.7 Income Redistribution by Country Group, 1980s–2010s *(difference in Gini points before and after taxes and transfers)*

Note: AEs = advanced economies; EMs = emerging market economies; LIDCs = low-income developing countries.

Sources: Standardized World Income Inequality Database (SWIID); and authors' calculations.

Factors and Markets

Employment of Factors

In the short and medium term, factors of production such as labor and capital are not necessarily fully employed. Recessions resulting from a variety of shocks, including financial distress and pandemics, can reduce long-term output (Cerra, Fatás, and Saxena forthcoming) and generate large spikes in unemployment and inequality and declines in capacity utilization (Heathcote, Perri, and Violante 2020). Unemployment creates income losses in the short term, especially for those in lower-income groups such as people with lower educational attainment, ethnic minorities, and women (Hoynes, Miller, and Schaller 2012). Unemployment often results in scarring effects on incomes over the longer term. As shown by von Wachter, Song, and Manchester (2009), 15 to 20 years after a layoff, earnings can be depressed by as much as 20 percent, as workers' skill set becomes outdated and they lose skills that are specific to the jobs lost in a specific industry. As described in Okun's Law (discussed in Chapter 3), unemployment varies inversely with cyclical growth (Ball, Leigh, and Loungani 2017). Higher growth generates employment, which improves inclusion. In general, economic volatility is associated with both lower growth and higher inequality (Chapter 11).

Another reason for unemployed or underemployed factors could be poverty traps that entail the inability of low-income individuals to pay any fixed costs of education, move to a booming region, or obtain collateral to obtain credit. Such individuals can be excluded from more remunerative productive activities or remain unable to meet a threshold of productivity. Those stuck in a poverty trap may not be able to benefit from growth in the absence of government intervention such as the provision of microcredit (see Banerjee et al. 2019).

Labor Supply Response

Growth that generates higher returns to labor would induce more work effort. If leisure is a normal good, then higher-income people would increase their work less than low-income people. Bick, Fuchs-Schündein, and Lagakos (2018) show empirically that this is the case across countries, where the average adult worker in a low-income country works 50 percent more hours than the adult workers in high-income countries. Moreover, within countries, on average, the number of hours worked decreases with the level of wages. The exception to these stylized facts occurs in very high-income countries, including the United States, where the number of hours increases with the wage rate.

Growth also leads to demographic changes, notably a decline in the number of children and investment in the upbringing of children (through parental efforts to educate them). Growth may induce women to enter the labor force, raising family incomes (and reducing poverty if women of poor families did not previously work outside the home). Becker (1992) analyses the interaction between fertility and growth. His economic framework shows how economic growth can result in a lower fertility rate, which reduces the labor supply and thus increases the return to labor.

Differentiated Labor

Labor is not homogeneous in practice. Educational attainment and skills vary across individuals. Technological progress has generally been more complementary to skilled and educated workers than to the unskilled and uneducated, leading to a higher demand for the former and a reduction in the demand for the latter. As a result of economic growth associated with skilled-biased technological change, the rising wage skill premium has increased inequality of labor income (Krusell et al. 2000).

In the United States, the observed increase in wage inequality since the 1980s can be attributed, at least partially, to the increase of the wage premium of college education. Autor (2014) and Autor, Katz, and Kearney (2008) show that the college wage premium roughly doubled between 1980 and 2012 for both male and female workers, in part due to skill-biased technological change that increased the demand for college-educated workers.[9] The relationship between growth and inequality through skill-biased technical change is not necessarily linear. Since the late 1980s, skill-biased technological change has led to job market polarization due to an increased demand for skilled and unskilled workers at expense of middle-class jobs, as new technologies are capable of performing routine tasks traditionally done by middle-wage workers (Goldin and Katz 2007).

Analyzing cross-country evidence, Brueckner, Dabla Norris, and Gradstein (2015) find that national income and distributional equity are positively related, with education as a possible channel. For a sample of 80 countries, the authors use two instruments for within-country variation of real GDP per capita, including international oil price fluctuations and countries' trade-weighted world income. The instrumental variables regressions show that, on average, a 1 percent increase in

---

[9] In addition, a slowdown in educational attainment starting in the early 1980s reduced the supply of skilled workers.

real GDP per capita reduces the Gini coefficient by around 0.08 percentage points. However, the importance of national income in explaining inequality is significantly reduced when education proxies are introduced, making education a probable channel.

Market Structure

Contrary to the assumptions in the Solow neoclassical growth model, many industries do not have perfectly competitive market structures. Natural monopolies, policy-induced monopolies, or industries supported by rents (particularly in the natural resource sectors) lead to high returns to owners without a commensurate rise in payments to labor. Returns to certain factors—entrepreneurship, capital, land, and resource ownership—rise faster than returns to labor (especially unskilled labor). Scale of market can be important—bigger markets provide higher returns to owners if competition can be avoided. There can also be network effects (such as in high-tech and communications sectors) and tournament effects (for instance, the best sport star earns much more than the second best; singers/actors benefit more from brand in large markets).

Diez, Leigh, and Tambunlertchai (2018) document that a generalized increase in market concentration (associated with higher markups) occurred across advanced economies and across industries. At high levels of markups and profitability, an increase in market concentration leads to lower investment and lower wages, which directly influences the income distribution and growth. De Loecker and Eeckhout (2018) also analyze the global evolution of market power from 1980 to 2016, based on data from Worldscope covering more than 60,000 firms located in 134 countries. They corroborate that the recent trend of rising markups and market power has been predominantly concentrated in advanced economies, while markups in most emerging economies have been either stable or declining.

For the United States, De Loecker, Eeckhout, and Unger (2020) show that markups nearly tripled between 1980 and 2016, increasing from 21 percent above marginal cost to 61 percent. The rise in markups was greatest for firms in the upper tail of the distribution: that is, with markups that were already high compared to the average. Those firms expanded at the expense of firms with low markups. This rise in markups can account for recent macroeconomic trends such as the secular decline in labor shares and the wage reduction of low-skilled workers. For a cost-minimizing firm, the labor share is inversely related to the markup. Greater market power also implies fewer firms, lower output, and reduced aggregate demand for labor, negatively affecting real wages and income inequality. Autor et al. (2020) also analyze the consequences of firm size on the labor market share by developing a framework for superstar firms characterized by a "winner takes most" feature. They provide evidence for the United States that industries that exhibited the largest increase in market concentration have also experienced larger declines in the labor market share. Chapter 6 discusses the role market structure plays in shaping inclusive growth in more detail.

Unbalanced Growth

For a variety of reasons, different sectors, industries, regions, and firms may grow at different rates. Many of the sources of growth, including technology and trade, could improve growth in some economic sectors more than in others. Uneven growth produces uneven returns. When some sectors boom but others lag, growth is not likely to raise incomes proportionately. Payments to factors may fall in some cases. As some industries emerge and others disappear in a process of "creative destruction" (Schumpeter 1942), some workers could be displaced or face stagnant wages. In addition, pecuniary externalities can cause an increase in market prices, such as housing rents, that may reduce real incomes of the poor.[10]

Economic development may entail unbalanced growth that affects inequality. For example, Kuznets (1955) postulated that inequality evolves as an inverted "U" shape function where inequality initially increases and eventually declines. In the initial stages of development, some workers migrate from rural agriculture to the fast-growing urban manufacturing sector. Workers in the manufacturing sector experience an increase in income, while the ones staying in the traditional sector remain with low wages, resulting in higher income inequality. As a larger share of workers shift to the manufacturing sector, inequality eventually declines at later stages of development.

Sectoral Composition

Empirical studies confirm that the sectoral composition of growth is important in determining poverty reduction. Loayza and Raddatz (2010) study a cross-section of 55 developing countries and find that growth in sectors that rely more intensively on unskilled labor have the greatest contribution to reducing poverty rates. The empirical results show that agriculture is the most effective poverty-reducing sector, followed by construction and manufacturing. Mining, utilities, and services do not have a statistically significant impact on poverty alleviation. These results highlight that in some countries, growth might be insufficient to reduce poverty if it is concentrated in sectors that are not intensive in unskilled labor, such as oil and mining.

Studies conducted for individual countries support the results of Loayza and Raddatz (2010). Ravallion and Datt (1996) find that for India in the second half of the twentieth century, growth in agriculture and services was correlated with declines in poverty in both rural and urban areas, while industrial growth did not have a systematic impact on poverty. Ravallion and Chen (2007) find that agriculture growth was the most important driver for poverty alleviation in China. For Indonesia, Suryahadi, Suryadarma, and Sumarto (2009) find that growth in the

---

[10] Matlack and Vigdor (2008), using Census data for US cities, show that an increase in income at the top of the income distribution leads to an overall increase in housing rents that disproportionally affect the poor, exacerbating inequality.

service sector was strongly correlated with poverty reduction in rural and urban areas, while agriculture growth was correlated with poverty declines in rural areas. Ivanic and Martin (2018) find that in poor countries, productivity gains in agriculture are generally—although not always—more effective in reducing global poverty than the productivity gains in industry or services of equivalent size. However, the effectiveness of the former fades as average income rises.

Capital Intensity

If growth is generated in sectors that are intensive in capital or innovative skill, such growth could provide higher returns to capital and entrepreneurs than to labor. Indeed, in recent years, the labor share of output across advanced and emerging market economies has fallen as a result of capital deepening and technological progress (Dao, Das, and Koczan 2019). Moreover, Piketty (2015) finds that the return on capital is higher than the growth rate of GDP in many country episodes, leading to higher inequality, as capital owners tend to be at the top of the income distribution. Using historical data from the United States and Europe, Piketty provides evidence that the difference between the return to capital (r) and the growth rate of GDP (g) has the effect of amplifying wealth inequality over time. Since wealth is highly concentrated at the top of the income distribution, the high return to capital relative to GDP growth increases the ratio of wealth to GDP, increasing the extent of inequality.

However, even if the driving sector is capital-intensive, it could have positive spillovers to the poor, provided it simulates enough growth in more labor-intensive sectors. Conversely, under some circumstances, strong productivity growth in labor-intensive agriculture could reduce demand for rural labor, thereby increasing poverty and the number of urban unemployed.

Technology and Innovation

The prospect of obtaining rents from new products drives innovation, and innovation contributes to growth. The rents created by successful innovations lead to a rising share of the top 1 percent of the distribution. However, innovations appear to have limited impact on inequality in the bottom 99 percent of the population, and there is some evidence that innovation is positively correlated with social mobility (Aghion et al. 2019). This may be consistent with the findings of Galor and Tsiddon (1997). They distinguish between "invention," which they assume draws on ability and leads to higher inequality and higher intergenerational mobility, versus a more accessible category of "innovation," which they model as depending on human capital correlated with parental human capital, and which thus leads to lower inequality but also lower intergenerational mobility.

The empirical evidence shows that investment in new technologies—such as information and communication technologies (ICT)—has important effects on the income distribution. Relying on a sample of 11 member-countries of the

Organisation for Economic Co-operation and Development (OECD) from 1980 to 2004, Michaels, Natraj, and Van Reenen (2014) find that industries that experienced the highest growth in the use of ICT technologies increased the demand for highly educated workers (such as physicians or engineers) at the expense of middle-educated workers (such as administrative or clerical occupations). The demand for low-skilled workers was not affected, since many of the tasks performed by these workers (such as janitors or farmworkers) are difficult to replace with new technologies. As a result, investment in ICT results in polarization of labor markets across OECD economies, as tasks of middle-educated workers are replaced by new technologies. ICT could also increase the bargaining power of large, financially strong and politically influential entities that are capable of collecting, storing and analyzing large amounts of individual data, to the detriment of individuals and smaller enterprises, raising inequality.

More recently, Graetz and Michaels (2018) study the impact of the adoption of robots across industries in 17 OECD countries from 1993 to 2007. As opposed to new ICT technologies, robots can perform a wide array of repetitive tasks typically done by low-skilled workers, such as wielding, painting, or packaging, with very little human intervention. The increased use of robots contributed to an increase in labor productivity and average wages and a decline in output prices that benefited consumers but reduced the employment shares of low-skilled workers. For the US labor markets, Acemoglu and Restrepo (2020) find that adopting robots has led to higher productivity gains, but lower aggregate employment and wages. The authors estimate that, on average, one robot displaces three workers, even after accounting for the positive effects via higher productivity and lower output prices. For the French manufacturing sector, Aghion et al. (2020) find net positive effects from automation technologies (including the adoption of robots) on employment, including of unskilled workers, and no discernible impact on wages. Chapters 3 and 5 look into the links between technology, labor markets, and inequality in more detail.

Trade

The simplest framework for understanding the impact of trade liberalization on inequality is the Stolper-Samuleson theorem (Stolper and Samuelson 1941) derived in the context of the Hecksher-Ohlin model of trade. In this framework of two countries, two goods, and two factors, a reduction of tariffs in a developing country abundant in unskilled labor will lead to an increase in exports of the good that uses labor intensively and higher labor compensation of unskilled workers in that country. Conversely, opening up to trade leads to higher imports of products from developed countries that use skills or capital intensively and a reduction in wages for high-skilled workers in the importing country. For developed countries that are abundant in skilled labor, the reverse will be true: trade liberalization will reduce the wages of unskilled workers relative to skilled ones.

Consequently, trade liberalization will lead to lower inequality in developing countries and higher inequality in advanced economies. In practice, however, the skill premium, or the gap between the wages of skilled and unskilled workers, has increased in both advanced and developing countries, mainly due to skill-biased technological change (see Chapter 7). This suggests that additional factors besides trade might be playing a role in driving inequality.

Financial Liberalization

Financial globalization can also influence income distribution through different channels (Chapter 8). For instance, foreign direct investment (FDI) typically flows to high-skilled sectors of the host economy (Cragg and Epelbaum 1996), which might raise the skill premium and increase inequality in that country. The impact of other capital flows (portfolio debt and equity flows) in principle can have an ambiguous impact on inequality. Some authors argue that higher global financial integration can improve financial intermediation and help the poor by providing funds that can be used to accumulate human and physical capital. On the other hand, capital account liberalization might increase the frequency of financial crises (Kaminsky and Reinhart 1999). Governments may also increase debt following financial market integration (Azzimonti, de Francisco, and Quadrini 2014), raising the likelihood of a debt crisis. Financial and debt crises often lead to severe recessions that disproportionately affect the poor and raise inequality (Chapter 11). The quality of institutions might also shape the direction in which financial flows influence income distribution. With strong institutions, financial flows might be channeled to the most productive uses and also would allow the poor to smooth consumption to better insure themselves against macroeconomic volatility. On the other hand, with weak institutions, those well connected to financial institutions might have disproportionate access to the financial flows to the detriment of the poor, which can exacerbate inequality.[11]

Empirical Estimates of Multiple Drivers of Growth and Inequality

Various empirical studies have estimated the impact of several factors mentioned above that concurrently affect growth and inequality. For instance, Jaumotte, Lall, and Papageorgiou (2013) focus on two important drivers of economic growth in recent decades—technological change and globalization—and evaluate their joint impact on inequality. Relying on a panel data set of 51 countries covering 1981 to 2003, they find that technological change has a greater impact on income inequality than globalization does. The overall impact of globalization on inequality is limited, reflecting two offsetting effects. Trade globalization reduces inequality by

---

[11] Globalization and technological change influence growth and inequality through different components of GDP. Trade globalization and technological change impact the income distribution through labor income and the skill premium, whereas financial flows affect capital income.

raising the income of the bottom four quintiles, while financial globalization—manifested through an expansion in FDI flows—increases inequality. Technological innovation is the key channel increasing inequality: it increases the demand for skilled workers and the returns to capital, and disproportionally boosts the income in the top quintile of the income distribution. The authors also find that an increase in access to education could offset the negative effects of technological change and financial globalization, thus reducing inequality.

More recently, Furceri and Ostry (2019) have corroborated the different roles of technological change and globalization in driving inequality. Using model-averaging techniques in a sample of 108 countries covering the more recent period of 1980 to 2013, they find econometric results consistent with Jaumotte, Lall, and Papageorgiou (2013): namely, that financial globalization and techno-logical improvements contribute to a rise in inequality while trade globalization is associated with lower inequality, especially in developing countries.[12]

IV. How Does Poverty and Inequality Affect Growth?

A. Empirical Estimates of the Impact of Poverty and Inequality on Growth

From Poverty to Growth

The empirical evidence shows that poverty is detrimental to long-term economic growth (Figure 2.8). Using panel data of 85 countries covering 1960 to 2000, López and Servén (2015) find that a 10 percentage-point increase in the poverty rate reduces the GDP per capita growth rate by 1 percentage point. In particular, an increase in the poverty rate reduces the investment rate for countries with low levels of financial development. There is also evidence that the negative impact of poverty on growth depends on the initial level of poverty. In a sample of 156 countries covering 1960 to 2010, Marrero and Servén (2018) find that for low levels of poverty (below the median), poverty has an insignificant impact on growth. In contrast, when the poverty rate is high, a 10 percentage-point decrease in headcount poverty is associated with an increase in economic growth ranging from 1 to 2 percent per year.

Related evidence comes from the observation that despite the global reduction in poverty rates, cross-country evidence indicates a lack of convergence in pov-erty rates. Studying 90 developing countries during the 1991–2004 period,

---

[12] More specifically, Furceri and Ostry (2019) estimate the drivers of inequality using weighted-average least square (WALS) techniques, whereby the reported coefficients are a weighted average of the estimated coefficients across all possible models. This technique addresses model uncertainty and endogeneity issues related to omitted variables typically present in empirical studies focused on income inequality.

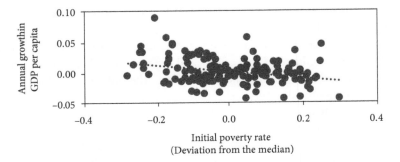

Figure 2.8 Growth in GDP per capita vs Initial Poverty, 1960–2010

Note: Data cover 156 countries and are controlled for initial income. The year of the initial poverty is 1960 and the average growth in GDP per capital is over the period 1960–2010. Initial poverty is expressed as deviation from the median.

Source: Marrero and Servén 2018.

Ravallion (2012) finds that two distinctive effects prevented the convergence of poverty rates. First, poverty reduces growth, consistent with the results from López and Servén (2015). Second, high initial poverty dulls the impact of growth in reducing poverty. The combination of these two channels makes it more difficult for the poorest countries to reduce their poverty rates.

From Inequality to Growth

As an illustration of the relationship from inequality to growth, Bénabou (1996) compares the growth outcomes of East Asian and Latin America economies conditional on the initial levels of income inequality. According to Bénabou (1996), the conventional wisdom among development economists is that the relatively equal distribution of income and land in East Asian economies contributed to their observed high economic growth rates. By the same token, the lack of a similar economic dynamism in Latin America has been attributed to the consequences of high concentration of wealth and income in that region.[13]

The left panel of Figure 2.9 reports the correlation between income inequality in 1980 and the average GDP per capita growth in the subsequent 30 years for selected Latin American and Asian economies. Consistent with Bénabou (1996), on average countries that exhibited lower levels of initial inequality also experienced higher rates of economic growth. While there are many other factors that might explain the economic dynamism of these Asian economies, such as the quality of institutions and high rates of saving and investment (Collins and Bosworth 1996), this figure illustrates that income distribution might be one key element for understanding differences in economic performance. An extended

---

[13] "Poverty trap" is a common narrative of economic development whereby some countries are stuck in poverty and would need external support (or a "big push") for them to escape it. Easterly (2006) rejects, however, the claim that "well-governed poor nations" are stuck in a trap just because they are poor. The author cannot statistically discern any effect of initial poverty on subsequent growth once bad governance is controlled for.

sample of advanced and developing countries (right panel) confirms the relation-ship between initial income inequality and subsequent growth.[14]

The empirical relationship between inequality and growth has been investi-gated formally in a number of cross-country growth studies, following Barro and Sala-i-Martin (1995). Many of these studies find that inequality, typically meas-ured by a Gini coefficient, enters with a negative and statistically significant sign in cross-country growth regressions, indicating that an increase in inequality leads to lower economic growth. In a survey of 23 different empirical studies on inequality and growth, for instance, Bénabou (1996) finds that despite differences in data sets, sample periods, and measures of income distribution, the studies consistently find that initial inequality is negatively associated with growth. In particular, the quantitative effects of inequality are quite robust across studies: a one-standard-deviation decrease in inequality raises the annual growth of GDP in the range of 0.5 percentage points to 0.8 percentage points.

Various studies examine different dimensions of the relationship. An early work by Alesina and Rodrik (1994) finds that income and land inequality are sta-tistically significant variables that decrease long-term growth in a sample of 70 advanced and developing countries. Perotti (1996) finds a negative and robust association between inequality, inversely related to the share of the middle class (third and fourth quantiles of the income distribution), and growth. He finds that social political instability and fertility rates could be driving the relationship between inequality and growth.

The impact of inequality on growth can also depend on the initial level of development. Barro (2000) estimates the impact of inequality on growth by splitting a sample of 100 countries into high- and low-income samples. In that specification, there is a negative relationship between inequality and growth for

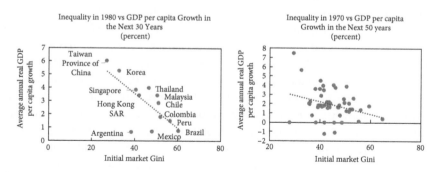

Figure 2.9 Growth in GDP per capita vs Initial Inequality

Note: Panel 1 shows a sample of selected Asian and Latin American economies. Panel 2 shows an extended sample of advanced economies and developing countries. Market Gini is before taxes and transfers.

Sources: Standardized World Income Inequality Database (SWIID); World Bank; and authors' calculations.

[14] The negative relationship between inequality and growth remains robust even when the analysis controls for the initial level of income, as is standard in growth regressions (see Barro 2000).

poor countries, similar to previous studies, while the relationship is positive for richer countries. The empirical results suggest that in the presence of credit constraints, inequality prevents low-income households from accumulating human and physical capital, resulting in lower growth in poor countries. On the other hand, the positive relationship observed in richer economies is consistent with the traditional growth-enhancing effects of inequality emphasized by Kaldor (1957).

The effects of inequality on output might also differ across economic sectors. For instance, Erman and te Kaat (2019) identify the effect of inequality on industry-level value added growth. The authors use a data set that includes 22 industries in 86 countries for the period between 1980 and 2012. They find that that higher income inequality increases the growth rates of industries that use physical capital intensively, while it decreases the growth rates of industries that use skilled labor intensively. Thus, the lower human capital stock associated with inequality drives its negative effect on growth. At the country level, these results are consistent with the theoretical predictions by Galor and Moav (2004).

Studies based on panel data techniques find conflicting results regarding the impact of inequality on economic growth. Forbes (2000) estimates the impact of inequality on growth in a panel of 45 advanced economies and emerging markets for the period between 1966 and1995. Contrary to the cross-country results, she finds that higher inequality leads to higher economic growth in the short and medium term. These results are robust to alternative samples and model specifications. Forbes mentions several theoretical models that are consistent with a positive relationship between inequality and growth. For example, Galor and Tsiddon (1997) find that a concentration of high-skilled workers in technologically advanced sectors allows a higher rate of technological innovation, promoting higher growth rates but also increasing inequality. More recently, using fixed effects panel data techniques, Cingano (2014) finds a negative effect of inequality on growth for a sample of 30 OECD countries for the period between 1970 and 2010. Berg et al. (2018) find that net inequality has a negative effect on growth in a sample of advanced and developing countries, and moderate redistribution through taxes and transfers does not have statistically significant effects on growth.

Evidence from panel data studies also indicates that the effect of inequality on growth might depend crucially on the level of the development and the time horizon of the growth spells (short term vs long term). Brueckner and Lederman (2018) find that income inequality may be beneficial for transitional growth in poor countries but becomes harmful for growth in economies with high average income, contradicting the results by Barro (2000). Regarding the time horizon, Halter, Oechslin, and Zweimüller (2014) find that higher inequality is beneficial for economic performance in the short term, but in the long term the net effect of the relationship tends to be negative. Inequality reduces the duration of growth spells (Berg, Ostry, and Zettelmeyer 2012; Berg and Ostry 2017), with most of the results coming from cross-country differences rather than changes over time.

Banerjee and Duflo (2003) find a nonlinear relationship between changes in inequality and growth. In particular, growth is an inverted U-shaped function of changes in inequality such that a change in the Gini coefficient in either direction is correlated with lower future growth. This empirical result strongly rejects the standard linear specification of cross-country growth regressions and suggests an explanation for the seemingly contradictory results obtained in the literature. However, the non-linear relationship could also reflect omitted variables in the empirical model. For instance, Aiyar and Ebeke (2020) show that the negative effect of inequality on growth largely depends on the degree of intergenerational mobility. In countries with higher intergenerational mobility, the negative impact of income inequality can be more easily reversed because the poor have more opportunities to improve their living standards. In particular, they show that in their specification, the nonlinear term proposed by Banerjee and Duflo (2003) is not statistically significant, suggesting that intergenerational mobility could be capturing the nonlinear relationship between inequality and growth.[15]

In sum, the mixed evidence of the impact of inequality on growth arises primarily based on whether the study used a cross-country approach (which includes between-country inequality) or a panel data approach (which includes only within-country variation over time). Given that some of the key mechanisms linking inequality to growth—such as institutional quality, credit constraints, and redistribution policies—do not change much over time, the influence of those channels are greater in the cross-country than the time series dimension. Given that channels such as political economy and credit constraints generate a negative impact of inequality on growth, this may explain the stronger negative results in cross-country regressions relative to the mixed results of panel data studies. In general, with many potential channels affecting the relationship, inconsistent findings may be expected with differences in country coverage, sample period, time horizon, model specification, and econometric method.

B. Channels from Poverty and Inequality to Growth

Channels by which Inequality Can Boost Growth
Incentives
Inequality provides incentives to work, save, and invest—those who do will receive higher returns than those who do not. Differential returns incentivize good behaviors that promote growth. Milton Friedman (Friedman 1962; Friedman and Friedman 1980) based his opposition to redistributive policies aimed at reducing inequality of outcomes on the grounds of efficiency, arguing

---

[15] The relationship between intergenerational mobility and growth is complex and may depend on inheritance laws and uncertainty of property rights. Chapter 18 examines these issues in more detail.

that they could distort incentives and induce an inefficient allocation of resources. In a capitalist system, the distribution of income is consistent with the ethical principle, "To each according to what he and the instruments he owns produces." This implies that in a free market economy, people should be rewarded according to their marginal productivity, resulting in some inequality of outcomes. Friedman emphasized that this inequality of outcomes could be necessary to provide incentives to perform certain types of tasks that could be risky or tedious (Friedman and Friedman 1980). Moreover, compensation schemes that reward relative performance and thus generate inequality can provide incentives for workers to invest in skills and exert strong efforts (Lazear and Rosen 1981).

Savings
Different savings rates between rich and poor can affect growth. Kaldor (1957) hypothesized that since the richer save more of their income, higher income inequality can lead to a higher national savings rate, a higher investment rate, and greater accumulation of capital, and consequently higher economic growth. Evidence for the United States (Dynan, Skinner, and Zeldes 2004), for instance, supports the notion that both saving rates and the marginal propensity to save are positively correlated with the level of income, suggesting that higher income inequality can lead to a higher savings rate, consistent with Kaldor's hypothesis.

Channels by which Inequality and Poverty Can Depress Growth
Poverty Traps and Human Capital
Poverty can undermine growth by hindering the accumulation of human capital through both health and education. Poverty is associated with high rates of malnutrition, especially in developing countries (Chapter 14). Stunting (a low height-to-age ratio)—an indicator of chronic malnutrition—and child survival rates are correlated with income across and within countries. Poor nutrition impairs children's capacity to learn. Poor children may also be kept out of school in order to support low family incomes through home production or informal work or because families cannot afford school fees. Students from poor households have higher learning gaps even when attending school (World Bank 2018). Empirical evidence shows that inequality of wealth, not just inequality of income, reduces the effectiveness of educational interventions (Deininger and Olinto 2000).

As described in Section II, lower-income countries experience higher poverty rates, partly reflecting the correlation between average country income and the income of the bottom of the distribution. Poor countries have weak capacity to supply public goods such as health and education. Indeed, public spending on health and education is lower for countries with high poverty rates (Figure 2.10, top left and right panels). Higher poverty is associated with lower access to doctors and higher illiteracy rates (bottom left and right panels).

Inequality in education attainment can undermine growth as economies develop (Galor and Moav 2004). In the initial stage of development when physical

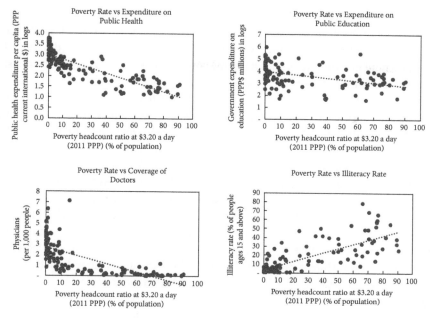

Figure 2.10 Access to Health and Education

Note: Data are for latest observation available including 142 countries from the World Bank's POVCALNET database. Poverty headcount ratio uses the poverty measure of $3.20 per day in 2011 purchasing power parity (PPP) terms.

Sources: World Bank; and authors' calculations.

capital is the prime source of growth, inequality raises growth because it channels resources to individuals with a higher propensity to save. This is reversed later in the development process: as human capital replaces physical capital as the main engine of growth, more equality leads to growth as it alleviates adverse effects of credit constraints on human capital accumulation.

Credit Market Imperfections

Weak credit markets can impede the poor from borrowing to invest in physical or human capital, thereby reducing growth. In the model proposed by Galor and Zeira (1993), wealthy individuals can invest in human capital using their own resources, while individuals with low levels of wealth can only invest in human capital if they have access to credit markets. However, financial frictions increase the interest cost for borrowers. Below a threshold of initial wealth, poor individuals find the cost of borrowing higher than the return to human capital and choose not to invest. In this economy, higher inequality reduces growth. However, redistribution provides the opportunity for the poor to invest in human capital, stimulating economic growth.

In their analysis of the impact of poverty on growth, López and Servén (2015) develop an endogenous growth model with learning-by-doing externalities and subsistence consumption. Poor consumers have a low endowment of wealth and no access to capital markets. The model predicts that in economies where the share of poor people is high enough, economic growth rates are lower because the poor are unable to invest and accumulate capital, resulting in a reduction of the potential growth rate of the economy. López and Servén (2015) report robust results consistent with this prediction.

Banerjee and Newman (1993) argue that, given credit constraints, wealth inequality can influence the occupational choice of individuals, thereby affecting growth. In their model, poor people decide to become (low-skilled) workers, rich people decide to become entrepreneurs, and the rest become self-employed. The model predicts that highly unequal societies stagnate since wages remain too low. Highly equal societies display a large share of self-employed workers. At an intermediate level of inequality, the society can "take off" and converge to a developed economy with a combination of entrepreneurs and workers receiving high wages.

Aghion and Bolton (1997) examine credit constraints where the accumulation of capital by the rich benefits the poor because more funds become available to the poor for investment purposes. Unlike Milton Friedman, they find that the laissez-faire outcome is not efficient because it does not allow the poor to invest amounts consistent with an optimal allocation of resources. Instead, a permanent redistribution of wealth can achieve the optimal allocation.

Demand and Structural Transformation
Inequality can shape the composition of demand and thereby impact growth and structural transformation. For goods produced with technologies subject to economies of scale, sales need to be large enough to cover fixed costs. If only high-income individuals can afford the price of the goods, a moderate level of inequality may be required so that there are enough rich people to make adoption of the technology feasible. Income generated by the sectors can spill over into demand for other goods and spur industrialization, but only if income is distributed broadly enough (Murphy, Shleifer, and Vishny 1989). In addition, productivity improvements through learning by doing can reduce the production costs and prices, making the goods affordable to more people. This can trigger mass production and industrialization provided that inequality is not too severe (Matsuyama 2002).

Risk Aversion and Decision-Making Capabilities
Inequality and poverty might also have a long-term impact on growth through the effects on individuals' decision-making processes. In order for people to overcome poverty, they must save and reinvest continually in order to earn higher wages, which also contributes to higher economic growth rates. However, living in impoverished conditions can prevent individuals from making the best decisions to escape poverty.

This faulty decision making can occur as a result of the particularly burdensome risks and uncertainty imposed by poverty. As noted by Banerjee (2000), the poor might be more risk averse than the rest of the population because they have more to lose if a bad shock materializes, even risking malnourishment or starvation. In the absence of developed financial and insurance markets, the poor will avoid investing in profitable investment opportunities that are intrinsically risky. That behavior self-perpetuates poverty, as the poor do not engage in risky activities that might boost their income. Dercon (2005) surveys several studies conducted in developing countries that support this hypothesis. He finds that if the poor could insure against risks in the same way as the rich, their income could be higher by at least 25 percent.

An alternative behavioral channel through which poverty is perpetuated and economic growth prospects is curtailed is through the lack of self-control in consumption and saving decisions. Banerjee and Mullainathan (2010) develop a model with "temptation" goods (such as cigarettes or alcohol) that provide utility in the present, but not in the future. Under the assumption that the share of expenditures on temptation goods declines with the level of income, the model can lead to poverty traps, whereby the poor overvalue the present and undervalue the future, and thus decide not to make investments that could yield a higher income later. Their model is consistent with the evidence that the poor spend a large fraction of their income on goods that are not survival necessities such as alcohol, tobacco, and festivities (Banerjee and Duflo 2007).

Shah, Mullainathan, and Shafir (2012) study an alternative mechanism through which poverty affects the decision-making process. Through several experiments, they illustrate how the poor devote a significant fraction of their attention span to satisfying basic needs, such as obtaining food, leaving them with less attention to handle other problems, such as investment decisions that would enable their businesses to expand and grow.

Lower aspirations induced by poverty is another channel through which poverty may affect the decision-making process of the poor, resulting in lower economic growth. La Ferrara (2019) reviews the theoretical literature on aspirations and provides empirical evidence on how they are correlated with poverty rates and income inequality. Data on aspirations are obtained from the tests on academic performance administered through the OECD's Programme for International Student Assessment (PISA), and are measured as the expectations of students as to what academic degree and job they will achieve in the future. The intuition of this channel is as follows. The poor have lower aspirations than the rich because they anticipate that the lack of resources (including financial buffers to withstand adverse shocks) will impede their success in the future. As result, the poor may lack the incentives to invest in their future income opportunities for their families, such as the education of their children or the adoption of new technologies. This in turn perpetuates their poverty, leading to a vicious cycle in which low growth breeds poverty and poverty promotes stagnation.

All these mechanisms share the common feature that poverty influences the behavior of poor individuals, with negative consequences on the accumulation of capital and long-term growth, hence self-perpetuating poverty. For instance, this behavioral channel is consistent with the empirical evidence that the poor borrow repeatedly at very high rates instead of self-financing through savings (Banerjee and Duflo 2005) or do not invest in profitable small-scale investment such as purchasing fertilizer (Duflo, Kremer, and Robinson 2011), preventing them from escaping poverty.

Political Economy
There are two key channels through which inequality has political economy effects that depress long-term growth. The first, the "redistribution" channel, is when inequality generates political pressures from voters for redistribution, which results in an increase in distortionary taxation, and consequently lower investment and growth. The second, "the institutional" channel, is when inequality leads the rich and powerful to influence institutions in such a way that laws benefit them but are not conducive to sustained growth for the population at large.

The redistribution channel is illustrated by Alesina and Rodrik (1994) based on the endogenous growth model of Barro (1990), where government spending is productive but is financed through distortionary capital taxation. Taxation and the growth rate of the economy exhibit an inverted "U" relationship. For low levels of tax rates, increasing the tax rate raises growth by funding the expansion of productive public infrastructure. After some point, however, further increasing the tax rate reduces growth because it reduces the incentives to accumulate private capital and may also provide declining marginal return to public expenditure. In the electoral process, the median voter prefers to impose a tax higher than the growth-maximizing tax rate, as they benefit from the public good while the tax falls disproportionately on capital owners. The model implies that the more unequal is the distribution of wealth or capital, the higher the tax rate chosen by the median voter, resulting in a lower rate of economic growth. Persson and Tabellini (1994) obtain similar theoretical results in an overlapping generations framework. Milanovic (2000, 2010) finds empirical support that more unequal countries redistribute more to the poor.

The view that redistribution harms growth was challenged by Saint-Paul and Verdier (1993). When tax revenues are invested in education, the growth rate is higher. The implication is that the growth effects of fiscal policy depend jointly on the tax distortions and expenditure benefits. Moreover, inequality does not necessarily imply demand for more redistribution; it depends on the position of the decisive voter's income relative to the mean (Meltzer and Richard 1981). In a democracy, redistribution depends on the skewness of the income distribution, which places the median voter below the mean (Saint-Paul and Verdier 1996).

The institutional channel is illustrated by Glaeser, Scheinkman, and Shleifer (2003). They propose that the wealthy and politically connected can subvert legal, political, and regulatory institutions, damaging growth through two distinctive mechanisms. First, the elite can weaken the protection of property rights of people at large, discouraging the accumulation of capital by the non-elite, with a negative impact on growth. Second, the elite can influence regulations in order to protect incumbents against entrant firms, with detrimental effects on technological innovation, capital accumulation, and growth. This implies that in countries with weak institutions geared toward the interests of the elite, only elite invest and accumulate wealth. The middle class can expand only when institutions are strong enough to protect them from the rich.

The causality between inequality and institutions goes in both directions. High initial inequality facilitates the elite's ability to subvert institutions toward their interests, but weak institutions can lead to higher inequality to the extent that only the rich and powerful can protect themselves. The authors find empirical support that inequality reduces growth only for countries with poor rule of law. Their results are also consistent with what Acemoglu and Robinson (2019) call "extractive political institutions." These institutions, where power is concentrated, benefit the elite at the expense of the rest of the society, leading to high inequality and low growth.[16]

Sociopolitical Unrest
Under this channel, inequality leads to a polarization of the society, social unrest, and violence, if the demands of the voters cannot be met through the traditional political system. Alesina and Perotti (1996) analyze this channel and find that an increase in inequality (inversely related to the income of the middle class, in their estimation) has a statistically negative effect on political stability. In the empirical analysis, the authors construct an index of political stability based on a dummy variable for democratic regimes, the number of assassinations and deaths, and the number of coups. In addition, they find that political instability negatively affects investment, a key determinant of long-term growth across countries. Their results are broadly consistent with three different mechanisms through which political stability affects investment. First, higher instability tends to shorten the horizon of the government in power; this, in turn, tends to be associated with higher taxation and lower investment, as the reputational costs of taxation are lower for regimes of short duration. Second, social unrest might lead to a disruption of

---

[16] Chapter 10 covers the impact of governance on inclusiveness in a society. Chapter 15 discusses the political economy factors that influence the supply and demand for reform and redistribution in more detail. Ostry, Loungani, and Berg (2019) highlight the impact of political choices in the relationship between inequality and growth.

productive activities and therefore a reduction in productivity. Third, political instability increases uncertainty, which can induce investors to postpone projects or to invest abroad.

Rodrik (1999) studies the interaction between social conflict (measured by inequality or ethnic and linguistic fragmentation) and the quality of government institutions in developing countries in response to external shocks (specifically, terms of trade shocks). Rodrik's analysis is intended to capture the experience in Latin America, the Middle East, and Sub-Saharan Africa, which had a sharp slowdown in growth after the negative shocks in the 1970s. The main channel through which social conflict exacerbates negative shocks is through macroeconomic mismanagement, in particular in the context of weak institutions. As societies become more polarized, the impact of the initial negative shock is exacerbated by the implementation of populist policies that have palliative short-term effects but result in uncertainty, low investment, and, consequently, poor long-term economic growth.

Gender Inequality

Galor and Weil (1996) develop a theory whereby gender inequality, measured as the wage gap between male and female workers, has a long-term impact on growth. In their model, an increase in the stock of capital per capita makes workers more productive, but more so for female than male workers (because as economies develop, the rewards to "brain relative to brawn" increase). The decline in the wage gap, in turn, increases the opportunity cost of raising children, and hence reduces the fertility rate and increases female labor force participation. Consequently, the reduction in the fertility rate leads to lower population growth and an increase in the stock of capital per capita, which in turns generates a positive feedback loop boosting growth and the relative wage of female workers.

This model accounts for the fact that some countries might experience development traps in which a low stock of capital per capita results in low wages for women, a high fertility rate, and high population growth, which further depresses the stock of capital per capita, generating an equilibrium of self-perpetuating stagnation. Kremer and Chen (2002) and de la Croix and Doepke (2003) corroborate that inequality is associated with higher fertility differentials within countries, with the poor having more children and achieving less education, which in turn leads to lower growth.

Several recent studies find that gender inequality reduces growth and has other adverse economic impacts (Malta 2021). Based on a difference-in-difference approach for advanced economies and emerging markets, Bertay, Dordevic, and Sever (2020) find that gender inequality reduces real economic growth at the industry level for the manufacturing sector. Cuberes, Newiak, and Teignier (2017) find that gender inequality in labor markets leads to income losses of 15.5 percent in OECD countries and 17.5 percent in non-OECD countries. Stotsky (2006) discusses the macroeconomic impacts of gender inequality. Chapter 16 examines gender and inclusive growth more extensively.

V. Conclusion and Policy Implications

This chapter traces the factors and policies that affect the nexus of growth, inequality, and poverty. Figure 2.11 presents an illustration of the main channels of this nexus. The relationships are complex, and a multitude of papers have been written to elucidate them. Bourguignon (2004) argues that creating development strategies for reducing poverty is challenging not because of its relationship with growth on the one hand and with inequality on the other. Rather, the difficulty lies in the two-way interaction between growth, inequality, and poverty.

Two main conclusions emerge from analyzing the impact of growth on inclusion.

- A nearly universal consensus in the empirical literature suggests that growth reduces poverty. Economic growth experienced in emerging and low-income economies has had a first-order effect on poverty reduction. Through various mechanisms, growth increases education, health, and job opportunities for the poor and improves their access to public goods and services, lifting their incomes and prospects for the future.
- On the other hand, the impact of growth on inequality (a relative measure of the well-being of the poor) is ambiguous and depends on the sources of growth. For example, growth propelled by skill-biased technological change can disproportionately benefit capital owners and skilled workers to the detriment of unskilled workers, whose earnings are generally low and who tend to be in the lowest quantiles of the income distribution. This type of technological innovation, while usually positive for economic growth, can induce an increase in inequality. Thus, identifying the underlying sectors driving economic growth is crucial for understanding the impact on inclusiveness. Most sources of growth generate unbalanced growth rates across sectors, industries, regions, and factors, so it is not possible to generalize about the distributional effects of growth.

Two conclusions also emerge from analyzing the impact of inclusion on growth: the reverse direction of causation.

- Most plausible mechanisms suggest that poverty impedes growth by reducing the ability and incentives of the poor to accumulate physical and human capital and assets. Poverty curtails access to markets and public services and distorts the incentives for entrepreneurship and forward-looking behavior,

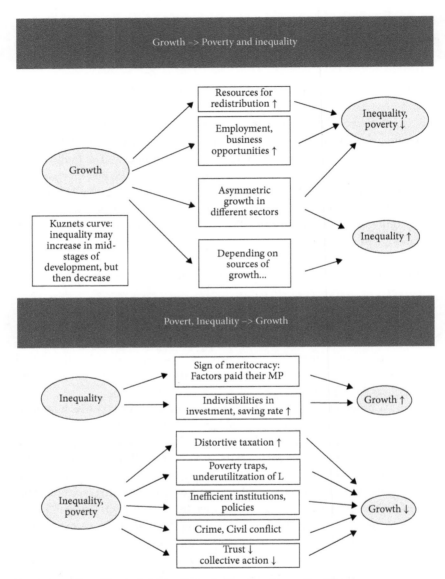

Figure 2.11 Key Channels in the Growth–Poverty–Inequality Nexus
Note: L = labor; MP = marginal product.
Source: Authors.

leading to individual and social stagnation. The empirical evidence amply supports the negative effect of poverty on economic growth.

- However, the impact of inequality on growth is less straightforward. A case can be made that inequality can serve as an incentive for effort and investment. However, other theoretical arguments and empirical evidence point to a negative effect of inequality on growth through a variety of channels, such as higher distributional pressures, lower institutional quality, greater social conflict, and higher fertility rates.

What are the implications of this analysis for the policy framework that should be adopted to promote inclusive growth?

- First, policies to promote growth are most relevant—crucially, because growth helps reduce poverty. An increase in growth is a necessary condition for lifting incomes; improving nutrition; and expanding access to health, education, and opportunities for high-quality jobs. While there is no single set of policies that will work in all countries, some general recommendations can be made. For instance, *The Growth Report* (Commission on Growth and Development 2008) describes a set of policies that has been adopted successfully in countries that have experienced large and sustained growth: an average rate of 7 percent per year or more for 25 years or longer. While the list of policies is not intended to be prescriptive, it provides a good benchmark of what has worked for supporting a successful growth strategy. The report explores policies falling into five broad categories: accumulation of human and physical capital; innovation and technology adoption; efficient allocation of resources; macroeconomic stabilization; and social inclusion.
- Second, economic growth is not an objective in itself, but a way to achieve human development. This requires that the benefits of growth are widely shared across society. Therefore, policy analysis must determine the distributional consequences as well as the growth consequences of policy interventions. Inevitably, market forces will not guarantee that growth is balanced. Thus, public measures will also be needed to ensure that the (absolute and relative) losers of any economic transformation have opportunities to move to better jobs, and support policies will be needed to provide social protection in the meantime.

Finally, is there a trade-off between inequality and growth? Or more precisely, must society tolerate inequality in order to spur growth? Considering the various channels from inequality to growth, the answer may reside in differentiating between *inequality of outcomes* and *inequality of opportunities*.

- The possibility of achieving high returns and higher incomes provides incentives to save, invest, acquire skills, innovate, and take risks, all of which can lead to higher growth. So, indeed some inequality of outcomes is necessary to motivate behavior that enhances growth.
- However, if the opportunity to save, invest, acquire skills, innovate, and take risks are thwarted by barriers (such as fixed costs) that depend on an individual's initial income/wealth/place of birth/race/ethnicity/sexual

orientation/disabilities, inequality can prevent many poor and marginalized people from contributing to growth. Moreover, if segments of the population do not perceive that growth is benefiting them, it can fuel discontent in the society and if not addressed can lead to political instability and social unrest.

The policy message is straightforward: policies to remove barriers to markets and public goods and services can improve growth and equity at the same time. In other words, equality of opportunity does *not* pose a trade-off with economic growth. Expanding access to health care, education, safety, justice, social protection, and finance, for example, can simultaneously boost growth and inclusion.

References

Acemoglu, D., and P. Restrepo. 2020. "Robots and Jobs: Evidence from US Labor Markets." *Journal of Political Economy* 128(6): 2188–44.

Acemoglu, D., and J.A. Robinson. 2019. "Rents and Economic Development: The Perspective of Why Nations Fail." *Public Choice* 181(1): 13–28.

Aghion, P., U. Akcigit, A. Bergeaud, R. Blundell, and D. Hemous. 2019. "Innovation and Top Income Inequality." *Review of Economic Studies* 86(1): 1–45.

Aghion, P., C. Antonin, S. Bunel, and X. Jaravel. 2020. "What Are the Labor and Product Market Effects of Automation? New Evidence from France." Documents de Travail de l'OFCE 2020–01, Observatoire Francais des Conjonctures Economiques (OFCE).

Aghion, P., and P. Bolton. 1997. "A Theory of Trickle-Down Growth and Development." *Review of Economic Studies* 64(2): 151–72.

Aiyar, S., and C. Ebeke. 2020. "Inequality of Opportunity, Inequality of Income, and Economic Growth." *World Development* 136 (December), 105115.

Alesina, A., and R. Perotti. 1996. "Income Distribution, Political Instability, and Investment." *European Economic Review* 40(6): 1203–28.

Alesina, A., and D. Rodrik. 1994. "Distributive Politics and Economic Growth." *The Quarterly Journal of Economics* 109(2): 465–90.

Autor, D.H. 2014. "Skills, Education, and the Rise of Earnings Inequality among the Other 99 Percent." *Science* 344(6186): 843–51.

Autor, D., D. Dorn, L.F. Katz, C. Patterson, and J. Van Reenen. 2020. "The Fall of the Labor Share and the Rise of Superstar Firms." *The Quarterly Journal of Economics* 135(2): 645–709.

Autor, D.H., L.F. Katz, and M.S. Kearney. 2008. "Trends in U.S. Wage Inequality: Revising the Revisionists." *The Review of Economics and Statistics* 90(2): 300–23.

Azzimonti, M., E. de Francisco, and V. Quadrini. 2014. "Financial Globalization, Inequality, and the Rising Public Debt." *American Economic Review* 104(8): 2267–302.

Ball, L., D. Leigh, and P. Loungani. 2017. "Okun's Law: Fit at 50?" *Journal of Money, Credit and Banking* 49(7): 1413–41.

Banerjee, A. 2000. "The Two Poverties." Working Paper 01–16, Department of Economics, Massachusetts Institute of Technology.

Banerjee, A., E. Breza, E. Duflo, and C. Kinnan. 2019. "Can Microfinance Unlock a Poverty Trap for Some Entrepreneurs?" NBER Working Paper 26346, National Bureau of Economic Research, Cambridge, MA.

Banerjee, A., and E. Duflo. 2003. "Inequality And Growth: What Can The Data Say?" *Journal of Economic Growth* 8: 267–99.

Banerjee, A., and E. Duflo. 2005. "Growth Theory through the Lens of Development Economics." *Handbook of Economic Growth*, Vol. 1A, edited by S. Durlauf and P. Aghion. Elsevier Science Ltd.-North Holland.

Banerjee, A., and E. Duflo. 2007. "The Economic Lives of the Poor." *Journal of Economic Perspectives* 21(1): 141–168.

Banerjee, A., and S. Mullainathan. 2010. "The Shape of Temptation: Implications for the Economic Lives of the Poor." NBER Working Paper 15973, National Bureau of Economic Research, Cambridge, MA.

Banerjee, A., and A. Newman. 1993. "Occupational Choice and the Process of Development." *Journal of Political Economy* 101(2): 274–98.

Barro, R. 1990. "Government Spending in a Simple Model of Endogenous Growth." *Journal of Political Economy* 98(5): 103–26.

Barro, R. 2000. "Inequality and Growth in a Panel of Countries." *Journal of Economic Growth* 5: 5–32.

Barro, R., and X. Sala-i-Martin. 1995. *Economic Growth.* New York: McGraw Hill.

Becker, G.S. 1992. "Fertility and the Economy." *Journal of Population Economics* 5(3): 185–201.

Bénabou, R. 1996. "Inequality and Growth." *NBER Macroeconomics Annual 1996*, Vol. 11, 11–92. Cambridge, MA: National Bureau of Economic Research.

Berg, A., and J.D. Ostry. 2017. "Inequality and Unsustainable Growth: Two Sides of the Same Coin?" *IMF Economic Review* 65(4): 792–815.

Berg, A., J.D. Ostry, C.G. Tsangarides, and Y. Yakhshilikov. 2018. "Redistribution, Inequality, and Growth: New Evidence." *Journal of Economic Growth* 23 (September): 259–305.

Berg, A., J.D. Ostry, and J. Zettelmeyer. 2012. "What Makes Growth Sustained?" *Journal of Development Economics* 98(2): 149–66.

Bergstrom, K.A. 2020. "The Role of Inequality for Poverty Reduction." Policy Research Working Paper 9409, World Bank, Washington, DC.

Bertay, A.C., L. Dordevic, and C. Sever. 2020. "Gender Inequality and Economic Growth: Evidence from Industry-Level Data." IMF WP 20/119, International Monetary Fund, Washington, DC.

Bick, A., N. Fuchs-Schündeln, and D. Lagakos. 2018. "How Do Hours Worked Vary with Income? Cross-Country Evidence and Implications." *American Economic Review* 108(1): 170–99.

Bloom, D.E., D. Canning, and G. Fink. 2010. "Implications of Population Ageing for Economic Growth." *Oxford Review of Economic Policy* 26(4): 583–61.

Blotevogel, R., E. Imamoglu, K. Moriyama, and B. Sarr. 2020. "Measuring Income Inequality and Implications for Economic Transmission Channels." IMF Working Paper 20/164, International Monetary Fund, Washington, DC.

Bluhm, R., D. de Crombrugghe, and A. Szirmai. 2018. "Poverty Accounting." *European Economic Review* 104 (C): 237–55.

Booth, C. 1891. *Life and Labour of the People in London* (4 volumes), revised edition. London and Edinburgh: Williams and Norgate.

Bourguignon, F. 2004. "The Poverty-Growth-Inequality Triangle" Working Paper 125, Indian Council for Research on International Economic Relations (ICRIER), New Delhi

Brueckner, M., E. Dabla Norris, and M. Gradstein. 2015. "National Income and Its Distribution." *Journal of Economic Growth* 20(2): 149–75.

Brueckner, M., and D. Lederman. 2018. "Inequality and Economic Growth: The Role of Initial Income." *Journal of Economic Growth* 23(3): 341–66.

Cerra, V., A. Fatás, and S. Saxena. Forthcoming. "Hysteresis and Business Cycles," *Journal of Economic Literature*. Also IMF WP/20/73.

Cingano. F. 2014. "Trends in Income Inequality and its Impact on Economic Growth." OECD Social, Employment and Migration Working Papers 163, Organization for Economic Co-operation and Development, Paris.

Collins, S.M., and B.P. Bosworth. 1996. "Economic Growth in East Asia: Accumulation versus Assimilation," *Brookings Papers on Economic Activity* 1996(2): 135–203.

Commission on Growth and Development. 2008. *The Growth Report: Strategies for Sustained Growth and Inclusive Development.* Washington, DC: World Bank.

Cragg, L., and M. Epelbaum. 1996. "Why Has Wage Dispersion Grown in Mexico? Is It the Incidence of Reforms or the Growing Demand for Skills?" *Journal of Development Economics* 51(1996): 99–116.

Cuberes, D., M. Newiak, and M. Teignier. 2017. "Gender Inequality and Macroeconomic Performance." In *Women, Work, and Economic Growth: Leveling the Playing Field*, edited by K. Kochhar, S. Jain-Chandra, and M. Newiak. Washington, DC: International Monetary Fund.

Dao, M. C., M. Das, and Z. Koczan. 2019. "Why is Labour Receiving a Smaller Share of Global Income?" *Economic Policy* 34(100): 723–59.

De la Croix, D., and M. Doepke. 2003. "Inequality and Growth: Why Differential Fertility Matters." *American Economic Review* 93(4): 1091–113.

Deininger, K., and P. Olinto. 2000. "Asset Distribution, Inequality, and Growth." Policy Research Working Paper 2375, World Bank, Washington, DC.

De Loecker, J., and J. Eeckhout. 2018. "Global Market Power." NBER Working Paper 24768, National Bureau of Economic Research, Cambridge, MA.

De Loecker, J., J. Eeckhout, and G. Unger. 2020. "The Rise of Market Power and the Macroeconomic Implications." *The Quarterly Journal of Economics* 135 (2, May): 561–644.

Dercon, S. 2005. "Vulnerability: A Micro-perspective." Paper presented at the Annual World Bank Conference on Development Economics, Amsterdam. World Bank, Washington, DC.

Diez, F. J., D. Leigh, and S. Tambunlertchai. 2018. "Global Market Power and its Macroeconomic Implications." IMF Working Paper 18/137, International Monetary Fund, Washington, DC.

Dollar, D., T. Kleineberg, and A. Kraay. 2015. "Growth, Inequality and Social Welfare: Cross-Country Evidence." *Economic Policy* 30(82): 335–77.

Dollar, D., T. Kleineberg, and A. Kraay. 2016. "Growth Still Is Good for the Poor." *European Economic Review* 81(C): 68–85.

Dollar, D., and A. Kraay. 2002. "Growth Is Good for the Poor." *Journal of Economic Growth* 7(3): 195–225.

Dollar, D., and A. Kraay. 2004. "Trade, Growth, and Poverty." *The Economic Journal* 114(493): 22–49.

Duflo, E., M. Kremer, and J. Robinson. 2011. "Nudging Farmers to Use Fertilizer: Theory and Experimental Evidence from Kenya." *American Economic Review* 101(6): 2350–90.

Duttagupta, R., and F. Narita. 2017. "Emerging and Developing Economies: Entering a Rough Patch or Protracted Low Gear?" *Journal of Policy Modeling* 39(4): 680–98.

Dynan, K.E., J. Skinner, and S.P. Zeldes. 2004. "Do the Rich Save More?" *Journal of Political Economy* 112(2): 397–444.

Easterly, W. 2006. "Reliving the 1950s: The Big Push, Poverty Traps, and Takeoffs in Economic Development." *Journal of Economic Growth* 11: 289–318.

Erman, L., and D.M. te Kaat. 2019. "Inequality and Growth: Industry-Level Evidence." *Journal of Economic Growth* 24: 283–308.

Fabrizio, S., D. Furceri, R. Garcia-Verdu, B. G. Li, S. V. Lizarazo, M. Mendes Tavares, F. Narita, and A. Peralta-Alva. 2017. "Macro-structural Policies and Income Inequality in Low-income Developing Countries." IMF Staff Discussion Notes No. 17/01, International Monetary Fund, Washington, DC.

Forbes, K.J. 2000. "A Reassessment of the Relationship between Inequality and Growth." *American Economic Review* 90(4): 869–87.

Fosu, A.K. 2017. "Growth, Inequality, and Poverty Reduction in Developing Countries: Recent Global Evidence." *Research in Economics* 71(2): 306–36.

Friedman. 1962. *Capitalism and Freedom.* Chicago, IL: University of Chicago Press.

Friedman, M., and R. Friedman. 1980. *Free to Choose: A Personal Statement.* New York: Harcourt Brace Jovanovich.

Furceri, D., and J.D. Ostry. 2019. "Robust Determinants of Income Inequality." *Oxford Review of Economic Policy* 35(3): 490–517.

Galor, O., and O. Moav. 2004. "From Physical to Human Capital Accumulation: Inequality and the Process of Development." *The Review of Economic Studies* 71(4): 1001–26.

Galor, O., and D. Tsiddon. 1997. "Technological Progress, Mobility, and Economic Growth." *American Economic Review* 87(3): 363–82.

Galor, O., and D.N. Weil. 1996. "The Gender Gap, Fertility, and Growth." *American Economic Review* 86(3): 374–87.

Galor, O., and J. Zeira. 1993. "Income Distribution and Macroeconomics." *Review of Economic Studies* 60(1): 35–52.

Glaeser, E., J. Scheinkman, and A. Shleifer. 2003. "The Injustice of Inequality." *Journal of Monetary Economics* 50 (1, January): 199–222.

Goldin, C., and L.F. Katz. 2007. "Long-Run Changes in the Wage Structure: Narrowing, Widening, Polarizing." *Brookings Papers on Economic Activity* 2 (2007): 135–68.

Gordon, R. J. 2018. "Why Has Economic Growth Slowed When Innovation Appears to Be Accelerating?" NBER Working Paper 24554, National Bureau of Economic Research, Cambridge, MA.

Graetz, G., and G. Michaels. 2018. "Robots at Work." *The Review of Economics and Statistics* 100(5): 753–68.

Halter, D., M. Oechslin, and J. Zweimüller. 2014. "Inequality and Growth: The Neglected Time Dimension." *Journal of Economic Growth* 19: 81–104.

Hausmann, R., D. Rodrik, and A. Velasco. 2005. *Growth Diagnostics.* The John F. Kennedy School of Government, Harvard University, Massachusetts.

Heathcote, J., F. Perri, and G. Violante. 2020. "The Rise of US Earnings Inequality: Does the Cycle Drive the Trend?" *Review of Economic Dynamics* 37 (Supp. 1): S181–S204.

Hoynes, H., D. L. Miller, and J. Schaller. 2012. "Who Suffers during Recessions?" *Journal of Economic Perspectives* 26(3): 27–48.

International Monetary Fund (IMF). 2020. "Measuring Economic Welfare: What and How?" IMF Policy Paper No. 20/028, International Monetary Fund, Washington, DC.

Ivanic, M., and W. Martin. 2018. "Sectoral Productivity Growth and Poverty Reduction: National and Global Impacts." *World Development* 109 (C, September): 429–39.

Jaumotte, F., S. Lall, and C. Papageorgiou. 2013. "Rising Income Inequality: Technology, or Trade and Financial Globalization?" *IMF Economic Review* 61(2): 271–309.

Johnson, P., and C. Papageorgiou. 2020. "What Remains of Cross-Country Convergence?" *Journal of Economic Literature* 58(1): 129–75.

Jones, C.I., and P.J. Klenow. 2016. "Beyond GDP? Welfare across Countries and Time." *American Economic Review* 106(9): 2426–57.

Kaldor, N. 1957. "A Model of Economic Growth." *The Economic Journal* 67(268): 591–624.

Kaminsky, G.L., and C.M. Reinhart. 1999. "The Twin Crises: The Causes of Banking and Balance-of-Payments Problems." *American Economic Review* 89 (3, June): 473–500.

Kraay, A. 2006. "When Is Growth Pro-Poor? Evidence from a Panel of Countries." *Journal of Development Economics* 80(1): 198–227.

Kremer, M., and D. L. Chen. 2002. "Income Distribution Dynamics with Endogenous Fertility." *Journal of Economic Growth* 7 (3, September): 227–58.

Krusell, P., L.E. Ohanian, J.V. Ríos-Rull, and G.L. Violante. 2000. "Capital-Skill Complementarity and Inequality: A Macroeconomic Analysis." *Econometrica* 68 (5, September): 1029–54.

Kuznets, S. 1955. "Economic Growth and Income Inequality." *American Economic Review* 45(1): 1–28.

La Ferrara, E. 2019. "Presidential Address: Aspirations, Social Norms, and Development." *Journal of the European Economic Association* 17(6): 1687–722.

Lazear, E.P., and S. Rosen. 1981. "Rank-Order Tournaments as Optimum Labor Contracts." *Journal of Political Economy* 89(5): 841–64.

Loayza, N. V., and C. Raddatz. 2010. "The Composition of Growth Matters for Poverty Alleviation." *Journal of Development Economics* 93 (1, September): 137–51.

López, H., and L. Servén. 2015. "Too Poor to Grow." Chapter 13 in *Economic Policies in Emerging-Market Economies Festschrift in Honor of Vittorio Corbo*, edited by R. J. Caballero and K. Schmidt-Hebbel, 1st edition 1, Vol. 21, 309–50. Central Bank of Chile.

Malta, V. 2021. "Gender issues," Chapter 3 in "Macroeconomic research in low-income countries: advances made in five key areas through a DFID-IMF collaboration," IMF RES-SPR joint Departmental Paper No. 21/06.

Marrero, G.A., and L. Servén. 2018. "Growth, Inequality, and Poverty: A Robust Relationship?" Policy Research Working Paper 8578, World Bank, Washington, DC.

Marx, K. 1867. Das Kapital: Kritik der politischen Oekonomie. Volume 1: Der Produktionsprozess des Kapitals,1 ed. Hamburg: Verlag von Otto Meissner.

Matlack, J.L., and J.L. Vigdor. 2008. "Do Rising Tides Lift All Prices? Income Inequality and Housing Affordability." *Journal of Housing Economics* 17(3): 212–24.

Matsuyama, K. 2002. "The Rise of Mass Consumption Societies." *Journal of Political Economy* 110(5): 1035–1070.

Meltzer, A., and S. Richard. 1981. "A Rational Theory of the Size of Government." *Journal of Political Economy* 89(5): 914–27.

Michaels, G., A. Natraj, and J. Van Reenen. 2014. "Has ICT Polarized Skill Demand? Evidence from Eleven Countries over Twenty-Five Years." *The Review of Economics and Statistics* 96(1): 60–77.

Milanovic, B. 2000. "The Median Voter Hypothesis, Income Inequality, and Income Redistribution: An Empirical Test with the Required Data." *European Journal of Political Economy* 16(3): 367–410.

Milanovic, B. 2010. "Four Critiques of the Redistribution Hypothesis: An Assessment." *European Journal of Political Economy* 26(1): 147–54.

Murphy, K., A. Shleifer, and R. Vishny. 1989. "Income Distribution, Market Size and Industrialization." *The Quarterly Journal of Economics* 104(3): 537–64.

Ostry, J., P. Loungani, and A. Berg. 2019. *Confronting Inequality*. Foreword by Joseph E. Stiglitz. New York: Columbia University Press.

Perotti, R. 1996. "Growth, Income Distribution, and Democracy: What the Data Say." *Journal of Economic Growth* 1 (2, June): 149–87.

Persson, T. and G. Tabellini. 1994. "Is Inequality Harmful for Growth?" *American Economic Review* 84(3): 600–21.

Piketty, T. 2014. "Capital in the Twenty-First Century." Harvard University Press.

Piketty, T. 2015. "About Capital in the Twenty-First Century." *American Economic Review* 105(5): 48–53.

Piketty, T., and E. Saez. 2014. "Inequality in the Long Run." *Science* 344(6186): 838–43.

Ravallion, M. 2012. "Why Don't We See Poverty Convergence?" *American Economic Review* 102(1): 504–23.

Ravallion, M., and S. Chen. 2007. "China's (Uneven) Progress against Poverty." *Journal of Development Economics* 82(1): 1–42.

Ravallion, M., and G. Datt. 1996. "How Important to India's Poor Is the Sectoral Composition of Economic Growth?" *World Bank Economic Review* 10 (1, January): 1–25.

Rodrik, D. 1999. "Where Did All the Growth Go? External Shocks, Social Conflict, and Growth Collapses." *Journal of Economic Growth* 4(4): 385–412.

Saint-Paul, G., and T. Verdier. 1993. "Education, Democracy and Growth." *Journal of Development Economics* 42 (2, December): 399–407.

Saint-Paul, G., and T. Verdier. 1996. "Inequality, Redistribution and Growth: A Challenge to the Conventional Political Economy Approach." *European Economic Review* 40(3–5): 719–28.

Schumpeter, J. 1942. *Capitalism, Socialism and Democracy*. New York; London: Harper & Brothers.

Shah, A., S. Mullainathan, and E. Shafir. 2012. "Some Consequences of Having Too Little." *Science* 338(6107): 682–85.

Smith, A. 1776. *An Inquiry into the Nature and Causes of the Wealth of Nations*. London: W. Strahan and T. Cadell.

Solow, R.M. 1956. "A Contribution to the Theory of Economic Growth." *The Quarterly Journal of Economics* 70(1): 65–94.

Solt, Frederick. 2020. "Measuring Income Inequality Across Countries and Over Time: The Standardized World Income Inequality Database." *Social Science Quarterly* 101(3):1183–1199. SWIID Version 9.0, October 2020.

Stolper, W., and P. Samuelson. 1941. "Protection and Real Wages." *Review of Economic Studies* 9(1): 58–73.

Stotsky, J. 2006. "Gender and Its Relevance to Macroeconomic Policy: A Survey." IMF Working Paper 06/233, International Monetary Fund, Washington, DC.

Suryahadi, A., D. Suryadarma, and S. Sumarto. 2009. "The Effects of Location and Sectoral Components of Economic Growth on Poverty: Evidence from Indonesia." *Journal of Development Economics* 89 (1, May): 109–17.

Tang, X. 2021. "Income inequality in low-income countries," Chapter 4 in "Macroeconomic research in low-income countries: advances made in five key areas through a DFID-IMF collaboration," IMF RES-SPR joint Departmental Paper.

von Wachter, T., J. Song, and J. Manchester. 2009. "Long-Term Earnings Losses due to Mass-Layoffs during the 1982 Recession: An Analysis Using Longitudinal Administrative Data from 1974 to 2004." Columbia University, New York. Unpublished.

Wagner, A. 1893. *Grundlegung der politischen Ökonomie*, 3rd ed. Leipzig, Germany: Winter.

World Bank. 2018. *World Development Report*. Washington, DC: World Bank.

3

Labor Markets

Asmaa El-Ganainy, Ekkehard Ernst, Rossana Merola,
Richard Rogerson, and Martin Schindler

I. Introduction

For the vast majority of individuals, payment from selling their labor services in the labor market is the single most important source of income and hence the dominant determinant of their material standard of living.[1] For this reason, the labor market has a key role to play in achieving inclusive growth.

Labor market inclusivity is inherently a multi-dimensional notion. Labor market opportunities encompass not only pay, but also the type of work; the working conditions, such as safety and ability to work flexible hours; arrangements for dealing with risk; and many other factors. This chapter embodies a collection of principles that capture the key aspects of an inclusive labor market and which also guide the structure of this chapter.

A key theme in this chapter is that while there may be cases where achieving inclusivity may entail a trade-off with economic efficiency, there are important areas where achieving inclusivity is a win-win proposition: that is, where making labor markets more inclusive also enhances economic efficiency and growth. Discrimination is an important such area.

The remainder of this chapter proceeds as follows. After outlining the principles of inclusivity in Section II, Section III provides measurements and stylized facts related to inclusivity in labor markets around the globe; Section IV provides a selected review of labor market policies and institutions that may enhance inclusivity; and Section V concludes.

[1] We thank Jaime Sarmiento Monroy for the excellent research assistance. We also thank Valerie Cerra, Romain Duval, Barry Eichengreen, Prakash Loungani, as well as participants in the Inclusive Growth book seminar series organized by the IMF Institute for Capacity Development for their comments.

Asmaa El-Ganainy, Ekkehard Ernst, Rossana Merola, Richard Rogerson, and Martin Schindler, *Labor Markets*
In: *How to Achieve Inclusive Growth*. Edited by: Valerie Cerra, Barry Eichengreen, Asmaa El-Ganainy, and Martin Schindler, Oxford University Press. © Asmaa El-Ganainy, Ekkehard Ernst, Rossana Merola, Richard Rogerson, and Martin Schindler 2022. DOI: 10.1093/oso/9780192846938.003.0003

II. Principles of Inclusive Labor Markets

We describe a set of four principles that serve as our guide for assessing labor market inclusiveness. In some cases, improving inclusivity along one dimension may be complementary to improvement along others, while in others, there may be trade-offs. The four principles are: (1) access, (2) fairness, (3) protection, and (4) voice.[2]

Access. At its simplest level, this principle stipulates that individuals should have access to employment opportunities. But more broadly, this principle also stipulates that an individual's access to specific jobs and occupations should be based on their ability to carry out the tasks associated with the activity and not on socioeconomic or demographic factors such as age, race, gender, or religion. Put differently, if the work environment is hostile to certain groups of workers, then this should be viewed as a barrier that limits access. Importantly, this principle applies not only to access to specific jobs, but also encompasses access to learning and development opportunities. Barriers to access can take many forms, including features like work arrangements. For example, if a job or occupation does not offer flexible work schedules despite it being economically feasible to do so, this would limit the access of productive individuals who require such flexibility. Similarly, not making adequate provisions that make work feasible for individuals with disabilities also serves as a barrier that limits access.

Fairness. This principle stipulates that workers should be rewarded based solely on their contributions and not based on factors such as age, race, gender or religion. Thus, an individual should not receive less than they merit based on productivity.

Protection. This principle stipulates that the labor market should provide insurance to protect individuals against negative shocks, such as temporary or permanent health shocks, or a job displacement shock due to downsizing or external trade competition. This insurance may take many forms—disability insurance, unemployment insurance, retraining programs, and many others. Viewed broadly, this principle would also extend to providing insurance to individuals who enter the labor market under poor initial conditions.

Voice. Every workplace has a large set of rules and practices that govern the range of activities that take place within it. These rules and practices describe how work is organized, how interactions take place between workers and management, and how work schedules and assignments are determined. The fourth principle stipulates that workers should have a voice in the process that determines these rules and practices. Formal collective bargaining agreements represent one means through which workers have voice, but workers may also maintain a voice

---

[2] This chapter focuses narrowly on features of the labor market per se. Many outcomes in life with important effects on labor market outcomes are realized prior to entering the labor market, such as the amount and quality of schooling. Such pre-labor market outcomes are outside the scope of this chapter.

without formal representation. Workers' voice can also be achieved at higher levels than the workplace through the political process.

Rather than trying to devise a single index, a useful approach to assessing the extent of inclusivity in a particular labor market is to examine the scope of departures from each of these four principles individually. In assessing these departures, it is important to assess the scope of the departure. For example, do the barriers to access reflect a widespread lack of access, or are they largely confined to a few subgroups? If workers are paid less than their productivity, does this describe the situation in general, or only of particular groups? If the departures are widespread, we will refer to them as *macro* departures, whereas if they are much narrower in scope, we will refer to them as *micro* departures. This distinction can have important implications for what sorts of policies will provide appropriate remedy, particularly for some dimensions of inclusivity.

III. Measures of Inclusivity

In this section we briefly discuss ways in which we can use available data to shed light on the extent to which labor markets differ in terms of achieving the four principles introduced earlier.

A. Access

Household labor force surveys represent the most widely available and comparable data on labor market outcomes. A key objective of these surveys is to divide the population into three mutually exclusive groups: the employed, the unemployed, and the non-participants. Data on these groups are commonly available and we discuss here how they can be used to shed light on the issue of access, while also noting some limitations of these basic data.

A key element of labor market access is the opportunity for employment. This suggests that the unemployment rate is a natural starting point; after all, in the labor market statistics individuals are unemployed if they are available for work and searching for work but not currently working. Modern theories of unemployment emphasize that some unemployment is inevitable in a dynamic economy, so one should not think that zero unemployment is the appropriate benchmark for assessing inclusivity. However, to the extent that these dynamic forces are broadly similar across economies, at least across those at similar stages of development, (large) differences in unemployment rates among countries are informative.

Figure 3.1 displays average unemployment rates over the period 2015–2019 for a large cross-section of countries, broken into three broad groups corresponding

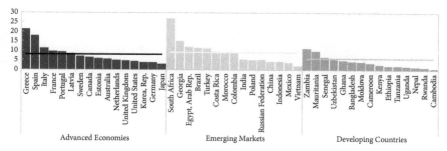

Figure 3.1   Unemployment Rate, Total (% of total labor force, averages of 2015–19)

Note: Averages are calculated based on all available countries in each group, respectively, including those not listed in the chart. Country groupings are based on the IMF WEO classification.

Sources: ILO and authors' calculations.

to categories of economic development.[3] The key message from this figure is that unemployment rates vary quite dramatically across countries. These differences are particularly noteworthy for the set of advanced economies (AEs) and emerging economies (EMs), a point we shall return to.[4]

While it is intuitively appealing to equate unemployment with a lack of access to employment, there are clearly exceptions to this rule. On the one hand, some unemployment may be voluntary in nature, in the sense that the individual has turned down some employment opportunity in favor of remaining unemployed. But on the other hand, it is important to note that an individual who desires work but does not search for work because there are no jobs available will not be counted as unemployed. For this reason, it is also of interest to examine the employment rate as a measure of opportunity. Figure 3.2 shows data for the employment rate that are comparable to those in the previous figure on the unemployment rate. Once again, there are striking differences across countries, but now the differences are particularly large for the less developed economies.[5] An important message is that the unemployment rate may be a much less accurate indicator of access in less developed countries.

---

[3] We report average values over several years to focus on longer run differences that do not simply reflect business cycle fluctuations. Country groups are based on the IMF's WEO classification.

[4] Important variations exist not only cross-sectionally, but also over time. For example, research estimating the so-called Okun's law—which, following Okun (1962), describes the empirical cyclical relationship between economic activity and unemployment—has shown that it can vary widely across countries, including especially between advanced economies and developing countries (Furceri et al. 2020). Related research has noted that adverse economic shocks can lead to persistent (scarring) effects on unemployment (Blanchard and Summers 1986) and economic activity (e.g., Cerra and Saxena 2008). This broader literature is suggestive of the role that labor market policies and institutions can potentially play not just for the level of unemployment, but also for how unemployment dynamically responds to adverse shocks.

[5] In the interest of space, we only present data for the overall population. Many factors can affect these aggregate numbers, including differences in demographic structure, but large differences remain even when focusing on more narrowly defined demographic groups.

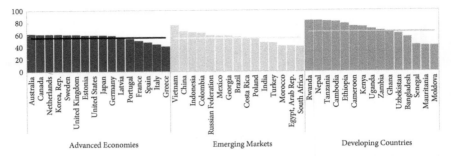

Figure 3.2 Employment to Population Ratio, Total (%, averages of 2015–19)

Note: Averages are calculated based on all available countries in each group, respectively, including those not listed in the chart. Country groupings are based on the IMF WEO classification.

Sources: ILO and authors' calculations.

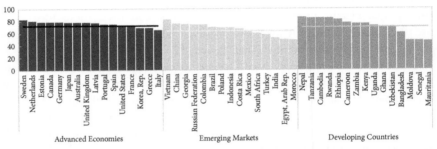

Figure 3.3 Labor Force Participation Rate, Total (% of total population ages 15–64, averages of 2015–19)

Note: Averages are calculated based on all available countries in each group, respectively, including those not listed in the chart. Country groupings are based on the IMF WEO classification.

Sources: ILO and authors' calculations.

To pursue this further, we examine the data for participation rates across the same set of countries (Figure 3.3). The participation rate tells us what fraction of the population is either working or looking for work. The key feature of this figure is the large variation in participation rates, both within and across groups. While there are many factors that can give rise to differences in participation rates, such large differences, especially among countries at a similar stage of development, is strongly suggestive of limited access.

The statistics we have presented for the aggregate labor market are best interpreted as reflecting macro departures from inclusivity. Standard labor force survey data also present these statistics for subgroups, which allows an examination of differences by gender, skill/education, age, and race/ethnicity. In the interest of space, we do not present any disaggregated data here, but we note that in many cases, differences across economies are much larger for some subgroups, even within country groupings by stage of development.

B. Fairness

One measure of fairness is whether workers are remunerated fairly. At the *macro* level, the labor income share has been falling in many countries over the past several decades. In AEs, labor income shares now are about five percentage points lower than they were in 1970 (Figure 3.4). Despite more limited data, similar trends have been observed since the 1990s in emerging markets and developing economies (EMDEs), especially among the largest EMs.

While there are important measurement issues in constructing the labor income share,[6] its downward trend indicates that average wage growth has fallen below average labor productivity growth.[7] Researchers have identified several contributing factors that are technological in nature: the form of technological progress along with a relative decline in investment goods prices (IMF 2017), automation (Acemoglu and Restrepo 2018; Martinez 2018; see also Chapter 5), and globalization and offshoring (Koh et al. 2000; IMF 2017; Elsby et al. 2013).

The technological factors noted in the previous paragraph could generate changes in the labor share even if labor and product markets were perfectly competitive. Another body of literature has emphasized the role of changes in

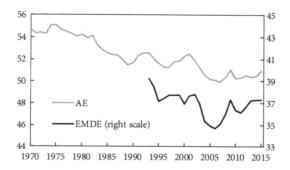

Figure 3.4 Evolution of the Labor Share of Income (%)
Source: IMF's World Economic Outlook (WEO) (April 2017), Figure 3.1.

---

[6] Two well-known measurement problems in the analysis of labor shares include: (1) the treatment of self-employment income, which is often incorrectly treated as capital income (Gollin 2002); and (2) the depreciation of capital, which should arguably be netted out from the calculation of income shares (Bridgman 2018).

[7] The labor share, defined as $W \cdot H/Y$ where W is compensation per hour, H is hours worked and Y is GDP (and hence, total income), can also be written as $W/(Y/H)$ which is in turn equal to W/APL where APL is the average product of labor. If the Marginal Product of Labor (MPL) is proportional to the APL (which is the case, e.g., for a Cobb-Douglas production function with a time-invariant capital share), then changes in the labor share can be used to infer changes in the ratio of wages to marginal productivity.

monopoly and monopsony power as factors leading to changes in the labor share (e.g., Eeckhout, 2021).[8] One strand of this literature notes the emergence of "superstar firms" (OECD 2018; Autor et al. 2017; Manyika et al. 2019) that has led to rising industry concentration, leading to rising market power, higher markups and thus greater profit shares (Chapter 6; Barkai 2020; Gutiérrez and Philippon 2017). Another strand has argued that deregulation of labor market institutions and weaker collective bargaining institutions have weakened the bargaining power of workers and thereby lowered wages relative to productivity (Ciminelli et al. 2020; Manyika et al. 2019; Bengtsson 2014). In a recent paper, Gouin-Bonenfant (2021) argues that changes in the distribution of firm-level productivity have effectively increased the degree of firm monopsony power in the labor market.

Changes in the labor income share are suggestive of how the experiences of workers on the whole have evolved over time. Here, we also consider whether different groups have had systematically different experiences—that is, fairness at the *micro* level. A large literature, going back at least to Mincer (1974), has attempted to establish whether individuals of different genders, racial, religious, or other groups have been paid significantly differently after controlling for observable characteristics that are believed to be related to productivity.[9] If so, this would suggest that factors other than an individual's contribution to output play a role.

In particular, this approach has been used to assess gender and racial wage gaps. Gender pay gaps are significant in most countries (Figure 3.5). Based on a recent cross-country study (ILO 2018b), factors such as education, age, work experience, workplace characteristics, working time, occupational categories, and other labor market attributes explain little of the gender pay gap at different points of the wage distribution, suggesting that other factors are at play.

Important pay gaps exist also across racial groups. Given different racial compositions, cross-country comparisons are challenging. However, for the case of the United States, Bayer and Charles (2019) find that in 2014 the median black man in the United States earned significantly less than the median white man (Figure 3.6). In addition to comparing median wages, Bayer and Charles also calculate the black-white earning gap for *all* individuals in the sample, whether employed or not, i.e., including the zero earnings of non-employed individuals.

---

[8] In a firm monopsony, firms can use their market power in employing labor to push wages below the marginal product of labor, collecting rents while reducing employment to below what would occur in a perfectly competitive benchmark.

[9] The Mincer model (Mincer 1974) provides a useful framework for understanding differences in earnings outcomes due to differences in schooling, labor market experience, and other factors. In its simplest form, it empirically estimates the relationship between an individuals' earnings and their education levels and labor market experience. Other models in a large related literature attempt to account for other productivity-related characteristics. See, e.g., Bowles et al. (2001).

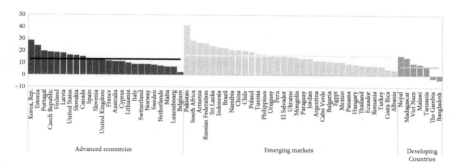

Figure 3.5 Median Gender Pay Gap (Factor-weighted gender pay gaps using hourly wages, averages of 2015–19)

Note: Averages are calculated based on countries shown in each group, respectively. Country groupings are based on the IMF WEO classification.

Sources: ILO and authors' calculations.

This calculation effectively combines differences in *access* (i.e., the likelihood of being employed) with *fairness* (i.e., wage differences). Applying this calculation widens the gap considerably—in fact, Bayer and Charles show that in real terms, relative to white men, black men are virtually no better off in 2014 than they were in 1950.

Importantly, differences in earnings are not necessarily evidence of a lack of inclusion. For example, based on the Mincer approach, empirical findings suggest that, on average, controlling for years of experience, one additional year of schooling raises average earnings by about 10 percent (Heckman et al. 2006; and Montenegro and Patrios 2014). That is, differences in education tend to translate into differences in earnings. There is evidence, however, that wage disparities have been widening over time across skill groups—average wages for workers with lower skill levels/educational attainment have remained nearly unchanged in real terms over the past 50–60 years, while those of workers with more than a college degree nearly doubled (Autor 2019). Much of the rise in skill premia can be attributed to rapid globalization and technological advancements, with many new technologies facilitating automation of routine and typically lower-skill tasks, while complementing many tasks that are often completed by higher-skilled workers.[10] Consistent with this, Heckman et al. (2006) estimate that the average return to schooling among males increased from about 10.5 percent during the 1980s to 14 percent during the 1990s.

---

[10] See Chapter 5 for further detail.

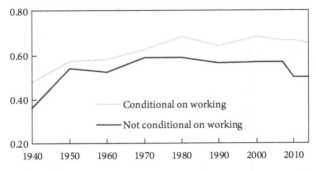

Figure 3.6 Median Black Male Wage for Every $1 Earned by White Men
Note: Men aged 25–54. Real wages are measured in thousands of 1980 dollars.
Source: Bayer and Charles, 2019.

Discrimination is an important candidate for explaining some of the pay differences that are not attributable to standard explanatory variables. It is a key challenge for policymakers striving for inclusive labor markets, often reflecting factors that originate outside the labor market (e.g., access to quality education). Discrimination can take many forms, ranging from individuals taking explicit actions against members of certain groups (e.g., racism) to more implicit or unintentional biases, sometimes rooted in (implicit or explicit) social norms (e.g., the notion that women should be the main childcare providers).

Increasingly, empirical work on discrimination has focused on field experiments, which are helpful in providing evidence that cannot be isolated using standard labor market data. While they leave unanswered the question as to whether the results apply more broadly, several such studies provide compelling evidence that discrimination is pervasive and important, in the United States and elsewhere.[11] For example, regarding gender discrimination, Goldin and Rouse (2000) assessed the extent of differential access between male and female symphony musicians. In a quasi-natural experiment, a change in hiring practices at symphony orchestras involved the move to "blind" auditions, in which the audition took place behind a screen, thereby preventing the jury from knowing the gender of the auditionee. Goldin and Rouse found that hiring was much more gender neutral when auditions were blind. More broadly, a consensus view from experimental research points to evidence of significant discrimination against women in high-status or male-dominated jobs as well as discrimination against men in female-dominated jobs (Azmat and Petrongolo 2014).[12]

---

[11] See Bertrand and Duflo (2016) for a survey of the broader literature.
[12] While research has focused on discrimination in hiring practices, one might hypothesize important general equilibrium effects in terms of how anticipated discrimination in the labor market might feed back into individuals' choices in human capital accumulation or job search. The experimental research summarized here does not offer insights on this dimension.

Other work has focused on racial discrimination. For example, Bertrand and Mullainathan (2004) assessed the extent to which race affects access to job opportunities. Their research design involved sending fictitious applications to real job openings, with applications identical except for varying names that suggested racial differences. They found large differences in callback rates: applicants with "white-sounding" names were 50 percent more likely to receive a callback than applicants with similar resumes but with "African-American-sounding" names.

Another set of studies examines the impact of bias on job performance. Glover, Pallais, and Pariente (2017) examined the performance of cashiers in a French grocery store chain. Cashiers worked with different managers on different days and their schedules were determined quasi-randomly. Minority cashiers that were scheduled to work with biased managers (as determined by an implicit association test) were absent more often and were less productive than majority cashiers.

C. Protection

Individuals are subject to various labor market risks, both cross-sectional and intertemporal. For example, search frictions imply that two *ex-ante* identical individuals may end up with different pay (e.g., Mortensen 2003), and earnings and unemployment risk mean that two *ex-ante* identical individuals with initially equal pay may experience different earnings profiles over time, independent of their individual actions. In this context, Jacobson et al. (1993) have documented that the earnings of displaced workers (i.e., those losing their job for reasons unrelated to their own performance or characteristics, such as plant closings) can remain 25 percent lower than those of similar non-displaced workers even five years after displacement.[13] The welfare losses of uninsured earnings risk can be large: Rogerson and Schindler (2002) calculate those associated with the earnings uncertainty of displacement on the order of up to one percent of output. Heathcote et al. (2007) consider more general types of labor market risk and calculate welfare costs that are up to an order of magnitude higher.[14]

Private insurance against these kinds of labor market risks is typically not available. However, there are several labor market policies and institutions that can help provide some insurance against earnings shocks that cannot otherwise be insured against. Unemployment insurance (UI) is a prime example of a

---

[13] Labor market risk, including persistent scarring effects, are often also the result of aggregate shocks. For example, the empirical literature suggests that negative shocks can lead to hysteresis, that is, output losses that persist long after the initial shock. See, e.g., Cerra and Saxena (2008) for an analysis of a broad set of macroeconomic crises, and IMF (2021) in the context of Covid-19.

[14] All of these welfare cost estimates are large when compared to Lucas's (1987) seminal examination of the welfare gain from eliminating all consumption fluctuations, which he estimated at less than 1/100th of one percent of consumption.

government-financed public insurance system. Other policies to deal with labor market risk include employment protection legislation (EPL) which is aimed at reducing the risk of unemployment, conditional on having a job.[15] These labor market policies will be discussed more in detail in Section IV.

Our goal in this subsection is to document the extent of differences in social protection that exist across countries. Later, we will discuss the efficacy of these measures and their potential adverse effects on other aspects of inclusivity. While almost all AEs have UI systems in place, they exist in only about 60 percent of EMDEs. In addition, recent estimates suggest that only about 22 percent of unemployed workers are covered by unemployment benefits (Duval and Loungani (2019) and ILO (2017)). Among those countries with an UI system, benefit coverage is much greater in AEs than in EMDEs—on average, close to half of the unemployed receive benefits in AEs, compared to less than a third in EMDEs (Figures 3.7 and 3.8).

The stringency of EPL and the coverage and level of MWs vary widely across countries. Among OECD countries, some countries such as the Netherlands employ strict EPL measures, while others, such as Canada and the United States, impose comparatively few restrictions on job dismissals, although the US experience rating premium in unemployment insurance taxes has similar effects on dismissals (Johnston 2021) (Figure 3.9). Similarly, MWs are widely used among

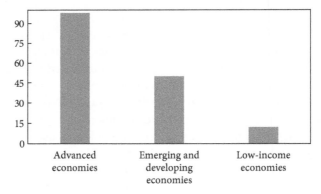

Figure 3.7 Share of Countries with an Unemployment Insurance System (2014, %)
Sources: ILO Statistics and Duval and Loungani, 2019.

---

[15] EPL refers to a set of regulations regarding individual and collective dismissals and the use of fixed term rather than open-ended contracts. It includes advance notice periods or severance payments in case of individual dismissals, prior announcement and authorization for collective dismissals and limits on the length and possibility for renewal of temporary contracts. In the United States, "experience rating" of unemployment insurance—where an unemployment insurance tax rate depends on the employer's history of layoffs—and strict anti-discrimination clauses—often enforced via class-action suits—have been shown to act as a dampening factor on layoffs over the business cycle (Ratner 2013; Johnston 2021).

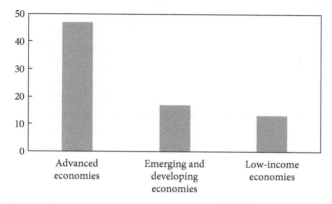

Figure 3.8 Unemployment Benefit Coverage (2013, Percentage of Unemployed Workers Receiving Benefits)

Sources: ILO Statistics and Duval and Loungani, 2019.

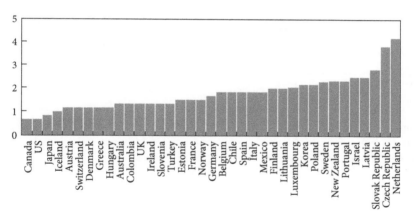

Figure 3.9 Procedural Requirements for Individual Dismissals of Regular Workers, (Indicator Score, 2019)

Note: Range of indicator scores: 0–6, with higher values indicating more procedural requirements. Procedural requirements consist of two components: notification procedures and time delay before notice can be given.

Source: OECD Employment Protection Legislation Database.

AEs, with nearly three-quarters having some MW, while only about 60 percent of EMDEs have a formal MW (Figure 3.10).

Most countries also have other complementary insurance systems, such as health, pension and disability insurance, as well as, in many cases, social welfare systems that provide a subsistence level of income. While a deeper discussion of these systems is beyond the scope of this chapter (see, however, Chapter 14 on health-related issues and Chapter 18 on generational issues), ILO (2017) concludes that such systems remain limited in terms of presence and coverage worldwide, and particularly in EMDEs—for example, globally only 41 percent of new mothers receive maternity benefits, while only about 28 percent of persons with severe disabilities receive disability benefits. However, Figure 3.11 indicates that the lack of social protection is not exclusively a matter of economic development—the most generous social protection systems in EMs exceed those at the lower end among AEs, while the least generous EMs fall short of some developing economies.

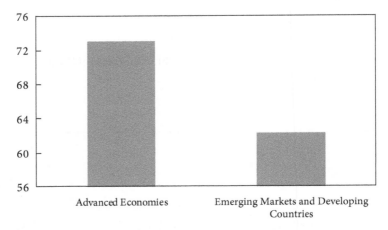

Figure 3.10 Share of Countries with Minimum Wage Legislation, by Country Groups (%)
Sources: ILO and authors' calculations.

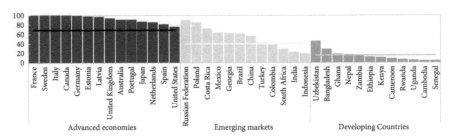

Figure 3.11 Proportion of Population Covered by Social Protection Floors (%, averages of 2015–18)
Note: Averages are calculated based on all available countries in each group, respectively, including those not listed in the chart. Country groupings are based on the IMF WEO classification.
Sources: ILO and authors' calculations.

D. Voice

Labor contracts—whether formal or informal—are never fully contingent and so allow for renegotiation after the realization of technological, preference or labor supply shocks. To facilitate such renegotiation and to protect match-specific investment, workers and firms often join trade unions and business associations, respectively, which can voice concerns over economic and social developments and engage in negotiations over wages and working conditions. Trade unions, in particular, play an important role as they can help strengthen workers' voice and their bargaining power. They have often contributed to a reduction in income disparities where they historically played an important role (Callaway and Collings 2018; Farber et al. 2018).

Forms of engagement and representation vary depending on the country context. For instance, workers can be represented by formally recognized trade unions or informal worker associations. Similarly, firms can be part of employers' associations or be members of chambers of commerce. In addition, many countries make provisions for firm-internal working conditions and grievance mechanisms, for instance, through work councils or ombuds(wo)men.[16] In many European countries, workers' wage and labor conditions are often covered by collective agreements despite not being member of a trade union (through voluntary or administrative extension of wage bargaining agreements).

The labor market effects of collective bargaining are shaped to a significant degree by how bargaining takes place. In some countries, collective bargaining is centralized, with both workers and businesses represented at the national level in tripartite structures to engage in negotiations over national development strategies. In others, bargaining is a decentralized system at the firm level, for example, with worker representatives being members of the board of certain (large) companies or organized through work councils. And in some, it takes a more intermediate form, with sectoral or occupational institutions bargaining over minimum standards for wages and working conditions for (covered) workers. In practice, collective bargaining institutions are more complex, and this can make clear-cut distinctions between these different types challenging. For example, while many European economies are classified as ones with predominantly sectoral bargaining, there is a great deal of variation among them in terms of extension agreements (i.e., the extent to which bargaining agreements are binding for non-participating firms); derogation (to what extent can individual firms opt out); and coordination through pattern bargaining (OECD 2013, Table 1).[17]

---

[16] To the best of our knowledge, no overall encompassing overview exists for cross-country comparison of different forms of such mechanisms of voice. Most comparable information is limited to rates of trade unionization and business associations.

[17] The possible impact of collective bargaining institutions on wage and (un)employment outcomes was summarized by Calmfors and Driffill's (1988) "hump-shaped hypothesis" which argued

Empirically, trade union density and collective bargaining coverage rates are much higher on average in AEs than EMDEs, with collective bargaining covering about half of salaried employees in AE on average, compared to about one-quarter in EMDEs (Duval and Loungani 2019), partly reflecting generally stronger organization of labor in AEs. However, trade union density, and collective bargaining coverage more generally, have been declining in most countries over recent decades, especially in comparison to business associations. For example, union density has roughly halved since 1980 in Germany, France, the UK, Austria, and the Netherlands, and it has declined substantially also in Central and Eastern European countries after the fall of central planning.[18] And since the early 2000s, union density and collective bargaining coverage have declined in almost all countries, mostly as a result of a rise in employment in non-covered sectors and occupations (Figures 3.12 and 3.13). Conversely, membership in business and employer associations has remained stable in all OECD countries (Cazes et al. 2017) except Slovenia and Portugal, having successfully adapted "their organizational structure as well as their activities to the changing needs of business" (Brandl and Lehr 2016). The decline in collective bargaining institutions may become

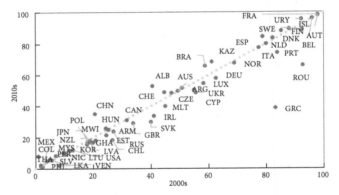

Figure 3.12 Evolution of Bargaining Coverage (%)

Note: Data are averaged across all available data points for a country in a given decade; data availability varies by country.

Source: ILO Statistics.

that highly centralized systems (by providing macro flexibility) and decentralized systems (by providing micro flexibility) would outperform sector-level bargaining in terms of unemployment outcomes. This is because under centralized systems, unions would be more likely to internalize the impact of negotiated wages on overall unemployment, while under firm-level bargaining, they would be cognizant of the firm's profitability so as to avoid layoffs—either of these constraining elements would be absent under intermediate systems, thus leading to relatively higher wage outcomes and lower production and employment. In practice, the hump-shaped hypothesis has had mixed empirical success, in part reflecting the complexity of collective bargaining institutions.

[18] The decline in union coverage in Germany arguably was one of the reasons for the introduction of a MW in 2015. In some other countries, union density has declined more moderately, such as Spain, Belgium, Iceland and the Nordic countries. For more details, see Visser (2013) and OECD (2017).

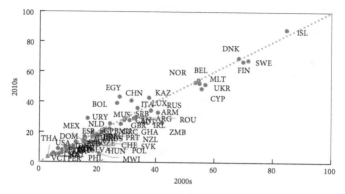

Figure 3.13 Evolution of Trade Unionization (%)

Note: Data are averaged across all available data points for a country in a given decade; data availability varies by country.

Source: ILO Statistics.

particularly worrisome in light of the technological and organizational changes that are transforming the labor market and generating new forms of employment. Importantly, a stronger voice of organized labor at the company level could help a more equitable introduction of new technologies that would improve the longer-term prospects for productivity and employment, for instance by strengthening incentives for worker training and supporting workforce reorganization (Genz et al. 2019).

E. Informality as a Cross-Cutting Issue

Informality is a cross-cutting example which touches on the aforementioned four pillars of inclusiveness.[19] While informal employment in many countries is often the only avenue for individuals to gain access to employment, it is frequently in the form of low-quality jobs with low pay (fairness).[20] Moreover, informal workers are insufficiently protected from risks such as job loss and health problems,

[19] The concept of informality ranges across several categories of activities and workers. Informality can refer to informal economic activity and informal employment. A first approach to defining informality, the enterprise-based approach, focused on the relationship between the enterprise and the government (e.g. registration status or recognition by a government). However, there are limits to this approach, since unregulated forms of employment may exist outside of informal enterprises. A second definition, resulting from the 17th International Conference of Labour Statistician, combines the concept of informal enterprises with a concept of informal jobs (Hussmanns 2004; Chen et al. 2005). Under this definition, paid employees are considered informal if they are not covered by any social protections. Still, the enterprise-based approach remains valid and is applied to self-employed (employers and own-account workers) who are considered to be in informal employment if the enterprise in which they work is informal. For a broader discussion, we refer to Diaz et al. (2018) and ILO (2018a).

[20] Workers with similar skills tend to earn more in the formal sector compared to their informal sector peers, with the wage gap widening at lower skill levels (Deléchat and Medina, 2020).

and hence face higher volatility in their income (protection). Finally, informal workers are typically not organized in trade unions and hence they do not have the opportunity to protect their labor rights, associated for instance with working hours or safety regulations, as well as to influence social and economic policies (voice).[21] Thus, in many EMDEs, providing formal employment opportunities is one of the main challenges to developing a more inclusive labor market, and in fact to inclusive growth more broadly.

Countries characterized by a high level of informality tend to experience higher poverty and inequality (World Bank 2019) and slower growth, with informal workers more vulnerable to shocks, since informal employment is often concentrated in low productivity activities that are more likely to be terminated in response to adverse shocks (Bacchetta et al. 2009). In this regard, informality can be a consequence of low levels of economic activity and volatile economic growth—lacking stable and productive employment opportunities and insufficient or absent social protection schemes, workers are forced into survival activities that make them particularly vulnerable to shocks. One of the main solutions to high levels of informality therefore is in many cases to create a dynamic and growing economy that provides sufficient formal employment opportunities. These broader policies are beyond the narrow scope of labor market policies (see Section IV for a discussion of some labor market policies to reduce informality).

According to the ILO, two billion of the world's employed population aged 15 and over work informally, representing 61.2 percent of global employment. The incidence of informality varies across countries and is positively correlated with the level of socio-economic development. In countries at a higher level of socio-economic development, namely North America, Europe, Australia, and New Zealand, informality rates are below 20 percent, while in emerging and developing countries more than 50 percent of the labor force is informal (Figure 3.14). Estimates for Sub-Saharan Africa and Asia are even higher.[22]

Despite the overall decline in informal employment across both AEs and EMDEs, substantial cross-country differences remain. In some countries, informal employment has increased, in contrast to much of Latin America, South Africa, Vietnam, and Indonesia, where its share has been declining (OECD 2011).[23,24] The increase in certain types of informal employment observed in some countries can be seen as the reaction to a failure on the part of governments to provide

---

[21] There are, nevertheless, examples of informal sector associations and trade unions are actively pursuing to reach out to informal workers. One example is WIEGO in India that has a global reach. For a strategy on how to extend social security to informal workers, see ILO (2020b).

[22] For more details, see also Gasparini and Tornarolli (2007) and Jütting et al. (2008).

[23] Heintz and Pollin (2005) show that within a data set of 23 countries, 19 showed increases in informality.

[24] In fact, the substantial decline in informality in Latin America over the past two decades was associated with large decline in inequality (Deléchat and Medina 2020).

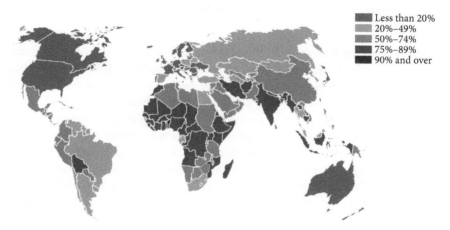

Figure 3.14 Share of Informal Employment (excluding Agriculture) (% of total employment, 2016)

Note: Country coverage is uneven. Countries for which no individual estimate exists are shaded according to their (sub-)regional average. In countries with large shares of agricultural employment, informality rates for total employment may be significantly higher.

Source: International Labour Organization.

proper social security or to difficulties faced by formal firms in surviving in world markets (see Bacchetta et al. 2009).

Several factors affect the level of informality or at least are correlated with it. Informality is highly correlated with own-account workers, the agricultural sector, rural areas, women, youth and elderly populations, and low educational attainment.[25]

Vicious cycles may arise and further exacerbate the problem. Facing unstable income, informal workers are unlikely to invest in human capital and move to higher-productivity jobs and very often they remain trapped in a vulnerable state. Moreover, high levels of informality also diminish public revenues and limit the State capacity to raise taxes that would allow it to finance public (primary and secondary) education and sustainable social security systems.[26]

Finally, the recent Covid-19 pandemic is likely to have a much more detrimental impact on informal workers. A large number of informal workers are engaged in manual tasks and service activities, which typically cannot be performed remotely and hence are more affected by the Covid-19 crisis.

[25] According to UN data, women are the overwhelming majority of informal workers in developing countries, accounting for 95 (90) percent of total employment in South Asia (Sub-Saharan Africa). Own-account work refers to self-employed workers who do not have any employees.

[26] In EMDEs, where informality is most pervasive, government revenues are, on average, lower by 5–10 percentage points of GDP, and expenditures are lower by 4–10 percentage points of GDP than in those with the lowest levels of informality (World Bank 2019).

IV. Policies for Inclusion

Departures from inclusivity in the labor market can arise from many factors, including demand and supply factors, cyclical or structural dynamics, and other market failures, such as incomplete insurance markets or non-competitive markets (e.g., market power). Devising the right policies to address shortcomings in labor market inclusiveness requires policymakers (1) to properly diagnose these challenges and (2) based on this diagnosis, design and implement appropriate policies.

Some standard labor market models and frameworks can be helpful in structuring such a diagnosis. For example, in some cases, it may be appropriate to consider perfectly competitive markets as a benchmark and ask if, and to what extent, market outcomes differ from such an outcome. Depending on the answer, policy implications can vary drastically: for example, in a perfectly competitive labor market equilibrium, imposing a (binding) MW will reduce employment and raise wages above the market level; by contrast, if the assessment is that firms have excessive market power (monopsony), a MW can raise employment and wages.

In other cases, it will be helpful to recognize that many labor market outcomes are shaped by frictions in the flow of job seekers and job vacancies. Job search and matching models are built on this notion (e.g., Mortensen and Pissarides 1994; Pissarides 2000; Layard et al. 1991; Ernst and Rani 2011). In particular, they provide a framework for examining the factors that affect the flows into and out of (un)employment, as well as the incentives for firms to create new jobs. Strong economic growth and high mobility of job seekers both across sectors and occupations allow for efficient labor reallocation and a fast return to low (equilibrium) unemployment, while frictions can, in times of recessions or when jobs are being destroyed for other reasons (e.g., automation or import competition), lead to more persistent increases in unemployment and slower adjustment to sectoral or other reallocation needs. Such frictions are particularly relevant in countries that are characterized by strong labor market segmentation arising, for instance, from lack of skills, tight regulation (e.g., occupational licensing, employment protection), lack of access to finance or lack of market access and slow growth (Fields 2005).

Based on the diagnosis, reform success depends on the state's capacity to identify challenges properly and its ability to design and implement appropriate policy reforms. Often, policy makers lack both. Regarding the first, many countries do not possess an independent employment observatory or a well-funded (national) statistical system that would allow to identify challenges and track policy impact and progress in implementation. Part of a successful transition to an inclusive labor market therefore will include strengthening labor market information and analysis systems.[27] In addition, policymakers must have the requisite

---

[27] Ideally, such systems should be removed from daily policy activities to provide for a systematic analysis of the challenges; given sufficient funding; and provided with political clout. Possibilities to

economic capacity to interpret data and devise appropriate policies. Even if policy needs are properly identified, countries with limited fiscal space and a reduced capacity to mobilize resources may not be able to prioritize policies that foster inclusiveness. Lastly, implementation also, importantly, hinges on the presence of sufficient legal and institutional frameworks to enforce policies.[28]

In the following, we discuss some policy measures that can help address some of the departures from inclusive labor markets suggested by the discussions so far.

A. Rebalancing Market Power

As discussed earlier, some recent research suggests that a rise in market power (firm monopsony) and a gradual erosion of effective labor market institutions, most notably a rapid decline in trade union membership and bargaining power, have played an important role in contributing to the substantial decline in labor income shares, i.e., a decline in wages relative to labor productivity. In this section we discuss some policy responses to these changes in market power.[29]

Minimum Wages

In the presence of monopsony on local labor markets (often found in retail or hospitality services), large employers offer both employment and wages below market clearing levels to maximize their profits (Manning 2021). Long treated as a theoretical peculiarity with little empirical relevance (Neumark and Wascher 2008), evidence for such market power has increasingly found empirical support in recent years, both economy-wide and for specific occupations and sectors.[30]

Against this backdrop, the debate on using MWs as a direct way for government to create a floor for working conditions has intensified, especially among AEs. In the presence of monopsony power, MWs can constitute a win-win policy,

strengthen such a function include linking it to institutions providing social security or setting up observatory groups within a (labor) ministry. To the extent that other institutions also collect information on (local) business conditions, it is also imperative to help connecting such information across institutions (e.g., the Beige Book by the US Federal Reserve Board).

[28] Resource mobilization is a constant challenge in many developing economies. Setting up a national development agency can help coordinate activities across ministries, ideally by including social partners, even though such efforts to coordinate policy actions face challenges of their own, as experienced in South Africa. Chapters 12 and 13 discuss in greater detail fiscal issues related to inclusive growth; Chapters 10 and 15 touch on some of aspects related to governance and political economy, respectively.

[29] We also noted that changes in the labor share could be due to the nature of technological change rather than changes in market power. Government policy might also be used to affect the nature of technological change and the extent to which labor-saving technology is adopted. Technology and policy are discussed in more detail in Chapter 5.

[30] See Davalos and Ernst (2021) for an overview of the current state of the discussion and microeconomic evidence on the extent of monopsonistic power in the United States and Peru. The importance of firm monopsonies has also received attention in recent discussions on raising the MW in the United States (CBO 2021). See also Chapter 6 on product markets and competition.

raising inclusion and efficiency. Even in the absence of firm power, the MW is a direct distributional tool and often seen as an appealing policy option for governments to help alleviate in-work poverty, and reduce income inequality, while imposing limited direct fiscal costs. MWs also interact with social security systems including pensions (Borgschulte and Cho 2019) and prevent the dilution of tax credits and wage subsidies (Rothstein and Zipperer 2020). The discussion regarding the impact of MW on restoring labor market inclusiveness hinges critically on the extent and scope of market power across sectors and occupations. That is, a single MW level may not be effective to help offset general firm monopsony power that plays out across the wage distribution.

Empirical estimates of the employment impact on low-wage earners remain inconclusive (Neumark and Shirley 2021; Dube 2019a) and show large variation across demographic groups (Cengiz et al. 2019).[31] Similar to the impact in AEs, adverse effects on employment of MWs in low- and middle-income countries are typically small and sometimes positive, depending on country circumstances.

The evidence does, however, point to strong positive effects on poverty alleviation (Dube 2019b). In OECD countries, an increase in the MW is likely to result in lower wage dispersion as it tends to benefit low-skilled workers (OECD 2011) and thus could help reduce earnings inequality. In developing countries with large shares of the workforce in informal employment, where statutory MWs cannot be enforced, they often tend to spill over nevertheless, raising incomes in both formal and informal employment relationships, suggesting significant market power of employers in the formal economy (Adam and Buffie 2020).

To maximize the effects on a reduction in poverty while limiting negative effects on jobs, the literature has identified a number of principles (Herr and Kazandziska 2011, provide a summary). For example, a (statutory) MW should be defined in consultation with social partners to achieve poverty alleviation objectives while minimizing possible adverse employment effects, and it should be regularly monitored and revised, for example, through a representative body and based on an evaluation of the economic and social evolution, to ensure it continues to have its intended impact (ILO 2015).[32] When collective bargaining agreements have sufficient coverage, they can be also be an effective mean to fix MWs.

---

[31] For example, Fedoretsa and Shupe (2021) find that the introduction of a MW in Germany in 2015 raised reservation wages by up to 16 percent, but only temporarily and only at the lower end of the wage distribution.

[32] As noted by the ILO in its *Minimum Wage Policy Guide*, "[s]etting and adjusting the level is perhaps the most challenging part of minimum wage fixing. If set too low, minimum wages will have little effect in protecting workers and [if] set too high, minimum wages [may] have adverse employment effects." The level that policymakers should set the minimum wage at will generally depend on country-specific factors and policy objectives, including, e.g., whether the aim of a MW is to achieve poverty objectives, address firm monopsonies, or counter discrimination.

Strengthening Collective Bargaining Institutions

Eroded bargaining power of (especially low-income) workers can be restored through stronger bargaining institutions. Policy intervention in this area is, however, less obvious as trade unionization relies heavily on political strategies of trade unions themselves, including whether they prefer to organize along sectoral or occupational delineations or coordinate at the regional or national level. In this regard, globalization, the rise in atypical work and a shift towards traditionally less unionized (private) service sector jobs has proved to be particularly damaging to trade unionization rates regardless of policy interventions, including in traditionally corporatist countries such as Germany where the number of trade union members halved between 1990 and 2010 (Bryson et al. 2011; Schnabel 2013). Such a reduction, while often promoted as a move towards a more flexible labor market, can come at the cost of making industrial relations more conflictual (Addison and Teixeira 2017). As discussed in Section III.D, trade unionization rates are low also, and especially, in developing countries where informality rates are high, despite an increasing effort of formal sector trade unions to reach out into the informal labor market (ILO 2019a).

The evidence on the impact of collective bargaining and unions on (un-) employment is mostly focused on AEs and is largely inconclusive. Most studies find, on balance, that unions either increase unemployment modestly or have no significant effect, although OECD data suggest that countries with high degree of coordination tend to have lower unemployment rates than others (Betcherman 2012). Consistent with theory, empirical studies also tend to find that union members and workers covered by collective bargaining earn higher wages than other workers, with a wage premium of around 5–15 percent in AEs, and up to 20 percent in some EMDEs (Betcherman 2012). Most studies show that the union wage effect is strongest for less skilled workers and is larger for women than for men, although the evidence on other typically low-wage groups, such as ethnic and racial minorities, is less clear. These effects are most prominent in systems where union density is high, and collective bargaining is centralized and/or coordinated. Thus, collective bargaining may reduce wage and income inequality (for example, Duval and Loungani 2019), although this impact tends to be moderate due to two competing effects: unions narrow wage differentials among their members but widen disparities between unionized and non-unionized workers (Betcherman 2012).

Policy makers have several ways of strengthening collective bargaining institutions. One frequently used intervention consists of extending collective agreements reached between management and unionized workers at the company- or sectoral-level to all employees, unionized or not.[33] Such administrative extensions

---

[33] See Hayter and Visser (2018) and Oesingmann (2016) for an overview of practices of administrative extension of collective agreements in Europe and some selected emerging economies.

have been shown to provide a fast and effective way of guaranteeing a protection floor, especially in low-wage sectors. They can also strengthen membership in business associations, giving employers a way to be involved in the collective bargaining process (Hayter and Visser 2018). At the same time, extending agreements administratively can lower incentives for unionization. It can also adversely affect market competition, as some firms may have an interest in pushing for higher wage agreements if coverage extension rules can be used to raise rivals' costs (Haucap et al. 2001; Villanueva 2015; Oesingmann 2016). Market concentration might therefore increase, further worsening labor market imbalances that such extensions of collective agreements try to address.

An alternative but more indirect way is to bolster industrial relations at the shop floor through works councils (Rogers and Streeck 1995). Depending on the specific institutional settings, worker representatives have to be consulted in cases of restructurings, investment or layoffs, thereby reducing labor turnover and layoffs (Hirsch et al. 2010). When combined with industry-level bargaining that prevents rent seeking at the shop floor, such works councils have been shown to raise firm-level productivity (Hübler and Jirjahn 2003) and to speed up the introduction of new technologies (Genz et al. 2019). Nevertheless, reaping such benefits from works councils might take time and require building up trust between management and workers representatives before contributing positively to profits and wages (Mueller and Stegmaier 2017).

Finally, some countries have managed to keep a high level of unionization through the "Ghent system," whereby trade unions rather than state agencies are responsible for administering a (voluntary) unemployment benefit system. These systems, while regulated and subsidized by the state, strengthen the ties between trade union organizations and employees, thereby increasing incentives for adherence to a union (Scruggs 2002). At the same time, younger workers and independent contractors often opt out of such systems if they have the choice, weakening both protection and union representation (Shin and Böckerman 2019).

B. Sharing Risk

Workers face a multitude of labor-market risks, most of which cannot (easily) be insured against. Such risks can include employment risk, technological change that makes existing skills (human capital) obsolete, and/or income risk. The absence of private insurance markets for many of these risks provides a rationale for governments to protect individuals.

Various approaches that are often chosen by governments include: (1) measures to restrict and/or regulate layoffs under certain conditions, for instance, in case of mass layoffs, but also more generally to prevent discrimination and unfair dismissals. Alternatively, (2) provision of replacement income through unemployment benefits either directly as a government-run support scheme or through subsidies to a voluntary insurance scheme. A third approach is (3) the use of labor market programs to facilitate search and retraining. The first two approaches seek to protect vulnerable households and prevent economic and social exclusion. However, they do not, per se, facilitate job mobility or provide jobseekers with the tools needed for access to, or re-entry into, the labor market. Moreover, various approaches to provide protection may contribute to labor market segmentation, thus providing protection at the expense of access. The third approach aims at limiting such segmentation by strengthening incentives for mobility and provide resources to switch occupations, sectors or locations. A proper design of the three protection mechanisms and their financing is therefore required to address such a trade-off. In addition, a successful strategy needs to rely on the joint implementation of income support and activation measures.

Employment Protection Legislation

As discussed in Section III.C, EPL coverage and enforcement vary significantly across countries.[34] In the majority of countries, some categories of (dependent) employees are excluded. For instance, in Turkey EPL does not cover domestic workers, agricultural workers, managers/executives, as well as employees in enterprises with fewer than 30 workers. Australia explicitly excludes casual workers from EPL legal coverage.[35] Moreover, and importantly, informally employed workers remain outside the reach of EPL.

EPL may reduce the risk of becoming unemployed for those individuals in protected jobs, but by reducing firms' incentives to create new jobs can reduce the probability for the unemployed of finding a job. Moreover, EPL has a mixed record of protecting workers against shocks. Research in AEs suggests that strict EPL reduces job destruction, as intended (Messina and Vallanti 2007), and workers in firms with less restrictive EPL are more likely to be dismissed (Boeri and Jimeno 2005). However, EPL can contribute to labor market segmentation between highly protected insiders and vulnerable outsiders and raises the risk of exclusion of youth and low-skilled (Betcherman 2012). Strict EPL also tends to encourage informal employment and to hinder productivity and economic growth (Bassanini et al. 2009). In the aggregate, EPL seems to slightly reduce employment, although more in EMDEs than in AEs (Duval and Loungani 2019; Betcherman 2012). Moreover, even though the impact of EPL on unemployment seems to be negligible (Heimberger 2020), by dampening labor market turnover

---

[34] See Gimpelson et al. (2010) and Aleksynska and Eberlein (2016).
[35] Casual workers are defined as persons "who have an explicit or implicit contract of employment which is not expected to continue for more than a short period, whose duration is to be determined by national circumstance" (see ILO 1993).

following an external shock, unemployment can become more persistent (Bassanini and Duval 2006).

EPLs can also affect wages. A report by the OECD (2011) argued that stricter EPLs compresses the wage distribution, and hence reduces wage inequality among the employed.

Differential EPL for different employment groups can lead to duality—in some labor markets, a significant share of workers is under temporary contracts, who are likely to receive less employer-sponsored training than workers under permanent contracts, where stricter EPL gives firms an incentive to invest more in their employees. Therefore, strict EPL reduces labor market opportunities of (more vulnerable) temporary workers relative to those under permanent contracts (Cabrales et al. 2014). Segmentation in the labor market may also lead to higher wage growth among more protected (permanent) workers, exacerbating wage inequality. Temporary contracts often involve a substantial wage penalty, for example, EU temporary workers earn on average 14 percent less than regular workers (European Commission 2010), further contributing to widening wage inequality (OECD 2011).

However, certain forms of EPL can have potentially beneficial effects. Ciminelli et al. (2020) suggest that strict EPL is associated with stronger workers' voice and hence low risk of exclusion (from employment). They argue that deregulation, by weakening workers' bargaining power, has been partially responsible for the declining labor income share in AEs. Moreover, strict EPL creates the expectation of long-lasting employment relationships and hence encourages investments by workers and firms in relationship-specific capital. Doepke and Gaetani (2020) point out that in those countries such as Germany where firms cannot easily fire workers because of strict EPL, in case of turbulence shocks firms are keen to invest to maintain workers' skills and productivity. Bassanini and Ernst (2002) find that strict EPL in combination with coordinated collective bargaining might have helped innovation and productivity by stimulating the accumulation of firm-specific capital.

Alternative forms of employment protection through worker retention and furloughing schemes have attracted increased attention especially following the outbreak of the Covid-19 pandemic (OECD 2020). Originally instituted in the chemical industry in Germany in 1910 to compensate workers for (temporary) interruptions of activity without laying them off, the German *Kurzarbeit* policy—which allows firms and workers to agree on hours reductions, with the shortfall in pay partially covered by the government—has been extended gradually to cover all sectors and workers. Other countries have expanded similar programs as well. By raising the elasticity of hours rather than of jobs, the policy has been shown to yield a significant reduction in job destruction, but also a reduction in the job-content of growth once the adverse shock is absorbed and a recovery sets in (Hijzen and Martin 2013). Arguably, however, an overly long extension of furloughing will slow down the reallocation of jobs, especially when the recovery is not symmetric across sectors and occupations (Cahuc 2019).

Income Support and Activation Measures

Unemployment insurance (UI) systems are intended to provide temporary income support during periods of joblessness, but often entail important trade-offs in balancing equity/insurance with efficiency considerations. For example, more generous UI can help offset the income losses from becoming unemployed (insurance) but may also lead to higher reservation wages and longer unemployment durations. Thus, at the most general level, UI systems should be neither too generous nor too low.[36] The empirical evidence on the impact of UI benefit duration on wages and unemployment durations is mixed: Arni (2017) finds that longer duration of UI benefits led to higher reservation (and realized) wages in Switzerland, while others find small negative effects of extending the duration of UI benefits on realized earnings in Germany (Schmieder and Von Wachter 2016) or modest effects in Austria (Nekoei and Weber 2017).

However, high replacement rates, especially if paid over an extended period, may reduce job search efforts and the incentive to return to work, lengthening unemployment spells, and eroding skills and labor market competencies (Van Ours and Vodopievic 2008; Tatsiramos 2009).

With regard to poverty and distributional effects, there does not seem to be a robust link between UI benefit levels and overall inequality in AEs (Jaumotte and Buitron 2015). In EMDEs, the low level of coverage limits the ability of UI systems to prevent unemployment-related poverty and inequality and increases the importance of informal coping mechanisms—that is, to seek informal employment to avert poverty (OECD 2011).

To strengthen incentives to return to work, some countries have reformed their UI systems by offering high initial replacement rates combined with obligations to accept certain job offers and a fast reduction in benefits as unemployment spells lengthen. The drawback is that a tapered scheme penalizes the most socially vulnerable groups who are the most adversely affected by unemployment, and is thus regressive (ILO 2000a). Moreover, the prospect of a cut in unemployment benefits may prevent jobseekers from devoting time to finding jobs that match their skills, with detrimental effects on overall productivity and growth.

Indeed, recent research (Farooq et al. 2020 for the United States, and Nekoei and Weber 2017 for Austria) suggests that by providing more time for job search,

---

[36] The design of UI schemes varies significantly across countries. E.g., the level of UI benefits may be calculated as a contributions-related benefit, as a flat rate, or as a percentage of the person's last wage. Some schemes also entail a combination of these options and the application of minimum and maximum thresholds.

extended UI benefits may significantly improve job matching. This ultimately benefits both workers and firms, another example of a "win-win" policy. On the one hand, workers have a higher probability to find the most suitable jobs—given their education, talents, and experience—and hence earn higher wages and have greater job satisfaction and thereby lower quit rates. On the other hand, a more efficient matching process also benefits firms and the overall economy because it lowers turnover and improves productivity. Moreover, in countries where unemployment benefit schemes are limited or absent, jobseekers are keen to accept any type of work, including informal employment. This can limit their opportunities for (re-)employment in the formal sector, for instance through an erosion of skills, adverse signaling of competencies or information barriers. Therefore, well-designed unemployment benefit schemes can strengthen incentives to work in the formal economy (Ernst 2015).

A successful strategy proposes the combination of income support and activation measures with a reduction in EPL as part of a "flexicurity" welfare reform (Bekker and Mailand 2019). The "flexicurity" model is characterized by the combination of three elements: generous social safety nets, an extensive system of activation policies and flexible hiring and firing. The most prominent example is Denmark's "flexicurity" model, which has resulted in low (long-term) unemployment rates and a high perception of job security among Danish workers (Andersen 2011). See also Chapter 21 for further discussion of the flexicurity model.

Social Protection

UI benefits are only one pillar of a larger package of programs to strengthen inclusiveness and provide protection against various forms of income loss due to illness, disability or old age. Common to all are several challenges to inclusiveness that tend to create a policy trade-off between protection and access. Contributory social security systems—financed through contributions by beneficiaries and their employers—create a duality in the labor market since they automatically exclude informal and (in most cases) self-employed workers.[37] Inefficiencies in social security systems often mean that the social protection benefits are small relative to contribution rates, discouraging individuals from seeking out formal employment, and similarly providing disincentives to formal job creation for firms.

Therefore, a successful policy strategy to address this trade-off needs to tackle both the lack of protection and the risk of labor market segmentation. Some governments, therefore, have started to expand non-contributory systems to promote inclusiveness by extending social protection systems to informal workers not

---

[37] In some countries, registered self-employed workers are also covered.

covered by any social mechanism. While this approach strengthens social protection, it further lowers incentives to work in the formal economy. A second pillar, therefore, consists of strengthening incentives to facilitate the way to formalization, for instance by broadening the tax base and lowering tax rates. In addition, a two-tier social protection system could extend unemployment benefits to all workers in the formal sector including those working part-time and/or on temporary contracts, lowering incentives for jobseekers to take up an informal job.[38]

In recent years, many governments have taken steps towards universalizing social protections combined with increased incentives to work formally.[39] Spain, for instance, lowered contribution rates for low-income workers to strengthen incentives to work formally. Similarly, Brazil, Thailand, and Uruguay provide subsidies for social security contribution of self-employed workers not previously covered by the compulsory social insurance system. Philippines, Uruguay and the Republic of Korea have extended legal coverage to specific occupations, such as domestic workers and construction workers. Some countries have reduced legal barriers to formality and modified eligibility conditions on the minimum period of employment or working hours (e.g., Netherlands and Vietnam).

Strengthening Resilience: Active Labor Market Policies

Social protections such as UI benefits play a key role in facilitating labor market inclusiveness by providing income support for jobless workers, but they do not necessarily equip them with the skills that they need to access better quality jobs or to achieve speedy re-entry into the labor market. In this regard, Active Labor Market Policies (ALMPs), if well designed, can equip jobseekers with the necessary support to transit to (better) job opportunities faster, thereby promoting inclusiveness.[40] Therefore, a successful strategy should rely on the joint implementation of ALMPs and income support measures. The combination of the Plan de Asistencia Nacional a la Emergencia Social (National Assistance Plan of Social Emergency, *PANES*) and *Trabajo por Uruguay* programs is an example of such a joint strategy. On the one hand, *PANES* aimed at providing monetary support to vulnerable households and preventing economic and social exclusion. On the other hand, *Trabajo por Uruguay* aimed at improving labor competencies of both dependent and self-employed workers and hence increasing their employability. However, the strategies have been criticized for not reaching their potential.[41]

---

[38] Cirelli et al. (2021) develop a model for middle-income developing countries and show that the introduction of a UI savings account system creates incentives to work in the formal sector.

[39] For an exhaustive discussion on strategies to extend social security to informal workers, see ILO (2020b).

[40] ALMPs include several tools, namely training provisions, Public Employment Service (PES) and job-search assistance, employment subsidies, start-up incentives, hiring incentives, direct job creation.

[41] One possible reason is the limited duration of *PANES* and *Trabajo por Uruguay*, which was capped to a maximum of five months (Escudero et al. 2020). Extending the duration of programs

Certain enabling conditions are required for the successful implementation of integrated approaches. First, a transparent and inclusive governance system is necessary for a rapid and efficient identification of the target of beneficiaries to ensure the participation of those in greatest need. Second, the involvement of social partners to address skills deficits and improve the delivery of training is important (see ILO 2019b).

There is evidence suggesting that certain programs are more effective than others. For example, job-search assistance and training tend to work well (Card et al. 2010) and well-designed wage subsidy schemes (Card et al. 2018; Estevão 2007), while public job creation (e.g., public works programs) appears less effective in helping workers over the long run (Bown and Freud 2019), though it could be helpful if linked with training.

Empirical evidence for Latin American countries demonstrates that ALMPs are more successful among low-skilled workers, women and youth, especially when implemented during periods of economic expansion (Escudero 2018 and Escudero et al. 2019). ALMPs are also associated with reduced informality: training programs increase both formal employment and earnings, while participating in the Public Employment Service increases the probability of having a formal job (Pignatti 2016).

C. Fighting Discrimination

Section III on measurement has summarized a subset of a large empirical literature documenting the importance of discrimination in determining labor market outcomes. Discrimination can take many forms, resulting in unfair differences in pay, in access to certain occupations, in working conditions, and many others. While there are indications that, along key dimensions, both racial and gender discrimination has declined over the past several decades, as measured by pay gaps or occupational misallocation, it remains an important obstacle to fully inclusive labor markets.

There is strong evidence that discrimination carries substantial economic costs. In their study on French grocery stores (see above), Glover, Pallais, and Pariente (2017) estimate that the performance losses due to discrimination reached up to nearly 10 percent. These losses also have an analogue at the macroeconomic level. For example, Hsieh et al. (2019) report that in 1960, over 90 percent of doctors and lawyers were white men, while by 2010, that share had come

---

might have helped reduce barriers faced by beneficiaries, particularly those associated with strengthening skills. Moreover, the World Bank estimate that about 60 percent of participants of the training activities appeared to have been trained to develop non-transferable skills, i.e. skills that were specific to the project in which the individual was involved. Developing transferable skills, based on vocational training could have increased the employability of participants (World Bank 2008).

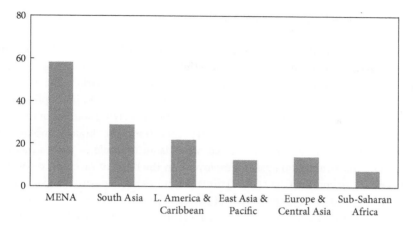

Figure 3.15 Output Losses from Gender Discrimination (%)
Note: Output gains are estimated based on a two-sector model assuming a closing of the female labor-force participation gap.
Source: Ostry et al., 2018.

down to just above 60 percent.[42] Assuming that there are no innate differences in the underlying talent distribution among different groups, this suggests that many women and black men were not in occupations where they could contribute most productively. The authors estimate that the improved allocation of talent across occupations between 1960 and 2010 has accounted for 20–40 percent of GDP growth during that time. Other research estimates benefits of reducing gender discrimination to be of a similar order of magnitude (Ostry et al. 2018 and Chapter 16).[43] See Figure 3.15. Thus, removing barriers to occupational choice, including through removing discrimination against workers of different race or gender, thus can have vast growth, productivity and equity benefits. Put differently, addressing discrimination is not only an ethical imperative, but is also of first-order importance from an economic perspective.

The large macroeconomic costs associated with discrimination suggest that this is an area of significant win-win outcomes: removing discriminatory occupational barriers and pay differences would benefit not only those discriminated against, but also the economy as a whole.

However, while the gains from addressing discrimination are potentially large, labor market policy options are complex. Much discriminatory behavior in the labor market is rooted in cultural and social norms that are formed outside the labor market. And important elements of unequal access arise from discrimination

[42] Anecdotally, as cited by Hsieh et al. (2019), Biskupic (2006) notes that Supreme Court Justice Sandra Day O'Connor graduated third in her class from Stanford Law School in 1952 yet could initially only find a job as a legal secretary.
[43] Relatedly, Page (2017) argued that diversity in teams carries a "bonus" in that their collective decision-making exceeds that of the group members' individual decision-making ability.

that has taken place prior to entering the labor market, such as access to quality education and training.[44]

While many of the above are issues that policymakers must address more broadly and beyond the labor market, the research literature suggests some options for addressing discrimination within the labor market. For example, making discrimination illegal is an important first step. While explicit legal requirements not to discriminate do not solve the underlying sources of discrimination, they are an important necessary condition. The Equal Employment Opportunity Act of 1972 in the United States is an example of such a measure forbidding discrimination against employees on the basis of race, sex, color, religion, or national origin. Chay (1998) finds that it has had a positive impact on the employment and earnings outcomes of African-American men.

The experimental studies mentioned earlier, including Goldin and Rouse (2000) and Bertrand and Mullainathan (2004), suggest that hiding the gender or racial background from recruiters can lead to less biased hiring decisions that are instead based on skills rather than other unrelated attributes, and hence to a more productive workforce. Similarly, the research by Glover et al. (2017) suggests that employers, by being more attuned to the dynamics of supervisor-supervisee relations across racial backgrounds, can achieve significantly higher productivity. While their study focused on racial aspects, similar effects may apply along the gender dimension. Implementing such policies is, again, a win-win for all involved, and policymakers and social partners can play a role in shaping an environment that encourages such practices.

Lastly, quotas can play an important role in achieving desirable outcomes. They can be an easily measurable, and thus easily enforceable, policy to achieve diversity. Gender quotas in particular have been increasingly adopted by many companies across the globe. In the case of European companies who implemented gender quotas on their corporate boards, Kuzmina and Melentyeva (2020) find that these companies experienced increases in firm value, suggesting that (gender) diversity and shareholder interests can go hand in hand—yet another win-win.[45,46]

---

[44] Among many examples, provision of public or subsidized childcare facilities could encourage higher female labor force participation with potentially large gains in terms of output (see Chapter 16).

[45] In the US state of California, a 2018 bill requires public companies with headquarters in California to name certain minimum number of female directors (varying by firm size) to their boards (Groves 2019).

[46] The policies listed here are of course not exhaustive, and standard labor market policies may also have an impact on discrimination. For example, Derenoncourt and Montialoux (2020) have argued that the extension of the federal minimum wage coverage under the 1966 Fair Labor Standards Act affected especially industries in which black workers were more strongly represented—the authors find that the broader minimum wage coverage lowered racial earnings gaps while finding no significant employment effects.

D. Addressing Labor Market Segmentation

As discussed in Section III.E, informality is one of the main obstacles to a more inclusive labor market in many countries. Policy solutions to reduce informality and labor market segmentation need to address their country-specific root causes (Loayza 2018). Frequently, stringent and burdensome regulation, such as strict labor regulations, high (marginal) taxes, and complicated tax payment procedures (Loayza et al. 2006; Schneider 2004; Perry et al. 2007), are a key cause of informality. A second cause is low institutional quality, such as corruption, weak rule of law, or lack of accountability, and low trust in institutions (Loayza 2007; Torgler and Schneider 2007; Van Elk et al. 2014). Finally, a lack of integration with the global economy, low educational levels and related low levels of productivity among formal sector firms limit gains from becoming formal (Bacchetta et al. 2009; de Paula and Scheinkman 2007; Perry et al. 2007; Jütting et al. 2008). Three key policy areas include strengthening labor productivity, tax measures, and administrative measures.

Encouraging Structural Change

Many factors prevent faster structural change towards high-productive, formal employment—in addition to weak overall economic demand, a lack of an educated workforce and low managerial competence are often to blame (Loayza 2018; Bloom et al. 2017). Frequently, low educational attainment translates into young workers not being able to enter the labor market other than through informal jobs, significantly reducing their long-term prospects (Shehu and Nilsson 2014).

Those shifting towards self-employment or entrepreneurship lack the skills and experience to create sustainable businesses. Overall, informal workers—whether self- or dependent employed—have significantly lower educational levels, preventing them from accessing high-productive, formal jobs (Maurizio and Vazquez 2019). General (public) investment in education infrastructure, quality teaching and the expansion of vocational training systems can help increase educational attainment and provide more opportunities for workers to transit to formal jobs (see also Chapter 14 on education for inclusive growth). This can include recognizing educational investment provided by the informal economy itself to facilitate occupational transition. Moreover, active labor policies and job reinsertion programs through (re-)training can contribute to facilitate the transition to formalization both on the current job and through job switch (Card et al. 2010 and 2018).

Taxation

An efficient tax system is an important tool for addressing rising inequality and informality and restoring robust economic growth. Taxation is a potential tool to lessen the costs of operating in the formal sector, since formality choices are highly elastic with respect to marginal tax rates.

Reducing the tax rate on formal businesses eases the migration of entrepreneurs from informal into formal activity, where productivity is higher, with positive effect on output and economic efficiency.[47] Higher tax rates among firm-owners induce not only substantial movements to the informal sector, but also under-reporting of taxable earnings and income shifting to tax-favored business forms, which may ultimately lead to inefficient allocation or resources.[48] Lowering payroll taxes is also a potential lever to increase formal employment and extend social insurance coverage among the labor force, although the effects may vary across countries.[49]

If informality is voluntary, lower tax rates should reduce firms' incentives to enter the informal sector. However, even if informality is involuntary, lower tax rates could reduce informality by encouraging formal sector firms to expand employment and create more formal jobs. The empirical literature suggests that the best approach to reduce the size of the informal sector is using taxation to reduce the costs of being formal and create the right incentives for companies and workers intending to switch to the formal sector.

Some countries in Europe have undertaken reforms to strengthen formalization. For example, reduced tax rates for low-wage earners (e.g., in Belgium, Bulgaria, the Netherlands, and France), as well as tax exemptions and reductions in sectors that rely on undeclared work (e.g., in Hungary, Sweden, Belgium, and France).

Some emerging economies, especially in Latin American countries, have also implemented policies aiming at removing obstacles to formalization, such as simplification to registration procedures and tax simplifications for small businesses.

Brazil is an illustrative example of an emerging country which, starting from a high level of informality in the late 1990s, has adopted a set of policy initiatives to facilitate the move to formality. The *Simples* and *Super Simples* programs, launched in 1996 and 2006 respectively, aimed at reducing the costs of formalization through a simplification and a reduction of tax rates and tax regulations for Brazilian micro firms with no more than five paid employees—most prevalent in the informal economy. Since the *Super Simples* came into force in July 2007, some 9 million businesses have joined this system of taxation and the formality rate has increased by 11 percentage points (see Fajnzylber et al. 2011).

Another example is the *Monotax* (or *Monotributo*) implemented in 1998 in Argentina. *Monotax* is a simplified tax collection/payment scheme for small taxpayers. People covered by the *Monotax* regime are entitled to the same social security benefits as salaried workers. The *Monotax* has proven to be an effective tool for the formalization of micro- and small enterprises, as well as for the

---

[47] For a case study on the Russian Federation, we refer to Slonimczyk (2012), while for a case study on Brazil see Araujo and Rodrigues (2016).

[48] See Waseem (2018) for an analysis of the Pakistani tax reform introduced in 2009.

[49] Pagés (2017) discusses pros and cons of payroll tax cuts in developing countries and analyzes the circumstances under which payroll tax cuts can pave the way to formalization.

extension of social security coverage to independent workers, especially women. While these types of programs could help foster formalization, they have their limits as they could hinder growth opportunities in EMs, since they increase the incentives for small enterprises to remain small (see Hsieh and Olken 2014).

In the same vein, tax reforms were implemented in Colombia in 2012 with the aim to increase employment and, in particular, formal employment. The reforms reduced payroll taxes for those with less than 10 employees and for self-employed who hired two employees or more. Empirical evidence suggests that the probability of formal employment and the likelihood of transitioning into registered employment increased for the affected groups after the reform (Kugler et al. 2017).

A more cautious view is provided by Langot et al. (2019), who analyze the effectiveness of a budget-neutral tax reform (that aims to reduce the tax burden for small enterprises) in fostering formalization. They find that tax policies might play only a minor role in improving formalization rates, especially in emerging countries. To reduce the incidence of informality, tax policy interventions should go hand in hand with other social protection policies as discussed earlier, and with administrative policies, which are discussed next.

Administrative (E-Formality) Policies

Administrative policies should support and strengthen the effectiveness of policies towards formalization by enhancing enforcement, promoting information sharing and elevating awareness, as well as establishing efficient and transparent administrative processes.

New technologies can enhance the impact of policies addressing informality. In recent years, an increasing number of governments have started promoting the application of new technologies. These so-called "e-formality" policies facilitate development of partnerships and sharing of information among tax, social security, and employment institutions, which ultimately simplify the transition to formal employment (Chacaltana et al. 2018).

An example of e-formality tools is the development of electronic solutions to facilitate tax filing and collection (e.g., *e-Tax* in Estonia), as well as to reduce time and costs for business registration (e.g., one-stop shops, such as *Ventanilla Única Empresarial* created in Colombia in 2017).

However, the registration of new firms does not necessarily imply the formalization of their workers (Deelen 2015). Therefore, a complementary tool is the electronic registration of workers (e.g., the *eSocial* project launched in Brazil in 2007 or the Electronic Payroll solution created in Peru in 2006 to replace the manual reporting of private business payrolls), as well as the development of electronic solutions, such as mobile apps, to simplify payment of social security contribution, especially for domestic workers. New technologies may also be used to enhance labor inspections (e.g., in the United Arab Emirates or the *Digital Inspector* scheme launched in Argentina in 2003).

Another aspect under which new technologies can contribute to formalization is improving access to information on and awareness of workers' human and social rights. In many countries, a large majority of workers in the informal economy has a low level of education and is often unaware of what social protection schemes are available to them and how they can access such schemes. Raising awareness is a catalyst for the extension of social security to the informal economy. Many countries have recently become more active in informing their members about their contribution records and entitlements. Turkey provides an illustrative example in this respect. Since 2012, an information system, combining the databases of three different social security institutions, allows users to obtain quick access to information on pension and health insurance status, registration and premiums by simply using their citizenship identification number (ILO 2019b).

Finally, tracking transactions is another important tool for the transition to the formal economy, since operators in the informal economy tend to use cash, because of their limited access to formal financial services and/or with the purpose to avoid paying taxes.[50] For instance, the Government of the Republic of Korea gives an incentive—in the form of a tax deduction in income tax—to those people reaching a certain amount in credit card transactions. Alternatively, some countries impose penalties instead of an incentive to discourage cash transactions. In Greece, for instance, taxpayers incur a penalty if they do not make enough electronic payments.

V. Conclusion

The labor market plays a key role in shaping the extent of inclusivity in the overall economy. While measuring inclusivity presents challenges, we have identified several dimensions along which there is substantial scope for improving inclusivity. We close this chapter by summarizing what we view as the four key takeaways for policy makers concerned with increasing the inclusivity of the labor market.

First, there is no uniform set of policy recommendations. Importantly, inclusivity is a multi-dimensional concept. The departures from inclusivity may differ across economies, and different economies may place different weights on the different dimensions of inclusivity. Drafting a course of action requires both assessing the various departures from inclusivity and assigning weights to the different dimensions of inclusivity.

Second, policy makers will often face important tradeoffs in terms of achieving the various dimensions of inclusivity. For example, as we have argued, employment

---

[50] See also Chapter 4 on financial inclusion.

protection may provide protection for currently employed workers while at the same time it diminishes access for young workers entering the labor market.

Third, and related, policy makers should view policies as a bundle and not individually. Some policies are substitutes while others are complements. Thus, policies should be assessed as part of a package and not in isolation. The Danish system of flexicurity stands out as an example of a package of policies that work together.

Fourth, departures from inclusivity occur both at the micro and the macro level. Many standard policy tools are best suited to addressing problems that are macro in scope, so addressing micro departures may require more novel approaches.

We close with two additional remarks. First, our analysis has focused somewhat narrowly on what happens in the labor market. But it is critical for policy makers to understand that much of what happens in the labor market is strongly influenced by outcomes and events outside of the labor market. Inequality in access to quality schooling translates almost directly into inequality of access to opportunities in the labor market. Cultural norms or discriminatory practices outside of the labor market will similarly translate into departures from inclusivity in the labor market.

Second, many labor market outcomes reflect changes in technology. While some aspects of technological change might best be viewed as exogenous, we think that an important area for future work is to understand how policy settings influence the extent and nature of technology adoption. Some tax policies, for example, might implicitly encourage firms to replace low skill labor with machines. As the impact of technology continues, we think it will become increasingly important to think about the potential for policy to shape the nature of technological innovation and adoption.

References

Acemoglu, D., and Restrepo, P. 2018. "The Race between Man and Machine: Implications of Technology for Growth, Factor Shares, and Employment." *American Economic Review* 108(6), June 2018: 1488–542.

Adam, C.S., and E.F. Buffie. 2020. "The Minimum Wage Puzzle in Less Developed Countries: Reconciling Theory and Evidence," IMF Working Paper No. 20/23 (Washington, DC).

Addison, J.T. and P. Teixeira. 2017. "Strikes, Employee Workplace Representation, Unionism, and Trust: Evidence from Cross-Country Data," IZA Discussion Paper No. 10575.

Aleksynska, M., and Eberlein, F. 2016. "Coverage of Employment Protection Legislation," *IZA Journal of Labor Policy*, ISSN 2193–9004, Springer, Heidelberg, Vol. 5, Iss. 17, pp. 1–20.

Andersen, T.M. 2011. "A Flexicurity Labour Market in the Great Recession: The Case of Denmark," IZA Discussion Papers 5710, Institute of Labor Economics (IZA).

Araujo, J., and M. Rodrigues. 2016. "Taxation, Credit Constraints and the Informal Economy." *Economia* 17: 43–55.

Arni, P. 2017. "What Drives Wage Effects of Unemployment Benefits? Evidence from Natural Experiments and Reservation Wage Data," Beiträge zur Jahrestagung des Vereins für Socialpolitik 2017: Alternative Geld- und Finanzarchitekturen. Conference paper. Available at: https://www.econstor.eu/handle/10419/168154.

Autor, D., D. Dorn, L. Katz, C. Patterson, and J. Van Reenen. 2017. "The Fall of the Labor Share and the Rise of Superstar Firms," IZA Discussion Paper 10756.

Autor, D. 2019. "Work of the Past, Work of the Future," NBER Working Paper No. 25588. Available at: https://www.nber.org/papers/w25588

Azmat, G., and Petrongolo, B. 2014. "Gender and the Labour Market: Evidence from Experiments," VoxEU Column, June 7, 2014. Available at: https://voxeu.org/article/gender-and-labour-market

Bacchetta, M., E. Ernst, and J. Bustamante. 2009. "Globalization and Informal Jobs in Developing Countries." A Joint study of the International Labour Office and the Secretariat of the World Trade Organization, Geneva.

Barkai, S. 2020. "Declining Labor and Capital Shares." *The Journal of Finance* 75(5): 2421–63, April 2020. Available at: https://onlinelibrary.wiley.com/doi/full/10.1111/jofi.12909.

Bassanini, A., and Duval, R. 2006. "Employment Patterns in OECD Countries: Reassessing the Role of Policies and Institutions," OECD Social, Employment and Migration Working Papers, No. 35. June 9, 2006. OECD Publishing, Paris. Available at: https://doi.org/10.1787/702031136412.

Bassanini, A., and E. Ernst. 2002. "Labour Market Regulation, Industrial Relations and Technological Regimes: A Tale of Comparative Advantage." *Industrial and Corporate Change* 11(3): 391–426.

Bassanini, A., L. Nunziata, and D. Venn. 2009. "Job Protection Legislation and Productivity Growth in OECD Countries [Appropriate Growth Policy: a Unifying Framework]." *Economic Policy*, CEPR; CES; MSH, 24(58): 349–402.

Bayer, P., and Charles, K. 2019. "Divergent Paths: A New Perspective on Earnings Differences Between Black and White Men Since 1940." *The Quarterly Journal of Economics* 133(3), August 2018: 1459–501. Available at: https://academic.oup.com/qje/article/133/3/1459/4830121.

Bekker, S., and M. Mailand. 2019. "The European Flexicurity Concept and the Dutch and Danish Flexicurity Models: How Have they Managed the Great Recession?" *Social Policy Administration* 53(1): 142–55.

Bengtsson, E. 2014. "Do Unions Redistribute Income from Capital to Labour? Union Density and Wage Shares since 1960." *Industrial Relations* 45(5) (September). First published: July 12, 2014. Available at: https://onlinelibrary.wiley.com/doi/10.1111/irj.12065.

Bertrand, M., and Mullainathan, S. 2004. "Are Emily and Greg More Employable Than Lakisha and Jamal? A Field Experiment on Labor Market Discrimination." *American Economic Review* 94(4): 991–1013.

Bertrand, M., and Duflo, E. 2016. "Field Experiments on Discrimination," NBER Working Paper No. 22014. Available at: http://www.nber.org/papers/w22014.

Betcherman, G. 2012. "Labor Market Institutions: A Review of the Literature," Policy Research Working Paper No.6276. November 2012. World Bank, Washington, DC: World Bank. Available at: https://openknowledge.worldbank.org/handle/10986/16382.

Biskupic, Joan. 2006. "Sandra Day O'Connor: How the First Woman on the Supreme Court Became Its Most Influential Justice," HarperCollins.

Blanchard, O. and Summers, L. 1986. "Hysteresis and the European unemployment problem," *NBER Macroeconomics Annual* 1986, Volume 1. Cambridge, MA: MIT Press.

Bloom, N., R. Sadun, and J. Van Reenen. 2017. "Management as a Technology?," NBER Working Paper No. 22327.

Boeri, T., and J.F. Jimeno. 2005. "The Effects of Employment Protection: Learning from Variable Enforcement." *European Economic Review* 49(8): 2057–77.

Borgschulte, M., and H. Cho. 2019. "Minimum Wages and Retirement." *ILR Review* 73(1): 153–77.

Bowles, S., Gintis, H., and Osborne, M. 2001. "The Determinants of Earnings: A Behavioral Approach." *Journal of Economic Literature* 39(4): 1137–76. Available at: https://www.aeaweb.org/articles?id=10.1257/jel.39.4.1137.

Bown, C., and C. Freud. 2019. "Active Labor Market Policies: Lessons from Other Countries for the United States," Peterson Institute for International Economics Working Paper No. 19–2.

Brandl, B., and A. Lehr. 2016. "The Strange Non-Death of Employer and Business Associations: An Analysis of their Representativeness and Activities in Western European Countries." *Economic and Industrial Democracy*, pp. 1–22.

Bridgman, B. 2018. "Is Labor's Loss Capital's Gain? Gross versus Net Labor Shares." *Macroeconomic Dynamics* 22(8), December 2018: 2070–87.

Bryson, A., B. Ebbinghaus, and J. Visser. 2011. "Introduction: Causes, Consequences and Cures of Union Decline." *European Journal in Industrial Relations* 17(2): 97–105.

Cabrales, A., J.J. Dolado, and R. Mora. 2014. "Dual Labour Markets and (Lack of) On-The-Job Training: PIAAC Evidence from Spain and Other EU Countries," CEPR Discussion Papers 10246, C.E.P.R. Discussion Papers.

Cahuc, P. 2019. "Short-time Work Compensation Schemes and Employment," IZA World of Labor, Institute of Labor Economics (IZA), pages 1–11.

Callaway, B., and W.J. Collings. 2018. "Unions, Workers, and Wages at the Peak of the American Labor Movement." *Explorations in Economic History* 68: 95–118.

Calmfors, L., and Driffill, J. 1988. "Bargaining Structure, Corporatism and Macroeconomic Performance." *Economic Policy* 3(6) (Apr. 1988): 14–61.

Card, D., J. Kluve, and A. Weber. 2010. "Active Labour Market Policy Evaluations: A Meta-Analysis." *Economic Journal, Royal Economic Society* 120(548): 452–77, November.

Card, D., J. Kluve, and A. Weber. 2018. "What Works? A Meta Analysis of Recent Active Labor Market Program Evaluations." *Journal of European Economic Association* 16(1): 894–931.

Cazes, S., Garnero, A., and Martin, S. 2017. "The State of Trade Unions, Employer Organisations, and Collective Bargaining in OECD Countries," VoxEU Column, July 10, 2017. Available at: https://voxeu.org/article/trade-unions-employer-organisations-and-collective-bargaining-oecd-countries

Cengiz, D., A. Dube, A. Lindner, and B. Zipperer. 2019. "The Effect of Minimum Wages on Low-Wage Jobs." *The Quarterly Journal of Economics* 134(3): 1405–54.

Cerra, V., and Saxena, S. 2008. "Growth Dynamics: The Myth of Economic Recovery." *The American Economic Review* 98: 439–57.

Chacaltana, J., V. Leung, and M. Lee. 2018. "New Technologies and the Transition to Formality: The Trend Towards E–Formality," ILO Employment Policy Department Working Paper 247, International Labour Organization.

Chay, K. Y. 1998. "The impact of federal civil rights policy on black economic progress: Evidence from the Equal Employment Opportunity Act of 1972." *Industrial and Labor Relations Review* 51(4), 608–32.

Chen, M.A., J.F. Vanek, F. Lund, J. Heintz, R. Jhabvala, and C. Bonner. 2005. "Progress of the World's Women 2005: Women, Work, and Poverty," United Nations Development Fund for Women (UNIFEM), New York.

Ciminelli, G., Duval, R., and Furceri, D. 2020. "Employment Protection Deregulation and Labor Shares in Advanced Economies." *Review of Economics and Statistics, forthcoming.* Available at: https://doi.org/10.1162/rest_a_00983.

Cirelli, F., E. Espino, and J.M. Sanchez. 2021. "Designing Unemployment Insurance for Developing Countries." *Journal of Development Economics* 148.

Congressional Budget Office (CBO). 2021. "The Budgetary Effects of the *Raise the Wage Act* of 2021," Congressional Budget Office, February 2021. Available at: https://www.cbo.gov/publication/56975.

Davalos, J., and E. Ernst. 2021. *How has labour market power evolved? Comparing labour market monopsony in Peru and the United States,* ILO Working Paper (Geneva), forthcoming.

Deelen, L. (Ed.). 2015. Políticas para la formalización de las micro y pequeñas empresas en América Latina (Santiago, International Labour Office).

Deléchat, C., and Medina, L. 2020. "What Is the Informal Economy?" *Finance and Development,* December 2020, IMF. Available at: https://www.imf.org/external/pubs/ft/fandd/2020/12/what-is-the-informal-economy-basics.htm.

Derenoncourt, E., and Montialoux, C. 2020. "Minimum Wages and Racial Inequality." *The Quarterly Journal of Economics* 136(1), February: 169–228. Available at: https://academic.oup.com/qje/article/136/1/169/5905427.

De Paula, A., and J. Scheinkman. 2007. "The Informal Sector." Second version. PIER Working Paper 07–035.

Diaz, J.J., J. Chacaltana, J. Rigolini, and C. Ruiz. 2018. "Pathways to Formalization: Going beyond the Formality Dichotomy," World Bank Policy Research Working Paper No. 8551.

Doepke, M., and R. Gaetani. 2020. "Why Didn't the College Premium Rise Everywhere? Employment Protection and On-the-Job Investment in Skills," mimeo.

Dube, A. 2019a. Impacts of Minimum Wages: Review of the International Evidence. (London, HM Treasury). Available at: https://www.gov.uk/government/publications/impacts-of-minimum-wages-review-of-the-international-evidence

Dube, A. 2019b. "Minimum Wages and the Distribution of Family Incomes." *American Economic Journal: Applied Economics* 11(4): 268–304.

Duval, R. and Loungani, P. 2019. "Designing Labor Market Institutions in Emerging Market and Developing Economies: Evidence and Policy Options," IMF Staff Discussion Note 19/04. May 21, 2019. Washington DC: IMF. Available at: https://www.imf.org/en/Publications/Staff-Discussion-Notes/Issues/2019/05/15/Designing-Labor-Market-Institutions-in-Emerging-and-Developing-Economies-Evidence-and-Policy-46855.

Eeckhout, J. 2021. "The Profit Paradox: How Thriving Firms Threaten the Future of Work," Princeton University Press.

Elsby, M., B. Hobijn, and A. Sahin. 2013. "The decline of the U.S. labor share," Brookings Papers on Economic Activity, Fall.

Ernst, E., and U. Rani. 2011. "Understanding Unemployment Flows," in *Oxford Review of Economic Policy* 27(2): 268–94.

Ernst, E. 2015. "Supporting jobseekers: How unemployment benefits can help unemployed workers and strengthen job creation." *International Social Security Review* 68(3).

Escudero, V. 2018. "Are Active Labour Market Policies Effective in Activating and Integrating Low-Skilled Individuals? An International Comparison." *IZA Journal of Labor Policy*, Springer; Forschungsinstitut zur Zukunft der Arbeit GmbH (IZA), 7(1): 1–26, December.

Escudero, V., E. López Mourelo, and C. Pignatti. 2020. "Joint Provision of Income and Employment Support: Evidence from a Crisis Response in Uruguay." *World Development*, Elsevier, Vol. 134(C).

Escudero, V., J. Kluve, E. López Mourelo, and C. Pignatti. 2019. "Active Labour Market Programmes in Latin America and the Caribbean: Evidence from a Meta-Analysis." *The Journal of Development Studies* 55(12): 2644–61.

Estevão, M. 2007. "Labor Policies to Raise Employment," *IMF Staff Papers*, Palgrave Macmillan, 54(1): 113–38.

European Commission. 2010. "Employment in Europe 2010," Chapter 3: Youth Segmentation in EU Labor Market. Available at: https://ec.europa.eu/employment_social/eie/chap3_en.html

Farber, H.S., D. Herbst, I. Kuziemko, and S. Naidu. 2018. "Unions and Inequality Over the Twentieth Century: New Evidence from Survey Data," National Bureau of Economic Research Working Paper no. 24587.

Fajnzylber, P., W.F. Maloney, and G.W. Montes-Rojas. 2011. "Does Formality Improve Micro-Firm Performance? Evidence from the Brazilian SIMPLES Program." *Journal of Development Economics* 94: 262–76.

Farooq, A., A. Kugler, and U. Muratori. 2020. "Do Unemployment Insurance Benefits Improve Match Quality? Evidence from Recent U.S. Recessions," NBER Working Paper No. 27574.

Fedorets, A., and Shupe, C. 2021. "Great Expectations: Reservation Wages and Minimum Wage reform." *Journal of Economic Behavior & Organization* 183: 397–419.

Furceri, D., Jalles, J. T., and Loungani, P. 2020. "On the Determinants of the Okun's Law: New Evidence from Time-Varying Estimates." *Comparative Economic Studies* 62: 661–700. Available at: https://link.springer.com/article/10.1057/s41294-019-00111-1.

Fields, G.S. 2005. *A Guide to Multisector Labor Market Models*, Social Protection Discussion Paper 0505. Washington, DC: World Bank.

Gasparini, L., and L. Tornarolli. 2007. "Labor informality in Latin America and the Caribbean: Patterns and trends from household survey microdata," CEDLAS Working Paper.

Genz, G., L. Bellmann, and B. Matthes. 2019. "Do German Works Councils Counter or Foster the Implementation of Digital Technologies? First Evidence from the IAB-Establishment Panel." *Jahrbücher für Nationalökonomie und Statistik* 239(3): 523–64.

Gimpelson, V., R. Kapeliushnikov, and A. Lukiyanova. 2010. "Employment Protection Legislation in Russia: Regional Enforcement and Labour Market Outcomes." *Comparative Economic Studies* 52(4): 611–36.

Glover, D., Pallais, A., and Pariente, W. 2017. "Discrimination as a Self-Fulfilling Prophecy: Evidence from French Grocery Stores." *The Quarterly Journal of Economics* 132(3), August 2017: 1219–60. Available at: https://doi.org/10.1093/qje/qjx006.

Goldin, C., and Rouse, C. 2000. "Orchestrating Impartiality: The Impact of 'Blind' Auditions on Female Musicians." *American Economic Review* 90(4): 715–41.

Gollin, D. 2002. "Getting Income Shares Right." *Journal of Political Economy* 110(2): 458–74.

Gouin-Bonenfant, E. 2021. "Productivity Dispersion, Between-Firm Competition, and the Labor Share," Unpublished Manuscript. Available at: https://sites.google.com/view/emilien/home

Gutiérrez, G., and Philippon, T. 2017. "Declining Competition and Investment in the US," NBER Working Paper No. 23583.

Groves, M. 2019. "How California's 'Woman Quota' is Already Changing Corporate Boards." Available at: https://calmatters.org/economy/2019/12/california-woman-quota-corporate-board-gender-diversity/.

Haucap, J., U. Pauly, and C. Wey. 2001. "Collective Wage Setting When Wages Are Generally Binding: An Antitrust Perspective." *International Review of Law and Economics* 21(3): 287–307.

Hayter, S., and J. Visser. 2018. "Collective Agreements: Extending Labour Protection." Geneva: ILO.

Heathcote, J., Storesletten, K., and Violante, G. L. 2007. "Insurance and Opportunities: A Welfare Analysis of Labor Market Risk," NBER WP No. 13673.

Heckman, J. J., Lochner, L. J., and Todd, P. E. 2006. "Earnings Functions, Rates, of Return and Treatment Effects: The Mincer Equation and Beyond," Chapter 7 in *Handbook of the Economics of Education*, Volume 1, edited by Eric A. Hanushek and Finis Welch, Elsevier B.V.

Heimberger, P. 2020. "Does Employment Protection Affect Unemployment? A Meta-analysis." *Oxford Economic Paper* 1–26.

Heintz, J., and R. Pollin. 2005. "Informalization, economic growth, and the challenge of creating viable labor standards in developing countries," in *Rethinking Informalization: Poverty, Precarious Jobs and Social Protection*, edited by N. Kudva and L. Beneria, Cornell University Open Access Repository.

Herr, H., and M. Kazandziska. 2011. *Principles of Minimum Wage Policy—Economics, Institutions and Recommendations*. Geneva: ILO.

Hijzen, A., and S. Martin. 2013. "The Role of Short-Time Work Schemes during the Global Financial Crisis and Early Recovery: A Cross-Country Analysis," IZA Discussion Papers 7291, Institute of Labor Economics (IZA).

Hirsch, B., T. Schank, and C. Schnabel. 2010. "Works Councils and Separations: Voice, Monopoly, and Insurance Effects." *Industrial Relations* 49(4): 566–92.

Hsieh, C-T., and B.A. Olken. 2014. "The Missing 'Missing Middle,'" *Journal of Economic Perspectives*, American Economic Association, 28(3): 89–108.

Hsieh, C. T., Hurst, E., Jones, C., and Klenow, P. 2019. "The Allocation of Talent and U.S. Economic Growth." *Econometrica* 87:5, 1439–74. Available at: https://onlinelibrary.wiley.com/doi/abs/10.3982/ECTA11427.

Hübler, O. and U. Jirjahn. 2003. "Works Councils and Collective Bargaining in Germany: The Impact on Productivity and Wages." *Scottish Journal of Political Economy*, Scottish Economic Society, 50(4): 471–91.

Hussmanns, R. 2004. "Measuring the Informal Economy: From Employment in the Informal Sector to Informal Employment," Working paper No. 53, Policy Integration Department, Bureau of Statistics. Geneva: ILO.

International Labour Organization (ILO). 1993. "*Resolution concerning the International Classification of Status in Employment* (ICSE-93)," January 1993. Available at: https://www.ilo.org/global/statistics-and-databases/standards-and-guidelines/resolutions-adopted-by-international-conferences-of-labour-statisticians/WCMS_087562/lang--en/index.htm

International Labour Organization (ILO). 2015. "Minimum Wage Policy Guide" (Geneva). Available at: https://www.ilo.org/global/topics/wages/minimum-wages/lang--en/index.htm

International Labour Organization (ILO). 2017. "World Social Protection Report 2017–19," November 2017 (Geneva). Available at: https://www.ilo.org/global/publications/books/WCMS_604882/lang--en/index.htm

International Labour Organization (ILO). 2018a. "Women and Men in the Informal Economy: A Statistical Picture," Third Edition, April 2018 (Geneva). Available at: https://www.ilo.org/global/publications/books/WCMS_626831/lang--en/index.htm

International Labour Organization (ILO). 2018b. "Global Wage Report 2018/19: What Lies Behind the Gender Pay Gaps," November 2018 (Geneva). Available at: https://www.ilo.org/global/about-the-ilo/mission-and-objectives/features/WCMS_650551/lang--en/index.htm

International Labour Organization (ILO). 2019a. "Organizing Informal Economy Workers into Trade Unions—A Trade Union Guide." June 19, 2019 (Geneva). Available at: https://www.ilo.org/actrav/pubs/WCMS_711040/lang--en/index.htm

International Labour Organization (ILO). 2019b. "What Works. Promoting Pathways to Decent Work," October 17, 2019 (Geneva). Available at: https://www.ilo.org/global/publications/books/WCMS_724097/lang--en/index.htm

International Labour Organization (ILO). 2000a. "Unemployment and Income Security" Discussion Paper prepared by Guy Standing for Geneva 2000: Follow-up to the World Summit on Social Development, Programme on Socio-Economic Security Papers No. 3 (Geneva).

International Labour Organization (ILO). 2020b. "Extending Social Security and Facilitating Transition from the Informal to the Formal Economy: Lessons from International Experience." June 29, 2020 (Geneva). Available at: https://www.ilo.org/secsoc/information-resources/publications-and-tools/Brochures/WCMS_749431/lang--en/index.htm

International Monetary Fund (IMF). 2017. "Understanding the Downward Trends in Labor Income Shares," Chapter 3, *World Economic Outlook*, April 2017. Washington, DC. Available at: https://www.imf.org/en/Publications/WEO/Issues/2017/04/04/world-economic-outlook-april-2017.

International Monetary Fund (IMF). 2021. "Recession and Recoveries in Labor Markets: Patterns, Policies, and Responding to the Covid-19 Shock," Chapter 3, *World Economic Outlook*, April 2021. Washington, DC.

Jacobson, Louis S., Robert J. LaLonde, and Daniel G. Sullivan. 1993. "Earnings Losses of Displaced Workers." *The American Economic Review* 83(4): 685–709. Available at: http://www.jstor.org/stable/2117574.

Jaumotte, F., and C. Buitron. 2015. "Inequality and Labor Market Institutions," IMF Staff Discussion Note No. 15/14. July 1, 2015. Washington DC: IMF. Available at: https://www.imf.org/en/Publications/Staff-Discussion-Notes/Issues/2016/12/31/Inequality-and-Labor-Market-Institutions-42987.

Johnston, A.C. 2021. "Unemployment Insurance Taxes and Labor Demand: Quasi-Experimental Evidence from Administrative Data." *American Economic Review: Economic Policy* 13(1): 266–93.

Jütting, J., J. Parlevliet, and T. Xenogiani. 2008. "Informal Employment Re-loaded," in IDS Bulletin, 39(2): 28–36.

Koh, D., Santaeulàlia-Llopis, R., and Zheng, Y. 2020. "Labor Share Decline and Intellectual Property Products Capital." *Econometrica* 88(6): 2609–28 November 2020. Available at: https://doi.org/10.3982/ECTA17477.

Kugler, A., M. Kugler, and L.O. Herrera-Prada. 2017. "Do Payroll Tax Breaks Stimulate Formality? Evidence from Colombia's Reform." *Economía Journal*, The Latin American and Caribbean Economic Association—LACEA, vol. 0 (Fall 2017), 3–40, November.

Kuzmina, O., and Melentyeva, V. 2020. "Gender Diversity in Corporate Boards: Evidence from Quota-Implied Discontinuities," CEPR Discussion Paper No. DP14942.

Langot, F., R. Merola, and S. Oh. 2019. "Can Taxes Help Ensure a Fair Globalization?," Policy Research Working Paper Series 8975, The World Bank.

Layard, R., S. Nickell, and R. Jackman. 1991. Unemployment, Macroeconomic Performance and the Labour Marke. Oxford: Oxford University Press.

Loayza, N.V., A.M. Oviedo, and L. Servén. 2006. "The Impact of Regulation on Growth and Informality: Cross-Country Evidence." In Unlocking Human Potential: Linking the Informal and Formal Sectors. EDGI-WIDER.

Loayza, N.V. 2007. "The causes and consequences of informality in Peru," Working Papers 2007–018, Banco Central de Reserva del Perú.

Loayza, N.V. 2018. "Informality: Why Is It So Widespread and How Can It Be Reduced?" World Bank Research and Policy Briefs No. 133110 (Washington, DC).

Lucas, R. 1987. *Models of Business Cycles*. Oxford: Basil Blackwell.

Manning, A. 2021. "Monopsony in Labor Markets: A Review," in *ILR Review* 74(1): 3–26.

Manyika, J., Mischke, J., Bughin, J., Woetzel, J., Krishnan, M., and Cudre, S. 2019. "A New Look at the Declining Labor Share of Income in the United States," Discussion Paper, McKinsey Global Institute.

Martinez, J. 2018. "Automation, Growth and Factor Shares," 2018 Meeting Papers 736, Society for Economic Dynamics. Meeting Paper 736, 2018.

Maurizio, R., and G. Vásquez. 2019. "Formal Salaried Employment Generation and Transition to Formality in Developing Countries: The case of Latin America," ILO Employment Working Paper No. 251 (Geneva).

Messina, J., and G. Vallanti. 2007. "Job Flow Dynamics and Firing Restrictions: Evidence from Europe." *The Economic Journal* 117(521): F279–F301.

Mincer, J. 1974. "The Human Capital Earnings Function," Chapter 5 in *Schooling, Experience, and Earnings*, edited by Jacob Mincer, NBER, pp. 83–96.

Montenegro, C. and Patrinos, H. 2014. "Comparable Estimates of Returns to Schooling around the World," World Bank, Washington D.C. Available at: https://elibrary.worldbank.org/doi/abs/10.1596/1813-9450-7020.

Mortensen, D. 2003. "Wage Dispersion: Why Are Similar Workers Paid Differently?," Cambridge: MIT Press.

Mortensen, D., and Pissarides, C. 1994. "Job Creation and Job Destruction in the Theory of Unemployment, *Review of Economic Studies* 61: 397–415.

Mueller, S., and J. Stegmaier. 2017. "The Dynamic Effects of Works Councils on Labour Productivity: First Evidence from Panel Data." *British Journal of Industrial Relations* 55(2): 372–95.

Nekoei, A., and A. Weber. 2017. "Does Extending Unemployment Benefits Improve Job Quality?" *American Economic Review* 107: 527–61.

Neumark, D., and W.L. Wascher. 2008. *Minimum Wages*. Cambridge, MA: MIT Press.

Neumark, D., and P. Shirley. 2021. "Myth or measurement: What does the new minimum wage research say about minimum wages and job loss in the United States?," NBER Working Paper, No. 28388.

Organisation for Economic Cooperation and Development (OECD). 2011. "Divided We Stand: Why Inequality Keeps Rising," Paris. Available at: https://www.oecd-ilibrary.org/social-issues-migration-health/the-causes-of-growing-inequalities-in-oecd-countries_9789264119536-en

Organisation for Economic Cooperation and Development (OECD). 2013. "The 2012 Labour Market Reform in Spain: A Preliminary Assessment," December 2013, Paris. Available at: https://www.oecd.org/employment/spain-labourmarketreform.htm

Organisation for Economic Cooperation and Development (OECD). 2017. "OECD Employment Outlook: Collective Bargaining in a Changing World of Work," Chapter 4, Paris. Available at: https://www.oecd-ilibrary.org/employment/oecd-employment-outlook-2017/collective-bargaining-in-a-changing-world-of-work_empl_outlook-2017-8-en

Organisation for Economic Cooperation and Development (OECD). 2018. "Market concentration," Issues paper, Paris, 2018. Available at: https://www.oecd.org/daf/competition/market-concentration.htm

Organisation for Economic Cooperation and Development (OECD). 2020. "Job Retention Schemes During the Covid-19 Lockdown and Beyond," OECD Policy Responses to Coronavirus (Paris). Available at: https://www.oecd.org/coronavirus/policy-responses/job-retention-schemes-during-the-covid-19-lockdown-and-beyond-0853ba1d/

Oesingmann, K. 2016. *Extension of Collective Agreements in Europe*, in CESifo DICE Report, Vol. 14, Nr. 2, pp. 59–64 (Munich, ifo Institute).

Okun, A. 1962. "Potential GNP: Its Measurement and Significance," American Statistical Association, Proceedings of the Business and Economics Statistics Section.

Ostry, J., Alvarez, J., Espinoza, R., and Papageorgiou, C. 2018. "Economic Gains from Gender Inclusion: New Mechanisms, New Evidence," IMF Staff Discussion

Note/18/06 October. https://www.imf.org/en/Publications/Staff-Discussion-Notes/Issues/2018/10/09/Economic-Gains-From-Gender-Inclusion-New-Mechanisms-New-Evidence-45543.

Page, S. E. 2017. "The Diversity Bonus: How Great Teams Pay Off in the Knowledge Economy," Princeton University Press.

Pagés, C. 2017. "Do payroll tax cuts boost formal jobs in developing countries?," *IZA World of Labor*, Institute of Labor Economics (IZA), pages 345–345, March 2017.

Perry, G., O. Arias, P. Fajnzylber, W. Maloney, A. Mason, and J. Saavedra. 2007. "Informality: Exit and Exclusion." Washington, DC: World Bank.

Pignatti, C. 2016. "Do Public Employment Services Improve Employment Outcomes? Evidence from Colombia," ILO Working Papers 994904833402676. Geneva: ILO.

Pissarides, C. 2000. *Equilibrium Unemployment Theory*. Cambridge, MA: MIT Press.

Ratner, D. 2013. *Unemployment insurance experience rating and labor market dynamics*, Finance and Economics Discussion Series (Washington, DC, Federal Reserve Board).

Rogers, J., and W. Streeck. 1995. Works Councils: Consultation, Representation, and Cooperation in Industrial Relations. Chicago, IL: University of Chicago Press.

Rogerson, R., and Schindler, M. 2002. "The Welfare Costs of Worker Displacement." *Journal of Monetary Economics*, 49(2002): 1213–34. Available at: https://www.sciencedirect.com/science/article/abs/pii/S0304393202001484.

Rothstein, J., and B. Zipperer. 2020. "The EITC and Minimum Wage Work Together to Reduce Poverty and Raise Incomes," EPI Report (Washington, DC., Economic Policy Institute). Available at: https://www.epi.org/publication/eitc-and-minimum-wage-work-together/

Schmieder, J.F., and T. Von Wachter. 2016. "The Effects of Unemployment Insurance Benefits: New Evidence and Interpretation." *Annual Review of Economics*, Annual Reviews, 8(1): 547–81, October.

Schnabel, C. 2013. "Union Membership and Density: Some (not so) Stylized Facts and Challenges." *European Journal of Industrial Relations* 19(3): 255–72.

Schneider, F. 2004. "The Size of the Shadow Economies of 145 Countries all over the World: First Results over the Period 1999 to 2003," IZA DP No. 1431.

Scruggs, L. 2002. "The Ghent System and Union Membership in Europe, 1970–1996." *Political Research Quarterly* 55(2): 275–97.

Shehu, E., and B. Nilsson. 2014. "Informal Employment Among Youth: Evidence from 20 School-to-Work Transition Surveys, (Geneva, ILO). Available at: https://www.ilo.org/employment/areas/youth-employment/work-for-youth/publications/thematic-reports/WCMS_234911/lang--en/index.htm

Shin, Y.-K., and P. Böckerman. 2019. "Precarious Workers' Choices About Unemployment Insurance Membership After the Ghent System Reform: The Finnish Experience." *Social Policy Administration* 53: 921–938.

Slonimczyk, F. 2012. "The Effect of Taxation on Informal Employment: Evidence from the Russian Flat Tax Reform," in "Informal Employment in Emerging and Transition

Economies," Vol. 34 of Research in *Labor Economics*, chapter 2, pp. 55–99, edited by Lehmann, H. and Tatsiramos, K.

Tatsiramos, K. 2009. "Unemployment Insurance in Europe: Unemployment Duration and Subsequent Employment Stability." *Journal of the European Economic Association* 7(6): 1225–60.

Torgler, B., and F. Schneider. 2007. "Shadow Economy, Tax Morale, Governance and Institutional Quality: A Panel Analysis," IZA DP No. 2563.

Van Elk, K., J. de Kok, J. Durán, and G. Lindeboom. 2014. "Enterprise formalization: Fact or fiction? A quest for case studies," Geneva: ILO.

Van Ours, J.C., and M. Vodopivec. 2008."Does Reducing Unemployment Insurance Generosity Reduce Job Match Quality?." *Journal of Public Economics* 92(3–4): 684–95.

Villanueva, E. 2015. "Employment and Wage Effects of Extending Collective Bargaining Agreements: Extending Provisions of Collective Contracts to All Workers in an Industry or Region May Lead to Employment Losses," in *IZA World of Labor*, Nr. 136 (Bonn, Institute for the Study of Labor).

Visser, J. 2013. ICTWSS: Database on Institutional Characteristics of Trade Unions, Wage Setting, State Intervention and Social Pacts in 34 countries between 1960 and 2007—Version 4. Available at: http://www.uva-aias.net/en/ictwss

Waseem, M. 2018. "Taxes, Informality and Income Shifting: Evidence from a Recent Pakistani Tax Reform." *Journal of Public Economics* 157(C): 41–77.

World Bank. 2008. "Del PANES al Plan de Equidad (Nota Técnica)."

World Bank. 2019. "Global Economic Prospects, January 2019: Darkening Skies," Chapter 3—Growing in the Shadows: Challenges of Informality," January 8, 2019. Washington, DC. Available at: https://openknowledge.worldbank.org/handle/10986/31066

4

Financial Inclusion

Adolfo Barajas, Thorsten Beck, Mohamed Belhaj,
and Sami Ben Naceur

The past two decades have seen a rapid increase in interest in financial inclusion, both from policymakers and researchers.[1] This chapter surveys the main findings from the literature, documenting the trends over time and gaps that have arisen across regions, income levels, and gender, among others. It points out that structural, as well as policy-related, factors, such as encouraging banking competition or channeling government payments through bank accounts, play an important role, and describes the potential macro and microeconomic benefits that can be derived from greater financial inclusion. It argues that policy should aim to identify and reduce frictions holding back financial inclusion, rather than targeting specific levels of inclusion. Finally, it suggests areas for future research.

I. Introduction

Financial inclusion has received increasing attention from both researchers and policymakers in the past two decades as a potential source of benefits to the economy. On the research side, the study of financial inclusion is partly a logical next step from the literature originating in the early 1990s, which uncovered positive micro and macroeconomic impacts from more efficient financial service provision in general.[2] For example, the broad process of *financial development* has been shown to promote economic growth at the national, industry, and firm levels, as well as to enhance productivity growth and resource allocation, with some effect on capital accumulation. It has also been shown to contribute to inclusive growth, reducing income inequality and poverty. As this chapter will discuss, financial inclusion can

[1] The authors thank Valerie Cerra, Barry Eichengreen, Mahvash Saeed Qureshi, Majid Bazarbash, Aidyn Bibolov, Héctor Cárcel Villanova, Esha Chhabra, Nicolas End, Yingjie Fan, Purva Khera, Elena Loukoianova, Ken Miyajima, Sumiko Ogawa, Andrea Presbitero, Kevin Wang Wagner, and seminar attendees at the Institute for Capacity Development for valuable comments
[2] See, for example, Levine (2005); Beck, Demirgüç-Kunt, and Levine (2007), and Beck, Levine, and Loayza (2000).

Adolfo Barajas, Thorsten Beck, Mohamed Belhaj, and Sami Ben Naceur, *Financial Inclusion* In: *How to Achieve Inclusive Growth.* Edited by: Valerie Cerra, Barry Eichengreen, Asmaa El-Ganainy, and Martin Schindler, Oxford University Press. © Adolfo Barajas, Thorsten Beck, Mohamed Belhaj, and Sami Ben Naceur 2022. DOI: 10.1093/oso/9780192846938.003.0004

be thought of as a dimension of financial development, and therefore potentially is associated with many of the benefits that are derived from this process.

As a result, policymakers have taken notice and action as well. According to the World Bank's 2014 Global Financial Development Report, about 50 countries had adopted explicit policies to boost financial inclusion. In its analysis of policy frameworks in 55 emerging market economies, the Economist Intelligence Unit's Global Microscope reported that about two-thirds of these countries had explicit national financial inclusion strategies in 2014. By 2019, all but one of the analyzed countries had them.

The purpose of this chapter is to give an overview of the trends and drivers of financial inclusion that incorporates the main findings from the research conducted to date, including the key insights for policymakers seeking to design strategies that will help to promote financial inclusion to its greatest advantage for the economy. Section II provides a working definition of financial inclusion that has proved useful for empirical work, takes stock of orders of magnitude and recent trends in the data, and introduces concepts that help to ascertain when there is an economically meaningful gap in financial inclusion. Section III reviews the main findings of theoretical and empirical research on the impacts of financial inclusion, that is, why it matters. Section IV zeroes in on the main findings regarding policies for promoting financial inclusion, with particular attention to households and micro, small, and medium-sized enterprises (MSMEs). Section V concludes and identifies directions for future research.

II. What Is Financial Inclusion?

There are many ways in which financial inclusion has been defined, each of which touches to some degree on one of several aspects: access of the population to financial services, the degree of use of these services, and their quality and cost. Similarly, there is a wide variety of financial services, such as payments, savings, credit, and insurance, and countries often differ quite sharply in how extensively each of these services is made available to and used by the population. An ideal measure should then incorporate the multidimensionality of financial inclusion across access, usage, quality, and cost; across different services; and across different agents, such as households and firms. In response, several recent studies have aimed at constructing multidimensional measures along these lines, which are described in the following section. Of course, the different dimensions are bound to be interrelated. For example, banking services will be used more extensively by the population the greater the ease of access—availability of ATMs or branches— the lower the cost, and the greater the quality of services.

As a first pass, one simple and easily observable definition was adopted by the World Bank's 2014 Global Financial Development Report: the proportion of individuals and firms that *use* financial services. However, as more detailed data

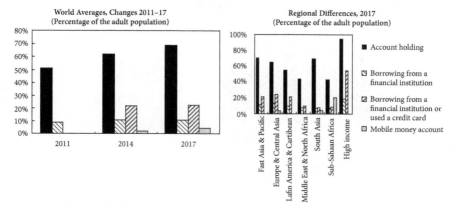

Figure 4.1 Household Financial Inclusion
Source: World Bank, Global Findex.

on specific aspects of financial inclusion have become available either within or across countries, this definition has been broadened to capture the multidimensionality of financial inclusion.[3]

A. Signs of Improvement

By most measures, financial inclusion has increased during the past decade. One prominent data source is the World Bank's Global Findex, a survey of about 150,000 households across 140 countries, covering account holdings, credit and savings activities, and whether wages or government transfers are paid directly into accounts. The Findex survey was first conducted in 2011 and has been conducted every three years since. One of its most often cited indicators, the percentage of the adult population holding a bank account, has experienced an impressive increase from a worldwide average of 51 percent in 2011 to 69 percent in 2017 (Figure 4.1).[4,5] Borrowing by households from formal financial institutions has also increased, although not at the same pace, from 9 to 11 percent if credit card use is excluded, and from 22 to 23 percent if it is included.

This still leaves an estimated 1.7 billion adults worldwide without an account, in other words, *unbanked*. Half of them live in seven developing economies

---

[3] In addition, the *intensity* of usage is another relevant dimension: for example, how often is a bank account used? How many transactions per month? Some datasets, such as the Global Findex, allow these differences to be captured for a wide sample of countries.

[4] Account holding refers specifically to whether the respondents reported having an account (by themselves or together with someone else) at a bank or another type of financial institution or report personally using a mobile money service in the past 12 months.

[5] Similar upward trends can be observed in financial inclusion indicators for firms (from the World Bank Enterprise Surveys) and from the percentage of the adult population who are depositors or borrowers from banking institutions (from the IMF Financial Access Survey).

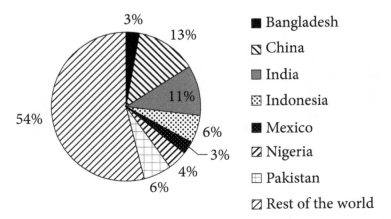

Figure 4.2 Nearly Half of All Unbanked Live in Just Seven Countries: Adults without an Account by the Economy (in %)
Source: World Bank, Global Findex.

(Figure 4.2).[6] Fifty-six percent are women, as there is a persistent gender gap, concentrated in three regions: the Middle East and North Africa, Sub-Saharan Africa, and South Asia. The poor are overrepresented, with half of the unbanked adults coming from the poorest 40 percent of households. Adults with low education or who are out of the labor force are also much more likely to be unbanked.

Moreover, the effective increase in financial inclusion may have been smaller. Rhyne and Kelly (2018) note that the 69 percent figure for banked individuals worldwide in 2017 becomes 55 percent once adjusting for inactive accounts, 48 percent for developing countries. Nearly 750 million people worldwide have accounts that they have not used in a year, the majority being in India and China.

The Findex survey identified the main reasons cited for not holding a formal bank account, as Figure 4.3 shows. The most cited is lack of money, followed by a family member having an account, opening an account being costly, banks being too far away, the respondent lacking proper documentation, little trust in financial institutions, or opting not to use financial services for religious reasons.

The data reveal other salient features. First, a key component of the increase in financial inclusion has been the result of fintech innovation, the introduction of mobile money accounts, which allow individuals and firms to use a mobile phone to send or receive money, make deposits, pay utility bills and, in some cases, apply for a loan. Adoption has occurred the most in Sub-Saharan Africa, where over one-fifth of the adult population now uses mobile money accounts, compared to 4 percent worldwide. While one might expect a strong negative correlation between the proliferation of mobile money and the use of conventional bank

---

[6] Bangladesh, China, India, Indonesia, Mexico, Nigeria, and Pakistan.

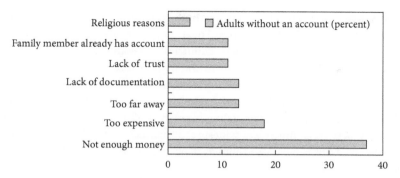

Figure 4.3 Reported Reasons for Not Having a Bank Account (percent)
Source: World Bank, Global Findex.

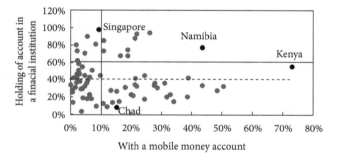

Figure 4.4 Mobile Money and Accounts in Financial Institutions (2017, percentage of adults)

Note: The solid vertical and horizontal lines denote the cross-country median values for account holding and mobile money usage, respectively.
Source: World Bank, Global Findex.

accounts, as the former substitutes for the latter, Figure 4.4 shows that this is not always the case. Kenya, the country with the highest mobile money penetration, at 73 percent, does contrast visibly with Singapore, a country with a much greater account holding and only 10 percent of adults with mobile money accounts. However, Namibia also has high mobile money penetration (43 percent) together with above-average account holding, while Chad has little presence of either. Finally, a large number of countries with widely varying levels of account holding have very little presence of mobile money.[7]

---

[7] Based on supplier-side data from the IMF's Financial Access Survey, Espinosa-Vega et al. (2020) find that mobile money penetration is negatively correlated with measures of access to traditional banking services, such as the number of ATMs per 100,000 adults. They also find a positive correlation with a broad index of enabling regulatory environment for mobile money. Sahay et al. (2020) document a rapid global expansion in fintech lending as well, from $125 billion in 2015 to $400 billion in 2017.

Second, as one might expect, levels of both account holding and borrowing are markedly higher in richer countries. For example, on average, account holding exceeds 90 percent in high-income countries, compared to 70 percent in the emerging and developing regions with the highest levels, East Asia and Pacific and South Asia. Differences in the use of bank borrowing are even more pronounced; 55 percent in high-income countries compared to 24 percent in Europe and Central Asia. Finally, it is notable that, across all regions and income levels, borrowing activity is much less widespread than account holding; even in rich countries, an adult is over four times as likely to have an account than to borrow from a formal financial institution.

Some studies have taken a multi-dimensional approach to measure financial inclusion, creating composite indicators from different sources and weighing each dimension by its statistical contribution to the total variation. The first in this vein was Svirydzenka (2016), who used a principal components methodology to construct a composite indicator of financial development (FD), a sub-component of which was itself a composite indicator of financial access (FA), combining aspects of household and firm access to services provided by financial institutions (FIA) and markets (FMA). Blancher and others (2019) used a similar procedure to construct a composite measure for small and medium enterprises (SMEs), and Loukoianova and Yang (2018) constructed composite indices based on individual indicators from the IMF's Financial Access Survey of financial institutions (FAS). Sahay and others (2020) construct indices of access to and usage of digital as well as traditional financial inclusion. All of these studies have used their measures in regressions aimed at assessing the macroeconomic impact of financial inclusion.

Financial inclusion has been affected by recent developments surrounding the Covid-19 crisis. First, the severe setbacks suffered by the real economy, both directly from the virus and as a result of the lockdowns and social distancing measures introduced, have weakened a wide spectrum of borrowers' ability to repay and, consequently, pose challenges for the survival of many financial institutions. These pressures have been particularly great for non-bank institutions such as microfinance lenders, who have experienced recent collapses in repayment rates, thus generating great uncertainty about their viability going forward.[8] This has the potential to leave a large number of MSMEs without access to finance. Fintech startups have been similarly affected, with venture capital and investors forced to withdraw funding.[9] On the positive side, there is evidence that individuals in many developing countries are accelerating their shift away from cash transactions and expanding the use of mobile money, given that cash transactions can be a medium of transmission of Covid-19. This shift has facilitated

---

[8] See,forexample,https://www.economist.com/finance-and-economics/2020/05/05/for-microfinance-lenders-covid-19-is-an-existential-threat.

[9] Zachariadis, Ozcan, and Dinckol (2020).

risk-sharing among families and friends and push-out of government support programs through mobile money networks, with Togo being a prime example.[10,11]

B. Structural Conditions Affecting Financial Inclusion

To some extent, the differences observed across countries, regions, and income levels are due to structural conditions in the economy. Extending financial services to a wide swath of the population entails certain costs that are likely to exhibit economies of scale, thus, it stands to reason that financial inclusion will be naturally higher in countries in which structural conditions are such that the per-person costs of providing financial services are lower.

One major structural condition is the income level; banks and other financial institutions will find it more cost-effective to provide services to higher-income potential customers, and therefore higher-income countries should be expected to have higher levels of financial inclusion, as reflected in the income group comparisons in Figure 4.1. More broadly, there is a positive association between a country's income per capita and different measures of financial inclusion, as illustrated in Figure 4.5, which shows a selection of financial inclusion indicators,

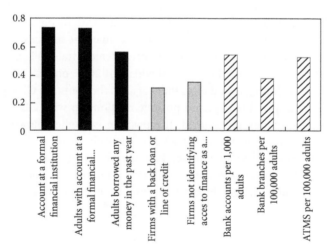

Figure 4.5 Financial Inclusion and Real GDP Per Capita Cross-Country Correlation, 2017 or latest date available

Sources: World Bank, Global Findex and Enterprise Surveys; IMF Financial Access Survey.

---

[10] Section II.F reviews evidence of how mobile money can enhance risk-sharing.
[11] See https://novissi.gouv.tg/en/home-new-en/.

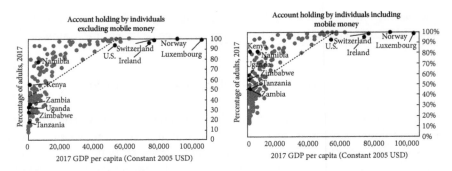

Figure 4.6 Mobile Money and Financial Inclusion

Sources: World Bank, Global Financial Development Database and authors' calculations.

from three sources.[12] The first indicator, of account holding and borrowing by individuals, has the highest correlation with income per capita, with a coefficient of over 0.70. The second type of indicator is focused on firms and is obtained from the World Bank's Enterprise Surveys (WBES): the percentage of firms that reported using bank credit and the percentage not identifying lack of finance as a major obstacle to their business. The third type of indicator involves supply-side information from the IMF's FAS, which collects data on access to and use of financial services across the globe.[13] The number of borrowers per 1,000 adults, and the extension of financial infrastructure—branches and ATMs—to the population, are both also shown to be positively correlated with income.

Innovation can reduce the costs of providing financial services, as the rapid proliferation of mobile money in some countries demonstrates. Figure 4.6 shows two measures of account holding by individuals in 2017, one excluding mobile money and one including it, and plots them against the country's GDP per capita. Both indicators display the expected positive relationship with GDP per capita, but once mobile money is included, the position of some countries changes markedly. While high-income countries are relatively unaffected, several low-income countries where mobile money has taken hold—a selection of which is displayed as black points in the figure—shift upward noticeably. For example, after including mobile money, Uganda and Zimbabwe exhibit levels of account holding

---

[12] It should be mentioned that the relationship between financial inclusion and income is likely to contain causality in both directions. Just as in the finance-growth literature surveyed by Levine (2005), care should be taken to account for reverse causality when estimating regressions that are meant to capture causal relationships.

[13] Espinosa-Vega and others (2020) provide a ten-year retrospective of the FAS. They show trends in the data, documenting how financial inclusion has expanded over the past decade in different regions, and by different modalities (for example, bank branches vs mobile and Internet banking) and income levels, as well as identifying major gaps that persist, for example, between income level, size of firms, or by gender.

markedly greater than the level predicted by their income, and Kenya, at over 80 percent, approaches the level of countries with many times its income per capita.

Using the World Bank's Finstats platform, observed levels of a wide range of indicators of financial development can be compared easily to benchmarks based on structural characteristics. As described in detail in Feyen, Kibuuka, and Sourrouille (2019), structural benchmarks for each of 46 indicators of financial depth, inclusion, or performance are estimated based on a set of structural explanatory variables reflecting income level, demographics, and special circumstances.[14] If the observed value of the indicator is above (below) the structural benchmark, one can say that the country is overperforming (underperforming) relative to what is typical for countries of similar structural conditions.[15]

Figure 4.7 illustrates the comparison for two emerging economies (India and Colombia) and two indicators, the percentage of account holding and the percentage of firms with a loan or line of credit with a formal financial institution. India, as a result of a massive government effort in recent years, managed to increase the percentage of account holders from 35 to 80 percent between 2011 and 2017, well surpassing its structural benchmark of 40 percent. However, firms' use of bank credit, at 21 percent in 2014, is well below the 35 percent level predicted by India's structural conditions. Colombia presents a contrasting case, with account holding underperforming its structural benchmark in 2017 while credit to firms appears to overperform.[16]

C. How to Interpret Gaps in Financial Inclusion

Data on financial inclusion reveals various gaps: for example, between rich and poor countries, between different regions, between partial and universal inclusion (particularly in the case of account holding), and between the observed levels and the structural benchmarks for a given country at a specific time. How should one interpret these gaps? Does the existence of a gap necessarily signal that there is a shortfall or deficiency that policymakers must aim to close? Is more financial inclusion necessarily better? The simple answer is no, more financial

---

[14] The full set of structural variables includes: economic development (GDP per capita and its square); population factors (total population and its density); demographic factors (young and old-age dependency ratios); "special circumstances" (dummies for oil exporters, offshore financial centers, transition countries, and landlocked countries); and the global cycle (time fixed effects).

[15] The Finstats database created by Feyen, Kibuuka, and Sourrouille (2019) provides observed values as well as estimated structural benchmarks for the 46 indicators. Using the Finstats Dashboard, graphical comparisons between observed levels and benchmarks, such as those shown in Figure 4.7, can be generated very easily.

[16] Note that, although the structural benchmarking regressions control for the global cycle, an individual country may seem to over-or underperform due to its own cyclical factors.

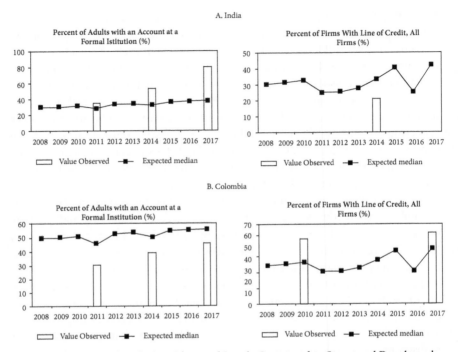

Figure 4.7 Financial Inclusion Observed Levels Compared to Structural Benchmarks
Source: World Bank, Finstats Database.

inclusion is not necessarily better, and not all gaps need to be eliminated. The main reasons for this argument are discussed below.

First, not all firms and households need all financial services. Consider that the Global Findex reveals that some financial exclusion is voluntary, that is, some individuals choose not to use financial services. For example, in Lithuania, a high-income country with a relatively high level of financial inclusion, while 83 percent of adults reported having a bank account in 2017, 8 percent stated that they did not have a bank account because they had access through another family member, and another 3 percent felt they had no need for financial services. An additional 1 percent cited religious reasons, a response that tends to be particularly high in countries with large Islamic populations.[17] Regarding Lithuanian firms, in the Enterprise Survey in 2013 about 33 percent reported having a bank loan or line of credit—very close to the global average—while 54 percent responded that

---

[17] For example, religious reasons were cited as the reason for not having in account in 12 percent of respondents in West Bank and Gaza, Pakistan, and Tajikistan, 10 percent in the Philippines and Tunisia, and 7 percent in Turkey.

they had not applied for bank credit because they had no need for it.[18] There may be a case for policy to affect voluntary exclusion, for example by encouraging financial education so that individuals may better understand the potential benefits of using financial services, or by providing financial services that are more compatible with individuals' religious beliefs. But there is an open question as to the cost-effectiveness of these types of policies, and it may be true that some individuals or firms simply do not need financial services.[19]

As for involuntary exclusion, there is a strong case against policymakers attempting to drive it to zero in all cases, for two main reasons: risks and costs. In the credit market, some borrowers may be too risky. As this market is characterized by having *information asymmetries*—lenders (banks) do not have perfect information on potential borrowers' riskiness—a situation emerges which was first described by Stiglitz and Weiss (1981). As interest rates rise, progressively riskier borrowers stay in the market. As a result of this *adverse selection*, banks will voluntarily choose to limit the interest rate charged on loans and ration borrowers out of the market, even some who would be willing to pay a higher rate. Thus, lack of inclusion, in this case, does not necessarily warrant a policy action to close the gap. In fact, it would be detrimental to society to include borrowers that are too risky.

Costs are also relevant. Some individuals or firms might be excluded due to the high costs of providing services to them. Focusing on the credit market, if transaction costs are large, lenders would need to charge a higher rate to cover them, and the quantity of credit in the economy would be small, as there would be fewer potential borrowers with projects whose return is high enough. Furthermore, also excluded are individuals with a demand for very small loans, since providing these loans has high fixed costs. Thus, some remote areas will not have a branch, for example, because the fixed cost cannot be covered by the low demand. That said, innovation can change the landscape of financial inclusion dramatically by reducing the fixed costs needed to provide some financial services. The examples cited of low-income countries recently boosting account holding through mobile money reflect this fact quite clearly, and it is becoming clear that some financial services, such as basic transactions and payments, can approach universality without undue costs or risks.

Structural benchmarks can serve as a useful guide to policymakers to assess a country's financial inclusion, providing a first pass comparison with peer countries. Evidence of underperformance with respect to the structural benchmark would suggest exploring the policies that have been successful in the overperforming peer countries. For example, Indian firms' use of credit—21 percent

---

[18] One possible reason for the reported lack of need for domestic bank loans in Lithuania is the direct support offered by the EU to SMEs through the Lithuanian Operational Program.

[19] Section IV discusses financial education and capability in greater detail.

compared with the structural benchmark of 35 percent—should suggest an examination of policies in the peer countries.

However, this framework has two main limitations that make it important not to read too much into comparisons with structural benchmarks. First, if a country is found to be performing above its structural benchmark, it is not immediately clear where the country lies relative to an optimal level of financial inclusion. That is, it is not clear whether Colombia's level of credit to firms or India's extent of account holding is close to, above, or below the optimal level of financial inclusion for a country of their structural characteristics. Thus, observing that a country is overperforming relative to the structural benchmark may not be informative for policymakers, and could lead to complacency. Second, it is possible for all, or most, countries sharing similar structural characteristics to be implementing suboptimal policies at the same time, and thus the median behavior would not be a good guide for policy. For example, in the run-up to the global financial crisis, many countries were experiencing unsustainable credit booms, so it is quite likely that the median behavior would also reflect the types of policies that permitted the booms to materialize. Aiming for the median would not be desirable.

Rather than targeting a level of financial inclusion directly, a policy should therefore focus its attention on involuntary exclusion driven by *frictions* in the markets and should aim to enact policies that reduce these frictions. One such friction is imperfect or incomplete information, as highlighted in the credit market example above. To the extent that it is both possible and cost-effective, a policy that helps to improve information on prospective borrowers—setting up a credit registry, for example—can help expand access to credit safely.[20]

III. Why Does Financial Inclusion Matter?

Implicit in the discussion up to now is that financial inclusion matters, that is, it has a potentially beneficial impact on the economy. This section will take stock of the main research on the economic relevance of financial inclusion, both in theoretical and empirical work, and both at the micro and macroeconomic levels. It focuses on a selection of studies that provide a useful overview of the main effects of financial inclusion on economic outcomes, and crucially, the channels through which these effects come about.

---

[20] In addition, De la Torre, Gozzi, and Schmukler (2017) propose a useful criterion to assess the need for policy actions, and Claessens and Rojas-Suárez (2020) argue for a "decision tree" approach to policy design for financial inclusion.

A. Financial Inclusion as a Dimension of Broad Financial Development

Critical to understanding why and how financial inclusion matters is to recognize that finance, or *financial development*, matters. As reviewed by Levine (2005), finance has a positive impact on the economy through the critical functions it undertakes: (i) to produce information; (ii) allocate capital to productive uses; (iii) monitor investments and exert corporate control; (iv) mobilize and pool savings; (v) facilitate trading, diversification, and management of risk; and (vi) ease exchange of goods and services. These functions can be carried out not only by banks and other financial institutions but also by firms markets, such as those for bonds or equity. Theoretical research has uncovered linkages between these functions and a variety of positive economic outcomes, such as higher economic growth and productivity. Thus, one can define a country's level of financial development as the extent to which the functions above are being carried out.

Empirical research has provided evidence of these positive linkages, relying on indicators that measure, at least approximately, the level of financial development. Until recently, the indicators used have reflected primarily the size or scale of financial activity: for banking, the ratio of credit to the private sector to GDP, and for markets, the ratio of stock market capitalization or volume of transactions per year to GDP. These measures are termed indicators of *financial depth* and are certainly related to financial development. For example, a country in which private credit and/or the volume of stock market transactions is very small clearly cannot be mobilizing a significant amount of savings, nor allocating capital, producing information about borrowers or issuers, or offering risk management tools for firms and individuals. Indeed, Levine (2005), and more recently, Popov (2018), review evidence from cross-country panel regressions showing that both financial depth measures are positively and significantly related to higher rates of long-run economic growth, capital accumulation, and productivity and that these relationships are likely to be causal, that greater depth leads to these better outcomes. Rajan and Zingales (1998) identify a key channel through which finance affects growth: easing the financing constraints in the sectors that naturally depend more heavily on external financing as opposed to their own funds. Therefore, through this mechanism, the financially dependent sectors may grow faster in countries with greater financial activity. More recent research has uncovered evidence supporting a "too much finance" hypothesis, whereby the relationship between growth and financial depth weakens at very high levels of financial depth and therefore tends to be hump-shaped rather than unambiguously increasing.[21]

---

[21] Arcand, Berkes, and Panizza (2015) find that the positive link between depth in banking and growth is not unlimited, and at sufficiently high levels of depth—private credit to GDP exceeding 100

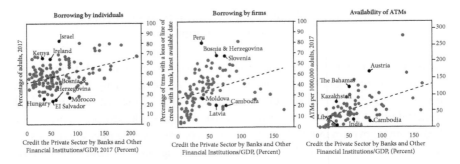

Figure 4.8 Financial Inclusion and Financial Depth

Sources: World Bank, Global Findex and Enterprise Surveys; IMF Financial Access Survey; and authors' calculations

Chapter 2 of this book discusses research exploring interrelationships between growth and inclusion, and there is also a body of empirical work investigating how financial development fits into these relationships. The main finding is that financial development is indeed associated with *inclusive growth*. Beck, Demirgüç-Kunt, and Levine (2007) present evidence that greater financial depth leads to lower income inequality and a smaller percentage of the population living in poverty. Zhang and Ben Naceur (2019) confirm these positive outcomes from greater stock market turnover, lower interest margins, and higher regulatory capital ratios of banks, although they also find that financial liberalization may have adverse effects on income equality and poverty.

Financial inclusion can be thought of as a *dimension* of financial development, in addition to the financial depth indicators that are imperfect and incomplete proxies. Of course, financial inclusion should be associated to some degree with financial depth; if a country mobilizes a large amount of funds, it is more likely to provide services to a large percentage of individuals and firms. However, this correlation is not perfect, as Figure 4.8 shows. Three financial inclusion measures are displayed together with the ratio of credit to GDP: the percentage of individuals with bank loans, the percentage of firms with a bank loan or line of credit, and the coverage of ATMs throughout the population. Several pairs of countries are highlighted in black to show that, although financial inclusion does tend to be greater in countries with greater banking depth, countries with similar depth can diverge quite dramatically in terms of financial inclusion. This suggests that financial development is more advanced, say, in Israel than in Bosnia and Herzegovina and

percent—the growth benefits begin to wane and may even become negative. Relatedly, Cecchetti and Kharroubi (2015) show that rapid growth of the banking sector can also have a negative impact on productivity. Rousseau and Wachtel (2017) show that the incidence of financial crises weakens the finance growth relationship as well.

that financial depth alone might be understating the possible benefits accruing from financial activity in Israel.

B. Macro-Level Relevance of Financial Inclusion

Suggestive Empirical Results Regarding Inclusive Growth

Viewed as a dimension of financial development, it follows that financial inclusion should have a measurable impact on macroeconomic outcomes such as fostering long-term growth, enhancing income equality, or reducing poverty, that is, contribute to *inclusive growth*. A small but growing literature examines the possible empirical links between financial inclusion and these outcomes, analogous to the previous body of work focusing on the inclusive growth implications of financial depth.

Sahay and others (2015a) use several FAS indicators as well as the Svirydzenka (2016) composite indicators along with the private sector credit-GDP ratio. Their results suggest that financial inclusion does have a measurable impact on 10-year growth, above and beyond that of financial depth.[22] The impact of depth on growth increases with the level of financial inclusion, measured by ATM coverage or the percentage of firms not considering lack of finance to be a significant obstacle. That is, Israel would be expected to derive greater growth benefits from finance than Bosnia and Herzegovina. The findings are also consistent with a "too much finance" hypothesis, with the growth impact weakening as both financial inclusion and depth become very large. Given the limited time series, however, this result is more suggestive than definitive in uncovering a financial inclusion-long run growth nexus.

Turning to broader issues of economic inclusion, Cihák and others (2020) also obtain encouraging results linking financial inclusion to lower inequality, based on panel regressions for 105 countries over the 2004–15 period. Payments services, as approximated by ATM coverage, are found to be associated with lower inequality, as measured by the Gini coefficient. Furthermore, this relationship is significantly stronger when economic growth is faster, when the financial system is more stable, and when financial depth is lower. For credit—the share of borrowers in the population—the differences in the negative financial inclusion-inequality relationship are even starker; while at low levels of depth this relationship is relatively strong, it weakens at progressively higher levels of depth, and eventually reverts, meaning that at high levels of depth an expansion in the use of credit can *increase* inequality. Using composite measures, Loukoianova and

---

[22] Sahay et al. (2020) find a positive association between *digital* financial inclusion and economic growth as well.

Yang (2018) also find beneficial effects of financial inclusion, reducing inequality and poverty in addition to increasing economic growth.

Tradeoffs Between Financial Inclusion and Financial Stability

There also has been empirical work exploring the relationship between financial inclusion and financial stability. This is motivated partly by the "too much finance" hypothesis, which argues that one reason why the finance-growth relationship exhibits the hump shape is that very large financial systems tend to become more prone to instability and crises. It is also related to work by Schularick and Taylor (2012) and others who find that rapid expansions in credit are often precursors to financial crises. Given the similar weakening relationship between financial inclusion and growth as inclusion increases, the question then is whether there is a tradeoff between financial inclusion and financial stability.

On the positive side, Han and Melecky (2013) find a stabilizing effect of greater inclusion in bank deposits; countries in which a larger share of the population had access to deposits prior to the 2008 global financial crisis suffered significantly smaller withdrawals when the crisis hit. Mehrotra and Yetman (2015) show that consumption volatility tends to be lower in countries where there is a larger percentage of adults that have accounts and save in formal financial institutions. Ahamed and Mallick (2019) studied a sample of 2,635 banks in 86 countries and found that financial inclusion contributes to a more stable banking system, an effect that is more pronounced when banks are mostly funded by deposits, display low marginal costs, and operate within a strong institutional environment.

Other studies have found more mixed results. In a panel data set including a sample of 150 countries, Cihák, Mare, and Melecky (2016) examine the inclusion-stability relationship more broadly, using measures of account ownership, payments, savings, credit, and insurance services, which they then relate to different indicators of financial stability. They find that the relationship is complex, with instances of tradeoffs between the two—in particular, with regard to expansions in credit access—but also instances of synergies between some aspects of financial inclusion and stability, primarily during non-crisis times. They also find that the relationship is also affected by country characteristics, such as financial openness, tax rates, education, and credit information depth. Sahay and others (2015b) and Cihák and others (2020) focus on credit inclusion and find that the relationship with financial stability depends crucially on the quality of bank regulation and supervision; the tradeoff emerges primarily when such quality is low. This suggests that sequencing is important in two respects: first, focusing initially on payment and savings inclusion allows to delay this tradeoff and build the necessary regulatory framework; and, second, credit inclusion should only be fostered where the necessary regulatory framework (including consumer protection) is in place.

C. Channels Through which Credit Affects Economic Outcomes

Relaxing Financing Constraints

The main consequence of financial activity is that it eases financing constraints to individuals and firms, thereby providing opportunities that would not be available if these agents were limited to their own funds. Recent theoretical work (Dabla-Norris et al. 2015 and 2019) has captured the workings of this channel. Some individuals have sufficient talent to become entrepreneurs, but because of their limited wealth, lack the capital required and must remain workers. Another group has sufficient talent and initial wealth to become entrepreneurs, but not sufficient wealth to operate their firms at the optimal scale. Credit allows some talented individuals to invest in the required capital and become entrepreneurs, and some entrepreneurs to increase their scale of production to the optimal level.

Therefore, overall GDP will most certainly increase, while effects on productivity and income distribution are a bit more complex. While some entrepreneurs are able to increase their productivity by reaching the optimal scale, access to credit also introduces small-scale firms that are initially not very productive, while the average entrepreneurial talent is likely to increase. Individuals becoming entrepreneurs will benefit, as will workers through upward pressure on wages—there is now a smaller supply of workers relative to entrepreneurs—but wealthy entrepreneurs who had been constrained will benefit as well.

Three main frictions inhibit an economy from increasing the availability and scale of credit. The first is *credit access* or entry cost friction that must be borne in order to obtain credit, reflecting such factors as the distance to the nearest bank, the documentation required, lack of knowledge about credit, cultural constraints, lack of trust in banks, and discrimination. The second friction is related to weak contract enforceability, which provides an incentive for borrowers to abscond with a portion of the loan and not invest it productively. In response, banks impose a *collateral constraint*, thus limiting the amount of leverage taken on by their borrowers. While prudent, this action also limits the quantity of credit or financial depth, therefore preventing some entrepreneurs from reaching their optimal scale. The final friction is related to the *efficiency* of financial intermediation, as reflected in the spread between the rate charged on loans and the rate paid on deposits. By increasing the cost of credit, this friction reduces the profitability derived from the debt-financed activity and therefore inhibits both the entry of new entrepreneurs and the scaling up of production by existing entrepreneurs.

Microfinance, Financial Frictions, and Poverty Traps

A large literature has emerged to examine the effects of microfinance. As reviewed and assessed by Buera, Kaboski, and Shin (2016), one key question posed by the literature is whether financial frictions play a role in generating "poverty traps" at the individual and economy-wide level. If so, then reducing these frictions—for example, by increasing access to credit, or by introducing targeted micro-credit programs or outright asset grants to poor entrepreneurs—might allow individuals and the economy to escape poverty traps. Indeed, in field studies, it has been shown that greater access to credit and targeted micro-credit and asset grant programs can have beneficial effects on income distribution.

Both theory and analysis of real-world experiments with micro-credit show that take-up tends to be relatively low, and therefore increases in entrepreneurship are modest. However, even individuals not directly participating in the programs—salaried workers—can benefit through upward pressure on wages. At the macro level, there does not seem to be a long-run poverty trap induced by financial frictions, partly because wealthier entrepreneurs can eventually escape financial constraints by generating sufficient funds internally to expand their scale of operation.

Although most micro-credit experiments are short-lived and do not offer the chance to assess their long-run impact, Banerjee and others (2019) analyzed an intervention in Hyderabad, India, in which micro-credit was randomly assigned to 52 neighborhoods and then withdrawn from all several years later. This allowed an assessment of the persistent impact of the program two years after it had been suspended and six years after the initial intervention. Relative to the "untreated" neighborhoods, where micro-credit was not offered, the study found significant increases in entrepreneurship, profits, business scale, turnover, and employment in the "treated" neighborhoods.

The experiment also found an important additional source of heterogeneity: between those who were already entrepreneurs when micro-credit was introduced ("gung ho entrepreneurs," GE), the new entrants ("reluctant entrepreneurs," RE), and those who did not become entrepreneurs, but rather used the micro-credit to finance consumption. The bulk of the positive business impacts of micro-credit was concentrated among the GEs. This suggests that there are dual technologies, one more productive and capital-intensive than the other. While the untreated GEs are essentially caught in a poverty trap due to lack of access to superior technology, those given access to credit were able to invest in this technology, grow their business, and escape poverty. The study even found evidence of *crowding in* of other sources of finance; GEs with access to micro-credit were also more likely to borrow from other sources. On the other hand, there was no significant impact of credit for either the REs or the consumption borrowers in relation to their credit-constrained counterparts.

Financial Inclusion for Households

There is evidence that shifting from cash payments into bank accounts lowers the cost of transactions and increases their speed. For example, in South Africa, the cost for the government to pay out social transfers using a smart card is equivalent to a third of the cost of cash payments. Shifting cash payments into accounts can also improve transparency and reduce corruption. Argentina introduced the *Jefes Program* in the midst of the 2002 economic and social crisis to shift government payments from cash to deposit accounts, which helped to reduce kickbacks, and delivered other beneficial effects (Duryea and Schargrodsky 2008). The shift also has been shown to help individuals build a payment history, which can then ease access to credit. In the United States, adding data on payment of utilities into credit files increased the number of adults for whom a credit score could be calculated (Turner and others 2012).

Mobile money allows people to access financial services including payments, transfers, savings, and, increasingly, credit, without the need for a bank account. These services can be performed through an electronic account linked to the SIM card in the phone. It has been shown that the M-PESA mobile money platform in Kenya has positive impacts on the ability to manage risk, aided by the fact that two-thirds of adults surveyed reported that M-PESA is the fastest way to send and receive money (GSMA 2014). Studies by Jack and Suri (2014) and Suri, Jack, and Stoker (2012) show that faced with a negative income shock, M-PESA users are more likely than non-users to receive a transfer from friends and family, receive more money in total, and receive it from a more diverse set of people in their network. In fact, a large share of transactions on M-PESA is between-person transfers across long distances. Figure 4.9 illustrates the risk-sharing advantages enjoyed by M-PESA users over non-users. In the event of shocks such as a natural disaster, the loss of a job, or an illness, they are less prone to cutting back on consumption (Panel a) and facing a health shock, they are able to spend more on medical expenses while also increasing expenses on food and maintaining their education expenditure (Panel b).[23]

Furthermore, mobile money provides other benefits. First, it can lower the cost of international remittances. Indeed, the Remittance Price Worldwide database

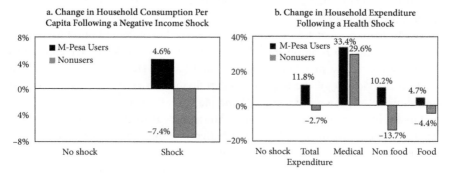

Figure 4.9 Risk Sharing through M-Pesa (Mobile Money) in Kenya
Source: Suri (2017).

---

[23] This figure is adapted from Figure 7 in the Suri (2017) survey paper.

shows that the average price of remittances is 6.67 percent in Q2 2020 compared to 4.42 percent when funds are sent from a mobile wallet. Second, mobile money transfers have further advantages including time savings, the ability to check instantly the exchange rate, limited risks compared to carrying cash, and the ability to keep cash in a mobile account. A recent study shows further evidence of the economic benefits of mobile money. Using granular data from Paytm, one of the largest providers of mobile money services in India, Patnam and Yao (2020) show that, at the district level, adoption is associated with greater resilience of economic activity and household consumption to adverse rainfall shocks. They also find that firm-level adoption of mobile money is associated with greater sales.

More recently, the Covid-19 crisis has seen an enhanced role for mobile money. In West Africa, where adoption still lags that of East African countries such as Kenya and Tanzania, individuals seeking to reduce the risk of contagion are shifting away from cash transactions. In some countries, the government or mobile money providers have aided in the process by lowering the barriers to opening mobile money accounts.[24] Penetration of these accounts has also facilitated the speed, efficiency, and safety with which governments can implement the social protection programs necessitated by the lockdowns and interruption of economic activity.[25]

The use of savings at a formal financial institution also has significant benefits. It can help reduce theft, improve household well-being, and reinforce women's economic empowerment. Brune and others (2016) analyzed a randomized control trial (RCT) of a program facilitating formal savings for Malawian tobacco farmers, finding that it not only increased banking activities but also household welfare, investments in inputs, and subsequent agricultural yields. Also using an RCT, Ashraf and others (2006) examine the impact of an individually held commitment savings product in the Philippines. They find that this saving product positively impacted the female decision-making power within the household.

Credit from a financial institution can benefit low-income households. They may gain access to funding for education or business under better conditions than from a family member or an informal lender. However, as discussed in Section II, evidence of the impact of microfinance on access to credit is mixed and shows, at most, a modest effect (Banerjee 2013; Banerjee and others 2015).

Finally, insurance products can help households manage financial risks, such as unexpected expenses, and provide better coverage than saving and credit. There is also evidence that individuals will adopt higher risk and return technologies if provided access to formal insurance (Rosenzweig and Binswanger 1993).

---

[24] See https://www.weforum.org/agenda/2020/04/coronavirus-set-to-spur-mobile-money-growth-in-w-africa/.

[25] See https://blogs.worldbank.org/africacan/covid-19-africa-how-can-social-safety-nets-help-mitigate-social-and-economic-impacts.

Using an RCT in China, Cai and others (2015) find that offering formal insurance to small pig farmers significantly increases the number of sows raised.

However, the benefits of expanding access to these services are not always clear-cut. Dupas and others (2018) find that, while programs to increase account ownership in Chile, Malawi, and Uganda did succeed in opening a large number of accounts, only a small fraction of them are used. In India, despite a massive government effort, three-quarters of the 222 million accounts opened are still inactive (Agrawal and others 2018).

D. Financial Inclusion for Micro, Small, and Medium Enterprises (MSMEs)

Given their economic relevance and the potential impact of financing constraints, the financial inclusion of MSMEs has been one major area of focus for research and policymakers alike. MSMEs comprise over 95 percent of firms around the world, and in low and middle-income countries they are particularly important in terms of employment; more than 50 percent of workers are in companies with fewer than 100 employees (Ayyagari, Demirgüç-Kunt, and Maksimovic 2011b). Further, there is ample evidence that smaller firms suffer more from financing constraints. Beck, Demirgüç-Kunt, and Maksimovic (2005), for example, show that financing obstacles constrain the growth of smaller firms more than that of larger firms and that this difference is larger in countries with more shallow financial systems.

Constraints to MSME Financial Inclusion

Several factors play a role in limiting access to and use of finance by MSMEs. First, fixed transaction costs in credit assessment, processing, and monitoring result in *economies of scale* which makes lending to MSMEs relatively costly. Second, compared with large firms, information asymmetries are likely to be more severe, as MSMEs are more *opaque*. They often do not have audited financial statements that allow a clearer picture of the enterprise and its projected profits, and are less likely to be able to post collateral. Third, MSMEs may voluntarily choose to be excluded due to cultural barriers or lack of financial literacy, or simply to a dearth of profitable investment projects in the economy. Fourth, financial institutions cannot rely as much on the law of large numbers to exploit scale economies and diversification benefits of SMEs, as there are fewer of them in a given sector, and their characteristics are harder to capture with a few quantitative indicators.[26] Fifth, the supply of financing may be limited further by regulatory

---

[26] See Beck and de la Torre (2007) and de la Torre, Martinez Peria, and Schmukler (2010) for a more in-depth discussion and references.

distortions or due to lack of competition, either of which can cause lenders to limit the availability of credit.

Note that there are relevant distinctions within this broad group of firms, which often require different policy approaches.[27] While micro-entrepreneurs are often self-employed individuals or household enterprises, with no separate business accounts and often no formal business license, medium-sized enterprises are often growth- and/or export-oriented, with formal accounts. These differences imply different financing needs and forms; while micro-entrepreneurs might be best served by microfinance institutions, medium-sized enterprises might look beyond bank finance to other sources, such as venture capital.

Another important distinction is between *subsistence* and *transformational* entrepreneurs. Subsistence entrepreneurs have businesses based on self-employment and informality and are almost exclusively micro-entrepreneurs. Many are established as a result of a lack of alternative employment options in the formal sector, and rely almost exclusively on the owner, maybe with support from family members and/or friends. On the other hand, transformational entrepreneurs often lead larger businesses that create jobs and are aimed at longer-term growth. De Mel, McKenzie, and Woodruff (2010) show that only 30 percent of microenterprise owners in Sri Lanka have characteristics similar to those of large firm owners, whereas 70 percent are more similar to wage workers. In a sample of micro-entrepreneurs in Mexico, Bruhn (2013) finds that about 50 percent are similar to wage workers. Thus, if the objective is to promote long-term aggregate growth and job creation, credit policy should focus on transformational enterprises, while non-credit policies should be targeted at vulnerable segments of the population (Fafchamps and Woodruff 2011).[28]

Impacts of Relaxing Financing Constraints of MSMEs

Even though there is no clear causal link between the share of MSMEs in manufacturing and per capita GDP growth rates, there is evidence that financial deepening can contribute to economic growth and ultimately poverty reduction by easing financing constraints of MSMEs (Beck, Demirgüç-Kunt and Levine 2005). Such effects are not always direct but act through improved resource allocation across the economy. Also, Pagano and Pica (2011) show a positive and significant relationship between financial development and job creation in developing countries, and Gine and Townsend (2004) show that in Thailand financial liberalization has contributed to a migration of subsistence agricultural workers into urban salaried jobs.

---

[27] There are different definitions of MSME. The MSME country indicator database, maintained by the IFC defines micro-enterprises as those with fewer than 10 employees, medium-sized as those with 50 to 249 employees and small enterprises with those between 10 and 49 employees. See Kushnir, Mirmulstein, and Ramalho (2010) for details.

[28] Among transformational enterprises, there is often a further emphasis on "gazelles," enterprises with exceptionally high growth rates over longer periods.

There are a variety of studies showing how financial development contributes to MSME growth, by alleviating financing constraints and leveling the playing field between firms of different sizes. The literature has identified three main channels, as shown below.

Financial development is positively associated with the number of start-ups—an important indicator of entrepreneurship—as well as with firm dynamism and innovation. Access to financial services can help new entrepreneurs survive beyond the first year, as evidence from a firm-level survey in Bosnia shows (Demirgüç-Kunt, Klapper, and Panos 2010). Interestingly, this effect operates through access to savings services, as shown by an RCT (Dupas and Robinson 2013), and can help enterprises innovate at a faster rate, as the World Bank ES data shows (Ayyagari, Demirgüç-Kunt, and Maksimovic 2011a). Finally, a more inclusive financial system, as proxied by more effective credit registries and higher branch penetration, is associated with a lower degree of tax evasion and thus lower informality, as shown with the World Bank's Enterprise Survey Data (Beck, Lin, and Ma 2014).

Finance also allows existing firms to exploit growth and investment opportunities, and to achieve a larger equilibrium size. Beck, Demirgüç-Kunt, and Maksimovic (2006) show in a cross-country sample that large firms—the most likely to be able to choose their boundaries—are larger in countries with more developed financial and legal systems.

Finance makes it possible for firms to acquire a more efficient productive asset portfolio and to choose more efficient organizational forms, such as incorporation. Demirgüç-Kunt, Love, and Maksimovic (2006) find that firms are more likely to operate in an incorporated form in countries with better-developed financial and legal systems, strong creditor and shareholder rights, and effective bankruptcy processes.[29] Incorporated firms have thus a comparative advantage in countries with institutions that support formal contracting, while unincorporated firms are more adapted to operate in countries with less developed formal institutions where firms have to rely on informal institutions and reputation.

Mobile money can also help small and micro enterprises expand access to trade credit, as shown by Beck, Ioannidou, and Schäfer (2018). Repayment to lenders via mobile money avoids the risk of theft but comes with transaction costs. Entrepreneurs with higher productivity and access to trade credit are more likely to use mobile money to pay their suppliers, which in turn expands the amount of trade credit they receive and lowers their interest rate. Calibrating the model to Kenyan firm-level survey data, the authors show that the adoption of M-PESA in 2007 can explain 10 percent of per capita income growth between 2007 and 2013.

---

[29] While these effects are tested separately, they are certainly interdependent with each other.

IV. Policies for Enhancing Financial Inclusion

A. For Households

Beck, Demirguc-Kunt, and Honohan (2008) were the first to investigate the barriers to financial inclusion, and proposed policies to overcome them. Using survey data from 209 banks in 62 countries, several factors arose as significant barriers to financial inclusion: minimum balances for deposit accounts and customer loans, annual fees, high documentation requirements, and the time required to process loans. Additional impediments included more stringent restrictions on bank activities, opaque banking systems, and a high incidence of government ownership of banks. Thus, the study suggested policies aimed at easing restrictions on banking entry and activities, enhancing bank transparency, improving the quality of physical infrastructure (such as electricity and Internet networks), lowering government ownership, and encouraging foreign bank entry.

Similar results were obtained by Allen and others (2012), using data on 124,000 individuals in 123 countries. They find ownership and use of a bank account are associated with lower fees to open an account, greater proximity to banks, a better enabling environment, and lower disclosure requirements. They also show that actions such as a requirement to offer free basic accounts, and exempting small or rural deposits from high disclosure requirements can help to increase access to financial services.[30] Aggarwal and Klapper (2012) proposed removing the barriers to open and use an account, to address the reason cited by 25 percent of Global Findex respondents in 2017 for not having an account. Along these lines, the Indian government has launched the Basic Savings Bank Deposit Accounts with no minimum balance requirements, provided a debit card, and allowed four free withdrawals per month.

Documentation requirements are another oft-cited barrier to account ownership. This generally takes the form of Know-Your-Customer (KYC) requirements to comply with Anti Money Laundering and Counter-Financing Terrorism (AML/CFT) guidelines. A number of countries have simplified these requirements, for example, for basic savings accounts in Brazil, or through the Indian "Aadhar" program that issues a biometric identification number and card for all Indian citizens.

One policy that has proven particularly effective in raising access for rural and poor populations is the requirement that government payments be made through bank accounts. The 2017 Global Findex data estimates that roughly 90 million adults opened their first bank account to collect public sector wages, 140 million to receive government transfers, 120 million to receive public sector pensions,

---

[30] The Financial Action Task Force (FATF) publishes recommendations and provides country examples on how to determine a threshold for disclosure requirements.

and 200 million to collect private sector wages. However, there is still room to build on this progress given that about 100 million unbanked adults still receive their government payments in cash and 230 million adults still receive their private-sector wages in cash.

Given that physical distance is another common barrier to financial inclusion— cited by 20 percent of Global Findex respondents as a reason for not having an account—several policies have been implemented to bring banking services closer to the population. The Reserve Bank of India required government-owned banks to open new branches in areas identified as unbanked, which resulted in the share of saving by rural banks increasing from 3 percent to 15 percent between 1969 and 1990 (Burgess and Pande 2005).[31] In the United States, the removal of barriers to intrastate bank branching in the 1970s was shown to lead to an expansion of bank branches which increased financial inclusion and wealth accumulation among the poorer households (Celerier and Matray 2019) and contributed to greater income equality (Beck, Levine, and Levkov 2010).

Since remotely located branches are generally costly to sustain, some countries have turned to agent or correspondent banking. Brazil is a case in point, with its Banco Postal partnering with local banks to open 10 million postal saving accounts between 2002 and 2011 (Anson and Gual 2008). In addition, more than 200 financial institutions in Brazil were bringing banking services to rural inhabitants in 340,000 locations across the country using local retail outlets as agents, which helped open 6.5 million new accounts (Aggarwal and Klapper 2013). The success of the Brazilian experience led many countries across the world (Bolivia, Chile, Kenya, Pakistan, among others) to introduce the correspondent-banking model.

Bruhn and Love (2014) examined the case of a market-driven innovation, Banco Azteca in Mexico, whose founding involved the simultaneous opening of over 800 bank branches in pre-existing Elektra department stores. It was able to take advantage of extensive purchase histories of the stores' customers to increase access to credit. The branch openings were shown to be linked to greater subsequent informal business activity, employment, and income for low-income households and residents in previously low-financial access areas.[32]

Credit reporting systems can also enhance the financial inclusion of households by reducing asymmetric information problems. Sharing of positive and negative credit information not only reduces moral hazard and thus default risk

---

[31] Burgess and Pande (2005) also linked this policy with a decline in poverty rates in the previously unbanked relative to the banked region. However, Kochar (2011) focuses on one state and uses more disaggregated data to examine the expansion of credit brought on by the policy, and finds that consumption inequality increased, as the effects of policy tended to favor the nonpoor over the poor.

[32] However, there has been anecdotal evidence questioning some of Banco Azteca's lending and collection practices. See for example, https://www.bloomberg.com/news/articles/2007-12-12/the-ugly-side-of-microlending.

with the threat of credit market exclusion for borrowers, but also allows borrowers to build up "reputation capital" that can be used across lenders, thus increasing competition. De Janvry, McIntosh, and Sadoulet (2010) document that the use of credit bureau services by a microfinance lender in Guatemala improved screening of new clients, increased the size of loans, but also led to an increase in the expulsion of existing clients. Agarwal and others (2018) showed that a microcredit program coupled with a well-functioning credit bureau in Rwanda improved individuals' access to commercial bank loans at favorable conditions.

As discussed earlier, financial innovations such as mobile banking can reduce the costs of providing financial services to the population. Recent research shows that M-PESA has helped lift 2 percent of Kenyans out of poverty by reducing transaction costs and enhancing consumption smoothing (Suri and Jack 2016). Extension of mobile banking into credit is also underway, with some early evidence of impact. Bharadwaj, Jack, and Suri (2019) find that M-Shwari, a digital bank service that offers a saving account and also a short-term loan, expanded access to credit and improved household's resilience to income shocks, but had no measurable effects on investments and savings.

However, Kenya's success with mobile banking has been difficult to replicate in other countries. Several factors led to the success of M-PESA, including high demand for domestic remittance services due to high internal immigration, the dominating position of Safaricom in the mobile phone market (not the case in many other SSA countries), rapid roll-out and marketing campaign by Safaricom, and willingness of the CBK to provide Safaricom with flexibility. Furthermore, early adopters played a crucial role in the adoption of mobile money in Kenya. Indeed, the majority of mobile users had a Nokia model. This made the transmission of technology knowledge from one person to another much easier.

Beyond Kenya's experience, researchers have found certain elements to be associated with greater mobile money adoption. An enabling approach to regulation can help; lowering barriers to entry into the financial sector, allowing both banks and mobile operators to provide mobile money, and for mobile money entrants to contract with agents to provide basic financial services with light regulation (Burns 2018). Certain reliable physical infrastructure is also required, such as electric and mobile networks and a well-functioning payment system, in addition to a network of bank agents or ATMs.[33] There would seem to be considerable scope to increase financial inclusion through mobile payments since the

---

[33] In particular, Davidovich and others (2019) identify preconditions in terms of physical and regulatory infrastructure that are necessary to spur growth in fintech applications in Pacific Island countries. Sahay and others (2020) find that better access to digital infrastructure—availability of the Internet and mobile phones—as well high usage of traditional financial services, quality of governance, and a consumer-friendly environment are all positively related to mobile money usage. As with traditional credit, digital credit inclusion is related to better information on borrowers.

digital penetration rate—the percentage of the population that use the Internet—is currently only 51 percent in 2019 (Statista 2019).

Lack of trust is another reason reported for not having an account. Policies to improve trust could include enhancing disclosure requirements for banks or introducing an explicit deposit insurance system to raise the confidence of depositors (Lovett 1989). One recent RCT study in rural Peru found that complementing a conditional cash transfer program with a training session aimed at building trust in financial institutions resulted in greater financial savings while having little impact on the use of transaction services (Galiani, Gertler, and Navajas Ahumada 2020).

Finally, although not directly linked to policy, there is evidence that international workers' remittances have a catalytic effect on financial inclusion. Earlier studies, such as Aggarwal, Demirguc-Kunt, and Martinez Pería (2011) analyzed the relationship with financial depth at the macro level, finding that the size of remittance flows into a country—scaled by its GDP—had a positive impact on the ratios of bank deposits and credit to GDP. More recently, Ben Naceur, Chami, and Trabelsi (2020) find a more nuanced relationship for financial inclusion at the macro level; when remittances are low, they act as a substitute for financial inclusion, but then complement or help to boost financial inclusion when they surpass a certain level.

Other studies examine the impact of remittances at the micro-level. For example, Anzoategui, Demirguc-Kunt, and Martínez-Pería (2014) analyze household survey data in El Salvador and find that remittance receipts increase the likelihood that a household will use deposit accounts, but may reduce the likelihood that they obtain credit from a financial institution, possibly because remittances may substitute for bank financing. Ayana Aga and Martínez Pería (2014) investigate household survey data in five countries in Sub-Saharan Africa and find that households receiving remittances are also more likely to open a bank account.

B. Enhancing Financial Education and Capability

Financial literacy has often been considered an essential skill to improve financial wellbeing and economic inclusion, given the increasing responsibility of individuals in taking financial decisions and the growing complexity of financial products. Indeed, sound financial behavior is associated with high financial knowledge levels (OECD/INFE 2013). Moreover, the lack of awareness and understanding of financial products may spur voluntary exclusion. For example, farmers with low ability to understand the terms of the insurance product are less likely to purchase it (Giné et al. 2008).

It is important to distinguish two key concepts—financial *literacy* and financial *capability*. Financial literacy refers to an understanding of basic financial information and concepts. Financial capability is a broader concept that includes knowledge, skills, attitudes, and ultimately, behaviors, the ability to use financial products to their best advantage. Thus, a financially capable individual not only has the requisite knowledge but also is able to make sound financial decisions: she saves enough for retirement or for her children's education, diversifies investment, borrows prudently, and manages risks. In this manner, she can contribute effectively to economic growth and stability. As one would expect, the two are correlated; for example, more financially educated households tend to hold more diversified portfolios (Von Gaudecker 2015) and obtain higher returns than less financially educated households (Bianchi 2018).

Lusardi and Mitchell (2008, 2011) were among the first to design a survey to evaluate basic financial literacy, consisting of three questions.[34] The initial results revealed a relatively low level of financial literacy in the United States, with only 30 percent of participants able to answer all three correctly, and less than half able to answer correctly the question on risk diversification, which would seem to be a prerequisite for sound investment decisions. The survey was repeated throughout the world, revealing similar gaps in financial knowledge in other regions

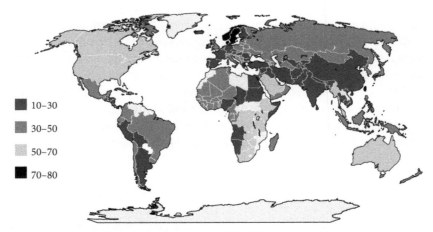

Figure 4.10 Financial Literacy Around the World (% of adults who are financially literate)

Note: A person is defined as financially literate when he or she correctly answers at least three out of the four financial concepts described in https://gflec.org/sp-global-finlit-survey-methodology/.

Source: S&P Global FinLit Survey.

---

[34] They were the following. (i) On compound interest: You deposit $100 in a savings account at 2 percent per year. Five years later you will have exactly $102, less than $102, or more than $102? (ii) On inflation: You deposit $100 in a savings account at 1 percent per year, and inflation is 2 percent per year. After one year, you will be able to take the amount in the savings account and purchase more, less, or the same amount of goods as you can today? (iii) On risk diversification: True or False: buying a single stock is safer than buying a stock mutual fund.

(Figure 4.10). Moreover, financial literacy was shown to be positively correlated with income and education and exhibited a gender gap across the developed and developing world. It also tends to follow an inverted U-shaped behavior with age, rising, then falling after a certain age. Finally, it varies by race and geographical location. For example, financial literacy scores in the United States are lower among Hispanics and African Americans than among Whites and Asians.

Many governments have put in place financial education programs—*interventions*—aimed at improving consumer awareness and promoting sound financial behavior, that is, greater financial capability. There is an ongoing debate about their effectiveness. Applying a meta-analysis approach, Miller and others (2014) and Fernandes and others (2014) conclude that, while they increase knowledge, interventions have little impact on behavior. However, Kaiser and Menkhoff (2017) and Kaiser and others (2020) find that they can impact financial behavior positively. Although the ultimate effectiveness is still under debate, some design features have been found to help, such as targeting the less literate groups, leveraging social networks, tailoring the interventions to participants' needs at "teachable moments," adapting the delivery mode to the audience, and simplifying the content and design of the interventions. [35],[36]

C. For Micro, Small, and Medium-Sized Enterprises

In order to foster greater financial inclusion of MSMEs, the policy should focus on alleviating the main access constraints. First are policies aiming to relax regulatory constraints and entry barriers into the financial system. Regulatory constraints include client documentation requirements and taxation issues (such as a VAT on leasing). These policies might also have an indirect impact by enabling the entry of new providers targeting previously unbanked entrepreneurs. Regarding AML/CFT, a risk-based approach that applies these requirements only on transactions and firms above a certain threshold can be useful.

Second are measures that aim to promote the financial capability of MSMEs, that is, to encourage the healthy use of financial products. The last few years have seen many interventions in the form of financial literacy RCTs for entrepreneurs. As with studies focused on households, there is a large variation in findings, with a general conclusion being that tailor-made interventions can have an impact on entrepreneurship and business expansion under certain circumstances.

---

[35] Examples of teachable moments are when a participant is about to make an important financial decision, such as buying a home or deciding to invest in education.

[36] See Bruhn and others (2013), Duflo and Saez (2003), Conley and Udry (2010), and Berg and Zia (2017) for examples of effective financial education interventions.

The final type of access constraint—too few projects generating sufficient returns to be financed externally—requires a set of policies that improve the business environment and institutional framework and are not necessarily specific to MSMEs. Macroeconomic stability is one such policy, as it affects the willingness and ability of entrepreneurs to invest in potentially profitable, longer-term projects. Other actions include introducing collateral registries, including registries of movable assets, as well as adopting accounting and auditing standards, and introducing or improving credit registries and bureaus to enhance information.[37]

There are also policies that intervene more directly into the market, trying to overcome market frictions. One oft-cited example is the partial credit guarantee (PCG) scheme, which figures prominently among "market-activist policies."[38] By providing guarantees to MSME loans, the opacity and lack of collateral offered by these firms can be overcome. However, certain design issues become relevant, for instance, their appropriate pricing, funding, and institutional structure. Ultimately, PCGs should be subjected to cost-benefit analysis. While such schemes could be run on a self-sustainable basis, they often involve significant subsidies and contingent fiscal liabilities in the event of losses, which may be difficult to compute ex ante. Furthermore, the main financial inclusion benefit should be *additionality*, that is, the share of borrowers that would not have gained access to finance were it not for the PCG.

Although there have been few rigorous impact assessments of PCGs, they seem to indicate a positive effect, as shown by Lelarge, Sraer, and Thesmar (2010) in the case of the French credit guarantee scheme. Two separate studies suggest that the Chilean scheme FOGAPE has generated additional loans for new and existing bank clients and that the additional loans have led to higher sales and profit growth (Cowan, Drexler, and Yañez 2009; Larrain and Quiroz 2006). However, another study questions the additionality effect, as approximately 80 percent of the firms that benefit from the guarantees had bank loans in the past (Benavente, Galetovic, and Sanhueza 2006). More evidence is needed to gauge what characteristics constitute a successful PCG scheme, exploiting the large variation in experiences across countries.

D. The Role of Competition and the Private Sector

Policies could also encourage greater competition in banking, although the theoretical and empirical literature is ambiguous on its effect on MSMEs' access to finance. While the traditional market efficiency view regards more competitive

---

[37] Love, Martínez Pería, and Singh (2013) analyzed firm-level data for a sample of 73 countries and found that the introduction of collateral registries for movable assets led to increases in firms' access to bank finance and that this effect was greater for smaller firms.

[38] For an overview of the literature on PCGs, see Beck, Klapper, and Mendoza (2010).

markets as conducive to greater access to external finance (e.g., Pagano 1993), other studies point to market power as providing necessary incentives to establish long-term lending relationships (Gerschenkron 1962; Petersen and Rajan 1995). Cetorelli and Gambera (2001) show that industries in which young firms rely more on external finance grow faster in countries with more concentrated banking systems. Similarly, di Patti and Dell'Ariccia (2004) show for Italy that bank concentration facilitates access to external finance in industries that are less transparent, thus more reliant on long-term relationships.

The effects of competition may depend on the institutional characteristics of countries. Beck, Demirgüç-Kunt, and Maksimovic (2004) show that bank concentration increases obstacles to external finance by MSMEs, but only in countries with low economic and institutional development. Similarly, Black and Strahan (2002) find for the U.S. that higher concentration is associated with lower new firm formation, while Kerr and Nanda (2009) find that greater competition after deregulation led to higher churn (entry *and* exit) among entrepreneurs in the U.S.. Using the Lerner index as a measure of market power, Carbo-Valverde, Rodriguez- Fernandez, and Udell (2009) find that greater competition improves credit availability for MSMEs in Spain.

Closely linked with the debate on competition and MSME finance is the discussion on different lending techniques—transaction-based versus relationship lending—that are appropriate for MSMEs. The traditional view argues that relationship lending is crucial, as longstanding relationships between a financial institution, or even a specific loan officer, and the borrower, allow problems of information asymmetry to be overcome.[39] This implies that smaller and local financial institutions are more effective in lending to MSMEs than large and foreign-owned banks. However, relationship lending tends to be costly, thus potentially putting financial services further out of reach.

A more nuanced view has also emerged, showing that large and foreign banks can have a comparative advantage at financing MSMEs through transaction-based lending techniques.[40] While relationship lending might thus be better carried out by small, community-based financial institutions, transaction-based lending is carried out more cost-effectively by large financial institutions that can exploit the necessary economies of scale that investment in technology implies. In many developing countries, this debate has an additional dimension, because smaller banks are often owned by domestic shareholders, while large financial institutions are often foreign-owned. However, there is no perfect mapping of size and ownership, a distinction exploited by Clarke and others (2005), who show across four Latin American countries that, relative to large domestic banks, large foreign banks often have a greater share and higher growth of lending to small

---

[39] Berger and Udell (1998).
[40] See Berger and Udell (2006) and de la Torre, Martinez Peria, and Schmukler (2010).

businesses, while smaller foreign banks have a smaller share and lower growth of lending to small businesses. It thus seems that both relationship- and transaction-based lending techniques can be appropriate for SME lending and that both domestic and foreign-owned banks can cater to SMEs.

Furthermore, more recent evidence suggests that foreign and domestic banks can cater to the same clientele, by using different lending techniques. Specifically, Beck, Ioannidou, and Schäfer (2018) find for Bolivia that foreign and domestic banks use different lending techniques for the same clientele, with foreign banks relying more on internal ratings, collateral, and shorter maturities as disciplining tools, while domestic banks rely more on relationship lending. However, this also suggests that transaction-based lending to MSMEs by foreign banks relies on several basic institutional pre-requisites, including collateral and credit registries, as discussed above.

There are also specific transaction-based lending techniques—leasing and factoring—that seem especially conducive to expanding MSMEs' access to finance. Leasing is attractive—from the perspective of both demand and supply—because it is based on the cash flow of the financed asset, such as machinery or a vehicle, rather than the reputation or asset value of the enterprise. It also often has tax advantages, and allows for easier recovery if the correct legal framework is in place. Factoring, the discounting of accounts receivable, is attractive for small suppliers of large credit-worthy buyers because it does not rely on information about the borrower, but rather about the obligor.[41] Both leasing and factoring rely on a legal framework to govern the transactions but rely to a lesser extent on the contractual framework of a country.

In summary, the degree of banking competition and structure of the banking system can be important factors for the financial inclusion of MSMEs. The evidence, however, is not clear-cut, although one could reach the tentative conclusion that competition and openness to foreign ownership can help ease MSMEs' financing constraints provided the necessary institutional and regulatory conditions prevail.

V. Conclusion

Interest in financial inclusion has increased very rapidly in the last two decades, as policymakers and researchers alike have sought to explore the potential economic benefits of expanding the outreach of financial services across the population. This chapter surveyed the main findings so far from the empirical and theoretical literature, based on a simple definition of financial inclusion: the

---

[41] Klapper (2006).

extent of access to and use of financial services. Using a variety of data sources, it documented the increase in the banked population worldwide over the past decade, but with persistent gaps between regions, income levels, and gender, among others. The chapter also showed that, given that providing financial services is costly, certain structural characteristics affect these costs and therefore help to explain why some countries have higher levels of inclusion than others. Of course, as innovation is introduced to reduce these costs, the relevance of some structural characteristics is bound to diminish, as the expansion of mobile banking in Sub-Saharan Africa illustrates.

The literature also showed that, beyond the structural characteristics, there are policy-related factors that work as obstacles to financial inclusion. In particular, frictions related to credit access, collateral requirements, and efficiency have been shown to impede financial inclusion and depth.

The chapter showed how financial inclusion matters, for households, MSMEs, and the macroeconomy in general. At a basic level, financial inclusion is one more dimension of financial development, thus it can be expected to contribute to the economy through the essential functions that financial activity undertakes. Among the benefits to the economy are the easing of financial constraints for potentially productive firms, and the ability to manage risk and smooth consumption for households. Empirical research has found evidence of these benefits at both the micro and macro levels.

The overriding message is that much good can come from advances in financial inclusion, and there are some areas in which policy can act effectively to bring this about. At the same time, there are notes of caution: policy should not operate mechanically, targeting a specific level, nor aiming to close a specific gap. Rather, the policy question should dig deeper, to identify the frictions that constitute the greatest constraints to a particular type of financial inclusion and explore the most cost-effective way of ameliorating them. Finally, tradeoffs should be considered when relevant, most notably between financial inclusion and fiscal costs, and between financial inclusion and stability.

This last consideration points to an area in which research can greatly contribute going forward, namely, improving our understanding of the possible tradeoffs involved in increasing financial inclusion. In most studies, policies are evaluated on their ability to increase households' or firms' access to financial services—the additionality effect—and the resulting impact on economic outcomes. Certainly, more empirical research is needed to assess the additionality of different policies. However, what is lacking most is a full cost-benefit analysis. One prominent example is PCGs, where the costs—both direct and contingent—are often not well understood or measured, let alone compared to the potential benefits of alternative uses of scarce fiscal resources. As for financial stability, the empirical literature appears to point to a meaningful tradeoff when expanding credit in situations with low-quality regulation and supervision. Thus, advances in theoretical models that incorporate financial stability effects would be welcome as well, to understand the mechanisms through which greater access to credit can eventually lead to undesirable outcomes, a "too much finance" phenomenon applied to inclusion. Further empirical work could draw on the literature linking credit accelerations to financial distress, exploring, for example, the financial inclusion implications of these accelerations.

Another important area for future research and policy work is the opportunity and risk stemming from fintech. While mobile money, discussed above, has already created alternatives to bank-based retail payment systems, stable coins (digital currencies, also known as cryptocurrencies, which are pegged to another asset, like the US dollar, and whose value is guaranteed by holding sufficient reserves in these assets) would allow the emergence of a parallel payment system outside the regulated banking system. As the reaction to the Libra proposal has shown, this has triggered regulatory responses and provided a push towards exploring central-bank denominated cryptocurrencies, which could also serve as a substitute for cash. The implications for financial inclusion of such a development are still unknown and might not be unambiguously positive, as certain digitally excluded or under-served groups might be permanently excluded.

Crowdfunding and peer-to-peer lending platforms are another important fintech trend that needs to be studied further. While starting from a low level across the globe, they have experienced quite high growth in some countries and have the potential to reach borrower groups that are excluded from the formal banking system (Rau 2019). However, it seems too early to draw conclusions on their long-term viability. China, one of the first countries with a boom in these platforms, has seen the failure and exit of many platforms and has adopted a tighter regulatory approach towards this intermediation form.

Finally, the financial inclusion agenda is also linked to the debate on the future of banking more broadly. With the entry of BigTech companies such as Alibaba and Tencent in China; Facebook and Google in the Western World and Mercado Libre in Latin America into financial services provision, the availability, variety, and efficiency of financial services stand to increase in many developing and emerging markets, but there are important implications for the regulatory framework (Carletti et al. 2020).

References

Agarwal, T.K., C. Minoiu, A.F. Presbitero, and A.F. Silva. 2018. "Financial Inclusion Under the Microscope." IMF Working Paper 18/208.

Aggarwal, R., A. Demirguc-Kunt, and M.S. Martinez Pería. 2011. "Do Workers' Remittances Promote Financial Development?" *Journal of Development Economics* 96: 255–64.

Aggarwal, S., and L. Klapper. 2012. "Designing Government Policies to Expand Financial Inclusion: Evidence from around the World." Unpublished working paper, World Bank, Washington, DC, 2012.

Ahamed, M.M., and S.K. Mallick. 2019. "Is Financial Inclusion Good for Bank Stability? International Evidence." *J. Econ. Behav. Organ.* 157: 403–27. https://doi.org/10.1016/j.jebo.2017.07.027.

Allen, F., A. Demirguc-Kunt, L. Klapper, and M.S. Martinez Peria. 2012. "Foundations of Financial Inclusion." Policy Research Working Paper 6290, World Bank, Washington, DC.

Ansón, J., and L.B. Gual. 2008. "Financial Access and Inclusion through Postal Networks: Evaluating the Experience of Brazil's Banco Postal." In *Postal Economics in Developing Countries*, edited by José Ansón and Joëlle Toledano. Universal Postal Union. Berne (Switzerland).

Anzoategui, D., A. Demirguc-Kunt, and M.S. Martínez Pería. 2014. "Remittances and Financial Inclusion: Evidence from El Salvador." *World Development* 54: 338–49.

Arcand, Jean-Louis, E. Berkes, and U. Panizza. 2015. "Too Much Finance." *Journal of Economic Growth* 20(2): 105–48.

Ashraf, N., D. Karlan, and W. Yin. 2006. "Tying Odysseus to the Mast: Evidence From a Commitment Savings Product in the Philippines." *Quarterly Journal of Economics* 121(2): 635–72.

Ayyagari, M., Demirgüç-Kunt, A., and Maksimovic, V. 2011a. "Firm Innovation in Emerging Markets: Role of Governance and Finance." *Journal of Financial and Quantitative Analysis* 46:1545–80.

Ayyagari, M., M. A. Demirgüç-Kunt, and V. Maksimovic. 2011b. "Small vs Young Firms Across the World: Contribution to Employment, Job Creation, and Growth." World Bank Policy Research Working Paper (No. 5631).

Ayana Aga, G., and M.S. Martínez Pería. 2014. "International Remittances and Financial Inclusion in Sub-Saharan Africa." World Bank Policy Research Working Paper 6991. Washington, DC: World Bank.

Banerjee, A. 2013. "Microcredit under the Microscope: What Have We Learned in the Past Two Decades, and What Do We Need to Know?" *Annual Review of Economics* 5(1): 487–519.

Banerjee, A., E. Breza, E. Duflo, and C. Kinman. 2019. "Can Microfinance Unlock a Poverty Trap for Some Entrepreneurs?" NBER Working Paper 26346.

Banerjee, A., E. Duflo, R. Glennerster, and C. Kinnan. 2015. "The Miracle of Microfinance? Evidence from a Randomized Evaluation." *American Economic Journal: Applied Economics* 7(1): 22–53.

Beck, T., and A. de la Torre. 2007. "The Basic Analytics of Access to Financial Services." *Financial Markets, Institutions and Instruments* 16: 79–117.

Beck, T., A. Demirguc-Kunt, and P. Honohan. 2008. *Finance for All? Policies and Pitfalls in Expanding Access.* Washington, DC: World Bank.

Beck, T., Aslı Demirgüç-Kunt, and Ross Levine. 2007. "Finance, Inequality and the Poor." *J Econ Growth* 12(1): 27–49.

Beck, T., Aslı Demirgüç-Kunt, and Ross Levine. 2005. "SMEs, Growth, and Poverty: Cross-Country Evidence." *Journal of Economic Growth* 10: 197–227.

Beck, T. A. Demirguc-Kunt, and V. Maksimovic. 2004. "Bank Competition and Access to Finance: International Evidence." *Journal of Money, Credit, and Banking* 36: 627–48.

Beck, T., Aslı Demirgüç-Kunt, Luc Laeven, and Vojislav Maksimovic. 2006. "The Determinants of Financing Obstacles." *Journal of International Money and Finance* 25: 932–52.

Beck, T., Vasso Ioannidou, and Larissa Schäfer. 2018. "Foreigners vs. Natives: Bank Lending Technologies and Loan Pricing." *Management Science* 64: 3792–820.

Beck, T., L. Klapper, and J. C. Mendoza. 2010. "The Typology of Partial Credit Guarantee Funds around the World." *Journal of Financial Stability* 6: 10–25.

Beck, T., R. Levine, and A. Levkov. 2010. "Big Bad Banks? The Impact of U.S. Branch Deregulation on Income Distribution." *Journal of Finance* 65: 1637–67.

Beck, T., R. Levine, and N. Loayza. 2000. "Finance and the Sources of Growth." *Journal of Financial Economics* 58: 261–300.

Beck, T., C. Lin, and Y. Ma. 2014. "Why Do Firms Evade Taxes? The Role of Credit Information Sharing and Banking Sector Outreach." *Journal of Finance* 69: 763–817.

Ben Naceur, S., R. Chami, and M. Trabelsi. 2020. "Do Remittances Enhance Financial Inclusion in LMICs and in the Fragile States?" IMF Working Paper 20/66. Washington, DC: International Monetary Fund.

Benavente, Galetovic & Sanhueza. 2006. *An Economic Analysis.* Chile: FOGAPE.

Berg, G., and B. Zia. 2017. "Harnessing Emotional Connections to Improve Financial Decisions: Evaluating the Impact of Financial Education in Mainstream Media." *Journal of European Economic Association* 15: 1025–55.

A.N. Berger, and G.F. Udell. 1998. "The Economics of Small Business Finance: The Roles of Private Equity and Debt Markets in the Financial Growth Cycle." *Journal of Banking and Finance* 22: 613–73.

Bharadwaj, P., W. Jack, and T. Suri. 2019. "Fintech and Household Resilience to Shocks: Evidence from Digital Loans in Kenya," NBER Working Paper 25604.

Bianchi, M. 2018. "Financial Literacy and Portfolio Dynamics." *The Journal of Finance* 73: 831–59.

Black S.E., and P.E. Strahan. 2002. "Entrepreneurship and Bank Credit Availability." *Journal of Finance* 57: 2807–33.

Blancher, N., M. Appendino, A. Bibolov, A. Fouejieu, J. Li, A. Ndoye, et al. 2019. "Financial Inclusion of Small and Medium-Sized Enterprises in the Middle East and Central Asia." IMF Middle East and Central Asia Department Paper No. 19/02.

Bruhn, M., L. de Souza Leao, A. Legovini, R. Marchetti, and B. Zia. 2013. "The Impact of High School Financial Education: Experimental Evidence from Brazil," Policy Research working paper; no. WPS 6723; Impact Evaluation series; no. IE 109. Washington, DC: World Bank Group.

Bruhn, M., and I. Love. 2014. "The Real Impact of Improved Access to Finance: Evidence from Mexico." *Journal of Finance* 69(3): 1347–76.

Brune, L., X. Giné, X., J. Goldberg, and D. Yang. 2016. "Facilitating Savings for Agriculture: Field Experimental Evidence from Malawi." *Econ. Dev. Cult. Change* 64 (2): 187–220.

Buera, F. J., J. P. Kaboski, and Y. Shin. 2016. "Taking Stock of the Evidence on Micro-Financial Interventions," NBER Working Paper 22674.

Burgess, R., and R. Pande. 2005. "Do Rural Banks Matter? Evidence from the Indian Social Banking Experiment." *American Economic Review* 95(3): 780–95.

Burns, S. 2018. M-PESA and the "Market-led" Approach to Financial Inclusion. *Econ. Aff.* 38: 406–21.

Cai, H., Y. Chen, H. Fang, and L.A. Zhou. 2015. "The Effect of Microinsurance on Economic Activities: Evidence from a Randomized Field Experiment." *Review of Economics and Statistics* 97: 287–300.

Carbó-Valverde, S., F. Rodríguez- Fernández, and G. Udell. 2009. "Bank Market Power and SME Financing Constraints." *Review of Finance* 13(2): 309–40.

Carletti, Elena, Stijn Claessens, Antonio Fatas, and Xavier Vives. 2020. *The Bank Business Model in the Post-Covid-19 World.* London: Centre for Economic Policy Research.

Cecchetti, Stephen G. and Enisse Kharroubi. 2015. "Why Does Financial Sector Growth Crowd Out Real Sector Growth?" BIS Working Paper No. 490.

Celerier, C., and A. Matray. 2019. "Bank Branch Supply, Financial Inclusion, and Wealth Accumulation." *Review of Financial Studies* 32(12): 4767–809.

Cetorelli, N., and M. Gambera. 2001. "Banking structure, Financial Dependence and Growth: International Evidence from Industry Data." *Journal of Finance* 56: 617–48.

Cihak, Martin, Davide S. Mare, and Martin Melecky. 2016. "The Nexus of Financial Inclusion and Financial Stability: A Study of Tradeoffs and Synergies." World Bank Policy Research Working Paper 7722. Washington, DC: World Bank Group.

Cihak, Martin, Ratna Sahay, Adolfo Barajas, Shiyuan Chen, Armand Fouejieu, and Peichu Xie. 2020. "Finance and Inequality." Staff Discussion Note 20/01. Washington, DC: International Monetary Fund.

Claessens, Stijn, and Liliana Rojas-Suárez. 2020. "A Decision Tree for Financial Inclusion Policymaking." Center for Global Development Working Paper 525.

Conley, Timothy G., and Christopher R. Udry. 2010. "Learning about a New Technology: Pineapple in Ghana," *American Economic Review,* American Economic Association, 100(1): 35–69, March.

Cowan, K., A. Drexler, and Á. Yañez. 2009. "The Effect of Credit Insurance on Liquidity Constrains and Default Rates: Evidence from a Government Intervention." Central Bank of Chile Working Papers No. 524.

Dabla-Norris, Yan Ji, Robert Townsend, and D. Filiz Unsal. 2015. "Identifying Constraints to Financial Inclusion and Their Impact on GDP and Inequality: A Structural Framework for Policy," IMF Working Paper 15/22.

Dabla-Norris, Yan Ji, Robert Townsend, and D. Filiz Unsal. 2019. "Distinguishing Constraints on financial inclusion and their impact on GDP, TFP, and the distribution of income." Washington, DC: Mimeo.

Davidovich, S., E. Loukoianova, C. Sullivan, and H. Tourpe. 2019. "Strategy for Fintech Applications in Pacific Island Countries." IMF Asian and Pacific Department Paper No. 19/14. International Monetary Fund: Washington, DC.

de la Torre, Augusto, Maria Soledad Martinez Peria, and Sergio L. Schmukler. 2010. "Bank Involvement with SMEs: Beyond Relationship Lending." *Journal of Banking and Finance* 34(9): 2280–93.

de la Torre, Augusto, Juan Carlos Gozzi, and Sergio L. Schmukler. 2017. *Innovative Experiences in Access to Finance: Market-Friendly Roles for the Visible Hand?* Washington, DC: World Bank Group.

de Janvry, A., C. McIntosh, and E. Sadoulet. 2010. "The Supply- and Demand-Side Impacts of Credit Market Information." *Journal of Development Economics* 93(2): 173–88.

De Mel, S., D. McKenzie, and C. Woodruff. 2010. "Who are the Microenterprise Owners?: Evidence from Sri Lanka on Tokman v. de Soto." In *International Differences in Entrepreneurship,* edited by J. Lerner, and A. Schoar. Boston, MA: National Bureau of Economic Research.

Demirgüc-Kunt, Asli, Leora F. Klapper, and Giorgios A. Panos. 2011. "Entrepreneurship in Post-Conflict Transition." *Economics of Transition* 19(1): 27–78.

Di Patti, E.B., and G. Dell' Ariccia. 2004. "Bank Competition and Firm Creation." *Journal of Money, Credit, and Banking* 36: 225–52.

Duflo, Esther, and Saez Emmanuel. 2003. "The role of information and social interactions in retirement plan decisions: Evidence from a randomized experiment," *Quarterly Journal of Economics* 118(3): 815–42.

Dupas, P., and J. Robinson. 2013. "Savings Constraints and Microenterprise Development: Evidence from a Field Experiment in Kenya." *American Economic Journal: Applied Economics* 5(1): 163–92.

Dupas, P., D. Karlan, J. Robinson, and D. Ubfal. 2018. "Banking The Unbanked? Evidence from Three Countries." *American Economic Journal: Applied Economics* 10 (2): 257–97.

Duryea, S., and E. Schargrodsky. 2008. "Financial Services for the Poor: Savings, Consumption, and Welfare." Processed.

Espinosa-Vega, M., K. Shirono, H. Carcel Villanova, E. Chhabra, B. Das, and Y. Fan. 2020. "Measuring Financial Access: Ten Years of the IMF's Financial Access Survey." IMF Statistics Department Paper No. 20/08.

Fafchamps, Marcel, David McKenzie, Simon R. Quinn, and Christopher Woodruff. 2011. "When Is Capital Enough to Get Female Microenterprises Growing? Evidence from a Randomized Experiment in Ghana." National Bureau of Economic Research Working Paper 17207.

Fernandes, Daniel, John G. Lynch, and Richard G. Netemeyer. 2014. "Financial Literacy, Financial Education, and Downstream Financial Behaviors," *Management Science, INFORMS* 60(8): 1861–83, August.

Feyen, Eric, Katie Kibuuka, and Diego Sourrouille. 2019. "Finstats 2019: A ready-to-use tool to benchmark financial systems across countries and over time," World Bank, Finance and Markets Global Practice.

Galiani, Sebastián, Paul Gertler, and Camila Navajas Ahumada. 2020. "Trust and Saving in Financial Institutions."

Gerschenkron, A. 1962. *Economic Backwardness in Historical Perspective.* Cambridge, MA: Belknap Press of Harvard University Press.

Gine, Xavier, and Robert Townsend. 2004. "Evaluation of Financial Liberalization: A General Equilibrium Model with Constrained Occupational Choice." *Journal of Development Economics* 74(2): 269–307.

Gine, Xavier, Robert Townsend, and James Vickery. 2008. "Patterns of Rainfall Insurance Participation in Rural India." *The World Bank Economic Review* 22(3): 539–66.

GSMA. "Digital Inclusion Report", 2014. http://www.gsma.org.

Han, Rui, and Martin Melecky. 2013. "Financial inclusion for financial stability: access to bank deposits and growth of deposits in the global financial crisis." World Bank Policy Research Working Paper 6577. Washington, DC: World Bank Group.

Jack, W., and T. Suri. 2014. "Risk Sharing and Transactions Costs: Evidence from Kenya's Mobile Money Revolution." *American Economic Review* 104(1): 183–223.

Kaiser, Tim, and Lukas Menkhoff. 2017. "Does Financial Education Impact Financial Literacy and Financial Behavior, and If So, When?" *The World Bank Economic Review* 31(3), October 2017, 611–30.

Kaiser, T., A. Lusardi, L. Menkhoff, and C. Urban. 2020. "Financial Education Affects Financial Knowledge and Downstream Behaviors," Pension Research Council Working Paper, WP2020-07.

Kerr, W.R., and Nanda, R. 2009. "Democratizing Entry: Banking Deregulations, Financing Constraints, and Entrepreneurship." *Journal of Financial Economics* 94: 124–49.

Klapper, Leora. 2006. 'Export Financing for SMEs: The Role of Factoring', Trade Note 26, International Trade Department, World Bank.

Kochar, A. 2011. "The Distributive Consequences of Social Banking: A Microempirical Analysis of the Indian Experience." *Economic Development and Cultural Change* 59(2): 251–80.

Kushnir, K., Mirmulstein, M.L., and Ramalho, R. 2010. *Micro, Small, and Medium Enterprises Around the World: How Many Are There, and What Affects the Count?* IFC.

Larraín, C. and J. Quiroz. 2006. *Study for the Guarantee Fund of Small Businesses.* State Bank.

Lelarge, Claire, David Sraer, and David Thesmar. 2008. *Entrepreneurship and Credit Constraints. Evidence from a French Loan Guarantee Program.* Mimeo: University of California Berkeley.

Levine, R. 2005. "Finance and Growth: Theory and Evidence, in *Handbook of Economic Growth*, edition 1, volume 1, chapter 12, edited by Philippe Aghion and Steven Durlauf. Amsterdam: Elsevier Science, pp. 865–934.

Loukoianova, E., and Y. Yang. 2018. "Financial Inclusion in Asia-Pacific." IMF Asia and Pacific Department Paper 17/18. Washington, DC: International Monetary Fund.

Love, I., M.S. Martínez Pería, and S. Singh. 2013. "Collateral Registries for Movable Assets: Does their Introduction Spur Firms' Access to Bank Finance?" World Bank Policy Research Working Paper 6477. Washington, DC: World Bank.

Lovett, W.A. 1989. "Moral Hazard, Bank Supervision and Risk-Based Capital Requirements."

Lusardi, A., and O.S. Mitchell. 2008. "Planning and Financial Literacy: How Do Women Fare?" *American Economic Review P&P* 98: 413–17.

Lusardi, A., and O. S. Mitchell. 2011. "Financial Literacy Around the World: An Overview." *Journal of Pension Economics and Finance* 10(4): 497–508.

Mehrotra A. N., and Yetman J. 2015. "Financial Inclusion: Issues for Central Banks." *BIS Quarterly Review*, March 2015: 83–96. Basel, Switzerland: Bank for International Settlements.

Miller, M. J., J. Reichelstein, C. Salas, and B. Zia. 2014, "Can You Help Someone be Financially Capable? A Meta-Analysis of the Literature," World Bank Policy Research Paper 6745.

OECD/INFE. 2013. Current Status of National Strategies for Financial Education: OECD/INFE Comparative Analysis and Relevant Practices. Paris: OECD.

Pagano, M. 1993. "Financial Markets and Growth: An Overview." *European Economic Review* 37: 613–22.

Pagano, M. and G. Pica, 2011. Finance and Employment. Centre for Studies in Economics and Finance. Working Paper No. 283.

Patnam, M., and W. Yao. 2020. "The Real Effects of Mobile Money: Evidence from a Large Scale Fintech Expansion. IMF Working Paper (forthcoming).

Petersen, M., and Rajan, R. 1995. "The Effect of Credit Market Competition on Lending Relationships." *Quarterly Journal of Economics* 110: 407–43.

Popov, A. 2018. "Evidence on Finance and Economic Growth." In *Handbook of Finance and Development*, edited by T. Beck and R. Levine. Cheltenham, UK and Northampton, MA, USA: Edward Elgar Publishing.

Rajan, R.G., and L. Zingales. 1998. "Financial Dependence and Growth." *American Economic Review* 88(3): 559–86.

Rau, R. 2019. "Law, Trust, and the Development of Crowdfunding." Working Paper.

Rhyne, E., and S.E. Kelly. 2018. *Financial Inclusion Hype vs Reality: Deconstructing the 2017 Findex Results*. Washington, DC: Center for Financial Inclusion.

Rosenzweig, M.R., and Binswanger, H.P. 1993. "Wealth, Weather Risk, and the Composition and Profitability of Agricultural Investments." *The Economic Journal* 103(416): 56–78.

Rousseau, P.L., and P. Wachtel. 2017. "Episodes of Financial Deepening: Credit Booms or Growth Generators?" In *Financial Systems and Economic Growth*, edited by Peter L. Rousseau and Paul Wachtel. Cambridge: Cambridge University Press.

Sahay, R., M. Cihak, P. N'Diaye, A. Barajas, S. Mitra, A. Kyobe, et al. 2015a. "Financial Inclusion: Can it Meet Multiple Macroeconomic Goals?," Staff Discussion Note 15/17. Washington, DC: International Monetary Fund.

Sahay, R., M. Cihak, P. N'Diaye, A. Barajas, R. Bi, Y. Gao, et al. 2015b. "Rethinking Financial Deepening: Stability and Growth in Emerging Markets," Staff Discussion Note 15/08. Washington, DC: International Monetary Fund.

Sahay, R., U. Eriksson von Allmen, A. Lahreche, P. Khera, S. Ogawa, M. Bazarbash, et al. 2020. "The Promise of Fintech: The Promise of Fintech in the Post Covid-19 Era." Monetary and Capital Markets Department Paper 20/09. Washington, DC: International Monetary Fund.

Schularick, Moritz, and Alan M. Taylor. 2012. "Credit Booms Gone Bust: Monetary Policy, Leverage Cycles, and Financial Crises, 1870–2008." *American Economic Review* 102(2): 1029–61.

Statista. 2019. "Internet Penetration Rate Worldwide 2019, by Region." New York, NY.

Stiglitz, Joseph, and Andrew Weiss. 1981. "Credit Rationing in Markets with Imperfect Information." *American Economic Review* 71(3): 393–410.

Suri, T. 2017. "Mobile Money." *Annual Review of Economics* 9: 497–520.

Suri, T., W. Jack, T.M. Stoker. 2012. "Documenting the Birth of a Financial Economy." *PNAS* 109(26):10257–62.

Suri, T., and W. Jack. 2016. "The Long-Run Poverty and Gender Impacts of Mobile Money." *Science* 354(6317): 1288–92.

Svirydzenka, Katsiaryna. 2016. "Introducing a New Broad-Based Index of Financial Development," IMF Working Paper 16/05.

Turner, M., P. Walker, C. Sukanya, and R. Varghese. 2012. "A New Pathway to Financial Inclusion: Alternative Data, Credit Building, and Responsible Lending in the Wake of the Great Recession." Durham, NC: PERC Press.

Von Gaudecker, H.-M. 2015. "How Does Household Portfolio Diversification Vary with Financial Literacy and Financial Advice?" *Journal of Finance* 70(2): 489–507.

World Bank. 2014. *Global Financial Development Report: Financial Inclusion.* Washington, DC.

Zachariadis, M., P. Ozcan, and D. Dinckol. 2020. "The Covid-19 Impact on Fintech: Now is the Time to Boost Investment." *LSE Business Review*, April 13.

Zhang, Ruixin, and Sami Ben Naceur. 2019. "Financial Development, Inequality, and Poverty: Some International Evidence." *International Review of Economics and Finance* 61: 1–16.

5

Technological Progress and Artificial Intelligence

Anton Korinek, Martin Schindler, and Joseph E. Stiglitz

Advances in artificial intelligence and automation have the potential to be labor-saving and to increase inequality and poverty around the globe.[1] They also give rise to winner-takes-all dynamics that advantage highly skilled individuals and countries that are at the forefront of technological progress. We analyze the economic forces behind these developments and delineate economic policies to mitigate the adverse effects while leveraging the potential gains from technological advances. We also propose domestic policy measures and reforms to the global system of governance that make the benefits of advances in artificial intelligence more inclusive.

I. Introduction

Advances in AI and related forms of automation technologies have led to growing fears about job losses and increasing inequality. This concern is widespread in high-income countries. Developing countries and emerging market economies should be even more concerned than high-income countries, as their comparative advantage in the world economy relies on abundant labor and natural resources. Declining returns to labor and natural resources as well as the winner-takes-all dynamics brought on by new information technologies could lead to further immiseration in the developing world. This could undermine the rapid gains that have been the hallmark of success in development over the past 50 years and threaten the progress made in reducing poverty and inequality.

For many decades, there was a presumption that advances in technology would benefit all—embodied by the trickle-down dogma that characterized

[1] We thank Avital Balwit, Andy Berg, Valerie Cerra, Barry Eichengreen, Katya Klinova and participants in the IMF IG seminar series for insightful comments and suggestions, David Autor, Adrian Peralta-Alva and Agustin Roitman for helpful data and charts, and Jaime Sarmiento for excellent research assistance. Financial support from the Institute for New Economic Thinking is gratefully acknowledged.

Anton Korinek, Martin Schindler, and Joseph E. Stiglitz, *Technological Progress and Artificial Intelligence* In: *How to Achieve Inclusive Growth*. Edited by: Valerie Cerra, Barry Eichengreen, Asmaa El-Ganainy, and Martin Schindler, Oxford University Press. © Anton Korinek, Martin Schindler, and Joseph E. Stiglitz 2022.
DOI: 10.1093/oso/9780192846938.003.0005

neoliberalism. And for some time, this presumption was in fact justified. For example, for the three decades following the Second World War, the US economy and many other high-income and developing countries experienced broadly shared increases in living standards. However, over the past half-century, output growth and median worker incomes started to decouple.

Moreover, economic theory cautions that technological progress is likely to create both winners and losers (see Korinek and Stiglitz 2019, for a review). As long as the winners and losers from technological progress are located within the same country, there is at least the possibility that domestic policy measures can compensate the losers. However, when technological progress deteriorates the terms of trade and thus undermines the comparative advantage of entire countries, then entire nations may be worse off except if the winners within one country compensate the losers in other countries, which seems politically very difficult.

This chapter argues that concerns about whether technological progress leads to inclusive growth are indeed justified—and that especially developing countries may face a stark new set of challenges going forward. However, we propose policies that can mitigate the adverse effects so that advances in technology lead to a world with greater *shared* prosperity. This will require new domestic polices and development strategies as well as strong international cooperation and a rewriting of the global rules governing the information economy.

We start by laying out the key properties of AI and related technologies that underlie the concerns about recent technological progress. AI is likely to be labor-saving and resource-saving, devaluing the sources of comparative advantage of many developing countries and deteriorating their terms of trade. Information technologies such as AI also tend to give rise to natural monopolies, creating a small set of so-called superstar firms that are located in a few powerful countries but serve the entire world economy. Moreover, under reasonable assumptions, the rate and direction of technological progress chosen by the market are generally suboptimal (Korinek and Stiglitz 2019). This creates the possibility of steering innovation in AI and other technologies in directions that are more beneficial to humanity at large, for example, preserving the planet or creating satisfying employment opportunities, rather than substituting for labor and creating more unemployment and inequality.

Taking a step back, we evaluate to what extent the discussed concerns about technological progress are justified, given what we know at present. There is vast uncertainty about the impact of artificial intelligence, even among experts in the field. Some argue that AI is less important than the big innovations of the twentieth century and will have rather limited impact on the economy, whereas others go as far as predicting that AI will lead to more rapid technological progress than mankind has ever seen before.

In this context, we discuss how to reconcile the buzz among technologists over the past decade with economic data that suggests rather modest productivity increases over the period—encapsulated by the so-called productivity puzzle. We also analyze how the forces generated by progress in AI interact with other recent developments, in particular with the recovery from Covid-19, with secular population dynamics, and with the need for a Green Transition.

Despite the uncertainties surrounding AI, its potentially dramatic consequences suggest that we should steer our own research in directions where the expected social value added of economic analysis is greatest: we need to think particularly hard about potential events that would be highly disruptive to our society.

To grasp the historical nature of what is going on, we look at the broader history of technological progress. Humanity spent much of its history at a Malthusian stage in which the vast majority of the population lived at subsistence levels. The Industrial Revolution that lifted living standards started a bit over two centuries ago, making it a mere blip in the history of human civilization. For developing countries, the era of manufacturing-based export-led growth that enabled the East Asian Miracle stretched over the past half-century—only one quarter of the history of the Industrial Revolution. It is conceivable that we are now going into another era. There is even a risk that the terms-of-trade losses generated by progress in AI may erase many of the gains that the developing countries have made in recent decades.

However, the Industrial Revolution also offers ample lessons on how to manage innovation in a positive way: technological revolutions are very disruptive, but collective action can mitigate the adverse effects and generate an environment in which the gains are shared broadly. The labor-using nature of the Industrial Revolution ushered in an *Age of Labor* in which the economic gains of workers also shifted political dynamics in their favor, but there is a risk that future labor-saving progress may do the opposite. The decline of manufacturing will require a new development model that follows a more multi-pronged strategy to replace the manufacturing-based export-led growth model.

The key policy question is how countries can improve the likelihood of benign outcomes from technological progress. This is especially pertinent for developing countries, but it is also a challenge for advanced economies to develop policies that ensure that technological advances lead to broadly shared prosperity and that their adverse effects are mitigated. We delineate here a number of such policies. Taxation and redistribution are a first line of defense to compensate the losers of progress, although the scope for redistribution may be limited in developing countries.

Targeted expenditure policies can serve double duty by providing both income to workers and a valuable social return—for example, investments in education or infrastructure are labor intensive and enhance human capital and the physical infrastructure of countries, both of which are important in bridging the digital divide and ensuring that all citizens can participate in the opportunities afforded by digital technologies.

To replace the manufacturing-based export-led growth model, developing countries will need to steer technological progress and technology adoption in new directions, in part by leveraging the opportunities that modern AI and other digital technologies afford in agriculture and services.

Finally, we describe a set of policies at the supra-national level to reform our global system of governance in a way that developing countries can benefit from advances in AI and other information technologies while addressing the downsides of these new technologies. We need to design a global tax regime for the digital age that enables countries to raise taxes on transactions that occur within their borders. Competition policy is also increasingly a question that transcends national borders as the footprint of the digital giants is global and authorities in their countries of origin do not face the correct incentives to ensure a competitive marketplace. Intellectual property regimes need to be adapted so they are attuned to the needs and circumstances of developing countries. Moreover, information policy including the regulation of data needs to be discussed at the supra-national level to provide a voice to developing countries that could otherwise not influence the design of such policies.

The remainder of this chapter is organized as follows. In the second section, we provide an overview of the downside risks of technological progress, with special emphasis on potential AI-induced economic disruptions; in the third, we discuss the uncertainties surrounding the nature and level of the impacts as well as the broader context. The fourth section reviews what we can learn from the bigger historical picture of technological progress. The fifth section distills the critical role of government policy in managing the effects of technological progress and in enabling the benefits of innovation to be widely shared. The sixth section analyzes how our global system of governance needs to be updated to allow developing countries to maximize the benefits and minimize the costs of advances in AI and other digital technologies.

II. Downside Risks of Technological Progress

Many technology optimists suggest that productivity gains go hand in hand with real wage gains. This presumption that technological progress would benefit all was also embodied by the trickle-down dogma that has characterized neoliberalism. However, the presumption was supported neither by theory nor evidence; indeed, economic theory has always held that advances in technology do not

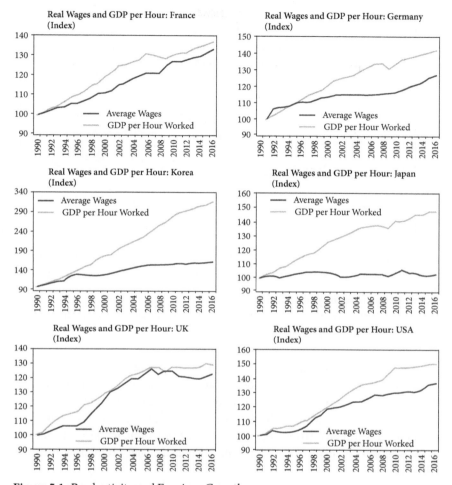

Figure 5.1 Productivity and Earnings Growth
Sources: OECD, Bureau of Labor Statistics, and IMF staff calculations.

necessarily benefit all and may create winners and losers. The data (Figure 5.1) show that in recent decades, many countries have experienced episodes during which wages lagged productivity growth. Moreover, as we argue below, even where average wages did keep up with productivity, median wages may not have, and there is a risk that any positive gains seen in the past may not continue.

Figure 5.2 illustrates that the income gains associated with technological progress have been highly unevenly distributed. In the United States and other high-income countries, most of the benefits of growth have gone to those at the top, resulting in widening income inequality in most advanced economies since the early 1980s, reversing an earlier downward trend in many countries.

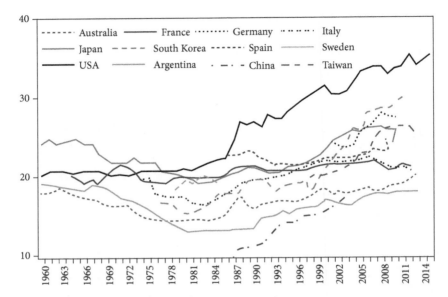

Figure 5.2 Income Inequality over Time, 1960–2015
Source: World in Data (WID, https://wid.world/). Data depict the cumulative share of national (pre-tax) income accruing to the top 5 percent of income earners.

How can we reconcile this with economic theory? In the context of a competitive economy, we can think of technological progress as moving out the production possibility frontier: one can get more of any output for a given amount of inputs. But this increase in production possibilities does not tell us how the gains from progress will be distributed. In our simplest economic models, for example, if we assume a competitive economy with a Cobb-Douglas production function, relative shares are fixed.

However, in the more general case, technical change may change the distribution of income, so that, for instance, labor gets a smaller share of a larger pie. If its share decreases enough, workers could even be worse off. Whether wages increase or decrease depends on what happens to the demand for labor at existing wages. Using the terminology first introduced by Hicks, technical change that leads to a decrease in the relative share of labor is called capital-biased; if it leads to a decrease in the share of unskilled labor, it is called skill-biased; if it leads to an outright reduction in wages, it is called labor-saving. The United States, for example, has experienced routine-biased technological change that has replaced workers engaged in both manual and cognitive routine activities since the 1980s and that has contributed to the hollowing out of the middle class (Autor et al. 2003). Korinek and Stiglitz (2019) show that the distributive effects of innovations can be seen as generating quasi-rents—the winners of progress (e.g., capitalists or skilled workers) experience gains without having contributed to the innovation, whereas others experience losses. For example, automation may lower the demand for labor and wages but lead to a corresponding increase in the return to capital that is in the nature of a quasi-rent. That, in turn, has an important implication: governments can capture some of the quasi-rents by taxing the winners and redistributing it; and given the nature of the gains, governments may even be able to raise taxes in ways that have no or limited distortionary effects. Thus, "managed" technological progress could allow for Pareto-improving outcomes.

However, there is a big difference between looking at the impacts of AI within a single country and from a global perspective. When the benefits are experienced in one country and the cost is borne in another, a Pareto improvement would require that the winners compensate the losers across national boundaries. Today, such cross-border transfers are voluntary and limited.

As a result, the fruits of technological progress will be unequally shared; but more troublesome is that while some countries may gain a great deal, others will lose. These differences will be reflected, respectively, in improvements and deteriorations of countries' terms of trade. In the following, we will analyze several of the specific forms of progress that the AI revolution and related automation technologies are likely to induce, with a particular focus on how they may hurt developing countries.

A. Labor-Saving Technological Progress

Many observers are concerned that AI may be labor-saving, that is, cause a decline in the demand for labor at existing factor prices. If this occurs, equilibrium wages will decrease and workers will be worse off.

As we have noted, over the past half-century, the United States and many other countries seem to have experienced technological progress that was biased against workers with lower levels of education performing routine tasks, sufficiently biased that it may even have been labor-saving in that segment, reducing such workers' real incomes. For example, Autor et al. (2003) observe that from the 1970s to the 1990s, while computerization was a substitute for an increasing number of routine tasks, technological change increased the productivity of workers in non-routine jobs that involved problem-solving and complex communications tasks. These changes in technology may have explained nearly two-thirds of the relative demand shift toward college-educated labor over that period. Similarly, more recently, Acemoglu and Restrepo (2020) estimated significant adverse employment and wage effects from the introduction of industrial robots in the United States, concentrated in manufacturing and among routine manual, blue-collar, assembly, and related occupations, helping to explain the dramatic

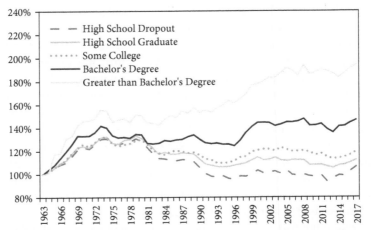

Figure 5.3 Rising Wage-Skill Premia in the US (Real Wages of Full-Time U.S. Male Workers, 1963 = 100)

Source: Autor (2019).

increase in wage dispersion across skill groups over the past five decades (Figure 5.3).

This job polarization in terms of wages has also been reflected in relative employment dynamics. Employment in nonroutine jobs has continued to grow steadily in the United States, while that in routine jobs has stagnated, or in some periods declined, since around 1990, contributing, as we have noted, to a "hollowing out of the middle" (Figure 5.4).[2] OECD (2019) note that middle-skilled jobs may be the most prone to both automation and offshoring, as they most encompass routine tasks that are relatively easy to automate (or offshore).

Standard models of aggregate production functions with skilled and unskilled labor-augmenting progress and capital-augmenting progress can generate the observed patterns of movements in factor prices and shares, depending on patterns of progress as well as elasticities and cross-elasticities of substitution. Acemoglu and Restrepo (2019a) formulate a particular model in which the displacement of workers by robots will reduce the labor share of income and may be labor-saving if the productivity gains from the robots are modest. Berg et al. (2018) focus on the differential effects of technological progress across worker groups and shows that technological progress may be unskilled-labor-saving because that type of labor is easily substituted for by robots; by contrast, high-skilled labor is likely complementary to robots and will benefit from technological progress; as a result, technological advances risk bringing about large increases

---

[2] As can be seen in the figure, the Covid shock in 2020 has clearly accelerated the trend, at least temporarily, giving rise to a large decline in employment in routine manual jobs but only a modest dip in nonroutine cognitive jobs.

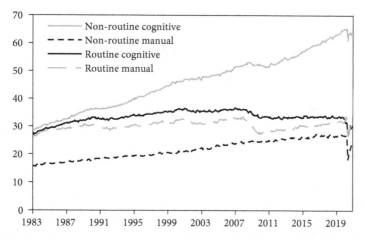

Figure 5.4 Employment in Routine vs. Non-Routine Jobs in the US (Persons, millions)
Source: Current Population Survey and Federal Reserve Bank of St. Louis.

in inequality. Automation may also worsen inequality along other dimensions—for example, in sectors where women occupy more routine jobs (Brussevich et al. 2018).

Even if technological progress is labor-saving in the short run, it may also trigger additional accumulation of capital that is complementary to labor, benefiting labor in the long run. For example, Stiglitz (2015) and Caselli and Manning (2019) show that in an economy with capital and labor only, in which long-run capital accumulation is determined by an exogenous interest rate, labor will always gain.[3] Ultimately, however, impacts on inequality depend on whether there are other scarce limiting factors in the economy, for example, natural resources or land, which would benefit from technological progress and ultimately become more scarce as the factors "capital" and "machine-replacing labor" become more abundant and cheaper. Indeed, Korinek and Stiglitz (2021a) show that if this is the case, then, without government intervention, labor may lose out from technological progress even in the long run.

At a global level, similar dynamics may play out. Although labor-saving technological progress would make the world as a whole richer, it would hit developing countries that have a comparative advantage in cheap labor particularly hard. If worldwide demand for labor, or for unskilled labor, declines, such countries would experience a significant deterioration in their terms of trade and lose a substantial fraction of their export income. Labor-saving progress may not only

---

[3] The result is intuitive: the dual to the production function is the factor price frontier. Technological change shifts out the factor price frontier, implying that if the interest rate is unchanged, wages must increase.

create winners and losers within the affected developing countries, but it may make entire countries on net worse off. Alonso et al. (2020) find that improvements in the productivity of "robots" could drive divergence, as advanced countries benefit from computerization more given their higher initial capital stock.

However, it is also conceivable that other forms of advances in technology could benefit workers: intelligence-assisting devices and algorithms (IA) may be complementary to labor rather than substituting for it, thus enhancing the prospects of labor. Innovations that fall into this category may include augmented reality (AR), machine learning (ML) algorithms that help analyze complex data, and other forms of integration of AI with humans.[4] Automation technologies frequently affect particular *tasks* but not (entire) jobs, which consist of multiple tasks (see, e.g., Acemoglu and Autor 2011)—IA innovations may help workers be more productive in their jobs by taking over, or improving, certain tasks. For example, a doctor is engaged in diagnosis but also in explaining the diagnosis to the patient. AI may do a better job in diagnosis—for example, in radiology—but it may not quite replace the doctor in communicating with the patient, at least not yet.

Driverless trucks provide another example: truck driving provides significant employment opportunities for men with only a high school education so there is understandably concern for the disruption that self-driving trucks might bring about. But truck drivers also perform a number of related tasks—they fill orders, load and unload, monitor the truck, and more—not all of which may be easily automated. More generally, most jobs have multiple dimensions and consist of multiple tasks. With some tasks automated, workers will be able to devote more attention to, and perform better at, those tasks that are not. Importantly, both AI and IA imply extensive restructuring of the economy.

The central concern of this chapter remains: there may be a reduction in the demand for labor, especially for unskilled labor. We will further evaluate whether or not these fears are justified below in Section III. If, however, it turns out that AI is labor saving, and especially if it is unskilled labor saving, the consequences for developing countries would be severe. This is the "resource" which constitutes their comparative advantage and in which they are relatively rich. The convergence in standards of living between developing countries and developed that has marked the past half-century would be arrested, even reversed. It would also present great challenges to domestic policy within developing countries. In many parts of the world, inequalities within developing countries are greater than in developed. AI would exacerbate those inequalities—and developing countries often lack the institutional capacities to counteract them.

---

[4] One extreme example is Elon Musk's *Neuralink,* which aims to achieve a symbiosis of humans and AI by surgically implanting technology into the brain.

B. Resource-Saving Technological Progress

Another type of progress that is of great concern to some developing countries is resource-saving technological progress. This has gotten less attention than labor-saving progress so far (e.g., Solow 2009), but AI and other digital technologies have often been praised for their potential to produce more output with fewer natural resources. For instance, they may help reduce the demand for depletable natural resources and lower carbon emissions. Examples include algorithms that optimize efficiency in data centers or that make transportation networks more efficient. Technologies that enable telework may also reduce the carbon footprint of workers.[5] Thus, such resource-saving innovations may have adverse distributional effects on developing countries that have a comparative advantage in natural resources, and that have specialized in exporting them. The impact on exporters of different types of natural resources may be quite different—for example, exporters of carbon-based energy will fare differently from exporters of rare earth metals.

Consider oil-exporting countries, which have already experienced many developmental challenges while being resource-rich. Resource-saving AI, while saving the planet, would make them resource-poor countries that still experience the same developmental challenges. The challenges of addressing global inequality under such a scenario would be an order of magnitude larger than they are even today, posing a test for the global community. A number of oil-exporting countries rely on their export revenue to buy food and other basic essentials—if they lose their ability to export oil, the consequences would be dire. Thus, as in the case of labor-saving technological progress, the world as a whole may be better off—in this case by undoing resource scarcity and reducing climate change—but not all countries would benefit.

C. Information, Digital Monopolies, and Superstars

The rise of AI and other information technologies may also lead to greater concentrations of market power. As a result, the economy may move to an equilibrium that is more distorted by market power, with greater rents for dominant

---

[5] As always, calculating the full consequences of a new technology on the demand for any natural resource, or carbon emissions, is complex. It must be done on a full life-cycle basis, incorporating initial investment, maintenance, as well as day-to-day operations. That said, for instance, data centers running cutting-edge AI applications are typically energy-intensive and may lead to increases in demand for electricity and depletable natural resources. Still, on net, it is likely that the demand for carbon-based energy sources will decrease. Some natural-resource-rich economies may benefit, such as those rich in rare earths or other metals that are inputs in the production of batteries, microchips, solar panels, wind turbines etc.

firms. Actors with market power will use that power to advantage themselves. The resulting distortions may offset part or all of the benefits of innovation, exacerbating the adverse distributive effects of labor-saving or resource-saving innovation. With any inequality-averse social welfare function, societal welfare could decrease.

While the assumption of competitive markets often provides a useful benchmark, that model becomes less appropriate as one considers an economy that is dominated by AI. It is hard to conceive of an AI economy being competitive, or at least well-described by the standard competitive equilibrium model.

There are several reasons why advances in AI intensify market power. First, AI is an information good, and information goods are different from other goods in that they are non-rivalrous—they can be used at close-to-zero marginal cost, implying that a single firm can serve a very large market. Moreover, the creation of AI codes or ML algorithms typically involves high sunk costs and/or fixed costs—in a private market, firms need to earn monopoly rents to recoup these costs. Moreover, even small sunk costs may result in markets not being contestable, i.e., there could be sustained rents and profits. In addition, AI applications and platforms typically involve significant network externalities. Some of these arise because firms accumulate vast amounts of data that allow them to train their algorithms better than those of the competition. All of these effects create large barriers to entry and a tendency towards creating large monopolies, sometimes also called "superstar" effects (see, e.g., Korinek and Ng 2019 and Greenwald and Stiglitz 2014a).

Some authors have identified a growing number of "superstar firms" in the economy that are "super profitable" (see, e.g., Autor et al. 2020). However, rather than reflecting "super-productive" technology, much of these profits may arise from the exercise of monopoly power that is derived from the nature of these information technologies. For example, in the US, a large fraction of the gains in the stock market over the past decade have been concentrated in digital giants, to an important extent driven by their market power. Moreover, algorithmic advances have also enabled digital firms to extract more consumer surplus through discriminatory pricing.

Such superstar and monopoly effects are likely to play out not only at a company level but also at a country level, and they are likely to be particularly severe in the context of AI. They may be exacerbated by agglomeration economies associated with R&D in AI. There is a risk that those countries that lead in the advancement in AI may reap all the benefits, becoming "superstar countries" and reaping all the rents associated with the development of AI. The rest of the world, and in particular most developing and emerging economies, may be left behind, with the notable exception of China—one of the leaders in artificial intelligence. Moreover, to the extent that firms or countries can protect their knowledge, the resulting monopolization of knowledge may also impede the catching-up process. Importantly, even if competitors could "steal" a superstar's knowledge, this may not necessarily be sufficient as the superstars can continuously improve their algorithms based on their users' data, thus remaining, perhaps permanently, ahead. In the past, advances in technology were driven to an important extent by basic research that was financed by governments in high-income countries and that was freely available to all—including developing countries. This too may change with AI.

Some observers suggest as a silver lining for developing countries that ML technologies are reliant on data and that more diverse data contain more information. Thus, selling data might generate some income for developing countries. However, this is unlikely to make up for their lost income as the marginal return to more diverse data may be limited. Moreover, future advances in ML algorithms may make them less reliant on large quantities of data and instead require more specific, tailored data.

D. Misguided Technological Progress

Economic theory has illuminated why the nature of innovation (e.g., the factor bias) may not be welfare maximizing. Much of economics takes the factor bias of technological change as exogenously given, and the standard economic welfare theorems assert the efficiency of competitive market economies for a given level of technology. However, the direction and rate of technological progress are themselves economic decisions, as emphasized by the literature on induced innovation (e.g., Kennedy 1964; von Weizsäcker 1966; Samuelson 1965; Atkinson and Stiglitz 1969; Acemoglu 1998, 2002; Stiglitz 2006). There is no analogue of the welfare theorems for innovation: markets on their own will not in general be efficient either in the level or direction (nature) of innovative activity and technological change. The market may even provide incentives for innovations that reduce efficiency by absorbing more resources than they create for society, as may be the case, for example, for high-frequency trading. This calls for policy to actively steer technological progress, as we will discuss further below.

The fundamental problem is that knowledge is a public good, in the Samuelsonian sense. If it is to be privately financed and produced, there must be inefficient restraints on the use of knowledge, and those restraints typically also give rise to market power. If there are no restraints on the use of knowledge, then innovators cannot appropriate the returns to their production of knowledge, and so they will have little incentive to innovate.[6] When knowledge is produced as a

---

[6] There is a large literature on the welfare economics of innovation, dating back to Arrow (1962a). Stiglitz (1975a, 1987a) drew attention explicitly to the public good aspects of knowledge, and the

by-product of learning or investing, the inability to fully appropriate all the learning benefits will lead to under production or underinvestment in sectors of the economy associated with high learning and learning spillovers. As Greenwald and Stiglitz (2006, 2014a) point out, this has important implications for developmental policy, providing a rationale for industrial and trade policies.[7]

More recent literature has drawn attention not only to biases in the level and pace of innovation but also to the direction. In economies with incomplete risk markets and imperfect and/or asymmetric information (i.e., in all real-world economies), the equilibrium is not constrained Pareto efficient, and prices do not necessarily give the "correct" signal to innovators on the direction of innovation. There are pecuniary externalities that matter.[8] For instance, in the Shapiro-Stiglitz (1984) efficiency wage model, where unemployment acts as a disciplining device to discourage shirking in the context of a labor market with imperfect and costly monitoring, there will be too much labor-augmenting technological progress, resulting in too high a level of unemployment (Stiglitz 2006). There are multiple other biases, for example, towards innovative activities in which intellectual property rights are more easily secured.

Markets do not care about income distribution. Market forces may drive economic decisions towards efficiency—in the narrow, microeconomic sense—but will not give any consideration to the distributive consequences. Recent contributions, however, have emphasized that overall economic performance can be affected by inequality (Ostry et al. 2019; Stiglitz 2013); obviously, individual entrepreneurs will not take into account this macroeconomic externality, and accordingly the market will be biased towards producing too much labor-saving innovation, creating a role for redistributive policies. In addition, Korinek and Stiglitz (2020) show that in the presence of constraints on redistribution, policy can improve welfare by steering innovation to take into account its distributive implications.

There are some self-correcting forces: for example, if labor is getting cheaper, innovators face smaller incentives to save on labor, providing a corrective mechanism within the market economy to an ever-decreasing share of labor, but this mechanism no longer works when wages are set by efficiency wage considerations or reach subsistence levels.[9]

---

similarity between the economics of information and the economics of knowledge. See also Romer (1986).

[7] The inefficiencies in economies with learning by doing were first noted by Arrow (1962b).

[8] See Greenwald and Stiglitz (1986). These, in turn, give rise to macroeconomic externalities; their consequences in the context of innovation have been studied by Korinek and Stiglitz (2019).

[9] More generally, the direction of innovation is affected by the *share* of the factor. If the elasticity of substitution is high, a lower factor price will be associated with an increased factor share, and this can induce greater efforts at increasing the productivity of that factor. In that case, the equilibrating force just described does not arise, and the opposite occurs (Stiglitz 2014).

What is most relevant for developing countries is that these distributive implications extend across borders, and so decisions made in one country have effects on other countries that the innovating country and the innovators within that country have no incentive to consider.

Even if markets were efficient in the choice of technology for the conditions of the country in which the innovation occurs, those conditions are markedly different from the conditions in other countries. In developing countries, a key question is about *adopting* appropriate technologies rather than innovating, but the same kind of analysis that argues for the need for government intervention in steering technological innovation also provides arguments for intervention in steering technology adoption. This is especially so if, after the initial adoption of technology from abroad, there is further adaptation to local circumstances, and the benefits and costs of the technological evolution are not fully appropriated, for example, in the process of learning by doing. These concerns have long been at the center of concern of industrial policy.

E. Broader Harms Associated with AI

There are also a number of broader harms associated with AI that have recently received a lot of attention—the ways in which new technology can affect security (including cybersecurity), privacy, incitement to "bad" behavior, including through hate speech, political manipulation, and, in the economic arena, price discrimination, sometimes exacerbating pre-existing societal divides.

While these matters affect both high-income and developing economies, an important concern is that the international community may address them in a way that does not reflect the priorities and needs of developing countries. Policymakers in many countries are beginning to discuss appropriate regulatory regimes and a set of rules to address these potential harms. It is unclear whether developing countries and emerging markets will be sufficiently represented at the table when these discussions take place. In fact, many of the standards, rules and regulations are likely to be set by high-income countries and China (e.g., Ding et al. 2018; Sacks 2018), even though the impacts may be larger, and potentially different, on developing countries and emerging markets.

Moreover, the institutional capacity of developing countries to counter these harms may be more limited—especially when facing off against the technology giants. Weaker institutional foundations may make some countries more prone to abuses of autocratic and totalitarian leaders using mis-/disinformation and surveillance technologies. Less educated populations may suffer more from the consequences of mis-/disinformation, such as those associated with the anti-vaccine movement.

III. Evaluating the Uncertainties and Opportunities

A. Uncertainty about the Pace and Scale of Progress

The impact of technological change depends heavily on its pace and scale. If it occurs slowly, there is time to adjust. If automation is limited to a few tasks or sectors at a time, the impacts will be limited. However, there is a great degree of uncertainty about the pace of change and the magnitude of the coming disruption, even among experts in this area. Some economists (e.g., Gordon 2016) assert that we are not in an era of unprecedented innovation, and that economic growth will be less rapid in the future than it has been over the past century. In fact, Gordon (2016) argues that indoor toilets and electricity had far bigger consequences on people's standards of living than more recent innovations.

Another view is that AI is a truly transformative technology—a General-Purpose Technology (GPT)—that has the potential to revolutionize every sector of the economy (e.g., Trajtenberg 2019). Like steam engines or electricity in previous technological revolutions, this view predicts that AI will lead to significant productivity gains and structural changes across the entire economy.

An even more radical perspective that goes back to John von Neumann is that AI may eventually advance to a point where AI systems reach human levels of general intelligence. This may imply that they can also do research, design better versions of themselves and thereby recursively self-improve, giving rise to accelerating technological progress and, in the words of von Neumann, "the appearance of approaching some essential singularity in the history of the race beyond which human affairs, as we know them, could not continue" (see Ulam 1958).[10] The concept of such a singularity has been popularized by Good (1965), Vinge (1993) and Kurzweil (2005), and is being increasingly discussed among economists (e.g., Nordhaus 2015; Aghion et al. 2017). Predictions of when such a chain of events might occur, however, continue to be perpetually revised—Armstrong et al. (2014) note that over the past six decades or so analysts have continued to expect "the development of [general] AI [to occur] within 15–25 years from whenever the prediction is made."[11]

This last perspective emphasizes that AI-driven machines may not only be physically stronger than humans and better and faster at processing information, but in an increasing number of domains, they may also learn better and faster

---

[10] As Vinge (1993) noted: "Within thirty years, we will have the technological means to create superhuman intelligence. Shortly after, the human era will be ended." However, it should be noted that general AI does not in itself imply the singularity (e.g., Walsh 2016).

[11] Responding to Kurzweil's (2005) thesis that "The Singularity is Near," Walsh (2016) provides arguments for why "The Singularity May Never Be Near."

than humans.[12] Thus, AI may be much more disruptive than a "mere" GPT; AI programs are increasingly replacing tasks previously performed by humans. If machines can engage in all tasks that have traditionally been performed by labor, and if they can do so at ever lower cost, then traditional labor would eventually become redundant, with the marginal product of human labor possibly falling so low that it no longer covers the subsistence cost necessary to keep a human alive (Korinek and Stiglitz 2019). This would represent the extreme case of labor-saving innovation: it is in fact labor-replacing innovation—employing labor would become a strictly dominated technology.[13]

We discussed earlier some studies examining which jobs may be replaced by automation and AI in coming decades, typically based on job- or task-level data. The predictions in these studies vary widely, ranging from a relatively small percentage of 14 percent of all jobs (OECD 2019) to an estimate of 20–25 percent (Harris, Kimson, and Schwedel 2018) and almost 50 percent by Frey and Osborne (2017) and McKinsey Global Institute (2017). Even the lower numbers suggest a significant effect, especially because the impact may be concentrated in certain industries and among certain groups of workers, specifically among unskilled and routine jobs. Knowing what fraction of all jobs will be lost to AI therefore does not necessarily provide a good metric of the impact on income distribution, especially in the short run.

Applying our earlier insights on steering innovation to economic research, economists should steer their research in directions where the expected social value added of economic analysis is greatest, that is, where it has the highest welfare impact.

Even if some of the described scenarios have a relatively low probability, it is important to think particularly hard about events that will be highly disruptive to society, to think through the consequences, and to prepare for how we might ameliorate some of the more adverse effects. Extensive labor replacing innovation would be such an event. Even if one places a relatively low probability on such an event—and one may argue that it is not actually a low-probability event—the associated social repercussions would be sufficiently large that it makes sense to focus attention on such an event. Studying scenarios that pose the most adverse social impacts would better prepare economies to deal with them when they occur—and they also provide valuable lessons for scenarios in which the impact is less stark.

---

[12] There is even a perspective that holds that AI-powered machines could become agents of their own (Korinek 2019).

[13] Note that this is in contrast to a long tradition in the traditional economics literature that viewed labor as an essential input for any production process.

B. The Productivity Puzzle: Are We Really in an Era of Unprecedented Innovation?

In relating the debate about the economic significance of AI-based innovation to recent economic data, we encounter a well-known puzzle: if we are really living in an era of significant technological disruption, why are the increases in innovation not showing up in GDP data? This is analogous to the puzzle of missing productivity growth from computerization that Bob Solow described in the 1980s when the GPT of the time—computers—spread throughout the economy (Solow 1987). It took until the following decade for US national accounts to show a pickup in productivity growth.

Part of the explanation for the productivity puzzle is that there are long lags, as was the case for computerization. At present, AI is influential in a limited number of sectors, like inventing better ways of advertising. Even if AI is transforming advertising, this will not transform our overall standard of living. (In this particular case, it may actually lower overall efficiency, as it may undermine the price system by enabling pervasive discriminatory pricing.) Going forward, many sectors of the economy will require complementary investments and changes in processes and organization as well as new skills among their workers to take full advantage of AI (see e.g., Brynjolfsson et al. 2019).

Another part of the explanation of the productivity puzzle is that there are difficult measurement problems. Many recent technologies may have led to increases in societal welfare that are not captured by GDP (see e.g., Brynjolfsson et al. 2020). For example, when online services are exchanged against "eyeballs," i.e., when users are exposed to advertisements instead of paying for services, the benefits to consumers are not included.[14]

C. Putting AI in the Broader Context of Development

There are several other important factors that are relevant when it comes to managing the potential adverse effects of AI on developing countries in coming decades.

---

[14] The measurement problems are still more complicated: advertising is an "intermediate" product and does not directly enter into the value of the final goods and service that constitutes GDP. If advertising were a normal input, and markets were competitive, an increase in the efficiency of production of an intermediate good would be reflected in a lowering of the final goods price, and that in turn would be associated with an increase in GDP. Better advertising engines may, as we noted earlier, actually increase market power and decrease overall economic efficiency. Moreover, they may induce an adverse redistribution, lowering welfare still more.

Covid-19

The Covid-19 pandemic has imposed an extra shadow cost on physical interaction with humans, which is likely to accelerate the automation of jobs that require physical interaction (see e.g., Korinek and Stiglitz 2021b). The resulting changes will have long-lasting effects on the economy, even after the pandemic is overcome. The new technologies that are introduced now will reduce the demand for labor worldwide for some time to come.[15]

Population Dynamics

Population dynamics will interact in important ways with labor-saving or -replacing technologies (see e.g., Varian 2020). In countries with rapidly growing working-age populations, such as in many African countries, lots of new jobs will have to be created to maintain a given employment rate. Advances in automation that are developed in high-income countries and easily deployed around the world will make this more difficult. However, the large supply of labor may slow down the development and adoption of automation technologies within such countries (although the evidence in several countries suggests that at least in large export-oriented manufacturing, the technologies employed are remarkably similar to those in advanced countries; see Rodrik 2011).[16] Moreover, young populations also generate significant demand for education, which in turn creates jobs. Overall, even countries like India face difficulties in creating enough formal sector jobs to keep pace with the growing working age population. The faster growth of population makes capital deepening more difficult, slowing the pace of growth in income per capita.

Conversely, in countries in which the working-age population is declining, such as China, the impact of job automation on the workforce is mitigated as workers that are replaced by technological progress can simply retire. Moreover, aging populations create large service sector needs, particularly in healthcare. Many of these service sector jobs are unlikely to be replaced by automation or AI in the near future. Overall, the evidence suggests that aging societies adopt new technologies and automate (Acemoglu and Restrepo 2019b and Figure 5.5).[17]

---

[15] Any innovations to deal with Covid-19 will still be available in the post-Covid-19 world. Moreover, the development of research strategies in response to Covid-19 may set in motion a process of "learning to learn," learning better how to innovate in human-replacing dimensions. See Atkinson and Stiglitz (1969) and Stiglitz (1987b).

[16] This would not, of course, be true if the factor price equalization theorem held. More generally, differences in domestic factor ratios do not necessarily align well with differences in factor prices.

[17] There are countervailing forces to the scarcity of labor associated with a declining working age population. A younger population may be more tech savvy, better able to pick up, adopt and adapt to new technologies. The figure suggests that the scarcity effect dominates. There are other factors too that play a role in robotization.

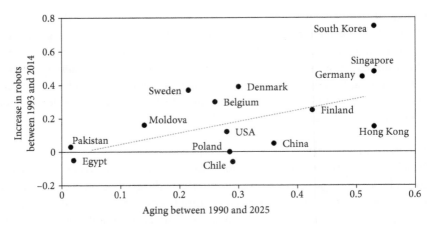

Figure 5.5 Population Aging and Automation

Note: Aging is measured as the change in the ratio of workers above 56 to workers aged 21–55; robots are measured as the number of industrial robots per thousand workers. Based on regression analysis in Acemoglu and Restrepo (2019b) controlling for a number of covariates.

Source: Reproduced from Acemoglu and Restrepo (2019b).

The Green Transition

A third important force affecting developing countries in coming decades is the threat of global warming, which calls for significant public policy interventions to facilitate the Green Transition, i.e., the transition away from an economy that is dependent on fossil fuels to one that is more environmentally sustainable and relies more on renewable energy. Without global policies to save our planet, developing countries will experience some of the largest losses from global warming.

There are many similarities between the effects of AI and the Green Transition. Both involve large changes in relative prices and generate significant redistributions, and many developing countries will be strongly affected. The Green Transition is similar to resource-saving innovation and risks undermining the standard of living of oil-exporting countries, among which there are a number of low-income countries.

There is also an important complementarity between the Green Transition and AI: the Green Transition is likely to increase the demand for labor which could offset some of the negative effects on labor demand of automation and AI. Indeed, given the labor needed for the Green Transition, the labor replacement due to automation and AI in many activities, including manufacturing, could be considered a fortunate development enabling countries to better address the challenges of climate change. There is thus an inherent tension in frequent claims that on the one hand economies cannot afford to mitigate climate change (i.e., that there are insufficient resources), and on the other hand concerns over a potential crisis with a surplus of labor arising from labor-saving AI.[18,19]

However, we do face challenges in how to channel surplus resources into what is required for the Green Transition. Some of the skill sets of those labor resources freed up by technological progress will differ from those needed in the Green Transition, although Louie and Pearce (2016) argue that the retraining costs would be moderate, and many of the investments (such as installing solar panels) require only limited skills.

There may be institutional constraints that make it difficult to reallocate capital towards green investment. While many sources of savings are long term (pension funds and sovereign wealth funds) and the investments needed for the Green Transition are long term, standing in between are short-term financial markets. Local, national, and multilateral Green Development Banks may be helpful in financing the private green transition. Better disclosure to investors of risks associated with "brown" investments (i.e., ones that contribute to pollution) and changes in fiduciary standards for asset managers towards their investors, would help move resources into green investments. Of course, without strong incentives, provided by price signals and environmental regulatory constraints, incentives for green investments and innovation will be greatly attenuated.

IV. Lessons from Past Technological Transformations

To grasp the historical nature of what is going on, it is necessary to put the advent of AI and related technologies in the context of the broader history of technological progress. Humanity spent much of its history at a Malthusian stage. The Industrial Revolution started a little over two centuries ago, and was but a blip in the history of mankind. The era of manufacturing-based export-led growth that enabled the East Asian Miracle stretched over the past half-century—one quarter of the history of the Industrial Revolution. It is easily conceivable that we are now going into another era.

Many are far more sanguine than we are about the disruptive potential of AI. They point to the automobile and other innovations at the end of the nineteenth

---

[18] There is a similar dissonance between those who argue that the economy faces secular stagnation and those who say there are not the resources required for a rapid green transition.

[19] Over the long run, the effect of the green transition on the demand for labor is more problematic. While many of the green technologies have higher upfront costs, maintenance costs are markedly lower, and not only are life-cycle carbon emissions lower, but so is labor usage.

century. Jobs were lost, making buggy whips and horse carriages obsolete, but overall, labor demand increased, and more jobs were created. Our analytical discussion made clear that there is no inherent reason that innovation has these effects. This time could well be different. Looking at the time before the Industrial Revolution and the early decades of the revolution itself serves as a reminder.

A. Pre-Industrial Revolution

Before the Industrial Revolution, innovation proceeded at a far slower pace than today. There were still many innovations, but the actual living standard of the vast majority of people was stagnant (Maddison 2003). The interpretation of Malthus (1798) was that every time an innovation took place, the population started to grow and absorbed the surplus that was generated.

This pre-industrial state of affairs may be still relevant in the least developed countries and is particularly problematic in some African countries, where the death rate has been greatly reduced by medical innovations, but reproductive rates have continued to be very high. The affected countries have been slow to go through the demographic transition that marked the rise of living standards in Asia. As a result, several countries are facing a difficult-to-manage explosion in population combined with stagnant living standards.

There is a risk that poor countries may see a return to Malthusian dynamics if technological progress undermines the source of their comparative advantage. Consider a country that exports manufacturing goods produced using cheap labor but is not very productive in agriculture, for example because of a shortage of land and a high population density. The country uses its export revenues to import food for workers in the manufacturing sector, granting them a living standard that is above subsistence levels. If a new technology produces the manufacturing goods more cheaply, the wages of the manufacturing workers will fall, and they may well fall below the subsistence cost of workers. If that is the case, the country may return to a Malthusian state of affairs in which part of the population suffers from hunger and deprivation. Increasing agricultural productivity may mitigate this dire state of affairs but the question is, would they be sufficient to support a population that was previously supported by imported food? Thus, populations may decline not as a result of choice, as in many developed countries, but from Malthusian dynamics. In today's globally connected world, that presents ugly alternatives: Will the rich countries simply look away, as they see this suffering and near-starvation in poorer countries? Will they create ever-increasing barriers to stave off the inevitable pressures of migration?

B. Industrial Revolution

The Industrial Revolution marked the beginning of rapid growth in high-income countries. After centuries in which standards of living had been stagnant, growth started to increase markedly. It transformed the world. The Industrial Revolution thus provides us with a number of lessons that are very relevant today:

Innovation Can Be Very Disruptive

Even when an innovation ultimately proves to be beneficial for society at large, not everyone benefits. It can give rise to very large disruptions during the transition. In the short run, there was significant social upheaval from the industrial revolution—Charles Dickens' novels make it clear that not everyone prospered. In the UK, some people were living under much worse conditions in the cities of the mid-nineteenth century than they had been in the rural areas prior to that. Even indicators such as life expectancy initially went down. Looking at those who suffered, the Industrial Revolution was clearly not a Pareto improvement.

Collective Action Can Mitigate the Adverse Effects

The onset of the industrial revolution posed many challenges that required collective action. However, it took time for societies to put in place the collective mechanisms to respond to these challenges. This is why the industrial revolution had significant negative effects on the masses for some time. Eventually, governments played an important role in mitigating the adverse effects, including the problems posed by urbanization, such as challenges in sanitation, environmental degradation, public health, infrastructure, and congestion.

Government took a strong role too in advancing the positive effects of the new economy. Education was an important element in creating a productive workforce—it was therefore also in the interests of capitalists, and public education received broad public support.

In high-income countries, institutions related to labor legislation, unionization, and social safety nets were not created until the end of the nineteenth century and beginning of the twentieth century. In the United States, the ready availability of land implied that labor was relatively scarce, limiting the extent to which labor could be exploited. Nonetheless, in the early years of the twentieth century, labor was not doing very well. It was only dramatic events like the 1911 Triangle Shirtwaist Factory fire in New York City that led to labor legislation that really protected workers. In most high-income countries, labor legislation today is taken for granted, but in 1900, it was not obvious if meaningful labor legislation would ever be enacted. Strikingly, some of the tough political battles that made the adoption of such legislation problematic a century ago are playing out once

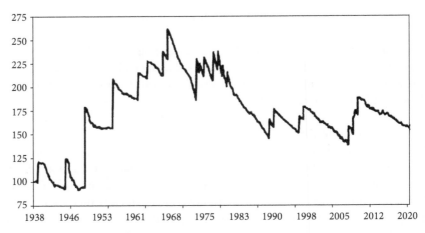

Figure 5.6 Federal Minimum Wage (adjusted for inflation) in the US, 1938–2020
Source: Federal Reserve Economic Data (FRED).

again in the United States, where there has been an erosion of protections, for example, those associated with minimum wages, health and safety standards, or overtime pay, among others.

These labor market reforms helped support the structural transformation that occurred with the rise of manufacturing, and they showed that equality and growth are complementary (e.g., Ostry et al. 2019). At a basic level, they were necessary to sustain social peace and democracy. And they ushered in what might be called an "Age of Labor." Most developing countries have not gone through this process yet.

This Age of Labor may not last forever. In the United States, minimum wages have declined in real terms in recent decades, below the level of 50 years ago (Figure 5.6), and many protections on hours and working conditions have been eviscerated. Advances in AI may further contribute to undermining labor's bargaining position and thus these social protections. And in developing countries, they may do so before workers have ever acquired similar levels of rights and protections as they have in high-income countries.

Politics and Political Economy

The Age of Labor conferred not only unprecedented economic returns upon workers in the form of rising wages, but also, in parallel, unprecedented political power. However, this power has been eroded more recently (see e.g., Boix 2019). In simple models of democracy, the median voter (or more broadly, the "majority") determines political outcomes. But the evidence is that that model provides a poor description of the outcomes of the political process. For instance, the majority of voters want a more egalitarian society (see Chapter 1). But in recent decades, in many countries, the political and economic rules have evolved in the opposite direction, giving more influence to the power of "money."[20],[21]

C. Manufacturing-Based Export-Led Growth

In developing countries, there has been a single model of development that has proved enormously successful over the past 50 years: manufacturing-based export-led growth (see Stiglitz 2018a). It enabled many East Asian countries to close the gap between themselves and high-income countries, increasing per capita incomes in these countries multifold.

One big change inherent in this development strategy was moving from discussions of static comparative advantage to more dynamic comparative advantage. This was central to the East Asia "Miracle." Half a century ago, South Korea was advised that its comparative advantage was growing rice. It rejected that advice and instead pursued a strategy of creating its own dynamic comparative advantage via an industrial policy that led it towards industrialization. That model served most of East Asia remarkably well, in a way few had anticipated (e.g., Myrdal (1968) who predicted that Asia would never develop). (See also Chapter 6.)

The path to development in East Asia has been via exports of cheap labor-intensive manufactured goods. This development strategy combined learning, the provision of employment opportunities, foreign exchange, tax revenue— everything that was needed for a quick developmental transition.

While their development trajectory began with taking advantage of their static comparative advantage in cheap labor, and especially cheap unskilled labor, over time, many East Asian countries moved up the "value" chain, producing higher value added and more complex products and developing their dynamic comparative advantage.

Earlier advances in technology have already reduced the importance of cheap labor; but now advances in AI may erode it further still. Going forward, growth led solely by exports of labor-intensive manufacturing goods will no longer be available as a strategy of development. Indeed, the share of manufacturing employment is decreasing globally. Moreover, the jobs that can be outsourced may be more easily automated. There may be reshoring of production that had

---

[20] For example, based on data for 1981–2002, Gilens (2005) finds that in the US actual policy outcomes strongly reflected the preferences of higher-income groups, with little relationship to the preferences of the poor or middle-income citizens. For a broader discussion of the interplay of economic and political inequality, see Stiglitz (2013, 2019).

[21] Harari (2017) also explores the implications of super-human artificial intelligence on society and politics.

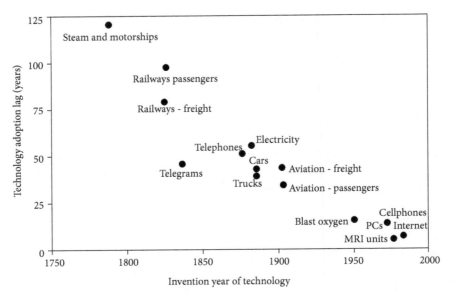

Figure 5.7 Technology Adoption Lags

Note: Technology adoption lag is a mean estimated lag in cross-country technology diffusion (Comin and Hobijn, 2010, Table 2).

Source: Comin and Hobijn (2010).

previously been outsourced, using highly automated production processes, and the process may have been accelerated by the Covid pandemic.

The forces that facilitated the development in East Asia may thus be going in reverse, making it difficult for other developing countries to follow the strategy.

One of the critical reasons for the success of the export-led growth model based on manufacturing goods was that it enabled developing countries to catch up in multiple domains.[22] Developing countries are poorer than developed countries not only because there is a gap in material resources but also because of a gap in knowledge (World Bank 1998). A quarter-century ago, the World Bank began thinking of itself as a knowledge bank, not only helping countries to catch up in resources but also to catch up in knowledge.

AI may have characteristics that will actually increase the gap in knowledge and make it more difficult to catch up. While technology adoption lags have declined over the past centuries (Comin and Hobijn 2010 and Figure 5.7; Peralta-Alva and Roitman 2018), the specific nature of AI may reverse that. Cutting-edge AI technology is highly specialized, and improvements are driven to a large degree by learning from large datasets, creating a winner-takes-all dynamic, as we

---

[22] The emphasis here is on (traded) goods rather than (non-traded) services—while learning by doing could occur in both, it is the former that drives export-led development. See, e.g., McMillan and Rodrik (2011) who note that non-traded service sector development on its own typically has not had a substantial impact on overall productivity.

noted earlier. In addition, a disproportionate share of the people working in AI are in private companies, and a significant share of the knowledge is not in the public domain and therefore not easily accessible to developing and emerging economies. (This contrasts with many past technologies, when publicly financed knowledge production was more central, so access to knowledge was more easily available to developing and emerging economies.) Moreover, an important resource input to AI is data, and access to data is concentrated and not globally public. The implication is that the nature of AI technology and how these advances are generated will make it more difficult to catch up than in the past. In fact, the exponential nature of growth in AI technology may imply that laggards not only cannot catch up, but that the gap between them and the front runners may grow, compounding the potential adverse effects that developing countries may suffer from labor-saving or resource-saving technological progress.[23]

D. What Is Different This Time

Not only may the AI revolution make it more difficult for developing countries to catch up, the AI revolution may also be more difficult to manage for economic policymakers than earlier technological transitions. The structural transformation from an agrarian rural economy to an industrial urban economy eventually led to a more egalitarian society. As we have noted, the reasons included that innovation associated with that transition overall was unskilled-biased, i.e., it increased the relative productivity of unskilled labor. Moreover, industrial production provided a strong force towards mass education. Furthermore, industrial production typically involved large establishments that could be unionized relatively easily, and the unions advocated for wage compression. All these forces led to greater equality.

In the current transition, what risks becoming our "destination"—a service sector economy, marked by greater inequality, with less support for public education and more concentrations of market power—may be less attractive in many ways than the current situation, and the process of getting there may be more disruptive; that is, unless countervailing policy interventions are made.

AI may be labor-saving and resource-saving, and it is likely more biased towards ever-higher skills so that general education becomes less important.[24]

---

[23] Stiglitz (2015) models the relationship between technological leaders and followers.

[24] We emphasize that the focus here is on the more adverse scenarios, to help prepare policies; should they not materialize, so much the better. We noted countervailing forces—the need for labor for the green transition, that even within advanced economies, people may still be needed for service jobs requiring physical proximity and/or the "human touch" (such as elderly care, housekeeping, etc.). Most important, these outcomes are not inevitable: we can steer innovation in a different direction and, as the discussion below will hopefully make clear, there are multiple actions that can be taken to mitigate some of the adverse effects.

This may reduce support for equality-enhancing public education, which has been one of the strong forces for more equalitarian outcomes in the past. Moreover, the service sector which is becoming an increasingly important part of the economy is marked by smaller establishments. In addition, worker tenure has declined, making it harder to unionize the workforce (Choi and Spletzer 2012). Digital technologies are likely to create more barriers to entry and give rise to more monopoly power and winner-takes-all dynamics, with rents going to a small number of extremely wealthy individuals and enterprises, disproportionately located in high-income countries.

Although for many developing countries, average income per capita may increase, large fractions of society may be left behind. Moreover, some developing countries may experience declines in income per capita as innovation erodes their comparative advantage. Unskilled workers in these countries may suffer the most.

Although greater inequality would increase the need for social protection, it may result in a less egalitarian politico-economic equilibrium, as the new concentrations of economic and political power may reduce support for the critical role of government in mitigating the adverse distributional consequences of technological change (see, e.g., Gilens 2005).

V. Domestic Policy Responses

We have seen how economic policy played a critical role in shaping economic outcomes in previous eras of innovation; the same will be true in the case of AI. In this section, we discuss what policy levers can be employed to address the effects of technological disruption, both in developing countries and to protect vulnerable segments in advanced economies. Some of these are similar to what worked in earlier periods of technological change; some are attuned to the special problems posed by AI and labor-replacing innovation. In section 6, we will discuss changes in global policies, norms and rules that would assist developing countries in their response to technological change. In this short chapter, we can only touch on a few of the more salient policies.

A. Taxation, Redistribution, and Government Expenditures

Among the critical policies to combat rising inequality are those of taxation and redistribution, with a particularly important role for progressive taxation. However, in recent years, a number of countries have actually made their tax systems more and more regressive. For example, many countries tax the returns to capital and rents (such as land rents, monopoly rents, and other forms of exploita-tion rents) at lower rates than workers. In the US, the rich pay a lower fraction of their income in taxes than the majority of the population (Saez and Zucman 2019).

Raising taxes is a particular challenge for developing countries, in which the informal sector is typically much larger than in high-income economies. Yet new digital tools and new data may actually give governments new policy tools to increase tax compliance. For example, when an activity becomes intermediated via centralized digital platforms, it becomes easier for governments to access business transactions and levy taxes on them. For example, governments have long found it difficult to monitor and tax the earnings of taxi drivers. But if driv-ing is intermediated via digital platforms, all their earnings—including most tips—are recorded.[25]

One of the dilemmas when it comes to taxation and redistribution is that labor-saving technological progress reduces tax revenue from labor—tradition-ally the most highly taxed factor in the economy—precisely at the time when the need for redistribution rises (see e.g., Korinek 2020). This necessitates that taxa-tion increasingly shifts towards other factors and rents. From the perspective of efficiency, the taxation of rents is particularly desirable (George 1879). Imposing taxes on fixed factors, such as land, acts like a lump sum tax, and taxing rents generated by market power and political activity may discourage such rent-seeking, enhancing efficiency.

We have argued earlier that technological progress creates winners and losers, and the gains of the winners are quasi-rents that governments may be able to tax without introducing distortions. In particular, some of the monopoly rents of dig-ital giants can be taxed without introducing major distortions into the economy.

In designing tax systems, an important concern is about incidence: the possi-bility that general equilibrium effects imply that taxes are ultimately borne by other factors and agents than those on whom they are levied, undermining the desired redistributive objectives. For example, a common result in simple models is that capital taxation discourages capital accumulation by capitalists. However, the adverse effects may be more than offset by public investments in human and physical capital (see e.g., Stiglitz 2018b). High on the list of what is desirable to tax are "bads" rather than goods, i.e., Pigouvian taxes on activities and goods that create negative externalities, for example, polluting or carbon-emitting goods. This would contribute to the Green Transition in a dual way, not only by provid-ing tax revenue for public investments but also by correcting market prices to reflect the negative externalities.[26]

---

[25] Some are justifiably concerned that digital platforms are in fact very efficient at exploiting work-ers. But platforms can also provide information on whether workers are exploited and, with proper regulation, make it easier to address such exploitation than it used to be before the digital age.
[26] See also Chapter 19.

Social Protection

If individuals could obtain insurance against the adverse effects of disruptive innovations, then it would be more likely that these innovations would be Pareto improvements (Korinek and Stiglitz 2019). But such insurance is not available. One of the functions of social insurance is to socialize these risks that otherwise would have been borne by individuals. But in developing countries, systems of social protection are typically less developed, making it even more likely that there be significant groups that are worse off.

Universal Basic Income

Many commentators have responded to concerns about the impact of technological progress on employment by advocating a universal basic income (UBI). While proposals differ in their detail, they typically entail that all individuals are paid a UBI independent of their employment or wealth status, and with a level of UBI payments geared above the poverty line. While such programs would imply formidable fiscal costs, and with it, possibly large distortionary taxes, those could be contained if a UBI replaced other social safety programs (such as social security, welfare, or unemployment insurance systems). By doing so, it would also reduce the overall administration costs.

From a global welfare perspective, a global UBI that was truly "universal" as the name suggests, i.e., that covers all citizens of the world equally, would be most desirable, given the potentially large global implications of AI. Currently, access to prototypes of a UBI is exclusive to people who were lucky to be born in specific locations that have the fiscal capacity to afford such programs (e.g., in Alaska where oil revenue is collected in the Alaska Permanent Fund and distributed to the residents of the state). But given the limitations on cross-border transfers that have been the center of attention of this chapter, a global UBI is clearly still in the realm of fantasy.[27,28]

However, in the short- to medium-run, the focus should be on creating jobs for everyone who is able and willing to work, especially in light of the earlier discussion of how much labor will be needed for the Green Transition, to provide

---

[27] Some countries have started to experiment with schemes that have some characteristics of a UBI. E.g., Spain introduced in early 2020 a "minimum vital income" to ensure a guaranteed minimum income for the poorest. However, it is not unconditional, but instead tops up incomes below the minimum income, which may create disincentive effects to continue work in jobs that pay below that threshold. Several other countries have run pilot programs, often on a small scale and/or for a limited time. Overall, these programs appear to indicate that such schemes tend to have little impact on labor supply (see, e.g., https://www.vox.com/future-perfect/2020/2/19/21112570/universal-basic-income-ubi-map). Earlier research on a negative income tax in the US suggested that by enabling individuals to search more for a better matching job may actually enhance productivity.

[28] UBI programs may turn out to be important policies in a future in which labor truly becomes redundant (Korinek and Juelfs 2021). There is uncertainty over when that future may arise, as the earlier discussions indicated—but given the complexities of transitioning to such a new regime, there may be a rationale for countries to start experimenting with UBI systems.

services to the young, the sick, and the elderly, and to invest in infrastructure. Governments may have a role to play in helping match the need for work and people willing and able to work. However, while a clear need for a UBI may be in a more distant future, there are other policies that may achieve similar objectives to a UBI. For example, one approach to ensuring a modicum of income for all over the long run, with co-benefits of perhaps increasing social cohesion and solidarity, is shared capital ownership (e.g., Solow 2009): as part of government assistance programs (such as those enacted in the wake of Covid-19 in 2020), firms receiving government help should contribute shares to a sovereign wealth fund—owned by everyone within the nation. Similarly, firms that build on or employ innovations that are based in part on government-funded research should be required to do the same.[29]

Starting with Keynes (1931), economists have argued that technological progress and automation would in principle enable people to work less and spend more time on more meaningful activities rather than tedious and repetitive tasks—a point also emphasized, for example, by Varian (2020). However, this requires either that wages go up in tandem with productivity growth, unlike in recent decades, or that the fruits of progress are shared more widely using transfers. If these questions of distribution can be solved satisfactorily, then individuals could indeed respond to productivity growth by working less without experiencing material losses. There is considerable evidence that many workers would prefer to work less and with more flexible work sessions. The Dutch model, which provides all workers with a right to part-time work (at pro-rated wages) could serve as an example, assuming that wages are sufficiently high.[30]

Expenditure and Infrastructure Policy

Expenditure policy can be as important in offsetting the adverse effects of AI as taxation and direct redistribution, and it carries several benefits over transfers that are particularly relevant in developing countries: government expenditures may be easier to target based on need, and for whom the social returns of those expenditures may be high. For instance, expenditures on human well-being, such as on education and health, are naturally targeted to those who need education and healthcare, rather than being spent on those who already are educated or on those who are healthy. Expenditures to protect the environment help those who

---

[29] Notably, some have discussed a "robot tax" that could help finance redistributive fiscal measures (e.g., Rubin 2020). However, such a robot tax may be difficult to implement (e.g., what distinguishes a "robot" from traditional capital?) and may discourage innovation (e.g., Summers 2017). Conceptually, government ownership of capital is equivalent to taxes on capital with exemptions on new investment that avoid any negative incentive effects of capital taxation, although it may be insufficient to provide funding for large-scale redistributive programs that may be needed in a long-term equilibrium with low employment levels. See also Korinek (2020).

[30] The reduced labor supply would itself help sustain higher wages.

bear the brunt of environmental degradation, including climate change, which disproportionately affect the poor.[31]

Expenditure policies that increase the demand for unskilled labor may serve double duty: they raise demand for unskilled labor, increasing the equality of market income (what is often now called pre-distribution), and sometimes they can be targeted so that the benefits of the expenditure go disproportionately to the less well-off. One important example is infrastructure investments in poorer neighborhoods, which are a labor-intensive expenditure that can be designed to be pro-egalitarian.

Of particular importance are investments in digital infrastructure that reduce the "digital divide" and allow citizens to access the vast services provided by the Internet. Recent advances in network technology allow developing countries to leapfrog older technologies in which high-income countries have invested fortunes, for example by using wireless 5G technologies instead of laying vast networks of cables.

Other infrastructure investments include public transportation systems that connect especially lower income workers with jobs and enhance the opportunities available to them. Another example of labor-demand increasing public expenditures is creating service sector jobs, for example in healthcare, caring for the elderly, and some aspects of education, which can again be designed to serve double duty—disproportionately benefiting the poor and needy as they increase wages by increasing the demand for labor.

B. Pre-Distribution

Our concern here is the distribution of consumption (or more broadly, of well-being) among the citizens of a country. That is affected by inequalities in market incomes and the extent of redistribution. The previous subsection discussed redistribution through tax and expenditure policies. But a society with a more equalitarian market distribution needs to place less burden on redistribution. Good policy entails an optimal mix of "pre-distribution"—actions to increase the equality of market income—and redistribution. This is especially so because some of the actions to increase the equality of market distribution are actually efficiency-enhancing, i.e., have a negative cost. These include, for instance, actions which reduce market power, the ability of firms to exploit information asymmetries, or to engage in a variety of other exploitive practices.

---

[31] For example, Colmer et al. (2020) find that while fine-particle air pollution has decreased overall in the US over the past four decades, whiter and richer neighborhoods have become relatively less polluted, while poor and minority communities are (still) the most polluted.

There are two categories of policies which affect the distribution of market incomes: (1) Policies that affect individuals' endowments of assets—human capital (education) and financial assets. These are affected by the public provision of education and more broadly, policies which affect the intergenerational transmission of advantage and disadvantage (such as inheritance taxes.) And (2) policies that affect the returns on factors, which include the laws and regulations that determine the "rules of the game." These include competition laws, labor legislation, and rules governing globalization, the financial sector, and corporate governance. These rules affect simultaneously efficiency and distribution.[32]

Education Regarding the first set of such policies, the fact that more educated workers receive higher incomes than less educated ones may invite the conclusion that education is the solution to inequality. While providing more equal access to high-quality education especially for the poor may reduce inequality—and is absolutely essential to avoid an education-based digital divide whereby some simply do not know how to access and benefit from the resources and opportunities offered by the Internet and related digital technologies—education is far from a panacea. Indeed, if there are large innate differences in ability, education can identify and amplify these differences, actually increasing inequalities in market income. (Stiglitz 1975b). Moreover, education cannot address the problems arising from the declining share of labor income overall.

Steering Innovation in AI in High-income Countries

The overall direction of innovation in AI will be set to a large extent by high-income countries plus China. This implies that the direction of technological progress in those countries—how labor-saving it is—also matters for developing countries that will be exposed to the new technologies.

Korinek and Stiglitz (2020) make the case for actively steering technological progress so that it is more labor-using. They show that whenever lump-sum transfers are not available, it is desirable to encourage technological progress that leads to higher demand for those types of workers with the lowest incomes. This can be done by nudging entrepreneurs, by considering the labor market implications of government-sponsored research, or by explicit incentives provided to the private sector. Klinova and Korinek (2021) and Partnership on AI (2021) describe how to develop and how to operationalize frameworks for steering advances in artificial intelligence towards greater shared prosperity.

Many governmental policies have indirect effects on incentives for innovation. For example, at least in the short run, the cost of capital is influenced by monetary policy, with the goal of stabilizing aggregate demand. In recent years, monetary

---

[32] For an extensive discussion of some of the critical "rules," see Stiglitz et al. (2015, 2019). Later, we discuss a particularly important set of policies that can affect the returns to factors—those associated with steering the development and adoption of technologies.

authorities in many countries have set interest rates such that real returns on safe assets have been very low or even negative, likely below the social shadow price of capital. Stiglitz (2014) shows that this encourages excessive automation in high-income countries. Acemoglu et al. (2020) observe that tax policies that favor capital over labor also distort the direction of progress towards saving labor.

And there are immediate implications for developing countries: once the cost of developing a labor-saving innovation has been incurred in high-income countries, it can frequently be rolled out globally at comparatively low cost, potentially imposing significant welfare costs on workers in developing countries. Examples include self-checkout kiosks that harm workers, whatever their benefits or costs may be for consumers and global corporates.

Pritchett (2019) observes that migration policies in high-income countries restrict labor supply and lead to comparatively high wages that do not reflect the abundance of labor, and in particular of unskilled labor, at the global level. The high wages then provide innovators in high-income countries with excessive incentives to invest in the automation of tasks that are performed by unskilled labor compared to what is desirable from the perspective of developing countries (or from the perspective of global efficiency).

Economists are also becoming increasingly aware of the importance of regional heterogeneity. Unlike in stylized models in which only national borders exist, labor does not move seamlessly across regions within countries. Even in high-income countries, large disparities between regions or between rural and urban areas persist, as illustrated, for example, by the case of northern and southern Italy or by the rural/urban differential in the United States and many other countries. Such disparities call for location-based policies in fostering development.

New Development Strategies

Developing countries will need a new multi-pronged development strategy to replace the manufacturing-led export-based growth model. Industrial policies have traditionally been among the most important aspects of countries' development strategies—interventions that shape the direction in which the economy is moving, with particular emphasis on the secondary sector. However, in an age of increasing automation in manufacturing, development strategies have to broaden their focus beyond manufacturing and the secondary sector to other sectors of the economy, including agriculture and services.[33]

Greenwald and Stiglitz (2014b) point out that every country has, in effect, a sectoral development policy—shaped by infrastructure and education investments

---

[33] Curiously, such policies have continued to be referred to as "industrial policies" even when they move the economy away from the industrial sector. We use the more generic term *sectoral policies*, but they are broader: they can also be used to change technology within a sector (e.g., towards green or more labor-intensive technologies).

and tax and regulatory policy. It is only that some countries do not know (or admit) that they have such policies. The danger then is that such policies can be more easily captured by special interests.[34] In developing countries development policies are much more at the center of economic policy. They need to be designed to manage innovations and mitigate the effects of and adapt to the disruptions that innovations may engender, to ensure that the net societal benefits, broadly defined, are maximized.

A lot of innovation in developing countries focuses on technology adoption and adaptation rather than developing entirely novel technologies. Whereas high-income countries focus on "steering innovation," developing countries need to pay attention to "steering the adoption of technologies." Their development strategy should intentionally focus on steering the adoption of labor-using technologies that have already been developed in high-income countries, adapting them to their own circumstances and needs, redesigning them, and building on them. Decisions on what type of inward FDI to encourage should also be informed by these objectives.

In designing the new development strategies, developing countries will need to think carefully about the rationale for public interventions: how can government improve upon the decisions made by decentralized agents? Of particular importance is that the direction of technological progress and technology adoption is endogenous, and there is no presumption that market decisions in this area are socially desirable. Decisions made at one date have effects in later periods, with firms making the decisions appropriating only a fraction of the benefits and bearing only part of the costs of their decisions. For example, this is clearly manifest when there are knowledge spillovers to other firms and when technology evolves over time, e.g., through learning by doing. Firms acting on their own will not fully consider the dynamic implications of their decisions today on others.

There are also market failures beyond the ability to appropriate the returns from current choices—for instance, imperfections of risk and capital markets. The capital market imperfections that impede the reallocation of labor in high-income countries in response to innovation—and that can result in innovations which decrease welfare—are even more important in developing countries, making it imperative to combine industrial policies with active labor market policies (see, e.g., Delli Gatti et al. 2012a, 2012b).

Relatedly, part of the problem is that market prices do not adequately reflect social shadow values. A well-known example is that, in the absence of appropriate regulation, the price of carbon in the market is zero, but this does not reflect the social cost of carbon.

---

[34] For example, US bankruptcy provisions favoring derivatives can be thought of a sectoral policy encouraging the growth of derivatives; but until the 2008 financial crisis, few outside of that sector were even aware of the favorable treatment that derivatives have received.

Similarly, market prices do not reflect the social value of an equitable distribution of resources and do not guide innovation in that direction. Given the constraints on redistribution, this leaves an important role for the government to steer innovation and foster economic development in a socially desirable direction (Korinek and Stiglitz 2020). For example, much could be gained from encouraging innovators to shift their focus from labor-saving towards more labor-using technologies.

Fortunately, while the new technologies necessitate a change away from the old and highly successful development strategies of the past half-century, they also open up new opportunities. In agriculture, AI offers the potential for large productivity increases based on algorithms that help farmers fine-tune and optimize a range of decisions that increase their yield. Such algorithms depend on crops, soil and weather conditions and need to be customized to local conditions. Just as agricultural extension services, which extended general knowledge about agriculture to local farmers, played a critical role in the development of the United States, there is an important role for government agricultural extension services today in developing countries.[35] Digital platforms can also enhance the ability of small farmers to trade their products at fair market prices, reducing the market power of middle men that frequently absorb a significant fraction of the surplus generated in agriculture.

Developing the service sector is crucial for economic development as the role of the primary and secondary sectors is declining. Many developing countries may carve out new areas of comparative advantage in services that will, however, depend on good Internet connections and a certain degree of education of the workforce. For example, call centers and similar business and consumer services rely on requisite language skills. There is also a growing market for simple human services that can be broken down into small components and fed into AI systems (e.g., labeling images). However, as we noted earlier, services that can be outsourced are often also more easily automated. Other services such as tourism have proven a more automation-resistant (although not pandemic-resistant) source of export revenue for countries that have managed to fashion themselves into desirable tourist destinations. Exporting services offers many of the potential growth benefits of the manufacturing-based export-led growth model.

Services that are aimed at a domestic audience, for example, healthcare, caring for the elderly, as well as education, may not deliver much export revenue but are important for economic development and welfare. There is much scope for employing AI to improve the delivery and efficiency of these services, and it requires government policy to do so since private service providers are frequently

---

[35] In 1914, the US Department of Agriculture created a system of "extension" services, with the aim of providing farmers with expert advice on agriculture and farming. See, e.g., https://www.almanac.com/cooperative-extension-services.

small in size and cannot afford the necessary investments. And even in these areas, there may be significant opportunities for cross-border trade, for example, via medical tourism and via retirees from advanced countries relocating to warmer climates, if adequate health care is available.

VI. Global Governance

In a globally integrated economy—from which developing countries and emerging markets have benefited enormously in many ways—global rules matter. The global rules have always been set to favor high-income countries; they are, to a large extent, set by the large powerful countries, and frequently by powerful special interests within them, whereas developing countries do not have a seat at the table, or are at least underrepresented.

The global rules have large effects on the ability of these countries to levy taxes in the digital era, on high-income countries' ability to extract rents from the developing countries (say through market power and intellectual property rights), and more broadly on the global terms of trade and distribution of income.[36] While developing countries may realize these inequities—and the inefficiencies—of our global economic system, it often seems that there is little they can do.

AI has provided a new arena in which rules need to be set, at the same time that it may exacerbate the imbalances in economic power, as our earlier discussion emphasized.

However, there are reasons for cautious hope when it comes to the rules governing information and AI. First, the rules in this area are still in the process of being set so there is hope that international institutions and civil society may have a positive impact on the shape of these rules. Still, the fact that recent trade agreements between the United States and other countries have contained provisions reflecting the interests of big-tech companies—with limited open debate and limiting the scope for these trading partners to design regimes that reflect a broader public interest—is of concern.

Secondly, it should be in the self-interest of high-income countries to avoid the possibility of a strong backlash to globalization in developing countries. The possibility of such a backlash is considerable: The United States and a number of other high-income countries, which have been big beneficiaries of globalization, have experienced such a backlash—in part because they have not ensured that the losers of globalization were compensated. In the past, there was at least some sense that globalization created mutual gains for high-income and developing countries. The backlash in developing countries would be even greater if they

---

[36] For a discussion of how this plays out in trade rules, see, e.g., Charlton and Stiglitz (2005).

come to see globalization as a mechanism of rent extraction from their economies (even if the truth may be that technological change is making them lose some of the earlier gains from globalization).

Moreover, international institutions, some of which are less and less dominated by high-income countries, may play a role in ensuring that the rules are set in a way that more adequately reflects the interests and concerns of all countries, including developing countries.

As the rules for new technologies are being written, there are several areas of particular concern in which reforms in global governance would help developing countries better adapt to advances in AI.

A. A Global Tax Regime for the Digital Age

The inadequacies in the global tax regime make it difficult for developing countries to capture much of the rents that the global digital giants earn within their borders, even as their activities take away business from domestic firms and thereby reduce the domestic tax base. Indeed, even high-income countries have had difficulty with adequately taxing global tech giants. Some of the issues are now being discussed at the OECD in an attempt to establish a global tax regime.

The current global tax regime allows multinational firms to avoid much taxation—often paying taxes at rates markedly lower than local small businesses. It also impairs the ability of developing countries and emerging markets to tax the economic activity which occurs within their territories. This system is both inefficient and inequitable.

The controversy over digital taxation has exposed the deeper problems of multinational corporate taxation based on transfer prices, which are easily manipulated. The issue could be addressed by moving to a formulary apportionment system, whereby the worldwide profits of a corporation are apportioned to different countries according to a formula (see, e.g., Clausing and Avi-Yonah 2007). The exact formula could have large distributive effects across countries. For instance, a simple formula based just on sales, while less manipulatable than other formulae, may disadvantage developing countries. A particular controversy associated with the digital economy is the value assigned to the data that are collected in the process of economic transactions and how and whether that value should be taxed.

The broader debate over international taxation has also led to renewed attention on closing down fiscal paradises, on international initiatives for transparency in capital ownership, which would help developing countries to increase their tax base, and on creating a global minimum multinational corporate tax rate, to prevent a race to the bottom.

B. Global Competition Policy

The tendency of digital technologies to give rise to natural monopolies makes competition policy especially important. One challenge is that the countries in which tech giants are based have incentives to protect their own tech firms since they share in the rents that these firms earn globally. For example, when the European Union investigated Google for anti-competitive practices or when Germany investigated the privacy practices of Facebook, the United States treated it as a political question rather than a matter of economic policy and responded by accusing Europe of being anti-American. While the policy remedies suggested by the Europeans may have reduced the rents the companies could earn in Europe, their purported aim was to ascertain that these firms' practices did not violate the norms on competition and privacy established in Europe. The tendency for matters of competition policy to turn into arguments over rents may get worse, given the global concentration of market power in AI in two countries, China and the United States.

Individual developing countries and emerging market economies stand little chance in reining in the behaviors of powerful global corporations on their own—in many instances, the corporations have a higher market capitalization than the GDP of the countries in question. This makes it important for developing countries to coordinate and develop competition policy together, for example, via a common competition authority for developing and emerging economies that can exert sufficient power over large global corporations, just as the countries of Europe would not be able to police the competitive behavior of American corporations on their own but are able to do so through the European Union.

Given the breadth and reach of the new digital giants, there is a need for stronger rules preventing conflicts of interest for companies that simultaneously own a marketplace and participate in it, and stronger rules preventing preemptive mergers, i.e., mergers and acquisitions designed to stifle the threat of a competitive marketplace in the future. There will also be a need for more ex-post remediation: breaking up mergers when they prove to be anti-competitive.[37] As the experiences cited above have shown, the countries in which digital giants are based may not have the correct incentives to police these companies' competitive practices, given the large global rents that are at stake.

---

[37] There is by now a large literature describing the new competition policies that may be required. See Stiglitz (2019) and Wu (2018).

C. Intellectual Property Rights

The current system of intellectual property (IP) rights is designed to give (tempo-rary) monopoly rents to innovators to compensate and reward them for their innovative activities. There has been much concern in recent years that the pre-vailing IP system gives excessive protection to innovators, with particularly adverse effects on developing countries. As the World Commission on the Social Dimensions of Globalization (2004) emphasized, there is a need to rebalance the international IP regime to ensure an equitable distribution of the gains from tech-nological progress. Korinek and Stiglitz (2019) demonstrated that reducing the length of patent protection can ensure that the gains from AI-based innovations are better shared among society and can thus lead to a welfare improvement.

The most efficient way of distributing technological advances is to keep them in the public domain, financed via governments, international organizations, donors or charities. This avoids restrictions in access to new technologies and the creation of monopolies that concentrate rents and power. There is much scope for publicly financed research and development to benefit developing countries, for example, in the areas of agriculture where new technologies increase the produc-tivity of crops, or in healthcare where developing countries face unique challenges that do not attract sufficient research by private corporations in high-income countries.

When research and development is financed privately, there is a strong case for granting different patent protection in developing countries than in high-income economies. The length of patent protection trades off how much surplus to allo-cate to innovators to compensate them for their efforts versus how much to let the broader public benefit from an innovation. Most patents are developed in high-income countries and are financed by the surplus that innovators extract from the patent protection there; innovators would not incur significant losses if develop-ing countries could use their technology for free before their patents expire in high-income countries. Indeed, in many sectors, including pharmaceuticals, there is extensive cross-border price discrimination; drug companies could offer life-saving drugs to some of the poorest countries at steeply discounted prices. Compulsory licenses (part of TRIPS and other international agreements) give the right to access such life-saving IP at appropriate royalties, but many developing countries do not have the capacity to exercise those rights; and those that do have the capacity are intimidated from doing so by threats from developed countries. Trade agreements have done everything they can to impede access to generic medicines, forcing developing countries to pay high prices for drugs.

Before the advent of AI, it was clear that there was a need for a developmentally oriented IP regime—in some ways markedly different from that currently prevail-ing (Cimoli et al. 2014).

But AI has made the challenge of access to knowledge even greater. Part of the nature of AI is that it may not even need much protection by the patent system. Algorithms can be kept proprietary, and they are always evolving. Requiring disclosure of certain key algorithms is imperative to ascertain whether algorithms are discriminatory, for example, by engaging in price discrimination.[38]

D. Data and Information Policy

Data is a critical input underlying the new AI economy. That is why information policy—the rules governing the control over and use of data—has moved to the top of the policy agenda. Global tech firms are setting the data regulatory agenda in their interest without sufficient public oversight. This has already happened in recent trade agreements. For instance, while the new trade agreement between Canada, Mexico, and the United States had stronger provisions protecting labor and access to healthcare as well as better investor-state dispute settlement provisions, rules on the digital economy moved in the opposite direction, providing better protection for the tech giants. Being part of an international agreement, it may be difficult to change the data regulation regime in the future. This is particularly important for developing countries: the rules are currently being set with little concern for the views of citizens in the high-income countries, let alone those in the rest of the world.

Moreover, the monopolization of data by global AI firms also makes it more difficult for developing countries to catch up and develop their own AI-based companies. Global firms can use their access to vast troves of data from across the world to refine their products and offerings to consumers ever further. This makes it more and more difficult for newcomers in developing countries to close the gap between themselves and the leading firms.

Europe has actively worked on rules to ensure that the benefits of new digital technologies are shared and the harms are minimized. For instance, the EU has put forward proposals to require data sharing, with the goal of preventing accretion of monopoly power by monopolizing data. But giving control rights over data to individuals will not suffice; without proper regulation, individuals turn their data over to the digital giants and Internet providers, receiving but a pittance: asymmetries in information and power are just too great to ensure an equitable outcome.

---

[38] It is sometimes argued that such disclosure is not possible because algorithms are always evolving. While they are always changing, they could still be disclosed as of a particular moment in time. There are other (often costly) ways of monitoring the behavior of algorithms at any point in time.

New transparency regulations, for example, regarding the algorithms and targeting of advertising, are necessary, but again not sufficient. Policymakers must be able to address the discriminatory impacts of pricing and advertising.

There is also a need for stronger rules protecting privacy and the rapid spread of misinformation and messages that promote violence and hate as well as other harmful messaging, even when conducted as part of a political campaign. In the United States, the Section 230 provision which reduces the accountability of Internet companies—unlike other publishers—is an example of a regulation that should be reconsidered.

As in the case of competition policy, the countries in which tech giants are based may not face the correct incentives to police the worldwide behavior of their companies since they share in the rents that these companies earn around the world. Developing countries need to cooperate and band together to have sufficient clout to impose regulation on global giants that reflects their developmental interests.

VII. Conclusion

Advances in AI and related technologies may, like the Industrial Revolution, represent a critical turning point in history. Increasing automation in manufacturing may lead to increases in wage inequality, declining labor demand, and increased skill premia in most countries; as well as to the demise of the manufacturing-export-led developmental model, which has historically had profound positive effects on many emerging market economies. The worst-case scenario is the unraveling of much of the gains in development and poverty reduction that could be observed over the last half-century.

While earlier technological advances were associated with more shared prosperity and increasing equality between and within countries, the new advances may result in increasing inequality along both dimensions unless policies are designed to counterbalance them.

The new era will be governed by different rules and will require a different kind of economic analysis. Just as the production functions that Ricardo used to analyze agrarian and rural economies are very different from those in the models of a manufacturing economy that dominated the mid-twentieth century, current economic frameworks must be adjusted and updated to think about the models that will describe the next 50 years. For instance, the competitive equilibrium model may be even less relevant to the twenty-first-century AI economy than it was to the twentieth-century manufacturing economy.

There is a particularly high degree of uncertainty across the possible scenarios of technological development and their impact, but what we do know is that there are large potential downside risks that should not be ignored. Economic analysis, based on models appropriate to this new era, has the potential to help in the development of policies—both at the global and national level—that can mitigate these adverse effects, to ensure that this new era of innovation will lead to increased standards of living for all, including the billions living in developing countries.

References

Acemoglu, Daron. 1998. "Why Do New Technologies Complement Skills? Directed Technical Change and Wage Inequality." *Quarterly Journal of Economics* 113(4): 1055–89.

Acemoglu, Daron. 2002. "Directed Technical Change." *Review of Economic Studies* 69(4): 781–809.

Acemoglu, Daron, and David Autor. 2011. "Skills, Tasks and Technologies: Implications for Employment and Earnings." *Handbook of Labor Economics* 4b: 1043–1171.

Acemoglu, Daron, Andrea Manera, and Pascual Restrepo. 2020. "Does the US Tax Code Favor Automation?" *Brookings Papers on Economic Activity* 2020(1).

Acemoglu, Daron, and Pascual Restrepo. 2019a. "Automation and New Tasks: How Technology Displaces and Reinstates Labor." *Journal of Economic Perspectives* 33(2): 3–30.

Acemoglu, Daron, and Pascual Restrepo. 2019b. "Demographics and Automation." Unpublished Working Paper, MIT. https://economics.mit.edu/files/16788

Acemoglu, Daron, and Pascual Restrepo. 2020. "Robots and Jobs: Evidence from US Labor Markets." *Journal of Political Economy* 128(6): 2188–244.

Aghion, Philippe, Benjamin F. Jones, and Charles I. Jones. 2017. "Artificial Intelligence and Economic Growth," NBER WP 23928.

Alonso, Cristian, Andrew Berg, Siddharth Kothari, Chris Papageorgiou, and Sidra Rehman. 2020. "Will the AI Revolution Cause a Great Divergence?" IMF Working Paper 20/184.

Armstrong, Stuart, Kaj Sotala, and Seán S. ÓhÉigeartaigh. 2014. "The Errors, Insights and Lessons of Famous AI Predictions—and What They Mean for the Future." *Journal of Experimental & Theoretical Artificial Intelligence* 26(3): 317–42. http://www.fhi.ox.ac.uk/wp-content/uploads/FAIC.pdf

Arrow, Kenneth. 1962a. "Economic Welfare and the Allocation of Resources for Invention." In *The Rate and Direction of Inventive Activity: Economic and Social Factors*, edited by R. Nelson. Princeton, NJ: Princeton University Press.

Arrow, Kenneth. 1962b. "The Economic Implications of Learning by Doing." *The Review of Economic Studies* 29(3) (June): 155–73.

Atkinson, Anthony, and Joseph Stiglitz. 1969. "A New View of Technological Change." *Economic Journal* 79 (315): 573–8.

Autor, David H. 2019. "Work of the Past, Work of the Future," AEA Papers And Proceedings, Vol. 109, May 2019, pp. 1–32.

Autor, David, David Dorn, Lawrence F Katz, Christina Patterson, and John Van Reenen 2020. "The Fall of the Labor Share and the Rise of Superstar Firms." *Quarterly Journal of Economics* 135(2): 645–709.

Autor, David, Frank Levy, and Richard J. Murnane. 2003. "The Skill Content of Recent Technological Change: An Empirical Exploration." *Quarterly Journal of Economics* 118(4): 1279–333.

Berg, Andrew, Edward F.Buffie, and Luis-Felipe Zanna. 2018. "Should We Fear the Robot Revolution? (The Correct Answer Is Yes)." *Journal of Monetary Economics* 97: 117–48.

Boix, Carles. 2019. *Democratic Capitalism at the Crossroads: Technological Change and the Future of Politics*. Princeton, NJ: Princeton University Press.

Brussevich, Mariya, Era Dabla-Norris, Christine Kamunge, Pooja Karnane, Salma Khalid, and Kalpana Kochhar. 2018. "Gender, Technology, and the Future of Work," IMF Staff Discussion Note, SDN/18/07, October 2018.

Brynjolfsson, Erik, Avinash Collis, Erwin Diewert, Felix Eggers, and Kevin Fox. 2020. "Measuring the Impact of Free Goods on Real Household Consumption," *AEA Papers and Proceedings* 110: 25–30.

Brynjolfsson, Erik, Daniel Rock, and Chad Syverson. 2019. "Artificial Intelligence and the Modern Productivity Paradox: A Clash of Expectations and Statistics," *The Economics of Artificial Intelligence: An Agenda, Agrawal, Gans, and Goldfarb.*

Caselli, Francesco, and Alan Manning. 2019. "Robot Arithmetic: New Technology and Wages." *American Economic Review: Insights 2019* 1(1): 1–12.

Charlton, Andrew, and Joseph E. Stiglitz. 2005. *Fair Trade for All.* Oxford: Oxford University Press.

Choi, Eleanor J., and James R. Spletzer. 2012. "The Declining Average Size of Establishments: Evidence and Explanations." *BLS Monthly Labor Review*, March 2012. https://www.bls.gov/opub/mlr/2012/03/art4full.pdf

Cimoli, Mario, Giovanni Dosi, Keith E. Maskus, Ruth L. Okediji, Jerome H. Reichman, and Joseph Stiglitz (Eds.). 2014. *Intellectual Property Rights: Legal and Economic Challenges for Development.* Oxford: Oxford University Press.

Clausing, Kimberley, and Reuben Avi-Yonah. 2007. "Reforming Corporate Taxation in a Global Economy: A Proposal to Adopt Formulary Apportionment," *The Hamilton Project, Brookings Institution.*

Colmer, Jonathan, Ian Hardman, Jay Shimshack, and John Voorheis. 2020. "Disparities in PM2.5 air pollution in the United States." *Science* 369(6503): 575–8.

Comin, Diego, and Bart Hobijn. 2010. "An Exploration of Technology Diffusion." *American Economic Review* 100(5): 2031–59.

Delli Gatti, Domenico, Mauro Gallegati, Bruce Greenwald, Alberto Russo, and Joseph E. Stiglitz. 2012a. "Sectoral Imbalances and Long Run Crises." In *The Global Macro Economy and Finance*, edited by Franklin Allen, Masahiko Aoki, Jean-Paul Fitoussi, Nobuhiro Kiyotaki, Roger Gordon, and Joseph Stiglitz, *IEA Conference Volume* No. 150-III, Palgrave, pp. 61–97.

Delli Gatti, Domenico, Mauro Gallegati, Bruce Greenwald, Alberto Russo, and Joseph E. Stiglitz. 2012b. "Mobility Constraints, Productivity Trends, and Extended Crises." *Journal of Economic Behavior & Organization* 83(3): 375–93.

Ding, Jeffrey, Paul Triolo, and Samm Sacks. 2018. "Chinese Interests Take a Big Seat at the AI Governance Table," New America blog, June 20, 2018. https://www.newamerica.org/cybersecurity-initiative/digichina/blog/chinese-interests-take-big-seat-ai-governance-table/

Frey, Carl Benedikt, and Michael A. Osborne. 2017. "The Future of Employment: How Susceptible Are Jobs to Computerisation?" *Technological Forecasting and Social Change* 114: 254–80.

George, Henry. 1879. *Progress and poverty: An inquiry into the cause of industrial depressions, and of increase of want with increase of wealth, the remedy*, D. Appleton and Company.

Gilens, Martin. 2005. "Inequality and Democratic Responsiveness." *Public Opinion Quarterly* 69(5): 778–96.

Good, Irving John. 1965. "Speculations Concerning the First Ultraintelligent Machine." *Advances in Computers* 6, 31–88.

Gordon, Robert. 2016. *The Rise and Fall of American Growth: The U.S. Standard of Living since the Civil War*. Princeton, NJ: Princeton University Press.

Greenwald, Bruce, and Joseph Stiglitz. 1986. "Externalities in Economies with Imperfect Information and Incomplete Markets." *Quarterly Journal of Economics* 101(2), May, 229–64.

Greenwald, Bruce, and Joseph Stiglitz. 2006. "Helping Infant Economies Grow: Foundations of Trade Policies for Developing Countries." *American Economic Review: AEA Papers and Proceedings* 96(2), May 2006, 141–6.

Greenwald, Bruce, and Joseph Stiglitz. 2014a. *Creating a Learning Society: A New Approach to Growth, Development, and Social Progress*. New York: Columbia University Press.

Greenwald, Bruce, and Joseph E. Stiglitz. 2014b. "Industrial Policies, the Creation of a Learning Society, and Economic Development." In *The Industrial Policy Revolution I: The Role of Government Beyond Ideology*, edited by Joseph E. Stiglitz and Justin Yifu Lin, Palgrave Macmillan, pp. 43–71.

Harari, Yuval Noah. 2017. *Homo Deus: A Brief History of Tomorrow*, Harper.

Harris, Karen, Austin Kimson, and Andrew Schwedel. 2018. "Labor 2030: The Collision of Demographics, Automation and Inequality," Bain and Company Reports.

Kennedy, Charles. 1964. "Induced Bias in Innovation and the Theory of Distribution." *Economic Journal* LXXIV: 541–7.

Keynes, John Maynard. 1931. *Essays in Persuasion*. London: Macmillan.

Klinova, Katya, and Anton Korinek. 2021. "AI and Shared Prosperity," forthcoming in *Proceedings of the 2021 AAAI/ACM Conference on AI, Ethics, and Society* (AIES '21).

Korinek, Anton. 2019. "The Rise of Artificially Intelligent Agents," working paper, University of Virginia.

Korinek, Anton. 2020. "Taxation and the Vanishing Labor Market in the Age of AI." *Ohio State Technology Law Journal* 16(1): 244–57.

Korinek, Anton, and Megan Juelfs. 2021. "Preparing for the (Non-Existent?) Future of Work," technical report, Darden School of Business.

Korinek, Anton, and Ding Xuan Ng. 2019. "Digitization and the Macro-Economics of Superstars," working paper, University of Virginia.

Korinek, Anton, and Joseph E. Stiglitz. 2019. "Artificial Intelligence and Its Implications for Income Distribution and Unemployment." In Agrawal et al., *The Economics of Artificial Intelligence*, NBER and University of Chicago Press.

Korinek, Anton, and Joseph E. Stiglitz. 2020. "Steering Technological Progress," working paper.

Korinek, Anton, and Joseph E. Stiglitz. 2021a. "Artificial Intelligence, Globalization, and Strategies for Economic Development," NBER Working Paper w28453.

Korinek, Anton, and Joseph E. Stiglitz. 2021b. "Will Covid-19 Drive Advances in Automation and AI that Exacerbate Economic Inequality?" *BMJ 372:n367*.

Kurzweil, Ray. 2005. *The Singularity is Near*. London: Penguin Group.

Louie, Edward P., and Joshua M. Pearce. 2016. "Retraining investment for U.S. transition from coal to solar photovoltaic employment." *Energy Economics* 57: 295–302.

Maddison, Angus. 2003. *Contours of the World Economy 1–2030 AD: Essays in Macro-Economic History*. Oxford: Oxford University Press.

Malthus, Thomas R. 1798. *An Essay on the Principle of Population*. London: John Murray.

McKinsey Global Institute. 2017. "Jobs lost, jobs gained: What the future of work will mean for jobs, skills, and wages," McKinsey Reports.

McMillan, Margaret S., and Dani Rodrik. 2011. "Globalization, Structural Change and Productivity Growth," NBER Working Paper 17143.

Myrdal, Gunnar. 1968. *Asian Drama: An Inquiry into the Poverty of Nations*. Pantheon Books.

Nordhaus, William. 2015. "Are We Approaching an Economic Singularity? Information Technology and the Future of Economic Growth," *NBER Working Paper* No. 21547.

Organisation for Economic Co-operation and Development (OECD). 2019. *The Future of Work*. OECD Employment Outlook 2019.

Ostry, Jonathan, Prakash Loungani, and Andrew Berg. 2019. *Confronting Inequality: How Societies Can Choose Inclusive Growth.* New York: Columbia University Press.

Partnership on AI. 2021. *Redesigning AI for Shared Prosperity: An Agenda.* Technical Report. Available at: partnershiponai.org/shared-prosperity

Peralta-Alva, Adrian, and Agustin Roitman. 2018. "Technology and the Future of Work," IMF Working Paper WP/18/207. Also published as IMF Staff Note to Group of Twenty: April 2018.

Pritchett, Lant. 2019. "The Future of Jobs is Facing One, Maybe Two, of the Biggest Price Distortions Ever." *Economic Research Forum Working Paper* 1370. https://erf. org.eg/app/uploads/2019/12/1370.pdf

Rodrik, Dani. 2011. "Unconditional Convergence," NBER Working Paper w17546.

Romer, Paul M. 1986. "Increasing Returns and Long-Run Growth." *Journal of Political Economy* 94(5) (October): 1002–37.

Rubin, Richard. 2020. "The 'Robot Tax' Debate Heats Up," *Wall Street Journal,* January 20, 2020. https://www.wsj.com/articles/the-robot-tax-debate-heats-up-11578495608.

Sacks, Samms. 2018. "Beijing Wants to Rewrite the Rules of the Internet," *The Atlantic,* June 18, 2018. https://amp.theatlantic.com/amp/article/563033/

Saez, Emmanuel, and Gabriel Zucman. 2019. *The Triumph of Injustice: How the Rich Dodge Taxes and How to Make Them Pay.* W.W. Norton & Company.

Samuelson, Paul. 1965. "A Theory of Induced Innovations along Kennedy-Weisäcker Lines." *Review of Economics and Statistics* XLVII: 444–64.

Shapiro, Carl, and J. E. Stiglitz. 1984. "Equilibrium Unemployment as a Worker Discipline Device." *American Economic Review* 74(3), June 1984, 433–444.

Solow, Robert. 1987. "We'd Better Watch Out." *New York Times Book Review,* July 12, pp. 36.

Solow, Robert. 2009. "Does Growth Have a Future? Does Growth Theory Have a Future? Are These Questions Related?" *History of Political Economy* 41: 27–34.

Stiglitz, Joseph E. 1975a. "Information and Economic Analysis." In *Current Economic Problems,* edited by J.M. Parkin and A.R. Nobay. Cambridge: Cambridge University Press, pp. 27–52. (Proceedings of the Association of University Teachers of Economics, Manchester, England, April 1974.)

Stiglitz, Joseph E. 1975b. "The Theory of Screening, Education and the Distribution of Income." *American Economic Review* 65(3), June 1975, 283–300.

Stiglitz, Joseph E. 1987a. "On the Microeconomics of Technical Progress." In *Technology Generation in Latin American Manufacturing Industries,* edited by Jorge M. Katz. New York: St. Martin's Press, pp. 56–77. (Presented to IDB-CEPAL Meetings, Buenos Aires, November 1978.)

Stiglitz, Joseph E. 1987b. "Learning to Learn, Localized Learning and Technological Progress." In *Economic Policy and Technological Performance,* edited by P. Dasgupta and Stoneman. Cambridge: Cambridge University Press, pp. 125–53.

Stiglitz, Joseph E. 2006. "Samuelson and the Factor Bias of Technological Change." In *Samuelsonian Economics and the Twenty-First Century*, edited by M. Szenberg et al. New York: Oxford University Press, pp. 235–51.

Stiglitz, Joseph E. 2013. *The Price of Inequality: How Today's Divided Society Endangers Our Future*. New York: W.W. Norton & Company.

Stiglitz, Joseph E. 2014. "Unemployment and Innovation," *NBER Working Paper* no. 20670.

Stiglitz, Joseph E. 2015. "Leaders and followers: Perspectives on the Nordic model and the economics of innovation." *Journal of Public Economics, Elsevier*, 127(C): 3–16.

Stiglitz, Joseph E. 2018a. "From Manufacturing-Led Export Growth to a Twenty-First-Century Inclusive Growth Strategy: Explaining the Demise of a Successful Growth Model and What to Do About It," *WIDER Working Paper 2018/176 Helsinki: UNU-WIDER*, accessible at https://www.wider.unu.edu/publication/manufacturing-led-export-growth-twenty-first-century-inclusive-growth-strategy

Stiglitz, Joseph E. 2018b. "Pareto Efficient Taxation and Expenditures: Pre- and Re-distribution." *Journal of Public Economics Special Issue in Honor of Sir Tony Atkinson (1944–2017)*, 162, 101–19.

Stiglitz, Joseph E. 2019. *People, Power, and Profits: Progressive Capitalism for an Age of Discontent*. W.W. Norton & Company.

Stiglitz, Joseph E., Nell Abernathy, Adam Hersh, Susan Holmberg, and Mike Konczal. 2015. *Rewriting the Rules of the American Economy: An Agenda for Growth and Shared Prosperity*. W.W. Norton & Company.

Stiglitz, Joseph E., Carter Daugherty, and the Foundation for European Progressive Studies. 2019. *Rewriting the Rules of the European Economy: An Agenda for Growth and Shared Prosperity*. W.W. Norton & Company.

Summers, Lawrence. 2017. "Picking on robots won't deal with job destruction," *The Washington Post Opinion*, March 5, 2017.

Trajtenberg, Manuel. 2019. "Artificial Intelligence as the Next GPT: A Political-Economy Perspective," pp. 175–86. In *The Economics of Artificial Intelligence: An Agenda*, edited by Ajay Agrawal, Joshua Gans, and Avi Goldfarb. National Bureau of Economic Research and University of Chicago Press.

Ulam, Stanislaw. 1958. "Tribute to John von Neumann." *Bulletin of the American Mathematical Society* 64, #3, part 2, pp. 5.

Varian, Hal. 2020. "Automation versus procreation (aka bots versus tots)," VoxEU, https://voxeu.org/article/automation-versus-procreation-aka-bots-versus-tots

Von Weizsäcker, Carl. 1966. "Tentative Notes on a Two-Sector Model with Induced Technical Progress." *Review of Economic Studies* 33: 245–51.

Vinge, Vernor. 1993. "The Coming Technological Singularity: How to Survive in the Post-Human Era." In *Vision-21: Interdisciplinary Science and Engineering in the Era of Cyberspace*, edited by Geoffrey Landis, *NASA Publication* CP-10129, pp. 11–22. https://edoras.sdsu.edu/~vinge/misc/singularity.html

Walsh, Toby. 2016. "The Singularity May Never Be Near," https://arxiv.org/abs/1602.06462v1.

World Bank. 1998. *World Development Report 1998/1999: Knowledge for Development*, Oxford University Press. https://openknowledge.worldbank.org/handle/10986/5981

World Commission on the Social Dimension of Globalization. 2004. *A Fair Globalization: Creating Opportunities for All*, https://www.ilo.org/public/english/wcsdg/docs/report.pdf

Wu, Tim. 2018. *The Curse of Bigness: Antitrust in the New Gilded Age*, Columbia Global Reports.

6

Competition and Innovation

Philippe Aghion, Reda Cherif, and Fuad Hasanov

I. Introduction

The recent decades have witnessed an erosion of competition in many countries with important implications for inclusive growth.[1] This decline in competition intensity can be seen in the increase of market concentration as well as the ability of firms to influence prices, or market power. It is also seen in the decreasing level of business dynamism, that is, the rate at which new firms enter and old ones exit the market. Evidence shows that this process is taking place in both advanced and developing economies and over a large array of sectors. The economic literature suggests that less competition disproportionately hurts the poor, especially in developing economies, and that it contributes to rising inequalities and less inclusive growth. Moreover, business dynamism is important for innovation and economic growth to lift people out of poverty.

This chapter reviews the different perspectives on how competition, innovation, and their interrelation affect inclusive growth in various ways. Achieving sustained broad-based growth, that is, growth that is shared by a majority, is paramount to tackle poverty. While in many cases more competition would help generate better growth outcomes, there are also contexts where limiting competition could be desirable. For instance, resource misallocation among firms as a result of barriers to entry or the ability of underperforming firms to survive can inflict a large cost on the economy in terms of productivity growth. In contrast, some monopoly power, in the form of patents, could be potentially needed to give enough incentives for firms to take the risky investment for innovation, which in turn would lead to growth. Moreover, taxation for redistribution in a country could reduce inequality. However, it could potentially accelerate the brain drain (see Akcigit, Baslandze, and Stantcheva 2016 for the top 1 percent of

[1] We are grateful to Valerie Cerra, Woon Gyu Choi, Sharmini Coorey, Ruud De Mooij, Federico Diez, Barry Eichengreen, Asmaa El-Ganainy, Shafik Hebous, Roshan Iyer, Francesco Luna, Samuele Rosa, and Martin Schindler for excellent discussions and suggestions. We would also like to thank participants in the Inclusive Growth book seminar series organized by the IMF Institute for Capacity Development for helpful comments.

Philippe Aghion, Reda Cherif, and Fuad Hasanov, *Competition and Innovation* In: *How to Achieve Inclusive Growth.*
Edited by: Valerie Cerra, Barry Eichengreen, Asmaa El-Ganainy, and Martin Schindler, Oxford University Press.
© Philippe Aghion, Reda Cherif, and Fuad Hasanov 2022. DOI: 10.1093/oso/9780192846938.003.0006

inventors), especially in developing economies, and limit the country's ability to innovate, compete, and achieve broad-based growth. At the same time, without redistribution, high inequality would make it difficult for potential inventors from the bottom part of the income distribution to undertake such careers, which would lead to entrenched inequalities and less innovation and growth.

There are also tradeoffs between market concentration and efficiency. Large firms, holding a large share of the market, are able to take advantage of economies of scale and access sufficient resources to incur R&D fixed costs. But not all large firms are equal in terms of the provision of employment, good jobs, and their contribution to growth and equity. Moreover, they could also erect barriers to entry to reap their monopoly rents, further stifling competition and inclusive growth.

The relationship between competition and innovation and growth policies to achieve inclusiveness is also multifaceted. The consensus has been that the state should focus on providing an enabling environment, which includes a legal framework, infrastructure, skills and fair competition. However, the existence of externalities may lead to suboptimal outcomes, requiring state intervention to alter the allocation of resources. Some state interventions, such as past import-substitution policies, curtail international and domestic competition to tackle those externalities and may be counterproductive in the medium to long-run. In general, policymakers should be cognizant of the differential impact of state interventions.

The recent rise in market power has renewed policymakers' focus on competition policy. Although competition policies in many countries may not necessarily be weak, they may need to be revamped to address not only consumer welfare but also inclusiveness, monopsony powers, and potential effects on innovation and knowledge diffusion. Examining the impact of the market power and overcharging on the bottom income quintiles may help the poor more. Leveling the playing field for workers and suppliers bargaining with large firms or digital platforms could be beneficial. Antitrust policies dealing with intellectual property rights of Big Tech could also be an important instrument in fighting market power, especially when network effects are present and breaking off large firms is difficult.

In this chapter, we explore the debate in the literature on the interaction of innovation and competition with inclusive growth. We suggest that theory and evidence show that innovation, as exemplified by Schumpeterian creative destruction, may lead to higher inequality at the top although it may also help raise wages of workers in innovative firms. Competition, an important ingredient of these growth models, is a key to keeping the corporate power in check, which if left uncontrolled, tends to reduce innovation and broad-based growth and increase inequality.

II. The Rise of Market Power

A. Competition, Market Power, and Inclusive Growth in Advanced and Developing Countries

Competition plays a key role in determining market outcomes, and it affects inclusiveness in multiple ways. It not only matters for driving growth but also can affect the distribution of profits among firms and ultimately the distribution of earnings among their workers. It can also affect the bargaining power of workers in the labor market as well as of firms in the supply chain. It can also affect the relative prices of certain goods hurting disproportionately the poor (e.g., food and communication). Competition can also affect income and productivity growth through its effect on the production structure of the economy as well as incentives or disincentives to invest and innovate (e.g., intellectual property). In addition, as discussed in the previous section, competition is one of the key elements needed to support high sustained broad-based growth, an important precursor for inclusive growth.

To measure the level of competition in a market, economists rely on the concept of market power, which is understood as the ability of a firm to influence the market for its product. It is usually measured in terms of deviation from the theoretical case of perfect competition where firms are assumed to be price takers. The intensity of competition, and ability of firm to influence the market, is difficult to measure directly. Instead, the literature relies on indirect measures such as concentration indexes (e.g., Herfindahl index of market shares) or price markups. Market concentration is an intuitive measure; however, it is not necessarily indicative of market power (Syverson 2019).[2] Moreover, in many developing economies a comprehensive census of firms, including their market shares, is difficult to obtain. In recent literature, price markups, the gap between the price charged and an estimate of the marginal cost, are the measure chosen to estimate market power. It is particularly useful for developing economies as survey information may suffice for the calculations. In practice, it can be proxied by the ratio of sales or revenue to a measure of variable cost, which is closely related to profitability.

Using a large sample of firms from developing economies, IMF (2019a) finds large markups in Sub-Saharan Africa compared to other developing economies. Notwithstanding potential measurement issues and bias, it finds that Sub-Saharan African economies have greater average markups compared to other developing and emerging economies in most sectors, and the gap is especially big in non-tradable industries (Figure 6.1). It also finds that average markups in non-tradable sectors in developing countries could be greater than in tradable industries, and in particular manufacturing. Using firm-level data, it shows that greater markups

---

[2] See OECD (2018) for a discussion of the definitions related to market concentration and market power.

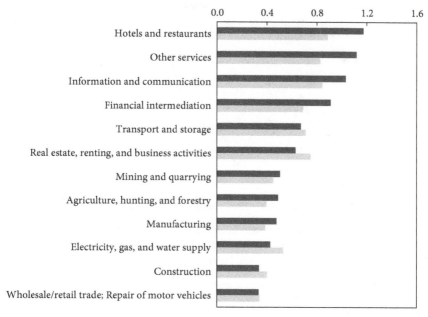

■ Sub-Saharan Africa   ▨ Emerging market economics and developing countries (excl. SSA)

Figure 6.1 Firm Markups by Sector: Emerging Markets and Developing Economies
Note: Based on Orbis data. Markup is defined as the log of the ratio of revenue turnover to costs.
Source: IMF (2019a).

are associated with lower labor share as well as lower investment, productivity growth and exports. These channels all point to an effect that is detrimental to the effort to decrease poverty and inequality.

There is also strong evidence of sizable and increasing market power in advanced economies (Figure 6.2). There is no corresponding rise in market power in emerging economies, although this does not preclude higher market power in these economies than that in advanced countries (IMF 2019b). De Loecker and Eeckhout (2020) document the rise in market power and profitability in the United States over the last decades and relate it to salient macroeconomic trends such as the decline in the labor income share and the decrease in labor market dynamics. Philippon (2019) argues that there exist extraordinary monopoly and oligopoly rents that are particularly detrimental to the interest of the poorest. In particular, he compares the United States to the EU, which have similar technologies. The dramatic change in communication costs in France after the entry of one additional operator (Free) in 2011 is a salient example. While costs were lower in the United States until 2011, they fell in relative terms by 40 percent within two years in France. Rising costs of communication, which represent a non-negligible share of the consumption basket (about 2 percent in the US

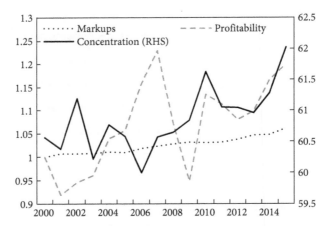

Figure 6.2 The Rise of Market Power in Selected Advanced Economies and Emerging Markets

Note: Based on Orbis data. The measure of profitability is the Lerner index, computed as the weighted average of firms' ratio of earnings before taxes to revenue. Concentration is computed as the ratio of sales of top four to top 20 firms within each country-sector bin and averaged across sectors (the median across countries is shown).

Source: IMF (2019b).

average) and is nowadays akin to a necessity, would hurt more the poor. A similar pattern would have an even stronger effect in developing economies.

The direct cost of anti-competitive behavior is high. Many studies estimate this cost by implied price overcharge, typically stemming from identified cartels. A common approach to estimating the price overcharge consists in applying a difference-in-difference technique, that is, by comparing prices in a market before and after an infringement was identified (e.g., a cartel) to a "counterfactual" market in a different location or product market where no infringement was identified.[3] The estimated price overcharges in advanced economies are found to be large on average, ranging from 15 to about 50 percent. Ivaldi et al. (2016) extends these estimations to 20 developing economies, using a database of over 200 major cartel episodes over 1995–2013. They estimate that the harm to the economy in terms of excess profits resulting from price overcharges could reach about 4 percent of GDP, accounting for the probability of undetected cartels. The cost of cartels could extend to overcharges in intermediate goods, ultimately affecting finished products, as well as procurement of public goods, or it could also affect the economy through a reduction in output (World Bank-OECD 2017). Even without cartels, anti-competitive behavior would result in higher prices and lower production.

---

[3] See World Bank-OECD (2017) for a summary of methods to estimate price overcharges resulting from anti-competitive behavior and for a review of empirical studies.

There is also growing evidence that the lack of competition not only affects more strongly the poorest countries but also hurts the poor more in each country. Higher market power in food, beverages and medicines was shown to be regressive, that is, they hurt more the poorest, as shown using Mexican data (Urzua 2013). Similar results exist in the context of advanced countries (e.g., Creedy and Dixon 1998 and 2000). There is also evidence that prices in Sub-Saharan Africa are higher than in other developing regions, controlling for income and other factors. The extra cost of living in this region is negatively correlated with aggregate measures of competition (IMF 2019a). Ennis et al. (2017), using a calibrated model on a selected group of advanced countries, find that market power could be responsible for a sizable increase in the wealth of the richest 10 percent and a large reduction in the income of the poorest 20 percent.

The decline in the labor share has also been interpreted as a sign of rising market power. Labor share has been decreasing in the United States and other advanced economies (IMF 2019b). This decline in labor share could be explained to a large extent as a result of the Information Technology (IT) revolution as argued by Aghion and others (2019). This revolution allowed superstar firms to expand into many sectors of the economy. As these firms have higher markups and lower labor shares than non-superstar firms, the decline in aggregate labor share and corresponding increase in aggregate markups reflect a "composition effect." In other words, it is not the result of a within-firm increase in markup or a decline in labor share. Evidence of the predominance of a "between-firm" (or "composition") effect over a "within-firm" effect is provided by De Locker and Eeckout (2019) and Baqaae and Farhi (2019). IMF (2019b) shows that the "reallocation" effect is pronounced in the United States but less so in other advanced countries. The long-term effect of this increasing hegemony of superstar firms has been to discourage innovation and entry by non-superstar firms, thereby leading to a decrease in aggregate productivity growth, broad-based growth, and business dynamism. This increasing hegemony, in turn, has been facilitated by an insufficient regulation of mergers and acquisitions, in other words by a competition policy, which has not adapted to the digital economy.

B. Tycoons and Big Firms: The Good and the Bad

Economic theory does not rule out situations where high concentration, and the associated high returns have benefits for society at large. In situations where there are economies of scale, concentration would lead to an overall increase in productivity. Alternatively, the hope of extracting monopoly rents from a dominant position, thanks to a patent for example, justifies the risk taken by innovators. In turn innovation would help increase productivity. Some argue that the rise of market concentration over the last decades in advanced countries reflects both the innovations and early investment in information technologies and the implied productivity gains (e.g., Bessen 2017; Aghion et al. 2019). If this is indeed the case, innovative firms should be investing more, and eventually other firms would use the same innovative processes and infrastructure. In turn, at the aggregate level, productivity and investment rates should be rising.

On a global level, domestic large firms in sophisticated sectors play a critical role in taking advantage of economies of scale and concentrating resources to absorb both frontier managerial and technological processes, especially when competing in international export markets (see Chandler 1991 and Cherif and Hasanov 2019). The sophisticated sectors are defined as highly R&D intensive such as advanced manufacturing and high-tech services (Cherif and Hasanov 2019). These firms provide directly a large number of good-paying jobs, but also support productivity gains and growth through their critical contribution to exports and spillovers (see Freund and Pierola 2016). Their success does not stem from generating rents from commodities or non-tradables, rather from producing and exporting. High broad-based growth helps achieve improvements in the living standards of workers in the rest of the economy, including non-tradable services. Samsung and Hyundai are very large and profitable firms relative to the Korean market. This success comes as a result of fierce competition on international markets in sophisticated sectors, requiring taking risks and investing substantially in both physical and human capital. They also employ a significant share of skilled and unskilled Korean workers at relatively high wages. More important, their success on international markets, representing more than a third of total exports, results in total productivity gains and rising incomes. This largely contributes to the difference in living standards between, for example, a taxi driver in Korea compared to the same in developing countries, although they provide exactly the same service with the broadly same productivity.

However, as observed by Baker (2019) and others, these developments have failed to show up in the aggregate investment and productivity numbers, at least in the US context, and the above explanation is only part of the story. It is also likely that the same dynamics are at work in many other advanced nations. In addition, a myriad of stylized facts, broadly described by the lack of business dynamism such as a decrease in the rate of creation of new enterprises, point to the other plausible reason for the rise of market concentration—an increase in market power as a result of hidden and explicit barriers to entry. These barriers could also be related to regulations, which could be partially encouraged by the same firms benefitting from them. The typical examples of a barrier to entry would be wireless phone licenses or zoning policies. Zoning policies limit the supply of housing in cities, leading to a rapid increase in the existing real estate assets as well as high returns for the few developers who have access to land (see Furman and Orszag 2015). This has implications on inequality on several levels. It prices out families with modest means, known as gentrification with its many social and psychological negative effects, and prevents others to move from less dynamic to more dynamic cities, where social lifts are more effective (see Hsieh and Moretti 2019).

A large firm dominating a domestic market in a developing economy, thanks to tariffs and other explicit or implicit barriers to entry, would be detrimental to both growth and its inclusiveness. Typically, large firms in low-income countries or resource-dependent ones would dominate a non-tradable service sector, such as telecommunication, construction or banking, without yielding significant employment, spillovers or productivity gains. The additional price they impose, and lower levels of investment, would lead to a bad quality of services as well as higher prices, directly harming the society's welfare. Higher prices could also harm international competitiveness and in turn keep the real exchange rate over-valued, reducing the prospects of improvements in living standards of workers.

An indirect way to study the issue of supernormal returns of large firms and inequality across the developing world is to study high-wealth individuals, who are behind those firms, or tycoons, (see Freund and Oliver 2016). To paraphrase their conclusions, all developing countries have tycoons with powerful connections to the state, but there is a fundamental difference between a tycoon whose wealth is derived from competing on international markets and supplying a good product and a tycoon benefitting from barriers to entry and focusing on the domestic market, for instance, an importer with exclusive rights or domestic producer of non-tradables such as construction (Freund and Oliver 2016). For the former kind of tycoons, international competition would also limit cronyism and encourage offering good salaries to skilled workers to retain them. It would also encourage long-term investment in domestic capabilities. For the latter kind of tycoons, the opposite is true.

C. The Rise of Big Tech

The important question is what explains these supernormal returns. On the one hand, as noted earlier, the rise of market power is a likely culprit as shown by different studies on the rise of market power in the last decades (see IMF 2019b). Evidence shows that most firms in the upper tail of the distribution are in the health and information technology sectors although there are also large firms in the retail and energy sectors (e.g., Walmart). This should not come as a surprise given the evidence about the high median wages in the top technology companies such as Google and Facebook, are more than four times the average wage in the same sector in the United States (see Autor et al. 2017 and Gutierrez and Philippon 2017). This confirms the largely shared view that the nature of certain sectors implies a "winner-takes-all" outcome. This in turn leads to a wide dispersion in wages among firms and workers even within the same sector and at comparable levels of technology and skills.

As large firms today are mostly in the information technology sector, one of the key issues of dealing with inequality is to a large extent related to the discussion about the rise of technology giants and how to deal with them. The increasing global interconnectedness contributed to the rise of Big Tech. Moreover, the presence of scale and uniqueness has also helped create "superstars" in many markets (Krueger 2019). In this regard, the current situation is similar to the rise of the telephone network in the United States in the first half of the twentieth century. A new technology was invented that led to what was described as a "network effect." That is, if an additional user joins the network, it benefits all the other users, encouraging newcomers and creating a feedback loop. Eventually, the sector which had several phone networks operating at the same time early on, came to be largely dominated by AT&T, as an early version of today's "tech giants."

The rise and dominance of FAANG (Facebook, Amazon, Apple, Netflix, and Google) and other tech giants stem from the same mechanism. A social network such as Facebook displays the typical network effect. Its value is enhanced when an additional user joins, and at the same time entices others to join as well. However, the feedback effect is not only limited to networks of users. It could also extend to platforms linking users and "suppliers" with potentially even stronger "winner-takes-all" effect and deeper economic implications. Suppose a platform links two networks: a network of users such as consumers or businesses to a network of suppliers of goods or services. Then, if an additional user joins the platform, in theory the value of the network for existing users does not necessarily *directly* increase. However, the value of the network of suppliers increases for all suppliers, encouraging more of them to join. In turn, the new suppliers would add to the value of the network of users to all users. This type of feedback effect would explain the dominance of platforms such as Amazon, linking consumers to goods' suppliers; Uber, linking passengers to drivers (service suppliers); or Alibaba, linking businesses in demand of intermediate goods and services to businesses supplying them.

D. The Consequences of Big Tech

The consequences of the rise of the giant platforms are multiple. The exclusive access to a large amount of data about users or suppliers in a network or platform can reinforce the market power of tech giants. The access to a large trove of personal data from a social network can help devise personalized advertisement methods, including in political campaigns, which is difficult to compete with without this access. Self-driving technology or personalized health services are other examples where the exclusive access to users' data can give a critical advantage to a firm and create monopolies. For example, while Tesla has accumulated millions of hours of drivers' data to develop its self-driving technology, other firms must rely on simulations to develop self-driving capabilities. Overall, this raises important questions about privacy, data ownership, and portability.

More important, the platforms give rise to a new type of "monopsony" power. A large set of freelance workers and suppliers must sell their goods and services through one or very few platforms to access their consumers. With a limited bargaining power for the suppliers, such a situation could lead to an increase in overall inequality although the price of the end-product or service could be competitive. For example, if the platform offers a luxury good or a service and it is mostly consumed by the upper middle-class or the rich, then a lower price would help their welfare. Meanwhile, small and medium-size suppliers and freelance or gig workers, providing the good or service, could see their welfare decrease substantially with low prices as payments for their services would be relatively low as well. If these suppliers are relatively poor or in the lower middle-class, then the result is an increase in inequality. One could argue that the platforms offer an efficiency gain to the economy, but it could be a one-time increase in efficiency followed by monopoly rents. If the platform generates supernormal returns, there could be room to use the efficiency of the platform technology while limiting the erosion of the welfare of suppliers. Ride-sharing services are likely to fall into this category.

One could argue that the issue of Big Tech is mostly relevant to advanced and some emerging economies. However, the dominance of these firms extends beyond borders and encompasses most of developing countries in environments where local institutions have little capacity to negotiate or enforce regulations. Several of these tech giants have annual revenues exceeding the GDP of most low-income countries. Platforms such as ride-sharing services have been cloned in many developing economies, potentially creating local monopolies.

At the same time, there are positive effects of platform economies. Increase in efficiency and decline in search costs, reduction in consumer prices for goods and services, decline in potential costs of doing business, and provision of opportunities for new businesses cannot be underestimated. What becomes clear is that policy intervention should target negative effects rather than use a broad-brush approach.

E. Big Agriculture and Inclusiveness

No other sector exemplifies better the links between efficiency gains and technological advancement, intra- and international market concentration and competition and their effect on inclusive growth than the agroindustry. Indeed, while agricultural production plays a key role in the economies of low-income countries, comprising mostly small-scale farms with little access to capital and inputs, these producers face an unsurmountable challenge to become internationally competitive. In contrast, modern agriculture in advanced and emerging economies has moved toward highly mechanized and large-scale producers, often financed by domestic agricultural development banks, to take advantage of economies of scale. This has generated formidable productivity gains in those countries over the last decades. For example, total factor productivity in the agricultural sector doubled in the United States over the last four decades (Wang et al. 2020). In developing countries, these large productivity gains and spillovers and linkages with the rest of the economy could be important for reducing poverty and producing shared prosperity.

Moreover, food producers in many advanced and emerging economies receive substantial production subsidies, and until relatively recently sizable export subsidies. For example, agricultural subsidies represent the biggest share of the budget of the European Union (more than a third in 2020). These policies have a strong rural development and food security rationale and they help the world be more resilient to shocks, but they also have important implications on inequality at both the national and international levels. For example, the provision of production subsidies in proportion to the size of the farm implies that smallest 25 percent of EU farmers receive less than 1.5 percent of total subsidies, while the largest 20 percent receive 80 percent, showing large disparities in the support received.[4] Moreover, given the large share of agricultural production in employment in low-income countries, usually the largest sector, these countries are not competitive enough and cannot develop their agricultural sectors, negatively affecting inclusive growth. In other words, although advanced economies' subsidies may be aiming at ensuring resilience in food production, they may also be undercutting agricultural production and employment in low-income countries. International coordination is warranted to reconsider food security policies of advanced countries and their implications on inequality and poverty in developing countries, without jeopardizing the resilience of the global food supply.

As an illustration, the rise of market concentration has been stark in the market of agricultural inputs.[5] In the United States, the market share of the four largest producers of seeds, fertilizers and farm pharmaceuticals have increased markedly since the 1990s reaching more than 50 percent. For corn and soy producers, for example, seeds represent a relatively large share of the cost, which means that an increase in price would affect them disproportionately. In this sector, concentration

---

[4] https://www.europeandatajournalism.eu/eng/News/Data-news/1.6-million-farmers-receive-almost-85-percent-of-the-EU-s-agricultural-subsidies.
[5] https://www.americanprogress.org/issues/economy/reports/2019/05/07/469385/fair-deal-farmers

of four firms reached more than 85 percent. Although investment in R&D has led to important innovations in biotechnology, the 6 largest players have been responsible for the vast majority of acquisitions of innovative biotechnology start-ups. As a result of a wave of consolidations and acquisitions, the bulk of important intellectual property rights in this domain is owned by few dominant actors.[6] There is growing evidence that those dominant actors are erecting steep barriers to entry through strategic licensing and protective patents. This implies less bargaining power for farmers as well as a curtailment of future innovation and competition by smaller firms. These developments have negative implications on firms and their workers along the whole supply chain that compete with giants of the industry.

In terms of inclusiveness in developing countries, the stakes are even higher, especially regarding genetically modified seeds. Although these new technologies would spur productivity gains providing more resistant crops, an extensive market power by a few dominant firms could undermine the returns to farmers, especially small farmers. The US market of soybean and corn gives an idea of the dynamics at play. Although soybeans and corn yield per acre have increased over the period 1985–2011 by about 19 and 30 percent, respectively, the prices of those seeds per acre have increased by 325 and 259 percent, respectively.[7] The late 1990s saw the rise of "terminator" gene-edited seed which yielded crops unable to produce a second generation of seeds. This is particularly worrying in terms of the potential negative effects on poverty alleviation and development in low-income countries. In Sub-Saharan Africa, two-thirds of the population consists of smallholder farmers. They would suffer tremendously if they lose access to replanting while facing the market power of dominant multinationals (Zerbe 2001). National antitrust policies, international coordination, and local initiatives to develop seed industries are urgently needed to tackle these far-reaching challenges.

III. Competition, Innovation, and Inequality

As discussed earlier, there could be a tradeoff between growth and innovation on the one hand and inequality on the other hand. One of the key ideas in growth theory is based on Schumpeter's insight of "creative destruction." According to this view, new entrants in a sector are innovators, which could take the form of a

---

[6] See Moss, "Testimony Before the U.S. Senate Judiciary Committee, Consolidation and Competition in the U.S. Seed and Agrochemical Industry" and Bryant and others, "Effects of Proposed Mergers and Acquisitions Among Biotechnology Firms on Seed Prices."
[7] National Agricultural Statistics Service, "Acreage" (Washington: U.S. Department of Agriculture, 1996), available at https://downloads.usda.library.cornell.edu/usda-esmis/files/j098zb09z/7w62fb474/zw12z7657/Acre-06-28-1996.pdf; National Agricultural Statistics Service, "Acreage" (Washington: U.S. Department of Agriculture, 2012), available at https://downloads.usda.library.cornell.edu/usda-esmis/files/j098zb09z/6395w898j/db78tf232/Acre-06-29-2012.pdf.

new good, technology or process. These innovators would capture a share of revenues eventually forcing incumbent firms to exit. The endogenous growth theory of Aghion and Howitt (1992) offers a framework in which a higher rate of entry and exit would lead to higher growth highlighting the crucial role of innovation in sustaining growth. A standard interpretation of this theory indicates that there is a link between innovation and intellectual property rights protection, which in turn curtails competition. Indeed, in standard models, the incentive to innovate stems from the perspective of extracting rents from a monopoly power, typically thanks to a patent or industrial secret. An increase in competition, for example by shortening a patent's life, would put a lid on these future rents, which could discourage innovation and growth. This is directly related to inclusive growth. A more stringent intellectual property right regime to spur innovation and growth, stifling competition to ensure more monopoly power, could in fact lead to more income concentration and inequality.

However, several firm-level empirical studies suggest a somewhat different picture. For example, Blundell, Griffith, and Van Reenen (1999) and Nickell and Van Reenen (2002) show that sectoral productivity growth increases with the level of competition. Moreover, Aghion and others (2005) and IMF (2019b) have shown that the relationship between competition, measured by the rates of entry and exit, and innovation, measured by the number of patents, follows an inverted-U relationship. In other words, at low levels of competition, increasing competition would lead to more innovation and the opposite would happen at very high levels of competition.

These results could be reconciled with economic theory once the heterogeneity of firms in terms of productivity is introduced. As shown by Aghion and others (2005), the distinction between frontier firms and laggards firms leads to a stark difference in terms of their respective reaction to heightened competition. The laggard firms, which are already far from the frontier, are discouraged from investing in innovation with more competition as it is harder to catch up. In contrast, best performers would increase their investment in innovation to keep their position close to the frontier. The models' prediction is confirmed by a study using UK firms (Aghion et al. 2009). They show that the relationship between the rate of entry by foreign firms, a proxy for competition, and innovation, measured by patents, differs for frontier firms and laggard ones. More competition would lead to more innovation among frontier firms and to less innovation among laggards, as predicted by the theory. Thus, to support innovation while minimizing concentration and potential negative implications on inclusive growth, both too little and too much competition may be counterproductive.

In addition, Aghion and coauthors (2016), using the Schumpeterian endogenous growth model, argue that although innovation by incumbents and entrants increases top income inequality, it does not increase the Gini coefficient while innovation by entrants increases social mobility. Higher innovation increases the entrepreneurial share of income, and new firms and employees not only provide more opportunities to be future business owners but also create role models to follow. They confirm in the cross-state and commuting zone data in the United States that innovation is positively related with top income inequality (1 percent) but has negative or no relationship with the broad measure of inequality like the Gini coefficient. More important, the authors find that creative destruction, or innovation by entrants, makes growth more inclusive and increases social mobility.

There is evidence pointing to the fact that inventors represent a sizable share of top income earners, and the rise in inequality observed over the last decades reflects the rapidly rising returns on innovation (Aghion et al. 2019). Therefore, studying the factors affecting inventors, such as parental income or taxation is key to understanding the dynamics of inequality and social mobility.

Income inequality among families could negatively affect innovation and in turn stifle social mobility. Studies show that there is a positive relationship between parental income and the chance of children becoming innovators (Bell et al. 2019 and Akcigit et al. 2018). These studies find a J-curve relationship such that the probability of a child becoming an inventor is mostly flat for parental income below the 20th percentile then it rises rapidly. More detailed analyses have shown that intrinsic abilities, such as math scores, do matter. But at the same time, for equivalent intrinsic abilities, parental income has a sizable influence on the chances of becoming an inventor.

Redistribution using taxation and transfers is a key tool in tackling inequality but increasing top personal income tax rates could potentially undermine the incentive to innovate although further research is needed. One plausible channel would be through the link between taxation and the "brain drain." Innovators and skilled workers, who depend mostly on their human capital as opposed to physical capital, are likely to be highly mobile and particularly sensitive to changes in the tax regime. This hypothesis is studied by Akcigit, Baslandze, and Stantcheva (2016). They construct an index to compare inventors in terms of the importance of their invention based on future citations. More citations indicate a greater value of a patent. They find that there is a negative relationship between the marginal tax rate of the highest income bracket and the fraction of "superstar" inventors, the top 1 percent according to their index, who remain in their country. This correlation disappears for the other inventors. This result was confirmed using quasi-natural experiments. For example, the dissolution of the Soviet Union in 1991 led to a massive migration of inventors and data show that they were more likely to immigrate to countries where the tax rate was lower. Moreover, Akcigit and others (2018) use a comprehensive dataset of US patents, citations, and inventors since 1920 to track the effects of variation in income and corporate tax rate among U.S. states and through time. They find that, everything else being equal, a greater tax rate decreases the number of patents, citations as well as inventors. At the same time, higher personal income taxes could support various redistribution programs and keep inequality and poverty lower, helping generate more superstar inventors.

But why would this have a meaningful effect on innovation if it concerns a minority of inventors? It is plausible that innovation follows the type of granularity observed in many fields where "superstars" dominate, including sports, music, and cities (Krueger 2019 and Gabaix 2009). Indeed, a minority of inventors are behind patents that are focal in the sense that they generate a lot of dynamic spillovers to the rest of the economy. The issue of the tradeoff between taxation and attracting innovators could be similar to the relationship between tax incentives and foreign direct investment (FDI). High personal income tax may or may not matter much, but a harmful inter and (intra) national race to the bottom would be detrimental to all.

IV. Competition and Growth Policies for Inclusive Growth

To promote inclusive growth, that is increasing broad-based growth and lowering inequality, considering innovation and competition is paramount. In the following section, we discuss salient competition and growth policies and highlight key elements needed for those policies to promote inclusive growth.

A. Competition Policies to Promote Inclusiveness

To tackle anti-competitive behavior and spur competition, World Bank-OECD (2017), adapting Kitzmuller and Martinez Licetti (2012), offers a comprehensive policy framework along two broad avenues. First, reforms should aim at tackling both regulations and government actions that represent implicit barriers to entry or are conducive to vested interests and collusion (e.g., licenses, tariffs, and access to public goods). Second, setting up the needed institutions with sufficient autonomy, resources, and authority to enforce rules and regulations is necessary.[8] One priority would be to improve the detection of anti-competitive behavior of local and international operators. Studies show that a non-negligible share of cartels are not identified in advanced countries every year, which makes the issue even more pressing in developing countries (in Europe, for example, more than 10 percent according to Combe, Monnier, and Legal 2008, compared to about 25 percent in the context of developing countries in Ivaldi et al. 2016, using the same

---

[8] See IMF (2019a) for a discussion in the context of Sub-Saharan Africa.

methodology). Another important role of competition authorities consists in the control of anti-competitive mergers to prevent the direct rise in market power or, indirectly, through increased collusions.

Given the limited resources of competition authorities, product markets affecting particularly the poor could be prioritized (IMF 2019a and World Bank-OECD 2017). For example, food and beverages represent a large share of the consumption basket of low-income households, especially in developing countries, that is typically 30–40 percent. The price of inputs that are key to the production of small firms, such as fertilizers for farmers, would also have a disproportionate effect on the poor. Moreover, these sectors have usually features that are conducive to anti-competitive behavior such as import barriers, concentration of importers, low price elasticity, and barriers to entry (see World Bank 2016).

It is also necessary to take into account the broader context of competition policies, including the international environment. For example, tariff reductions on staple food that is highly subsidized in advanced countries could wipe out large numbers of small producers, ultimately leading to unemployment and even more pressure on wages in the absence of dynamic sectors. Moreover, a small share in the consumption basket could be a misleading indicator of potential welfare gains. For example, medicines have typically a low share among low-income households but the introduction of regulation encouraging the entry of generic drugs could massively decrease their price with potentially large effects on health outcomes (see Tenn and Wendling 2014). Finally, instead of focusing on sectors representing a large share of consumption among low-income households, it could be more effective to identify the anti-competitive behaviors (e.g., in energy sector or the imports of machinery in manufacturing) that limit the growth of dynamic sectors that have high paying jobs.

Since the 1980s, most developing countries have followed comprehensive "liberalization" policies to let markets emerge, mostly by tackling price controls, lowering tariffs, dismantling SOEs, and deregulating capital and financial markets. In parallel, there has also been progress in the adoption of competition laws and the establishment of competition agencies, especially in the 2000s. However, the intensity of competition in many developing countries remains significantly lower than in emerging and developed economies (IMF 2019a).

A major obstacle faces developing economies in ensuring competition while liberalizing. Beyond the legal framework, the institutions in charge of competition need to be well funded, staffed with competent and non-corrupt civil servants, and bestowed with full autonomy. These conditions are drastic for countries that suffer from weak institutions and lack of resources and capabilities in the first place. Privatization without proper competition regulation and oversight could be counterproductive in critical natural monopoly sectors such as power utilities if it leads to under-investment and over-charging. As argued by Armstrong and Sappington (2006), one must distinguish between liberalization policies that "generally are procompetitive from corresponding anticompetitive liberalization policies." Moreover, with the advent of Big Tech, competition agencies should be better equipped to be able to regulate the digital economy while preserving efficiency gains.

As for advanced economies, many have argued that there was a shift in the 1980s toward a different understanding of undue market power in the United States, focusing on consumer welfare and prices (Phillips Sawyer 2019). If companies charge low prices, or even provide free services, it cannot be argued that a monopoly is harming consumer welfare. This is in contrast with the older view, or the Harvard interpretation, that competition was a goal aiming at minimizing undue concentration of political power, among others. There is evidence that over this period anticompetitive practices and non-competitive market structures have contributed to the dominance of large firms in key industries of the US economy. This dominance was also translated into political influence, further entrenching their position (Khan and Vaheesan 2017). The recent trend indicates that there could be a need to recalibrate antitrust regulation. Some argue that the latter should adopt tackling inequality as an explicit aim instead of the narrow understanding of consumer welfare based on prices in a single sector (Baker and Salop 2015). However, it is not clear how to impose more competition in sectors exhibiting network externalities.

Beyond strengthening competition laws and competition agencies in charge of applying them, there is also a need to formulate a new paradigm to incorporate specifically inequality in the competition framework. In most economies, it means more funds and incentives to prosecute anti-trust cases even when they involve local or foreign firms with powerful backing.

The information technology and artificial intelligence revolutions may not only have a positive impact but also produce large negative effects on the economy, and there is a need for competition policy to tackle them. Indeed, these technological developments may contribute to a rise in aggregate rents, the fall in aggregate labor share, and the fall in growth and business dynamism. Gilbert (2020) argues that in the United States, competition policy should tackle this issue as it did not prevent the hegemony of superstar firms. Going forward, it should move away from a "static" view of competition policy, largely focused on market definition and market power to a more "dynamic" view focused on spurring innovation and encouraging the entry of new firms.

Gilbert (2020) also argues that instead of overhauling anti-trust legislation, it should be adapted to spur "dynamic competition," and market definition should not be based on existing markets. Moreover, when assessing a merger or acquisition, the potential effects on innovation, firm entry, and on other markets should also be considered.

The case of AT&T, which established Bell Labs in the early century to conduct its R&D in communication technology to showcase its contribution to society and avoid antitrust actions illustrates the importance of antitrust policy to spur technology diffusion. In 1958, the US government took an antitrust decision giving Bell Labs' existing patents for free to all national companies and imposed a small license fee for future ones. Facklet et al. (2017) showed that this decision had a sizable effect on innovation in the United States. It is remarkable that Bell Labs contributed directly to the invention of many far-reaching technologies such as radar, transistors, and satellite technologies, and its mathematicians and statisticians contributed with important theories such as information theory and quality control. The antitrust policy of the time helped through the implicit pressure to engage in significant R&D at Bell Labs. The decision of 1958 accelerated the diffusion of the technologies created to the rest of the economy, contributing to the creation of new sophisticated sectors and good-paying jobs.

In general, going beyond pricing, the issue of size is important to tackle and has been a central issue already by the turn of the twentieth century as argued by Lamoreaux (2019) with cases such as Standard Oil. Indeed, policymakers managed a balancing act to protect society against the dangers of size without punishing firms that grew large because they were innovative. The key to success of the antitrust regime of the time was to focus on large firms' conduct toward competitors and banning practices that were anticompetitive or exclusionary. In this regard, a stakeholder approach to corporations, beyond a narrow shareholder view, may also produce fairer outcomes.

B. Growth Policies to Alleviate Poverty and the Role of Competition

There is a positive correlation between long-term growth and poverty alleviation. More specifically, Lant Pritchett argues, based on cross-country patterns, that "broad-based growth, defined as the process that raises median income, is far and away the most important source of poverty reduction."[9] The sharp decline in poverty rates in China (about 800 million people escaped poverty) amid the two decades of break-neck growth is the starkest illustration. As discussed, innovation-based growth based on Schumpeterian creative destruction is key to productivity gains and sustained growth. The question is how to achieve broad-based, high and sustained growth which means to spur the emergence of good-paying jobs. This is perhaps one of the most difficult and debated questions in economics.

The standard view shared by most economists over the last few decades is that "horizontal policies," that is improvements in education, the quality of institutions, infrastructure, business environment, and regulations are key. Many of these policies tackle what is known as "government failures" as described in

---

[9] See https://econofact.org/poverty-reduction-and-economic-growth.

Rodrik (2005). In other words, state intervention should limit itself to providing public goods and the provision of a good environment while crucially ensuring an adequate level of competition. In this context, firms would have the incentive to invest and deploy efforts to be competitive through improvements in productivity and innovation to offer new and better-quality goods among others.

However, growth can be harmed by anti-competitive behaviors or distortive policies which can take different and subtle forms and are not always easy to gauge. Among these, imposing barriers to entry or helping non-performing firms remain in business, could have a substantial negative effect. Hsieh and Klenow (2009) emphasize the importance of input reallocation effects. They show that aggregate productivity differentials can be explained by differences in terms of the distribution of firms' productivity. This means that firms that are relatively less productive have access to a considerable share of the resources. They argue that it is harder for a more productive firm to grow but also easier for a less productive firm to survive in India than in the United States. In the same vein, Aghion (2016) suggests that that there is more business dynamism in the United States than India, that is, more firms enter and exit, which would explain input misallocation and differences in income per capita.

Compared to the United States, potential constraints in developing economies such as India include more rigid capital markets and labor/product markets, the lower supply of skills, the poorer quality of infrastructure, and the lower quality of institutions to protect property rights and to enforce contracts. However, even if markets are perfectly competitive and an adequate environment is ensured, the economy may still not reach its full potential. This is because of "market failures," which typically happen in the presence of externalities. They are at play when firms and workers do not fully internalize the effects of their decisions on the broader economy and their dynamic implications. Typically, they are learning externalities, coordination failures, or information asymmetries (Rodrik 2005).

As argued by many (e.g., Arrow 1962 and Matsuyama 1992), some activities entail higher productivity gains, or more learning potential, for an economy compared to other traditional activities such as non-tradable services or agriculture. Firms may not be fully aware of these productivity gains, leading to lower output in high-productivity sectors and lower relative incomes over time. The coordination failure is based on the idea that a critical size of the modern sector is needed for a firm to enter it. It would be profitable for a firm to invest in a modern sector only if there are enough firms investing simultaneously in other modern sectors. If many firms invest together in modern sectors, described as the "big push," economy reaches a higher level of productivity and development (Rosenstein-Rodan 1943; Murphy et al. 1989). Lastly, information asymmetries exist if there is imperfect information about new markets and products, and firms underinvest as a result (Hausmann and Rodrik 2003). This is clearly seen in firms trying to export and penetrate new geographical markets with their products.

In theory, tackling these externalities would necessitate a state intervention, broadly defined as industrial policy. However, the scope, the tools and whether it could in practice be superior to a more "laissez-faire" approach, leaving the outcome to unfettered competition, is the object of an ongoing debate. At the heart of the debate lies the definition of what constitutes a "modern" sector, which is conducive to productivity gains and spillovers to the rest of the economy. While it is typically associated with manufacturing (Matsuyama 1992 and Krugman 1987) or related to the concept of sophistication (Hausmann, Hwang, and Rodrik 2007 and Cherif and Hasanov 2019), others argue that service sectors could also play a role (IMF 2018). More important for inclusive growth, if a sector is to be targeted, it should help achieve broad-based growth to contribute to poverty alleviation. In practice it means that it should also generate (directly or indirectly) enough employment, and the level of skills to fill those jobs should be realistically met over the medium term.

The other key question relates to how state intervention to tackle externalities could curtail or distort competition. Indeed, state interventions of the past typically followed the model of import-substitution policies. The main idea was to protect domestic producers from international competition by imposing barriers to trade, such as high tariffs. In many cases, the curtailment of competition went further and encompassed the domestic market as countries relied on one or very few "champions" to achieve import-substitution goals. The many past failed cases in Latin America and the Middle East imply that such policies may be counterproductive in general (Cherif and Hasanov 2019b). The comparison of Malaysia's foray into automotive industry in the 1970s with its champion Proton to the success of Korea's Hyundai is a case in point (Cherif and Hasanov 2019c). After decades of support and protection from domestic and international competition, Proton depended on imports of critical inputs, including the engine. The high tariffs to protect it also meant that consumers had to pay higher prices for lower quality products. In comparison, although Hyundai benefitted from state support as well, it was also forced early on to compete both on the domestic and international markets. It could be argued that competition provided Hyundai with an incentive to innovate and take advantage of economies of scale.

Moreover, support for firms could be pursued without necessarily implying less competition. Aghion and others (2015) develop a simple model showing that targeted subsidies can be used to induce several firms to operate in the same sector, and that the more competitive the sector is, the more it will induce firms to innovate in order to "escape competition" (Aghion et al. 2005). Of course, a lot depends upon the design of industrial policy. Such policy should target sectors, not particular firms (Aghion 2016). Using Chinese firm-level panel data, Aghion and others (2015) look at the interaction between state subsidies to a sector and the level of product market competition in that sector. They show that TFP, TFP growth, and product innovation (defined as the ratio between output value generated by new products to total output value) are all positively correlated with the interaction between state aid to the sector and market competition in the sector. In other words, the more competitive the recipient sector is, the more positive the effects of targeted state subsidies to that sector are. In fact, for sectors with low degree of competition the effects are negative, whereas the effects become positive in sectors with sufficiently high degree of competition. Finally, the interaction between state aid and product market competition in the sector is more positive when state aid is less concentrated.

Yet, there are externalities that can be tackled without curtailing competition with the potential to have a sizable contribution to broad-based growth and poverty alleviation. These are typically related to informational asymmetries. Bloom and Van Reenen (2010), for example, show that interventions to improve management practices in Indian small firms can significantly improve productivity. So did the productivity missions of the Marshall Plan in Europe after the Second World War (Giorcelli 2019). In the same vein, Atkin et al. (2017) showed that Egyptian rug producers can be helped to access export markets by tackling informational asymmetries and coordination failures. In other words, they showed that interventions such as export promotion agencies can help SMEs advertise their products in foreign markets and act as a communication channel between them and customers. They also showed that export activities helped small producers improve their quality and value added which confirms the importance of export orientation. This focus on SMEs can help increase productivity and tackle inequality at the same time.

The trade-off between the benefits and costs of state intervention suggests that the way the state intervenes in the economy is crucial. This intervention needs to be cognizant of exacerbating government failures such as rent-seeking and corruption. Moreover, even if these interventions are successful in the sense that they create competitive industries and contribute to growth, they should avoid creating "islands" of relatively advanced sectors. If these sectors are disconnected from the rest of the economy, broad-based growth may not be sustained, and it would exacerbate inequality. For example, thanks to interventions and targeted policies, Costa Rica managed to foster a high-tech sector in electronics and health instruments (Spar 1998). Although it led to higher growth and declining poverty as well as productivity improvements in agricultural sectors, high inequality persisted while growth policies for inclusiveness were missing (Ferreira, Fuentes, and Ferreira 2018).

V. Conclusion

The broad implication of this chapter is that competition and innovation influence inclusive growth through different channels. Policies for inclusiveness should consider these channels and the implied tradeoffs. More important, policies should keep in mind the dynamic effects on growth, especially the incentives on innovation and the ability of firms to harness economies of scale. In theory, encouraging more innovation tends to increase inequality at the top while improving wages of the workers in productive firms and improving social mobility. In addition, policies to support innovation could also improve business dynamism and reduce market power that would be overall beneficial for inclusive growth. We further argue there is a role for a new competition policy both to encourage competition and innovation and tackle inequality.

First, in this new competition policy, there is a need for a reappraisal of the laws and regulations such that the effect on current and future inequality is explicitly considered. In practice, this would mean studying the tradeoff between consumer welfare in the relevant market, the wider effect on inequality (e.g., ride-sharing), and the implications of the dominance of a firm in the future on related sectors (e.g., data access and use). It would also mean weighing the effects of policies on transaction costs and future innovation. Moreover, discretion could be given to competition agencies to prioritize sectors and goods affecting poor and middle-class families (Baker and Salop 2015).

Second, policies to encourage technology diffusion should be considered as part of the competition framework. Given the major role played by supernormal returns, and the associated inequality in wage income, a special attention to these firms is needed. As noted earlier, it is difficult to determine to what extent these firms either hold a superior technology, operate in a sector with network effects and scale economies naturally leading to a monopoly, or are benefitting from hidden barriers to entry. An alternative policy would encourage the big firms to set-up independent industrial research labs, allowing all firms to access the technologies produced in exchange for a relatively cheap license fee or for free. The associated technology creation and diffusion could help revive business dynamism and in turn mitigate the rise of inequality.

References

Aghion, Philippe. 2016. "Growth Policy Design for Middle-Income Countries." In *Breaking the Oil Spell: The Gulf Falcons' Path to Diversification*, edited by Cherif, Reda, Fuad Hasanov, and Min Zhu. Washington, DC: International Monetary Fund Press.

Aghion, Philippe, Ufuk Akcigit, Antonin Bergeaud, Richard Blundell, and David Hemous. 2016. "Innovation and Top Income Inequality." Working paper.

Aghion, Philippe, Antonin Bergeaud, Timo Boppart, Peter J. Klenow, Huiyu Li. 2019. "A Theory of Falling Growth and Rising Rents." Working paper.

Aghion, Philippe, Nick Bloom, Richard Blundell, Rachel Griffith, and Peter Howitt. 2005. "Competition and Innovation: An Inverted-U Relationship." *The Quarterly Journal of Economics* 120(2): 701–28.

Aghion, Philippe, Richard Blundell, Rachel Griffith, Peter Howitt, and Susanne Prantl. 2009. "The Effects of Entry on Incumbent Innovation and Productivity." *The Review of Economics and Statistics* 91(1): 20–32.

Aghion, Philippe, Jing Cai, Mathias Dewatripont, Luosha Du, Ann Harrison, and Patrick Legros. 2015. "Industrial Policy and Competition." *American Economic Journal: Macroeconomics* 7(4), October: 1–32.

Aghion, Philippe, and Peter Howitt. 1992. "A Model of Growth Through Creative Destruction." *Econometrica* 60: 323–51.

Akcigit, Ufuk, Salomé Baslandze, and Stefanie Stantcheva. 2016. "Taxation and the International Mobility of Inventors." *American Economic Review* 106(10): 2930–81.

Akcigit, Ufuk, John Grigsby, Tom Nicholas, and Stefanie Stantcheva. 2018. "Taxation and Innovation in the 20th Century." NBER Working Papers, September 2018, No. 24982.

Armstrong, Mark and David Sappington. 2006. "Regulation, Competition and Liberalization." *Journal of Economic Literature* 44(2): 325–66.

Arrow, Kenneth. 1962. "The Economic Implications of Learning by Doing." *The Review of Economic Studies* 29(3), June: 155–73.

Atkin, Davis, Amit K. Khandelwal, and Adam Osman. 2017. "Exporting and Firm Performance: Evidence from a Randomized Experiment." *The Quarterly Journal of Economics* 132(2): 551–615.

Autor, David, David Dorn, Lawrence F. Katz, Christina Patterson, and John Van Reenen. 2017. "Concentrating on the Fall of the Labor Share." *American Economic Review* 107(5), May: 180–5.

Baker, Jonathan B. 2019. *The Anti-Trust Paradigm*. Cambridge, MA: Harvard University Press.

Baker, Jonathan B., and Steven C. Salop. 2015. "Antitrust, Competition Policy, and Inequality." Georgetown Law Faculty Publications and Other Works, 1462.

Bessen, James. 2017. "Information Technology and Industry Concentration." Law and Economics Paper No 17–41. Boston University School of Law.

Bloom, Nicholas, and John Van Reenen. 2010. "Why Do Management Practices Differ across Firms and Countries." *Journal of Economic Perspectives* 24(1): 203–24.

Blundell, Richard, Rachel Griffith, and John van Reenen. 1999. "Market Share, Market Value and Innovation in a Panel of British Manufacturing Firms." *Review of Economic Studies* 66(3): 529–54.

Chandler, Alfred D., Jr. 1991. *Scale and Scope: The Dynamics of Industrial Capitalism.* Cambridge, MA: Belknap Press.

Cherif, Reda, Marc Engher, and Fuad Hasanov. 2020. "Crouching Beliefs, Hidden Biases: The Rise and Fall of Growth Narratives." IMF Working Paper 20/228.

Cherif, Reda, and Fuad Hasanov. 2016. "Soaring of the Gulf Falcons: Diversification in GCC Oil Exporters in Seven Propositions." In *Breaking the Oil Spell: The Gulf*

Falcons' Path to Diversification, edited by Cherif, Reda, Fuad Hasanov, and Min Zhu. Washington, DC: International Monetary Fund Press.

Cherif, Reda, and Fuad Hasanov. 2019. "Principles of True Industrial Policy." *Journal of Globalization and Development* 10(1): 1–22.

Cherif, Reda, and Fuad Hasanov. 2019b. "The Return of the Policy that Shall Not Be Named: Principles of Industrial Policy." IMF Working Paper 19/74.

Cherif, Reda, and Fuad Hasanov. 2019c. "The Leap of the Tiger: Escaping the Middle-Income Trap to the Technological Frontier." *Global Policy* 10(4): 497–511.

Cherif, Reda, Fuad Hasanov, and Min Zhu (eds). 2016. *Breaking the Oil Spell: The Gulf Falcons' Path to Diversification*. Washington, DC: International Monetary Fund Press.

Combe, E., C. Monnier, and R. Legal. 2008. "Cartels: The Probability of Getting Caught in the European Union." Bruegel European Economic Research Papers no. 12.

Creedy, J., and R. Dixon. 1998. "The Relative Burden of Monopoly on Households with Different Incomes." *Economica* 65(258): 285–93.

Creedy, J., and R. Dixon. 2000. "Relative Welfare Losses and Imperfect Competition in New Zealand." *New Zealand Economic Papers* 34(2): 269–86.

De Loecker, Jan, and Jan Eeckhout. 2020. "The Rise of Market Power and the Macroeconomic Implications." *Quarterly Journal of Economics*.

Ennis, Sean, Pedro Gonzaga, and Chris Pike. 2017. "Inequality: A hidden Cost of Market Power." Available: http://www.oecd.org/daf/competition/inequality-a-hidden-cost-of-market-power.htm.

Fackler, Thomas A., Markus Nagler, and Monika Schnitzer, and Martin Watzinger. 2017. "How Antitrust Enforcement Can Spur Innovation: Bell Labs and the 1956 Consent Decree," CEPR Discussion Papers 11,793, C.E.P.R. Discussion Papers.

Ferreira, Gustavo Filipe Canle, Pablo Antonio Garcia Fuentes, and Juan Pablo Canle Ferreira. 2018. "The Successes and Shortcoming of Costa Rica Exports Diversification Policies." Background paper to the UNCTAD-FAO Commodities and Development Report 2017.

Freund, Caroline, and Sarah Oliver. 2016. *Rich People Poor Countries: The Rise of Emerging-Market Tycoons and their Mega Firms*. Peterson Institute Press: All Books, Peterson Institute for International Economics, 7038, July.

Freund, Caroline, and Martha Denisse Pierola. 2016. "The Origins and Dynamics of Export Superstars," Working Paper Series WP16-11, Peterson Institute for International Economics.

Furman, Jason, and Peter Orszag. 2015. "A Firm-Level Perspective on the Role of Rents in the Rise in Inequality." Presentation at "A Just Society" Centennial Event in Honor of Joseph Stiglitz, Columbia University.

Gabaix, Xavier. 2009. "Power Laws in Economics and Finance." *Annual Review of Economics* 1(1): 255–94.

Gilbert, Richard. 2020. *Innovation Matters: Competition Policy for the High-technology Economy.* Cambridge, MA: MIT Press.

Giorcelli, Michela. 2019. "The Long-Term Effects of Management and Technology Transfers." *American Economic Review* 109(1): 121–52.

Gutiérrez, Germán, and Thomas Philippon. 2017. "Declining Competition and Investment in the U.S." NBER Working Papers 23,583, National Bureau of Economic Research, Inc.

Hausmann, Ricardo, Jason Hwang, and Dani Rodrik. 2007. "What You Export Matters." *Journal of Economic Growth* 12(1), March: 1–25.

Hausmann, Ricardo, and Dani Rodrik. 2003. "Economic Development as Self-discovery." *Journal of Development Economics* 72(2): 603–33, December.

Hsieh, Chang-Tai, and Peter Klenow. 2009. "Misallocation and Manufacturing TFP in China and India." *The Quarterly Journal of Economics* 124(4), November: 1403–48.

Hsieh, Chang-Tai, and Enrico Moretti. 2019. "Housing Constraints and Spatial Misallocation." *American Economic Journal: Macroeconomics* 11(2), April: 1–39.

International Monetary Fund (IMF). 2018. "Manufacturing Jobs: Implications for Productivity and Inequality." *World Economic Outlook*, Chapter 3, April.

International Monetary Fund (IMF). 2019a. "Competition, Competitiveness, and Growth in Sub-Saharan Africa." *Sub-Saharan Africa Regional Economic Outlook*, October. Washington, DC.

International Monetary Fund (IMF). 2019b. "The Rise of Corporate Market Power and Its Macroeconomic Effects." *World Economic Outlook*, April. Washington, DC.

Ivaldi, Marc, Frédéric Jenny, and Aleksandra Khimich. 2016. "Cartel Damages to the Economy: An Assessment for Developing Countries."

Khan, Lina, and Sandeep Vaheesan. 2017. "Market Power and Inequality: The Antitrust Counterrevolution and its Discontents." *Harvard Law and Policy Review* 235.

Kitzmuller, M., and M. Martinez Licetti. 2012. "Competition Policy: Encouraging Thriving Markets for Development." Viewpoint: Public Policy for the Private Sector, Note 331 (August), World Bank Group, Washington, DC.

Krueger, Alan B. 2019. *Rockonomics: A Backstage Tour of What the Music Industry Can Teach Us About Economics and Life.* New York: Currency.

Krugman, Paul. 1987. "The Narrow Moving Band, the Dutch Disease, and the Competitive Consequences of Mrs. Thatcher: Notes on Trade in the Presence of Dynamic Scale Economies." *Journal of Development Economics* 27(1–2): 41–55.

Lamoreaux, Naomi R. 2019. "The Problem of Bigness: From Standard Oil to Google." *Journal of Economic Perspectives* 33(3): 94–117.

Matsuyama, Kiminori. 1992. "Agricultural Productivity, Comparative Advantage, and Economic Growth." *Journal of Economic Theory* 58(2): 317–34.

Murphy, Kevin M., Andrei Shleifer, and Robert W. Vishny. 1989. "Industrialization and the Big Push." *Journal of Political Economy* 97(5): 1003–26.

Nickell, Stephen and John van Reenen. 2002. "Technological Innovation and Economic Performance in the United Kingdom." In *Technological Innovation and Economic Performance*, edited by Richard Nelson, Benn Steil, and David Victor. Princeton, NJ: Princeton University Press, pp. 178–99.

Organisation for Economic Co-operation and Development (OECD). 2018. "Market Concentration." Issues Paper. Prepared by the OECD Secretariat for the Hearing on Market Concentration at the 129th Meeting of the OECD Competition Committee, 6–8 June.

Philippon, Thomas. 2019. *The Great Reversal: How America Gave Up on Free Markets*. Cambridge, MA: Belknap Press.

Phillips Sawyer, Laura. 2019. "U.S. Antitrust Law and Policy in Historical Perspective." Harvard Business School Working Paper, No. 19–110, May.

Rodrik, Dani. 2005. "Growth Strategies." In *Handbook of Economic Growth*, edition 1, volume 1, chapter 14, edited by Philippe Aghion and Steven Durlauf. Oxford: Elsevier, pp. 967–1014.

Rosenstein-Rodan, Paul. 1943. "Problems of Industrialization of Eastern and South-Eastern Europe." *Economic Journal* 53(210/211): 202–11.

Spar, Debora. 1998. "Attracting high technology investment: Intel's Costa Rican plant." Foreign Investment Advisory Service occasional paper; no. FIAS 11. Washington, DC: World Bank Group.

Syverson, Chad. 2019. "Macroeconomics and Market Power: Context, Implications, and Open Questions." *Journal of Economic Perspectives* 33(3), Summer: 23–43.

Tenn, S., and B.W. Wendling. 2014. "Entry Threats and Pricing in the Generic Drug Industry." *Review of Economics and Statistics* 96(2): 214–28.

Urzua, C.M. 2013. "Distributive and Regional Effects of Monopoly Power." *Economia Mexicana Nueva Epoca* 22(2): 279–95.

Wang, Sun Ling, Roberto Mosheim, Richard Nehring, and Eric Njuki. 2020. "Agricultural Productivity in the U.S." USDA, Economic Research Service, January.

World Bank. 2016. "Markets and Competition Policy Assessment Tool" (MCPAT).

World Bank and Organisation for Economic Co-operation and Development (OECD). 2017. "A Step Ahead: Competition Policy for Shared Prosperity and Inclusive Growth," World Bank Publications, The World Bank, number 27527.

Zerbe, Noah. 2001. "Seeds of Hope, Seeds of Despair: Towards a Political Economy of the Seed Industry in Southern Africa." *Third World Quarterly* 22(4): 657–73.

7

Trade

Marc Bacchetta, Valerie Cerra, Roberta Piermartini,
and Maarten Smeets

I. Introduction

A. Trade and Inclusion Concerns

Inequality and trade have both increased in many developed and developing countries since 1990.[1] Over the past few decades, inequality has risen in most advanced countries but also in several developing and emerging economies, especially in Eastern Europe and Asia (Figure 7.1). At the same time, trade openness has expanded until the Global Financial Crisis, in part due to trade liberalization and integration from emerging market countries such as China (Figure 7.2). These developments have raised questions of whether trade has been a culprit for the rising inequality. Concerns over globalization contributed to the passage of the UK's Brexit, the trade tensions between the United States and China, the US withdrawal from the Trans-Pacific Partnership, other increases in protectionism, and a rise in economic nationalism (Autor et al. 2020; Colantone and Stanig 2018a, 2018b; Ravallion, JEL 2018).

In a number of mostly rich countries, trade and trade agreements have been blamed for causing manufacturing job losses and for harming the poor. However, this sentiment may reflect the public's search for an explanation of slower growth in advanced economies, particularly in the decade following the global financial crisis (ILO and WTO 2011). In fact, there are many other forces, such as technological advances, that contributed to the increase in inequality, as discussed in other chapters. Nonetheless, weak economic conditions and job losses in manufacturing industries in advanced economies, in particular, have soured perceptions of trade for some politically sensitive groups, although the perceived impact of trade became more favorable in the second half of the 2010s (Antras 2020). Indeed, according to Pew Research Center's Spring 2018 Global Attitudes Survey,

[1] We thank Jaime Sarmiento for research assistance. We also thank Barry Eichengreen, Sharmini Coorey, Andy Berg, Karim Barhoumi, Moya Chin, Maksym Ivanyna, Francesco Luna, Nikola Spatafora, as well as participants in the Inclusive Growth book seminar series organized by the IMF Institute for Capacity Development for their comments.

Marc Bacchetta, Valerie Cerra, Roberta Piermartini, and Maarten Smeets, *Trade* In: *How to Achieve Inclusive Growth*. Edited by: Valerie Cerra, Barry Eichengreen, Asmaa El-Ganainy, and Martin Schindler, Oxford University Press. © Marc Bacchetta, Valerie Cerra, Roberta Piermartini, and Maarten Smeets 2022. DOI: 10.1093/oso/9780192846938.003.0007

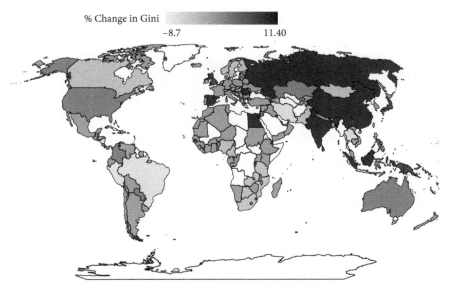

Figure 7.1 Change in Net Gini, 1990s–2010s
Note: white stands for no data
Sources: SWIID and authors' calculation.

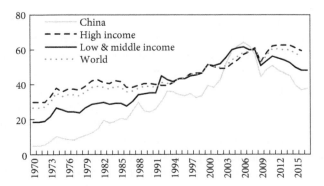

Figure 7.2 Trade Openness, 1970–2017
Sources: World Bank and authors' calculations.

public views on trade depend on the economic performance in the respondent's country, with a high correlation between the country's GDP growth rate and the belief that trade will increase wages (Figure 7.3). More generally, most people consider trade to be good for their countries and to create employment opportunities, with somewhat more optimism in emerging countries. In most countries, individuals with higher education and above median incomes are more likely to think trade creates jobs.

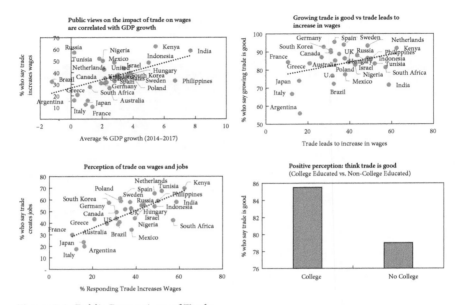

Figure 7.3 Public Perceptions of Trade

Sources: Pew Research Center and authors' calculations.

This chapter examines the relationship between international trade and inclusive growth. To set the stage, we describe the underlying trends driving trade and its composition in the recent decades and as projected into the future. We then turn to trade's relationship with growth and inclusion, where inclusion is defined broadly to encompass outcomes across the socio-economic spectrum. We assess the theoretical and empirical literature on the impact of trade, both in terms of aggregate economic outcomes and the relative impact on different population segments in a country. Although many countries have already reduced tariffs to low levels in past liberalizations episodes, scope remains to reduce non-tariff barriers and other trade costs, as well as addressing inclusion and sustainability in trade agreements. We thus delve into the debate on policy design for reaping the advantages of integration while minimizing or compensating any adverse impacts on sub-groups.

B. International Trade Trends

Global trade has responded to changes in technology, economic conditions, and policy. Trade grew by over 300 percent between 1870 and the start of the First World War due to declining trade and communication costs prompted by technological innovations such as the steamship and telegraph (Figure 7.4). Trade

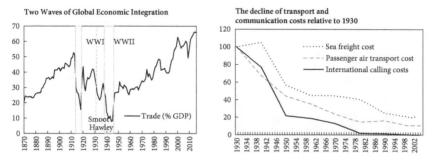

Figure 7.4 Trade Integration and Trade Costs
Sources: Jorda-Schularick-Taylor Macrohistory database, WDR-OECD Economic Outlook (2007), and authors' calculations.

collapsed during the two world wars and the Great Depression, due to the disruptions of conflict, the weak economic conditions, and a rise in protectionism (e.g., Smoot Hawley Act). Trade volumes surged by 7 percent per annum from 1950 to a high of roughly 60 percent of GDP (summing exports and imports) by the 2008–09 Global Financial Crisis (GFC). In addition to technological change that significantly reduced transportation and communication costs (e.g., containerization), the post-war period also witnessed major changes in trade policy. High-income countries reduced tariffs to less than 5 percent by the 1980s in early GATT rounds, while developing countries undertook major unilateral liberalizations in the 1980s and 1990s (Pavcnik 2017). Regional trading agreements and arrangements (e.g., the European Union, NAFTA, ASEAN) also proliferated over recent decades since the 1980s.

In recent decades, the country and industry composition of trade has shifted. In the early 1990s, merchandise trade between advanced countries comprised about 2/3 of global trade, but this share has fallen to only about 1/3, as trade between emerging market and developing economies (EMDEs) and advanced economies (AEs) has increased sharply (Figure 7.5). China's accession to WTO led rising shares from Asian countries in the 2000s. China's share of world merchandise exports grew from 1.2 percent in 1983 to 13.1 percent in 2018, which also explains Asia's share in world merchandise exports that grew from 19.1 percent to 33.6 percent in the same period. During this period, EMDEs have expanded their share of world manufacturing exports. Global value chains (GVCs)—in which the production process is broken up and firms in different countries specialize in specific tasks rather than producing the entire good or service—rose from about 37 percent of total trade in 1970 to above 50 percent by the mid-2000s (WDR 2020). Trade in services, despite relatively high policy barriers, has expanded faster than trade in goods between 2005 and 2017, at 5.4 percent per year on average, and now accounts for about one-quarter of total trade (IMF, World Bank, and WTO 2018).

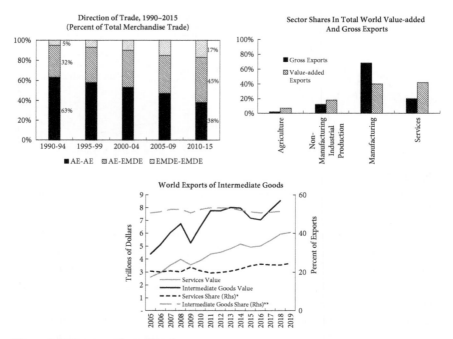

Figure 7.5 Composition of Trade

Note: *Service share is defined as world exports of goods and commercial services. **Intermediate Goods share is defined as world merchandise exports excl. fuels.

Sources: IMF Direction of Trade Statistics, WTO, and Johnson (2014) using WIOS with data as of 2008.

Recent global crises have slowed the rise in trade relative to GDP. The growth of trade was disproportionately concentrated in the period 1986–2008, owing to the IT revolution and articulation of supply chains, the fall in trade costs, and political developments such as the fall of communism and emergence of China (Antras 2020). However, trade growth decelerated dramatically following the Global Financial Crisis, due to diminished growth and investment, rising protectionism, and maturation of global value chains (IMF 2016). Due to the Covid-19 pandemic, world merchandise trade was projected to fall by 9 percent in 2020 (WTO 2020), and services trade to plummet due to transport and travel restrictions. Global foreign direct investment flows fell by 49 percent in the first half of 2020 (UNCTAD 2020a) and a further additional decline of 5–10 percent for 2021 (UNCTAD 2020b) is likely to exacerbate the contraction in trade flows, given the close interlinkages between trade and investment. Developing countries will be the hardest hit given their strong reliance on GVCs intensive industries and extractive industries, which have been severely affected by Covid-19. A 2021 recovery in trade is expected, depending on the duration of the outbreak and the effectiveness of the policy responses. Trade will likely fall steeper in sectors with complex value chains, particularly electronics and automotive products, which may be intensified by calls for and policies stimulating re-shoring of production. On the positive side, new services are provided through on-line shopping, e-commerce transactions and digital trade.

Looking ahead, underlying trends point to a continued increase in services trade, and growth areas such as e-commerce and digital trade, although this is difficult to document. The value of e-commerce transactions is estimated at US$27.7 trillion in 2016, up 44 percent from 2012 (USITC 2017; WTO 2018). There is also evidence of growing international opportunities for leading digital economy firms.[2] Three main trends are likely to affect the growth of services trade: (i) generally lower trade costs due to digital technological innovation; (ii) a reduced need for face-to-face interaction; and (iii) a lowering of the policy barriers. Simulations using the WTO's Global Trade Model project that, as a result of these trends, the services sector share of global trade may grow by 50 percent by 2040 (World Trade Report 2019). The reduction of trade costs induced by digital technologies is likely to foster trade in time-sensitive goods, certification intensive goods and contract intensive goods. Trade in customizable goods is also likely to increase and the advent of 3D printing technology may well prolong the decreasing trend in the trade of certain digitizable goods. Finally, the "sharing economy" business model could affect trade in durable consumer goods. Digital technologies may affect the international fragmentation of production. However, the overall impact on GVC trade is difficult to predict. In combination with innovations in logistics, the reduction of transaction costs through the Internet has led to an enormous expansion of GVCs. Yet new technologies can also bring a reversal of this process through reshoring and 3D printing (WTO 2018), though production location decisions tend to be sticky due to large sunk costs. Moreover, while technological improvements and automation may lead some inputs to be produced in domestic economies, increased productivity may increase the firm's optimal scale, thereby increasing their demand for intermediate inputs from abroad (Antras 2020).

II. Aggregate Impact of Trade on Growth and Inclusion

A. Standard Theories

Standard trade theories have mixed predictions for the impact of trade openness on inclusive growth. Trade occurs due to differences in sectoral technology, factor endowments, economies of scale, and firm productivity differences. Theories

---

[2] For example, international streaming revenue for Netflix grew from US$4 million to US$5 billion between 2010 and 2017 (WTO 2018).

focus on the welfare effects of trade, predicting that there will be gainers and losers from trade but that the gains will exceed the losses if adjustment costs are not too high. Because trade theories typically assume full employment and costless adjustment of labor from declining to growing industries and firms, they typically suggest that trade should not have a major effect on the aggregate level of employment. They tend to predict that trade has second order effects by shifting resources across firms and sectors, which can affect aggregate employment if labor-market frictions are sector or firm-specific (Helpman and Itskhoki 2010; Davis and Harrigan 2011; Carrère et al. 2016).

Technological differences between countries could confer mutual trading benefits. Ricardo (1817) espoused the idea that countries would export goods in which they had a comparative advantage due to higher relative productivity (a lower opportunity cost of production). Each country could potentially consume more of everything due to the global gains from specialization, which makes production more efficient. Within each country, sectors of comparative disadvantage would contract, but Ricardian theory assumes costless reallocation of workers to the growing domestic sector, abstracting from transitional or structural unemployment. Trade allows higher aggregate productivity, generating higher real wages, consumption, and welfare for everyone.

Trade based on differences in resource endowments is expected to benefit most the owners of the country's abundant factors. Heckscher-Ohlin theory (Ohlin 1933; Samuelson 1939) attributes trade to differences in countries' endowments of land, high- and low-skill labor, capital and any other factors of production. Trade induces a country to export goods that are produced using its abundant factors intensively relative to the trading partner, since the factor input costs would be lower. Stolper-Samuelson (1941) showed that since trade opening raises the demand for the abundant factor as the sector that uses it intensively expands, the returns to that factor (e.g., wages, profits, or rents) would rise. This suggests that low-skilled workers would benefit most from trade liberalization in low-skilled labor-abundant developing countries, while capital and high-skilled labor would benefit most in advanced economies. Consequently, inequality would be expected to fall in developing economies and rise in advanced economies. Thus, while net gains would be positive, some people could be worse off from trade unless compensated through redistribution.

Imperfect labor mobility could alter some of the predictions of these trade theories. Sectors that contract as a result of trade—those with comparative disadvantage or those employing scarce factors—could experience short-term unemployment if wages are not fully flexible, job creation in the expanding sector is slow, or laid off workers are unable to find rapid job matches elsewhere. In the long-run, trade is expected to reduce unemployment if driven by Ricardian comparative advantage or if the country is labor abundant (Dutt, Mitra, and Ranjan 2009).

Trade based on economies of scale and product differentiation provide benefits of competition and product variety. Until recent decades, global trade was dominated by trade between advanced countries in similar industries, rather than between advanced and developing countries based on comparative advantage or different factor endowments. Intra-industry trade accounted for about half of trade in advanced countries in the mid-1990s. Deemed "new" trade theory, Krugman (1981) showed that countries could take advantage of economies of scale in producing differentiated goods in the same industry. Access to new markets would permit an increase in production and decline in average costs. This form of trade provides welfare gains from greater variety of products without requiring any substantial contraction of industries or decline in returns to factors. The integrated market could spur competition, boosting innovation and growth. However, it could also force less competitive firms to go out of business.

Productivity differences between firms in the same industry play an important role in trade and appear to induce within industry dispersion in wages and profits. In the "new new" trade theory pioneered by Marc Melitz (2003), the most productive firms in an industry find it profitable to export. As trade expands, profits and wages in exporters rise while the less productive firms contract production or exit, leading to a rise in average industry productivity. Empirical evidence confirms that exporters are larger and more productive than non-exporters (Lileeva and Trefler 2010). Evidence also suggests that inequality within an industry rises. Firm productivity differences also impact firms' decisions to engage in FDI and to offshore stages of the production process (Antras and Helpman 2004).

Trade can also generate dynamic gains. Beyond the static benefits of increasing production efficiency and product variety, theory provides several channels through which trade can encourage sustained growth and welfare improvements. Opening up to trade affects growth positively because trade improves resource allocation by allowing countries to exploit comparative advantages. In some industries, the rise in production associated with specialization could lead to learning by doing that raises productivity. Higher competition could generate incentives to innovate (Alvarez, Benavente, and Crespiand 2019; Wacziarg and Welch 2008) and prompt improvements in institutions and government policies to ensure competitiveness (Krueger 1974; Tong and Wei 2014; Amiti and Khandelwal 2013). Trade and FDI may also lead to knowledge spillovers across countries (De Loecker 2013; Coe, Helpman, and Hoffmaister 1997). Trade allows firms that extend their market size beyond national borders to exploit economies of scale and become more productive and profitable, creating incentives to accumulate capital faster and to invest in R&D. Small open economies may also sustain rapid capital accumulation without a decline in the return to capital, which is determined in world financial markets. As a case in point, the East Asian tigers achieved fast export-led growth and rapid capital accumulation during the 1970s and 1980s, gradually shifting into more capital-intensive industries (Ventura 1997).

B. Evidence for Aggregate Net Benefits of Trade

Empirical evidence supports a number of net societal benefits of trade. According to the theories described in Section II.A., trade generates net benefits for an economy by taking advantage of specialization and comparative advantage in technology, resources, factor abundance, and differentiation. Empirical evidence finds overall benefits of trade, including higher growth, productivity, innovation, and technological upgrading; learning by exporting; reduction of corruption and discrimination; lower prices, especially for the poor; increased variety; and reduced input costs. This section summarizes the evidence for these effects, mainly at the aggregate level.

Trade openness is positively correlated with per capita income and economic growth (Figure 7.6). Empirical studies confirm the positive relationship between trade and growth, controlling for other factors (Sachs and Warner 1995; Busse and Koniger 2012). However, some critics debate the direction of causation (see reviews by Hanson and Harrison 1999, and Rodriguez and Rodrik 2001). To address this concern, a few studies use the exogenous component of trade openness based on geography and find that more open countries tend to have higher average per capita incomes (Frankel and Romer 1999; Cerdeiro and Komaromi 2020). An increase in trade openness of 1 percent of GDP is associated with 2–6 percentage points higher per capita GDP. Some research finds that countries that liberalized trade in the 1980s and 1990s achieved higher growth (1.5 percentage points) than countries that did not liberalize (Wacziarg and Welch 2008; Estevadeordal and Taylor 2013). The analysis may not be definitive given shortcomings associated with each research approach (e.g., geography may affect growth through other channels besides trade, and trade liberalization episodes coincided with other reforms), but a variety of research methods consistently find a positive impact of trade on growth. The success of several Asian countries in industrializing through export-led growth lent further evidence to development through openness rather than import substitution (World Bank 1987).

Evidence shows that trade increases productivity and innovation, key channels for raising growth. The literature provides robust evidence that trade liberalization increases industry productivity, both through reallocation to more productive firms and to improvements within firms (see surveys by Harrison and Rodriguez-Clare (2010), De Loecker and Goldberg (2014), and Melitz and Redding (2014)). Trade openness raises productivity across countries (Alcala and Ciccone 2004), and particularly benefits sectors where lower tariffs reduce inputs costs (Ahn et al. 2016). For example, the Canada-US FTA raised productivity in Canadian export and import-competing sectors most impacted by the agreement (Trefler 2004) and in US manufacturing industries (Bernard, Jensen, and Schott 2006). Trade reforms in Brazil during 1988–90 improved productivity in industries

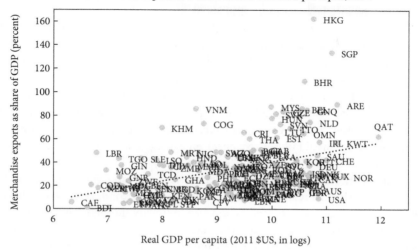

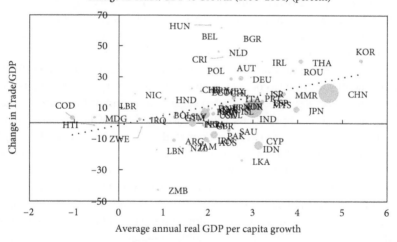

Figure 7.6 Trade vs Income and Growth
Sources: World Bank, and authors' calculations.

(Ferreira and Rossi 2003). Trade shifts production toward sectors that have the highest comparative advantage (Ricardo 1817; De Loecker and Goldberg 2014). It also increases competition and the size of the market, spurring firms to innovate and upgrade technology (Lileeva and Trefler 2010; Bustos 2011; Bloom, Draca, and Van Reenenet 2015). Trade and FDI facilitate diffusion of technology across trading partners (De Loecker 2013; Coe and Helpman 1995; Coe et al. 2009; Lumenga-Neso, Olarreaga, and Schiff 2005).

Trade openness appears to be correlated with slightly higher employment in the long run. The initial impact of trade liberalizations depends on country specific factors and vary by episode and most economists attribute differences in long-run unemployment to labor market institutions and other structural factors (ILO and WTO 2007; Blanchard 2006). Cross-country studies find that trade liberalizations and openness reduce long-run unemployment (Dutt et al. 2009; Felbermayr et al. 2009). A review of recent country level studies also confirms that trade has a small but positive effect on aggregate labor market outcomes in advanced economies (Feenstra and Sasahara 2017).

Trade liberalization leads to lower prices and a greater variety of consumer goods, increasing the real income of households. Lower goods prices arise directly through the lower price of imports and also indirectly through improvements in productivity (Costinot and Rodriguez-Clare 2014). Some studies suggest that the poor spend a higher share of their income on tradeable goods, especially food and beverages (Cravino and Levchenko 2017) and have higher welfare gains on average, estimated at 63 percent for the poorest 10th percentile of the income distribution (Faijgelbaum and Khandelwal 2016). Lowering tradeable goods prices therefore also reduces poverty and inequality. Reducing trade barriers also exerts competitive pressure that lead to lower markups and lower prices and helps reduce rents earned by monopolies and cartels (Levinsohn 1993; Harrison 1994; Edmond, Midrigan, and Xu 2015). For example, Argent and Begazo (2015) estimate that 40,000 families could be brought out of poverty by removing trade barriers that protect Kenya's concentrated sugar market and its high prices. Likewise, replacing Nigeria's import bans with an average level of tariffs could allow 3.3 million people to escape poverty (Cadot et al. 2018). Trade also had a very large impact on the introduction of new varieties in the United States (Broda and Weinstein 2006) and India (Topalova 2010; De Loecker et al. 2016), and to a lesser extent in Costa Rica (Klenow and Rodriguez-Claire 1997; Arkolakis et al. 2008).

Trade openness is associated with poverty reduction (Figure 7.7), at least indirectly by raising growth and income, although the impact depends on institutions and complementary policies (WTO 2008). Increases in real incomes of the poorest quintile of the population is strongly correlated with increases in trade openness (IMF, World Bank, and WTO 2017). Trade raises average real income, which in turn leads to an almost one-for-one rise in the real incomes of the poor (Dollar and Kraay 2004; Dollar, Kleineberg, and Kraay 2016).

At the aggregate level, trade improves the income distribution for EMDEs and has an insignificant impact in AEs (Figure 7.8). Panel regressions on Gini coefficients show that trade openness reduces inequality in emerging and developing countries and has no significant impact in advanced economies, in contrast to financial integration which increases inequality (Beaton, Cebotari, and Komaromi

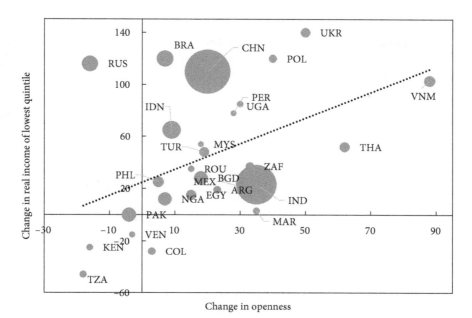

Figure 7.7 Change in Openness and Income of the Poor, 1993–2008

Sources: World Bank and authors' calculations. EMDEs with average population greater than 20 million. Dot size is proportional to population.

(BCK) 2017; and Jaumotte, Lall, and Papageorgiou (JLP) 2013).[3] Event studies of liberalization episodes, mainly reflecting emerging market countries, corroborates the beneficial impact of trade. In addition to boosting growth, investment, and FDI, trade liberalization prevented the steep rise in inequality experienced by countries that remained relatively closed to international trade (Beaton, Cebotari, and Komaromi, 2017). Cerdeiro and Komaromi (2020) exploit countries' exogenous geographic characteristics to estimate the causal effect of trade on inequality; they find the positive impact of trade on income is highest for the poorest income deciles and a one-percentage point higher openness is associated with a 0.2–0.6 points lower net Gini coefficient.

The impact of trade integration may depend on macroeconomic policies as well as cyclical conditions and structural trends. Most trade theories are set in the context of balanced trade, but actual trade integration seldom occurs in isolation. For example, high government deficits contribute to current account deficits if

---

[3] The significance of the results depends on sample and controls. BCK (2017) find trade significantly reduces market inequality in EMDEs, but is not significant for net inequality. JLP (2013) appear to find a significant reduction in net inequality for a pooled sample of AEs and EMDEs. The lack of an increase in inequality in AEs suggests that trade occurs for reasons other than differences in factor endowments as in the H-O model.

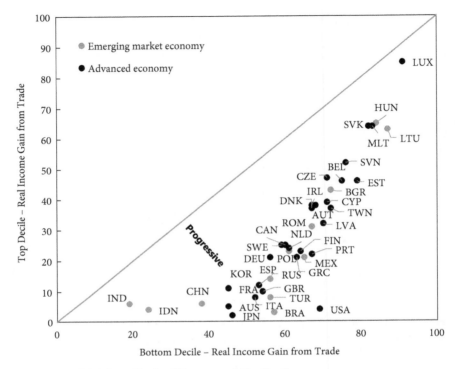

Figure 7.8 Gains from Trade of Bottom and Top Deciles

Note: Real gains from trade are relative to counterfactual of no trade.

Sources: Faijgelbaum and Khandelwal (2016, Table V) and authors' calculations.

not offset by greater private sector saving.[4] The associated low export growth may impede workers laid off in contracting import-competing industries from being hired into export-oriented industries. Evidence suggests that rising trade with China contributed to the decline in US manufacturing jobs after 2000 (Pierce and Schott 2016a; Autor, Dorn, and Hanson 2013). But the US current account deficit rose sharply as a percentage of GDP over 2000–2006. In contrast, while Germany also faced import competition from China and other emerging countries, its overall current account surplus seems to have protected manufacturing jobs (Dauth, Findeisen, and Suedekum 2017).

Trade substantially improves economic outcomes for women. Trade driven by comparative advantage is probably the driving force of the increase in female participation in the labor force in developing countries, especially as some

---

[4] Current account deficits are best viewed as equilibrium outcomes of other drivers of trends, including fiscal deficits. Nonetheless, they represent a deviation from assumptions of balanced trade used in many models.

developing countries specialized in the textile industry. In the Republic of Korea, for example, the share of women employed in manufacturing grew from 6 percent in the 1970s to 30 percent in the 1990s (Berik 2011). More broadly, economic theory suggests that trade reduces firms' incentive to discriminate through its competition effects. Evidence shows that trade is associated with more, better paid and better-quality jobs for women at the country, sector and firm level. Open economies have lower rates of informality and higher levels of gender equality, including from smaller gender wage gaps (Black and Brainerd 2004; Klein et al. 2010). Firms that engage in international trade employ substantially more women than non-exporting firms (World Bank and WTO 2020).

Trade has increased female bargaining power, allowing women to delay marriage and increase investments in education. Female employment empowers women in household, social, and political spheres, which has knock-on effects through decisions that support girls' nutrition, health, and education. In Bangladesh, for example, young women in villages that have been exposed to the export-intensive garment sector have delayed marriage and childbirth, and young girls have gained an additional 1.5 years of schooling.

Global trade trends, such as growing trade in service, e-commerce and participation in GVCs offer new opportunities to access foreign markets (World Bank and WTO 2020). Small producers—many of which are women—can indirectly access the world market by producing a small component of a product or providing a service to a multinational. E-commerce facilitates access to international markets and finance and lowers costs of doing business, as well as reducing women's exposure to discrimination. For example, new technologies can allow digital payment, even without a bank account, thus reducing time and mobility constraints by generating a more transparent and faster shopping process especially for imports. Blockchain technology may boost participation in international trade (Bahri 2020). Blockchain's anonymity and efficiency could particularly enable financial and business transactions by women, who otherwise would be constrained by law, custom, lack of identification documents, or high costs. It can be used to prove their ownership of assets without interventions from male family members. Blockchain can help micro-, small- and medium-sized enterprises (MSMEs), more than 30 percent of which are owned by women, to overcome costs associated with exporting and importing, and interact easily with consumers, other businesses engaged in the supply chain, customs officers and regulatory bodies. In fact, women-owned companies are more present online than offline (World Bank 2020; AliResearch 2017). Services—where most women work—are increasingly important in the global economy and are becoming increasingly tradable. Increasingly, education and health services are becoming tradable. This is likely to generate new job opportunities for women in sectors where they have a relative advantage.

III. Relative Impact and Adjustment

Despite the aggregate benefits of trade, the gains are distributed unevenly across sectors, industries, firms, regions, factors of production, and workers. Trade may induce absolute losses for some groups, especially in the hard-hit manufacturing sector of AEs (Figure 7.9). Workers in contracting industries and occupations and less productive firms may experience job losses or declining wages. In theory, they could find employment in expanding industries and firms, but in practice there are many barriers to smooth adjustment. Industries are often concentrated regionally and there are high costs of moving to another region especially for those whose family network remains in the local region. Likewise, switching occupations or improving skills may require costly retraining. Information on job openings may also be limited. Thus, trade is similar to technological change, which also spurs aggregate growth but entails significant distributional changes and dislocations.

Studies show that adjustment to trade and other macro shocks is often slow. Geographic regions vary in their industry composition and exposure to trade integration, with the adverse impact typically concentrated in import-competing sectors. Labor mobility is limited across geographic regions in developed countries (Autor et al. 2013; Hanson 2019) and in developing countries (Topalova 2007, 2010; McCaig 2011; Kovak 2013). The shock has persistent long-term effects, with regional wage gaps widening over time rather than declining (Dix-Carneiro and Kovak 2015). Earnings and job losses can have negative long term effects on the economic, social, health, and psychological well-being of individuals and their children (Pierce and Schott 2016; Davis and von Watcher 2011; Oreopoulos et al. 2008; Giuliano and Spilimbergo 2009; Altindag and Mocan 2010). Trade may

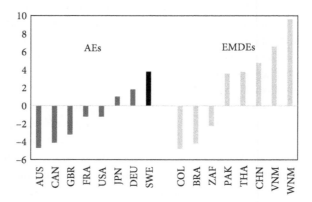

Figure 7.9 Change in Manufacturing Share of GDP in Constant 2000 Prices, Selected Economies, 1995–2004

Sources: World Bank, WTO, and authors' calculations.

also increase the sensitivity of employment and wages to international business conditions and raise the elasticity of demand for labor, leading to more earnings instability and lower bargaining power of workers (OECD 2017; Krebs et al. 2005). Sections III.A. and III.B. review the literature on the impacts of and adjustments to trade shocks in AEs and EMDEs, respectively.[5]

A. Impact and Adjustment in Advanced Economies

Trade integration had adverse effects on some industries and localities. In an influential study, Autor et al. (2013) showed that the rapid growth in Chinese manufacturing exports following its accession to the WTO in 2001 had a larger negative impact on those industries and communities in the United States that were most exposed to this import competition shock. Their results were interpreted as suggesting that the "China shock" accounted for about one-quarter of US manufacturing job losses. Likewise, across 18 OECD countries with diverse labor market institutions, employment fell in sectors that are more exposed to imports from China (Thewissen and van Vliet 2019). Subsequent research, however, showed that once exports, input-output linkages and value-added trade statistics are accounted for, trade's contribution to the decline in manufacturing employment in advanced economies, if any, is very small (Magyari 2017; Feenstra, Ma, and Xu 2017; Feenstra and Sasahara 2017). Similarly, with regard to localities, the picture got more nuanced once the effects of export expansion, cheaper inputs, and value chain linkages were taken into account. Available evidence suggests that the effect of trade can differ markedly by region. Areas that benefit from export expansion or cheaper inputs experience wage and employment growth while areas that compete with imports or have no access to foreign markets might fall behind. Moreover, employment declines more in less productive firms when facing import competition (Bernard, Jensen, and Schott 2006; Trefler 2004).

Employment losses have led to some prolonged economic and social consequences. Due to limited mobility to other geographic regions and industries, workers who lost their jobs due to import competition from China suffered significant and prolonged unemployment. Displaced workers tended to be older, with lower skills, and less education, making it harder to find reemployment, especially if facing an "identity mismatch" that deters them from seeking jobs in alternative industries (OECD 2005, 2012; Kletzer 2001; Autor et al. 2014; Notowidigdo 2013). Long-term unemployment had knock-on effects, such as poorer health outcomes, higher mortality, and lower educational achievements by their children (Pierce and Schott 2016b; Autor et al. 2015; Davis and von Watcher 2011).

---

[5] Previous surveys include Wood (1999), Feenstra and Hanson (2003), Goldberg and Pavcnik (2007), Harrison, McLaren, and McMillan (2011), Pavcnik (2012), and Goldberg (2015).

Trade integration seems to have had only a modest contribution to rising skill premium and wage dispersion. According to literature surveys by Cline (1997) and Bivens (2008), studies found that trade contributed between 10 to 40 percent of the rise in US wage inequality during the 1980s and 1990s, with most findings at the low end of the range. However, a large share of trade in this earlier period was between AEs. Bivens (2013) finds that growing trade with EMDEs reduced wages of non-college educated US workers by 5.5 percent in 2011. Research on the effect of the China shock on wages found either no impact or a small impact (Autor, Dorn, and Hanson 2013; Feenstra, Ma, and Xu 2017; Rothwell 2017). Ebenstein et al. (2015) found occupational wages rather than industry wages declined slightly due to import competition.

Trade may increase the skill bias indirectly by incentivizing technological innovation. Most studies attribute rising skill premia and wage inequality to technological change rather than to trade (Machin and van Reenen 1998; Berman et al. 1997; Baldwin and Cain 2000). However, technology and trade are intertwined since trade induces an increase in market share that can motivate firms to innovate or adopt technology, which is typically a complement to skilled labor (Thoenig and Verdier 2003). Trade can also boost the earnings of superstar firms, especially in high-tech industries that benefit from network externalities (Haskel et al. 2012).

Trade has increasingly been associated with offshoring of some activities and jobs as production becomes fragmented into global value chains (GVCs). Offshoring can increase production efficiency, but it is another channel that impacts the skill premium. Matched employer-employee data from Denmark show offshoring increased (decreased) wages of skilled (unskilled) workers, with routine task workers suffering the largest wage losses (Hummels et al. 2014). Firm and worker-level evidence shows that offshoring and import competition have a small positive impact on the demand for non-routine occupations and thus on job polarization in advanced economies (Becker et al. 2013; Keller and Utar 2016). Confirming findings from the 1990s, however, a number of studies find that technology is significantly more important in driving polarization than import competition or offshoring in value chains (Autor et al. 2015; Zhu 2017). Outsourcing accounted for 15 percent of the rise in relative wages of skilled workers in the United States, while computer use contributed about 35 percent (Feenstra and Hanson 1999). Goos et al. (2014) differentiate technology (using the routine task index of Autor and Dorn 2013) from offshorability (using the index from coder assessments in Blinder and Krueger 2009) and find that technology had a substantially more important impact than offshoring.

But the studies of local and industry impacts of trade tell only a partial story. The China Shock led exposed firms to cut back on employment in localities and industries for which China had a competitive advantage. But the lower production costs allowed the same firms to expand in other localities and industries. On balance, exposed firms expanded employment by 2 percent more per year, creating more manufacturing and non-manufacturing jobs than non-exposed firms (Magyari 2017).

Expansion of trade also leads to export growth and job creation in export industries and supply chains. General equilibrium effects can provide offsetting benefits. Indeed, job losses from the China Shock were roughly offset by job gains due to merchandise export growth in the United States during 1991–2011 (Feenstra, Ma, and Xu 2017). In addition, US service sector exports generated a few million jobs, leading to net job gains from trade (Feenstra and Sasahara 2017). In Germany, rising trade exposure from China and Eastern Europe during 1990–2010 led to net earnings gains in manufacturing, although there was relatively little reallocation of workers from declining import-competing industries to the expanding export-oriented ones (Dauth, Findeisen, and Suedekum 2014). The composition of local labor markets and the skill set of workers also matter. Local labor markets in Germany with a high share of industries requiring skills similar to those of the contracting industries were able to reallocate the workers more quickly and with less earnings loss (Yi, Muller, and Stegmaier 2017). Adverse employment effects of the China Shock may also be offset by trade with other countries, as in the case of German trade with China and Central Eastern Europe that led to net job creation (Dauth et al. 2014).

The impact of trade liberalization also depends on concurrent macroeconomic developments. Crinò and Epifani (2017) attribute the rise in skill premium and wage inequality in AEs to global trade imbalances, particularly the US trade deficit. Likewise, Borjas et al. (1991) attributes one-quarter of the rise in the college premium between 1980 and 1985 to the US trade deficit. Layoffs associated with the 2001 dot-com recession may also have exacerbated the negative employment impacts of import competition (Davis and von Wachter 2011).

Uncertainty of trade policy can have strong economic impacts. Firms' investment and exporting decisions depend on their expectations of trade policy. China's entry in the WTO reduced uncertainty since it no longer needed annual renewal of MFN status. US import-competing industries that experienced the largest fall in uncertainty also had the largest employment changes (Handley and Limao 2017). Likewise, the reduction in uncertainty of bound tariffs in Australia led to a rise in imports from new import destinations (Handley 2014) and the reduction in trade policy uncertainty from Portugal's entry into the EU increased export participation of Portuguese firms (Handley and Limao 2015). In fact, the uncertainty of trade policies triggered much of countries' interest in joining the WTO and making binding commitments. Separately, the uncertainties that resulted from trade tensions between major trading nations, including the United States, China, EU, Russian Federation, have undermined the trust in trade and led to significant policy efforts to restoring the trust in support of inclusive growth (Smeets and Mashayekhi 2019).

Gains and losses from trade shape political pressure on trade policies. Consistent with the Heckscher-Ohlin and Stolper-Samuelson theorems, research finds that pro-labor governments adopt more protectionist policies in capital-rich countries and more pro-trade policies in labor-rich countries (Dutt and Mitra 2006). Well-organized lobbies for trade protection also featured in earlier episodes of the passage of the Smoot-Hawley Act (Eichengreen 1986) and nineteenth-century "iron and rye" tariffs in Germany (Gerschenkron 1943). Regions more exposed to import competition from low-wage countries became more polarized in the United States (Autor et al. 2016) and in Germany and France (Malgouyres 2017; Dippel, Gold, and Heblichet 2015). Anti-globalization and nativist pressures intensify following weak economic conditions (Mian et al. 2014; Funke et al. 2016).

B. Impact and Adjustment in Developing Economies

The impact of trade is geographically concentrated. In EMDEs, as with AEs, the adverse impacts of trade on economic and social outcomes depend on the region's exposure to import competition. Topalova (2010) finds that rural districts in India with a higher concentration of import-competing industries had worse outcomes on poverty than other districts following tariff reductions. Likewise, Baldarrago and Salinas (2017) find that districts in Peru competing with liberalized imports experienced significantly lower growth in per capita consumption in response to increased import competition. Literature surveys by Goldberg (2015) and Goldberg and Pavcnik (2007, 2016) highlight similar findings in other studies. Other social indicators in exposed local communities also deteriorated, with crime increasing, and output and tax revenue falling (Dix-Carneiro, Soares, and Ulyssea 2018). The impact is transmitted to the next generation through lower school attendance relative to other regions (Edmonds, Pavcnik, and Topalova 2010).

Inter-regional worker mobility is very low and the impact of the shock is highly persistent. Studies document low labor mobility across regions and industries in EMDEs, such as India, Brazil, and Mexico (see Goldberg and Pavcnik 2007, and Pavcnik 2017 for a review). For example, less than 1 percent of rural Indians and 5 percent of urban Indians moved across districts for jobs in the 1980s and 1990s (Topalova 2010). Low inter-regional labor mobility is due to costs of moving, housing costs, imperfect capital markets for borrowing, imperfect insurance markets, low levels of public safety nets and retraining, informal familial and community-based social systems, skill mismatches, and sometimes government restrictions. The effects of the shock magnify over time, due to slow adjustment of capital away from the region and a decline in firm entry, perhaps due to agglomeration economies at a regional level. Some laid off workers are absorbed by the informal sector, while others leave the labor force (Dix-Carneiro and Kovak 2017).

Labor mobility is lower and adjustment costs are higher in EMDEs with lower per capita GDP and educational attainment (Artuç, Lederman, and Porto 2015).

In contrast, regions with a high concentration of export-oriented industries benefit significantly from trade. Vietnam's bilateral trade agreement with the United States led to very large reductions in regional poverty from exporting. Provinces experiencing the largest tariff reductions for export to the US experienced fast wage growth for low-education workers, and a reduction in child labor (McCaig 2011). In India, IT call centers led to higher schooling in associated regions because the jobs required more education (Oster and Steinberg 2013). Other studies corroborate the positive relative impact for export-exposed regions. Brazilian locations benefiting from rising Chinese commodity demand observed faster wage growth than other locations (Costa, Garred, and Pessoa 2016), as did Mexican regions exposed to NAFTA (Chiquiar 2008) and Chinese regions most exposed to export opportunities following China's WTO accession (Erten and Leight 2017). In addition, while tariff reductions on final goods have adverse effects on import-competing firms, tariff cuts on intermediate goods lead to substantial increases in wages for workers in importing firms (Amiti and Davis 2012).

The losses associated with import competition were *second order effects*. As in AEs, the studies of the impact of tariff reduction on final goods in import-competing regions, industries, and firms demonstrated that the losses are offset by gains in other sectors and regions. Aggregate outcomes were favorable. For example, poverty was declining in India, Peru, and other country cases, so the import competition merely attenuated the decline in exposed regions. In addition, many of the studies of liberalization episodes were associated with unilateral tariff reductions given that AEs had already reduced tariffs on final goods to low levels prior to the 1980s. More generally, the impact of trade reform would depend on the pattern of reform to both import and export sectors.

The impact of trade on labor markets and on the poor in developing countries needs to account for informality. Informal workers (those insufficiently covered by formal arrangements (ILO 2015) typically account for a large share of the workforce in developing countries (La Porta and Schleifer 2014; Schneider et al. 2010). Empirical studies find mixed effects of trade opening on informality (Becker 2018; ILO and WTO 2009). Some studies find that trade opening reduces informal employment. Large reductions in US tariffs on Vietnamese exports led to a contraction of informal employment as workers transitioned to the formal sector (McCaig and Pavcnik 2018). In Brazil, the informal share of employment decreased as a result of the combined effect of improved access to export markets and domestic tariff cuts on imports (Paz 2014). Also, NAFTA was shown to have reduced informal employment, by pushing informal firms to exit the market (Aleman-Castilla 2006). Other studies find that trade opening has either no effect or increases informal employment (Goldberg and Pavcnik 2003). In Brazil, for example, after long periods of non-employment, trade-displaced formal sector workers eventually fall back into informal employment (Dix-Carneiro and Kovak 2019). In South Africa, Erten et al. (2019) find evidence that workers in districts facing larger tariff reductions experience a relatively more significant decline in both formal and informal employment than workers in districts less exposed to these reductions (Erten et al. 2019). Along the same line, McCaig and McMillan (2019) find that in Botswana, trade liberalization increased the prevalence of working in an informal firm or of being self-employed.

Wage inequality increased after some liberalization episodes. In Colombia's unilateral trade liberalization of the 1990s, wages fell in industries with larger tariff reductions, which were also the industries with the lowest initial wages such as textiles, apparel, footwear. This contributed to a rise in wage inequality, albeit only a marginal component (Attanasio, Goldberg, and Pavcnik 2004; Goldberg and Pavcnik 2005).

Wage inequality was associated with a rise in the skill premium in many EMDEs. Empirical evidence showed that trade led to an increase in earnings of better educated workers relative to less educated ones in developing countries, contrary to the predictions of the Stolper-Samuelson theory. Several factors were at play. Technological adoption increased skill premia globally, not just in AEs. But trade has also contributed to skill-biased technical change (Costinot and Vogel 2010; Pavcnik 2017). Trade has also been correlated with capital inflows, which tend to be complementary to skilled labor (Goldberg and Pavcnik 2007). Evidence suggests that the rise in skill premium may be more pertinent to emerging market economies which are relatively skill-abundant compared to LICs (Goldberg and Pavcnik 2007; Meschi and Vivarelli 2009).

The rise in skill premia may also be associated with offshoring and global value chains. With the fragmentation of the production process along global supply chains, workers in developing countries move into earlier stages of production. For example, AEs outsource activities that are unskilled relative to their average skill level, but represent higher than average skill levels for the destination EMDE. Outsourcing of this type can simultaneously raise the average skill content in both sets of countries. Relatedly, globalization facilitates cross-border teams. Low-skilled workers do routine tasks, while high-skilled workers do knowledge-intensive tasks. The result is a non-monotonic effect on wage inequality (Antràs, Garicano, and Rossi-Hansberg 2006; Costinot, Vogel, and Wang 2012).

EMDEs' exports to AEs induce quality upgrading. Export destination influences the skill premium and wage inequality. High-income countries demand higher quality products, which requires EMDEs to upgrade the skills of their labor force. The rise in demand for skills raises the skill premium leading to higher wage inequality. For example, the 1994 Mexican devaluation increased exports to the United States and led to quality and skill upgrading (Verhoogen 2008). Export to high-income countries also entails other services that are skill intensive. For example, Argentine firms exporting to high-income countries hired more skilled workers than other exporters or domestic firms (Brambilla, Lederman, and Porto 2012).

Much of wage inequality occurs between firms. According to the "new new" trade theory, firms that are larger and more productive pay higher wages and are more likely to export. Exporting raises wages, increasing the wage gap with non-exporters and within firms between more and less educated workers (Helpman, Itskhoki, and Redding 2010). Empirical evidence corroborates the theory as around two-thirds of wage dispersion in Brazil during 1986–1995 occurred between firms within the same sector and among workers with the same occupation (Helpman et al. 2017).

Trade has brought many people out of poverty in EMDEs, though the impact depends on the sectoral pattern of liberalization. Aside from the decline in poverty associated with higher growth, the aggregate impact on poverty will also depend on whether the sectors that expand have a higher concentration of poor compared with the sectors that contract. There is evidence that the US-Vietnam FTA has reduced poverty in Vietnam. Poverty decreased the most for families living in provinces that benefited from the largest cuts in the cost of exporting to the US (McCaig and Pavnick 2014). Following trade liberalization, poverty declined in India, but less so for regions affected more by tariff reductions, which contained some of the poorest households. Still, evidence demonstrates that trade reduces poverty on average, especially in the long run (Winters et al. 2004). Outward-oriented countries, especially those in Asia, achieved remarkable success in bringing hundreds of millions of people out of severe poverty over the span of a few decades.

Trade liberalization does not affect all poor equally. At the individual level, the effects on trade will depend on where the poor live (rural versus urban areas), their individual characteristics (skill, gender), the type of trade policy change (increased import competition or export opportunities) and where they work (type of industry, size firm, formal/informal sector). In her study of the effects of India's liberalization in 1991, Topalova (2010) finds evidence of slower decline in poverty in rural districts, among the least geographically mobile at the bottom of the income distribution, and in Indian states where inflexible labor laws impeded factor reallocation across sectors. In general, the literature finds that not only sectoral patterns of liberalization, but also worker mobility costs—costs to move across sectors, regions or tasks play a key role in the effect of trade on poverty (World Bank and WTO 2015, 2018).

The direct participation of SMEs in international trade in developing countries is not in line with their importance at the domestic level. Evidence suggests that direct exports represent just 7.6 percent of total sales of SMEs in the manufacturing sector, compared to 14.1 percent for large manufacturing enterprises. Among developing regions, Africa has the lowest export share at 3 percent, compared to 8.7 percent for developing Asia. Indirect exports of manufacturing SMEs (i.e., the supply of goods to domestic firms that export) account for another 2.4 percent of total sales, compared to 12.6 percent for large manufacturing enterprises. Even in developing Asia, the region with the highest forward and backward participation of SMEs in GVCs (considering only developing countries), most manufacturing SMEs have both low forward and backward GVC participation rates compared to those of large enterprises (WTO 2016a). A lower participation of SMEs on trade compared to large firms is to be expected, as firms are small because they are less productive. However, the better performance of SME in online international markets suggests there are also trade costs that impede SMEs adequate participation to trade. For example, data from eBay covering 22 countries show that the vast majority of eBay-enabled small firms export—97 percent (eBay 2012, 2014, 2016). There is therefore a potential for more inclusive participation of SMEs in trade.

Trade contributes to structural transformation and development for EMDEs. As with other types of structural transformation, some industries and jobs are lost while others are gained. But people gradually move to industries and regions with better opportunities. Export-led growth contributed to China's structural transformation. People migrated from rural to urban areas and from agriculture to manufacturing. The impact on inclusive growth was mixed. Incomes of manufacturing workers rose, while masses were left behind in agriculture, thus driving up inequality (as in theories of Lewis 1955, and Kuznets 1955). But exporting increases wages of workers, encourages innovation, technology adoption, and product quality upgrading. So, it contributed to China's extraordinary growth and poverty reduction. Over time, China and other export-oriented countries have been able to move up the value chain in production and export. However, this process has been uneven, with the rising manufacturing competitiveness of the Asian exporters coming largely at the expense of developing countries in other regions, especially Latin America and Africa, and with possible trends toward "premature deindustrialization" (Rodrik 2015). Even so, the tradability of services has been increasing over time, leading to new export opportunities (Antras 2020).

Trade reforms are entangled with the political process. The distributional impact of trade integration depends on the pre- and post-reform pattern of protection across sectors. Porto (2006) finds that the regional trade agreement Mercosur provided benefits across the income distribution in Argentina, but especially for the poor. Prior to Mercosur, tariffs were higher on relatively skill-intensive goods, which tended to protect the rich more than the poor. The tariff removals therefore had a pro-poor bias.

IV. Policies to Share Trade Gains

Policy intervention is required to mitigate adverse trade impacts, especially on disadvantaged groups. While theory and evidence point to many gains from trade at the aggregate level and a limited or benign impact on the overall income distribution, there is also ample evidence for significant and sometimes long-lasting losses for some groups in both advanced and developing countries. Whether the relative or absolute losses most impact the well-off or poor in a country depends on the pattern of trade liberalization and initial conditions. Trade policies need to be designed to minimize adverse distributional effects; using the increase in resources (such as higher government revenue associated with higher growth) to provide social safety nets and invest in public services to facilitate adjustment; and employing other government policies to smooth the impact of the trade shock and ease adaptation to it.

A. Trade-related Policies

Lowering tariffs and non-tariff barriers between countries is an essential element for inclusive growth. High trade costs undermine firms' participation into global value chains—a powerful channel for flows of knowledge and know-how between the foreign and the domestic firm. This is particularly harmful for low-income countries, where trade opens up opportunities for new and better jobs for the poor, that are often women, low-skilled workers and workers in the informal sectors. The specific impact of trade on economic and social outcomes of the poor will inevitably depend on its impact on the industries and firms in which the poor employment is concentrated. However, lowering trade costs is essential for countries that seek to take advantage of global value chains to integrate into global markets.

There is evidence that tariff barriers are inversely related to income and are higher for women and people living in rural areas and in the informal sector (Mendoza, Nayyar, and Piermartini 2018). This underlines the need to do more on this front. People with lower levels of income tend to be employed in sectors that face higher barriers to export than people who earn more (Figure 7.10). Women face higher barriers "at the border"—such as higher tariffs in goods that women produce and consume, such as in agriculture and textiles. For India, a pink tariff (the gap between what women pay and what men pay) exists of 6 percentage points (Mendoza et al. 2018). Although the gap is lower in developed countries, there is also a pink tariff for the United States and Germany (World Bank and WTO 2020).

Trade and regulatory barriers in countries with a large poor and rural population represent a big obstacle to increasing farmers' productivity. The agricultural sector is critical to inclusive development, since it employs most of the poor. Tariffs and subsidies create large distortions in the sector. In addition, lack of competition in some segments of the supply chains can make it hard for the poor to capture the benefits of trading. Poor farmers also lack the capacity to comply

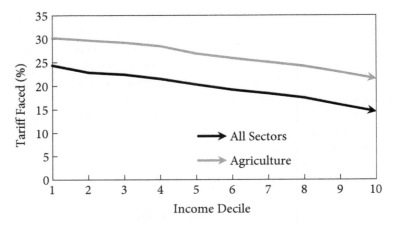

Figure 7.10 Tariff Faced by Income Decile in Agriculture and Averaged Across All Sectors (India)

Source: Mendoza, Nayyar, and Piermartini (2018), based on Indian household survey data collected from July 2011 to June 2012.

with standards. Sanitary and phytosanitary standards, even when well-designed to pursue legitimate objectives, increase production costs and can impede access to international markets (Janssen et al. 2014). Agricultural development will depend on reducing barriers to the imports of seeds and fertilizers, which significantly limit farmers' productivity, and also increasingly to access to a variety of services that are key inputs in production chains (WTO 2019).

Facilitating procedures to cross the border can be particularly beneficial for the poor, especially for women. Long waiting times at the border are particularly disadvantageous for women who are more likely to being discriminated against and who are more time-constrained due to the higher burden of work at home (World Bank and WTO 2018, 2020). In addition, trade facilitation is also more generally important for trade of perishable goods, that are often the products that the poor produce.

Fixed trade costs adversely affect the ability of SMEs to participate in trade, to a greater extent than large enterprises. Evidence suggests that a lack of information about foreign distribution networks, border regulations and standards represent the main obstacles to trade for SMEs (WTO 2016a; Fontagné, Orefice, and Piermartini 2020). Large firms can more easily adapt to new costly requirements, but small firms are driven out of business if a new restrictive standard is introduced into a market (Fontagné et al. 2015). There is also evidence that SMEs perceive high tariffs as a more significant obstacle to trade than large firms (WTO 2016a). This may be because SMEs' trade flows are more sensitive (elastic) to tariff changes (Spearot 2013) and/or because SMEs appear to be relatively more concentrated in sectors facing higher tariff barriers than large firms (WTO 2016a).

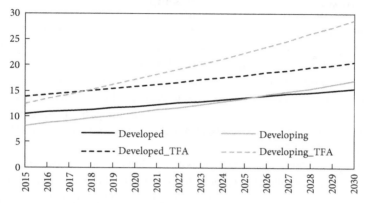

Figure 7.11 Trade Facilitation: Projected Exports 2015–2030
Source: WTO (2015a), in trillions constant $US 2007.

Trade facilitation plays a key role in reducing transaction costs and facilitating inclusive growth. High trade costs isolate poor economies from international markets and stand in their way of benefiting from greater specialization, accessing new technologies, and generating economies of scale. Several studies estimate that the full implementation of the Trade Facilitation Agreement (TFA) could reduce global trade costs by an average of 14 percent (WTO 2015a) and up to 23 percent (Moise and Sorescu 2013).[6] Low and lower-middle income countries are likely to see the biggest reduction in trade costs (Teh et al. 2016). Developing countries implementing the TFA have a significantly higher forecast of exports growth between 2015–2030 (Figure 7.11).

How a country implements its own trade policies can play a role in easing adjustment and spreading the gains from trade. For example, advanced announcement and gradual phasing of trade liberalization can help to avoid labor market bottlenecks and congestion, and can buy time to put in place domestic cost mitigating policies (Bacchetta and Jansen 2003). This is especially true when a rapid increase in import competition is concentrated in a sector or region. At the same time, these policy decisions are not one-size-fits-all, and potential advantages should be weighed against the costs of delaying the benefits (Trebilcock 2014). Multilateral trade liberalization is by its very nature a gradual process and in this respect leaves room for adjustment processes to take place smoothly. Many WTO agreements contain more or less explicit provisions that aim to facilitate their adoption. In particular, they often specify phased in implementation periods, with developing and least-developed countries usually being granted longer

---

[6] The Trade Facilitation Agreement (TFA) was negotiated and adopted during the Ninth WTO Ministerial Conference (MC-IX) in December 2013 and entered into force in February 2017. It aims at expediting the movement, release and clearance of goods, improving cooperation between customs and other authorities and enhancing technical assistance and building capacity for its implementation.

implementation periods than industrialized countries. Temporary import safeguards are another policy measure that may be appropriate in exceptional circumstances, and when consistent with a country's WTO obligations. However, any consideration of invoking safeguards should take into account their adverse effects on domestic workers in downstream industries, the additional costs to consumers, and the impact on policy uncertainty. Also, enhanced communication by governments on the benefits of trade may broaden engagement, strengthen public support for trade, and make trade more inclusive (IMF, World Bank, and WTO 2018).[7]

Specific provisions addressing various dimensions of inclusiveness are included in an increasing number of regional trade agreements. A growing number of RTAs include provisions that explicitly relate to some of the dimensions of inclusiveness, including human rights, sustainable development, gender equality and SMEs participation. Provisions in RTAs are known to be heterogenous and inclusiveness-related provisions are no exception. While many provisions on inclusiveness promote cooperation activities, some other provisions establish specific level playing field disciplines or exemptions. Relatively common provisions related to the social dimension of sustainable development require the parties to effectively enforce, and in some cases, adopt and improve labor standards (Raess and Sari 2018 and 2020). Often, a related provision further requires the parties not to relax their labor standards in order to attract investment and promote exports. Some gender-related provisions refer to specific international conventions and call for or require the adoption and effective implementation of gender-related policies (Monteiro 2018). Some inclusiveness-related provisions target firms, by promoting voluntary best practices of corporate social responsibility (Monteiro, 2021). Several provisions found in recent RTAs aim at improving SMEs access to trade-related information, including through the creation of a publicly accessible website (Monteiro 2016a), exempting SMEs and/or programs supporting SMEs from specific trade obligations set out in the RTA.

But little is known about the actual effectiveness of these provisions on inclusiveness. Although some RTAs have established institutional arrangements to monitor the progress of implementation of some of these inclusiveness-related provisions, most of the available evidence on the effectiveness of inclusiveness-related provisions remains anecdotal and limited. This is in large part due to the lack of disaggregated data (for instance by gender and firm size), which hinders the ability of researchers to identify the differential effect of these inclusiveness-related provisions.

Some trade agreements contain chapters to deal with environmental issues or climate change, though there is scope for more ambitious action. A few RTAs

---

[7] IMF, World Bank, and WTO (2017) Making trade an engine of growth for all, Paper for discussion at the meeting of G20 sherpas, March 23–24, 2017, Frankfurt, Germany.

make binding environmental commitments (Monteiro 2016b; Monteiro and Trachtman 2020). Trade policy can facilitate environmental goals in a number of ways (WEF 2020).[8] Tariffs can be reduced on environmentally friendly goods and services and agreements reached on regulatory standards that affect them. Governments could commit to phase out inefficient environmentally unfriendly fossil-fuel subsidies that mostly benefit high income consumers. Climate policies, such as carbon pricing regimes and border carbon adjustments, can be aligned with trade rules. Governments can pivot towards green procurement practices, including by signing on to the WTO Government Procurement Agreement.

Technological innovation is expected to boost trade growth, as a result of both falling trade costs and the more intensive use of ICT-services. Technological innovation, including robotization, artificial intelligence, servicification of the production process, and the rise of online markets and platforms, is projected to increase global trade growth by an average of 2 percentage points per year between now and 2030, with higher growth for developing countries and services exports (Bekkers et al. 2021).

Digital trade can play a significant role in supporting inclusive economic growth and enhancing the development perspectives of developing countries (Smeets 2021). Of critical importance is the need to put the right infrastructure in place and to facilitate IT and reduce transaction costs, thus allowing a better connection to markets. The further adoption of digital technologies is expected to increase developing countries' trade, in part by facilitating connections to GVCs. This requires adequate domestic regulatory systems as well as harmonization and coordination of such policies at the international level (Smeets 2021). Based on a review of the literature and experience from Africa, Parry et al. (2021) find that digital advances (the quickening pace of the Fourth Industrial Revolution (4IR)) can serve to accelerate inclusive growth. However, international trade is increasingly determined by the competitive and enabling environment created by countries at the national (i.e., domestic) level, including well-informed policies, regulations and institutions to drive the necessary changes. Developing countries that lack the tools to compete in the new digital environment are in danger of being left even further behind. The areas requiring special attention by policymakers include: the problem of data inadequacy; uneven and costly digital connectivity; and education systems that are not preparing entrepreneurs for in-demand jobs or for the workplace of the future. Two of the prerequisites for leveraging digital technologies in order to drive more inclusive growth are an effective legal and regulatory framework and a commercial environment that is both trade- and investment-friendly.

---

[8] The US-Mexico-Canada Agreement and the Comprehensive and Progressive Agreement for Trans-Pacific Partnership include mechanisms for dispute resolution (WEF 2020).

Domestic reforms help countries to benefit from trade liberalization.[9] For example, WTO accession requires countries

> to put in place a set of norms and institutions, which support the liberalization of markets and increase transparency and promote the rule of law, contract enforcement and the evolution of an independent judicial system. In principle, nothing would prevent government from putting in place these norms and regulations on a unilateral basis. The role of the WTO in this process is to facilitate the introduction of effective reforms not only by reinforcing the credibility of the government's trade policies but also help introduce the policies that are based on best-practices and that must be harmonized.
>
> (Bacchetta and Drabek 2002)

This hypothesis of the importance of domestic reforms has been analyzed and validated in the case of Georgia (Arveladze and Smeets 2017) and in the case of the Kyrgyz Republic (Smeets and Djumaliev 2019).

Multilateral cooperation through accession to the WTO has significantly lowered overall levels of protection and expanded trade opportunities over the past 20 years (WTO 2015b).[10] Acceding members have made binding commitments on virtually all their tariffs, thus significantly improving the certainty and predictability of their trade regimes and creating a more competitive environment. As a result of their domestic reforms and more liberal commitments, trade of acceding countries has grown almost double that of original members (12½ percent versus 7½ percent), including after the global financial crisis of 2008. Multilateral cooperation also provides a forum for continued dialogue on inclusion and sustainability issues.

B. Adjustment Policies

Adjustment policies are justified on three grounds: economic efficiency, fairness and/or political support. Though not specific to trade, government interventions aimed at reducing adjustment costs speed up the transition towards an efficient allocation of resources and improve economic efficiency. Adjustment policies can also be justified on the basis of fairness as many gain from trade, while adjustment costs are borne by a small number of workers and firms. Finally, the political argument in favor of adjustment policies, particularly trade-specific adjustment programs, is that they may increase support for further trade opening (Trebilcock 2014).

---

[9] WTO accessions Annual report by the Director General December 2016 (WTO 2016b).

[10] WTO at Twenty, challenges and achievements, 2015, chapter 5. Accession refers to Article XII members and has been especially beneficial for large economies like China.

Policies that governments can implement to lower the cost of adjustment typically involve some combination of active and passive labor market policies. Countries have a variety of tools at their disposal to facilitate adjustment. While passive and active labor market policies are the instruments of choice, countries can also facilitate adjustment with other complementary policies that have more of an indirect effect on the labor market. Passive labor market policies usually refer to unemployment benefit systems and social insurance programs which help workers with temporary income support, while active labor market policies cover a wide range of policies aimed at helping workers find a job as quickly as possible (Chapter 3). From a theoretical perspective, wage subsidies seem to be the best way to compensate workers who switch sectors (Davidson and Matusz 2000, 2006; Kletzer and Litan 2001; Kletzer 2016). Available evidence on the effectiveness of adjustment policies suggests that there is no "one-size-fits-all" recipe to reduce trade-related adjustment costs (WTO 2017).

In addition to social protection programs, place-based policies may be needed to increase geographic mobility and support the economies of hard-hit regions. Chapter 17 elaborates on the policy options. When "spatially-blind" policies such as universal social safety nets and adjustment policies operating at the national level are insufficient, "spatially-connective" policies to integrate lagging regions or "spatially-targeted" policies aimed at regional interventions may be warranted. Public investment in infrastructure, information, and communication networks can reduce transportation and communications costs to connect peripheral regions to markets and jobs in leading regions. Spatially targeted interventions— such as regionally focused public-investment projects, the relocation of government agencies and research institutions, and location-specific tax incentives and regulatory relief—could support local demand and business conditions in peripheral regions. The appropriate policy mix will be country- and context-specific. It will depend on the characteristics of a country's leading and lagging regions, and the key drivers of regional disparities. Ultimately, policy makers must strike the right balance between fostering rapid but regionally uneven growth on the one hand and promoting more inclusive regional development outcomes on the other. There is a similarity between intranational and international trade in the way they affect the geography of economic activity within and across borders. On one hand, this means that it is difficult to identify the specific cause of a certain inclusiveness issue. On the other hand, this also means some of the policy recommendations may hold whether geographical inequalities occur because of domestic market integration or international trade.

Only a small number of countries provide special assistance to workers who lose their jobs due to increased imports or international shifts in production. The United States' Trade Adjustment Assistance (TAA) was introduced in 1962 to compensate workers negatively affected by tariff cuts negotiated as part of the GATT's Kennedy Round and help address domestic resistance to trade liberalization. Its scope has since been broadened and its efficiency improved through successive revisions (Rosen 2008; Guth and Lee 2017). The TAA includes both active and passive assistance components (Collins 2018). Overall, empirical evidence about the effectiveness of TAA is mixed (D'Amico and Schochet 2012). A recent review of evaluations of the TAA by Guth and Lee (2018) concludes that targeting of the program has improved over time, that TAA has had neutral to slightly positive effects on employment and mixed effects on wages (depending upon which assumptions and methodologies were employed and which version of the program was evaluated) and that TAA training has generally been beneficial for workers. A recent study finds that the TAA works as a short-term cushion for workers by providing them with the skills they need to find jobs quicker, but that these skills become obsolete or are less in demand 10 years later (Hyman 2018).

Multiple features of the TAA program explaining its limited efficiency have been identified and addressed over the years. Among the reasons behind the mixed success of successive versions of the TAA program are restrictive eligibility criteria, long deadlines for eligibility, limited awareness of the existence of the programs, technical problems relating to access to the benefits or waiting periods, the bureaucratic petition process or the artificial strictures it places on workers' re-employment options (Rosen 2008; Autor 2018). According to Rosen (2008), despite a significant increase in import penetration in the US economy over the years, efforts to assist workers adversely affected by increases in imports and shifts in production have remained modest at best and implementation of useful reforms has been uneven. In Rosen's view, expanding labor-market adjustment programs remains a low priority in the United States, but this should change. Along the same line, Autor argues that making assistance more accessible, flexible, and supportive rather than constraining of labor market re-entry would be a first constructive step towards mitigating adjustment costs and sharing the gains from trade integration more broadly (Autor 2018).

So far, the European Globalization Adjustment Fund (EGF), launched in 2007 by the European Union (EU) to help support workers made redundant by international trade, has also had a limited impact. The Fund provides member States with additional funding to carry out active labor market policies in situations where major structural changes in world trade patterns lead to a serious economic disruption. The current annual budget of the Fund is €150 million, which is much less than the €12 billion allocated to the European Social Fund (ESF), which deals with long-term labor adjustment. As the EGF is a new program, it is not currently possible to determine whether those who benefited from EGF financing did better than those who did not. Claeys and Sapir (2018) estimate that the EGF helped only about 4 percent of workers adversely affected by globalization between 2007 and 2016. This could be due to the Fund's relatively high eligibility threshold of 500 workers, to the fact that intra-EU competition or offshoring is not an eligibility criterion, to the relatively slow administrative process which can take up to 12 months between application and approval of funds, and/or to the co-financing rate of 60 percent which may be too low for some countries (Puccio 2017).

Most countries implement general adjustment policies which aim at addressing adjustment problems independently of their cause. For one, special or targeted programs are often difficult to access for workers for reasons discussed previously. General adjustment policies appear to be more effective than specific trade adjustment policies for facilitating workers' adjustment to trade, particularly in the presence of global value chains. As a result of increasing input-output linkages, trade shocks spread more widely in an economy indirectly affecting workers up and down the value chains, making it more difficult for them to claim trade adjustment assistance. Non-specific adjustment programs also support workers adversely affected by technological and other shocks which generate effects that are difficult to disentangle from and similar to those induced by trade (Bacchetta and Stolzenburg 2019). Finally, providing specific support to workers made redundant by globalization can be seen as an unfair practice (Baicker and Rehavi 2004). General adjustment policies typically involve passive and active labor market policies and adequate social protection systems (Chapter 13).

While policy knowledge is lamentably incomplete, training assistance and education programs have an increasingly important role to play in facilitating adjustment to trade in the presence of global value chains. Autor (2018) emphasizes the importance of wage insurance and wage subsidies as well as of explicitly engineering adjustment policies to be rigorously evaluated as they go into effect as policy levers that appear promising for mitigating adjustment costs such as those associated with the China shock. With the rise of global value chains, comparative advantage has shifted towards the level of production stages and specific tasks within value chains. As their old task might disappear altogether as a result of a trade shock, workers need to upgrade their skill set to perform a different task or to transition without training into low wage jobs (Keller and Utar 2016). Effective training assistance and education policies (Chapter 14) promote skills that are relevant for multiple industries, increasing workers' flexibility and resilience in an unpredictable job market (Humlum and Munch 2019; Baldwin 2016). Recruitment campaigns that provide information about job opportunities have proven effective for increasing labor force participation and mobility in rural India (Jensen 2012).

C. Complementary Policies

The poor, women and SMEs also face high "behind the border" constraints like limited access to finance, education and technology. For example, women's access to the Internet remains significantly lower than men's (in developing countries the Internet access gap is 7.6 percent on average) and tech-related jobs remain male-dominated. A challenge in GVCs is to ensure that women have better access to high-skill tasks and occupations. This would require more inclusive management organizations. For women to capture full potential benefit from trade, the barriers that hold women back need to be lifted and appropriate policies to deal with adjustment costs are to be put in place (World Bank and WTO 2020).

Lack of competition in the distribution sector, high domestic transport costs can significantly limit the extent to which the benefits from trade reach the poor. Trade openness and trade growth alone may not suffice to end extreme poverty. Often the poor live in rural areas, far from ports. If inland transport costs are high, say, only a part of the beneficial price changes that trade bring will pass on to the poorest in a country. Trade reduces poverty also because it reduces the price of the goods they consume, including for example fertilizers used in agricultural production. The extent to which households benefit from trade liberalization on the consumption side depends on a range of factors that influence the pass-through of price changes from the border to consumers. Transport costs matter. For example, a study finds that tariff pass-through was significantly higher in the Mexican states closest to the United States border, and thus, households living in these states benefited relatively more from the reductions in tariffs (Nicita 2004). Another important factor shaping the extent to which the poor benefit from trade is market frictions. If domestic industries are imperfectly competitive, changes in tariffs may be absorbed by profit margins or mark-ups (Campa and Goldberg 2002). There is evidence the market power of intermediaries in domestic industries affects the mark-ups and results in different rates of tariff pass-through within sub-Saharan Africa (Atkin and Donaldson 2015).

Macroeconomic stabilization policies are also a critical part of the toolkit for reducing adjustment costs and sharing the benefits of trade. Recessions impede opportunities for re-employment following job displacement due to trade or other structural reasons, triggering large, persistent earnings losses for affected workers (Davis and von Watcher 2011). In addition to preventing or ameliorating crises and downturns, stable sustainable macroeconomic policies can create fiscal space for financing social insurance, education and retraining, and labor market programs. Strong public finances—especially low fiscal deficits—can also improve the country's savings-investment position, thus avoiding current account deficits that accelerate deindustrialization in AEs and invite destabilizing capital inflows in EMDEs. Strong macroeconomic management can also avoid overvalued real exchange rates that weaken trade competitiveness, reduce economic growth (Rodrik 2008; Berg and Miao 2010), and contribute to balance of payments crises (Kaminsky, Lizondo, and Reinhart 1998), all of which undermine inclusive growth.

V. Conclusion

International trade is strongly associated with improvements in inclusive growth. While each research approach has its merits and shortcomings, studies using a variety of methodologies find that trade integration increases growth and, in EMDEs, lowers inequality at the aggregate level. Trade improves productivity, contributes to knowledge diffusion and innovation, incentivizes skill accumulation, and increases product variety while reducing prices. A predictable and transparent environment is essential to support business and sustainable development. At this regard, the World Trade Organization plays a critical role in underpinning an open and inclusive global trading system.

More can be done to foster more inclusive trade. At the multilateral level, for instance, addressing distortions in agriculture to improve market access and reduce food price volatility can benefit both poor farmers and poor consumers. An agreement to limit fisheries subsidies will be crucial for the livelihoods of coastal communities and the preservation of fish stocks (IMF, World Bank, and WTO 2017, 2018). Finally, addressing barriers to trade in services and e-commerce can also open up new opportunities for inclusive growth by benefiting for example MSMEs and women (World Bank and WTO 2020).

Actions at the multilateral level need to be complemented by more targeted action to remove the constraints that the MSMEs, women and the poor face in benefiting from trade. Farmers and firms in rural areas face particularly high transport costs and delays when shipping to international—and national—markets. Workers in informal firms, women and small business typically have limited access to finance, including trade finance, that limit their ability to access international markets trade.

Trade, like other structural change—notably change triggered by technological progress—has heterogeneous effects on regions, industries, firms, and workers, depending on their orientation toward import competing versus export markets. In both AEs and EMDEs, those regions, industries, and firms most vulnerable and exposed to import competition suffer relative declines in labor market conditions and other socio-economic outcomes. But these are only relative and partial effects. Trade induces job growth in other areas. Moreover, those regions, industries, and firms most oriented and exposed to export opportunities experience relative improvements in labor market and socio-economic outcomes. And studies find the latter beneficial effects outweigh the losses of import competition, consistent with the aggregate benefits.

Policies are nonetheless needed to ensure the net benefits of trade are shared with those left behind by the structural changes. Policy actions to improve labor mobility—across sectors, regions, and skills—are particularly important. These include labor market policies aimed at retraining workers and helping them to transition into new job opportunities. Wide-range education policies that support the development of the right skills in a rapidly changing economic and technological environment, credit policies to help fund self-employment or human capital investment, housing market policies to improve geographical mobility, or regional policies that help re-orient the economies of the harder-hit regions are all needed to support adjustment. And, for those who suffer long-term losses from economic change redistributive policies may be necessary.

References

Ahn, J., Dabla-Norris, E., Duval, R., Hu, B., and Njie, L. 2016. "Reassessing the Productivity Gains from Trade Liberalization." International Monetary Fund Working Paper No. 16/77.

Alcalá, F., and Ciccone, A. 2004. "Trade and Productivity." *The Quarterly Journal of Economics*, 119(2): 613–46.

Aleman-Castilla, B. 2006. "The Effect of Trade Liberalization on Informality and Wages: Evidence from Mexico." Centre for Economic Performance (CEP), Discussion Paper 763, London: London School of Economics.

AliResearch. 2017. "Inclusive Growth and E-Commerce: China's Experience." Prepared for a meeting on Inclusive Development and E-Commerce: The Case of China, UNCTAD, April 2017.

Altindag, D.T., and Mocan, N.H. 2010. "Joblessness and Perceptions about the Effectiveness of Democracy." NBER Working Paper No. 15994.

Álvarez, R., Benavente, J.M., and Crespi, G. 2019. "Foreign Competition and Innovation in Latin America." IDB Discussion Paper IDB-DP-00728.

Amiti, M., and Davis, D. 2012. "Trade, Firms, and Wages: Theory and Evidence." *Review of Economic Studies* 79(1): 1–36.

Amiti, M., and Khandelwal, A. 2013. "Import Competition and Quality Upgrading." *Review of Economics and Statistics* 95(2): 476–90.

Antràs, P. 2020. "De-Globalisation? Global Value Chains in the Post-Covid-19 Age." NBER Working Paper No. 28115.

Antràs, P., Garicano, L., and Rossi-Hansberg, E. 2006. "Offshoring in a Knowledge Economy." *The Quarterly Journal of Economics*, Oxford University Press, 121(1): 31–77.

Antras, P., and Helpman, E. 2004. "Global Sourcing." *Journal of Political Economy* 112(3): 552–80.

Argent, J., and Begazo, T. 2015. "Competition in Kenyan Markets and its Impact on Income and Poverty: A Case Study on Sugar and Maize." World Bank Policy Research Working Paper, 7179.

Artuç, E., Lederman, D., and Porto, G. 2015. "A Mapping of Labor Mobility Costs in the Developing World." *Journal of International Economics* 95(1): 28–41.

Arveladze, G., and Smeets, M. 2017. Georgia's Post-Accession Structural Reform Challenges', *WTO Working Paper Series*, (WTO), ERSD-2017–10.

Atkin, D., and Donaldson, D. 2015. "Who's Getting Globalized? The Size and Implications of Intra-national Trade Costs." CEPR Discussion Papers 10,759.

Attanasio, O., Goldberg, P., and Pavcnik, N. 2004. "Trade Reforms and Wage Inequality in Colombia." *Journal of Development Economics* 74(4): 331–66.

Autor, D. 2018. "Trade and Labor Markets: Lessons from China's rise." IZA World of Labor, 2018: 431.

Autor, D., and Dorn, D. 2013. "The Growth of Low-Skill Service Jobs and the Polarization of the US Labor Market." *American Economic Review* 103(5): 1553–97.

Autor, D.H., Dorn, D., and Hanson, G.H. 2013. "The China Syndrome: Local Labor Market Effects of Import Competition in the United States." *American Economic Review* 103(6): 2121–68.

Autor, David, David Dorn, and Gordon Hanson. 2015. "Untangling Trade and Technology: Evidence from Local Labour Markets." *The Economic Journal* 125 (May): 621–46.

Autor, D.H., Dorn, D., and Hanson, G.H. 2016. "The China Shock: Learning from Labor-Market Adjustment to Large Changes in Trade." *Annual Review of Economics* 8: 205–40.

Autor, D., Dorn, D., Hanson, G., and Majlesi, K. 2020. "Importing Political Polarization? The Electoral Consequences of Rising Trade Exposure." *American Economic Review* 110(10): 3139–83.

Autor, D., Dorn, D., Hanson, G.H., and Song, J. 2014. "Trade Adjustment: Worker Level Evidence." *Quarterly Journal of Economics*, 129(4): 1799–860.

Bacchetta, M., and Drabek, Z. 2002. "Effects of WTO Accession on Policy-Making in Sovereign States: Preliminary Lessons from the Recent Experience of Transition Economies," *WTO Working Paper Series*, (WTO), April 2, 2002.

Bacchetta, M., and Jansen, M. 2003. "Adjusting to Trade Liberalization, the Role of Policy, Institutions and WTO Disciplines." World Trade Organization, Special Studies no 7, Geneva: World Trade Organization.

Bacchetta, M., and Stolzenburg, V. 2019. "Trade, Value Chains and Labor Markets in Advanced Economies." In *Global Value Chain Development Report 2019— Technological Innovation, Supply Chain Trade, and Workers in a Globalized World.* Geneva: World Trade Organization, pp. 45–62.

Bahri, A. 2021, "Blockchaining International Trade: A Way Forward for Women's Empowerment?" In Smeets (Ed.), pp. 300–15.

Baicker, K., and Rehavi, M. 2004. "Policy Watch: Trade Adjustment Assistance." *Journal of Economic Perspectives* 18(2): 239–55.

Baldarrago, E., and Salinas, G. 2017. "Trade Liberalization in Peru: Adjustment Costs Amidst High Labor Mobility." IMF Working Paper No. 17/47. Washington: International Monetary Fund.

Baldwin, R. 2016. *The Great Convergence: Information Technology and the New Globalization*. Cambridge, MA: Belknap Press.

Baldwin, R., and Cain, G. 2000. "Shifts in Relative U.S. Wages: The Role of Trade, Technology, and Factor Endowments." *Review of Economics and Statistics* 82(4): 580–95.

Beaton, K., Cebotari, A., and Komaromi, A. 2017. "Revisiting the Link between Trade, Growth and Inequality: Lessons for Latin America and the Caribbean," IMF Working Paper No. 17/46. Washington: International Monetary Fund.

Becker, D. 2018. "Heterogeneous Firms and Informality: The Effects of Trade Liberalization on Labour Markets." *Oxford Economic Papers* 70(1): 47–72.

Becker, S., Ekholm, K., and Muendler, M.A. 2013. "Offshoring and the Onshore Composition of Tasks and Skills." *Journal of International Economics* 90(1): 91–106.

Bekkers, E., Koopman, R., Sabbadini, G., and Teh, R. 2021. "The Impact of Digital Technologies on Developing Countries' Trade." In Smeets (Ed.), pp. 36–53.

Berg, A., and Miao, Y. 2010. "The Real Exchange Rate and Growth Revisited: The Washington Consensus Strikes Back?" IMF Working Paper No. 10/58.

Berik, G. 2011. "Gender Aspects of Trade." In *Trade and Employment: From Myths to Facts*, edited by Jansen, M. Geneva: ILO.

Berman, E., Bound, J., and Machin, S. 1997. "Implications of Skill-Biased Technological Change: International Evidence." NBER Working Papers, no. 6166.

Bernard, A., Jensen B., and Schott, P.K. 2006. "Survival of the Best Fit: Exposure to Low-Wage Countries and the (Uneven) Growth of US Manufacturing Plants." *Journal of International Economics* 68: 219–37.

Blinder, A.S., and Krueger, A.B. 2009. "Alternative Measures of Offshorability: A Survey Approach." NBER Working Paper 15,287, August.

Bivens, J. 2008. *Everybody Wins, Except for Most of Us: What Economics Teaches About Globalization*. Washington, DC: Economic Policy Institute.

Bivens, J. 2013. "Using standard models to benchmark the costs of globalization for American workers without a college degree," Washington, DC: Economic Policy Institute Briefing Paper No. 354.

Black, S.E., and Brainerd, E. 2004. "Importing Equality? The Impact of Globalization on Gender Discrimination." *Industrial and Labor Review* 57.

Blanchard, O. 2006. "European Unemployment: The Evolution of Facts and Ideas." *Economic Policy*, CEPR, CES, MSH, 21(45): 5–59.

Bloom, N., Draca, M., and Van Reenen, J. 2015. "Trade Induced Technical Change: The Impact of Chinese Imports on Innovation, Diffusion, and Productivity." *Review of Economic Studies* 83(1): 87–117.

Borjas, G., Freeman, R., and Katz, L. 1991. "On the Labor Market Effects of Immigration and Trade," NBER Working Papers 3761, National Bureau of Economic Research, Inc.

Brambilla, I., Lederman, D., and Porto, G. 2012. "Exports, Export Destinations, and Skills." *American Economic Review* 102(7): 3406–38.

Broda, C., and Weinstein, D. 2006. "Globalization and the Gains from Variety." *Quarterly Journal of Economics* 121(2): 541–85.

ABusse and Koniger. 2012. "Trade and Economic Growth: A Re-examination of the Empirical Evidence," HWWI Research Paper, No. 123, Hamburgisches WeltWirtschaftsInstitut (HWWI), Hamburg.

Bustos, P. 2011. "Trade Liberalization, Exports, and Technology Upgrading: Evidence on the Impact of MERCOSUR on Argentinian Firms." *American Economic Review* 101.

Cadot, O., Ferrantino M., Gourdon, J., and Reyes, D. 2018. "Reforming Non-Tariff Measures: From Evidence to Policy Advice." Washington, DC: World Bank.

Campa, J.M., and Goldberg, L. 2002. "Exchange rate pass-through into import prices: a macro or micro phenomenon?" Staff Reports 149, Federal Reserve Bank of New York.

Carrère, C., Fugazza, M., Olarreaga, M., and Robert-Nicoud, F. 2016. "On the Heterogeneous Effect of Trade on Unemployment," CEPR Discussion Paper No. DP11540.

Cerdeiro, D.A., and Komaromi, A. 2020. "Trade and Income in the Long Run: Are There Really Gains, and Are They Widely Shared?" *Review of International Economics.* https://doi.org/10.1111/roie.12494.

Chiquiar, D. 2008. "Globalization, Regional Wage Differentials and the Stolper-Samuelson Theorem: Evidence from Mexico." *Journal of International Economics* 74(1): 70–93.

Claeys, G., and Sapir, A. 2018. The European Globalisation Adjustment Fund: Easing the pain from trade? Breugel Policy Contribution No. 5. Brussels: Breugel.

Cline, W. 1997. "Trade and Income Distribution," Peterson Institute Press: All Books, Peterson Institute for International Economics, number 58, October.

Coe, D., and Helpman, E. 1995. "International R&D Spillovers." *European Economic Review* 39(5): 859–87.

Coe, D., Helpman, E., and Hoffmaister, A.W. 1997. "North-South R&D spillovers." *The Economic Journal* 107(440): 134–49.

Coe, D., Helpman, E., and Hoffmaister, A. 2009. "International R&D Spillovers and Institutions." *European Economic Review* 53(7): 723–41.

Colantone, I., and Stanig, P. 2018a. "The Trade Origins of Economic Nationalism: Import Competition and Voting Behavior in Western Europe." *American Journal of Political Science* 62(4): 936–53.

Colantone, I., and Stanig, P. 2018b. "Global Competition and Brexit." *American Political Science Review* 112(2): 201–18.

Collins, B. 2018. Trade Adjustment Assistance for Workers and the TAA Reauthorization Act of 2015, Congressional Research Service, 7–5700.

Costa, F., Garred, J., and Pessoa, J.P. 2016. "Winners and Losers from a Commodities-for- Manufactures Trade Boom." *Journal of International Economics* 102: 50–69.

Costinot, A., and Rodríguez-Clare, A. 2014. "Trade Theory with Numbers: Quantifying the Consequences of Globalization." In *Handbook of International Economics (Vol. 4)*, edited by Gopinath, G., Helpman, E., and Rogoff, K. Amsterdam: Elsevier.

Costinot, A., and Vogel, J. 2010. "Matching and Inequality in the World Economy." *Journal of Political Economy* 118(4): 747–86.

Costinot, A., Vogel, J., and Wang, S. 2012. "Global Supply Chains and Wage Inequality." *American Economic Review* 102(3): 396–401.

Cravino, J., and Levchenko, A. 2017. "The Distributional Consequences of Large Devaluations." *American Economic Review* 107(11): 3477–509.

Crinò, R., and Epifani, P. 2017. "The Skill Bias of the US Trade Deficit." In *The Factory-Free Economy: Outsourcing, Servitization, and the Future of Industry*, edited by Lionel Fontagné and Ann Harrison. Oxford: Oxford University Press.

D'Amico, R., and Schochet, P.Z. 2012. The Evaluation of the Trade Adjustment Assistance Program: A Synthesis of Major Findings: Final Report Prepared as Part of the Evaluation of the Trade Adjustment Assistance Program, Oakland (CA): Social Policy Research Associates, Mathematica Policy Research.

Dauth, W., Findeisen, S., and Suedekum, J. 2014. "The Rise of the East and the Far East: German Labor Markets and Trade Integration." *Journal of the European Economic Association*, 12(6): 1643–75.

Dauth, W., Findeisen, S., and Suedekum, J. 2017. "Trade and Manufacturing Jobs in Germany." *American Economic Review* 107(5): 337–42.

Davidson, C., and Matusz, S.J. 2000. "Globalization and Labour-Market Adjustment: How Fast and at What Cost?" *Oxford Review of Economic Policy* 16(3): 42–56.

Davidson, C., and Matusz, S.J. 2006. "Trade Liberalization and Compensation." *International Economic Review* 47(3): 723–47.

Davis, D., and Harrigan, J. 2011. "Good Jobs, Bad Jobs, and Trade Liberalization." *Journal of International Economics* 84: 26–36.

Davis, S., and von Watcher, T. 2011. "Recessions and the Costs of Job Loss," NBER Working Paper no. 17638.

De Loecker, J. 2013. "Detecting Learning by Exporting." *American Economic Journal: Microeconomics* 5(3): 1–21.

De Loecker, J., and Goldberg, P. 2014. "Firm Performance in a Global Market." *Annual Review of Economics* 6: 201–27.

De Loecker, J., Goldberg, P.K., Khandelwal, A., and Pavcnik, N. 2016. "Prices, Markups and Trade Reform." *Econometrica* 84(2): 445–510.

Dippel, C., Gold, R., and Heblich, S. 2015. "Globalization and Its (Dis-)Content: Trade Shocks and Voting Behaviour." NBER Working Paper 21812.

Dix-Carneiro, R., and Kovak, B. 2015. "Trade Reform and Regional Dynamics: Evidence from 25 Years of Brazilian Matched Employer-Employee Data." NBER Working Paper 20908.

Dix-Carneiro, R., and Kovak, B.K. 2017. "Trade Liberalization and Regional Dynamics." *American Economic Review* 107(10): 2908–46.

Dix-Carneiro, R., and Kovak, B.K. 2019. "Margins of Labor Market Adjustment to Trade." *Journal of International Economics* 117: 125–42.

Dix-Carneiro, R., Soares, R.R., and Ulyssea, G. 2018. "Economic Shocks and Crime: Evidence from the Brazilian Trade Liberalization." *American Economic Journal: Applied Economics* 10(4): 158–95.

Dollar, D., and Kraay, A. 2003. "Institutions, Trade and Growth." *Journal of Monetary Economics* 50(1): 133–62.

Dollar, D., and A. Kraay. 2004. "Trade, Growth, and Poverty." *The Economic Journal* 114: F22–F49.

Dollar, D., Kleineberg, T., and Kraay, A. 2016. "Growth Still Is Good for the Poor." European Economic Review 81(C): 68–85.

Dutt, P., Mitra, D., and Ranjan, P. 2009. "International Trade and Unemployment: Theory and Cross-National Evidence." *Journal of International Economics*, 78(1): 32–44.

Dutt, P., and Mitra, D. 2006. "Labor Versus Capital Trade-Policy: The Role of Ideology And Inequality." *Journal of International Economics* 69(2): 310–20.

eBay. 2012. Small Online Business Growth Report 2012. San Jose, CA: eBay Inc.

eBay. 2014. Small Online Business Growth Report 2014. San Jose, CA: eBay Inc.

eBay. 2016. Small Online Business Growth Report 2016. San Jose, CA: eBay Inc.

Ebenstein, A., Harrison, A., and McMillan, M. 2015. "Why Are American Workers Getting Poorer? China, Trade and Offshoring." NBER Working Paper No. 21027.

Edmond, C., Midrigan, V., and Xu, D. 2015. "Competition, Markups, and the Gains from International Trade." *American Economic Review* 105(10): 3183–221.

Edmonds, E., Pavcnik, N., and Topalova, P. 2010. "Trade Adjustment and Human Capital Investment: Evidence from Indian Tariff Reforms." *American Economic Journal: Applied Economics* 2(4): 42–75.

Eichengreen, B. 1986. "The Political Economy of the Smoot-Hawley Tariff." NBER Working Paper No. 2001.

Erten, B., and Leight, J. 2017. "Exporting out of Agriculture: The Impact of WTO Accession on Structural Transformation in China," mimeo.

Erten, B. Leight, J., and Tregenna, F. 2019. "Trade Liberalization and Local Labor Market Adjustment in South Africa." *Journal of International Economics* 118: 448–67.

Estevadeordal, A., and Taylor, A. 2013. "Is the Washington Consensus Dead? Growth, Openness, and the Great Liberalization, 1970s–2000s." *Review of Economics and Statistics* 95: 1669–90.

Faijgelbaum, P., and Khandelwal, A. 2016. "Measuring the Unequal Gains from Trade." *The Quarterly Journal of Economics* 131(3): 1113–80.

Feenstra, R.C., and Hanson, G.H. 2003. "Global Production Sharing and Rising Inequality: A Survey of Trade and Wages." In *Handbook of International Trade*, edited by Choi, E.K. and Harrigan, J. London: Basil Blackwell, pp. 146–85.

Feenstra, R.C., and Hanson, G.H. 1999. "The Impact of Outsourcing and High-Technology Capital on Wages: Estimates for the United States, 1979–1990." *Quarterly Journal of Economics* 114(3): 907–40.

Feenstra, R., Ma, H., and Xu, Y. 2017. "US Exports and Employment." NBER WP 24056.

Feenstra, R., and Sasahara, A. 2017. "The 'China Shock', Exports, and US Employment: A Global Input-Output Analysis." NBER WP 24022.

Felbermayr, G., Prat, J., and Schmerer, H.J. 2009. "Trade and Unemployment: What Do the Data Say?" IZA Discussion Papers 4184. Institute for the Study of Labour.

Ferreira, P., and Rossi, J. 2003. "New Evidence from Brazil on Trade Liberalization and Productivity Growth." *International Economic Review*, 44(4): 1383–405.

Fontagné, L., Orefice, G., and Piermartini, R. 2020. "Making (Small) Firms Happy. The Heterogeneous Effect of Trade Facilitation Measures." *Review of International Economics*, doi.org/10.1111/roie.12463.

Fontagné, L., Orefice, G., Piermartini, R., and Rocha, N. 2015. "Product Standards and Margins of Trade: Firm-level Evidence." *Journal of International Economics* 97(1): 29–44.

Frankel, J.A., and Romer, D. 1999. "Does Trade Cause Growth?" *American Economic Review* 89(3): 379–99.

Funke, M., Schularick, M., and Trebesch, C. 2016. "Going to Extremes: Politics after Financial Crises, 1870–2014." *European Economic Review* 88(C): 227–60.

Gerschenkron, A. 1943. "Bread and Democracy in Germany." Berkeley and Los Angeles: University of California Press.

Giuliano, P., and Spilimbergo, A. 2009. "Growing up in a Recession: Beliefs and the Macroeconomy." NBER Working Paper No. 15321. Cambridge, MA: National Bureau of Economic Research.

Goldberg, P. 2015. "Review Article: Trade and Inequality." In *Elgar Research Reviews in Economics*. Cheltenham, UK: Edward Elgar.

Goldberg, P., and Pavcnik, N. 2007. "Distributional Effects of Globalization in Developing Countries." *Journal of Economic Literature* XLV(1): 39–82.

Goldberg, P., and Pavcnik, N. 2003. "The Response of the Informal Sector to Trade Liberalization." *Journal of Development Economics* 72(2): 463–96.

Goldberg, P.K., and Pavcnik, N. 2005. "Trade, Wages, and the Political Economy of Trade Protection: Evidence from the Colombian Trade Reforms." *Journal of International Economics* 66(1): 75–105.

Goldberg, P., and Pavcnik, N. 2016. "The Effects of Trade Policy." NBER Working Paper No. 21957. Cambridge, MA.

Goos, M., Manning, A., and Salomons, A. 2014. "Explaining Job Polarization: Routine-Biased Technological Change and Offshoring." *American Economic Review*, August, 2509–26.

Guth, J., and Lee, J. 2017. Evaluations of the Trade Adjustment Assistance Program for Workers: A Literature Review. USITC Executive Briefings on Trade, Washington, DC: United States International Trade Commission (USITC).

Guth, J., and Lee, J. 2018. A brief history of the U.S. Trade Adjustment Assistance Program for workers. USITC Executive Briefings on Trade, Washington, DC: United States International Trade Commission (USITC).

Handley, K. 2014. "Exporting Under Trade Policy Uncertainty: Theory and Evidence." *Journal of International Economics* 94(1): 50–66.

Handley, K., and Limão, N. 2014. "Policy Uncertainty, Trade and Welfare: Theory and Evidence for China and the U.S." NBER Working Papers No. 19376.

Handley, K., and Limão, N. 2015. "Trade and Investment under Policy Uncertainty: Theory and Firm Evidence." *American Economic Journal: Economic Policy* 7(4): 189–222.

Handley, K., and Limão, N. 2017. "Policy Uncertainty, Trade, and Welfare: Theory and Evidence for China and the United States." *American Economic Review* 107(9): 2731–83.

Hanson, G. 2019. "Economic and Political Consequences of Trade-Induced Manufacturing Decline." In *Meeting Globalization's Challenges: Policies to Make Trade Work for All*, edited by L. Catão and M. Obstfeld. Princeton, NJ: Princeton University Press.

Hanson, G., and Harrison, A. 1999. "Who Gains from Trade Reform? Some Remaining Puzzles." *Journal of Development Economics* 59(1): 125–54.

Harrison, A.E. 1994. "Productivity, Imperfect Competition and Trade Reform: Theory and Evidence." *Journal of International Economics* 36(1): 53–73.

Harrison, A., McLaren J., and McMillan, M. 2011. "Recent Perspectives on Trade and Inequality." *Annual Review of Economics* 3: 261–89.

Harrison, A., and Rodríguez-Clare, A. 2010. "Trade, Foreign Investment, and Industrial Policy for Developing Countries." In *Handbook of Development Economics*, edited by Rodrik, D. and Rosenzweig, M.R., (Vol. 5, pp. 4039–214). Amsterdam, Netherlands: Elsevier.

Haskel, J., Lawrence, R.Z., Leamer, E.E., and Slaughter, M.J. 2012. "Globalization and U.S. Wages: Modifying Classic Theory to Explain Recent Facts." *Journal of Economic Perspectives* 26(2): 119–40.

Helpman, E., and Itskhoki, O. 2010. "Labour Market Rigidities, Trade and Unemployment." *The Review of Economic Studies* 77(3): 1100–37.

Helpman, E., Itskhoki, O., and Redding, S. 2010. "Inequality and Unemployment in a Global Economy." *Econometrica* 78(4): 1239–83.

Helpman, E., Itskhoki, O., Muendler, M.A., and Redding, S. 2017. "Trade and Inequality: From Theory to Estimation." *The Review of Economic Studies* 84(1), January 2017, pp. 357–405.

Humlum, A., and Munch, J.R. 2019. "Globalization, Flexicurity and Adult Vocational Training in Denmark." In *Making Globalization More Inclusive—Lessons from Experience with Adjustment Policies*, edited by M. Bacchetta, Milet, E., and Monteiro, J.-A. Geneva: World Trade Organization.

Hummels, D., Jørgensen, R., Munch, J., and Xiang, C. 2014. "The Wage Effects of Offshoring: Evidence from Danish Matched Worker-Firm Data." *American Economic Review* 104(6): 1597–629.

Hyman, B. 2018. "Can Displaced Labour Be Retrained? Evidence from Quasi-random Assignment to Trade Adjustment Assistance. Philadelphia, PA: The Wharton School, University of Pennsylvania.

International Labour Organization (ILO). 2015. Transition from the informal to the formal economy recommendation no 204.

International Labour Organization (ILO) and World Trade Organization (WTO). 2007. Trade and Employment: Challenges for Policy Research.

International Labour Organization (ILO) and World Trade Organization (WTO). 2009. Globalization and Informal Jobs in Developing Countries.

International Labour Organization (ILO) and World Trade Organization (WTO). 2011. Making Globalization Socially Sustainable.

International Monetary Fund (IMF). 2016. "Global Trade: What's Behind the Slowdown," World Economic Outlook (October), Chapter 2.

International Monetary Fund (IMF), World Bank, and World Trade Organization (WTO). 2017. "Making Trade an Engine of Growth for All: The Case for Trade and for Policies to Facilitate Adjustment," Prepared for the meeting of the G20 Sherpas, March 23–24, Frankfurt, Germany.

International Monetary Fund (IMF), World Bank, and World Trade Organization (WTO). 2018. "Reinvigorating Trade and Inclusive Growth."

Janssen, M., Sadni Jallab, M., and Smeets, M. (Eds.) 2014. Connecting to Global Markets, Challenges and Opportunities: Case Studies Presented by WTO Chairholders (WTO).

Jaumotte, F., Lall, S., and Papageorgiou, C. 2013. "Rising Income Inequality: Technology, or Trade and Financial Globalization?" *IMF Economic Review* 61(2): 271–309.

Jensen, R. 2012. "Do Labor Market Opportunities Affect Young Women's Work and Family Decisions? Experimental Evidence from India." *The Quarterly Journal of Economics* 127(2): 753–92.

Johnson, R. 2014. "Five Facts about Value-Added Exports and Implications for Macroeconomics and Trade Research." *Journal of Economic Perspectives* 28(2): 119–42.

Jordà, Ò., Schularick, M., and Taylor, A.M. 2017. "Macrofinancial History and the New Business Cycle Facts." In NBER Macroeconomics Annual 2016, Volume 31, edited by Martin Eichenbaum and Jonathan A. Parker. Chicago, IL: University of Chicago Press.

Kaminsky, G., Lizondo, S., and Reinhart, C. 1998. "Leading Indicators of Currency Crises," IMF Staff Papers, 45(1): 1–48.

Keller, W., and Utar, H. 2016. "International Trade and Job Polarization: Evidence at the Worker Level," CESIFO Working Paper No. 5978.

Klein, M.W., Moser, C. and Urban, and Dieter M. 2010. "The Contribution of Trade to Wage Inequality: The Role of Skill, Gender, and Nationality," NBER Working Papers 15,985, National Bureau of Economic Research, Inc.

Klenow, P. and Rodriguez, C. 1997. "Quantifying Variety Gains from Trade Liberalization," unpublished manuscript.

Kletzer, L.G. 2001. "Job Loss from Imports: Measuring the Costs," Institute for International Economics.

Kletzer, L. 2016. Why the U.S. Needs Wage Insurance. Harvard Business Review, https://hbr.org/2016/01/why-the-u-s-needs-wage-insurance.

Kletzer, L.G., and Litan, R.E. 2001. "A Prescription to Relieve Worker Anxiety", Policy Brief No. 73, Washington, DC: Brookings Institute.

Kovak, B. 2013. "Regional Effects of Trade Reform: What Is the Correct Measure of Liberalization?" *American Economic Review* 103(5): 1960–76.

Krebs, T., Krishna, P., and Maloney, W. 2005. "Trade Policy, Income Risk, and Welfare," Policy Research Working Paper Series 3622. Washington, DC: World Bank.

Krueger, A. 1974. "The Political Economy of the Rent-Seeking Society." *American Economic Review* 64(3): 291–303.

Krugman, P. 1981. "Intraindustry Specialization and the Gains from Trade." *Journal of Political Economy* 89(5): 959–73.

Kuznets, S. 1955. "Economic Growth and Income Inequality." *The American Economic Review* 45(1): 1–28.

La Porta, R., and Schleifer, A. 2014. "Informality and Development." *Journal of Economic Perspectives* 28(3): 109–26.

Levinsohn, J. 1993. "Testing the Imports-as- Market-Discipline Hypothesis." *Journal of International Economics* 35(1–2): 1–22.

Lewis, W.A. 1955. *Theory of Economic Growth.* London: Allen and Unwin.

Lileeva, A., and Trefler, D. 2010. "Improved Access to Foreign Markets Raises Plant-level Productivity...For Some Plants." *The Quarterly Journal of Economics* 125(3): 1051–99.

Lumenga-Neso, O., Olarreaga, M., and Schiff, M. 2005. "On 'Indirect' Trade-Related R&D Spillovers," European Economic Review, 49(7): 1785–98.

Machin, S., and Van Reenen, J. 1998. "Technology and Changes in Skill Structure: Evidence from seven OECD countries." *Quarterly Journal of Economics* 113(4): 1215–44.

Magyari, I. 2017. Firm Reorganization, Chinese Imports, and US Manufacturing Employment. US Census Bureau, Center for Economic Studies.

Malgouyres, C. 2017. "The Impact of Chinese Import Competition on the Local Structure of Employment and Wages: Evidence from France," *Journal of Regional Science* 57(3): 411–41.

McCaig, B. 2011. "Exporting out of poverty: Provincial poverty in Vietnam and U.S. market access." *Journal of International Economics* 85(1): 102–13.

McCaig, B., and McMillan, M. 2019. "Trade Liberalisation and Labour Market Adjustment in Botswana." *Journal of African Economies* 29(3): 236–70.

McCaig, B., and Pavcnik, N. 2014. "Export Markets and Labor Reallocation in a Low-Income Country." NBER Working Paper No. 20455.

McCaig, B., and Pavcnik, N. 2018. "Export Markets and Labor Allocation in a Low-Income Country." *American Economic Review* 108(7): 1899–941.

Melitz, M. 2003. "The Impact of Trade on Intra-Industry Reallocations and Aggregate Industry Productivity." *Econometrica* 71(6): 1695–725.

Melitz, M.J., and Redding, S.J. 2014. "Heterogeneous Firms and Trade." In *Handbook of International Economics* (Vol. 4: 1–54), edited by Gopinath, G., Helpman, E., and Rogoff, K. Amsterdam: Elsevier.

Mendoza, A., Nayyar, G., and Piermartini, R. 2018. "Are the 'Poor' Getting Globalised?" Forthcoming in World Bank/WTO Trade and Poverty Reduction: New Evidence of Impacts in Developing Countries.

Meschi, E., and Vivarelli, M. 2009. "Trade and Income Inequality in Developing Countries." *World Development* 37(2): 287–302.

Mian, A., Sufi, A., and Trebbi, F. 2014. "Resolving Debt Overhang: Political Constraints in the Aftermath of Financial Crises." *American Economic Journal: Macroeconomics* 6(2): 1–28.

Moise, E., and Sorescu, S. 2013. "Trade Facilitation Indicators: The Potential Impact of Trade Facilitation on Developing Countries," OECD Trade Policy Papers (No. 144).

Monteiro, J.-A. 2016a. "Provisions on Small and Medium-sized Enterprises in Regional Trade Agreements," WTO Staff Working Paper, No. ERSD-2016–12.

Monteiro, J.-A. 2016b. "Typology of Environment-related Provisions in Regional Trade Agreements," WTO Staff Working Paper, No. ERSD-2016–13.

Monteiro, J.-A. 2018. "Gender-related Provisions in Regional Trade Agreements," WTO Staff Working Paper No. ERSD-2018–15.

Monteiro, J.-A. 2021. "Buena Vista: Social Corporate Responsibility Provisions in Regional Trade Agreements," WTO Staff Working Paper No. ERSD-2021–11.

Monteiro, J.-A., and Trachtman, J.P. 2020. "Environmental Laws", in *Handbook of Deep Trade Agreements*, edited by Mattoo, A., Rocha, N., and Ruta, M. Washington, DC: World Bank.

Nicita, A. 2004. "Who Benefited from Trade Liberalization in Mexico? Measuring the Effects on Household Welfare." World Bank Policy Research Working Paper Series, no. 3265.

Notowidigdo, M.J. 2013. "The Incidence of Local Labor Demand Shocks," mimeo and NBER Working Paper 17,167.

Organisation for Economic Co-operation and Development (OECD). 2005. "Trade-adjustment Costs in OECD Labour Markets: A Mountain or a Molehill?" OECD Employment Outlook, Paris: Organization for Economic Cooperation and Development.

Organisation for Economic Co-operation and Development (OECD). 2012. "Trade, Growth and Jobs," Summary of the OECD/ICITE report on Policy Priorities for International Trade and Jobs, Paris: Organization for Economic Cooperation and Development.

Organisation for Economic Co-operation and Development (OECD). 2017. "Enhancing the Contributions of SMEs in a Global and Digitalized Economy." Meeting of the OECD Council of Ministers, June 2017.

Ohlin, B. 1933. *Interregional and International Trade*. Cambridge, MA: Harvard University Press.

Oreopoulos, P., Page, M., and Stevens, A.H. 2008. "The Intergenerational Effects of Worker Displacement." *Journal of Labour Economics* 26(3): 455–83.

Oster, E., and Steinberg, B. 2013. "Do IT Service Centers Promote School Enrollment? Evidence from India." *Journal of Development Economics* 104: 123–35.

Parry, A., Van Rensburg, A.J., and Viviers, W. 2021. "Are digital advances and inclusive growth compatible goals? Implications for trade policy in developing countries." In *Adapting to the Digital Trade Era, Challenges and Opportunities (WTO)*, edited by Smeets, M., pp. 280–95.

Pavcnik, N. 2012. "Globalization and Within-Country Inequality." In *Making Globalization Socially Sustainable*, edited by Bacchetta, M. and Jansen, M., pp. 233–59. Geneva, Switzerland: ILO/WTO.

Pavcnik, N. 2017. "The Impact of Trade on Inequality in Developing Countries," NBER Working Paper No. w23878.

Paz, L.S. 2014. "The impacts of trade liberalization on informal labor markets: a theoretical and empirical evaluation of the Brazilian case," *Journal of International Economics* 92: 330–48.

Pew Research Center. Spring 2018 Global Attitudes Survey.

Pierce, J.R., and Schott, P.K. 2016a. "The Surprisingly Swift Decline of US Manufacturing Employment." *American Economic Review* 106(7): 1632–62.

Pierce, J.R., and Schott, P.K. 2016b. "Trade Liberalization and Mortality: Evidence from U.S. Counties," NBER Working Paper No. 22849.

Porto, G. 2006. "Using Survey Data to Assess the Distributional Effects of Trade Policy." *Journal of International Economics* 70(1): 140–60.

Puccio, L. 2017. "Policy Measures to Respond to Trade Adjustment Costs," Briefing, Brussels: European Parliamentary Research Service, European Union.

Raess, D., and Sari, D. 2018. "Labor Provisions in Trade Agreements (LABPTA): Introducing a New Dataset." *Global Policy* 9(4): 451–66.

Raess, D., and Sari, D. 2020. "Labor Market Regulations." In *Handbook of Deep Trade Agreements*, edited by Mattoo, A., Rocha, N., and Ruta, M. Washington, DC: World Bank.

Ravallion, M. 2018. "Inequality and Globalization: A Review Essay." *Journal of Economic Literature* 56(2): 620–42.

Ricardo, D. 1817. *On the Principles of Political Economy and Taxation.* (1 ed.), London: John Murray.

Rodríguez, F., and Rodrik, D. 2001. "Trade Policy and Economic Growth: A Skeptic's Guide to the Cross-National Evidence," NBER Macroeconomics Annual 2000, Volume 15, pp. 261–338.

Rodrik, D. 2008. "The Real Exchange Rate and Economic Growth," Brookings Papers on Economic Activity, 2, pp. 365–412.

Rodrik, D. 2015. "Premature Deindustrialization," NBER Working Paper No. 20935.

Rosen, H.F. 2008. "Strengthening Trade Adjustment Assistance," Policy Brief PB08-2, Washington, DC: Peterson Institute for International Economics.

Rothwell, J. 2017. Cutting the Losses: Reassessing the Costs of Import Competition to Workers and Communities, manuscript, Available at SSRN: https://ssrn.com/abstract=2,920,188.

Sachs, J., and Warner, A. 1995. "Natural Resource Abundance and Economic Growth," NBER Working Paper No. w5398.

Samuelson, P. 1939. "The Gains from International Trade." *Canadian Journal of Economics and Political Science* 5: 195–205.

Schneider, F. Buehn, A., and Montenegro, C.E. 2010. "New Estimates for the Shadow Economies All Over the World." *International Economic Journal* 24: 443–61.

Smeets, M. (Ed.) 2021. *Adapting to the Digital Trade Era, Challenges and Opportunities.* Geneva: WTO.

Smeets, M., and Djumaliev, M. 2019. Kyrgyz Republic and Structural Reforms: Twenty Years of WTO Membership, St Petersburg University, *Journal of Economic Studies* 35(4): 513–42.

Smeets, M., and Mashayekhi M. 2019. Trade policies in support of inclusive growth to the benefit of all in "Restoring Trust in Trade", Liber Amicorum in honour of Peter van den Bossche; D, Prevost, I. Alexovicova, J. Hillebrand Pohl (ed.). Hart Publishing, pp. 5–50.

Solt, Frederick. 2020. "Measuring Income Inequality Across Countries and Over Time: The Standardized World Income Inequality Database." *Social Science Quarterly* 101(3): 1183–99. SWIID Version 9.0, October 2020.

Spearot, A. 2013. "Market Access, Investment, And Heterogeneous Firms." *International Economic Review* 54(2): 601–27.

Stolper, W.F., and Samuelson, P.A. 1941. "Protection and Real Wages." *The Review of Economic Studies* 9(1): 58–73.

Teh, R., Smeets, M., Sadni Jallab, M., and Chauhdri, F. (Eds). 2016. Trade Costs and Inclusive Growth, Case Studies Presented by WTO chair-holders (WTO).

Thewissen, S., and van Vliet, O. 2019. "Competing with the Dragon: Employment Effects of Chinese Trade Competition in 17 Sectors Across 18 OECD Countries." *Political Science Research and Methods* 7(2), April 2019, 215–32.

Thoenig, M., and Verdier, T. 2003. "A Theory of Defensive Skill-Biased Innovation and Globalization." *American Economic Review* 93(3): 709–28.

Tong, H., and Wei, S.J. 2014. "Does Trade Globalization Induce or Inhibit Corporate Transparency? Unbundling the Growth Potential and Product Market Competition Channels." *Journal of International Economics* 94(2): 358–70.

Topalova, P. 2007. "Trade Liberalization, Poverty and Inequality: Evidence from Indian Districts." In *Globalization and Poverty*, edited by Harrison, A. Chicago, IL: University of Chicago Press.

Topalova, P. 2010. "Factor Immobility and Regional Impacts of Trade Liberalization: Evidence on Poverty from India." *American Economic Journal: Applied Economics* 2(4): 1–41.

Trebilcock, M.J. 2014. *Dealing with Losers: The Political Economy of Policy Transition*. Oxford: Oxford University Press.

Trefler, D. 2004. "The Long and Short of the Canada-U. S. Free Trade Agreement." *American Economic Review* 94(4): 870–95.

US International Trade Commission (USITC). 2017. "Global Digital Trade 1: Market Opportunities and Key Foreign Trade Restrictions."

United Nations Conference on Trade and Development (UNCTAD). 2020a. Global Trade Update (October). Geneva.

United Nations Conference on Trade and Development (UNCTAD). 2020b. World Investment Report 2020. Geneva.

Ventura, J. 1997. "Growth and Interdependence." *The Quarterly Journal of Economics* 112(1): 57–84.

Verhoogen, E. 2008. "Trade, Quality Upgrading, and Wage Inequality in the Mexican Manufacturing Sector." *Quarterly Journal of Economics* 123(2): 489–530.

Wacziarg, R., and Welch, K.H. 2008. "Trade Liberalization and Growth: New Evidence." *World Bank Economic Review* 22(2): 187–231.

World Economic Forum (WEF). 2020. The U.S.-Mexico-Canada Agreement and the Comprehensive and Progressive Agreement for Trans-Pacific Partnership include mechanisms for dispute resolution.

Winters, A., McCulloch, N., and McKay, A. 2004. "Trade Liberalisation and Poverty: The Evidence so Far." *Journal of Economic Literature* 42(1): 72–115.

Wood, A. 1995. "How Trade Hurt Unskilled Workers." *Journal of Economic Perspectives* 9(3): 57–8.

Wood, Adrian. 1999. "Openness and Wage Inequality in Developing Countries: The Latin American Challenge to East Asian Conventional Wisdom." In *Market Integration, Regionalism and the Global Economy*, edited by R. Baldwin et al. Cambridge; New York and Melbourne: Cambridge University Press, pp. 153–81.

World Bank. 1987. World Development Report. Washington, DC.

World Bank. 2020. World Development Report.. Trading for Development in the Age of Global Value Chains. Washington, DC.

World Bank and World Trade Organization (WTO). 2015. "The Role of Trade in Ending Poverty." Washington, DC: World Bank; Geneva: World Trade Organization.

World Bank and World Trade Organization (WTO). 2018. Trade and Poverty Reduction: New Evidence of Impacts in Developing Countries. Washington, DC: World Bank; Geneva: World Trade Organization.

World Bank and World Trade Organization (WTO). 2020. Women and Trade: The Role of Trade in Promoting Gender Equality. Washington, DC: World Bank; Geneva: World Trade Organization.

World Trade Organization (WTO). 2008. World Trade Report: Trade in a Globalizing World. Geneva.

World Trade Organization (WTO). 2015a. World Trade Report. Speeding up trade: benefits and challenges of implementing the WTO Trade Facilitation Agreement. Geneva.

World Trade Organization (WTO). 2015b. The WTO at Twenty: Challenges and Achievements. Geneva.

World Trade Organization (WTO). 2016a. World Trade Report: Levelling the Trading Field for SMEs. Geneva.

World Trade Organization (WTO). 2016b. Accessions Annual Report by the Director General. Geneva.

World Trade Organization (WTO). 2017a. World Trade Report: Trade, Technology and Jobs. Geneva.

World Trade Organization (WTO). 2017b. "20 Years of the Information Technology Agreement. Boosting Trade, Innovation and Digital Connectivity." Geneva.

World Trade Organization (WTO). 2018. World Trade Report: The Future of World Trade: How Digital Technologies are Transforming Global Commerce. Geneva.

World Trade Organization (WTO). 2019. World Trade Report: The Future of Services Trade. Geneva.

World Trade Organization (WTO). 2020. Trade Forecast. Press release October 6: "Trade Shows Signs of Rebound from Covid-19, Recovery Still Uncertain." Geneva.

Yi, M., Mueller, S., and Stegmaier, J. 2017. "Transferability of Skills across Sectors and Heterogeneous Displacement Costs." *American Economic Review* 107(5): 332–6.

Zhu, W. 2017. "Heterogeneous Technological Changes and Their Impacts on Income Inequality and Productivity Growth." Kingston, Ontario: Queen's University.

8

Financial Globalization

Barry Eichengreen, Balazs Csonto, and Asmaa El-Ganainy

I. Introduction

In this chapter, we focus on the relationship of financial globalization to income inequality and the implications for policy.[1,2] Our point of departure is the contrast between trade liberalization and financial liberalization. Standard logic suggests that trade liberalization will have opposing effects on distribution in high- and low-income countries. The Stolper-Samuelson theorem predicts that trade opening will increase demands for the services and therefore the relative incomes of a country's abundant factors of production, those used intensively in the exportables sector. In high-income countries, these abundant factors are well-compensated capital and skilled labor; in low-income countries they are less-skilled labor. It follows that the impact of trade liberalization on inequality will vary with economic development: income inequality will increase in high-income countries, as the well compensated become even better compensated, but fall in low-income economies, where opening disproportionately benefits low-wage workers.[3]

---

[1] We thank Jaime Sarmiento Monroy for the excellent research assistance. We also thank Valerie Cerra, Rupa Duttagupta, Rishi Goyal, Swarnali Ahmed Hannan, Olivier Jeanne, Samira Kalla, Amine Mati, Monique Newiak, Marco Pani, Charalambos Tsangarides, Jiaxiong Yao, Jiae Yoo, as well as our colleagues at Banco de México, and participants in the Inclusive Growth book seminar series organized by the IMF Institute for Capacity Development, and at the 3rd Joint IMF-OECD-World Bank Conference on Structural Reforms (Improving the Income Distribution Effect of Market Reforms in a Post-Covid-19 World) for their comments.

[2] Unless otherwise indicated, inequality throughout this chapter is measured by the Gini coefficient from The Standardized World Income Inequality Database (SWIID) (see Solt 2020 for a description of SWIID and Chapter 1 for more details on various measurements of inequality). Although there exist alternatives, recent research pointed to uncertainty about the accuracy of wealth inequality estimates, as well about alternative income inequality indicators such as the top 1 percent income share. For example, while Piketty et al. (2018) find that the top 1 percent income share increased by two-thirds since 1960 and doubled since 1980 in the United States, Auten and Splinter (2018) show that there has been only a little change since 1960 and a modest increase since 1980 using a different allocation of underreported tax income.

[3] A substantial number of early studies (reviewed in Krueger 1983) confirmed or were not inconsistent with these predictions. The subsequent literature then qualified these findings, especially as they pertained to developing countries. Wood (1997) showed that trade liberalization could be unequalizing rather than equalizing for some emerging markets, notably middle-income countries whose labor-intensive export sectors were squeezed by low-wage competition from China. (We would observe that this conclusion is by no means inconsistent with the Stolper-Samuelson logic of the

Barry Eichengreen, Balazs Csonto, and Asmaa El-Ganainy, *Financial Globalization* In: *How to Achieve Inclusive Growth*. Edited by: Valerie Cerra, Barry Eichengreen, Asmaa El-Ganainy, and Martin Schindler, Oxford University Press.
© Barry Eichengreen, Balazs Csonto, and Asmaa El-Ganainy 2022. DOI: 10.1093/oso/9780192846938.003.0008

A theorem in international economics, due to Mundell (1957), suggests that trade flows and capital flows have the same distributional effects. Yet this does not appear to be the case in practice.[4] Recent studies suggest that inequality, as measured by the Gini Coefficient, has risen with financial globalization in *both* advanced and developing countries.[5] They show that different kinds of capital flows can have different effects and that those effects are context-specific—multiple types of capital and multiple contexts of course not being part of the classic Mundellian framework.

Evidently, even when financial globalization supports economic growth, it can be unequalizing, depending on situation and circumstances. This creates a dilemma for policymakers. Living standards can be raised by making the pie as large as possible, something that financial globalization promotes in countries with strong institutions and effective policy and regulatory frameworks. At the same time, it is desirable that the increase be widely shared, something that is by no means guaranteed. It is important therefore to couple international financial liberalization with other social and economic policies that help to level the distributional playing field.

This chapter shows that the distributional impacts of capital flows depend on countries' initial conditions. The relevant conditions include the level of human capital, the depth of financial markets, and the strength of institutional and policy frameworks. Higher levels of educational attainment, stronger creditor rights, and more effective rule of law in countries on the receiving end of capital flows can help to reap the benefits in terms of growth while minimizing the costs in terms of distribution.

Moreover, different financial flows have different distributional implications:

FDI: The distributional effects of *inward FDI* will depend on its sectoral composition and on the variation in labor intensity and skills across sectors. In general, the adverse distributional effects will be greatest when FDI flows into sectors characterized by strong complementarities between capital and skill. In this case, a better-educated labor force will facilitate wider sharing of the benefits.[6]

Outward FDI, which is sourced mainly from high-income countries and now increasingly from middle-income countries such as China, tends to be associated with a decline in the demand for less-skilled labor in the source country. Such

previous paragraph.) Pavcik (2017) showed that the impact on developing countries varied by region or locale. The safest conclusion would appear to be that the impact of trade opening in developing countries is not uniform. In contrast, recent work has reinforced the view that trade openness has been a factor behind rising inequality in advanced countries. Autor et al. (2016) is probably the most influential such study.

[4] For a comprehensive discussion on the distributional impact of trade, see Chapter 7.

[5] For developing countries in particular, this evidence differs, to a large extent, from that of trade (see Chapter 7 for a full treatment of this literature).

[6] Over the long term, the inequality increasing effect of FDI tends to diminish with rising educational levels; see for example Mihaylova (2015).

effects diminish insofar as competitiveness gains from the extension of global supply chains support growth and job creation in the sending country. But there is growing evidence that adverse distributional consequences in the source country persist. In addition, the threat of relocating production abroad may reduce the bargaining power of labor and thus its income share, further accentuating inequality.

Portfolio financial capital flows: These may affect inequality through several channels, including by accentuating macroeconomic volatility, which disproportionately hurts the poor. Financial flows can also be vehicles for tax avoidance and other illicit flows that disproportionately benefit high earners. But portfolio capital inflows can reduce inequality insofar as they help to deepen and develop the financial sector and in so doing boost financial inclusion and entrepreneurial opportunity for the poor. Strong institutions, policies to manage capital flow surges and reversals, and well-developed financial markets that are capable of efficiently intermediating funds are similarly important for mitigating the inequality-raising effects of portfolio capital flows.

Official development assistance: Official flows have the potential to reduce inequality where institutions are sufficiently strong. However, aid may induce officials and well-connected individuals in the private sectors, who already enjoy relatively high incomes, to engage in rent-seeking activities aimed at appropriating resource windfalls where institutional checks are lacking (Svensson 2000; Hodler 2007; Economides et al. 2008). Moreover, donors may allocate aid in a way that deviates from pro-poor growth rhetoric and rather serves their politically-motivated self-interest. In addition, official flows tend to be procyclical, which can amplify volatility that disproportionately hurts the poor. All this suggests that ODA will tend to reduce inequality only when it is timed and targeted appropriately by the donor and when the recipient has in place institutions adequate for limiting diversion and appropriation.

Other official flows include those associated with *reserve accumulation*—when a government uses some of its resources to acquire foreign assets. Higher reserves could reduce macroeconomic and financial volatility, thereby mitigating the disproportionate impact of downturns on low-income households. However, reserve accumulation can be expensive, since the opportunity cost of funds (the typical government's funding costs) are a multiple of the interest income earned from holding US treasury bonds or other similar "safe assets" (Rodrik 2006).

The rest of the chapter is organized as follows. Sections II and III discuss some stylized facts about the evolution of capital flows and inequality, respectively, over the last few decades. Section IV probes deeper with a discussion of the main channels through which different types of capital flows could affect income distribution. Section V discusses the role of capital flows in shaping developments in inequality in Mexico since the 1970s. Finally, Section VI draws policy implications for maximizing the benefits from financial globalization for all, while Section VII provides a few concluding remarks.

II. Facts about Capital Flows

In the early 1990s, the flow of capital across borders accelerated, rising faster than global trade and output (Figure 8.1). On the policy side, the growth of financial flows was facilitated by capital account liberalization, in emerging and developing countries (EMDCs) in particular (again, see Figure 8.1).[7] There was a tenfold increase between 1970 and 2015 in cross-border investment, which rose from 20 to 200 percent of global GDP, with the bulk of the increase following the liberalization waves of the 1990s and the early-2000s run-up to the Global Financial Crisis (GFC).

Cross-border financial flows also responded to changes in technology and market structure (Häusler 2002). New technologies, such as electronic trading, relaxed geographic constraints and facilitated interaction among financial market participants (Allen et al. 2001). Building out the global network of submarine fiber-optic cables allowed market participants to communicate with global financial centers in real time (Eichengreen et al. 2016). Advances in computer technology enhanced access to information while facilitating risk assessment and asset valuation. Liberalization and development of domestic financial markets in EMDCs opened

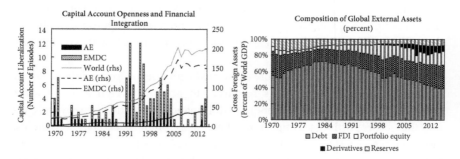

Figure 8.1 Capital Account Openness and Financial Integration, 1970–2015
Note: Similar to other studies (e.g., Furceri et al. 2018), we assume that capital account liberalization occurs when the change in the Chinn-Ito index exceeds its average by at least two standards deviations. Our approach further assumes that there is no reversal of liberalization over the following ten years.
Sources: Chinn and Ito (2006), Lane and Milesi-Ferretti (2018), and authors' calculations.

---

[7] Of 135 episodes of capital account liberalization over the last five decades, 95 took place in EMDCs. Most of the EMDC episodes took place in emerging markets. Specifically, 69 and 26 episodes were identified in emerging markets (EMs) and low-income developing countries (LIDCs), respectively.

new opportunities for market participants (Lane and Milesi-Ferretti 2007; Levy-Yeyati and Williams 2011).[8] New technologies providing alternatives to bank wire transfers and traditional platforms such as Western Union similarly encouraged remittance flows.

Meanwhile, regulatory changes allowed a broader range of financial entities, including mutual funds, hedge funds and insurance companies, to engage in cross-border intermediation. As Häusler (2002) argues, these investors sought to diversify their portfolios internationally, with the aim of maximizing risk-adjusted returns. The emergence of additional investors and the deepening of financial markets could thus have contributed to a decline in home bias (i.e., the tendency for investors to hold a disproportionately high share of funds in domestic assets and neglect foreign investment opportunities).[9]

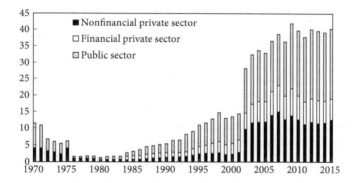

Figure 8.2 External Debt Securities, 1970–2015
(percent of GDP)
Sources: IMF World Economic Outlook, and authors' calculations.

Relatedly, production was increasingly fragmented across countries with the emergence of global value chains, a process related to cross-border investments both directly and indirectly. Cross-border FDI by multinational companies motivated by these outsourcing opportunities could take the form of offshoring of portions of the production process or acquisition of host-country firms. By positively affecting the domestic business environment (e.g., through higher demand for local inputs and the transfer of knowledge to local suppliers), a country's participation in global value chains could also enable it to attract additional foreign investors (Amendolagine et al. 2017).

---

[8] For example, since the late 1990s, a growing number of EMDCs participated as issuers on sovereign bond markets (Presbitero et al. 2015).
[9] Indeed, there is some evidence that home bias is smaller, the larger the assets managed by institutional investors (Darvas and Schoenmaker 2017).

Different types of flows dominated in different periods. In the 1970s, capital flows were predominantly debt flows to the public sector, which accounted for the bulk of the increase in cross-border positions (Figures 8.1 and 8.2). This was followed in the 1980s with an increasing importance of FDI and portfolio equity. The share of portfolio equity in total flows then rose further in the 1990s. The period between the GFC and the Covid-19 pandemic then saw a decline in debt flows, offset by an increase in FDI (Lane and Milesi-Ferretti 2018).

Overall, from 6–10 percent of world GDP in the 1970–1980s, the stock of FDI reached nearly 60 percent of global GDP in 2015, at which point FDI assets amounted to 37 and 4 percent of GDP in advanced economies (AEs) and EMDCs, respectively. Although some 80 percent of the stock of global FDI is held by investors in AEs, there has been some increase in the FDI assets of EMDCs since the 1990s, driven by increased outward FDI by China.[10]

In AEs, the dominance of debt inflows in the 1970 and 1980s was followed by an increase in portfolio equity inflows and derivatives in the 1990s and the 2000s, respectively. In EMDCs, in contrast, there was an increase in private debt inflows in the 1970s, when the combination of abundant petrodollars, favorable global interest rates and deregulation of banks' international activities led to an increase in cross-border bank loans—which constituted more than half of all capital flows to emerging markets in 1973–1982 (Eichengreen 2004). The Latin American debt crisis, which erupted in 1982, interrupted debt inflows and prompted debt rescheduling and restructuring. Private capital inflows then picked up again in the 1990 and 2000s following initiation of the Brady Plan. In lower-income EMDCs, by comparison, the increase in portfolio flows was more gradual, with an acceleration in non-FDI capital inflows and the emergence of sovereign bond issuances in the 2000s (Araujo et al. 2015a; Presbitero et al. 2015).

Official flows include official development assistance (ODA), comprised of aid, concessional loans and debt relief, as well as transactions related to the management of international reserves.[11] Notwithstanding a moderate decline in the 1990s, net ODA, typically directed at low-income EMDCs, has risen more than threefold expressed at constant prices, and has been broadly stable expressed relative to the Gross National Income of the OECD Development Assistance Committee (DAC) between the early 1970s and the late 2010s.[12]

Reserve accumulation has been a major "uphill" capital flow from EMDCs to AEs. Foreign official holdings of US Treasuries increased from some US$200 billion in the early 1990s to US$4 trillion (around 30 percent of total marketable US

---

[10] Chinese cross-border FDI now accounts for fully 25 percent of total outward FDI by EMDCs.

[11] Although aid is in the current account (i.e., it is not capital flow), we discuss it as in many cases its behavior is similar to that of concessional loans.

[12] ODA is measured here at constant prices. Based on OECD data. DAC is the international forum of major providers of aid, with 30 members.

Treasury debt securities) in the mid-2010s.[13] The increase was driven by EMDCs, which accumulated reserves in two waves: during the pre-GFC period with either precautionary motives or on the back of high commodity prices, and during the post-GFC period as a result of foreign exchange interventions taken in response to surging capital inflows (Csonto and Tovar 2017).

III. Facts about Inequality

Other more favorable effects of capital account liberalization notwithstanding, the policy has been accompanied by rising within-country income inequality across a variety of country groups.[14,15] Simply put, the increase in the Gini

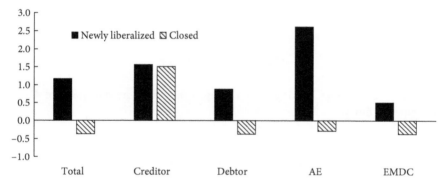

Figure 8.3 Financial Globalization and Inequality, 1970–2015
(change in the Gini index after capital account liberalization, percent)

Note: The figure shows the median change in the average market Gini index during the 10-year periods before and after capital account liberalization. Newly liberalized countries correspond to those liberalizing their capital account according to the methodology described in Figure 8.1. Closed countries are those with Chinn-Ito Index that is below the lowest value of the index at the time of capital account liberalization across episodes and those that do not liberalize their capital account over the following ten years. Creditor (debtor) countries are those with positive (negative) average net foreign assets over the next ten years. The sample includes 173 countries where a total of 135 episodes were identified (of which data were available for 111 episodes).

Sources: Chinn and Ito (2006), Solt (2020), Lane and Milesi-Ferretti (2018), and authors' calculations.

---

[13] Based on data by Bertaut and Tryon (2007) and Bertaut and Judson (2014).
[14] To be clear, financial globalization and financial liberalization are not one and the same. Our fundamental concern in this chapter is the effects of financial globalization, as indicated by our title. But financial liberalization episodes may be particularly informative, as they allow for a before and after comparison. Hence our focus here and elsewhere in the chapter on the evidence they provide.
[15] Of the 135 episodes mentioned earlier, inequality data were available for 111 episodes. Although the limited number of episodes in LIDCs (only 13 episodes) does not allow for the breakdown of EMDCs into EMs and LIDCs, it is worth noting that more than half of LIDC episodes were characterized by decreasing inequality.

coefficient in newly liberalized countries was higher than in countries that remained financially closed, as shown in Figure 8.3.

This increase was pronounced among AEs that liberalized their capital accounts, whereas in EMDCs the picture was more mixed. About 40 percent of newly liberalized EMDCs, including Latin American countries in the early 2000s, experienced a decline in inequality following capital account liberalization. In some EMs where inequality increased, particularly in Central and Eastern Europe (CEE), liberalization took place during the transition from central planning to the market economy, so it is hard to know whether the observed increase is the product of financial liberalization and opening or of other changes that accompanied enterprise privatization and restructuring.

Income inequality appears to have risen following liberalization episodes in both creditor and debtor countries.[16] There is no clear relationship between the sign of net international investment positions and inequality, in other words.[17]

IV. Probing Deeper

We now probe deeper, looking more closely at the distributional effects of different types of flows.

A. Foreign Direct Investment

We identified 14 episodes since 1995 when EMDCs reduced restrictions on inward FDI and calculated the change in the Gini index following each.[18] The results suggest that increased openness to FDI was followed by rising income inequality, absolutely and relative to countries that maintained their restrictions

---

[16] In the case of creditor countries, however, inequality also increased in closed countries over the same period.

[17] There is no major difference, for example, in income inequality between a major advanced creditor country, such as Germany (with a positive NIIP of 48 percent of GDP, and Gini coefficient of 51), and the largest advanced debtor country, the United States (with a negative NIIP of 41 percent of GDP, and Gini coefficient of 52). Similarly, two major EMDCs, China and Mexico, face similar outcomes in terms of income inequality (both have a Gini coefficient of 0.47) against the backdrop of NIIP of +15 and -53 percent of GDP, respectively.

[18] Of the 14 episodes, data for inequality and investment were available for 12 and 13 episodes, respectively. The small sample does not allow for a breakdown into EMs (7 and 7 episodes with data on inequality and investment, respectively) and LIDCs (5 and 6 episodes with data on inequality and investment, respectively).

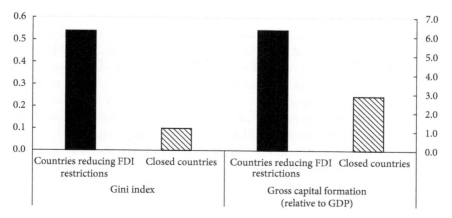

Figure 8.4 Openness to FDI, Inequality and Investment, Emerging Markets and Developing Countries, 1995–2015

(change in the Gini index and investments after FDI liberalization, percent)

Note: The figure shows the median change in the average market Gini index and gross capital formation (as share in GDP) during the 10-year periods before and after inward FDI liberalization in 68 EMDCs between 1995 and 2015. Inward FDI liberalization is defined on the basis of a decline in the direct investment inflow restrictions sub-index of the Fernandez-Klein-Rebucci-Schindler-Uribe index. Change in Gini and gross capital formation/GDP is shown on the left- and right-hand-side axis, respectively.

Sources: Fernandez et al. (2016), Solt (2020), IMF World Economic Outlook Database, and authors' calculations.

(Figure 8.4). Many studies using more sophisticated methodologies similarly find a positive relationship between inward FDI and inequality.[19]

A first possibility is that by raising the *capital-labor ratio*, inward FDI will increase the return to labor relative to capital.[20] As foreign and domestic capital compete for workers, there will be upward pressure on wages. This reduces income inequality, insofar as ownership of capital is concentrated in the hands of high-income groups (Wolff 2010).

---

[19] See, for example, Tsai (1995); Gopinath and Chen (2003); Te Velde (2003); Te Velde and Morrissey (2003); Lee (2006); Basu and Guariglia (2007); Jaumotte et al. (2008); Asteriou et al. (2014); Herzer et al. (2014); Suanes (2016). Some, however, find mixed or even no such evidence. See, for example, Te Velde and Morrissey (2004); Milanovic (2005); Sylwester (2005). Differences in methodologies, in measures of inequality, in country sample and in period plausibly explain these differences.

[20] There is some evidence that FDI inflows into manufacturing lead to more total investment in developing countries, especially in the case of investments by residents of advanced economies (Amighiani et al. 2017). This means that any crowding out effect on domestic investment would be more than offset by the positive impact of FDI. Amighiani et al. (2017) also suggest that the direct impact on investment, and thus capital stock depends on whether FDI takes the form of greenfield investments, i.e. the establishment of foreign operations by a company (e.g., by creating a new factory) that has direct positive impact on capital stock, or whether it is in the form of mergers and acquisitions, which involve the transfer of the ownership of existing assets. FDI may also exercise indirect effects on domestic investment, both positive and negative. It may create additional demand for inputs provided by local suppliers, thereby encouraging investment, but also push domestic firms out of the market, in an obvious sense discouraging investment.

But if capital *substitutes* for unskilled labor and/or *complements* skilled labor, then FDI inflows will increase the relative demand for skilled labor and thus the skill premium (Krusell et al. 2000; Larrain 2017; Jaumotte et al. 2008).[21] Here it is important to differentiate between horizontal and vertical FDI. Horizontal FDI means that firms undertake the same activities at their foreign affiliates as in their home country, typically motivated by the promise of obtaining improved market access. Since the FDI decision is not prompted by the promise of lower labor costs, it is not clear that horizontal FDI will affect the skill premium.

Vertical FDI, in contrast, will almost certainly affect the skill premium, although in what direction will depend on the context. Vertical FDI involves outsourcing segments of the production process, typically to locations where costs, notably those of labor, are lower. The impact on the relative demand for low-skilled labor and thus the skill premium in the recipient country varies across countries, depending on, among other factors, the skill composition of outsourced activities and that of the labor force in recipient countries. For example, the outsourcing of skill-intensive activities by German and Austrian firms to cheaper skilled-labor-abundant CEE economies in the 1990s raised the skill premium in the recipient countries, aggravating inequality (Marin 2004). Similarly, Feenstra and Hanson (1997) found that FDI, accompanied by rapid technological change that places a premium on skills, increased the demand for skills and thus the skill premium in Mexico in the 1980s.[22] In contrast, vertical FDI flows following the advent of NAFTA in the mid-1990s contributed to the decline in inequality observed in Mexico starting from the mid-1990s by raising the demand for low-skilled relative to high-skilled labor.[23] Robertson (2007) provides some evidence that the changing nature of foreign investments in the 1990s that favored less skill-intensive activities (e.g., an expansion of assembly activities made possible by NAFTA) led to higher demand for low-skilled workers in Mexico, thereby reducing the skill premium.

The extent to which capital account liberalization leads to additional investment and thereby affects the skill premium will also depend on external financial dependence. External financial dependence varies widely across sectors, with manufacturing (especially chemicals) and certain services (post and telecommunications, real estate, hotels and restaurants) having large needs for external finance, in contrast to other services (such as education and health care) (see

---

[21] The mechanism is similar to that of skill-biased technological change, i.e. when advances in technology favor high-skilled labor (Berman et al. 1998). Goldberg and Pavcnik (2007) provides a comprehensive overview of the different channels through which globalization affects inequality, including the impact of outsourcing on the skill premium.

[22] They noted, however, that these outsourced activities are less skill-intensive in the United States. As they point out, even if relocated activities are low-skill intensive in the home country, they can still lead to an increase in the relative demand for skilled labor in the recipient country, provided their skill intensity is higher than that of domestic production.

[23] See Section V for a more comprehensive discussion about the case of Mexico.

Larrain 2017). In economies where access to external finance is otherwise limited, inward FDI can relax that constraint and allow the sectors in question and their derived demand for factor services to expand. To the extent that FDI flows into sectors where both external financial dependence and capital-skill complementarity are high (e.g., telecommunications), opening the capital account do more to raise the demand for skilled labor, the skill premium, and thus wage inequality.

FDI may also affect inequality through its impact on *product markets and prices*. For example, FDI has been one of the main drivers of the "de-fragmentation" of the retail sector in EMDCs, i.e. of the shift to larger, centralized wholesale and retail markets (Reardon et al. 2003). Although the presence of foreign retailers could put a downward pressure on prices via their higher productivity and more intense competition, the crowding-out of local stores could also allow foreign retailers to use their market power to raise prices over time (Durand 2007). To the extent that the first factor dominates, and these goods constitute a larger share of the consumption basket of low-income households, this would have favorable distributional effects. In addition, however, against the backdrop of low levels of unionization in low-skilled services sectors such as retail, entry by foreign firms could intensify competition in the product market, thereby lowering the bargaining power of labor and encouraging race-to-the-bottom wage dynamics. This was the case in Mexico, where real wages in retail fell by 18 percent between 1994 and 2003 following the entry of Walmart (Durand 2007).[24]

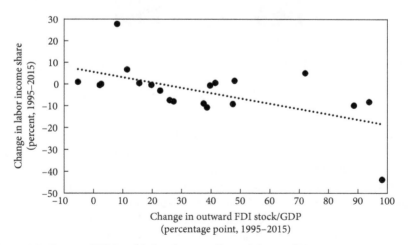

Figure 8.5 Outward FDI and Labor Income Share, Advanced Economies
Sources: Lane and Milesi-Ferretti (2007, 2018), and authors' calculations

---

[24] During the same period, however, overall inequality fell in Mexico, partly driven by FDI (see Section V).

Turning to outward FDI, some studies find that this is positively associated with inequality because it lowers the capital/labor ratio, reduces the demand for less skilled labor disproportionately, or weakens labor's bargaining power (see e.g., Choi 2006; Jaumotte et al. 2008). The evidence suggests a negative relationship between outward FDI and the labor income share in AEs (Figure 8.5). Analyzing the US experience with outsourcing less-skill intensive activities to Mexico in the 1980s, for example, Feenstra and Hanson (1997) find that the skill premium increased in the United States as outsourcing such activities reduced the demand for less skilled workers. In contrast, Marin (2004) shows that Austrian and German multinationals in the 1990s outsourced skill-intensive stages of production to CEE region, thereby exerting downward pressure on the skill premium in Austria and Germany (while raising the skill premium in CEE region, as mentioned above).

In addition, capital account liberalization could lower the bargaining power of labor and thus its income share, by creating a credible threat to relocate production

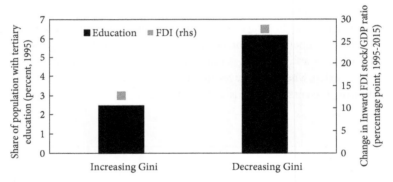

Figure 8.6 Inward FDI, Education and Inequality, Emerging Markets and Developing Countries
Sources: Barro and Lee (2013), Lane and Milesi-Ferretti (2018), Solt (2020), and authors' calculations

and jobs abroad (Rodrik 1998; Furceri et al. 2018; Ostry et al. 2019).[25] As Rodrik (1998) argues, "employers can pack up and leave, but workers cannot," implying that workers "have to receive lower wages and benefits whenever bargaining is an element in setting the terms of employment." Consistent with this observation, Blinder (2009) finds that "the 5.7 million most offshorable jobs seem to pay a wage penalty—estimated to be about 14 percent" in the United States.

FDI can also facilitate *tax avoidance* by multinational companies. "Phantom FDI," defined as investments with no real links to the local economy, accounts for an estimated 40 percent of global FDI (Damgaard et al. 2019). These investments pass

---

[25] Using a panel of 23 AEs and 25 industries over the period 1975–2010, for example, Furceri et al. (2018) find that capital account liberalization tends to reduce the labor income share to a larger extent in sectors with higher natural layoff rate with the mechanism possibly operating through the lower bargaining power of labor.

through corporate shells with a view to minimizing multinationals' global tax bills.[26] Such tax avoidance will likely raise returns for capital owners, accentuating income inequality in source countries.[27]

Finally, the inequality-increasing effects of inward FDI appear to be less in countries with higher levels of educational attainment. Mihaylova (2015) argues that this is related to the fact that the technologies transferred by FDI often require the use of relatively skilled labor in the recipient country. A higher level of human capital in the FDI recipient country will thus tend to limit the impact on the skill premium. As we show in Figure 8.6, between 1995 and 2015, more than 6 (slightly more than 2) percent of the population completed tertiary education in EMDCs that observed a decline (an increase) in inequality, with no major difference in terms of inward FDI across these groups.[28,29]

B. Non-FDI Private Capital Flows

Insofar as portfolio capital flows and FDI have similar impacts on investment in the recipient country, they will have similar distributional effects.[30] In addition, however, the impact of portfolio flows is likely to reflect their implications for aggregate volatility. Several studies find pronounced negative distributional consequences when capital account liberalization increases macroeconomic volatility (Chauvet et al. 2017) and especially when it is followed by a crisis (Ernst and Escudero 2008; Furceri et al. 2018) (Figure 8.7).[31,32,33]

[26] A few well-known tax havens host the vast majority of the world's FDI through special purpose entities. Globally, phantom investments amount to $15 trillion, or the combined annual GDP of China and Germany. Despite international attempts to curb tax avoidance, the growth of phantom FDI continues to outpace that of genuine FDI. Investments in foreign empty shells could indicate that domestically controlled multinationals engage in tax avoidance that benefits the rich, with potential adverse implications for inequality in the source countries (i.e., where the owners of these companies reside) (see also Chapter 12 on taxation).

[27] At the same time, tax payments generate fiscal revenue in recipient countries. If such revenues finance redistributive policies, they might help to reduce inequality. However, if the revenues are captured by the elites, they will aggravate inequality.

[28] It is worth noting that the first group also attracted higher FDI relative to the size of their economies.

[29] Out of 53 EMDCs, there were only 14 LIDCs, with around 2.5 (1.7) percent of the population having completed tertiary education in countries with a decline (increase) in inequality.

[30] Non-FDI private capital flows include portfolio debt and equity flows and other investments such as bank funding, and trade credit/deposits. Portfolio debt flows include flows where the debtor is government and the creditor is private sector entity as these flows are considered market-driven.

[31] Specifically, Chauvet et al. (2017) finds that income volatility has an adverse impact on inequality for a panel of 142 countries between 1973 and 2012. Ernst and Escudero (2008) finds the inequality-raising impact of crisis in a sample of 102 countries between 1960–2006, while Furceri et al. (2018) examining a sample of 23 countries over the period 1975–2010 show that the distributional impact of capital account liberalization is magnified when liberalization is followed by crisis.

[32] We identified 22 episodes, of which data are available for 16 episodes. There is only one crisis episode in AEs in the sample. The EMDC group is dominated by EMs (11 episodes), whereas there are only 4 LIDC episodes.

[33] The Committee on International Economic Policy and Reform (2012) similarly concluded that "the procyclical nature of cross-border bank-intermediated credit flows have given rise to serious economic and financial instabilities."

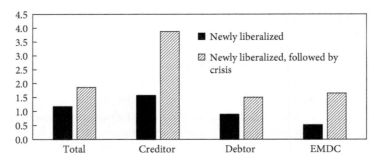

Figure 8.7 Capital Account Liberalization, Crises, and Inequality, 1970–2015
(Gini coefficient, percent change, before and after capital account liberalization)

Note: Newly liberalized, followed by crisis indicates those capital account liberalization episodes that are followed by either currency, banking or sovereign debt crisis within ten years. See Figure 8.3 for the country sample.

Sources: Chinn and Ito (2006), Solt (2020), Lane and Milesi-Ferretti (2018), Laeven and Valencia (2012), and authors' calculations.

The procyclicality of portfolio inflows in EMDCs is well established: net flows rise in good times and fall in bad times, amplifying business-cycle fluctuations.[34] Relatedly, there is a literature linking financial liberalization and capital inflow surges on the one hand to crises on the other.[35] But the pro-cyclicality of capital flows differs across countries and borrowers. Capital inflows into developing countries are less pro-cyclical than those into more developed countries (Araujo et al. 2015b). This could be the result of the less pronounced financial accelerator in developing countries, given smaller banking systems and a less pronounced leverage cycle (Geanakoplos 2009). The cyclical properties of inflows also reflect the type of borrower: sovereign borrowing is countercyclical in EMs and acyclical in AEs, while borrowing by banks and corporates is uniformly pro-cyclical (Kalemli-Ozcan et al. 2017).

Gross flows are more procyclical than net flows, making them a better indicator of financial vulnerabilities.[36,37] Both gross inflows by non-residents and gross outflows by residents decline during crises (Broner et al. 2013), so their respective impacts on net flows offset one another. This implies that the degree of global

---

[34] See, for example, the literature on sudden stops (e.g., Calvo and Reinhart 2000, or Kaminsky et al. 2004).

[35] See, for example, Eichengreen (2004); Reinhart and Reinhart (2008); Reinhart and Rogoff (2009).

[36] See, for example, Lane and Milesi-Ferretti (2007); Forbes and Warnock (2011); Broner et al. (2013).

[37] A higher degree of complementarity between gross inflows and outflows reduces the volatility of net inflows in AEs, i.e., given relatively stable current account balance and reserve positions in these countries, changes in gross capital inflows are typically mirrored by changes in gross capital outflows (Bluedorn et al. 2013).

financial market integration (as proxied by gross flows) is more important for inequality than whether a country is a net creditor or debtor.[38]

Aggregate volatility is associated with higher inequality, because poorer households suffer more in economic downturns (see also Chapter 11).[39,40] The mechanisms here are several:

- Recessions disproportionately affect wages and employment for poor households, since firms are more reluctant to lay off their skilled workers due to higher hiring and training costs (Agenor 2001).
- Credit rationing by banks, which is more prevalent during downturns, disproportionately affects poorer households, since their loans are considered riskier. For example, Choudhary and Jain (2017) show that when facing an increase in their funding costs due to an exogenous shock caused by flooding, banks in Pakistan disproportionately reduce credit to less-educated, poorer borrowers.
- Poor households may be forced to interrupt the education of their children (Hausmann and Gavin 1996).[41] Consequently, recessions may have long-lasting impacts on human capital formation, resulting in an "asymmetric hysteresis effect on poverty" (Agenor 2001).

Negative distributional effects can thus be limited by policy frameworks that help countries to effectively manage capital flows, and reduce the associated volatility. The IMF has suggested a variety of capital flow measures (CFMs) that might be deployed in this connection, though such measures should not be substitute for warranted macroeconomic adjustment. Strengthening financial regulation and supervision are important here as well (IMF 2012).[42] So too are macroprudential policies, which can mitigate the impact of global financial shocks (Bergant et al. 2020). Improved access to financial services can also allow households to borrow as a way of mitigating the consequences of downturns.

---

[38] This last implication is consistent with the earlier discussion pointing to the absence of a clear relationship between income inequality on the one hand and countries' net external positions as debtors or creditors on the other.

[39] See, for example, Heathcote et al. (2010); Atkinson and Morelli (2011); Guillaumont Jeanneney and Kpodar (2011); Agnello and Sousa (2012); and Chauvet et al. (2017).

[40] Financial crises however could reduce wealth inequality as bankruptcies and falling asset prices may have greater impact on those who are better off (Atkinson and Morelli 2011).

[41] For example, the 1998 crisis in Indonesia was followed by a decline in the school enrollment of young children in the poorest households (Thomas et al. 2004). In contrast, children were found not more likely to drop out from school during recessions in Brazil (Neri and Thomas 2000). Similarly, the Great Recession was found to have a long-term negative impact on employment in the United States, with larger effects among older and lower-income individuals (Yagan 2019).

[42] Bumann and Lensink (2016) focus on financial depth as the main channel through which capital account liberalization (a particular form of financial liberalization) affects income inequality. They find that capital account liberalization only tends to lower income inequality if the level of financial depth, as measured by private credit over GDP, is high, in excess of 25 percent.

Here the composition of flows again matters. While a surge in capital inflows increases the probability of a banking or a currency crisis in immediately succeeding years, this effect may be less when flows take the form of portfolio equity or FDI than when it takes the form of debt (Furceri et al. 2011a). Again, capital flow and regulatory measure can be used to shape tilt the composition of flows in more stable directions.

Capital flows may also affect inequality through their impact on financial inclusion.[43,44] The development of mobile money services, facilitated by foreign portfolio investment, could enhance access to credit. For example, equity investment by the foreign-owned Safaricom contributed to the introduction of M-PESA in Kenya in 2007, leading to a significant increase in access to finance.[45] Wider access to financial services (e.g., payments services, savings accounts) helped make financial transactions more efficient, and facilitated investment in small enterprise by households that did not previously have access to such services. Improved access to loans also helped with the management of income shocks due to loss of employment and thus protect households from falling into poverty (Demirguc-Kunt et al. 2017).[46]

Portfolio capital flows may further influence inequality through their fiscal impact, making it easier for the sovereign to finance its spending but also leading to rising debt. The distributional impact will then depend on how the additional resources are used and additional liabilities are managed: for example, on whether the resources are used to support pro-poor programs and whether the debt is prudently managed (see Chapter 11).

Opening the capital account can also create a foreign demand for domestic assets (Azis and Shin 2015; Kim and Yang 2009; Ananchotikul and Zhang 2014). For example, portfolio equity, portfolio debt and net bank inflows may also be associated with a boom in housing prices (Jara and Olaberría 2013); the impact on distribution will depend on who owns the housing stock. By comparison, an increase in equity prices driven by capital flows will almost certainly increase wealth inequality insofar as stocks typically constitute a larger share of asset holdings of high-income households.[47]

---

[43] For an overview of the link between financial inclusion and inequality, see Chapter 4.

[44] For example, the use of external funds by banks to lend to the private sector could enhance financial inclusion. On the other hand, capital flows to countries where targeted lending by banks to specific groups of interest is prevalent could result in higher inequality. In general, the literature on capital flows and financial inclusion is scarce.

[45] Ultimately, this technology spread to other countries in the region, reaching 30 million users, significantly boosting financial inclusion (Sy 2019).

[46] In their study of towns in Mexico where bank branches were rapidly opened, Bruhn and Love (2014) argue that increased access to financial services leads to an increase in income for low-income individuals by allowing informal business owners to keep their businesses open and creating an overall increase in employment.

[47] For example, in the context of the distributional impact of quantitative easing in the euro area, Lenza and Slacalek (2018) discuss the potential role of the portfolio composition channel,

Portfolio flows may further alter net wealth through their impact on the exchange rate. For example, currency depreciation due to outflows will tend to reduce the net wealth of households with foreign-currency-denominated liabilities and raise the cost of repaying foreign-currency-denominated debt. This effect was evident in Central/Eastern European countries where the majority of mortgage debt was financed by foreign-domiciled banks and denominated in euros and Swiss francs.

Finally, openness to capital flows can facilitate tax evasion and illicit financial flows, much as in the case of the phantom FDI discussed above.[48] An additional motive for turning to offshore centers is to avoid prosecution for fraud and corruption.[49] Comparing information from offshore financial institutions with administrative wealth records in Denmark, Norway, and Sweden, Alstadsæter et al. (2019) find that offshore tax evasion is mainly engaged in by the rich. They estimate that the 0.01 percent richest households thereby evaded around 25 percent of their taxes.[50]

In sum, portfolio capital flows may raise inequality through their impact on volatility, tax avoidance, illicit flows, and asset prices—all of which tend to benefit the rich. Such flows may be inequality reducing, however, when they boost financial inclusion. Strong institutions and pro-active policies help to mitigate the potential inequality-raising effects, however, and to share the benefits more widely.

C. Official Capital Flows

Studies that analyze the distributional impact of ODA reach conflicting conclusions. Chong et al. (2009), using cross-section and system GMM panel techniques, find no robust effect of aid on inequality. Shafiullah (2011), in contrast, estimates fixed and random effects models and finds that aid reduces income inequality. Calderón et al. (2006) find that foreign aid reduces inequality so long as institutional quality exceeds a critical threshold. Conversely, weak institutions in recipient countries enhance the ability of local authorities to engage in corruption and rent-seeking activities aimed at appropriating resource windfalls and diverting aid funds, resulting in greater inequality (Chong and Gradstein 2007). Herzer and

highlighting that self-employed business and stock market wealth constitute a substantially larger share of total assets in the top net wealth quintile of households.

[48] Compared with tax avoidance in the case of FDI, tax evasion refers to illegal activities.

[49] Relatedly, capital account openness could also encourage organized crime by providing opportunities for money laundering.

[50] Ndikumana and Boyce (2018) estimate that capital flight, inferred from capital flows not recorded in the balance of payments, amounted to a cumulative US$1.4 trillion in 30 African countries between 1970 and 2015. According to estimates by the United Nations Office on Drugs and Crime, money laundering was close to 3 percent of world GDP in 2009 (UNODC 2011).

Nunnenkamp (2012), using panel cointegration estimators to examine long term effects of aid, also find that aid increases inequality on balance.

When foreign donors are not purely altruistic, they may use aid to buy political support by the local elite, in which case aid benefits the rich rather than the poor in the recipient country. Similarly, there may be a heightened risk that aid is diverted into inter alia foreign bank accounts in countries where political institutions are weak. Two conditions thus must be met in order for ODA to be effective in reducing inequality: first, donors must allocate aid in line with their rhetoric on pro-poor growth; and both they and the local authorities must ensure that aid reaches the poor—in this regard, strong institutions are a pre-condition for aid to reach those in need and for it to reduce inequality.

Finally, there is the problem that official aid is procyclical (Pallage and Robe 2002). This may reflect the fact that recipient countries may have less ability during downturns to meet the matching requirements set by donors. This implies that instead of playing a stabilizing role, aid flows can exacerbate aggregate volatility, with potential adverse effects for inequality, as discussed above.

The second form of official capital flows we consider is reserve accumulation, when capital flows out of countries, including EMDEs, seeking to augment their reserves and into the safe reserve assets issued by, inter alia, the US government. The rapid build-up of international reserves by emerging market countries in the pre-GFC period, for example, had the potential to affect inequality through two channels. First, larger reserves augmented the capacity of central banks and governments to insulate the domestic economy from the effects of capital flow reversals; this helped to help mitigate growth volatility associated with changing global financial conditions, thereby also lowering possible adverse distributional consequences as discussed in the previous section. Second, as "reserves were accumulated in the context of foreign exchange interventions intended to promote export-led growth by preventing exchange-rate appreciation" (Bernanke 2005), the impact on inequality also depends on how evenly the gains from the export-led growth are distributed across skilled- and unskilled labor, as well as labor and capital owners.[51]

D. The Case of Mexico

In this section, we consider Mexico as a way of illustrating aspects of the capital flows-inequality nexus.

---

[51] For a comprehensive discussion on trade and inequality, see Chapter 7.

Geographer and explorer Alexander von Humboldt, who visited in 1803–1804, described Mexico as "a country of inequality."[52] Nowadays, Mexico has one of the highest levels of income inequality among OECD countries. The country's modern history has encompassed increasing levels of external integration, including joining the GATT in 1986 and adopting NAFTA in 1994.

Trends in inequality since the 1970s fall into three distinct periods. Inequality first fell in the 1970s from high initial levels (Figure 8.8). This was followed by an increase from the mid-1980s through the mid-1990s, with both gross and disposable-income Ginis rising steadily.[53] Inequality then declined again from the mid-1990s (coincident with the implementation of NAFTA) through the late 2000s (which closed with the GFC). This last phase was especially evident in terms of disposable income, with the decline being widespread across states.

The first period of declining inequality coincided with the end of Mexico's post-World War II period of "state-led development, rapid industrialization" (Bleynat et al. 2017). The new economic policy announced in 1970, the start of *Desarrollo Compartido* (Shared Development), had the express objective of reducing income inequality (Kehoe and Meza 2012). The discovery of sizeable oil fields in 1978 then financed increased public investment. All this was strongly equalizing.

However, given that the widening fiscal deficit was partly financed with borrowing from abroad, external debt increased sharply during this period (Figure 8.8). When hit by tightening global financial conditions and declining oil prices, the Mexican government was forced to announce in 1982 that it could not

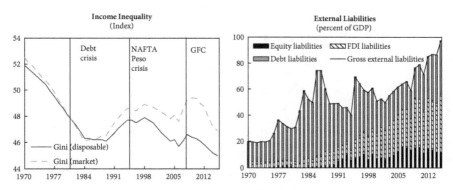

Figure 8.8 Mexico: Income Inequality and External Liabilities, 1970–2015
Sources: Solt (2020), Lane and Milesi-Ferretti (2018), and authors' calculations.

[52] "Mexico is a country of inequality. Nowhere does there exist such a fearful difference in the distribution of fortune, civilization of the soil, and population." (http://www.worldeconomicsassociation.org/newsletterarticles/inequality-in-mexico/)
[53] Disposable income refers to income after taxes and transfers.

service its debt. The economy entered a severe recession, during which inequality worsened.

Mexico regained access to international markets following a debt restructuring agreement with foreign lenders in 1990. FDI had already picked up in response to reforms in the second half of the 1980s. This foreign investment together with skill-biased technological change contributed to the increase in the relative demand for skilled labor, as noted above in section IV (Cragg and Epelbaum 1996; Feenstra and Hanson 1997). The increase in the skill premium, reflected in the relatively rapid rise of wages at the upper part of the income distribution, in turn contributed to rising inequality (Esquivel 2010).

Foreign capital market access led in practice to the rapid build-up of short-term, dollar-indexed debt, culminating in the 1994–1995 crisis which resulted in devaluation of the peso and a spike in interest rates, followed by a sharp economic contraction and significant rise in unemployment. Income inequality fell between 1994 and 1996, as the top 10 percent of the income distribution comprised a large share of high-skilled workers in the non-tradable sectors such as financial services, which were the hardest hit by the crisis (Lopez-Acevedo and Salinas 2000).[54]

Several potential drivers of the post-NAFTA fall in wage inequality have been suggested. The supply of skilled workers rose following an increase in college enrollment starting in 1995 (Campos-Vázquez 2013). In addition, wages rose at the bottom of the income distribution, suggesting a role for demand-side factors (Esquivel 2010). In particular, the demand for unskilled labor increased as a result

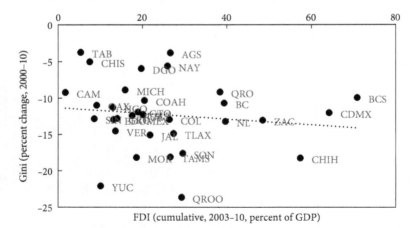

Figure 8.9 Mexico: Income Inequality and FDI, by States
Sources: CONEVAL, INEGI, and authors' calculations.

[54] Notwithstanding the decline in income inequality, the poor were seriously hit by the crisis, with a 24 percent increase in the poverty headcount during the crisis (Pereznieto 2010).

of the expansion of assembly activities by foreign investors (Robertson 2007). Chiquiar (2008) shows that wage developments in this period were in line with the prediction of the Stolper- Samuelson Theorem. Specifically, the increase in low-skilled wages was larger in states closer to the US-Mexico border where there is a higher concentration of manufacturing production and FDI. This spatial pattern reinforced the heterogeneous regional impact of NAFTA.

These wage developments were linked in part to FDI inflows. Jensen and Rosas (2007) find that Mexican states receiving larger FDI inflows experienced larger declines in inequality between 1990 and 2000.[55] Using industry-level data for the period 1994–2005, Waldkirch (2008) also finds evidence that FDI into maquiladora industry (factories serving industries operating under preferential tariff regimes established by Mexico and the United States) benefited unskilled workers disproportionately. Our data for 2003–2010, in Figure 8.9, also indicate that inequality decreased more in regions that received higher inflows of FDI.

V. Policy Implications

Our survey points to six sets of measures that governments can take in order to derive benefits from financial globalization while mitigating adverse implications for income distribution.

Macroeconomic policies: Limiting the macroeconomic volatility associated with capital flows through the application of countercyclical macroeconomic policies will have favorable distributional consequences, since such volatility disproportionately hurts the poor. Monetary policy is unlikely to be helpful in this connection. Raising interest rates to damp down demand when capital is flowing in will only attract more capital, while lowering interest rates to damp down the capital inflow will only aggravate the problem of excess demand. In practice, this mainly means using fiscal policy to lean against the capital-flow-induced wind. Countries opening the capital account should therefore first strengthen their automatic fiscal stabilizers. Strengthening fiscal institutions (creating an independent agency to construct fiscal forecasts for example) can similarly strengthen the conduct of discretionary fiscal policy.

Capital-flow management policies: CFMs could be deployed as part of a broader policy package to limit the risk of capital-flow reversals and crises that disproportionately hurt the poor.[56] However, CFMs should not be a substitute for warranted macroeconomic adjustment. In addition, distributional and social objectives

---

[55] At the same time, Rivera and Castro (2013) find that FDI raised inequality between regions but not within them.

[56] The recent IMF IEO report on capital flows recommends that the IMF considers the distributional effects as part of the strategy for capital account liberalization within the IMF's Institutional View on CFMs (IMF 2012). However, any changes to the Institutional View would need to be decided by the IMF Executive Board.

could be considered explicitly, for example by allowing for housing-related restrictions on non-resident investments could be considered in countries where housing affordability is an issue (IMF 2020). In response to the increased role of non-residents in the housing sector, a number of advanced economies that generally maintain very open capital accounts have adopted policy measures to influence capital flows into the real estate sector to mitigate concerns about affordability and financial stability. Since 2011, five advanced economies—Australia, Canada, Hong Kong SAR, New Zealand, and Singapore—have all adopted or tightened measures discriminating between residents and non-residents with respect to investment in domestic real estate, mostly in the form of stamp duties and other transaction taxes. Some countries (e.g., Australia) have outright prohibitions on non-residents' purchases of real estate (e.g., Australia) or quotas and/or limitations on portfolio investment in real estate (e.g., China, India, Indonesia, and Switzerland).

Education: The adverse distributional effects of liberalization are smaller, or even absent, in EMDCs where the population has a relatively high level of educational attainment, such that the increase in the skill premium resulting from inward FDI in particular is more widely shared. Reaping the benefits of higher levels of education means avoiding skill mismatch. Achieving those higher levels requires getting an early start—that is, aligning the pace of enhancing the educational attainment with the capacity of the education system in order to avoid a decline in quality.

Business Climate: Reliable contract enforcement and business-enabling regulation can help to make EMDCs more attractive destinations for FDI. Promoting competition in product markets, streamlining regulation, reducing bureaucratic discretion, and increasing transparency (e.g., through developing information portals to make laws and regulations publicly accessible) all encourage long-term investors and help shift the composition of capital inflows toward forms with more favorable distributional consequences (Furceri et al. 2011b). The activities of investment-promotion agencies can further contribute to efforts to attract FDI by, among other things, providing information and assistance in obtaining approvals, licenses, utilities, etc. Morisset (2003) argues that political visibility of such agencies (e.g., a direct link of the agency to the highest government official such as the president or the prime minister) and private sector involvement (e.g., private participation in the agency's supervisory board) are important for "strengthening the government's commitment and reinforcing the agency's credibility and visibility."[57]

Financial sector policies, including macroprudential policies: Ensuring the prudent use of external funds by banks through sound micro- and macro-prudential policies could enhance the resilience of the banking sector, thereby enhancing

---

[57] Also, a well-designed feedback process needs to be in place to assess the performance of the agency.

financial stability, moderating business cycle fluctuations and reducing the potential adverse distributional of economic and financial volatility. For example, imposing a macroprudential levy on bank flows could be considered to manage risk taking by banks, particularly in the case of increased bank-led flows (Azis and Shin 2015). Similarly, regulatory frameworks that foster competition in the banking and finance can facilitate access to credit, and ultimately allow the benefits of more abundant credit to be more widely shared. For example, abolishing credit and interest-rate controls and strengthening banking supervision (e.g., higher powers for the banking supervisory authority, more stringent capital regulation, more monitoring of bank activities) could positively affect financial inclusion and reduce inequality (Delis et al. 2012).[58] At the same time, some macroprudential policies could have adverse direct distributional effects: e.g., loan-to-value (LTV) and debt-to-income (DTI) limits on mortgages can, for instance, restrict the ability of households with limited financial wealth to purchase a house, and to use a house as collateral for small business investment. This may prevent low-income households from increasing their income or benefiting from price increases, adversely affecting income distribution (Frost and van Stralen 2018).

Redistributive policies and social safety nets: Inequality in disposable incomes increased by less than inequality in market incomes following capital account liberalization episodes, suggesting that redistribution mitigated some of the adverse effects (Figure 8.10). But because financial globalization shifts the burden of taxation from more mobile factors (capital and highly-skilled labor) to less mobile

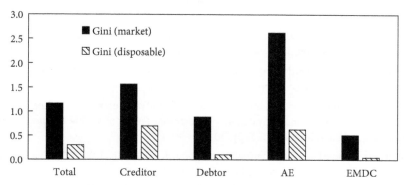

Figure 8.10 Capital Account Liberalization, and Gross and Net Income Inequality, 1970–2015
(Gini coefficient, percent change, before and after capital account liberalization)
Sources: Chinn-Ito (2006), Solt (2020), Lane and Milesi-Ferretti (2018), and authors' calculations.

---

[58] Credit and interest-rate controls lower liquidity and work against the poor as higher restrictions tend to produce less competitive markets. Under these conditions, it is possible that relationship lending or lending to well-established firms with high levels of collateral and strong credit history prevails, constraining access to credit for the relatively poor. As higher supervisory power is usually related to more effective supervision of financial-intermediation services, this could facilitate more competition in banking sector, which could in turn drive funds to the best investment ideas and thus provide equal opportunities to the relatively poor.

factors (low-skilled labor), proactive changes in tax and transfer policies may be needed to achieve the desired effect (Razin and Sadka 2019).[59] Strengthening social safety nets can also help consumption smoothing, thereby mitigating potential adverse implications of crises for the poor.

VI. Concluding Remarks

Financial globalization has a tendency to foster economic growth but also to raise inequality, where the first effect presumably is desired, whereas the second is not. But neither result is foreordained. The tendency for capital flows to encourage growth is likely to be evident only in countries that first make progress in strengthening policies and institutions, thereby limiting the volatility of those flows and creating some assurance that they will be directed toward appropriate uses and sectors. The tendency for capital flows to raise inequality can be limited by policies that shape their composition and timing and thereby prevent any associated rise in aggregate volatility and increased incidence of crises. That tendency can be further limited or even reversed by taking ex ante steps to increase educational attainment so that more workers benefit from foreign capital-skill complementarities, and by ex post measures that redistribute income to the disadvantaged.

References

Agenor, Pierre-Richard. 2001. "Macroeconomic Adjustment and the Poor: Analytical Issues and Cross-Country Evidence," The World Bank, First Draft: October 3.

Agnello, Luca, and Ricardo Sousa. 2012. "How Do Banking Crises Impact on Income Inequality?," *Applied Economics Letters* 19(15): 1425–9.

Allen, Helen, John Hawkins, and Setsuya Sato. 2001. "Electronic Trading and Its Implications for Financial Systems." In *Electronic Finance: A New Perspective and Challenges*, edited by BIS, Vol. 7, pp. 30–52.

Alstadsæter, Annette, Niels Johannesen, and Gabriel Zucman. 2019. "Tax Evasion and Inequality." *American Economic Review* 109(6): 2073–103.

Amendolagine, Vito, Andrea F. Presbitero, Roberta Rabellotti, Marco Sanfilippo, and Adnan Seric. 2017. "FDI, Global Value Chains, and Local Sourcing in Developing Countries," IMF Working Paper 17/284.

---

[59] See Chapter 12 on taxation for a discussion on policies related to corporate income taxation and multinationals, as well as tax administration issues related to tax evasion and avoidance as well as transfer pricing.

Amighiani, Alessia A., Margaret S. McMillan, and Marco Sanfilippo. 2017. "FDI and Capital Formation in Developing Economies: New Evidence from Industry-Level Data," NBER Working Paper 23,049.

Ananchotikul, Nasha, and Longmei Zhang. 2014. "Portfolio Flows, Global Risk Aversion and Asset Prices in Emerging Markets," IMF Working Paper 14/156.

Araujo, Juliana D., Antonio C. David, Carlos von Hombeeck, and Chris Papageorgiou. 2015a. "Non-FDI Capital Inflows in Low-Income Developing Countries: Catching the Wave?," IMF Working Paper 15/86.

Araujo, Juliana D., Antonio C. David, Carlos von Hombeeck, and Chris Papageorgiou. 2015b. "Joining the Club? Procyclicality of Private Capital Inflows in Low Income Developing Countries," IMF Working Paper 15/163.

Asteriou, Dimitrios, Sophia Dimelis, and Argiro Moudatsou. 2014. "Globalization and income inequality: A panel data econometric approach for the EU27 countries," *Economic Modelling* 36(2014): 592–9.

Atkinson, A.B., and Salvatore Morelli. 2011. "Economic Crises and Inequality," UNDP-HDRO Occasional Papers No. 2011/6. Available at: https://ssrn.com/abstract=2351471

Auten, Gerald, and David Splinter. 2018. "Income Inequality in the United States: Using Tax Data to Measure Long-term Trends," version as of August 23, 2018.

Autor, David, David Dorn, and Gordon Hansen. 2016. "The China Shock: Learning from Labor Market Adjustment to Large Changes in Trade," *Annual Review of Economics,* 8, 205–40.

Azis, Iwan J., and Hyun Song Shin. 2015. "Capital Flows and Income Distribution," In *Managing Elevated Risk.* Chapter 4, 79–99. Singapore: Springer.

Barro, Robert, and Jong-Wha Lee. 2013. "A New Data Set of Educational Attainment in the World, 1950-2010." *Journal of Development Economics* 104: 184–98.

Basu, Parantap, and Alessandra Guariglia. 2007. "Foreign Direct Investment, Inequality, and Growth." *Journal of Macroeconomics* 29(2007): 824–39.

Bergant, Katharina, Francesco Grigoli, Niels-Jakob Hansen, and Damiano Sandri. 2020. "Dampening Global Financial Shocks: Can Macroprudential Regulation Help (More than Capital Controls)?," IMF Working Paper 20/106.

Berman, Eli, John Bound, and Stephen Machin. 1998. "Implications of Skill-biased Technological Change: International Evidence." *The Quarterly Journal of Economics* 113: 1245–79.

Bernanke, Ben S. 2005. "The Global Saving Glut and the U.S. Current Account Deficit," Homer Jones Lecture, Federal Reserve Bank of St. Louis, St. Louis, Missouri, April 14, 2005.

Bertaut, Carol C., and Ruth Judson. 2014. "Estimating U.S. Cross-Border Securities Positions: New Data and New Methods," International Finance Discussion Papers No. 1113, Board of Governors of the Federal Reserve System.

Bertaut, Carol C., and Ralph W. Tryon. 2007. "Monthly Estimates of U.S. Cross-Border Securities Positions," International Finance Discussion Papers No. 910, Board of Governors of the Federal Reserve System.

Bleynat, Ingrid, Amílcar Challú, and Paul Segal. 2017. "Inequality, Living Standards and Growth: Two Centuries of Economic Development in Mexico," ESRC GPID Research Network Working Paper 4, September 19, 2017.

Blinder, Alan. S. 2009. "How Many US Jobs Might be Offshorable." *World Economics* 10(2): 41–78, April–June 2009.

Bluedorn, John, Rupa Duttagupta, Jaime Guajardo, and Petia Topalova. 2013. "Capital Flows are Fickle: Anytime, Anywhere," IMF Working Paper 13/183.

Broner, Fernando, Tatiana Didier, Aitor Erce, and Sergio L. Schmukler. 2013. "Gross Capital Flows: Dynamics and Crises." *Journal of Monetary Economics* 60(2013): 113–33.

Bruhn, Miriam, and Inessa Love. 2014. "The Real Impact of Improved Access to Finance: Evidence from Mexico." *Journal of Finance* 69(3): 1347–76.

Bumann, Silke, and Robert Lensink. 2016. "Capital Account Liberalization and Income Inequality." *Journal of International Money and Finance* 61: 143–62.

Calderón, María Cecilia, Alberto Chong, and Mark Gradstein. 2006. "Foreign Aid, Income Inequality, and Poverty," Inter-American Development Bank Working Paper 547.

Calvo, Guillermo A., and Carmen M. Reinhart. 2000. "When Capital Inflows Come to a Sudden Stop: Consequences and Policy Options." MPRA Paper 6982, University Library of Munich, Germany.

Campos-Vázquez, Raymundo M. 2013. "Why Did Wage Inequality Decrease in Mexico after NAFTA?" *Economia Mexicana* XXII(2): 245–78.

Chauvet, Lisa; Marin Ferry; Patrick Guillaumont; Sylviane Guillaumont Jeanneney; Sampawende J.-A. Tapsoba; and Laurent Wagner. 2017. "Volatility Widens Inequality. Could Aid and Remittances Help?", FERDI Development Policies, Working Papers P158.

Chinn, Menzie D., and Hiro Ito. 2006. "What Matters for Financial Development? Capital Controls, Institutions, and Interactions." *Journal of Development Economics* 81(1): 163–92.

Chiquiar, Daniel. 2008. "Globalization, Regional Wage Differentials and the Stolper-Samuelson Theorem: Evidence from Mexico." *Journal of International Economics* 74(2008): 70–93.

Choi, Changkyu. 2006. "Does Foreign Direct Investment Affect Domestic Income Inequality?," *Applied Economics Letters* 13(12): 811–14.

Chong, Alberto, and Mark Gradstein. 2007. "Inequality and Institutions." *The Review of Economics and Statistics* 89(3): 454–65.

Chong, Alberto, Mark Gradstein, and Cecilia Calderon. 2009. "Can Foreign Aid Reduce Income Inequality and Poverty?" *Public Choice* 140: 59–84.

Choudhary, M. Ali, and Anil Jain. 2017. "Finance and Inequality: The Distributional Impacts of Bank Credit Rationing," Board of Governors of the Federal Reserve System, International Finance Discussion Papers Number 1211, July 2017.

Committee on International Economic Policy and Reform. 2012. "Banks and Cross-Border Capital Flows: Policy Challenges and Regulatory Responses," September 2012.

Cragg, Michael Ian, and Mario Epelbaum. 1996. "Why Has Wage Dispersion Grown in Mexico? Is It the Incidence of Reforms or the Growing Demand for Skills?" *Journal of Development Economics* 51(1): 99–116.

Csonto, Balazs, and Camilo E. Tovar Mora. 2017. "Uphill Capital Flows and the International Monetary System," IMF Working Paper 17/174.

Damgaard, Jannick, Thomas Elkjaer, and Niels Johannesen. 2019. "What is Real and What Is Not in the Global FDI Network?," IMF Working Paper 19/274.

Darvas, Zsolt, and Dirk Schoenmaker. 2017. "Institutional Investors and Home Bias in Europe's Capital Markets Union," Bruegel Working Paper Issue 2.

Delis, Manthos D., Iftekhar Hasan, and Pantelis Kazakis. 2012. "Bank Regulations and Income Inequality: Empirical Evidence," Bank of Finland Research Discussion Papers, No. 18/2012, ISBN 978-952-462-805-1, Bank of Finland, Helsinki.

Demirguc-Kunt, Asli, Leora Klapper, and Dorothe Singer. 2017. "Financial Inclusion and Inclusive Growth," World Bank Group, Policy Research Working Paper 8040.

Durand, Cédric. 2007. "Externalities from Foreign Direct Investment in the Mexican Retailing Sector." *Cambridge Journal of Economics* 2007(31): 393–411.

Economides, George, Sarantis Kalyvitis, and Apostolis Philippopoulos. 2008. "Does Foreign Aid Distort Incentives and Hurt Growth? Theory and Evidence from 75 Aid-recipient Countries." *Public Choice* 134(3): 463–88.

Eichengreen, Barry. 2004. *Capital Flows and Crises*. Cambridge, MA: MIT Press.

Eichengreen, Barry, Arnaud Mehl, and Romain Lafarguette. 2016. "Cables, Sharks and Servers: Technology and the Geography of the Foreign Exchange Markt," NBER Working Paper no. 21884.

Ernst, Ekkehard, and Verónica Escudero. 2008. "The Effects of Financial Globalization on Global Imbalances, Employment and Inequality," International Institute for Labour Studies Discussion Paper 191/2008.

Esquivel, Gerardo. 2010. "The Dynamics of Income Inequality in Mexico Since NAFTA," Centro de Estudios Economicos, Documento de Trabajo IX-2010.

Feenstra, Robert C., and Gordon H. Hanson. 1997. "Foreign Direct Investment and Relative Wages: Evidence from Mexico's Maquiladoras." *Journal of International Economics* 42 (1997): 371–93.

Fernandez, Andres, Michael Klein, Alessandro Rebucci, Martin Schindler, and Martin Uribe. 2016. "Capital Control Measures: A New Dataset." *IMF Economic Review* 64: 548–74.

Forbes, Kristin J., and Francis E. Warnock. 2011. "Capital Flow Waves: Surges, Stops, Flight, and Retrenchment," NBER Working Paper 17,351.

Frost, Jon, and Rene van Stralen. 2018. "Macroprudential Policy and Income Inequality." *Journal of International Money and Finance* 85: 278–90.

Furceri, Davide, Stéphanie Guichard, and Elena Rusticelli. 2011a. "Episodes of Large Capital Inflows and the Likelihood of Banking and Currency Crises and Sudden Stops," OECD Economics Department Working Papers No. 865.

Furceri, Davide, Stéphanie Guichard, and Elena Rusticelli. 2011b. "Medium-Term Determinants of International Investment Positions: The Role of Structural Policies," OECD Economics Department Working Papers No. 863.

Furceri, Davide, Prakash Loungani, and Jonathan D. Ostry. 2018. "The Aggregate and Distributional Effects of Financial Globalization: Evidence from Macro and Sectoral Data," IMF Working Paper 18/83.

Geanakoplos, John. 2009. "The Leverage Cycle," Cowles Foundation Discussion Paper No 1715.

Goldberg, Pinelopi Koujianou, and Nina Pavcnik. 2007. "Distributional Effects of Globalization in Developing Countries," NBER Working Paper 12,885.

Gopinath, Munisamy, and Weiyan Chen. 2003. "Foreign Direct Investment and Wages: A Cross-country Analysis." *Journal of International Trade & Economic Development* 12(3): 285–309.

Guillaumont Jeanneney, Sylviane, and Kangni Kpodar. 2011. "Financial Development, Financial Instability and Poverty," CERDI Etudes et Documents, E.2006.7.

Häusler, Gerd. 2002. "The Globalization of Finance." *Finance and Development* 39(1), March 2002.

Hausmann, Ricardo, and Michael Gavin. 1996. "Securing Stability and Growth in a Shock Prone Region: The Policy Challenge for Latin America," Working Paper 315, Office of the Chief Economist, Inter-American Development Bank.

Heathcote, Jonathan, Gianluca Violante, and Fabrizio Perri. 2010. "Inequality in Times of Crisis: Lessons from the Past and a First Look at the Current Recession," February 2, 2010, https://voxeu.org/article/economic-inequality-during-recessions

Herzer, Dierk, and Peter Nunnenkamp. 2012. "The Effect of Foreign Aid on Income Inequality: Evidence from Panel Cointegration." *Structural Change and Economic Dynamics* 23(3): 245–55.

Herzer, Dierk, Philipp Hühne, and Peter Nunnenkamp. 2014. "FDI and Income Inequality – Evidence from Latin American Economies." *Review of Development Economics* 18(4): 778–93.

Hodler, Roland. 2007. "Rent Seeking and Aid Effectiveness." *International Tax and Public Finance* 14(5): 525–41.

International Monetary Fund (IMF). 2012. "The Liberalization and Management of Capital Flows—An Institutional View," available at: https://www.imf.org/en/

Publications/Policy-Papers/Issues/2016/12/31/The-Liberalization-and-Management-of-Capital-Flows-An-Institutional-View-PP4720

International Monetary Fund (IMF). 2020. Independent Evaluation Office of the IMF, "IMF Advice on Capital Flows," Evaluation Report, 2020. Available at: https://ieo.imf.org/en/our-work/Evaluations/Completed/2020-0930-imf-advice-on-capital-flows

Jara, Alejandro, and Eduardo Olaberría. 2013. "Are all Capital Inflows Associated with Booms in House Prices? An Empirical Evaluation," Banco Central de Chile, Documentos de Trabajo No. 696.

Jaumotte, Florence, Subir Lall, and Chris Papageorgiou. 2008. "Rising Income Inequality: Technology, or Trade and Financial Globalization?" IMF Working Paper 08/185.

Jensen, Nathan M., and Guillermo Rosas. 2007. "Foreign Direct Investment and Income Inequality in Mexico, 1990–2000." International Organization 61(3): 467–87.

Kalemli-Ozcan, Sebnem, Luis Servén, Stefan Avdjiev, and Bryan Hardy. 2017. "Gross Capital Inflows to Banks, Corporates and Sovereigns," CEPR Discussion Paper DP11806.

Kaminsky, Graciela L., Carmen M. Reinhart, and Carlos A. Végh. 2004. "When It Rains, It Pours: Procyclical Capital Flows and Macroeconomic Policies," NBER Working Paper 10,780.

Kehoe, Timothy J., and Felipe Meza. 2012. "Catch-up Growth Followed by Stagnation: Mexico, 1950-2010," Federal Reserve Bank of Minneapolis, Working Paper 693.

Kim, Soyoung, and Doo Yang Yang. 2009. "Do Capital Inflows Matter to Asset Prices? The Case of Korea." Asian Economic Journal 23(3): 323–48.

Krueger, Anne. 1983. Trade and Employment in Developing Countries, Volume 3: Synthesis and Conclusions. Chicago, IL: University of Chicago Press.

Krusell, Per, Lee E. Ohanian, José-Víctor Ríos-Rull, and Giovanni L. Violante. 2000. "Capital-Skill Complementarity and Inequality: A Macroeconomic Analysis." Econometrica 68(5): 1029–53.

Laeven, Luc, and Fabián Valencia. 2012. "Systemic Banking Crises Database: An Update," IMF Working Paper 12/163.

Lane, Philip R., and Gian Maria Milesi-Ferretti. 2007. "The External Wealth of Nations Mark II: Revised and extended Estimates of Foreign Assets and Liabilities, 1970–2004." Journal of International Economics 73(2007): 223–50.

Lane, Philip R., and Gian Maria Milesi-Ferretti. 2018. "The External Wealth of Nations Revisited: International Financial Integration in the Aftermath of the Global Financial Crisis." IMF Economic Review 66: 189–222.

Larrain, Mauricio. 2017. "Capital Account Opening and Wage Inequality." Review of Financial Studies 26: 555–87.

Lee, Jong-Eun. 2006. "Inequality and Globalization in Europe." Journal of Policy Modeling 28: 791–6.

Lenza, Michele, and Jiri Slacalek. 2018. "How Does Monetary Policy Affect Income and Wealth Inequality? Evidence from Quantitative Easing in the Euro Area," ECB Working Paper Series No 2190, October 2018.

Levy-Yeyati, Eduardo, and Tomas Williams. 2011. "Financial Globalization in Emerging Economies: Much Ado About Nothing?" Latin America Initiative at Brookings.

Lopez-Acevedo, Gladys, and Angel Salinas. 2000. "How Mexico's Financial Crisis Affected Income Distribution," The World Bank Policy Research Working Paper 2406.

Marin, Dalia. 2004. "'A Nation of Poets and Thinkers'—Less So with Eastern Enlargement? Austria and Germany," Munich Discussion Paper No. 2004–6.

Mihaylova, Svilena. 2015. "Foreign Direct Investment and Income Inequality in Central and Eastern Europe." Theoretical and Applied Economics XXII(2015), 2(603): 23–42.

Milanovic, Branko. 2005. "Can We Discern the Effect of Globalization on Income Distribution? Evidence from Household Surveys." The World Bank Economic Review 19(1): 21–44.

Morisset, Jacques. 2003. "Does a Country Need a Promotion Agency to Attract Foreign Direct Investment?," The World Bank Policy Research Working Paper 3028.

Mundell, Robert. 1957. "International Trade and Factor Mobility." American Economic Review 47: 321–35.

Ndikumana, Léonce, and James K. Boyce. 2018. "Capital Flight from Africa: Updated Methodology and New Estimates," PERI Research Report, June 2018.

Neri, Marcelo C., and Mark R. Thomas. 2000. "Household Educational Responses to Labor-Market Shocks in Brazil, 1982–99," May 31.

Ostry, Jonathan, Prakash Loungani, and Andrew Berg. 2019. Confronting Inequality: How Societies Can Choose Inclusive Growth. New York: Columbia University Press.

Pallage, Stéphane, and Michel A. Robe. 2002. "Foreign Aid and the Business Cycle." Review of International Economics 9(4): 641–72.

Pavcik, Nina. 2017. "The Impact of Trade on Inequality in Developing Countries," NBER Working Paper no. 23878.

Pereznieto, Paola. 2010. "The Case of Mexico's 1995 Peso Crisis and Argentina's 2002 Convertibility Crisis," UNICEF Social and Economic Policy Working Paper, December 2010.

Piketty, Thomas, Emmanuel Saez, and Gabriel Zucman. 2018. "Distributional National Accounts: Methods and Estimates for the United States." The Quarterly Journal of Economics 131(2): 519–78.

Presbitero, Andrea F., Dhaneshwar Ghura, Olumuyiwa S. Adedeji, and Lamin Njie. 2015. "International Sovereign Bonds by Emerging Markets and Developing Economies: Drivers of Issuance and Spreads," IMF Working Paper 15/275.

Razin, Assaf, and Efraim Sadka. 2019. "Welfare State, Inequality, and Globalization: Role of International-Capital-Flow Direction," NBER Working Paper 25,772.

Reardon, Thomas, C. Peter Timmer, Christopher B. Barrett, and Julio Berdegué. 2003. "The Rise of Supermarkets in Africa, Asia, and Latin America." *American Journal of Agricultural Economics* 85(5): 1140–6.

Reinhart, Carmen M., and Vincent R. Reinhart. 2008. "Capital Flow Bonanzas: An Encompassing View of the Past and Present," NBER Working Paper 14,321.

Reinhart, Carmen M., and Kenneth S. Rogoff. 2009. "The Aftermath of Financial Crises." *American Economic Review* 99(2): 466–72.

Rivera, Carmen Guadalupe Juárez, and Gerardo Ángeles Castro. 2013. "Foreign Direct Investment in Mexico: Determinants and Its Effect on Income Inequality." *Contaduría y Administración* 58(4), August–December: 201–22.

Robertson, Raymond. 2007. "Trade and Wages: Two Puzzles from Mexico," *The World Economy* 30(9): 1378–98.

Rodrik, Dani. 1998. "Capital Mobility and Labor," Draft paper prepared for the NBER workshop on Trade, Technology, Education, and the U.S. Labor Market, April 30–May 1, 1998.

Rodrik, Dani. 2006. "The Social Cost of Foreign Exchange Reserves," CEPR Discussion Paper Series No. 5483.

Shafiullah, Muhammad. 2011. "Foreign Aid and its Impact on Income Inequality." *International Review of Business Research Papers* 7(2): 91–105.

Solt, Frederick. 2020. "Measuring Income Inequality Across Countries and Over Time: The Standardized World Income Inequality Database." *Social Science Quarterly* 101(3): 1183–99, SWIID Version 9.0, October 2020.

Suanes, Macarena. 2016. "Foreign Direct Investment and Income Inequality in Latin America: A Sectoral Analysis." *CEPAL Review* 118, April.

Svensson, Jakob. 2000. "Foreign Aid and Rent-seeking." *Journal of International Economics* 51(2): 437–61.

Sy, Amadou N.R. 2019. "Fintech in Sub-Saharan Africa: A Potential Game Changer," IMFBlog, February 14, 2019.

Sylwester, Kevin. 2005. "Foreign Direct Investment, Growth and Income Inequality in Less Developed Countries." *International Review of Applied Economics* 19(3): 289–300.

Te Velde, Dirk. 2003. "Foreign Direct Investment and Income Inequality in Latin America," Overseas Development Institute, April 2003.

Te Velde, Dirk, and Oliver Morrissey. 2003. "Do Workers in Africa Get a Wage Premium if Employed in Firms Owned by Foreigners?" *Journal of African Economies* 12(1): 41–73.

Te Velde, Dirk, and Oliver Morrissey. 2004. "Foreign Direct Investment, Skills and Wage Inequality in East Asia." *Journal of the Asia Pacific Economy* 9(3): 348–69.

Thomas, Duncan, Kathleen Beegle, Elizabeth Frankenberg, Bondan Sikoki, John Strauss, and Graciela Teruel. 2004. "Education in a Crisis." *Journal of Development Economics* 74(2004): 53–85.

Tsai, Pan-Long. 1995. "Foreign Direct Investment and Income Inequality: Further Evidence." *World Development* 23(3): 469–83.

United Nations Office on Drugs and Crime. 2011. "Estimating Illicit Financial Flows Resulting from Drug Trafficking and Other Transnational Organized Crimes," Research Report, October 2011.

Waldkirch, Andreas. 2008. "The Effects of Foreign Direct Investment in Mexico since NAFTA," MPRA Paper No 7975.

Wolff, Edward N. 2010. "Recent Trends in Household Wealth in the United States: Rising Debt and the Middle-Class Squeeze—an Update to 2007," Levy Economics Institute Working Paper No. 589.

Wood, Adrian. 1997. "Openness and Wage Inequality in Developing Countries: The Latin American Challenge to East Asian Conventional Wisdom." *World Bank Economic Review* 11: 33–57.

Yagan, Danny. 2019. "Employment Hysteresis from the Great Recession." *Journal of Political Economy* 127(5): 2505–58.

9

Migration

Zsoka Koczan, Giovanni Peri, Magali Pinat, and Dmitriy Rozhkov

I. Introduction

International migration is an important channel of material improvement for individuals and their offspring.[1,2] The movement of people across country borders, especially from less developed to richer countries, has a substantial impact in several dimensions. First, it affects the migrants themselves, by allowing them to achieve higher income, as a result of their higher productivity in the destination country. It also increases the expected income for their offspring. Second, it affects the destination country through the impact on labor markets, productivity, innovation, demographic structure, fiscal balance, and criminality. This is due in large part to the fact that immigrants are different from natives, differentiated among themselves. Third, it can have a significant impact on the countries of origin. It may lead to loss of human capital, amplified by the fact that migration can beget more future migration (the so-called chain or network effect) but it also creates a flow of remittances and increased international connections in the form of trade, FDI, and technological transfers.

This chapter will survey our understanding of how migration affects growth and inequality in the world, through the impact on migrants themselves as well as on the destination and origin countries. Before doing that, it is useful to frame the discussion within a few important facts, relative to international migration and its evolution in the last 30 years.

Total migrants as a percentage of the world population have remained rather stable at around 3 percent since 1990. While a lot of attention in the media and among the politicians in recent years has focused on migration from Africa and the Middle East to Europe and North America, most migration in the world is in fact intra-regional (Figure 9.1). Large regional migration hubs have emerged in

---

[1] We thank Valerie Cerra and Barry Eichengreen, as well as participants in the Inclusive Growth book seminar series organized by the IMF Institute for Capacity Development for their comments.
[2] While internal migration is also a very important phenomenon with significant economic and social consequences, we focus on international movements as data for those are more accurate, differences in economic performance between origin and destination countries are larger and issues like language barriers and human capital costs of transfer more important.

Zsoka Koczan, Giovanni Peri, Magali Pinat, and Dmitriy Rozhkov, *Migration* In: *How to Achieve Inclusive Growth*.
Edited by: Valerie Cerra, Barry Eichengreen, Asmaa El-Ganainy, and Martin Schindler, Oxford University Press.
© Zsoka Koczan, Giovanni Peri, Magali Pinat, and Dmitriy Rozhkov 2022. DOI: 10.1093/oso/9780192846938.003.0009

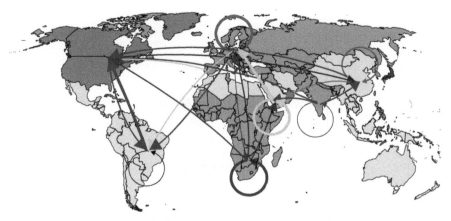

Figure 9.1 Migration Flows between 2010 and 2020

Note: Migrants are defined as the foreign-born population in a destination region. The figure shows migration flows larger than 200,000 people between 2010 and 2020. The width of flows is proportional to the number of migrants.

Source: IMF (2020).

Africa (Cote d'Ivoire, South Africa), Asia (Hong Kong, Singapore), and the Middle East (GCC countries), and there is also significant migration within the European Union. The only exception is Latin America, where there is relatively little intra-regional migration (possibly because some migration, for example from Venezuela to neighboring Colombia and Ecuador, is not captured by statistics). That said, the impact on various countries in terms of population growth has been quite different. While mobility among developing economies has grown less than their population, mobility from developing to advanced economies has significantly increased, especially as a share of the advanced economies' population (which has not increased much in the recent decades). In the last 30 years, the share of migrants from developing to advanced economies has increased from 4 to 9 percent of the population of advanced economies (IMF 2020), and this has generated strong social and political reactions and increased attention to the phenomenon in most advanced countries.

Another important fact is that most of the increased migration from developing to advanced economies can be defined as "economic migration," meaning driven by people looking for better economic opportunities. While migration driven by wars, natural disasters, and political turmoil has increased in numbers, most of it is internal or between developing countries close to each other. Accordingly, most of the discussion in this chapter refers to economic migration, although in some instances we will note the special case of refugees and the way their impact is likely to differ from that of economic migrants.

Following the common practice for most studies, we define "migrants" as individuals who are foreign-born residents of a recipient country. Consequently, we will not distinguish between permanent migrants (intending to stay in the receiving country indefinitely) and temporary migrants (those who plan to return to their country of origin). Such definitions are themselves rather arbitrary, as migrants who move to a country on a temporary basis may end up staying for long periods, while migrants who arrive as permanent may return or re-migrate. We will note the instances where this distinction is likely to be important.

The ability to measure the stock and flows of migrants across countries has improved significantly in the recent decades, mainly thanks to careful work using population censuses that infer net migration from the change in stocks of people born in a country and residing in a different one. These data usually include people who are "undocumented," i.e. present in a country without a proper title for staying, as they are based on counts of resident (and not citizen) population. However, measures of gross flows of migrants, which are based on arrival records, can significantly underestimate migration due to the flows of undocumented migrants.

With this background, we will review what recent research has found in terms of the economic effects of international migration and what we have learned about policy instruments that can be used to manage migration to maximize its benefits for receiving and sending countries.

II. Consequences of Migration for Migrants

As noted in Chapter 1, the decomposition of global inequality into between-country and within-country inequality is sensitive to data measurement issues. But the consensus holds that within-country inequality has been rising around the world over the past several decades, while between-country inequality has declined moderately. Nevertheless, large and persistent gaps in mean income between countries remain. Unskilled workers' wages in rich and poor countries often differ by a factor of 10 to 1. This substantial difference in incomes between countries is certainly the main driver of economic migration.

As a consequence, many migrants experience a large increase in income when they move to richer economies. Clemens, Montenegro, and Pritchett (2019) estimate the real (purchasing power parity, PPP) wage gaps between immigrants in the United States and their observably equivalent national counterparts in 42 home labor markets in developing countries. They calculate the average lower bound on this wage ratio (weighted by the working-age (15–49) population of the home countries) to be 5.7. This ratio exceeds 16 for some developing countries in the sample. There is therefore a very large potential monetary gain from migration.

The gains from migration are larger the younger the migrant is because younger migrants have a longer lifetime ahead of them to benefit from the extra income, hence the present discounted gains from migration are higher (IMF WEO 2020). Other factors include the level of education and skills that are in high demand in the destination countries. These factors drive the selection of people who migrate, with younger, more educated, and more skilled individuals being among those with a higher probability of emigration. Large potential monetary gains have developed an industry around migration, with recruiting firms and brokers engaging in fraudulent and abusive practices. Regulating better the migration industry would protect migrants' workers from exploitation and substantial loss of savings and assets (World Bank 2014).

At the same time, the ability to integrate into the receiving country is a key element of whether migrants are able to fully realize the potential gains from migration. Figure 9.2, taken from OECD and EU (2018), shows that in the EU and in other OECD countries migrants tend to have much higher poverty rates than the native population. OECD and EU (2018) also shows that they are more likely to be unemployed or overqualified in their jobs, more likely to live in over-crowded housing, have worse health outcomes, and worse educational outcomes for their children compared to native. The ability of migrants to assimilate depends on their origin, skills, and characteristics (Ho and Turk-Ariss 2018; Abramitzky et al. 2019). In many OECD countries, immigrants report high levels of discrimination and abuse based on their nationality, ethnicity, or race.

While discrimination and prejudice leading to incomplete integration are significant hurdles to the economic success of immigrants, the revealed preference argument suggests that, in most cases, by moving and remaining in the destination country, migrants are willing to withstand these difficulties, in order to achieve the significant income gain. In this respect, refugees are different, in that for this group the gains are more likely to take the form of escape and safety from violence, persecution, and famine.

The decision to return to their home country is quite common among emigrants. However, the rate of return depends, among other things, on the destination country, with a substantially higher rate of return from European destinations compared with Australia, Canada, New Zealand, and the United States. The time spent in the destination country is also an important factor in the decision to return. Return migration rates are highest during the first decade from arrival and then level off (Dustmann and Görlach 2016). Some migrants decide to return to their home country because they did not achieve the success they anticipated in terms of employment, wages, or quality of life. For other migrants, the decision to return can be part of the initial strategy: migrants move temporarily to accumulate savings and human capital and return to their home country to benefit from it. Barrett and Goggin (2010) find that wage premia affect Mexican, Albanian, Hungarian, and Irish migrants' decision to return. Dustmann (1996) and Dustmann and Görlach (2016) develop theoretical models of temporary

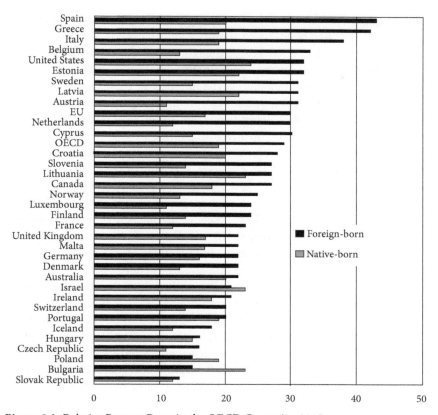

Figure 9.2 Relative Poverty Rates in the OECD Countries, 2015
Percentages of the population aged 16 years and over
Source: OECD (2018).

migration in which migrants working abroad acquire additional skills that are rewarded in the home country.

III. Impact of Migration on Destination Countries

International migration is both a challenge and an opportunity for destination countries. On the one hand, especially in the short run, immigrants can create challenges in local labor markets, potentially affecting wages and displacing some native workers who compete with them. Their arrival may also impose a short-term fiscal cost. On the other hand, especially in the medium and long run, immigrants can boost output, create new opportunities for local firms and native workers, supply abilities and skills needed for growth, generate new ideas, stimulate international trade and contribute to long-term fiscal balance, by making the age distribution of advanced countries more balanced. Moreover, both in the short and long run, different groups (high or low educated workers, owners of capital, owners of houses, young or old individuals) may benefit to a different extent from the inflow of immigrants. The interplay of these factors affects the political economy of migration: public perceptions of migration and policies chosen by the governments often depend on which groups gain more, less, or possibly lose from migration, and on their relative political weight.

This section will discuss the existing evidence about the channels through which immigration affects the labor market, economic growth, public finances, incidence of crime, and inequality in the destination country and the characteristics, both of immigrants and of the receiving economies, that affect such impacts. Two important factors affecting those outcomes are the type of migrants moving to a destination country and their speed and degree of integration in the local economy and the formal labor market. Immigration inflows including a large number of highly skilled and working immigrants will have a particularly beneficial impact on the economic and employment growth of the receiving country and on its public finances.

We start by considering a few statistics to illustrate the reality of immigration. From the viewpoint of destination countries, migration flows tend to be a highly concentrated phenomenon, in the sense that the top destinations for migrants account for a large share of them. Figure 9.3 from World Bank (2019) shows the largest destinations of international migrants in absolute numbers and as a proportion of the resident population. Countries in Europe, North America, and the Persian Gulf region as the largest recipients of international migrants. The main reason for this concentration of migrants is the tendency to move to economically successful countries, and to the dense and fast-growing urban areas within

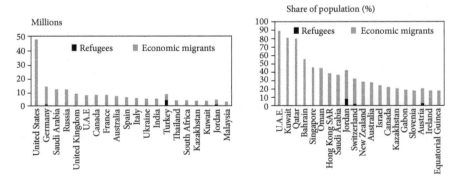

Figure 9.3 Top 20 Destination Economies by Number of International Migrants and Refugees and by Share of the Population, 2018
Source: World Bank (2019) based on UNDESA (2017) and UNHCR.

those countries. The top 10 destination countries account for 60 percent of global immigration (World Bank 2018). Within the United States, two-thirds of arrivals settle in six states, within them in only a handful of counties. Cities like New York, Los Angeles, London, and Vancouver have become important migration hubs, with a share of foreign-born in their population significantly larger than in the rest of the country, sometimes as large as 40 or 50 percent of their residents.

A. Impact on the Labor Market

While the flow of migrants, especially from developing to advanced economies, tends to follow economic success, the question is whether migrants themselves contribute to the success of the receiving economy, or whether their presence deprives natives of job opportunities and/or it represents a burden to citizens. A simplistic model of labor demand and supply, as the one shown in Diagram 9.1a, would suggest that immigration, represented as a simple shift in labor supply, with a downward-sloping labor demand curve and keeping everything else equal, would reduce wages of natives, or crowd out their employment if wages are rigid. Some studies, such as Borjas (2003) have argued that this "wage depressing effect" is significant and not negligible.

Several considerations and extensive empirical evidence, however, suggest that the inflow of immigrants may affect the receiving economy through other channels, which would shift the labor demand curve to the right, and as a result produce an overall impact on wages and employment of natives that could be null or even positive (as represented in Diagram 9.1b). Abundant empirical evidence, especially in recent years, suggests that those channels are important.

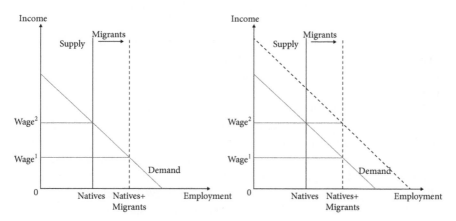

Diagram 9.1 Wage Effect of Migration
Source: Authors.

First, immigrants often take jobs that are different and complementary to (rather than in competition with) those of natives (Peri and Sparber 2009). Second, they increase local demand as they consume and invest, and this can in turn increase labor demand to produce local goods and services (Peri, Rury, and Wiltshire 2020). Third, firms often respond quickly to immigration, by both expanding and moving to where new immigrants arrive, generating investments and more opportunities for natives (Beerli et al. 2018). Fourth, many immigrants are entrepreneurs themselves and they create firms and opportunities for natives (Fairlie and Lofstrom 2015). Vandor and Franke (2016) report that immigrants represent 27.5 percent of the country's entrepreneurs but only around 13 percent of the population in the United States. Similarly, about a quarter of all technology and engineering companies started in the United States between 2006 and 2012 had at least one immigrant co-founder. Finally, in the longer run, the variety of skills and ideas of immigrants is highly correlated with innovation and growth (Kerr and Lincoln 2010; Docquier et al. 2018).

The combination of these effects implies that it is important to analyze the relation between immigration and wages empirically. In a review of literature, Peri (2014) concludes that the effects of immigrants on average native wages are close to zero. Based on 27 empirical studies corresponding to more than 270 baseline estimates, the estimated elasticities range from -0.8 to 0.8, with about 80 percent of the studies showing an elasticity of local wages to immigration concentrated between -0.1 and 0.2. Such a large sample of elasticity estimates around zero is consistent with the idea that the negative competition-crowding out effects are balanced by positive demand/complementarity/productivity effects of immigrants that we will discuss below.

These studies vary in terms of countries considered, a unit of analysis (local areas, states, or countries), and an identification strategy. Typically, most of them use local area-level variation in immigrants' inflows and in wages and adopt an instrumental variable strategy to address endogeneity issues. The fact that migrants tend to go to locations where wages are growing can bias the OLS estimates. Using historical enclaves of country-specific immigrants as a predictor of where new immigrants locate, in a shift-share instrumental variable, usually reduces such endogeneity bias.

Besides analyzing cross-sectional and panel evidence on the impact of immigrants on wages, many economists have also studied specific events, to try to isolate the short-run effect of immigration and possibly find the negative wage impact suggested by the simple labor supply shift, all else equal. Considering sudden, push-driven, and "quasi-experimental" events can also alleviate the problem of endogeneity. In those events, migrants were not attracted by economic conditions but were fleeing events in the place of origin, hence there is no reason to think that their sudden arrival was correlated with local wage growth.

One of the first and extensively studied natural experiments was the Mariel Boatlift.[3] In April 1980, Fidel Castro opened the port of Mariel in Cuba to enable anyone who wanted to emigrate to do so. Between April and September of that year, 125,000 Cuban refugees arrived on the coast of Florida in the United States and many of them settled in Miami, where there was already a large Cuban community. The labor supply in this metropolitan area increased by about 8 percent, and this increase was concentrated among less-skilled workers, as most migrants had low levels of schooling. This event provides an opportunity to identify the short-run impact of a large, exogenous, and sudden influx of low-skilled migrants, as researchers can compare the labor market conditions in Miami versus other American cities that did not experience a similar arrival of migrants. The sudden occurrence and exogeneity of the event provide good identification.

Despite the sudden nature and large inflow of immigrants in Miami, this case does not provide clear evidence of a negative effect of immigrants on wages. While a study by Borjas (2017) finds that wages decreased significantly for the group of non-Hispanic native workers with no high school degree, Card (1990) and Peri and Yasenov (2017) find that the event left the wages and employment of most native groups unaffected, and only when considering very small groups, whose wages are likely to have large measurement error in the Current Population Survey (CPS) sample, one can find some negative (imprecisely estimated) effects. The estimated effects on most groups for which there are enough observations are very small and often non-negative. The following sections will detail the different potential channels through which immigration may affect native wages.

The Substitution/Complementarity Effect

The effect emphasized by Borjas (2017) when analyzing the Mariel Boatlift and in most of his other studies of immigration (for instance Borjas 2003, 2014) is the competition (substitution) effect of immigrants, especially for natives with less than a high school degree. Such effect can be represented as adding more identical workers to the supply of less-educated natives and as a shift of the supply curve to the right, illustrated in Diagram 9.1a above. This effect, by itself, would result in downward pressure on wages for less-skilled natives.

Such an effect assumes, however, that immigrants and natives supply the same type of labor, i.e. are substitutes, and that nothing else changes in the local economy, specifically that firms do not adjust their physical capital. Several recent

---

[3] Some other natural experiments studied in the literature include the return of French expatriates to their home country after Algeria declared its independence in 1962 (Hunt 1992); the repatriation of Portuguese from Angola and Mozambique in the 1970s following their independence (Carrington and De Lima 1996); ethnic Germans living in Eastern Europe and in the former Soviet Union returning to Germany after the fall of the Berlin Wall in 1989 (Glitz 2012); the flow of refugees from Burundi and Rwanda to Tanzania following the civil war and genocide in those countries (Maystadt and Verwimp 2014); and the large wave of migration from Central American countries to the United States following Hurricane Mitch in 1998 (Kugler and Yuksel 2008).

studies have pointed out that immigrants, because of their different specialization, skills, and language ability, are not substitutes of natives, even for similar levels of schooling (Peri and Sparber 2009; Card 2009; Cattaneo, Fiorio, and Peri 2014; D'Amuri and Peri 2014). If immigrant labor is a different type of labor relative to natives, then the increase in its supply may increase the marginal productivity of native labor and shift its demand to the right. Moreover, firms and investment seem to respond relatively quickly to the opportunities created in a local economy by new workers (Olney 2013), so that physical capital increases and the short-run labor demand curve may shift to the right, as illustrated in Diagram 9.1b above.

One group that may feel the competition of new immigrants more than natives are previous immigrants. Some studies (e.g. D'Amuri, Ottaviano, and Peri 2010) find a sizeable competition effect on previous immigrants: ten new immigrants in the Western German labor market drive three to four old immigrants out of employment while having no effect on natives. The high degree of substitutability between new and previous migrants (Beine et al. 2011), the tendency of new migrants to cluster in areas in which previous migrants are already over-represented (World Bank 2018) and wage rigidity contribute to this effect.

The Productivity and Demand Effect

One reason that makes the Mariel Boatlift episode rather dated and not very representative of the impact of immigration is that those migrants were mainly uneducated. In the last 20 years, in most OECD countries (Docquier, Ozden, and Peri 2014) including the United States, immigrants on average were more skilled than natives. In this case, immigration would result in an increase in the relative abundance of skilled people with further positive complementarity effects on less educated and, potentially, with important productivity effects. This type of immigration would increase the relative wages of low-skilled workers and potentially also reduce inequality in the long run. Moreover, if high-skilled immigrants have a positive effect on innovation and productivity (e.g. Kerr and Lincoln 2010; Peri 2012) in the long run, this will help economic growth and wage growth for the whole economy.

Another channel through which immigration may increase native employment is through providing services that increase native labor supply. Cortes and Tessada (2011) and Jaumotte, Koloskova, and Saxena (2016) find that the availability of relatively low-cost workers in the services or health care sector may allow high-skilled women to join the labor force or work longer hours, increasing the country's productivity. Highly skilled native women can join the labor market because they can employ lower-skilled immigrants. Conde Ruiz, Ramón Garcia, and Navarro (2008) find that the rapid increase in immigration in the early 2000s in Spain led to growth in the personal services sector, which in turn had a positive impact on female labor force participation.

Furthermore, immigration, by covering some specific manual labor-intensive jobs, encourages high-skilled native workers to specialize in more complex occupations, thus raising their productivity and wages through "occupational upgrading" (Cattaneo, Fiorio, and Peri 2014; Foged and Peri 2016). If migrants fill sectoral labor shortages, then immigration might have a positive effect on native workers.

Immigration also has a demand (or scale) effect. Immigrants demand goods and services, and their presence leads to an increase in overall production. The scale effect of immigration generates an increase in employment among native workers due to the rise in output (Ozden and Wagner 2014). Bodvarsson and Van den Berg's (2006) study of a flow of Hispanic immigrants to a meatpacking plant in Dawson County in Nebraska shows that immigration can substantially boost local consumer demand. Bodvarsson et al. (2008) find strong evidence that immigrants increased consumption and demand for local services in Miami after the Mariel Boatlift event.

The demand and productivity effects aggregate to generate the shift of the labor demand line to the right, as shown in Diagram 9.1b. The shift in demand can be smaller, as large, or larger than the shift in supply, generating a net decrease, no change, or increase in natives' wages. The shifts of demand and supply in Diagram 9.1b, generating roughly no wage change, correspond to what most studies find as the effect of immigration on average and low-skilled native wages.

Finally, studies show that migrant networks foster trade and FDI (Cohen, Gurun, and Malloy 2017; Parsons and Vezina 2016; Burchardi, Chaney, and Hassan 2016), contributing to economic growth. For instance, Javorcik et al. (2011) find that US FDI abroad is positively correlated with the presence of migrants from the host country. While this is likely to have a beneficial impact primarily on the country of origin, it can benefit the destination country as well. Immigrants lower informational barriers through the knowledge of their home country's language, regulations, market opportunities, and informal institutions.

In summary, one can understand the overall impact of immigration on native workers' wages and employment only by combining the substitution, complementarity, productivity, and demand effects. Most studies find close to zero overall effects on average wages, suggesting that the negative substitution effect is offset by the positive effects on native wages. The impact on wages of low-skilled, high-skilled, and wage inequality also depends on the skill composition of immigrants and the response to it. Most studies do not find much effect on native wage inequality from immigration, suggesting that the other factors compensate for the pure substitution effect.

B. Impact on Public Finance

Another significant concern in the public opinion toward immigrants is their impact on public finances, specifically whether they are net contributors or net recipients of welfare transfers. Dustmann and Preston (2007) show that this concern is even more salient in people's minds than the impact of migration on wages and employment. The perception that immigrants pose a burden on public finances may explain why, in many developed countries, wealthier individuals are often in favor of restricting migration, despite the fact that the owners of capital are likely to gain from the inflow of labor.

In the short term, migrants tend to impose a cost on the destination country, especially in the area of social integration and assistance and as they may take some time to find a job. These costs are higher for refugees and lower for economic immigrants. In terms of health care immigrants tend to be less costly than natives for a long time, as they tend to move when they are young. Over time, migrants have a net positive effect on government budgets if they successfully integrate into the labor market. In aging societies, the immigration of young workers could ease the fiscal sustainability pressure of pension systems as well as help paying the medical costs of retirees.

Short-term Fiscal Impact

The short-term fiscal costs of immigrants are likely to be mainly for social assistance, labor market integration, unemployment benefits, as well as administrative costs. These costs depend on the generosity and the coverage of the social protection system in the receiving country, as well as on the type and skills of immigrants. As a consequence, the calculation of the fiscal costs of immigrants can be quite country-specific. In addition to these differences, in some countries, asylum seekers receive accommodation, subsistence, and integration support (such as language classes), and these add to the fiscal cost. As refugees account for only around 10 percent of migrants to OECD countries, these costs are small for most advanced economies. In the case of a country like the United States, where immigrants work at high rates and there is a balance between high and low skilled, Flavin et al. (2011) estimate that the fiscal cost per capita of foreign-born is between half to two-thirds that of US-born individuals.

A different picture would emerge if we focus on the countries (mainly developing) shouldering the costs of significant flows of refugees. These flows can be unexpected, affect most countries near the origin of refugees, and may imply a large short-term cost, including the setting up of refugee camps. For instance, the recent refugee wave from Syria in 2012–2015 has brought millions of refugees, especially to the neighboring countries of Jordan, Lebanon, and Turkey (in the case of Jordan, the inflow was equivalent to about 10 percent of the population). The estimated fiscal cost of these refugees was 2.4 percent of GDP for Jordan, 3.2 percent for Lebanon, and 1.3 percent for Turkey (Rother et al. 2016). In 2018, the estimated fiscal costs associated with migration flows from Venezuela were 0.5 percent of the GDP of neighboring countries.

So, in the case of fiscal impact in the short run, it is crucial to distinguish between economic migrants, mostly moving to advanced economies, who have small initial costs and are distributed over a longer time period, and refugees, mostly moving to neighbor developing countries, which may represent a significant short-run fiscal transfer.

Long-term Fiscal Impact

Over time, migrants contribute to the destination country's revenues by paying taxes. The long-term fiscal impact of immigration depends on the generosity, design, and coverage of the tax and benefit system. To estimate the long-term fiscal impact of immigrants in destination countries, we need to evaluate the equation in Diagram 9.2.

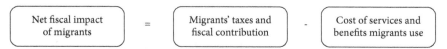

Diagram 9.2 The Net Fiscal Impact of Immigrants
Source: Authors.

Integration into the formal labor market is the key to generating a positive long-term fiscal impact. Migrants' skill composition is also important: higher-skilled migrants are expected to contribute more to the tax system because of their higher income. Dustmann and Frattini (2014) show that migrants who arrived in the United Kingdom after 2000 were on average highly skilled and had a higher positive net fiscal contribution than did the native population. Similarly, Orrenius (2017) show a positive net fiscal contribution of immigrants in the US over their lifetime, especially for more recent migrants.

Another important component in assessing the fiscal impact of immigrants is the demographic structure of the native and immigrant population. In countries with an aging native population, like in most advanced economies, immigrants (who are usually young) increase the size of the labor force and reduce the old-age dependency ratio, i.e. the number of retired people relative to those of working age. This demographic effect helps reduce the adverse fiscal impact of an aging population. Pension and healthcare spending in developed economies is projected to reach 24.8 percent of GDP by 2100, up from 16.4 percent in 2015 simply because of population aging. Clements (2015) show that allowing for more immigration could help reduce old-age dependency ratios, and thus age-related expenditures by 2 percent of GDP by 2100. Immigration flows will have to increase substantially to fully address the effects of population aging. Nevertheless, moderate inflows of immigrants can alleviate the burden on the pension system, preventing drastic cuts in benefits.

As for native workers, immigrants tend to have a negative net fiscal balance during youth and old age, and a positive fiscal balance during their working age. As immigrants arrive in the destination country early in their working age, they tend to have a higher net positive fiscal impact. The receiving countries save the cost of their education and benefit from the many contributing years before retirement.

The OECD (2013) presents an overall picture of the net fiscal impact of immigrants in a cross-country study based on a static accounting model. The impact of immigration on public finances is calculated to be typically ±0.5 percent of GDP for advanced economies. In the cases in which immigrants compare less favorably to the native-born population in terms of net fiscal balance, this is mainly due to lower tax contributions rather than greater demand for benefits. This emphasizes the crucial role of immigrants' formal employment rate in determining their economic and fiscal contribution.

C. Impact on the Incidence of Crime

Another major public concern about the impact of migration on receiving countries is the connection between immigration and crime. Statistically, cities with high rates of crime tend to have more immigrants. However, controlling for the demographic characteristics of the cities or using instrumental variables, immigration appears to have little to no significant causal effect on crime rates. Earlier work by Butcher and Piehl (1998, 2007) finds no effect of immigration on crime rates in the United States. Youth born abroad are significantly less likely than native-born youth to be criminally active and are also less likely to be incarcerated. Using the immigration status of those who are arrested, Miles and Cox (2014) find similar results. Bianchi, Buonanno and Pinotti (2012) find that only the incidence of robberies in Italy has increased due to immigration, but since robberies represent a small fraction of total criminal offenses, the effect on the overall crime rate is not significantly different from zero.

Labor market opportunities are a key determinant of the criminal behavior of individuals, including immigrants. In the Becker-Ehrlich model of crime (Becker 1968; Ehrlich 1973), individuals rationally choose between crime and legal labor market work depending on the potential returns of each option. The "return" from crime is weighted by the probability of getting caught and sanctioned and compared to the earnings from formal employment. If the former outweighs the latter, an individual will engage in crime. Translated into the context of migration, the model suggests that integration into formal employment reduces the probability that migrants commit crimes. Bell, Fasani, and Machin (2013) compare two large waves of immigration in the UK (the late 1990s/early 2000s asylum seekers and the post-2004 inflow from EU accession countries), and find that only immigrants in the former group caused a modest but significant increase, and only in property crime. The former group was also characterized by limited access to the official labor market.

Both in the United States and in Europe, undocumented immigrants cannot officially work or start a new economic activity. In the United States, nevertheless, undocumented immigrants have been shown to have very high employment rates in the legal economy, presumably due to lax enforcement, and a nearly zero labor supply elasticity (Borjas 2017). When immigrants can only participate in the informal economy, they face inferior earnings opportunities relative to their legal counterparts (Kossoudji and Cobb-Clark 2002; Lozano and Sørensen 2011). In line with the findings that migrants with a formal job tend to commit less crime, legal immigrants also have much lower crime rates than illegal immigrants (Mastrobuoni and Pinotti 2011). Pinotti (2017) shows that legalization reduces the crime rate of immigrants by 0.6 percentage points on average, on a baseline crime rate of 1.1 percent in Italy.

D. Adopting Reasonable Immigration Policies and Fostering Integration

Given our description of the potential economic, labor market, and fiscal benefits from immigration with some evidence of potential short-term costs on native-born, we now discuss some policies that may help ease the initial cost and enhance and redistribute the economic benefits of migration so that policies chosen by the government are supported by the citizens.

Immigration policies based on forward-looking considerations, such as the country's population projection and expectation of labor force needs, are more likely to succeed.

Reaping the Benefits of Immigration

When looking at policies in countries with large numbers of immigrants, those based on selecting immigrants for their skills, such as Canada and Australia, seem to have succeeded in selecting a large number of immigrants with skills in line with the economic needs of the countries. Those more centered on family ties and reunification, such as the United States, have often produced bottlenecks (oversubscription of the H-1B) or generated other, less efficient channels of the entry (undocumented inflows). Also, the level of public support for immigration has remained higher in Canada than in the United States.

Integrating migrants into the labor market is a key to achieving their full productive contribution and to limiting their potential burden on public finances. This suggests that an immigration system centered around working visas and permits is more likely to be economically successful for the immigrants and for the receiving country. At the same time, reducing the opportunities to access formal work, as done in some cases for asylum seekers, leads to a loss of tax revenue, a likely deterioration of their human capital, and, in the long run, to higher welfare benefit bills.

While it is not easy to find policies that are effective in integrating refugees and non-economic migrants into the domestic labor market, there is evidence that some basic education, including basic health care and especially language training (see Arendt 2020) could be effective in increasing their long-run employment and earnings potential. Extremely important is the schooling of the second generation. Children of immigrants have the opportunity of full integration if given the right schooling opportunities. On the other hand, Helbling, Simon, and Schmid (2020) show on the evidence of 22 European countries that immigration restrictions do not lead to better integration of migrants.

In helping their chances in the labor market, governments should provide timely work permit authorizations and a swift process for certificate, degree, and license recognition across countries in order to tap into the full potential of migration. According to OECD and EU (2018), the average overqualification rate of the foreign-born population in the EU was over 33 percent, compared to 21 percent for native-born workers (over-qualification is defined as the share of tertiary-educated employees who work in a job that is ISCO-classified as low or medium-skilled, i.e. ISCO levels 4 to 9). Employment rates for migrants are higher in countries with low entry-level wages and less employment protection (Ho and Shirono 2015). Encouraging migrant entrepreneurship could help foster competitiveness and innovation and create positive spillovers. Securing access to financial services, such as bank accounts and financial transactions, can also broaden their opportunities.

Once migrants have a job, it is important to provide a clear path to residency and employment security. Uncertainty leads to inefficiency and long-term cost for both migrants and their employers (World Bank 2018). This is particularly important for highly skilled workers, as firms tend to invest more in their positions. A system in which a temporary visa can be converted to a permanent one if employers are willing to sponsor the immigrants, as it is for H1-B visas in the US, may offer the flexibility and the certainty needed.

Minimizing the Impact on Native Workers

A large body of research finds that natives will respond to immigration by upgrading and adjusting their occupation and job (Peri and Sparber 2009; Cattaneo, Fiorio, and Peri 2015). Policies to help native workers during their adjustment and relocation may further help reduce the costs and increase the benefits from immigration. *Adjustment assistance mechanisms* target native workers who compete with migrants, to provide them with more relevant skills. *Relocation assistance* can include assistance with changing occupations, cities, or sectors of employment. This can also include transitory welfare benefits or unemployment insurance payments. However, both mechanisms require that authorities identify the impacted native population, which is very difficult. It may be best just to promote efficient and flexible labor markets, where the cost of changing jobs is small and workers can transition easily across occupations. By moving to complex jobs, natives protected their wages from the immigrant competition and took advantage of the creation of those jobs that complement the manual tasks provided by immigrants. Letting this mechanism work may benefit less-educated natives, in particular through more hiring in those occupations. Strong protection of labor hurts this mechanism and reduces labor markets' ability to absorb immigrants through the occupational upgrading of natives (D'Amuri and Peri 2014). If there is a concern of competition effects on a group of vulnerable native workers, such as low educated manual workers, *Minimum income schemes*, as in Denmark, or minimum wage could be alternatives, but more research is needed to fully understand their implications.

In this context, encouraging immigration fees rather than quotas can be a sensible approach to the issue. To finance adjustment or relocation, policymakers could impose a fee on employers hiring foreign workers, so that those who are getting the surplus from such hires are also responsible for paying some of the costs. Both Singapore and Malaysia have such a scheme in place but to our best knowledge, no compelling assessment of its efficiency has been conducted. Immigration quotas, especially when the cap is determined by the bureaucratic assessment, rather than by employers and the market, lead to misallocation, increase the risk of rent-seeking and corruption (by government officials), and do not generate any revenue. Instead, a visa fee or a visa auction system has the advantage of letting firms choose the workers while providing extra revenue to the government that could be used to alleviate transitional costs.

Paying Special Attention to Refugees

While most economic migration flows are gradual enough for destination economies to plan and absorb, the case can be different for refugees. Sometimes, a large number of people move over a short period of time to countries with limited resources. Policies that are related to hosting refugees introduce different challenges and require additional attention. The reasons to admit them are humanitarian, rather than economic. However, especially if accompanied by the right policies, refugees can turn into a valuable economic asset for the receiving country in the medium and long run.

First, as mentioned above, asylum seekers should be allowed to work early on in the process of requesting asylum. Given their likely trauma and skill deterioration due to the circumstances that caused their migration, they may be in particular need of policies to improve skills and language before accessing the labor market. Encouraging refugees to move to places with labor demand for their skills can ease integration. Introducing temporary wage subsidies can create incentives for employers and improve migrants' integration.

Monitoring countries that are becoming unstable and offering their citizens an option of orderly migration for labor purposes before a crisis erupts can be an important mitigation mechanism. A solution, when a migration crisis is under-way, could be to spread the burden of refugees across countries. Compared to the population of advanced countries or to economic migrants, the number of refu-gees remains small. World Bank (2018) suggests establishing an active large-scale refugee settlement policy and coordinating financial assistance.

IV. Impact of Migration on Origin Countries

On a global scale, emigration is more dispersed between countries than immigra-tion. In most countries, the share of emigrants relative to the countries' total pop-ulation does not exceed 10 percent. Notable exceptions include some fragile states, and also clusters of countries with high emigration in Eastern Europe, Central Asia, and Latin America.

In some regions, in particular Europe, Central Asia, and Sub-Saharan Africa, a large part of emigration (70–80 percent of the migrants) goes to countries in the same region (Figure 9.4, from World Bank 2019). The share of emigrants moving intra-regionally is much lower in Asia and the Americas.

A. Impact on the Labor Market in Origin Countries

On the theoretical level, the impact on the labor markets in the origin countries can be seen as a mirror image of the impact in destination countries. An outflow of labor can be expected to reduce the supply of the workforce, but also reduce

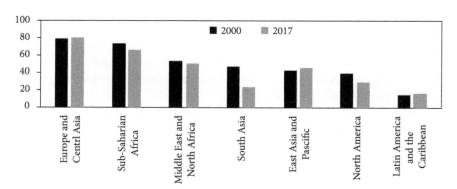

Figure 9.4 Share of Emigrants Moving Intra-regionally, by World Region, 2000 and 2017

Source: World Bank (2018) based on UN DESA 2017.

demand, human capital, and entrepreneurship with ambiguous overall effects on wages. In countries that are suffering from chronic unemployment (or underemployment), emigration can ease tensions in the labor market and improve the availability of jobs, as long as the demand and human capital effects do not depress local labor demand. As emigrants are usually positively selected in terms of skills (Grogger and Hanson 2011), their loss can contribute to a loss of productivity, ability to innovate, and net loss in fiscal balance. Furthermore, symmetric to the case of destination countries, emigration can create negative demand and productivity effects.

Perhaps not surprisingly, empirical evidence on the labor market impact in origin countries is somewhat contradictory. Dustmann and Görlach (2015) argued that large-scale emigration did in fact raise employment and wages in Poland following its entry into the European Union. At the same time, IMF (2016, SDN/16/07) noted that, as emigrants are primarily high-skilled workers, emigration creates a negative externality, which leads to a reduction in productivity. This can also lead to other negative consequences, which are described in more detail later, in the section on brain drain.

B. The Role of Remittances

Remittances are perhaps the most highly visible and tangible benefit of emigration to the origin countries. On a global level, the World Bank estimates officially recorded remittances at $548 billion in 2019, more than three times the volume of official development assistance and comparable in size to total FDI flows. Not surprisingly, remittances have become a major source of inflows in many countries. They are often in the range of 15–20 percent of GDP, and in some exceptional cases can reach 30–40 percent of GDP (Tonga, Haiti, Kyrgyz Republic).

These large volumes are transferred, even though sending money across borders remains expensive, with fees often surpassing 5 percent. Costs vary widely across corridors and providers. They tend to be highest in small markets with little competition and through commercial banks. Recent advances in mobile technology will likely help bring remittance costs down (Cecchetti and Schoenholtz 2018; Schmitz and Endo 2011).

In many countries in Asia and Africa, remittances have helped to significantly reduce poverty levels and improve nutritional and educational outcomes, in particular by reducing the need to send children to work (Binci and Giannelli 2018; Bargain and Boutin 5).

Remittances can also foster consumption smoothing, not only through their own counter-cyclicality but also by supporting financial inclusion and access to credit. Remittances allow recipients to save in good times and tap into these resources in periods of falling domestic income. They facilitate access to credit by endowing borrowers with collateral and strengthening their capacity to repay. These effects are likely to be especially important for liquidity constrained, poorer households.

There is an emerging consensus in the literature that migration and remittances are part of an overall livelihood strategy through which households try to cope with shocks. For instance, contrary to private international capital flows, remittance flows do not depend on interest rate differentials. They remain stable or even increase after the onset of natural disasters (World Bank 2006). Increased remittances helped smooth household consumption and compensate for the loss of assets after earthquakes (Halliday 2006; Suleri and Savage 2006), tsunamis and cyclones (Fagen 2006; Wu 2006), floods and droughts (Arouri et al. 2015; Davies 2008; Mohapatra et al. 2009). Their role as insurance has also been documented in relation to shocks to the individual income (De Brauw et al. 2013) or health (Ambrosius and Cuecuecha 2013).

There is also some evidence that migrants transfer funds to their countries of origin at times of conflict when other flows have all but disappeared. Weiss, Fagen, and Bump (2005) document the increasing role of migration and remittances during crises in Afghanistan, Somalia, and Eritrea. Koczan (2016) shows that remittances from Germany to ex-Yugoslavia increased during the conflict of the early 1990s, despite the breakdown of formal intermediation channels.

The impact of remittances on various macroeconomic outcomes in the countries of origin is far from simple. Abdih et al. (2012a) show that (unsurprisingly) remittances improve fiscal balance, by increasing the aggregate private demand and thus expanding the tax base, especially for VAT and sales taxes. This in principle provides additional revenue for the government to pay for social spending that benefits the poor. However, the expansion of private demand happens mainly through increased consumption. To the extent that remittances are not consumed, they are saved in the form of assets such as gold and real estate and do not typically increase private investment.

Remittances can also have other negative effects that can hurt development in the countries of origin in the long term. Abdih et al. (2012b) argue that remittances negatively affect governance by creating a moral hazard problem. Remittances ensure the households against adverse economic shocks and insulate them from government policies, and thus reduce the incentives to pressure the government to implement necessary reforms to facilitate economic growth. In turn, this reduces incentives for the governments to implement reforms and can erode fiscal and debt discipline. Moreover, by providing large substitute income for families, remittances can reduce labor force participation rates, especially for women.

The impact of remittances on inequality will generally depend on which households receive them and how much they receive. As long as families who are on the receiving end of remittance transfers are disadvantaged and low-income, remittances have the potential to lower inequality. Beyond their direct effects on income, remittances could also affect inequality through their indirect macroeconomic effects, insofar as they facilitate setting up businesses, resulting in employment creation which tends to be pro-poor.

Most early studies examined the distributional effects of remittances by comparing income distributions with and without remittances (simply subtracting remittance amounts from income for remittance-receiving households) or by using income-source decompositions of inequality, computing Gini coefficients separately for non-remittance income and remittance income (Adams and Alderman 1992; Stark et al. 1988, and Taylor et al. 2009). This approach implicitly assumes that there would be no behavioral changes in the absence of remittances. It would, however, seem likely that, given the drop in income, other household members would start working or increase their working hours. To take this into account, several recent studies have created counterfactual income distributions, designed to capture what a migrant's income would be in the home country in the absence of migration, as well as what the participation decisions and earnings of other household members would be.

Although they rely on similar methodologies, these studies nonetheless reach different conclusions. Möllers and Meyer (2014) find that remittances increase inequality in Kosovo, while Mughal and Anwar (2012) and Koczan and Loyola (2018) find that they lower it in Pakistan and Mexico, respectively.

These conflicting findings may be driven by differences in the "migration stage" of a country. As highlighted by Stark et al. (1988) and Taylor et al. (2009), "pioneer" migrants who lack pre-existing migrant networks and therefore face higher costs of migration may come from wealthier households. In contrast, later migrants, who come from poorer households, may benefit from falling costs as migrant networks expand. If so, migration and associated remittance receipts will first increase then reduce inequality in sending countries.

This interpretation is consistent with the findings of Acosta et al. (2008), who identify different effects across Latin American countries depending on their migration histories, the extent of migrant networks, and proximity to migrant destinations. Migrants and remittance-receiving households are more likely to be from the bottom of the income distribution in Mexico and Paraguay, with longer migration histories and lower costs of migrating to their main migrant destinations, whereas migrants tend to be drawn from higher-income portions of the population in Haiti, Peru, and Nicaragua. Brown and Jimenez (2007) find larger poverty- and inequality-reducing effects of remittances and migration in Tonga, an economy with a relatively long migration history and high remittances, than in Fiji, an economy with a more recent migration history.

Margolis et al. (2013) similarly point to larger inequality-reducing effects in Algerian regions with more migrants and remittance-receiving households. Further consistent with this view, McKenzie and Rapoport (2007) find that migration and remittances reduce inequality in rural Mexican communities with high levels of past migration. Acharyaa and Leon-Gonzalez (2012) argue that remittances from India (unlike remittances from elsewhere) reduce inequality in Nepal due to the greater participation of the poor in the Nepal-India migration process. Möllers and Meyer's (2014) contrasting finding that migration and remittances increase inequality in rural Kosovo similarly could be explained by the country's recent migration history and consequently high costs of migration.

Thus, while the findings of different studies are mixed, their differences may reflect changing effects over time and indicate that any inequality-reducing effects of remittances are more pronounced in countries with longer migration histories, where the fixed costs of migration are lower and migration and remittances are more accessible to poorer households.

C. Impact Through Trade and Investment

Emigration can also help the origin countries through better and easier integration into global trade and investment. Parsons and Vezina (2016) demonstrate that, following the lifting of trade restrictions in 1994, US exports to Vietnam grew most in US states with larger Vietnamese populations, which resulted from large exogenous refugee inflows 20 years earlier. Burchardi, Chaney, and Hassan (2016) show that the impact on investment from the receiving country can be long-lasting. They use 130 years of historical data on migration to the US to show that the ancestry composition of US counties has a causal effect on foreign direct investment sent and received by local firms. Their results show that doubling the number of residents with ancestry from a given foreign country relative to the mean increases the probability that at least one local firm directly invests in that country by 4 percentage points. This effect appears to be primarily driven by a reduction in information frictions, and not by better contract enforcement, taste similarities, or convergence in factor endowments.

The strength of the impact on trade and investment would depend on the skill composition of migrants, and on the cohesion and attitude of emigrants. A strong emigrant network that is business-oriented can facilitate trade between destination and origin countries, and increase investment flows, by leveraging their newly acquired information, business skills, and the knowledge of business and investment environment in the countries of origin. This can also lead to easier and cheaper transfers of technology, potentially stimulating convergence and growth of countries of origin.

The investment activity of emigrants can also provide an impulse to the development of capital markets in the countries of origin. These investors can help to diversify the investor base and bring a reliable source of funding into the country. Furthermore, these investors are likely to be able to undertake riskier projects than foreign investors, because they can better evaluate the risks and possess contacts and local knowledge that can reduce the risks and that are not available to foreigners.

D. Costs of Emigration Associated with the Brain Drain

Brain drain, i.e. the emigration of highly skilled and highly productive individuals, is the primary source of concern for origin countries. Data shows that this is, in fact, a valid concern, with the share of highly skilled workers that have left the country reaching 40 percent in some small low-income countries (Artuç et al. 2014) and in general with highly educated being two to three times more likely to migrate than less educated (Grogger and Hanson 2011).

Brain drain can affect the origin countries in many ways. On the most obvious level, it lowers the human capital of the origin country and produces a shortage of high-skilled labor, thereby reducing productivity. This may be accompanied by increases in wages, driven both by the overall shortage of labor and by rising reservation wages due to remittance inflows (IMF 2016b). The combination of these factors can have a significant negative impact on potential growth. IMF (2016) simulates that emigration may have reduced annual growth rates by 0.6–0.9 percentage points in some countries in South-Eastern Europe (Albania, Montenegro, and Romania) and the Baltics (Latvia and Lithuania), also slowing income convergence as a consequence.

Brain drain may also have large implications for public finance. This channel works in particular through shifting tax revenue from income taxes (which decline because of lower high skilled labor) in favor of consumption taxes (which increase because of remittances inflows). Less obviously, it also often shifts the balance of public expenditures, with lower spending on education (which can be explained by lower demand with the outflow of high skilled workers) and higher spending on social assistance programs. The argument on education spending can go the other way, however—Beine, Docquier, and Rapoport (2008) argue that the possibility of migrating increases demands for schooling, generating in net higher skills. On balance, IMF (2016) estimates that emigration during 1990–2012 has been linked to an average increase of overall government spending relative to GDP of 6.2 percentage points in Central European and South-Eastern European countries.

Furthermore, brain drain can have a long-lasting damaging impact on the quality of institutions in the origin countries. Departing high-skilled workers are an important potential political force advocating for improvements in business and investment climate and better control of corruption (Omar Mahmoud et al. 2013). With their departure, there is a danger that a country may turn into a passive recipient of remittances, with a large majority uninterested in changing the status quo.

E. Country Case: Kyrgyz Republic

The case of the Kyrgyz Republic illustrates many of the points made in this part of the chapter.[4] While the exact number of migrants out of the Kyrgyz Republic is somewhat hard to pin down because of informality and the temporary status of many emigrants, the country has been an important source of migrants in the region for many years. The importance of migration is evident in the size of remittances, which increased spectacularly from virtually zero in 2000, reaching 10 percent of GDP by 2005 and 30 percent of GDP in 2011. Remittances averaged almost 30 percent of GDP during the last decade.

IMF (2016a) analyzed the impact of remittances on the Kyrgyz economy and found little evidence of any positive impact on growth, confirming that remittances are typically used for basic consumption and not investment. At the same time, the study found a significant impact of remittances on real effective exchange rate appreciation, suggesting a possibility of Dutch disease-like effects.

During the period of high emigration (beginning around 2000), extreme poverty has been reduced, but overall poverty levels remain high compared to regional peers. Income inequality in the Kyrgyz Republic fluctuated a lot, with civil conflict, political instability, and the banking crisis wiping out the hard-won gains. Nevertheless, inequality has been on a steady declining trend since 2006 (the period that coincided with high emigration), and the Gini coefficient fell by about 10 points during that period.

The outflow of labor did not bring tangible benefits to the labor market. Unemployment remains high, especially among youth and women, and the country lags behind its neighbors in terms of primary school enrolment and youth literacy levels. IMF (2016a) emphasized the need to improve the business environment, promote formal employment and build human capital among the key measures to reduce inequality.

F. Country Case: Mexico

Mexico is one of the world's largest recipients of remittances.[5] While in the early years, remittance-receiving households were typically in the middle of the income distribution, there has been a clear shift over time: as the fixed costs of migration fell and migration opportunities became more widespread, remittances became increasingly pro-poor. Remittance-receiving households are on average poorer than non-remittance-receiving households, even when taking remittances into

---

[4] This section is based on IMF Country Report No. 16/56 (Kyrgyz Republic: Selected Issues).
[5] This section draws on Koczan and Loyola (2018).

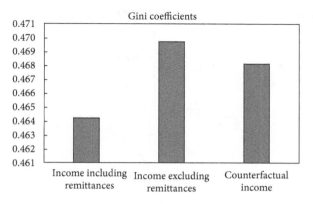

Figure 9.5 Remittances and Income Inequality

Note: Counterfactual income uses actual income for non-remittance-receiving households and an estimated counterfactual income for remittance-receiving households based on propensity score matching. Based on 2002, 2008, and 2014 surveys.

Sources: INEGI, and authors' calculations.

account. Remittances also tend to constitute a larger share of income for poorer households.

This pro-poor pattern of remittances is visible in Mexico's Gini coefficient. The Gini coefficient of households' "no-migration" counterfactual income is higher than that of actual income, suggesting that inequality would be higher in the absence of remittances, even when taking into account that remittance-receiving households adjust their behavior (Figure 9.5). The behavioral response is also reflected in the counterfactual inequality being lower than that based on income excluding remittances. This pattern holds up over time and is especially pronounced in rural areas, which are on average poorer and have more remittance-receiving households.

Remittances also become more pro-poor during economic crises, such as the peso crisis (1994) and the Global Financial Crisis (2008–2009). Figure 9.6 shows that during both crises, the likelihood of receiving remittances as well as their amount as a share of income fell for the top income deciles, consistent with falling investment motives. During the peso crisis, there was little change for the lower-income deciles. However, for poorer households, the likelihood of receiving remittances and their amount as a share of income actually *increased* during the Global Financial Crisis. This may reflect falling fixed costs of migration, which make migration more accessible to poorer households. Alternatively, this effect could be driven by migrants' better integration in the United States (with higher incomes, more stable jobs, a regularized status), allowing them to better cushion the shock. This insurance effect is quite striking in a context where both the sending and receiving countries were hit by a common shock.

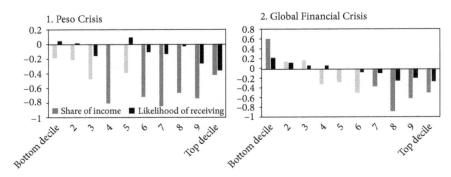

Figure 9.6 Crisis Effects

Note: The figure plots crisis year dummy coefficients. Darker colors denote statistically significant coefficients at the 10 percent level.

Sources: INEGI, and authors' calculations.

G. Policies that Can Help the Origin Countries to Maximize the Benefits and Minimize the Costs of Emigration

There are virtually no theoretical or empirical studies that look at potential policies that can be recommended to origin countries or analyze their impact in cases where these policies were implemented. The policies suggested below follow from the discussion of the benefits and costs of migration. Some policies can be aimed at reducing high-skilled emigration and the associated brain drain, by addressing the root problems that caused the brain drain in the first place. Others can focus on maximizing the benefits and mitigating the potential negative consequences of outward migration. The former essentially boils down to creating more and better employment opportunities in the origin countries, which can have the triple benefit of slowing emigration, reversing some outflows of labor, and attracting some immigrants from third countries.

- Creating a better business and investment environment can be achieved by improving institutions, maintaining macroeconomic and financial stability, supporting job creation, and improving education. All these measures would strengthen the labor market by creating employment opportunities, and thus help to mitigate the negative effect of emigration, as well as to reduce emigration itself.
- Replenishing the stock of high skilled workers is essential for mitigating the negative impact of brain drain. This can be done by encouraging emigrants to return or facilitating high skilled immigration from other countries. Both can be achieved by creating a welcoming environment, easing (re)integration, removing labor market barriers by recognizing degrees from other countries, etc.

- Better utilizing the remaining workforce, by increasing labor force participation and improving labor quality through education and on-the-job training would also reduce the costs of emigration.

In addition, given their impact on poverty and inequality, policy measures should aim at maximizing the gains from remittances. Increasing competition among remittance service providers, helping migrants compare costs across different providers, and facilitating mobile technologies can help reduce transaction costs. While remittances may not be very cost-sensitive, this would nonetheless constitute a welfare gain by increasing amounts received by households. At the same time, policies should help mitigate risks arising from the large dependence on remittances, including by improving investment opportunities, financial inclusion, and access to high-quality productive jobs in the home countries.

V. Conclusion

Migration is an important phenomenon largely driven by powerful economic and labor market forces: Large differentials in wages and employment opportunities, both between advanced and developing countries and within developing regions, create powerful incentives for individuals to migrate, in order to achieve a higher income and to increase the expected income for their offspring.

Migration presents both challenges and opportunities for both receiving countries and countries of origin. Policymakers' task is to overcome the challenges and to take advantage of the opportunities. For destination countries, immigrants can create challenges in local labor markets, potentially depressing wages in the short run and displacing some native workers who compete with them. They can also impose short-term fiscal costs and in some cases increase the crime rate. But immigrants also tend to boost output, create new opportunities for native workers, provide skills needed for growth, generate new ideas, stimulate international trade and contribute positively to long-term fiscal balances. Integrating migrants into the labor market is key to achieving their full productive contribution, limiting their potential burden on public finances, and reducing their potential impact on crime rates.

For the origin countries, emigration may lead to a loss of much-needed human capital (the so-called brain drain) and create upward pressure on wages, thereby reducing competitiveness. But emigration also creates a flow of remittances, an important source of income for many poor families (albeit their overall macroeconomic impact can be ambiguous). It can also increase international connections in the form of trade, FDI, and technological transfers. For policymakers in countries of origin, the optimal strategy is to improve business and employment opportunities, take advantage of the financial and technological inflows and reduce the loss of highly skilled labor.

References

Abdih, Y, Barajas, A, Chami, R, and Ebeke, C. 2012a. "Remittances Channel and Fiscal Impact in the Middle East, North Africa, and Central Asia (April 2012)," IMF Working Paper No. 12/104.

Abdih, Y., Chami, R., Dagher, J., and Montiel, P. 2012b. "Remittances and Institutions: Are Remittances a Curse?" *World Development* 40: 657–66.

Abramitzky, R., Boustan, L.P., Jácome, E., and Pérez, S. 2019. Intergenerational Mobility of Immigrants in the US over Two Centuries (No. w26408). National Bureau of Economic Research.

Acharyaa, C.P., and Leon-Gonzalez, R. 2012. "The Impact of Remittances on Poverty and Inequality: A Micro-simulation Study for Nepal." GRIPS Discussion Paper 11–26.

Acosta, P, Calderon, C, Fajnzylber, P, and Lopez, H. 2008. "What Is the Impact of International Remittances on Poverty and Inequality in Latin America?" *World Development* 36(1): 89–114.

Adams, R, and Alderman, H. 1992. "Sources of Inequality in Rural Pakistan: A Decomposition Analysis." *Oxford Bulletin of Economics and Statistics* 54(4): 591–608.

Ambrosius, C., and Cuecuecha, A. 2013. "Are Remittances a Substitute for Credit? Carrying the Financial Burden of Health Shocks in National and Transnational Households." *World Development* 46(C): 143–52.

Arendt, J.N. 2020. "Labor Market Effects of a Work-first Policy for Refugees." *Journal of Population Economics*: 1–28.

Arouri, M., Nguyen, C., and Youssef, A.B. 2015. "Natural Disasters, Household Welfare, and Resilience: Evidence from Rural Vietnam." *World Development* 70, pp. 59–77.

Artuç, E., Docquier, F., Özden, Ç., and Parsons, C. 2014. *A Global Assessment of Human Capital Mobility: The Role of Non-Oecd Destinations.* Washington, DC: World Bank.

Bargain, O., and Boutin, D. 2015. "Remittance Effects on Child Labour: Evidence from Burkina Faso." *Journal of Development Studies* 51(7): 922–38.

Barrett, A., and Goggin, J. 2010. "Returning to the Question of a Wage Premium for Returning Migrants." *National Institute Economic Review* 213(1): R43–51.

Becker, G.S. 1968. "Crime and Punishment: An Economic Approach." In *The Economic Dimensions of Crime*, edited by N.G. Fielding, A. Clarke, and R. Witt (pp. 13–68). London: Palgrave Macmillan.

Beerli, A., Ruffner, J., Siegenthaler, M., and Peri, G. 2018. The abolition of immigration restrictions and the performance of firms and workers: evidence from Switzerland (No. w25302). National Bureau of Economic Research.

Beine, M., Docquier, F., and Oden-Defoort, C. 2011. "A Panel Data Analysis of the Brain Gain." *World Development* 39(4): 523–32.

Beine, M., Docquier, F., and Rapoport, H. 2008. "Brain Drain and Human Capital Formation in Developing Countries: Winners and Losers." *Economic Journal* 118(528): 631–52.

Bell, B., Fasani, F., and Machin, S. 2013. "Crime and Immigration: Evidence from Large Immigrant Waves." *Review of Economics and Statistics* 21(3): 1278–90.

Bianchi, M., Buonanno, P., and Pinotti, P. 2012. "Do Immigrants Cause Crime?" *Journal of the European Economic Association* 10(6): 1318–47.

Binci, M., and Giannelli, G.C. 2018. "Internal versus International Migration: Impacts of Remittances on Child Labor and Schooling in Vietnam." *International Migration Review* 52(1): 43–65.

Bodvarsson, O., and Van den Berg, H. 2006. "Does Immigration Affect Labor Demand? Model and Test." *Research in Labour Economics* 24: 135–66.

Bodvarsson, Ö.B., Van den Berg, H.F., and Lewer, J.J. 2008. "Measuring Immigration's Effects on Labor Demand: A Reexamination of the Mariel Boatlift." *Labour Economics* 15(4): 560–74.

Borjas, G.J. 2003. "The Labor Demand Curve Is Downward Sloping: Reexamining the Impact of Immigration on the Labor Market." *The Quarterly Journal of Economics* 118(4): 1335–74.

Borjas, G.J. 2014. *Immigration Economics.* Cambridge, MA: Harvard University Press.

Borjas, G.J. 2017a. "The Wage Impact of the Marielitos: A Reappraisal." *ILR Review* 70(5): 1077–110.

Borjas, G.J. 2017b. "The Labor Supply of Undocumented Immigrants." *Labor Economics* 46: 1–13.

Brown, R. P.C., and Jimenez, E. 2007. "Estimating the Net Effects of Migration and Remittances on Poverty and Inequality: Comparison of Fiji and Tonga." UNU-WIDER Research Paper 2007/23, United Nations University World Institute for Development Economics Research, Helsinki.

Burchardi, K.B., Chaney, T., and Hassan, T.A. 2016. Migrants, ancestors, and investments (No. w21847). National Bureau of Economic Research.

Butcher, K.F., and Piehl, A.M. 1998. "Cross-city Evidence on the Relationship Between Immigration and Crime." *Journal of Policy Analysis and Management: The Journal of the Association for Public Policy Analysis and Management* 17(3): 457–93.

Butcher, K.F., and Piehl, A.M. 2007. "Why Are Immigrants Incarceration Rates so Low? Evidence on Selective Immigration, Deterrence and Deportation." NBER Working Paper w13229, National Bureau of Economic Research.

Card, D. 1990. "The Impact of the Mariel Boatlift on the Miami Labor Market." *ILR Review* 43(2): 245–57.

Card, D. 2009. "Immigration and Inequality." *American Economic Review* 99(2): 1–21.

Carrington, W.J., and De Lima, P.J.F. 1996. "The Impact of 1970s Repatriates Africa on the Portuguese Labor Market." *Industrial and Labor Relations Review* 49(2): 330–47.

Cattaneo, C., Fiorio, C.V., and Peri, G. 2015. "What Happens to the Careers of European Workers when immigrants 'take their jobs'"? *Journal of Human Resources* 50(3): 655–93.

Cecchetti, Stephen, and Schoenholtz, Kim. 2018. "The Stubbornly High Cost of Remittances," VoxEU, March 27, 2018.

Clemens, M.A., Montenegro, C.E. and Pritchett, L. 2019. "The Place Premium: Bounding the Price Equivalent of Migration Barriers." *Review of Economics and Statistics* 101(2): 201–13.

Clements, B., Dybczak, K., Gaspar, V., Gupta, S., and Soto, M., 2015. "The Fiscal Consequences of Shrinking Populations." International Monetary Fund Staff Discussion Note No. SDN/15/21.

Cohen, L., Gurun, U.G., and Malloy, C. 2017. "Resident Networks and Corporate Connections: Evidence from World War II Internment Camps." *The Journal of Finance* 72(1): 207–48.

Conde-Ruiz, J.I., García, J.R., and Navarro, M. 2008. "Inmigración y crecimiento regional en España." *Colección estudios económicos*, 09(08): 1–36.

Cortes, P., and Tessada, J. 2011. "Low-skilled Immigration and the Labor Supply of Highly Skilled Women." *American Economic Journal: Applied Economics* 3(3): 88–123.

D'Amuri, F., and Peri, G. 2014. "Immigration, Jobs, and Employment Protection: Evidence from Europe Before and During the Great Recession." *Journal of the European Economic Association* 12(2): 432–64.

D'Amuri, F., Ottaviano, G., and Peri, G., 2010. "The Labor Market Impact of Immigration in Western Germany in 1990s." *European Economic Review* 54(4): 550–70.

Davies, S. 2008. "Remittances as Insurance for Household and Community Shocks in an Agricultural Economy: The Case of Rural Malawi," Unpublished manuscript. Available online at http://siteresources.worldbank.org/INTTRADERESEARCH/Resources/544824-1323963330969/8322197-1323963818018/Davies.pdf.

De Brauw, A., Mueller, V., and Woldehanna, T. 2013. "Motives to Remit: Evidence from Tracked Internal Migrants in Ethiopia." *World Development* 50(C): 13–23.

Docquier, F., Dao, T.H., Parsons, C., and Peri, G. 2018. "Migration and Development: Dissecting the Anatomy of the Mobility Transition." *Journal of Development Economics* 132(1): 88–101.

Docquier, F., Ozden, Ç., and Peri, G., 2014. "The Labour Market Effects of Immigration and Emigration in OECD Countries." *The Economic Journal* 124(579): 1106–45.

Dustmann, C. 1996. "The Social Assimilation of Immigrants." *Journal of Population Economics* 9(1): 37–54.

Dustmann, C., and Frattini, T. 2014. "The Fiscal Effects of Immigration to the UK." *The Economic Journal* 124(580): F593–643.

Dustmann, C., and Görlach, J.S. 2015. "Selective Out-migration and the Estimation of Immigrants' Earnings Profiles. In *Handbook of the Economics of International Migration* (Vol. 1, pp. 489–533). North-Holland.

Dustmann, C., and Görlach, J.S. 2016. "The Economics of Temporary Migrations." *Journal of Economic Literature* 54(1): 98–136.

Dustmann, C., and Preston, I.P. 2007. "Racial and Economic Factors in Attitudes to Immigration." *The BE Journal of Economic Analysis & Policy* 7(1): 1–39.

Ehrlich, I. 1973. "Participation in Illegitimate Activities: A Theoretical and Empirical Investigation." *Journal of Political Economy* 81(3): 521–65.

Fagen, P. (2006). "Remittances in Crises: A Haiti case study," Humanitarian Policy Group Background Paper, London: ODI.

Fairlie, R.W., and Lofstrom, M. 2015. "Immigration and Entrepreneurship. In *Handbook of the Economics of International Migration* (Vol. 1, pp. 877–911). North-Holland.

Flavin, P., Pacek, A.C., and Radcliff, B. 2011. "State Intervention and Subjective Well-Being in Advanced Industrial Democracies." *Politics & Policy* 39(2): 251–69.

Foged, M., and Peri, G. 2016. "Immigrants' Effect on Native Workers: New Analysis on Longitudinal Data." *American Economic Journal: Applied Economics* 8(2): 1–34.

Glitz, A. 2012. "The Labor Market Impact of Immigration: A Quasi-experiment Exploiting Immigrant Location Rules in Germany." *Journal of Labor Economics* 30:1(2012): 175–213.

Grogger, J., and Hanson, G.H. 2011. "Income Maximization and the Selection and Sorting of International Migrants." *Journal of Development Economics* 95(1): 42–57.

Halliday, T. 2006. "Migration, Risk and Liquidity Constraints in El Salvador." *Economic Development and Cultural Change* 54(4): 893–925.

Helbling, M., Simon, S., and Schmid, S.D. 2020. "Restricting Immigration to Foster Migrant Integration? A Comparative Study across 22 European Countries." *Journal of Ethnic and Migration Studies* 46(13): 2603–24.

Ho, G., and Shirono, K. 2015. "The Nordic labor market model and the role of labor mobility and migration." International Monetary Fund Working Paper No. 15/254.

Ho, G., and Turk-Ariss, R. 2018. "The Labor Market Integration of Migrants in Europe: New Evidence from Micro Data." International Monetary Fund Working Paper No. 18/232.

Hunt, J. 1992. "The Impact of the 1962 Repatriates from Algeria on the French Labor Market." *Industrial and Labor Relations Review* 45(3): 556–72.

International Monetary Fund (IMF). 2016a. Kyrgyz Republic: Selected Issues. IMF Country Report No. 16/56.

International Monetary Fund (IMF). 2016b. World Economic Outlook. Chapter 4: Spillovers from China's Transition and from Migration.

International Monetary Fund (IMF). 2020. World Economic Outlook: The Great Lockdown. Chapter 4: The Macroeconomic Effects of Global Migration. Washington, DC, April.

Jaumotte, M.F., Koloskova, K., and Saxena, M.S.C. 2016. "Impact of Migration on Income Levels in Advanced Economies." International Monetary Fund Spillover Notes No. 16.08.

Javorcik, B.S., Özden, Ç., Spatareanu, M., and Neagu, C. 2011. "Migrant Networks and Foreign Direct Investment." *Journal of Development Economics* 94(2): 231–41.

Kerr, W.R., and Lincoln, W.F. 2010. "The Supply Side of Innovation: H-1B Visa Reforms and US Ethnic Invention." *Journal of Labor Economics* 28(3): 473–508.

Koczan, Z. 2016. "Remittances During Crises: Evidence from Ex-Yugoslavia." *Economics of Transition* 24(3): 507–33.

Koczan, Z., and Loyola, F. 2018. "How Do Migration and Remittances Affect Inequality? A Case Study of Mexico," IMF Working Paper No. 18/136.

Kossoudji, S.A., and Cobb-Clark, D.A. 2002. "Coming Out of the Shadows: Learning about Legal Status and Wages from the Legalized Population." *Journal of Labor Economics* 20(3): 598–628.

Kugler, A., and Yuksel, M. 2008. "Effects of Low-Skilled Immigration on U.S. Natives: Evidence from Hurricane Mitch." IZA Discussion Paper No. 3670, 2008.

Lozano, F., and Sørensen, T.A. 2011. The Labor Market Value to Legal Status.

Margolis, D., Miotti L., El Mouhoub M, and J. Oudinet. 2013. "To Have and Have Not: Migration, Remittances, Poverty and Inequality in Algeria." IZA Discussion Paper 7747, Institute for the Study of Labor, Bonn.

Mastrobuoni, G., and Pinotti, P. 2011. "Migration Restrictions and Criminal Behavior: Evidence from a Natural Experiment." *Economy and Society*, No. 115723.

Maystadt, J.-F., and P. Verwimp. 2014. "Winners and Losers among a Refugee-hosting Population." *Economic Development and Cultural Change* 62(4): 769–809.

McKenzie, D., and Rapoport, H. 2007. "Network Effects and the Dynamics of Migration and Inequality: Theory and Evidence from Mexico." *Journal of Development Economics* 84(1): 1–24.

Miles, T.J. and Cox, A.B. 2014. Does immigration enforcement reduce crime? evidence from secure communities. *The Journal of Law and Economics* 57(4): 937–73.

Mohapatra, S., Joseph, G., and Ratha, D. 2009. "Remittances and Natural Disasters: Ex-post Response and Contribution to Ex-ante Preparedness," Policy Research Working Paper Series No. 4972. Washington, DC: The World Bank.

Möllers, J, and Meyer, W. 2014. "The Effects of Migration on Poverty and Inequality in Rural Kosovo." *IZA Journal of Labor & Development* 3(16): 1–18.

Mughal, M, and Anwar, Amar Iqbal. 2012. "Remittances, Inequality and Poverty in Pakistan: Macro and Microeconomic Evidence." CATT Working Paper 2, Centre d'Analyse Théorique et de Traitement des données économiques, Cedex.

Organisation for Economic Co-operation and Development (OECD). 2013. *International Migration Outlook 2013*. Paris.

Organisation for Economic Co-operation and Development (OECD) and European Commission (EU). 2018. "Settling in 2018: Indicators of Immigrant Integration." Paris/European Union, Brussels.

Olney, W.W. 2013. "Immigration and Firm Expansion." *Journal of Regional Science* 53(1): 142–57.

Omar Mahmoud, T., Rapoport, H., Steinmayr, A., and Trebesch, C. 2013. "The Effect of Labor Migration on the Diffusion of Democracy: Evidence from a Former Soviet Republic." *American Economic Journal: Applied Economics* 9(3): 36–69.

Orrenius, P. 2017. "New Findings on the Fiscal Impact of Immigration in the United States." Federal Reserve Bank of Dallas Working Paper No. 1704.

Özden, Ç., and Wagner, M. 2014. *Immigrant versus Natives? Displacement and Job Creation*. Policy Research Working Paper No. 6900, Washington, DC: World Bank.

Parsons, C., and Vezina, P. 2016. "Migrant Networks and Trade: The Vietnamese Boat People as a Natural Experiment." *The Economic Journal* 128(612): 210–34.

Peri, G. 2012. "The Effect of Immigration on Productivity: Evidence from US States." *Review of Economics and Statistics* 94(1): 348–58.

Peri, G. 2014. *Do Immigrant Workers Depress the Wages of Native Workers?* IZA World of Labor.

Peri, G., Rury, D., and Wiltshire, J. 2020. "The Economic Impact of Migrants from Hurricane Maria." National Bureau of Economic Research Working Paper No. 27718.

Peri, G., and Sparber, C. 2009. "Task Specialization, Immigration, and Wages." *American Economic Journal: Applied Economics* 1(3): 135–69.

Peri, G., and Yasenov, V. 2017. "The labor market effects of a refugee wave: Applying the synthetic control method to the Mariel Boatlift." NBER Working Paper No. 21801.

Pinotti, P. 2017. "Clicking on Heaven's Door: The Effect of Immigrant Legalization on Crime." *American Economic Review* 107(1): 138–68.

Rother, M.B., Pierre, M.G., Lombardo, D., Herrala, R., Toffano, M.P., Roos, M.E., et al. 2016. The Economic Impact of Conflicts and the Refugee Crisis in the Middle East and North Africa. International Monetary Fund Staff Discussion Note No. SDN/16/08.

Schmitz, Kai, and Isaku Endo. 2011. "Lowering the Cost of Sending Money Home." *Finance and Development*, June 2011.

Stark, Oded, J. Edward Taylor, and Shlomo Yitzhaki. 1988. "Migration, Remittances and Inequality: A Sensitivity Analysis using the Extended Gini Index." *Journal of Development Economics* 28: 309–22.

Suleri, A.Q., and Savage, K. 2006. "Remittances in Crises: A Case Study from Pakistan," Humanitarian Policy Group Background Paper. London: Overseas Development Institute.

Taylor, J. Edward, Richard Adams, Jorge Mora, and Alejandro López-Feldman. 2009. "Remittances, Inequality and Poverty: Evidence from Rural Mexico." Available at http://essays.ssrc.org/acrossborders/wp-content/uploads/2009/08/ch6.pdf.

Vandor, P., and Franke, N. 2016. "Why Are Immigrants More Entrepreneurial?" *Harvard Business Review* 10(1): 1–7.

Weiss Fagen, P., and Bump, M.N. 2005. "Remittances in conflict and crises: How remittances sustain livelihoods in war, crises, and transitions to peace," International Peace Academy Policy Paper, Washington, DC: International Peace Academy. Georgetown University.

World Bank. 2006. *Global Economic Prospects: Economic Implications of Remittances and Migration.* Washington, DC.

World Bank. 2014. *International Migration and Development in East Asia and the Pacific.* Washington, DC.

World Bank. 2018. *Moving for Prosperity Global Migration and Labor Markets.* Washington, DC.

World Bank. 2019. *Leveraging Economic Migration for Development.* Washington, DC.

Wu, T. 2006. "The Role of Remittances in Crisis: An Aceh Research Study," Humanitarian Policy Group Background Paper, London: ODI.

10

Governance

Maksym Ivanyna and Andrea Salerno

I. Introduction

Through the provision of basic public services and goods, the state plays a key role in promoting inclusive and sustainable growth.[1] Central to the state's role is the quality of its governance. Defined broadly, governance refers to institutions, mechanisms, and practices, through which governmental power is exercised (IMF 2017a).

There is growing recognition that poor governance undermines the role of the state and negatively affects lives and livelihoods (IMF 2016a; North et al. 2008; North 1991). Poor governance weakens fiscal performance by limiting revenue collection and distorting expenditure. Distortions in expenditure (for instance, neglect of proper spending on health and education programs) exacerbate poverty and inequalities. The cost and uncertainty that poor governance generates undermine the business climate, hence limiting domestic and foreign investments and opportunities for growth. When some or all these problems become sufficiently systemic, they can increase distrust in the state, ultimately leading to state fragility, civil strife, or conflict—thus turning the state from a solution to inclusive growth into a major obstacle.

This chapter explores two key causes of poor governance—corruption and lack of institutional and human capacity. It offers a brief review of how they can erode governance, with substantial adverse effects on (inclusive) growth, poverty, and inequality. It then reviews the key policies to improve governance, linking them into a simple theoretical framework. The policies include (1) structural reform, automation, improving rules and procedures (including for fiscal and monetary policies) to limit the discretion and hence the space for policy errors; (2) human resource policies, capacity building, effective anti-corruption frameworks to incentivize public officials to make decisions in the best public interest; and (3)

[1] With contributions by Chady Adel El Khoury, Francisca Fernando, Maksym Markevych, and Joel Turkewitz. We thank Jaime Sarmiento Monroy for the research assistance. We also thank Olivier Basdevant, Valerie Cerra, Moya Chin, Sharmini Coorey, Barry Eichengreen, Alice Flora French, Torben Steen Hansen, Ashraf Khan, Sebastian Pompe, Keyra Primus, as well as participants in the Inclusive Growth book seminar series organized by the IMF Institute for Capacity Development for their comments.

Maksym Ivanyna and Andrea Salerno, *Governance* In: *How to Achieve Inclusive Growth*. Edited by: Valerie Cerra, Barry Eichengreen, Asmaa El-Ganainy, and Martin Schindler, Oxford University Press. © Maksym Ivanyna and Andrea Salerno 2022. DOI: 10.1093/oso/9780192846938.003.0010 transparency, accountability, and inclusive political institutions to inform and monitor policymaking.

II. Causes of Poor Governance: Corruption and Lack of Capacity

Two broad factors stand in the way of good governance: corruption and lack of institutional and human capacity to enact good policies.

Corruption is a complex, multidimensional problem (Basu and Cordella 2018) and, to a varying degree, affects economies at all stages of development (IMF 2016a). While a comprehensive definition of corruption can be difficult to formulate given the variations in corrupt behavior and its concealed nature (IMF 2017a), "the abuse of public office for private gain" is one of the most widely accepted definitions in the literature and among practitioners. It implies a focus on corrupt practices involving civil servants or elected officials that are detrimental to the public interest, even though corruption is often enabled by the supply side—the bribe givers. An act can be corrupt even if it does not result in direct financial gain for the public official, as for example in case of negligence, absenteeism, clientelism, or cronyism/nepotism.[2]

Acts of corruption can be classified into different categories. The most common distinction is between petty and grand corruption. Petty corruption usually occurs when the state restricts market mechanisms or when bureaucracy interacts with the public and is easier for ordinary citizens to observe or experience. Grand corruption involves a small number of powerful players and large sums of money. The corrupt seek government contracts, privatized firms, and concessions; they bribe legislators to pass favorable laws, and cabinet ministers and agency heads to enact beneficial regulations.

The extent of corruption around the world is staggering. In 2017 nearly one in four people in developing countries said that they paid a bribe for public services (Transparency International 2017). The percentage of firms identifying corruption as the largest obstacle to do business is 6–10 percent depending on a geographical region (Figure 10.1).

Yet, poor governance is possible even in the absence of significant corruption (IMF 2017a; World Bank 2017). The rapid pace of globalization and the expanded role of the state requires governments to make decisions in a global environment of uncertainty, heterogeneity, and a high level of complexity. Governments, therefore, need to always invest in the institutional and human capacity to avoid the decay of their existing institutions and to adequately react to new policy challenges.

---

[2] Absenteeism is a practice of missing work without a legitimate reason. Clientelism is a practice of exchanging goods and services for political support. Cronyism/nepotism is a practice of giving favors or hiring friends and associates for a government position.

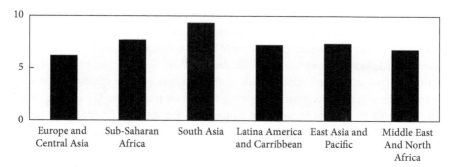

Figure 10.1 Corruption as a Major Obstacle To Do Business: Percent of Firms Choosing Corruption as Top Business Environment Obstacle
Source: World Bank Enterprise Surveys, average over all surveys in 2009–2019.

Capacity refers to the capability to deliver on an envisioned task at the agency or government level and can differ significantly even in countries with similar levels of corruption. For example, there are large differences among countries in the efficiency of their public investment. While part of the efficiency loss can be explained by corruption, another plausible explanation is inefficiency in public investment management: some governments may not have a systemic approach to project selection, some may not have multi-year planning procedures. It is therefore important to go beyond corruption and analyze governance through a broader set of lenses. These include fiscal governance, financial sector oversight, central bank governance, quality of market regulation, rule of law, and others.

Corruption and lack of capacity are highly interconnected. Corruption begets a lack of capacity as public resources—including investment in capacity development—are stolen, misallocated or spent inefficiently, and political will to improve capacity is low. In turn, lack of capacity begets corruption, as governments do not utilize the best available frameworks and practices to restrain corruption and promote integrity. As a result, it is often the case that when the state is most needed, i.e. when people depend on the most on basic public goods and services, it is often least capable of carrying through its functions in an efficient way (Tanzi 1998).

III. Effect of Poor Governance on Inclusive Growth

Poor governance can severely hamper the government's ability to deliver inclusive growth. Efficiency-enhancing views of corruption, namely that it may be able to "grease the wheels of the economy," do not consider the systemic impact of corruption on growth, ignore its permanent distortions, and its adverse effect on inequality and poverty. Even if in some cases bribery may be a way to bypass a particularly distorting regulation, the regulation itself is a manifestation of poor governance. Dozens of peer-reviewed empirical studies show that poor governance and corruption are associated with lower economic growth, lower investment, and lower tax revenue (IMF 2018a; Ugur 2014). For example, the EBRD estimates that in Ukraine closing half of the gap between the quality of the economic institutions (i.e. its governance level) and the corresponding G7 average would lift the country's income growth per capita by an average of 1.2 percentage points a year (EBRD 2019).[3] Worsening in the corruption index of an average country by one standard deviation is associated with the same increase in income inequality as a reduction in average secondary schooling of 2.3 years (Gupta, Davoodi, and Alonso-Terme 1998).

Following are some of the main effects of poor governance on inclusive growth (Figure 10.2).[4]

Impaired provision of public goods and services. The provision of core public goods and services can be severely hampered. Corruption increases their costs and can create additional inefficiencies through market distortions (Olken and Pande 2012). For example, public procurement in Latin America accounts for an average of 10 to 15 percent of gross domestic product, and it is also the government activity that is the most vulnerable to corruption (Pimenta and Pessoa 2015). Inflated public procurement costs have been an issue in advanced economies as

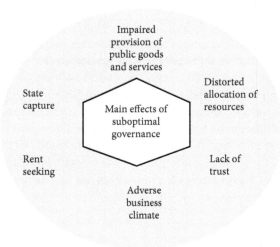

Figure 10.2 Main Effects of Poor Governance: Summary

---

[3] Note that cross-country empirical studies may underestimate the negative effect of poor governance on economy, not least due to a measurement error—likely to be significant for governance—which biases estimated coefficients towards zero (Svensson 2005).

[4] Check out (IMF 2016a, 2019) for more details.

well. Research showed that corruption raised the costs of a public project by 13 percent on average in eight European countries (PwC 2013). Efforts to contain the Covid-19 health crisis have been undermined by public officials and local entrepreneurs accused of personal enrichment by price-gouging hospitals and governments for medical supplies (Kitroeff and Taj 2020). Exacerbating the matter, poor governance in revenue management enables tax evasion, diversion of grants and borrowed funds, and theft from unmonitored treasury accounts, thus effectively reducing the amount of public resources available to spend (IMF 2019a).

Inadequate provision of public goods and services hampers the government's ability to support inclusive growth, as the poor effectively receive a lower level of social services, suffer weaker protection of their property and other rights, are more affected by uncorrected negative externalities (e.g. polluted air and water), and have less education or business opportunities. Women tend to be disproportionately affected, as they tend to spend more time in unpaid labor, such as caring for children or sick family members, and so tend to rely more on social services (IMF 2016a).

Distorted allocation of resources. Public resources can be allocated to activities where bribes or political gains can be more easily extracted. For instance, public funds get diverted from current expenditure to public investment. This can increase public investment in unproductive projects (IMF 1998), and hamper core services such as health and education (IMF 2019a), which again disproportionately affect the poor. Countries with poor governance do allocate lower share of government spending for health and education (Figure 10.3). Governments can also engage in excessive borrowing (at the cost of high debt) and seigniorage (at the cost of high inflation) in order to increase the pool of resources for embezzlement (Ivanyna, Mourmouras, and Rangazas 2018; IMF 2016a).

Erosion of trust. Trust is a key element for good governance. Corruption can undermine trust in the state, erode social capital, and weaken the impact of

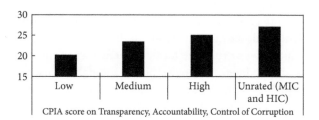

Figure 10.3 Less Education and Health Spending in Countries with Poor Governance

Education and health government spending, % total

Note: CPIA—Country Policy and Institutional Assessments by the World Bank, mostly covering low income countries. MIC—middle-income countries, HIC—high-income countries

Source: World Bank World Development Indicators; averages over 2015–019.

policies and public spending. In addition, crises (economic, health, social, etc.) test people's trust in government and institutions, as ethical behavior becomes even more salient when state services are in high demand. As a result, corruption can deepen the impact of crises, and threaten political and social cohesion (IMF 2020a). Distrust in state capacity also discourages entrepreneurs from starting new businesses in the formal economy, therefore eroding the revenue base (IMF 2016a). As the rule of law is weakened, distrust of the state can fuel and justify acts of corruption, resulting in a negative cycle (Rose-Ackerman and Palifka 2016).

Adverse business climate. High and rising corruption contributes to increasing uncertainty in the business climate and acts as a tax on economic activities, raising transactional costs. Corrupt or inefficient courts and law enforcement institutions also effectively diminish property rights protection and the ability of businesses to enforce contracts. Uncertainty, higher cost of doing business, and lower property rights protection can, in turn, reduce the willingness of enterprises to invest, lead more productive firms to exit the market, and drive activities towards the informal economy (Rose-Ackerman and Palifka 2016). The capacity of the state to attract foreign direct investments is also negatively affected. Increased uncertainty and lower effective return decrease incentives not only for investment but also for the accumulation of human capital (IMF 2016a).

Rent-seeking. There are instances in which the government's restrictions on the market and economic activities can give rise to a variety of rents (Rowley, Tollison, and Tullok 1978), i.e. largely unproductive, expropriative activities that bring a positive return to an individual but not to society (Abed and Gupta 2002). These restrictions facilitate rent-seeking activities, in particular when they require the government's approval (IMF 2016a). Rent-seeking can take many forms, from lobbying to bribery (Krueger 1974). The result, however, remains a waste of resources as these are diverted from productive activities, such as investments or human capital development (Rowley, Tollison, and Tullok 1978).

State capture. State capture refers to a situation in which influential firms or special interests "buy" laws and policies (Konucová 2006), i.e. they shape and affect the "rules of the game." While other forms of corruption distort how laws or rules are implemented, state capture refers to the efforts to influence, in the first instance, how such laws or rules are formed. There is a variety of mechanisms by which firms and elite interests capture policy through collusive arrangements, from bribes to political donations and kickbacks to hiring friends and family for lucrative positions (World Bank 2017). Being so pernicious, state capture is a fundamental cause of poor governance and weak institutions (Hellman and Kaufmann 2001), generating a vicious cycle. The "privatization of public policy" leads to inefficient allocation of public resources, a higher degree of insecurity of property rights, and rent-generating advantages for a selected few. The selected few, in turn, undermine reforms that limit their power, thus lowering growth, exacerbating inequalities, and contributing to accelerated state capture. Breaking this vicious cycle is a key milestone on the way to inclusive growth.

IV. Policies to Improve Governance: Overview

Improving governance is the basis for sustainable and inclusive growth, but is not an easy task. Many politicians declare war on corruption, yet it is still widespread around the world. Political and economic institutions, both formal and informal, are shaped by centuries of history—colonial heritage, legal origin, ethnic fractionalization—as well as by climatic and geographic conditions, and natural resource endowments.[5] Institutions change very slowly, and not always in the right direction. This is because major political and economic actors are often interested in keeping and expanding their privileges, including access to grand corruption schemes. At the same time, active civil engagement is often inhibited by a lack of income, education, or infrastructure, especially in countries where governance reform is most needed. Long-lasting improvements are more likely after "critical junctures"—major historical events like crises, conflicts, political scandals, natural or technological disasters—but those are rare, largely accidental, and hardly desirable (Acemoglu and Robinson 2012).[6]

Despite the headwinds, improving governance is possible. Western Europe and the United States eliminated most of the widespread corruption practices in the early twentieth century. Singapore and Hong Kong SAR did so in the post-Second World War era (Dixit 2018). Georgia and Rwanda made major advances in the 2000s (IMF 2019a). While progress on grand corruption is notoriously hard to measure and achieve, petty bribery can be reduced relatively more quickly. For instance, over the past ten years, quite a few developing countries have been able to reduce bribery incidence among firms (Figure 10.4).

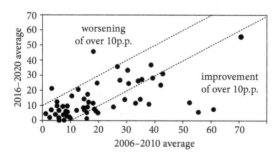

Figure 10.4 Bribery Dynamics Around the World
Percent of Firms Reporting Bribery Demand, Country Average
Source: World Bank Enterprise Surveys.

---

[5] Resource sector often generates significant economic rents (e.g. above-normal profits), which can give rise to corruption and inefficiency. Also see Chapter 19.
[6] The example of a "critical juncture" is the Pendleton Act of 1883 in the United States, which ended a long-standing practice of hiring political supporters to lucrative positions in the government. The act was adopted after the assassination of the newly elected President James A. Garfield by a would-be office seeker (Fukuyama 2018).

The history of governance reforms offers several general lessons. First, reform's success crucially depends on the political will at the top. International cooperation, active civil engagement, and broad support by the public are essential too. Second, the reform process can be slow and its progress hard to observe and measure. Proper communication about it is extremely important. Perception of governance may even worsen at the beginning of an anti-corruption campaign if expectations are not properly managed. Third, even if the communication is proper, and there is political will for change, there are no simple one-size-fits-all strategies to improve governance that work for all countries. Reaching the best policy mix is a process of trial and error, which depends on a country's social, political, and economic circumstances, and the capacity of its policymakers. Yet, adherence to international standards and agreements is an important step to guide the reforms.[7]

What follows is a broad overview of policies to improve governance, provided there is a political will to go ahead. To understand the rationale behind these policies and linkages between them, let us start from a simple theoretical framework.

In a nutshell, governance is shaped by a series of everyday policy decisions by public officials. Some decisions are made at a grand or macro level—by presidents, ministers, parliamentarians, supreme court judges, central bank governors, or heads of major state-owned companies. Other decisions are more local, such as those made by a traffic police officer deciding whether to issue a fine for speeding.

Each of these policy decisions could potentially be suboptimal, meaning that their outcomes are not in the best public interest, thus constituting poor governance. For example, the winner of a procurement contract could offer an inferior price-to-quality ratio, because public officials lack the capacity to organize the procurement process in the most efficient way. Or the procurement law could impose too many restrictions to participate in the bidding process because some parliamentarians took bribes to introduce inferior changes.

Improving governance means less of the policy decisions being suboptimal. This can be done by pursuing two broad avenues.

The first is to reduce discretion by public officials when the policy decision is made or decide whether the policy decision is needed at all. If there is no clear case for government intervention, government regulation is "excessive" or corruption risks are too high, we could streamline, simplify or do away with the policy decision altogether. This is essentially the case of structural reform. If there is a clear case for the government's intervention, can the policy decision be outsourced or automated? An automated speed enforcement system—radar equipment combined with a camera—may do a better job than the traffic police if

---

[7] For example, the UN Convention Against Corruption (UNCAC) or standards and codes by the IMF and World Bank—discussed in more detail in subsequent sections.

the latter is known to be corrupt. Alternatively, and importantly, the policy decision could be subject to a set of rules and procedures to guide public officials and limit the space for possible error, whether deliberate or not. All key state functions and institutions are guided by some sort of rules and procedures, be it a constitution—the key law in any country—public finance management procedures to inform fiscal policy, or guidelines for central bank operations and financial supervision, among others.

For most policy decisions, discretion by public officials cannot be avoided. In fact, we need discretion when policy decisions require judgment and agile government reaction to unexpected circumstances—something that cannot be fully outlined by a set of rigid rules, let alone automated. Hence the second broad avenue is to reduce the likelihood of poor governance, at the time when discretionary policy decisions are made.

How to induce public officials to make decisions in the best interest of their country? The key is to set the right incentives.[8] First, encourage and facilitate good governance: for instance, through competitive salaries, career prospects, or capacity building. Second, discourage poor governance, in particular corruption. The key instrument is punishment of corruption—for both bribe-takers and bribe-givers, which requires quality law enforcement. One can also employ political instruments, such as regulation of lobbying and political contributions, or behavioral nudges—emphasis on reputational risks and elimination of culture of corruption in society. Making it difficult to use the proceeds of corruption is also a way to effectively reduce benefits, and the primary instrument for this is anti-money laundering enforcement.

For these incentives to work, it is crucial to have quality monitoring and informing the policymaking process. The key element is transparency—opening data about government operations and making them easily accessible. Transparency sheds light on government operations and thus enables their external scrutiny. It also enables governments to make informed, evidence-based and, thus, better policy decisions. Monitoring and informing the policymaking process also requires engaging official anti-corruption institutions and, importantly, the general public and civil society. This engagement is necessary for a participatory, informed, and thus inclusive decision-making process.

Pursuing both avenues is critical, but so is the right policy sequence. Quite often "prevention" is better than "treatment"—the priority is to reduce discretion, and hence the space for errors, when a policy decision is made, rather than to ensure and monitor, whether this decision is optimal. For example, if a procurement law does not provide an adequate set of guidelines for the procurement

---

[8] As in general crime-punishment framework of (Becker 1968). See also (Allingham and Sandmo 1972) and (Olken and Pande 2012).

process, it might be very costly or even futile to design incentives for public officials to follow the law. In some cases, the enforcement of a poorly formulated policy can be counterproductive, giving rise to the argument that bribery (in order to evade this policy) "greases the wheels of the economy." For example, cracking down on tax evasion in an environment of particularly high tax rates and inefficient public financial management may result in lower economic growth (Ivanyna, Mourmouras and Rangazas 2015). Fighting medical staff absenteeism is costly and non-effective if policy-prescribed job requirements and benefits are inadequate (Banerjee and Duflo 2011). Creating a proper legal and regulatory framework to improve policymaking, and getting the policy right, are the priorities in such cases. Nevertheless, poor governance and, in particular, corruption can thrive even if policies are well-formulated, so it is important to complement the policy frameworks with appropriate monitoring and account-ability mechanisms.

Figure 10.5 provides an overview of the governance policies and in the follow-ing sections we discuss them in more detail.

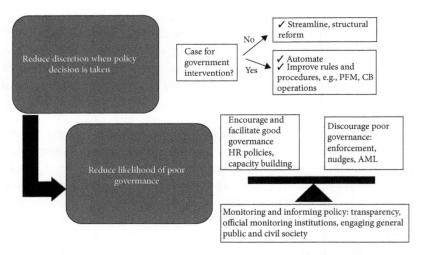

Improving government involves two broad avenues to pursse. First is reducing discretion when policy decision is made -via structural reform, rules and procedures, automation, Seconds is reducing likelihood of poor governance (when discretionary policy decision is made) - via appropriate incentives for public officials. Abbreviations: PFM - public finance management, CB - central bank, HR - human resource, AML- anti-mony laundering
Source: authors' preparation

Figure 10.5 Improving Governance Decomposed

V. Reducing Discretion when a Policy Decision Is Made

The broad prescription is to implement structural reforms to streamline and simplify policies if there is no strong case for government intervention or if cor-ruption risks are too high. If the case for the government intervention is strong—market failures need to be addressed—then the priority is to improve rules and procedures, explore the potential for automation, or outsource some of the government functions.

A. Structural Reforms to Reduce Government Discretion

Structural reforms are defined as policy measures that reduce impediments to the efficient allocation of resources (Ostry, Prati, and Spilimbergo 2009). In the context of governance, the reforms often include streamlining, simplifying, or removing excessive government regulation and oversight. Structural reforms reduce the need for contacts between the private sector and public officials and, with it, the number of discretionary policy decisions. Removing a cap on trucking licenses means that there is no need for a public official to decide who should receive the license. Reducing the number of tax payments means fewer visits to the tax collection agency. In a cross-section of countries, less burdensome government regulation is indeed associated with a.smaller shadow economy and lower corruption.[9]

Examples of structural reforms include:

- For businesses: reducing the number of documents, procedures, and cost to open and close firms, license new products, start construction, receive loans, fire and hire workers, comply with safety and other standards, or pay taxes and fees.
- For exporters and importers: removing impediments to trade and move capital across borders.
- For individuals: reducing licensing to enter a new profession or limiting requirements to sell a house or receive a driver's license, among others.
- Removing the asymmetrical treatment of similar economic agents: for example, export subsidies, import quotas, special economic zones or favorable tax treatment of foreign investment, food or energy subsidies, different custom tariffs for similar products.
- Reducing regulatory overlap, when different agencies can issue regulations, permits, or licenses over similar matters. This can reduce the unpredictability and magnitude of bribery (Schleifer and Vishny 1993).
- Privatization of state-owned enterprises (SOEs), with the caveat that the privatization process itself can be subject to corruption and capacity constraints.
- Strengthening the independence of public institutions, including SOEs and in particular central banks (Barro and Gordon 1983), subject to effective accountability frameworks. This includes less government discretion over

---

[9] See for example (Djankov et al. 2002), or (Besley 2015) for a broader overview.

the appointment and dismissal of management, recruitment within institutions, internal rules and procedures, and financial autonomy.

Removing and streamlining government regulations can reduce the space for policy error, yet the most challenging part is to identify which regulations are excessive. For example, some countries require over 20 procedures to issue a construction permit. In some countries, it takes years to enforce contracts or resolve insolvencies. These extreme outcomes of regulation are hardly justifiable. But very often the answer is less clear. Some government regulations are essential. Even the most business-friendly countries take time to enforce contracts, grant construction permits or resolve insolvency. They do require businesses to register or obtain construction permits. Very often, the choice is between addressing a governance failure versus addressing a market failure or achieving other societal goals (e.g., eradication of poverty or environmental sustainability).

How much regulation is too much? The answer ultimately depends on each country's circumstances. Lower quality of governance makes the case for more deregulation. Georgia, for example, abolished 20 inspection agencies during 2005–2011, including food and fire safety inspections. At the time, these agencies were deemed too corrupt to perform even their basic functions (World Bank 2012). This strategy would probably not work for all countries, including Georgia, in the long term. On October 30, 2015, a Colectiv nightclub fire in Bucharest, Romania, took the lives of 64 people, the main cause being blatant fire safety violations by the club that went unchecked by the responsible inspection agency (Barberá 2019). Having no agency at all would not have saved lives. What could have helped was an agency, which would adequately perform its functions. Deregulation could be the first line of defense against poor governance, but it would not help solve many issues.

B. A Case for Government Intervention: Automation, Outsourcing, Rules, and Procedures

Where the role of the government is essential, governance reforms must go beyond streamlining. In order to reduce discretion and space for policy error, some policy decisions can be delegated to computer algorithms or, in other words, automated. Some can be delegated to third parties, which are more trusted or capable—a case of so-called "regulatory outsourcing." Lastly and importantly, policy decisions can be constrained and guided by a set of rules and prescribed procedures.

Automation of government operations is becoming an increasingly viable solution thanks to rapid progress in information technology. Well-designed computer algorithms can remove human errors in decision-making and so reduce opportunities for poor governance.[10] They can be used to:

- Automatically assign tax audits, like in Estonia or France among other countries—a part of the so-called risk-based approach (IMF 2018b; World Bank 2011). This not only helps detect tax evasion more effectively but also removes potentially erroneous (or corrupt) policy decisions on whom to audit. The same risk-based approach is used at customs, for financial supervision, or to assign judges to court cases.
- Automatically identify eligible recipients of social transfers. For example, in South Africa, all social security recipients must periodically present proof of life—automatically by fingerprint or voice verification (IMF 2018b). This not only reduces the compliance cost for the recipients but also removes the opportunity for "leakages"—i.e. collusion between non-eligible recipients and Social Security Agency clerks.
- Automatically detect traffic violations, charge for parking or public transport, regulate congestion (through the pricing of road use).
- Provide government services online: pay taxes, utilities, fines; register businesses, vehicles; apply for birth, marriage, or death certificate; apply for driver's license, etc. (Figure 10.6). The Covid-19 pandemic highlighted the importance of digital solutions, enabling governments to efficiently deploy funds within their social assistance programs.
- Automate the procurement process: online announcement, bidding process, monitoring, evaluation, and results.

Automation helps improve governance, yet it comes with several risks. First, setting up automatic systems may require significant initial investment and building up capacity to operate these systems. Second, the most vulnerable can be excluded. While over 60 percent of countries offer online services for the poor (Figure 10.6), billions of people—often the poorest—still do not have Internet access or lack digital literacy to be able to benefit from these services. Without major investments in education and infrastructure, the poor can disproportionately be exposed to government inefficiencies, including extortion by public officials (UN 2018). Third, the more services become automatized, the larger is the potential cost of a cyber-security breach or identity theft.

The second solution to limit discretion and space for policy decision error is outsourcing—the delegation of selected policy decisions to an institution with

---

[10] Progress in IT (digitization) also creates new governance challenges, such as, for example, regulation of data privacy protection or taxation in times when cross-border movement of capital becomes easier and harder to detect (IMF 2018b).

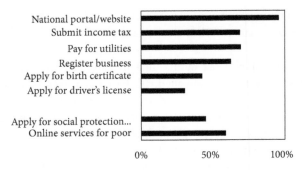

Figure 10.6 E-Government on Rise
Percent Countries Offering Government Services Online in 2018
Source: UN E-Government Survey 2018.

better capacity or less corruption.[11] For example, national regulatory authorities in 40 countries (as of 2019) collaborate with the World Health Organization's Prequalification Program to accelerate the approval of medicines ('t Hoen et al. 2014; WHO 2019). Since 2016 Ukraine has outsourced the procurement of medicines to UNICEF and UNDP, which helped save $66 million of state budget funds (UNDP 2019). Even high-level anti-corruption law enforcement can be outsourced, as in the case of Guatemala's Commission against Impunity (UN 2019). Nevertheless, outsourcing has its limits, as third-party dependency may have low political acceptability.

The third and the most universal solution is to guide policy decisions by rules and prescribed procedures. For example, a rule that sets strict time limits to issue or refuse a license may deter public officials' attempts to require a bribe to "grease the wheels" of the bureaucratic process. A well-established routine for procurement or a budgetary process may help even inexperienced public officials perform their job well.

The most fundamental policies and institutions are guided by rules, starting with the constitution. The conduct of key macroeconomic policies—fiscal policy, monetary policy, financial sector regulation—is also increasingly subject to rules and procedures. Central banks in many countries set an explicit inflation objective to guide their monetary policy actions and communications (IMF 2015). Fiscal policy is often anchored by fiscal rules in the form of lasting constraints on key fiscal indicators (Eyraud et al. 2018). Financial sector regulation includes, for instance, the so-called stress-testing—a procedure to check whether banks can sustain adverse economic conditions (Ong 2014). The set of guidelines for all three policies is not limited to these examples. A broader overview is presented in the following subsections.

A successful inclusive growth strategy requires a governance framework—a set of appropriate rules and procedures—at the highest levels of government (OECD

---

[11] Check (Ivanyna and Salerno 2021) for more details on regulatory outsourcing.

2016). It should feature a whole-of-government approach, including mechanisms to coordinate between line ministries. It should also employ tools to assess the government performance based on a dashboard of indicators measuring not only average economic growth—a traditional approach—but also the distribution of its benefits across the population as well as the quality of education, health services, and environmental sustainability. The framework should also align spending decisions with medium- and long-term inclusive growth objectives, combined with comprehensive ex-ante and ex-post policy evaluation procedures. Finally, to enhance the design, implementation, and evaluation of inclusive growth policies, the framework should feature instruments for inclusive political institutions, e.g. those that facilitate the participation of all stakeholders—including to most vulnerable ones—in the decision-making process.

Well-functioning rules and procedures are key to good governance, but they involve trade-offs. Rules should be rigid enough to limit the discretion of public officials where appropriate, but flexible enough to perform equally well under different circumstances. This leaves two options. Rules can be made extremely complex, specifying all potential courses of action, though this raises the question of how well such rules can be enforced and complied with. Or alternatively, rules can be made less specific and less rigid—a case of "principles-based" regulation, allowing more discretion to public officials (Khan 2018; Eyraud et al. 2018).

The balance between flexibility and rigidity of rules ultimately depends on each country's circumstances and the policy issue at hand. For example, Norway's fiscal rule limits government spending to no more than 3 percent (as of 2020) of the value of its sovereign wealth fund—on average over the medium term. The government is permitted to adjust the spending over the economic cycle to help stabilize the economy. The rule performed very well for Norway: it is almost 20 years old and has survived major economic shocks—the financial crisis of 2008 and the collapse of oil prices in 2015. But it is flexible, and it has required a high level of government discipline.

The search for optimal rules is an ongoing exercise. The key point, however, is that for most policy decisions at least some level of discretion by public officials is unavoidable and often necessary, for example, to ensure the independence of key public institutions such as courts or central banks. It is therefore essential to incentivize public officials to do what is in the best interest of their country, that is to reduce the likelihood of poor governance.

Rules and Procedures: Examples of Public Financial Management and Tax Administration

The effectiveness of fiscal policy is key to inclusive and sustainable growth, and it crucially depends on the quality of fiscal governance—institutional frameworks and practices that broadly encompass tax administration on the government revenue side, public financial management on the expenditure side, and fiscal transparency (IMF 2018a).[12]

Broadly defined, public financial management (PFM) deals with rules and procedures that cover all aspects of managing public resources, and in particular how governments manage the budget in its established phases—formulation, approval, and execution (Allen, Hemming, and Potter 2013, Cangiano, Curristine, and Lazare 2013). Strong PFM plays a key role in maintaining a sustainable fiscal position, effective allocation of resources, and efficient delivery of public goods and services.

The Public Expenditure and Financial Accountability (PEFA), launched in 2001 by the international community, has become the acknowledged standard for PFM assessments, both at the national and sub-national levels. It evaluates PFM rules and procedures along seven key pillars:[13]

- Budget reliability: whether the budget is realistic and implemented as intended.
- Transparency of public finances: comprehensive, consistent, and accessible information on government budget including budget classification, intergovernmental transfers, and service delivery performance; consistency of the reporting with international standards; public access to fiscal and budget documentation.
- Management of government assets and liabilities: reporting and monitoring of fiscal risks (e.g. publicly-guaranteed debt, projected future social security, and health spending, the projected fiscal cost of natural disasters); effective public asset and debt management; effective public investment management—procedures for projects' planning, allocation, and implementation. IMF's Public Investment Management Assessment (PIMA) is a widely-used comprehensive framework to assess the quality of infrastructure governance and identify reform priorities (IMF 2019b; Schwartz et al. 2020).[14]
- Policy-based fiscal strategy and budgeting: orderly and timely budget preparation with the effective participation of relevant stakeholders; legislative scrutiny of budget; medium-term perspective in expenditure budgeting; robust fiscal forecasts and procedures to assess the economic impact of fiscal policy proposals.
- Predictability and control in budget execution: procedures to administer government revenue; procedures to record, report, and consolidate revenue collected; reliable projections of cash commitments and requirements; measures to address arrears; effective payroll controls; effective procurement—transparency of arrangement, open and competitive procedures, monitoring of results; procedures and agencies for internal audit.

---

[12] Fiscal transparency is covered in Section 10.7.
[13] https://www.pefa.org/
[14] https://infrastructuregovern.imf.org/content/PIMA/Home/PimaTool.html

- Accounting and reporting: financial data integrity, in-year budget reports to monitor budget performance and introduce corrective measures if needed; annual financial reports.
- External scrutiny and audit: significant, timely, transparent, and independent.

On the government revenue side, IMF's Tax Administration Diagnostic Assessment Tool (TADAT) covers most critical tax administration functions, procedures, and institutions along nine performance outcome areas: (i) integrity of the registered taxpayers base; (ii) effective risk management (in particular, compliance risks); (iii) supporting voluntary compliance; (iv) timely filing of tax declarations; (v) timely payment of taxes; (vi) accurate reporting in declarations; (vii) effective tax dispute resolution; (viii) efficient revenue management; and (ix) accountability and transparency.

Rules and Procedures: Example of Central Bank Safeguards Assessment

Central banks are responsible for monetary and exchange rate policy, and often for financial regulation. The effectiveness of these policies crucially depends on the central bank governance, in particular as it pertains to the central bank's mandate, its decision-making, autonomy, transparency and accountability (IMF 2015, 2020).

IMF's Central Bank Safeguards Assessment is a diagnostic of the central bank's governance with the main objective to mitigate the risks of misuse of IMF resources and misreporting key monetary data to the IMF (IMF 2020d; Bossu and Rossi 2019; Kabwe et al. 2019). It focuses on five key areas:

1. External audit mechanism: are the bank's financial statements independently audited and how are external auditors selected?
2. Legal structure and autonomy: do current laws and regulations ensure the central bank's independence from government interference?
3. Financial reporting: does the central bank adheres to international standards of accounting and financial reporting?
4. Internal audit mechanism: does the audit have enough capacity and organizational independence?
5. System of internal controls: is there a proper oversight of the central bank's operations by the bank's board? How good are the controls in foreign exchange management, currency and vault operations, etc?

Rules and Procedures: Example of Financial Sector Assessment Program (FSAP)

The Financial Sector Assessment Program (FSAP) is a comprehensive and in-depth analysis of the financial sector. A joint program of the IMF and the World Bank, its goal is to gauge the stability and soundness of the financial sector and assess its contribution to economic development.[15] The essential component of FSAP is a detailed analysis of governance in the financial sector.

To assess financial stability, FSAPs:

- Design and conduct procedures to examine the resilience of the financial sector, including stress-tests and analysis of systemic risks.
- Examine microprudential and macroprudential frameworks.
- Review the quality of financial sector supervision.
- Evaluate the procedures to respond effectively in case of systemic stress.

To assess development aspects, FSAPs examine the quality of the legal framework and of payments and settlements systems, as well as institutional obstacles to financial development, inclusion, and technological progress.

VI. Reducing the Likelihood of Poor Governance

Most policy decisions cannot be fully automated, outsourced, or defined by a rule and so it is important to incentivize public officials by increasing their net benefit (benefit less cost) of good governance, i.e. making policy decisions in the best public interest, and decreasing their net benefit of poor governance, in particular corruption.

How to incentivize public officials to make policy decisions in the best public interest?

- Design human resource policies—public salaries, hiring and firing practices, performance assessment, codes of ethics—to reward integrity and best effort.
- Build inclusive political institutions. The possibility of being elected into office is an incentive for good governance.
- Develop capacity. Doing the job well is easier if one knows how to do it, and has the means to do it.

How to disincentivize poor governance and corruption in particular?

- Punish and discourage it using tangible and non-tangible means. Possibilities to be fined or imprisoned are deterrents of corruption. So are concerns about reputation, or social norms about corruption's unacceptability.
- Address both demand (bribe-takers) and supply (bribe-givers) sides of corruption, and make it harder to coordinate between them. Corruption is costlier if it is harder to extract bribes, or if potential bribe-givers are less willing to pay.

---

[15] https://www.imf.org/external/np/fsap/fssa.aspx

- Make it harder to use the illicit proceeds. The benefit of corruption is effectively lower if it is costly or risky to use or "launder" its proceeds.

Key to reducing the likelihood of poor governance is monitoring and informing policy decisions. Effective law enforcement and auditing agencies are more likely to detect corruption. Actively engaged and informed public helps detect corruption too—a case of grassroots monitoring. But both the official agencies and the grassroots monitoring can only thrive if there are transparency and accountability of government operations. Transparency and accountability, as well as engagement of civil society, are also key to inform policy decisions, making them more inclusive, and so closer to optimal.

Figure 10.7 provides a summary of all these incentives. In the following sections, we will go over them one by one.

A. Encouraging Good Governance: Human Resource Policies, Political Institutions, Capacity Building

All else equal, a higher public salary increases the reward for good governance (Becker and Stigler 1974). It also attracts better talent and hence more capacity in the public sector (Klitgaard 1989). In practice, countries where public officials are paid more on average experience less corruption (Van Rijckeghem and Weder 2001; IMF 2019a).[16]

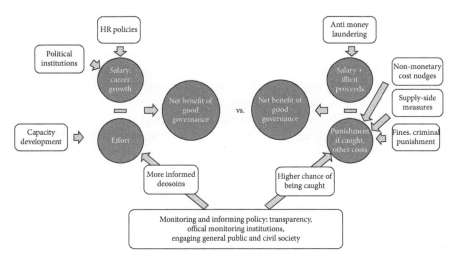

Figure 10.7 Reducing Likelihood of Poor Governance

---

[16] Also see (Di Tella and Schargrodsky 2003; van Veldhuizen 2013).

Table 10.1 Public Wage Statistics from Around the World, 2008–2016

	10th percentile	Median	90th percentile	Number of observations
Public wage bill, %GDP	4.4	7.2	11.9	179
Public employment, % total	13.8	22.8	44.3	236
Public wage premium, all employees				
Countries with low corruption	0	22.9	41.6	35
Countries with high corruption	−15.5	25.7	43.4	39
Public wage premium, employees with tertiary education				
Countries with low corruption	−0.1	8.8	28.4	17
Countries with high corruption	−60	−6.1	23.3	10

Source: Public wage statistics - Worldwide Bureaucracy Indicators (World Bank 2018); corruption - Transparency International's Corruption Perception Index (CPI) (Transparency International 2019). Countries with low corruption are those above 75th percentile by the CPI in 2008-2016 (CPI above 44). Countries with high corruption are those below the 25th percentile (CPI below 27). Public wage premium indicates by how many percent is average wage in the public sector higher than the average wage in private sector, controlling for education, age, gender, and location.

Raising public salaries is costly, though. The public wage bill is a sizeable part of government spending (Table 10.1). A major public salary raise can also affect wages in the private sector and reduce the country's competitiveness at least in the short run (Afonso and Gomes 2014). Finally, if the hiring process is not transparent, higher public salaries may invite nepotism and corruption at the hiring stage (Shah 2006). These costs should be carefully weighed against the presumed benefits.

Overall, a competitive public salary is a necessary but not sufficient condition to improve governance. In most low corruption countries public employees can earn at least as much as they would in the private sector (Table 10.1). In high corruption countries, this is not always the case, especially for employees with tertiary education. At the same time, many high corruption countries pay their public employees large premia, yet this does not seem to help (Table 10.1).[17]

Other human resource policies should complement a competitive salary:

- Open contests at the hiring stage can impede bribery and nepotism.
- Meritocratic working environment, for example clearly specified procedures for performance assessment or bonus payments that are tied to performance.

---

[17] See also (Quah 2002; IMF 2016b).

- Properly designed and implemented Codes of Conduct at government institutions set expectations as to what constitutes appropriate behavior of staff to prevent corruption and conflict of interest.[18] A well-functioning code should clearly specify within-institution ethics rules and values, definitions of corruption offenses, and rules to prevent conflict of interest (IMF 2020c).

Inclusive political institutions can also encourage good governance. Politicians tend to be less corrupt if they can run for re-election (Ferraz and Finan 2011). While the optimal design of political institutions is still an open question (Kunicova 2006), two features seem to matter the most: high degree of political competition, including low barriers to entry, and minimized electoral fraud, making it harder to misrepresent the public choice.

Even with inclusive political institutions and adequate human resource policies, good quality policy decisions may still be hard to make if the government capacity is low. Developing the capacity requires adequate physical infrastructure, high quality of general education, and continuous investments in job training for government officials. Capacity development programs at the IMF are an example of the latter.

B. Discouraging Poor Governance: Tangible and Non-tangible Cost, Supply-Side measures, Anti-Money Laundering

Decent salaries, the prospect of career growth, and capacity development may not be enough. Some public officials may still lean towards engaging in corruption, so it is important to discourage it.

All else equal, more severe punishment should discourage corruption. In most countries, prison sentences are generally a norm even for petty bribery, but whether this deters corruption depends on the quality of law enforcement.[19] Capacity constraints in law enforcement can be mitigated by the prosecution of illicit enrichment (also called unexplained wealth orders). The idea is to track public officials' wealth and criminalize the increases that cannot be explained by the income from official sources—no need to prove that the unexplained wealth is linked to a particular illegal activity (Dornbierer 2019). In Italy elements of it were in place already in the 1950s, Ireland adopted a comprehensive law in 1996, and many more countries followed in the 2000s.

---

[18] Also known as Codes of Ethics.
[19] Disciplinary liability (reprimands, warnings) are also usually applicable in milder cases. Additional measures generally include fines, confiscation of assets, temporary or permanent ban on government employment and taking part in elections (Baker McKenzie 2017).

Punishment should extend to bribe-givers—the supply side of corruption. Since both supply and demand sides carry the risk of penalty the coordination between the two becomes more complicated, effectively increasing the cost of corruption. The UN Convention Against Corruption (UNCAC), signed and ratified by 186 countries as of 2019, requires all parties to criminalize the bribery of foreign public officials as well as to cooperate on extradition of offenders and return of stolen assets. The OECD Convention on Combating Bribery of Foreign Public Officials in International Business Transactions, signed by 44 countries as of 2019, contains even stricter and more obliging requirements on the prosecution of bribery abroad (Clifford Chance 2019). Proper implementation of these agreements would effectively increase the cost of poor governance.

Political institutions are key to hinder the coordination between potential bribe-takers and bribe-givers. Many countries, for example, limit the size of political contributions, make the lobbying process more transparent, and restrict the pre/post-government employment to avoid the "revolving door" phenomenon, when former policymakers land lucrative jobs in the lobbying industry and vice versa.

Prohibitions and punishments are not the whole story though: often a motivation for public officials to abstain from corruption is its high intangible cost—a motivation to do their job well. This motivation often depends on prevailing social norms, acceptability of corruption in society, as well as a perception of what others do (Innes and Mitra 2013; Ivanyna, Mourmouras, and Rangazas 2015).

The presence of corruption's intangible costs carries at least four policy implications:

1. The same anti-corruption frameworks (salaries, punishment, and monitoring procedures) may have different results in different countries or institutions. Some countries may require tougher tangible incentives to reduce corruption, while others may rely more on existing social norms and trust.

2. Big institutional crackdowns on corruption—the creation of so-called "islands of excellence," as for example in the case of traffic police reforms in Georgia and Ukraine—can have a long-lasting effect. The crackdowns wipe out corrupt public officials and, in addition, change the culture and social norms within the institution.

3. Promoting gender equality can also disrupt the culture-of-corruption environment, as experimental and survey-based studies show that women tend to be less willing to engage in bribery, and gender equality within households promotes social trust (Stensöta and Wängnerud 2018).

4. Social and educational initiatives promoting integrity increase the intangible cost of and hence discourage illicit behavior. The initiatives include social advertisement, implementing codes of conduct for public employees, as well as senior public officials leading by example.

Preventing Criminals from Benefiting from the Proceeds of Corruption:
Anti-Money Laundering Frameworks

A further way to disincentivize corruption is to make it more difficult for criminals to benefit from the proceeds of their criminal behavior. Criminals typically
launder their illicit income so that it appears to come from legitimate sources. In
order to prevent this, countries should put into place an effective anti-money
laundering (AML) framework.

The Financial Action Task Force (FATF) is the inter-governmental body
responsible for developing the policies for combating money laundering, terrorist
financing, and proliferation financing. The FATF has developed 40 recommendations covering a range of measures that countries should adopt with respect to
AML/CFT frameworks—referred to as the AML/CFT international standard.

The FATF recommendations encompass both preventive as well as enforcement measures. On the preventive side, financial institutions and other businesses
(e.g. lawyers, real estate agents, accountants) are required to "know their customer." This includes identifying customers, verifying the beneficial owners of
legal entities, and due diligence measures on politically exposed persons (PEPs).[20]
Financial institutions and others should also report transactions, where there is
suspicion of illegal activity related to corruption. On the enforcement front,
money laundering and corruption activities should be properly investigated;
offenders prosecuted and subject to effective, proportionate, and dissuasive sanctions; and proceeds of corruption confiscated. Where necessary, countries should
cooperate internationally: deliver appropriate information, financial intelligence,
and evidence, and facilitates action against criminals and their assets.

VII. Monitoring and Informing the Policy

Creating incentives for good governance is futile if there is no effective monitoring framework in place. It starts with effective official anti-corruption and audit
institutions. They can investigate and prosecute corruption, thus raising its cost,
and they can introduce measures to prevent corruption, such as defining national
anti-corruption strategies and supporting integrity practices at government
institutions.

But official institutions alone are not enough; engagement of civil society, or
so-called grassroots monitoring, is also critical. Civil society can provide useful

---

[20] PEPs are individuals who are or have been entrusted with prominent public functions either
domestically or by a foreign country, for example Heads of State or of government, senior politicians,
senior government, judicial or military officials, senior executives of state-owned corporations,
important political party officials. PEPs also include persons who are or have been entrusted with a
prominent function by an international organization.

signals to official anti-corruption institutions, and boost the political cost of corruption, even if formal investigations are delayed or blocked.

Civil society also informs policy decisions. Active public and NGOs are often in contact with public officials regarding their concerns and ways to solve them. Independent institutes and councils, as well as international organizations, scrutinize government policies and provide their recommendations. These inputs enhance the government's capacity and make sure the decision-making process, and its results, are truly inclusive (OECD 2016).

Underpinning the ability to monitor and inform policy are transparency and accountability of government operations.

A. Transparency and Accountability

"Without transparency corruption is inevitable" (Collier 2010). So are policy errors, even if public officials have no special interests. Shedding light on government operations is key to monitoring, both by official institutions and civil society. It is also critical to informing the policy.

The key policy measure to boost transparency is to open data. Opening data is about making it both available and usable. This means data must be clearly defined, reliable, comprehensive, and easy to compare over time and across units (firms, households, local governments, countries). It should also be easy to use—downloadable and stored in a machine-readable format and feature a simple and convenient user interface with flexible search and low barriers (registration or payment) to access.

The crucial step towards opening data is complying with data dissemination standards, which are routinely set, maintained, and updated by various international organizations. UN's System of National Accounts sets the standards on measuring basic macroeconomic aggregates (economic output, prices, etc.) at the country level (UN 2009). The IMF's and World Bank's standards and codes elaborate further on government finance, financial statistics, transparency in fiscal and monetary and financial policy among others (IMF 2017b).[21] The International Labour Organization sets standards on labor market indicators (ILO 2018).

IMF's Fiscal Transparency Code (FTC) focuses directly on the public sector, which makes it one of the most important standards for improving governance (IMF 2012). For example, one of its guidelines for advanced transparency is to cover the fiscal operations of the central government, but also local governments and state-owned enterprises. This means shedding light in areas where misuse of public funds is usually more common (Baum et al. 2019).

---

[21] Also see IMF's Factsheet on Good Governance—https://www.imf.org/en/About/Factsheets/The-IMF-and-Good-Governance

Another important set of transparency standards are those covering the natural resource sector. With its often above-normal profits and large government revenues, the risk of corruption is high if transparency is not adequately addressed. Resource revenue management is one of the main pillars of the IMF's FTC; it is also the focus of the Extractive Industry Transparency Initiative (EITI). As of 2019, 51 countries joined the EITI, though only seven achieved EITI-validated satisfactory progress on the standard as of 2019 (EITI 2019). Among other things, the standard requires countries to disclose all contracts and licenses at a project level, beneficial ownership of all private developers who receive a license, and all government resource revenues.

Transparency and accountability of the central bank's actions are key to the effectiveness of the monetary policy.[22] IMF's Central Bank Transparency Code (IMF 2020f) is a comprehensive, central bank-focused set of principles and practices encompassing transparency in:

- Governance: legal structure, mandate, autonomy, decision-making arrangements.
- Policies: policy frameworks, policy decisions, supporting analyses.
- Operations: instruments, coverage, access.
- Outcomes: reports on governance actions, policies, operations.
- Official relations: with government, other agencies, and internationally.

Monitoring corruption can be enhanced by maintaining and opening land and company registers. First, if data is open, real estate and business ownership become harder to manipulate. Second, proceeds from corruption and tax evasion are usually invested in real estate or businesses. So, opening land and company registers makes illicit enrichment more visible. However, it is only recently and only a handful of countries, notably the UK, started to publish information on beneficial ownership—a necessary piece needed to identify real asset owners behind no-name shell companies (Open Government Partnership 2019).

Asset declarations by public officials represent another critical information to track illicit enrichment and prevent potential conflict of interests. Changes in declared wealth can be compared to public officials' income, and then cross-checked with land and company registers. Even if illicit enrichment is not considered a crime, it can still have political cost if asset declarations are open to the public. Besides, public officials can also be criminally liable for non-declaring or declaring false information. Open asset declarations can also expose conflicts of interest in areas like state contracts, licenses, or procurement—when public officials arrange favorable conditions for the companies they own (Rossi, Pop, and Berger 2017).

---

[22] For example, public's trust is necessary to anchor the inflation expectations.

The benefits of transparency can be enhanced by international cooperation, which includes:

- Shared data that enables governments to make policy decisions based on international experience, which is why complying with the international data dissemination standards is so important.
- Exchange of information on tax payments, beneficial ownership that helps with monitoring corruption.
- Sharing data between custom offices, which helps detect trade fraud.

Transparency is crucial, but it involves trade-offs. First, collecting and maintaining data can be costly. Complying with international data dissemination standards requires extensive capacity building and full-time staff working on it. Reporting beneficial ownership down to the smallest owner can be quite expensive too. And millions of public officials have to submit their asset declarations, in many cases as often as once per year (Rossi, Pop, and Berger 2017). Second, transparency may conflict with privacy and, sometimes, safety. For example, the information from open land or company registers, or asset declarations, could be potentially used by organized crime groups for extortion or identity theft.

Ultimately, the balance between privacy, transparency, and its cost depends on each country's circumstances. The case for transparency is stronger for countries with lower governance quality and in areas where corruption risks are higher. For example, in the case of disclosing beneficial owners, the priority is likely higher for license-wining companies in the natural resource sector, or for companies that win state procurement contracts. As for the balance between privacy and transparency, for instance, the UK and Denmark publish in their beneficial ownership registers only what's necessary for a meaningful public investigation and exempting those with legitimate safety concerns.[23] The UK publishes only owners' names, months, and year of birth—not enough to identify a person exactly, but enough to "flag" a suspicious case and hand it down to official law enforcement (Open Ownership 2019).

The effectiveness of transparency can be greatly enhanced, and its cost reduced, if governments harness and embrace IT advances. Not only policy decisions themselves can be automated, as discussed above in this chapter, but also monitoring and informing policymaking can be made more effective. Examples abound:

- Big data is now widely used to do short-term projections of key macroeconomic indicators—GDP, trade, inflation, etc. (Buono et al. 2018).

---

[23] In the UK, six months after the opening of company register, over one million companies provided beneficial ownership information, and only 270 individuals applied for an exemption. Of these only five were granted it (Open Ownership 2019).

- Satellite imaging offers new ways to measure economic activity, inequality, land use, air pollution, etc. at a high-resolution level (Donaldson and Storeygard 2016). These measures are then used as key inputs for various policies.
- In Boston, USA, Yelp restaurant reviews have been used to identify potential food safety violations, thereby increasing the efficiency of restaurant inspections (e.g., number of violations per inspection) by 25 percent since 2017 (DrivenData Labs 2020).[24]
- In Estonia and France, machine-learning algorithms analyze tax payments to identify potential evasion (IMF 2018b).
- Romania's PREVENT system automatically cross-checks procurement contracts with asset declarations by public officials to flag potential conflicts of interest (Dragos and Neamtu 2018).
- Instagram photos of public officials' luxurious lifestyles are being used in investigations of illicit enrichment (Kreamer 2019).[25]

B. Official Anti-Corruption Institutions

A key element of anti-corruption efforts is the establishment or designation of specialized anti-corruption agencies.[26] One of the main functions of anti-corruption agencies is preventive, which includes anti-corruption policy development, monitoring, and coordination, prevention of conflicts of interests, raising public awareness. Another key function is law enforcement—investigation and prosecution of corruption and related offenses.

Anti-corruption agencies can be represented by a separate specialized institution (e.g. Independent Commission against Corruption in Hong Kong) or be a part of a broader body (e.g. public prosecutors in Germany). The case to establish a separate and independent specialized anti-corruption agency is stronger in countries where corruption is pervasive, potentially extending to law enforcement, and trust in the existing institutions is low. Such an agency could focus exclusively on high-level corruption, which is particularly damaging to inclusive and sustainable growth.

An effective anti-corruption agency requires:

---

[24] Yelp is a popular US website to share user reviews of various businesses.

[25] Instagram is a popular US website to share user photos.

[26] Establishment of specialized anti-corruption agencies is featured in United Nations Convention Against Corruption (Articles 6 and 36), Council of Europe's Criminal Law Convention on Corruption (Article 20), Inter-American Convention against Corruption (Article III), African Union Convention on Preventing and Combatting Corruption (Articles 4 and 20). Colombo Commentary on the Jakarta Statement on principles for Anti-Corruption Agencies, Vienna, 2020.

- A transparent process for the selection of the agency's leadership, which would enhance public trust in anti-corruption institutions. The leadership should enjoy the security of tenure and their removal should be based on a limited set of criteria in a clearly defined procedure.
- Strong internal controls and accountability, as well as periodic reporting of the agency's activities.
- Independence, including sufficient resources and budgetary autonomy, authority over the selection, promotion, and dismissal of personnel, operational autonomy. The agency should also have a clear mandate and powers, including unobstructed and timely access to various state databases, the ability to request and share information with other agencies, and a wide range of investigative tools.

The judiciary plays a crucial role in the anti-corruption criminal justice system and is necessary to ensure that anti-corruption investigations lead to convictions. Considering the complexity of high-level corruption cases, judges should have the necessary skills and expertise that are required to understand, for example, financial analysis, opaque corporate structures, and evidence received from abroad. Therefore, countries could consider establishing a specialized anti-corruption judiciary, either as specialized chambers in existing courts or as separate courts.

An important role in the detection, investigation, and confiscation of corruption proceeds belongs to the Financial Intelligence Units (FIUs)—national agencies in charge of collection and analysis of suspicious transaction reports from the financial institutions and other businesses. FIUs disseminate the results to law enforcement agencies that can use it to initiate or support ongoing corruption investigations.

As corruption and laundering of its proceeds in many cases expand across country borders, countries should adopt legislative measures to allow for effective international cooperation of anti-corruption institutions. This cooperation should include mutual legal assistance in investigations, prosecutions, and adjudication, extradition, information exchanges between law enforcement, and international cooperation in confiscation. Overall, confiscation of proceeds of corruption, including recovery of assets hidden abroad, is one of the key policy goals of anti-corruption efforts aimed at reducing the potential benefits of corruption.

C. Engaging Civil Society

An inclusive decision-making process is critical to improving governance for inclusive growth. Policy decisions are informed by the feedback from the active public and independent councils, as well as by international experience. Official anti-corruption institutions are more effective with the input from investigative journalists or whistleblowers.

Engagement of civil society is more likely if it is easy and safe to self-organize, monitor, and communicate with public officials, and when these efforts find feedback in policy decision making. Key policy recommendations in this space include:

Create and use official channels of communication. Two-sided communication of government and the public is essential to good governance. Governments need to know public preferences and concerns to prioritize their policies. In turn, policy reforms can only be successful and sustainable if they are understood and accepted by the public. The channels of communication include official meetings with voters, press conferences, collaboration with mass media, and possibilities to submit official requests to government agencies, household and business surveys to gauge public opinion, and ensuring the right for peaceful assembly (e.g. protest) and petition.

Go beyond the traditional channels of communication. An example is participatory budgeting in local governments, with direct public oversight over discretionary public spending—in the form of public hearings, discussions, and up to direct vote by elected representatives of civil society (Shah 2007). Another example is direct civil society participation in the design of politically sensitive reforms or appointments to key non-elected government positions. In 1996, Namibia's National Deregulation Task Force, comprised of various stakeholders across the economy, formulated the key principles of the energy subsidy reform, then implemented by the government and contributed to the reform's sustainability (IMF 2013).

Harness progress in IT to make government-public communications less expensive and more efficient. Examples include national government web-portals; electronic contact forms; platforms to report bribery and other transgressions (e.g. Indian web-platform "I Paid A Bribe"); platforms for e-participatory budgeting (e.g. D-Brain in South Korea); platforms to submit and sign petitions; communication through social networks.

Inform citizens about the government's functions and responsibilities. Freedom and availability of mass media are associated with lower corruption and better governance (Strömberg 2015). For example, the gap between budgeted and actual spending in Uganda's local school grant program fell significantly (and student enrollment increased) after the government introduced a newspaper campaign informing parents and teachers about the funding their schools were supposed to get (Reinikka and Svensson 2011).

Bring governments closer via properly designed decentralization, i.e. giving more political, financial, and administrative power to local governments (Boadway and Shah 2009). Decentralization makes governments more accountable, government-public communication more direct, and requires less coordination effort for civil activity. Properly designed decentralization—that is, when local public officials are elected and have significant autonomy both to spend and collect taxes—is indeed associated with less corruption (Ivanyna and Shah 2011; Fisman and Gatti 2002).

Make civil participation safe. This includes proper investigation of crimes against investigative journalists, who cover politics and corruption: 426 murder cases have been confirmed between 2009 and 2019 (Committee to Protect Journalists 2020). This also includes encouraging and not restricting the activity of anti-corruption civil society organizations, the latter being an unfortunate global trend after 2009 (Freedom House 2019; Transparency International 2018).

Protect whistleblowers—those who expose poor governance from within their institutions. Protection includes measures like introducing channels for the disclosure (for example, a hotline), guarantee of confidentiality or anonymity, and penalties for potential retaliation.

Cooperate with independent councils and institutes. For example, as of 2016, 39 countries operated independent fiscal councils (Beetsma et al. 2018). The main objective of these is to oversee fiscal policy: whether government conforms with fiscal rules, whether the underlying government's forecasts are realistic, etc. Adding independent experts to state-owned enterprise boards is also a good corporate governance practice (IMF 2020b).

Seek help from the international community. The IMF, for example, monitors economic developments of its member countries and provides their authorities with recommendations on key macroeconomic and structural policies—the so-called Article IV consultations (IMF 2020e). Similarly, other international organizations, as well as academic and research institutions, provide their advice to governments. The policy advice menu includes the governance reform itself, as in, for example, Transparency International's National Integrity System Assessment (Transparency International 2012) or IMF's Governance Diagnostics (IMF 2017a, 2020).

Examples of IMF's Governance Policy Advice in Selected Countries

IMF's policy advice on governance is an integral part of the design of its programs and communication with country authorities (IMF 2020c).

In Mexico's 2019 Article IV report, the government policy advice included:

- On fiscal governance: centralizing and digitizing public procurement processes.
- On anti-corruption measures: appointing constitutionally mandated anti-corruption judges and prosecutors, implementing asset declarations.
- On AML/CFT: improving the effectiveness of AML/CFT authorities (e.g., through interagency performance agreements) and enhancing the transparency of beneficial ownership.

- On rule of law: training and protecting staff of judicial institutions and law enforcement.
- On financial sector oversight: enhancing definitions of "related party" and increasing the operational independence and budget autonomy of financial-sector supervisors.

In the Sri Lanka's 2016 program and subsequent reviews, the mutually agreed upon governance reform plan included:

- On fiscal governance: recording the fiscal cost of non-commercial obligations (including subsidies) for SOEs in the central government budget; compiling fiscal statistics in accordance with the 2014 Government Finance Statistics Manual (GFSM).
- On anti-corruption measures: approving the National Action Plan for Combating Bribery and Corruption, which envisages (i) prevention measures; (ii) value-based education and community engagement; (iii) institutional strengthening of Sri Lanka's anti-corruption commission and other law enforcement agencies; and (iv) law and policy reforms to strengthen anti-corruption efforts and compliance with international obligations.
- On central bank governance: establishing a sound legal and institutional infrastructure for the implementation of flexible inflation targeting and strengthening the central bank's governance, accountability, and transparency frameworks.

Other examples are discussed in detail in (IMF 2020c).

VIII. Conclusion

Quality of governance defines the government's ability to promote inclusive growth. In countries where governance quality is particularly low—corruption is rampant and the state is captured—governments may turn from a solution into a problem, creating a vicious cycle of increasing inequality, worsening institutions, and lack of inclusive growth. But governance is not just a fashionable term. Neither it is a destiny that cannot be changed. Behind it are thousands of public officials making hundreds of policy decisions every day. It is their capacity and their willingness to rightly make these decisions that underpins governance. The recipe to improve governance is therefore to boost human and institutional capacity and strengthen the incentives for public officials to act in the best public interest. This chapter looks at the policy mix behind this advice. It covers the most important pieces of the puzzle: structural reforms, policy rules, and procedures, human resource policies, transparency and accountability, monitoring and punishment of corruption, engaging civil society. It presents policy options in each area, their rationale, costs, and benefits. By no means is it exhaustive of details of all policies, but it hopefully enables readers to see the big picture, identify main policy gaps and priorities in their countries and communities, and find additional references to elaborate on the issues of interest. Improving governance is not easy, but it is certainly possible.

References

Abed, George T. and Sanjeev Gupta. 2002. *Governance, Corruption, and Economic Performance*. Washington DC: IMF.

Acemoglu, Daron, and James A. Robinson. 2012. *Why Nations Fail: The Origins of Power, Prosperity, and Poverty*. New York: Crown.

Afonso, Antonio, and Pedro Gomes. 2014. "Interactions Between Private and Public Sector Wages." *Journal of Macroeconomics* 39(A): 97–112.

Allen, Richard, Richard Hemming, and Barry H. Potter. 2013. *The International Handbook of Public Financial Management*. London: Palgrave Macmillan.

Allingham, Michael G., and Agnar Sandmo. 1972. "Income Tax Evasion: A Theoretical Analysis." *Journal of Public Economics* 1: 323–38.

Baker McKenzie. 2017. *Global Overview of Anti-Corruption Laws*. Accessed December 12, 2019. https://globalcompliancenews.com/anti-corruption/anti-corruption-laws-around-the-world/.

Banerjee, Adhijit V., and Esther Duflo. 2011. *Poor Economics: A Radical Rethinking of the Way to Fight Global Poverty*. New York: Public Affairs.

Barberá, Marcel Gascón. 2019. "Romania Convicts 13 People over Deadly Nightclub Fire." *BalkanInsight*. December 16. Accessed September 30, 2020. https://balkaninsight.com/2019/12/16/romanian-convicts-13-people-over-deadly-nightclub-fire/.

Barro, Robert J., and David B. Gordon. 1983. "A Positive Theory of Monetary Policy in a Natural Rate Model." *Journal of Political Economy* 91(4): 589–610.

Basu, Kaushik, and Tito Cordella. 2018. *Institutions, Governance and the Control of Corruption*. Cham: Palgrave Macmillan.

Baum, Anja, Clay Hackney, Paulo Medas, and Sy Mouhamadou. 2019. "Governance and State-Owned Enterprises: How Costly is Corruption?" IMF Working Paper 19/253.

Becker, Gary. 1968. "Crime and Punishment: An Economic Analysis." *Journal of Political Economy* 78: 169–217.

Becker, Gary S., and George J. Stigler. 1974. "Law Enforcement, Malfeasance and Compensation of Enforcers." *Journal of Legal Studies* 3(1): 1–18.

Beetsma, Roel, Xavier Debrun, Xiangming Fang, Young Kim, Victor Lledó, Samba Mbaye, et al. 2018. "Independent Fiscal Councils: Recent Trends and Performance." IMF Working Paper 18/68.

Besley, Timothy. 2015. "Law, Regulation, and the Business Climate: The Nature and Influence of the World Bank Doing Business Project." *Journal of Economic Perspectives* 29(3): 99–120.

Boadway, Robin, and Anwar Shah. 2009. *Fiscal Federalism: Principles and Practice of Multi-order Governance.* New York: Cambridge University Press.

Bossu, Wouter, and Arthur D.P. Rossi. 2019. "The Role of Board Oversight in Central Bank Governance: Key Legal Design Issues." IMF Working Paper 19/293.

Buono, Dario, George Kapetanios, Massimiliano Marcellino, Gianluigi Mazzi, and Fotis Papailias. 2018. "Big Data Econometrics: Now Casting and Early Estimates." BAFFI CAREFIN Centre Research Paper No. 2018–82.

Cangiano, Marco, Teresa Curristine, and Michel Lazare. 2013. *Public Financial Management and Its Emerging Architecture.* Washington, DC: IMF.

Clifford Chance. 2019. *An International Guide to Anti-Corruption Legislation.* Accessed December 13, 2019. doi:https://www.cliffordchance.com/content/dam/clifford-chance/hub/Risk/An_international_guide_to_anti_corruption_legislation.pdf.

Collier, Paul. 2010. *Plundered Planet: How to Reconcile Nature with Prosperity.* Oxford: Oxford University Press.

Committee to Protect Journalists. 2020. Accessed January 14, 2020. https://cpj.org/.

Di Tella, Rafael, and Ernesto Schargrodsky. 2003. "The Role of Wages and Auditing during a Crackdown on Corruption in the City of Buenos Aires." *The Journal of Law and Economics* 46(1): 269–92.

Dixit, Avinash. 2018. "Anti-corruption Institutions: Some History and Theory." In *Institutions, Governance and the Control of Corruption*, edited by Kaushik Basu and Tito Cordella, pp. 15–49. Cham: Palgrave Macmillan.

Djankov, Simeon, Rafael La Porta, Florencio Lopes-de-Silanes, and Andrei Shleifer. 2002. "The Regulation of Entry." *Quarterly Journal of Economics* 117(1): 1–37.

Donaldson, Dave, and Adam Storeygard. 2016. "The View from Above: Applications of Satellite Data in Economics." *Journal of Economic Perspectives* 30(4): 171–98.

Dornbierer, Andrew. 2019. "Quick Guide to Illicit Enrichment." *Basel Institute on Governance.* Accessed December 14, 2019. https://www.baselgovernance.org/blog/andrew-dornbierers-quick-guide-illicit-enrichment.

Dragos, Dacian, and Bogdana Neamtu. 2018. "Transposition of EU Procurement Directives in Romania: Complex Issues of Implementation and Control." In *Modernizing Public Procurement: The Approach of EU Member States*, edited by Steen Treumer and Mario Comba, pp. 173–200. Cheltenham: Edward Elgar.

DrivenData Labs. 2020. "Using Yelp Reviews to Flag Restaurant Health Risks." *DrivenData Labs.* Accessed January 4, 2020. http://drivendata.co/case-studies/using-yelp-reviews-to-flag-restaurant-health-risks/.

European Bank for Reconstruction and Development (EBRD). 2019. "Transition Report 2019–20 Better Governance, Better Economies." EBRD report.

Extractive Industry Transparency Initiative (EITI). 2019. *Extractive Industry Transparency Initiative: Who We Are.* Accessed December 30, 2019. https://eiti.org/who-we-are.

Eyraud, Luc, Xavier Debrun, Andrew Hodge, Viktor Duarte Lledo, and Catherine A. Pattillo. 2018. *Second-Generation Fiscal Rules: Balancing Simplicity, Flexibility, and Enforceability.* Staff Discussion Note No. 18/04, IMF.

Ferraz, Claudio, and Frederico Finan. 2011. "Electoral Accountability and Corruption: Evidence from the Audits of Local Governments." *American Economic Review* 101(4): 1274–311.

Fisman, Raymond, and Roberta Gatti. 2002. "Decentralization and Corruption: Evidence Across Countries." *Journal of Public Economics* 83(3): 325–45.

Freedom House. 2019. "Freedom in the World." Report by Freedom House

Fukuyama, Francis. 2018. "Corruption as a Political Phenomenon." In *Institutions, Governance and the Control of Corruption*, edited by Kaushik Basu and Tito Cordella, pp. 51–73. Cham: Palgrave Macmillan.

Gupta, Sanjeev, Hamid Davoodi, and Rosa Alonso-Terme. 1998. *Does Corruption Affect Income Inequality and Poverty?* Working Paper WP/98/76, IMF.

Hellman, Joel, and Daniel Kaufmann. 2001. "Confronting the Challenge of State Capture in Transition Economies." Finance & Development 38(3).

International Labour Organization (ILO). 2018. *Decent Work and the Sustainable Development Goals: A Guidebook on SDG Labour Market Indicators.* Geneva.

International Monetary Fund (IMF). 1998. "Does Corruption Affect Income Inequality and Poverty?" IMF Working Paper 98/76.

International Monetary Fund (IMF). 2012. "Fiscal Transparency, Accountability, and Risk." IMF Board Paper.

International Monetary Fund (IMF). 2013. *Energy Subsidy Reform in Sub-Saharan Africa: Experiences and Lessons.* Washington, DC.

International Monetary Fund (IMF). 2015. *Evolving Monetary Policy Frameworks in Low-Income and Other Developing Countries.* IMF Staff Report.

International Monetary Fund (IMF). 2016a. "Corruption Costs and Mitigating Strategies." IMF Staff Discussion Note 16/05

International Monetary Fund (IMF). 2016b. "Managing Government Compensation and Employment—Institutions, Policies, and Reform Challenges." IMF Policy Paper.

International Monetary Fund (IMF). 2017a. The Role of the Fund in Governance Issues—Review of the Guidance Note—Preliminary Considerations. IMF Policy Paper.

International Monetary Fund (IMF). 2017b. "Joint Review of the Standards and Codes Initiative." IMF Policy Paper.

International Monetary Fund (IMF). 2018a. Review of 1997 Guidance Note on Governance—A Proposed Framework for Enhanced Fund Engagement. IMF Policy Paper.

International Monetary Fund (IMF). 2018b. "Fiscal Monitor, April 2019." IMF Report, Chapter 2.

International Monetary Fund (IMF). 2019a. "Fiscal Monitor, April 2019." IMF Report, Chapter 2.

International Monetary Fund (IMF). 2019b. "Public Investment Management Assessment: Strengthening Infrastructure Governance." FAD note

International Monetary Fund (IMF). 2020a. *Corruption and Covid-19*. July 28. https://blogs.imf.org/2020/07/28/corruption-and-covid-19/.

International Monetary Fund (IMF). 2020b. "Fiscal Monitor, April 2020." IMF Report, Chapter 3.

International Monetary Fund (IMF). 2020c. "Progress in Implementing the Framework for Enhanced Fund Engagement on Governance." Policy Paper.

International Monetary Fund (IMF). 2020d. "Protecting IMF Resources—Safeguards Assessments of Central Banks." Accessed January 16, 2020. https://www.imf.org/en/About/Factsheets/Sheets/2016/08/02/21/43/Protecting-IMF-Resources-Safeguards.

International Monetary Fund (IMF). 2020e. "Surveillance." Accessed January 15, 2020. https://www.imf.org/external/about/econsurv.htm.

International Monetary Fund (IMF). 2020f. "The Central Bank Transparency Code." IMF Policy Paper.

Innes, Robert, and Arnab Mitra. 2013. "Is Dishonesty Contagious?" *Economic Inquiry* 51(1): 722–34.

Ivanyna, Maksym, Alexandros Mourmouras, and Peter Rangazas. 2015. "The Culture of Corruption, Tax Evasion, and Economic Growth." *Economic Inquiry* 54(1): 520–42.

Ivanyna, Maksym, Alexandros Mourmouras, and Peter Rangazas. 2018. *Macroeconomics of Corruption*. New York: Springer.

Ivanyna, Maksym, and Andrea Salerno. 2021. "Governance." IMF Working Paper.

Ivanyna, Maksym, and Anwar Shah. 2011. "Decentralization and Corruption: New Cross-Country Evidence." *Environment and Planning C: Politics and Space* 29(2): 344–62.

Kabwe, George M., Elie Chamoun, Riaan van Greuning, Mowele Mohlala, and Julia Cardoso. 2019. "Safeguards Assessment—2019 Update." IMF Policy Paper 19/041.

Khan, Ashraf. 2018. *A Behavioral Approach to Financial Supervision, Regulation, and Central Banking*. IMF Working Paper 18/178.

Kitroeff, Nathalie, and Mitra Taj. 2020. "Latin America's virus villains: Corrupt officials collude with price gougers for body bags and flimsy masks." *The New York Times*, June 20.

Klitgaard, Robert. 1989. "Incentive Myopia." *World Development* 17(4): 447–59.

Kreamer, Justin. 2019. "Real-World Social Media Investigations: Omar and Jenny Ambuila." *Hanzo*. Accessed January 4, 2020. https://www.hanzo.co/blog/real-world-social-media-investigations-omar-and-jenny-ambuila.

Krueger, Anne O. 1974. The Political Economy of the Rent-Seeking Society. *The American Economic Review* 64(3): 291–303.

Kunicova, Jana. 2006. "Democratic Institutions and Corruption: Incentives and Constraints in Politics." In *International Handbook on Economics of Corruption*, edited by Susan Rose-Ackerman, pp. 140–60. Cheltenham: Edward Elgar.

New York Times, The. 2020. *Latin America's virus villains: Corrupt officials collude with price gougers for body bags and flimsy masks*. Newspaper article.

North, Douglass, Daron Acemoglu, Francis Fukuyama, and Dani Rodrik. 2008. *Governance, Growth, and Development Decision-Making*. Working paper, World Bank.

North, Douglass. 1991. "Institutions." *Journal of Economic Perspectives* 5(1): 97–112.

Organisation for Economic Co-operation and Development (OECD). 2016. *The Governance of Inclusive Growth*. OECD Report.

Olken, Benjamin A., and Rohini Pande. 2012. "Corruption in Developing Countries." *Annual Review of Economics* 4: 479–509.

Ong, Li, ed. 2014. *A Guide to IMF Stress Testing: Methods and Models*. Washington, DC: IMF.

Open Government Partnership. 2019. "Beneficial Ownership." https://www.open-govpartnership.org/wp-content/uploads/2019/05/Global-Report_Beneficial-Ownership.pdf.

Open Ownership. 2019. "Data Protection and Privacy in Beneficial Ownership Disclosure." https://www.openownership.org/uploads/oo-data-protection-and-privacy.pdf.

Ostry, Jonathan D., Alessandro Prati, and Antonio Spilimbergo. 2009. *Structural Reforms and Economic Performance in Advanced and Developing Countries*. Occasional Paper No. 268, IMF.

Pimenta, Carlos, and Mario Pessoa. 2015. *Public Financial Management in Latin America: The Key to Efficiency and Transparency*. Washington, DC: IADB.

PwC. 2013. "Identifying and Reducing Corruption in Public Procurement in the EU."

Quah, Jon S.T. 2002. "Combating Corruption in Singapore: What Can Be Learned?" *Journal of Contingencies and Crisis Management* 9(1): 29–35.

Reinikka, Ritva, and Jacob Svensson. 2011. "The Power of Information in Public Services: Evidence from Education in Uganda." *Journal of Public Economics* 95(7–8): 956–66.

Rose-Ackerman, Susan, and Bonnie J. Palifka. 2016. *Corruption and Government*. Cambridge: Cambridge University Press.

Rossi, Ivana M., Laura Pop, and Tammar Berger. 2017. *Getting the Full Picture on Public Officials: A How-To Guide for Effective Financial Disclosure*. Washington, DC: World Bank.

Rowley, Charles K., Robert D. Tollison, and Gordon Tullok. 1978. *The Political Economy of Rent-Seeking*. Boston: Springer.

Schleifer, Andrei, and Robert W. Vishny. 1993. "Corruption." *Quarterly Journal of Economics* 108(3): 599–617.

Schwartz, Gerd, Manal Fouad, Torben S. Hansen, and Genevieve Verdier. 2020. *Well Spent: How Strong Infrastructure Governance Can End Waste in Public Investment*. Washington, DC: IMF.

Shah, Anwar. 2006. *Corruption and Decentralized Public Governance.* Policy Research Working Paper, World Bank.

Shah, Anwar, ed. 2007. *Participatory Budgeting.* Washington, DC: World Bank.

Stensöta, Helena, and Lena Wängnerud. 2018. *Gender and Corruption: Historical Roots and New Avenues for Research.* New York: Palgrave Macmillan.

Strömberg, David. 2015. "Media Coverage and Political Accountability: Theory and Evidence." In *Handbook of Media Economics*, edited by Simon P. Anderson, Joel Waldfogel, and David Strömberg, pp. 595–622. Amsterdam: North-Holland.

't Hoen, Ellen F. M., Hans V. Hogerzeil, Jonathan D. Quick, and Hiiti B. Sillo. 2014. "A Quiet Revolution in Global Public Health: The World Health Organization's Prequalification of Medicines Programme." *Journal of Public Health Policy,* January 2014, pp. 1–25.

Tanzi, Vito. 1998. *Fundamental Determinants of Inequality and the Role of Government.* IMF Working Paper 98/178.

Transparency International. 2012. "National Integrity System Assessment Toolkit." Report

Transparency International. 2017. "Global Corruption Barometer." Report

Transparency International. 2018. "Europe and Central Asia: More Civil Engagement Needed." February 21. Accessed January 14, 2020. https://www.transparency.org/news/feature/europe_and_central_asia_more_civil_engagement.

Transparency International. 2019. "Corruption Perception Index 2018." Accessed November 25, 2019. https://www.transparency.org/cpi2018.

Ugur, Mehmet. 2014. "Corruption's Direct Effect on Per-Capita Income Growth: A Meta-Analysis." *Journal of Economic Surveys* 28(3): 472–90.

United Nations (UN). 2009. "System of National Accounts 2008." New York.

United Nations (UN). 2018. *E-Government Survey: Gearing E-Government to Support Transformation Towards Sustainable and Resilient Societies.* New York: United Nations.

United Nations (UN). 2019. *CICIG (International Commission against Impunity in Guatemala).* online article, United Nations. Accessed November 7, 2019. https://www.un.org/undpa/es/node/183334.

United Nations Development Programme (UNDP). 2019. *Procurement Support Services to the Ministry of Health of Ukraine.* online article, United Nations Development Program Ukraine. Accessed November 7, 2019. https://www.ua.undp.org/content/ukraine/en/home/projects/procurement-support-services-to-the-MOH.html.

Van Rijckeghem, Caroline, and Beatrice Weder. 2001. "Bureaucratic Corruption and the Rate of Temptation: Do Wages in the Civil Service Affect Corruption, and By How Much?" *Journal of Development Economics* 65(2): 307–31.

van Veldhuizen, Roel. 2013. "The Influence of Wages on Public Officials' Corruptibility: A Laboratory Investigation." *Journal of Economic Psychology* 39: 341–56.

World Health Organization (WHO). 2019. *Accelerated Registration of Prequalified FPPs.* online article. Accessed November 7, 2019. https://extranet.who.int/prequal/content/collaborative-registration-faster-registration.

World Bank. 2011. *Risk-Based Tax Audits: Approaches and Country Experiences.* Edited by Munawer S. Khwaja, Rajul Awasthi and Jan Loeprick. Washington, DC.

World Bank. 2012. *Fighting Corruption in Public Services: Chronicling Georgia's Reforms.* Washington, DC.

World Bank. 2017. "World Development Report." Report by World Bank.

World Bank. 2018. *Worldwide Bureaucracy Indicators.* Accessed November 25, 2019. https://www.worldbank.org/en/topic/governance/brief/size-of-the-public-sector-government-wage-bill-and-employment

11

Macroeconomic Stability, Adjustment, and Debt

Hamid R. Davoodi, Peter Montiel, and Anna Ter-Martirosyan

I. Introduction

Macroeconomic volatility has considerable impacts on growth and inclusiveness.[1] The absence of inclusiveness, in turn, can both be a source of macroeconomic volatility and amplify the macroeconomic effects of shocks. Evidence suggests, for example, that there is a positive relationship between macroeconomic volatility and inequality. The conventional wisdom prevailing before the Global Financial Crisis (GFC) of 2008–2009 considered macroeconomic volatility, driven primarily by productivity shocks, as an important driver of inequality (Krusell and Smith 1998; Quadrini and Rios-Rull 2015). However, causation can also run in the opposite direction; namely, high and rising inequality or lack of inclusiveness could be the cause of macroeconomic volatility and economic crises (Kumhof, Ranciere, and Winant 2015; Mian and Sufi 2018).

Not surprisingly, a new literature in macroeconomics has emerged since the GFC that tackles these complex interactions in novel ways. This literature goes beyond the traditional representative agent models of macroeconomics by explicitly incorporating income and wealth heterogeneity among households. It shows analytically that macroeconomic aggregates and national well-being depend on income and wealth distribution in non-trivial ways. These new models often deliver strikingly different implications for macroeconomic policies and economic fluctuations and, conversely, allow a serious study of the distributional implications of macro policies (Yellen 2016; Ahn et al 2018).

In a similar vein, and from a policy point of view, distributional and inclusive growth implications of macroeconomic policies have been incorporated increasingly in the design and implementation of IMF-supported adjustment programs as well as in the annual consultations of the IMF staff with the IMF's 190 member

[1] We thank Jaime Sarmiento for his research assistance. We also thank Barry Eichengreen, Andy Berg, Valerie Cerra, as well as participants in the Inclusive Growth book seminar series organized by the IMF Institute, for Capacity Development for their comments.

Hamid R. Davoodi, Peter Montiel, and Anna Ter-Martirosyan, *Macroeconomic Stability, Adjustment, and Debt* In: *How to Achieve Inclusive Growth*. Edited by: Valerie Cerra, Barry Eichengreen, Asmaa El-Ganainy, and Martin Schindler, Oxford University Press. © Hamid R. Davoodi, Peter Montiel, and Anna Ter-Martirosyan 2022.
DOI: 10.1093/oso/9780192846938.003.0011

countries (Georgieva 2019, 2020). This understanding has gone beyond traditional macroeconomic policies to include structural reforms that support inclusiveness in many areas, including Covid-related financial assistance in excess of $100 billion that was awarded by the IMF to more than 80 countries in 2020.[2]

In this chapter, we analyze the dynamic relationship between macroeconomic volatility and inclusiveness. First, we look at the impact of economic fluctuations on several measures of inclusiveness, focusing separately on advanced and developing economies (Section II). Then, we study the effects of inequality on macroeconomic volatility (Section III). In both sections, we separately look at the effects of economic crises—an extreme case of economic volatility—on inclusiveness and vice versa. Finally, we shift the discussion to an analysis of the role of fiscal, monetary, macroprudential, and exchange rate policies in supporting inclusiveness (Section IV).

II. Impact of Macroeconomic Volatility on Inclusiveness

A. Impact of Volatility on Inclusiveness in Advanced Economies

There is extensive evidence that higher output volatility tends to widen income disparities. This positive output volatility-inequality relationship holds across countries, within countries, and across regions within a country (Breen and Garcia-Penalosa 2005; Chauvet et al. 2019; Huang et al. 2015; Aye et al. 2019). Similarly, business cycle fluctuations have significant effects on poverty and unemployment, two important measures of inclusiveness. For example, earnings volatility in the United States is highly cyclical and closely tracks the unemployment rate, and markedly so during the Great Recession (Carr and Wiemers 2018).[3] More generally, looking across a broad sample of countries, income volatility tends to vary positively with the volatilities of both poverty and unemployment. Moreover, the cyclical components of unemployment and poverty account for a significant share of their total volatility (Camarena et al. 2019).

The GFC underscored an often-overlooked fact that macroeconomic instability can have large distributional consequences. The evidence shows that countries with larger output and employment losses in the initial aftermath of the GFC on average registered greater increases in income inequality compared with their pre-crisis average. (Figure 11.1.)

Generally, business cycles affect inclusiveness at many levels. During recessions, income losses are often accompanied by deterioration in numerous indicators of inclusiveness, from inequality (of income or consumption) to inequality of health and education outcomes, such as infant mortality and school enrollments,

---

[2] See https://www.imf.org/en/Topics/imf-and-covid19/Covid-Lending-Tracker
[3] The Great Recession refers to the recession following the GFC.

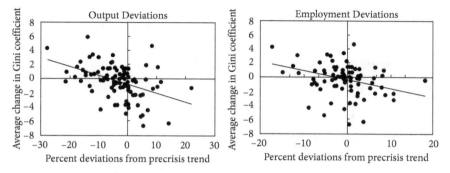

Figure 11.1 Post-crisis changes in income inequality

Note: The Gini coefficient is based on income before taxes and transfers and ranges from 0 to 100. The change in the Gini coefficient is calculated as the difference between the average during 2005–08 and 2014–15. Movement from left to right on the x-axis indicates less negative/more positive average deviations from the pre-crisis trend in 2011–13.

Sources: SWIID (Solt 2020) and authors' calculations.

from job losses to physical dislocation of individuals, loss of dignity and skewed gender disparities (Vegh et al. 2019).

There are many studies of business cycles in the United States that provide a rich view of how recessions influence the evolution of income and its distribution. These studies offer valuable insights that may be representative of the experiences in other developed economies. One key insight is that recessions—defined as periods of negative output growth rates—on average lead to permanent output and income losses, regardless of the cause (Cerra and Saxena 2008, 2017).

Another important insight is that there are sizable short-run and long-run impacts of US post-war recessions on many measures of inclusiveness—such as unemployment, earnings inequality, intergenerational disparities, socioeconomic status, and mortality rates.[4] Conceptually, unemployment matters for income distribution because increases in the unemployment rate happen faster than declines in the unemployment rate, and the fact that unemployment disproportionately affects the youth, the less skilled, and the less educated.

The history of the labor market in the United States provides a good example of inequality dynamics. Figure 11.2 shows the evolution of earnings inequality between 1969 and 2018 for two measures of inequality. Inequality at the top end of the distribution is captured by the ratio of the earnings in the 90th percentile to that of the 50th percentile (90/50 ratio). Inequality at the bottom end of the distribution is captured by the ratio of the earnings in the 50th percentile to that of the bottom 20th percentile (50/20 ratio).

First, inequality is captured by the increasing trend in both ratios but also that the cyclical properties of earnings inequality are different at the bottom and the top. Second, inequality at the top (the 90/50 ratio) increases steadily and does not

[4] See Dupraz, Nakamura, and Steinsson (2020), Schwandt and von Wachter (2020) and Case and Deaton (2020).

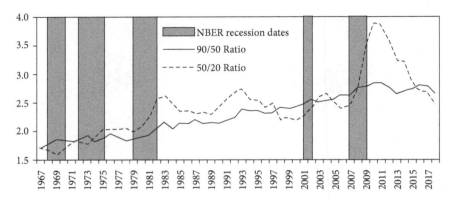

Figure 11.2 Earnings Inequality and Business Cycles in the United States

Source: Heathcote, Jonathan, Fabrizio Perri, and Giovanni L. Violante. 2020. "The Rise of US Earning Inequality: Does the Cycle Drive the Trend." *Review of Economic Dynamics* 37: S181–S204.

exhibit any particular cyclical pattern. In contrast, inequality at the bottom (the 50/20 ratio) increases sharply in each recession. Third, the longer the expansion, the more inequality declines. However, despite improvements in inequality during expansions, the cumulative increase in the 50/20 ratio that happened during all US recessions exceeds the overall increase in the same ratio over the entire 1968–2018 period.

Some of these findings also extend to the dynamics of wealth and income inequality. A study of the US economy that also takes into account different heterogeneous experiences in the labor market finds that business cycle fluctuations can account for about 50 percent of the rise in US wealth inequality, and virtually for the entire increase in income inequality between 1980 and 2015 (Bayer et al. 2020).

Changes in earnings inequality over the business cycle in advanced economies are also reflected in asymmetries in unemployment as steep rises in layoffs during recessions are followed by slow hiring during recoveries and slower wage gains for those at the bottom end of the income distribution (McKay and Reis 2008). The longer workers remain unemployed, the greater is the attenuation in their skills and loss of human capital. Business cycle volatility and its asymmetric effects on unemployment during recessions and recoveries tend to disproportionately affect wage earners at the low end of the income distribution. As a result, recessions can have long-run effects on inequality of income and earnings.

In fact, models of business cycles with hysteresis demonstrate that cyclical fluctuations in inequality are connected to trend movements. In other words, cycles and trends cannot be analyzed independently of each other. For example, Barlevy and Tsiddon (2006) develop a model in which recessions amplify long-run trends in earnings inequality and provide empirical support for this amplification effect from the first half of the twentieth century in the United States.

More recent studies of the United States provide more direct evidence and insight into the long-run effects of cyclical changes in inequality. One observation is that there has been a marked trend decline in relative wages of low-skilled workers in the United States. Recessions imply a double whammy for these workers as they are hit disproportionately more during recessions. The higher the unemployment rate among these workers, the further are declines in their skills and potential earnings, known as a scarring effect. As a result, the cycle tends to drive the trend, with recessions having long-run adverse effects on inequality (Heathcote, Perri, and Violante 2020). These findings mirror arguments made by Cerra et al. (2021) on the scarring effects of business cycles. Permanent income losses may therefore be associated with permanent setbacks for inclusiveness.

These findings have important policy implications. Welfare gains from stabilization policies (to smooth output fluctuations) are likely to be larger than those estimated in the traditional business cycle analysis (Lucas 2003) because stabilization also has the beneficial effect of reducing income inequality. These welfare gains are expected to be even larger under a hysteresis view of the business cycle whereby a crisis or recession delays investment in human capital and spending on research and development, which in turn diminishes long-run growth (Stiglitz 2012; Cerra, Fatás, and Saxena forthcoming).

B. Impact of Volatility on Inclusiveness in Developing Economies

Low-income countries and emerging market economies tend to experience more frequent crises (economic, political, and climate-related), as well as deeper recessions than rich countries (Naoussi and Tripier 2013; Cerra and Saxena 2008, 2017). As a result, the impact of recessions and volatility on measures of inclusiveness is more pronounced for low-income countries and emerging market economies than for advanced countries.

For example, terms-of-trade shocks are an important source of volatility for developing and emerging market economies and can drive both growth and inclusiveness. Cross-country evidence shows that higher terms of trade volatility affect growth adversely by reducing investment in human and physical capital (Cavalcanti, Mohaddes, and Raissi 2014). On perhaps a more positive side, during the commodity boom of 2003–2014, poverty in Latin America and the Caribbean region declined by almost 19 percentage points. Much of the progress reflected real labor income gains for lower-skilled workers, especially in services, with a smaller but positive role for government transfers (IMF 2018b). However, besides the trend decline, cyclical income volatility accounted for about 40 percent of the decline in poverty (Camarena et al. 2019).

The global coronavirus pandemic recession caused massive income losses as measured by the drop in labor income due to layoffs, shorter hours worked, and furloughs. According to the International Labour Organization, labor income losses (excluding income support measures) at the global level are estimated to have declined by 35 percent during the first three quarters of 2020 (from the fourth quarter of 2019), a loss of 1 billion full-time equivalent jobs. This is equivalent to US$3.5 trillion or 5.5 percent of global GDP (International Labour Organization 2020).

The pandemic-induced collapse in output and employment in 2020 also had devastating effects on many measures of inclusiveness. For example, a World Bank study estimates that the Covid-19 pandemic may have driven some 70 million people into extreme poverty (those living on less than US$1.90 a day) under the baseline scenario of 5 percent global GDP contraction in 2020 (Mahler et al. 2020).[5] Under a downside scenario of a global contraction of 8 percent in 2020, an additional 46 million will join the ranks of the extreme poor in 2020. By comparison, the number of extreme poor has declined by about 30 million between 2015 and 2019.

C. Impact of Economic Crises on Inclusiveness

Economic crises affect all countries as evidenced, in this section, by a review of the experiences of advanced economies, developing economies, and emerging market economies. Economic crises are episodes of severe macroeconomic instability, representing an extreme form of volatility. Macroeconomic crises generally result in severe recessions, with accompanying job losses. The depth of output losses and human suffering tends to be much larger and more acute in recessions induced by the crisis than in non-crisis recessions. Crises originate from various sources and are of different types. They include financial sector, currency (or balance of payments), and debt (public or private) crises. Crises of different types sometimes can also occur together, with "twin crises" of currency/banking and currency/debt more common than a banking/debt twin crisis (Laeven and Valencia 2018). Unfortunately, crises afflict countries at all income levels. The evidence from across more than 180 countries during 1960–2014 shows that the persistent output losses relative to the pre-crisis trend were as high as 5 percent for the balance of payment crises, 10 percent for banking crises, and 15 percent for twin banking/balance of payment crises (Cerra and Saxena 2008).

Financial sector crises appear to have a more adverse effect on inequality than crises of other types. These crises do not occur in a vacuum. They are often accompanied by credit booms fuelled by fickle capital flows, loose lending standards, financial liberalization, capital account liberalizations, and excessive risk-taking. During booms that precede a financial sector crisis, individuals at the

---

[5] By comparison, during the GFC, global GDP contracted by 0.07 percent in 2009. The estimate of a 5 percent contraction in global output is close to that projected in the October 2020 projection of the IMF's World Economic Outlook.

bottom end of the income distribution often incur large amounts of debt to finance current consumption, purchase houses, or acquire other assets. For example, rising income inequality since 1980 in the United States generated a rise in household borrowing by non-rich households, financed by rich households (Mian, Straub, and Sufi 2020).

A common observation is that systematic differences in asset portfolios and leverage among households at different income levels, also mean that the booms and busts associated with financial sector crises tend to affect inclusiveness in part through their effects on the distribution of wealth (Kuhn, Schularick, and Steins 2020). Since in most advanced economies portfolios of rich households are dominated by stocks, whereas portfolios of middle-class households are concentrated in real estate and are highly leveraged, other things being equal, housing booms lead to substantial wealth gains for leveraged middle-class households and tend to decrease wealth inequality, while stock market booms primarily boost the wealth of households at the top of the wealth distribution.

The postwar American history provides a good example of the effects of the economic crisis on wealth distribution in advanced economies. In the United States, portfolio valuation effects have been predominant drivers of shifts in the distribution of wealth. During the four decades before the GFC, the US middle class (50th–90th percentiles) lost ground to the top 10 percent with respect to income, but it largely maintained its wealth share due to substantial gains in housing wealth. However, following the collapse in the housing market in the GFC, the middle class suffered substantial wealth losses, whereas the quick turn-around in stock markets boosted wealth at the top. The housing market did recover but this occurred much later than the rise in the stock market.

More generally, aside from their effects on the distribution of wealth, financial sector crises tend to increase poverty and inequality. Their immediate effects are unemployment, loss of income, delayed loan repayments, foreclosures on real estate, and outright debt default. The larger the debt overhang, the deeper is the ensuing recession (Mian, Sufi, and Verner 2017). As the size of the debt overhang increases, those in the bottom end of the income distribution are hit harder, and inequality, poverty, and unemployment deteriorate more. A number of studies across broad samples of countries have found that banking and currency crises tend to increase income inequality and poverty, though causality is far from clear (Baldacci et al. 2002; De Haan and Jan-Egbert Sturm 2017).

The impact of the GFC on income inequality and poverty in OECD countries has been the subject of many studies (Jenkins et al. 2013).[6] A study based on a

---

[6] To date, there are no systematic cross-county studies of the impact of economic crises on a comprehensive set of social indicators. See Easterly (1999) for a study of the impact of growth on social indicators at decade-long frequencies and Camarena and others (2019) for a study impact of business cycles on social indicators at business cycle frequencies, focusing mostly on Latin America and the Caribbean.

survey of 100,000 US households shows that income losses imposed by the GFC were disproportionately borne by low- to middle-income groups (Almeida 2020). Income losses experienced by richer households were relatively modest and transitory, while those experienced by poorer households were not only large but also highly persistent.[7] The bottom 10 percent of the distribution experienced a 70 percent drop in earnings relative to the pre-crisis year of 2007, long after the official end of the recession, while the top 10 percent experienced a drop of less than 5 percent (Almeida 2020). The effects of the GFC on inclusiveness have been worldwide. One study estimated that the GFC added some 64 million people to the population living below the poverty line of $2 dollar a day, an international benchmark at the time (Ravallion and Chen 2009).

A sovereign debt crisis is another type of macroeconomic crisis that may have significant effects on inclusiveness. Such crises arise when sovereign debt evolves on a trajectory that cannot be sustained as creditors are unwilling to refinance maturing debt. Common reasons for unsustainable sovereign debt, among many, include rising interest rates that increase debt service costs, unexpected external or domestic shock that leads to persistent fiscal deficits, an exchange rate devaluation that raises the domestic currency cost of servicing foreign-currency-denominated debt. These situations can trigger sovereign default or the need to reschedule debt, requiring a large fiscal adjustment or fiscal consolidation to restore fiscal sustainability.

The direct distributional consequences of high debt or debt crisis have not received much attention in the literature. However, the *indirect* distributional consequences of unsustainably high debt or debt crisis have received more attention, as unsustainably high debt or debt crises can influence income distribution through many channels, including low or negative growth, higher inflation, greater inflation instability, higher output volatility, large exchange rate devaluations, abandonment of a pegged exchange rate regime or a large depreciation, and debt write-offs or haircuts in which only a fraction of the debt is repaid to domestic or foreign debt holders.

There is substantial evidence both within countries and across countries that recessions are often preceded by a buildup of sovereign debt and other vulnerabilities (Kumhof, Ranciere, and Winant 2015; IMF 2017a; Mian and Sufi 2018) and that high debt is a good predictor of low or negative economic growth and higher unemployment (Reinhart and Rogoff 2010; Mian and Sufi 2018; Kim and Zhang 2019). An important channel through which high debt and debt crises may exert such contractionary effects is often through the subsequent fiscal adjustments or fiscal consolidation.

---

[7] Income is defined as the sum of (pre-tax, pre-transfer) earnings, private transfers, and net asset income, based on person-equivalized household income with individual weights (Almeida 2020).

Fiscal consolidation measures usually include some combination of tax increases and expenditure cuts aimed to reduce fiscal deficits and improve fiscal sustainability. These measures affect aggregate demand, employment, income, consumption, and investment. They can also change income distribution through their impacts on transfers, public sector wages, and unemployment. The magnitude and direction of these effects are likely to vary depending on the composition of fiscal measures, the state of the economy, and potentially other factors. Understanding these effects can help policymakers in designing consolidation packages that minimize the negative impacts on the economy and inclusiveness.

Although some studies report expansionary consolidations (e.g., Alesina et al. 2019), it is generally accepted that fiscal austerity measures negatively affect output and economic growth, at least in the short run.[8] The magnitude of these effects depends on the composition of the adjustment and its persistence. It also matters whether the adjustment was anticipated and whether other macroeconomic policies were able to cushion some of the impacts.

Tax-based fiscal consolidations tend to have a larger negative impact on economic output than spending-based ones, particularly over the medium term. Most estimates show multipliers around -2 to -3 for tax measures but only around or below one for spending. There are several explanations for these findings. First, with expenditure-based austerity, forward-looking households may anticipate that future taxes will not rise as much as previously expected and raise their consumption. Similarly, investors would also expect a smaller tax burden in the future and thus increase their investment today. On the supply side, tax distortions may affect the supply of labor, particularly for second earners in a family and younger people who may delay their entry into the labor market, which in turn would have a long negative impact on output (Alesina et al. 2019; Ramey 2019).

The range of estimated multipliers for fiscal consolidations, however, becomes much wider when considering country-specific characteristics, such as the type of an exchange rate regime, initial tax coverage, and tax rates. For example, the negative effects of spending cuts tend to be larger for countries with a fixed exchange rate regime and higher debt levels. Evidence based on fiscal consolidations in 10 OECD countries during 1978–2014 shows that if tax-based consolidations are achieved by broadening the tax base, the negative impact on output and employment tends to be much smaller than if they are based on tax rate increases (Dabla-Norris and Lima 2018). In addition, tax multipliers could be essentially zero under relatively low initial tax rate levels (Gunter et al. 2019).

---

[8] Alesina et al. (2019) find a few cases of "expansionary austerity" in which the output costs associated with an expenditure-based austerity plan produce output gains. Examples include Ireland, Denmark, Belgium, and Sweden in the 1980s and Canada in the 1990s.

In addition, as austerity measures are rarely implemented in isolation, other macroeconomic policies can cushion their impact on the economy. For instance, by lowering interest rates, monetary policy can support investment and consumption during consolidation episodes (Ramey 2019). Thus, a negative impact of fiscal consolidation can be particularly severe during recessions or periods at the zero lower bound of interest rates, when support from other policies is constrained.[9] In these situations, countries could enter a negative loop when their attempts to lower government debt through spending cuts or tax increases result in lower growth and even higher debt-to-GDP ratios. These episodes are called hysteresis episodes of self-defeating fiscal consolidations (Fatás and Summers 2018).

Most studies of the output effects of fiscal consolidation rely on consolidation episodes in advanced economies and limited research in developing countries. This is in part due to data limitations and difficulties in identifying fiscal policy shocks.[10] Available empirical studies suggest that the impact of fiscal policy on output in developing countries is lower than in advanced economies and perhaps more short-lived.[11] Specifically, government consumption cuts have a temporary impact on output, but public investment shocks have a larger and longer-lasting effect, as the private sector is small and public investment is essential for economic growth. In addition, as with advanced economies, the output effects appear to be larger during recessions (Honda et al. 2020).

Fiscal adjustments affect inequality through their output and employment effects as well as through distributional effects of spending cuts and tax increases. The overall effect on inequality depends on the composition of fiscal adjustment, stage of the business cycle, and labor market conditions (Woo et al. 2013). Fiscal consolidations are often accompanied by an increase in long-term unemployment and a decline in the labor share of income. This decline tends to increase inequality because of the relatively high share of wages in the incomes of lower-income groups.[12] In addition, it is generally found that unemployment losses fall disproportionately upon low-income groups (OECD 2015). Frontloaded adjustments and consolidations were undertaken during recessions tend to have especially strong effects on social welfare if they are implemented when unemployment is already high (Blanchard and Leigh 2013).

One study found that IMF program conditionalities may have led to higher income inequality (Forster et al. 2019). However, another study found out the nature of reforms and initial conditions matter to the evolution of inequality.

---

[9] Unconventional monetary policy can and has been used to mitigate possible negative effects of fiscal consolidation particularly when the interest rate is at the zero lower bound; see section IV.

[10] Fiscal shocks are discretionary changes in government spending and taxes that are not correlated with contemporaneous macroeconomic shocks.

[11] Kraay (2014) estimates fiscal spending multipliers to be around 0.4 for a large sample of developing countries over the period 1970–2010.

[12] Low-income households typically rely on labor income, whereas high-income households tend to receive a relatively larger share of their income from capital income.

For example, fiscal reforms such as improving the efficiency of public investment, pursued in many IMF-supported programs, tend to reduce income inequality but financial sector reforms neither increased nor decreased inequality (Fabrizio et al. 2017).

There is a broad consensus that in advanced economies adjustments based on spending cuts have larger effects on income inequality than those based on tax hikes. Based on more than 100 episodes of fiscal consolidation in advanced economies, Woo et al. (2013) show that on average inequality increased about 2 percent after the spending-based consolidations, while it rose about 1 percent in the case of the tax-based episodes. Other studies find a similar pattern (Ball 2014). This could be explained by the fact that most of the redistribution in advanced economies is conducted through government spending. Also, lower-income earners are typically more affected by spending cuts as a larger portion of their disposable income comes from public spending and they are more vulnerable to job losses. Furceri et al. (2018) report *a medium-term inequality multiplier* for government spending and find significant and long-lasting effects of spending cuts on inequality and poverty, suggesting a unit elasticity.

The net effect of fiscal consolidation on inequality also depends on the specific composition of the spending or revenue adjustment.[13] Reductions in social benefits tend to worsen inequality more than other spending cuts. Proportional reductions in pensions across all beneficiaries are regressive because pensioners in the lower-income groups lose a greater share of their total income (Clements et al. 2015). Finally, cuts in education and health spending have a greater impact on inequality in the longer term (Woo 2013).

There is less evidence on the distributional effects of fiscal consolidation for developing economies. Several factors suggest a potentially lower impact for spending cuts. First, social spending is on average much lower than in advanced economies and not well-targeted. Further, in-kind social spending—such as education and health spending—is often not well targeted which exacerbates post-transfer inequality because the poor have limited access to public services. In cases when consolidation is achieved by cuts in fuel price subsidies, the net effect on inequality and poverty depends on the design of those measures. Across-the-board cuts often hurt the poor more often than the rich unless they are accompanied by mitigating measures such as temporarily maintaining universal subsidies on commodities that are more important in the budgets of the poor while improving targeting that corrects the flaws in the initial design of such

---

[13] For example, fiscal consolidations in Spain (1992–1998) and Norway (1993–1997) consisted of across-the-board spending cuts, while protecting social benefits. Tax-based consolidations that rely more on indirect taxes or are combined with expenditure cuts tend to worsen inequality (Iceland, 2004–2006). Also, addressing tax evasion and tax loopholes is an alternative way to generate public savings without necessarily elevating the income inequality (Germany 1992–1999); Woo (2013) for more details.

programs (Coady et al. 2015). On the revenue side, a larger share of revenues comes from indirect taxes, which tend to be regressive. Therefore, tax hikes could be detrimental to welfare, especially for the poor.[14] In terms of the timing, similar to cases for advanced economies, fiscal consolidation undertaken during recessions tends to have a larger impact on unemployment and inequality (Honda, Miyamoto, and Taniguchi 2020).

Both spending and revenue measures could be designed to mitigate the negative impact of fiscal consolidation on lower-income groups. In particular, a larger share of fiscal adjustments could be achieved through revenue measures targeted at the higher income segments of the population. Also, broad spending cuts could be accompanied by targeted social benefits and subsidies designed to offset some of the adverse distributional impacts of consolidation (Clements et al. 2015; Fabrizio et al. 2017).[15]

In short, fiscal consolidation in response to unsustainable sovereign debt and sovereign debt crises has costs for both economic output and inequality. Evidence suggests that spending-based consolidation measures tend to be less contractionary for output than tax hikes. Yet, many studies also show that spending cuts can have a large negative impact on inequality. There is scope for further research about the net effects of consolidation, particularly for developing economies. In the meantime, countries should aim to develop consolidation packages that minimize effects on growth without widening inequality.

III. Impact of Inclusiveness on Macroeconomic Volatility and Crises

A. Macroeconomy and Inequality: A Paradigm Shift

The macroeconomics literature until the GFC was dominated by the view that income distribution did not matter for macroeconomic fluctuations. If anything, a widely held perspective was that macroeconomic aggregates affect income distribution, but not vice versa, a view challenged by Stiglitz (2012). However, there has been a notable paradigm shift in macroeconomics. According to the new

---

[14] Fabrizio et al. (2017) find that in LICs increases in value-added tax is associated with an increase in the Gini coefficient by about 1.5 percent in the medium term. Peralta-Alva et al. (2018) show that hikes in the value-added tax rate can substantially reduce welfare in Ethiopia by widening the rural-urban gap, despite having the least efficiency costs in terms of implementation.

[15] Analysis of several consolidation episodes in selected European economies in the aftermath of the GFC shows that the overall impact of consolidation could be progressive (Clements et al. 2015). Likewise, for developing countries, in Honduras, negative distributional effects from increases in value added tax were offset –among other factors—by a targeted cash transfer program, conditional on households' enrolling their children in schools, resulting in the overall progressive distributional impact (Fabrizio et al. 2017).

paradigm, inequality matters for the macroeconomy, and the macroeconomy matters for inequality (Ahn et al. 2018). The key to this paradigm shift was the rising inequality leading up to the GFC as well as better data and computational capabilities for macroeconomic modeling, but more importantly, the incorporation of heterogeneity, especially in income and wealth, into models that shifted away from representative agent models that are silent on distributional issues.

Moreover, the new literature also underscores the need to employ better methods and economic theory to establish causality that at least recognizes the two-way relationship between inequality and the macroeconomy. In this regard, recent methods for the identification of causal relationships are promising (Nakamura and Steinsson 2018; Gabaix and Koijen 2020). However, these novel methods are yet to be fully embraced in the literature. These observations caution us about reading too much into causality in many studies reviewed in this section although some studies, as we see shortly, do a good job of using an array of standard causality tests.

B. Impact of Inequality on Growth and Growth Volatility

The impact of inequality on economic growth has been the subject of many empirical studies that have at times produced conflicting results.[16] For example, Forbes (2000) finds a positive association between inequality and growth. Panizza (2002) finds a negative relationship across a sample of 50 US states. Banerjee and Duflo (2003) find the association to be non-linear. In a dynamic model of 77 countries, Grigoli, Paredes, and Di Bella (2018) allow for cross-country heterogeneity and find that higher income inequality leads to lower growth in three-quarters of the 77 countries in their sample. In general, studies that focus on short-run relationships (e.g., 5-year averages) tend to find a positive association. The results vary due to differences in methodologies, transmission channels, measures of inequality, functional relationships (linear and non-linear), and data frequencies.

With respect to volatility, one line of research has investigated the impact of inequality on the durability of growth. A key finding in this area is that high-income inequality results in a shorter and more fragile growth spell, that is, output growth is only sustained for short periods. In other words, high inequality leads to high output volatility. Conversely, low inequality is associated with faster and more durable growth spells. These findings hold even after controlling for

---

[16] The growth-inequality relationship discussed in Chapter 2 complements the analysis in this section though the focus in this chapter is confined to short- and medium-run growth horizons and output growth volatility. The impact of inclusive growth on other aspects of the macroeconomy (financial inclusion, new technologies, liberalization, and globalization) are covered in previous chapters.

various determinants of output growth (Berg et al. 2018). Low inequality contributes to the durability of growth (lower output volatility) by (i) relaxing credit market imperfections, easing financing for investment in human capital, (ii) reducing incentives for distortionary taxation to finance public spending; and (iii) reducing political instability and uncertainty and thereby raising incentives for investment.

Capital market imperfections combined with unequal access to investment opportunities across individuals have also been shown to generate endogenous and permanent fluctuations in output, investment, and interest rates (Aghion, Banerjee, and Piketty 1999). In some periods, savings are plentiful and underutilized because of investors' borrowing constraints, resulting in slow output and investment growth, and low-interest rates. Following deleveraging and rising profitability, investment demand and growth increase and interest rates climb. As debt burdens become high, profits net of debt payments falls, eventually leading to collapse in investment, taking the economy into recession or slow growth. This implies that economies with less developed financial markets and credit-constrained investors will tend to be more volatile and to grow more slowly. Therefore, improving financial inclusion may be a necessary condition for macro-economic stabilization. A second-best policy may be to use tax policy to absorb idle savings and provide investment subsidies or tax cuts for investors.

More broadly, weak institutions amplify the impact of high-income inequality on growth and growth volatility. Evidence from a broad sample of countries shows that drops in growth are sharper in countries with divided and socially polarized societies—as measured by high-income inequality and high ethnic fragmenta-tion—and with weak institutions of conflict management, such as quality of gov-ernmental institutions, rule of law, and social safety nets (Rodrik 1999; Woo 2011; Grigoli, Paredes, and Di Bella 2018). In these studies, the issue of causality is tack-led by using data on income inequality that preceded the growth collapse.

C. Impact of Inequality on Economic Crises

There is a extensive literature that examines whether inequality is a cause of the economic crisis. The literature considers different theories about the relationship between various types of economic crises and inequality and investigates empiri-cally the relationship across time periods and countries, using different method-ologies and measures of inequality.

A study of financial crises among 14 advanced countries between 1920 and 2000 found that credit booms increased the probability of a banking crisis but found no evidence that a rise in top income shares led to credit booms. Instead, the pattern of the financial crisis seems to fit the standard boom-bust pattern of declines in interest rates, followed by strong growth, credit booms, asset price booms, and crises (Bordo and Meissner 2012). However, this study excluded the GFC. When the sample includes the GFC, higher top income shares are found to be positively associated with credit booms, given other determinants of credit booms (Perugini et al. 2016). The study uses some widely-used econometric techniques to argue that the relationship is causal, running from inequality to financial crisis. Empirically, the impact of inequality on credit booms and the likelihood of financial crises is also found to depend on the extent of financial deregulation; the more deregulated financial markets are, the greater the impact of inequality on financial fragility and financial crises (Perugini et al. 2016).

However, to conclude that income inequality can contribute to causing an economic crisis, empirical studies invariably need to address the difficult challenge of identifying changes in income inequality that are truly exogenous with respect to an economic crisis.

Recent empirical studies have shied away from the difficult task of establishing causality and have turned their attention instead to the simpler task of assessing the predictive power of income inequality for crisis episodes. Studies have found that slow-moving trends such as rising top income inequality and prolonged periods of low productivity growth have strong predictive power for both the onset and severity of financial crises. This evidence holds across many developed countries and various historical episodes, given other determinants of crisis (Kirschenmann, Malinen, and Nyberg 2016; Paul 2020). Moreover, the available evidence also shows that when crises are preceded by these slow-moving trends, the subsequent recoveries also tend to be slower, with significant output and labor productivity effects (Paul and Pedtke 2020).

A number of studies have used formal theoretical models to show that income inequality can be a cause of the economic crisis.[17] Motivating such models is the important stylized fact that a persistently rising trend in inequality in the United States culminated in the two highest top income shares in US history since 1920. One was in 1928, on the eve of the Great Depression, and the other in 2007, on the eve of the Great Recession. In both episodes, there was also a simultaneous large increase in debt-to-income ratios among lower- and middle-income households as these segments of the population have little savings and must borrow to finance their spending. Therefore, high leverage and economic crisis may have been the endogenous result of growing income inequality (Kumhof, Ranciere, and Winant 2015).

The transmission mechanism may work as follows. The rapid rise in the share of top incomes, a shock to income inequality, results in a larger supply of savings in the economy. The wealthy with top income shares have higher savings rates and lend their accumulated savings to lower- and middle-income households

---

[17] See Rajan (2010); Kumhof, Ranciere, and Winant (2015); Mian and Sufi (2018); Coibion et al. (2020).

through the financial system. A greater supply of savings lowers the interest rate. This in turn encourages households in the lower and middle segment of the income distribution to borrow to compensate for the loss of consumption entailed by their lower-income share. Low interest rates may also fuel a credit bubble, in which case borrowing rises even further, leading to higher household debt-to-income ratios. The resulting financial fragility eventually leads to debt default, a financial crisis, and a collapse in real output. High inequality can continue to deepen the scarring from the crisis, including a slower recovery, as low-income but highly leveraged households reduce their purchases in order to avoid further default and bankruptcy.

Others argue heuristically that the rising inequality exacerbates banking and financial crises but does not cause them (Piketty and Saez 2013). The fact that debt rose so much and so fast is probably not a coincidence. Piketty and Saez (2013) argue that modern financial systems are highly fragile and can crash by themselves even without rising inequality to push them over the edge.

IV. Macroeconomic Policies and Inclusiveness

Section II analyzed the adverse effects of macroeconomic instability—and specifically of recessions—on inclusiveness. However, recessions may not necessarily lead to adverse long-run effects on inequality if the policy response is sufficiently aggressive. In fact, this is a key policy implication of the hysteresis literature. "The reason why the Great Depression was followed by huge inequality decline is not the depression, but rather the large political shocks and policy responses—in particular the tremendous changes in institutions and tax policies and rise of the welfare state—which took place in the 1930s–1940s" (Piketty and Saez 2013). Taking into account business cycle asymmetries and hysteresis, recent studies show that in addition to stabilizing the economy, macroeconomic policies can also raise the average level of economic activity, thereby reducing the natural level of unemployment (Dupraz, Nakamura, and Steinsson 2020). In this section, we provide an overview of the effects of stabilization policies on inclusiveness.

A. Fiscal Policy

Fiscal policy is often seen as the governments' most powerful tool to promote inclusiveness by pursuing its main objectives of efficiency and macroeconomic stabilization with a concern for their equity implications. Changes in the level and types of taxes, the scale of spending and its composition, the size of the budget deficit, and the modalities of its financing, can all have implications for inclusiveness.

Fiscal policy can help lower inequality through fiscal redistribution, which can operate on both sides of the budget. On the tax side, a progressive income tax structure, whereby richer individuals face higher tax rates, can reduce the inequality of pre-tax incomes (Chapter 12). On the expenditure side, governments provide direct cash transfers such as social security payments, disability payments, unemployment benefits, food stamps as well as in-kind transfers such as spending on education and health and other targeted transfers (Chapter 13). Over the long run, spending on education and health (Chapter 14) also helps reduce inequality because it increases the skill set of individuals, boosts long-term earning capacity, and improves opportunities for social mobility across generations (see Chapter 18). On the financing side, central bank financing of large deficits can increase the inflation tax, which potentially has more adverse effects on the poor, who tend to hold more of their savings in form of cash balances than the rich.

Fiscal policy in advanced economies, on average, reduces income inequality (measured by the Gini coefficient) by about 33 percent. Two-thirds of this reduction is achieved by public transfers—such as pension and other social benefits—and about one-third comes from progressive taxation. Developing and emerging economies have much lower distributive capacity because of the lower level of taxes and spending (Clements et al. 2015). In contrast to advanced economies, fiscal redistribution in Latin America, the region with the highest average level of income inequality, on average reduces income inequality by about 10 percent (Clements et al. 2015).

The overall effects of fiscal policy on inclusiveness depend, of course, on the joint effects of tax and expenditure policies. If progressive taxes are used to finance progressive, pro-poor public expenditures, the net incidence of fiscal policy favors the poor. In this case, fiscal policy would contribute to lower disposable income inequality relative to the inequality that arises from market incomes.[18]

As argued previously, lower output volatility tends to go hand in hand with lower income inequality. The contribution that fiscal policy makes to reducing or aggravating macroeconomic instability thus provides a separate link between fiscal policy and inclusiveness. One important vehicle through which fiscal policy influences macroeconomic volatility is through the operation of automatic stabilizers. These are components of taxes and spending that are designed to respond automatically to economic cycles. Automatic stabilizers are generally regarded as the most efficient tool for fiscal stabilization of output and employment fluctuations. Thus, countries with strong automatic stabilizers tend to have lower output volatility (IMF 2015). Indeed, automatic stabilizers are estimated to account for up to two-thirds of the overall fiscal stabilization effort in advanced countries, a

---

[18] Pre-tax, pre-transfer income inequality, and post-tax, post-transfer inequality are also referred to as gross and net inequality, respectively, or market and disposable income inequality, respectively.

contribution that is twice as large as in emerging markets and developing economies (IMF 2015).

Besides automatic stabilizers, fiscal policy also has a component referred to as discretionary fiscal policy. Discretionary countercyclical fiscal policy occurs when the government actively raises taxes and/or reduces spending during booms and cuts taxes and/or increases spending during recessions. To the extent that such policies reduce macroeconomic volatility, they can be expected to have favorable effects on inclusiveness. These effects can be enhanced if the specific spending and revenue measures are pro-poor, in the form of progressive tax-and-transfer policies or spending on infrastructure, health, and education that favors the poor.

Unfortunately, not all countries manage to use countercyclical fiscal policy for stabilization. Some countries have procyclical fiscal policies characterized by expansions during economic booms and contractions during busts. Fiscal procyclicality tends to exacerbate economic cycles by magnifying economic expansions and prolonging economic downturns. Brueckner and Carneiro (2017), for example, show that the negative effects of terms-of-trade shocks are significantly higher in countries with procyclical government spending. This magnification of volatility resulting from procyclicality is likely to have negative effects on inclusiveness through the channels discussed in Section II.

The procyclicality of fiscal policy has also been linked more directly to poor social outcomes. Vegh and Vuletin (2015) show that procyclical fiscal policy causes a deterioration of poverty rate, income inequality, and the unemployment rate in a number of Latin American and European countries. In a related study of 30 Sub-Saharan economies, the effect of procyclical fiscal policy on income inequality is shown to vary by type of spending. Procyclical government investment is associated with a higher level of inequality than procyclical government consumption (Ouedraogo 2015). This appears to be driven by the fact that cuts in government investment in recessions happen more frequently than cuts in government consumption.

Why do some countries pursue procyclical fiscal policies that are detrimental to economic stability and inclusiveness? Explanations in the literature tend to focus on lack of access to credit markets in bad times as well as political pressures in good times.[19] High levels of public debt, limited fiscal space, and low quality of institutions also affect governments' ability to conduct countercyclical fiscal policy (Aizenman et al. 2019; Frankel et al. 2013). A separate strand of literature

---

[19] Credit constraints compel governments to cut spending and raise taxes during downturns, while political pressures for additional spending in good times prevents governments from savings, particularly when there is a need for more spending in critical social areas. In addition, Alesina et al. (2008) offer the "starve-the-Leviathan" reasoning, arguing that distrust in the government and fear that resources will be "wasted" cause the general public to demand tax cuts in good times, resulting in procyclical fiscal policies and higher levels of public debt.

notes that causation between non-inclusiveness and procyclicality may be bidirectional, since social polarization may promote fiscal procyclicality. For example, Woo (2011) presents strong evidence that countries with high initial income inequality tend to have greater fiscal policy volatility and procyclicality.[20] All of these factors tend to be more prominent in developing economies. Not surprisingly, therefore, IMF (2015) shows that while about three-fourths of advanced economies can conduct countercyclical stabilizing fiscal policies, only slightly more than a quarter of the emerging market and developing economies have countercyclical fiscal policies.

Strengthening institutions and building fiscal space during economic upturns would allow countries to pursue more stabilizing fiscal policies and move away from fiscal procyclicality, supporting more sustainable and equitable economic growth. Many countries would also benefit from building deeper safety nets, which would strengthen the operation of automatic stabilizers as well as add a countercyclical fiscal buffer, thereby mitigating the adverse income effects of recessions and reducing income inequalities over time. The good news is that a growing share of developing economies has been graduating from procyclical fiscal policies in the last two decades as the result of improvements in their fiscal institutions (Frankel et al. 2013).[21]

Besides fiscal policy, the government has other macroeconomic policy instruments for stabilization, especially monetary policy, macro, and micro-prudential policies, and exchange rate policy, all of which may affect growth and the distribution of income and wealth.

B. Monetary Policy

Many central banks employ monetary policy to achieve low and stable inflation with the objective of promoting high and sustainable growth. Countercyclical monetary policy (i.e., raising interest rates during booms and episodes of rising inflation, while cutting them during recessions) can reduce business cycle fluctuations and volatility of output and inflation. However, as is true of fiscal policy, many developing countries have traditionally pursued procyclical monetary policies, thereby magnifying volatility, in part because of their pursuit of exchange rate objectives. As it is true of fiscal policy, this situation is also changing in desirable directions during recent years, as one-third of developing countries have

[20] Woo (2011) uses empirical cross-country data over the period 1960–2000 to show that more unequal societies are more likely to use procyclical fiscal policies that are detrimental to growth. In the study, social polarization is measured by income and educational inequality.

[21] Frankel et al. (2013) argue that Chile is a good example of a country that has succeeded in developing stronger fiscal institutions over time and, as a result, has been able to conduct countercyclical fiscal policy.

transitioned to pursuing counter-cyclical monetary policy over the last decade (Vegh and Vuletin 2013).

Monetary policy can affect inequality and poverty through various channels.[22] Monetary policy expansion can increase growth and contribute to employment creation, at least in the short run, and thereby favor the poor and the middle class, for whom labor income constitutes a higher share of their total income than for the rich. Expansionary monetary policy can increase inflation and inflation expectations, eroding the real value of debt to the benefit of debtors, who are generally poorer than creditors. However, higher inflation may disproportionately hurt the poor too, as they tend to hold a higher share of their savings in cash. Likewise, lower interest rates reduce debt service costs to the benefit of middle- and lower-income groups who tend to be borrowers, but also increase equity and property values owned disproportionately by the wealthy. Given these multiple channels, the theoretical net effect of monetary policy on inequality is ambiguous (Bernanke 2015).

Empirical studies examining the impact of monetary policy shocks on income inequality generally find modest effects. A study of 32 advanced and emerging market economies over the 1990–2013 period found that expansionary monetary actions reduce income inequality and vice versa. The effect, however, varies over time and depends on the state of the business cycle as well as country characteristics such as the share of labor income and fiscal redistribution policies (Furceri, Loungani, and Zdzienicka 2018). However, Coibion et al. (2017) looked at the US experience since 1980 and found that contractionary monetary policy systematically increased inequality in labor earnings, total income, consumption, and total expenditures. Furthermore, monetary policy shocks accounted for a non-trivial component of the historical cyclical variation in income and consumption inequality.

The differential response across income distribution underscores the need to look at heterogeneity of labor earnings and to go beyond a summary statistic of the income distribution such as the Gini coefficient. Models that incorporate wealth and income heterogeneity better disentangle the transmission channels of monetary policy. One such study found that a monetary policy rule that emphasizes price stability redistributes income towards rich households, while one that stresses output stability redistributes it towards poor households who are more exposed to unemployment risk, and that the median household prefers output stability (Gornemann, Kuester, and Nakajima 2016). Another study showed that

---

[22] Although central banks' mandates do not typically involve distributional considerations, they have begun to engage the public about income inequality and social issues such as unemployment, regional disparities, and access to education, especially since the GFC. For the US Federal Reserve, see Yellen (2014) and Bank of England, see Financial Times (August 20, 2017). This trend has increased significantly during the Covid-19 pandemic.

when marginal propensities to consume vary, three channels affect aggregate spending: an earnings heterogeneity channel from unequal income gains, a Fisher channel from unexpected inflation, and an interest rate exposure channel from real interest rate changes. Italian and US data suggest that all three channels are likely to amplify the effects of monetary policy (Auclert 2019).

A recent review of the evidence concludes that empirical research yields mixed findings on the effects of conventional monetary policy on income and wealth inequality. However, there seems to be a consensus that higher inflation, at least above some threshold, increases inequality. Similarly, conclusions regarding the impact of unconventional monetary policies on inequality are also not clear cut. To better understand policy effects on inequality, future research should focus on the estimation and analytics of general equilibrium models with heterogeneous agents (Kaplan, Moll, and Violante 2018; Colciago, Samarina, and de Haan 2019). One such recent study found that making consumption equality an explicit target for monetary policy, particularly if central banks follow standard Taylor rules, can increase welfare compared with the case in which inequality is not part of the mandate of a central bank (Hansen, Lin, and Mano 2020). Clearly, more work is needed in this area.

C. Macroprudential Policies

Macroprudential policy is part of a country's macroeconomic framework designed to limit systemic risk and ensure financial stability. It, therefore, contributes to macroeconomic stability while complementing monetary policy. Macroprudential policy limits systemic risks by addressing two externalities: the interconnectedness of financial entities and the financial accelerator. The first occurs when different financial entities do not internalize their risk to the financial system as a whole through their transactions with other entities. The financial accelerator is the phenomenon of amplifying feedbacks within the financial sector and between the financial sector and the macroeconomy, which can generate unsustainable credit booms. As an economic boom turns to bust, the financial markets can magnify the disruption and cause a deep economic recession. So, like fiscal and monetary policies, a macroprudential policy can in principle contribute to inclusiveness by mitigating financial sector vulnerabilities and reducing macroeconomic volatility.

An extensive literature has documented procyclicality in financial markets and systemic risk (Cerutti, Claessens, and Laeven 2017). Macroprudential policy instruments such as a cap on loan-to-value ratio (LTVs) ratio, loan-to-income ratio (LTI), and debt service-to-income ratios (DSTI) are often used to contain the build-up of systemic vulnerabilities by reducing the procyclical feedback between credit and asset prices and by containing unsustainable increases in leverage.

Moreover, a successful macroprudential policy can enhance the volatility-reducing effectiveness of monetary policy by reducing the frequency and intensity of financial disruptions that amplify economic fluctuations and by lowering the pressure to cut interest rates unduly in order to address threats to financial stability during downturns. A recent empirical study showed the complementarity between monetary policy and macroprudential policy. A study of 37 emerging and advanced economies over 2000–2014 found that (i) an overall tightening in macroprudential policies is associated with a reduction in credit growth; (ii) a restrictive monetary policy enhances the impact of macroprudential tightening on credit growth; and (iii) monetary policy helps to reduce the transmission delay of macroprudential policy actions (Garcia Revelo, Lucotte, and Pradines-Jobet 2020).

There are limited studies that look at the relationship between macroprudential policy and inequality. One study finds that higher concentration limits, macro-prudential reserve requirements, and interbank exposure limits are positively associated with the higher market and net income inequality in the subsequent year, while LTV and DTI limits are positively associated with net inequality though not statistically significant (Frost and van Stralen 2018). Another study found that high LTV ratios at the time of asset acquisition contributed to wealth inequality, while house price increases reduced it. The cost of credit did not exhibit a significant link to the distribution of wealth (Carpantier, Olivera, and Van Kerm 2018).

D. Exchange Rate Management

Policymakers also rely on exchange rate policy as part of a macroeconomic policy toolkit when responding to shocks, especially those that generate large trade or current account imbalances which undermine macroeconomic stability. Much like other macroeconomic policies, the choices of an exchange rate regime and exchange rate policy have both direct and indirect effects on measures of inequality.

It may be useful to distinguish the inclusiveness effects of exchange rate regimes from those of specific exchange rate movements. To the extent that macroeconomic stability promotes inclusiveness, a fixed or floating regime is more likely to be conducive to inclusiveness if it is more successful in stabilizing the economy in response to shocks. The automatic stabilizing effects of fixed or floating regimes, however, are not clear-cut: they depend on a variety of factors, such as the sources of shocks to the economy, the nature of the country's financial links to the rest of the world, the country's monetary policy regime, and the effectiveness of domestic prudential policies, which can influence the balance-sheet effects of exchange rate fluctuations.

However, in spite of this theoretical ambiguity empirical evidence finds that flexible exchange rate regimes tend to be more effective in stabilizing output (Hausmann and Gavin 1996; Levy-Yeyati and Sturzenegger 2003; Aizenman et al. 2018). Flexible rate regimes can also help countries recover more quickly from commodity price shocks and global recessions than pegs (Roch 2019; Terrones 2020) and mitigate the transmission of global financial shocks to domestic financial markets (Obstfeld, Ostry, and Qureshi 2019). In this sense, flexible exchange rates can reduce output volatility and be an income-equalizing force during the recovery stage of the business cycle.

On the other hand, pegs are associated with lower inflation, which may benefit the poor (Levy-Yeyati 2019). In the long run, pegs help monetary policy not only by anchoring inflation expectations but also by disciplining monetary policy. However, floating exchange rate regimes may also be able to protect the poor, if they have a credible inflation-targeting framework that anchors inflation at low levels.

Large discrete exchange rate movements can arise either under fixed or flexible exchange rate regimes, but are more likely under fixed exchange rates, in the form of currency crises. The effects of such movements on inclusiveness are also likely to depend on country characteristics. Large exchange rate depreciations tend to favor the expansion of the traded goods sector relative to nontraded goods, and to the extent that the export and import-competing sectors are dominated by large firms owned by the rich, while the poor are concentrated in the nontraded goods sector, such movements may promote wealth inequality by increasing the value of firms producing traded goods and increase income inequality by reducing real wages in the nontraded goods sector. On the other hand, to the extent that firms owned by the rich in the nontraded goods sector are characterized by balance sheet mismatches, the effects of large depreciations on wealth inequality may not be clear.

So, in general, it is difficult to state conclusively whether fixed or flexible exchange rate regimes help inclusive growth as this depends on many factors. New research in this area should be able to throw additional light on this important question (Berg and Kpodar 2019) but it must also pay attention to the role of exchange rate policy in amplifying or attenuating balance sheet vulnerabilities (Finger and Lopez Murphy 2019) which can affect macroeconomic volatility and inclusiveness.

V. Conclusion

This chapter analyzed the relationship between macroeconomic stability and macroeconomic policies, on the one hand, and measures of inclusiveness such as income inequality, wealth inequality, poverty, and unemployment, on the other. Macroeconomic instability and inclusion have a complex relationship, affecting each other through multiple channels. Macroeconomic policies can play a key role in promoting economic stability while minimizing the adverse consequences for inclusiveness when the economy faces aggregate shocks and uncertainty. However, at times, aggregate fluctuations can also originate from poor policies, weak macroeconomic frameworks, and weak institutions. Mitigating macroeconomic volatility and avoiding procyclical policies should be on the agenda of all policymakers concerned with promoting inclusive growth as these policies have first-order economy-wide effects. This is imperative since the evidence shows many countries continue to pursue procyclical macro policies.

The chapter also described the evolving paradigm in macroeconomics of inequality, an important aspect of inclusive growth. This includes emerging macroeconomic models that incorporate heterogeneity in income and wealth and use of "big data," large surveys of income and wealth distribution, and surveys of labor markets that are typically used in microeconomics. Nonetheless, we need to be upfront about the limitations of our knowledge of the macroeconomics of inclusive growth. Policymakers faced with tradeoffs, uncertainty, and political economy considerations may not be as much aware of these limitations and gaps in our knowledge as the experts are.

The emerging empirical and theoretical literature demonstrates that the macroeconomy affects inequality and inequality affects the macroeconomy. Heterogeneity can magnify business cycle fluctuations and initial wealth disparities can have short-run and long-run effects. This implies that there is a stronger role for macroeconomic stabilization policies than thought previously. A review of the evidence and theory showed that many seemingly short-run temporary fluctuations or cycles in fact have long-run effects. Specifically, the chapter summarized evidence on the scarring effects of recessions, across a diverse set of countries, on unemployment, human capital formation, and health conditions as well as the skewed and the fanning effects of recessions on the earnings of those in the bottom and top ends of the income distribution. These findings are bound to show up even more strongly when we take stock of the scarring effects of the global coronavirus pandemic on an array of measures of inclusiveness.

Moreover, to make more progress on the crucial role of macroeconomic policy in contributing to inclusiveness, we must employ more innovative methods and economic theory that can more effectively establish causality between measures of inclusiveness and macroeconomic policies. At a minimum, we must recognize the two-way relationship between inequality and the macroeconomy. In this regard, recent research has identified methods for establishing causal relationships, but these methods are yet to be fully embraced in the literature.

This is particularly relevant on the crisis-inequality nexus where disagreements on causes and effects are plentiful. Policymakers must constantly watch for their actions on a buildup of economic vulnerabilities and take steps to avoid them as these can lead to costly economic crises with adverse consequences for inclusiveness. Specifically, a build-up of vulnerabilities can happen in the financial sector as manifested through policies that fuel credit booms; it can happen in the fiscal sector as manifested through pursuing procyclical fiscal policies and adopting a deficit bias; it can happen in the currency market as manifested through active involvement of the public and private sector involved in external borrowing or encouraging capital flows in the face of possibly misaligned exchange rates, and in the area of monetary policy and macroprudential policy as manifested through following excessively accommodative and excessively tight monetary policy as well as through macroprudential policies that encourage excessive risk-taking in the financial sector.

Finally, more research is needed to better understand the relationship between macroeconomic policies such as monetary policy, macroprudential policies, and exchange rate policy on the one hand and measures of inclusiveness on the other.

References

Adrian, Tobias, Nina Boyarchenko, and Domenico Giannone. 2019. "Vulnerable Growth." *American Economic Review* 109(4): 1263–89.

Aghion, Philippe, Abhijit Banerjee, and Thomas Piketty. 1999. "Dualism and Macroeconomic Volatility." *The Quarterly Journal of Economics* 114(4): 1359–97.

Ahn, SeHyoun, Greg Kaplan, Benjamin Moll, Thomas Winberry, and Christina Wolf. 2018. "When Inequality Matters for Macro and Macro Matters for Inequality," *NBER Macroeconomics Annual*, Vol. 32, edited by Martin Eichenbaum and Jonathan A. Parker, National Bureau of Economic Research.

Aizenman, Joshua, Yothin Jinjarak, Gemma Estrada, and Shu Tian. 2018. "Flexibility of Adjustment to Shocks: Economic Growth and Volatility of Middle-Income Countries." *Emerging Markets Finance and Trade* 54(5): 1112–31.

Aizenman, Joshua, Yothin Jinjarak, Hien Thi Kim Nguyen, and Donghyun Park. 2019. "Fiscal Space and Government-spending and Tax-rate Cyclicality Patterns: A Cross-country Comparison, 1960–2016." *Journal of Macroeconomics* 60: 229–52.

Alesina, A., F.R. Campante, and G. Tabellini. 2008. "Why Is Fiscal Policy Often Procyclical?" *J. Eur. Econ. Assoc.* 6(5): 1006–36.

Alesina, Alberto, Carlo Favero, and Francesco Giavazzi. 2019. *Austerity: When It Works and When It Doesn't*. Princeton, NJ: Princeton University Press.

Almeida, Vanda. 2020. "Income Inequality and Redistribution in the Aftermath of the 2007–2008 Crisis: The US Case." *National Tax Journal* 73(1): 77–114.

Auclert, Adrien. 2019. "Monetary Policy and the Redistribution Channel." *American Economic Review* 109(6): 2333–67, June.

Aye, Goodness C., Giray Gozgo, and Rangan Gupta. 2019. "Dynamic and Asymmetric Response of Inequality to Income Volatility: The Case of the United Kingdom." *Social Science Research* 147: 747–62.

Baldacci, Emmanuel, Luiz de Mello, and Gabriel Inchauste. 2002. "Financial Crises, Poverty and Income Distribution," IMF Working Paper 02/4, International Monetary Fund, Washington.

Ball, Laurence. 2014. "Long-term Damage from the Great Recession in OECD countries." *European Journal of Economics and Economic Policies: Intervention* 11(2): 149–60.

Banerjee, Abhijit V., and Esther Duflo. 2003. "Inequality and Growth: What Can the Data Say?" *Journal of Economic Growth* 8(3): 267–99, September.

Banerjee, Abhijit V., and Andrew F. Newman. 1991. "Risk-Bearing and the Theory of Income Distribution." *The Review of Economic Studies* 58(2), April 1991: 211–35, https://doi.org/10.2307/2297965.

Barlevy, Gadi, and Daniel Tsiddon. 2006. "Earnings Inequality and the Business Cycle." *European Economic Review* 50: 55–89.

Bayer, Christian, Benjamin Born, and Ralph Luetticke. 2020. "Shocks, Frictions, and Inequality in US Business Cycles" VOXEu.org https://voxeu.org/article/shocks-frictions-and-inequality-us-business-cycles

Berg, Andrew, and Roland Kpodar. 2019. "Exchange Rate Policy and Inequality," https://www.banque-france.fr/sites/default/files/session-2_berg.pdf

Berg, Andrew, and Jonathan Ostry. 2017. "Inequality and Unsustainable Growth: Two Sides of the Same Coin?" *IMF Economic Review* 65(4): 792–815.

Berg, Andrew, Jonathan Ostry, Charalambos Tsangarides, and Yarbol Yakhshilikov. 2018. "Redistribution, Inequality, and Growth: New Evidence." *Journal of Economic Growth* 23: 259–305.

Bernanke, Ben. S. 2015. "Monetary Policy and Inequality," https://www.brookings.edu/blog/ben-bernanke/2015/06/01/monetary-policy-and-inequality/

Blanchard, Olivier J., and Daniel Leigh. 2013. "Growth Forecast Errors and Fiscal Multipliers." *American Economic Review* 103(3): 117–20.

Blanchard, Olivier, David Romer, Michael Spence, and Joseph Stiglitz. 2012. *In the Wake of the Crisis: Leading Economists Reassess Economic Policy.* Cambridge, MA: MIT Press.

Blanchard, Olivier, and Lawrence H. Summers. 2019. *Evolution or Revolution? Rethinking Macroeconomic Policy after the Great Recession.* MIT Press and the Peterson Institute for International Economics.

Bordo, Michael D., and Christopher M. Meissner. 2012. "Does Inequality Lead to a Financial Crisis?" *Journal of International Money and Finance,* Elsevier, 31(8): 2147–61.

Breen, Richard, and Cecilia Garcia-Penalosa. 2005. "Income Inequality and Macroeconomic Volatility: An Empirical Investigation." *Review of Development Economics* 9(3): 380–98.

Brueckner, Markus, and Francisco Carneiro. 2017. "Terms of Trade Volatility, Government Spending Cyclicality, and Economic Growth." *Review of International Economics* 25(5): 975–89.

Business Cycle Dating Committee. 2010. *National Bureau of Economic Research*, https://www.nber.org/cycles/recessions.html

Camarena, José Andrée, Luciana Galeano, Luis Morano, Jorge Puig, Daniel Riera-Crichton, Carlos Vegh, et al. 2019. "Fooled by the Cycle: Permanent vs Cyclical Improvements in Social Indicators, " NBER *WP* 26199.

Carpantier, Jean-Francois, Javier Olivera and, Philippe Van Kerm. 2018. "Macroprudential Policy and Household Wealth Inequality." *Journal of International Money and Finance* 85(2018): 262–77.

Carr, Michael D., and Emily E. Wiemers. 2018. "New Evidence on Earning Volatility in Survey and Administrative Data." *American Economic Review* 108: 287–91.

Case, Anne, and Angus Deaton. 2020. *Deaths of Despair and the Future of Capitalism*. Princeton: Princeton University Press.

Cavalcanti, Tiago V. De V, Kamiar Mohaddes, and Mehdi Raissi, 2014. "Commodity Price Volatility and the Sources of Growth." *Journal of Applied Econometrics* 30 (6): 857–73.

Cerra, Valerie, and Sweta Chaman Saxena. 2008. "Growth Dynamics: The Myth of Economic Recovery." *American Economic Review* 98(1): 439–57.

Cerra, Valerie, and Sweta Chaman Saxena. 2017. "Booms, Crises, and Recoveries: A New Paradigm of the Business Cycle and its Policy Implications," *IMF Working paper* WP/17/250.

Cerra, Valerie, Antonio Fatás, and Sweta C. Saxena. Forthcoming "Hysteresis and Business Cycles," *Journal of Economic Literature*. Also IMF WP/20/73.

Cerutti, Eugenio, Stijn Claessens, and Luc Laeven. 2017. "The Use and Effectiveness of Macroprudential Policies: New Evidence." *Journal of Financial Stability* 28, February: 203–24.

Chauvet, Lisa, Marin Ferry, Patrick Guillaumont, Sylviane Guillaumont Jeanneney, Sampawende J.-A. Tapsoba, and Laurent Wagner. 2019. "Volatility Widens Inequality: Could Aid and Remittances Help." *Review of World Economics* 155: 71–104.

Clements, Benedict, Ruud de Mooij, Sanjeev Gupta, and Michael Keen. 2015. *Inequality and Fiscal Policy*. Washington, DC : International Monetary Fund. https://www.elibrary.imf.org/view/IMF071/22448-9781513531625/22448-9781513531625/22448-9781513531625.xml

Coady, David, Valentina Flamini, and Louis Sears. 2015. "Fuel Subsidies Revisited: Evidence for Developing Countries," IMF Working Paper.

Coibion, Olivier, Yuriy Gorodnichenko, Marianna Kudlyak, and John Mondragon. 2020. "Does Greater Inequality Lead to More Household Borrowing? New Evidence from Household Data." *European Economic Review*, January: 1–50.

Coibion, Olivier, Gorodnichenko, Yuriy, Kueng, Lorenz, and Silvia, John. 2017. "Innocent Bystanders? Monetary Policy and Inequality." *Journal of Monetary Economics*, Elsevier, 88(C): 70–89.

Colciago, Andrea, Anna Samarina, and Jakob de Haan. 2019. "Central Bank Policies and Income and Wealth Inequality: A Survey." *Journal of Economic Surveys* 33(4): 1199–231.

Dabla-Norris, Era, and Frederico Lima. 2018. "Macroeconomic Effects of Tax Rate and Base Changes: Evidence from Fiscal Consolidations." IMF Working Paper.

De Haan, Jakob, and Jan-Egbert Sturm. 2017. "Finance and Income Inequality: A Review and New Evidence." *European Journal of Political Economy* 50, December: 171–95.

Dupraz, Stephane, Emi Nakamura, and Jon Steinsson. 2020. "A Plucking Model of Business Cycles," forthcoming in the *Journal of Political Economy* https://eml.berkeley.edu/~enakamura/papers.html

Easterly, William. 1999. "Life During Growth." Journal *of Economic Growth* 4(3) (September 1999): 239–75.

Fabrizio, Stefania, Davide Furceri, Rodrigo Garcia-Verdu, Bin Grace Li, Sandra V. Lizarazo, Marina Mendes Tavares, et al. 2017. "Macro-Structural Policies and Income Inequality in Low-Income Developing Countries," *IMF Staff Discussion Note* SDN/17/01. International Monetary Fund.

Fatás, Antonio, and Lawrence H. Summers. 2018. "The Permanent Effects of Fiscal Consolidations." *Journal of International Economics* 112: 238–50.

Financial Times, Aug 20. 2017. "Bank of England's Andy Haldane goes on a tour of the UK," https://www.ft.com/content/f87a585a-829b-11e7-a4ce-15b2513cb3ff

Finger, Harold, and Pablo Lopez Murphy. 2019. "Facing the Tides: Managing Capital Flows in Asia," International Monetary Fund.

Forbes, K.J. 2000. "A Reassessment of the Relationship Between Inequality and Growth." *American Economic Review* 90: 869–87.

Forster, Timon, Alexander E. Kentikelenis, Bernhard Reinsberg, Thomas H. Stubbs, and Lawrence P. King. 2019. "How Structural Adjustment Programs Affect Inequality: A Disaggregated Analysis of IMF Conditionality, 1980–2014." Social *Science Research* 80, May: 83–113.

Frankel, Jeffrey A., Carlos A. Vegh, and Guillermo Vuletin. 2013. "On Graduation from Fiscal Procyclicality." *Journal of Development Economics* 100(1): 32–47.

Furceri, Davide, and Prakash Loungani. 2018. "Distributional Effects of Capital Account Liberalization." *Journal of Development Economics* 130: 127–44.

Furceri, Davide, Prakash Loungani, and Aleksandra Zdzienicka. 2018. "The Effects of Monetary Policy Shocks on Inequality." *Journal of International Money and Finance*, Elsevier 85(C): 168–86.

Furceri, Davide, Gabriele Ciminelli, Jun Ge, Jonathan D. Ostry, and Chris Papageorgiou. 2019. "The Political Costs of Reforms: Fear or Reality?" IMF Staff Discussion Note No. 19/08.

Furceri, Davide, Jun Ge, Prakash Loungani, Giovanni Melina, and Chris Papageorgiou. 2018. "The Distributional Effects of Government Spending Shocks in Developing Economies," IMF Working Papers 2018/057, International Monetary Fund.

Gabaix, Xavier, and Ralph S.J. Koijen. 2020. "Granular Instrumental Variables," NBER WP.

García-Peñalosa, Cecilia, and Stephen J. Turnovsky. 2005. "Production Risk and the Functional Distribution of Income in a Growing Economy: Tradeoffs and Policy Responses." *Journal of Development Economics* 76(1): 175–208.

Garcia Reveloa, Jose, Yannick Lucotte, and Florian Pradines-Jobet. 2020. "Macroprudential and Monetary Policies: The Need to Dance the Tango in Harmony." *Journal of International Money and Finance* 108.

Georgieva, Kristalina. 2019. "The IMF's Purpose: Delivering for People." Speech delivered at the Plenary IMF-World Bank Annual Meetings https://www.imf.org/en/News/Articles/2019/10/18/sp101819-md-am-plenary-speech

Georgieva, Kristalina. 2020. "The Global Economic Reset—Promoting a More Inclusive Recovery" https://blogs.imf.org/2020/06/11/the-global-economic-reset-promoting-a-more-inclusive-recovery/

Gornemann, Nils, Keith Kuester, and Makoto Nakajima. 2016. "Doves for the Rich, Hawks for the Poor? Distributional Consequences of Monetary Policy." Federal Reserve Board, International Finance Discussion Papers 1167.

Grigoli, Francesco, Evelio Paredes, and Gabriel Di Bella. 2018. "Inequality and Growth: A Heterogeneous Approach." *Journal of Income Distribution* 27(3–4): 18–49.

Gunter, Samara, Daniel Riera-Crichton, Carlos A. Vegh, and Guillermo Vuletin. 2019. "Policy Implications of Non-linear Effects of Tax Changes on Output." Policy Research Working Paper Series 8720, The World Bank.

Hansen, Niels-Jacob H., Alessandro Lin, and Rui Mano. 2020. "Should Inequality Factor into Central bank Decisions?" IMF Working Paper 20/196.

Hausmann, Ricardo, and Michael Gavin. 1996. "Securing Stability and Growth in Shock-Prone Region: The Policy Challenge for Latin America," *Inter-American Development Working Paper* no. 315.

Heathcote, Jonathan, and Fabrizio Perri. 2018. "Wealth and Volatility." *Review of Economic Studies* 85: 2173–213.

Heathcote, Jonathan, Fabrizio Perri, and Giovanni L. Violante. 2020. "The Rise of US Earning Inequality: Does the Cycle Drive the Trend." *Review of Economic Dynamics* 37: S181–204.

Honda, Jiro, Hiroaki Miyamoto, and Mina Taniguchi. 2020. "Exploring the Output Effect of Fiscal Policy Shocks in Low-Income Countries." IMF Working Papers 20.

Huang, Income Inequality and Macroeconomic Volatility: An Empirical Investigation et al. 2015. "The Effect of Growth Volatility on Income Inequality." *Economic Modelling* 45: 212–22.

International Labour Organization (ILO). 2020, September 23. "ILO Monitor Covid-19 and the World of Work" Sixth edition https://www.ilo.org/global/about-the-ilo/newsroom/news/WCMS_755875/lang--en/index.htm

International Monetary Fund (IMF). 2015. Fiscal Monitor. Chapter 2, "Can Fiscal Policy Stabilize Output."

International Monetary Fund (IMF). 2016. "Debt: Use it Wisely," *Fiscal Monitor*, October.

International Monetary Fund (IMF). 2017a. "Unbundling the Downward Trend in Labor Income Share," Chapter 3 in *World Economic Outlook*, April.

International Monetary Fund (IMF). 2017b. Tackling Inequality, *Fiscal Monitor*, October.

International Monetary Fund (IMF). 2017c. "Household Debt and Financial Stability." Chapter 2 in *Global Financial Stability Report: Is Growth at Risk*. October.

International Monetary Fund (IMF). 2018a. "The Global Economy Recovery 10 Years After The 2018 Financial Meltdown," Chapter 2 in *World Economic Outlook*, October.

International Monetary Fund (IMF). 2018b. "Poverty and Inequality in Latin America: Gains During the Commodity Boom but an Uncertain Outlook," Chapter 5 in *Western Hemisphere Department Regional Economic Outlook*, May.

International Monetary Fund (IMF). 2019. *World Economic Outlook*. October. Washington DC: International Monetary Fund.

International Monetary Fund (IMF). 2020a. G-20 Surveillance Note. International Monetary Fund, Washington DC.

International Monetary Fund (IMF). 2020b. "G-20 2020 Report on Strong, Sustainable, Balanced, and Inclusive Growth." Washington DC: International Monetary Fund.

International Monetary Fund (IMF). 2020.c Enhancing Access to Opportunities. Washington DC: International Monetary Fund.

Jenkins, Steven P., A.Brandolini, J. Micklewright, and B. Nolan. 2013. *The Great Recession and the Distribution of Household Income*. Oxford: Oxford University Press.

Jon Frost, and René van Stralen. 2018. "Macroprudential Policy and Income Inequality." *Journal of International Money and Finance* 85(2018): 278–90.

Kaplan, Greg, Benjamin Moll, and Giovanni L. Violante. 2018. "Monetary Policy According to HANK." *American Economic Review* 108(3), March, 697–743.

Kim, Yun Jung, and Jing Zhang. 2019. "Debt and Growth," Twentieth Jacques Polak Annual Research Conference, IMF November 7–8, 2019.

Kirschenmann, Karolin, Tuomas Malinen, and Henry Nyberg. 2016. "The Risk of Financial Crises: Is There a Role for Income Inequality?" *Journal of International Money and Finance* 68(C): 161–80.

Kraay, Aart. 2014. "Government Spending Multipliers in Developing Countries: Evidence from Lending by Official Creditors." *American Economic Journal: Macroeconomics* 6(4): 170–208.

Krusell, Per, and Anthony A. Smith, Jr. 1998. "Income and Wealth Heterogeneity in the Macroeconomy." *Journal of Political Economy*, October, 106(5): 867–96.

Kuhn, Moritz, Moritz Schularick, and Ulrike I. Steins. 2020. "Income and Wealth Inequality in America, 1949–2016." *Journal of Political Economy* 128(9): 3469–519.

Kumhof, Michael, Romain Rancière, and Pablo Winant. 2015. "Inequality, Leverage, and Crisis." *American Economic Review* 105(3): 1217–45.

Laeven, Luc, and Fabian Valencia. 2018. "Systemic Banking Crisis Revisited," IMF Working Paper WP/18/206.

Lakner, Christoph, Daniel Gerszon Mahler, Mario Negre, and Espen Beer Prydz. 2020b. "How Much Does Reducing Inequality Matter for Global Poverty? Global Poverty Monitoring Technical Note." World Bank, Washington, DC. https://open-knowledge.worldbank.org/handle/10986/33902

Levy-Yeyati, Eduardo. 2019. "Exchange Rate Policies and Economic Development," *Oxford Research Encyclopedias*.

Levy-Yeyati, Eduardo, and Federico Sturzenegger. 2003. "To Float or to Fix: Evidence on the Impact of Exchange Rate Regimes on Growth." *American Economic Review* 93(4): 1173–93.

Lucas, Robert E. 2003. "Macroeconomic Priorities." *American Economic Review* 93(1): 1–14.

Mahler, Daniel Gerszon, Christoph Lakner, Mario Negre, and Espen Beer Prydz. 2020. "Updated Estimates of the Impact of Covid-19 on Global Poverty," https://blogs.worldbank.org/opendata/updated-estimates-impact-covid-19-global-poverty

McKay, Alisdair, and Ricardo Reis. 2008. "The Brevity and Violence of Contractions and Expansions." *Journal of Monetary Economics* 55: 738–51.

Mian, Atif, and Amir Sufi. 2018. "Finance and Business Cycles: The Credit-Driven Household Demand Channel." *Journal of Economic Perspectives* 32(3): 31–58.

Mian, Atif, Amir Sufi, and Emil Verner. 2017. "Household Debt and Business Cycles Worldwide." *The Quarterly Journal of Economics* 132(4), November 2017: 1755–817, https://doi.org/10.1093/qje/qjx017

Mian, Atif, Amir Sufi, and Emil Verner. 2020. "How Does Credit Supply Expansion Affect the Real Economy? The Productive Capacity and Household Demand." *Journal of Finance* LXXV: 949–94.

Mian, Atif R., Ludwig Straub, and Amir Sufi. 2020. "The Saving Glut of the Rich and the Rise of In Household Debt," NBER WP 26941.

Mitchell, W.C. 1927. *Business Cycles: The Problem and Its Setting.* New York: National Bureau of Economic Research.

Nakamura, Emi, and Jón Steinsson. 2018. "Identification in Macroeconomics." *Journal of Economic Perspectives* 32(3): 59–86.

Naoussi, Claude Francis, and Fabien Tripier. 2013. "Trend Shocks and Economic Development." *Journal of Development Economics* 103: 29–42.

Obstfeld, Maurice, Jonathan D. Ostry, and Mahvash S. Qureshi. 2019. "A Tie That Binds: Revisiting the Trilemma in Emerging Market Economies." *Review of Economics and Statistics*, May 101(2): 279–93.

Organisation for Economic Co-operation and Development (OECD). 2015. *In It Together: Why Less Inequality Benefits All.* Paris: OECD Publishing.

Ouedraogo, Rasmane. 2015. "Does Pro-cyclical Fiscal Policy Lead to More Income Inequality? An Empirical Analysis for Sub-Saharan Africa." *Economics Bulletin* 35(2): 1306–17.

Panizza, Ugo. 2002. "Income Inequality and Economic Growth: Evidence from American Data." *Journal of Economic Growth* 7: 25–41.

Paul, Pascal. 2020. "Historical Patterns of Inequality and Productivity around Financial Crises" March, Federal Reserve Bank of San Francisco Working Paper 2017–23.

Paul, Pascal, and Joseph H. Pedtke. 2020. "Historical Patterns around Financial Crises," Federal Reserve Bank of San Francisco Economic Letter, May 4.

Peralta-Alva, Adrian, Xuan Song Tam, Xin Tang, and Marina Mendes Tavares, 2018," The Welfare Implications of Fiscal Consolidations in Low Income Countries", IMF Working Papers. 18/146.

Perugini, C., J. Hölscher, and S. Collie. 2016. "Inequality, Credit and Financial Crises." *Cambridge Journal of Economics* 40(1): 227–57.

Piketty, Thomas, and Emmanuel Saez. 2013. "Top Incomes and the Great Recession: Recent Evolutions and Policy Implications." *IMF Economic Review* 61: 456–78.

Quadrini, Vincenzo, and Jose-Victor Rios-Rull. 2015. "Inequality and Macroeconomics." In *Handbook of Income Distribution*, Volume 2B, edited by Anthony B. Atkinson and Francois Bourguignon. Amsterdam: North-Holland.

Rajan, Raguraman. 2010. *Fault Lines*. Chicago, IL: University of Chicago Press.

Ramey, Gary, and Valerie A. Ramey. 1995. "Cross-Country Evidence on the Link Between Volatility and Growth." *American Economic Review* 85(5): 1138–51.

Ramey, Valerie. 2016. "Macroeconomic Shocks and their Propagation." In *Handbook of Macroeconomics*, edited by John B. Taylor and Harold Uhlig, Elsevier Science, and Technology.

Ramey, Valerie. 2019. "Ten Years After the Financial Crisis: What Have We Learned from the Renaissance in Fiscal Research?" *The Journal of Economic Perspectives* 33(2): 89–114.

Ravallion, Martin, and Shaohua Chen. 2009. "The Impact of the Global Financial Crisis on the World's Poorest," http://www.voxeu.org/article/impact-global-financial-crisis-world-s-poorest.

Reinhart, Carmen M., and Kenneth S. Rogoff. 2010. "Growth in a Time of Debt." *American Economic Review* 100(2): 573–8.

Roch, Francisco. 2019. "The Adjustment to Commodity Price Shocks." *Journal of Applied Economics* 22(1): 437–67.

Rodrik, Dani. 1999. "Where Did All the Growth Go? External Shocks, Social Conflict, and Growth Collapses." *Journal of Economic Growth* 4: 385–412.

Schwandt, Hannes, and Till M. von Wachter. 2019. "Unlucky Cohorts Estimating the Long-Term Effects of Entering the Labor Market in a Recession in Large Cross-Sectional Data Sets." *Journal of Labor Economics* 37: S161–98.

Schwandt, Hannes, and Till M. von Wachter. 2020. "Socioeconomic Decline and Death: Midlife Impacts of Graduating in a Recession," *NBER WP* 26638.

Solt, Frederick. 2020. "Measuring Income Inequality Across Countries and Over Time: The Standardized World Income Inequality Database." *Social Science Quarterly* 101(3):1183–99. SWIID Version 9.0, October 2020.

Stiglitz, Joseph E. 2012. "Macroeconomic Fluctuations, Inequality, and Human Development." *Journal of Human Development and Capabilities* 13(1): 31–58.

Terrones, Marco E. 2020, "Do Fixers Perform Worse than Non-fixers During Global Recessions and Recoveries." *Journal of International Money and Finance* 104, June: 1–16.

Vegh, Carlos, and Guillermo Vuletin. 2013. "Overcoming the Fear of Free-falling: Monetary Policy Graduation in Emerging Markets." In *The Role of Central Banks in Financial Stability: How Has It Changed?*, edited by Douglas Evanoff, Cornelia Holthausen, George Kaufman, and Manfred Kremer, pp. 105–31, Federal Reserve Bank of Chicago and European Central Bank.

Vegh, Carlos, and Guillermo Vuletin. 2015. "How Is Tax Policy Conducted over the Business Cycle?" *American Economic Journal: Economic Policy* 7 (August 2015), pp. 327–70.

Vegh, Carlos A., et al, 2019, "Effect of the Business Cycle on Social Indicators in Latin America and the Caribbean: When Dreams Meet Reality," The World Bank.

Woo, Jaejoon. 2011. "Growth, Income Distribution, and Fiscal Policy Volatility." *Journal of Development Economics* 96(2): 289–313.

Woo, Jaejoon, Elva Bova, Tidiane Kinda, and Yuanyan Zhang, 2013., "Distributional Consequences of Fiscal Consolidation and the Role of Fiscal Policy: What Do the Data Say?". IMF Working Papers. 13/195.

Yellen, Janet L. 2014, "Perspectives on Inequality and Opportunity from the Survey of Consumer Finances," https://www.federalreserve.gov/newsevents/speech/yellen 20141017a.htm

Yellen, Janet. 2014. "Many Targets, Many Instruments: Where Do We Stand?" In *What Have We Learned? Macroeconomic Policy after the Crisis*, edited by Akerlof, George, Olivier Blanched, David Romer, and Joseph Stiglitz. Cambridge, MA: MIT Press.

Yellen, Janet. 2016. "Macroeconomic Research After the Crisis," https://www.federalreserve.gov/newsevents/speech/yellen20161014a.htm

12

Tax Policy

Khaled Abdel-Kader and Ruud De Mooij

I. Introduction

Taxation is at the heart of the inclusive growth debate.[1] Taxes are known to affect employment and investment and empirical studies find that taxes have important implications for GDP growth. Yet, taxes are also known to affect inequality or "inclusiveness," mainly through the progressivity of the tax system—a tax burden that rises with a taxpayer's income or wealth, but also through affecting other dimensions of equality, such as equal treatment by gender, equality of opportunity, intergenerational equity and by treating people in similar circumstances the same (horizontal equity).

Both the level and composition of taxes matter for inclusive growth. Regarding the level of taxation, there is widespread consensus that a minimum level of tax revenue is necessary for countries to ensure that the state can provide its essential functions that support redistribution and growth. Gaspar et al. (2016a) find, for instance, that, once tax-to-GDP levels reach 12.75 percent, economic growth increases sharply and in a sustained manner over the following decade. However, while tax ratios in advanced economies (excluding social contributions) average around 25 percent of GDP, those in developing economies are often below the tipping point estimated by Gaspar et al.

The composition of taxes is also important for inclusive growth. For instance, empirical studies have established a so-called growth-ranking of taxes, with income taxes found to be more harmful for growth than consumption and property taxes.[2] However, opposite results are found for the ranking on inequality, namely income taxes tend to reduce inequality more than consumption taxes. This suggests that there must ultimately be a trade-off between efficiency and equity in choosing the tax composition. Yet, this trade-off might be relaxed by improving the design of taxes. For instance, measures to broaden the VAT base

[1] The authors are grateful to the valuable comments and suggestions provided by Valerie Cerra, Barry Eichengreen, Nikolay Gueorguiev, Alex Klemm, Miguel Pecho, and Steve Vesperman as well as participants in the Inclusive Growth book seminar series organized by the IMF Institute for Capacity Development. We thank Jaime Sarmiento Monroy for the excellent research assistance.

[2] Arnold et al. 2011 and Acosta-Ormaechea, Sola, and Yoo 2019.

Khaled Abdel-Kader and Ruud De Mooij, *Tax Policy* In: *How to Achieve Inclusive Growth*. Edited by: Valerie Cerra, Barry Eichengreen, Asmaa El-Ganainy, and Martin Schindler, Oxford University Press. © Khaled Abdel-Kader and Ruud De Mooij 2022. DOI: 10.1093/oso/9780192846938.003.0012

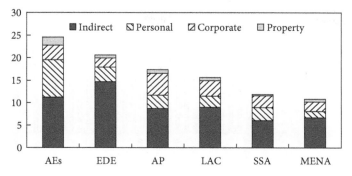

Figure 12.1 Composition of Tax Revenue by Region, 2018

Source: Authors' calculations.

AEs = Advanced Economies (39)
EDE = Emerging and Developing Europe (12)
AP = Asia and Pacific (38)
LAC = Latin America and Caribbean (32)
SSA = Sub-Saharan Africa (49)
MENA = Middle East and North Africa (20)

are found to be less harmful for growth than raising VAT rates; and corporate taxes can be redesigned to eliminate their distortions to growth. These issues are addressed in more detail below.

The composition of taxes varies considerably between advanced and developing economies, with a notably larger role for personal income taxes and property taxes in advanced economies (Figure 12.1).

Tax-benefit systems in advanced economies achieve significant redistribution, as can be inferred from the difference in the Gini coefficient between market incomes and disposable incomes, that is the difference after applying income taxes and social benefits (Figure 12.2).

The average reduction in the Gini coefficient is 18 percent, of which around one quarter is due to progressive taxation and three quarters are due to social benefits.[3] While analysis for developing countries is scarcer, the redistributive impact of fiscal policy is generally much smaller than in advanced economies due to lower social transfers and lower income taxes.

The debate on taxation and inclusive growth has recently received ample interest from scholars, commentators and politicians. For instance, Thomas Piketty's book *Capital in the 21st Century* (2014) on the growing wealth inequality in advanced economies, has sparked a wave of calls for more progressive tax

---

[3] Note that incomes are generally measured on an annual basis. A significant fraction of the redistribution in annual incomes reflects redistribution over the lifecycle, for example through pensions or social insurance. Bovenberg, Hansen, and Sorenson (2012) estimate this share at three quarters in Denmark. Only one quarter would thus represent redistribution from the lifetime rich to the lifetime poor.

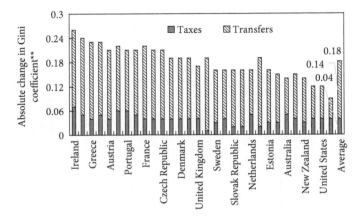

Figure 12.2 Redistributive Impact of Tax*

Source: OECD Income Distribution Database.

* Data as of *2015* or latest av*ailable*.

** Calculated as Gini coefficient for market income minus Gini coefficient for disposable income.

systems. Similar calls are made in a recent book by Martin Sandbu, *The Economics of Belonging* (2020), which discusses political-economy aspects of state intervention. In the United States, candidates for the 2020 Democratic Presidential nomination proposed wealth taxes on millionaires. This issue is controversial, however, and economists such as Larry Summers have downplayed expectations of the revenue-raising ability of wealth taxes (e.g., due to valuation problems and widespread tax avoidance and evasion).

Taxation and inclusive growth has received further impetus from the Covid-19 crisis.[4] Indeed, questions arise for the post-Covid-19 phase as to how to provide prospects and support to vulnerable individuals and struggling but viable businesses hit hard by the crisis while, at the same time, ask for a larger contribution from those who are doing well. There is a great clamor for specific levies on wealth, top income earners and profitable businesses to cover the costs of fiscal interventions during and after the pandemic. At the same time, tax policies should be designed so as not to impede growth during the recovery phase.

This chapter discusses the theory and practice of tax design in support of inclusive growth.[5] It starts with a discussion of the key principles from tax theory to

---

[4] See, for example, the IMF Special Covid-19 series note "Taxation and Inclusive Growth After the Pandemic."

[5] An extensive analysis of the topics addressed in this chapter can be found in the two volumes of the Mirrlees Review: Dimensions of Tax Design (2010) and Tax by Design (2011). Examples of the IMF contributions to the discussions on taxation and inclusive growth can be found in Boadway and Keen (2000); Bastagli, Coady, and Gupta (2012); IMF (2014); Clements, De Mooij, Gupta and Keen (2015); and the Fiscal Monitor of October 2017.

guide practical tax design (Section II). Then, it elaborates on the practice of tax policy making, thereby discussing key choices in the structure of the personal income tax on labor (Section III), capital income (Section IV), wealth (Section V), the corporate income tax (Section VI), and consumption taxes (Section VII). Finally, the chapter elaborates on how to make tax reform happen (Section VIII).

II. Taxation Principles

A. Efficiency

Part of the public finance theory concentrates on the efficiency effects of taxation, typically assuming economies with identical representative agents. These theories teach us some important lessons about efficient tax design. By transferring resources from the private to the public sector, taxes inescapably impose a loss on society that goes beyond the revenue generated (except when taxes are "lump sum"). This is because taxes drive a wedge between the price a buyer pays for something and the amount the seller receives. As a result, a tax can prevent some mutually beneficial transactions. For example, a firm will demand labor up to the point where the wage cost (inclusive of tax) equals its marginal product; but a worker will supply labor effort such that its opportunity costs (foregone leisure or home production) equals the after-tax wage. The difference between the wage cost and the after-tax wage is called the labor-tax wedge, which reflects the gap between the value of extra production and the foregone leisure. The reduction in working hours is a pure welfare loss for society over and above the loss from the direct transfer to the public sector. This deadweight loss (or excess burden) is what determines a tax distortion.

Efficient tax design aims to minimize the total deadweight loss of taxes. The size of this loss depends on two main factors. First, losses are bigger the more responsive the tax base is to taxation. Second, the loss increases more than proportionately with the tax rate: adding a distortion to an already high tax rate is more harmful than adding it to a low tax rate. Two prescriptions for efficient tax policy follow: (i) it is efficient to impose taxes at a higher rate if things are in inelastic demand or supply; and (ii) it is best to tax as many things as possible to keep rates low. The latter forms the basis for several policy prescriptions, such as for base broadening and rate reduction.

B. Equity

Any meaningful tax analysis of equity considerations requires a theory that departs from the representative agent assumption and allows for heterogeneity.

Tax theory typically does this by assuming variation in people's "innate ability," or "talent." The impact of a tax system on the distribution of after-tax incomes then depends on the progressivity of the tax-benefit system—that is, how rapidly the share of income taken by tax increases with the level of income. Thereby, theory generally allows for the possibility of negative taxes (i.e., transfers). The welfare impact of income redistribution is reflected in the social welfare function, which generally adds the utilities of individuals. Redistribution is desirable for two reasons: first, declining marginal utility of income implies that transferring a dollar from a rich to a poor person will increase the sum of the utilities; second, there is a possibility of social aversion against inequality by assigning higher welfare weights to people with low ability. One extreme here is the pure utilitarian approach that assigns equal weights to individual utilities; the other extreme is the Rawlsian approach that assigns only value to the utility of individuals with the lowest ability.

Income redistribution through a progressive tax-benefit system becomes more complicated if other dimensions are considered. For instance, should redistribution be based on individual or family income? And should progressivity be assessed in terms of annual income—an arbitrary period of measurement—or lifetime income? People may reasonably disagree on these matters and designing an equitable tax-benefit system becomes less straightforward than it may seem. It also raises important related equity issues, such as gender equality and intergenerational equity, which should be taken into account when designing the tax system.

Another important issue for equity is tax incidence. The person who ultimately bears the real burden of a tax may not be the one legally responsible for remitting payment, since taxes can affect market prices (including before-tax wages). The principle is that the burden of a tax—its effective incidence—falls more heavily on the side of the transaction with the least elastic response—that is, the one that finds it more difficult to shift out of the activity being taxed. These price changes as well as general equilibrium effects on the prices in other markets, are often ignored but can matter significantly for the distributional impact of tax policies.

C. Trade-off Between Equity and Efficiency

Optimal tax theory emphasizes the trade-off between equity and efficiency. Ideally, governments should implement a progressive tax-benefit system that is based on the exogenous innate ability of people.[6] This would be efficient as it induces no distortions in behavior. Unfortunately, the government cannot

---

[6] Human capital of individuals is of course not exogenous, as it depends on education, health and other choices which can all be influenced by taxation. The emphasis here is on the innate talent.

observe the talent of people. Instead, it can only observe their income, which is the product of talent and effort (in e.g., education, training, work). By setting a tax that is based on income, the tax-benefit system discourages this effort and inevitably creates a distortion that is associated with welfare loss. This gives rise to a fundamental trade-off in designing the tax-benefit system, namely between equity and efficiency.

Pioneered by Mirrlees (1971) and advanced by Diamond (1998) and Saez (2001), optimal income tax theory explores how the tax-benefit system can strike an optimal balance between the two. Irrespective of the social welfare weights assumed in the social welfare function, it appears that the average tax burden at the bottom is negative—reflecting transfers provided to those with the lowest income. Then, marginal tax rates should optimally feature a U-shaped form as a function of income—that is, they should be high at the bottom, then fall between the bottom to the middle of the income distribution, and subsequently rise from the middle to the top of the distribution. The high marginal tax rate at the bottom is because the transfers being given to the lowest income groups are phased out for middle incomes, as it would be too costly to provide them universally. The low marginal tax rate for the densely populated middle-income groups aims to avoid large aggregate distortions in labor effort. Then, a progressive tax rate structure should be imposed from the middle towards the top of the distribution to increase progressivity. Interestingly, this structure roughly resembles how most systems of means-tested benefits and personal income tax schedules have currently been shaped.[7]

The assumptions underlying optimal income tax theory have been challenged, however. The view that progressive taxes are bad for efficiency is based on "first-best" analysis in an economy without other, non-fiscal distortions. In practice, however, the world is full of other distortions. For example, markets may be missing (e.g., because of high transaction costs) or fail (externalities, asymmetric information, imperfect competition). In such a "second-best" world, progressive taxes can make a positive contribution to social welfare if they reduce distortions associated with missing and failing markets (yet, they could also exacerbate these distortions). Indeed, efficiency improvements have been emphasized in case of imperfections in labor, capital, and insurance markets (Abdelkader and De Mooij 2020).

D. Enforcement

A critical element for equity and efficiency is to minimize both tax avoidance (legal) and evasion (illegal). The dividing line between them is not as clear-cut as it may sound, but both are major concerns for governments. Tax avoidance

---

[7] For an overview of these models and various extensions, see Piketty and Saez (2013).

should be addressed by good tax design, for example by minimizing opportunities for tax arbitrage such as income shifting or by imposing tight anti-avoidance measures. Minimizing tax evasion requires a good implementation and enforcement by the tax administration. This can be facilitated by making things simple for taxpayers who want to comply through self-assessment. Ultimately, tax administrations should ensure that the probability of detecting noncompliance—and the penalties that follow—is high enough to encourage compliance while supporting and reflecting widespread willingness to follow the rules.

There are special concerns on tax compliance in developing countries, where constraints on the implementation and enforcement of taxes are often more binding due to limited capacity. Moreover, underdeveloped capital markets and a large fraction of the population in informal self-employment render the opportunities for tax design more limited. In fact, constraints have often kept aggregate tax ratios very low. Simplicity in tax law design, easy tax collection from a limited number of sources, and ample self-assessment is therefore important to deal with these enforcement constraints and provide a rationale for corporate income taxes, for example (especially to collect tax from retained corporate earnings that are otherwise hard to tax), value-added tax (for which the self-enforcing mechanism provides incentives for voluntary compliance), withholding taxes (exploiting administrative powers of large corporations and banks to reduce collection costs), excises (which can often be levied from just a few large businesses, such as breweries, tobacco companies and oil companies) and import tariffs (which can easily be collected on physical goods at the border).

The rest of this chapter discusses how the lessons from tax theory inform the practice of tax policy making, thereby focusing on the design of various taxes in support of inclusive growth.

III. Taxation of Labor Income

In advanced economies, the personal income tax (PIT) raises around 10 percent of GDP. In developing countries, this is much lower, generally not more than 3 percent of GDP. Moreover, these PIT liabilities in developing countries come from a small portion of the population, often comprising of salaried employees in the public sector. In general, designing an efficient, equitable, and enforceable PIT system requires considering the following aspects.

A. Use Individual Income as the Tax Unit

The unit of income taxation can be either family or individual income. Traditional family-based taxation is often based on income splitting, which means that incomes of both partners in a couple are first aggregated and then split in two equal halves that are taxed at the prevailing progressive rate structure. This system is neutral with respect to the choices made within the household, as the tax due for the family does not depend on which partner generates the income. However, if the incomes of two partners vary (perhaps being zero for one of them) they could significantly reduce their joint tax liability by marrying and filing jointly (a "marriage bonus").[8] In a progressive tax system, income splitting reduces the marginal tax rate of the primary earner (the partner with the highest income) and increases it for the secondary earner (the partner with the lowest income). Since the latter are often women, family-based tax systems implicitly create a gender bias. As the elasticity of labor supply is generally found to be considerably higher for women than for men, these systems also discourage overall labor supply.[9] For instance, Jaumotte (2003) finds for OECD countries that eliminating tax discrimination against secondary earners (relative to singles) could raise the labor-force participation rate of women by 3.9 percentage points.

Many advanced economies have transformed their PIT into an individualized system. They are now in place in most European countries following initial reforms in the 1970s and 1980s in Scandinavia, Austria, the Netherlands and in 1990 in the UK. Other countries with predominantly individualized systems have maintained some elements of family-based taxation, such as a transferable tax deduction from the non-working spouse to the breadwinner, family-based deductions, dependent spouse deductions, or options for joint filing. Countries have also introduced other features to improve the labor market participation of secondary earners, such as tax credits or deductions for childcare expenses or targeted deductions for the income of secondary earners.

B. Choose an Appropriate PIT Threshold

A threshold—either in the form of a zero-tax bracket, a basic deduction or a general tax credit—supports tax progression by reducing or eliminating the tax burden on people with the lowest incomes.[10] Thresholds vary significantly across economies. In the OECD, the median is approximately 25 percent of the average wage. In developing countries, they are generally higher as a percentage of the average wage, which helps ease administration. However, thresholds sometimes significantly exceed the average wage, which shrinks the tax coverage and turns

---

[8] For an analysis of the impact of the U.S. income tax on the marriage bonus (or penalty), see for example https://www.taxpolicycenter.org/briefing-book/what-are-marriage-penalties-and-bonuses.

[9] Compared to men, women take on a larger share of home duties relative to paid labor, which makes them more flexible in adjusting formal working hours, see for example Alesina et al. (2011). Evers et al. (2008) provide a meta-analysis of estimated labor-supply elasticities for men and women.

[10] Tax credits are in principle more progressive than tax deductions, since the value of a credit does not depend on the marginal tax rate faced by the taxpayer, as is the case with a deduction.

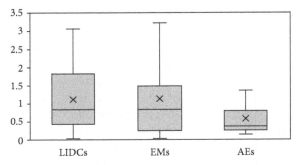

Figure 12.3 Personal Income Tax Threshold (Percent of GDP per capita), 2019
Source: Authors' calculations.

LIDCs = Low-Income and Developing Count*ries* (57)
EMs = Emerging Markets (96)

the PIT into a tax on top-income earners only, thereby raising little revenue. In several developing economies, for instance, the threshold exceeds two times GDP per capita (Figure 12.3). Common advice is not to set the threshold above the average wage, although higher levels can be envisaged where this average is below a reasonable subsistence level.

C. Provide Relief for Low-income Wage Earners

Optimal income tax theory provides a rationale for subsidizing earnings of low-wage workers. In many advanced economies, these take the form of a refundable tax credit, which constitutes a net transfer to the individual when they exceed income tax liabilities.[11] These benefits increase the net income gain from accepting a job relative to the alternative of being out of work, which can encourage participation; they also provide income support to low-wage earners, which can be good for inclusion. In-work benefits are usually phased out as incomes rise, with the steepness of phase-out depending on the primary objective of the program. In countries that emphasize the labor force participation objective, benefits are usually gradually phased out with individual income (Belgium, Finland, Germany, the Netherlands, and Sweden).[12] In countries that emphasize the income support objective, benefits are often conditional on the presence of children in the household and generally phased out more steeply with family income

---

[11] In-work tax credits require a strong tax administration and work best if taxpayers are already filing tax returns. This makes them less suitable for many developing countries.
[12] For schemes in the UK. and the United States, evaluation studies find that programs have a positive net effect on employment, especially for single women with children. Although negative labor supply effects have been found for those with income levels within the phase-out range, these were generally small.

so as to prevent leakage of benefits to higher income families and reduce fiscal costs (Canada, France, Korea, New Zealand, the Slovak Republic, the United Kingdom, and the United States). In the United States in 2017, 27 million eligible workers and families nationwide received about $65 billion in tax credits under the earned income tax credit. The federal government estimates that it lifted 9.4 million people out of poverty, including 5 million children.[13]

D. Rationalize Tax Deductions

Many countries—including developing ones—adopt various tax allowances in the PIT related to children, education, housing, health insurance, commuting, and charitable donations. Some of these accrue disproportionately to the rich, such as deductions for mortgage interest, because households with high incomes are more often homeowners. More generally, PIT tax expenditures (defined as specific provisions in the tax code that allow certain people or companies to pay less tax) in several countries accrue disproportionally to people with high incomes. For example, Toder and Baneman (2012) find that if all individual income tax expenditures in the United States had been eliminated in 2011, the outcome would have been broadly progressive, with a 19.8 percent decline in after-tax income for the top 1 percent of the income distribution, compared to only a 7.5 percent decrease for the bottom quintile, with additional revenue available for pro-inclusive tax and expenditure changes.

E. Use a Stepwise Rising PIT Rate Schedule

Flat PIT schedules often have appeal to policy makers as they signal simplicity and efficiency. Both arguments are flawed, however. The former requires designing a simple tax base, for example by minimizing deductions, credits and exemptions. The rates that are applied to this tax base will then be a simple calculation. The latter, as we have seen above, requires a non-linear structure of the PIT with rising marginal tax rates towards the top—not a flat tax.

Nevertheless, since the mid-1990s 27 countries—especially in Central and Eastern Europe and Central Asia—have introduced flat PIT systems, usually with a low marginal rate (Figure 12.4). When combined with a threshold, these schemes are still progressive in the sense that the average tax burden rises with income. However, significantly more progression can be achieved by using a piecewise linear tax system whereby marginal tax rates increase with income.[14]

---

[13] See https://www.eitc.irs.gov/eitc-central/about-eitc/about-eitc.
[14] The IMF (2020) provides an illustration of such an assessment.

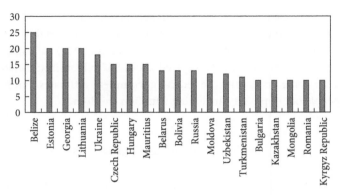

Figure 12.4 Countries with Flat PIT Rates (Percent), 2019
Source: Authors' calculations.

F. Set the Top PIT Rate at an Appropriate Level

Income tax progressivity has declined steeply in the 1980s and 1990s and has remained broadly stable since (IMF 2017). For instance, the median top PIT rate (across various country groups) dropped from 47 percent in 1990 to 30 percent in the past decade (Figure 12.5). The choice of the top PIT rate is usually a contentious policy issue, but optimal tax models provide some guidance. For instance, if one assigns zero welfare weight to top income earners (Rawlsian social welfare), it would be optimal simply to maximize revenue collected from them. This requires balancing the revenue gain from a higher marginal top PIT rate at the initial base against the revenue loss induced by behavioral responses that a higher tax rate would induce—such as reduced labor effort, avoidance or evasion. The latter can be measured by the elasticity of taxable income (see Saez et al. 2012 for a review). Studies estimating this revenue-maximizing rate find that it generally ranges between 50 and 60 percent (IMF 2013).[15] Some argue that it may be higher—up to 80 percent—as higher top rates can help discourage rent seeking by top-income earners (e.g., managers who might be able to partly set their own pay by bargaining harder or influencing compensation committees) (Piketty, Saez, and Stantcheva 2014). Others, however, emphasize that high marginal rates cause other economic costs as well, for example on innovation and entrepreneurship (Akcigit et al. 2019). Moreover, the calculations rely on the extreme assumption of a zero welfare weight for the very rich. If a positive welfare weight is assigned to them, the optimal top PIT rate will be lower. Nevertheless, the results of these models suggest that some countries seem to have room to increase their top PIT rate to boost revenue and strengthen progressivity.

---

[15] Revenue-maximizing rates in developing countries with notably weaker administrative capacity, might be lower than in advanced economies. Top PIT rates in developing countries are indeed generally lower than in advanced economies.

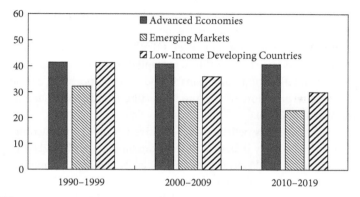

Figure 12.5 Average Top PIT Rates (Percent), 1990–2019
Source: Authors' calculations.

IV. Taxation of Capital Income

An important aspect of efficient redistributive taxation is how capital income is treated. To understand this, it is useful to make a distinction between two components of capital income: the normal return to capital and economic rent. The normal return is defined as the minimum return required to make investors indifferent between investing in the asset and investing in some benchmark investment (adjusted for risk), such as a government bond. The remaining profit, over and above the normal return, is called rent.

The public finance literature is unanimous in advocating taxes on rents for both efficiency and equity reasons. Rent taxes are in principle non-distortionary and a classic result from the literature is that they can in fact be taxed at 100 percent without inducing behavioral change. In practice, tax burdens are generally lower, in part because rents are often "quasi rents," arising from specific long-term investments with a fixed cost. These investments might be distorted if tax rates become too high. Moreover, some factors that generate rents (such as intellectual property rights) might be mobile internationally in terms of where they are held and managed from. Taxation can thus induce a distortion in the location of these factors.

The literature is divided on the question whether the normal return to capital should be taxed or not. Capital income—interest, dividends and capital gains—is used for future consumption so that taxes on it correspond to a differentiated consumption tax on present versus future consumption—one that compounds if the time horizon expands. Prudent people who prefer to postpone consumption to later in life (or transfer it to their heirs) will thus be taxed more than those who do not, even though they have the same life-time earnings. This violates horizontal equity principles. Moreover, it causes a distortion by encouraging individuals to substitute future with current consumption, that is, they reduce savings. The tax is therefore also inefficient. A classical result, formalized by Chamley (1986) and Judd (1985), is that the optimal tax on capital is zero and that redistribution could better be achieved by a progressive tax on labor income. This result has led several economists to argue for a tax exemption of the normal return. However, there is fundamental criticism on this zero-capital income tax result, focused on the empirical validation of assumptions in the models, practical considerations and even the interpretation of the model results (Banks and Diamond 2010; Straub and Werning 2020).

While most economists believe that a positive tax on capital income is desirable, there remains a lively debate as to how capital income should be taxed. For some, the theoretical ideal is to tax the sum of labor and capital income at a progressive rate structure, consistent with the ability-to-pay principle. This "global income tax" prevents arbitrage between labor and capital that could otherwise arise in the taxation of self-employed. However, others support separate taxation of labor and capital income under a "dual income tax." Typically, a progressive rate scheme then applies to labor income, while a flat rate applies to capital, usually at a relatively lower rate. The motivation for this is twofold: first, it mitigates distortions in saving and investment, which tend to be relatively severe; and second, capital income taxes do not need to be personalized, which eases enforcement by using final withholding schemes. Whatever system is chosen, the following design recommendations are universal.

A. Ensure Neutral Taxation of Entrepreneurial Income

One reason for taxing capital income is that it provides a necessary backstop in the taxation of entrepreneurial income. Indeed, it is often difficult (or even impossible) for tax administrations to distinguish labor income from capital income earned by self-employed entrepreneurs. Businesses organized as sole proprietorships are therefore generally taxed on their total income through the prevailing PIT—and no distinction is made between the labor and capital components of that income. However, entrepreneurs might also opt to run their business as a closely-held corporation. The business then pays its owner-director some fixed remuneration for its labor, which would be subject to the PIT scheme. The remainder of its business income would be seen as capital income and taxed under the corporate income tax (CIT) and complemented by a tax on dividend distributions. However, if there is a large difference between the PIT and the CIT treatments, these entrepreneurs will have an incentive to manipulate the share of labor and capital income so as to minimize their overall tax liability. As this will be hard to verify by the government, such arbitrage looms large. To avoid this, it is important to broadly harmonize the rates of the PIT and the combined burden of the CIT and dividend taxation.

B. Tax Different Types of Investment Income Uniformly

In many countries, different forms of investment income are taxed at different tax rates. For instance, interest payments are usually deductible for the CIT, whereas returns on equity are not. As a result, interest received by individuals is more lightly taxed than equity returns. At the personal level, moreover, dividends are often taxed at much higher rates than capital gains—with the latter sometimes being left entirely untaxed. This induces firms to retain earnings in the firm or distribute profit by buying back shares. Many countries also have some form of preferential treatment for certain investors or investments by exempting them from PIT. For example, capital returns of pension funds are often untaxed; and some countries exempt interest on government bonds or other types of returns. All these differences induce changes in asset portfolios of investors that erode the capital income tax base and create economic distortions. A neutral, uniform treatment of all investment income without exemptions is the best way to mitigate this and enhance the progressivity of taxation.

C. Minimize Tax Evasion

Taxing capital income at the individual level can be administratively challenging because people can often hide their income from the tax administration, for example by holding their assets abroad. The key challenge for tax administrations is to collect and use third-party information to implement taxes on capital income. For instance, the implementation challenges provide a very strong rationale for withholding taxes at the level of the firm, that is, through the CIT. Moreover, withholding taxes on interest and dividends can, to some extent, further circumvent administrative difficulties as they utilize banks and large corporations to collect taxes. Some Latin American countries also impose withholding taxes on capital gains.

An important development for the enforcement of capital income taxes is the increasing prevalence of arrangements to exchange information between countries for tax purposes. Especially automatic exchange of information (AEOI) under the initiative of the G20 and the US Foreign Account Tax Compliance Act (FATCA) hold the prospect of facilitating the enforcement of both capital income taxes and net wealth taxes. A recent IMF study by Beer et al. (2019) finds that the introduction of these standards has already reduced deposits held in low-tax jurisdictions by 25 percent—indicating their effectiveness in curbing tax evasion. Global adoption of these standards is necessary, however, as otherwise deposits might be shifted elsewhere where they can remain hidden. Moreover, for developing countries, there remains a challenge to effectively utilize such information to enforce the taxation of capital income.

V. Taxation of Wealth

Wealth is more unevenly distributed than income, both across and within countries. In the OECD for example, the average share of wealth held by the top
10 percent of households is 50 percent, which by far exceeds the average share of
income (24 percent) earned by the top 10 percent (Figure 12.6). In the United
States, the top 0.1 percent of the population holds nearly 22 percent of total net
wealth, a similar share as the bottom 90 percent. These large and growing inequalities have sparked debate on the taxation of wealth.[16] Figure 12.7 shows the revenues raised by such taxes. In advanced economies, it ranges between 1 and
4 percent of GDP; in developing countries, it is on average much lower than that.
The following points guide policy makers on their use.

A. Strengthen Recurrent Property Taxes

Real property taxes are imposed on gross values.[17] They are among the least distortive
for economic growth as their base is immobile. Given that they are paid mainly by
residents, and property values likely reflect the value of local public services, property
taxes can resemble a benefit tax which can support accountability of local authorities.

Property taxes raise on average around 1 percent of GDP in advanced economies;
their yield goes up to 3 percent of GDP in the UK and Canada. In developing
countries, they generally raise less than 0.5 percent of GDP. In many countries,
there is scope to exploit this tax more fully by raising tax rates, updating property
values to current market prices and, especially in developing countries, improving
cadasters and scaling up administrative capacity. Where market-based valuation

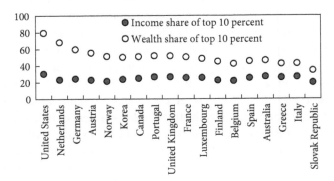

Figure 12.6 Income and Wealth Shares (Percent)*
Sources: World Bank WDI and OECD Wealth Distribution Database.
Data from 2012 or latest available year.

---

[16] See for example the IMF Fiscal Monitor October 2017.
[17] Norregaard (2013).

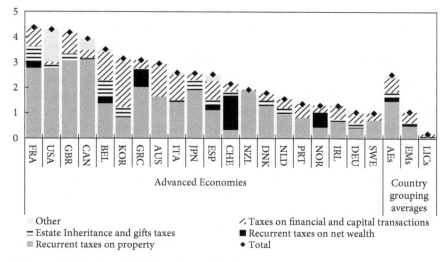

Figure 12.7 Taxes on Wealth (Percent of GDP), 2017

Note: Recurrent taxes on property include taxes levied on the use or ownership of immovable property, including land and buildings. Debts are not taken into account. Taxes paid by households and other entities are included. Recurrent taxes on net wealth cover taxes levied regularly on net wealth, which includes a wide range of movable and immovable property, net of debt. Includes taxes paid by individuals and corporate enterprises. Estate taxes are charged on the amount of total estate, whereas inheritance taxes are charged on the shares of individual recipients. Taxes on financial and capital transactions include taxes on the issue, transfer, purchase and sale of securities, as well as taxes levied on specific transactions such as the sale of immovable property. Other includes other non-recurrent taxes on property.

Source: OECD Global Revenue Statistics Database.

is hard, simplified approaches based on property areas can produce reasonable outcomes at lower administrative costs.

B. Consider a Net Wealth Tax (NWT) if other Capital Income Taxes are Hard to Impose

NWTs are imposed on the sum of financial and non-financial wealth minus liabilities. They target the same base as capital income taxes to the extent that assets generate a flow of income. The base of a NWT might be broader if non-income generating assets are included. However, difficulties often arise with the valuation of such assets, which is one reason why these have often been exempt from NWTs (e.g., primary residences, pension assets; farm and business assets, artwork, jewelry, shares in unlisted businesses).

Tax evasion by the wealthy has been particularly difficult to uncover through traditional means, such as random audits and self-reporting. Hence, the introduction of a NWT will require increased resources for enforcement.[18] The key to

---

[18] In many advanced economies, tax administrations have separate units to deal with the compliance of high net wealth individuals, a group that is considered extremely high risk (McLaughlin and

enforcing a NWT is information reporting by third parties. For instance, financial institutions should provide end-of-year wealth balances for interest-bearing assets, publicly-listed stocks, assets held by mutual funds, and mortgage or student loans; pension funds should report the value of individual retirement accounts; and local governments should share information about the value of real estate and registered vehicles. These issues likely make a NWT less feasible for countries with weak administrative capacity.

The value of wealth held offshore is especially hard to ascertain, as information is more difficult or even impossible to obtain. Zucman (2013) estimates the portion of global financial wealth that is held in offshore low-tax jurisdictions at 8 percent—much of which is likely to go untaxed. These enforcement challenges of a NWT might be mitigated by the increasing prevalence of arrangements to exchange information between countries for tax purposes.

A handful of studies have estimated the extent to which NWTs induce behavioral responses in the form of reduced saving/investment, avoidance behavior (i.e., legal shifts toward exempt or tax-preferred assets) and tax evasion (illegal misreporting of wealth) (Scheuer and Slemrod 2020). This is reflected in the tax elasticity of reported wealth. In Denmark, Spain, and Switzerland effects are estimated to be very large, in order of a decline in reported wealth between 32 and 44 percent in response to a 1 percent tax on wealth. Using evidence from the Panama papers, it appears that a significant portion of these behavioral responses is due to evasion; and this response tends to increase with the level of wealth, namely evasion is much larger for the ultra-wealthy (Alstadsæter et al. 2019).

The prevalence of comprehensive NWTs has declined over time. Several countries that had a NWT in the 1990s, for instance, have repealed it (e.g., Australia, Canada, Pakistan and several European countries, including recently France)—in some cases due to limited revenue relative to administrative effort or for constitutional reasons. However, NWTs have survived in Italy, Norway, and Switzerland and have been reinstated by Belgium and Spain. In Switzerland, all cantons levy a NWT on a relatively broad base, which yields around 1 percent of GDP. In other countries, revenue from NWTs has generally been lower as the base has been narrower.

C. Tax Inheritances and Gifts

Inheritance or estate taxes can be effective redistributive tools to limit intergenerational wealth inequality and enhance equality of opportunity—an important dimension of inclusiveness. Although most advanced economies impose them, these taxes have not proved easy to implement due to ample tax exemptions, sometimes very high thresholds, and widespread avoidance and evasion.

Buchanan 2017). The number of tax administrations focusing on this segment has been increasing in the higher-income countries, but not in developing countries.

The average revenue in countries that have such a tax is 0.1 percent of GDP in 2017. However, revenues are higher in Belgium and France (up to 0.7 percent of GDP), suggesting that often improvement is feasible.

VI. Corporate Income Taxation (CIT)

A positive tax on capital income doesn't mean countries should tax corporations. Indeed, capital income taxes can be levied directly on the people that ultimately receive that income, namely shareholders and creditors. So: why is there a need for a CIT?

It is hard to justify a CIT on efficiency grounds. For instance, with mobile capital after-tax returns on investment are fixed on world capital markets. Any source-based tax will then lead to adjustment in the amount of capital such that before-tax return rises enough to restore equilibrium. Less capital means lower wages so that the incidence of a source-based capital tax will fall on workers. Empirical evidence suggests that, indeed, the lion's share of the corporate tax burden falls on wages (Arulampalam, Devereux, and Maffini 2012)—although this conclusion is not undisputed (Gravelle 2013). Since it is more efficient to tax labor directly than indirectly, the optimal CIT is then found to be zero. This is an application of the Diamond-Mirrlees (1971) production efficiency theorem, one of the most powerful precepts in public finance: transactions between businesses should never be taxed because firms will choose different inputs than they would in the absence of the tax and end up producing less than they could. Thus, there are no efficiency reasons for a tax on the normal return earned by businesses. There are yet two reasons why a CIT can still be desirable for countries:

- *The CIT imposes tax on economic rents, including those earned by foreign owners.* For an individual country, taxing these rents has significant appeal. This is especially important for rents arising from extractive industries that exploit natural resources—which is particularly important for several developing countries. Fiscal regimes are generally in place to ensure that a fair share of these natural resource rents accrues to the governments of the country where the resources are located. Aside from the CIT, such regimes generally rely on a combination of specific rent taxes and royalties.
- *The CIT has administrative appeal due to its withholding function.* Corporations are convenient collection agents for governments as they hold proper books and records that can effectively be monitored by tax inspectors. Relying entirely on individuals to pay their tax based on filed tax returns would be considerably costlier to enforce. The withholding role of the CIT is especially important for profits that are retained in the company, which lead to higher share prices and, therefore, to capital gains for the owners. However, for practical reasons capital gains are rarely taxed on an

accrual basis at the individual level (e.g., a cash-constrained owner would have to sell stock to pay its tax) but rather upon realization. Capital owners can thus postpone their tax payment by not realizing these gains. The attraction of the CIT is that it withholds tax on all profits as they arise, thus eliminating the difficulty in taxing capital gains.

On average across the world, the CIT raises around 3 percent of GDP. Especially for low-income countries, they provide for a relatively large share of total revenue (Figure 12.8). CIT revenue has been stable for quite some time, despite a reduction in rates. Indeed, over the past three decades, CIT rates have tumbled from an average of around 40 percent in 1990 to slightly more than 20 percent today (Figure 12.9). That this has not induced a reduction in revenue is because countries have simultaneously broadened their corporate tax bases.

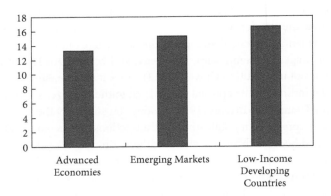

Figure 12.8 Tax Share of CIT (In Percent of Total Tax Revenue)
Source: Authors' calculations.

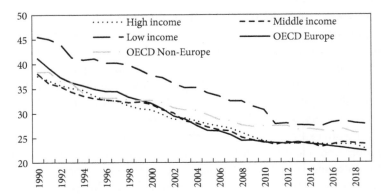

Figure 12.9 Combined CIT Rates (Percent)
Source: Authors' calculations.

A. Design the CIT as a Rent Tax

The key drawback of how CIT systems are currently designed in most countries is that they create two major economic distortions. First, by raising the cost of capital on equity CIT systems distort investment. This hurts economic growth and adversely affects efficiency. Second, by differentiating between debt and equity, the CIT creates a bias toward debt finance. This not only causes an additional direct welfare loss, but also threatens financial stability.[19]

Both distortions can be eliminated by designing the CIT as a rent tax.[20] There are different ways of doing this. First, one class of rent taxes is known as cash-flow taxes, which allow for full expensing of investment instead of deductions for tax depreciation. The simplest form is a real-base cash-flow tax, defined as the net sum of all real receipts and payments, excluding financial flows such as interest payments, net debt issuance, and net dividends. A second type of cash-flow tax is levied on real and financial cash-flows, which adds inflows from issuing loans or interest received and deducts outflows, such as repayments and interest costs. In practice, pure cash-flow taxes are rare. However, there are many examples of countries implementing some of their features. Some countries, for example, have temporarily allowed expensing of investment, but without restricting interest deductibility, such as the United States does since its latest reform in 2017. Other countries use cash-flow tax features on surtaxes, for example in the natural resource sector, to capture resource rents (IMF 2012).

An alternative rent-based tax system keeps the current CIT but adds a deduction for a notional return on corporate equity—to equalize the treatment of interest. Similarly, the so-called allowance for corporate capital (ACC) replaces the deductibility of actual interest with a notional interest rate applied on all capital, namely debt and equity, to obtain neutrality. Allowance for corporate equity systems have been implemented, sometimes only for a few years, in several countries (Belgium, Croatia, Cyprus, Italy, Latvia, Liechtenstein, Malta, Turkey). Studies generally find powerful effects of these systems on corporate debt levels. ACC-like systems were in place in several countries during the world wars, known as excess profits taxes, to finance extraordinary spending.

B. Consider Cost-Based Rather than Profit-Based Tax Incentives

Most countries use some form of tax incentives to mitigate the distortionary impact of the CIT on investment. In advanced economies, especially investments in research and development (R&D) are incentivized. In developing countries,

---

[19] For a more in-depth discussion, see IMF (2016a).
[20] Normal returns can still be taxed at the personal level.

incentives often focus on attracting foreign direct investment (FDI). For both, their design can often be improved by focusing the incentives on reducing the cost of investment, rather than incentives that relief tax on profits.[21]

Many advanced countries encourage R&D by special tax credits or super deductions. These policies can be efficient due to the positive externalities associated with R&D. Empirical evidence suggests that these policies have worked well in many countries and that they hold the prospect of generating significant positive long-term growth effects. The April 2016 Fiscal Monitor, for example, finds that efficient pricing of R&D can boost GDP by 5 percent on average. Yet, they require strong enforcement capacity to limit abuse. Recently, some countries—most notably in Europe—have adopted patent boxes that reduce the tax on the profits generated by innovation. Evaluation studies indicate that these regimes either had no discernible impact on R&D or, where they did have an impact, had significant fiscal costs. Indeed, incentives that reduce the costs of R&D investments directly are more cost-efficient than profit-based measures.

Many developing countries aim to attract FDI by providing outright tax exemptions, for example in special economic zones, or through time-bound tax holidays. However, these incentives are generally found to be ineffective and inefficient. Indeed, their fiscal cost can be high, while surveys indicate that these tax incentives generally rank low in the list of relevant location factors for multinationals. Investment tax incentives that directly reduce the cost of investment, such as investment tax credits, accelerated depreciation or outright expensing of investment yield more investment per dollar spent. The governance and management of tax incentives can often be improved by relying on objective rules-based criteria embedded in the tax law, as opposed to discretionary granting on a case-by-case basis.[22]

C. Adopt Tailored Anti-Tax Avoidance Measures

A major risk for the CIT base of countries is due to profit shifting by multinational companies. For instance, international businesses can use transfer pricing techniques, international debt shifting and treaty shopping to reduce their tax liability in a country (see Beer et al. 2020 for a review of evidence on profit shifting). These risks are particularly important for developing countries (Crivelli et al. 2016). The G20/OECD project on base erosion and profit shifting (BEPS) agreed upon common international rules and guidance for countries to protect their tax base, while avoiding double taxation. However, distinct problems and capacity limitations in developing countries require more tailored or simplified solutions that strike a balance between being administrable without infringing

---

[21] See IMF 2016b.
[22] IMF, OECD, World Bank, and UN (2015), Options for Low Income Countries' Effective and Efficient Use of Tax Incentives for Investment.

upon legitimate business undertakings.[23] For instance, an alternative minimum tax can be imposed, based on simplified indicators, such as turnover or assets.[24] Similarly, simple caps can be imposed on deductible payments to mitigate tax avoidance. Developing countries should also exercise caution in signing double tax treaties and pay close attention to their terms and conditions. For instance, they should avoid tight restrictions on the use of withholding taxes on foreign payments (e.g., on royalties, interest or intra-company services), which can be effective instruments to mitigate tax avoidance.

VII. Consumption Taxation

The distinction between direct taxes on income and indirect taxes on consumption is less important than it may seem. A uniform tax on consumption is broadly equivalent to a uniform tax on income, the only difference being that the consumption tax excludes the normal return on capital (hence it is equivalent to a tax on wages and economic rents).[25] However, an important difference in implementing the tax is that the government can generally observe individual incomes but not individual consumption. Therefore, if it wants to efficiently design a redistributive tax-benefit system, it can better use a progressive individualized income tax than a non-individualized consumption tax (Atkinson and Stiglitz 1976). Nevertheless, consumption taxes are a major revenue source for most governments, in part due to their relative ease of enforcement and collection.

Empirical studies generally find that consumption taxes are relatively growth friendly, for example compared to income taxes. At the same time, consumption taxes are often claimed to be regressive, namely richer households pay less tax as a percentage of their income than poorer households. Nevertheless, claims about regressivity should be qualified, as they mainly reflect higher savings by the rich. When the consumption tax burden is considered as a proportion of total current expenditure—which many would argue is likely a better indicator of economic wellbeing—consumption taxes are often found to be neutral for the income distribution—or even slightly progressive (IMF 2019c; Bachas, Gadenne, and Jensen 2020). Moreover, if the revenue is used for progressive spending, the net impact on the poor can be positive.

---

[23] For a more in-depth discussion, see IMF 2014 and 2019b. These papers also discuss options for the design of the international tax framework and the importance of international coordination on these matters.

[24] Aslam and Coelho (2021).

[25] The equivalence only holds under restrictive assumptions regarding the utility structure of households. In more general settings, consumption taxes should minimize distortions between taxed and untaxed goods and services (such as leisure and home production) (Corlett and Hague 1953). Empirically, however, there is little consensus among economists as to the precise optimal rate differentiation. As a rule of thumb, therefore, a uniform consumption tax is generally seen as a proper benchmark for the optimal tax on consumption.

A. Design an Efficient VAT

Today, more than 160 countries have a VAT system in place, which resembles a broad-based consumption tax.[26] These systems typically account for around one-quarter or more of total tax revenue. A VAT is imposed on every transaction in the production process. When goods are purchased by a VAT-registered business, the tax paid on inputs is credited or refunded. This ensures that VAT is ultimately only levied on final consumption, where no credits or refunds are provided. This design has the attraction of encouraging voluntary tax compliance, since each business has an incentive to register in order to claim credits on their inputs. Moreover, those who operate in the informal sector are still charged on their inputs, without them being able to claim credits. Nevertheless, VAT design in many countries can be full of exemptions and differential rates, which reduces these advantages and induces economic distortions. Acosta Ormaechea, and Morozumi (2019) find that this can be damaging for economic growth. To effectively raise revenue from VAT while doing the least damage to inclusive growth, VAT systems can best be designed with a high threshold, a broad base, and a single rate.

- *A sufficiently high threshold* aims to reduce the compliance costs of VAT for small traders. At the same time, the revenue foregone can be minimal, in part because unregistered businesses cannot claim input credits. A VAT threshold can also strengthen the progressivity of the VAT by reducing the tax on small traders in rural areas where the poorest often buy their goods (Jenkins, Jenkins, and Kuo 2006).
- *Minimize VAT exemptions.* Some countries exempt certain goods and services from VAT to mitigate its distributional effects. However, exemptions are inefficient to achieve a more equitable outcome. First, they cause distortions due to cascading effects (tax on tax) if applied to intermediate stages of the supply chain, as exempt businesses cannot claim credits on their inputs. Second, exemptions create a bias against outsourcing by businesses, since the tax burden can be reduced by producing inputs in-house rather than purchasing taxable inputs from third parties. This creates another inefficiency. Third, by exempting suppliers, the incentives for voluntary compliance with the VAT are reduced. A limited number of well-defined exemptions is quite common, however, for practical reasons. Standard exemptions are applied for example for margin-based financial services, basic health care, and education.

---

[26] A deeper analysis and discussion can be found in Ebril et al. (2001) or the Tax Policy Assessment Framework on https://www.imf.org/en/Data/TPAF. Some countries refer to the value-added tax as "goods and services tax" (GST)—for example Australia, Canada, India, New Zealand and Singapore.

- *Use a single VAT rate.* Some countries tax necessities such as food and medicine at special reduced VAT rates to pursue redistributive policies. The idea is that the poor spend a large proportion of their income on them so that a reduced or even zero rate offers relief.[27] However, this policy is inferior to pursuing redistribution through other tax and spending policies since it is poorly targeted. For instance, as the rich spend a larger absolute amount on such goods, a large portion of the benefits from a reduced rate accrue to them. Moreover, differential rates significantly complicate VAT administration and cause complexity in defining what goods precisely fall under the reduced rate. Spending measures, such as transfers in cash or in kind, are considerably more efficient to achieve distributional objectives than reduced VAT rates. In developing countries, where the availability of these spending instruments is less common, some reduced VAT rates can be justified on equity grounds—albeit at a high revenue cost.[28]

B. Impose Environmental Taxes

A key efficiency reason for differential consumption taxation is due to externalities. They arise if the consumption of a good affects the wellbeing of those not involved in the underlying transaction. Environmental damage, such as climate change, is the leading example of a negative externality. The corrective tax, also called a Pigouvian tax, is designed to internalize the external cost of a transaction in the price (i.e., "setting the price right") so that agents change their behavior in the desired direction, for example by reducing pollution.[29] Pigouvian taxes generally come on top of broad-based consumption taxes and should be imposed per unit of consumption, at a level directly related to the external costs—such as the social cost of carbon emissions in the case of climate externalities.

As environmental taxes can be regressive, their introduction may require offsetting tax or spending measures to compensate poor households. In advanced economies, environmental taxes (including on energy) raise around 1.5 percent of GDP in revenue; in developing countries this is usually lower. In many

---

[27] Under a zero VAT rate, suppliers can claim credits for input VAT. This is different from a VAT exemption, in which case no credits can be claimed. Exports should be zero-rated and imports taxed under a destination-based VAT. As VAT credits can exceed VAT liabilities for zero-rated suppliers (including exporters), this gives rise to VAT refunds. Managing such refunds has been challenging in many developing countries; for a discussion, see Pessoa et al. (2021).

[28] Sometimes, reduced VAT rates can have the opposite distributional effect. For example, OECD/KIPF (2014) finds that reduced VAT rates on restaurant food and hotel accommodation tend to benefit the rich more than the poor.

[29] Instead of a corrective tax, externalities can also be priced through a cap and trade scheme, such as the emission trading scheme in the European Union.

countries, there is significant potential for these taxes to yield more revenue while also improving environmental quality. For example, in the EU, environmental taxes raise around 2.5 percent of GDP. This seems to have had no negative impact on economic growth. For instance, a recent study by Metcalf and Stock (2020) finds no evidence for negative growth effects of carbon taxes in Europe.[30] A carbon tax of $75 per ton, necessary to meet the Paris climate objectives, has been estimated to yield more than 1.5 percent of GDP in revenue in G20 countries.

C. Use Specific Excises

Excises on alcohol, tobacco and unhealthy food ("sin goods") are generally motivated by related social concerns—although not strictly speaking externalities. Bounded rationality of households and lack of self-control may justify government intervention in the pricing of these addictive commodities—although such arguments are not undisputed. Most countries use excises on these products as part of their policy to improve health outcomes, but revenue raising objectives are important as well. For developing countries, these excises can have special appeal as concentrated production and high import shares make administration relatively easy. Revenue from excises (including on fuel products) varies from an average of 1 percent of GDP in low-income countries to around 2.5 percent of GDP in advanced economies. Over time, revenue has often declined in several countries due to a lack of indexation of the specific (i.e., per unit) rates, which causes real revenue to fall with inflation. In many countries, there is scope to raise significantly more revenue from excises without adverse distributional effects (Cnossen 2020). Indeed, while excises tend to bear relatively more heavily on people with low incomes, this only holds in advanced economies and not for developing countries. Special excises on luxury goods, such as yachts, jewelry or perfumes usually contribute little to achieving equity objectives, raise little revenue, and add to administrative costs. The exception is excises on motor vehicles, which can raise sizable amounts and are generally progressive.

VIII. How to Make It Happen?

This chapter suggests that many countries have scope to promote inclusive growth through tax reform. Policy recommendations vary by country, yet some reform options are common. For advanced and some emerging market economies, promising options include a more progressive PIT system, more neutral taxation

---

[30] For a more in-depth analysis and discussion of pricing climate externalities, see IMF (2019a).

of capital and corporate income, improvements in VAT design, and more/better use of carbon taxes, property taxes and taxes on inheritances. Developing countries should first and foremost enhance their administrative capacity. Yet, they could also often improve and simplify their VAT and excise policies, better protect their income taxes against avoidance and evasion, reduce discretionary tax incentives, enhance their fiscal regimes for extractive industries, and better exploit taxes on property and pollution.

Successfully achieving a welfare-improving tax reform is a difficult task, however, due to complex political-economy dynamics and various institutional constraints. Indeed, large discrepancies can be observed between prescriptions by tax theory and the actual tax practice of countries. Recently, surveys have been used to better understand these discrepancies, thereby looking at the determinants of people's support for redistributive tax policies (Stantcheva 2020). It appears that this depends critically on people's perceptions and beliefs and how that differs from reality due to limited knowledge. Also mistrust in government plays an import role for people's views on redistribution. These findings point to a critical role of the management of tax policy reform by governments.

Managing a successful tax reform strategy in support of inclusive growth requires at least consideration of the following ten issues:[31]

A. Ensure Strong Political Commitment and Leadership

Tax reform affects all factions of society and will need the support from the entire government—calling for a "whole-of-government approach." The Minister of Finance is usually responsible for the management of the tax system and should have the clear and unconditional leadership of the reform effort. In many countries, a permanent or temporary committee chaired by the Minister of Finance and supported by technical working groups, brings together all stakeholders from the public sector to reflect the different interests.

B. Build Consensus and Generate Public Support

Gaspar et al. (2016b) find that, aside from credible leadership, inclusive politics and constitutive institutions are vital elements of tax capacity building. Indeed, it is essential to hold extensive political consultation with multiple stakeholders in

---

[31] The management of tax system reform is one component of the so-called Medium-Term Revenue Strategy (MTRS), a concept developed by the Platform for Collaboration on Tax (PCT) and being implemented by several countries with support from PCT partners, see https://www.tax-platform.org.

society, such as businesses, tax professionals, civil society organizations, local governments, academic researchers, think tanks, etc. Consultative discussions might not create unanimous approval or support, but will instill in society a sense of country-wide ownership. Some groups in society might not be well-organized or integrated into the formal economy—often low-income groups that could benefit most from measures to support inclusion. This may require special attention from the government. Other groups can be very well organized and could even become a stumbling block to the reform if they aim to protect vested interests— often the more affluent who can, for example, oppose increases in tax progression. Managing these political differences requires forceful leadership and strong communication.

C. Develop a Clear and Broad Communication Strategy

The communication campaign should develop a narrative to position the tax reform as a government-led and country-owned strategy that aims to support inclusive growth, emphasizing the benefits to society at large. The government should mobilize representatives from the public sector, the private sector, business associations, religious leaders, community representatives and the mass media, to signal broad consensus across the wider community and involve them in the communication.

D. Emphasize the Joint Impact of Taxes and Expenditures

It is generally difficult to pursue a revenue-raising structural tax reform due to opposition from those who will be taxed more. Sometimes, this is due to a too narrow focus on the tax burden, without looking at the broader implications on the spending side. To convince the general public of the need and desirability of revenue-raising tax reform, it is critical to emphasize the additional expenditures they help finance. This joint impact of tax and spending can be progressive and supportive of inclusive growth, even if some of the individual taxes are regressive. Earmarking of taxes for specific expenditures should be avoided, however, since it can lead to inefficient spending decisions.

E. Quantify the Impact of the Reform

An evidence-based quantitative impact assessment is essential for several reasons. Quantification will help structure the debate and rationalize discussions among stakeholders—which might otherwise be dominated by vague statements, loose beliefs and ill-informed perceptions. Analysis of the impact on revenue, the income distribution and the economy will also help policy makers design the reform in the best possible manner. This enables the government to convince stakeholders that the reform is both inclusive and growth friendly. Quantitative analysis also supports the transparency and accountability of the reform process and ultimately helps build trust in government.

F. Sequence Reforms Well

Tax reforms can be either incremental or comprehensive. Incremental reforms have the advantage that they avoid large shocks in incomes or asset prices and that people can anticipate them. For instance, reforms in the taxation of housing are often incremental to avoid large disruptions in house prices. However, incremental tax reforms might not be credible if their time span is too long as they can be hard to be sustained politically. Indeed, interest groups will have time to mobilize opposition and find ways to block those reforms. A comprehensive reform might be more difficult to achieve, however, although has the appeal of creating package deals whereby the income effects of some tax measures can be offset against others. Especially when there is space for tax relief, structural improvements might thus be achieved. Some sequencing in the reform process, even under a comprehensive reform, might still be desirable to avoid too many changes for taxpayers and tax administrations at the same time, which can impose a large burden on them.

G. Recognize Institutional Constraints

Revenue agencies responsible for the implementation of the tax system should participate in the reform process, for example as core members of the tax reform committee. This ensures that concerns about enforcement of a reformed tax system are recognized and accounted for in the reform strategy. For instance, some reforms may introduce excessive complexity, impose undue compliance costs, or require (third-party) information that is not yet available. Legal drafting experts are also essential for the reform process to ensure that tax laws are clear and unambiguous and that they ensure tax certainty. In some countries, decentralized fiscal powers (e.g., States, provinces or municipalities) can create obstacles to the reform process or for its implementation and their interests should also be integrated into the reform management process.

H. Build Effective Administrative Capacity

Capacity constraints in tax and custom administrations are often major obstacles to revenue mobilization in developing countries. Clearly, revenue administrations should have sound management and governance arrangements and modern process/systems to manage core tax functions. And enforcement generally benefits from simple, clear, and transparent legislation (including procedural and administrative regulations), remittance and withholding regimes at adequate point of collections, taxpayer segmentation strategies, and large scale information cross-matching based on extensive use of third-party information. Administrative considerations should play a key role in the design of tax reform, for example with major focus on simplicity, voluntary compliance mechanism and easy collection by use of withholding. Reforming the tax administration to deal with new or modified tax laws usually takes time to bear fruit, especially if they require major changes in how people work and in administrative processes. Experience therefore teaches us that revenue effects of tax reform often occur with a time lag.

I. Use Opportunities During Good Times

Tax reforms have been most successful when undertaken during good times, when a reduction in the overall tax burden can be used to compensate losers. For example, growth-friendly tax reforms—characterized by rate reductions and base broadening—took place in the 1980s in the United States and UK. Countries in continental Europe successfully moved their tax burdens in the 1990s away from direct toward indirect taxation. While growth friendly, not all these reforms were inclusive, however, and some may have increased income inequality.

J. Use Opportunities During Bad Times

During or after a crisis, policymakers under pressure may rush into measures that risk damaging inclusive growth, for example through quick fixes like tax rate increases or the introduction of new distortive transaction taxes. However, in some countries a crisis paved the way for the introduction of long-lasting structural reforms that support inclusive growth. Indeed, crisis times may offer an opportunity for reform as the urgency facilitates political agreement among different actors. Special temporary levies on top income earners and corporate profits, for instance, have been introduced in Germany to cover the costs of unification and in Japan to finance the reconstruction efforts after the 2012 earthquake. Also, the Covid-19 crisis triggered a debate on the use of such levies to cover the increased debt—perhaps as a structural measure to increase tax progression.

References

Abdelkader, K., and R. de Mooij, 2020, Tax Policy and Inclusive Growth, IMF Working paper No. 2020/271, International Monetary Fund, Washington DC.

Acosta-Ormaechea, S., and A. Morozumi. 2019. "The Value Added Tax and Growth: Design Matters." IMF Working Paper No. 19/96, International Monetary Fund, Washington DC.

Acosta-Ormaechea, S., S. Sola, and J. Yoo. 2019. "Tax Composition and Growth: A Broad Cross-Country Perspective." *German Economic Review* 20(4): 70–106.

Akcigit, U., J. Grigsby, T. Nicholas, and S. Stantcheva. 2019. "Taxation and Innovation in the Twentieth Century." NBER Working Paper No. 24982.

Alesina, A., A. Ichino, and L. Karabarbounis. 2011. "Gender-Based Taxation and the Division of Family Chores." *American Economic Journal: Economic Policy* 3(2): 1–40.

Alstadsæter, A., N. Johannesen, and G. Zucman. 2019. "Tax Evasion and Inequality." *American Economic Review* 109: 2073–103.

Arnold, J., B. Brys, C. Heady, Å. Johansson, C. Schwellnus, and L. Vartia. 2011. "Tax Policy for Economic Recovery and Growth." *Economic Journal* 121(550): 59–80.

Arulampalam, W., M.P. Devereux, and G. Maffini. 2012. "The Direct Incidence of Corporate Income Tax on Wages." *European Economic Review* 56(6): 1038–54.

Aslam A., and M. Coelho. 2021. "A Firm Lower Bound: Characteristics and Impact of Corporate Minimum Taxation." IMF Working Paper No. 21/161, International Monetary Fund, Washington DC.

Atkinson, A.B., and J.E. Stiglitz. 1976. "The Design of Tax Structure: Direct Versus Indirect Taxation." *Journal of Public Economics* 6(1–2): 55–75.

Bachas, P., L. Gadenne and A. Jensen. 2020. "Informality, Consumption Taxes, and Redistribution.", NBER Working Paper No. 27429.

Banks, J., and P. Diamond. 2010. "The Base for Taxation." In *Dimensions of Tax Design: The Mirrlees Review*, Chapter 6, Institute for Fiscal Studies.

Bastagli, F., D. Coady, and D. Gupta. 2012. "Income Inequality and Fiscal Policy." IMF Staff Discussion Note 12/08, International Monetary Fund, Washington, DC.

Beer, S., M. Coelho, and S. Leduc. 2019. "Hidden Treasures: The Impact of Automatic Exchange of Information on Cross-Border Tax Evasion." IMF Working Paper 19/286, International Monetary Fund, Washington, DC.

Beer, S., R. de Mooij, and L. Liu. 2020. "International Corporate Tax Avoidance: A Review of the Channels, Magnitudes, and Blind Spots." *Journal of Economic Surveys* 34(3): 660–88.

Boadway, R., and M. Keen. 2000. "Redistribution." In *Handbook of Income Distribution*, edited by Anthony Atkinson and François Bourguignon, Chapter 12. Amsterdam: Elsevier.

Bovenberg, A.L., M.I. Hansen, and P.B. Sorenson. 2012. "Efficient Redistribution of Lifetime Income through Welfare Accounts." *Fiscal Studies* 33(1): 1–37.

Chamley, C. 1986. "Optimal Taxation of Capital Income in General Equilibrium with Infinite Lives." *Econometrica* 54(3): 607–22.

Clements, B., R. De Mooij, S. Gupta, and M. Keen. 2015. *Inequality and Fiscal Policy*. Washington DC: International Monetary Fund.

Cnossen, S. 2021. "Excise Taxation for Domestic Resource Mobilization." CESifo Working Paper No. 8442.

Corlett, W.J., and D.C. Hague. 1953. "Complementarity and the Excess Burden of Taxation." *Review of Economic Studies* 21(1) 21–30.

Crivelli, E., R. de Mooij, and M. Keen. 2016. "Base Erosion, Profit Shifting and Developing Countries." *FinanzArchiv* 72: 268–301.

Diamond, P.A. 1998. "Optimal Income Taxation: An Example with a U-shaped Pattern of Optimal Marginal Tax Rates." *American Economic Review* 88(1): 83–95.

Diamond, P.A., and J.A. Mirrlees. 1971. "Optimal Taxation and Public Production I: Production Efficiency, and II: Tax Rules." *American Economic Review* 61: 8–27, 261–78.

Ebrill, L., M. Keen, J.P. Bodin, and V. Summers. 2001. *The Modern VAT*. Washington DC: International Monetary Fund.

Evers, M., R. de Mooij, and D. Van Vuuren. 2008. "The Wage Elasticity of Labor Supply: A Synthesis of Empirical Estimates." *De Economist* 156: 25–43.

Gaspar, V., L. Jaramillo, and P. Wingender. 2016a. "Tax Capacity and Growth: Is There a Tipping Point?" IMF Working Paper 16/234, International Monetary Fund, Washington DC.

Gaspar, V., L. Jaramillo, and P. Wingender. 2016b. "Political Institutions, State Building, and Tax Capacity; Crossing the Tipping Point." IMF Working Paper 16/233, International Monetary Fund, Washington DC.

Gravelle, J. 2013. "Corporate Tax Incidence: Review of General Equilibrium Estimates and Analysis." *National Tax Journal* 66(1): 185–214.

International Monetary Fund (IMF). 2012. "Fiscal Regimes for Extractive Industries: Design and Implementation." Washington DC. www.imf.org/external/np/pp/eng/2012/081512.pdf.

International Monetary Fund (IMF). 2013. *Fiscal Monitor: Taxing Times*. Washington DC. https://www.imf.org/en/Publications/FM/Issues/2016/12/31/~/media/Websites/IMF/imported-flagship-issues/external/pubs/ft/fm/2013/02/pdf/_fm1302pdf.ashx.

International Monetary Fund (IMF). 2014. "Fiscal Policy and Income Inequality." IMF Policy Paper. Washington DC. https://www.imf.org/en/Publications/Policy-Papers/Issues/2016/12/31/Fiscal-Policy-and-Income-Inequality-PP4849

International Monetary Fund (IMF). 2016a. "Taxation, Leverage and Macroeconomic Stability." IMF Policy Paper. Washington DC. https://www.imf.org/en/Publications/Policy-Papers/Issues/2016/12/31/Tax-Policy-Leverage-and-Macroeconomic-Stability-PP5073

International Monetary Fund (IMF). 2016b. *Fiscal Monitor: Acting Now, Acting Together.* Washington DC. https://www.imf.org/~/media/Websites/IMF/imported-full-text-pdf/external/pubs/ft/fm/2016/01/pdf/_fm1601.ashx

International Monetary Fund (IMF). 2017. *Fiscal Monitor: Tackling Inequality.* Washington DC. https://www.elibrary.imf.org/doc/IMF089/24492–9781484312483/24492–9781484312483/Other_formats/Source_PDF/24492–9781484317419.pdf.

International Monetary Fund (IMF). 2019a. *Fiscal Monitor:* How to Mitigate Climate Change. Washington DC. https://www.imf.org/~/media/Files/Publications/fiscal-monitor/2019/October/English/text.ashx

International Monetary Fund (IMF). 2019b. Corporate Taxation in the Global Economy, IMF Policy Paper. Washington DC. https://www.imf.org/~/media/Files/Publications/PP/2019/PPEA2019007.ashx

International Monetary Fund (IMF). 2019c. Macroeconomic Developments And Prospects In Low-Income Developing Countries—2019, IMF Policy Paper. Washington DC. https://www.imf.org/en/Publications/Policy-Papers/Issues/2019/12/11/Macroeconomic-Developments-and-Prospects-in-Low-Income-Developing-Countries-2019–48872

International Monetary Fund (IMF). 2020. Finland: Staff Report for 2019 Article IV Consultation, IMF Country Report 20/5. Washington DC. https://www.imf.org/~/media/Files/Publications/CR/2020/English/1FINEA2020001.ashx.

International Monetary Fund (IMF), Organisation for Economic Co-operation and Development (OECD), World Bank, and United Nations (UN). 2015. *Options for Low Income Countries' Effective and Efficient Use of Tax Incentives for Investment: A Report to the G-20 Development Working Group.* https://www.imf.org/external/np/g20/pdf/101515.pdf

Jaumotte, F. 2003. "Female Labor Force Participation: Past Trends and Main Determinants in OECD Countries." OECD Economics Department Working Paper No. 376, OECD, Paris.

Jenkins, G., H. Jenkins, and C.-Y. Kuo. 2006. "Is the Value Added Tax Naturally Progressive?" Working Paper 1059, Queen's University, Kingston.

Judd, K.L. 1985. "Redistributive Taxation in a Simple Perfect Foresight Model." *Journal of Public Economics* 28(1): 59–83.

McLaughlin, L., and J. Buchanan. 2017. "Revenue Administration: Implementing a High-Wealth Individual Compliance Program." Technical Notes and Manuals, International Monetary Fund, Washington, DC.

Metcalf, G.E., and J.H. Stock. 2020. "Measuring the Macroeconomic Impact of Carbon Taxes." *American Economic Association Papers and Proceedings* 110: 101–6.

Mirrlees, J. A. 1971. "An Exploration in the Theory of Optimum Income Taxation." *Review of Economic Studies* 38(2): 175–208.

Mirrlees, J., S. Adam, T. Besley, R. Blundell, S. Bond, R. Chote, M., et al. 2010. *Dimensions of Tax Design: The Mirrlees Review*, Institute for Fiscal Studies.

Mirrlees J., S. Adam, T. Besley, R. Blundell, S. Bond, R. Chote, et al. 2011. *Tax by Design: The Mirrlees Review*. Oxford: Oxford University Press.

Norregaard, J. 2013. "Taxing Immovable Property: Revenue Potential and Implementation Challenges." IMF Working Paper 13/129, International Monetary Fund, Washington DC.

Organisation for Economic Co-operation and Development (OECD)/KIPF. 2014. *The Distributional Effects of Consumption Taxes in OECD Countries*. Paris: OECD Publishing.

Piketty, T. 2014. "Capital in the Twenty-First Century." Harvard University Press.

Piketty, T., and E. Saez. 2013. "Optimal Labor Income Taxation." In *Handbook of Public Economics* (Volume 5, Chapter 7), edited by A.J. Auerbach, R. Chetty, M. Feldstein, and E. Saez, pp. 391–474. North Holland: Elsevier.

Piketty, T., E. Saez, and S. Stantcheva. 2014. "Optimal Taxation of Top Labor Incomes: A Tale of Three Elasticities." *American Economic Journal: Economic Policy* 6(1): 230–71.

Pessoa, M., A. Okello, A. Swistak, M. Muyangwa, V. Alonso-Albarran and V. Koukpaizan. 2021. How to Manage Value-Added Tax Refunds. How-To Note No. 2021/4. International Monetary Fund, Washington DC.

Saez, E., 2001. "Using Elasticities to Derive Optimal Income Tax Rates." *Review of Economic Studies* 68(1): 205–29.

Sandbu, M. 2020. "The Economics of Belonging." Princeton University Press.

Scheuer, F., and J. Slemrod. 2020. "Taxing Our Wealth," mimeo, University of Zurich and University of Michigan.

Stancheva, S. 2020. "Understanding Tax Policy: How do People Reason," NBER Working Paper 27,699.

Straub, L. and Werning, I. 2020. "Positive Long-Run Capital Taxation: Chamley-Judd Revisited." *American Economic Review* 110(1): 86–119.

Toder E., and D. Baneman. 2012. "Distributional Effects of Individual Income Tax Expenditures: An Update." Urban-Brookings Tax Policy Center.

Zucman, G. 2013. "The Missing Wealth of Nations: Are Europe and the U.S. Net Debtors or Net Creditors?" *Quarterly Journal of Economics* 128(3): 1321–64.

13

Public Expenditure

Younes Zouhar, Jon Jellema, Nora Lustig, and Mohamed Trabelsi

I. Introduction

Public expenditure policy is a critically important tool for promoting inclusive growth.[1] Public expenditure policy affects economic growth and the distribution of income both in the short run and the long run. For example, social spending provides a minimum income level and increases access to valuable public services. In the short run, public spending on cash transfers reduces income poverty and inequality directly. In the long run, cash transfers, especially if targeted to the poor, can be both growth-enhancing and improve distributional outcomes because of their positive impact on the human capital of children from disadvantaged backgrounds. Spending on education and healthcare services improves the quality of life, is growth-enhancing (through the human capital channel) and can, if targeted to those most in need, increase equality of opportunity and social mobility, which may lead to greater equality in social outcomes. Social spending also provides a risk-mitigation tool: vulnerable segments of the population will be at least partially protected from the global or local macroeconomic, financial, social, and environmental shocks that buffet them. Public investment in infrastructure is equally important as it raises long-term economic growth and overall productivity which in turn generate higher employment overall while improving living standards and reducing poverty. Furthermore, spending on certain types of infrastructure—such as water and sewerage—improves living standards in multiple dimensions in the short term as well.

The impact of public expenditure on inequality and poverty depends on its size, composition, progressivity and the way it is funded. The redistributive impact of public expenditure tends to be lower among developing countries than among advanced countries, reflecting differences in levels of development, spending

[1] We thank Jaime Sarmiento Monroy and Beenish Amjad for the excellent research assistance. We also thank Valerie Cerra, Barry Eichengreen, Zhiyong An, Boele Bonthuis, Tewodaj Mogues, Randa Sab, Marina M. Tavares, Joseph Thornton, Claude Wendling, Yuan Xiao as well as participants in the Inclusive Growth book seminar series organized by the IMF Institute for Capacity Development.

Younes Zouhar, Jon Jellema, Nora Lustig, and Mohamed Trabelsi, *Public Expenditure* In: *How to Achieve Inclusive Growth.* Edited by: Valerie Cerra, Barry Eichengreen, Asmaa El-Ganainy, and Martin Schindler, Oxford University Press. © Younes Zouhar, Jon Jellema, Nora Lustig, and Mohamed Trabelsi 2022. DOI: 10.1093/oso/9780192846938.003.0013

magnitudes, and the composition of spending.[2] In developing countries, social spending is generally low—with limited social protection coverage—and tends to be procyclical. Pro-poor public spending often reduces poverty and inequality, even though it is paid for with regressive taxes. However, when consumption taxes are too high, the poor can end up being net payers into the fiscal system, reducing their purchasing power and welfare (Lustig 2018, chapter 10). The capacity of budget institutions to deliver an "inclusive" spending program varies widely among countries and across levels of development; the quality of budget institutions matters not only for the cost-effectiveness of public service delivery, but also for how well public resources are protected from corruption and waste.

Public expenditure policy is shaped by preferences with respect to the role of the government; levels of development; available fiscal space; and ability to raise taxes. In order to foster more inclusive growth in advanced economies where tax and debt burdens are already high, the focus should be on better targeting benefits and ensuring the sustainability of the pension system (Clements et al. 2014, 2015). In contrast, in developing countries, given the large gaps in public services and infrastructure, the priority should be on extending the coverage of social safety nets, and improving access to basic public services. Equal emphasis should be placed on reducing nonproductive spending (such as subsidies that benefit disproportionately the nonpoor) and improving tax mobilization to preserve fiscal sustainability.

The distributional impact of expenditure policies must be analyzed jointly with those of revenue policy and tax collection measures.[3] The impact of revenue policy can be—and often is!—large enough to either counterbalance or enhance expenditure policy's impact. For example, consumption taxes like VAT or excises can be regressive (when considered in a vacuum); despite this, the impact of fiscal policy *overall* may be still progressive when benefits from public expenditures are distributed in a progressive manner. Therefore, it is theoretically possible that increasing the revenue from regressive taxes to fund more progressive public expenditures is the best approach to supporting redistribution. On the spending side, cash transfers may seem generous and pro-poor, but if the poor pay more taxes, transfers net of taxes received by the poor could be nil or even negative (see, for example, Lustig 2018, chapter 10). Therefore, the design of taxes to finance social spending should ensure that the poor do not end up being net payers.[4]

---

[2] As shown in Lustig (2015), when advanced countries were as poor as some of today's developing countries, the level of spending of the former on education or health, for example, was considerably smaller.

[3] Lustig (2018), chapters 1–4. Also, see Lustig (2020).

[4] See Abdel-Kader and De Mooji (2020) for the design elements of tax policy that fosters inclusive growth.

Drawing from theory and empirical evidence, this chapter will describe when and how public expenditure promotes inclusive growth. The central role of public expenditure has further gained prominence during the Covid-19 pandemic with the scaling up of spending to increase health capacities, mitigate the effects on the vulnerable segments of the population, and support the private sector. The Covid-19 crisis has also underscored the need to have in place adequate social safety nets and to accelerate the development agenda in order to address the large gaps in the social sector and inclusive infrastructure.[5] The second section presents stylized facts about public expenditure. In the third section, we lay out a conceptual framework describing the connections between public expenditure and inclusive growth and discuss the design of "inclusive" public expenditure policies. The following section reviews evidence of the impact of public expenditure and its different components on inequality and poverty, as well as inequities in accessing public services. The fifth section will discuss policy options for enhancing inclusive growth via public spending.

II. Public Expenditure—Stylized Facts

Government spending has expanded globally, increasing from 29 percent of GDP in 2000 to 33 percent in 2019; this overall increase hides significant differences in terms of levels and trends between advanced and developing economies (Figure 13.1). In advanced economies government spending has hovered just below 40 percent of GDP (notwithstanding a spike in 2009). The composition of spending changed slightly with the increase in social benefits being offset by

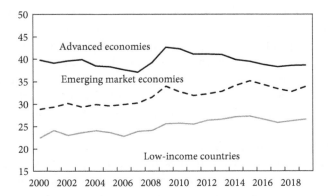

Figure 13.1 General Government Expenditure (percent of GDP)
Source: IMF WEO Database

---

[5] The chapter does not cover the Covid-19 pandemic period and its specific implications on public expenditure and inclusive growth.

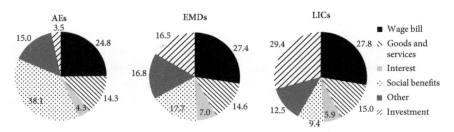

Figure 13.2 Public Expenditure by Expenditure Category
Source: IMF WEO Database.

wage containment and cuts in public investment. In emerging and low-income economies, government spending has by contrast risen to 34 and 27 percent of GDP, respectively, driven up by higher wage bills, social benefits, and public investment.

There are significant differences in the spending structure by income levels (Figure 13.2). The share of the wage bill in total spending ranges from 25 percent in advanced economies to 28 percent in low-income countries (LICs) while the relative share of goods and services tends to be about the same (14–15 percent) in both groups. However, advanced economies allocate a larger proportion of public spending to social benefits (38 percent) than emerging economies (18 percent) and LICs (9.4 percent). Conversely, the share of public investment is lower in advanced economies (4 percent) than in emerging economies (17 percent) and LICs (29 percent).

There are also noticeable differences in trends and composition of social spending over the last two decades (Figure 13.3).[6] Social spending amounted to about 26.5 percent of GDP among advanced economies in 2016–2018 against 25 percent of GDP in 2000–2003. This increase has been driven by social benefits and healthcare spending. Social spending is significantly lower in emerging economies and LICs. It increased in emerging economies from 11 percent to 13.8 percent of GDP, due to higher spending on healthcare and social protection. In LICs, social spending rose by 1.5 percentage point to 8 percent of GDP, reflecting a slight increase in spending on social protection and education while health spending stagnated. During the same period, advanced economies steadily reduced their spending on defense and security from 3.4 percent of GDP in 2000–2003 to 3 percent of GDP in 2016–2018. Spending on defense decreased in emerging economies but was more than offset by higher spending on public order and safety. Spending on both items rose in LICs, totaling 3.7 percent of GDP in 2016–2018 against only 2.7 percent during 2000–2003.

---

[6] Social spending comprises public spending on social protection, education, and health.

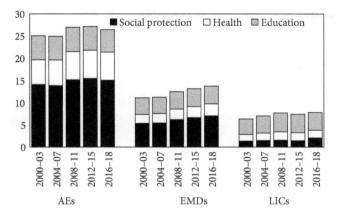

Figure 13.3 Social Spending (percent of GDP)
Sources: IMF, World Bank, and national authorities.

Public spending tends to be procyclical.[7] Public expenditures should be contained during good times in order to build fiscal buffers so that increased spending can boost aggregate demand and foster macroeconomic stability during downturns or in the face of unanticipated shocks. Empirical evidence shows, however, that public spending and social spending are subject to procyclicality in most countries. The issue is more pronounced for developing countries, reflecting the notably smaller size of automatic stabilizers (e.g., unemployment benefits) as well as political economy factors such as the common pool problem and policy myopia (Del Granado et al. 2010; Frankel et al. 2011).[8] By exacerbating economic fluctuations, procyclical spending has adverse effects on both growth and equity objectives. In some developing countries and especially in resource-rich countries, the cyclicality of public spending can be asymmetric (Abdih et al. 2010) with spending procyclical during good times as windfalls are shared with the population in the form of higher wages, increased public sector employment, and larger subsidies; and counter-cyclical or neutral during bad times. When persistent, this often leads to excessive debt accumulation and breeds macroeconomic instability and with it higher inflation and a reduction in the purchasing power of the most vulnerable.

There are significant inefficiencies in public spending, particularly among developing countries.[9] For example, at least 20–40 percent of health spending is

---

[7] When analyzing procyclicality, one should look at the overall stance of the fiscal policy. However, and following many studies, we focus here on the cyclicality of public spending, because tax receipts tend to be endogenous with respect to the business cycle (Frankel et al. 2011).

[8] Capital spending is often the first item to be curtailed in the face of rising fiscal pressures during downturns, reflecting an anti-investment bias. For more detail, see Essama-Nssah and Moreno-Dodson (2011).

[9] Efficiency means the adequate use of the available resources in order to obtain the maximum outcome. Inefficiencies of public spending are measured as a difference between the actual spending and the theoretically possible minimum spending that is sufficient to produce the same level of actual outcome. In practice, identifying the extent of spending inefficiency is difficult. For example,

typically wasted (the World Health Organization 2010). Grigoli and Ley (2012) estimate that GDP losses due to wasteful spending on education and health were substantial, reaching more than 4 percent of GDP, among a set of 24 advanced and emerging economies. An IMF study has estimated that the average country loses about 30 percent of the value of its public investment due to inefficiencies (IMF 2015). Examples of prevalent inefficiencies include quasi-fiscal activities related to inefficient and unprofitable state-owned enterprises and generalized energy subsidies.

The capacity of budget institutions to deliver efficient public spending varies widely across countries.[10] Strong budget institutions reinforce the sustainability of fiscal policy and the country's ability to implement sound fiscal policies. The IMF assesses the quality of budget institutions based on 12 indicators that fall under three broad areas: (i) understanding the fiscal challenge; (ii) developing a credible fiscal strategy; and (iii) implementing the fiscal strategy (IMF 2014a). Advanced economies score consistently high in all three areas, while emerging economies and LICs tend to lag—albeit at different degrees—in the capacity to understand fiscal challenges and develop a credible fiscal strategy. The assessment of the quality of public investment management (PIMA) shows similar patterns (IMF 2015). Government effectiveness is stronger in advanced economies than in emerging economies, with LICs lagging significantly.[11] While public spending (as a share of GDP) rose among LICs over the last decade, government effectiveness ratings have slightly receded.

III. Public Spending and Inclusive Growth—An Analytical Framework

It is useful to start with a framework that lays out the channels through which public spending can help achieve inclusive growth objectives. The broader concept of inclusive growth encompasses dimensions such as equity, poverty reduction, and inclusion in the labor market. It emphasizes generation of productive employment and the accumulation of human capital over time, rather than solely direct short-term income redistribution, as a means of increasing incomes.

---

measuring inefficiencies in the health sector typically involves comparing a particular health system to an "efficient" one. However, because many factors other than spending affect health, and they vary across countries, it is difficult to identify the minimum spending required to achieve given health outcomes (Coady et al. 2014).

[10] Budget institutions refer to the standing requirements, procedures and processes applied when deciding and implementing public policies.

[11] The government effectiveness indicator compiled by the World Bank captures perceptions of the quality of public services, the quality of the civil service and the degree of its independence from political pressures, the quality of policy formulation and implementation, and the credibility of the government's commitment to such policies. It ranges from -2 to 2, with 2 being the most effective.

Promoting inclusiveness means also that the government should provide a risk management mechanism to help individuals absorb risks to income or welfare that materialize and prevent vulnerability to shocks from becoming a constraint on productive, human-capital-seeking behaviors.

Public spending is a powerful instrument to promote inclusive growth. Public spending can contribute to the creation of opportunities in society through factor accumulation and productivity. It is also key in ensuring that individuals are ready and able to take advantage of the opportunities created by growth dynamics. To justify public action to achieve inclusive growth objectives (rather than relying on markets) and lay out the connections between public spending and inclusiveness, it is useful to examine the basics—the threefold rationale for fiscal policy proposed by Musgrave (1959). Under that framework, fiscal policy should aim at (i) promoting macroeconomic stabilization by focusing on countercyclical measures in the short term while preserving debt sustainability in the medium and long term; (ii) improving resource allocation by providing public goods in a cost-effective manner; and (iii) addressing distributional disparities and promoting equal opportunities.

Recurring crises have further refocused interest in public spending as an instrument for inclusive growth. Following the 2007–2008 financial crisis, advanced economies and developing countries have strived to address the economic challenge of low growth and productivity slowdown and rising inequality. The 2020 global Coronavirus pandemic reinforced the central role of public spending in many ways. In the short term, spending on health and emergency services was fully accommodated to save lives and find and roll out vaccines and there were widespread countercyclical stimulus packages targeted at workers and firms. The 2020 health and economic crisis has also brought to the surface long-standing challenges of the capacity and the quality of healthcare systems and of social protection measures targeting the unemployed. Furthermore, it has uncovered and magnified the distributional effects of the digital gap—prevailing across countries and within countries—in terms of unequal or limited access to essential services such as remote learning, teleworking, telemedicine, and E-government services.

All three of these rationales for fiscal policy may have an impact on the nature or extent of inclusive growth. As noted by Brahmbhatt and Canuto (2011), "fiscal policy undertaken under one or more rationales will typically affect the different development objectives." Similarly, a spending measure undertaken under one rationale may affect some or all dimensions of inclusive growth, resulting in favorable or adverse effects (Figure 13.4). In fact, many areas of public spending offer possibilities to foster inclusive growth by focusing on reducing poverty and inequality and promoting quality employment. As such, they entail complementarities as they can achieve both efficiency and equity. Other measures, however, involve trade-offs that cannot be systematically avoided (Figure 13.5).

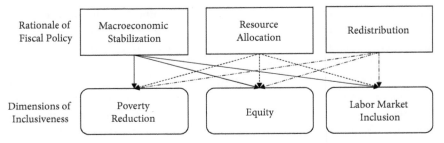

Figure 13.4 From Musgrave's Framework of Fiscal Policy to Inclusiveness
Source: Authors' illustration.

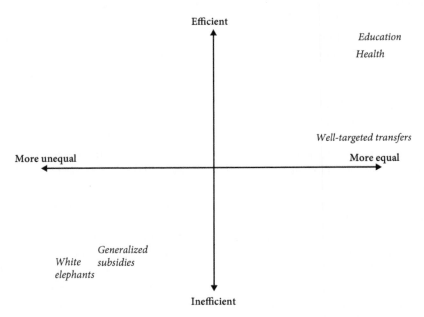

Figure 13.5 Examples of Complementarities and Trade-offs Involved in Spending Measures
Source: Authors' illustration.

- In one extreme, there are win-win measures that can enhance long-term growth and labor market participation while reducing inequality. For example, expanding equal access to education will boost both growth and equity.
- At the other extreme, there are lose-lose policies that tend to generate inefficiencies and more inequality. Generalized energy subsidies are a good example of such policies as they tend to undermine economic growth and diversification and benefit disproportionally upper-income households.
- Across this efficiency-equity spectrum, there are growth-enhancing public spending measures that can make a significant contribution to growth and poverty reduction but with adverse effect on income distribution. Although,

there are measures that can promote growth with no significant effect on income distribution.

- There are also redistributive spending measures that aim mainly at reducing inequality and poverty, but can also be good for growth, particularly when inequality is initially high. However, relying mainly on redistribution to reduce poverty and inequality can be a source of distortions and can crowd out resources for growth-enhancing spending policies. This may lead to lower growth and higher unemployment, and in some cases, to unsustainable fiscal deficits and macroeconomic instability, all of which undermine inclusiveness.

Policies entailing an efficiency-equity trade-off should be complemented by mitigating measures. Achieving higher growth is crucial to reduce poverty. However, structural or fiscal measures that improve productivity and long-term growth can entail near-term burdens for some groups leading to higher inequality and greater wage dispersion. These anticipated negative distributional effects can be mitigated through the introduction or the scaling up of social protection such as well-targeted anti-poverty measures and social safety nets.

The analysis of the effects of spending measures on inclusiveness needs to consider how they were financed. Public expenditures are made possible by the raising of taxes, borrowing, or a reallocation of resources.

- *Taxation*: Taxes generate distortions and they have costs for efficiency. The distributional impact of tax burdens depends on the design of the tax system (Abdel-Kader and De Mooji 2020). For example, a personal income tax with a progressive marginal rate structure and a threshold that protects poor and vulnerable populations can reduce income inequality; a flat value-added tax can increase income inequality because consumption expenditures typically represent a larger share of income among poorer households than among richer households. However, when a regressive tax funds a highly progressive spending measure (such as a means-tested cash transfer), the net position (post-tax and post-transfer) of low-income households will be enhanced relative to their pre-tax, pre-transfer position. In other words, it is important to consider jointly the net effects of spending and taxes on social welfare and inclusiveness.

- *Borrowing*: More borrowing needs to be consistent with a sustainable fiscal policy. Large fiscal deficits are a source of macroeconomic instability (see Chapter 11). Moreover, high levels of debt lead to a higher interest burden on the budget, reducing thereby the fiscal space for productive and inclusive spending. For example, in Egypt, interest payments increased threefold between 2009 and 2017, from 15.2 percent to 42.6 percent of government revenue in lockstep with the rise in the debt-to-GDP ratio. If left unattended, higher debt-servicing burdens will affect long-term growth and undermine

inclusiveness as the negative effects of, for example, increased inflation and interest rate tend to disproportionally affect low-income households.
- *Spending reallocation*: Fiscal space for productive and inclusive spending can be created through reductions in other expenditures. For example, removing generalized and untargeted subsidies can free up substantial resources that can be used to expand inclusive infrastructure and design better targeted social safety nets. Boosting capital spending by excessively reducing current spending may, however, be counterproductive and generate a negative impact (Gemmell et al. 2011). It would be important to be selective as capital spending and some components of current spending (e.g., operations and maintenance) tend to be complements rather than substitutes (IMF 2020b).

The package of spending measures should be cost-effective, consistent with fiscal sustainability and take into account country-specific circumstances. The nature and number of constraints on truly inclusive growth differ from country to country. The appropriate mix of public spending measures will depend on (i) the starting point with regard to the prevalence of poverty and the degree of inequality and the nature of their drivers; (ii) the initial coverage and adequacy of the social protection system; and (iii) the administrative quality and capacity. Countries with high poverty rates may prioritize decreasing poverty rather than inequality and costs (including the efficiency costs of taxation); countries with relatively low poverty and inequality might instead emphasize growth-enhancing fiscal measures to reverse low productivity trends and boost long-term growth and generate jobs. In most developing countries, income inequality tends to reflect sizeable informal sector and rural-urban disparities. Deprivations and exclusion tend to be strongly correlated: for example, a lack of access to piped water may lead to poor health outcomes and more frequent high school dropouts; or poor market access and a lack of adequate roads may prevent farmers from netting the highest price for any harvest surplus. Governments should focus on areas where there are substantial weaknesses and potential low-hanging fruits. For example, in countries where there is low and unequal access to education, notably for girls, and weak labor market participation of women, priorities may be given to expand school infrastructure and enhance provision of quality childcare facilities.

IV. Public Spending and Inclusiveness—Evidence

Public expenditure has been more effective than taxation in reducing inequality.[12] In advanced economies, personal income taxation and direct transfer spending have contributed to the reduction of prefiscal (i.e., before taxes and transfers)

---

[12] These findings are based on the use of a sequential method for the assessment of fiscal measures. The use of marginal contribution may lead to different findings (see Lustig 2018 for differences between these two methods).

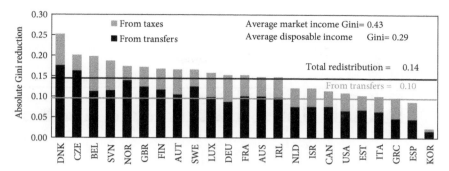

Figure 13.6 Redistributive Impact of Fiscal Policy in Advanced Economies, Mid-2000s

Sources: Paulus, Figari, Hegedus, and others (2009), except for Australia, Canada, the Czech Republic, Korea, Norway, Israel, and the United States for which data are from Caminada and others (2012). Figure 2.9 in IMF (2014c).

income inequality by 14 percentage points or about 25 percent (OECD 2017a).[13] The effect varies widely: there is a 3 percentage points reduction in income inequality in Korea and a 26 percentage point reduction in Denmark (Figure 13.6). Approximately two-thirds of this redistribution is due to public expenditures, but because the analysis does not include the distributional effects of indirect taxation—rates of which are generally high in advanced economies (about 20 percent)—the estimates are not complete.[14] Taking indirect taxes and subsidies into account might cause an increase in the impact of expenditure-side policy on redistribution overall. Within transfers, assistance transfers (e.g., family benefits) account for the bulk of the redistribution (Causa and Hermansen 2017).

The redistributive effect of taxes and transfers has declined over the last two decades.[15] The downward trend has been particularly evident between mid-1990 and 2007, reflecting less generous transfers and, to some extent, less progressive income taxation. However, this result showing retrogression may be driven in part by the higher progressivity observed in the mid-1990s when the crises then experienced by Finland, Sweden, and Norway, which caused a cyclical rise in transfers minus taxes.[16] During the 2007–2008 crisis, the redistributive effect increased owing to automatic stabilizers and discretionary measures to cushion the impact of the financial crisis on the population and the economy. However, since then, as automatic stabilizers have phased out (given recovery, albeit slow) and benefit eligibility has been narrowed (to support fiscal consolidation), the redistributive effect receded again (Causa and Hermansen 2017).

[13] Redistribution is quantified as the relative reduction in prefiscal income inequality achieved by personal income taxes, employees' social security contributions, and cash transfers; estimates are based on household-level micro data.
[14] Were indirect taxes and subsidies taken into account this might reduce the redistributive effect overall while causing an increase in the relative impact (on overall redistribution) of expenditure-side policies.
[15] See Lindert (2017) for an historical perspective of the redistributive role of fiscal policy.
[16] See Lindert (2021) page 376, fn 12.

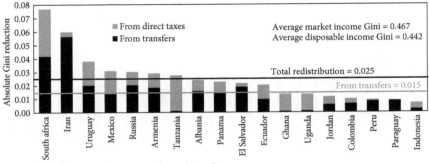

*Contributory pensions are consided as deferred income

Figure 13.7 Redistributive Impact of Fiscal Policy in Developing Countries

Sources: Albania (Dávalos et al 2018); Armenia (Younger & Khachatryan 2017); Colombia (Melendez & Martinez 2019a, 2019b); Ecuador (Llerena Pinto et al 2015); El Salvador (Beneke et al 2018); Ghana (Younger et al 2017); Indonesia (Jellema et al 2017); Iran (Enami et al 2017); Jordan (Alam et al 2017); Mexico (Scott 2014); Panama (Martinez-Aguilar 2019); Paraguay (Gimenez et al 2017); Peru (Jaramillo 2019); Russia (Lopez-Calva et al 2017); South Africa (Inchauste et al 2017); Tanzania (Younger et al 2016); Uganda (Jellema et al 2018); Uruguay (Bucheli et al 2014).

The redistributive effect of fiscal policy is much smaller in developing countries. In the fiscal incidence studies summarized in the Commitment to Equity (CEQ) Assessment archive (housed at the CEQ Institute), fiscal redistribution via personal income taxation and direct transfers (excluding public pensions) reduces the inequality in prefiscal incomes by 2.5 Gini points (or 5.5 percent on average) (Figure 13.7). Transfers have a marginal impact that amounts to approximately 60 percent of the overall reduction in inequality. CEQ Assessments also estimate the incidence and impact of indirect taxation (e.g., VAT) and indirect subsidies (e.g., food, energy, and agricultural inputs). These two factors tend to offset each other, combining for a very small net reduction in the Gini coefficient. The meagre redistributive impact of public spending is not surprising given the low levels of public spending and social protection in the (mostly) developing countries covered by the CEQ Assessment archive.[17]

In-kind transfers have a substantial effect on inequality (Figure 13.8). Public spending on education and health reduces the Gini coefficient by 2.1 and 3.3 percentage points, respectively in advanced economies. For developing countries, the redistributive effect is estimated at 2.4 percentage points for education and 1.6 percentage points for health. However, this assessment doesn't fully capture the role of education and health spending on inequality for at least two reasons. First, the redistributive effects may be smaller given that the incidence analysis values public services at their cost of provision, which may not correspond to the real benefits received by the population. Inefficiencies would indeed erode their

---

[17] The CEQ archive also demonstrates that countries which have allocated proportionally more resources to social spending (not including public pension spending) have witnessed a larger reduction in inequality.

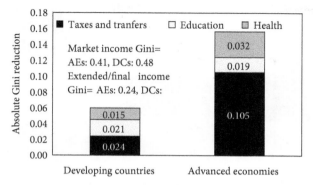

Figure 13.8 Redistributive Effects of In-Kind Transfers

Sources: Armenia (Younger & Khachatryan 2017); Brazil (Higgins et al 2014); Colombia (Melendez & Martinez 2019a, 2019b); Dominican Republic (Aristy-Escuder 2018); Ecuador (Llerena Pinto et al 2015); El Salvador (Oliva 2018); Ghana (Younger et al 2017); Indonesia (Jellema et al 2017); Iran (Enami et al 2017); Jordan (Alam et al 2017); Mexico (Scott 2014); Panama (Martinez-Aguilar 2019); Paraguay (Gimenez et al 2017); Peru (Jaramillo 2019); Russia (Lopez-Calva et al 2017); South Africa (Inchauste et al 2017); Sri Lanka (Arunatilke 2010); Tanzania (Younger et al 2016); Uganda (Jellema et al 2018); Uruguay (Bucheli et al 2014). Advanced economies (OECD 2011).

redistributive effects. Furthermore, upper-income households tend to extensively use private education and healthcare services given the poor quality of public services.[18] In some countries, the related charges can be tax deductible, reducing the redistributive effect of taxation. If this is not the case, it is likely that upper-income households may be less tax-compliant given that they are not using public education services.

The direct effect of transfers on poverty varies widely across developing countries. Fiscal policy reduces poverty headcount ratios by 2.3 percentage points (on average, from 23.9 percent at prefiscal income to 21.6 percent at disposable income) in a sample of 16 developing countries, using the international $PPP 3.20 per person per day poverty line. This reflects overwhelmingly the role of transfers as direct taxation tends to increase poverty in most countries. The effect of public expenditure on poverty reduction ranges from negligible levels in Uganda to 10.5 percentage points in South Africa.

Inequality reduction from fiscal policy does not always translate into better social welfare for the poor and vulnerable (Lustig 2018). While fiscal policy reduces inequality, it may not always lead to poverty reduction. For example, using a sample of 35 emerging economies and low-income countries, fiscal policy was found to reduce inequality for all countries. At the same time, it increased the poverty headcount ratio (based on $PPP 3.20 poverty line) in 12 out of 35 countries. The role of taxes and the low level of transfers and subsidies that can be smaller in magnitude than consumption taxes, may indeed lead to a deterioration of the purchasing power of some vulnerable households.

---

[18] For example, in Morocco, 50 percent of the students in the highest income decile attend a private school against only 4 percent for the lowest decile (Ezzarari 2018).

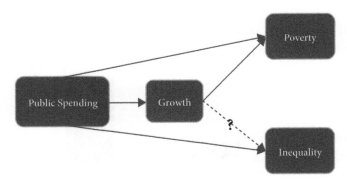

Figure 13.9 Public Spending, Growth, and Inclusiveness
Source: Authors' illustration.

In some cases, even when fiscal policy reduces the poverty rate, not all poor or vulnerable households will benefit uniformly. While the aggregate impact of pro-poor fiscal measures on the poverty is favorable, some vulnerable individuals and households can still be worse off; Higgins and Lustig (2016) refer to this phenomenon as "Fiscal Impoverishment." This can happen when anti-poverty programs like direct cash transfers have low rates of coverage (among the poor and vulnerable) while indirect taxes like VAT are levied on most goods and services.[19] In this case, many poor and vulnerable individuals will end up being "net payers" into the fiscal system even while there is no net increase in the number of individuals measured as poor.[20] Pro-poor programs that focus mainly on those just below the poverty line may lead also to the same phenomenon.

In addition to the mechanical effects above, the impact of public spending on inclusiveness is also mediated through economic growth (Figure 13.9). The pathways from public expenditure to overall economic growth is well documented (e.g., Gemmell et al. 2011). An increase in productive spending results in higher growth and employment which in turn will lift income and reduce poverty. India and China in particular demonstrate how rapid economic growth can lead to a significant reduction in poverty. However, there is no clear-cut answer on how growth affects inequality. Growth may reduce inequality or exacerbate it (Chapter 2; and Bourguignon 2003).

V. Policy Options

This section discusses public spending measures that can help in improving one or more dimensions of inclusiveness. These policies may entail complementarities

---

[19] The tendency of the poor to rely more on informal markets may mitigate the regressive impact of consumption taxes (Bachas et al. 2020).

[20] Higgins and Lustig (2016) also show the converse: *some* poor individuals and households can experience fiscal gains even while the impact of fiscal policy on the poverty headcount ratio, the poverty gap, the squared poverty gap, or other anonymous poverty measures is negative.

or trade-offs between growth and equity objectives. We identify measures that can reduce both inequality and promote economic growth and highlight those that may entail trade-offs. This section draws mainly from the work done at the IMF (notably IMF 2014c, 2014d, 2017a), the World Bank (2018), the OECD (notably OECD 2011, 2017a, 2017b, 2018), the CEQ Institute (Lustig 2018), and the ILO (2017). There are three major policy areas that have the largest scope to make growth more inclusive: (i) social protection; (ii) human capital; and (iii) government effectiveness and budget institutions. We will focus in this chapter on the social safety nets, the pensions as well as budget institutions. Public spending policies pertaining to labor market and human capital are covered in Chapter 3 and Chapter 14, respectively.[21]

A. Social Protection

Social protection is an important element of social welfare and represents a key pillar of the social contract. It helps individuals minimize the negative effects of shocks, natural disasters, and unfavorable life events and protect them from poverty and destitution. It also provides opportunities to build skills necessary to access jobs and return to the labor market. There are three broad categories of social protection interventions: (i) social safety nets (SSN)/social assistance programs (SA); (ii) social insurance programs; and (iii) labor market programs (Table 13.1).

Table 13.1 Types of Social Protection Instruments

Social Safety Nets/Social Assistance (Non-Contributory)	Social Insurance (Contributory)	Labor Market Programs
Unconditional/conditional cash transfers	Contributory old-age, survivor, disability pensions	*Active labor market programs*
Social pensions	Sick leave	Training
Food and in-kind transfers	Maternity/paternity benefits	Employment intermediation services
School feeding programs	Health insurance coverage	Wage subsidies
Pubworks		*Passive labor market programs*
Fee waivers and targeted subsidies		Unemployment insurance
		Early retirement incentives

Source: The State of Social Safety Nets 2018, World Bank.

---

[21] See also Zouhar et al. (2021) for an analysis of the effects of public spending on education and health on inequality and poverty.

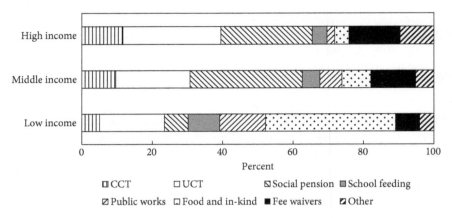

Figure 13.10 Social Safety Nets Spending by Instrument
Source: ASPIRE database, World Bank.

Social Safety Nets (SSNs)

Developing countries allocate smaller budget resources to social safety nets. Spending on SSN programs varies between 1.4 percent of GDP in low-income countries and 2 percent of GDP in emerging economies, while it reaches 2.7 percent in OECD countries.[22] Social protection systems in advanced economies are mature and comprehensive and comprise tax-financed universal social assistance schemes. By contrast, the social protection system in developing countries is fragmentated and has insufficient administrative capacity, limited coverage, and inadequate benefit levels (Grosh et al. 2008). Close to half of developing countries allocates less than 1 percent of GDP to social assistance.

An analysis of SSN spending by type of instrument indicates significant differences across countries (Figure 13.10):

- *Cash transfer programs* are the most common mechanism used by governments to provide social assistance to the vulnerable population (representing one-third of reported SSN programs). They account for two thirds of SSN spending in high- and middle-income countries and only 30 percent in low-income countries. They can be unconditional (UCT) or conditional (CCT) with the eligibility contingent upon certain behaviors (e.g., the use of specific health and education services for children). CCT tend to be more effective in reducing inequality and enhancing long-term growth given their impact on raising school enrollment and improving health outcomes. They can also contribute to reducing gender equality by (i) improving the school enrollment of girls, and (ii) strengthening women's role in the allocation of households' resources (OECD 2011).

---

[22] The analysis of the magnitude and the incidence of spending on social protection in this section relies on the ASPIRE database compiled by the World Bank.

- *Food and in-kind transfers* are an important component of the social assistance, particularly among low-income countries, accounting for 37 percent of total SSN spending. They are often funded by donors and consist mainly of food rations, clothes, school supplies, fertilizers, among others. Their objectives are usually to provide food security, improve nutrition, increase agricultural productivity, and deliver emergency relief. Given their self-targeting feature, their coverage rate of the poor tends to be high. This is the case of India where they cover 94 percent of the poor (World Bank 2018).
- *Public work programs*: These programs typically provide income support to the poor through labor-intensive public works. The related spending ranges from 2.2 percent of total SSN spending among high-income countries to 13 percent among low-income countries. The activities under these programs consist in general of community projects that contribute to local development (e.g., through road construction and maintenance, drainage projects, and public building maintenance) (Grosh et al. 2008). To avoid misuse and ensure the beneficiary's self-selection, wages under these programs should be set up at relatively low levels. To increase their effectiveness, some countries have included a training component with the objective of improving beneficiaries' skills and their job opportunities. In Argentina, the public work program gives participants the option of either working or attending training courses or educational classes in exchange for benefits.

The SSN coverage of the poor is low among developing countries. Social assistance programs cover 33 percent of the total population in developing countries. However, the coverage is only 18 percent in low-incomes countries against 43 percent in emerging economies. Close to 60 percent of the poorest 40 percent of individuals (so approximately 24 percent of the total population) in emerging economies benefit from an SSN program against only 20 percent (so approximately 8 percent of the total population) among LICs. The coverage rate of the poor is the highest for school feeding programs in both LICs and emerging economies. LICs lag in all other areas of social assistance. For example, the coverage of the poor is 6 percent and 11 percent, respectively for unconditional and conditional cash transfers among LICs while in emerging economies both types of cash transfer achieve 35 percent coverage rates. Family and child benefits cover only 9 percent of households in LICs against 54 percent in emerging economies and 90 percent in advanced economies (ILO 2017).

Moreover, SSN programs are not well targeted towards the poor. The poorest 40 percent of individuals represent, respectively, 46 percent and 57 percent of SSN beneficiaries among LICs and emerging economies. This means that leakages are significant: 34 (24) percent of SSN beneficiaries among LICs (emerging economies) belong to richest 40 percent of individuals. The share of all SSN benefits accruing to the same 40-percent-poorest and 40-percent-richest groups among

LICs (emerging economies) is 43 percent (64 percent) and 42 percent (21 percent), respectively. Conditional cash transfer benefits are more pro-poor than general SSN benefits, with 54 percent and 75 percent of benefits accruing to the poorest 40 percent of individuals among LICs and EMEs respectively. By contrast, untargeted subsidies and other social assistance programs provide only one-third of benefits to the poorest 40 percent of the population.

SSN programs have limited impact on poverty and inequality. In addition to low coverage and poor targeting, the level of SSN transfers is small, representing 6.4 percent of total consumption of beneficiaries among LICs and 12 percent among emerging economies. The empirical literature suggests the size of transfers should not be too large (which could imply fewer beneficiaries and reduced incentives to work) but also large enough to ensure a meaningful welfare impact for beneficiaries. For example, cash transfer programs were found to be more impactful when the transfer is set at least at 20 percent of a household's consumption (World Bank 2018; Handa et al. 2014). Based on the World Bank's ASPIRE database, the average SSN transfer amounts in LICs represents 10.8 percent of the welfare of a beneficiary in the poorest quintile and in emerging economies the average SSN transfer amounts to 24 percent of the welfare of a beneficiary in the poorest quintile. In LICs, the redistributive effect of SSN programs is barely perceptible while they reduce poverty rates by just less than 2.5 percent. In emerging economies, SSN programs reduce inequality by 4.2 percent and poverty by 13 percent.

SSN programs need to be carefully designed to avoid misuse and leakages and increase their impact on poverty and inequality. The appropriate set of SSN programs will depend on the administrative capacity and the targeted segments of the population. Options to improve the effectiveness and the scope of social assistance programs include (mainly for developing countries):

- Scaling up spending on SSN programs in order to increase their scope and their coverage. Measures may consist, for example, of introducing family and child allowances, extending coverage to the informal workers, and providing more public work programs. Appending a training component to the latter could help enhance job opportunities for the beneficiaries;
- Developing multi-dimensional programs that cover many areas such as health, education, and nutrition. As administrative capacity improves, social assistance programs can embed a mutual obligation in benefits by combining the transfer with the requirement to maintain investment in human capital and child health (e.g., conditional cash transfer programs); and
- Improving the targeting performance of the social programs. This would entail the consolidation of the myriad of existing social assistance programs as well as a better coordination between the different stakeholders. Developing biometric identification schemes and establishing a national social registry (unique identifier) are also key.

Pensions

Public spending on pensions and coverage varies considerably across the world (see Chapter 18). Advanced economies allocate close to 9 percent of GDP to public spending on social protection for the elderly, with a coverage rate of 97 percent. The coverage of social protection for the elderly has also expanded (ILO 2017) in developing countries, with some countries achieving universal coverage (e.g., Argentina, Bolivia). Notwithstanding this, LICs and emerging economies achieve effective coverage rates of only 24 percent and 57 percent, respectively of the elderly populations, reflecting notably smaller spending (1 percent and 4 percent of GDP, respectively).

Pension systems in advanced economies pose challenges in terms of sustainability and equity, but issues are complex. Pensions are often the largest single expenditure in the budget. Increasing shares of the elderly in total populations means high and rising public spending on pensions, which tends to crowd out other growth-enhancing spending and constrain resources for redistribution to the working-age population (Causa and Hermansen 2017; Clements et al. 2014).[23] Cournède et al. (2018) found that pension reforms will increase long-term growth via reduced incentives for early withdrawal from labor markets which will expand labor supply. The simulated impact of such reforms on the income distribution of the working-age population was not significant. However, it is estimated that they will entail in the future a 20 percent reduction in replacement rates—the average pension benefit divided by the average wage—and may cause potentially a significant increase in the elderly poverty rate (Shang 2014).[24] Parametric reforms that emphasize an extension of the retirement age instead of a reduction in the replacement rate tend to increase employment rates among the elderly, which helps in containing or reducing old-age poverty. However, higher statutory retirement age is not by any means exempt from equity concerns as it may benefit more those with high economic status who often have longer life expectancy, better health status, as well as jobs with less hardship and high tele-workability.

In developing economies, contributory pensions schemes are marked by low coverage and adequacy. Contributory pension systems exclude large segments of the population, which may exacerbate inequality. The share of the population

---

[23] However, care must be taken regarding this assertion because a portion of what is paid in contributory pensions at any moment in time is implicitly paid by the workers′ contributions during their working years (Lustig, ed., 2018, chapter 1). Even in a pay-as-you-go system, income from pensions is a form of deferred income. Whether individuals are recipients of a transfer embedded in their income from pensions or not depends on the history of their contributions, their retirement age and the age at time of death. In fact, in pay-as-you-go systems that put a cap on benefits, high wage earners could end up being taxed: that is, their pension income from retirement age to death is lower than what they contributed during their working years (plus the standard return). This means that assessing whether pensions are in fact crowding out other forms of spending is a more complex issue that cannot be answered by just looking at spending on pensions to GDP at any point in time.

[24] Shang (2014) estimates an elasticity of the elderly poverty rate to replacement rate of −0.4, which implies that a 10 percent reduction in the aggregate replacement rate would increase the elderly poverty rate by about 4 percent.

above the statutory pensionable age receiving an old-age pension is 13 percent among LICs and 29 percent among emerging economies (ILOSTAT), but coverage is often limited to public sector employees and (in some countries) formal sector workers, leaving out workers in the informal sector and many if not all of the self-employed. For these uncovered groups, voluntary savings are often not feasible given their low income and lack of access to financial services. Some countries have, however, taken steps to include the workers in these sectors in the pension systems. For example, Morocco has recently extended the public pension scheme to self-employed workers and workers with low and irregular earnings.

Assessing the impact of pensions on poverty and inequality is challenging. Pensions allow individuals to defer current income to future selves; treating public pensions as purely government transfers will inflate their impact on poverty and inequality.[25] Enrolling in a public pension system entails often deferring a portion of current working-age income to a future, retired self. Therefore, even were there no public pension scheme, today's pension system income recipients would likely have used other savings vehicles to defer working-age incomes to a future, non-working self.[26] Assuming instead that today's pension system incomes are entirely a *transfer* from the government (and not deferred income) would then overstate the impact of that transfer on income poverty or inequality (see Chapter 2, Lustig 2018). Using a set of 19 developing countries, Lustig (2018) shows that if pensions are accounted for as government transfers, the *average* impact of fiscal policy would be a reduction of the poverty headcount ratio by 47.4 percent; while if instead pensions are treated as deferred income, the reduction would be only 26.2 percent.[27] The reduction in inequality (for a set of 45 developing countries), meanwhile, is 8.9 percentage points on average when pensions are accounted for as government transfers and 6.9 percentage points when pensions are accounted for as deferred income (Lustig 2018). This large difference is mainly explained by the fact that considering pension incomes as a government transfer leads to the creation of many "false poor" at prefiscal income; and thereby leads to an overestimation of the impact of fiscal poverty on reduction of poverty and inequality.[28] The reality most likely lies somewhere between these two extremes. Countries often have a hybrid pension system where the contributory

---

[25] This will be true system for any pension system and regardless of whether the system in question is "actuarially fair" or not.

[26] Such individuals would also have had access to appropriate and efficient old-age savings vehicles during their productive years as well.

[27] When poverty is estimated at the $PPP (2011) 1.90 per person per day line and over the postfiscal income concept Consumable Income, which includes indirect tax burdens and indirect subsidy benefits.

[28] "False poor" individuals are those who have zero or near-zero incomes without public pension system incomes; but who would have generated income for their pension-age selves (i.e., deferred income) using, for example, private pension or voluntary savings vehicles, if the public pension system had not been available.

pension system is in deficit and part of pensions are tax-funded out of general revenue. In this case, it is more accurate to assume that a portion of pensions is a deferred income and a portion is a government transfer.[29]

Many developing countries have introduced social pension schemes to address the low social insurance coverage of the elderly. Social pensions are non-contributory benefits that are tax-funded and target the old-age population. They can be universal or means-tested. They globally cover close to 35 percent of the old-age population. In several countries, social pension schemes are universal and constitute the main component of the pension system (e.g., Bolivia, Botswana, Thailand). They cover 50 percent of the poorest 40 percent of the population in LICs and 63 percent in emerging economies. They also tend to be progressive, representing a significant proportion of the welfare for elderly people in the poorest quintile (12 percent in LICs and 35 percent in emerging economies). Social pensions contribute to poverty reduction and inequality, albeit the outcomes are different across countries. For instance, in Bolivia, where a universal social pension exists, the pension benefit is well below the $2.5 a day poverty line, which makes only a small dent in the high elderly poverty rate (Dethier et al. 2010).

Policy options that can be considered to make pensions more equitable, while ensuring their sustainability, include:

- In countries where the pension system is relatively developed, monitoring the trends in the pension benefits and ensuring that the parametric pension reforms don't translate into a substantial decline in pension benefits. Mitigating measures should be considered to ensure that the pension reform doesn't increase the elderly poverty;[30]
- Expanding pension coverage in developing countries to workers in the informal sector and leveraging it to facilitate their transition to the formal sector. For example, a number of countries in Latin America have extended coverage to the self-employed population by a subsidy combined with a simplified tax and social security contribution mechanism (Ortiz 2018);
- Ensuring that the design of the pension scheme is appropriate, notably by setting the pension benefit at an adequate level that addresses the poverty risk without weakening incentives to work;

---

[29] For a more detailed analysis, see Lustig, chapter 1, in Lustig et al. 2018.

[30] Pension reforms fall into two broad categories: parametric and structural. Parametric adjustments are the most common type of the pension reform and consist mainly of adjusting the retirement age, the contribution rates and bases, the benefit assessment periods, or the indexation rules. Structural reforms involve changing the relative importance of defined-benefit versus defined-contribution benefit assessment, funding versus pay-as-you-go (PAYG) financing, or private versus public management. Structural reforms introduce profound changes in the way risks are distributed across the government and individuals, and the manner in which the system's components are financed and governed and pay benefits (Clements et al. 2014).

- In countries with no pension or low pension coverage, examining options to introduce or expand non-contributory means-tested social pensions;
- Enhancing employment opportunities for the old-age population by promoting lifelong learning and upskilling. This will maintain skills and facilitate the adaptation to technological change (OECD 2019); and
- Providing adequate support through other mechanisms for old-age individuals whose health status prevents them from working or searching for jobs.

Universal Basic Income

Challenges with existing forms of social protection have renewed interest in the universal basic income. Even in advanced economies with mature social protection systems, some groups are still not adequately covered (e.g., the long-term unemployed) by the social protection system, especially when jobs are not available. In developing countries, the development of social protection systems has focused on those at both ends of the income distribution, leaving the "middle," including those at risk of poverty and workers in the informal sector with little social protection (ILO 2017). [31] Moreover, the global aging and the transformation of the nature and organization of work—towards more temporary and contractual jobs—have highlighted the limits of the traditional social provisions in ensuring high coverage and adequacy. In this context, universal basic income (UBI) programs are increasingly suggested (and piloted or tested) in both developing and advanced economies.

There is a robust debate regarding a UBI's potential benefits and costs. Proponents argue that a UBI provides income security and guarantees a minimum standard of living in the face of job *precarization* and high unemployment.[32] UBIs require little administrative capacity and in particular they generate no administrative costs as eligibility determination is not needed. Coverage gaps in the existing social protection system would be eliminated. However, opponents underscore that covering everyone in society would entail large fiscal costs, crowd out productive spending, and cause unwarranted leakages to upper-income households. It will also weaken incentives to work and delink benefits from job search behaviors with adverse effects on the labor supply. Moreover, if UBIs replace unemployment benefits, for example, fiscal policy may become less counter-cyclical with fewer automatic stabilizers.

---

[31] On the one hand, the introduction of contributory mechanisms (social insurance) tends to start with employees in the public and formal private sectors and on the other hand, there are non-contributory mechanisms in the form of social assistance to cover the needs of people living in extreme poverty.

[32] Job *precarization* refers to the rise of non-standard or temporary employment that may be poorly paid, insecure, unprotected, and unable to support a household.

Simulations and field experiments help shed some light on potential costs and benefits of UBI and identify winners and losers. For example, in a scenario of a budget-neutral substitution of an UBI to the current social protection in OECD, the UBI would represent only a fraction of the relative poverty line. Thus, it will have a limited and mixed impact on poverty as some individuals would be lifted out, but others may fall into poverty (OECD 2017c). However, setting the UBI close to the poverty line will be very costly and would require significant tax increases and reductions in other benefits and tax exemptions. An UBI set at 25 percent of median per capita income would entail a fiscal cost of 6–7 percent of GDP in advanced economies—which is around the current cost of social protection—and 3–4 percent in developing countries (IMF 2017a). For the latter, the impact on poverty would be substantial (10.4 points) given the low coverage and adequacy of existing social protection programs. UBI programs entail also distributional effects. Losers include early retirees and low-income households as the UBI would be lower than the pension or the benefit under the current system. But overall, it will lead to a reduction in inequality, with a magnitude depending on how it is financed.

The financing scheme matters. Financing UBIs through higher domestic revenues may lead to negative social outcomes. Lustig, Jellema, and Pabon (2019), for example, demonstrate in a sample of nine countries in Sub-Saharan Africa, that providing income floors by raising domestic taxes on individuals would imply such large increases in taxes that significant labor-market disincentives would arise which would then produce negative impacts on tax collection.[33] When fewer individuals are covered or the income floor is made less generous, such scenarios require fewer additional resources; even so, the imposition of more or higher taxes to fund these income floors often leads to negative incomes and extreme re-ranking—those at the top of the pre-fiscal income distributions end up with negative incomes after taxes and, thus, move from being the pre-fiscal richest to the post-fiscal poorest.

The desirability of a UBI hinges on many factors, notably the comprehensiveness of the current social protection programs. Given the potential large fiscal costs associated with UBI schemes, OECD (2017c) suggests to consider instead (i) a "partial" form of basic income, receipt of which is tied to mild eligibility conditions (e.g., a participation income proposed by Atkinson) or (ii) a gradual roll-out (e.g., only to new cohorts of young adults) of a full-fledged UBI.[34] A framework developed by the IMF assesses the desirability of a UBI for a country

---

[33] The sample covers four low-income, three lower-middle-income, and two upper-middle-income countries in Sub-Saharan Africa.

[34] Atkinson (1996) proposed that a basic income would be paid conditional on a social contribution. This could include engaging in education, training, caring for the young, elderly or disabled dependents or undertaking other forms of voluntary work.

based notably on (i) the current coverage of the poor and (ii) the current adequacy of benefits (Francese 2018; IMF 2020a).

B. Government Effectiveness and Budget Institutions

High levels of social spending are not enough by themselves to foster inclusive growth. Unfavorable distributional effects stem from inefficiencies and political economy factors. Ensuring a better design of public programs and reducing waste will enhance their impact on inequality and poverty. Priorities include public wage containment, better targeting of subsidies, enhancing public investment efficiency, and strengthening budget institutions.

Rationalization of the Remuneration Policy in the Public Sector
In a context of a declining labor income share, a large public sector wage bill may increase income inequality. The wage bill in the public sector tends to be among the largest components of the budget. In advanced economies public sector wages (as a share of GDP) have declined somewhat from 10.7 percent in 2000–2003 to 10.3 percent in 2016–2018, reflecting wage containment measures in the context of fiscal consolidation following the 2008 financial crisis. The wage bill increased by 0.5 percentage points in emerging economies, reaching about 9 percent of GDP in 2016–2018. The increase was more substantial for LICs (1.5 points); however the wage bill in LICs—at 7 percent of GDP in 2016–2018—is still lower on average than for emerging or advanced economies. In many countries, the large size of the wage bill is not matched by the availability and quality of public services, in particular among LICs (IMF 2018). Moreover, given the secular decline in the share of labor income in the economy in most countries (ILO 2019; IMF 2017b), a stable or rising share of the public sector wage bill implies that the burden of rising income inequality was borne out by workers in the private sector.

Large wage gaps between public and private sector undermine inclusiveness. The average public sector wage premium—the amount by which public sector wages exceed those in the private sector after controlling for skills and education— is significant, reaching on average 5 percent for advanced economies and 13 percent for developing countries. This may be due to the fact that the remuneration policy in the public sector tends to be disconnected from productivity. Indeed, wage increases tend be sometimes politically motivated to glean the political support of the civil servants, which often represent a large segment of the middle class. They can also be driven by social pressures and, where social protection systems are weak, by the need to cushion the impact of shocks on the population; that is "excess" civil servant labor employed or higher civil servant wages may be a partial substitute for social protection in these countries. In addition, the public sector tends in general to be highly unionized and the resulting collective bargaining power and proximity to public policy debates may give civil servants an outsized influence on public policy. All of this may exacerbate inequality and crowd out productive spending. It also makes the budget more rigid as wage increases implemented in good times are difficult to reverse in bad times. For example, in Mauritania, the government doubled the salaries of civil servants between 2004 and 2008 to mitigate the impact of the commodity price shock. In a context of centralized administration (about 50 percent of civil servants are located in the capital), this has worsened income inequality and spatial disparities (Zouhar 2012). In the MENA region, countries with higher public wages tend to display higher inequality (IMF 2014b). Also, large civil servant wage premiums tend to be associated with higher inequality (Zouhar et al. 2021). The disconnect between public compensation and productivity fragments labor markets, discourages accumulation of skills, and cultivates dependence and resistance to reforms. Furthermore, large wage premiums exacerbate perceived social inequities, especially where more equitable social transfers are small or absent (IMF 2018). They also lead to higher reservation wages, causing longer unemployment spells. Similarly, high rates of public employment, which is often associated with substantial fiscal costs, have a large negative impact on private employment rates and do not reduce overall unemployment rates (Behar and Mok 2013).

Containing the public wage bill is key to reducing expenditure rigidities and creating fiscal space for productive and social spending. Pressures for higher public sector wage bill stem mainly from the need to adjust for the inflation and for more hiring in the social sectors such as education and health, notably in developing countries.[35] However, the upward trend in the wage bill (as percentage of GDP) observed in the past has not always be matched by an improvement in the government effectiveness or social outcomes. Measures to keep the public sector wage bill under check could include: (i) avoiding using the public sector as an employer of last resort, and (ii) rationalizing compensation policy by tightening the link between pay and performance.[36]

Replacing Generalized Subsidies by Targeted Transfers

Subsidies are pervasive and costly. Many countries provide generalized price subsidies with the intention to shield consumers from large swings in commodity prices and to boost certain economic sectors. Universal subsidies can function as a form of social protection and can partially compensate for the lack of adequate social safety nets. As a matter of fact, in many countries, subsidies have been in place for a relatively long period of time and are perceived as a de facto

---

[35] One should note that the adjustment of wages for inflation is not always warranted in the private sector, and other considerations may come into play such the degree of tightness in the labor market and the trends in the profitability. This may contribute to the wage gap between the public and private sector.

[36] See IMF (2016) for detailed recommendations to manage and contain the public sector wage bill.

entitlement. The cost of subsidies can be large. For example, post-tax energy sub-sidies were estimated globally at \$5.2 trillion (6.5 percent of global GDP) in 2017 (Coady et al. 2019).

Subsidies can be important for enhancing poor households' purchasing power, but larger shares of subsidy expenditures are captured by richer households. Though they may reach the poor to some extent, those who consume more—i.e., the better off—will always capture more of the subsidy benefits available. For example, for energy, IMF calculations for 32 developing countries found that 45 percent of subsidies accrue to the richest 20 percent of households against only 7 percent for the poorest 20 percent (Coady et al. 2015).

By distorting real comparative advantages, prolonging the viability of ineffi-cient production, and by reducing the capacity of the government to provide other productivity-enhancing services, subsidies undermine longer-term growth. Although they can be used to provide short-term support to the productive sec-tor, in the long run subsidies have a dampening effect on growth potential. For example, energy subsidies lead to under-investment in labor-intensive and energy-efficient sectors, which affects adversely the diversification of the econ-omy[37]. Subsidies also crowd out productive spending on human and physical capital. For example, water subsidies can be substantial and may exceed total spending on public investment in some countries (Lipton 2016; Andres 2019). A 2015 IMF study (Ebeke and Ngouana 2015) found that a 1 percentage point increase in energy subsidies to GDP leads, on average, to a reduction of public spending in education and health by 0.6 percentage point of GDP. The crowding out effect tends to be larger in the presence of weak domestic institutions and narrow fiscal space. Often, decisions about subsidies take place in an opaque manner (the so-called quasi-fiscal activities of SOEs such as utilities) hence escaping the standard budget preparation process necessary for enhancing alloca-tive efficiency.[38]

Nonetheless, current subsidies represent a sizeable share of the purchasing power of poor and vulnerable households, so subsidy reform should proceed cau-tiously. For example, in the case of fuel, a 2015 IMF study simulated the impact of a \$0.25 dollar liter increase in fuel prices on the real income of households in about 40 developing countries around the world and found that that on average a household in the poorest 40 percent of the population will witness a 5.4 percent reduction of its real income (Coady et al. 2015). Lustig et al. (2019) found in a

[37] Energy subsidies can also lead to underinvestment in the fossil fuel sector. For example, in Egypt, generous consumer subsidies contributed to the accumulation of arrears to foreign partners in that sector and to significant losses for public energy enterprises. The ensued negative feedback loop led to a structural decline in energy production (Jarvis et al. 2015).

[38] Enhancing the transparency of the quasi-fiscal activities in the utilities sector and fully reflecting them in the budget would be a first step towards an assessment by the budget central authority and budget decision makers of their magnitude as well as the merits of such policies as compared to other spending alternatives.

sample of 11 countries in Africa that a budget-neutral transformation of current subsidy expenditure into targeted or universal cash transfers would actually create a net loss (relative to the status quo) for some poor and vulnerable households, indicating that subsidies captured often represent a greater share of income than do social transfers.

Introducing mitigating measures is a key component of any subsidy reform strategy. Governments need to preserve access of poor households to basic goods and services (e.g., energy) and protect their purchasing power from the direct and indirect effects of subsidy reform. This is critical for building public support for subsidy reform and minimizing the risk that the reform is derailed after it is introduced. There is no single recipe for success in subsidy reform, and governments should tailor reform strategies to their individual country circumstances; however, there are a number of measures that can contribute to the success of subsidy reforms including: (i) thorough preparation, including careful planning of the pace and breadth of reform, with technical assistance from international stakeholders; (ii) strong commitment of the government to reform, which can be achieved by building pro-reform consensus, through communication and coalition building; (iii) introduction or scaling-up of effective social safety nets to mitigate the impact of subsidy reform on the vulnerable; and (iv) building consensus and the case for reform by reaching out and consulting with different stakeholders (Clements et al. 2013; Sdralevich et al. 2014).

Building Inclusive Infrastructure

Public investment affects inclusive growth through many channels. The effect of public investment materializes, first, in the short-term by boosting aggregate demand (through the short-term fiscal multiplier) during the implementation phase of projects. More importantly, public investment increases long-run growth by expanding the productive capacity of the economy, facilitating human capital accumulation, and enhancing returns on private investment as well as productivity gains. However, the magnitude of the supply-side effect depends largely on how efficient the investment is. Also, the growth gains tend to be lower at high levels of public capital stock (OECD 2018b). The potential impact on inequality and poverty can be considerable. Public investment can facilitate human capital accumulation and acquisition of skills and increase the participation of the poor in the growth process. For example, infrastructure investment such as schools and hospitals in underserved areas can reduce inequities in access to education and health services. It can help improve the living standards of the population by generalizing access to water and sanitation. Expanding rural roads improves labor mobility and allows access to markets. Public investment improves the overall productivity of the economy which can have a mixed effect on inequality depending on whether it leads to a divergence or not of intra-firm productivity. If the location of infrastructure projects is unduly influenced by political factors, this will widen regional disparities. Overall, public investment expansions are associated with lower inequality among LICs. An exogenous increase in public investment of 1 percent of GDP was found to reduce the Gini coefficient by about 0.3 percent one year after the increase and about 2.3 percent five years after the increase (Fabrizio et al. 2017). The beneficial impact vanishes, however, when investment efficiency is poor. For OECD countries, larger public investment could increase growth without significant impact on inequality (OECD 2018).

Public investment can play a central role to achieve inclusive growth. Preserving public investment and improving efficiency are key. The declining trend in public capital stock should be reversed to avoid adverse effects on long-term growth. This will require addressing the anti-investment bias by nesting the planning and the execution of public projects in the context of a medium-term expenditure framework that is consistent with fiscal sustainability. This will help also minimize problems arising from excessive political discretion. Sound institutional processes, including better project appraisal and selection that identifies and targets infrastructure bottlenecks, and improved project execution should be in place to ensure productive and quality investment (IMF 2015). Improving public investment management would help also contain the fiscal cost and mitigate the trade-off between growth and debt.[39] There is a need to scale up public investment on school and health infrastructure in order to expand access to education and healthcare services and address the social gaps. Investment strategies should cover areas that enable the largest possible number of poor people to engage in productive activities and access social services. Priorities could focus on: (i) expanding the road network especially in underserved areas; (ii) improving access to water and sanitation; (iii) preserving access to affordable energy services through subsidies targeted to poor households; (iv) ensuring an equal access to affordable Internet in order to reduce the digital divide between rural and urban areas and between low- and upper income households; (v) expanding fair access to E-government services; and (vi) supporting the adoption by smaller firms of new technologies.

Role of Budget Institutions

Weak budgetary institutions hamper economic development and limit equal opportunity. Decisions about public spending and redistribution are ultimately determined through a political process (Musgrave 1959). Weak public institutions will more likely lead to a failure to incentivize government and government officials to allocate resources towards achieving *inclusive* growth. There is no shortage of anecdotal evidence of how the politically connected capture the policy process

---

[39] Improving investment management (to the 90th percentile of best performers in each income group) could halve the size of investment inefficiencies across countries (Baum et al. 2020).

to acquire rents and tilt the policies and rules in their favor.[40] The formulation and the implementation of fiscal policy are, indeed, besieged with many challenges of political economy, such as the common pool problem and political myopia. This can be particularly acute during the election cycles, with adverse effects on fiscal sustainability. For example, Ebeke and Ölçer (2013) found in the case of LICs that government consumption tends to significantly increase during election years. The ensuing higher fiscal deficits impose harsh adjustment during the two years following elections in the form of higher taxes and capital spending cuts.

By contrast, good budget institutions reduce political discretion and help contain the spending bias. They are also conducive of more efficiency and reinforce the counter-cyclical feature of public spending, reflecting prudent policies during good times that allow to build fiscal buffers for the bad times. This, in turn, will help limit the severity of recessions and their impact on the population and speed up recoveries. A 2014 IMF analysis of policy responses to the 2009 global crisis among G20 countries found that strong budget institutions are associated with more timely fiscal policy response, reflecting notably the ability of governments to quickly identify and understand the economic challenges (IMF 2014a). Another key finding is that countries with weak budget institutions fail to protect public investment during fiscal consolidation episodes. Moreover, strong institutions lead to more stable and predictable investment flows (IMF 2015).

Strengthening public financial management can reduce rent-seeking, improve efficiency of public spending and lead to more inclusion. Improvements in public financial management (proxied by PEFA scores) are associated with declining inequality in developing countries (Zouhar et al. 2021). For OECD countries, Fournier and Johansson (2016) found that greater government effectiveness may reduce inequality, as a result of better targeting of disadvantaged groups and more cost-efficient delivery of transfer programs. Strategies to strengthen budgetary institutions need to focus on enhancing fiscal transparency, enforcing expenditure controls, strengthening accountability and audit, and improving governance of state-owned enterprises. Priorities could also include:

- *Enacting fiscal responsibility laws*: This encompasses the agreed-on set of policies, processes, or arrangements intended to improve fiscal outcomes, discipline, transparency, and accountability by requiring governments to commit to fiscal policy objectives and strategies that can be monitored (Van Eden, Khemani, and Emery 2013). Adopting fiscal responsibility laws are beneficial in many ways. It helps smoothing out fiscal policy over time by taking into account longer-term considerations; as such a fiscally responsible

---

[40] See for example Rijkers, Freund, and Nucifora (2014) for the case of Tunisia during the Era of President Ben Ali.

government will not resort to policies which may put an excessive burden on future generations. Fiscal responsibility reinforces macroeconomic stability and growth as fiscally disciplined governments tend to implement sound fiscal policies and are in a better position to react to unexpected events. Governments can also better focus on designing efficient spending and implementing strategic priorities as they spend less time to worry about how to make the ends meet (peace of mind).

- *Improving public procurement procedures.* Given the large funds involved, procurement is potentially vulnerable to fraud and corruption. It can also alter fair competition and equal opportunities to companies as it can be captured by politically connected firms. Promoting transparent bidding processes and competitive procurement should improve efficiency (value-for-money) and effectiveness.
- *Operationalizing medium-term budgeting.* Understanding the future implications of current policy decisions on fiscal sustainability requires a multi-year budget framework. However, to be effective, multi-year budget frameworks need to be consistently articulated with the annual budget and well embedded in the decision-making process (not just an accounting exercise). By emphasizing a strategic perspective, medium-term budgeting allows to align inclusive growth objectives with resource allocation over time (OECD 2011). It also helps enforce fiscal discipline and reduce the deficit bias. Moreover, a credible medium-term fiscal framework anchors investor confidence and preserve government access to financial markets during downturns, which helps curb procyclical pressures. The transition from a line-item budgeting to program budgeting would increase accountability and reinforce the link between resources and outcomes.[41]
- *Involving citizens and NGOs in the budget process.* There are plenty of examples of politicians using public spending for their own political gains, including by providing benefits to their favored groups. Giving citizens a say in the design and implementation of the budget can support inclusiveness by improving the quality of the service delivery and ensuring more accountability. For example, de Renzio and Wehner (2015) shows that greater citizen participation and budget openness can help tackle leakage and corruption and improve public resource allocation by ensuring that the selection of public programs takes into account the needs and preferences of the most disadvantaged. Conducting incidence analysis of fiscal policy options can better inform policy choices and the design of mitigating measures to protect the vulnerable and those adversely impacted by reforms. For example, Spain

---

[41] The budgeting framework can further be adapted and refined to increase focus and accountability on key socio-economics areas. For example, many countries have adopted gender budgeting in their efforts to promote gender equality (IMF 2017c). Experiments to explicitly integrate the SDGs in the budget processes (SDG budgeting) are being considered (Gouzien 2020).

conducts impact assessments of policies and regulations on gender and regional distribution (OECD 2011). Some countries, such as the United Kingdom and New Zealand, require a distributional analysis of the public projects, in which, at a minimum, appraisers quantify how project costs and benefits accrue to different socioeconomic groups (Taliercio and Estrada 2020).

VI. Conclusion

Public expenditure is the most powerful instrument at hands of governments to achieve their objectives of economic development and social welfare. The central role of public expenditure has been further ascertained by the global Covid-19 pandemic crisis in view of the widespread and massive rolling out of spending measures to scale up health capacities, protect the population and support businesses.

Public expenditure policy is shaped by country-specific circumstances such as the country's preferences with respect to the role of the government, the country's development level, its available fiscal space, and the government's ability to raise taxes. In advanced economies, where tax and debt burdens are already high, the focus could be on better targeting the benefits through means-testing and ensuring the sustainability of the pension system. In developing countries, given the large gaps in public services and infrastructure, the priority should be on extending the coverage of well-targeted social safety nets, and improving access to basic public services. Equal emphasis should be put on reducing nonproductive spending (such as universal subsidies), enhancing public investment efficiency, and improving tax mobilization to preserve fiscal sustainability.

Understanding the trade-offs and complementarities of fiscal measures with regard inclusiveness is key. Many areas of public spending offer possibilities to achieve both efficiency and equity. Examples of win-win measures include expanding equal access to education and promoting access to maternal health services. Other measures (e.g., subsidy reform), however, involve trade-offs that cannot be systematically avoided, and would require mitigating measures. The right policy choices require assessing the incidence on different population groups, particularly the poor.

The "right" package of spending measures should be cost-effective, consistent with fiscal sustainability and take into account country specific circumstances. The nature and number of constraints on truly inclusive growth differ from country to country. The appropriate mix of public spending measures will depend on (i) the starting point with regard to the prevalence of poverty and the degree of inequality and the nature of their drivers; (ii) the initial coverage and adequacy of social protection system; and (iii) administrative quality and capacity. Countries with high poverty rates may prioritize decreasing poverty rather than inequality and costs (including the efficiency costs of taxation); countries with relatively low poverty and inequality might instead emphasize growth-enhancing fiscal measures to reverse low productivity trends and boost long-term growth and generate jobs.

Strengthening the institutions and governance is necessary to improve the quality of spending and its efficiency. Some measures that can be considered cover the areas of public financial management, procurement, and fiscal transparency laws. It is also important to improve fiscal transparency and ensure a better involvement of the civil society throughout the different stages of the budget process. Equally important are the establishment of effective independent audit institutions and anti-corruption agencies.

References

Abdel-Kader, Khaled, and Ruud De Mooji. 2020. "Tax Policy and Inclusive Growth." IMF Working Paper, WP/20/271. Washington, DC: International Monetary Fund.

Abdih, Yasser, Pablo Lopez-Murphy, Agustin Roitman, and Ratna Sahay. 2010. "The Cyclicality of Fiscal Policy in the Middle East and Central Asia: Is the Current Crisis Different?" IMF Working paper WP/10/68. Washington, DC: International Monetary Fund.

Alam, Shamma A., Gabriela Inchauste, and Umar Serajuddin. 2017. "The Distributional Impact of Fiscal Policy in Jordan," chap. 6 in *The Distributional Impact of Taxes and Transfers. Evidence from Eight Low- and Middle-Income Countries*, edited by Gabriela Inchauste and Nora Lustig. Washington, DC: World Bank.

Andres, Luis A., Michael Thibert, Camilo Lombana Cordoba, Alexander V. Danilenko, George Joseph, and Christian Borja-Vega. 2019. *Doing More with Less Smarter Subsidies for Water Supply and Sanitation*. Washington, DC: World Bank.

Aristy-Escuder, Jaime, Maynor Cabrera, Blanca Moreno-Dodson, and Miguel E. Sanchez-Martin. 2018. "Dominican Republic: Fiscal Policy and Redistribution," chap. 14 in *Commitment to Equity Handbook. Estimating the Impact of Fiscal Policy on Inequality and Poverty*, edited by Nora Lustig (Brookings Institution Press and CEQ Institute, Tulane University).

Arunatilake, Nisha, Gabriela Inchauste, and Nora Lustig. 2017. "The Incidence of Taxes and Spending in Sri Lanka," chap. 9 in *The Distributional Impact of Taxes and Transfers. Evidence from Eight Low- and Middle-Income Countries*, edited by Gabriela Inchauste and Nora Lustig. Washington, DC: World Bank.

Atkinson, A.B. 1996. "The Case for a Participation Income." *The Political Quarterly* 67: 67–70. doi:10.1111/j.1467-923X.1996.tb01568.x

Bachas, Pierre, Lucie Gadenne, and Anders Jensen. 2020. "Informality, Consumption Taxes and Redistribution." Policy Research Working Papers no. 9267. Washington, DC: World Bank.

Baum, Anja, Tewodaj Mogues, and Genevieve Verdier. 2020. "Getting the Most from Public Investment." In *Infrastructure Governance: From Aspiration to Action*, edited by Gerd Schwartz, Manal Fouad, Torben Steen Hansen, and Genevieve Verdier. Washington, DC: International Monetary Fund.

Behar, Alberto, and Junghwan Mok. 2013. "Does Public-Sector Employment Fully Crowd Out Private-Sector Employment?" IMF Working paper, WP/13/146. Washington, DC: International Monetary Fund.

Beneke, Margarita, Nora Lustig, and Jose Andres Oliva. 2018. "El Salvador: The Impact of Taxes and Social Spending on Inequality and Poverty," chap. 15 in *Commitment to Equity Handbook. Estimating the Impact of Fiscal Policy on Inequality and Poverty*, edited by Nora Lustig (Brookings Institution Press and CEQ Institute, Tulane University).

Bourguignon, François. 2003. "The Poverty-Growth-Inequality Triangle," Paper prepared for a Conference on Poverty, Inequality and Growth, Agence Française de Développement/EU Development Network, Paris, November 13, 2003.

Brahmbhatt, Milan, and Otaviano Canuto. 2011. "Fiscal Policy for Growth and Development." In *Is Fiscal Policy the Answer? A Developing Country Perspective*. Washington, DC: World Bank.

Bucheli, Marisa, Nora Lustig, Maximo Rossi, and Florencia Amabile. 2014. "Social Spending, Taxes and Income Redistribution in Uruguay," in *Analyzing the Redistributive Impact of Taxes and Transfers in Latin America*, edited by Nora Lustig, Carola Pessino and John Scott, Special Issue, *Public Finance Review* 42(3): 413–33. Available at: DOI: 10.1177/1091142113493493

Cabrera, Maynor, and Hilcias E. Moran. 2015. "*CEQ Master Workbook: Guatemala (2011)*," CEQ Data Center on Fiscal Redistribution (CEQ Institute, Tulane University, Instituto Centroamericano de Estudios Fiscales (ICEFI) and International Fund for Agricultural Development (IFAD)).

Caminada, K., K. Goudswaard, and C. Wang. 2012. "Disentangling Income Inequality and the Redistributive Effect of Taxes and Transfers in 20 LIS Countries Over Time." LIS WorkingPaper Series No. 581. Luxembourg: Luxembourg Income Study.

Cancho, Cesar, and Elena Bondarenko. 2017. "The Distributional Impact of Fiscal Policy in Georgia," in *The Distributional Impact of Taxes and Transfers. Evidence from Eight Low- and Middle-Income Countries*, edited by Gabriela Inchauste and Nora Lustig. Washington, DC: World Bank.

Causa, Orsetta, and Mikkel Hermansen. 2017. "Income Redistribution Through Taxes and Transfers Across OECD Countries." Economics Department Working Papers No. 1453. Paris: OECD.

Clements, Benedict J., David Coady, Stephania Fabrizio, Sanjeev Gupta, Trevor Alleyne, and Carlo Sdralevich. 2013. "Energy Subsidy Reform: Lessons and Implications." IMF Policy Paper. Washington, DC: International Monetary Fund.

Clements, Benedict, Frank Eich, and Sanjeev Gupta. 2014. *Equitable and Sustainable Pensions: Challenges and Experience*. Washington, DC: International Monetary Fund.

Clements, Benedict, Ruud de Mooij, Sanjeev Gupta, and Michael Keen. 2015. *Inequality and Fiscal Policy.* Washington, DC: International Monetary Fund.

Coady, David, Maura Francese, and Baoping Shang. 2014. *Finance & Development,* December 2014. Washington, DC: International Monetary Fund.

Coady, David, Ian Parry, Nghia-Piotr Le, and Baoping Shang. 2019. "Global Fossil Fuel Subsidies Remain Large: An Update Based on Country-Level Estimates". IMF Working Paper WP/15/250. Washington, DC: International Monetary Fund.

Coady, David, Valentina Flamini, and Louis Sears. 2015. "The Unequal Benefits of Fuel Subsidies Revisited: Evidence for Developing Countries." IMF Working Paper WP/15/250. Washington, DC: International Monetary Fund.

Cournède, Boris, Jean-Marc Fournier, and Peter Hoeller. 2018. "Public Finance Structure and Inclusive Growth." OECD Economic Policy Paper No. 25.

Davalos, Maria E., Monica Robayo-Abril, Esmeralda Shehaj, and Aida Gjika. 2018. "The Distributional Impact of the Fiscal System in Albania," Policy Research Working Paper, WPS 8370. Washington, DC: World Bank.

de Renzio, Paolo, and Joachim Wehner. 2015. *The Impacts of Fiscal Openness: A Review of the Evidence. Global Initiative for Fiscal Transparency and the International Budget Partnership.* Washington, DC: International Budget Partnership.

Del Granado, Javier Arze, Sanjev Gupta, and Alejandro Hajdenberg. 2010. "Is Social Spending Procyclical?" IMF Working Paper WP/10/234. Washington, DC: International Monetary Fund.

Dethier, Jean-Jacques, Pierre Pestieau, and Rabia Ali, 2010. Universal Minimum Old Age Pensions Impact on Poverty and Fiscal Cost in 18 Latin American Countries. Policy Research Working Paper 5292. Washington, DC: World Bank.

Ebeke, Christian, and Constant Lonkeng Ngouana. 2015. "Energy Subsidies and Public Social Spending: Theory and Evidence." IMF Working Paper WP/15/101. Washington, DC: International Monetary Fund.

Ebeke, Christian, and Dilan Ölçer. 2013. "Fiscal Policy over the Election Cycle in Low-Income Countries." IMF Working Paper WP/13/153. Washington, DC: International Monetary Fund.

Enami, Ali, Nora Lustig, and Alireza Taqdiri. 2017. "Fiscal Policy, Inequality and Poverty in Iran: Assessing the Impact and Effectiveness of Taxes and Transfers." CEQ Working Paper 48 (CEQ Institute, Tulane University and the Economic Research Forum).

Essama-Nssah B., and Blanca Moreno-Dodson. 2011. "Fiscal Policy for Growth and Social Welfare." In *Is Fiscal Policy the Answer? A Developing Country Perspective,* edited by Blanca Moreno-Dodson. Washington, DC: World Bank.

Ezzarari, Abdeljaouad. 2018. Dépenses Publiques et dépenses des Ménages en Education. Les Brefs du Plan, Haut Commissariat au Plan, Rabat, Morocco.

Fabrizio, Stefania, Davide Furceri, Rodrigo Garcia-Verdu, Bin Grace Li, Sandra V. Lizarazo Ruiz, Marina Mendes Tavares, et al. 2017. "Macro-Structural Policies and Income Inequality in Low-Income Developing Countries." IMF Staff Discussion Note No. 17/01. Washington, DC: International Monetary Fund.

Fournier, Jean-Marc, and Åsa Johansson. 2016. "The Effect of the Size and the Mix of Public Spending on Growth And Inequality." OECD Economics Department Working Paper No. 1344.

Francese, Maura, and Delphine Prady. 2018. "Universal Basic Income: Debate and Impact Assessment." IMF Working Paper WP/18/273. Washington, DC: International Monetary Fund.

Frankel, Jeffrey A., Carlos A. Végh, and Guillermo Vuletin. 2011. "On Graduation from Fiscal Procyclicality." NBER Working Paper No. 17619.

Gemmell, Norman, Florian Misch, and Blanca Moreno-Dodson. 2011. "Public Spending and Long-Run Growth in Practice: Concepts, Tools, and Evidence." In *Is Fiscal Policy the Answer? A Developing Country Perspective* edited by Blanca Moreno-Dodson. Washington, DC: World Bank.

Gimenez, Lea, Maria Ana Lugo, Sandra Martinez-Aguilar, Humberto Colman, Juan Jose Galeano, and Gabriela Farfan. 2017. "Paraguay: Analisis del Sistema Fiscal y su Impacto en la Pobreza y la Equidad." CEQ Working Paper 74 (Ministerio de Hacienda de Paraguay, World Bank and CEQ Institute, Tulane University).

Gouzien, Quentin. 2020. "Integrating the SDGs into the Budget: The Experience of African Countries," IMF blog. Washington, DC: International Monetary Fund.

Grigoli, Francesco, and Eduardo Ley. 2012. "Quality of Government and Living Standards: Adjusting for the Efficiency of Public Spending." IMF Working Paper WP/12/182.

Grosh, Margaret; del Ninno, Carlo; Tesliuc, Emil; Ouerghi, Azedine. 2008. *For Protection and Promotion : The Design and Implementation of Effective Safety Nets.* Washington, DC: World Bank.

Handa, S., M. Park, R. Osei Darko, I. Osei-Akoto, B. Davis, and S. Daidone. 2014. *Livelihood Empowerment against Poverty Program: Impact Evaluation.* Chapel Hill: UNC Carolina Population Center.

Higgins, Sean, and Nora Lustig. 2016. "Can a Poverty-Reducing and Progressive Tax and Transfer System Hurt the Poor?" *Journal of Development Economics* 122(C): 63–75.

Higgins, Sean, and Claudiney Pereira. 2014. "The Effects of Brazil's Taxation and Social Spending on the Distribution of Household Income," in *Analyzing the Redistributive Impact of Taxes and Transfers in Latin America,* edited by Nora Lustig, Carola Pessino and John Scott, Special Issue, *Public Finance Review* 42, 3, pp. 346–67. Available at: DOI: 10.1177/1091142113501714

Hill, Ruth, Gabriela Inchauste, Nora Lustig, Eyasu Tsehaye, and Tassew Woldehanna. 2017. "Fiscal Incidence Analysis for Ethiopia," chap. 3 in *The Distributional Impact of Taxes and Transfers. Evidence from Eight Low- and Middle-Income Countries,* edited by Gabriela Inchauste and Nora Lustig. Washington, DC: World Bank.

ILO. 2017. World Social Protection Report 2017–19: Universal social protection to achieve the Sustainable Development Goals. Geneva: International Labour Office.

ILO. 2019. "The Global Labour Income Share and Distribution." Geneva: International Labour Office.

IMF. 2014a. "Budget Institutions in G-20 Countries: An Update." IMF Policy Paper. Washington, DC: International Monetary Fund.

IMF. 2014b. "Toward New Horizons Arab Economic Transformation Amid Political Transitions." MCD Departmental Paper Series. Washington, DC: International Monetary Fund.

IMF. 2014c. "Public Expenditure Reform: Making Difficult Choices," April 2014 Fiscal Monitor. Washington, DC: International Monetary Fund.

IMF. 2014d. "Fiscal Policy and Income Inequality." IMF Policy Paper. Washington, DC: International Monetary Fund.

IMF. 2015. "Making Public Investment More Efficient." IMF Policy Paper. Washington, DC: International Monetary Fund.

IMF. 2016. "Managing Government Compensation and Employment—Institutions, Policies, and Reform Challenges." IMF Policy Paper. Washington, DC: International Monetary Fund.

IMF. 2017a. "Tackling Inequality," October 2013 Fiscal Monitor. Washington, DC: International Monetary Fund.

IMF. 2017b. "Understanding the Downward Trend in Labor Income Share." In *World Economic Outlook*, April 2017. Washington, DC: International Monetary Fund.

IMF. 2017c. "Gender Budgeting in G7 Countries." IMF Policy Paper. Washington, DC: International Monetary Fund.

IMF. 2018. "Public Wage Bills in the Middle East and Central Asia." MCD Departmental Paper Series. Washington, DC: International Monetary Fund.

IMF. 2020a. "Managing the Impact on Households: Assessing Universal Transfers (UT)." Special Series on Fiscal Policies to Respond to COVID-19. Washington, DC: International Monetary Fund.

IMF. 2020b. "Public Investment for the Recovery," October 2020 Fiscal Monitor. Washington, DC: International Monetary Fund.

Inchauste, Gabriela, Nora Lustig, Mashekwa Maboshe, Catriona Purfield, and Ingrid Woolard. 2017. "The Distributional Impact of Fiscal Policy in South Africa," chap. 8 in *The Distributional Impact of Taxes and Transfers. Evidence from Eight Low- and Middle-Income Countries, edited by Gabriela Inchauste and Nora Lustig* (Washington, DC: World Bank).

Instituto Centroamericano de Estudios Fiscales. 2017a. "Incidencia de la fiscal en la desigualdad y la pobreza en Honduras." CEQ Working Paper 51 (CEQ Institute, Tulane University, IFAD and Instituto Centroamericano de Estudios Fiscales).

Instituto Centroamericano de Estudios Fiscales. 2017b. "Incidencia de la fiscal en la desigualdad y la pobreza en Nicaragua." CEQ Working Paper 52 (CEQ Institute, Tulane University, IFAD and Instituto Centroamericano de Estudios Fiscales).

Jaramillo, Miguel. 2014. "The Incidence of Social Spending and Taxes in Peru," in Analyzing the Redistributive Impact of Taxes and Transfers in Latin America, edited by Nora Lustig, Carola Pessino and John Scott, Special Issue, *Public Finance Review* 42(3): 391–412. Available at: DOI: 10.1177/1091142113496134.

Jaramillo, Miguel. 2019. "*CEQ Master Workbook: Peru (2011),*" CEQ Data Center on Fiscal Redistribution (CEQ Institute, Tulane University). February 11, 2019.

Jarvis, Chris, Oussama Kanaan, Younes Zouhar, and Chadi Abdallah, 2015. "Policies to Promote Growth and Create Jobs over the Next Decade in Egypt." IMF Selected Issues Paper. Washington, DC: International Monetary Fund.

Jellema, Jon, Astrid Haas, Nora Lustig, and Sebastian Wolf. 2018. "Uganda: The Impact of Taxes, Transfers, and Subsidies on Inequality and Poverty," chap. 19 in *Commitment to Equity Handbook. Estimating the Impact of Fiscal Policy on Inequality and Poverty*, edited by Nora Lustig (Brookings Institution Press and CEQ Institute, Tulane University).

Jellema, Jon, Matthew Wai-Poi, and Rythia Afkar. 2017. "The Distributional Impact of Fiscal Policy in Indonesia," chap. 5 in *The Distributional Impact of Taxes and Transfers. Evidence from Eight Low- and Middle-Income Countries*, edited by Gabriela Inchauste and Nora Lustig. Washington, DC: World Bank.

Jouini, Nizar, Nora Lustig, Ahmed Moummi, and Abebe Shimeles. 2018. "Tunisia: Fiscal Policy, Income Redistribution and Poverty Reduction," chap. 18 in *Commitment to Equity Handbook. Estimating the Impact of Fiscal Policy on Inequality and Poverty*, edited by Nora Lustig (Brookings Institution Press and CEQ Institute, Tulane University).

Lindert, Peter H. 2017. "The Rise and Future of Progressive Redistribution." CEQ Working Paper 73. CEQ Institute at Tulane University New Orleans.

Lindert, Peter H. 2021. *Making Social Spending Work.* Cambridge: Cambridge University Press.

Lipton, David. 2016. "The Case for Reforming the Price of Water." IMF Blog: https://blogs.imf.org/2016/03/22/the-case-for-reforming-the-price-of-water/. Washington, DC: International Monetary Fund.

Llerena Pinto, Freddy Paul, Maria Cristhina Llerena Pinto, Maria Andrea Llerena Pinto, and Roberto Carlos Saa Daza. 2015. "Social Spending, Taxes and Income Redistribution in Ecuador," CEQ Working Paper 28 (Center for Inter-American Policy and Research and Department of Economics, Tulane University and Inter-American Dialogue).

Llerena Pinto, Freddy Paul, Maria Cristhina Llerena Pinto, Roberto Carlos Saa Daza, and Maria Andrea Llerena Pinto. 2017. "*CEQ Master Workbook: Ecuador (2011–2012),*" CEQ Data Center on Fiscal Redistribution (CEQ Institute, Tulane University).

Lopez-Calva, Luis Felipe, Nora Lustig, Mikhail Matytsin, and Daria Popova. 2017. "Who Benefits from Fiscal Redistribution in the Russian Federation?," chap. 7 in *The Distributional Impact of Taxes and Transfers. Evidence from Eight Low- and Middle-Income Countries*, edited by Gabriela Inchauste and Nora Lustig (Washington, DC: World Bank).

Lustig, Nora. 2015. The Redistributive Impact of Government Spending on Education and Health: Evidence from 13 Developing Countries in the Commitment to Equity Project, In Sanjeev Gupta, Michael Keen, Benedict Clements and Ruud de Mooij (Eds.), Inequality and Fiscal Policy, Washington: International Monetary Fund. 2015.

Lustig, Nora (ed). 2018. *Commitment to Equity Handbook—Estimating the Impact of Fiscal Policy on Inequality and Poverty*. Brookings Institution Press and CEQ Institute at Tulane University New Orleans.

Lustig, Nora, Jon Jellema, and Valentina Martinez Pabon. 2019. "Leaving No One Behind: Can Tax-funded Transfer Programs Provide Income Floors in Sub-Saharan Africa?" CEQ Working Paper 85. CEQ Institute at Tulane University New Orleans.

Martinez-Aguilar, Sandra, Alan Fuchs, Eduardo Ortiz-Juarez, and Giselle del Carmen. 2018. "Chile: The Impact of Fiscal Policy on Inequality and Poverty," chap. 13 in *Commitment to Equity Handbook. Estimating the Impact of Fiscal Policy on Inequality and Poverty*, edited by Nora Lustig (Brookings Institution Press and CEQ Institute, Tulane University).

Martinez-Aguilar, Sandra. 2019a. *"CEQ Master Workbook: Panama (2016),"* CEQ Data Center on Fiscal Redistribution (CEQ Institute, Tulane University and the Economic Co-operation and Development).

Melendez, Marcela, and Valentina Martinez. 2019b. *"CEQ Master Workbook: Colombia (2010),"* CEQ Data Center on Fiscal Redistribution (CEQ Institute, Tulane University and Inter-American Development Bank).

Melendez, Marcela, and Valentina Martinez. 2019. *"CEQ Master Workbook: Colombia (2014),"* CEQ Data Center on Fiscal Redistribution (CEQ Institute, Tulane University and Inter-American Development Bank).

Molina, Emiro. 2016. *"CEQ Master Workbook: Venezuela (2012),"* CEQ Data Center on Fiscal Redistribution (CEQ Institute, Tulane University). April 5, 2018.

Musgrave, Richard. 1959. *The Theory of Public Finance: A Study in Public Economy*. New York: McGraw Hill.

OECD. 2011. *Divided We Stand: Why Inequality Keeps Rising*. Paris: OECD.

OECD. 2017a. "Bridging the Gap: Inclusive Growth 2017 Update Report." Paris: OECD.

OECD. 2017b. Update Report 2017—Inclusive Growth. Meeting of the OECD Council at Ministerial Level Paris, June 7–8, 2017. Paris: OECD.

OECD. 2017c. "Basic Income as a Policy Option: Can It Add Up?" OECD Policy Brief on the Future of Work. Paris: OECD.

OECD. 2018. Public Finance Structure and Inclusive Growth. OECD Policy Paper. December 2018 No. 2. Paris: OECD.

OECD., 2019. Economic Policy Reforms—Going for Growth 2019.

Oliva, Jose Andres. 2019. "CEQ Master Workbook: El Salvador (2011)," CEQ Data Center on Fiscal Redistribution (CEQ Institute, Tulane University and Inter-American Development Bank).

Ortiz, Isabel. 2018. "The Case for Universal Social Protection." In *Finance and Development*, December 2018. Washington, DC: International Monetary Fund.

Paulus, A., M. Čok, F. Figari, P. Hegedüs, N. Kump, O. Lelkes, et al. 2009. "The Effects of Taxes and Benefits on Income Distribution in the Enlarged EU." EUROMOD Working Paper EM8/09. Essex: University of Essex.

Paz Arauco, Veronica, George Gray-Molina, Ernesto Yañez Aguilar, and Wilson Jimenez Pozo. 2014. "Explaining Low Redistributive Impact in Bolivia," in *Analyzing the Redistributive Impact of Taxes and Transfers in Latin America*, edited by Nora Lustig, Carola Pessino and John Scott, Special Issue, *Public Finance Review* 42(3): 326–45. Available at: DOI: 10.1177/1091142113496133

Rijkers, Bob, Caroline Freund, and Antonio Nucifora. 2014. "All in the Family: State Capture in Tunisia." World Bank Policy Research Working Paper 6810. Washington, DC: World Bank.

Rossignolo, Dario. 2018. "Argentina: Taxes, Expenditures, Poverty, and Income Distribution," chap. 11 in *Commitment to Equity Handbook. Estimating the Impact of Fiscal Policy on Inequality and Poverty*, edited by Nora Lustig (Brookings Institution Press and CEQ Institute, Tulane University).

Sauma, Pablo, and Juan Diego Trejos. 2014. "Social Public Spending, Taxes, Redistribution of Income, and Poverty in Costa Rica," CEQ Working Paper 18 (Center for Inter-American Policy and Research and Department of Economics, Tulane University and Inter-American Dialogue).

Scott, John. 2014. "Redistributive Impact and Efficiency of Mexico's Fiscal System," in *Analyzing the Redistributive Impact of Taxes and Transfers in Latin America*, edited by Nora Lustig, Carola Pessino, John Scott, Special Issue, *Public Finance Review* 42(3): 368–90. Available at: DOI: 10.1177/1091142113497394

Sdralevich, Carlo, Randa Sab, Younes Zouhar, and Giorgia Albertin. 2014. *Subsidy Reform in the Middle East and North Africa: Progress and Challenges Ahead.* MCD Departmental Paper Series. Washington, DC: International Monetary Fund.

Shang, Baoping. 2014. "Pension Reform and Equity: The Impact on Poverty of Reducing Pension Benefits." In *Equitable and Sustainable Pensions: Challenges and Experience.* Washington, DC: International Monetary Fund.

Taliercio, Robert, and Eduardo Andrés Estrada. 2020. "Getting the Most from Public Investment." In *Well Spent—How Strong Infrastructure Governance Can End Waste in Public Investment*, edited by Gerd Schwartz, Manal Fouad, Torben Steen Hansen, and Genevieve Verdier. Washington, DC: International Monetary Fund.

Van Eden, Holger, Pokar Khemani, and Richard P. Emery Jr. 2013. "Developing Legal Frameworks to Promote Fiscal Responsibility: Design Matters." In *Public Financial Management and Its Emerging Architecture.* Washington, DC: International Monetary Fund.

World Bank. 2018. *The State of Social Safety Nets 2018.* Washington, DC: World Bank.

World Health Organization. 2010. *The World Health Report: Health Systems Financing—The Path to Universal Coverage.* Geneva: World Health Organization.

Younger, Stephen D., and Artsvi Khachatryan. 2017. "Fiscal Incidence in Armenia," chap. 2 in *The Distributional Impact of Taxes and Transfers. Evidence from Eight Low- and Middle-Income Countries*, edited by Gabriela Inchauste and Nora Lustig. Washington: World Bank.

Younger, Stephen, Flora Myamba, and Kenneth Mdadila. 2016. "Fiscal Incidence in Tanzania." *African Development Review* 28(3): 264–76. Available at: DOI: 10.1111/1467-8268.12204.

Younger, Stephen, Eric Osei-Assibey, and Felix Oppong. 2017. "Fiscal Incidence in Ghana." *Review of Development Economics* 21(4): 47–66. Available at: DOI: 10.1111/rode.12299

Zouhar, Younes. 2012. "Inclusive Growth in Mauritania, Islamic Republic of Mauritania: Selected Issues Paper." IMF Country Report No. 12/249. Washington, DC: International Monetary Fund.

Zouhar, Younes, Jon Jellema, Nora Lustig, and Mohamed Trabelsi. 2021. "Public Expenditure and Inclusive Growth—A Survey." IMF Working Paper WP/21/83. Washington, DC: International Monetary Fund.

14

Education and Health

Deon Filmer, Roberta Gatti, Halsey Rogers, Nikola Spatafora, and Drilona Emrullahu

Education then, beyond all other devices of human origin, is the great equalizer of the conditions of men, the balance-wheel of the social machinery.

—Horace Mann

I. Introduction

Economies prosper when people are well educated and healthy, two key prerequisites for inclusive growth. Education and health, beyond their undeniable intrinsic value, enable people to realize their potential as productive members of society. More human capital—knowledge, skills, and health—leads to higher earnings for individuals, increased social mobility, and faster and more sustainable growth for countries.[1] People across the world see education and health as a priority. And human capital is particularly important for disadvantaged households, who rely on it to escape deprivation. But in practice the accumulation of human capital has often become a mechanism for the perpetuation of inequality and poverty.

Substantial human-capital shortfalls and equity gaps persist. Worldwide, a child born in early 2020, just before the Covid-19 pandemic struck, could on average expect to achieve just 56 percent of her potential human capital—her productivity as a future worker were she to enjoy complete education and full health (World Bank 2020a).[2] Human capital increases systematically with income, both across and within countries, reflecting inequalities in the access to, quantity, and quality of education and health care. Gaps in human capital remain especially

---

[1] Flabbi and Gatti (2018) and Rossi (2019) review the literature linking human capital with earnings, income, and growth.

[2] "Complete education" is defined as 14 learning-adjusted years of schooling, and "full health" as 100 percent child-survival rates and no childhood stunting. They do not imply equal productivity or outcomes across individuals. Kraay (2019) and D'Souza et al. (2019) provide details on, respectively, the construction of this human capital index and its socioeconomic disaggregation. World Bank (2020) summarizes the key messages from analyzing the index.

Deon Filmer, Roberta Gatti, Halsey Rogers, Nikola Spatafora, and Drilona Emrullahu, *Education and Health* In: *How to Achieve Inclusive Growth*. Edited by: Valerie Cerra, Barry Eichengreen, Asmaa El-Ganainy, and Martin Schindler, Oxford University Press. © Deon Filmer, Roberta Gatti, Halsey Rogers, Nikola Spatafora, and Drilona Emrullahu 2022. DOI: 10.1093/oso/9780192846938.003.0014

deep in low-income countries (LICs) and those affected by institutional fragility, armed conflict, and violence. In the poorest countries, a child will on average grow up to be only about 30 percent as productive as she could be. And, within any given country, rich households accumulate greater overall human capital than poor ones (Figure 14.1).[3] Similar income gradients emerge when analyzing specific education outcomes, such as school completion rates (Figure 14.2), and health outcomes, including various measures of mortality and morbidity (Figure 14.3 and Figure 14.4) (see also O'Donnell et al. 2014). Some of these within-country differences by income level coincide with rural-urban or ethnic divides, further threatening social cohesion. And these opportunity gaps have displayed only a weak tendency to decrease over time.

The Covid-19 pandemic highlighted the fragility and inequity of many education and health systems. School closures and family hardship put pressure on students, teachers, and parents, and left millions at risk of dropping out of school.

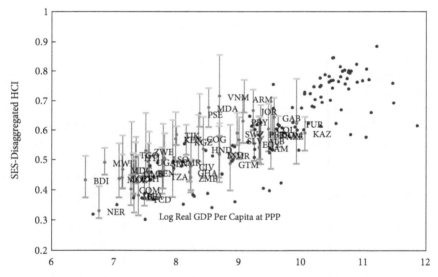

Figure 14.1 Human Capital and Income Within and Across Countries

Note: The figure depicts the World Bank Human Capital Index (HCI) disaggregated by socioeconomic-status quintiles (SES-HCI) on the vertical axis, against log real GDP per capita on the horizontal axis, for the 51 countries in the SES-HCI dataset. For each country, the solid dot denotes the average across quintiles, and the top (respectively, bottom) of the vertical bar denotes the value for the top (respectively, bottom) quintile. Light-grey points show the HCI for countries where the SES-HCI is not available.

Source: D'Souza et al. (2019), figure 6. License: CC BY 3.0 IGO.

---

[3] In Madagascar, shortfalls in education and health, and their differential impact across socioeconomic groups, imply that the expected productivity as future workers of children born into the poorest and richest quintile equals, respectively, 40 percent and 58 percent of its potential level. In richer Vietnam, the corresponding values equal 58 percent and 85 percent.

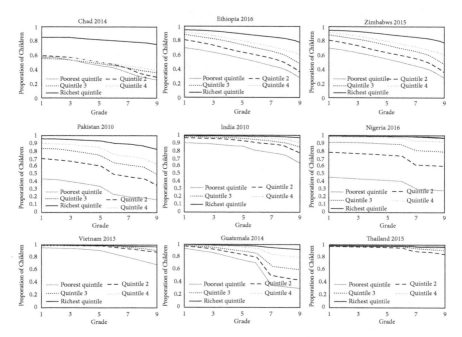

Figure 14.2 Proportion of 10–19-year-old Children who Attain Each Grade, by Wealth Quintile

Source: Avitabile et al. (2020), figure 2.4. License: CC BY 3.0 IGO.

The disruption in health services and losses in income acted to increase child mortality and chronic malnutrition. In both cases, the impact will be felt for decades, and will prove especially severe among already disadvantaged groups.

Within-country differences across socioeconomic quintiles account for roughly one-third of the total variation in human capital in low- and middle-income economies (D'Souza et al. 2019).[4] In fact, average human capital outcomes increase with income at roughly the same rate across socio-economic groups *within* countries as they do across countries. This suggests that national social protection and other programs aimed at mitigating human-capital risks affecting poor households are relatively ineffective—no better than the mechanisms for sharing risk across countries.

Governments have a vital role to play in reducing this inequality of opportunity. Inequalities in education and health matter intrinsically, and are likely to be transmitted across generations. These inequalities stem at least partly from barriers to investment in human capital which, by preventing the full development of individual talents, constrain overall growth (Flabbi and Gatti 2018). Intervention

---

[4] In both Madagascar and Vietnam, the within-country rich-poor gap equals roughly half the gap in average human capital between the highest- and lowest-performing country.

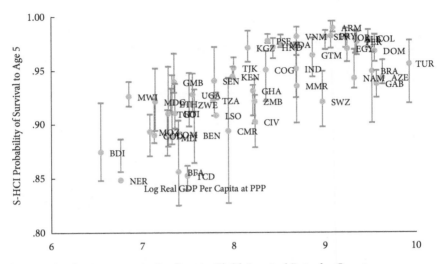

Figure 14.3 Socioeconomic Gradient in Child-Survival Rates by Country Income Level

Note: The figure depicts child-survival rates (probability of survival until age 5) disaggregated by socioeconomic quintile on the vertical axis, against log real GDP per capita on the horizontal axis, for the 51 countries in the SES-HCI dataset. Solid dot denotes average across quintiles, and top (bottom) of vertical bar denotes value for the top (bottom) quintile. Country average (dot) may fall below value for lowest quintile (bottom end of vertical bar) when middle quintiles have values below lower quintiles (for instance, Niger).

Source: D'Souza et al. (2019), figure 1. License: CC BY 3.0 IGO.

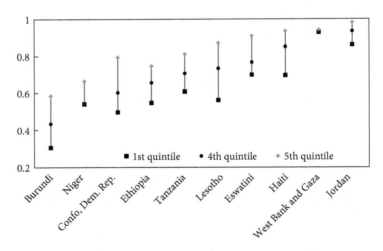

Figure 14.4 Socioeconomic Gradient in Non-Stunting Rates by Country Income Level

Note: Stunting, an indicator of chronic malnutrition, means that a child has low height-for-age. It is defined as a height-for-age more than 2 standard deviations below the median of a healthy reference population.

Source: Avitabile et al. (2020), figure 2.3. License: CC BY 3.0 IGO.

is further justified by important externalities and public goods—in public health and health research, but also in education, which yields positive economic and social spillovers through faster technological innovation and adoption (Huang et al. 2020), lower crime (Bell et al. 2018), a vibrant press (Guseva et al. 2008), and the creation of shared values, high levels of political engagement, trust, and tolerance (Chong and Gradstein 2015). Critically, appropriate interventions can boost both efficiency *and* equity; there is no inherent trade-off between these goals when addressing inequality of opportunity in education and health.

Education and health policies should reflect certain common principles. The broad policy *goals* should be to improve:

- The *quality*, and not just the quantity, of education and health care.
- Outcomes for *disadvantaged groups*, who are worse served by current systems. The return to investing in these groups is especially high, particularly in countries with the largest equity gaps, and especially for measures early in life.
- *Lifelong outcomes*, especially because (working) lives are steadily lengthening.

The *means* to achieve these goals, while maximizing value for money, include:

- Focusing on *results—learning and good health*—rather than just inputs, such as education and health spending.
- Moving from narrow, piecemeal interventions to *systemic reform*, centered on efforts to increase accountability and improve incentives, including by empowering citizens.
- Adopting a *"whole-of-society"* approach. Government departments largely function along discrete lines, often with minimal inter-sectoral cooperation. Coordinating efforts within government to reflect important interactions between policies, and sustaining such efforts across political cycles, can foster policy coherence and effectiveness. Partnership with the private sector and civil society can, in turn, complement government action in helping improve the coverage and quality of service delivery. In particular,
  - Supply-side measures to strengthen education and health systems must be complemented by demand-side measures to help families accumulate human capital by easing financial constraints—for instance, through conditional cash transfers, or reconnecting workers with jobs.
  - Different dimensions of human capital reinforce each other—"skills beget skills." There are therefore important complementarities among different policy measures (Cunha and Heckman 2007). For instance, improvements in sanitation and nutrition that enhance children's health complement teacher training in boosting learning.

Reforms must be underpinned by a robust evidence base. Evidence helps stakeholders judge system performance, reveals opportunity gaps, and catalyzes action. It shines a light on constraints, enabling policymakers to design effective interventions and target support to the most vulnerable. It shows whether reforms are working and suggests ways to refine them. Its importance is multiplied during crises: governments that use relevant real-time data can better respond to both immediate and long-term challenges.

These themes do play out differently with regard to education and to health care. We explore these two policy areas in turn, summarizing key messages from the academic and policy literature.

II. Education

A. The Learning Crisis and Its Causes

In many education systems, children learn very little—a true learning crisis.[5] Even after several years, they remain unable to read a simple story or do basic addition and subtraction. Fifty-three percent of all 10-year-old children in low- and middle-income countries, and 93 percent of those in LICs, cannot read and understand a simple age-appropriate story ("learning poverty"; World Bank 2019a). In rural India, only half of grade-5 students fluently read grade-2 text, such as "It was the month of rains." In Ghana and Malawi, more than three-fifths of students ending grade-2 cannot read a single familiar word such as "the" or "cat." In Nicaragua, only half of grade-3 students can solve "5 + 6" (World Bank 2018a).

While not all developing countries suffer from such extreme shortfalls, many fall far short of the levels they aspire to. International assessments of literacy (PIRLS) and numeracy (TIMSS) show the average student in LICs performs worse than 95 percent of students in high-income countries. Many high-performing students in middle-income countries, who rank in the top quarter of their cohorts, would rank in the bottom quarter in a wealthier country. In Algeria, the Dominican Republic, and Kosovo, test scores of students at the cutoff for the top quarter of students are well below the bottom-quarter cutoff in OECD countries, as measured by the PISA assessment (Figure 14.5). Even in Costa Rica, a relatively strong performer, performance at the cutoff for the top quarter of

---

[5] This section draws heavily on World Bank (2018, 2020b, 2020f). It focuses on foundational skills, such as literacy, numeracy, and basic reasoning, acquired from birth through secondary school. These skills provide the critical foundation for higher-order reasoning, creativity, and socioemotional skills like perseverance and teamwork. They allow adaptability and lifelong learning.

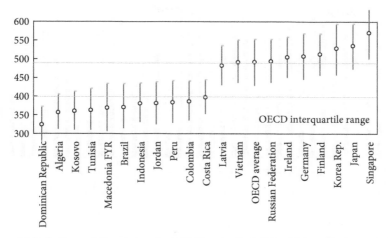

Figure 14.5 In Several Countries, the 75th Percentile Of Test-Takers Performs Below the 25th Percentile of the OECD Average (2015 PISA Mathematics Assessment)
Source: World Bank (2018a), figure O.2. License: CC BY 3.0 IGO.

students equals performance at the bottom-quarter cutoff in Germany. While some countries are making progress, this is typically slow.

The learning crisis amplifies inequality: it hobbles especially severely the disadvantaged youths who most need a good education. The most disadvantaged suffer from the worst access to schooling, highest dropout rates, and largest learning deficits. Differences by income level are stark (Figure 14.6). At the end of primary school, only 5 percent of girls in Cameroon from the poorest quintile had learned enough to continue schooling, compared with 76 percent of girls from the richest quintile. Learning outcomes are also highly unequal along disability, gender, and ethnic lines; displaced children typically fare worse even when in school. These learning gaps often grow with more years in school. And learning inequalities are particularly high in more unequal societies, partly reflecting a greater learning gap between public and private schools and greater socio-economic sorting across school types (Patel and Sandefur 2020). On the TIMSS assessment, the gap between the top and bottom quarter of US students is larger than the median-score gap between the United States and Algeria.

Millions of disadvantaged children remain out of school, because of conflicts, poverty, and the learning crisis itself. Enrollment gaps in basic education between high- and low-income countries are closing. But even before Covid-19 one-fifth of children of primary- and secondary-school age, and 10 percent of primary-school age children in lower-middle-income countries, remained out of school (UNESCO 2019). Worldwide, only half of all three- to six-year-olds have access to pre-school education; in LICs, just one-fifth do. Conflict-affected countries account for a disproportionate one-third of out-of-school children. But almost all

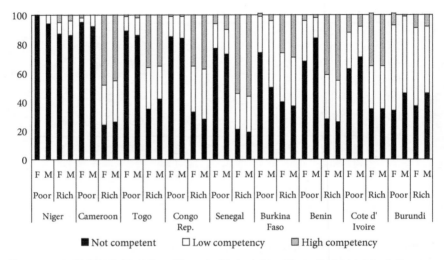

Figure 14.6 Children from Poor Households in Africa Typically Learn Much Less

Percentage of grade-6 PASEC test-takers who score above ("high competency") and below ("not competent") the sufficiency level on reading achievement: poorest and richest quintiles by gender

Note: Quintiles are nationally defined. Not competent refers to levels 0–2 in the original coding, and is below the sufficiency level for school continuation; low competency refers to level 3; high competency refers to level 4.

Source: World Bank (2018a), figure O.3. License: CC BY 3.0 IGO.

developing countries have pockets of out-of-school children from excluded groups. Poverty most consistently predicts failing to complete schooling; gender, disability, caste, and ethnicity contribute. And, when poor parents perceive education to be of low quality, they become less willing to sacrifice to keep children in school.

The Covid-19 pandemic both exposed and magnified existing inequalities. Disadvantaged groups, including poor and rural children, were disproportionately affected by school closures (OECD 2020a; Lustig et al. 2020; Garcia Jaramillo 2020). They had less capacity to learn at home: they suffered from the digital divide, including differences in access to hardware, connectivity, the right software, teachers with digital skills, and schools with the resources to provide remote learning;[6] less educated parents could provide less support; and poorer parents could not afford private tutors. And the disadvantaged, including in particular adolescent girls and the disabled, were at greater risk of dropping out (UN 2020). The impact on learning will likely prove large (World Bank 2020e) and persistent (Andrabi et al. 2020).

---

[6] Around one-third of schoolchildren worldwide lack all access to remote learning via radio, television, or online content (UNICEF 2020).

Immediate Causes of the Learning Crisis

Struggling education systems typically lack some key school-level learning ingredients:

- *Children arrive in school unprepared to learn.* Malnutrition, illness, low parental investments, and the harsh environments associated with poverty undermine early childhood learning and weaken developmental foundations.[7] These deprivations have long-lasting effects because they impair infants' brain development, and the brain becomes less malleable with age.
- *Teachers lack the skill, motivation, or support to be effective.* Teachers are the most important factor affecting learning in schools (Schleicher 2018). US students with great teachers advance three times faster than those with a poor teacher; in developing countries, teacher quality can matter even more (Bau and Das 2017). And teacher salaries are the largest single education-budget item, taking up three-quarters of the primary-level budget in developing countries. Yet many systems struggle to attract strong candidates into teaching (Bruns and Luque 2014), and to provide a solid foundation of subject or pedagogical knowledge before they start teaching.[8] Continuing professional development is inconsistent, overly theoretical, and often expensive. There are few mechanisms in place to mentor, support, and motivate teachers. Substantial learning time is lost because classroom time is spent on other activities or teachers are absent (Bold et al. 2017). The problems are particularly severe in rural or remote communities.
- *Inputs fail to affect learning.* Often, inputs do not even reach the frontlines. In Sierra Leone, textbooks were distributed to schools, but most were locked up unused in cupboards (Sabarwal et al. 2014). In Brazil, the One Laptop per Child initiative faced years of delays. One year after the laptops finally made it to classrooms, more than 40 percent of teachers had never or rarely used them (Lavinas and Veiga 2013).
- *Management and governance are weak.* Effective school leadership improves teaching quality, ensures effective resource use, and boosts student performance, even after controlling for student and school characteristics (Adelman and Lemos 2021; Robinson et al. 2008). School principals can actively help teachers solve problems, provide instructional advice, and set goals that prioritize learning. But management capacity is substantially lower in schools than in manufacturing, and particularly weak in LICs (Bloom et al. 2015). And schools often lack decision-making autonomy, while community engagement fails to provide oversight (Bruns et al. 2011).

---

[7] McCoy et al. (2016), Schady et al. (2015). Thirty percent of under-5 children in developing countries are physically stunted, typically reflecting chronic malnutrition.

[8] In Sub-Saharan Africa, less than 20 percent of grade-4 teachers have mastered the curriculum they teach.

These quality problems are concentrated among disadvantaged children, amplifying social inequalities. In LICs, among children under 5, stunting rates, an indicator of chronic malnutrition, are almost three times higher in the poorest quintile than the richest. Problems with teacher absenteeism, lack of inputs, and weak management are most severe in poorer communities.

Systemic Causes of the Learning Crisis

Low learning levels ultimately reflect both technical and political challenges, which help explain poor learning conditions in schools and communities.

Technical Challenges

Many countries, and particularly LICs, collect little systematic information on learning; this makes it difficult to monitor and manage learning activities. Teaching involves significant discretion and regular, repeated interactions, making it challenging to manage learning (Andrews, Pritchett, and Woolcock 2017). Many systems lack the reliable, timely assessments of student learning and of teaching quality needed to provide feedback on performance. More than one-fifth of children in low- and middle-income countries, and 54 percent of children in Sub-Saharan Africa, live in countries with no or dated learning assessment data (World Bank 2019a). One-third of countries lack information on reading and mathematics proficiency of children at the end of primary school. Even more lack it for the end of lower secondary. Available data are often from one-time assessments that do not allow tracking over time.

All parts of the education system must be coherent. A new curriculum that emphasizes active learning and creative thinking will not change much per se. Teachers must be trained and motivated to use active learning methods, which are more demanding than rote learning. Unreformed exams can weaken the effect of curriculum reform through misaligned incentives: in Korea, the curriculum now focuses on students' creativity and socioemotional skills, but many parents still send their children to private "cram schools" to prepare for high-stakes university-entrance exams (Park 2016).

The need for coherence makes it risky to borrow system elements from better-performing countries. Finland's high-performing system gives considerable autonomy to its well-educated teachers, who tailor teaching to student needs. But in lower-performing systems, where teachers are poorly educated, unmotivated, and loosely managed, giving them more autonomy may worsen outcomes (Chisholm and Leyendecker 2008).

Political Challenges

Many education actors have interests beyond learning. Politicians may focus benefits on their base, for example awarding education jobs through patronage rather than based on merit. Bureaucrats may protect their position by keeping politicians and teachers happy. Private education suppliers may act against students' interests to boost profits. Teachers may fight to protect employment and incomes. Higher-income urban families press for investments to benefit their children, diverting funding from poorer communities. Families in private schools are less willing to pay for public schools. Various actors use education to promote particular ideologies. Especially in poorly managed systems, policy choices are determined by who the more powerful actors are—not by what improves learning.

Potential beneficiaries of learning—students, parents, and employers—face difficulties in organizing themselves or acquiring the information needed for reforms. Parents are usually not organized to participate in system-level debates, may lack knowledge of potential reform gains, and may fear opposing teachers, bureaucrats, and politicians. Students may ignore how little they are learning. Employers facing skilled-worker shortages may lobby for lower taxes rather than quality education. Conversely, potential losers from reform are aware of what is at stake and are better organized to act collectively. Particularly in low-trust, risky environments, it is often in each individual's interest to maintain the status quo.

B. Three Policy Responses

Education systems must make learning a serious goal, through three complementary strategies. These will both improve short-term service delivery for current students, and establish systemic changes to boost long-term outcomes (World Bank 2020f).

- *Assess learning*: measure student learning to spotlight inequalities and spur action.
- *Make schools work for learners*: use evidence to guide innovation and practice.
- *Reform the system*: tackle technical and political barriers to learning.

The relationship between public spending per se and educational outcomes is often weak. Public spending does not correlate strongly with learning, or even access to education, even among countries at similar development levels (World Bank 2018a, spotlight 6; Al-Samarrai et al. 2019). Across systems and schools, similar levels of resources are associated with vast differences in outcomes. Likewise, increases in spending have limited effects on learning.[9] Spending has

---

[9] Kenya and Lesotho both increased public spending per primary-school student during the 2000s; learning improved in Lesotho but decreased in Kenya. Guatemala reduced per-student spending during 2006–2013, as did Bulgaria during 2009–2015; in both cases, learning improved significantly.

particularly weak effects in countries with weak governance (Suryadarma 2012; Rajkumar and Swaroop 2008). Adopting a more granular approach, specific interventions focused on providing inputs alone, such as more teachers or greater salaries, generally boost neither access nor learning (Angrist et al. 2020; Global Education Evidence Advisory Panel 2020). Direct school grants have often increased student enrollment and retention, but with limited effects on learning.

However, increased financing can support improvements in learning, *if* it is complemented by and supports broad reforms—that is, "spending more *and* better" (Gaspar et al. 2019). Currently, funds sometimes fail to reach schools, or pay for inputs that do not improve teacher-learner relationships. And financing is allocated inequitably, reducing overall learning (IMF 2017): poor and rural communities receive fewer education resources, including materials and staff (Jackson 2020; Lafortune et al. 2018), and relatively large amounts are devoted to secondary and tertiary education, which marginalized children are less likely to complete than primary education. More financing for business-as-usual will not change outcomes. But where countries seriously tackle barriers to learning for all, education spending is a critical investment. Good teachers, conducive learning environments, reliable assessment systems, and innovative learning technologies all cost money. Even with greater efficiencies, more children staying in school longer will require more financing, especially in countries that currently invest little in education.

A short-term step towards the goal of improved learning is to ensure a sustained commitment to financing education in the wake of the Covid-19 crisis, with funding prioritized based on both need and effectiveness (World Bank 2020b). Sharp cuts in public education spending, at a time when households are less able to support children's education, would further widen outcome gaps and cause long-term damage. To prevent this, it is important to support those with the greatest need, for instance through formula-based funding that prioritizes support to disadvantaged households and areas. At the same time, tight post-crisis budgets make it even more important to engage in proven, high-return interventions.

We now discuss the three complementary strategies that will greatly increase the likelihood that education spending leads to learning for all.

Assess Learning

Better data on learning gaps will help catalyze reforms. Germany's "PISA 2000 shock"—when new international learning comparisons showed mediocre scores and large achievement gaps in that country—led to successful reforms. In Bangladesh, India, and Tanzania, widely publicized results from citizen-led learning assessments shifted the government's focus toward learning.

Many different learning metrics are required. *Assessment by teachers in classrooms* helps tailor teaching to students' needs. Singapore identifies lagging grade-1 students through screening tests, then gives them intensive support. *National and subnational learning assessments* provide system-level insights on students' learning, lagging groups, drivers of achievement, and progress over time. *International assessments* raise awareness of how a country falls short of its peers, and can be powerful tools politically. *Other learning metrics* can strengthen the quality and equity of assessments. Grassroots accountability movements—led by civil-society organizations like ASER in India and UWEZO in East Africa— have deployed citizen-led assessments to measure the foundational learning of young children in their communities, using the data to advocate for reform. Some household surveys collect learning data, enabling assessment of out-of-school children, and analysis of how learning correlates with income and community variables. All these learning metrics can function as a check on each other's accuracy.

Metrics must be designed and used judiciously, or they could prove misleading. They may not capture important educational dimensions; the MDG of universal primary education did not capture foundational literacy and numeracy skills, let alone other life skills (the SDGs have filled this gap). If assessments are poorly designed or implemented, they may encourage shallow forms of learning such as rote memorization, or provide administrators or educators incentives to cheat.

The barriers to better measurement of learning are both technical and political. Teachers may lack the training to assess learning effectively, and especially to capture higher-order skills—through project-based assessment, say. Education ministries may lack capacity to design and implement valid assessments. Policymakers may prefer to avoid testing and be assumed ineffective, rather than to test and remove all doubt; or they may decline to publish test results (like Mexico with the 1995 TIMSS assessment).

Make Schools Work for Learners

There are three entry points for policy to improve school-level outcomes: prepared learners, effective teaching, and inputs and management that affect learning. Hundreds of systematic evaluations from multiple contexts demonstrate that many educational interventions substantially improve learning and boost earnings, and identify the channels (Angrist et al. 2020; Evans and Yuan 2017). Some of the most cost-effective programs deliver the equivalent of three additional years of high-quality schooling for just $100 per child. Specific solutions do need to be tailored to local contexts. The key is to use evidence to guide local innovation, and monitor learning to evaluate what works in a given setting.

Preparing children for learning is the critical first step. Priorities include:

- *Early childhood development services*, including nutrition, stimulation, and care. In Jamaica, a program to improve cognitive and socioemotional development led to lower crime rates, better mental health, and earnings that were 25 percent higher 20 years later (Gertler et al. 2014). Working through parents and across ministries is essential here.

- *Lower school costs* to get children into school, but then use other tools to boost motivation and effort. Fee reductions and conditional cash transfers are highly effective in getting children to school, even in fragile contexts, but design matters as to whether they affect learning (Barrera-Osorio and Filmer 2016). Groups with high dropout risk, such as girls or students from marginalized communities, and their parents and teachers, should receive targeted support and communications, including socioemotional support (World Bank 2020b).
- Since many youths leave basic education lacking skills, provide *remedial education* before further education and training. Universities in both Mexico and Chile have developed structured programs to assist students in their transition to higher education.

To boost teacher skills and motivation, the teaching profession must be reshaped as a meritocratic, socially valued career. Teachers must be held to high professional standards, and be given the corresponding tools and support. Key principles include:

- *Teacher training* should provide sufficient subject-content knowledge and mastery of core pedagogical practices. It must recognize that the role of teachers is increasingly to facilitate learning, including teaching students how to learn, and not simply to deliver content. Pre-service training should allow extensive practice; in-service professional development must be individually tailored, practical, repeated, with follow-up coaching—often around a specific pedagogical technique (Kraft et al. 2018; Darling-Hammond et al. 2017; Popova et al. 2016, 2019). Teachers should be supported with proven, structured lesson plans (Béteille and Evans 2019). Training systems should incorporate an integrated, diversified set of measures to evaluate teachers' practices and effectiveness, including evidence of learning, direct observation, videotapes, artifacts, and student surveys (Bill and Melinda Gates Foundation 2010). Value-added measures of student achievement tied to individual teachers must take into account potential differences in student and school characteristics, and as a result should not generally be used for high-stakes decisions (Darling-Hammond et al. 2012).
- *Target teaching to the level of the student*, to keep learners from falling behind to the point where they cannot catch up (J-PAL 2018). Effective tactics include improved classroom assessment, to identify learning gaps; having community teachers provide remedial lessons (Banerjee et al. 2007, 2010); reorganizing classes by ability (Banerjee et al. 2016, Duflo et al. 2011); teaching

students in their first language—globally, 40 percent of children are still taught in a language they do not fully speak or understand (Lyytinen et al. 2019); and using technology to adapt lessons to individual needs, including computer software (Muralidharan et al. 2019) or text messages (Angrist et al. 2020b). These efforts need clear system-level guidance and materials; focused, practical training for principals and teachers; and substantial resources.

- Use pecuniary and nonpecuniary incentives to improve *teacher motivation*, ensuring that the incentivized actions are within teachers' capacity. Linking teacher pay or career progression to learning outcomes is often effective (Brazil, India, Israel, Kenya, and Peru). However, design details matter (Bruns et al. 2011). And it is important to secure buy-in from teachers, as shown by Chile's successful, long-running, national-level "pay-for-performance" scheme.

Effective teaching also requires engaging parents. Parents play a critical role in supporting children's learning, and need to be involved from the earliest years (Shonkoff and Fisher 2013). Parents should therefore be provided with appropriate guidance and resources, including through coaching on positive discipline and how to engage in stimulating activities with their children, and effective parent-teacher connections (Vegas and Winthrop 2020).

School inputs, management, and governance must focus on improving learning. To this end,

- *New technology, including for remote learning, must be implementable in current systems and reach all learners* (World Bank 2020b, 2020d). Education technology (including hardware, software, digital content, data, and information systems) can enhance system performance, equity, and resilience. It can help assess learning, improve teacher skills, customize instruction, manage service delivery, and ensure that resources reach all (J-PAL 2019). It can foster new connections between teachers, students, parents, and broader communities to create learning networks. It can strengthen lifelong learning and reach out-of-school children. And it can assist in implementing change at scale, quickly, and cost-effectively. But many technology interventions fail because they are ill-adapted to their setting—complementary infrastructure or the knowledge on how to use technology is missing. And effectiveness hinges on incorporating feedback from parents, teachers, and school-leaders, as seen in Peru (Vegas and Winthrop 2020). In particular, remote learning should be designed for scale for all children, using technology already widely available in-country. In LICs, this may involve low-tech solutions, such as radio or TV. More generally, it will require multi-modal delivery—for instance, radio, text-messaging, print materials, and online learning. And scaling up effectively requires a whole-of-government, multi-stakeholder approach, bringing together the entire education ecosystem including telecom companies, publishers, local EdTech startups, and radio and TV stations.

- *Inputs, including technology, must complement rather than substitute for teachers* (Snilstveit et al. 2016). Credible plans for integrating technology into teaching are critical. Technology should enhance teachers' access to content, data, and expertise, allowing for real-time adaptation. When a computer-assisted learning program in India complemented regular lessons, it increased learning, especially for initially poorer-performing students. When it substituted for lessons, it *decreased* learning. As a corollary, countries should invest in teacher (and student) digital skills.
- *School-management and governance reforms should foster innovation in learning; decision-making autonomy must be framed by clear mandates and accountability structures.* School-leaders should be pedagogical leaders, closely involved in student learning, mentoring teachers, and engaging with the wider community, rather than simply performing administrative duties. Student learning is significantly increased by programs that train principals in providing feedback to teachers on lesson plans, regular learner assessments, action plans to improve student performance, and teachers' classroom performance (Fryer 2017). Mentoring and coaching of principals from experienced school leaders is also effective (Nannyonjo 2017), as is clarifying the respective management roles of district officers, school principals, and teachers (Lassibille 2016). Involving parents and communities in school governance, supported by solid learning metrics, can complement such efforts (Beasley and Huillery 2017).

Reform the System

Deploying effective school-level programs is insufficient. Replicating experimental interventions across the entire school system often fails because of systemwide constraints. Cambodia scaled up early childhood development centers and preschools—programs that had worked in some parts of the country when implemented by NGOs. But there were no improvements in child development, as parents' demand for the services remained low, reflecting: limited ability to absorb the associated costs (for instance, new clothing or school supplies); lack of information on the benefits; and the low quality of the programs provided, in terms of location, hours of operation, and/or intensity (Bouguen et al. 2013). Kenya tried to lower student-teacher ratios by hiring contract teachers—an intervention that improved student outcomes when implemented by NGOs. But the results were negligible, reflecting implementation and political-economy constraints (Bold et al. 2013). When Indonesia tried to increase teacher effectiveness by nearly doubling the salaries of certified teachers, political pressures watered down the certification process but left the pay increase in place. The result: much larger expenditure, but no increase in teacher skills or student learning (De Ree et al. 2017).

School-level interventions boost learning and equity systemwide only if countries tackle the system-level technical and political barriers to change discussed earlier. Reformers can use two sets of tools: form coalitions to advocate for learning and to rebalance political incentives; and innovate flexibly, using evidence to identify where to start, and metrics to adapt.

Coalitions and Incentives

Mobilize everyone with a stake in learning. Many countries have used wide-ranging consultations to build support for reforms. Malaysia used a "lab" model to bring together coalitions of stakeholders and involve them in all stages of reform, from design to implementation. Communication campaigns can mobilize citizens. In Peru, information on poor learning mobilized support for strengthening teacher accountability. It catalyzed action by businesses, which funded campaigns highlighting the importance of quality education for economic growth. And parents protested teacher strikes that disrupted schooling (Bruns and Luque 2014). Another coalition-building tool is bundling reforms, so that everyone achieves a top priority. Modernizing vocational training can buy employers' support for broader reforms.

A negotiated, gradual approach to reform is more promising than confrontation. Fostering collaboration around shared goals boosts the chances of success. In Chile, successive negotiations between the government and the teachers' union built broad support for reforms that linked pay and career development more closely to performance, while also improving teachers' working conditions, raising overall salaries, and boosting resources for education (Mizala and Schneider 2012). Regular discussions on the implementation of reforms further increased trust. Several countries have compensated actors who might lose from reforms, or phased in changes to protect incumbents; in Peru and Washington, DC, pay-for-performance schemes were initially voluntary.

Form strong partnerships between schools and their communities. Local-level community engagement can complement national change efforts, or substitute for them where political and bureaucratic reform incentives are weak (Mansuri and Rao 2012). In South Africa, political and economic constraints hampered efforts to improve national education performance. Yet progress was made in improving outcomes at some local levels through strong parent–school partnerships.

Innovation and Agility

Innovation and adaptation are critical to developing learning approaches that fit different contexts and changing circumstances. The better-performing parts of any system can suggest feasible approaches. Argentina's Misiones Province had high dropout rates, but some schools bucked the trend, reflecting more constructive teacher-parent relationships. When other schools adopted this approach, dropouts fell significantly (Green 2016). As Burundi recovered from civil war, an adaptive approach to getting textbooks to schools reduced delivery times in some areas from over a year to sixty days—and was then replicated in other areas (Campos et al. 2015).

Incentives determine whether systems innovate and adopt emerging solutions at scale. Closed systems that limit teacher and school autonomy, and judge performance by compliance with resource-use rules, provide little room for innovation. Open systems that focus on results rather than inputs, and provide flexibility in using financing, will see greater innovation and diffusion of new approaches (Andrews et al. 2013). But innovations must be supported by good metrics and system-level coalitions—otherwise, improvements will prove short-lived or geographically limited.

III. Health Care

A. The Challenges

Living long, healthy lives is a common aspiration across all societies; but significant challenges stand in the way of achieving this goal, particularly for the disadvantaged. The past few decades represented a golden era for global health. During 1950–2019, global life expectancy increased from 46 years to 73 years; mortality from infectious diseases fell especially sharply. Developing countries in particular saw vast increases in access to health services (including antenatal care, vaccinations, and HIV treatments) and other health determinants (such as clean water and sanitation). But the world faces both an unfinished health agenda, and emerging challenges. In LICs and lower middle-income countries (LMICs), poor and rural households still experience high rates of infectious disease; reproductive, maternal, newborn, and child health disorders; and malnutrition. Meanwhile, most countries face a rapidly growing burden from non-communicable diseases (NCDs; for instance, cardio-vascular disease, cancer, chronic respiratory conditions, diabetes, and mental health), reflecting rising exposure to behavioral and environmental risk factors and the impact of population aging.[10] NCDs are diseases of slow progression and long duration. Their initial onset is occurring at increasingly younger ages, implying that people will spend more years living with

---

[10] NCDs now account for 71 percent of all deaths globally, and more than half of all lost disability-adjusted life-years (Global Burden of Disease Study 2017). Their prevalence has increased rapidly across all advanced and developing regions. Risk factors include unhealthy diets, physical inactivity, smoking, alcohol misuse, and air pollution, also through their impact on obesity, cholesterol, and hypertension.

chronic conditions and disability and will face greater health-care needs. At older ages, NCDs are associated with comorbidities that interact with them and complicate treatment and care. Looking ahead, the world is underprepared for emerging health threats, including new pandemics, as illustrated by the Covid-19 crisis (Bill and Melinda Gates Foundation 2020; Winskill et al. 2020; UNDP 2020a, UNDP 2020b); antimicrobial resistance (Prestinaci et al. 2015); and global climate change (Lancet Commission on Health and Climate Change 2015). In general, poor populations are most exposed to these challenges, reflecting greater vulnerability to risks and less ability to access or afford preventive services and treatment. Late diagnosis, owing to delays in seeking care, often leads to more chronic illness and complications.

Building health systems that achieve better outcomes for all, and are resilient to crises, requires making significant progress towards *universal health coverage (UHC)* (UHC2030 2020). There are three key dimensions to UHC (WHO and World Bank 2013):

- Coverage for the entire population, regardless of socioeconomic status, geographic location, gender, age, or preexisting conditions—including coverage for groups, such as poor, rural, and informal-sector workers, that in many developing countries are largely uncovered.
- Financial protection from direct payment for health services—in particular, protection from catastrophic or impoverishing health expenditures.[11]
- Access to a full spectrum of essential, quality health services according to need.

A pro-poor pathway to UHC, which prioritizes expanding coverage and financial protection for all groups including the disadvantaged (a "progressive universalism"), will deliver large benefits (Lancet Commission on Investing in Health 2013; WHO 2014). Indeed, coverage expansion should target the most vulnerable first: better-off households have more options for obtaining coverage and are more resilient in the face of unexpected medical bills. The emphasis should be on health interventions that provide good value for money, address a significant disease burden, are feasible to implement in a range of countries, prioritize the worse-off, and increase protection against financial risks. Examples include a wide range of maternal and child health services, interventions against HIV/AIDS and tuberculosis in adults, and various interventions to address NCDs and injuries (Watkins et al. 2017).

---

[11] Health expenditures are described as "catastrophic" if they exceed some significant share (say, 10 percent) of total household expenditure, and "impoverishing" if they push households below the poverty line.

Many developing economies are far from achieving UHC, which generates deep inequalities. Less than half the world's population is covered by essential health services (WHO 2019). Each year, approximately 90 million people fall into poverty, and 900 million people encounter serious hardship, from paying for health services; lower-income households are far more likely to have to spend a large income share on out-of-pocket payments; and many others forgo care because of prohibitive costs (WHO and World Bank 2019). Conversely, achieving UHC will help households both prevent and better manage health shocks and their financial consequences.

Improving health outcomes, and meeting growing health-care demands, must be achieved without unduly burdening household or government budgets. This is possible, given that similar levels of health expenditure translate into vastly different outcomes in different health systems—just as was true of education (Figure 14.7; Barber et al. 2020). Relatedly, greater health expenditure does not automatically translate into improved outcomes. Still, in some countries, public health expenditure must clearly increase (Gaspar et al. 2019). It currently averages less than $10 per capita in LICs, and $30 in LMICs, reflecting both their low capacity to mobilize revenues and the relatively small share of government spending allocated to health (World Bank 2019c). The annual cost of a package of essential, high value-for-money services that could facilitate the achievement of the health-related SDG targets equals on average $79 per capita in LICs, and $130 per capita in

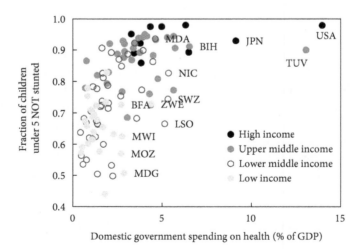

Figure 14.7 Relationship Between Childhood Stunting and Health Expenditure

Note: CAN = Canada; ETH = Ethiopia; GEO = Georgia; JPN = Japan; KAZ = Kazakhstan; KOR = Republic of Korea; LBR = Liberia; LSO = Lesotho; NAM = Namibia; NGA = Nigeria; SWZ = Swaziland; TCD = Chad; TLS = Timor-Leste; TUV = Tuvalu; USA = United States; VNM = Vietnam; ZAF = South Africa; ZWE = Zimbabwe.

Source: Andrews et al. (2019), figure 13. License: CC BY 3.0 IGO.

LMICs.[12] Providing this package would on average require additional investments of 8 percent of national income in LICs, and 4.2 percent of national income in LMICs.

A focus on both improving efficiency, and raising revenues equitably, will help improve health outcomes (Lancet Commission on Investing in Health 2013; Smith and Nguyen 2013). There are two priorities. First, making health systems perform more efficiently, and with a greater emphasis on the quality of care; for instance, by creating effective multifunctional delivery platforms that can treat a range of health concerns and provide lifelong care. Second, raising financing in a manner that does not depress utilization or worsen outcomes, particularly among the disadvantaged. Broad institutional reforms are required to underpin both agendas.

Using information systems to capture and analyze relevant data on health processes and outcomes, and to transmit information to policymakers and the public in a timely, digestible fashion, is essential to effective policy making. Measurement is key to accountability and improvement, but available metrics do not capture much of what matters most to people, such as competent care, user experience, health outcomes, and confidence in the system (Lancet Global Health Commission 2018). Conversely, inputs such as medicines and equipment are commonly recorded, but are only weakly related to quality of care. Robust vital registries, trustworthy routine health-information systems, financial-protection indicators, and real-time measures of health facilities and populations are all prerequisites for good performance assessment. Investing in better measurement, in the institutions and professionals with the skills to generate and interpret data, including through new research, yields high returns.

Reforms will prove successful and sustainable only if underpinned by improved governance. Decision-making processes must be viewed as fair, encourage public involvement, ensure accountability in policy development and implementation, and track progress (Kurowski 2018). Accountability requires that decisions be transparent and justified by legitimate criteria. At the same time, public-health officials across all levels of government should enjoy appropriate autonomy and well-aligned incentives. Mechanisms that both allow beneficiaries to appeal decisions, and which review them based on new information, strengthen the accountability link between service providers and beneficiaries.

B. Building a High-Performing Health System

A policy priority, in health as in education, is to obtain greater value-for-money through systems reform, rather than just raising expenditure. Current health-care

---

[12] Watkins et al. (2020). Stenberg et al. (2017) provide comparable estimates.

service delivery structures are often low-value and high-cost. They over-provide potentially clinically ineffective treatments in inappropriate settings, and under-provide more effective treatments (Lancet Global Health Commission 2018). Low-quality care raises costs for both governments and households and reduces health gains. Efficiency and resilience to crises can be significantly boosted by complementary reforms focused on five key areas (Somanathan et al. 2015; Kruk et al. 2015; Maeda et al. 2014).

Moving Away from Hospital-Centric Structures, by Increasing the Availability, Effectiveness, and Quality of Primary Care

High-quality primary care, including preventive care, remains one of the most efficient and cost-effective ways to achieve UHC (UN 2019). Such care is accessible, can address more than 80 percent of a person's lifetime health needs, and is affordable: many interventions cost less than $100 per additional healthy life-year (McKinsey Global Institute 2020). Prevention in particular is often more clinically- and cost-effective than treatment. The Covid-19 pandemic re-emphasized the need to invest in these services, with strong frontline delivery systems. In LICs and LMICs, priorities include perinatal care; childhood immunizations and nutrition (section IV provides case studies of reductions in child stunting); infectious disease control programs for HIV/AIDS, tuberculosis, and malaria; and community-based health promotion and disease prevention, including sanitation. Upper-middle-income and high-income countries should focus on reducing the growing NCD burden and promoting healthy longevity. This involves a life-course perspective to health care, both reducing behavioral risk factors at all ages, and increasing the early detection and management of diseases.

Primary care should tackle a greater range of low-acuity conditions; hospitals should only provide complex services that need advanced expertise, with clear pathways for referral and consultation ("right-placing care"). Reorganizing services so that care is provided at the right level, and available resources are optimized, is in the interests of both health systems and patients. Better health is often incorrectly attributed to more consultations, admissions, drugs, and procedures. Meanwhile, too little attention is paid to prevention, early diagnosis and treatment, and control of conditions.[13] Once a diagnosis is made, care is rarely coordinated across provider levels, resulting in service duplication and lack of continuity. Often, health care is sought too late, leading to high-cost treatment in expensive acute-care hospitals. The lack of effective referrals, gatekeeping, and post-discharge care contributes to avoidable or unnecessarily long admissions that

---

[13] Many developing countries are characterized by hypertension that is rarely brought under control; limited programs to prevent and treat substance abuse, including smoking; little emphasis on weight management; little testing for high cholesterol; low screening rates for the most treatable cancers (breast, cervical, colon, and prostate); and rare flu vaccinations for the elderly (Lancet Global Health Commission 2018).

prove costly.[14] For instance, with better patient-centric care models, primary-care centers would provide long-term care for chronic conditions; conversely, some labor and delivery services could be relocated to hospitals. Right-placing care presupposes a significant strengthening of primary care, with support from community health workers: currently, primary care is often rudimentary and low-quality (see below), and the public therefore bypasses it.

Pandemics including Covid-19 have also highlighted the need for stronger, more resilient, and equitable public-health systems. Priorities include:

- *Strengthening national and global disease-surveillance systems*, by boosting the ability to collect, analyze, and interpret relevant data from public and private providers, including primary-care practitioners. This will enable authorities to better plan, implement, and evaluate actions to prevent and control disease outbreaks (Revenga and Galindo 2020). Effective disease surveillance is feasible even in low-resource settings, based on standardized sets of symptoms.
- *Building early-response capacity*. Responsiveness calls for preparedness before outbreaks occur. This requires years of planning and investing in the institutional and technical capacity to rapidly step in and manage crises (Fernandes 2020). Other ingredients include teams with decision-making autonomy to respond swiftly, and emergency-procurement procedures in the event of shortages.
- *Ensuring a "whole-of-society," multi-sectoral approach*. Local leaders and community volunteers are critical to effective community outreach, social-services delivery, and support for quarantined households (WHO 2020). Partnerships with the private sector are equally important: in many developing countries, private facilities are the first health-care contact point and deliver most services. With most pandemics being of zoonotic origin, closer coordination between the health and agriculture sectors is instrumental to preventing future outbreaks. Boosting public health involves complementary investments in infrastructure, including safely managed sanitation, clean drinking water, and handwashing facilities.

Improving Quality of Care in Treating Both Chronic and Acute Illness

The care that people receive is often inadequate, with disadvantaged groups faring the worst. High-quality care involves thorough assessment, detection of asymptomatic and co-existing conditions, accurate diagnosis, appropriate and timely treatment, referral when needed for hospital care and surgery, and the ability to

---

[14] Many developing countries have high rates of hospitalization for hypertension, a condition that should be controlled at lower levels of care.

follow the patient and adjust treatments as needed. But low-quality care is common across countries and conditions. Audits of patient-provider encounters find a high frequency of incorrect diagnosis or treatment, even for common, serious conditions including tuberculosis, pneumonia, myocardial infarction, and newborn asphyxia (WHO, World Bank, and OECD 2018). There are major system-level deficiencies in infection control, prevention, and continuity and timeliness of care. Patients frequently complain about poor communication by providers, lack of attention and respect, and excessively short consultations. Sometimes, providers are simply absent; in Togo and Uganda, almost half of primary-care providers were absent from their health facility in 2013 (Andrews et al. forthcoming). And worse health outcomes for the disadvantaged frequently reflect inequalities in the quality of care, rather than in access or financial coverage. Even where coverage for some health services is seemingly equal, the effective coverage, with services of quality sufficient to achieve the expected health gains, often remains highly unequal.[15] Patients may seek higher quality by bypassing designated health providers, but this will force them to pay in full for services and increase the incidence of catastrophic expenditures. In LMICs, poor-quality care is now a larger barrier to reducing mortality than insufficient access. Quality of care will become an even more important driver of population health as the burden of disease shifts to more complex conditions such as NCDs.

Structural, foundational change is needed to improve the quality of care, and ensure that it is evidence-based and both clinically- and cost-effective. Health-system leaders should adopt a shared vision of quality care, backed by a clear quality strategy, incorporating multiple, complementary measures (Lancet Global Health Commission 2018):

- Boosting provider skills, through rigorous pre-service education and early clinical exposure, specialty training, and an emphasis on continuous, active, problem-based learning. Better performance measurement, linked to professional recognition or compensation, may improve motivation (see below).
- Increasing management capacity at all levels, including through training programs and adoption of electronic health records.
- Strengthening regulation and accountability, including through clinical treatment protocols, inspector training, and legal-redress mechanisms. In hospitals, specific reforms may include dedicated quality-of-care committees, using checklists for supervision and inventory-control purposes, and auditing the medical register routinely or after deaths.

---

[15] In the Democratic Republic of Congo, coverage for antenatal care, defined as attending a consultation, does not vary significantly by household wealth. But effective coverage, including appropriate tests, treatments, and communication, remains much more unequal (Fink, Kandpal, and Shapira 2021).

Coordination with the private sector and other public sectors, such as education and infrastructure, will help boost outcomes. Partnerships with civil society, for instance through community monitoring programs (Björkman and Svensson 2009) and informational campaigns (Pandey et al. 2007), will increase accountability and raise user satisfaction. At the same time, quality improvements may require increased inputs, including staffing and physical resources. Primary-care facilities in lower-income countries, especially in disadvantaged communities, often lack access to clean water, electricity, and improved toilets; refrigerator temperatures may not comply with standards for storing vaccines.

Reforming Mechanisms for Paying Health-Care Providers

In many high- and some middle-income countries, the incentives embedded in provider-payment systems have encouraged physicians to overprovide services, driving up costs. This applies especially to fee-for-service systems without budget caps or other cost-containment measures; these reward quantity over quality, and discourage prevention and patient education. Experience with payment reforms points toward reimbursing hospitals on the basis of expected costs for clinically defined episodes of care, and reimbursing primary-care providers at least partly through a "lump sum" per patient. Possibly, measured risk factors could be used as a basis for reimbursement to incentivize physicians through pay-for-performance schemes. In all cases, appropriate incentives must also ensure quality of care. Depending on the institutional setting, measures to boost competition among hospitals, physicians, pharmacists, and/or insurance providers, within a strong government regulatory framework, may help reduce costs and/or raise quality (Propper 2018; Gaynor and Town 2011).

Most LICs and LMICs, conversely, are struggling with under-provision of essential services; incentives are needed to boost access, utilization, and quality, particularly for the disadvantaged. Uptake remains very low among the disadvantaged groups that would benefit most from such services, including family planning and maternal and child health. Here, some level of fee-for-service can be beneficial. Again, pay-for-performance schemes can be highly clinically- and cost-effective in improving delivery of targeted services (Kandpal 2016). They may also promote general health-system strengthening, and increase efficiency and accountability, through more active supervising and monitoring, more quantifiable involvement with communities, and increased health-worker satisfaction. Such supply-side incentives work best when combined with demand-side financing measures to boost health-seeking behavior, including cash or in-kind transfers, transportation, and community outreach.

Improving the Price and Availability of Critical Medical Products

Inefficiencies in purchasing pharmaceuticals result in high prices for drugs, driving up costs for governments and users. The price of common, off-patent statins (cholesterol-lowering drugs critical for pharmacological management of cardiovascular disease) varies significantly across countries. For example, in Vietnam, a highly decentralized and complex procurement system, involving more than 1,000 entities, results in wide differentials in medicine prices across facilities (Somanathan et al. 2015). Purchasing strategies used to reduce drug prices include:

- *Therapeutic reference pricing*: purchasers set fixed reimbursement levels for the price of drugs by referencing a base drug within that therapeutic class.
- *Risk-sharing arrangements for high-cost drugs*, such as price-volume arrangements where the manufacturer pays for any volume over the agreed threshold.
- *Sole-source tendering*, where the winning bidder is the sole supplier for a fixed term.
- *Bulk-buying of drugs*, where a lead agency consolidates purchases by different entities.

Building diversified, resilient global medical supply chains remains critical. The Covid-19 crisis underscored existing vulnerabilities, generating shortages and potentially excessive pricing for key medical products (OECD 2020b). Suppliers struggled to meet growing global demand for personal protective equipment, ventilators, and other supplies, including because of severe disruptions to global supply chains. Developing countries remain vulnerable to partner countries' restrictions on exports of medical products, also reflecting some exporting countries' high global market share in specific products (Espitia et al. 2020).

Accelerating Technological Transformation, while Prioritizing Among Available Interventions and Technologies

Continued innovation in health-care delivery and medical technology, underpinned by global cooperation to ensure equitable access, has proven essential to improving long-run outcomes. Telemedicine, including virtual care platforms and digital monitoring, is proving an increasingly cost-effective delivery mechanism. For many NCDs, including some cancers, mental-health disorders, and dementia, more in-depth knowledge is required on the underlying biology; and further innovation in medicines, procedures, medical devices, and delivery models will help improve the range and availability of treatments (McKinsey Global Institute 2020). For many promising technologies, small-scale pilots and applications already exist; many are preventive in nature and enabled by digital technology. The Covid-19 pandemic also exposed the need to bolster research into infectious diseases, including therapeutics and vaccines, even before an outbreak occurs. Digital technology and machine learning can assist with pandemic containment and mitigation processes, including the diagnosis and prognosis of patients. Developing countries, given resource constraints, will need to partner with the international community and private sector to leverage the latest technology. The global deployment of new vaccines requires significant financing and the coordinated use of financial instruments including grants, concessional loans, and advance market commitments (Yamey et al. 2020).

However, prioritizing which new technologies are adopted is vital to controlling health-expenditure growth. Many OECD countries have introduced explicit prioritization systems, through health-technology assessments (HTA) that systematically and transparently assess the value-for-money of new technologies, devices, and procedures. Developing the capacity to undertake HTA is costly and time-consuming. Developing countries could start by using the findings from more established HTA agencies to inform prioritization.

C. Efficient, Equitable Financing

Financing measures to support UHC should not burden the disadvantaged and further depress their low health-services utilization rate. One option: publicly financed insurance could cover only essential health-care interventions, which disproportionately benefit the poor, with no user fees. Alternatively, a larger benefit package could be funded through a range of financing mechanisms, including tax revenue but also mandatory insurance premiums and/or copayments, with the poor exempted from all payments (Lancet Commission on Investing in Health 2013). This latter approach assumes sufficient administrative capacity to identify the poor, and levy payments from the non-poor. In either case, taxation of tobacco, alcohol, and other harmful substances, and the removal of fossil-fuel subsidies that encourage pollution, can both raise revenue and directly curb NCDs, with disproportionate health benefits for the poor.

Less reliance on contributory funding mechanisms, and de-linking entitlements to coverage from users' direct health-insurance contributions and employment status, can often help broaden health coverage. General revenues can instead be used to fully cover contributions, at least for those who cannot afford to pay or whose contributions would be administratively difficult to collect (the approach being adopted in Indonesia, the Philippines, Thailand, and Vietnam). Historically, it has proved extremely difficult to enroll through contributory means the poor and other vulnerable groups, such as informal-sector workers (Bitran 2014); even small out-of-pocket payments depress utilization rates among disadvantaged groups. Premiums, even when apparently low, remain unaffordable for many. The very process of having to enroll in contributory schemes and/or apply for subsidies is often associated with administrative complexities that create additional barriers to access (Alfers 2013; Barasa et al. 2017). And there is widespread lack of information about, or trust in, the benefits of enrollment

(Dartanto et al. 2016). As a result, partial subsidies, even when combined with assistance in enrolling (such as information and reminders), have proven less effective than anticipated; often they have resulted in adverse selection, as only those with high anticipated health needs were willing to pay to enroll (World Bank 2019c). All this is a particular concern in regions, such as Africa or Asia, where the informal sector remains large. However, there are examples of success. Among the very few countries that have been successful in enrolling all or most informal-sector workers are Thailand (100 percent premium subsidy) and China (90 percent premium subsidy under the National Cooperative Medical Scheme). In the case of pharmaceuticals, and especially outpatient drugs (for instance, beta-blockers for heart disease, and antiretroviral and anti-tuberculosis drugs), out-of-pocket payments may reduce adherence to treatment regimens and increase downstream systemwide costs owing to more hospitalizations.

Reducing fragmentation of health-insurance schemes can deliver important benefits. In many countries, current arrangements are often fragmented, inequitable, inefficient, and costly. Governments frequently initiate coverage with the formal sector, providing privileged access to a politically influential group (Somanathan et al. 2015). Those initially covered resist extending the same entitlements to the rest of the population, resulting in multiple insurance schemes being created with varying levels of coverage.[16] Such schemes have proved politically difficult to integrate, since any such measure would redistribute resources across organized interest groups. However, multiple risk pools are both inequitable and inefficient. Moreover, the relatively generous benefits for the formal sector threaten cost-containment. That said, in countries with fledgling schemes, fragmentation may initially be inevitable. Efforts to expand health coverage may have to rely on a variety of financing sources and coverage packages. Even here, it remains important to ensure that everyone is entitled to a basic coverage level.

IV. Reasons for Optimism: Case Studies of Successful Reform

The experience of countries at all development levels demonstrates that significant progress is possible.[17] Countries can draw on systematic knowledge about what works at the micro level and how to sustain system-wide improvements. Any given intervention may not pay off in all contexts, and successful interventions cannot be imported wholesale into new contexts. Nonetheless, countries can use them as starting points for their own innovations. We now present some illustrative case studies.

---

[16] In Mexico, prior to deep reforms, per-capita funding for social health-insurance beneficiaries was 6 times larger than for those dependent on national health services. Coverage for hypertension control was 20 percentage points higher among the former than among the latter group.

[17] This section draws on World Bank (2018a, 2019b, 2020 section 2.3, 2020c).

A. Overall Human-Capital Development

Singapore, Morocco, Ghana, and the Philippines have all experienced, to varying degrees, notable human-capital improvements. Singapore has built a world-class education system, which balances creativity with the increasing need for analytical skills and teamwork. Life expectancy is among the highest and infant mortality among the lowest in the world. Morocco has experienced remarkable gains in both urban and rural primary enrollment. Child and maternal mortality have declined sharply, and most children are fully immunized. In Ghana, primary enrollment has increased sharply, with an influx of students from disadvantaged families, and child stunting, an indicator of chronic malnutrition, has almost halved. The Philippines has seen a dramatic expansion in school enrollment since the 1970s, but quality remains an issue.

Successful reforms in these countries have adopted a "whole-of-society" approach, involving:

- *Coordination*—between sectoral programs, and among different levels and branches of government.
- *Continuity*—sustaining effort across many political cycles.
- *Evidence*—building an evidence base to improve and update human-capital strategies.

Multisectoral strategies that also involve local actors are more likely to succeed, particularly in lower-income countries. Integrated efforts are especially beneficial in countries with limited public funds and technical and administrative capacity, which cannot afford to waste resources. In the *Philippines*, successive governments have adopted multi-sectoral programs, promoted integrated approaches, and encouraged greater participation by stakeholders in service delivery. A conditional cash transfer program integrates human-capital development with poverty reduction. It assists chronically poor households with children under 14 living in deprived areas. Beneficiaries must undertake activities to improve their children's health and education, including prenatal checkups, pediatric visits, and regular school attendance. Multiple agencies, including state-owned banks, implement the program; efforts are coordinated with regional offices. Local service providers, including school principals and midwives, verify household compliance with program conditions. This enables the program to reach targeted households across hundreds of islands. A range of other policies, including poverty-reduction efforts, recognize that human-capital development is affected by multiple factors including clean air, a safe water supply, and sanitation services.

Ghana's success in reducing stunting also largely reflects a multi-sectoral approach. The school-feeding program brings together community leaders with local caterers and farmers to supply food to children. The program is linked to local agricultural development, especially smallholder production, helping to create new markets for locally grown food. Monitoring and evaluation rely on local head-teachers and caterers. Likewise, initiatives to improve water sanitation and hygiene in schools have boosted both health and education indicators. *Morocco* has developed a variety of social safety nets that cover multiple sectors and support a range of human-capital outcomes. Complementary programs aim to achieve universal education and reduce school drop-out, especially in rural areas and among girls, by providing school bags, subsidized transport, food, and school supplies for students. There are also programs for disabled individuals, social protection centers, and centers for training and education that support disadvantaged girls. A range of sub-national committees help select development projects and monitor implementation. *Singapore* has integrated health and education goals into many facets of government. Urban planning stresses health outcomes, since these are affected by all aspects of urban life—including housing, water supply, air quality, waste disposal, and traffic. Coordination between government institutions enables the country to track trends in labor demand, and match the skills taught in the education system with market needs.

Continuity of commitment and effort over successive governments is key to growing human capital, a process which can take generations. Such continuity is easier when a country enjoys political stability and consensus. In *Ghana*, a stable multiparty democracy since 1992, successive governments from different parties have made human capital a priority, with broad social support. By contrast, in the *Philippines*, while successive administrations did adopt strategies to build human capital, they did not make the sustained effort to build the capacity and governance necessary to implement these strategies. And although *Morocco* showed sustained political commitment to education, this commitment did not extend to other policies critical to improving human capital.

Adequate, sustainable funding is crucial, as is using resources efficiently. *Singapore* ensured that expenditures were managed effectively, including through severe sanctions for corruption. In *Ghana*, domestic resource mobilization enabled a large expansion of primary-care insurance coverage, including prenatal and postnatal care, vaccinations, and health and nutrition education. Inequity in access was reduced by exempting disadvantaged groups from premiums. By contrast, the *Philippines* have generally failed to provide adequate financing, leading to understaffed, overcrowded clinics and schools, underpaid providers, inadequate infrastructure, and a lack of administrative and technical capacity, especially at the local level. Weak governance led to widespread fraud in textbook distribution, theft of funds or supplies, and ghost workers in municipal health facilities. All this particularly affects low-income households and more remote regions, which lag in terms of access.

Reliable, timely administrative and survey data is critical to effective policy design and implementation. *Singapore*'s digital infrastructure, tech-savvy administrators, and experienced teachers form a robust data-collection system that generates critical real-time information on schools, training institutions, and skills in demand. Policymakers use these data to assess school and student performance, control costs, help managers and teachers to make decisions at every level, and enable workforce planning. In *Ghana*, national poverty statistics and a food security and vulnerability analysis established that school-feeding programs were not effectively reaching vulnerable groups. The data were combined to refine targeting and reduce leakages. The *Philippines* implemented a data-driven system that supported a range of social programs and enabled effective beneficiary targeting. Conversely, in *Morocco*, limited data has prevented evaluation and stymied improvements to the conditional cash transfer program.

B. Successes in Education

Several countries have implemented reforms that led to sustained improvements in learning. Their success reflects varying combinations of the approaches discussed earlier: new pedagogical methods, ways to ensure that students and teachers are motivated, new approaches to school management, and technologies to enhance learning.

- *Korea* had very low literacy rates in the 1950s, but by 1995 was performing at the highest levels on international assessments. It first prioritized universal basic education and vocational learning, to supply the skilled workers necessary for economic development. It then targeted universal secondary education, and rapidly expanded higher education and private education as the economy became more knowledge-based. This sequential educational expansion helped solve the constraint of limited resources.
- *Finland*'s major education reform in the 1970s increased quality and equity at reasonable cost, helping it top the 2000 PISA assessment. Key measures included investments in teacher education, and a major overhaul of the curriculum and assessment system to ensure access to a "thinking curriculum" for everyone.
- *Vietnam* and *Shanghai* today show that it is possible to perform far better than income levels would predict. A generation ago, Vietnam was far from even universal primary schooling, but today learning poverty has been virtually eliminated, and secondary schools achieve PISA scores on par with Germany's. National strategies focused first on free primary education, particularly for the disadvantaged. Greater attention was then given to vocational education to meet the demand for trained workers, particularly in key sectors. New pre- and in-service training programs were initiated at massive scale for all teachers. Shanghai topped the 2012 PISA rankings, as policies

ensured every classroom had a prepared, supported, and motivated teacher, and key system elements, including a well-focused curriculum, were all aligned toward learning   (Liang et al. 2016).

Even in countries stuck in low-learning traps, some teachers, schools, and regions successfully promote learning. In the state of Ceará in Brazil, the municipality of Sobral in 2005 ranked 1,366th among 5,570 Brazilian municipalities on the country's synthetic indicator of education quality. A decade later, it ranked first in the country in both primary and lower-secondary education, achieving learning outcomes comparable to world-class education systems (Cruz and Loureiro 2020; World Bank 2019a). This success occurred despite a relatively low GDP per capita and a high student-to-teacher ratio, suggesting high system efficiency. It reflected a focus on four pillars: continuous use of student assessments; a focused curriculum with a clear learning sequence and prioritization of foundational skills; developing a pool of well-prepared and motivated teachers; and autonomous and accountable school management, with school principals appointed through a meritocratic technical selection process. Underlying this, state political leaders insulated education from partisan politics.

C. Successes in Health Care

Case studies confirm that improving health outcomes requires cross-cutting, "whole-of-society" solutions; chronic malnutrition provides a clear example. Successful health reform typically demands that governments "put forward a multi-sectoral approach for health at all government levels, to address NCD risk factors and underlying determinants of health comprehensively and decisively" (UN 2011). Multiple interventions from both within and outside the health sector are required to tackle chronic malnutrition, or stunting, among children, with its large, permanent effects on health and cognitive development (Bhutta et. al. 2020). Peru, in less than a decade, more than halved its rate of stunting among children under five. This success reflected a shift in focus away from simply providing food assistance to poor households, and towards a multi-sectoral approach to nutrition that included better provision of public services; cooperation between multiple national ministries, regional and municipal governments, and NGOs; and improved incentives for government and households (Marini et al. 2017). Government agencies were given monetary incentives to expand health and nutrition services, especially for the most vulnerable. Conditional cash transfers to poor households, increased health-insurance coverage, and public-outreach campaigns boosted demand for these health and social services. Comprehensive data-monitoring systems and strong local accountability mechanisms enhanced program effectiveness. And persistent lobbying by civil society convinced four successive governments to continue the effort. A similar multi-sectoral approach enabled Senegal to reduce sharply child stunting, anemia, and obesity, and chronic malnutrition (Ruel-Bergeron 2018).

The benefits of multi-sectoral strategies are evident for child development more generally, and for public health. Chile enjoyed remarkable progress in child development through the integrated deployment of a broad range of health, nutrition, education, and social programs and benefits, coordinated by a national-level body and municipalities. Direct transfer funding agreements, and the systematic collection of data for program management, promoted local accountability (World Bank 2018b; BMJ 2018; Clarke et al. 2018). Similarly, tobacco and alcohol control require coordination across sectors such as finance (taxation strategies), agriculture (crop substitution programs), and preventive care (tobacco cessation programs). Such coordination is easiest with formal inter-agency cooperation agreements (Lencucha et al. 2015). Agreements in these areas, as in nutrition policy, must be structured to avoid regulatory capture by private interests (Carey et al. 2015).

V. Conclusion

More and better investments in education and health can help realize their full promise as drivers of poverty elimination and inclusive growth. Education and health are basic human rights. Done right, they yield huge payoffs, improving social outcomes in many spheres of life. For individuals and families, they expand economic opportunities and agency. For societies, they promote social mobility and make institutions function more effectively. They increase a country's resilience, and allow it to take advantage of technological change or economic integration. These benefits depend on the skills that students acquire and on the population's health, not just on the number of years in the classroom or total health-care spending.

The Covid-19 pandemic presents an opportunity to "build back better," creating stronger, more resilient, and more inclusive education and health systems. There is an opening to mobilize a consensus for tackling existing inefficiencies and inequities. Most households now share the long-standing concerns of the vulnerable: having access to safe, good schools and health care. The pandemic galvanized new actors across the community—parents, community health and social welfare organizations, media and technology companies, local nonprofits and businesses—to work together with schools and health facilities to support learning and good health (World Bank 2020b; Vegas and Winthrop 2020).

Significant progress is possible with a commitment to spending not only more, but better. A commitment to improving delivery systems by strengthening accountability and incentives. A commitment to an evidence-based, whole-of-society approach to policymaking and action. A commitment to reform that is maintained across political cycles. Countries at every income level have shown such commitment, and now reap the rewards.

References

Adelman, M., and R. Lemos. 2021. *Managing for Learning: Measuring and Strengthening Education Management in Latin America and the Caribbean. International Development in Focus.* Washington, DC: World Bank.

Al-Samarrai, S., P. Cerdan-Infantes, and J. Lehe. 2019. "Mobilizing Resources for Education and Improving Spending Effectiveness." World Bank Policy Research WP 8773.

Alfers, L. 2013. "The Ghana National Health Insurance Scheme: Barriers to Access for Informal Workers." WIEGO WP 30.

Andrabi, T., B. Daniels, and J. Das. 2020. "Human Capital Accumulation and Disasters: Evidence from the Pakistan Earthquake of 2005." RISE WP 20/039.

Andrews, K., C. Avitabile, and R. Gatti. 2019. "Domestic Government Spending on Human Capital: A Cross-Country Analysis of Recent Trends." World Bank Policy Research WP 9033.

Andrews, K., R. Conner, R. Gatti, and J. Sharma. Forthcoming. "The Average Citizen's Experience with Primary Care: Levels and Distribution of Quality Care in 9 Countries in Sub-Saharan Africa." World Bank Policy Research WP.

Andrews, M., L. Pritchett, and M. Woolcock. 2013. "Escaping Capability Traps through Problem Driven Iterative Adaptation (Pdia)." *World Development.* Volume 51.

Andrews, M., L. Pritchett, and M. Woolcock. 2017. *Building State Capability: Evidence, Analysis, Action.* Oxford University Press. 1st Edition.

Angrist, N., D. Evans, D. Filmer, R. Glennerster, F.H. Rogers, and S. Sabarwal. 2020. "How to Improve Education Outcomes Most Efficiently?" World Bank Policy Research WP 9450.

Angrist, N., P. Bergman, C. Brewster, and M. Matsheng. 2020b. "Stemming Learning Loss During the Pandemic: A Rapid Randomized Trial of a Low-Tech Intervention in Botswana." CSAE WP 2020–13.

Avitabile, C., R. D'Souza, R. Gatti, and E.W. Chapman. 2020. *Insights from Disaggregating the Human Capital Index.* Washington, D.C.: World Bank Group.

Banerjee, A., S. Cole, E. Duflo, and L. Linden. 2007. "Remedying Education: Evidence from Two Randomized Experiments in India." *Quarterly Journal of Economics* 122(3).

Banerjee, A., R. Banerji, E. Duflo, R. Glennerster, and S. Khemani. 2010. "Pitfalls of Participatory Programs: Evidence from a Randomized Evaluation in Education in India." *American Economic Journal: Economic Policy* 2(1): 1–30.

Banerjee, A., R. Banerji, J. Berry, E. Duflo, H. Kannan, S. Mukherji, et al. 2016. "Mainstreaming an Effective Intervention: Evidence from Randomized Evaluations of 'Teaching at the Right Level' in India." NBER WP 22746.

Barasa, E.W., N. Mwaura, K. Rogo, and L. Andrawes. 2017. "Extending Voluntary Health Insurance to the Informal Sector: Experiences and Expectations of the Informal Sector in Kenya." *Wellcome Open Research* 2(94).

Barber, S., S. O'Dougherty, L. Torres, T. Tsilaajav, and P. Ong. 2020. "Other Considerations Than: How Much Will Universal Health Coverage Cost?" *Bulletin of World Health Organization*, 98 (2): 95 – 99.

Barrera-Osorio, F., and D. Filmer. 2016. "Incentivizing Schooling for Learning: Evidence on the Impact of Alternative Targeting Approaches." *Journal of Human Resources* 51(2).

Bau, N., and J. Das. 2017. "The Misallocation of Pay and Productivity in the Public Sector: Evidence from the Labor Market for Teachers." World Bank Policy Research WP 8050.

Beasley, E., and E. Huillery. 2017. "Willing but Unable? Short-Term Experimental Evidence on Parent Empowerment and School Quality." *World Bank Economic Review* 31(2).

Bhutta, Z., N. Akseer, E. Keats, T. Vaivada, S. Baker, S. Horton, et al. 2020. "How Countries Can Reduce Child Stunting at Scale: Lessons from Exemplar Countries." *American Journal of Clinical Nutrition* 112(Supplement_2).

Bell, B., R. Costa, and S. Machin. 2018. "Why Does Education Reduce Crime?" CEPR DP 13162.

Béteille, T., and D. Evans. 2019. "Successful Teachers, Successful Students: Recruiting and Supporting the World's Most Crucial Profession." World Bank Policy Approach to Teachers.

Bill and Melinda Gates Foundation. 2010. *Learning about Teaching—Initial Findings from the Measures of Effective Teaching Project.* MET project. Research Paper.

Bill and Melinda Gates Foundation. 2020. *Covid-19: A Global Perspective.* Goalkeepers Report.

Bitran, R. 2014. *Universal Health Coverage and the Challenge of Informal Employment: Lessons from Developing Countries.* Washington, DC: World Bank.

Björkman, M., and J. Svensson. 2009. "Power to the People: Evidence from a Randomized Field Experiment on Community-Based Monitoring in Uganda." *Quarterly Journal of Economics* 124(2): 735–769.

Bloom, N., R. Lemos, R. Sadun, and J. Van Reenen. 2015. "Does Management Matter in Schools?" *Economic Journal* 125(584): 647–74.

BMJ. 2018. "Scaling Up an Early Childhood Development Programme Through a National Multisectoral Approach to Social Protection: Lessons Learned from *Chile Crece Contigo*."

Bold, T., D. Filmer, G. Martin, E. Molina. C. Rockmore, B. Stacy, et al. 2017. "What Do Teachers Know and Do? Does It Matter? Evidence from Primary Schools in Africa." World Bank Policy Research WP 7956.

Bold, T., M. Kimenyi, G. Mwabu, A. Ng'ang'a, and J. Sandefur. 2013. "Scaling up What Works: Experimental Evidence on External Validity in Kenyan Education." CGD WP 321.

Bouguen, A., D. Filmer, K. Macours, and S. Naudeau. 2013. "Impact Evaluation of Three Types of Early Childhood Development Interventions in Cambodia." World Bank Policy Research WP 6540.

Bruns, B., D. Filmer, and H. Patrinos. 2011. *Making Schools Work: New Evidence on Accountability Reforms. Human Development Perspectives*. World Bank.

Bruns, B., and J. Luque. 2014. *Great Teachers: How to Raise Student Learning in Latin America and the Caribbean*. Washington, DC: World Bank.

Campos, J. E., B. Randrianarivelo, and K. Winning. 2015. "Escaping the 'Capability Trap': Turning 'Small' Development into 'Big' Development." *International Public Management Review* 16(1).

Carey, R., M. Caraher, M. Lawrence, and S. Friel. 2015. "Opportunities and Challenges in Developing a Whole-of-Government National Food and Nutrition Policy." *Public Health Nutrition*.

Chisholm, L., and R. Leyendecker. 2008. "Curriculum Reform in Post-1990s Sub-Saharan Africa." *International Journal of Educational Development* 28(2).

Chong, A., and M. Gradstein. 2015. "On Education and Democratic Preferences." *Economics and Politics* 27(3).

Clarke, D., G. Cortés Méndez, and D. Vergara Sepúlveda. 2018. "Growing Together: Assessing Equity and Efficiency in an Early-Life Health Program in Chile." IZA DP 11847.

Cruz, R., and L. Loureiro. 2020. "Achieving World-Class Education in Adverse Socioeconomic Conditions: The Case of Sobral in Brazil." Washington, DC: World Bank.

Cunha, F., and J. Heckman. 2007. "The Technology of Skill Formation." *American Economic Review* 97 (2): 31–47.

D'Souza, R., R. Gatti, and A. Kraay. 2019. A Socioeconomic Disaggregation of the World Bank Human Capital Index."

Darling-Hammond, L., A. Amrein-Beardsley, E. Haertel, and J. Rothstein. 2012. "Evaluating Teacher Evaluation." *Phi Delta Kappan* 93(6).

Darling-Hammond, L., M. Hyler, and M. Gardner. 2017. "Effective Teacher Professional Development." Learning Policy Institute.

Dartanto, T., J. Rezki, W. Pramono, C. Siregar, U. Bintara, and H. Bintara. 2016. "Participation of Informal Sector Workers in Indonesia's National Health Insurance System." *Journal of Southeast Asian Economies* 33(3).

De Ree, J., K. Muralidharan, M. Pradhan, and H. Rogers. 2017. "Double for Nothing? Experimental Evidence on the Impact of an Unconditional Teacher Salary Increase on Student Performance in Indonesia." *Quarterly Journal of Economics* 133(2).

Duflo, E., P. Dupas, and M. Kremer. 2011. "Peer Effects, Teacher Incentives, and the Impact of Tracking: Evidence from a Randomized Evaluation in Kenya." *American Economic Review* 101(5).

Espitia, A., N. Rocha, and M. Ruta. 2020. "Trade in Critical Covid-19 Products."

Evans, D., and F. Yuan. 2017. "The Economic Returns to Interventions that Increase Learning."

Fernandes, G. 2020. "Overhauling Health Systems." *Finance & Development.* International Monetary Fund. Fall 2020 Issue.

Fink, G., E. Kandpal, and G. Shapira. 2021. "Inequality in Quality of Health Services: Wealth, Content of Care, and Price of Antenatal Consultations in the Democratic Republic of Congo." *Economic Development and Cultural Change* 69(4).

Flabbi, L., and R. Gatti. 2018. "A Primer on Human Capital." World Bank Policy Research WP 8309.

Fryer, R. 2017. "Management and Student Achievement: Evidence from a Randomized Field Experiment." NBER WP 23437.

Garcia Jaramillo, S. 2020. "Covid-19 and Primary and Secondary Education: The Impact of the Crisis and Public Policy Implications for Latin America and the Caribbean." UNDP Covid-19 Policy Document 20.

Gaspar, V., D. Amaglobeli, M. Garcia-Escribano, D. Prady, and M. Soto. 2019. "Fiscal Policy and Development: Human, Social, and Physical Investment for the SDGs." IMF Staff Discussion Note 19/03.

Gaynor, M., and R. Town. 2011. "Competition in Health Care Markets." In *Handbook of Health Economics 2* (Volume 2, Chapter 9), edited by Pauly, M., T. Mcguire, and P. Barros. Elsevier B.V.

Gertler, P., J. Heckman, R. Pinto, A. Zanolini, C. Vermeersc, S. Walker, et al. 2014. "Labor Market Returns to an Early Childhood Stimulation Intervention in Jamaica." *Science* 344(6187).

Global Education Evidence Advisory Panel. 2020. "Cost-Effective Approaches to Improve Global Learning."

Green, D. 2016. *How Change Happens.* Oxford: Oxford University Press.

Guseva, M., M. Nakaa, A. Novel, K. Pekkala, B. Souberou, and S. Stouli. 2008. "Press Freedom and Development." United Nations Educational Scientific and Cultural Organization.

Huang, Z., G. Phillips, J. Yang, and Y. Zhang. 2020. "Education and Innovation: The Long Shadow of the Cultural Revolution." NBER WP 27107.

International Monetary Fund (IMF). 2017. *IMF Fiscal Monitor: Tackling Inequality.* October.

Global Burden of Disease Study 2017. *The Lancet* 392(10159): 1683–2138.

Jackson, C. 2020. "Does School Spending Matter? The New Literature on an Old Question." In *Confronting Inequality: How Policies and Practices Shape Children's*

Opportunities, edited by Tach, L., R. Dunifon, and D. L. Miller. *American Psychological Association.*

J-PAL. 2018. "Teaching at the Right Level to Improve Learning."

J-PAL. 2019. "Evidence Review: Will Technology Transform Education for the Better?"

Kandpal, E. 2016. "Completed Impact Evaluations and Emerging Lessons from the Health Results Innovation Trust Fund Learning Portfolio." Washington, DC: World Bank.

Kraay, A. 2019. "The World Bank Human Capital Index: A Guide." *World Bank Research Observer* 34(1): 1–33.

Kraft, M., D. Blazar, and D. Hogan. 2018. "The Effect of Teacher Coaching on Instruction and Achievement: A Meta-Analysis of the Causal Evidence." *Review of Educational Research* 88(4).

Kruk, M., M. Myers, S.T. Varpilah, and B. Dahn. 2015. "What Is a Resilient Health System? Lessons from Ebola." *Lancet* 385(9980).

Kurowski, C. 2018. "Equity on the Path to UHC: Deliberate Decisions for Fair Financing." 3rd Annual UHC Financing Forum. Background Report (Conference Version).

Lafortune, J., J. Rothstein, and D. W. Schanzenbach. 2018. "School Finance Reform and the Distribution of Student Achievement." *American Economic Journal: Applied Economics* 10(2): 1–26.

Lancet Commission on Health and Climate Change. 2015. "Health and Climate Change: Policy Responses to Protect Public Health." *Lancet* 386(10006).

Lancet Commission on Investing in Health. 2013. "Global Health 2035: A World Converging Within a Generation." *Lancet* 382(9908).

Lancet Global Health Commission. 2018. "High-Quality Health Systems in the Sustainable Development Goals Era: Time for a Revolution." *Lancet Global Health* 6(11).

Lassibille, G. 2016. "Improving the Management Style of School Principals: Results from a Randomized Trial." *Education Economics* 24(2).

Lavinas, L., and A. Veiga. 2013. "Brazil's One Laptop Per Child Program: Impact Evaluation and Implementation Assessment." *Cadernos de Pesquisa* 43(149): 542–69.

Lencucha, R., J. Drope, and J. Chavez. 2015. "Whole-of-Government Approaches to NCDs: The Case of the Philippines Interagency Committee—Tobacco." *Health Policy and Planning* 30(7).

Liang, X., H. Kidwai, and M. Zhang. 2016. *How Shanghai Does It: Insights and Lessons from the Highest-Ranking Education System in the World.* Directions in Development—Human Development. Washington, DC: World Bank.

Lustig, N., G. Neidhöfer, and M. Tommasi. 2020. "Short and Long-Run Distributional Impacts of Covid-19 in Latin America." CEQ WP 96.

Lyytinen, H., E. Ojanen, J. Jere-Folotiya, S. Ngorosho, F. Sampa, P. February, et al. 2019. "Challenges Associated with Reading Acquisition in Sub-Saharan Africa:

Promotion of Literacy in Multilingual Contexts." In *Improving Early Literacy Outcomes*, edited by Spaull, N., and J. Comings. Leiden: Brill Sense.

Maeda, A., C. Cashin, J. Harris, N. Ikegami, and M. Reich. 2014. *Universal Health Coverage for Inclusive and Sustainable Development: A Synthesis of 11 Country Case Studies*. Directions in Development; Human Development. Washington, D.C.: World Bank Group.

Mansuri, G., and V. Rao. 2012. *Localizing Development: Does Participation Work?*. *Policy Research Report*. Washington, DC: World Bank.

Marini, A., C. Rokx, and P. Gallagher. 2017. *Standing Tall: Peru's Success in Overcoming Its Stunting Crisis*. Washington, DC: World Bank.

McCoy, D.C., E. Peet, M. Ezzati, G. Danaei, M. Black, C. Sudfeld, et al. 2016. "Early Childhood Developmental Status in Low- and Middle-Income Countries: National, Regional, and Global Prevalence Estimates Using Predictive Modeling." *PLOS Medicine*.

McKinsey Global Institute. 2020. *Prioritizing Health: A Prescription for Prosperity*. McKinsey & Company.

Mizala, A., and B. R. Schneider. 2012. "Negotiating Education Reform: Teacher Evaluations and Incentives in Chile (1990–2010)." *Governance* 27: 87–109.

Muralidharan, K., A. Singh, and A. Ganimian. 2019. "Disrupting Education? Experimental Evidence on Technology-Aided Instruction in India." *American Economic Review* 109(4).

Nannyonjo, H. 2017. *Building Capacity of School Leaders: Strategies that Work— Jamaica's Experience*. Washington, DC: World Bank.

O'Donnell, O., E. Van Doorslaer, and T. Van Ourti. 2014. "Health and Inequality." In *Handbook of Income Distribution* 2B, edited by Atkinson, A., and F. Bourguignon. Elsevier.

Organisation for Economic Co-operation and Development (OECD). 2020a. *The Economic Impacts of Learning Losses*. Education Working Papers, No. 225, Paris.

Organisation for Economic Co-operation and Development (OECD). 2020b. *Exploitative Pricing in the Time of Covid-19*. Tackling Covid-19: Contributing to a Global Effort.

Pandey, P., A. Sehgal, M. Riboud, D. Levine, and G. Madhav. 2007. "Informing Resource-Poor Populations and the Delivery of Entitled Health and Social Services in Rural India: A Cluster Randomized Controlled Trial." *JAMA* 298(16):1867–75.

Park, R. K. E. 2016. "Preparing Students for South Korea's Creative Economy: The Successes and Challenges of Educational Reform." Asia Pacific Foundation of Canada.

Patel, D., and J. Sandefur. 2020. "A Rosetta Stone for Human Capital." CGD WP 550.

Popova, A., D. Evans, and V. Arancibia. 2016. "Training Teachers on the Job: What Works and How to Measure It." World Bank Policy Research WP 7834.

Popova, A., D. Evans, M. Breeding, and V. Arancibia. 2019. "Teacher Professional Development Around the World: The Gap Between Evidence and Practice." CGD WP 517.

Prestinaci, F., P. Pezzotti, and A. Pantosti. 2015. "Antimicrobial Resistance: A Global Multifaceted Phenomenon." *Pathogens and Global Health* 109(7): 309–18.

Propper, C. 2018. "Competition in Health Care: Lessons from the English Experience." *Health Economics, Policy and Law.*

Rajkumar, A., and V. Swaroop. 2008. "Public Spending and Outcomes: Does Governance Matter?" *Journal of Development Economics* 86(1).

Revenga, A., and J. Galindo. 2020. "Responding to Global Systemic Shocks: Applying Lessons from Previous Crises to Covid-19." EsadeEcPol Insight #5.

Robinson, V., C. Lloyd, and K. Rowe. 2008. "The Impact of Leadership on Student Outcomes: An Analysis of the Differential Effects of Leadership Types." *Educational Administration Quarterly* 44(5).

Rossi, F. 2019. "Human Capital and Macro-Economic Development: A Review of the Evidence." World Bank Policy Research WP 8650.

Ruel-Bergeron, J. 2018. *The Case for Investment in Nutrition in Senegal*: Analysis and Perspective—15 Years of Experience in the Development of Nutrition Policy in Senegal. Washington, DC: World Bank.

Sabarwal, S., D. Evans, and A. Marshak. 2014. "The Permanent Input Hypothesis: The Case of Textbooks and (No) Student Learning in Sierra Leone." World Bank Policy Research WP 7021.

Schady, N., J. Behrman, M. Araujo, R. Azuero, R. Bernal, D. Bravo, et al. 2015. "Wealth Gradients in Early Childhood Cognitive Development in Five Latin American Countries." *Journal of Human Resources* 50(2).

Schleicher, A. 2018. *World Class: How to Build a 21st-Century School System, Strong Performers and Successful Reformers in Education.* Paris: OECD Publishing.

Shonkoff, J., and P. Fisher. 2013. "Rethinking Evidence-Based Practice and Two-Generation Programs to Create the Future of Early Childhood Policy." *Development and Psychopathology. 25(4 Pt 2):1635–53.*

Smith, O., and S. Nguyen. 2013. *Getting Better: Improving Health System Outcomes in Europe and Central Asia Reports.* Washington, DC: World Bank.

Snilstveit, B., J. Stevenson, R. Menon, D. Philips, E. Gallagher, M. Geleen, et al. 2016. *The Impact of Education Programmes on Learning and School Participation in Low- and Middle-Income Countries: A Systematic Review Summary Report.* International Initiative for Impact Evaluation (3ie).

Somanathan, A., C. Bredenkamp, E. Pambudi, and A. Tandon. 2015. *Macrofiscal Implications of Achieving Universal Health Coverage in East Asia and Pacific.* In *East Asia and Pacific Economic Update*, World Bank, April.

Stenberg, K., O. Hanssen, T. Tan-Torres Edejer, M. Bertram, C. Brindley, A. Meshreky, et al. 2017. "Financing Transformative Health Systems towards Achievement of the Health Sustainable Development Goals." *Lancet Global Health* 5(9).

Suryadarma, D. 2012. "How Corruption Diminishes the Effectiveness of Public Spending on Education in Indonesia." *Bulletin of Indonesian Economic Studies* 48(1): 85–100.

UHC2030. 2020. "Living with Covid-19: Time to Get Our Act Together on Health Emergencies and UHC."

United Nations (UN). 2011. *Political Declaration of the High-Level Meeting of the General Assembly on the Prevention and Control of Non-Communicable Diseases. UN General Assembly (66th sess.: 2011–2012).*

United Nations (UN). 2019. *Universal Health Coverage (UHC): Fact Sheet.* World Health Organization.

United Nations (UN). 2020. *Education During Covid-19 and Beyond.* Policy Brief.

United Nations Development Programme (UNDP). 2020a. "Coronavirus Versus Inequality."

United Nations Development Programme (UNDP). 2020b. "Covid-19: Are Children Able to Continue Learning During School Closures?"

United Nations Educational, Scientific and Cultural Organization (UNESCO). 2019. New Methodology shows that 258 Million Children, Adolescents and Youth are out of School. Fact Sheet no.56. UIS/2019/ED/FS/56

Vegas, E., and R. Winthrop. 2020. "Beyond Reopening Schools: How Education can Emerge Stronger than Before Covid-19."

Watkins, D., D. Jamison, A. Mills, R. Atun, K. Danforth, A. Glassman et al. 2017. "Universal Health Coverage and Essential Packages of Care." In: Jamison, D., H. Gelband, S. Horton, et al. (eds). In *Disease Control Priorities, 3rd Edition: Volume 9, Improving Health and Reducing Poverty:* Ch. 3. Washington, DC: World Bank.

Watkins, D., J. Qi, Y. Kawakatsu, S. Pickersgill, S. Horton, and D. Jamison 2020. "Resource Requirements for Essential Universal Health Coverage: A Modelling Study Based on Findings from *Disease Control Priorities, 3rd Edition.*" *Lancet Global Health* 8(6).

World Health Organization (WHO). 2014. "Making Fair Choices on the Path to Universal Health Coverage: final report of the WHO consultative group on equity and universal health coverage." *World Health Organization.*

World Health Organization (WHO). 2019. *Primary Health Care on the Road to Universal Health Coverage: 2019 Monitoring Report. Conference Edition.* World Health Organization.

World Health Organization (WHO). 2020. "Responding to Covid-19—Learnings from Kerala." Feature Stories. World Health Organization.

World Health Organization (WHO) and World Bank. 2013. *Monitoring Progress towards Universal Health Coverage at Country and Global Levels: A Framework.*

World Health Organization (WHO) and World Bank. 2019. *Global Monitoring Report on Financial Protection in Health 2019.*

World Health Organization (WHO), World Bank, and Organisation for Economic Co-operation and Development (OECD). 2018. *Delivering Quality Health Services: A Global Imperative for Universal Health Coverage.*

Winskill, P., C. Whittaker, P. Walker, O. Watson, D. Laydon, N. Imai, et al. 2020. "Equity in Response to the Covid-19 Pandemic." Imperial College, London (12-05-2020).

World Bank. 2018a. *World Development Report 2018: Learning to Realize Education's Promise*. A World Bank Group Flagship Report. Washington, DC.

World Bank. 2018b. *10 Years of* Chile Grows with You*: Key Components and Lessons Learned for the Setting Up of Comprehensive Child Development Support Systems*. Washington, DC.

World Bank. 2019a. *Ending Learning Poverty: What Will It Take?* Washington, DC.

World Bank. 2019b. *Human Capital Project: How Countries Nurture Human Capital – Implement a Whole of Government Approach; Coordination Across Government; Policies and Programs that Use and Expand the Evidence Base; Sustained Efforts Across Political Cycles*. Washington, DC.

World Bank. 2019c. *High-Performance Health Financing for Universal Health Coverage: Driving Sustainable, Inclusive Growth in the 21st Century*. Washington, DC.

World Bank. 2020a. *The Human Capital Index 2020 Update*: Human Capital in the Time of Covid-19. Washington, DC.

World Bank. 2020b. *The Covid-19 Pandemic: Shocks to Education and Policy Responses*. Washington, DC.

World Bank. 2020c. *Human Capital Project Case Studies Series*. Washington, DC.

World Bank. 2020d. *Reimagining Human Connections: Technology and Innovation in Education at the World Bank*. Washington, DC.

World Bank. 2020e. *Learning Poverty in The Time of Covid-19: A Crisis Within A Crisis*. Washington, DC.

World Bank. 2020f. *Realizing the Future of Learning: From Learning Poverty to Learning for Everyone, Everywhere*. Washington, DC.

Yamey, G., M. Schäferhoff, M. Pate, M. Chawla, K. Ranson, F. Zhao, et al. 2020. "Funding the Development and Manufacturing of Covid-19 Vaccines." Duke Global WP 20.

15

The Political Economy of Inclusive Growth

Barbara Dutzler, Simon Johnson, and Priscilla Muthoora

I. Introduction

Inclusive growth, or rather the lack of it, has become a recurring theme in political discourses.[1] Economic growth has lifted millions of people out of poverty and led to higher living standards worldwide in the decades following the Second World War. Yet, there remains a sense that growth increasingly serves a privileged few and that countries' national institutions and politics are not sufficiently responsive to the needs of all citizens. This has motivated civil protest movements and nationalist sentiments, led to greater political polarization, and fueled a new wave of populism across the globe. Increasing economic inequality, the argument goes, leads to more divided societies with worse outcomes for all citizens.

In most advanced economies, income inequality is now at its highest level since the late 1970s. Among developing countries, the picture is mixed with several exceptions to the trend of increasing inequality. However, even in countries where inequality declined, progress on other dimensions of inclusiveness has been limited. Access to education, health care, finance, and employment opportunities, for example, remain unequal (Dabla-Norris et al. 2015; IMF 2020).

Several factors explain the widening gap within countries between the rich and poor. They include technological changes that favor the highly-skilled; the decline of unions and thus of worker protection and wage bargaining power; the deregulation of financial markets; the rising market power of a few superstar firms and individuals; globalization with its integrated value chains of production and relocation of production factories to low-cost developing countries; and migration on an unprecedented scale (Atkinson 2015; Bourguignon 2018a; Sandbu 2020).

Importantly, policy decisions by national governments and other economic agents play a major role in shaping the effect of these factors on economies

[1] We thank Valerie Cerra, Moya Chin, Hamid Davoodi, Barry Eichengreen, participants in the Inclusive Growth book seminar series organized by the IMF Institute for Capacity Development, and colleagues from the IMF for useful comments and suggestions. We also thank Christina Fong, Vincent Mahler, and Piotr Paradowski for permission to reproduce their data.

Barbara Dutzler, Simon Johnson, and Priscilla Muthoora, *The Political Economy of Inclusive Growth* In: *How to Achieve Inclusive Growth*. Edited by: Valerie Cerra, Barry Eichengreen, Asmaa El-Ganainy, and Martin Schindler, Oxford University Press. © Barbara Dutzler, Simon Johnson, and Priscilla Muthoora 2022. DOI: 10.1093/oso/9780192846938.003.0015

(Atkinson 2015). Thus, Ostry, Loungani, and Berg (2019) argue that increased inequality has been a choice, not an inevitable outcome.

In this chapter, we discuss the role of the political economy—the relationships between individuals, society, markets, and the state—in inclusive growth. While interpersonal disparities related to gender, race, ethnicity, health, and education are critical for inclusive growth, we mainly focus on the income inequality dimension for which political economy assessments are more prevalent.[2] Research has shown that a wide set of public policies affects income inequality (and vice versa) through complex interactions with politics and political institutions, historical legacies, and endowments.[3] This includes policies pertaining to labor markets, property laws, the financing of education and health care, and the provision of public goods (implicit redistribution or "pre-distribution" policies), on one hand, and explicit redistribution through taxes and transfers, on the other.

We organize our review into three broad questions. First, what determines the demand for and supply of redistribution, and can these determinants explain recent trends in inequality? Second, is there a robust link between political ideologies and inequality? Third, is the trend increase in inequality self-sustaining, or is there a tipping point, especially with the Covid-19 pandemic? To answer each of these questions, we draw on theoretical and empirical studies in the political economy literature, on historical evidence, and contemporary country experiences.

Our review suggests that political economy forces on the demand and supply side have weakened redistribution over time and contributed to the new wave of populism in many countries. Experience with populist experiments, however, casts doubt on the ability of this new populism to provide lasting solutions. The Covid-19 pandemic is widening economic inequalities and will test inclusive growth models. A rethink of the social contract is thus a policy imperative. This new social contract will necessarily reflect country-specific circumstances, but both the "what" and the "how" are important. First, in terms of content, there is growing consensus around three areas for policy interventions: investing in "local communities," where possible; helping the creation of "good jobs"; and improving deliberations and communications to rebuild trust in public institutions. Second, in terms of process, input matters as much as output for legitimacy. Thus, participation in decision-making through truly representative and democratic processes is key to ensure broad support by the population.

The chapter is organized as follows. Section II discusses the demand for redistribution, while Section III focuses on the supply-side. While demand and supply are interrelated, as supply-side institutions such as the welfare state are formed by

---

[2] As are spatial disparities across these dimensions.
[3] See, for example, McCarthy and Pontusson (2011); Acemoglu and Robinson (2013); and Morgan and Kelly (2013).

and respond to citizens' demands, for analytical purposes they are reviewed separately. Section IV examines which political regimes deliver more redistribution. Section V discusses the when and how of redistribution, including how to transition towards new social and political arrangements when trust in the government has been eroded.

II. Demand for Redistribution: Theory and Practice

One of the most widely known results in political economy theory is that democracy leads to more redistribution and lower inequality. This result derives from the median voter model of Meltzer and Richard (1981), who showed that the decisive preference of the voter at the median of the income distribution, whose income is below the mean, will result in a preference for higher taxes and redistribution.[4,5]

History provides some support for this proposition. In a study of the extension of the franchise in the West during the nineteenth century, Acemoglu and Robinson (2000a) documented that the broadening of voting rights in England, France, Sweden, and Germany was accompanied by significant redistributive reforms financed by an increase in taxation. Social spending emerged at the same time as the expansion of political voice, enfranchising middle- and lower-income groups and women from the 1880s to the 1960s (Lindert 2017).[6]

Recent empirical evidence is more nuanced. Taxes are higher and inequality is lower, *on average*, in democracies (Acemoglu et al. 2015), but the experience of the former communist economies (Milanovic 1998) or South Africa in the post-apartheid era (Leibbrandt et al. 2010) shows that inequality is not necessarily self-correcting in democracies. Some scholars have documented a "Robin Hood Paradox," whereby countries with high levels of inequality tend to have less redistributive policies than more egalitarian ones (Lindert 2004).

How can theory be reconciled with practice? Extensions to the basic median voter setting can alter the conclusions of the model. Benabou (2000), for example, demonstrates that there can be a non-linear relationship between the level of inequality and redistribution. This is because support for efficient redistributions, notably for social insurance, tends to be higher in more homogenous societies. Acemoglu et al. (2015) explain the empirical failure of the median voter

---

[4] This is the case if there are more poor people in the population than rich ones, namely, if the respective distributions of income and wealth are skewed to the right, with thick upper tails.

[5] A related result, in this set-up, is that greater initial inequality should lead to more redistribution given electoral competition.

[6] Aidt et al. (2006) find that social welfare only emerged relatively late and to a lesser extent, with public spending as a percentage of GDP shifting out of defense, administration, police, and judiciary first into transport, construction, and communication, and subsequently into public schooling and health.

hypothesis by factors that constrain democracies. These include constitutions, conservative political parties, capital flight, or widespread tax evasion by the elite. Political inequality and other factors shaping demand for redistribution also matter in practice.

A. Political Participation and Inequality

A key assumption of the median voter model is that every person who is eligible to vote does so. Another is that every vote carries the same weight. If the political influence of individuals increases with their incomes, the rate of redistribution will be lower than in the median voter model and fall with increasing inequality (Przeworski 2015). In terms of the median voter model, if the income of the *likely* voter is close to or above the mean income, this reduces demand for redistribution. Net inequality may then rise with market inequality, with only a partial correction by redistributive policies.

How relevant is this in practice? In the United States, Gilens (2009) finds that there are significant differences in income-based preferences on many social and welfare policies. Thus, the sharp increases in incarcerated Americans and ineligible ex-felons since the 1970s and in immigration, which have reduced voter turnout at the lower tail of the income distribution, may have steered policy towards the preferences of wealthier voters and away from redistribution.[7] The turnout gap between the richest and poorest voter in the United States was 23.6 percentage points, versus 8.4 percentage points on average in the 13 other OECD states in the years 2001–2004 (Mahler et al. 2015).

More generally, whether the poor are less likely to vote than the rich depends on additional factors. These include the government's capacity to tax and the political salience of redistribution or strategic spending by politicians, especially during election years. In developing countries, high levels of inequality can coexist with high electoral participation of the poor if electoral parties mobilize them through targeted goods, and the capacity to monitor such strategic spending by incumbents is weak.[8] This can contribute to creating and maintaining bad equilibria characterized by high inequality and low state capacity.

Would a higher, and more equal, voter turnout in fact increase redistribution? Robust empirical evidence for this proposition is missing, likely because voters also care about non-economic issues (Finseeras 2007). In a third of the sample of 14 OECD countries studied by Mahler et al. (2015), the turnout gap between the

---

[7] See, for example, Rosenthal (2004) for a discussion of the effect of "felony disenfranchisement" and immigration on voter turnout. Further, a substantial share of eligible voters in the United States remains unregistered due to the responsibility of registering resting with the individual, not the state, unlike most countries in the sample of Mahler et al. (2015).

[8] Kasara and Suryanarayan (2014) find the relative turnout of the rich to be higher than the poor, where rich individuals oppose redistribution and governments have a high ability to tax the rich. Amat and Beramendi (2020) study the issue of strategic spending by politicians.

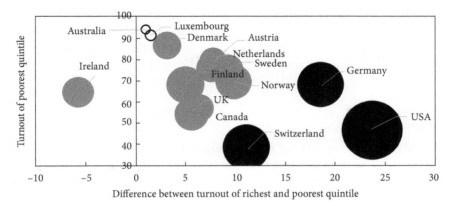

Figure 15.1 The Income Skew of Voter Turnout in Advanced Economies

Note: The size of the bubble is distribution of electoral turnout across income groups–the bigger, the more unequal.

Source: Mahler, Jesuit, Paradowski(2015).

richest and the poorest quintile is bigger than 10 percentage points. There is some evidence of a positive relationship between turnout and redistribution, but this effect is stronger for the 11 European countries in the study. The United States is an outlier, with the second-lowest voter turnout values for the bottom quintile, a significant skew of voter turnout towards high-income groups (Figure 15.1), and low social transfers. Two other non-European countries in the study, Australia and Canada, have low redistribution shares but, compared to the United States, lower voter inequality. A study by Fujiwara (2015) shows that the enfranchisement of the poor, through electronic voting, which improves their electoral participation, leads to greater health spending in Brazilian municipalities. Overall, these studies, although they cover a small sample of countries, provide suggestive evidence that voting rules do not imply a linear mapping of voter preferences to policy and that income is not the only factor driving preferences for redistribution.

Regardless of the income levels of voters, in contexts of greater inequality, "money-magnified voices" can shape the political debate and reduce the participation of all citizens (Ritter and Solt 2019). Elite capture can reduce support for redistribution when economic elites promote policies in their business interests (Gilens and Page 2014).[9] Voting behavior and political participation of poor and rich people are likely biased by inequality through many other channels, including limited resources of the poor to engage in politics; privileged access of the rich to campaign contributions; party financing and political representation; or incentives of political parties to target the poor (Cagé 2018; Dabla-Norris et al. 2015; Milanovic 2017; UN DESA 2020a).

---

[9] On the drivers of the bargaining process among self-interested elite actors and its effect on policy formulation and implementation in developing countries, see World Bank (2017).

Over time, this can result in a high share of disenfranchised citizens, or a sense of "not belonging" (Sandbu 2020). Thus, political inequality and economic inequality tend to go together, in ways more complex than the classical dichotomy between the median voter model and the Robin Hood paradox implies.

B. What Other Factors Shape Preferences?

In addition to the location of the voter along with the distribution of income, various other factors can shape preferences for redistribution. A growing literature in political economy and behavioral economics emphasize the following factors:

- *Expectations about net financial gains*: From a common pool perspective, redistribution creates benefits for well-defined groups, with the cost borne by society at large. This can limit support for redistribution. Durante, Putterman, and van der Weele (2014) conclude from an experimental study that income maximization, risk aversion, and concerns about inefficient taxation all matter for redistribution.
- *Economic conditions and risk aversion to economic shocks*: Job losses and perceptions of heightened economic insecurity increase support for welfare spending (Margalit 2013, for the United States; Martén 2019, for Sweden). This increased support does not persist in good times, however. Further, the sensitivity of preferences for redistribution to economic conditions is higher for those between the ages of 18 and 24 (Giuliano and Spilimbergo 2014).
- *Habituation effects*: Experiences of high inequality can increase or decrease demand for redistribution, depending on whether these lead to habituation by shifting the reference point or to rejection due to the first-hand experience. An experimental study by Charité, Fisman, and Kuziemko (2015) confirms the role of reference points. Roth and Wohlfart (2018) find that individuals living in highly unequal societies favor less redistribution, after controlling for income, demographics, unemployment experiences, and current macroeconomic conditions. Inequality experiences thus affect redistribution preferences, most likely by changing the level of inequality people accept as fair. This mechanism could explain the manifest lack of self-correction in many countries in the face of increasing inequality. But it also implies a role for culture and the state to shape attitudes towards redistribution.
- *Beliefs about the determinants of success*: Support for redistribution seems to stem from powerful commitments to fairness and reciprocity, that is the propensity to cooperate and share but to punish those who violate

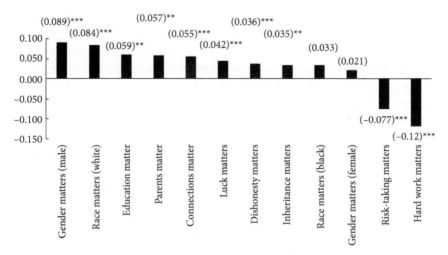

Figure 15.2 Determinants of Support for or Opposition to Redistribution

Note: The chart depicts the values of the estimated coefficients (significant at 1% level) from an OLS regression using the 1998 Gallup Social Audit Survey with 5001 US respondents, predicting support for redistribution depending on beliefs about causes for poverty/wealth.

Source: Fong, Bowles, and Gintis (2003) "Reciprocity, Self-interest, and the Welfare State" in the Handbook on the Economics of Giving, Reciprocity and Altruism (2004) Part II, edited by Jean Mercier-Ythier and Serge Kolm.

cooperative social norms.[10] If the beneficiaries of economic advantages believe their individual characteristics (gender, race) or luck to matter for success, they are much more likely to support redistribution than if they think the key to success is hard work and risk-taking (Figure 15.2).[11] This explains why support for redistribution is higher when people are more pessimistic about social mobility (Alesina, Stantcheva, and Teso 2017). On the other hand, rejection of redistribution may reflect the apparent violation of reciprocity norms by welfare programs where the recipients are perceived to be undeserving (Fong, Bowles, and Gintis 2003).

- *Perceptions about inequality*: There is increasing evidence that perceptions matter sometimes more than facts in shaping demand for redistribution

---

[10] Opposing individual motives towards redistribution like self-oriented income maximization and other-oriented social affinity can co-exist, nevertheless. Cavaillé and Trump (2015) find that differentiating between redistribution as taking from the rich and redistribution as giving to the poor helps to explain this puzzling concomitance in attitudes towards redistribution.

[11] Empirically, another factor which decreases willingness to redistribute is a high degree of racial or ethnic fractionalization. This is especially true in contexts where the bottom of the income distribution comprises mostly racial or ethnic minorities (Alesina, Baqir, and Easterly 1999; Alesina, Glaeser and Sacerdote 2001; Alesina and Glaeser 2004; Alesina and Giuliano 2011; Dahlberg et al. 2012; Mollerstrom 2016). Alesina and Glaeser (2004), using data from 1990–2000, found that about half of the difference in the extent of redistribution, measured by the amount of social spending to GDP, between Europe and the United States could be attributed to variations in the degree of racial and ethnic fractionalization.

(Cruces, Perez-Truglia and Tetaza 2013; Alesina, Miano, and Stantcheva, 2018; Bussolo et al. 2019; Cavaillé and Ferwerda 2018; Karadja, Mollerstrom, and Seim 2017). These perceptions reflect objective macroeconomic conditions such as unemployment, the poverty rate, local and national inequality, as well as personal experience with insecurity. Experiments show that changes in perceptions are crucial in increasing support for redistributive policies (Bastani and Waldenstrom 2019). However, support for redistributive policies is not elastic. Kuziemko et al. (2013) use randomized online survey experiments to provide information on US income inequality, the link between top income tax rates and economic growth, and the estate tax. They find that this informational treatment strongly affects views about inequality but does not shift preferences on tax and transfer policies much. The exception is the estate tax, where extreme *ex-ante* misinformation seems to drive the results. The small effects for all other policies are driven by the respondents' low trust in government. Decreasing trust lowers support for all poverty-alleviation policies.

The above factors may explain why there can be inconsistencies between the perceived level of income inequality, the actual level of income inequality, and demand for redistribution.[12] After examining the supply side of redistribution, we will discuss the factors hindering the transmission of preferences into policy-making and inhibiting government responsiveness.

III. The "Supply" of Redistribution

The mix of redistributive policies and instruments used to address economic inequality reflects various "supply" factors. These include the policy objectives of and trade-offs to governments; administrative capacity constraints; political systems; and the legacy of the welfare state institutions in place. These, in turn, are shaped by societal preferences for redistribution. Moreover, there are inevitably groups who stand to lose from redistribution. The extent of redistribution may partially reflect their respective influence in the policy choice. Thus, the questions of why some governments redistribute more, and what drives their capacity to do so, can be understood in this supply and demand framework.

The largest differences in the supply of redistribution are between advanced and developing economies. These reflect variations in the use of tax instruments, and fiscal and administrative capacity (Bourguignon 2018b). Even within advanced economies, however, there are significant variations in social contracts. The weight placed on implicit and explicit redistribution policies, and on the respective roles

---

[12] See Kenworthy and McCall (2007) for an examination of patterns over time for 8 OECD countries.

of the government and other entities (charities, churches) in improving distributional outcomes, differs. The effectiveness of redistribution (coverage, progressivity, generosity) also varies, but it is difficult to establish given the scarcity of data, including on in-kind benefits, which would be required to enable a full incidence analysis (Lustig 2017).

Recent policy debates highlight the importance of implicit redistribution ("pre-distribution") policies to correct the market income generation process. These include the role of governments in incentivizing capital formation and helping create good jobs (Collier 2018; Gruber and Johnson 2019; Rajan 2019; Sandbu 2020).[13] Minimum wage and anti-discrimination laws can also foster inclusive growth by improving work and training incentives for various groups (women and minority groups, for example). The role of anti-corruption strategies in reducing rent-seeking has also been emphasized.

Explicit redistribution policies nevertheless remain relevant. Theory and evidence suggest that who is taxed and who benefits from transfers matter for equality outcomes. The taxation of wealthy individuals and corporations is hotly contested because of the possible disincentive effect of high taxes on capital gains and profits on savings. This could reduce investment, and, thus, productivity and economic growth (Jones 2019). From this perspective, the worldwide trend to reduce direct taxes exemplifies countries' internal redistributive struggles as a function of their social stratification. When upper-income groups can resist direct taxation, the capacity of governments for redistribution is limited (Kaufman and Stallings 1991).

A. Setting the Stage for Redistribution: Welfare States

The modern welfare state, or how states assume responsibility for social welfare and thereby fulfill the social contract, varies widely among countries. Historical and cultural legacies of conservative, liberal, and social democratic principles shape welfare states in their current form. Important differences across welfare systems include the conditions of eligibility; the quality of benefits and services; the emphasis on means-testing versus universal access; and the rights of citizens to employment (Esping-Andersen 1989).

A widely used approach distinguishes between at least three models of Welfare States ("Nordic," "corporatist," and "Anglo-Saxon"). These models differ according to reliance on universalism vs targeting; reliance on markets vs government; or

---

[13] Interestingly, already in 1955, Simon Kuznets observed that when governments limit wealth accumulation through policy instruments such as inheritance taxes and other capital levies, they act on a societal preference against income inequalities. He also argued for regulation to prevent capital flight as this reduces the capital formation required for economic growth.

the role of churches and voluntary means. The Nordic countries can be grouped in the social democratic model, which emphasizes universal access and the limited role of the private market. Anglo-Saxon countries belonging to the liberal group tend to favor minimal public intervention and a decisive role for the market, while continental European countries making up the conservative or corporatist group historically rely extensively on social insurance and family and churches as means of welfare delivery (Causa and Hermansen 2017).

Welfare institutions are a key "intervening variable" shaping distributional outcomes. The capacity of different welfare models to reduce inequality and poverty is likely shaped by coalitions of interest groups, while they, in turn, affect the formation of "interests, preferences, and coalitions among citizens" (Korpi and Palme 1998).

Whereas the level of social spending differs considerably between these welfare models, compared to social expenditure in developing countries, the differences appear trivial. Abstracting from differences in spending ability, which are reviewed below, the historical institutional dimension helps to shed light on the persistence of high levels of inequality in developing countries. A rich literature shows how welfare institutions, as other institutional structures, are influenced by colonial history, ethnolinguistic heterogeneity, and conflict and political instability. Examples include exploitative institutions in the Americas triggered by colonialization, which continued to advantage elites by providing them privileged access to political power or economic opportunities (Engerman and Sokoloff 2002). Angeles (2007) confirms that colonialization is a major explanation for today's higher level of inequality in former colonies, by influencing how institutions were created. However, Haller et al. (2016) find that a well-functioning welfare state as measured by the level of social spending can cancel out the effect of high ethnic fractionalization and a history of slavery on inequality. These findings have important implications for the development of welfare institutions in developing countries.

B. Measuring Pro-Poorness of Redistribution

Determining whether countries that redistribute more share common features in terms of their political and welfare systems is complicated. There are difficulties in assessing both the pro-poorness of redistribution (this section) and classifying political regimes beyond the democracy-dictatorship dichotomy (Section IV).

Beyond the size of government tax take and social spending, key qualitative features of redistribution efforts are population coverage, progressivity, and generosity (Francese and Prady 2018).[14] The volume of social spending is not

---

[14] Social spending comprises both social protection and expenditure on health and education (IMF, 2019a). Social protection encompasses programs on (i) social assistance or social safety nets

sufficient to qualify as a welfare-state commitment as it may disproportionately benefit a privileged few or powerful interest groups. Low expenditure on unemployment programs may reflect an effective welfare state delivering full employment. A high share of social expenditure may be due to administrative inefficiencies rather than high quality. However, size matters, as do the composition of government spending, financing, and the progressivity taxes and government spending (Lustig 2017).

Assessing the effect of public social spending on household income is complicated. In-kind benefits, indirect transfers, and indirect taxes and co-payments for health are typically not recorded in household surveys. The difference between market and net Gini, a widely used proxy for redistribution, only considers the effect of direct taxes and transfers. This underestimates the true effort and impact of government spending on the ability of a household to maintain a living standard beyond its market income.[15] An important element lies in the primary purpose of in-kind transfers: to ensure equal access to good education, healthcare, and other public goods. Their effect is thus to equalize inequality's long-term effects and to prevent transmission of poverty across generations. Among OECD countries, despite little targeting of in-kind transfers to low-income households, their substantive size and their progressive incidence make them highly equalizing instruments (Causa and Hermansen 2017).

In advanced economies, taxes on personal income and cash transfers to the poor, as a share of GDP, are on average about ten times higher than in low-income countries (Bourguignon 2018b). In-kind transfers are generally progressive. Among OECD countries, social spending expenditure, which contains government expenditure on social protection in cash and in-kind, on average is above 20 percent of GDP, with considerable variation across countries (Figure 15.3). This is almost twice the level as in low-income and middle-income economies. In conformity with the worldwide trend, social spending—namely, the welfare state—as a proportion to GDP has risen over the last 20 years. The largest public spending item is pensions, worth 8 percent of GDP across the OECD.

In 2018 in the 28 EU Member States, expenditure on social protection represented 18.6 percent of GDP or 40.6 percent of total expenditure.[16] Around 90 percent of this expenditure was cash benefits and services in kind. In terms of effectiveness,

---

(cash transfers, non-contributory pensions, food and in-kind programs, fee waivers, social care services, etc.) (ii) social insurance (contributory pensions, health, and other insurance such as maternity leave, paid sick leave, etc.), and (iii) labor market programs (passive such as unemployment benefits, active such as training and employment incentives). Programs typically encompass both tax incentives as well as expenditure.

[15] Based on experimental Distributional National Accounts analysis, Causa and Hermansen (2017) report that with social transfers in kind, total household income would be 22 percent higher, on average, across the nine OECD countries included in their analysis.

[16] The Eurostat definitions on social expenditure are similar to the ones used by OECD, but there are differences in coverage and categorizations that explain the differences in reported shares of GDP. While the OECD-SOCX database uses ESSPROS-Eurostat data for the EU member states, OECD has its own databases for health, childcare, and ALMPs (OECD SOCX Manual, 2019Th).

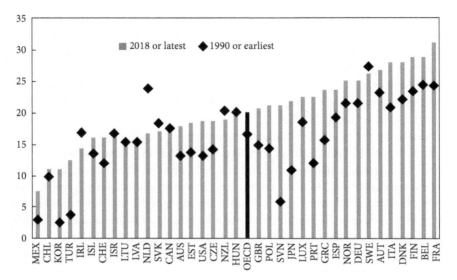

Figure 15.3 Public Social Spending in the OECD

Note: Social spending includes cash benefits, in-kind services, and tax breaks with social purposes.
Source: OECD.

a higher share of GDP on social protection tends to be associated with a lower level of inequality, consistent with the negative relationship found in the literature (IMF 2019b).[17]

From a cursory overview, without investigation into structural policy changes at the country level, changes in social spending are not associated with a consistent pattern of inequality changes (Figure 15.4). Between 2000–2018, social protection spending rose in half of this sample of EU countries and fell in the remaining half. Inequality increased equally in both groups approximately two-thirds of the time.[18] A more detailed analysis for seven EU countries of the effect of changes in taxes and transfers on poverty and inequality reveals that structural reforms tended to increase inequality, especially during 2007–2011—implying the drawing back of safety nets at the time when they were needed and demanded most (Hills et al. 2014; Eurobarometer 2011).[19]

At the same time, the composition of social spending was changing. Cash transfers on average were reduced and in-kind support, foremost health care, increased (Causa and Hermansen 2017). Limited fiscal space coupled with

[17] However, low inequality also exists in countries with relatively low spending on social protection, for example in the Slovak and the Czech Republic.

[18] Spending-to-GDP reflects changes in economic trends (unemployment spending) as well as contraction of GDP; in Ireland GDP in 2015 expanded by 25 percent due to relocation of intellectual property.

[19] The highest political priority for European citizens in repeated special surveys between 2009 and 2011 was "tackling exclusion and poverty."

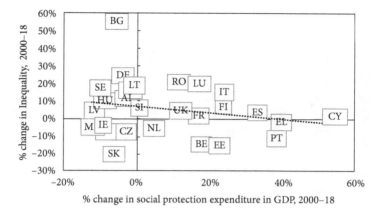

Figure 15.4 Changes in Inequality and Social Protection: 2000–2018
Note: General government total expenditure on social protection as defined by COFOG.
Source: Eurostat.

population aging may require more emphasis on health and pension spending at the expense of other social protection programs. Any reduction in inequality from in-kind support would not be captured in the disposable income at the household level, as discussed above.

More generally, both the level and composition of social spending matter for the net progressivity of government budgets. In the United States, Argentina, and Uruguay, increased social transfers offset declining top tax rates over time. In Japan, South Korea, and Taiwan Province of China, where direct transfers to the poor are limited, significant redistribution occurs via public education spending and subsidies. In countries where increased public pension benefits in social transfers crowded out equalizing expenditure on children and working-age adults, progressivity declined (Lindert 2017).

In developing countries, in addition to historical, political, and administrative constraints, limited redistribution also reflects the composition of taxes and spending. Tax policy is typically not as effective in altering the post-tax distribution of income as in developed countries. Further, social protection is much lower, and the composition of spending and the coverage of the population through social assistance, social insurance, or labor market programs is very different (Figure 15.5). For low-income countries, the dominant source of social protection is domestic private, rather than public, transfers. Without those, coverage of the population is below 20 percent. Similarly, adequacy of benefits, namely, the total benefits received by all beneficiaries in the population as a share of the total welfare of beneficiaries, is much lower in developing countries. There is thus limited redistribution through fiscal policy for developing countries (IMF 2017).

Developing countries thus mostly attempt to alter welfare through in-kind transfers such as education or health care (Davoodi et al. 2003). Using the average

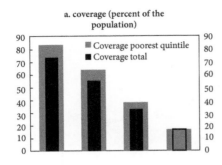

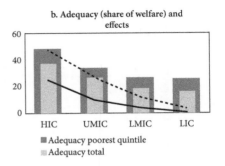

Figure 15.5 Social Protection and Labor Programs (SPL)

Note: Coverage is the percentage of the population participating in social insurance, social safety net, unemployment benefits, and active labor market programs. Adequacy is the total transfer amount received by all beneficiaries in a population group as a share of the total welfare of beneficiaries in that group.

Source: WB ASPIRE. Latest available data 2008–2018.

cost of provision to value the benefits to individuals from free education and health services, Lustig (2017) shows that, for 19 developing countries, social spending and spending on education and health increase with market-income inequality. This improves inequality outcomes for all countries, but many of the poor are, to varying degrees, net payers into the fiscal system based on post-fiscal income (after direct cash transfers, direct taxes, and net indirect taxes).

An important takeaway, therefore, is that the fiscal system can be inequality reducing, but poverty increasing. The overall impact on household wellbeing as a token of welfare state effectiveness depends on the combined effect of taxation and social spending. On this account, structural factors can make the joint objectives of equality and prosperity more challenging for developing countries. The design of these policies in a mutually reinforcing way, on the other hand, reflects government choices that are dependent on the political system and institutional environment, as discussed in Section IV.

IV. Which Political Regimes Deliver More Redistribution?

Political regimes, institutions, and processes play a key role in influencing demand for and supply of redistribution by aggregating voter preferences and matching them with the size and scope of redistributive policies offered by different political regimes. In this section, we examine this relationship, focusing on two hypotheses. The first is that electoral systems matter for coalition formation and hence outcomes. The second posits that the dynamics of inequality affect, and is affected by, changing political cleavages. In this context, we discuss the recent rise of populism and its likely sustainability.

A. Redistribution under Proportional and Majoritarian Representation

Elections are the core mechanism shaping and translating preferences in a democracy. Electoral systems affect electoral competition, the formation of coalitions, the partisan composition, and, ultimately, redistributive outcomes (Persson and Tabellini 1999, 2000, 2003; Iversen and Soskice 2006). Proportional representation systems tend to favor governments that redistribute more than majoritarian systems. This is because proportional systems encourage coalition formation among a broad group of parties, including those catering to the poor and labor unions.[20] Majoritarianism, on the other hand, makes the entry of new parties difficult. Most European countries, except for France and the United Kingdom, have proportional representation systems. In the past, this has favored parties supporting more extensive redistribution and larger welfare states, traditionally voted for by voters with lower income. The United States has a majoritarian system with a greater degree of federalism and decentralization. This latter characteristic also plays a role as redistribution undertaken by lower levels of governments tends to be more fragmented. Alesina, Glaeser, and Sacerdote (2001) and Alesina and Glaeser (2004) concluded that up to half of the difference in redistribution between Europe and the United States between 1990 and 2000 could be explained by their electoral systems.

B. Redistribution with Changing Political Cleavages

Political parties represent coalitions of interest groups with shared views on government policies influencing redistribution, capital formation, or migration, amongst others. For Piketty (2018), the recent failure of the democratic processes to rein in inequality is a departure from the relatively egalitarian period between 1950–1980. A hypothesis is that political cleavages may have shifted and no longer resemble traditional class-based coalitions.[21] Analyzing long-run transformations of party systems by the level of income and education of voters in France, the United Kingdom, and the United States, he diagnoses a dissociation of lower education and lower-income voters from their traditional political representations, which today mainly represent elite voters (high income or high education). This could explain the lack of democratic response to rising

---

[20] See, for example, Chin (2019) for recent empirical evidence that proportional representation favors broader coalitions using data for Brazil municipalities.

[21] Economic and identity cleavages are also emphasized by Mukand and Rodrik (2019) and Gennaioli and Tabellini (2019).

inequality and the rise of populist parties supported by "abandoned" non-elite voters, as new cleavages between "globalists" (high-education, high-income) and "nativists" or "populist" (low-education, low-income) have emerged. A way out of the predicament requires uniting low-education, low-income voters from different backgrounds, which is the type of political coalition that provided egalitarian policies in the past; but how and under which circumstances this is possible is less than clear.

C. Redistribution under Populism: Then and Now

Populist movements are hardly new, but history suggests that populists are rarely elected in good economic times. Instead, they seem to be brought about by a combination of economic, social, and political circumstances: economic insecurity, threats to national identity, and an unresponsive political system (Eichengreen 2018).

There is no universally accepted definition of populism. Central to the populist ideology, however, is the programmatic distinction between the "pure people" versus the "others," such as elites, established political parties, state institutions (court, parliament, a central bank, etc.), or immigrants.[22] When the excessive influence of the rich becomes a frequent narrative, voters rally behind populist parties that denounce a country's elite as evil.

Populism can be prevalent both at the right as well as at the left of the political spectrum. Right-wing populist movements tend to be characterized by nativism, or the belief that non-native inhabitants are threatening to the homogenous nation-state. Left-wing populism typically calls for a major redistribution of resources to counter economic inequality.

Between the 1940s and 1980s, left-wing populist governments were widespread in Latin America, but rarer in advanced economies (Dornbusch and Edwards 1991). The recent surge in populism in many advanced and emerging economies, by contrast, has been driven by right-wing populists. In Europe, not only has the number of parties classified as a populist (Figure 15.6) doubled in numbers since 2000 but so has the number of governments with populist participation.[23] Whereas in early 2000, populist parties accounted for just 7 percent of votes across the continent, in 2018, one in four voted for a populist party.[24]

Rising inequality is a possible explanation for the rise of populism. Tabellini (2019) emphasizes inequality associated with new divisions along specific social

---

[22] Authoritarianism or the belief in a strictly ordered society with severe punishment for those opposing the order can also be a feature. See for example, Mudde (2004), Weyland (2001), Dahrendorf (2003), and Kaltwasser (2014).

[23] https://institute.global/insight/renewing-centre/european-populism-trends-threats-and-future-prospects#article-footnote-2

[24] https://www.theguardian.com/world/ng-interactive/2018/nov/20/revealed-one-in-four-europeans-vote-populist

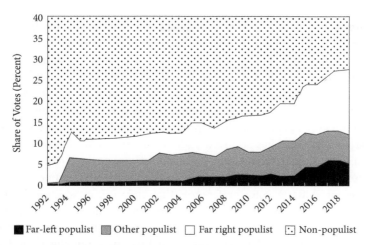

Figure 15.6 Vote Shares in European Countries
Source: ParlGov(European countries), classifications from the PopuList-www.popu-list.org.

dimensions including education, geography, exposure to technology, and globalization. He suggests two behavioral mechanisms to explain the success of populist
parties: disappointed expectations and switching social identities. Disappointed
expectations favor political risk-taking by voters, leading to the emergence of
more extremist parties and new parties, including populists. Populist parties seek
to broaden their base by adopting platforms of lower taxes and conservative cultural and social policies, which end up being supported by an unlikely coalition of
"very disappointed" and "very rich" voters.[25]

Moreover, as losers from technology and globalization tend to be less educated
and more socially conservative, economic conflicts transform into social conflicts
over immigration and civil rights. These new social identities, fostered by economic dislocations, are exploited by populist parties. This proposition is partly
borne out in empirical evidence. Dal Bó and others (2019) find, for example, that
the rise of the Sweden Democrats, a far-right party, can be explained by the growing support of voters facing greater income decline and job insecurity over time.
Inglehart and Norris (2016), on the other hand, using data from the pooled
European Social Survey 1-6 (2002–2014), find evidence of a "cultural backlash"
largely fueled by immigration. Redistributive concerns still matter, though:
insofar as adverse economic conditions increase competition for government
funds, nativism will object to granting economic benefits to outsiders.

---

[25] This idea echoes Algan et al. (2018) who argue that the 2017 French presidential elections illustrate a collapse of the traditional left-right axis. Using monthly survey data from 17,000 panelists, they
show that this phenomenon can be explained by subjective variables such as life satisfaction and interpersonal trust.

D. Redistribution under Populism: The Outcome

As to the consequences of populism, a study of Latin America's history is instructive. Edwards (2019) draws a distinction between past "classical" populist episodes, mostly occurring before the 1990s, and the "new" populism, which appeared after the 1990s in Latin America and is now gaining momentum in other parts of the world. Classical populists mostly came to power and were forced out by non-democratic means. Their focus was on redistribution through money creation and expansionary fiscal policies. The "new" populism is different, Edwards argues, in that it has occurred under democracy and focuses on microeconomic issues such as regulations; protectionist measures; expansion of the public sector; and, mandatory minimum wages. De Bolle and Zettelmeyer (2019) also note recent shifts in voter preferences that embrace, in addition to trade restrictions, other policies classified as "economic nationalism" such as restrictions of foreign direct investment, bans on immigration, and withdrawal from multilateral organizations. Another feature of this "new populism" in Latin America has been the recourse to constitutional amendments to achieve distributional objectives.

The final days of the "classical" populist experiences in Argentina, Brazil, Chile, Mexico, Peru, and Nicaragua display "the self-destructive feature of populism". Expansionary policies and inflationary spending brought immediate gains, but they ended with macroeconomic crises characterized by high inflation, capital flight, and sharp declines in real wages and per capita income (Dornbusch and Edwards 1991). Ultimately, these policies hurt growth and did not achieve lasting redistribution and inequality reduction (Cardoso and Hellweger 1991; Edwards 2019).

The inclusive growth record of "new" populist regimes in Latin America remains mixed. In Bolivia, under populist leadership between 2006–2019 extreme poverty nearly halved; growth and infrastructure investment were strong; the currency was stable, and; inflation remained low. It is noteworthy however that poverty and inequality outcomes improved broadly during this period in Latin America, including in countries with non-populist governments. Importantly, subsequent political developments in Bolivia cast doubt on the ability of the "new" populism to sustain inclusive growth. [26] While it is too early to assess the effects on growth outcomes, and much depends on country circumstances, policy design, and actual implementation, the historical experience would weigh the risks to inclusive growth higher than the opportunities.

---

[26] https://www.theguardian.com/world/2019/mar/07/how-a-populist-president-helped-bolivias-poor-but-built-himself-a-palace; https://www.theguardian.com/world/2019/nov/17/bolivia-more-volatile-than-ever-as-president-flees-and-leaders-denounce-a-coup

E. A Tipping Point?

Is the growing attraction of voters to populist parties reversible? If their rise was predominantly driven by economic forces, stronger growth and rising wealth for the left- behind segments of the population could help restore votes to the political middle. The underlying dynamics, however, do not make this outcome likely.

Political betrayal of the voters appears widespread, under both "classical" and "new" populism. Redistributive rhetoric camouflages policies in line with the interests of the elite (Acemoglu et al. 2013). To raise voter turnout, populist movements behave opportunistically or use strategic extremism, for example, division on religious values (Glaeser et al. 2005).

Paradoxically, the lack of results can make populism self-sustaining as populist governments are able to harness popular discontent against the media, immigrants, or experts. Angry voters are more easily distracted (Johnson 2019a and 2019b), and as individuals adjust to prevailing circumstances, discontent with populist politicians grows only moderately despite rising inequality (Roth and Wohlfart, 2018).

This may explain why populism is associated with leaders' prolonged stay in power, weakened checks on government powers, and restrained civil rights such as freedom of the press or political participation (Kyle and Gultchin 2018; Kyle and Mounk 2018). Shifts in economic and identity cleavages through economic shocks or political strategies by groups contending for power lead to conflicts.[27] To the extent that these overshadow redistributive concerns, political systems can enter a bad equilibrium. In this environment, government policies do not counter the underlying economic forces driving market inequality, as voters are distracted by identity conflicts. Increasing inequality can reinforce the identification of the voters with new platforms against their economic interests and stabilize the political regime.

Taking a long-term perspective, for the first time in history, there are more democracies than non-democracies. The number of countries that score the maximum value on the respective indicator, however, has been stagnant and recently declining (Figure 15.7). Consequently, the gap between high-scoring democracies and democracies just above the threshold has been growing.

Inclusive political strategies will be decisive for lowering economic and identity cleavages and keeping the very fabric of liberal democracies alive. Governments' willingness to address inequality needs to be matched by their ability to deliver a better livelihood for their citizens. Safeguarding against a potential democratic backslide, from this perspective, requires not only strengthening political representation and democratically debating and solving essential policy issues. Capably

---

[27] See Mukand and Rodrik (2019). Guiso et al. (2017) find that economic insecurity destroys trust and fosters adverse attitudes towards immigrants. Further, voters change their beliefs and preferences when economic shocks create new cleavages (Gennaioli and Tabellini 2019).

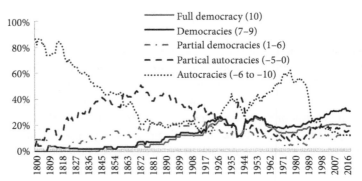

Figure 15.7 Evolution of Democracies and Autocracies since 1800

Note: The maximum score for democracy is 10; a full autocracy scores-10.

Source: Polity IV Database (http://www.systemicpace.org/inscrdata.html" www.systemicpace.org/inscrdata.html), polity 2 indicators.

addressing the needs of the most vulnerable segments of society inclusively and sustainably, while managing existing constraints and questions of political feasibility will be an important part of the answer to the populist challenge.

V. The "How" and "When" of Redistribution

The degree of inequality in an economy depends on its structure, or people's endowments and the value earned with these endowments. Latin America's proneness to populist cycles, for example, has been attributed to the formation of a landed elite or export oligarchies in the second half of the nineteenth century that led to a persistently high concentration of income and assets (Kaufman and Stallings 1991).

A. "Pre-distribution" versus Redistribution

"Pre-distribution," or implicit redistribution, affects endowments. It can be influenced by "market reforms that encourage a more equal distribution of economic power and rewards even before government collects taxes or pays out benefits" (Hacker 2012).

Redistribution, in contrast, hinges on taxing "winners" in order to fund programs that compensate "losers." Such measures, Kuttner (2018) observes, are only "second bests. They do not foster social cohesion: winners resent the loss of earnings; losers, the loss of dignity." This view is echoed by Rodrik and Sabel (2019): "Ex post redistribution through taxes and transfers accepts the productive structure as given, and merely ameliorates the results through handouts."

In his 15-point proposal in response to *Inequality: What Can Be Done?*, the late Sir Tony Atkinson called for several pre-distribution policies.[28] He emphasized public employment; minimum wages; innovation that increases employment opportunities; and competition policies with a distributional dimension. Renewed calls have been made recently for greater weight on pre-distribution policies relating to technological change (Acemoglu 2020); competition policies (Aghion, Cherif, and Hasanov 2021); and minimum wages, education, and retraining for workers (Sandbu 2020).

The appropriate mix of policies will necessarily vary across countries, reflecting their specific circumstances. Rodrik (2019) offers a useful taxonomy, suggesting that pre-distributive and redistributive measures depend on whether countries target inequality at the bottom, middle, or top of the income or wealth distribution. Universal basic income, health, and education increase endowments, consistent with pre-distribution interventions, focus on the bottom of the distribution. By contrast, greater anti-trust regulation and wealth taxes target the top of the distribution.

In practice, there can be important financing and political feasibility constraints for both pre-distribution and redistribution. In what follows, we discuss some of these constraints.

B. What Are the Constraints?

Are there limits to redistribution? From an economic point of view, the obvious starting point is the potential trade-off between economic performance (efficiency) and income equality in the sense of Okun's "leaky bucket" metaphor. Efficiency losses due to redistribution tend to rise with the amount of redistribution. Andersen and Maibom (2016) revisit the issue and find that, along the efficiency frontier (under stochastic frontier analysis), for a sample of OECD countries between 1980 and 2010, the trade-off exists. For countries below the efficiency frontier, they confirm the positive correlation between income equality and economic performance found by Ostry, Berg and Tsangarides(2014). This implies scope for most countries to improve both economic performance and equality.

Turning to political limits, a theory relating to elite capture is the "political-loser hypothesis" (Acemoglu and Robinson 2000b). It predicts that those groups that stand to lose political power from a technological or economic change and have power will block it. Those agents that are economic losers but have no political power cannot prevent the change. Thus, reforms that may be beneficial to many can be resisted by few. Applied to changing an existing redistributive

---

[28] https://www.tony-atkinson.com/the-15-proposals-from-tony-atkinsons-inequality-what-can-be-done/

system, the distribution of political power is important, as well as identifying winners and losers from a proposed reform. Concentrated losses and dispersed benefits are obstacles to reform. Uncertainty about the distribution of gains and losses similarly leads to a status quo bias (Fernandez and Rodrik 1991).

Climate policy brings into sharp relief these issues. Climate change generates significant externalities at the national and global levels, requiring international agreements on mitigation supported by country-level measures. Poorer households and countries, which contribute less to climate change, are most at risk from its effects. Climate change also has important implications for intergenerational equity as climate inaction now adversely affects future generations. Conversely, the costs of climate mitigation will be primarily borne by current generations while its benefits will mostly accrue in the future. Concentrated losses and dispersed benefits, coupled with the short policy horizons of national governments, dampen the effectiveness of collective action at the national and global level.[29] Ideological divides on the science of climate change among political parties seem to play a lesser role in explaining differences in legislative climate action. Fankhauser, Gennaoili, and Collins (2015), for example, find no significant differences in climate legislation between left-wing and right-wing governments, except in a few Anglo-Saxon countries where right-wing governments have affected the passing of climate legislation.

C. Lessons from International Experience

Political feasibility continues to be the biggest obstacle to reforms. In the short run, their distributional consequences can dwarf the expected gains, making them politically costly (Ciminelli et. al 2019; Chen et al. 2019). Thus, in practice, politicians often implement reforms strategically: using crises as windows of opportunity to push through reforms; sequencing reforms to identify winners and losers and implement the easiest ones first; or using divide-and-rule tactics that involve building coalitions with the winners (Roland 2002).

A selective review of country experiences suggests that the careful timing and design of reforms and a good communications strategy can reduce political barriers to reforms:

- *Economic crises can favor reforms, but not always.* An influential study by Alesina and Drazen (1991) modeled economic stabilization as a distributional conflict, explaining delays by a war of attrition between various interest groups. The model implies that crises can help reconcile political views and generate support for reform. Alesina, Ardagna, and Trebbi

---

[29] See, for example, IMF (2019c), "How to mitigate Climate Change," *Fiscal Monitor* (October).

(2006), analyzing inflation and fiscal stabilization, find empirical support for this idea. Subsequent research suggests that there is no systematic evidence on the catalyzing effect of crises: history abounds with examples of crises that spurred reforms and those which did not.[30] Much depends on the effect of the crises on the political equilibrium (Robinson 2009) and the type of reform (Ciminelli et al. 2019). Long-lasting tax reforms, for example, are mostly observed in "good times" (IMF 2013b; Chen et al. 2019), and weak macroeconomic conditions, especially low growth, and high inflation are frequent barriers to energy subsidy reforms (Clements et al. 2013).

• *Adapting the sequence and pace of reforms to the level of social consensus and government commitment can help.* Limited social consensus and government commitment act as powerful barriers to reform, and weak institutions hinder implementation (World Bank 2000). Thus, focusing on delivering only key interventions in periods of low public support and government commitment while laying the groundwork for further reforms and waiting for windows of opportunities can be viable strategies. Elections can create such windows as reforms tend to be less costly early in an incumbent's term (Ciminelli et al. 2019). In the Philippines, for example, the World Bank (2015) notes that the aftermath of the 2010 Presidential elections opened the way for greater focus on poverty and the successful expansion of a pilot conditional cash transfer program.

• *Reforms that include mitigating measures tend to generate more support.* Opposition to reforms can arise from uncertainty about the distributional effects of reforms or low confidence in the ability of the government to protect the most vulnerable. Compensating measures can thus help reduce resistance. In Indonesia, for example, the implementation of fuel subsidy reforms in 2005 and 2008, after unsuccessful previous attempts, was aided by mitigation measures, including an unconditional cash transfer program (Clements et al. 2013). The ability to do so, however, depends on a country's fiscal situation. The bundling of reforms into comprehensive packages can also help the distributional effects from individual measures net out. This was the case for example in Italy's 2014 labor market reform, which combined more flexible employment regulations, increased coverage and duration of unemployment benefit, and more effective active labor market policies (European Commission 2020).

• *Reform design can make a difference.* Some reforms can both reinforce growth and reduce inequality, others involve trade-offs. For instance, fiscal consolidation without increasing inequality has proven to be challenging. A review of 27 fiscal adjustments in advanced and emerging Europe between 2002 and 2007 showed that market inequality typically increased, due to

---

[30] Robinson (2009) and European Commission (2020).

lower output and employment. The composition and pace of the fiscal consolidation determined the effect on disposable income inequality. The increase in inequality was greater when more regressive taxes were raised and progressive spending was cut (IMF 2014). Inequality tends to rise as lower-income groups are disproportionately affected by cuts in social benefits and lower public sector wages. Progressive taxation, protection of social benefits for vulnerable groups, or promoting education and training for low- and middle-income workers, can mitigate these effects (IMF 2013a).

- *Broad public consultations underpinned by a good communications strategy are crucial.* Consultations and communications are no substitute for good policies, but reforms are more likely to be derailed if they are not properly understood or accepted (Stankova 2019). Wide public consultations, supported by clear and transparent communications, are critical to building political cohesion and buy-in for reforms. This is especially important in an environment characterized by low trust in government; hyper-connectedness and increasing expectations about transparency; and widespread fake news. The strategic use of public consultations and communications was a key success factor behind the 2010 Danish tax reform. The reform was announced years in advance, creating time for consultations; a tax commission was established to champion the reform; and public communication was broadly used—including by presenting the tax commission's report live on TV (OECD 2010, Annex A). In Iran, a broad public relations campaign was used to explain that the 2010 subsidy removal aimed to reduce excessive consumption and smuggling and that cash transfers would be introduced to mitigate its impact (Clements et al. 2013; Coady, Parry, and Shang 2018).

D. The Covid-19 Pandemic: A Game Changer?

Before the Covid-19 pandemic, the context for redistributive reform was one in which a series of global forces would further widen economic inequalities. Mckinsey Global Institute (2017) identified six megatrends that would severely test inclusive growth models and the social contract in the European Union: demographics; digital technology, automation, and artificial intelligence (AI); increased global competition; migration; climate change and pollution; and shifting geopolitics. In developing countries, population growth, the dislocating effects of structural transformation, and vulnerability to climate change were seen as threats to the position of lower-income groups.

The Covid-19 crisis has exposed and exacerbated long-standing societal inequities (Case and Deaton 2020). The virus has exacted a heavy toll across the world, in terms of loss of human lives and economic disruptions. Moreover, its impact has fallen disproportionately on lower-income individuals and groups and those whose jobs are less amenable to teleworking (Brussevich, Dabla-Norris, and Khalid 2020). Projections suggest inequities could rise further, with significant increases in the number of people living in poverty (Furceri, Loungani, and Ostry 2020; Sumner, Ortiz-Juarez and Hoy 2020). There is uncertainty about how long-lasting the pandemic's effect will be, however (IMF 2020). Experience with the Great Depression and the Great Recession shows that when governments increased health care and social protection, inequality declined after the initial increase (UN DESA 2020b). Indeed, the response of the public benefits scheme in Spain substantially mitigated the effect of Covid-19 on inequality (Aspachs et al. 2020).

Governments' policy responses are likely to be constrained in many countries by low growth, high government debt, and declining trust in public institutions. The resulting unmet demand or disappointed expectations can compound existing discontent and distrust and fuel social unrest. Nevertheless, this need not be an inevitable outcome. Florini and Sharma (2020) suggest that societal responses to Covid-19, including notably growing attention to the social value and compensation of service workers, provide some indications on how to achieve more resilient polities based on renewed social trust. Many economists have also argued that the recent public discontent could lead to a rethink of capitalism (Collier 2018; Wolf 2020). In turn, this could generate a new consensus about the role of the post-pandemic government and social contracts, in developed and developing economies alike (Acemoglu and Robinson 2019; Buiter 2020; De Bolle 2020; Case and Deaton 2020; Mazzucato and Skidelsky 2020; Rajan 2019).

E. Policy Options

The precise shape of new social contracts will be country-specific, but there are a few common elements. From the growing literature, we identify emerging support for a welfare state that invests in people, stimulates them to be active, and protects them when needed.[31] This necessitates policy interventions in three areas: investing in "local communities"; helping the creation of "good jobs"; and, improving processes of deliberations and communications to rebuild trust in public institutions.

Greater recognition of the limitations of conventional policy tools has led to increasing calls for local solutions. McChrystal et al. (2015), for example, emphasize "empowered self-organization," that is bottom-up, self-organized action by individuals to complement responses of central governments. Rajan (2019) argues that big technological revolutions upset the equilibrium between three

---

[31] http://www.gini-research.org/articles/home

pillars: the political structure (governments); the economic structure (markets and firms); and the sociological or human structure (communities). The resulting anxiety and conflict can lead to populism. The idea that populism may be the response to weakened social ties or solidarity between individuals is also articulated in Collier (2018).

Local communities (neighborhoods, villages, local governments) have a pivotal role to play in providing safety nets to individuals and reducing spatial disparities. Empirical analysis by Boeri et al. (2018), based on European and Latin American Barometer data, provides indirect evidence in support of this hypothesis and highlights the importance of civil society. Rajan (2019) gives the example of Pilsen, an area of Chicago that was once crime and drug-ridden but attracted new residents following revitalization through community efforts. In the United Kingdom, until 2013, the city Preston faced severe challenges of deindustrialization and destitution, but its fortunes improved noticeably when the local city council started investing in local businesses and job creation to fill in the gap for a dwindling private sector.[32] This "inclusive localism'" investing in communities with economically viable opportunities and lowering barriers to entry into those, Rajan suggests, is an alternative to the new populism.

Job creation is another essential ingredient. Gruber and Johnson (2019) argue for the need for massive public investment in breakthrough science outside of the five urban cores or superstar cities in the United States.[33] They suggest that investment in other cities with a high concentration of educated young people, inexpensive housing, short commutes, low crime rates, and strong university science and engineering education can help create industries of the future and support broad-based job creation and growth. Rodrik and Sabel (2019) make a similar call for government intervention to build "a good jobs economy"—increasing overall employment opportunities in the formal sector and providing key labor protection.

Good communication on policies and reforms to the political system that encourages broad participation has also been emphasized. "Multi-layered governance" or "whole-of-society solutions" where policymakers collaborate with experts, the public, and other stakeholders (Florini and Sharma 2020) is especially important at a time of declining trust in public institutions (Stankova 2019).

VI. Conclusion

The interactions between individual preferences, politics, and economics are complex and multifaceted. Disentangling them is important to explain patterns of

---

[32] https://www.theguardian.com/commentisfree/2018/jan/31/preston-hit-rock-bottom-took-back-control?CMP=share_btn_tw

[33] Silicon Valley, the New York City area, Greater Boston, Los Angeles, and Washington, DC.

inequality and redistribution and to inform debates on inclusive growth. The growth that is more equitably distributed and creates opportunities for all is a key ingredient to prevent lasting damage from populist movements (Eichengreen 2018). Evidence suggests that the best-performing countries in terms of economic, employment, social cohesion and equality outcomes have in common a welfare state that invests in people, stimulating and supporting them to be active and adequately protecting them and their children.[34]

A widening of the income distribution is a failure of the political and social systems to protect the already weak position of the low-income shares (Kuznets 1955). People's experience of deprivation matters and these are concrete, not abstract (Piven and Cloward 1993). The core challenge, then, lies in creating a political system where all who benefit from such high social cohesion have a say in shaping it and continue to do so over decades. A big part of this requires education, mobilization, and organization of voters to prioritize their economic interests (Berman 2019).

While there are more open questions than definite answers, part of the way forward is to actively search for solutions that work. Some of those may be local, but they will need to be complemented by policies that favor the creation of "good jobs" and improve deliberations and communications to rebuild trust in public institutions.

References

Acemoglu, Daron. 2020. "Remaking the Post-Covid World." Sixth Richard Goode Lecture. Washington: International Monetary Fund. https://www.imf.org/external/mmedia/view.aspx?vid=6214241193001

Acemoglu, Daron, Georgy Egorov, and Konstantin Sonin. 2013. "A Political Theory of Populism." *The Quarterly Journal of Economics* 128(2): 771–805.

Acemoglu, Daron, Suresh Naidu, Pascual Restrepo, and James A. Robinson. 2015. "Democracy, Redistribution and Inequality." Chapter 21 in *The Handbook of Income Distribution*, Volume 2B: 1885–1966, edited by Anthony Atkinson and Francois Bourguignon. The Netherlands: North-Holland.

Acemoglu, Daron, and James A. Robinson. 2000a. "Why Did the West Extend the Franchise? Democracy, Inequality, and Growth in Historical Perspective." *The Quarterly Journal of Economics* 15(4): 1167–99.

Acemoglu, Daron, and James A. Robinson. 2000b. "Political Losers as a Barrier to Economic Development." *The American Economic Review* 90(2): 126–30.

Acemoglu, Daron, and James A. Robinson. 2013. *Why Nations Fail: The Origins of Power, Prosperity, and Poverty.* New York: Crown Books.

---

[34] http://www.gini-research.org/articles/home

Acemoglu, Daron, and James A. Robinson. 2019. *The Narrow Corridor: States, Societies and The Fate of Liberty*. New York: Penguin Press.

Aghion, Philippe, Reda Cherif and Fuad Hasanov. 2021. "Fair and Inclusive Markets: Why Dynamism Matters." IMF *Working Paper 21/29*. Washington: International Monetary Fund.

Aidt, Toke, Dutta, Jayasri, and Loukoianova, Elena. 2006. "Democracy Comes to Europe: Franchise Extension and Fiscal Outcomes 1830–1938." *European Economic Review* 50(2): 249–83.

Alesina, Alberto, Silvia Ardagna, and Francesco Trebbi. 2006. "Who Adjusts and When? The Political Economy of Reforms." IMF *Staff Papers 53 (Special Issue)*: 1–29. Washington: International Monetary Fund.

Alesina, Alberto, Reza Baqir, and William Easterly. 1999. "Public Goods and Ethnic Division." *The Quarterly Journal of Economics* 114(4): 1243–84.

Alesina, Alberto, and Allan Drazen. 1991. "Why Are Stabilizations Delayed?" *The American Economic Review* 81(5): 1170–88.

Alesina, Alberto, and Edward Glaeser. 2004. *Fighting Poverty in the US and Europe: A World of Difference*. Oxford: Oxford University Press.

Alesina, Alberto, Edward Glaeser, and Bruce I. Sacerdote. 2001. "Why Doesn't the United States Have a European-Style Welfare State?" *Brookings Papers on Economic Activity* 2: 187–254.

Alesina, Alberto, and Paola Giuliano. 2011. "Preferences for Redistribution." In *Handbook of Social Economics* 1: 93–131. Edited by Jess Benhabib, Mattehw O. Jackson and Alberto Bisin. The Netherlands: North-Holland.

Alesina, Alberto, Armando Miano, and Stefanie Stantcheva. 2018. "Immigration and Redistribution." No w24733. *National Bureau of Economic Research*.

Alesina, Alberto, Stefanie Stantcheva, and Edoardo Teso. 2017. "Intergenerational mobility and preferences for redistribution." No w23027. *National Bureau of Economic Research*.

Algan, Yann, Elisabeth Beasley, Daniel Cohen, and Martial Foucault. 2018. "The Rise of Populism and the Collapse of the Left-Right Paradigm: Lessons from the 2017 French Presidential Election," *CEPR Discussion Paper 13,103*.

Amat, Francesc, and Pablo Beramedi. 2020. "Democracy under High Inequality: Capacity, Spending, and Participation." *The Journal of Politics* 82(3): 859–78.

Andersen, Torben M., and Jonas Maibom. 2016. "The Big Trade-Off Between Efficiency and Equity—Is It There?" *CEPR Discussion Paper 11,189*.

Angeles, Luis. 2007. "Income Inequality and Colonialism." *European Economic Review*, Elsevier, 51(5): 1155–76.

Aspachs, Oriol, Ruben Durante, Alberto Graziano, Josep Mestres, Jose G. Montalvo, and Marta Reynal-Querol. 2020. "Real-Time Inequality and the Welfare State in Motion: Evidence from Covid-19 in Spain." *CEPR Discussion Paper 15,118*.

Atkinson, Anthony B. 2015. *Inequality: What Can Be Done?* Cambridge, MA: Harvard University Press.

Bastani, Spencer, and Daniel Waldenström. 2019. "Salience of Inherited Wealth and the Support for Inheritance Taxation," *CEPR Discussion Paper 13,484.*

Benabou, Roland. 2000. "Unequal Societies: Income Distribution and the Social Contract." *American Economic Review* 90(1): 96–129.

Berman, Sheri. 2019. "The Downsides and Dangers of Economic Determinism," Social Europe, September 23, 2019; https://www.socialeurope.eu/the-downsides-and-dangers-of-economic-determinism

Boeri, Tito, Prachi Mishra, Chris Papageorgiou, and Antonio Spilimbergo. 2018. "Populism and Civil Society." *IMF Working Paper 18/245.* Washington: International Monetary Fund.

Bourguignon, François. 2018a. *The Globalization of Inequality.* Princeton, NJ: Princeton University Press.

Bourguignon, François. 2018b. "Spreading the Wealth." *Finance and Development* 55(1): 22–4. https://www.imf.org/external/pubs/ft/fandd/2018/03/pdf/bourguignon.pdf

Brussevich, Mariya, Era Dabla-Norris, and Salma Khalid. 2020. "Who Will Bear the Brunt of Lockdown Policies? Evidence from Tele-workability Measures Across Countries." *IMF Working Paper* 20/88. Washington: International Monetary Fund.

Buiter, Willem H. 2020. "Paying for the Covid-19 pandemic Will Be Painful," *Financial Times*, May 15, 2020.

Bussolo, Maurizio, Ada Ferrer-i-Carbonell, Anna Barbara Giolbas, and Ivan Torre. 2019. "I Perceive Therefore I Demand: The Formation of Inequality Perceptions and Demand for Redistribution," *Policy Research Working Paper Series 8926.* The World Bank.

Cagé, Julia. 2018. *Le prix de la Démocratie.* Paris: Fayard.

Cardoso Eliana, and Ann Hellweger. 1991. "Populism, Profligacy, and Redistribution." Chapter 3 in *The Macroeconomics of Populism in Latin America*, edited by Rudiger Dornbusch and Sebastian Edwards. Chicago: University of Chicago Press, pp. 45–74.

Case, Anne, and Angus Deaton. 2020. "The United States of Despair." Project Syndicate, June 15, 2020.

Causa, Orsetta, and Mikkels Hermansen. 2017. "Income Redistribution through Taxes and Transfers across OECD Countries," OECD Economics Department Working Papers, No. 1453. http://www.ecineq.org/ecineq_paris19/papers_EcineqPSE/paper_154.pdf

Cavaillé, Charlotte, and Jeremy Ferwerda. 2018. "How Distributional Conflict over In-Kind Benefits Generates Support for Anti-Immigrant Parties." Working Paper. Georgetown University.

Cavaillé, Charlotte, and Kris-Stella Trump. 2015. "The Two Facets of Social Policy Preferences." *Journal of Politics* 77(1): 146–60.

Charité, Jimmy, Raymond Fisman, and Ilyana Kuziemko. 2015. "Reference Points and Redistributive Preferences: Experimental Evidence." No. w21009. *National Bureau of Economic Research.*

Chen, Chuling, Era Dabla-Norris, Jay Rappaport, and Alekzandra Zdzienicka. 2019. "Political Costs of Tax-based Consolidations." IMF *Working Paper 19/298*. Washington: International Monetary Fund.

Chin, Moya. 2019. "When Do Politicians Appeal Broadly? The Economic Consequences of Electoral Rules in Brazil." https://scholar.harvard.edu/files/moyachin/files/moyachin_jmp.pdf

Ciminelli, Gabriele, Davide Furceri, Jun Ge, and Jonathan D. Ostry. 2019. "The Political Cost of Reforms." *Staff Discussion Note SDN19/08*. Washington: International Monetary Fund.

Clements, Benedict, David Coady, Stefania Fabrizio, Sanjeev Gupta, Trevor Alleyne, and Carlo Sdralevich. 2013. *Energy Subsidy Reforms: Lessons and Implications.* Washington: International Monetary Fund.

Coady, David, Ian W.H. Parry, and Baoping Shang. 2018. "Energy Price Reform: Lessons for Policymakers." *Review of Environmental Economics and Policy* 12: 197–219.

Collier, Paul. 2018. *The Future of Capitalism: Facing the New Anxieties.* United Kingdom: Allen Lane.

Cruces, Guillermo, Ricardo Perez-Truglia, and Martin Tetaza. 2013. "Biased Perceptions of Income Distribution and Preferences for Redistribution: Evidence from a Survey Experiment." *Journal of Public Economics* 98, Feb. 2013, 100–112.

Dabla-Norris, Era, Kalpana Kochhar, Nujin Suphaphiphat, Frantisek Ricka, and Evridiki Tsounta. 2015. "Causes and Consequences of Income Inequality: A Global Perspective." *Staff Discussion Note SDN15/13*. Washington: International Monetary Fund.

Dahlberg, Matz, Karin Edmark, and Heléne Lundqvist. 2012. "Ethnic Diversity and Preferences for Redistribution." *Journal of Political Economy* 120(1): 41–76.

Dahrendorf, Ralf. 2003. "Acht Anmerkungen zum Populismus." Transit 25. Europäische Revue. Published 18 September 2007. https://www.eurozine.com/acht-anmerkungen-zumpopulismus/

Dal Bó, Ernesto, Fredeico Finan, Olle Folke, Torsten Persson, and Johanna Rickne. 2019. "Economic Loser and Political Winners: Sweden's Radical Right." Working Paper. http://perseus.iies.su.se/~tpers/papers/CompleteDraft190301.pdf

Davoodi, Hamid, Edwin R. Tiongson, E.R., and Sawitree S. Asawanuchit. 2003. "How Useful Are Benefit Incidence Analyses of Public Education and Health Spending?" IMF *Working Paper 03/227*. Washington: International Monetary Fund.

De Bolle, Monica. 2020. "Basic Income Scheme for the Developing World." Financial Times, May 18, 2020.

De Bolle, Monica, and Jeromin Zettelmeyer. 2019. "Measuring the Rise of Economic Nationalism." *Working Paper 19–15*. Washington: Peterson Institute for International Economics.

Dornbusch, Rudiger, and Sebastian Edwards. 1991. "The Macroeconomics of Populism." In *The Macroeconomics of Populism in Latin America*, 7–13. Edited by Rudiger Dornbusch and Sebastian Edwards. Chicago: University of Chicago Press.

Durante, Ruben, Louis Putterman, and Joel van der Weele. 2014. "Preferences for Redistribution and Perception of Fairness: An Experimental Study." *Journal of the European Economic Association* 12(4), August 1, 1059–86.

Edwards, Sebastian. 2019. "On Latin American Populism, and Its Echoes around the World." *Journal of Economic Perspectives* 33(4): 76–99.

Eichengreen, Barry. 2018. *The Populist Temptation: Economic Grievance and Political Reaction in the Modern Era.* New York: Oxford University Press.

Engerman, Stanley L., and Kenneth Sokoloff. 2002. "Factor Endowments, Inequality, and Paths of Development Among New World Economics." No. w9259. *National Bureau of Economic Research.*

Esping-Andersen, Gosta. 1989. "The Three Political Economies of the welfare state." *Canadian Review of Sociology* 26(1): 10–36.

Eurobarometer. 2011. *Europeans and the Crisis.* Special Eurobarometer Report 75.2, European Parliament.

European Commission. 2020. "Understanding the Political Economy of Reforms: Evidence from the EU." Technical note for the Eurogroup (03 September). https://www.consilium.europa.eu/media/45511/ares-2020-4586969_eurogroup-note-on-political-economy-of-reforms.pdf

Fankhauser, Sam, Caterina Gennaioli, and Murray Collins. 2015. "The Political Economy of Passing Climate Change Legislation: Evidence from a Survey." *Global Environmental Change* 35: 52–61

Fernandez, Raquel, and Dani Rodrik. 1991. "Resistance to Reform: Status Quo Bias in the Presence of Individual Specific Uncertainty." *American Economic Review* 81(5): 1146–55.

Finseeras, Henning. 2007. "Voter Turnout, Income Inequality, and Redistribution." Paper prepared for presentation at the ECPR conference in Pisa, September 2007.

Florini, Ann, and Sunil Sharma. 2020. "Reckoning with Systemic Hazards." *Finance and Development* 57(2): 48–51. https://www.imf.org/external/pubs/ft/fandd/2020/06/pdf/reckoning-with-systemic-hazards-florini.pdf

Fong, Christina M., Samuel Bowles, and Herbert Gintis. 2003. "Strong Reciprocity and the Welfare State." In *Handbook on the Economics of Giving, Reciprocity, and Altruism*, Part II, edited by Jean Mercier-Ythier, and Serge Kolm. The Netherlands: North-Holland.

Francese, Maura, and Delphine Prady. 2018. "Universal Basic Income: Debate and Impact Assessment." IMF *Working Paper 18/273*. Washington: International Monetary Fund.

Fujiwara, Thomas. 2015. "Voting Technology, Political Responsiveness, and Infant Health: Evidence from Brazil." *Econometrica* 83(2) (March), 423–64.

Furceri, Davide, Prakash Loungani, and Jonathan D. Ostry. 2020. "How Pandemics Leave the Poor Even Farther Behind." https://blogs.imf.org/2020/05/11/how-pandemics-leave-the-poor-even-farther-behind/

Gennaioli, Nicola, and Guido Tabellini. 2019. "Identity, Beliefs and Political Conflict," https://voxeu.org/article/identity-beliefs-and-political-conflict

Gilens, Martin. 2009. "Preference Gaps and Inequality in Representation." *PS: Political Science and Politics* 42(2): 335–41.

Gilens, Martin, and Benjamin I. Page. 2014. "Testing Theories of American Politics: Elites, Interest Groups, and Average Citizens." *Perspectives on Politics* 12(3): 564–81.

Giuliano, Paola, and Antonio Spilimbergo. 2014. "Growing Up in a Recession: Beliefs and the Macroeconomy." No. w15321. *National Bureau of Research.*

Glaeser, Edward L., Giacomo A.M. Ponzetto, and Jesse M. Shapiro. 2005. "Strategic Extremism: Why Republicans and Democrats Divide on Religious Values." *The Quarterly Journal of Economics* 120(4): 1283–330.

Gruber, Jon, and Simon Johnson. 2019. "Jump-Starting America. Policy summary." https://www.jump-startingamerica.com/policy-summary

Guiso, Luigi, Helios Herrera, Massimo Morelli, and Tommaso Sonno. 2017. "Populism: Demand and Supply." *CEPR Discussion Paper 11,871.*

Hacker, Jacob. 2012. "The Institutional Foundations of Middle-Class Democracy," cited in https://www.theguardian.com/commentisfree/2012/sep/12/ed-miliband-predistribution

Haller, Max, Anja Eder, and Erwin Stolz. 2016. "Ethnic Stratification and Patterns of Income Inequality Around the World: A Cross-National Comparison of 123 Countries, Based on a New Index of Historic Ethnic Exploitation." *Social Indicators Research* 128: 1047–84.

Hills, John, Alari Paulus, Holly Sutherland, and Iva Tasseva. 2014. "A Lost Decade? Decomposing the Effect of 2001–2011 Tax-Benefit Policy Changes on the Income Distribution in EU Countries." *ImPRovE Discussion Paper* No. 14/03, June 2014. http://improve-research.eu/

International Monetary Fund (IMF). 2011. *Regional Economic Outlook: the Middle East and Central Asia.* World Economic and Financial Surveys. Washington, DC.

International Monetary Fund (IMF). 2013a. "Who Let the Gini Out?" *Finance and Development* 50(4): 25–7. https://www.imf.org/external/pubs/ft/fandd/2013/12/furceri.htm

International Monetary Fund (IMF). 2013b. "Taxing Times." *Fiscal Monitor* (October).

International Monetary Fund (IMF). 2014. "Fiscal Policy and Income Inequality." *Policy Paper* (January).

International Monetary Fund (IMF). 2017. "Tacking Inequality." Chapter 1, Fiscal Monitor (October).

International Monetary Fund (IMF). 2018. "Age of Insecurity: Rethinking the Social Contract." *Finance and Development* 55(4): 4–8.

International Monetary Fund (IMF). 2019a. "A Strategy for IMF Engagement on Social Spending." *Policy Paper* No. 19/016.

International Monetary Fund (IMF). 2019b. "Reallocating Public Spending to Reduce Income Inequality: Can It Work? Working Paper.

International Monetary Fund (IMF). 2019c. "How to Mitigate Climate Change." *Fiscal Monitor* (October).

International Monetary Fund (IMF). 2020. "Box 1.2 Inclusiveness in Emerging and Developing Economies and the Impact of Covid-19." *World Economic Outlook* (October).

Inglehart, Ronald, and Pippa Norris. 2016. "Trump, Brexit, and the Rise of Populism: Economic Have-Nots and Cultural Backlash." *HKS Working Paper* No. RWP16-026, Harvard Kennedy School.

Iversen, Torben, and David Soskice. 2006. "Electoral Institutions and the Politics of Coalitions: Why Some Democracies Redistribute More Than Others." *American Political Science Review* 100(2): 165–81.

Johnson, Simon. 2019a. "The Populist Paradox." Project Syndicate. May 31.

Johnson, Simon. 2019b. "Angry Voters Are Easier to Distract." https://www.business-times.com.sg/opinion/angry-voters-are-easier-to-distract

Jones, Charles I. 2019. "Taxing Top Incomes in a World of Ideas." No. w25725. *National Bureau of Economic Research.*

Kaltwasser, Cristóbal Rovira. 2014. "The Responses of Populism to Dahl's Democratic Dilemmas." *Political Studies* 62(3): 470–87.

Karadja, Mounir, Johanna Mollerstrom, and David Seim. 2017. "Richer (and Holier) Than Thou? The Effect of Relative Income Improvements on Demand for Redistribution." *Review of Economics and Statistics* 99(2), May 2017, 201–12.

Kasara, Kimuli, and Pavithra Suryanarayan. 2014. "When Do the Rich Vote Less Than the Poor and Why? Explaining Turnout Inequality across the World." *American Journal of Political Science* 59(3): 613–27.

Kaufman Robert, and Barbara Stallings. 1991. "The Political Economy of Latin American Populism." Chapter 2 in *The Macroeconomics of Populism in Latin America*, 15–43. Edited by Rudiger Dornbusch and Sebastian Edwards. Chicago: University of Chicago Press.

Kenworthy, Lane, and Leslie McCall. 2007. "Inequality, Public Opinion, and Redistribution." *Socio-Economic Review* 6(1): 35–68.

Korpi, Walter, and Joakim Palme. 1998. "The Paradox of Redistribution and Strategies for Equality: Welfare State Institutions, Inequality, and Poverty in Western Countries." *American Sociological Review* 63/5: 661–87.

Kuttner, Robert. 2018. *Can Democracy Survive Global Capitalism.* New York: W.W. Norton & Company.

Kuziemko, Ilyana, Michael I. Norton, Emmanuel Saez, and Stefanie Stantcheva. 2013. "How Elastic Are Preferences for Redistribution? Evidence from Randomized Survey Experiments." No. w18865. *National Bureau of Economic Research.*

Kuznets, Simon. 1955. "Economic Growth and Income Inequality." *The American Economic Review* 45(1): 1–28.

Kyle, Jordan, and Limor Gultchin. 2018. "Populists in Power Around the World. Tony Blair Institute for Global Change." http://institute.global/insight/renewing-centre/populists-power-around-world

Kyle, Jordan, and Yascha Mounk. 2018. "The Populist Harm to Democracy: An Empirical Research." Tony Blair Institute for Global Change. http://institute.global/insight/renewing-centre/populist-harm-democracy

Leibbrandt, Murray, Ingrid Woolard, Arden Finn, and Jonathan Argent. 2010. "Trends in South African Income Distribution and Poverty Since the Fall of Apartheid." OECD Social, Employment and Migration papers, No. 101.

Lindert, Peter H. 2004. *Growing Public: Social Spending and Economic Growth since the Eighteenth Century*. Cambridge: Cambridge University Press.

Lindert, Peter H. 2017. "The Rise and Future of Progressive Redistribution." Commitment to Equity (CEQ) Working Paper Series 73, Tulane University, Department of Economics.

Lustig, Nora. 2017. "Fiscal Policy, Income Redistribution, and Poverty Reduction in Low- and Middle-Income Countries." Tulane University Working Paper 1701.

Mahler, Vincent, David K. Jesuit, and Piotr Paradowski. 2015. "Electoral Turnout and State Redistribution: A Cross-National Study of Fourteen Developed Countries. *Political Research Quarterly* 67(2): 361–73.

Margalit, Yotam. 2013. "Explaining Social Policy Preferences: Evidence from the Great Recession." *American Political Science Review* 107(1): 80–103.

Martén, Linna. 2019. "Demand for Redistribution: Individuals' Responses to Economic Setbacks." *The Scandinavian Journal of Economics* 121(1): 225–42.

Mazzucato, Mariana, and Robert Skidelsky. 2020. "Toward a New Fiscal Constitution." Project Syndicate. July 10, 2020.

McCarthy, Nolan, and Jonas Pontusson. 2011. "The Political Economy of Inequality and Redistribution." Chapter 26 in *The Oxford Handbook of Inequality*, edited by Wiemer Salverda, Brian Nolan and Timothy M. Smeeding. New York: Oxford University Press.

McChrystal, Gen. Stanley, Tantum Collings, David Silverman, and Chris Fussell. 2015. *Team of Teams: New Rules of Engagement for a Complex World*. New York: Portfolio/Penguin.

McKinsey Global Institute. 2017. "Six Global Megatrends Testing the Resilience of Europe's Inclusive Growth Model."

Meltzer, Allan H., and Scott F. Richard. 1981. "A Rational Theory of the Size of Government." *Journal of Political Economy* 89(5): 914–27.

Milanovic, Branko. 1998. "Income, Inequality, and Poverty During the Transition from Planned to the Market Economy." World Bank regional and sectoral studies. World Bank.

Milanovic, Branko. 2017. "The Higher the Inequality, the More Likely We Are to Move Away from Democracy." https://www.theguardian.com/inequality/2017/may/02/higher-inequality-move-away-from-democracy-branko-milanovic-big-data

Mollerström, Johanna. 2016. "Ethnic Fractionalization and the Demand for Redistribution." *Nordic Economic Policy* (1): 219–43.

Morgan, Jana, and Nathan Kelly. 2013. "Market Inequality and Redistribution in Latin America and the Caribbean." *The Journal of Politics* 75(3): 672–85.

Mudde, Cas. 2004. "The Populist Zeitgeist." *Government and Opposition* 39(4): 541–63.

Mukand, Sharun W., and Dani Rodrik. 2019. "The Political Economy of Liberal Democracy." http://j.mp/2oSx0v3

Organisation for Economic Co-operation and Development (OECD). 2010. *Making Reforms Happen: Lessons from OECD Countries.* Paris.

Ostry, Jonathan David, Andrew Berg, and Charalambos G. Tsangarides. 2014. "Redistribution, Inequality, and Growth." *Staff Discussion Note SDN 14/02.* Washington: International Monetary Fund.

Ostry, Jonathan David, Loungani Prakash, and Andrew Berg. 2019. *Confronting Inequality: How Societies Can Choose Inclusive Growth.* New York: Columbia University Press.

Persson, Torsten, and Guido Tabellini. 1999. "The Size and Scope of Government: Comparative Politics with Rational Politicians." *European Economic Review* 43(4–6): 699–735.

Persson, Torsten, and Guido Tabellini. 2000. *Political Economics: Explaining Economic Policy.* Cambridge, MA: MIT Press.

Persson, Torsten, and Guido Tabellini. 2003. *The Economic Effects of Constitutions: What do the Data Say?* Cambridge, MA: MIT Press.

Piketty, Thomas. 2018. "Brahmin Left vs. Merchant Right: Rising Inequality and the Changing Structure of Political Conflict. Evidence from France, Britain and the US, 1948–2017)" WID.world *Working Paper Series 2018/7*, World Inequality Lab.

Piven, Frances F., and Richard Cloward. 1993. *Regulating the Poor: The Functions of Public Welfare.* New York: Vintage Books.

Przeworski, Adam. 2015. "Economic Inequality, Political Inequality, and Redistribution." Draft. Department of Politics. New York University.

Rajan, Raghuram. 2019. *The Third Pillar: How Markets and the State Leave the Community Behind.* U.S.A.: Penguin Press.

Rajan, Raghuram. 2020. "Which Post-Pandemic Government?" Project Syndicate. May 22, 2020.

Ritter, Michael, and Frederick Solt. 2019. "Economic Inequality and Campaign Participation." *Social Science Quarterly* 100(3): 678–88.

Robinson, James A. 2009. "Good Crises? Implications for Developing Countries." https://scholar.harvard.edu/jrobinson/publications/good-crises-implications-developing-countries

Rodrik, Dani. 2019. Concluding Remarks at the Peterson Institute for International Economies' conference on "Combating Inequality: Rethinking Policies to Reduce Inequality in Advanced Economies": 17–18 October. https://www.piie.com/system/files/documents/2019-10-18-s6-rodrik-close-ppt.pdf

Rodrik, Dani, and Charles Sabel. 2019. "Building a Good Jobs Economy." https://drodrik.scholar.harvard.edu/publications/building-good-jobs-economy

Roland, Gérard. 2002. "The Political Economy of Transition." *Journal of Economic Perspectives* 16(1): 29–50.

Rosenthal, Howard. 2004. "Politics, Public Policies, and Inequality: A Look Back at the Twentieth Century." Chapter 23 in *Social Inequality*, edited by Kathryn M. Neckerman. U.S.A.: Russel Sage Foundation.

Roth, Christopher, and Johannes Wohlfart. 2018. "Experienced Inequality and Preferences for Redistribution." *Journal of Public Economics* 167: 251–62.

Sandbu, Martin. 2020. *The Economics of Belonging*. Princeton, NJ: Princeton University Press.

Stankova, Olga. 2019. "Frontiers of Economic Policy Communications." IMF Departmental Paper 19/08. Washington: International Monetary Fund.

Sumner, Andy, Eduardo Ortiz-Juarez, and Chris Hoy. 2020. "Precarity and the Pandemic: Covid-19 and Poverty Incidence, Intensity, and Severity in Developing Countries." WIDER Working Paper 2020/77. Helsinki: UNU-WIDER.

Tabellini, Guido. 2019. "Changing Dimensions of Political Conflicts and the Rise of Populism," Fifth Annual Richard Goode Lecture, International Monetary Fund.

United Nations Department of Economic and Social Affairs (UN DESA). 2020a. World Social Report 2020. Inequality in a Rapidly Changing World. New York: United Nations. https://www.un.org/development/desa/dspd/world-social-report/2020-2.html

United Nations Department of Economic and Social Affairs (UN DESA). 2020b. "Covid-19 Recovery Measures Could Prevent Widening Inequalities due to the Pandemic." https://www.un.org/fr/desa/covid-19-recovery-measures-could-prevent-widening-inequalities-due-pandemic

Weyland, Kurt. 2001. "Clarifying a Contested Concept. Populism in the Study of Latin American Politics." *Comparative Politics*, 34(1).

Wolf, Martin. 2020. "Democracy Will Fail if We Don't Think as Citizens." *Financial Times Series*, July 6, 2020.

World Bank. 2000. "The Effectiveness of the World Bank's Poverty Reduction Strategy: An Evaluation." Washington, DC.

World Bank. 2015. "The Poverty Focus of Country Programs: Lessons from World Bank Experience." Washington, DC.

World Bank. 2017. "World Development Report 2017. Governance and the Law." Washington, DC.

16

Gender Equality

Raquel Fernández, Asel Isakova, Francesco Luna,
and Barbara Rambousek

This chapter is divided into three sections.[1] The first section sets out the current levels of gender inequality that exist across various dimensions worldwide. The second one lists the key drivers and underlying causes of persisting gender gaps, and the final section presents and analyzes examples of policies that have been proposed and implemented to address them. The central argument of the chapter is that sustained and inclusive growth can only be achieved if women, who make up 50 percent of the world's population, are fully able to contribute towards and benefit from the economic gains that are being created. Effective policy measures to promote gender equality need to take into consideration and reflect the specific cultural and social norms of a country as well as its level of economic development.

I. Gender Gaps Persist

Countries around the globe have made considerable progress in narrowing or sometimes closing, gender gaps across many dimensions. For example, female labor force participation and employment have increased and the wage gap relative to men has narrowed globally, lowering gender inequality as shown by the UNDP Gender Inequality Index (GII) (Figure 16.1).[2] This important change reflects many factors, including achievements in education and a growing proportion of women who join and stay in the labor market. However, despite this progress, challenges still persist across all aspects of life.

There is a growing body of literature suggesting that gender equality—in addition to being a moral imperative – has important implications for growth. This is based on a positive association between gender equality and per capita GDP, even

[1] The authors would like to thank Valerie Cerra, Asmaa ElGanainy, and Martin Schindler for their continuous support as well as Barry Eichengreen and participants in the Inclusive Growth book seminar series organized by the IMF Institute for Capacity Development for their poignant comments, plus Jaime Sarmiento for his excellent assistance.
[2] Overall, historical gender gap data tends to be only available for certain countries or specific indicators.

Raquel Fernández, Asel Isakova, Francesco Luna, and Barbara Rambousek, *Gender Equality* In: *How to Achieve Inclusive Growth*. Edited by: Valerie Cerra, Barry Eichengreen, Asmaa El-Ganainy, and Martin Schindler, Oxford University Press.
© Raquel Fernández, Asel Isakova, Francesco Luna, and Barbara Rambousek 2022.
DOI: 10.1093/oso/9780192846938.003.0016

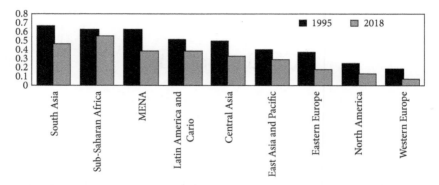

Figure 16.1 Gender Inequality Index[3]

Note: Average by region, with a higher value corresponding to a higher level of gender inequality.

Source: UNDP Gender Inequality Index, regional averages are authors' calculations

though the direction of causality of this association is difficult to ascertain. The argument is that gender inequality in economic participation restricts the pool of talent in the labor market and can lead to a less efficient allocation of resources and, hence, lower GDP growth (Hsieh et al. 2019). At the same time, gender equality can lead to economic gains through greater diversity and complementarity of male and female labor in production as well as sectoral reallocation (Ostry et al. 2018). A resulting higher efficiency and productivity can contribute towards growth also result in better development outcomes (Duflo 2012). Equally important is that improving women's absolute and relative status can help achieve better outcomes for their children (Adato et al. 2000).

II. Understanding the Reasons Behind Gender Gaps

A. Income Inequality, Inequality of Opportunity, and Poverty

The level of gender equality has implications for how incomes are distributed within society. A number of studies look at the relationship between income inequality and economic growth, and some suggest that an unequal income distribution undermines growth (Ostry et al. 2014).

Inequality of income can stem from either the level of effort and choices that a person makes in terms of their education or career or from circumstances at birth, which are beyond their direct control. Inequality of opportunity describes

---

[3] Gender Inequality Index (GII) measures gender inequalities in three aspects of human development: reproductive health (measured by maternal mortality ratio and adolescent birth rates), empowerment (measured by proportion of parliamentary seats occupied by females and proportion of adult females and males aged 25 years and older with at least some secondary education), and economic status (measured by labor force participation rate of female and male populations aged 15 years and older). See http://hdr.undp.org/sites/default/files/hdr2020_technical_notes.pdf.

the share of income inequality that can be attributed to such circumstances, including gender or parental background. According to the EBRD, in countries of Eastern Europe, Central Asia, and the Caucasus region, between 20 and 50 percent of income inequality is due to circumstances at birth. Gender explains between a quarter and a half of the overall inequality of opportunity in these countries (EBRD 2016).

The gender earnings gap directly adds to a country's overall income inequality, while unequal access to education, health services, and financial resources as well as legal barriers result in unequal chances of accessing better jobs and opportunities over the life cycle.

Gender inequality also leads to the greater vulnerability of women to poverty (Nieuwenhuis et al. 2018). Disparities in labor market outcomes are a reflection of lower female labor force participation (Figure 16.2) and lead to gender wage and earnings gaps. Women perform more unpaid care work than men. For women, the existence and number of children and dependents are an important factor that defines their ability to pursue economic activities, especially during their reproductive years (Munoz Boudet et al. 2018). Even in wealthy households, the lack of an own income and economic independence may affect not only the well-being of women but also their lifetime earnings, including more limited access to social security or dedicated pension entitlements later in life (Nieuwenhuis et al. 2018). Furthermore, the majority of single parents are women, with data suggesting an increased risk of poverty for single-parent households, that often only have access to a single income and less access to social protection coverage or childcare support (de Vilhena and Olah 2017). Among widowed, divorced, or separated women, the rate of extreme poverty is twice that for men (UN Women 2020a). Migrant women and older women living alone are also more vulnerable to impoverishment than men in similar types of households. As poverty tends to be

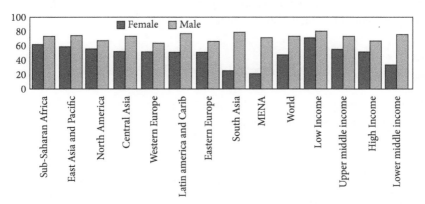

Figure 16.2 Labor Force Participation Rate (in percent)

Note: Population-weighted averages are authors' calculations, except for the world average, data for 2019.

Sources: The World Bank: World Development Indicators: International Labor Organization, ILOSTAT database, authors' calculations.

transmitted from parents to children, targeting gender inequality also has important intergenerational implications (European Parliament 2015). Thus, tackling gender inequalities can have a direct impact on poverty levels.

Finally, women can also be more vulnerable to climate change as they tend to be poorer, less educated, and unable to participate equally in decision-making related to climate change policies and measures (UNDP 2012). It is also harder for women to gain the necessary skills and be able to access new types of jobs that emerge from the transition to a green economy (UNFCCC).[4] Hence, the future is likely to increase poverty levels further if these gender inequalities are not tackled now.

B. Violence Against Women

Domestic violence, largely suffered by women, is recorded in most countries.[5] It is also another possible source of poverty. Violence against women can take many forms, including physical, sexual, verbal, or emotional abuse, reproductive coercion as well as digital or financial abuse. It has a devastating impact on women's physical and mental health, leading to repercussions in their performance in the workplace and on firm productivity (Hess and Del Rosario 2018). A recent survey conducted by the Institute for Women's Policy Research in the US showed that the average financial cost for survivors of domestic violence is over $100,000 for medical and legal expenses—but four times higher for women than for men.[6] Other consequences include interruptions in education, difficulties in obtaining a job (in about 80 percent of the cases), or the loss of a job (in 50 percent of the cases). Most survivors had money "taken" by their partners, which translated into unpaid bills, poor credit scores, and the inability to create financial security. Increasing women's outside options, ranging from easier access to divorce and child support to reducing the gender gap in employment and pay, can help reduce the prevalence of intimate partner violence.[7]

C. Gender Gaps in Labor Market Participation

Women's participation rate in labor markets reflects various factors, including differences in economic development.

---

[4] UNFCCC https://unfccc.int/gender

[5] In some countries, 80 percent of women say that they have experienced physical and/or sexual violence from an intimate partner at some time in their life. See https://data.oecd.org/inequality/violence-against-women.htm.

[6] https://iwpr.org/iwpr-publications/report/dreams-deferred-a-survey-on-the-impact-of-intimate-partner-violence-on-survivors-education-careers-and-economic-security/

[7] For example, in the context of the United States, increased ease of divorce was found to lead to important decreases in intimate partner violence (Stevenson and Wolfers 2006).

There is considerable variation in women's participation in labor markets, nonetheless, within regions and for similar income levels. For example, in Nepal, the participation rate of women in the labor market stands at over 80 percent, while it is only at 26 percent on average in South Asia, the second-lowest in the world.[8] This may be explained by both higher poverty rates and less restrictive social norms in Nepal. Indeed, in Pakistan, another middle-income economy, female labor participation stands at around 22 percent.[9] The analysis of the evolution of women's labor force participation reveals the role of access to modern contraception as an important factor in determining women's economic status. According to Goldin and Katz (2002), the introduction of the contraceptive "pill" in the United States enabled young women to better plan their careers and place a greater emphasis on their professional success, leading to a shift in the occupations they chose and a delay in the age of marriage.

D. Gender Gaps in Health

Healthy lives and the well-being of both men and women are essential in order to achieve growth and sustainable development (SDG3).[10] Still, gender disadvantages in health persist in all regions of the world, with the underlying reasons for the gaps as well as the age profiles of affected women and girls varying. China, India, and Sub-Saharan Africa account for 87 percent of excess female mortality and "missing girls" (World Bank 2012). This phenomenon of missing or unborn girls measured as male-to-female sex ratios at birth is one of the results of sex-selective abortions due to son preference in some regions of the world. The WHO assesses that the natural average global sex ratio at birth stands at 105 males born for every 100 females.[11] In China, this ratio stands at 112.6, in India at 110.[12] Another reason for the gender health gap is the excess mortality of women during their reproductive years, reflecting health issues due to pregnancy or childbirth. In Sub-Saharan Africa, especially in countries with high HIV/AIDS rates, this accounts for 78 percent of overall excess female mortality. Finally, young girls are five times more likely to be affected by child marriage, compared to boys (UNICEF).[13]

Life expectancy at birth is higher for women than it is for men, however, and globally female survival to the age 65 years exceeds that for men. This difference is partly due to biological factors, but also reflects social norms as well as

---

[8] ILOSTAT database; estimates for 2019.
[9] ILOSTAT database; estimates for 2019.
[10] US Sustainable Development Goal 3 https://www.un.org/sustainabledevelopment/health/
[11] World Health Organization, http://origin.searo.who.int/entity/health_situation_trends/data/chi/sex-ratio/en/#:~:text=Population%20sex%20ratio%20(males%20per,males%20for%20every%20,100 percent20females.
[12] World Bank, Sex Ratio at Birth (male births per female births).
[13] https://www.unicef.org/protection/child-marriage

behavioral differences between men and women. According to the WHO, the biological advantage of women is overridden by gender-based discrimination in some regions, notably in parts of Asia, reducing female life expectancy at birth to levels equal to or below that of men.[14]

Women are generally less likely to engage in risky health behavior but make up the majority of victims of sexual abuse and domestic violence. Men are more likely to be victims of traffic accidents. Certain diseases affect only men (prostate cancer) or women (cervical cancer). Women are also more likely to be employed in health care sectors, constituting 70 percent of global health care workers (UNFPA).[15] They shoulder the bulk of care responsibilities for sick family members, which may expose them to a heightened risk of infection during outbreaks of epidemic-prone diseases (such as Covid-19 or Ebola) (The Washington Post, 2014).[16,17] Pregnant women are likely to be especially vulnerable. Taken together, these factors are key to understanding the role of gender in health outcomes.

Increased access to preferred contraception methods can also bring significant health and other benefits to women, beyond being a basic human right. The use of contraception helps reduce health risks related to pregnancy, especially for adolescent girls, and decreases infant mortality rates (WHO 2020). It also offers non-health benefits and strengthens women's agency. A recent study demonstrates that women are more likely to have their demand for modern contraceptive methods satisfied in countries that achieved more gender equality and improved women's education opportunities (Slaymaker et al. 2020).

E. Legal Barriers and Social Norms

Legal barriers and social norms create further barriers for women to access economic opportunities the same way that men do. According to the World Bank "Women, Business and the Law" survey, ninety countries in the world still have at least one restriction on the professions that women can enter and most have no legislation mandating equal remuneration for work of equal value (World Bank 2019). In addition to legal barriers, social norms and attitudes further restrict opportunities for women and girls. According to the OECD Social Institutions and Gender Index (SIGI) report, the role of women across all countries and regions of the world is still often restricted to traditional reproductive and caring responsibilities, and they often face the highest level of discrimination at home (OECD 2019a).

---

[14] WHO https://www.who.int/gho/women_and_health/mortality/situation_trends_life_expectancy/en/
[15] https://www.unfpa.org/news/pandemic-rages-women-and-girls-face-intensified-risks
[16] https://www.unfpa.org/news/pandemic-rages-women-and-girls-face-intensified-risks
[17] https://www.washingtonpost.com/national/health-science/2014/08/14/3e08d0c8-2312-11e4-8593-da634b334390_story.html

The labor force participation and fertility of women are further influenced by their aspirations and expectations. As shown by Fernández and Fogli (2009), married women born in the same country (e.g., the United States) have different degrees of participation in the labor market according to the beliefs that were once prevalent in their parents' country of ancestry, even after controlling for the city in which these women live, their age and education, as well as the age, education, and income of their husband. This shows that neither formal institutions nor underlying economic conditions are sufficient to explain the variation in women's work and fertility choices, highlighting the importance of culture (here transmitted by their parents).

F. Implicit Gender Bias

In addition, prevailing social norms, culture, values, and past experiences form stereotypes and result in implicit, or unconscious, biases against women. Unconscious gender bias is an unintentional (automatic) mental association that leads to a quick assessment of an individual according to their gender. Stereotypes influence expectations about acceptable behavior of women and men. Unconscious bias can impede the advancements of women in their professional careers (Nosek et al. 2009). The UN Gender Social Norm Index (GSNI) estimates that 91 percent of men and 86 percent of women in 75 countries covered by the survey, demonstrate at least one bias against gender equality in areas such as politics, economic, education, intimate partner violence, and women's reproductive rights (UNDP 2020).[18] The ILO's "Women in Business and Management" report finds that gender stereotypes are among the top three barriers to women's leadership together with unpaid care responsibilities and male-dominated corporate cultures (ILO 2015a).

G. Financial Inclusion

Gaps in access to financial services can shape women's entrepreneurship opportunities and labor market participation. Worldwide, only 37 percent of women have a formal bank account compared with 46 percent of men, a difference that is persistent across all income groups in developing countries (Delechat et al. 2018). These gaps also limit entrepreneurship opportunities for women as they restrict women's access to finance and wider economic opportunities. Indeed, studies

---

[18] The GSNI is a social norms index that captures how social beliefs can obstruct gender equality along four dimensions: political, educational, economic and physical integrity. It reflects how prevalent are biases from social norms in these dimensions as well as how are they evolving. It is constructed based on responses to seven questions which are used to create seven indicators. See more http://hdr.undp.org/sites/default/files/frequently_asked_questions_gsni.pdf

highlight the disproportionate barriers for women entrepreneurs to obtain start-up assistance, entrepreneurship training, angel and venture capital investments, and finance to further expand and grow their businesses (Gonzalez et al. 2015).

H. Sectoral Segregation and Type of Work

Data on labor force participation may hide important differences between the type and quality of work performed by men and women as well as their working arrangements. On average, men are more likely to be employed in the production of goods and construction, while women tend to work in social and personal service sectors. Women tend to work part-time, in lower-quality jobs, with less job security and low pay. According to the ILO, women are significantly more likely to be in vulnerable and informal employment in developing countries (ILO 2018a).

Digitalization and changes in the future of work can create further challenges for women. Women tend to perform more repetitive and less analytical tasks even when they perform similar roles to men (Brussevich et al. 2018). In health and public administration—sectors where women are relatively overrepresented, and where jobs are at a lower risk of being automated – women tend to perform more routine tasks and are thus more exposed to potential displacement compared to men in the same sectors. Women are less likely to work on the design and application of new technologies, including artificial intelligence, and are therefore more at risk of remaining behind in the race to take advantage of the associated opportunities.

Women and girls remain underrepresented in science, technology, engineering, and mathematics (STEM) fields and gaps in mathematics and numeracy remain (OECD 2017). Globally, only 35 percent of STEM graduates were women in 2016. Factors determining these choices can have long-term consequences for the economic outcomes of women, including stereotypes about which types of careers are suitable for women or men. Since jobs based on STEM skills tend to be in growing and highly-paid sectors such as computer science or engineering, this difference in choices further exacerbates the persistent global gender pay gap. Additionally, new technology solutions often reflect the needs of men rather than women (for instance, airbags in cars were initially designed based on the physiognomies of adult men).

I. The Glass Ceiling

The "glass ceiling" phenomenon refers to an invisible ceiling blocking the entry of women into leadership positions within firms and organizations. For example, in Japan, gender inequalities in managerial positions are highest among OECD countries (ILO 2015a). There, the disparity in promotions between men and women that cannot be explained by educational level, experience, or other human capital, constituted between 70 and 79 percent in 2009. In Korea, the same unexplained portion of promotion decisions increased from 72 percent to 84 percent between 1990 and 2013 (Yamaguchi and Youm 2020). The glass ceiling effect also persists in other countries, including Sweden (Albrecht et al. 2003). Policies to address these challenges in Japan included a pledge in 2013 that 30 percent of civil service and local government leadership positions would be filled by women by 2020. However, progress has not kept pace with this aspiration, and these goals were reduced to less than half only two years later (Aoki 2015).

J. Unpaid Work

Women perform the bulk of unpaid work globally. The ILO finds that women perform 76.2 percent of total hours of unpaid care work globally, more than three times as much as men (ILO 2018c). In Asia and the Pacific, this rises to 80 percent. Unpaid work includes such care provided for children, the elderly, as well as routine housework, and shopping, representing a large share of economic activity by women which is not factored into GDP calculations. Various methodologies suggest that the estimated value of unpaid activities could range between 11 and up to 66 percent of GDP across G7 economies (OECD 2018). This contribution is only marginally recognized in those countries where the retirement age for women is lower than for men. However, unpaid care work leaves less time for girls and women to spend on education and participate in the formal labor market, thereby further restricting their prospects to access paid work and hence, widening the gender pay gap. Unpaid care can also lead women to engage more in low-paid or informal work to allow them to balance between their unpaid care responsibilities and paid employment. This reduces women's bargaining power and contributes to gender gaps in political participation.

Globally, women lag behind men in relation to political empowerment, as reflected in the low numbers of women in political leadership roles. According to UN Women, fewer than 7 percent of heads of states globally were women in 2020, while the average representation of women in parliaments was only 25 percent (UN Women 2020b).

K. Gender Gaps Across a Woman's Life Cycle

Specific gender gaps throughout different stages of a woman's life are important determinants to shape policy solutions (UNDP 2018). At the early stages of life, educational enrollment and the proportion of girls in STEM programs should be considered to provide equal opportunities for girls and boys. Adulthood and, in particular, the start of parenthood represents the stage when gender gaps are widening, especially in relation to economic participation rates. During the reproductive

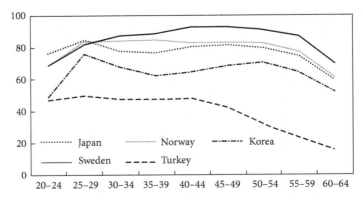

Figure 16.3 Age-employment Profiles for Women (in percent)

Note: Estimates for 2019.

Source: International Labor Organization. "Employment by sex and age — ILO modelled estimates." ILOSTAT. Accessed 14-02-2020. https://ilostat.ilo.org/data.

years, the labor force participation of women declines, reflecting a substantial and continuing "child penalty." In Japan and Korea, the age-employment profile of women exhibits an M-shaped line, showing a drop in labor force participation during the time when women have children (Figure 16.3). This coincides with a critical stage of career development and can therefore have a long-term impact on the professional development. The resulting drop in lifetime earnings can range from 21 to 26 percent for mothers in Scandinavian countries to 51 to 61 percent in Austria and Germany, whilst earnings of fathers remain virtually unchanged (Kleven et al. 2019).

L. The Gender Gap in Pensions

The inequalities that women face over the course of their lives, such as interrupted careers, part-time jobs, or early withdrawals from the labor force, results in lower lifetime earnings and a larger gender pension gap. Women tend to live longer but are less likely to have a pension: 10 percent more men receive a pension than women (UNDP).[19] When women do receive a pension, it is likely to be smaller than that of men. According to EIGE, the gender gap in pensions exceeded the overall gender pay gap and stood at around 37 percent across EU member states in 2018. The pensions gap was similar or above 40 percent across six EU countries and below 10 percent in only three member states (EIGE 2019). Estimating the gender pension gap for emerging market economies and developing countries is not always possible due to a lack of data. According to UNDP, only six out of 41 countries with low Human Development Index rankings report pension data. In these countries, 17 percent of men and 11 percent of women have access to

[19] http://hdr.undp.org/en/content/closing-gender-gaps-throughout-life-course

pensions, and women typically receive a smaller pension compared to men (UNDP).[20] Since women tend to accumulate fewer savings than men over their lifetimes, they are also more vulnerable to poverty in their retirement (WEF 2018).

M. Gender-Relevant Data

A key challenge for tackling gender inequality is the lack of gender-relevant data, without which governments and companies struggle to assess the differential needs and the impact of policies on men and women. This applies to macroeconomic measures and infrastructure planning, education and labor market regulations as well as health and safety policies. Moreover, a lack of women in leadership positions can shape the type of decisions that are taken by governments and enterprises. Perez (2019) explores the critical role of sex-disaggregated data gaps and biases in affecting the potential for women's economic and social advancement. Importantly, macroeconomic policy experience highlights that quality-driven data collection leads to analytical and policy reforms that exceed the initial costs of the data collection. The World Bank is spearheading these efforts through the introduction of its Gender Data Portal (http://datatopics.worldbank.org/gender/), a comprehensive source of sex-disaggregated data and gender statistics covering demography, education, health, labor participation, economic opportunities, public life and decision-making, and agency. Data2X is another leading gender data resource platform established by UN agencies, governments, civil society, academics, and the private sector.

N. Focus on Gender Data Enhancing Financial Inclusion of Women in Egypt

The promotion of a gender-inclusive financial system that addresses the specific needs of women is an important policy aim of the Central Bank of Egypt (CBE). Guidelines to banks require the collection and reporting of gender-disaggregated data to track the progress of women's financial inclusion and map relevant demand and supply-side data. Together with the Alliance for Financial Inclusion (AFI) and Data2X, a gender data platform, the CBE is building a national sex-disaggregated supply-side data collection framework.[21]

In addition, the CBE strengthened financial consumer protection regulations, enhanced awareness of and access to financial literacy programs

---

[20] In http://hdr.undp.org/en/content/closing-gender-gaps-throughout-life-course
[21] https://data2x.org/about-us/

through the Egyptian Banking Institute (EBI), and invested in enhanced digital financial infrastructure to capitalize on increasing mobile phone ownership rates, including amongst women. The CBE is also co-leading AFI's Financial Inclusion Data (FID) Working Group. It analyses data and indicator definitions, develops adequate data collection methodologies, advises on objective policy targeting, and guides data analysis to enable evidence-based financial inclusion policymaking and regulation.[22]

III. Policies to Close Gender Gaps

The third section of this chapter reviews policy proposals designed to reduce or eliminate gender gaps in order to achieve enhanced economic benefits.[23]

Which tools are best employed to address the gender gap in its many dimensions? In large part, the solution cannot abstract from the need for a cultural revolution to enfranchise women from their traditional roles as mothers and caregivers and extol those qualities in men. There are, however, many instruments that can help in that transition. The first section reviews fiscal policies starting from gender-sensitive Public Financial Management practices then addresses taxes and finally expenditures. The second one is devoted to more general structural reforms. It focuses on reforms of the legal framework to protect the safety of women at home and their rights to education, to abolish discriminatory laws in terms of inheritance, access to jobs and careers, and to promote financial inclusion for women.

A. Fiscal Policy

Gender Budgeting and Public Financial Management (PFM) Reforms
In broad terms, gender budgeting is a way to commit a government explicitly to "weigh the benefits and costs of policies that would promote gender equality" (Stotsky 2016). Not just explicit measures (i.e., taxes or specific expenditures), but also procedures in the budget cycle affect the gender gap and can be designed to address and help correct existing biases. The goal is to amplify women's voices in the political discussion and guarantee that fair action is taken in response to such cost-benefit evaluations. This is done in the context of enhancing overall equality

---

[22] https://www.afi-global.org/publications/2330/Financial-Inclusion-Data-FID-Working-Group-factsheet

[23] Case studies include Holmes et al. (2014) for fragile states, Stotsky et al. (2016) for sub-Saharan Africa, Chakraborty (2016) for Asia, IMF (2017b) for G7 countries, and OECD (2017) for OECD members and a few non-OECD countries.

rather than disadvantaging boys and men. It is also set to correct any recognized discrimination against lesbian, gay, bisexual, transgender, intersex, and questioning (LGBTIQ) and other communities. Indeed, the Canadian Government's Gender Budget Statement, introduced in 2017, includes a gender-based analysis that covers factors such as ethnicity, age, income and sexual orientation to be considered in public policy making in association with gender (IMF 2017b).

However, it is not always obvious how to put these ideas into practice. As Welham (2018) points out, "gender budgeting" could imply that (i) public services programs should be *equally accessed* by men and women; or (ii) that *equal amounts* of public spending are spent on men and women, or even that *public spending should be biased* in favor of women and girls. Or perhaps, (iii) that it should require the *identification of specific "women and girls" spending programs* and the allocation of more funding in their favor. This latest option seems the one pursued more often.

Public Financial Management (PFM) procedures can be devised to give due attention to gender issues at each stage of the budget process. They contribute to operationalizing gender-responsive fiscal policies. The first step occurs at the setting of policy goals and targets, then in the actual preparation of the budget law, to be followed up in the control and execution stage, the preparation of the reports, and finally with the independent ex-post audit of the budget.

For example, with the goal of supporting women's labor participation, a cost-benefit analysis of a "universal childcare" option (like in Denmark) could be compared with a "universal child benefit" (like the one in the UK). Once the choice has been made taking into consideration budget constraints and relative pros and cons, attention to gender issues continue at each step. In the case of the UK, which opted for the "universal child benefit," the measure, it was argued, reaches all households irrespective of income or employment status. At the policy goal level, several aspects were considered: (i) it benefits women who, in general, are the primary child care givers; (ii) does not seem to affect labor market participation since it is not based on employment status; but (iii) it may incentivize the traditional role of women making it less attractive to look for a job or a more remunerative one. In the preparation of the specific law, attention should be paid in the text, for example, to how "household" is defined, to make sure that single-parent families (predominantly with single mothers) are included without any limitation. At the control stage, what ministry is going to be in charge? The Ministry for Children and Family? The Ministry of Labor? How are the benefits going to be paid? Do all households have access to the payment instruments or are women negatively affected as they may have less access to a bank account (for example)? Are the reports transparent about the portion of eligible households that have been reached? How well-publicized are these reports? Finally, the audit process should point at any irregularities that have impacted single mothers (or women in general).

Numerous tools and practices have been designed to support gender-focused PFM. In 2017, the IMF organized a survey among OECD countries to assess the adoption of these measures. The results indicated that Austria and Spain in particular have introduced many of these tools and practices and should be taken as an example by G7 countries.[24]

Revenue Policies for Gender Equality

The more recent literature on gender biases focuses on the expenditure side of fiscal policies. However, some explicit discriminations were part of tax laws of European countries until recently and some implicit ones still exist.[25] Clearly, the first step in designing effective reforms is the study of the specific tax code to identify the explicit and implicit biases in it.

Gender Analysis of Tax Policy

Stotsky (1996) contains many examples of explicit and implicit discrimination with direct and potential economic effects. Clearly, correcting explicit biases is the obvious starting point. Explicit discrimination with only potential/indirect economic adverse consequences is the case of the UK, prior to the 1990 reform: all property income was attributed to the husband if the married couple filed separately (see for example Andrienko et al. 2014). In case of divorce or marriage dissolution, the asset attribution could be contentious. This problem is still relevant for land ownership in Latin America as we will see below.

Examples of explicit discrimination with direct economic consequences were found in South Africa until 1995 where a married woman would pay a higher tax rate than a married man, and still in Morocco, where a man is granted a tax deduction if married with children, but a woman will be given the same deduction only if she can prove to be the children's legal guardian.

Due to various reasons documented in previous sections of this chapter, women tend to be the secondary earner in most households. According to the most recent Global Wage Report 2018/2019, the average wage gap is still about 20 percent (ILO 2018b). This implies that in countries that tax incomes at the household level or pooled among spouses, the lower or secondary income earner is effectively taxed at a higher marginal rate unless the rate is flat for all income levels.

However, as noted in Stotsky (2017), a reduction in progressivity (suggested in many countries under the banner of "flat tax" as a way to simplify the system), is most likely to translate into an increased gender bias if designed to maintain the same overall budget revenue. Indeed, the less wealthy part of taxpayers—and women earners are mostly in this category—will have to bear a larger portion of

---

[24] It would be too long to list the sets of all indicators and tools surveyed. We invite the interested reader to consult the full survey description and results in IMF 2017.

[25] See for example the analysis of the taxation of household's income proposed by Andrienko et al. (2014).

the collection. It is, obviously, a political decision how to "share" the tax burden, but there are various methods to alleviate the progressivity effect on second earners. In particular, in the United States and other countries, it is possible for each spouse to file separately hence avoiding the cumulation of income and higher marginal tax brackets. In other cases, a couple filing jointly obtains an automatic standard deduction that is larger than twice the deduction allowed for a single filer.

As for indirect taxes like VAT and excises, there is theoretically no explicit bias. However, different VAT rates on products typically consumed by women may indeed result in biases.[26] As reported also by the OECD, "women in developing countries tend to purchase more goods and services that promote health, education, and nutrition compared to men. This creates the potential for women to bear a larger VAT burden if the VAT system does not provide for exemptions, reduced rates, or zero-rating."[27]

Enhanced Public Education on the Revenue System

The government can and should play an essential role in disseminating information on revenue policy, on how taxes are calculated and levied. The process may employ different channels in order to reach men and women: where women represent a large part of the television audience, for example, instructional TV programs tend to be effective. In India, the government's and NGOs' efforts to educate women are often thwarted by the physical distance between the rural areas and the institutions (banks, insurance companies, post offices) that provide the instruction.[28] However, the increased availability of mobile technology is promising and should be harnessed to support these initiatives.

Methods for Tax Collection

Revenue collections procedures can be improved to ensure fair treatment of female taxpayers that often (especially, but not exclusively in developing countries) are harassed by tax collecting agents.

Methods for Payments of Social Transfers

As women tend to be un-banked or under-banked in some parts of the world, it has been shown that social transfer payment procedures that are not based on

---

[26] On January 15, 2019 the EU parliament issued a report inviting member countries to adopt a 0 percent VAT rate on feminine hygiene products such sanitary towels and tampons. Indeed "VAT (the Value Added Tax), [...] does not take into consideration women's specific consumption patterns. The most common example is feminine hygiene products [...], but there are also other goods and services that women consume more than men and which promote "health, education, and nutrition." See https://www.forbes.com/sites/anagarciavaldivia/2019/01/16/fiscal-justice-for-women-the-european-parliament-encourage-individual-taxation-to-fight-gender-bias/#2b8e27856ab7

[27] https://www.oecd.org/dac/gender-development/44896295.pdf

[28] See https://savvywomen.tomorrowmakers.com/wise/how-financial-literacy-can-empower-women-develop-financial-identity-expert-article

cash payments—for example based on the mobile network—can have a wider beneficial impact.[29]

Gender-Related Public Expenditures

Gender-related public expenditure management (GRPEM) is sometimes referred to as "gender-responsive budgeting" (GRB). Following Welham et al. (2018) these expenditures can be classified as:

Gender-Related Equal Opportunities Programs

These typically focus on support for mothers' parental leave, subsidized childcare to allow women labor participation, and help for victims of domestic abuse.[30] In addition, they often include campaigns to increase public awareness and change traditional behavior to foster gender equality.

General Public Services Targeted at or Mostly Used by Women

These can include health programs for pregnant women or for psychological support to new mothers. In other cases, general programs may have a particularly strong impact on women like those focused on education or directed at the support for female entrepreneurship: the experience with micro-finance in South Asia is of course emblematic and some studies seem to confirm that microfinance directed at women entrepreneurs may have positive effects on reducing gender inequality when the cultural environment welcomes (or is not hostile to) a woman's active economic role. Hence, according to Zhang and Posso (2017), microfinance in Ghana appears more effective than in Bangladesh.

"Gender-Blind" Public Services/Policies

Even when considered gender-neutral or "blind," certain programs may result in entrenching gender inequality or possibly even exacerbating it. Gender budgeting insists on the need for a full examination of the effects of all policy measures.[31] An example of "not-so-blind" policies is provided by OXFAM (2019) in its analysis of the policies pursued after the food crisis of 2008 in rural Africa. A combination of export bans and investments that "mostly targeted staple grain productivity, rather than horticulture crops that could boost the livelihoods, food security and nutrition of smallholders, particularly women" had the effect of benefiting market-ready farmers, usually men.

---

[29] The role of financial inclusion is covered in Chapter 4.

[30] The important role of paid parental leave for fathers is addressed below.

[31] The report *The Gendered Impact of IMF Policies in MENA*, prepared for OXFAM by Abdo (2019) demonstrates that the reduction of fuel subsidies—a generally welcome and encouraged measure—ended up increasing the price of cooking oil hence having a negative impact on women.

Further Complexity in Low-Capacity Countries

Although many of the factors affecting the gender gap are common to all countries at every level of development, they are even more pronounced in low-capacity countries. In such contexts, social norms and cultural obstacles are coupled with what is perceived as a more stringent use of scarce resources. The literature has identified such factors as limited resources and economic uncertainty, the political economy of public expenditure, and competing budget reform objectives.

B. Structural Policies

Structural reforms are particularly difficult to implement as the institutions that they target are often the result of long-standing social norms and cultural beliefs. These though can change sometimes rapidly, responding to incentives, institutional changes, and the diffusion of information and revised beliefs.[32]

Legal Framework

Explicit gender discrimination can be addressed by a change in the legislative framework. *De facto*, the results may not be immediate as the enforcement may be lacking, but in many cases, this is nonetheless a powerful step in triggering a cultural evolution of social norms. The "Legislation online" web portal, offers a wealth of law on gender-related issues organized by international organizations and by country.[33]

The OECD's SIGI Global Report (2019) recommends that governments take actions across three dimensions:[34]

 i. *Translate international conventions into national legal frameworks.* This would abolish discriminatory laws, notably on women's workplace rights and reproductive autonomy.
 ii. *Implement laws more forcefully [...], while inviting community leaders and citizens to join in publicly recognizing the discriminatory nature of harmful norms and practices.*
 iii. *Report publicly and regularly on progress towards gender equality, even when objectives are not met.*

---

[32] See Fernández (2013) for a calibrated model of the evolution of social beliefs about married women's labor force participation. She shows how beliefs respond at different rates leading to periods of rapid social change.

[33] https://www.legislationline.org/topics/topic/7

[34] OECD Social Institutions and Gender Index, 2019.

Historically, reforms expanding women's rights and legal protection have been associated with greater female labor force participation, women's greater movement out of agricultural employment, larger shares of women in wage employment, lower adolescent fertility, lower maternal and infant mortality, and higher education enrollment among girls. Furthermore, such correlation was the strongest for lower-income countries (Hallward-Driemeier, Hasan, and Bogdana Rusu 2013; Markus and Harper 2014). Education and awareness campaigns as well as sensitization of the population can help legal reform bring more benefits (ODI 2015).

Explicit Legal Provisions to Protect Women
There are several macroscopic improvements in the legal provisions that have been recently introduced in many countries and should become pervasive and more stringent for the positive repercussions they appear to have on the gender gap.

Sakhonchik et al. (2015) stressed the importance of the following actions in those areas of the world where these problems are still present:

i. *Increase in the minimum legal age to marry.* Effects include, for example, a higher secondary enrolment of girls of almost 15 percentage points. Furthermore, female employment in relation to population is almost twice as high (at 50 percent).
ii. *Punish marital rape.*
iii. *Punish domestic violence.* In countries where domestic violence is punished, the women mortality rate is significantly lower and, for children under 5 years of age, the mortality rate is lower than one half.

Access to Justice
Lack of access and unequal treatment by the justice system undermines women's legal capacities as well as the distribution of resources, especially when economic rights are at stake. The justice system is therefore a vital component of smooth business operations, with implications for enforcing contracts, opening and closing businesses, resolving employment disputes, and upholding the rights of women.

Focus on the Access to Justice for Women Entrepreneurs in Jordan
Women entrepreneurs in Jordan often lack awareness about their legal rights, how to access legal advice, or the costs and risks involved. According to findings by the European Bank for Reconstruction and Development (EBRD), the International Development Law Organization (IDLO), and the Centre for Women's Studies at the University of Jordan,

these challenges are exacerbated by a low degree of gender sensitivity among justice actors, leading to unintended biased decisions that can adversely affect women-owned businesses.[35]

Policy responses need to focus on the capacity building of actors across the judiciary system (including judges, prosecutors, mediators, and bar associations) and the development of legal aid on civil and family matters. Furthermore, selection processes within the judicial system need to be transparent and open to all, with a focus on promoting career advancement for women to top-level positions in the sector. Thirdly, the use of mediation in commercial disputes needs to be strengthened and the availability and quality of legal aid services enhanced.[36] *The affordability of legal representation should be improved and legal awareness training offered to women entrepreneurs. More equitable gender composition of legal professionals is key, requiring the active promotion of legal careers to influence the educational and career choices of women.*[37]

The Recent Wave of Legal Reforms

Several reforms have been implemented along the lines indicated above, especially among developing countries. G7 and other advanced economies, where many types of disparities were corrected or reduced during the final decades of the twentieth century, are now focusing more on PFM and implicit bias.

Frameworks for Land Tenure

In several countries, inheritance laws favor male children (World Bank).[38] Deere and Leon (2003) report on the situation in Latin America. There, the recent introductions of i) the legal figure of dual-headed household; ii) partible inheritance; and iii) mandatory joint titling of land for married couples have much improved the previous legal provisions that would assign all non-labor income to the husband as well as the de facto management of the property. In addition, thanks to growing literacy rates, women have become more aware of their rights as widows or daughters.

Nevertheless, even where the path to land ownership through inheritance has improved, the gender gap tends to persist as "market acquisition" of property is still biased in favor of men. In many countries, it is, therefore, necessary to

---

[35] https://www.idlo.int/sites/default/files/pdfs/publications/report-we_atoj-jordan-final.pdf
[36] https://www.idlo.int/sites/default/files/pdfs/publications/report-we_atoj-jordan-final.pdf
[37] Chile, for example, created a Working Group on Gender Issues composed of members of the judiciary as well as ministers, judges and trade union representatives. The Working Group analyses and evaluates gender-based discrimination in the exercise of jurisdictional activity as well as identifying gender mainstreaming objectives in the judiciary (OECD 2019b).
[38] See https://blogs.worldbank.org/opendata/where-world-do-women-still-face-legal-barriers-own-and-administer-assets

introduce pro-active measures to guarantee equal access to financial resources: access to credit is essential especially for poor rural households, typically headed by women.

Labor Market Policies

Due to its positive impact on women's bargaining positions within the family, increasing labor force participation among married women can potentially lead to changes in public policies as well as to a gradual deconstruction of traditional gender roles in the sharing of caring work (Korpi 2000).

Numerous gender gaps can be reduced by improving labor market conditions for women. It is necessary not only to guarantee equal access to the labor market but also to obtain equal pay.

The "wage gap" was already the focus of the Equal Remuneration Convention promoted by the ILO in 1951.[39] Not long after that, in 1958, the ILO organized a Convention on Discrimination (Employment and Occupation).[40]

The recent global recession and the subsequent recovery have provided further support to the perception that the link between growth and employment has become more tenuous. The consensus is now that policies to promote growth must be explicitly designed to foster employment. An integrated approach to development is necessary and the design of National Employment Policies (NEP) is recommended to make explicit the importance of job creation in the desired economic growth path.

In this context, the ILO "Resource Guide on Gender Issues in Employment and Labor Market Policies" (2014), contains a number of explicit recommendations to overcome the gender disadvantage in the labor force. Active Labor Market Policies (ALMPs) have a greater positive effect on the employment of women compared to men (Bergemann and van der Berg 2008). These policies include support for the unemployed by creating and financing institutions that provide training and help with job search, subsidies for taking up jobs, and job-creation initiatives in the local communities.[41] The ALMPs are typically integrated with "passive" labor market policies like unemployment benefits so as to promote re-entry into the labor market, especially for women after interruptions due to childbirth and child-rearing (Auer et al. 2008). Other measures specifically targeted at reducing the labor market participation gap include family benefits, (e.g., paid parental

---

[39] https://www.ilo.org/dyn/normlex/en/f?p=NORMLEXPUB:12100:0::NO::P12100_ILO_CODE:C100

[40] https://www.ilo.org/dyn/normlex/en/f?p=NORMLEXPUB:12100:0::NO::P12100_ILO_CODE:C111

[41] The Austrian program "Frauen in Handwerk und Technik FiT" that offers certified apprentice-ships, technical vocational schools and universities of applied science in non-traditional professions has been particularly successful according to subsequent surveys.

leave), subsidized childcare, and subsidies to businesses to encourage the hiring of women.

On the revenue side, typical policies encompass tax benefits to promote the supply of labor, tax reliefs on the household's second or single earner. Indeed, as stressed in OECD's study on 30 countries over 1980–2007, women's labor participation is still discouraged by high taxes on household's secondary earners (OECD 2012).

Labor participation and type of employment are affected by globalization and trade liberalization/export-promotion. Women are heavily employed in the textile and apparel sectors that are entry industries for poor countries undergoing export-oriented industrialization. Working in a textile factory and in other assembly operations is presumably a step up from rural agriculture and household work. Furthermore, as mentioned in Chapter 7 of this book, women in open, export-oriented economies, on average, enjoy better-paid jobs, are in school for more years, while the overall wage gap is smaller. At the same time, many of these jobs are repetitive, strenuous, and prone to be automatized as robots are introduced in the production chain.

Automation and artificial intelligence present potential benefits and challenges. Flexible and remote working based on enhanced Internet connectivity and ICT skills can open up global markets for women across divides of social norms and geography. Job portals and Internet platforms can assist in enhancing access to markets for micro-businesses, but these contractual workers' rights must be well protected.[42] According to some studies, female workers face a higher risk of automation compared to male workers. Less well-educated, and older female workers (aged 40 and above), as well as those in low-skills clerical, service, and sales positions are disproportionately exposed to automation. According to the IMF, globally, 180 million jobs that are mostly held by women are at risk (Brussevich et al. 2018). Policy responses focus on enhanced access to ICT connectivity and skills, a stronger focus on lifelong learning, particularly for lower-skilled women in the workforce, the introduction of regulation of digital jobs platforms, and the use of artificial intelligence.

Value Domestic Activities as Unpaid Work
Wage gaps are linked to the disregard of the rights of and contributions made by unpaid domestic work. For most households in poor countries and for a large part also in advanced economies, outsourcing unpaid care activities, such as cooking, cleaning, or fetching water is simply not an affordable option. As mentioned above, the burden of performing these tasks continues to fall predominantly on women in these households, reducing their time for education or economic activity and substantially reducing their lifetime earnings. There are various factors

---

[42] An interesting case is that of Kenya: https://www.un.org/africarenewal/magazine/april-2019-july-2019/technology-liberating-force-african-women

behind the unequal distribution of unpaid care work between women and men. For example, Ferrant et al. (2014) conclude that culturally engrained "gender inequality in unpaid care work is the missing link in the analysis of gender gaps" affecting labor force participation, quality of employment, and wages. Lack of appropriate infrastructure and public services or family policies (e.g., paternity leave), as well as legal institutions, also influence the burden of unpaid work borne by girls and women. There are various policy measures that could help effectively address this important issue.

Reduce the Burden of Care and Domestic Work

The reduction of the unpaid burden of caregiving and domestic work may translate into a boost for economic growth. According to a study by De Henau et al. (2016) for the UK Women's Budget Group, the impact of investing 2 percent of GDP in public provision of childcare and elder care services in seven OECD countries would have a significantly larger growth impact than an equally sized investment in construction. For the US, for example, such an investment would create 13 million new jobs, most of which would be taken by women.

Redistribute These Tasks More Equally Between Men and Women

In some economically more developed countries that Korpi (2000) defines as "dual-earner" welfare states, the desire on the part of men to get involved in the care of children and family members is growing.[43] Hence, on the path to gender equality, social norms will record a progressively more even distribution of these tasks.

Measures to encourage such a process have been implemented and move along two parallel routes. The first one is a substantial investment in household-related infrastructure like day-care facilities and nursing homes for the elderly.[44] The second is the provision of tax-funded paid parental leave for fathers or male carers. To be effective, parental leave needs to be well paid, sufficiently long in duration (i.e., somewhat longer period than 5 days for fathers or male carers compared to 98 days for mothers or female carers) (Figure 16.4), and non-transferable. This latter aspect is important. For example, in Denmark (one of the countries with the highest score in gender equality) "only" 24 percent of fathers or male carers take parental leave, which is otherwise transferred to mothers or female carers, while in Sweden, where paternal leave is "use it or lose it," for the first three months, 90 percent of fathers use it (OECD 2016).[45]

---

[43] An extended coverage of these aspects is offered in Elson (2017).

[44] It is noteworthy that in Denmark the wage gap (on average) at less than 10 percent is one of the lowest among OECD countries, child care provision is the responsibility of local government, and all children, starting from 6 months of age are entitled to a full-time place and fees are related to the earnings of parents.

[45] https://www.oecd.org/els/family/Backgrounder-fathers-use-of-leave.pdf. https://www.washingtonpost.com/lifestyle/2019/09/07/what-would-parenting-be-like-if-fathers-took-six-months-parental-leave-take-look/

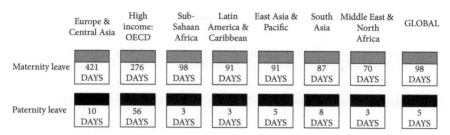

	Europe & Central Asia	High income: OECD	Sub-Sahaan Africa	Latin America & Caribbean	East Asia & Pacific	South Asia	Middle East & North Africa	GLOBAL
Maternity leave	421 DAYS	276 DAYS	98 DAYS	91 DAYS	91 DAYS	87 DAYS	70 DAYS	98 DAYS
Paternity leave	10 DAYS	56 DAYS	3 DAYS	3 DAYS	5 DAYS	8 DAYS	3 DAYS	5 DAYS

Figure 16.4 Parental Leave According to Women Business and the Law Database

Note: Maternity leave refers to the sum of paid maternal leave and paid parental leave, excluding any parental leave specifically reserved for fathers. Paternity leave refers to the sum of paid paternity leave and any paid parental leave specifically reserved for fathers. of the econromes covered, 184 guarantee at least one day of maternity leave and 105 guarantee at least one day of paternity leave.

Source: Women, Business and the Law databse.

Education, Training, and Skills

Promoting the accumulation of women's human capital helps to close gender gaps.[46] Legal and financial literacy plays an essential role in reducing asset owner-ship and wage gaps. In general, budget expenditures in education narrow the edu-cation gap (Jain-Chandra et al. 2018). In many cases vocational training is supply-driven: it focuses on activities and sectors where women tend to be over-represented and therefore contributes little towards eliminating gender gaps. To break occupational segregation, it is necessary to diversify the educational choices women make—and the opportunities that they see—towards subjects that tend to attract fewer numbers of female students (including STEM). This requires tar-geted education and skills policies that start at the early years' stage and continue throughout primary, secondary, and tertiary education. They are critical to help-ing social norms shape the educational decisions that girls and young women take.

The cooperation between education authorities and employers is paramount. Public-private sector partnerships can provide female role models from indus-tries where women are underrepresented, improve the quality and relevance of career advice and guidance, as well as introduce better work-based learning mod-els (such as apprenticeships, traineeships, or similar) to smooth school to work transition, especially in STEM areas.

Focus on Enhancing Women Employment in Central Asia

In Kazakhstan, the Commission for Families, Demographics, and Gender,
the Ministries for Labor and Education established close cooperation

---

[46] Hui (2011) links the increase in the numbers of women in the United States obtaining a college education in the last five decades with the rise in the college wage premium. Clearly it is not possible to ascertain the causation direction, but the finding is suggestive of the synergies between economic and social norms development.

with the private sector via the Foreign Investment Council (i) to introduce better career guidance and progression routes from STEM education / vocational training into jobs for women and young people, specifically in the Power & Energy and Natural Resources Sectors where women continue to be underrepresented in technical and higher-paid roles, (ii) to enhance national-level skills standards so that they reflect the needs of employers, and (iii) to remove labor market restrictions that currently bar women from performing a wide range of (largely technical) roles.

In 2018, a reform of the Kazakh Labor Code removed 96 types of work from a list of 287 jobs that women are barred from accessing due to perceived adverse working conditions and the performance of hard physical work.

Financial Inclusion

Financial inclusion at the micro-level improves women's lives by enhancing their agency and improving their access to economic opportunity. Studies suggest that women are more likely to be excluded from the formal financial sector in countries where laws and norms discriminate against women. This includes countries with lower female labor market participation, weaker collateral and bankruptcy laws, and where state-owned banks have a bigger share in the banking system (Morsy et al. 2017).

Health

Policy priorities to abate gender disparities in health outcomes change with an economy's level of development. In low-income countries and emerging market economies, better provision of basic public infrastructures such as clean water and sanitation, access to health services to prevent maternal mortality, and fight against HIV/AIDS will be key to help reduce excess girls and female mortality.

In countries and regions where sex-selective abortions and preference for sons over daughters drive gender disadvantage for children already born, changes to informal institutions and household behavior are the keys to the solution. The case of South Korea is paradigmatic. A patriarchal tradition compounded with an authoritarian regime (after the Korean war of the early 50s) pursuing an accelerated economic development resulted in a dramatic increase in the newborn boy/girl ratio.[47] Only more recently, thanks to urbanization, higher levels of education for women, and higher labor participation, gender equality has recorded significant improvements (Chung and Gupta 2007).[48] Other policies such as public campaigns aimed at changing people's perception about the role of daughters and sons, and legislation to enhance gender equity have promoted a change in social norms.

---

[47] Medical advances made it easier to detect and determine the sex of the foetus.
[48] With the provision of services and support network beyond the close family relations.

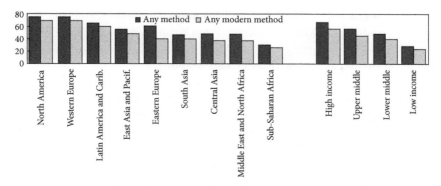

Figure 16.5 Contraceptive Prevalence (percent)

Note: averages across regions are authors' calculations.

Source: United Nations, Department of Economic and Social Affairs, Population Division (2020). World Contraceptive Use 2020 (POP/DB/CP/Rev2020).

Child marriages that disproportionately affect girls are still pervasive. The roots of the practice vary across countries—poverty, lack of educational opportunities, and poor access to health services make it difficult to eradicate. Here, too, changing cultural beliefs and stereotypes around gender roles at the national and community levels are deemed necessary.

Similarly, proactive measures should be implemented to educate how to use (and guarantee easy access to) cheap and effective contraception. According to the UN in 2019, only 30 percent of women (married or in a union) in Western Africa (compared with 50 percent around the world) could make their own decision about contraception.[49] Figure 16.5 demonstrates contraceptive prevalence across the world. Significantly, the SDGs aim to meet 75 percent of the global demand for contraception by 2030. Bailey et al. (2012), records that when in the 1960s in the United States, independent access (i.e., without the consent of a guardian) to contraception was given to women at 18 (rather than 21), both participation and wage gaps decreased significantly, even after controlling for other factors like civil rights movement, technological progress, and so on.

Practice shows that health plans often do not recognize the different needs of men and women. Many drugs are deemed effective in clinical tests that often do not include women; similarly, tools and work spaces were designed for men. The World Health Organization (2006) report on work-related health issues is an important source of information and policy recommendations in this area.

Gender is often an ignored factor during health emergencies. However, recognizing the extent to which disease outbreaks affect women and men differently is a fundamental step to understanding the primary and secondary effects of a

---

[49] Spotlight on Sustainable Development Goal 5. https://www.unwomen.org/en/digital-library/multimedia/2017/7/infographic-spotlight-on-sdg-5

health emergency on different individuals and communities, and for creating effective, equitable policies and interventions (Wenham et al. 2020).

Focus on Gender as Part of Health Crisis Responses

Policies and public health efforts to combat pandemics rarely address the gendered impacts of disease outbreaks. However, gender influences both patterns of exposure to and the treatment of infectious disease. Differences in the provision of health care as well as scientific knowledge about the effects of treatments on men and women shape the course and outcomes for those infected (WHO 2007).

In most societies, women are more likely to be caregivers for the sick as part of the health care system as well as through unpaid care at home. More women are in informal jobs without social protection and at a higher risk of wage loss or unemployment. Jobs held by women are 1.8 times more vulnerable to the Covid-19 crisis than those held by men (McKinsey Global Institute, May 2020). School closures also impact dropout rates among girls and particularly affect single parents, 90 percent of whom are women worldwide (Subrahmanyam 2016). Incidents of domestic violence against women tend to increase, and women's participation in decision-making as part of crisis responses is insufficient (Wenham et al. 2020).

Effective gender-sensitive responses need to focus on collecting and analyzing gender- and age-disaggregated data in all surveillance and monitoring efforts, gender-sensitive health care and labor market policies, dedicated support to women entrepreneurs, as well as specific measures to counteract gender-based violence and harassment.

Aid in Education and Health

Especially in developing countries, it is essential to provide women with the appropriate support with "scheduling times for training; provision of transport or grants/subsidies; and additional basic skills where necessary (e.g., literacy and numeracy training)" (Kring 2017). ILO's sponsored programs like the Training for Rural Economic Empowerment (TREE) in Pakistan or the Technical and Vocational Training (TVET) project in Bangladesh promoted demand-driven skills as inferred through an assessment of the labor market demand and by introducing stronger links with the private sector (ILO 2014c).

Culture of Gender Inequality and Implicit Bias

The eradication of stereotypes that perpetuates a gender cultural bias is the ultimate goal and certainly cannot be attained in the very short term. It requires a conscious effort in education from a very early age with personnel (early childhood educators) that are well trained. However, other mechanisms have emerged as a potent tool of gender equality: television and imposed quotas.

Indeed, in rural Indian states, television has proven to be a strong advocate against gender bias and the ingrained stereotypical perception of women.[50] Households owning a connected TV set are less likely to accept domestic violence as "normal" and express a less pronounced preference for sons. The response of the state government to the initial findings was that of distributing free TV sets to hundreds of households.

Similarly, in rural areas of Brazil, the impact of telenovelas typically telling stories of small families has led to a drop in fertility rates with the smaller number of newborns often named after the telenovelas' protagonists.

The analysis of the effect of quotas on social norms is more complicated. Many countries have used quota systems to increase the number of women in political and corporate leadership.[51]

Political quota systems can be mandated by the constitution and/or electoral law or introduced on a voluntary party basis (Vargas-Valente 2001). Figure 16.6 shows countries that have adopted legislative quotas.

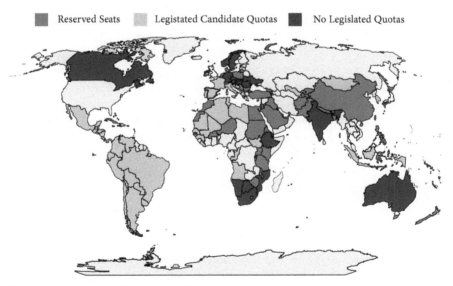

Figure 16.6 Gender Quotas in Parliaments

Note: Light gray stands for no data.

Sources: International IDEA, Inter-Parliamentary Union and Stockholm University, Gender Quotas Database, https://www.idea.int/data-tools/data/gender-quotas, accessed March 18, 2021.

[50] See Jensen and Oster (2009) for a case study in India and La Ferrara (2012) for similar results in Brazil.

[51] International IDEA, Inter-Parliamentary Union and Stockholm University, Gender Quotas Database https://www.idea.int/data-tools/data/gender-quotas

Quotas have proved to be a relatively efficient tool to increase gender diversity in parliaments and on company boards. Gender diversity increases the talent pool and improves the quality of decision-making both in politics and in the corporate world. Furthermore, women leaders can be role models and help change traditional expectations about gender roles and stereotypes. This point is also supported by some social/anthropological studies.

Using data from artefactual field experiments and surveys conducted in 61 villages in India, Gangadarhan et al. (2016) find that in the short run, there is a backlash against women in leadership positions from men that initially see this as a "transgression of social norms." However, in time, these roles are internalized as "normal." Hence, quotas can have a positive education effect despite the initial frictions. Similar conclusions are reached (again for rural India) by Beaman et al. (2009). After ten years of quotas, women are more likely to participate and win elected positions when quotas are lifted: "Prior exposure to a female chief councilor improves perceptions of female leader effectiveness and weakens stereotypes about gender roles in the public and domestic sphere."

However, women sometimes express their opposition to the idea of quotas as they expect their leadership position (political or economic) to be accepted because of recognized talent, skills, and competence rather than the result of a kind concession. This attitude has been recorded especially in advanced economies.[52]

Focus on Corporate Gender Quotas

According to a report by Deloitte (2019), only 17 percent of corporate board seats globally are held by women.[1] To increase this share, countries have used mandatory or voluntary systems of quotas. A widely cited example is Norway, a country that has mandated listed companies to reserve at least 40 percent of board seats for women since 2007 (mission of Norway to the EU. 2017). Many other countries in Europe followed (The Economist 2018).

As shown below, these policies have proved effective in making boards more gender diverse (Figure 16.7). At the same time, some criticized quotas for issues like the lack of experienced women, "tokenism"—a mainly symbolic practice to fulfill obligations, rather than a true effort, and more pressures on "golden skirts"—a small number of highly qualified women stretched across many boards (Bertrand et al. 2017).

Furthermore, so far quotas have not led to more women in senior and managerial positions or among top executives, i.e., those who would make a pipeline to take board seats. Globally, less than 5 percent of

---

[52] As a curiosum, it is interesting to note that in December 2020 the Paris Municipality was fined by the French government for hiring too many women in senior positions at the local government. This is because the number of women exceeded the 60 percent maximum for one gender as determined by law in 2012. https://www.nytimes.com/2020/12/16/world/europe/paris-too-many-women-fine.html

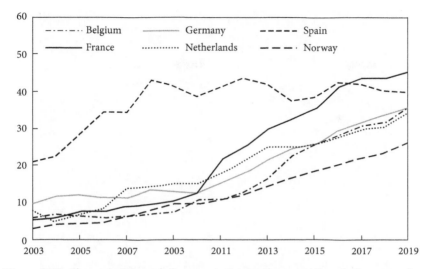

Figure 16.7 Change in Women's Representation on Company Boards (in percent)
Note: women board members in largest listed companies, percent of total.
Source: European Institute for Gender Equality, Gender Statistics Database

company CEOs are women (ILO 2015c). Experience shows that quotas, on their own, will not remove all the barriers, but contribute to eliminating some obstacles that prevent women from advancing in their careers or becoming political leaders.

IV. Conclusion

Inclusive growth cannot be achieved without gender equality. Countries around the globe have made considerable progress in narrowing gender gaps. Female labor force participation and employment have increased and the wage gap relative to men has narrowed. This important change reflects many factors, including achievements in education and a growing proportion of women who join and stay in the labor market while combining their work with raising children.

Despite this progress, however, gender inequality persists. Gender gaps vary across countries, areas, and age profiles. While lower-income countries are still struggling in achieving gender parity in educational attainment and experience excess female mortality, countries across all regions of the world experience slow progress in bringing more women into the labor force, and face persistent gender earnings gaps and stubbornly high barriers for female career progression and political empowerment. Certain policies or lack of appropriate support for families and working mothers, social norms and informal institutions, and legal barriers are among the main factors exacerbating gender gaps.

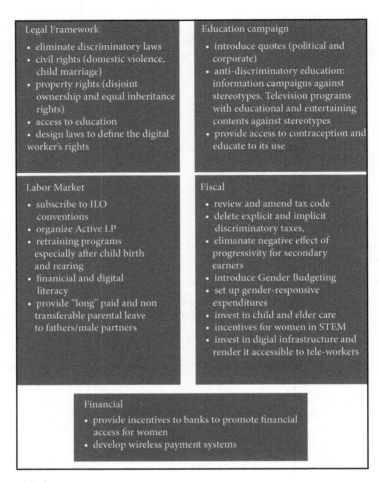

Figure 16.8 Summary

As summarized in Figure 16.8, governments must step up their effort in achieving gender equality through policies such as removing gender-based legal restrictions, introducing gender-responsive budgeting, revising tax policies and creating space for priority spending, supporting families, incentivizing paternal leave, collecting data on and punishing domestic violence, making streets and public transportation safe for women, and making finance accessible for women. Public intervention and campaigns aimed at changing people's perceptions (informal institutions and social norms) can be instrumental in eliminating gender stereotypes that are often at the core of gender disparities. Empowering women through opening up increased participation in government and corporate decision-making will shape policy reforms to reflect the specific experiences, challenges, and needs of women. Resolving the problems of today—from inequality and poverty, climate change, and health emergencies to economic shocks—will not be possible without the empowerment and full participation of women across all aspects of life.

References

Abdo, N. 2019. "The Gendered Impact of IMF Policies in MENA," OXFAM Briefing. Oxfam GB, Oxfam House, John Smith Drive, Cowley, Oxford, OX4 2JY, UK. Note. Available at: https://oxfamilibrary.openrepository.com/bitstream/handle/10546/620878/bn-imf-gendered-impact-policies-mena-081019-en.pdf

Adato, M., B. de la Briere, D. Mindek, and A. Quisumbing. 2000. "The Impact of PROGRESA on Women's Status and Intrahousehold Relations," Final Report, http://ebrary.ifpri.org/utils/getfile/collection/p15738coll2/id/125438/filename/125439.pdf

Albrecht, J., A. Bjorklund, and S. Vroman. 2003. "Is There a Glass Ceiling in Sweden?" *Journal of Labor Economics* 21(1): 145–77.

Andrienko, Y., P. Apps, and R. Rees. 2014, "Gender Bias in Tax Systems Based on Household Income," IZA Discussion Paper No. 8676. Available at https://www.iza.org/publications/dp/8676/gender-bias-in-tax-systems-based-on-household-income

Aoki, M. 2015. "Japan drastically lowers its goal for female managers in government and private sectors, "The Japan Times, December 25, 2015. Available at https://www.japantimes.co.jp/news/2015/12/25/national/japan-drastically-lowers-its-goal-for-female-managers-in-government-and-private-sector/#.Xlan7MhKhaQ

Ashraf, Quamrul, and Oded Galor. 2013. "The 'Out of Africa' Hypothesis, Human Genetic Diversity, and Comparative Economic Development." *American Economic Review* 103(1): 1–46. Also available at https://www.nber.org/papers/w17216

Auer, P., U. Efendioglu, and J. Leschke. 2008. *Active Labor Market Policies Around the World: Coping with the Consequences of Globalization.* 2nd ed. Geneva: ILO.

Bailey, M.J., B. Herbein, and A.R. Miller. 2012. "The Opt-In Revolution? Contraception and the Gender Gap in Wages." *American Economic Journal: Applied Economics* 4(3): 225–54, http://dx.doi.org/10.1257/app.4.3.225

Bergemann, A., and G. van den Berg. 2008. "Active Labor Market Policy Effects for Women in Europe: A Survey." *Annals of Economics and Statistics* 91–92: 385–408. Available at http://www.jstor.org/stable/27917252

Beaman, L., R. Chattopadhyay, E. Duflo, R. Pande, and P. Topalova. 2009. "Powerful Women: Does Exposure Decrease Bias?" *The Quarterly Journal of Economics* 124(4): 1497–540.

Bertrand, M., S.E. Black, S. Jensen, and A. Lleras-Muney. 2017, "Breaking the Glass Ceiling? The Effect of Board Quotas on Female Labor Market Outcomes in Norway," NBER Working Paper No. 20256. Available at https://www.nber.org/papers/w20256.pdf

Brussevich, M., E. Dabla-Norris, Ch. Kamunge, P. Karnane, A. Khalid, and K. Kochhar. 2018. "Gender, Technology, and the Future of Work," IMF Staff Discussion Note 18/07. Available at https://www.imf.org/en/Publications/Staff-Discussion-Notes/Issues/2018/10/09/Gender-Technology-and-the-Future-of-Work-46,236

Carter, David, A. Frank D'Souza, Betty J. Simkins, and W. Gary Simpson. 2010. "The Gender and Ethnic Diversity of US Boards and Board Committees and Firm Financial Performance." *Corporate Governance: An International Review* 18(5): 396–414. Available at http://www.wedc-online.net/Resources/WEDC-Documents/Women%20On%20Board/Gender%20Diversity%20and%20Boards.pdf

Chakraborty, Leka. 2016. "Asia: A Survey of Gender Budgeting Efforts," IMF Working Paper WP/16/150.

Chung, W., and M. Gupta. 2007. "The Decline of Son Preference in South Korea: The Roles of Development and Public Policy." *Population and Development Review* 33(4): 757–83. Available at https://www.researchgate.net/publication/4917046_The_Decline_of_Son_Preference_in_South_Korea_The_Roles_of_Development_and_Public_Policy

Deere, C.D., and M. Leon. 2003. "The Gender Asset Gap: Land in Latin America." *World Development* 31(6): 925–47. Available at: https://www.amherst.edu/media/view/92212/original/gender%20asset%20gap.pdf

De Henau, J., S. Himmelweit, Z. Łapniewska, and D. Perrons. 2016. "Investing in the Care Economy. A Gender Analysis of Employment Stimulus in Seven OECD countries," report by the UK Women's Budget Group, Brussels. Commissioned by the International Trade Union Confederation. Available at https://www.ituc-csi.org/IMG/pdf/care_economy_en.pdf

Delechat, C., M. Newjak, R.X. Fan Yang, and G. Aslan. 2018. "What Is Driving Women's Financial Inclusion Across Countries?" IMF Working Paper 18/38. Available at https://www.imf.org/en/Publications/WP/Issues/2018/03/05/What-is-Driving-Womens-Financial-Inclusion-Across-Countries-45,670

Deloitte. 2019. "Women in the Boardroom." Available at https://www2.deloitte.com/global/en/pages/risk/articles/women-in-the-boardroom-global-perspective.html

Duflo, E. 2012. "Women Empowerment and Economic Development." *Journal of Economic Literature* 50(4): 1051–79. Available at https://economics.mit.edu/files/7417

The Economist. 2018. "Ten years on from Norway's quota for women on corporate boards," https://www.economist.com/business/2018/02/17/ten-years-on-from-norways-quota-for-women-on-corporate-boards

Elson, D. 2017. "Recognize, Reduce, Redistribute Unpaid Care Work: How to Close the Gender Gap," *New Labor Forum*. Available at: https://newlaborforum.cuny.edu/2017/03/03/recognize-reduce-redistribute-unpaid-care-work-how-to-close-the-gender-gap/

European Bank for Reconstruction and Development (EBRD). 2016. Transition Report 2016/17. "Transition for All: Equal Opportunities in an Unequal World."

Available at https://www.ebrd.com/news/publications/transition-report/transition-report-201,617.html

European Institute for Gender Equality (EIGE). 2019. "Tackling the Gender Pay Gap: Not Without a Better Work-Life Balance." Available at https://eige.europa.eu/publications/tackling-gender-pay-gap-not-without-better-work-life-balance. Gender Statistics Database. Available at https://eige.europa.eu/gender-statistics/dgs

European Parliament. 2015. "Workshop on Main Causes of Female Poverty." Available at https://www.europarl.europa.eu/RegData/etudes/STUD/2015/519193/IPOL_STU(2015)519193_EN.pdf

Fernández, Raquel. 2013. "Cultural Change as Learning: The Evolution of Female Labor Force Participation over a Century." *American Economic Review* 103(1): 472–500.

Fernández, R., and A. Fogli. 2009. "Culture: An Empirical Investigation of Beliefs, Work, and Fertility." *American Economic Journal: Macro* 1(1): 146–77.

Ferrant, G., L.M. Pesando, and K. Nowacka. 2014. "Unpaid Care Work: The missing link in the analysis of gender gaps in labor outcomes," OECD Development Centre, Issues paper, December 2014. Available at https://www.oecd.org/dev/development-gender/Unpaid:care_work.pdf

Gangadharan, L., T. Jain, P. Maitra, and J. Vecci. 2016. "Social Identity and Governance: The Behavioral Response to Female Leaders." *European Economic Review* 90: 302–25.

Goldin, C., and L. Katz. 2002. "The Power of the Pill: Oral Contraceptives and Women's Career and Marriage Decisions." *Journal of Political Economy* 110(4): 730-70. https://dash.harvard.edu/bitstream/handle/1/2624453/Goldin_PowerPill.pdf?sequence=4_1

Gonzales, Ch., S. Jain-Chandra, K. Kochhar, M. Newiak, and T. Zeinullayev. 2015. "Catalyst for Change: Empowering Women and Tackling Income inequality," IMF Staff Discussion Note 15/20. https://www.imf.org/external/pubs/ft/sdn/2015/sdn1520.pdf

Hallward-Driemeier, M., T. Hasan, and A. Bogdana Rusu. 2013. "Women's Legal Rights over 50 Years: What Is the Impact of Reform?" Policy Research Working Paper 6617. http://documents.worldbank.org/curated/en/340791468151787181/pdf/WPS6617.pdf

Hess, C., and A. Del Rosario. 2018. "Dreams Deferred: A Survey on the Impact of Intimate Partner Violence on Survivors' Education, Careers, and Economic Security," Institute for Women's Policy Research. Washington DC. Available https://iwpr.org/wp-content/uploads/2020/09/C475_IWPR-Report-Dreams-Deferred.pdf

Holmes, R., R. Slater, A. Acker, and A. Berezovskaja. 2014. "Gender-responsive Budgeting in Fragile and Conflict-Affected States: A Review," London: Overseas Development Institute. Available at https://securelivelihoods.org/wp-content/uploads/Gender-responsive-budgeting-in-fragile-and-conflict-affected-states-a-review.pdf

Hsieh, C., E. Hurst, Ch. I Jones, and P.J. Klenow. 2019. "The Allocation of Talent and US Economic Growth." *Econometrica* 87(5): 1439–74. Available at http://klenow. com/HHJK.pdf

Hui, H. 2011. "Why Have Girls Gone to College? A Quantitative Examination of the Female College Enrollment Rate in the United States: 1955–1980." *Annals of Economics and Finance* 12(1): 43–66.

International Labour Organization (ILO). 2014. "The Gender Divide in Skills Development: progress, Challenges and Policy Options for Empowering Women." Geneva. Available at https://www.ilo.org/skills/pubs/WCMS_244380/lang—en/ index.htm

International Labour Organization (ILO). 2015a. "Women in Business and Management: Gaining Momentum." Geneva. Available https://www.ilo.org/wcmsp5/groups/ public/—dgreports/—dcomm/—publ/documents/publication/wcms_334882.pdf

International Labour Organization (ILO). 2015b. "Women and the Future of Work: Beijing +20 and Beyond." Geneva. Available at https://www.ilo.org/wcmsp5/ groups/public/—dgreports/—dcomm/documents/briefingnote/wcms_348087.pdf

International Labour Organization (ILO). 2015c. "Women on Boards—Building the female talent pipeline," Geneva. Available at https://www.ilo.org/gender/ Informationresources/Publications/WCMS_410200/lang—en/index.htm

International Labour Organization (ILO). 2018a. World Employment Social Outlook: Trends for Women. Geneva. Available at https://www.ilo.org/global/research/global-reports/weso/trends-for-women2018/WCMS_619577/lang—en/index.htm

International Labour Organization (ILO). 2018b. Global Wage Report 2018/19: What Lies Behind Gender Pay Gaps. Geneva. Available at https://www.ilo.org/global/ about-the-ilo/newsroom/features/WCMS_650551/lang—en/index.htm

International IDEA, Inter-Parliamentary Union and Stockholm University, Gender Quotas Database https://www.idea.int/data-tools/data/gender-quotas

International Monetary Fund (IMF). 2017b. "Gender Budgeting in G7 Countries," IMF Policy Paper. Available at: https://www.imf.org/en/Publications/Policy-Papers/ Issues/2017/05/12/pp041917gender-budgeting-in-g7-countries

Jain-Chandra, Sonali, K. Kochhar, M. Newiak, Y. Yang, and E. Zoli. 2018. "Gender Equality: Which Policies Have the Biggest Bang for the Buck?" IMF Working Paper 18/105. Also available at https://www.imf.org/en/Publications/WP/Issues /2018/05/10/Gender-Equality-Which-Policies-Have-the-Biggest-Bang-for-the-Buck-45,823

Jensen, R., and E. Oster. 2009. "The Power of TV: Cable Television and Women's Status in India." *The Quarterly Journal of Economics* 124(3): 1057–94.

Kleven, H., C. Landais, J. Posch, A. Stenhauer, J. Zweimuller. 2019. "Child Penalties Across Countries: Evidence and Explanations." *American Economic Association: Papers and Proceedings* 109: 122–26, https://www.aeaweb.org/articles?id=10.1257/ pandp.20191078

Korpi, W. 2000. "Faces of Inequality: Gender, Class, and Patterns of Inequalities in Different Types of Welfare States." *Soc. Polit. Int. Stud. Gend. State Soc.* 7(2): 127–91. Available at: https://www.researchgate.net/publication/31268455_Faces_of_ Inequality_Gender_Class_and_Patterns_of_Inequalities_in_Different_Types_of_ Welfare_States

Kring, Sriani Ameratunga. 2017. "Gender in Employment Policies and Programmes: What Works for Women?" *Employment* ILO Working Paper No. 235.

La Ferrara, E., A. Chong, and S. Duryea. 2012. "Soap Operas and Fertility: Evidence from Brazil." *American Economic Journal: Applied Economics* 4(4): 1–31.

Markus, R., and C. Harper. 2014. "Gender Justice and Social Norms—Processes of Change for Adolescent Girls: Towards a Conceptual Framework," Overseas Development Institute, London. Available at https://www.odi.org/sites/odi.org.uk/ files/odi-assets/publications-opinion-files/8831.pdf

McKinsey Global Institute MGI. 2020. "Covid-19 and Gender Equality: Countering the Regressive Effects." July 15, 2020. Available at https://www.mckinsey.com/featured-insights/future-of-work/covid-19-and-gender-equality-countering-the-regressive-effects

Mission of Norway to the EU. 2017. "Sharing Norway's experience with gender quotas for boards," Available at https://www.norway.no/en/missions/eu/about-the-mission/ news-events-statements/news2/sharing-norways-experience-with-gender-quotas-for-boards/

Morsy, H., and H. Youssef. 2017. "Access to Finance—Mind the Gender Gap," EBRD Working Paper No 202. Available at https://www.ebrd.com/publications/working-papers/access-to-finance

Munoz Boudet, A., P. Buitrago, B. Leroy De La Briere, D. Newhouse, E. Rubiano Matulevich, K. Scott, et al. 2018. "Gender Differences in Poverty and Household Composition Through the Life-Cycle: A Global Perspective," World Bank Policy Research Working Paper 8360.

Nieuwenhuis, R., T. Munzi, J. Neugschwender, H. Omar, and F. Palmisano. 2018. "Gender Equality and Poverty Are Intrinsically Linked: A Contribution to the Continued Monitoring of Selected Sustainable Development Goals," UN Women Discussion Paper No. 26 https://www.unwomen.org/en/digital-library/publications /2018/12/discussion-paper-gender-equality-and-poverty-are-intrinsically-linked

Nosek, B.A., F.L Smyth, N. Sriram, N.M. Lindner, T. Devos, A. Ayala, et al. 2009. "National Differences in Gender–Science Stereotypes Predict National Sex Differences in Science and Math Achievement." *PNAS* 6(26): 10,593–7, http://www. people.fas.harvard.edu/~banaji/research/publications/articles/2009_Nosek_ PNAS.pdf

Organisation for Economic Co-operation and Development (OECD). 2012. "Closing the Gender Gap: Act Now," Paris. Available at https://www.oecd.org/gender/ closingthegap.htm

Organisation for Economic Co-operation and Development (OECD) 2016. "Background Brief on Fathers' Leave and Its Use," Paris. Available at https://www.oecd.org/els/family/Backgrounder-fathers-use-of-leave.pdf

Organisation for Economic Co-operation and Development (OECD). 2017. "The Pursuit of Gender Equality: An Uphill Battle," Paris. Available at https://www.oecd.org/gender/the-pursuit-of-gender-equality-9,789,264,281,318-en.htm

Organisation for Economic Co-operation and Development (OECD). 2018a. "Including unpaid household activities: An estimate of its impact on macro-economic Indicators in the G7 economies and the way forward," Paris. Available at http://www.oecd.org/officialdocuments/publicdisplaydocumentpdf/?cote=SDD/DOC(2018)4&docLanguage=En

Organisation for Economic Co-operation and Development (OECD). 2019a. *SIGI 2019 Global Report: Transforming Challenges into Opportunities*, Social Institutions, and Gender Index, OECD Publishing, Paris. Available at https://doi.org/10.1787/bc56d212-en.

Organisation for Economic Co-operation and Development (OECD). 2019b. Promoting Gender Equality in Eurasia: Better Policies for Women's Economic Empowerment. Draft Background Note, February 2019. Available at https://www.oecd.org/eurasia-week/Promoting-Gender-Equality-Eurasia-Feb2019.pdf

Ostry J., J. Alvarez, R. Espinoza, and C. Papageorgiou. 2018. "Economic Gains From Gender Inclusion: New Mechanisms, New Evidence," IMF Staff Discussion Note 18/06. Available at https://www.imf.org/en/Publications/Staff-Discussion-Notes/Issues/2018/10/09/Economic-Gains-From-Gender-Inclusion-New-Mechanisms-New-Evidence-45543

Ostry, J., A. Berg, and C. Tsangarides. 2014. "Redistribution, Inequality, and Growth." Staff Discussion Note, IMF Staff Discussion Note 14/02. Available at https://www.imf.org/external/pubs/ft/sdn/2014/sdn1402.pdf

Overseas Development Institute. 2015. *The Law as a Tool for Changing Gender Norms Affecting Adolescent Girls: The Case of Child Marriage Laws*. London. Available at https://www.odi.org/sites/odi.org.uk/files/odi-assets/publications-opinion-files/9811.pdf

OXFAM. 2019. "Gender Inequalities and Food Insecurity," Briefing Paper July 2019. Available at: https://www.oxfamamerica.org/explore/research-publications/gender-inequalities-and-food-insecurity/

Perez, C.C. 2019. *Invisible Women: Exposing Data Bias in a World Designed for Men*. London: Chatto & Windus.

Sakhonchik, Alena, I. Santagostino Recavarren, and P. Tavares. 2015. "Closing the Gap—Improving Laws Protecting Women from Violence," *Women, Business and the Law*, World Bank group. Available at: http://pubdocs.worldbank.org/en/349811519938655769/Topic-Note-Protecting-Women-from-Violence-EN.pdf

Slaymaker, E., R. Scott, M. Palmer, L. Palla, M. Marston, L. Gonsalves, et al. 2020. "Trends in sexual activity and demand for and use of modern contraceptive methods in 74 countries: a retrospective analysis of nationally representative surveys," Lancet Glob Health 2020; 8: e567–79. Published Online March 9, 2020. https://doi.org/10.1016/S2214-109X(20)30060-7

Stevenson, B., and J. Wolfers. 2006. "Bargaining in the Shadow of the Law: Divorce Laws and Family Distress." *Quarterly Journal of Economics* 121(1): 267–88.

Stotsky, Janet G. 1996. "Gender Bias in Tax Systems," IMF Working Paper 96/99.

Stotsky, Janet G. 2016. "Gender Budgeting: Fiscal Context and Current Outcomes", IMF Working Paper 16/149. Available at: https://www.imf.org/en/Publications/WP/Issues/2016/12/31/Gender-Budgeting-Fiscal-Context-and-Current-Outcomes-44132

Stotsky, J. G., L. Kolovich, and S. Kebaj, 2016, "Sub-Saharan Africa : A Survey of Gender Budgeting Efforts" IMF Working Paper 16/152. Available at https://www.imf.org/en/Publications/WP/Issues/2016/12/31/The-Influence-of-Gender-Budgeting-in-Indian-States-on-Gender-Inequality-and-Fiscal-Spending-44411

Stotsky, Janet G. 2017. "Tax Proposals: A Missed Opportunity for Addressing Implicit Gender Bias," *The Gender Policy report*, November 2017. Available at: https://genderpolicyreport.umn.edu/tax-proposals-a-missed-opportunity-for-addressing-implicit-gender-bias/

Subrahmanyam, G. 2016. "Gender perspectives on causes and effects of school drop-outs." SIDA Available at http://www.ungei.org/Final_Paper_on_Gender_perspectives_C2.pdf

United National Development Program (UNDP). 2012. "Overview of Linkages Between Gender and Climate Change," New York. Available at https://www.undp.org/content/dam/undp/library/gender/Gender%20and%20Environment/PB1_Africa_Overview-Gender-Climate-Change.pdf

United National Development Program (UNDP). 2020. "Tackling Social Norms: A game-changer for gender inequalities." New York. Available at http://hdr.undp.org/sites/default/files/hd_perspectives_gsni.pdf

UN Women. 2020a. "Progress of the world's women 2019–2020: Families in a changing world," https://www.unwomen.org/en/digital-library/progress-of-the-worlds-women

UN Women. 2020b. Women in Politics: 2020. Available at https://www.unwomen.org/-/media/headquarters/attachments/sections/library/publications/2020/women-in-politics-map-2020-en.pdf?la=en&vs=827

United Nations World Contraceptive Use Database. 2020. https://www.un.org/en/development/desa/population/publications/dataset/contraception/wcu2020.asp

Vargas-Valente, Virginia. 2001. "Municipal Budgets and Democratic Governance in the Andean Region," Gender Budget Initiatives: Strategies, Concepts, and Experiences, ed K. Judd, (UNIFEM).

de Vilhena, D., and L. Olah. 2017. "Family Diversity and its Challenges for Policy Makers in Europe," Population Europe, Discussion Paper no. 5. Available at https://population-europe.eu/sites/default/files/famsoc_discussionpaper5_final_web.pdf

The Washington Post. 2014. "Ebola striking women more frequently than men," https://www.washingtonpost.com/national/health-science/2014/08/14/3e08d0c8-2 312-11e4-8593-da634b334390_story.html

Welham, Bryn. 2018. "How to Make 'Gender Budgeting' Work in Practice," Overseas Development Institute, *Insights*. https://www.odi.org/blogs/10671-how-make-gender-budgeting-work-practice

Welham, Bryn, K. Barnes-Robinson, Mansour-Ille, and R. Okhadiar. 2018. "Gender-responsive public expenditure management. A public finance management introductory guide," Overseas Development Institute. https://www.odi.org/publications/11123-gender-responsive-public-expenditure-management-public-finance-management-introductory-guide

Wenham, C., J. Smith, and R. Morgan. 2020. "Covid-19: the gendered impacts of the outbreak. The Lancet," March 6. https://www.thelancet.com/journals/lancet/article/PIIS0140-6736(20)30526-2/fulltext#%20

World Bank. 2012. World Development Report 2012: Gender Equality and Development. Washington, DC. Available at https://openknowledge.worldbank.org/handle/10986/4391

World Bank. 2019. "Women, Business and the Law. Washington, DC. Available at https://openknowledge.worldbank.org/bitstream/handle/10986/31327/WBL2019.pdf?sequence=4&isAllowed=y

World Economic Forum. 2018. The Global Gender Gap Report. Geneva. https://www.weforum.org/reports/the-global-gender-gap-report-2018

World Health Organization (WHO). 2006. "Gender equality, work, and health: a review of the evidence." Geneva. Available at https://www.who.int/occupational_health/publications/genderwork/en/

World Health Organization (WHO). 2007. Addressing sex and gender in epidemic-prone infectious diseases. Available at https://www.who.int/csr/resources/publications/SexGenderInfectDis.pdf

World Health Organization (WHO). 2020. "Family planning/contraception methods," https://www.who.int/news-room/fact-sheets/detail/family-plan

Yamaguchi, K., and Y. Yoosik. 2020. "Gender Gaps in Japan and Korea: A comparative study on the rates of promotions to managing positions." The Research Institute of Economy, Trade and Industry Discussion Paper 16-E-011, Japan. Available at: https://www.rieti.go.jp/jp/publications/dp/16e011.pdf

Zhang, Q., and A. Posso. 2017. "Microfinance and Gender Inequality: Cross-Country Evidence." *Applied Economics Letters* 24(20): 1494–8. Available at: https://www.tandfonline.com/doi/full/10.1080/13504851.2017.1287851

17

Regional Disparities

Holger Floerkemeier, Nikola Spatafora, and Anthony Venables

I. Introduction

Many countries are characterized by significant regional disparities in economic performance and living standards, as reflected in income, education, or health outcomes.[1] These regional disparities raise equity concerns: they contribute to overall within-country inequality, and they are linked to inequality of opportunity, as measured by, say, intergenerational mobility.[2] Regional disparities may also have harmful implications for economic efficiency, as limited opportunities for those stuck in the wrong place lead to the underutilization of potential and constrain overall growth.[3] More broadly, regional disparities, including urban-rural differences, can fuel social tensions and pathologies (Case and Deaton 2020), promote political polarization (Wilkinson 2019), increase populism and resentment towards urban elites (Rodríguez-Pose 2018; Kessler 2018; Muro and Liu 2016; Shearer 2016), threaten countries' social fabric and national cohesion, and in extreme cases lead to conflict, particularly where the disparities reinforce existing ethnic, racial, linguistic, or religious divisions.

Large and/or rising regional disparities may arise in different contexts. In some cases, they may be a normal feature of growth. The concentration and specialization of production can boost overall economic productivity but will do so unevenly across regions: "development does not bring economic prosperity everywhere at once; markets favor some places over others" (World Bank 2009). Favored areas will then pull away from other regions, which may experience an economic decline in relative and possibly absolute terms; but dispersing production more broadly across regions could lower aggregate productivity and reduce economic growth. In other cases, regional disparities may be a consequence of

---

[1] We are grateful for comments provided by Andy Berg, Carlos Caceres, Valerie Cerra, Gilles Duranton, Barry Eichengreen, John Spray, Zhongxia Zhang, and participants in the Inclusive Growth book seminar series organized by the IMF Institute for Capacity Development.

[2] A child born in San Francisco in the bottom 20 percent of the national income distribution has twice as much chance of ending up in the top 20 percent as an adult as a similar child born in Detroit (*Equality of Opportunity* project).

[3] Countries with larger regional disparities experience lower long-term growth (Che and Spilimbergo 2012).

Holger Floerkemeier, Nikola Spatafora, and Anthony Venables, *Regional Disparities* In: *How to Achieve Inclusive Growth.*
Edited by: Valerie Cerra, Barry Eichengreen, Asmaa El-Ganainy, and Martin Schindler, Oxford University Press.
© Holger Floerkemeier, Nikola Spatafora, and Anthony Venables 2022. DOI: 10.1093/oso/9780192846938.003.0017

adverse economic shocks that have impacted particular regions. Adjustment to these shocks can be very slow, giving rise to persistent disparities.

All this raises three broad sets of questions. First, what economic forces will dampen, or conversely amplify, regional disparities? Second, if market forces alone do not bring about convergence across regions, are the resulting regional disparities, in fact, efficient, or do they instead reflect market and/or policy failures? As a corollary, will policy attempts to reduce regional disparities necessarily involve a trade-off between spatial equality and growth, between equity and efficiency? Finally, should there be a policy response, and if so what form should it take? Is geographically "balanced growth" a precondition for inclusiveness, and should policy focus on boosting the economic performance of lagging regions? Or should policymakers accept the presence of regional disparities in productivity, and instead assist households in lagging regions through transfer payments, investments in education, health, and other basic services, and by facilitating out-migration?

This chapter first presents some key stylized facts regarding regional disparities. It then sets out a conceptual framework to interpret these facts and analyze the drivers of disparities and concludes with a discussion of potential policy responses.

II. Key Facts

Levels of economic activity and welfare differ sharply across sub-national regions, in both advanced and developing economies. This inequality is evident when looking at output or income. In advanced economies, real GDP per capita in leading regions is now on average 70 percent higher than in lagging regions (Figure 17.1, left panel).[4] In developing economies, regional disparities are even larger, about twice the size of those in advanced economies (Figure 17.1, right panel). Such regional disparities are also reflected in labor-market performance (for instance, labor productivity, employment, and wages) and indicators of human development (for instance, education and health outcomes) (Figure 17.2; see also Avitabile et al. 2020).

In advanced economies, regional disparities have broadly increased since the late 1980s, as affluent places, in particular, large, well-connected cities, pulled away from poorer ones. This represents a marked contrast to the steady decrease in disparities between the end of the Second World War and the 1980s (Figure 17.1, left panel). In the OECD, the average labor productivity gap between the most productive 10 percent of regions and the bottom 75 percent widened by nearly 60 percent over the past 20 years.[5] In the United States, inter-regional

---

[4] "Leading" and "lagging" regions are defined here as those at, respectively, the 90th percentile and the 10th percentile of the within-country distribution. Subnational regions are the TL2 regions as defined in OECD (2018); these are typically the first-level administrative units within a country, corresponding roughly to US states or German Länder.
[5] From US$15,200 to US$24,000 (OECD 2016).

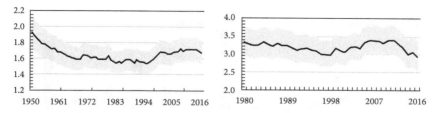

Figure 17.1 90th percentile / 10th percentile of regional real GDP per capita, the average across advanced economies, 1950–2016 (left panel), and emerging markets, 1980–2016 (right panel).

Note: The 90/10 ratio for a country is defined as real GDP per capita in the region at the 90th percentile of the country's regional real GDP per capita distribution relative to that in the region at the 10th percentile. The solid line shows the year fixed effects from a regression of country-specific 90/10 ratios on year fixed effects and country fixed effects; this procedure accounts for entry and exit during the period and level differences in the 90/10 ratios. The shaded areas indicate the associated 90 percent confidence interval.

Source: IMF (2019), figure 2.1. License: CC BY 3.0 IGO.

income inequality is at its highest point in a century (Kemeny and Storper 2020). The share of output generated by the top four metropolitan areas has risen across a wide range of industries, the gap in employment rates between leading and lagging regions has steadily widened (Austin et al. 2018), and innovative sectors have grown fastest in those areas where they were relatively large, to begin with (Atkinson et al. 2019).[6] Relatedly, the average pace of convergence between leading and lagging regions has decreased markedly over the past five decades and is now close to zero (Figure 17.3, left panel). Again, this contrasts markedly with the remarkably broad and uniform spatial convergence previously observed within the United States (Barro et al. 1991; Barro and Sala-i-Martin 1992), Canada (Coulombe and Lee 1995), the European Union (both as a whole and within individual countries; Neven and Gouymte 1995; Persson 1997; De La Fuente 2002), and Japan (Sala-i-Martin 1996). The rate of economic convergence across U.S. states during 1990–2010 was less than half that observed during 1880–1980, and it has since fallen close to zero; likewise, convergence across EU regions largely stopped after the mid-1980s (Martin 2001). However, while the wage premium associated with working in large cities has increased sharply for skilled workers, it has mostly disappeared for the less skilled (Gaubert et al. 2021b; Autor 2019; Abel and Deitz 2019; Giannone 2019; Vanheuvelen and Copas 2019; De La Roca and Puga 2017). Relatedly, cities with more vibrant labor markets have a lower share of less-skilled, low-wage workers (Ross and Bateman 2019); and, at least in the United States, while college-educated workers have been steadily moving into affluent cities, non-college workers have been moving out (Ganong and

---

[6] Between 2002 and 2014, it rose from 18 percent to 29 percent for financial services, and from 15 percent to 21 percent for trade and logistics.

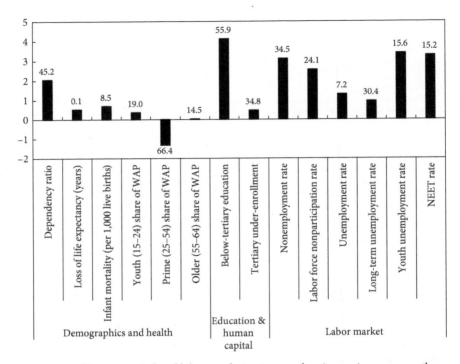

Figure 17.2 Human capital and labor market outcomes, lagging regions versus other regions, the average across advanced economies, latest available year (percentage point difference, unless otherwise noted).

Note: For each variable, bars show the difference between lagging regions and other regions; numbers above bars show the sample average of a variable. Lagging regions are defined as those with real GDP per capita below their country median in 2000 and with average growth below the country's average over 2000–16. Results based on regressions of each variable on an indicator for whether a region is lagging, controlling for country-year fixed effects, with standard errors clustered at the country-year level. Solid bars indicate estimated coefficient on the lagging indicator is statistically significant at a 10% level. Positive estimated coefficients indicate worse performance by lagging regions. Tertiary under-enrollment = difference in the percent of the population enrolled in tertiary education in other regions versus lagging regions. Nonemployment rate = 100 - employment rate. Labor force nonparticipation rate = 100 - labor-force participation rate of working-age (15–64) population. Unemployment rate = share of the working-age labor force that is unemployed. Long-term unemployment rate = share of working-age labor force unemployed for one year or more. Youth unemployment rate = share of youth (15–24) labor force that is unemployed. NEET rate = percent of the youth population that is not in education, employment, or training. WAP = working-age population.

Source: IMF (2019), figure 2.4. License: CC BY 3.0 IGO.

Shoag 2017). That said, the trends in regional disparities vary sharply across countries, and regional disparities account for a much larger share of overall inequality in some countries than in others.[7]

---

[7] The regional component of household disposable income inequality is less than 1 percent in Austria, but more than 10 percent in Italy (IMF 2019). Again, subnational regions here are typically the first-level administrative units within a country, corresponding roughly to US states or German Länder.

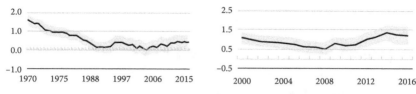

Figure 17.3 Speed of regional convergence (percent), the average across advanced economies, 1970–2016 (left panel), and emerging markets, 2000–2016 right panel)

Note: The figure depicts the coefficient on initial regional log real GDP per capita from a cross-sectional regression of average regional real purchasing power parity GDP per capita growth on initial regional log real GDP per capita, estimated over a 20-year rolling window. The regression includes country-fixed effects, so it indicates average within-country regional convergence. The coefficient is expressed in annualized terms, indicating the average annual speed of convergence.

Source: IMF (2019), figure 2.1. License: CC BY 3.0 IGO.

Further, in advanced economies, the rise in regional disparities appears to be associated with negative economic *shocks* and de-industrialization since the 1980s. Lagging regions are typically more concentrated in slow-growing manufacturing and agriculture, and less concentrated in the faster-growing service sectors, than leading regions. Much research highlights the impact of trade shocks. For instance, China's rapid export growth had a particularly adverse impact on those advanced-economy regions initially specialized in the manufacturing industries that became subject to increased import competition (Autor et al. 2013, 2013b). Other research suggests a large impact from automation, particularly on smaller, more rural regions (Muro et al. 2019). Under either interpretation, some regions fell behind because of their failure to adjust to adverse shocks; for instance, advanced-economy regions that experienced closures of automotive manufacturing plants after 2000 saw their unemployment rate rise relative to other regions within the same countries (IMF 2019). And the impact of shocks proved larger where the adjustment was hampered by less open and flexible labor and product markets.

In developing economies, as discussed, regional disparities in GDP per capita are even larger. Further, such differences in economic activity translate even more directly into differences in living standards.[8] However, the limited data available do not point to broad-based increases in disparities (Figure 17.1, right panel), and on average suggest continued convergence between leading and lagging regions (Figure 17.3, right panel), over the past two decades. Similar conclusions emerge when analyzing disparities within individual large emerging markets such as Brazil and India (Nagaraj et al. 2000).

---

[8] In developing countries, real household consumption levels are approximately 75 percent higher in leading regions than in lagging regions. For advanced economies, the corresponding consumption gap is less than 25 percent (World Bank 2009).

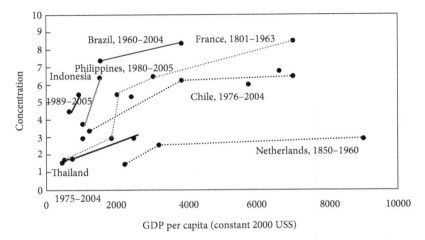

Figure 17.4 As economies develop, GDP concentrates in cities and leading regions.

Note: The concentration measure is defined as follows. First, an area's hypothetical share of national GDP is estimated under the assumption that national GDP exhibits a uniform spatial distribution. Second, the area with the highest actual share of national GDP is identified. Third, the actual GDP share of this leading area is divided by its hypothetical (uniformly spatially distributed) share to yield a measure of spatial concentration. For example, if the leading area has an actual share of 10 percent and a hypothetical share of 2 percent, then the concentration measure equals 5. See World Bank (2009) for details.

Source: World Bank (2009), figure 2.2. License: CC BY 3.0 IGO.

Importantly, in developing economies, economic *takeoffs* are often associated with the emergence of regional disparities. That is, regional disparities here may be symptomatic of positive rather than negative shocks. Economic development, in its early stages, leads to the rapid concentration of economic activity in locations close to markets. Such favored locations include cities, often capitals and primary cities in particular, and leading regions (Figure 17.4), for instance, areas near large cities, as well as coastal areas that are more open to international trade. As Thailand industrialized, activity rapidly concentrated in the Bangkok metropolitan area; in Brazil, concentration in the Sao Paulo metropolitan area also rose. These leading regions diversify out of agriculture and into higher-productivity manufacturing, with significant changes in both sectoral employment mixes and sectoral productivity.

As economic development proceeds, regional disparities in living standards between leading and lagging regions at first widen, but then typically stabilize and eventually decline (World Bank 2009). Regional differences in wages, income, and access to public services typically prove long-lived. However, over time, prosperity tends to spill over to other areas that are, or are made, well connected to the leading regions. The divergence and re-convergence are likely to occur faster in more dynamic areas and countries. This is an important mechanism behind the *Kuznets curve*—the hypothesis that as an economy develops, market forces first increase and then decrease economic inequality, including across regions. This pattern was evident in today's advanced economies as they are industrialized. In the United Kingdom, regional disparities (as measured by the coefficient of variation of GDP per capita) increased by almost 40 percent between 1871 and 1911, before stabilizing and then slowly converging until the late 1970s (Crafts 2005). In the United States, disparities in GDP per capita across states increased between 1840 and 1880, but then slowly began to narrow. In France, the dispersion of wages across *départements* increased between 1855 and 1900, when convergence set in. In Canada, the dispersion of gross value added per capita between provinces increased between 1890 and 1930 but then started falling. And a similar pattern can be seen in today's developing economies. For instance, regional inequality widened sharply in the fast-growing East Asian economies between the early 1990s and the late 2000s (Kanbur et al. 2014). China experienced the most dramatic increase in regional disparities, with output per capita in the coastal regions rising to more than twice the level in the inland regions. More recently, these regional disparities in living standards have started to stabilize. In India, coastal states have also fared better than inland states over the past two decades. And, across Eastern Europe, regional disparities widened sharply after the beginning of a transition. That said, in these fast-growing economies, all subnational areas generally experienced gains in wages and income, even though leading regions benefited the most. And in relatively closed, slower-growing economies, such as Brazil and Colombia, regional disparities have decreased over time, even where the population continued to concentrate.

Are current trends intensifying economic concentration, and both amplifying regional disparities and making them more persistent? Rising spatial concentration and typically rising regional disparities characterized today's developed economies when they industrialized; for instance, Korea after 1970. But globalization and technological progress, including improved transportation and communications infrastructure, maybe increasing the market potential of leading versus lagging regions over time. To make sense of such issues, we now develop a conceptual framework.

III. Drivers of Regional Disparities: Conceptual Framework

Spatial unevenness in economic activity is startling, with 55 percent of the world population concentrated in 1 percent of the world land area. This is partly natural, driven by soil fertility, rainfall, natural resources, and trade possibilities. And it is partly driven by the costs and benefits of clustering people and activity together, and the tension between forces for dispersion versus clustering of economic activity. The dispersion forces arise, in the broadest terms, from diminishing returns: if putting more activity in a particular place runs into diminishing returns, then the activity will spread out. The clustering forces are driven by increasing returns: these mean that the more activity there is in a place, the higher the value of moving there.

Spatial unevenness is a particular concern when it reflects disparities in the distribution of not just economic activity, but also income per capita and well-being. Such disparities are widespread and quite persistent. Standard economic models suggest that, within a country or region where labor and firms are mobile, there should be little spatial variation in the real income of people with similar attributes. Two mechanisms would ensure this. First, jobs would move to lower-wage regions—or, in a growing economy, new job creation will be slanted towards such regions. Second, people would move to higher-wage regions. Why do these mechanisms not work, or at least only work slowly? We discuss first the movement of jobs, and then that of workers and households.

A. Firms, Jobs, and Capital

Firms' location decisions are shaped by multiple forces. In many sectors proximity to customers is all-important, as goods or services do not travel well or have to be supplied face-to-face. Other sectors, such as natural-resource intensive sectors, are located close to raw materials. In sectors not dominated by these forces, location decisions depend on factors including wages, productivity, the supply of suitably skilled labor, and ease of access to customers and to suppliers of intermediate goods and services.

These factors have a spatial dimension, particularly as firms derive advantages from proximity to other firms and to households—"agglomeration economies." Agglomeration effects reflect the economies of scale that arise between firms, and also between firms, households, and workers (Duranton and Puga 2004, 2020; Puga 2010; Rosenthal and Strange 2004). Some of these benefits arise simply from cost savings. If your customers and suppliers are close by, they can be reached at low cost; just-in-time operation requires both frequent and reliable deliveries, easier to secure if suppliers are nearby. Other benefits arise as there are often knowledge spillovers between firms.[9] These effects are manifest particularly in the tendency of firms in R&D-intensive sectors to cluster together.

Agglomeration benefits also arise because of scale and specialization. Larger and denser markets allow for scale, scope, and specialization. Specialist suppliers and workers represent a good example. The larger the market, the more likely it is that a firm or worker will find it worthwhile to specialize and hone skills in producing a particular good or service. This specialization creates high productivity.

---

[9] "The mysteries of the trade become no mysteries; but are as it were, in the air"; Marshall (1920), writing about the nineteenth-century Sheffield metals cluster.

And, while customers pay for the product, they are likely to also receive some net benefit, over and above what they pay. This creates positive feedback. Customers will be attracted to a place with multiple suppliers, thereby growing the size of the market, and making it attractive for further and more specialized suppliers to set up operations. This is the classic process of growing a "business ecosystem" and of cluster formation.[10]

The agglomeration process operates at several different levels. In the supply of intermediate goods between firms, it is the basis of the "linkages" discussed in an old development economics literature, and in the "new economic geography" research (Fujita et al. 1999). Between firms and final consumers, it is the basis of Krugman's core-periphery model (Krugman 1991). And in the labor market, it takes the form of thick market effects that allow for better matching of firms to workers. In some contexts, these agglomeration economies are based on overall economic activity in an area—the size and diversity of the labor force, and the level of demand for goods and services. In others, they involve sector-specific knowledge spillovers, specialist labor skills, and demand and supply linkages in related sectors. The strength of different effects varies widely across sectors.

Agglomeration implies spatial differences in productivity. There is significant research on the extent to which firm productivity varies with access to economic size. Economic size typically refers to an area such as a city or travel-to-work area and is measured in different ways, such as urban population, or more sophisticated measures of market access or the effective density of a city or region. A consensus view is that, after controlling for variation in labor-force characteristics (skills, age, and in some cases occupation), the elasticity of productivity with respect to economic size is around 3–6 percent in advanced economies (Combes and Gobillon 2015; Rosenthal and Strange 2004). This means that each doubling of economic size raises productivity by around 5 percent so that a city of 5 million has productivity 20–30 percent higher than one of 200,000, numbers that align well with the casual observation of London or New York as compared to smaller towns and cities. Of course, these are average numbers, and the productivity advantage of urban areas will show up in different degrees in different sectors, and affecting different types of labor. For example, in advanced countries, regional disparities in the wages of skilled labor have increased much more in recent years than has been the case for unskilled labor.

Agglomeration effects are possibly much larger in developing countries. There, weaknesses and wide variation in the provision of physical infrastructure (such as transportation, communications, and power), in education, and in the provision of public services, significantly reduce the attractiveness of lagging places for investment unless offset by correspondingly large wage differentials (World

---

[10] Technically, these are positive pecuniary externalities between firms, not internalized by market decision-taking.

Bank 2009). Estimates based on variations in productivity across urban areas in developing countries suggest an elasticity of productivity with respect to city size of around 8 percent, twice that in developed economies (Chauvin et al. 2017; Glaeser and Xiong 2017). Regional productivity and earnings differentials are amplified further by the presence of informal sectors and traditional agricultural activities, whose productivity maybe four or five times lower than that of modern sector urban activities (Gollin et al. 2014).

Agglomeration economies imply that regional disparities may prove persistent. There is a "first-mover" or coordination problem: no firm wants to leave an existing cluster and forego the associated productivity benefits. Coordinated movement by many firms might be collectively profitable, but the market mechanism cannot achieve this. This is because, while each firm creates benefits for other firms, these do not enter its decision taking. It follows that even large wage differences between regions may be insufficient to induce firms to locate in a lagging region, rather than in an established center. A further implication is that there are threshold effects and "tipping points." Policy changes below some threshold may be wholly ineffective, while a big push of policy across a range of actions may stand a greater chance of success (Murphy et al. 1989).

Agglomeration effects also imply that transport and infrastructure improvements, and "connectivity" more broadly, have ambiguous effects—but at some point, are likely to reduce disparities. Reducing the cost of shipping goods and services—globalization—enables clusters of activity to form, since production no longer has to take place close to consumption. This allows regional disparities to develop, particularly if clusters are associated with high productivity. But in the limiting case where connectivity is perfect, and goods, services, capital, and knowledge are equally accessible from all places, then geography is immaterial—the "death of distance." We are back in the textbook model of firms moving to the lowest-wage places, thus removing regional wage disparities and securing factor price equalization (Fujita et al. 1999). This ambiguity makes it difficult to generalize about the effects of improving connectivity.

Moreover, the effects are highly sector-specific. In finance and some creative sectors, improved information and communications connectivity has promoted the concentration of activity. A few centers can supply services to much of the world, while at the same time benefiting from the agglomeration economies of thick local labor markets and a cluster of providers of specialist services. In other sectors, the emergence of global value chains means that value-added in the production of a final product has become more dispersed, helping reduce inequalities across countries. Yet different stages of production ("tasks" or functions such as R&D and inputs of financial and legal services) have become more spatially concentrated, sometimes in just a few cities, so creating disparities within countries. While these global changes in connectivity will affect different regions in different ways, it is nevertheless likely that a lagging region is more likely to be an attractive destination for inwards investment, the better connected it is.

In summary, the potential movement of jobs and capital does not imply equalization of productivity but does place bounds on spatial productivity differences. In an advanced economy with good connectivity and little variation in public capital, productivity in booming areas may be up to 60 percent higher than in lagging regions (as in Figure 17.1, left panel). In developing countries connectivity is probably weaker, variation in public capital is much greater, and agglomeration effects may be more powerful, yielding larger productivity variation (Figure 17.1, right panel).

B. Migration and Labor

The second mechanism that should act to equalize real incomes across regions is the migration of workers to places with higher real income. Returns to mobile factors will then tend to be equalized and productivity differences will show up in the returns to immobile factors. For example, suppose that labor is perfectly mobile while land and housing are immobile and fixed. Labor mobility then tends to equalize real incomes (utility), because people leave a low-wage region until the price of land and housing has fallen to a low enough level to compensate for low nominal wages. At the same time, the price of land and housing is bid up in the destination region (Combes et al. 2019), and it is landowners who capture much of the agglomeration benefits of booming cities.

But migration may fail to iron out spatial differences in real incomes. First, the gains from moving to higher productivity areas vary across individuals. Spatial wage differentials are much higher for some skill types, often skilled as opposed to unskilled workers, so migration tends to change the skill and occupational mix of different places. Second, migration is costly, financially and also because of social networks and other amenities that are lost in migration. These costs vary widely across individuals in the population. Migration from lower- to higher-wages areas is, therefore, income-equalizing for the marginal worker but, across the population at large, leaves spatial variation in productivity, wages, and real income. Those left behind in lower productivity areas, for whom moving costs exceed the expected present value of gains from relocation, are likely to be older and less-skilled workers.

Declining areas are often subject to a vicious circle of further decline. As young, skilled workers migrate away, the local tax base and hence tax revenues diminish. In turn, this implies a deterioration in public services, such as schools, public safety, and cultural amenities (Florida 2014), and/or an increase in local tax rates (Pallagst et al. 2014). A shrinking local market may reduce any local agglomeration benefits; for instance, the "brain drain" of skilled workers decreases the region's ability to attract clusters of skilled, innovative activities (Davis and Dingel 2020; Berry and Glaeser 2005). Falling land and property prices may lock-in older residents (as owner-occupiers are unable to finance moves, particularly if capital markets are imperfect), but also cause a deterioration in standards of property maintenance and upgrading. Under these circumstances, it becomes even harder to retain or attract skilled workers (including public sector employees, such as teachers) and inward investment by firms. The region may become locked in a downward spiral (Holmes and Ohanian 2014; Weaver et al. 2018), characterized by a persistent urban decline (Glaeser and Gyourko 2005).

C. Spatial Equilibrium

Spatially uneven outcomes may represent a "spatial equilibrium." Because of agglomeration effects, productivity is higher in a cluster or booming region than in a poorly connected lagging region. If wages are correspondingly higher in the high productivity area, then no individual firm has an incentive to move. Workers and households may have little incentive to move either if land and property prices are low enough in the lagging region to compensate for lower nominal wages.

The nature of the spatial equilibrium poses several problems. First, this equilibrium is not generally efficient. There are multiple externalities; for example, growing a city brings positive externalities from agglomeration and negative ones from congestion and pollution. Coordination failures mean that efficient outcomes are not achieved (see examples below). Second, as we have noted, real incomes are not fully equalized across space, for several reasons. Most importantly, migration is slow, causes adverse changes in the skill and age structure of places experiencing substantial out-migration, and creates large social costs for the left-behind. In addition, there are limits to the extent to which low land and property prices can compensate for low wages—once such prices fall far enough, then housing is left vacant as the place depopulates.

D. Growth and Regional Disparities in Developing Countries

It is almost inevitable that a process of rapid growth and structural change starts in a few places, rather than uniformly across a country. Agglomeration forces are likely to be strong, as firms, skilled workers, large markets, and the network of supplier firms that support agglomeration are concentrated in a few large centers. This is likely to be reinforced by the spatial distribution of public capital. Transport infrastructure, power grids, and other utilities are all expensive and lumpy investments that will initially serve some regions better than others. It is efficient to concentrate them in areas of high population density and incipient, if not actual, economic activity. In addition, political institutions and policies may encourage over-concentration in excessively large cities, through a skewed allocation of public services and under-investment in inter-regional transport and communications (Davis and Henderson 2003). In such circumstances the first-mover problem is acute, meaning that firms and workers will concentrate in the economic center, even if spatial wage differences are large. This is manifest in, amongst other things, the growth of developing country megacities and the problem of "excess primacy," that is the dominance of the largest city in the overall urban hierarchy (World Bank 2009; Henderson 2002).

From these beginnings, how is convergence likely to be achieved? Jobs are likely to spread out of central areas, as costs in these areas increase. Wages and land rents increase, and so too may costs of congestion and pollution. This spread of activity can be promoted by the provision of transport and other infrastructure. At the same time, there will be movement of people towards prosperous areas, further boosting the mega-cities, and possibly creating demographic and social problems in places experiencing out-migration. It is unsurprising that countries should want to manage the balance of these two different processes but doing so is difficult. Direct controls of population movement—the Chinese *hukou* system—may be effective but are viewed as impractical or undesirable in many countries. Appropriate measures will be country-specific, but should generally support the growth of secondary cities, while at the same time accepting that some regions are likely to face population decline.

E. Lagging Regions in Advanced Economies

International competition and technical change have created large and persistent regional disparities in a number of advanced economies. The shocks are typically sector- and place-specific, hitting a sector in which some areas have had a traditional comparative advantage, such as textiles, shipbuilding, extractive industries, and, in some cases, the automobile industry. That is, regional disparities are relatively more likely to be symptomatic of negative shocks in advanced economies than in developing countries. How do places adjust to these shocks, and how is it that, in some cases, the impacts are so persistent?[11]

In this context, adjustment mechanisms may fail for several reasons. We have already discussed some of these issues, and two further points need to be made. First, there may be downwards rigidity in nominal wages, arising from both institutional frictions and the setting of national, rather than regional, norms. This has

---

[11] Austin et al. (2018) analyze this issue for the United States.

resulted in high levels of unemployment in many affected regions (Figure 17.2). More fundamentally, even with wage flexibility and full employment, there remains the question of what sectors are likely to replace those that have been lost. Many of the traditional industries that have been hit by these changes involved highly sector-specific skills that are not attractive to potential inward investors. And, fundamentally, agglomeration economies often operate at the sectoral level ("economies of localization"). This means that sectoral clusters form (for instance, in finance, technology, and the creative industries) and that the first-mover problem is strong in such sectors. Those areas that have lost traditional tradable sectors do not offer an internationally competitive environment for these new sectors. These areas do, however, if wages are low enough, offer an environment for non-tradable sectors supplying the domestic economy—for instance, back-office operations, warehousing, local food processing, and public sector administration. Such areas have therefore tended to fill up with these non-tradable sectors, often offering low-skill and low-wage jobs. The difficulty of setting up new tradable sectors (especially those with localization economies) means that it is possible for a country to end up both with regional disparities and with an inefficiently small tradable goods sector. This is a low-level equilibrium trap, brought about by the first-mover problem.

IV. Policy Response

A. Spatially Blind, Spatially Connective, and Spatially Targeted Policies

The geography of economic activity within countries has changed fundamentally in recent decades, in particular in advanced economies. Following a long period of regional convergence, international economic integration, and technological progress that favors economies of scale and agglomeration have triggered deep structural changes within national economies, including an increasing concentration of value creation in a number of metropolitan areas. Is it possible to withstand the forces of skill-biased technological change, globalization, and agglomeration that have driven regional disparities in recent decades? Moreover, is it desirable to do so, as these same forces have also been key drivers of overall economic growth and prosperity? Hence, is there an inherent trade-off between economic efficiency and regionally inclusive growth, or are there effective policies that can revive economic activity in declining areas without jeopardizing aggregate growth and welfare?

Traditional economic orthodoxy suggests that governments should care about people rather than places. Economic policy should focus on macroeconomic stability and building strong economic institutions that allow an efficient allocation of resources and smooth adjustment to shocks through free flows of labor and capital while ensuring the provision of public goods and affordable access to basic services such as primary health care, education, sanitation, and security. Policymakers should focus on attaining spatial inclusiveness by promoting equality of opportunity rather than even economic activity across regions. Progressive taxation systems and social protection could help achieve more equal outcomes in terms of disposable real incomes and living standards.

As a result, *spatially blind*, people-based policies would generally be the first choice to address regional disparities in countries where labor and capital are mobile (World Bank 2009). These are universal policies applied on a national level, which do not explicitly focus on lagging regions, but which can nevertheless assist them by assisting lagging *households*. Such policies could include measures to:

- Strengthen public services such as health, education, and utilities (for instance, rural electrification).
- Ensure that interregional transfers, stemming for instance from a progressive tax system and social protection, as well as nationwide economic regulations, all assist lagging households.

Spatially connective policies could complement spatially blind policies, by connecting peripheral areas to markets, facilitating the movement of goods, services, people, and ideas, integrating lagging and leading areas, and thereby promoting interregional convergence. Such measures could include:

- Infrastructure investment in highways, railroads, ports, airports, and public transportation, as well as in information and communication networks. The return to these policies will be especially high where lagging regions nevertheless enjoy relatively high economic density.
- Efforts to facilitate the movement of people from lagging regions to more prosperous ones ("mobility towards opportunity").

However, the experience of recent decades raises some doubts as to whether these standard policy prescriptions are sufficient to overcome regional divides and promote opportunity. While spatially blind and connective policies may help many skilled, young, and ambitious people in lagging regions move toward better opportunities in booming regions, the majority of the population is less mobile and may remain stuck in their declining home regions. In some (mostly developing) countries, inter-regional mobility is inherently hindered by geographic, social, cultural, or ethnolinguistic divisions. Moreover, mobility is not always towards opportunity: while mobility in most OECD countries is indeed towards urban metro centers (OECD 2018), for the United States a much higher share of moves has been between lagging (low vitality) regions rather than from less to more dynamic regions (Nunn et al. 2018). In many advanced economies, the declining demand for lower-skilled labor and steep increases in housing costs in booming regions have further reduced migration from lagging regions (Nunn et al. 2018; Bayoumi and Barkema 2019; Hsieh and Moretti 2019). This limited mobility has contributed to high and persistent non-employment rates in some regions that have experienced deindustrialization and economic decline (Austin et al. 2018). In this context, unemployment is a far more important determinant of discontent than low earnings—increasing social strains in economically depressed regions are linked to a lack of jobs rather than disposable income (Austin et al. 2018; Neumark 2018).

All this suggests a case for *spatially targeted*, place-based policies that make lagging regions more attractive places in which to create jobs, for instance by supporting local demand and improving business conditions, as opposed to people-based redistributive policies that aim to address skewed economic outcomes. Regionally focused incentives could encompass:

- Location-specific favorable tax treatments, investment subsidies, special regulations, and investment climate reforms.
- The targeted location of public employment, and public funding of research and higher education facilities or local infrastructure.

Economists have traditionally been skeptical about the effectiveness of spatially targeted policies and concerned about their distortionary side-effects. The conventional wisdom is that such policies have at best mixed-effects (Neumark and Simpson 2015). Their impacts have often been limited and not sustainable. Sometimes, they largely amount to beggar-thy-neighbor policies that shift activity and employment from one place to another (Ehrlich and Overman 2020). That said, infrastructure policies seem to work better than tax exemptions, or employment and investment subsidies. For instance, in the United States, the Tennessee Valley Authority generated significant improvements in that region's infrastructure, with a lasting impact on its development. But even in this case, the local manufacturing agglomerations it engendered were offset by losses in the rest of the country (Kline and Moretti 2014). The fiscal costs of interventions can be high and favoring some regions over others generates horizontal-equity concerns (Gbohoui et al. 2019). Other possible side-effects include distorted migration and the capitalization of the benefits into housing costs (Austin et al. 2018). Moreover, the case for place-based policies was historically weak against the backdrop of a long period of regional convergence and high inter-regional mobility.

Nevertheless, spatially targeted policies never completely fell out of policymakers' favor, and the case for them has strengthened over time, given persistently high and/or widening regional disparities, lower inter-regional mobility, and the social and political costs of the deindustrialization and economic decline of entire regions. Some market failures may be best addressed at the local level—for instance, localized productivity spillovers, or when not-working rates and employment elasticities are both comparatively large in distressed regions (Austin et al. 2018). Even where efficiency arguments for such policies are weak, they could help ensure individual regions against place-based shocks, and address equity concerns (Gaubert et al. 2021).

B. Firms, Jobs, and Capital

We now examine the case for some of these policies in greater detail. We focus first on measures to boost job creation, including both spatially connective policies, and place-based policies such as the localization of public investment and public employment, tax or spending benefits for businesses and/or individuals, and regulatory relief measures. Policy measures can be explicitly spatial (such as the US Appalachian Regional Commission, the *Mezzogiorno* tax credit for Italy's South, or the solidarity surcharge for East Germany) or implicitly spatial, for instance, sectoral support for an industry that is highly concentrated in specific regions.

Public capital: infrastructure and connectivity. Spatially connective infrastructure, for instance, highways, railroads, and metropolitan transit networks can promote mobility, either by facilitating long-distance moves or by reducing economic distance, allowing commuters from further afar to participate in the economic activity of a leading region (Neumark 2018; Smith 2018). In the latter case, a metropolitan area enlarges by integrating its hinterland. A good example of a spatially connective policy initiative that goes beyond mere transport infrastructure is the concept of "rural-urban integrated cities" developed in South Korea. Launched in the mid-1990s, the policy aimed at reducing rural-urban disparities by integrating rural counties with cities in a unified spatial framework. Such frameworks encompass joint planning of transport links, land use, public service provision, and local administration (World Bank 2009).

At the same time, the physical and digital infrastructure helps connect different regions, improving the access of entrepreneurs and firms in lagging areas to the larger and thriving markets of leading areas. While better access to a large and growing market may boost some economic activity in the lagging area, it also allows companies from leading areas to compete in the periphery. Furthermore, firms from the lagging area may be lured to relocate to the leading area themselves. Thus, better infrastructure links could also further increase the concentration of economic activity. Most likely, industries that exhibit agglomeration economies would relocate to the center, while those that do not might benefit from the lower labor costs in the periphery.

Spatially targeted public investment projects are generally the most popular tool for promoting local economic development. Empirically, their record is mixed. Generally, they have been successful when they identified and targeted regional interventions with high returns, such as the electricity supply capacity created by the *Tennessee Valley Authority*. Such projects produced durable employment impacts and agglomeration economics, serving as incubators for private investment. However, public investment programs have failed to make a lasting impact where they did not target high return interventions, their scale was too modest, or their scope too broad. Moreover, there are risks that political pressures, limited local ownership, and the lack of thorough cost-benefit analysis produce white elephant projects with marginal benefits and possibly high follow-up costs for operation and maintenance. Policymakers can mitigate such risks through close coordination and collaboration with local authorities, businesses, and citizens, together with rigorous cost-benefit and impact analyses. The European Union's *Smart Specialization Strategy* is a promising approach in this regard.

To some extent, governments can also support structurally weak regions through the targeted location of government agencies, public research institutions, technology parks, or military installations. Some developing and emerging economies have gone as far as relocating the country's administrative capital in an effort to both develop the hinterland and to reduce congestion in the traditional center (for instance, Brazil, Indonesia, Kazakhstan, Myanmar, Egypt). While proximity to federal or state capitals may be important for some government agencies, others are quite insensitive to the location (Yglesias 2016). Stable public or publicly funded white-collar employment could serve as a solid demand base for local economies that lack agglomeration economies and other competitive advantages. Moreover, colleges, universities, research institutions, and technology parks can also have substantial local externalities in terms of symbiotic public-private training and research partnerships, entrepreneurial start-ups, and the diffusion of knowledge, ideas, and technologies to local firms (Baron et al. 2018; Link and Scott 2018). The broad distribution of federal and state government agencies, as well as research institutions, has in many cases successfully contributed to the mitigation of regional disparities in Germany, sustaining the local economies of small- and mid-sized cities and creating symbiotic partnerships. Examples are the network of *Fraunhofer Gesellschaft* research institutes or Baden-Württemberg's *universities of cooperative education*, with their close links to regional small and medium enterprises.

The regional targeting of corporate tax incentives and subsidies could be attractive if there are large regional differences in unemployment (for instance owing to the decline of a localized industry), and measures supporting employment promise to have a high return in lagging places. Many developing countries have introduced special export-processing zones, some of which have been very successful as incubators for broader industrial development (such as the *Special Economic Zones* in China). Policymakers in advanced economies have introduced corporate investment and employment incentives in the form of tax credits, subsidies, preferential credit, or funding for workforce training to support disadvantaged regions (Neumark 2018). Examples include the United Kingdom (*Enterprise Zones*), United States (*Empowerment Zones* and *Opportunity Zones*), France (*Zones Franches Urbaines*), and the European Union's Cohesion Policy. Their results have been mixed, with both the size and the sustainability of impact being very sensitive to the time period and individual approach (Austin et al. 2018; Busso et al. 2013; Ham et al. 2011; Neumark and Kolko 2010; Greenbaum and Engberg 2004; O'Keefe 2004; Bondonio and Engberg 2000). Case studies suggest that interventions are more likely to prove successful if they build on existing comparative advantages, focus on innovative and high value-added activities, and display close coordination between national and regional authorities and the private sector.

Region-specific tax incentives or subsidies for individuals are less common than for corporations. They are generally regressive (with benefits accruing mostly to higher-income earners), poorly targeted for regional redistribution, and may result in distorted migration to subsidized areas without incentivizing concomitant job creation. Moreover, horizontal equity concerns are likely to be more serious for individuals than for corporate subsidies. That said, spatially blind national tax policy can have implicit spatial effects, as with the 2017 US tax reform, which combined lower individual tax rates with caps on the deductibility of home mortgage interest, thus penalizing coastal high-tax states.

In numerous cases, spatially targeted regulatory relief measures have been combined with corporate employment subsidies in special enterprise zones. They include relaxed zoning and environmental regulations, one-stop permitting, and other simplified bureaucratic procedures. In other cases, stringent urban zoning and building regulations, such as minimum lot sizes, maximum lot occupancy rates, height and unit restrictions, or historic preservation districts have contributed to an inelastic housing supply with steep housing cost increases, restricting the population growth in booming areas (for instance the San Francisco Bay area or London).

C. Migration and Labor

Several factors have negatively affected interregional labor mobility, often rooted in policies that have created market distortions. The most important are housing costs and social benefits (Bayoumi and Barkema 2019; Hsieh and Moretti 2019; Nunn et al. 2018; Ganong and Shoag 2017). Sometimes, discriminatory policies and residential segregation along ethnic/racial lines have contributed to and manifested inequalities on the regional or local levels (Hardy et al. 2018; Pietila 2010). Moreover, there are also social costs to moving and leaving family and friends behind, and these costs are likely rising given aging societies and the high cost of elderly care and childcare.

Housing Costs

In some countries, stringent municipal zoning regulations, building codes, and land-use conversion rules have contributed to an increasingly constrained and inelastic housing supply in booming areas (Hsieh and Moretti 2019). The resulting steep increases in housing costs have made it unaffordable for many people to move from lagging to leading regions.[12] Disincentives from high housing costs dominate the incentives from higher potential earnings, especially for people in lower-wage professions (Bayoumi and Barkema 2019). In many developing countries, insecure property rights, high transaction costs due to the lack of titles and cadasters, and limited access to credit are additional deterrents to regional mobility (World Bank 2009). Consequently, strengthening property rights and making land use, zoning, and building regulations more flexible could help make housing supply more elastic, transactions smoother, and housing more affordable. Support for investment in social housing could help increase the availability and affordability of housing in booming urban areas.[13] Finally, some cities rely on rent-control regulations; these may limit the cost of existing living space but are also likely to deter investment in new housing units.

Social Benefits

The non-portability of state and local social benefits is a major deterrent to labor mobility. Public pension schemes, often explicitly designed to incentivize long-term job commitment, create strong incentives for public employees not to leave (Economist 2017). Municipal-level social benefits, such as housing vouchers, as well as federal social programs that are administered at local or regional levels (for instance, Medicaid in the United States) equally, encourage people to stay put, as they may lose or have to reapply for the benefits when they move between counties or states (Austin et al. 2018). Lower living costs in lagging regions may motivate people that rely on fixed social benefits, such as unemployment insurance, not to relocate. The granting of a universal basic income could have a similar effect, reducing labor supply in booming regions (Waldman 2016). On the

---

[12] At the same time, depressed real estate values and slow-moving housing markets have made leaving more difficult for people that live in regions that are in economic decline.

[13] For instance, Vienna, Austria, has a long tradition of providing affordable public housing; it owns or operates more than 420,000 housing units.

other hand, it would also help support demand in lagging regions. That said, both effects are likely modest.

D. Choice of Measures and Implementation Considerations

There are trade-offs between spatially connective policies that strengthen mobility and spatially targeted policies that directly support local economies. Measures that improve mobility reinforces regionally unbalanced growth and geographical concentration, withdraw the most productive workers from lagging regions, and thereby further diminish the economic prospects of the less skilled and mobile workers that are left behind. In contrast, place-based policies foster more balanced economic activity across regions but may hamper overall economic growth by inhibiting an efficient spatial allocation of capital and labor. This is because the same forces that lead to a concentration of economic activity and inequality are important drivers of growth: technological progress has favored economies of scale and agglomeration, while international economic integration has created opportunities but also brought about structural change and dislocation in many local and regional economies. Misguided place-based policies could result in unproductive capital investment and discourage efficiency-enhancing labor mobility by distorting workers' incentives to move towards opportunity. Thus, policymakers need to strike the right balance between fostering rapid but regionally uneven growth on the one hand, and promoting more inclusive regional development outcomes on the other.

Ultimately, the choice of policies must be country- and context-specific. One-size-fits-all policy interventions are not appropriate for vastly different regional economies, and there is merit in place-sensitive policies tailored to particular locales. The right mix of measures may differ between advanced and developing economies, or between higher- and lower-income regions. Spatially blind and spatially targeted policy strategies can complement or counteract each other, depending on the context. The goal is always to release the development potential of all regions and counter the under-utilization of skills and resources (Iammarino, Rodriguez-Pose, and Storper 2018). To this end, "economic development policy should be both sensitive to the need for agglomeration and the need to occur in as many places as possible," to foster dynamic efficiency and maximize the aggregate economy's future innovation potential.

The appropriate policy mix will depend on the characteristics of a country's leading and lagging regions, and the key drivers of regional disparities. Sparsely populated lagging areas may be best served by people-based policies focused on providing basic public services. In contrast, large-scale infrastructure investment would likely generate low returns, and spatially targeted policies aimed at attracting business investment would be handicapped by the limited market size and shallow local labor markets. Densely populated lagging areas, on the other hand, could benefit from spatially connective infrastructure if there are no significant structural impediments to mobility, and otherwise from spatially targeted incentives and local infrastructure investment (World Bank 2009). In this context, policymakers should consider to what extent disparities reflect strong agglomeration economies, low interregional mobility, or weak interconnectedness of regional markets. The policy should also take into account the specific regional economic structures, resource endowments, and employment elasticities, as well as the presence of positive or negative externalities, and any regional targeting challenges. More broadly, in advanced regions, policies should focus on maintaining the innovative edge to keep abreast with the routinization, imitation, and geographic spread as technologies mature. In lagging lower-income regions suffering from limited skill pools and productive capital, policies should exploit wage competitiveness, and boost local capacity through active labor market policies, education reforms, and university-industry linkages to foster skill development and innovation absorption. Policymakers must also bear in mind the potential for reforms to trigger out-migration of the skilled and young, resulting in negative demographic dynamics that further undermine economic and social creativity.

Authorities should also consider fiscal costs, policy space, and implementation capacity, and quality of governance at both the national and regional levels (EBRD 2019). Large-scale infrastructure projects and spatially targeted policies to boost local markets, business investment, and employment are costly. They must be weighed against the expected social returns, using thorough cost-benefit analysis. This is all the more important where fiscal policy space is constrained, and spending needs to be prioritized. Even where the economic returns from spatially connective or place-based policies are in principle high, if the quality of governance and the government's implementation capacity are weak, then actual outturns will likely suffer from delays, wasteful spending, rent-seeking behavior, or outright corruption. In such contexts, the focus should be first on strengthening governance and institutions, including property rights, land regulations, economic management, and planning and implementation capacity at the national and sub-national levels. Related considerations include the design of intergovernmental financial relations, the presence of vertical fiscal imbalances, and the level of fiscal and political decentralization, which will determine which level of government should be responsible for the design, implementation, and monitoring of policy measures (Bartolini et al. 2016; Gbohoui et al. 2019).

Governments must also take into account political economy considerations, including society's preferences regarding interregional redistribution. Where the public's appetite for spatial redistribution is low in general or limited by the existence of cultural, ethnic, or political divisions between regions, the focus should be on spatially blind national policies with the potential to assist disproportionately lagging regions. These could be complemented by spatially connective measures to help reduce regional divisions over time.

E. Case Studies: German Reunification, and the Italian *Mezzogiorno*

We now illustrate the arguments through two case studies of place-based policies. The first, German reunification, proved relatively successful. The second, the Italian *Mezzogiorno* (South), less so.

German Reunification

When Germany was reunified in 1990, the East lagged far behind the West in economic performance and living standards. Labor productivity in the East was 30 percent of that in the West. The conversion of East Germany's currency into West Germany's at parity, rapid wage increases in the East stemming from the national bargaining system and generous public-sector salaries, and the adoption of Western labor regulations created a massive revaluation shock for East German firms. The short-term result was large-scale deindustrialization and mass unemployment.

But over time the East largely converged with the West. Manufacturing grew rapidly, and new industrial clusters emerged. In 2019, GDP per capita and disposable income in the East stood at, respectively, approximately 75 percent and 85 percent of Western levels, and the cost of living was lower. Indeed, growth in the East outstripped that in most eastern European countries, despite starting from a higher base. Unemployment fell from a post-reunification high of 20 percent to 7 percent. Life also improved drastically across a range of other measures: the life-expectancy gap closed, and the air became cleaner. That said, convergence has largely stalled since 2000 and remains incomplete, in terms of productivity as well as educational attainment and unemployment.

The East benefited from significant assistance from the West. Financial transfers from the West to the East equaled, for extended periods, about one-third of the East's GDP, and are still on the order of 10 percent of GDP. Most transfers took the form of pension and unemployment benefits, supporting consumption. But there was also significant investment in infrastructure (20 percent of all transfers), support to companies, including investment subsidies (9 percent), and investment in technical universities.

This regional policy faced challenges, but also enjoyed successes. Capital invested in the East was substantially less productive and profitable than in the West (Schalk and Untiedt 2000). A disproportionate share of investment went into capital-intensive sectors, such as chemicals, automotive, and microelectronics, resulting in relatively little value-added and employment creation. Relatedly, the East experienced significant net emigration toward the West, especially among the young. Nevertheless, investment incentives were effective in boosting regional investment, employment, and growth, especially in manufacturing but also in business services (Demary and Röhl 2009). The regional policy also promoted growth in labor productivity, particularly in the less developed regions (Alecke et al. 2013).

The Italian *Mezzogiorno*

In contrast, Italy's *Mezzogiorno* has suffered from extended economic under-performance. Italy's regional divide has proved extremely persistent. Its South has displayed little convergence with the North over the past century. The South's GDP per capita remains a little over half that of the North, its unemployment exceeds 20 percent, and it only attracts 1 percent of Italy's inward FDI. One consequence is continued large emigration from the South, particularly of the young and skilled. Political integration has delivered some convergence in consumption, supported by large transfers, although poverty rates remain twice as high in the South. But productivity convergence ultimately requires a catch-up in the production of increasingly complex tradables. And this remains hampered by poor institutional quality, as well as labor market rigidities including nationwide centralized wage bargaining (Boeri et al. 2019; Boltho et al. 2018).

Regional policy in Italy only enjoyed short-lived successes. The period after the Second World War saw massive assistance to southern Italy through the State-owned *Cassa per il Mezzogiorno* (1950–1984), modeled on the Tennessee Valley Authority. It concentrated first on agriculture and infrastructure; after the late 1950s, it turned towards industry and especially capital-intensive sectors. It proved effective in the first two decades, thanks to its remarkable technical autonomy in planning initiatives and distributing funds (Felice and Lepore 2017). Indeed, the 1951–1973 period saw the only episode of convergence of the South towards Italian and European averages. But starting in the 1970s the agency lost its autonomy, progressively becoming an instrument of waste and misallocation, and the South once more fell behind. Subsequently, the EU "Structural and Investment Funds" for regional policy, and the *Patti Territoriali* community development policies which emphasized local autonomy in designing interventions, have not, in general, helped raise productivity or employment in the South (Ciani and de Blasio 2015; Accetturo and de Blasio 2012; Aiello and Pupo 2012; Percoco 2005). Spending on infrastructure and in highly urbanized areas did prove relatively more successful than subsidies to firms or purchases of goods and services.

Weak institutions largely underlie the failure of regional policy towards the *Mezzogiorno*. Difficulties persist in managing public money and in identifying clear objectives. Poor governance, manifested in political clientelism and pervasive corruption, turns regional development funds into instruments of patronage. Regional policy is captured by local and national elites and distorts incentives by encouraging rent-seeking rather than entrepreneurship (Felice 2018). Organized crime, feeding off development programs, compounds the challenges (Leonardi 1995). As a result, despite large regional development expenditure, the South continues to suffer from relatively poor physical and digital connectivity, and lower-quality education. And, within the South, regional investments were more likely to raise productivity in areas characterized by higher institutional quality (Albanese et al. 2020).

V. Conclusion

Levels of economic activity and welfare differ sharply across sub-national regions, in both advanced and developing economies. In advanced economies, the rise in regional disparities appears to be associated with economic shocks and de-industrialization since the 1980s. In developing economies, regional disparities are instead often associated with economic takeoffs that spread unevenly across regions. These persistent disparities largely reflect clustering forces ("economies of agglomeration"), which generate spatial differences in productivity and living standards. The differences may be especially large in developing countries, reflecting wide variation in the provision of public services. The movement of jobs to lower-wage regions, and of people to higher-wage regions, may fail to iron out such differences while plunging declining areas into a vicious "death spiral." Such regional disparities raise equity concerns. They may have harmful implications for economic efficiency, as limited opportunities for those stuck in the wrong place leading to the underutilization of potential. And they can fuel social tensions.

It remains uncertain how future technological and societal trends will affect these regional disparities. Advances in communications technology, whose adoption was sharply accelerated by the Covid-19 pandemic, have increased the scope for remote work, especially in high-skilled sectors and occupations (Clancy 2020). In response, workers and firms may increasingly move out of large, expensive, congested, commuter-driven conurbations towards smaller cities and towns, while still reaping the benefits of a broadened pool of potential employers and employees. Geographic inequality would then diminish. However, it remains unclear how large-scale, full-time remote work would affect productivity (Choudhury et al. 2021; Bloom et al. 2015), and in particular learning and innovation (Sandvik et al. 2020; Cornelissen et al. 2017). More broadly, large cities have a long history of adapting to overcome challenges such as epidemics or the decline of manufacturing districts (Glaeser 2020). They may yet again prove resilient (Florida et al. 2020).

If market forces alone do not bring about convergence across regions, the first line of action lies in *spatially blind*, people-based policies, which address regional disparities by assisting lagging households. Examples include measures to strengthen basic services such as health and education and to ensure that national tax and social benefits systems assist underprivileged households.

Such measures may be usefully complemented by *spatially connective* policies, which aim to connect peripheral areas to markets, facilitating the movement of goods, services, people, and ideas, and thereby promoting interregional convergence. Examples include infrastructure investment in transportation, as well as information and communication networks, and measures to facilitate migration by reducing housing costs in leading regions and enhancing the geographic portability of social benefits.

In addition, there is a role for *spatially targeted*, place-based policies, focused on creating regional employment, particularly where there are significant obstacles to factor mobility—whether of workers to more dynamic areas or of firms to lower-wage regions. Examples include regionally focused public-investment projects, the relocation of government agencies and research institutions, and location-specific tax incentives and regulatory relief.

The appropriate policy mix will be country- and context-specific. It must depend on the characteristics of a country's leading and lagging regions, and the key drivers of regional disparities. Ultimately, policymakers must strike the right balance between fostering rapid but regionally uneven growth on the one hand and promoting more inclusive regional development outcomes on the other.

References

Abel, J., and R. Deitz. 2019. "Why Are Some Places So Much More Unequal Than Others?" *Federal Reserve Bank of New York Economic Policy Review* 25(1): 58–75.

Accetturo, A., and G. de Blasio. 2012. "Policies for Local Development: An Evaluation of Italy's 'Patti Territoriali.'" *Regional Science and Urban Economics* 42: 15–26.

Aiello, F., and V. Pupo. 2012. "Structural Funds and the Economic Divide in Italy." *Journal of Policy Modeling* 34(3): 403–18.

Albanese, G., G. de Blasio, and A. Locatelli. 2020. "Does EU Regional Policy Promote Local TFP Growth? Evidence from the Italian Mezzogiorno." *Papers in Regional Science* 100(2).

Alecke, B., T. Mitze, and G. Untiedt. 2013. "Growth Effects of Regional Policy in Germany: Results from a Spatially Augmented Multiplicative Interaction Model." *Annals of Regional Science* 50: 535–54.

Atkinson, R., M. Muro, and J. Whiton. 2019. *The Case for Growth Centers: How to Spread Tech Innovation Across America*. Washington, DC: Brookings Metropolitan Policy Program & ITIF.

Austin, B., E. Glaeser, and L. Summers. 2018. "Jobs for the Heartland: Place-Based Policies in 21st-Century America." *Brookings Papers on Economic Activity* 49(1): 151–255.

Autor, D. 2019. "Work of the Past, Work of the Future." *AEA Papers and Proceedings* 109: 1–32.

Autor, D., D. Dorn, and G. Hanson. 2013. "The Geography of Trade and Technology Shocks in the United States." *American Economic Review* 103(3): 220–5.

Autor, D., D. Dorn, and G. Hanson. 2013b. "The China Syndrome: Local Labor Market Effects of Import Competition in the United States." *American Economic Review* 103(6): 2121–68.

Avitabile, C., R. D'Souza, R. Gatti, and E.W. Chapman. 2020. *Insights from Disaggregating the Human Capital Index*. Washington, DC: World Bank Group.

Baron, J., S. Kantor, and A. Whalley. 2018. "Extending the Reach of Research Universities: A Proposal for Productivity Growth in Lagging Communities." In *Place-Based Policies for Shared Economic Growth*, edited by J. Shambaugh and R. Nunn. Policy Proposal 2018-11. Washington, DC: Brookings Institution.

Barro, R., X. Sala-i-Martin, O. Blanchard, and R. Hall. 1991. "Convergence Across States and Regions." *Brookings Papers on Economic Activity* 22(1): 107–82.

Barro, R., and X. Sala-i-Martin. 1992. "Convergence." *Journal of Political Economy* 100: 223–51.

Bartolini, D., S. Stossberg, and H. Blöchliger. 2016. "Fiscal Decentralisation and Regional Disparities." Economics Department Working Paper 1330. OECD, Paris.

Bayoumi, T., and J. Barkema. 2019. "Stranded! How Rising Inequality Suppressed US Migration and Hurt Those 'Left Behind.'" IMF Working Paper 19/122.

Berry, C., and E. Glaeser. 2005. "The Divergence of Human Capital Levels Across Cities." *Papers in Regional Science* 84(3): 407–44.

Bloom, N., J. Liang, J. Roberts, and Z. Ying. 2015. "Does Working from Home Work? Evidence from a Chinese Experiment." *Quarterly Journal of Economics* 130(1): 165–218.

Boeri, T., A. Ichino, E. Moretti, and J. Posch. 2019. "Wage Equalization and Regional Misallocation: Evidence from Italian and German Provinces." NBER Working Paper 25,612.

Boltho, A., W. Carlin, and P. Scaramozzino. 2018. "Why East Germany Did Not Become a New Mezzogiorno." *Journal of Comparative Economics* 46(1): 308–25.

Bondonio, D., and J. Engberg. 2000. "Enterprise Zones and Local Employment: Evidence from the States' Programs." *Regional Science and Urban Economics* 30(5): 519–49.

Busso, M., J. Gregory, and P. Kline. 2013. "Assessing the Incidence and Efficiency of a Prominent Place-Based Policy." *American Economic Review* 103(2): 897–947.

Case, A., and A. Deaton. 2020. *Deaths of Despair and the Future of Capitalism*. Princeton University Press.

Chauvin, J., E. Glaeser, Y. Ma, and K. Tobio. 2017. "What is Different about Urbanization in Rich and Poor Countries? Cities in Brazil, China, India, and the United States." *Journal of Urban Economics* 98: 17–49.

Che, N., and A. Spilimbergo. 2012. "Structural Reforms and Regional Convergence." IMF Working Paper 12/106.

Choudhury, P., C. Foroughi, and B. Zepp Larson. 2021. "Work-from-Anywhere: The Productivity Effects of Geographic Flexibility." *Strategic Management Journal* 42: 655–83.

Ciani, E., and G. de Blasio. 2015. "European Structural Funds During the Crisis: Evidence from Southern Italy." *IZA Journal of Labor Policy* 4.

Clancy, M. 2020. "The Case for Remote Work." Iowa State University, Economics Working Papers 20,007.

Combes, P-P., G. Duranton, and L. Gobillon. 2019. "The Costs of Agglomeration: House and Land Prices in French Cities." *Review of Economic Studies* 86(4): 1556–89.

Combes, P-P., and L. Gobillon. 2015. "The Empirics of Agglomeration Economies." In *Handbook of Regional and Urban Economics 5:* Ch. 5, edited by G. Duranton, J.V. Henderson, and W. Strange. Amsterdam: Elsevier, pp. 247–348.

Cornelissen, T., C. Dustmann, and U. Schönberg. 2017. "Peer Effects in the Workplace." *American Economic Review* 107(2): 425–56.

Coulombe, S., and F. Lee. 1995. "Convergence across Canadian Provinces, 1961 to 1991." *Canadian Journal of Economics* 28(4a): 886–98.

Crafts, N. 2005. "Regional GDP in Britain, 1871–1911: Some Estimates." *Scottish Journal of Political Economy* 52(1): 54–64.

Davis, D., and J. Dingel. 2020. "The Comparative Advantage Of Cities." *Journal of International Economics* 123: 103291.

Davis, J.C., and J.V. Henderson. 2003. "Evidence on the Political Economy of the Urbanization Process." *Journal of Urban Economics* 53(1): 98–125.

De La Fuente, A. 2002. "On the Sources of Convergence: A Close Look at the Spanish Regions." *European Economic Review* 46(3): 569–99.

De La Roca, J., and D. Puga. 2017. "Learning by Working in Big Cities." *Review of Economic Studies* 84(1): 106–42.

Demary, M., and K. Röhl. 2009. "Twenty Years after the Fall of the Berlin Wall: Structural Convergence in a Slow-Growth Environment." *Applied Economics Quarterly* 60: 9–34.

Duranton, G., and D. Puga. 2004. "Micro-Foundations of Urban Agglomeration Economies." In *Handbook of Regional and Urban Economics 4:* Ch. 48, edited by J.V. Henderson and J-F. Thisse, pp. 2063–117. Amsterdam: Elsevier.

Duranton, G., and D. Puga. 2020. "The Economics of Urban Density." *Journal of Economic Perspectives* 34(3): 3–26.

EBRD. 2019. *Transition Report 2019–20: Better Governance, Better Economies.* London.

The Economist. 2017. "Globalization has Marginalized Many Regions in the World." The briefing, Oct. 21.

Ehrlich, M., and H. Overman. 2020. "Place-Based Policies and Spatial Disparities across European Cities." *Journal of Economic Perspectives* 34(3): 128–49.

Felice, E. 2018. "The Socio-Institutional Divide: Explaining Italy's Long-Term Regional Differences." *Journal of Interdisciplinary History* 49(1): 43–70.

Felice, E., and A. Lepore. 2017. "State Intervention and Economic Growth in Southern Italy: The Rise and Fall of the *Cassa Per Il Mezzogiorno* (1950–1986)." *Business History* 59(3): 319–41.

Florida, R. 2014. *The Rise of the Creative Class—Revisited*. New York: Basic Books.

Florida, R., A. Rodríguez-Pose, and M. Storper. 2020. "Cities in a Post-Covid World." Utrecht University Papers in Evolutionary Economic Geography 20.41.

Fujita, M., P. Krugman, and A. Venables. 1999. *The Spatial Economy; Cities, Regions and International Trade*. Cambridge, MA: MIT Press.

Ganong, P., and D. Shoag. 2017. "Why Has Regional Income Convergence in the US Declined?" *Journal of Urban Economics* 102: 76–90.

Gaubert, C., P. Kline, and D. Yagan. 2021. "Place-Based Redistribution." NBER Working Paper 28,337.

Gaubert, C., P. Kline, D. Vergara, and D. Yagan. 2021b. "Trends In US Spatial Inequality: Concentrating Affluence and a Democratization of Poverty." NBER Working Paper 28,385.

Gbohoui, W., R Lam, and V. Lledo, 2019. "The Great Divide: Regional Inequality and Fiscal Policy." IMF Working Paper 19/88.

Giannone, E. 2019. "Skill-Biased Technical Change and Regional Convergence." Pennsylvania State University.

Glaeser, E. 2020. "Cities and Pandemics Have a Long History." *City Journal Magazine. Spring 2020*.

Glaeser, E., and J. Gyourko. 2005. "Urban Decline and Durable Housing." *Journal of Political Economy* 113(2): 345–75.

Glaeser, E., and W. Xiong. 2017. "Urban Productivity in the Developing World." *Oxford Review of Economic Policy* 33: 373–404.

Gollin, D., D. Lagakos, and M. Waugh. 2014. "The Agricultural Productivity Gap." *Quarterly Journal of Economics* 129(2): 939–93.

Greenbaum, R., and J. Engberg. 2004. "The Impact of State Enterprise Zones on Urban Manufacturing Establishments." *Journal of Policy Analysis and Management* 23(2): 315–39.

Ham, J., C. Swenson, A. Imrohoroglu, and H. Song. 2011. "Government Programs Can Improve Local Labor Markets: Evidence from State Enterprise Zones, Federal Empowerment Zones, and Federal Enterprise Community." *Journal of Public Economics* 95(7): 779–97.

Hardy, B., T Logan, and J. Parman. 2018. "The Historical Role of Race and Policy for Regional Inequality." In *Place-Based Policies for Shared Economic Growth*, edited by J. Shambaugh and R. Nunn. Washington, DC: Brookings Institution.

Henderson, J.V. 2002. "Urbanization in Developing Countries." *World Bank Research Observer* 17(1): 89–112.

Holmes, T., and L. Ohanian. 2014. "Pay with Promises or Pay as You Go? Lessons from the Death Spiral of Detroit." FRB Minneapolis Staff Report 501.

Hsieh, C., and E. Moretti. 2019. "Housing Constraints and Spatial Misallocation." *American Economic Journal: Macroeconomics* 11(2): 1–39.

Iammarino, S., A. Rodriguez-Pose, and M. Storper. 2018. "Regional Inequality in Europe: Evidence, Theory, and Policy Implications." *Journal of Economic Geography* 19(2).

IMF. 2019. "Closer Together or Further Apart? Subnational Regional Disparities and Adjustment in Advanced economies." *World Economic Outlook*, October: Ch. 2.

Kanbur, R., C. Rhee, and J. Zhuang. 2014. *Inequality in Asia and the Pacific: Trends, Drivers, and Policy Implications*. Asian Development Bank and Routledge.

Kemeny, T., and M. Storper. 2020. "Superstar Cities and Left-Behind Places: Disruptive Innovation, Labor Demand, and Interregional Inequality." LSE III Working Paper 41.

Kessler, J. 2018. *How the Concentration of Opportunity Elected Trump*. Third Way. Available at: https://www.thirdway.org/report/how-the-concentration-of-opportunity-elected-trump

Kline, P., and E. Moretti. 2014. "Local Economic Development, Agglomeration Economies, and the Big Push: 100 Years of Evidence from the Tennessee Valley Authority." *Quarterly Journal of Economics* 129(1): 275–331.

Krugman, P. 1991. "Increasing Returns and Economic Geography." *Journal of Political Economy* 99: 483–99.

Leonardi, R. 1995. "Regional Development in Italy: Social Capital and the Mezzogiorno." *Oxford Review of Economic Policy* 11(2): 165–79.

Link, A., and J. Scott. 2018. "Geographic Proximity and Science Parks." *Oxford Research Encyclopedia: Economics and Finance*.

Martin, R. 2001. "EMU Versus the Regions? Regional Convergence and Divergence in Euroland." *Journal of Economic Geography* 1(1): 51–80.

Marshall, A. 1920. *Principles of Economics*. London: Macmillan.

Muro, M., and S. Liu. 2016. "Another Clinton-Trump Divide: High-Output America vs Low-Output America." The Avenue Blog, Brookings Institution.

Muro, M., R. Maxim, and J. Whiton. 2019. *Automation and Artificial Intelligence: How Machines are Affecting People and Places*. Washington, DC: Brookings Institution.

Murphy, K.M., A. Shleifer, and R. Vishny. 1989. "Industrialization and the Big Push." *Journal of Political Economy* 97(5): 1003–26.

Nagaraj, R., A. Varoudakis, and M.-A. Véganzonès. 2000. "Long-run Growth Trends and Convergence across the Indian States." *Journal of International Development* 12: 45–70.

Neumark, D. 2018. "Rebuilding Communities Job Subsidies." In *Place-Based Policies for Shared Economic Growth*, edited by J. Shambaugh and R. Nunn. Washington, DC: Brookings Institution.

Neumark, D., and J. Kolko. 2010. "Do Enterprise Zones Create Jobs? Evidence from California's Enterprise Zone Program." *Journal of Urban Economics* 68(1): 1–19.

Neumark, D., and H. Simpson. 2015. "Place-Based Policies." In *Handbook of Regional and Urban Economics 5*: Ch. 18, edited by G. Duranton, J.V. Henderson, and W. Strange, pp. 1197–287.

Neven, D., and C. Gouymte. 1995. "Regional Convergence in the European Community." *Journal of Common Market Studies* 33(1): 47–65.

Nunn, R., J. Parsons, and J. Shambaugh. 2018. "The Geography of Prosperity." In *Place-Based Policies for Shared Economic Growth*, edited by J. Shambaugh and R. Nunn. Washington, DC: Brookings Institution.

O'Keefe, S. 2004. "Job Creation in California's Enterprise Zones: A Comparison Using a Propensity Score Matching Model." *Journal of Urban Economics* 55(1): 131–50.

OECD. 2016. *OECD Regional Outlook 2016: Productive Regions for Inclusive Societies.* Paris: OECD Publishing.

OECD. 2018. *OECD Regions and Cities at a Glance 2018.* Paris: OECD Publishing.

Pallagst, K., T. Wiechmann, and C. Martinez-Fernandez. 2014. *Shrinking Cities: International Perspectives and Policy Implications.* New York: Routledge.

Percoco, M. 2005. "The Impact Of Structural Funds On The Italian Mezzogiorno, 1994–1999." *Région et Développement* 21: 141–53.

Persson, J. 1997. "Convergence Across the Swedish Counties, 1911–1993." *European Economic Review* 41: 1835–52.

Pietila, A. 2010. *Not in My Neighborhood. How Bigotry Shaped a Great American City.* Chicago, IL: Ivan R. Dee.

Puga, D. 2010. "The Magnitude and Causes of Agglomeration Economies." *Journal of Regional Science* 50(1): 203–19.

Rodríguez-Pose, A. 2018. "The Revenge of the Places that Don't Matter (and What to Do About It)." *Cambridge Journal of Regions, Economy, and Society* 11(1).

Rosenthal, S., and W.C. Strange. 2004. "Evidence on the Nature and Sources of Agglomeration Economies." In *Handbook of Regional and Urban Economics 4*: Ch. 49, edited by J.V. Henderson, and J-F. Thisse, pp. 2119–71. Amsterdam: Elsevier.

Ross, M., and N. Bateman. 2019. *Meet the Low-Wage Workforce.* Washington, DC: Brookings Institution.

Sala-i-Martin, X. 1996. "Regional Cohesion: Evidence and Theories of Regional Growth and Convergence." *European Economic Review* 40(6): 1325–52.

Sandvik, J., R. Saouma, N. Seegert, and C. Stanton. 2020. "Workplace Knowledge Flows." *Quarterly Journal of Economics* 135(3): 1635–80.

Schalk, H.J., and G. Untiedt. 2000. "Regional Investment Incentives in Germany: Impacts on Factor Demand and Growth." *Annals of Regional Science* 34(2): 173–95.

Shearer, C. 2016. "The Small Town-Big City Split that Elected Donald Trump." The Avenue Blog, Brookings Institution.

Smith, S. 2018. "Development Economics Meets the Challenges of Lagging U.S. Areas: Applications to Education, Health and Nutrition, Behavior, and Infrastructure." In *Place-Based Policies for Shared Economic Growth*, edited by J. Shambaugh and R. Nunn. Washington, DC: Brookings Institution.

VanHeuvelen, T., and K. Copas. 2019. "The Geography of Polarization, 1950 to 2015." *Russell Sage Foundation Journal of the Social Sciences* 5(4): 77–103.

Waldman S. 2016. "The Economic Geography of a Universal Basic Income." Interfluidity Blog.

Weaver, R., S. Bagchi-Sen, J. Knight, and A. Frazier. 2018. *Shrinking Cities: Understanding Urban Decline in the United States*. London: Routledge.

Wilkinson, W. 2019. "The Density Divide: Urbanization, Polarization, and the Populist Backlash." Research Paper. Washington, DC: Niskanen Center

World Bank. 2009. *World Development Report 2009: Reshaping Economic Geography*. Washington, DC: World Bank.

Yglesias, M. 2016. "Let's Relocate a Bunch of Government Agencies to the Midwest." Vox. Available at: https://www.vox.com/new-money/2016/12/9/13881712/move-government-to-midwest

18

Generational Aspects of Inclusive Growth

Benedicte Baduel, Asel Isakova, and Anna Ter-Martirosyan

Inclusive growth refers to sharing economic benefits equitably across all segments of society, such as groups of people from different genders, ethnicities, and regions.[1] Another important aspect of inclusion is the sharing of economic benefits across generations, both in the static dimension of people in different age groups at a point in time and the dynamic dimension of people from different generations over time. This chapter analyzes the challenges and policy options to promote both static and dynamic generational inclusion.

At a point in time, the two main generational groups that are most vulnerable are the youth and the elderly. The youth have higher poverty rates and they have significantly worse labor market outcomes than other groups in many countries. The elderly often rely on income and health care support from public systems that are under increasing strains due to demographic and other trends.

Turning to the intergenerational dimension, a key issue is the dependence of economic opportunity on resources and advantages passed from parents to their children. In some countries, intergenerational mobility has been falling in recent times, exacerbating the impact of inequality by thwarting opportunities for social advancement.

I. Youth Poverty and Unemployment

Youth worldwide are a vulnerable group. The transition from childhood to adulthood, and especially from school to work, presents multiple challenges that are critical for long-term livelihood outcomes. Young adults' prospects and outcomes are largely influenced by socioeconomic factors during their childhood such as opportunities in terms of access to quality education and health services, geography, and so on. As a result, disadvantaged youth are more at risk of being marginalized.

[1] We thank Jaime Sarmiento Monroy and Amine Yaaqoubi for the excellent research assistance. We also thank Boele Bonthuis, Valerie Cerra, Barry Eichengreen, Asmaa El-Ganainy, Martin Schindler, and Nikola Spatafora, as well as participants in the Inclusive Growth book seminar series organized by the IMF Institute for Capacity Development for their comments.

Benedicte Baduel, Asel Isakova, and Anna Ter-Martirosyan, *Generational Aspects of Inclusive Growth* In: *How to Achieve Inclusive Growth.* Edited by: Valerie Cerra, Barry Eichengreen, Asmaa El-Ganainy, and Martin Schindler, Oxford University Press. © Benedicte Baduel, Asel Isakova, and Anna Ter-Martirosyan 2022.
DOI: 10.1093/oso/9780192846938.003.0018

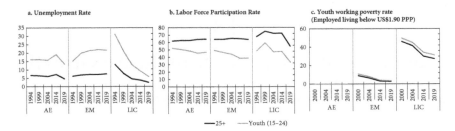

Figure 18.1 Youth Vulnerabilities
Sources: World Development Indicators Database, and authors' calculations.

Youth are particularly vulnerable to poverty. Youth unemployment and inactivity rates are higher than those of the adult population (Figure 18.1a–b) and young workers are more likely to live in poverty than their adult peers (Figure 18.1c). Globally, 30 percent of working youth live in extreme or moderate poverty conditions (i.e., living with less than $3.20 a day). Even in countries with well-developed social safety nets, these often target different groups (e.g., elderly, families with children, etc.), leaving working-age youth vulnerable to poverty. For example, in the United States, young adult poverty has increased over the past decades and is among the highest for any age cohort (Hawkins 2019).

Poor labor market prospects and lack of opportunities are a major source of concern for young people and have spurred social discontent in many countries. Surveys of young adults around the world highlight youth concerns regarding difficult labor market prospects. For example, 45 percent of Arab youth saw high unemployment as the biggest obstacle facing the Middle East (2019 ASDA'A Burson-Marsteller Arab Youth Survey); 69 percent of young African cited unemployment as their main concerns (2016 IPSOS African Youth survey); and 42 percent of youth surveyed in the European Union (EU) in 2017 said that employment should be a priority for the EU.

The Covid-19 crisis disproportionately affected the youth. Recent survey-based research in the UK shows that young people were among the hardest hit by the coronavirus shock (Adam-Prassl et al. 2020). In particular, they were more likely to have worked fewer hours, earned less than usual, and lost their job in the four weeks through March 25, 2020, than adults. Data for the United States shows that although the 16–24 years old cohort only represents 12 percent of all workers, they represent 24 percent of those employed in industries vulnerable to Covid-19 (Kochhar 2020). In addition, extended containment measures may affect educational outcomes and accentuate inequalities as online schooling content appears inadequate and sometimes inexistent. This is especially a risk in EMDEs where poorer populations do not have reliable access to the Internet, increasing the risk of school dropouts, especially young girls.

The transition from education to work is a critical period for youth that has implications for long-term employment outcomes. Technology is rapidly changing work, requiring new skills and increased adaptability among workers. How youth fare in their first transition has implications for future job opportunities in an evolving labor market (World Bank 2019). Entrenched youth exclusion deteriorates human capital which in addition to creating a lost generation, can ultimately affect growth and productivity, hampering future economic prospects of countries.

A. Young People in the Labor Market

Youth unemployment is high at the global level and inactivity is a persistent challenge. According to International Labor Organization (ILO) data, the unemployment rate of youth was nearly 14 percent as of 2019, more than three times higher than that of the adult population, and reached a high of 27 percent in the Middle East and North Africa (ILO 2020a; Matsumoto and Elder 2010). Based on the broader concept of inactivity, about 22 percent of youth globally are not in employment, education, or training (NEET) ranging from 12 percent in AEs to above 25 percent in some large EMs (for example Nigeria, South Africa, Turkey, and the MENA region, Figure 18.2a).

Young people tend to have lower-quality jobs (Ahn et al. 2019; Cho et al. 2012; Quintini and Martin 2014; Shehu and Nilsson 2014). Wage employment remains high, around 54 percent globally (ILO 2020b), on par with the adult population. However, it is not anymore systematically associated with job security and social protection as non-standard forms of work (temporary, part-time contracts, "gig" economy) have been increasing. Globally, the share of underemployed youth (Figure 18.2b) is three times as high as the equivalent share among adults (ILO

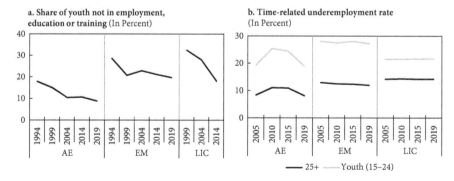

Figure 18.2 Educational Enrollment
Sources: ILO data and authors' calculations.

2020b) ranging from around 18 percent in AEs to over 25 percent in EMs. In EMDEs, absent adequate social safety nets, a disproportionate share of young workers are still employed in informal jobs (around 55 percent on average in EMDEs, excluding agriculture sector informal jobs according to Ahn et al. 2019).[2]

Wage inequality tends to be higher among youth. The youngest cohorts, with less education, typically work in the lowest-paying jobs. As a result, in the United States, for example, the mean wage of 16–24 years old is about 65 percent that of 25–34 years old. Underemployment is also associated with lower earnings. Because the most disadvantaged youth combine low education and low skills or experience, they find themselves at the bottom of the wage distribution and are more likely to experience poverty. As a consequence, wage inequality tends to be higher among youth than among the adult population. However, it has decreased since the global financial crisis, mostly driven by falling returns on tertiary education (ILO 2020b).

Despite converging education rates, young women are still at a disadvantage in the labor market. Educational gaps have broadly closed but young women still have more difficulties finding jobs (Figure 18.3) than young men (see Chapter 16) and they are disproportionately represented among NEET (70 percent of youth NEET are young women). Progress has been achieved in recent years to reduce the gender gap in participation in EMDEs, but it remains significantly higher than in AEs (Ahn et al. 2019). Additionally, even for young women who do find a job, evidence suggests that they take longer to find their first job than young men (Manacorda et al. 2017). There is also a gender pay gap among young cohorts reflecting, in part, the fact that young women are more likely to be

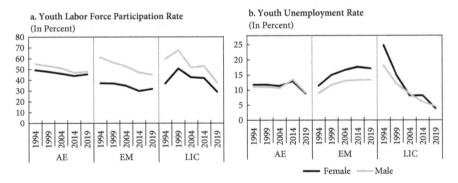

Figure 18.3 Gender Gaps

Sources: ILO Database, and authors' calculations.

---

[2] A measure developed by the ILO to capture labor market deficiencies such as people working less hours and earning less income than they would like and are available to or using their occupational skills incompletely.

under-employed and are more represented in low pay jobs than young men. However, it is lower than for the adult population, as single young men and women tend to appear very similar to employers, although not everywhere, often influenced by cultural factors.

B. Causes of Youth Vulnerability

Young people are more vulnerable than adults to economic downturns because they have fewer buffers. Because young adults are more financially constrained than adults, economic downturns that translate into deteriorating living conditions often lead youth to make decisions that further affect their prospects such as prematurely ending their education or transitioning into low-quality jobs with poor working conditions and low wages. Because they are less experienced, have shorter employment tenures, and are more likely to have less secure contracts than adults, youth are often the "last in—first out." In AEs, the youth unemployment rate increased by 5 percentage points between 2007 and 2013 in the context of the global financial crisis. Studies have found that these negative effects can be persistent, especially for youth entering the labor market during recessions (e.g., Cockx and Ghirelli 2016). In EMDEs with weak social protection and widespread informality rates, the informal sector tends to act as a shock absorber when formal labor market demand decreases in downturns (Ahn et al. 2019).

But structural constraints explain a significant share of youth unemployment. All over the world, evidence suggests that youth take a long time, around two years, to find their first job, translating into high rates of long-term unemployment among people who have never worked (Manacorda et al. 2017; Krafft and Assaad 2016). On the demand side, the lack of dynamism of the private sector in a context of dynamic demographic trends and slow economic transformations in EMDEs, at a time where educational attainment is increasing, present specific challenges for youth to transition to jobs that match their qualifications (Fox and Kaul 2017). On the supply side, in some regions duality such as preference toward public sector jobs also explains low youth employment rates among educated youth as those who can afford to stay unemployed (supported by their families) "queue" for these jobs.

A rigid labor market can make the transition to employment more difficult. As new entrants into the labor market, young people can be disproportionately affected by high labor costs (e.g., high minimum wages) and rigid employment protection (e.g., large severance payments) that are likely to discourage employers to hire them in stable jobs (Quintini and Martin 2014). There is evidence that this is associated with lower youth employment (Duval and Loungani 2019). In addition, in AEs, this often translates into an increase in temporary contracts for youth while in EMDEs, which offer fewer benefits and protection to workers, it often leads youth into informal jobs.

In general, longer education is associated with better labor market outcomes. Better education is associated with lower unemployment and inactivity rates, higher-quality jobs, and a better chance to transition to formal work in EMDEs (Shehu and Nilsson 2014). However, the returns to education have been decreasing in some parts of the world, either through a weaker transition to work as labor demand has not kept pace with growingly educated labor supply (EMDEs) or through a combination of lower job quality and more expensive education (AEs). In this context, young people find it more difficult to get jobs than their parents (see the section on intergenerational mobility). As social mobility declines, transitioning to employment is growingly challenging for disadvantaged youth. In some countries, the quality of education has not always kept up with the changing labor demand, making young people ill-equipped to succeed in the labor market.

Gaps in opportunities explain the gender gap in labor market outcomes. Young women still disproportionately face distortions and discriminations in the labor market, mobility constraints, the brunt of family obligations, and restrictions on their rights (ILO 2020b; Elborgh-Woytek et al. 2013; Gonzales et al. 2015; Shehu and Nilsson 2014). Young women are also still underrepresented in some education and career streams such as STEM or vocational education and training programs. Gender gaps tend to widen with marriage and more so with parenthood reflecting the penalty for women in the labor market associated with their disproportionate contribution to household and family obligations. In addition, the lack of networks and role models, which in some regions play a particularly important role in successful labor market transitions for youth amplifies the constraints for young women.

C. Policy Options

Designing and implementing reforms to support youth transition into the labor market is critical to foster sustainable and inclusive growth. Evidence suggests that to be most effective, strategies need to be broad-based, including education, labor market, and product market reforms, aiming at facilitating school-to-work transitions into good-quality jobs.

Some critical areas of reform can be outlined for AEs and EMDEs. If some areas are common to all countries, the starting point is not the same. In AEs, educational attainments are higher, and social protection systems are stronger. Demographics trends are also more favorable for young people as the aging population retires. In these countries, reforms should aim at fine-tuning institutions and policies to better prepare and protect youth, especially disadvantaged ones, in rapidly evolving labor market environments. In EMDEs, there is a need to

continue to improve the educational attainment of young people as well as to foster economic transformations that create enough jobs for increasingly educated
youth, a multi-dimensional challenge that is particularly relevant for resource-
rich countries (see Chapter 19). In the context of high informality and often weak
social protection systems, supporting youth transition to good-quality jobs early
in their career is critical.

Everywhere, young people need to be equipped with better and broader skills.
This requires better education throughout their youth, starting with early childhood development and good quality primary education. This is especially important for disadvantaged youth for which policies should aim at extending their stay
in formal education as long as possible, for example by providing direct cash
transfers to their families (ILO 2011). In EMDEs, it also means improving access
to and quality of secondary education and in AEs focusing on retention through
high school (Quintini and Martin 2014). Given the changes associated with automation and the need to build resilience in the face of pandemics, policies need to
support young people in being rapidly adaptable to changing labor market needs
and demand. In this context, tertiary education and vocational studies especially,
need to modernize to provide youth with those needed skills. Although there is
mixed evidence on the outcomes of vocational training, some studies have found
that in countries such as Germany or Denmark, it has had positive impacts on
youth integration into the labor market (Zimmermann et al. 2013). Generally,
strengthening the link between education, training and work would support
youth integration (ILO 2011).

Flexible labor markets with social safety nets that aim to protect workers—not
jobs—can support youth employment. More flexible labor market institutions are
associated with better outcomes for youth (Ahn et al. 2019; Banerji, et al. 2014;
Purfield, et al. 2018). In general, labor market regulations that reduce duality,
facilitate workers' mobility, and unemployment protection systems that support
workers' transition without raising the opportunity cost of work would all contribute to limit distortions to youth's integration (see Chapter 3 for more details).
In all countries, addressing legal impediments for women's integration into the
labor market and promoting family-friendly labor regulations is critical to reducing gender gaps (see Chapter 16 for more details).

Targeted active labor market policies (ALMPs) can support youth employment, particularly those more at risk of unemployment such as disadvantaged
youth.[3] These programs are common in AEs and have increased significantly in
Europe in the aftermath of the global financial crisis. In EMDEs, wage subsidy
programs are less developed than in AEs. Given that on average youth in EMDEs

---

[3] Active labor market policies are public programs aimed at helping a target population of
unemployed people find work, for example through income support, job search services or training
and skills building, or public works.

have lower education than in AEs, training programs that help young people acquire skills (as in Latin America for example) can be more effective for their integration into the labor market (O'Higgins 2017). In LICs, wage subsidy programs are rare and ALMPs mostly take the form of public employment programs in specific sectors such as public infrastructure maintenance (O'Higgins 2017). In this context, they have low efficiency in improving employment prospects when they do not contribute to building skills (and they sometimes carry a negative stigma) but have also been used as a transitory income support mechanism. Programs aimed at promoting self-employment and entrepreneurship have shown the most positive results among ALMPs in EMDEs, especially when they are combined with other policies in the areas of social protection, access to finance, and so on (O'Higgins 2017; Levy-Yeyati, et al. 2019). Successful implementation of cost-efficient programs tends to require a high administrative capacity to target, implement, monitor, and evaluate outcomes which can be more challenging in EMDEs than in AEs (Angel-Urdinola and Leon-Solano, 2013)). In general, ALMPs also have weaker results where job creation is lackluster (see Chapter 3 on labor market policy for a detailed discussion on ALMPs).

Reducing informality should be part of a broader policy strategy to improve job quality in EMDEs. Informal jobs in EMDEs are the norm for many youths. Evidence shows that policies aimed at reducing informality work best when combined with policies to improve the quality of formal employment and broaden the coverage of social protection (O'Higgins 2017). Because of the "signaling" effect of early labor market experiences, policies aimed at reducing informality should target interventions into preventing youths entry into informal jobs by aiming at improving young people's first experience in the labor market. First jobs programs have been developed, in Latin America for example, focusing on providing young people with good quality apprenticeship, internship opportunities, hiring subsidies, and special arrangements for youth employment (O'Higgins 2017).

Fostering private sector development in EMDEs, especially SMEs, is critical to creating more jobs for growing working-age populations. In many parts of the world, growingly educated youth has been discouraged by the lack of job opportunities. Creating enabling environments for private sector activity to thrive and create jobs is critical. Measures targeted at SMEs and promoting entrepreneurship, such as access to finance, could help support youth transition to work. Young people are tech savvy and they can also benefit from technology-driven change if given adequate incentives and opportunities. In EMDEs, improving the productivity of the informal sectors (including agriculture), by implementing measures to support human capital build-up and to create an enabling environment towards formality (market access, regulations, access to finance, etc.) could also contribute to decreasing youth exclusion and poverty.

II. Elderly Poverty

A. Why Elderly Poverty

The share of elderly people in the world population is now higher than ever and rising. The world population over the age of 65 is projected to increase from 9 percent in 2019 to 16 percent by 2050 (UN 2019). Elderly people face greater risks of becoming or remaining poor due to reduced options to work and more health issues. If elderly people have inadequate savings and social benefits, they can be vulnerable to economic insecurity and poverty, with limited options to escape.

The Covid-19 crisis amplified the existing vulnerabilities of the elderly across the world. With the fatality rates for older people several times the global averages and limited access to essential health services in many countries, elderly people face a range of additional risks from the pandemic, including age discrimination in accessing health care service, neglect, and violence (UN 2020, Policy Brief: The Impact of Covid-19 on older persons). The pandemic may also lead to a scaling back of critical services unrelated to Covid-19, further increasing risks to the lives of older persons (WHO 2020).

B. Measuring Elderly Poverty

There are several measures of elderly poverty and inequality. Absolute poverty rates show the percentage of elderly people living below the poverty line, whereas relative measures assess the distribution of poverty within the elderly group (horizontal inequality) or relative to other age groups (vertical inequality). For instance, horizontal inequality by income tends to be higher for countries with large informal sectors and relatively generous formal pensions.[4] Vertical inequality can provide an insight into the relative situation of older people, as many low-income countries with a high absolute elderly poverty rate may have an even higher poverty rate for other age groups (Evans and Palacios 2015).

Global estimates of poverty rates among older people are limited. With the absence of an international harmonized database on age-related poverty, the evidence is mainly limited to regional or country-level databases. In addition, most of the measures rely on country-specific thresholds which are not easily comparable across countries, particularly when comparing developed and developing countries. For example, the OECD defines elderly poverty as income below half

---

[4] Low pension coverage exacerbates income inequality and may result in a regressive redistribution of resources from low- to high-income individuals.

of the national median household income, which does not necessarily imply a low standard of living.

C. Facts on Elderly Poverty

The poverty rates for older people vary significantly across countries. In OECD countries, elderly poverty rates (over 65) averaged 13.5 percent in 2017, compared with 12 percent for the population as a whole (OECD 2019) (Figure 18.4). However, there are significant differences across countries. The poverty rates exceeded 40 percent in Korea, were above 30 percent in Estonia and Latvia, and more than 20 percent in Mexico and the United States. By contrast, in the Czech Republic, Denmark, and some other countries relative poverty rates were below 5 percent. These differences reflect many factors, including overall poverty rates in a country, pension coverage, family structure, and societal preferences in designing social transfer schemes. Although no harmonized databases exist for developing economies, higher overall poverty rates, larger informal sectors, and lower pension coverage suggest that elderly poverty rates on average are higher than in developed countries.

Incomes of older people relative to the rest of the population also differ depending on pension coverage and the adequacy of old-age social protection systems. For the OECD countries, older people fare relatively better than the rest of the population in 20 countries, including France, Slovakia, and the Netherlands. In Greece, Italy, and Spain incomes for the elderly are above 90 percent of the national average because of the relatively generous pension schemes (Figure 18.5). By contrast, in Korea, Estonia, Latvia, and Australia, older people are much more likely to be poor. For G20 counties beyond OECD, elderly poverty rates are high

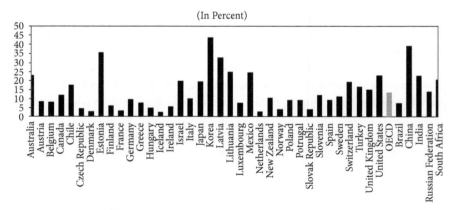

Figure 18.4 Elderly Poverty Rates (Over 65), 2019
Source: OECD Income Distribution Database.

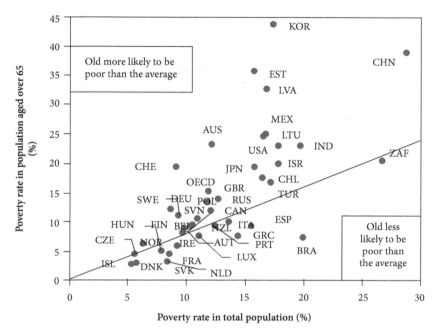

Figure 18.5 Income Poverty Rates by Age: Elderly vs Total Population
Source: OECD Income Distribution Database.

in China and India, 39 percent and 23 percent, respectively, while Brazil has much lower elderly poverty rates (OECD 2019).

For developing countries, relative poverty levels depend on demographics, pension coverage, and cultural arrangements. Older persons tend to be poorer than the general population in many African countries and are more often less poor in Latin America (UNCTAD 2017, Ageing report). Kakwani and Subbarao (2005) find that for Sub-Saharan African countries older persons are poorer than other age groups. In Zambia, for example, 80 percent of people aged 60 years or over were below the poverty line compared to 67 percent national average. In contrast, Evans and Palacios (2015), found that in a majority of countries—out of their sample of 60 developing countries—elderly people are less likely to be poor than children.

Within the elderly group, women and "very old" are more likely to be poor, and there are significant income inequalities in many countries:

- Older women are at greater risk of poverty than older men in all OECD countries where breakdowns are available (except Chile), with the average old-age poverty rate for women at nearly 16 percent versus about 10 percent for men (OECD, 2019). This likely reflects longer life expectancy and a lower labor force participation because of shorter and interrupted careers due to childbearing and caring.

- As the very old (over 75) people are more likely to have spent their savings, have fewer opportunities to work, and more need age-appropriate health services, in most OECD countries the poverty rates are higher for "very old," averaging 16 percent. In Korea, Estonia, and Latvia this difference is particularly high, reflecting low pension indexation. In addition, in Korea, where the pension system is still maturing, younger generations get higher pension benefits.
- While for the majority of OECD countries income inequality among the elderly is lower than for the general population due to redistributive features of first-tier pension benefits and other schemes, in Mexico, Korea, and the US elderly inequality is higher than that for the general population. For China and India, income inequality for the elderly also markedly exceeds that of the total population.

D. Sources of Income for Elderly People

Pensions remain the main source of income for elderly people in most countries. The main sources of income for old can be broadly classified into five categories: public transfers (pensions, resource-tested benefits, etc.), occupational transfers (pensions based on employment), savings, work, and intra-family transfers (Figure 18.6). For the OECD countries, public and occupational transfers account for about two-thirds of the total income (OECD 2019). For some countries, public pensions and transfers account for more than 80 percent of income (Hungary, Belgium). In contrast, in Mexico, public transfers are as low as 6 percent (as only 35 percent of workers are covered by public pensions). Work is important in many countries (Mexico, United States, Korea) due to several factors. For some countries the pension age is higher than 65 years (United States), for others, people keep on working to fill gaps in contribution histories or to obtain better incomes over retirement. Also, as incomes are measured for households, older people draw on the earnings of younger family members in multi-generational households (Korea). However, intra-family transfers to the elderly have been declining in many countries. In Korea, for example, fewer young people believe that they are obliged to support their parents (Kim 2014).[5] A study for advanced economies shows that in the United States, Germany, and Italy, elderly parents are more likely to support their adult children than vice versa. There are also sharp differences across income groups. It is more likely for adults with lower annual household incomes to support their aging parents than for those with higher incomes (Pew Research Center 2015).

---

[5] In Korea, the proportion of private transfers in total retirement income among the elderly decreased from 55 to 45 percent between 1990 and 2008.

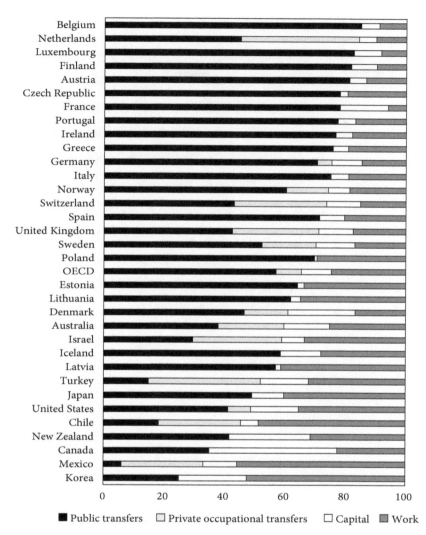

Figure 18.6 Income Sources of Elderly People
Source: OECD Income Distribution Database.

At the global level, 68 percent of people above retirement age receive some pension, either contributory or non-contributory (ILO 2017) (Figure 18.7).[6] However, the coverage varies significantly across the regions and income levels. While the coverage rates are close to 100 percent in developed countries, in Sub-Saharan Africa, and in Southern Asia less than one-quarter of elderly people

[6] Coverage for women is somewhat lower than that for entire population at 64.1 percent, largely reflecting lower labor force participation and overrepresentation among self-employed (ILO 2017).

(In percent)

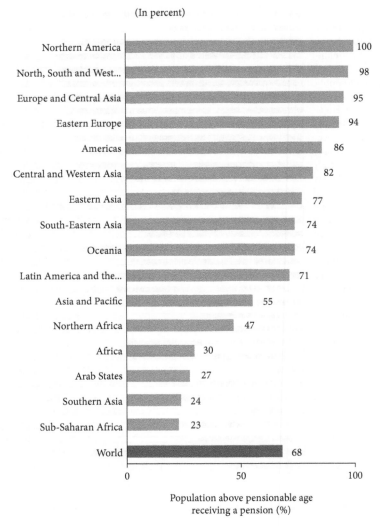

Figure 18.7 Pension Coverage for Older Persons
Source: ILO, World Social Protection Database.

receive pensions, depending heavily on family support arrangements. In addition, the level of pensions—and other social benefits in general—also vary across countries. For OECD pensions, the average replacement rate is around 53 percent at the age of retirement, falling to 47 percent at the age of 80 due to below wage growth indexation.[7] Many developing countries have introduced social pensions

---

[7] Defined as a ratio of pension to pre-retirement earnings.

to address the low insurance coverage of the elderly (Zouhar et al, 2021).[8] Social pensions globally cover almost 35 percent of the old-age population.

Income sources can largely explain the variation of poverty rates and income levels for older people across countries. The elderly are relatively better off in countries with higher levels and broader coverage of public and occupational pensions and higher social transfers related to health care. Income composition also changes along with the income distribution: older people at the bottom of the income distribution are more likely to derive their income entirely from public transfers, while the capital and private pensions are more important for the top of the income distribution. The adequacy of retirement benefits depends not only on cash benefits provided but also on the costs of essential services such as health care. Countries with large informal sectors, not covered by universal retirement benefits, experience higher elderly poverty rates.[9]

E. Demographic Trends and Their Impact on Elderly

Demographic and economic trends, such as longevity and population aging, can have a significant impact on elderly poverty in the future:

- The pace of world population aging is accelerating. Projections indicate that between 2019 and 2050, the number of elderly people will double. Population aging that has already affected most developed economies is expected to spread to developing countries, with a substantially faster rate than it occurred in developed countries. The number of people aged 80 years or over—the "oldest-old"—is growing even faster and is expected to almost triple by 2050. In the middle of the century, two out of every three oldest-old persons will be living in developing regions, countries with still large informal sectors, not covered by public pensions and transfers (UN 2019 Ageing report).
- Each successive cohort of older persons is expected to live longer and possibly also have fewer adult children as potential sources of support in old age. In 2015 there were seven people in the traditional working age for each older person aged 65 years and over in the world. By 2050, this number will be halved. At the same time, with urbanization and the transformation of many traditional family ties, more elderly are expected to live in nuclear households without family support (Kim 2014).

---

[8] Social pensions are non-contributory benefits that are tax-funded and target the old-age population. They can be universal or means-tested.
[9] Universal retirement benefits are usually granted based on age and residence.

- Population aging costs put pressure on public pension and health care systems, affecting fiscal sustainability. As a result, many countries are reassessing elderly benefits and transfers, making them less generous (EU 2012; Shang 2014). These reforms often include raising retirements' ages or lengthening required years of service, as well as reducing replacement rates. The potential negative impact of these reforms on elderly poverty can be sizable (Shang 2014).[10] Longevity will also increase demand for health care services, particularly long-term care, which is not adequate in many countries (ILO 2017; WHO 2015).[11]

F. Policies to Reduce Elderly Poverty

Policies needed to alleviate elderly poverty vary substantially across countries. In countries with comprehensive and mature systems of social protection and aging populations, policies should maintain a good balance between financial sustainability and pension adequacy. In countries with still limited pension coverage for elderly people and high levels of informality, policies should aim to broaden the coverage while ensuring the sustainability of social schemes. Polices to facilitate employment opportunities for elder workers and to reduce gender inequality in pensions are relevant across all countries. Finally, improving health care affordability and services is essential to maintain living standards for elderly people (ILO 2017; UN 2017, 2020).

- Countries that are planning or undergoing austerity pension reforms can mitigate the adverse impact on older people by adjusting the design of social security systems to support the elderly with lower incomes. This could be done, for instance, by reducing replacement rates for public pensions only for higher-income retirees, introducing universal social benefits, such as social pensions (Zouhar et al. 2021), or by targeting assistance to the poor. However, these policies should be weighed against potential adverse effects on labor markets (Shang 2014).
- Countries with a large informal sector and low pension coverage could rely on a number of measures to broaden the coverage in a sustainable way. These measures can include policies to increase the formal sector by, for example, incentivizing firms to use formal contracts, or by designing social

---

[10] Shang estimates relationship between public pension replacement rate s and elderly poverty and finds an elasticity of about -0.4. In addition, Shang finds that reforms will disproportionally affect the poorest part of elderly population.

[11] In many countries access to health services is limited and health workers may have inadequate training to deal with issues common in old age.

assistance in a way that makes contributory schemes more beneficial for workers (Figliuoli et al. 2018).[12] Also, efforts could be made to increase coverage for the lower-skilled and less-educated by, for example, automatic enrollment in voluntary pension plans (Benartzi and Thaler 2013).

- With increasing longevity, policy measures should also support labor force participation for older people. These policies should focus not only on postponing the formal retirement age but also on creating incentives and opportunities to keep older workers with accrued pension rights in employment and on facilitating flexible working arrangements. Health care and training can maintain the productivity and employability of older workers (Figliuoli et al. 2018).

- As in many countries, women are disadvantaged in the wages they earn, policies should aim to reduce gender gaps in pensions. Potential measures could include using more progressive pension schemes, and compensating women for "lost" years due to childbearing and caring. In addition, policies that help to promote labor force participation by women—for example, by improving child care benefits—could result in higher contributions and higher replacement rates upon retirement (Shang 2014).

- Policies to improve access to universal health coverage, including long-term care protection, are essential for maintaining living standards for elderly people. Even before the Covid-19 crisis, as many as half of older persons in some developing countries did not have access to essential health services. The pandemic may also lead to a scaling back of critical services unrelated to Covid-19, further increasing risks to the lives of older persons (WHO 2020). A simple increase in coverage may not be sufficient to address the needs of the aging population. Even in high-income countries, health systems are often better designed to cure acute conditions than to manage and minimize the consequences of the chronic states prevalent in old age.

III. Intergenerational Mobility

Socio-economic status at birth influences prospects of employment, health, and education outcomes, as well as other opportunities that are important for our well-being. This is shown by a number of studies about social mobility. For example, in OECD countries, children whose parents did not complete secondary school have only a 15 percent chance of going to university. At the same time,

---

[12] Since workers may choose between formal and informal employment opportunities based on the perceived value of future benefits from formal employment relative to current contributions, pension schemes may be designed in a way that increases incentives to participate.

children with at least one parent with tertiary-level education have a 60 percent chance of making it to university (OECD 2018).

The relationship between the parents and adult children's socioeconomic positions describes intergenerational social mobility. There is a difference between *absolute* and *relative* intergenerational mobility:

- *Absolute* intergenerational mobility compares the living standards across generations and looks at the share of children with higher living standards as adults compared with their parents.
- *Relative* mobility, or social mobility or fluidity, measures the probability that a child will attain a different economic status than that of their parents.

In this sense, social mobility is about ensuring that every individual has the opportunity and a fair chance of achieving their potential regardless of their family background. Relative intergenerational mobility and social mobility are used interchangeably and are the main focus of this section.

Citizens and governments are increasingly worried that younger generations will have fewer opportunities for upward social mobility than preceding generations. For example, in the UK, according to the Social Mobility Bathometer, a national survey of over 5 thousand people, revealed that 40 percent of respondents think that it is getting harder for people from less advantaged backgrounds to move up in British society, while only 21 percent think the opposite is true (Social Mobility Commission 2018). In the United States, data suggests that the chances of out-earning parents have been declining, too, especially for those from the middle class (Lu 2020). The data on historic trends supports these concerns. OECD estimates that it could take on average four to five generations for children from a family in the bottom decile of the income distribution to reach the average income in OECD countries. This estimate ranges from two generations in Denmark to nine and eleven generations in Brazil and South Africa (OECD 2018).

Social mobility goes both upward and downward. "Sticky floors" refer to the low upward mobility at the bottom of the income distribution. At the same time, children from privileged families are much less likely to experience downward mobility: the ceilings are "sticky," too (OECD 2018).

Intergenerational mobility is closely related to equality of opportunity. Economies with more unequal opportunities tend to have lower intergenerational mobility. Intergenerational mobility can be used as one of the possible indicators of inequality of opportunity (Stiglitz et al. 2018).

Countries with higher income inequality tend to be countries with low intergenerational mobility. This relationship is commonly referred to as "The Great Gatsby Curve" (Figure 18.8).

There is limited knowledge of the causal relationship between the two. Low mobility can be both a cause and a consequence of greater inequality. For

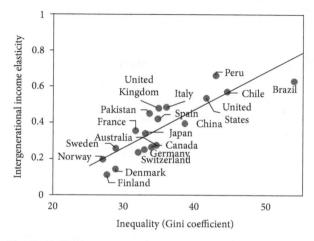

Figure 18.8 The Great Gatsby Curve

Sources: Gini coefficient from the World Bank Development Indicators, latest available. Accessed September 2020; IGE from the World Bank Intergenerational Mobiliyu database (GDIM), 2018. Development Research Group, World Bank.

example, inequalities in socioeconomic outcomes determine access to opportunities in education, health, and the labor market, and, thus, influence the potential for social mobility.

Lack of social mobility can have a negative impact on economic growth. As the OECD explains, a lack of upward mobility among individuals at the bottom of the income distribution means a loss of potential talents and investment opportunities (OECD 2018). In other words, inequality of opportunity prevents people from realizing their economic potential. The World Economic Forum estimates an opportunity cost of low social mobility based on the findings of its Global Social Mobility Report (WEF, 2020). This report suggests that if countries improved their performance by 10 points in the WEF's Global Social Mobility Index the global economy would gain an additional US$514 billion per year (in PPP terms), all else being equal. This gain could be as large as US$14.5 billion in Brazil, US$103 billion in China, US$18.5 billion in Germany, US$42.8 billion in India, US$17.8 billion in Russia, and US$3.4 billion in South Africa.

Perceived and actual mobility affects life satisfaction, social cohesion, and policy preferences. Studies suggest that prospects of upward social mobility positively influence people's life satisfaction and well-being. Perceptions about equality of opportunities can reduce the likelihood of social conflict (OECD 2018), while inequality of opportunity is associated with lower levels of support for the market economy and democracy (EBRD 2016). Pessimism and optimism about social mobility are significantly correlated with people's preferences for redistribution policies (Alesina et al. 2018).

A. Measuring Intergenerational Social Mobility

Intergenerational mobility can be analyzed in terms of various outcomes, such as earnings, education, occupation, wealth, or health. It is also a concept that may be difficult to measure with a single indicator. Social and economic mobility should be considered in combination with measures of poverty and inequality.

Intergenerational mobility of earnings measures the persistence of income between generations. Relative mobility in earnings can be measured by calculating the elasticity of intergenerational earnings (IGE). For example, consider the linear parent-child regression of the form:

$$y_{i,child} = a + by_{i,parent} + e_i \tag{1}$$

The coefficient b represents the elasticity with a higher number implying that it is more difficult for an individual to move outside their income class. An elasticity of zero means the highest social mobility where a child's adult outcomes are not related to the status of their parents at all. If elasticity is 100 percent, all life outcomes of a child are fully linked to the socioeconomic status of their parents.

According to the World Bank Global Database of Intergenerational Mobility (GDIM), income mobility appears to be lower in low and middle-income countries and higher in high-income countries (Figure 18.9). For example, in high-income countries, an average IGE was estimated at around 35 percent. The highest income persistence was estimated in countries in Latin America and the Caribbean with an IGE of around 90 percent.

There are notable differences within income or regional groups. The elasticity in OECD countries varies from below 20 percent in the Nordic countries to

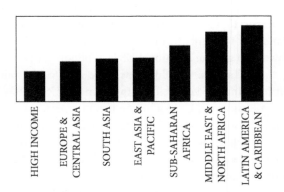

Figure 18.9 Intergenerational Mobility in Income

Note: The graph shows estimates of persistence in income as measured by intergenerational income elasticity from the World Bank GDIM; regional averages are authors' calculations.

Source: GDIM. 2018. Global Database on Intergenerational Mobility. Development Research Group, World Bank.

70 percent or more in emerging market economies (OECD 2018). Among high-income economies in Europe and North America, the estimates of earnings persistence for Germany, the UK, France, and the United States were above 40 percent. Income persistence in Turkey was estimated at 30 percent, which is below the average in Europe and Central Asia, and much lower than in its emerging market peers, such as Brazil and South Africa with income persistence of above 60 percent (World Bank GDIM 2018). In Asia, where the average IGE is around 50 percent, estimates for Taiwan and Singapore suggest relatively high-income mobility in these two countries—18 and 26 percent, respectively (World Bank 2018).

Intergenerational educational mobility has a strong association with intergenerational persistence in wages. A World Bank study estimates the lowest education mobility in Sub-Saharan Africa and South Asia, and highest in Western Europe, Canada, Australia, and Japan (Figure 18.10) (Narayan et al. 2018). This measure is based on a coefficient from the regression of children's years of education on the education of their parents (World Bank 2018).

As in the case with income mobility, there is significant variation within regions. For example, in Africa, intergenerational mobility in education was relatively high in South Africa and Botswana, and low in Sudan, Mozambique, Burkina Faso, and Malawi (Alesina et al. 2019). There is generally a positive correlation between mobility in earnings and in education, but some notable exceptions exist.

Social mobility in occupational status reflects social inequalities and has an impact on individuals' life chances and life choices. Studies of mobility across

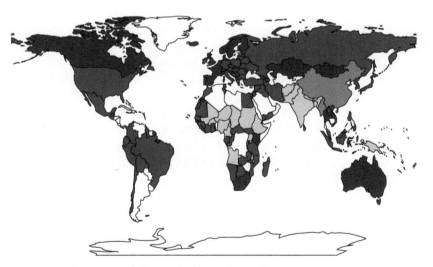

Figure 18.10 Intergenerational Mobility in Education

Note: darker shades indicate higher intergenerational education mobility; white color indicates that data was not available.

Sources: Narayan, A. et al. 2018; GDIM 2018. Global Database on Intergenerational Mobility. Development Research Group, World Bank.

social classes represent more established literature on this topic. Such mobility is often captured by the occupational status of fathers and sons. There are several ways to study social mobility based on occupation or social class (OECD 2018). Relative social mobility in occupation can be defined as the probability that a child born to parents from a particular social class remains in the social class. In their analysis for presentational purposes, the OECD aggregates social classes based on occupation into three broad categories: manual workers, routine workers, and managers. Their findings show that about a third of children from manual workers remain manual workers themselves, while half of the children with parents in managerial class become managers.

Prospects of social mobility can vary within a country, where the chances of being successful are linked to where a person lives. Chetty et al. (2014) establish that there is substantial variation in intergenerational mobility across different areas in the United States. In the UK, according to Social Mobility Commission, the population living in London and the commuter belt areas around it are more socially mobile in comparison to the rest of the country. In these areas, children, including those from disadvantaged backgrounds, demonstrate excellent results at school and have better higher education opportunities. In contrast, young people from some of the isolated rural and coastal towns have poorer chances of achieving good educational outcomes and have lacked access to further education and employment opportunities (Social Mobility Commission 2017). Alesina et al. (2019) show that proximity to the coast and the capital city in Africa within a country leads to higher mobility, even after conditioning on the initial level of literacy. They also find that malaria-prone regions tend to have lower mobility.

Studies suggest some differences in social mobility between women and men. Women are more likely than men to achieve a higher level of education than that of their parents. OECD finds that there is a gender gap in upward educational mobility in favor of women, which is particularly wide in Denmark, Estonia, Finland, and Italy (OECD 2017). At the same time, the mobility of educational attainments between mothers and daughters tends to be lower than the mobility between fathers and sons. OECD finds such patterns in southern Europe and the emerging market economies (OECD 2018). Some studies suggest women tend to have greater occupational mobility than men (ILO 2018). However, occupational segregation by gender remains a barrier to many women. Relative earnings mobility tends to be similar for daughters and sons (OECD 2018). Although certain patterns of social mobility emerge, the estimates are likely to be country-specific, and as we suggested earlier, can also vary within countries.

B. Barriers and Drivers of Social Mobility

People can face barriers to social mobility at different stages of their life. At the early stage, early childhood education and care give children a good start in life.

Certain features of a secondary and tertiary education system can create obstacles for upward social mobility. For example, early selection and tracking can explain limited educational mobility in some of the EU member states (Eurofound 2017). The transition from school to employment poses challenges related to youth unemployment and may leave a large number of youth among those who are not in employment, education, or training (NEET). Lack of access to certain occupations is linked to parental background, and in some instances to discrimination, elitism, and nepotism. Especially affected are women and ethnic minority groups. Various shocks related to health, changes in marital and job status in absence of effective social protection mechanisms may damage the life prospects of the most vulnerable.

The Global Social Mobility Report by the World Economic Forum identifies main drivers of social mobility as policies, practices, and institutions across the following dimensions: health, education, technology, work, and social protection, and inclusive institutions (WEF 2020). On a global level, the report suggests that such areas as fair wage distribution and deficiencies in social protection coverage are challenges among several countries, while the lack of opportunities for life-long learning are challenges faced by all countries analyzed in the report. Looking at findings across regions can offer several insights. While countries in North America are doing relatively well in such areas as access to technology, education quality, and health, as well as work opportunities and inclusive institutions, they could improve in such areas as high incidence of low wages, working conditions, and social protection that could help protect workers from adverse personal shocks. In Sub-Saharan Africa, countries could improve in several areas, including access and quality of education, fair wage distribution, and social protection.

C. Policies to Promote Intergenerational Mobility

Policies can have an impact on how advantages or disadvantages are transmitted from parents to children. Such policies may include a wide range of measures including policies to support health and education mobility, policies to support families, labor market policies, tax and transfer policies, local and urban development and planning and housing policies, access to technology, and, more broadly, policies and reforms aimed at building more inclusive institutions.

Policy interventions starting from one's early childhood to their transition to the labor market can bring positive returns in supporting social mobility. The phenomenon of sticky floors tends to emerge from a very early age and matter for opportunities later in life. Young people, in particular those from disadvantaged backgrounds, may struggle at school, drop out from formal education, and encounter difficulties in the labor market. Policy options outlined in the section on "Youth Poverty and Unemployment" provide an overview of measures that can help support families and youth and promote social mobility, including the need to provide life-learning opportunities and effective social protection schemes. Moreover, policies should also emphasize the need to tackle various forms of discrimination in the labor market. Such measures can facilitate job access to professions based on candidates' ability rather than their socioeconomic background or social network.

Policies to support working parents can also be instrumental. Such policies can focus both on providing flexible working hours to parents, financial support for childcare as well as providing support in developing parental skills. For example, the Parenting Early Intervention Program (PEIP) in the UK focuses on parents from socially disadvantaged backgrounds emphasizing the role of such skills.[13] Promotion of access to childcare for ethnic minorities is another measure to promote social mobility.

Social mobility also requires policies to reduce spatial segregation and inequalities between neighborhoods in cities. Measures to improve access to good-quality education, health, jobs, and affordable housing as well as the development of transport infrastructure on a local level have been recommended as policies to address regional or spatial divide within countries. Measures to improve access to jobs and creating job opportunities at the local level may include tax breaks and creating enterprise zones as employment support programs. Such measures may need to be considered carefully not to undermine the tax base and thus make it difficult to support the needed public infrastructure.

Tax policies that affect wealth accumulation can also affect social mobility. Wealth is more unequally distributed than income, and wealth deprivation can cause "sticky floors," while wealthier parents are likely to pass on their advantage to their children ("sticky ceilings").

In short, social mobility and social inequalities are not set in stone. Policies can help in promoting equality of opportunity to avoid passing the socio-economic disadvantages from one generation to another.

IV. Conclusion

Sharing economic benefits equitably across all segments of society includes addressing the specific challenges of different generations. The youth, who are trying to establish themselves in the labor market, and the elderly, who in some countries have limited incomes after completing their working lives, are typically more vulnerable to poverty relative to adults in their middle years.

---

[13] Think Family Toolkit (2010), Guidance note 07, 2010; https://dera.ioe.ac.uk/9475/17/Think-Family07.pdf

Strategies to foster youth integration into the labor market need to be broad-based. They include good quality primary education all the way up to tertiary education, vocational training, and apprenticeships. Additional policies would include flexible labor markets with social safety nets to protect workers and active labor market policies to support employment along with measures to foster private sector development and entrepreneurship.

The elderly often rely on income and health care support from public systems that are under increasing strains due to demographic and other trends. In countries with comprehensive and mature systems of social protection and aging populations, policies should maintain a good balance between financial sustainability and pension adequacy. In many developing countries with large informal sectors, the policy objective is to broaden coverage and increase formalization.

There might not be a general consensus on the acceptable level of inequality of outcomes, but there is widespread agreement on the need to promote equality of opportunities. Everyone should have the same chances in life, regardless of their initial socioeconomic positions and that of their parents. In that sense, equality of opportunity is closely related to relative intergenerational mobility or social mobility. There is an increasing concern that social mobility has been declining and it can have a negative impact on economic growth, affect life satisfaction, and social cohesion. Policies that may help promote social mobility include early interventions such as supporting early childhood education and care; labor market policies to better integrate the young and improve access to certain jobs, measures to tackle spatial segregation and concentration of poverty, and investment in housing and infrastructure. Effective social protection schemes can also protect against unexpected income losses, especially for those most vulnerable and in precarious employment.

The pressing issues of climate change and public debt that have important implications for intergenerational equity and justice are discussed in other chapters of the book.

References

Ahn, J., A. Zidong, J.C. Bluedorn, G. Ciminelli, Z. Koczan, D. Malacrino, et al. 2019, "Improving Youth Labor Market Outcomes in Emerging Market and Developing Economies," IMF Staff Discussion Note 19/02. Washington, DC.

Alesina, A., S. Stantcheva, and E. Teso, 2018, "Intergenerational Mobility and Preferences for Redistribution," American Economic Review, Vol. 108, No. 2, 521–54

Alesina, A, S. Hohmann, S. Michalopoulos, and E. Papaioannou. 2019. "Intergenerational mobility in Africa," CEPR Discussion Paper 13,497.

Angel-Urdinola, D. and R. Leon-Serano, 2013, "A Reform Agenda for Improving the DElivery of ALMPs in the MENA region", *IZA Journal of Labor Policy* 2:13.

Banerji, A., S. Saksonovs, H. Lin, R. Blavy, et al. 2014. "Youth Unemployment in Advanced Economies in Europe: Searching for Solutions", IMF Staff Discussion Note, December 2014.

Benartzi, Shlomo, and Richard Thaler. 2013. "Behavioral Economics and the Retirement Savings Crisis." *Science* 339(6124): 1152–3.

Chetty, R., N. Hendren, P. Kline, and E. Saez. 2014. "Where Is the Land of Opportunity? The Geography of Intergenerational Mobility in the US," NBER Working Paper 19,843.

Cho, Y., D. Margolis, D. Newhouse, D. Robalino, and David, A. 2012. "Labor Markets in Low- and Middle-Income Countries: Trends and Implications for Social Protection and Labor Policies", Social Protection and Labor Discussion Paper, No. 1207. Washington, DC: World Bank Group. Available at https://openknowledge. worldbank.org/handle/10986/13550 License: CC BY 3.0 IGO.

Cockx, B. and C. Ghirelli (2016): "Scars of Recessions in a Rigid Labor Maket". *Labour Economics* 41: 162–76. Available at: https://www.sciencedirect.com/science/article/abs/pii/S0927537116300239?via%3Dihub

Duval, R., and P. Loungani. 2019. "Designing Labor Market Institutions in Emerging and Developing Economies: Evidence and Policy Options," IMF Staff Discussion Note 19/04. Washington, DC.

Elborgh-Woytek, K. et al. 2013. "Women, Work, and the Economy: Macroeconomic Gain from Gender Equity," Staff Discussion Note 13/10. Washington, DC: International Monetary Fund.

Eurofound. 2017. *Social Mobility in the EU.* Luxembourg: Publications Office of the European Union, https://www.eurofound.europa.eu/sites/default/files/ef_publication/field_ef_document/ef1664en.pdf

European Bank for Reconstruction and Development (EBRD). 2016. Transition Report 2016–17. Available at https://www.ebrd.com/news/publications/transition-report/transition-report-201617.html

European Commission (EU). 2012. *The 2012 Ageing Report: Economic and Budgetary Projections for the 27 EU Member States.* Brussels: Directorate-General for Economic and Financial Affairs, European Commission.

Evans, B., and P. Palacios. 2015. "Who is Poorer? Poverty by Age in the Developing World" (No. 18), Social Protection & Labor Policy Note. Washington, DC: World Bank.

Figliuoli, Lorenzo U., Valentina Flamini, Misael Galdamez, Frederic Lambert, Mike Li, Bogdan Lissovolik, et al. 2018. "Growing Pains; Is Latin America Prepared for Population Aging?" IMF Departmental Paper.

Fox, L., and U. Kaul., 2017., "How Should Youth Employment Programs in Low-Income Countries be Designed?", Policy Research Working Paper 8500, World Bank Group.

GDIM. 2018. *Global Database on Intergenerational Mobility*. Development Research Group, World Bank. Washington, DC: World Bank Group.

Gonzales, C., S. Jain-Chandra, K. Kochhar, and M. Newiaket. 2015. "Fair Play: More Equal Laws Boost Female Labor Force Participation," IMF Staff Discussion Note.

Hawkins, J. 2019. "The Rise of Young Adult Poverty in the US," Issue Brief.

International Labour Organization (ILO). 2017. *World Social Protection Report 17–19*. Available at: ps://gspp.berkeley.edu/assets/uploads/page/poverty_FINAL_ formatted.pdf

International Labour Organization (ILO). 2011. "Increasing the Employability of Disadvantaged Youth," Skills for Employment Policy Brief Series.

International Labour Organization (ILO). 2018. "Intergenerational Mobility: A Dream Deferred?" Research Paper, ILO Future of Work Research Paper Series. Available at https://www.ilo.org/wcmsp5/groups/public/—dgreports/—cabinet/documents/ publication/wcms_649496.pdf

International Labour Organization (ILO). 2020a, "World Employment and Social Outlook – Trends 2020." Geneva: International Labour Office.

International Labour Organization (ILO). 2020b. "Global Employment Trends for Youth 2020: Technology and the Future of Jobs." Geneva.

Kakwani, Nanak, and Kalanidhi Subbarao. 2005. "Ageing and Poverty in Africa and the Role of Social Pensions," Working Papers 8, International Policy Centre for Inclusive Growth.

Kim, Seong Sook. 2014. "Providing Adequate Old-Age Pensions in the Republic of Korea." In *Equitable and Sustainable Pensions. Challenges and Experience*, edited by Benedict Clements, Frank Eich, and Sanjeev Gupta. Washington, DC: International Monetary Fund.

Kochhar, R., and A. Barroso: "Young Workers Likely to be Hard Hit as COVID-19 Strikes a Blow to Restaurants and Other Service Sector Jobs", Pew Research Center, March 27, 2020. https://pewrsr.ch/3bxQNs1.

Krafft, C., and Assaad, R. 2016. "Inequality of Opportunity in the Labor Market for Higher Education Graduates in Egypt and Jordan," In *The Middle East Economies in Times of Transition*, edited by I. Diwan and A. Galal. International Economic Association Series. London: Palgrave Macmillan. Available at: https://doi. org/10.1007/978-1-137-52977-0_6

Levy-Yeyati, E., and others (2019): "What Works for Active Labor Market Policies?", Center for International Development, CID Faculty Working Paper No. 358. Available at: What Works for Active Labor Market Policies? | Harvard Kennedy School

Lu, Markus. 2020. "Is the American Dream over? Here's What the Data Says," World Economic Forum. This article is published in collaboration with Visual Capitalist. September 2, 2020. Available at https://www.weforum.org/agenda/2020/09/ social-mobility-upwards-decline-usa-us-america-economics/

Manacorda, M., F. C. Rosati, M. Ranzani, and G. Dachille. 2017. "Pathways from School to Work in the Developing World." *IZA Journal of Labor Development* 6(1). Available at: https://doi.org/10.1186/s40175-016-0067-5

Matsumoto, M. and S. Elder., 2010,. "Characterizing the School-to-Work Transition of Young Men and Women: Evidence from the ILO School-to-Work Surveys", Employment Working Paper 51. Geneva: ILO.

Narayan, Ambar, Roy Van der Weide, Alexandru Cojocaru, Christoph Lakner, Silvia Redaelli, Daniel Gerszon Mahler, et al. 2018. *Fair Progress? Economic Mobility Across Generations Around the World*. Equity and Development. Washington, DC: World Bank. https://openknowledge.worldbank.org/handle/10986/28428 License: CC BY 3.0 IGO.

O'Higgins, N. 2017. "Rising to the Youth Employment Challenge: New Evidence on Key Policy Issues," ILO. Geneva: International Labour Office.

OECD. 2017. "The Pursuit of Gender Equality: An Uphill Battle," http://www.oecd.org/publications/the-pursuit-of-gender-equality-9,789,264,281,318-en.htm

OECD. 2018. "A Broken Social Elevator? How to Promote Social Mobility," http://www.oecd.org/social/broken-elevator-how-to-promote-social-mobility-9789264301085-en.htm

OECD. 2019. *Pensions at a Glance 2019: OECD and G20 Indicators*. Paris: OECD Publishing.

Adams-Prassl, Abi, Teodora Boneva, Marta Golin, and Christopher Rauh. "Inequality in the Impact of the Coronavirus Shock: Evidence from Real Time Surveys." *Journal of Public Economics* 189: 104245, ISSN 0047-2727.

Pew Research Center. 2015. "Family Support in Graying Societies: How Americans, Germans, and Italians Are Coping with an Aging Population." Washington, DC: Pew Research Center. Available at: https://www.pewresearch.org/social-trends/2015/05/21/family-support-in-graying-societies/

Purfield, C., H. Finger, K. Ongley, B. Baduel, C. Castellanos, G. Pierre, et al. 2018. "Opportunity for All: Promoting Growth and Inclusiveness in the Middle East and North Africa", IMF Departmental Paper, Middle East and Central Asia Department.

Quintini, G., and S. Martin. 2014. "Same Same but Different: School-to-work Transitions in Emerging and Advanced Economies," OECD Social, Employment and Migration Working Papers, No. 154, OECD Publishing. Available at: https://doi.org/10.1787/5jzbb2t1rcwc-en.

Shang, Baoping. 2014. "Pension Reform and Equity: The Impact on Poverty of Reducing Pension Benefits." In *Equitable and Sustainable Pensions. Challenges and Experience*, edited by Benedict Clements, Frank Eich, and Sanjeev Gupta. Washington, DC: International Monetary Fund.

Social Mobility Commission. 2017. "State of the Nation: Social Mobility in Great Britain," November 2017. Available at https://assets.publishing.service.gov.uk/government/uploads/system/uploads/attachment_data/file/662744/State_of_the_Nation_2017_-_Social_Mobility_in_Great_Britain.pdf

Social Mobility Commission. 2018. Social Mobility Barometer, "Public attitudes to social mobility in the UK," December 2018. Available at: https://assets.publishing. service.gov.uk/government/uploads/system/uploads/attachment_data/file/766797/ Social_mobility_barometer_2018_report.pdf

Stiglitz, J., J. Fitoussi, and M. Durand (Eds.). 2018. *For Good Measure: Advancing Research on Well-being Metrics Beyond GDP*. Paris: OECD Publishing. https://doi. org/10.1787/9789264307278-en

Sun, F., and A. Ueda. 2013. "Intergenerational Earnings Mobility in Taiwan." *Economic Bulletin* 35(1), http://www.accessecon.com/Pubs/EB/2015/Volume35/EB-15-V35-I1-P21.pdf

Think Family Toolkit. 2010. Guidance note 07, 2010, https://dera.ioe.ac.uk/9475/17/ Think-Family07.pdf

United Nations. 2019. United Nations, Department of Economic and Social Affairs, Population Division. World Population Prospects 2019: Highlights. ST/ESA/ SER.A/423.

United Nations. 2020. "Policy Brief: The Impact of Covid-19 on Older Persons."

United Nations Conference on Trade and Development (UNCTAD). 2017. "Robots, Industrialization, and Inclusive Growth," in "Trade and Development Report 2017: Beyond Austerity.—Towards a Global New Deal," Chapter 3, United Nations, New York and Geneva. Available at: Trade and Development Report 2017—Beyond Austerity: Towards a Global New Deal (unctad.org)

United Nations, Department of Economic and Social Affairs, Population Division. 2017. *World Population Ageing 2017* (ST/ESA/SER.A/408).

World Bank. 2018. Global Database on Intergenerational Mobility (GDIM). Development Research Group, World Bank. Washington, DC: World Bank Group. Available at: https://www.worldbank.org/en/topic/poverty/brief/what-is-the-global-database-on-intergenerational-mobility-gdim

World Bank. 2019. "World Development Report: The Changing Nature of Work". Washington, DC: World Bank. Available at: doi:10.1596/978-1-4648-1328-3

World Economic Forum. 2020. "The Global Social Mobility Report 2020." Available at https://reports.weforum.org/social-mobility-report-2020/

World Health Organization. 2015. World Report on Aging and Health. Luxemburg: World Health Organization. Available at: https://apps.who.int/iris/handle/10665/ 186463

World Health Organization. 2020. "Covid-19 Strategy Update, 14 April 2020." https:// www.who.int/publications-detail/covid-19-strategy-update—14-april-2020

Zimmermann, K., C. Biavaschi, W. Eichhorst, C. Giulietti, M.J. Kendzia, A. Muravyev, et al. 2013. "Youth Unemployment and Vocational Training." *Foundations and Trends in Microeconomics* 9(1–2): 1–157.

Zouhar, Y., N. Lustig, J. Jellema, and M. Trabelsi, 2021 "Public Expenditure and Inclusive Growth—A Survey". IMF Working paper 21/083. Washington, DC.

19

Sharing Resource Wealth
and Addressing Fragility

Nathalie Pouokam

I. Introduction

The fast-paced global economy of the post-Second World War era has led many countries to harness their natural capital at an unprecedented fast pace.[1] Unfortunately, in many cases, the harnessed returns from natural resources have not been conducive to inclusive growth (Sachs and Warner 2011) which requires that growth equitably benefits society, within and across generations. Rather, the depletion of many types of natural resources has often mostly benefitted a handful of people from the extracting generations. This chapter discusses the main challenges faced by resource-rich nations in promoting equity, describes some of the policy tools available for managing exhaustible natural resources, and analyzes the relationship between resource wealth and state fragility.

Natural resource wealth often constitutes a large share of economic wealth, but contributes little to inclusive growth, especially in developing countries. In 2014, natural capital (including both exhaustible and non-exhaustible resources) accounted for about 50 percent of the total wealth of low-income countries. In the same year, it accounted for 3 percent of the total wealth of high-income OECD countries (World Bank 2018). Yet, over the period 1995–2014, natural capital only contributed to 10 percent of growth in low-income countries. In advanced economies, it contributed to 3 percent of growth during that period (World Bank 2018). The fact that advanced economies have been getting relatively higher returns from their resource wealth suggests that with appropriate policies, most resource-rich developing countries could grow faster than they currently do. The experience of Botswana supports this hypothesis.

[1] I thank Jaime Sarmiento Monroy for excellent research assistance. I am also grateful for comments received from Valerie Cerra, Barry Eichengreen, Andrew Warner, Maksym Ivanyna, Nikola Spatafora, Christian Henn, Olivier Basdevant, John Hooley, Paulo Medas, Joseph Procopio, and participants in the Inclusive Growth book seminar series organized by the IMF Institute for Capacity Development.

Nathalie Pouokam, *Sharing Resource Wealth and Addressing Fragility* In: *How to Achieve Inclusive Growth.*
Edited by: Valerie Cerra, Barry Eichengreen, Asmaa El-Ganainy, and Martin Schindler, Oxford University Press.
© Nathalie Pouokam 2022. DOI: 10.1093/oso/9780192846938.003.0019

Despite being plagued with persistent inequality, Botswana is one example of a developing and resource-rich country which has been successful at avoiding the vicious cycle of resource dependence and economic stagnation.[2] Over the last three decades that preceded the 2008 financial crisis, Botswana remarkably grew by an average growth rate of 7.5 percent, with 40 percent of this growth being attributed to mining (Iimi 2007). According to Acemoglu et al. (2012), the factors behind this outstanding performance were: efforts to improve governance, commitment to strong fiscal discipline, and strong investment in education and public infrastructure, all of which were possible thanks to Botswana's strong institutions which protect investors' property rights, provide political stability, and ensure broad citizens' participation in the policy making process.[3] Between 1998 and 2007, Botswana invested on average 8 percent of GDP in education, well above the average of 3 percent seen in resource-rich countries over the same period. This chapter posits that if resource-rich societies manage to strengthen their institutions and implement sound policies, they could achieve the successful performance of Botswana, and with less inequality.

Harnessing natural resources comes with several challenges. These challenges include: the eminent exhaustibility of key natural resources; the risk that myopic governments favor the fast depletion of natural resources over a longer-term development strategy that would be conducive to a productive business climate; the risk that resource wealth fuels corruption and leaves the country trapped in a vicious cycle of poor governance and low growth; the risk of a decline in the competitiveness of non-resource based exports; and for hydrocarbon producers, the new constraints imposed by a carbon-conscious global economy. Overcoming the challenges imposed by natural resources comes with sizeable opportunities for developing countries, which in many cases are plagued with widespread poverty despite holding significant resource wealth.

In the case of fragile countries, resource wealth poses an additional challenge. Often, it serves to fuel conflict by providing a funding base for military spending that is given priority over basic social and physical infrastructure needs. For this reason, resource wealth often undermines the ability of countries to exit fragility. But fortunately, this paradoxical role of resource wealth can be avoided by committing to a transparent and sound management of the resource wealth.

[2] According to Hillbom and Bolt (2015), income inequality in Botswana peaked in the 1970s, at the time of the shift between the cattle economy established during the colonial era, and the diamond economy. Since then, inequality has been declining in Botswana, driven by targeted government transfers and growing incomes generated by fast and sustained growth. Albeit still very high, Botswana's income Gini index fell from 0.61 to 0.53 between 2010 and 2015.

[3] Acemoglu et al. (2012) argues that Botswana owes its strong institutions to the fact that British colonialism did not destroy its pre-colonial institutions which were relatively inclusive institutions, to strong political leadership since independence, and to the elite's interests in reinforcing institutions.

Most of the challenges associated with harnessing resource wealth can indeed be overcome with an adequate policy framework. This requires: (1) adopting a resource wealth management framework that serves the joint interests of both current and future generations; (2) sustaining investment in human capital with earnest commitment to using resource wealth for educating masses; and (3) diversifying away from natural resources to curb resource dependence. As the experiences of Botswana and Norway discussed in this chapter suggest, strong institutions and sustained citizen participation in the policy-making process are of paramount importance in making governments accountable and ensuring the inclusive management of resource wealth. To understand how economic diversification could be achieved in resource-rich countries, this chapter further proposes lessons learned from the economic diversification experiences of Malaysia and Chile. For what follows, discussions are focused on exhaustible (non-renewable) natural resources.

II. The Challenges of Natural Resource Wealth

A. The Challenge of Measuring Resource Wealth

Quantifying natural resource wealth is a daunting task for two reasons: (1) existing estimates of the amounts of resources still in the ground are based on approximative methods with various degrees of confidence (Satter and Iqbal 2016); and (2) forecasting commodity prices has proved to be bound to large errors caused by the highly volatile nature of shocks to commodity prices (IMF 2015). Accounting for this uncertainty requires a resource wealth management framework which provides regular estimates of the value of the country's resource reserves under different price and extraction scenarios (IMF 2015).

In practice, economists usually keep track of two measures when estimating resource wealth. These measures are the annual resource rents-to-GDP and the time left to depletion. Resource wealth is then estimated as the net present value of current and future natural resource rents over the time left to depletion, also known as exhaustion time (World Bank 2011). Following a methodology used by the World Bank, the exhaustion time is typically calculated as the ratio of reserves remaining at the end of a given year, to the production level recorded in that particular year. Because this approximation of the time to depletion does not account for the possibility of future discoveries, it provides only a basic and crude estimate for the exhaustibility of key natural resources. This is an imperfect, yet useful, starting point in assessing the urgency to transform from a resource-based economy to a more diversified economic structure.

The exhaustibility of major types of natural resources is a binding constraint. For many resource-rich countries, the exhaustion of proven reserves of key natural resources is in fact expected to happen in the foreseeable future, given current

Time to depletion of oil reserves, 2019
(Years)

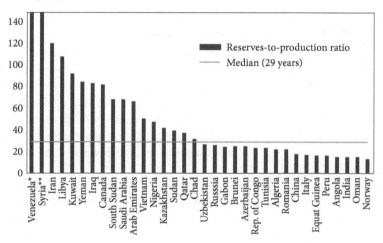

Time to depletion of Cobalt reserves, 2019
(Years)

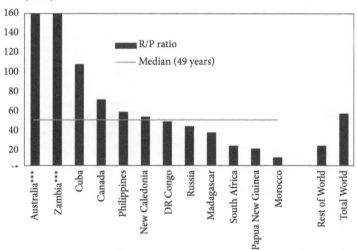

Figure 19.1 Exhaustibility of Natural Resources: Number of Years Left to Depletion

Note: *Venezuela reported 906 years; **Syria exhibited 291 years to depletion; and ***Australia and Zambia reported 234 and 213 years respectively.

Source: Author's calculations using data from the BP Statistical Review.

production rates (Figure 19.1). For instance, in 2019, the world median expected number of years to depletion was 29 years for oil reserves, and 49 years for cobalt reserves. In other words, many countries dependent on either oil or cobalt could take less than one generation to become resource-poor.

B. The Challenge of Political Myopia

The abundance of natural resources has lured many countries into delaying efforts to promote a business climate favorable to growth in the non-resource sector. When governments are short-sighted because of political instability or a lack of government accountability, they are often unwilling to champion reforms to improve the business climate and support an expansion of non-resource-based sectors. This could explain in part why so many resource-rich developing countries continue to lag behind their resource-poor peers, both in terms of export diversification and export quality (Figure 19.2). Unfortunately, specialization in natural resources has also usually hindered macroeconomic stability in these countries.

Indeed, most commodity exporters have been at the mercy of fluctuations in global commodity prices. For instance, in resource-rich countries, government revenues over the last two decades have almost perfectly mirrored fluctuations in global commodity prices (Figure 19.4), reflecting heavy dependence on resource windfalls. Likewise, real exchange rates have also been driven by commodity price swings (Pouokam 2021), often to the detriment of competitiveness and the ability to develop export capacity in non-commodity traded goods. Such

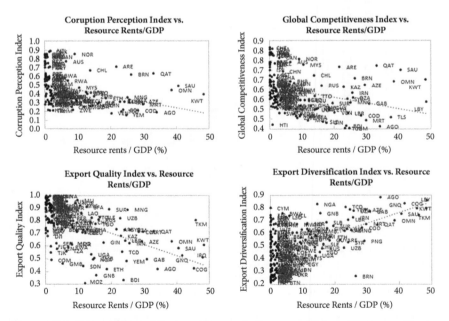

Figure 19.2 Corruption and Competitiveness in Resource-Rich and Resource-Poor Countries

Sources: Author's calculations using data from the World Development Indicators, World Economic Forum, and Transparency International databases.

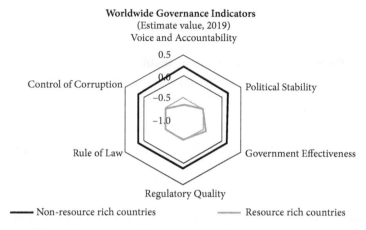

Figure 19.3 Natural Resources and Governance Indicators
Note: values between -2.5 to 2.5 (best).
Source: Author's calculations using data from the Worldwide Governance Indicators database.

economic volatility has contributed to further weakening growth and exacerbating inequality (Goderis and Malone 2011).

If not properly managed, natural resource wealth could fuel corruption and leave the country trapped in a quagmire of poor governance, resource dependence, and slow growth. The data indeed suggests a negative association between governance quality and resource abundance (Figure 19.3).[4] Two mechanisms may explain this negative correlation. First, weak institutions and poor governance create opacity in public financial management and support corruption which polarizes the ownership of the resource capital, ultimately creating long-lasting vested interests for resource dependence. Second, natural resource rents fuel corruption and slow down institutional reforms, undermining the long-term growth potential. The abundance of natural resources therefore creates even higher stakes for reinforcing political accountability and committing to policy frameworks that would help ensure that corruption does not stand in the way of institutional reforms and long-term growth.

C. The Challenge of Falling Global Demand for Hydrocarbon Exports

Greater global awareness of the negative impact of fossil fuel energy consumption on the environment has created new challenges for carbon-rich countries. These challenges include the risk of a permanent fall in global carbon prices if global demand for these resources (essentially oil, gas, and coal) were to plummet in

---

[4] The positive association between corruption and resource wealth is discussed in Veisi 2017.

response to increased carbon taxes (IMF 2019) while global supply were to surge, caused by hydrocarbon companies extracting faster in anticipation of higher future carbon taxes—the green paradox (World Bank 2018; Sinn 2008). In the process, speedy efforts to increase carbon production would also imply a misallocation of resources away from promising sectors for which returns on investment would be perceived as less immediate.

III. Resource Curse, Dutch Disease, and Exchange Rate Policies

A. The Resource Curse and the Dutch Disease

Resource wealth tends to be associated with slower economic growth. A large body of the economic literature has documented the negative association between resource dependence and per capita GDP growth, a phenomenon known as the "resource curse." The seminal empirical study of Sachs and Warner (1995) establishes that countries starting with relatively higher ratios of natural resource-based exports to GDP in 1971 had relatively lower average growth rates over the subsequent period 1971–1989, including after controlling for initial per capita income, trade policy, government efficiency, investment rates, and other variables relevant for economic growth. Papyrakis and Gerlagh (2007) confirms this empirical finding for the United States, suggesting that US states with relatively large natural resource wealth endowments grew less over the period 1986–2000 than the rest of the country, because they not only had poorer growth-promoting outcomes in terms of investment, schooling, openness, and R&D expenditure, but also had more corruption. James and Aadland (2011) similarly finds a negative correlation between resource wealth and economic growth at the more disaggregated US county level, including for more recent periods.

If the existence of a negative relationship between resource wealth and growth is usually accepted as a given, there is much less consensus about the underlying reasons explaining such a relationship (see James 2015 for a detailed review). The mechanisms highlighted in the economic literature to explain the resource curse to a large extent echo the previous discussion of challenges associated with resource wealth. Explanations for the resource curse include that: (1) resource wealth tends to prolong anti-growth policies such as autarkic trade policies (Auty 1994); (2) resource wealth creates opportunities for rent-seeking behaviors which diverts entrepreneurial talent away from productive business enterprise (Torvik 2002); (3) resource wealth raises the stake for social conflict as factions of society compete to take control of the natural resource (Collier and Hoeffler 1998); (4) resource wealth creates a false sense of economic security, leading to underinvestment in human capital (Gylfason 2001); and (5) resource wealth crowds out other growth-promoting industries such as manufacturing, a phenomenon known as the Dutch disease (Matsuyama 1992; Sachs and Warner 1999).

The term "Dutch disease" refers to the decline in traditional industries that often follows commodity booms.[5] The common explanation for the Dutch disease phenomenon is that commodity booms create a reallocation of resources toward the commodity sector which bids up wages, causing the non-resource tradable sector (typically manufacturing and agriculture) to become less competitive (Corden and Neary 1982). Usually, the real exchange rate appreciates as domestic demand for both tradable and non-tradable goods (typically services) increases, pushing non-tradable goods prices up while tradable goods prices remain fixed at international levels. The increase in the relative price of non-tradable-to-tradable goods in a context of booming commodity prices causes factors of production to move from the non-resource tradable sector to the non-tradable sector, which leads to an expansion in non-tradable services and a decline in tradable manufacturing and agriculture sectors (Ismail 2010). Evidence for the manifestation of the Dutch disease in the manufacturing sector in response to unanticipated changes in real commodity prices has been established at quarterly frequency for Canada (Charnavoki and Dolado 2014) and Australia (Dungey et al. 2014), and at an annual-frequency using cross-country data (Ismail 2010).

Theory and evidence suggest that exchange rate policies are not the most effective way to address the Dutch disease for which there seems to be no short-term cure. In fact, neither a fixed, nor a floating exchange rate regime provides complete insulation against the Dutch disease, which in the first case manifests through domestic inflation, and in the latter comes mainly through nominal exchange rate appreciation (Lama and Medina 2012). Also, neither the policy of real exchange rate stabilization, nor that of pegging the export price of a major commodity as suggested by Frankel (2003) provides a cost-free solution to the Dutch disease (Pouokam 2021). Stabilizing the real exchange rate in the context of booming commodity prices can provide welcome support to a dragging tradable non-resource sector, but at the cost of higher macroeconomic volatility (Lama and Medina 2012). This is because when policy intervention after a surge in commodity prices limits the appreciation of the real exchange rate to support the tradable non-resource sector, the role of the nominal exchange rate as a shock absorber is partially lost, and resources are inefficiently reallocated away from the booming commodity sector, despite welcome support provided to falling non-commodity exports. Similarly, a peg to the export price does not resolve the Dutch disease threat. For instance, with a peg to the export price, if the nominal exchange rate appreciates in response to a surge in the price of the commodity that the country specializes in, non-resource-based exports could become less competitive, and the standard Dutch disease symptoms could ensue. The key strategy to address the Dutch disease is instead to diversify the economy over time, so that Dutch

---

[5] The term "Dutch disease" was initially used to describe the decline in traditional industries in the Netherlands after the discovery and development of natural gas industries in the 1960s (see Pouokam 2021 for a discussion).

disease symptoms could be reduced as the economy becomes less dependent on natural resources. This is discussed later.

IV. Fiscal Policy Frameworks for Managing Resource Wealth

The fiscal policy framework should be tuned to ensure that the management of the resource wealth promotes an equitable sharing of the resource dividend across and within generations, limits the impact of fluctuations in commodity prices on the rest of the economy, and fully supports human capital accumulation and social cohesion. As examples, the Permanent Income Hypothesis (PIH) and the Bird-in-Hand (BIH) frameworks have often been used to institutionalize savings for future generations. This has usually been done in combination with fiscal rules that help to shelter the economy from the deleterious impact of large fluctuations in commodity prices.

A. Two Frameworks for Saving Resource Wealth: the PIH and BIH

The management of natural resource wealth to promote intergenerational equity can be achieved with fiscal frameworks designed to smooth the spending of natural resource windfalls over time. Two examples of such frameworks are the Permanent-Income Hypothesis (PIH) and the Bird-in-Hand (BIH) which specify how much of the resource rents should be spent (as measured by the non-resource primary deficit) and how much should be saved for future generations. The PIH framework restricts spending to the interest income generated by the net present value of current and future resource windfalls—the permanent income, while the BIH framework restricts spending to the interest gains on the natural resource investment fund itself. These frameworks are useful commitment devices for ensuring that the benefits of natural resource windfalls get spread out across generations. Both frameworks offer predictability and a clear understanding of the weight given to future generations in the allocation of resource wealth. However, to serve their purposes, they require unequivocal transparency. Full disclosure of all operations related to the management of savings funds for future generations is needed to help create the foundation for a check and balance system capable of bringing strong discipline to the management of natural resource wealth.

The PIH and BIH frameworks could be modified to accommodate developing countries' needs for investment in human capital and public infrastructure. In fact, the PIH and BIH frameworks assume that the long-term rate of return on the savings fund intended for future generations exceeds the marginal social return on other assets. But in most developing countries, the marginal returns to investments in human capital and public infrastructure are still very high

(Humphrey et al. 2007). The successful experiences of Botswana suggest a practical approach to accounting for these investment needs: institutionalizing a savings fund for future generations (the Pula Fund) to enforce the proper use of natural resource windfalls, while also prioritizing spending to favor human capital and public infrastructure investments.

In Botswana, the prioritization of development-promoting spending is institutionalized in the Sustainable Budget Index (SBI) rule which requires that mineral revenues finance "investment expenditure" exclusively (Iimi 2007). The rule defines investment expenditure as development expenditure and recurrent spending on education and health. The SBI rule works in tandem with the Pula Fund in which financial assets are invested on a long-term basis.

Iimi (2007) recognizes three institutional pillars supporting Botswana's sound management of resource wealth: (1) in recognition of the need for government accountability, Botswana's Ministry of Minerals, Energy and Water Resources is charged with responsibility for natural resource regulation and management; (2) the Directorate of Corruption and Economic Crime established in 1994 serves as an independent anticorruption authority, reporting corruption cases directly to the president; and (3) there is independence between the attorney general and the government, as established by the constitution.

B. Country Examples of PIH and BIH Frameworks

São Tomé and Príncipe and the PIH Framework

São Tomé and Príncipe was the first country in Africa to formally adopt the Permanent Income Hypothesis (PIH) framework. In December 2004, São Tomé and Príncipe promulgated the Oil Revenue Management Law for the management of oil revenues (Segura 2006). The law required the central bank to open the National Oil Account (NOA) with a custodian foreign bank, on behalf of the government, for the purpose of managing resource wealth. The NOA was to be divided into two subaccounts: the "Unrestricted Part of the National Oil Account" in which all oil revenues would be deposited, and a "Permanent Fund" for future generations, into which the remaining balance of the Unrestricted subaccount would be transferred once a year, after the annual single transfer to the budget. It was established that the resources deposited in the NOA would be managed by the Management and Investment Committee composed of five members, among them the Minister of Finance and the President of the central bank. The Petroleum Oversight Commission including representatives of the civil society was created to ensure permanent monitoring and auditing of all transactions related to oil revenues and resources. To protect the fund from political pressures that can lead to its depletion, a rule was established to limit withdrawals from the Permanent Fund in any single year to a maximum of 20 percent of the accumulated assets (IMF 2012).

São Tomé and Príncipe's Oil Revenue Management Law stipulates that the amount of oil revenues to be saved in the Permanent Fund would be decided annually, based on a PIH framework aiming to support government spending, including after the exhaustion of oil resources. Namely, the law requires that every year, the amount of oil revenues transferred to fund the national budget does not exceed the lesser of:

(1) the sum of (A) the long-term real rate of return multiplied by the balance of the Permanent Fund on June 30 of the previous year, and (B) the long-term real rate of return multiplied by the expected present value of future oil revenues on June 30 of the previous year; and

(2) the sum of: (A) the long-term real rate of return multiplied by the balance of the Permanent Fund on June 30 of the previous year, and (B) the balance of the "Unrestricted" subaccount of the NOA—in which current oil revenues are deposited—on June 30 of the previous year (Sao Tome and Principe 2004). This second term reflects a conservative approach which helps limits the downside risks from overly optimistic forecasts of future revenues in the calculation of the net present value.

For the purpose of oil revenue management, the long-term real rate of return used is the real rate of return expected on a portfolio composed of assets proportionate to the assets held in the Permanent Fund during the same period, and is capped at 5 percent.

Timor-Leste and the Modified Permanent Income Hypothesis Framework

Timor-Leste's approach to oil wealth management under the Petroleum Fund law follows the PIH but with some flexibility. Specifically, the saving policy adopted makes it possible to spend more than the level of sustainable spending, but with authorization from Parliament (Kim et al. 2005). The level of sustainable spending is calculated every fiscal year, as the product of a long-term real rate of return of 3 percent on the one hand, and the sum of the current balance of the Petroleum Fund and the net present value of all current and expected future income flows from oil reserves on the other hand. Parliament could for instance authorize an increase in spending above the sustainable level to meet urgent needs for public infrastructure. Parliament could also require a level of spending below the sustainable level if warranted by limited absorption capacities.

The Modified Permanent Income Hypothesis (MPIH) Framework adopted by Timor-Leste can help accommodate a more front-loaded spending path than a traditional PIH framework. In principle, the flexibility of the spending rule allows financial assets to be drawn down for a few years during the scaling up of public investment projects, the goal being to later offset the impact on the oil savings fund with fiscal adjustment (IMF 2012). If the scaling up of investment later leads to increasing non-resource revenues, the need for fiscal adjustment to compensate for the initial drawdown could be eliminated. The requirement to provide justification to parliament when the amount of spending planned is higher than the level indicated by a PIH helps to discipline the choice of investment projects that are undertaken as part of the national development strategy. For instance, to ensure that the public investment scaling up program produces the benefits expected under the MPIH, the government of Timor-Leste has created institutions that are responsible for project appraisal, procurement, and monitoring within the budget process (IMF 2012).

Timor-Leste's flexible approach shows how the PIH could be modified to address development needs in a manner that is consistent with the well-being of both current and future generations. However, this approach does not fully offset the risk that the expected returns to the investment projects undertaken could fail to materialize. If the level of fiscal adjustment later needed to compensate future generations is gauged unsustainable by future governments due to a poor economic outlook, future generations could be permanently made worse off.

Norway and the BIH Framework

Norway is one of the largest oil and gas producers in the world, and a pioneer of the Bird-in-Hand approach with its sovereign wealth fund, the Government Pension Fund Global (GPFG). The GPFG was originally named the Government Petroleum Fund. It was established by the Government Petroleum Fund Act of 1990 which stipulated that its operational management was to be carried out by Norges Bank, under a management agreement with Norway's Ministry of Finance which would exercise oversight, including setting guidelines for benchmark and risk limits (Backer 2009).

Since receiving its first transfer in 1996 (Government of Norway 2015), the GPFG has been one of the fastest-growing Sovereign Wealth Funds in the world. In October 2019, its value reached 10 trillion Kroner (US$1.15 trillion) (Norges Bank Investment Management 2020). This success has been attributed to a governance framework featuring a high degree of transparency in the management of the GPFG, to Norway's commitment to its fiscal rule, and to a carefully chosen investment strategy (IMF 2008).

The Norwegian model of sovereign wealth fund management has been applauded as an exemplary model of transparent governance (IMF 2008). The GPFG's institutional framework sets clear guidelines and expectations for the roles of the Ministry of Finance and Norges Bank. The Ministry of Finance reports regularly on the GPFG's governance framework, its goals, its investment strategy and results, and its ethical guidelines. As the Fund's operational manager, Norges Bank publishes quarterly and annual reports on the fund's management. These reports include information on the fund's performance and an annual listing of all investments. Regularly, information is also made available on how the fund voted during shareholders' meetings.

Norway's fiscal rule has facilitated the integration of the Fund's net allocation decision with fiscal policy (IMF 2008). The fiscal rule sets the limit on the central government's non-oil structural deficit at around 4 percent of the assets of the GPFG. Because 4 percent is the estimated long-run real rate of return (Government of Norway 2015), the rule therefore amounts to saving the fund's capital and spending only its return, as typical in a BIH approach. The integration of the GPFG's saving and spending rule with the fiscal rule is one of the praised features of Norway's approach to sovereign wealth fund management (IMF 2008). It provides a unified accountability framework for the government to the people of Norway regarding the use of petroleum revenues and the rentability of the GPFG.

The GPFG's successful investment strategy builds on four pillars. First, the fund has a stake in sustainable global development because it targets long-term returns that are environmentally and socially responsible (Government of Norway 2020b). Second, the fund follows clear guidelines for risk limits (for instance, a minimum of 7.5 percent of the net asset value of the fund is to be held in treasury bonds issued by the governments of France, Germany, Japan, the United Kingdom, and the United States of America (Government of Norway 2020b). Third, the fund diversifies its investment portfolio by setting a limit to how much may be invested in a single company's equity (Government of Norway 2020b). As of 2020, the GFPG holds equity in about 9,000 companies with head-quarters in 74 countries (Government of Norway 2020a). Finally, to help protect the krone against large foreign exchange fluctuations generated by the petroleum industry, the fund invests exclusively abroad (Government of Norway 2020a).

C. Fiscal Rules for Dealing with Volatile Resource Revenue

Large fluctuations in commodity prices undermine the ability of resource-rich countries to leverage their resource wealth to sustain long periods of stability and prosperity. In the absence of countercyclical fiscal policy which builds buffers during commodity booms, fluctuations in commodity prices directly translate into fluctuations in natural resource revenues and spending. Studies have shown that government revenues are particularly vulnerable to terms-of-trade shocks in resource-rich countries (Figure 19.4), due to the significant dependence on the resource sector and also to the high elasticity of non-resource revenues with respect to GDP (von Haldenwang and Ivanyna 2018). Countercyclical fiscal policy is therefore particularly useful in resource-dependent countries as it helps provide a stable base for spending, therefore helping to avoid the temptation of increasing distortionary taxes in the face of negative shocks to commodity prices.

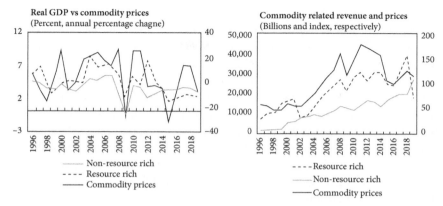

Figure 19.4 Natural Resource Wealth Causes Volatility in Government Revenues
Sources: Author's calculations using data from the World Development Indicators and the World
Economic Outlook databases.

Unfortunately, experience shows that fiscal policy in most resource-rich countries
has been mainly procyclical, due to overoptimism in good times, but also to rent-
seeking behaviors (IMF 2015).

Fiscal rules could be a powerful commitment device for the countercyclical
management of natural resource wealth. Fiscal rules in resource-rich countries
have typically been formulated either as a floor on the fiscal balance—as in Chile
and in the Central African Economic and Monetary Community (CEMAC)—or
as a constraint on the flows of revenues to and from natural resource funds as in
Norway (IMF 2015). Empirically, countries that have been successful at effectively
using fiscal rules to promote countercyclical fiscal policy typically have strong
institutions (IMF 2015).

A weak institutional framework challenges the enforcement of fiscal rules and
leaves fiscal policy decisions at the mercy of political pressure and off-budget
spending. For instance, Chad, Ecuador, and Papua New Guinea all had unsuccessful
experiences with fiscal rules. In these countries, weak enforcement and increased
spending pressures ultimately led to the abandonment of the sovereign funds which
were judged incompatible with the budget needs (Keiko Takahashi 2010; IMF 2015).

Country Examples of Fiscal Rules for Managing Natural Resource
Revenue Volatility

Botswana, Norway, and Chile are examples of countries that have used fiscal rules
to promote countercyclical fiscal policy. The experiences of Botswana and Norway
were met with success because: (1) they were successful at striking the right balance between flexibility and credibility in the design of their fiscal rules; and (2)
they have achieved credibility in the implementation of their fiscal rules by limiting the number of deviations from the rules. Consequently, both countries have

not only enjoyed solid growth over extended periods, but they have also managed to keep public debt at relatively low levels (Pouokam 2021). In the case of Chile, success has been to some extent mixed, as the global financial crisis has complicated the ability of the country to commit credibly to its fiscal rule.

Botswana's fiscal framework includes an institutionalized ceiling rule on public debt that is achieved with two fiscal targets: a balanced budget fiscal rule and a spending rule (Lledó et al. 2017). The debt limit rule was introduced by the Stock, Bonds, and Treasury Bills Act of 2005. It caps both total domestic debt and total foreign debt at 20 percent of GDP. The spending rule was introduced in 2006 as a limit of 40 percent of GDP on government spending. By 2018, the spending rule had been breached only once, during the 2008 global financial crisis; and public debt had remained below 15 percent of GDP.

Although Norway's ceiling on the non-oil structural deficit in principle allows for some flexibility, the rule has been implemented as a de facto commitment to a positive budget balance. In principle, Norway's fiscal framework allows for deviations from the fiscal rule, during both expansions and recessions. For instance, in the event of large changes influencing the structural non-oil deficit, it is expected that the pace of adjustment to petroleum revenue spending would be spread across several years, based on the projected future real returns on the fund (Official Norwegian Reports 2015). An expert commission reporting on the application of the fiscal rule is required to advise on how the fiscal rule should adapt to the exceptional circumstances (Government of Norway 2020c). Yet, despite the fact that deviations from the fiscal rule would be tolerated if warranted by exceptional circumstances, Norway has consistently accumulated fiscal surpluses, including during the global financial crisis (Pouokam 2021). This has helped keep the Norwegian public debt consistently below 25 percent of GDP, as of 2018.

Analysis of the financial position of Norway's public sector suggests that its stellar natural resource management framework and fiscal rules have put it into a strong position to face aging pressures, though some limited fiscal consolidation would eventually be needed. It has been estimated that although the public sector's assets exceeded liabilities by some 340 percent of GDP in 2018, the intertemporal net worth remained negative at about 240 percent of GDP when accounting for future liabilities related to old age pensions (Cabezon and Henn 2020). This is mainly because over the last 15 years, non-oil fiscal deficits have risen steadily from below 2 to above 7 percent of non-oil GDP (Cabezon and Henn 2020). However, estimates suggest that complementing Norway's BIH framework with fiscal consolidation targeting a fiscal balance of 5 percent of non-oil GDP by the mid-2020s would make it possible to finance future pensions from the country's oil wealth (Cabezon and Henn 2020). One important takeaway from Norway's experience is that resource funds are the most effective at promoting fiscal sustainability when they are properly integrated with both the budget and the fiscal anchor, as has been stressed by Poplawski-Ribeiro et al. (2012).

The Chilean fiscal rule experience has mainly had mixed success. Established in 2001, the Chilean fiscal rule requires a positive structural balance. The structural balance is defined as the central government balance evaluated at potential output and using the long-term copper price. The rule initially led to the accumulation of fiscal surpluses which helped contain the public debt to GDP ratio below 7 percent, prior to the onset of the global financial crisis. In fact, Chile's net asset position strengthened from 3.25 percent of GDP in 2000 to 19.5 percent in 2008, against the background of increasing copper prices. Since then, public debt-to-GDP has increased relatively rapidly, reaching the level of 25 percent of GDP in 2018. However, by all standards, Chile's debt level still remains relatively low for a middle-income country.

Chile's experience has proved that fiscal rules can become ineffective in difficult times if they are not sufficiently constraining. In practice, Chile's fiscal framework allows the government's administrations to change the structural balance target as desired. In fact, the structural target has been modified multiple times, despite the requirement by the Fiscal Responsibility Act of 2006 that incoming governments should announce structural fiscal targets for the full length of their mandates within the first 90 days of their administration (Lledó et al. 2017). From 2001 to 2007, the structural balance target was a surplus of 1 percent of GDP. In 2008, the target was brought down to a surplus of 0.5 percent of GDP. In 2009, the target was changed to a zero structural balance, and a de facto escape clause was introduced to accommodate the countercyclical measures implemented in the context of the global financial crisis. In 2010, an adjustment path was specified to get the structural balance to converge to 1 percent of GDP by 2014. In 2015, the fiscal rule of a balanced structural budget was temporarily abandoned with the plan that it would be reinstated in 2018 after a gradual adjustment path of fiscal consolidation that would continue to support pro-growth expenditure in infrastructure and education.

One lesson from Chile's experience is that more predictability and a stronger anchor for fiscal policy, especially after deviations, can enhance commitment to the fiscal rule. It is good practice to embed clear guidance on medium-term objectives for the structural balance and net assets in the fiscal rule itself. An explicit escape clause to allow discretionary policy in the event of large, clearly defined shocks usually helps enhance clarity while preserving flexibility.

V. Natural Resources, Poverty, and Inequality

Most often, resource-rich countries have been unable to transfer an appropriate share of the resource dividend to those at the bottom of the market income distribution. In fact, many households in resource-rich countries still live below the US$1.90 a day poverty line (Figure 19.5). The evidence also suggests that higher resource rents have generally not been associated with less market income inequality (Pouokam 2021), except for a few countries in the Middle East and North Africa (MENA) region and the Central Asia region which have usually used government employment as a means of keeping people out of poverty (Adams and Page 2003; IMF 2018). This indicates that resource-rich countries are generally not more successful than resource-poor countries at addressing inequality in opportunities. Equally surprisingly, the disposable income Gini in resource-rich countries has usually not been substantially lower than the market income Gini, suggesting that fiscal policy has not achieved much redistribution in these economies (Pouokam 2021).

Empirical studies suggest that resource wealth exacerbates rather than alleviates inequality. Eicher and Turnovsky (2003) documents a positive association, albeit weak, between the share of natural resource wealth in total wealth, and Gini market income inequality. Hartwell et al. (2019) finds evidence of a positive correlation between the lags of resource rents and market income inequality among countries with low levels of democracy, and a negative correlation among countries with relatively high levels of democracy.[6] Lessmann and Steinkraus (2019) provides evidence of a strong and positive association between spatial inequality in the distribution of resource wealth and intergroup market income inequality.

The impact of resource abundance on education outcomes could be one fundamental reason why resource wealth does not seem to reduce inequality. To explain why market income inequality is higher in resource-rich Latin American countries compared to resource-poor East Asian countries, Leamer et al. (1999) propose the explanation that natural resource-intensive sectors absorb capital that might otherwise flow to manufacturing, hence delaying industrialization by depressing workers' incentives to accumulate skills, and by the same token contributing to increasing inequality.

To explain the nexus between resource dependence, the level of democracy, and inequality, Hartwell et al. (2019) propose that the influence of democracy operates through three distinct channels affecting equity. First, democracies allow a broader number of checks and balances, thus preventing the concentration of power over the control of resource rents into the hands of a few economic and political players. Second, because it allows citizens to sanction an unsatisfactory distribution of resource windfalls and indirectly decide over social spending programs, democracy may help spread the resource wealth more equitably than autocracy. Third, by enabling the diffusion of power and by encouraging social spending, democracy encourages citizens to maximize their own potential and invest to improve their human capital.

Bhattacharyya and Hodler (2014) propose an alternative explanation linking resource abundance to a lack of will power to promote financial development.

---

[6] In the study of Hartwell et al. (2019), democracy is measured by the democratic accountability score from the International Country Risk Guide (ICRG) dataset.

They argue that in countries with poor political institutions, easy access to resource rent makes incumbent governments unwilling to take on the challenge of improving contract enforcement. In the absence of strong contract enforcement, the private sector finds it difficult to obtain credit and undertake otherwise productive activities. Resource wealth therefore hinders financial development which, as discussed in Chapter 4, is one channel to reduce inequality.

Resource-rich countries tend to have relatively lower spending in equity-promoting areas such as health and education. In fact, resource-rich developing countries invest markedly less in health and education (in terms of shares of GDP) than their resource-poor peers (Figure 19.5). Resource abundance has actually been shown to be negatively correlated with spending on education (Cockx and Francken 2016) and spending on health (Cockx and Francken 2014), including after controlling for GDP and other relevant factors. One possible explanation is that resource-rich countries tend to have opaque public finances and a lack of government accountability, both of which allow government officials to self-appropriate the economy's resources and conduct inefficient policies that serve their own interests. These government failures are not unique to resource-rich countries, but are exacerbated by the rent-seeking opportunities

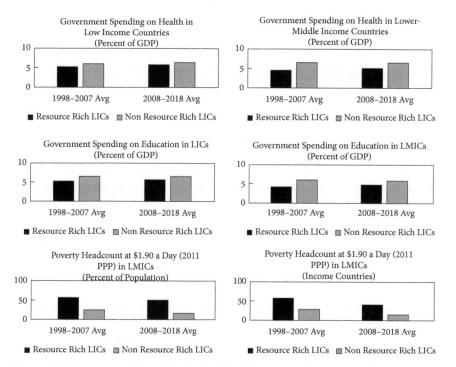

Figure 19.5 Poverty and Spending in Health, Education in Resource-Rich Countries

Sources: Author's calculations using data from the World Development Indicators and Standardized World Income Inequality databases.

created by resource wealth. Thus, resource-rich societies need to build institutions capable of supporting human capital accumulation, which is fundamental for development and inclusive growth.

Tackling poverty and inequality requires investing earnestly in human capital, and creating budget space to assist the poor and vulnerable. This requires commitment to strong fiscal discipline to make sure that the funding base for education and health spending, but also social protection measures, is not eroded by commodity busts. It also requires a reprioritization of spending to focus on measures that effectively reach the poor. This could for instance involve abandoning costly fuel subsidies that primarily benefit the wealthy, and freeing up resources to invest more in health, education, unemployment insurance, school feeding programs, and cash transfers. The pioneering experience of Latin America with cash transfers that are conditioned on children's attendance to school or health clinic programs has shown that well designed cash transfers programs could be an effective approach to reducing inequality (Lustig, Pessino, and Scott 2013).

VI. Structural Policy: Making the Case for Economic Diversification

Effective diversification policies can help countries sustain high long-term growth and escape the trap of resource dependence. The experiences of Malaysia and Chile present two tales of economic diversification that other resource-rich countries could learn from.

A. The Experience of Malaysia with Economic Diversification

Early on, Malaysia shifted away from its import substitution strategy. In the early 1960s, Malaysia' s trade policy focused on an import substitution strategy (Lim 1987). Malaysia's exports at the time relied heavily on tin and rubber production which was declining. This prompted the government to promote the development of new exports markets, but also to pursue vertical policies toward higher-value-added activities related to natural resource industries, including to support the export of oil refinery by the state company after oil was discovered in the 1970s. In fact, in the 1970s, Malaysia was one of the earliest oil exporters to scale down its import substitution strategy to rely more on an export promotion policy (Cherif and Hasanov 2015).

One key feature of Malaysia's diversification program was the strong involvement of the government which fiercely promoted Malaysian exports. To diversify Malaysia's export base, the government rallied the efforts of the private sector, initially focusing on promoting the development of the palm oil industry (agricultural diversification), but later supplementing this with industrialization policies focused on export promotion. Agricultural diversification policies in Malaysia consisted in providing cash, tax incentives, and direct government support to promote the cultivation, processing, and exports of palm oil and palm oil products. Industrialization policies mainly focused on an export-oriented development strategy centered around free-trade zones, and were accompanied with trade liberalization and the promotion of human capital accumulation through support for education and skills development (Friska 2013).

These strategies initially produced spectacular results. Manufacturing exports rose from about 6 percent of total exports in the early 1970s to more than 70 percent in the early 2000s. Following the creation of the Multimedia Super Corridor (MSC) in 1996 to promote tax incentives favoring the IT sector, the share of the IT industry rose to more than 70 percent of manufacturing exports by the early 2000s (Friska 2013). However, since then, the process of structural transformation has stalled, indicating the need for a new strategy to reach higher value-added markets.

One reason which may explain why Malaysia's progress has stalled is the lack of innovation and technology diffusion. In Malaysia, the process of industrialization has been mainly carried out by multinationals not keen on transferring technology to local firms, unlike in South Korea and Taiwan Province of China where innovation has been mainly carried out by local firms (Cherif and Hasanov 2015). As a result, growth in total factor productivity in Malaysia has lagged behind that of these two Asian Tigers, making it difficult for Malaysia to continue its process of structural transformation by further moving up the value-added ladder. The Malaysian experience hence suggests that a government-led diversification program can effectively promote new export markets early on, but would require research and development, along with technology diffusion to take the country to the technological frontier. The examples of "spin off" firms in Taiwan Province of China and "chaebols" in South Korea illustrate how close collaboration and long-term relationships with international firms can nurture innovation by local firms.

The approach of the government of Taiwan Province of China to technology diffusion has been summarized in two pillars (Cherif and Hasanov 2015): (1) an active participation of public and quasi-public research institutes which would spin off firms introducing new technologies; and (2) massive public investment in training engineers abroad to support the formation of a "technical community" with valuable technical experience and informal connections with the Silicon Valley. As explained in Cherif and Hasanov (2015), The Industrial Technology Research Institute (ITRI) was created in 1973 to negotiate licenses or technology-sharing agreements with US electronics firms. Typically, ITRI's staff would be sent for training in the production facilities of US partners and upon their returns, would set up an experimental production unit within ITRI's facilities. Once this stage was passed, the team of engineers and technicians involved in the new technology would then form a "spin-off" firm with about 40–50 percent of the initial capital coming from the government. When the government of Taiwan Province of China ended its spin-off program in the mid-1990s, the leading firms in the electronics sector were already investing heavily in R&D and were using the best technologies available (Cherif and Hasanov 2015).

South Korea led an export-driven and very ambitious strategy to promote technology diffusion. The strategy mainly consisted of providing pecuniary incentives for South Korean firms to create global brands (chaebols) with strong footholds in several industries. These industrial conglomerates were encouraged to export immediately, and this, according to Cherif and Hasanov (2015) would be precisely the reason why the automaking industry expanded more rapidly in South Korean than it did in Malaysia, despite facing initially similar challenges in terms of technology acquisition and skills adequacy. Chaebols would receive loans with low and often negative real interest rates that were often made conditional on explicit and quantified exports targets (Cherif and Hasanov 2015). Stiff international competition therefore forced the chaebols to operate at the technological frontier very early on. Knowledge spillovers across the different industries in which the chaebols operated further supported overall productivity growth.

B. The Experience of Chile with Economic Diversification

Economic diversification effectively took off in Chile in the 1980s after trade liberalization reforms and successful efforts to bring technological innovation into strategic sectors. Starting in the mid-1970s, Chile pursued aggressive unilateral trade liberalization by slashing out imports tariffs and turning away from the import substitution strategy that had been in place since 1934 (Friska 2013). This set the stage for an export-oriented growth strategy focused on creating new export markets by introducing and disseminating new technologies in selected sectors. Large-scale technology diffusion was made possible by foreign direct investments, especially in the wine sector, but also by the work of Fundación Chile as a "do tank" in the fish and fruits sectors (World Bank, 2014). The Innovation for Competitiveness Fund (ICF) created in 2006 played a catalytic role as well, by establishing a framework for the use of windfalls from copper exports to support different programs for science and research and development (R&D). This helped finance and monitor high growth start-up firms, and led to significant investments in advanced skills, including scholarships to enroll Chileans into top global universities (OECD/WTO 2019).

What made Fundación Chile successful as a vehicle for technology transfer was its role as a not-for-profit venture capitalist. Technology transfer in Chile usually worked as a two-stage process (Lebdioui 2019). Initially, Fundación Chile would create firms to demonstrate the new technologies. Then, after the industry had become viable, these firms would be sold to the private sector. From the very beginning, Fundación Chile would share its knowledge with private entrepreneurs, which in this way could freely access innovative technologies. Overall, Fundación Chile created around 70 firms (Lebdioui 2019).

In essence, Fundación Chile demonstrated viable business models through the companies it created. In the case of the salmon industry, the acquisition of the American company Domsea Farms and the creation of Salmones Antarctica by Fundación Chile in 1981 helped bring production levels from very low levels up to around 1,000 tonnes by 1988 when Salmones Antarctica was sold (Lebdioui 2019). Most importantly, this helped demonstrate to the private sector that the large-scale farming, breeding, and production of salmon in Chile was technically and commercially feasible (United Nations 2006). By the early 2000s, annual salmon production had surpassed 500,000 tonnes and salmon had become Chile's second largest source of export revenues after copper (Lebdioui 2019). Similarly, in the fruits industry, Berries la Union, a company created by Fundacion Chile in 1980, helped elaborate a profitable business model for the cultivation of berries in Chile by disseminating the technology of cold storage systems (Agosin et al. 2010).

Overall, Chile's diversification strategy has met with only partial success as merchandise exports remain essentially resource-based. In 1980, Chile's merchandise exports were poorly diversified: mining accounted for 64 percent of total merchandise exports; the agro-industry for 24 percent; and manufacturing for 9 percent. As of 2019, the overall picture shows only moderate improvements: the share of the agro-industry in Chile's total merchandise exports is relatively large at around 33 percent; but the share of the mining sector continues to be high at around 53 percent, while that of manufacturing continues to be low at around 13 percent. By comparison, in Malaysia the export share of the agro-industry sector fell from 46 percent in 1980 to 11 percent in 2019, while that of the nonrenewable resource sector (essentially fuel and mining) fell from 35 percent in 1980 to 18 percent in 2019, contrasting sharply with an increase from 19 percent to 70 percent for the manufacturing sector. In South Korea and Taiwan Province of China (herein "Taiwan"), which are both resource-poor economies, the share of manufacturing products in total merchandise exports which was already very high in 1980 (at 89 percent for South Korea and 88 percent for Taiwan) continues to be very high by all standards (at 87 percent for South Korea and 91 percent for Taiwan, as of 2019).

As a result of the focus on the agro-industrial sector, Chile's diversification strategy has led to slow total factor productivity growth. In fact, despite the multiple innovations introduced in the Chilean wine, fishing, fruits, and meat industries, total factor productivity growth has stagnated since the 1970s, with Chile lagging significantly behind the Asian Tigers, but also behind Malaysia (Cherif and Hasanov 2015). Chile's slow productivity growth has been attributed in part to significant entry barriers and regulatory complexity (OECD 2018) which prevents small and medium enterprises (SMEs) from innovating and competing in sectors in which the Chilean government is not leading with a top-down approach to innovation and growth. For instance, in 2018, only 2 percent of Chilean SMEs participated in international trade (OECD 2018). More so, the concentration of Chile's innovation efforts in the agro-industrial sector has not allowed the country to fully benefit from cross-sectoral knowledge spillovers catalyzed by exporting manufacturing firms (Herzer et al. 2006; Wei and Liu 2006). This could explain why productivity growth in Chile has been much lower than it has been in Malaysia, South Korea, and Taiwan in which the manufacturing sector has grown more rapidly.

VII. Conflict and Fragility

Conflict and fragility exacerbate the risk of misuse of resource wealth. Of the 36 countries identified as fragile in 2019, half were resource-rich countries in the 2000s, in the sense that they had an average ratio of natural resource rents-to-GDP that exceeded 10 percent.[7] Of these 18 resource-rich fragile countries, only five were not low-income countries (Iraq, Libya, Myanmar, Papua New Guinea, and Timor-Leste). This tight nexus between resource wealth, economic development, and state fragility has been explained by a negative impact of natural resources on the institutional climate and the state capacity in fragile countries (Chami et al. 2021). The effect of natural resources on state capacity operates through two channels.

First, natural resource windfalls fuel military spending and conflict. The basic mechanism is that natural resource wealth not only heightens the stake for conflict in institutionally weak countries, but it also contributes to the opacity of budget processes, thereby allowing for the prioritization of military spending over human capital development needs. In fact, in fragile states, resource wealth tends to be associated with a higher ratio of military spending over GDP (Figure 19.6). Consistent with this fact, Deléchat et al. (2018) shows that a relatively high level of natural resource rents is associated with a relatively low probability that a fragile country would eventually exit fragility by reaching a Country Policy and Institutional Assessment (CPIA) score above what could be considered a threshold for institutional resilience.[8]

---

[7] The list of fragile and conflict-affected situations (FCS) is released annually by the World Bank Group (WBG). Fragile countries are countries with high levels of institutional and social fragility, identified based on CPIA scores, and countries affected by violent conflict, identified based on a threshold number of conflict-related deaths relative to the population. https://www.worldbank.org/en/topic/fragilityconflictviolence/brief/harmonized-list-of-fragile-situations

[8] The CPIA—Country Policy and Institutional Assessment—rates countries against a set of 16 criteria grouped in four clusters: (a) economic management; (b) structural policies; (c) policies for social

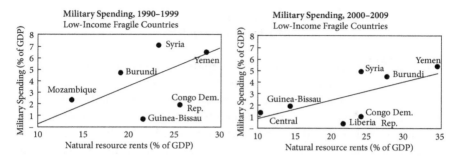

Figure 19.6 Military Spending and Resource Wealth in Low-Income Countries
Source: Author's calculations using data from the World Development Indicators database.

Second, dependence on natural resources weakens fiscal capacity in fragile countries. Natural resource wealth undermines efforts to collect non-resource revenues—particularly VAT, corporate, and trade taxes (Crivelli and Gupta 2014). In doing so, natural resource wealth contributes to weakening fiscal capacity in fragile countries (Deléchat et al. 2018). Weak capacity in turn challenges the management of government revenues. This for instance creates hurdles for the completion of public infrastructure projects in the face of reversals in commodity booms, leading to additional inefficiencies. More generally, fragility makes a strong case for strengthening institutional capacity to promote sound fiscal policy and a conscious sharing of the resource wealth across generations.

History teaches us that improving governance and investing in human capital would be the way out of the vicious cycle of resource dependence and poverty. Of the 52 countries classified by the World Bank as low-income in 1995, only 28 had become middle-income countries by 2014, while the 24 other countries had remained low-income countries, including among them 12 resource-rich countries of which 8 are currently classified as fragile-conflict states (World Bank 2018). The 24 countries that were unable to graduate to the status of middle-income countries also had the lowest rankings on most dimensions of institutions and governance quality as measured by the World Governance Indicators—voice and accountability, political stability and absence of violence, government effectiveness, regulatory quality, rule of law, and control of corruption (World Bank 2018). Among the 28 countries that successfully made the transition to the middle-income status, 15 countries considered resource-rich effectively invested in other forms of assets than natural capital. However, among these 15 countries, only those which invested significantly in human capital were able to cut their poverty rates by half.

inclusion and equity; and (d) public sector management and institutions. https://ida.worldbank.org/financing/resource-management/ida-resource-allocation-index

VIII. Strengthening Governance in the Management of Resource Wealth

The positive role of good governance in the management of natural resource wealth cannot be overstated. Strong institutions are essential to establishing effective regulatory frameworks and promoting accountability and transparency which together condition a country's capacity to exit the vicious cycle of resource dependence and poverty discussed earlier. Steps usually taken by governments in resource-rich countries to promote accountability and transparency include joining the Extractive Industries Transparency Initiative (EITI) and endorsing the Santiago Principles for the management of Sovereign Wealth Funds (SWFs).

The Santiago Principles

The Santiago Principles are a voluntary code of 24 guidelines for the management of SWFs. These guidelines were proposed in 2008 through a joint effort between the IMF and the International Working Group of SWFs. They are organized in three blocks aiming at three different objectives: (1) encouraging SWFs to publicly disclose their legal frameworks and policy purposes; (2) promoting a sound governance framework that clearly and effectively divides roles and responsibilities among a SWF's constituents; and (3) supporting appropriate investment and risk management frameworks for SWFs (Tapsoba, 2014). As of 2020, 33 countries have signed up to the Santiago Principles.[9]

The Extractive Industries Transparency Initiative

Established in 2003, the Extractive Industries Transparency Initiative (EITI) is a global standard to support transparency and accountability in the management of extractive resources in resource-rich countries.[10] The EITI promotes transparency by publishing independent reports on resource revenues, and by requiring that governments engage with civil societies as a way of disseminating information on the revenues collected. EITI reports compare company information on payments from of oil, gas, and mining operations with government information on revenues from these sectors. Signatories countries lose credibility in the management of their natural resource wealth if they fail to produce information on resource revenues that can be reconciled with payments data from extractive industry (EI) companies. Adhering to the EITI therefore provides additional incentives for governments to truthfully report on the revenues collected. Ultimately, greater

---

[9] These countries are: the United Arab Emirates, Rwanda, the United States, France, Mexico, Italy, China, Spain, Panama, Senegal, Angola, Australia, Singapore, Nauru, Ireland, Morocco, Kazakhstan, Malaysia, South Korea, Kuwait, Libya, Iran, New Zealand, Nigeria, State of Palestine, Qatar, Russia, Oman, Azerbaijan, Trinidad and Tobago, Botswana, Timor-Leste, and Turkey.
https://www.ifswf.org/our-members
[10] https://eiti.org/who-we-are

transparency on the amount of resource revenues collected by the government could lead to more inclusive spending policies as informed citizens make the government accountable for its poor choices. As of 2020, 53 countries are members of the EITI; three countries have lost their membership for failing to meet EITI standards (Equatorial Guinea, Gabon, and Yemen); and four have withdrawn from the EITI (Azerbaijan, the United States, Niger, and Solomon Islands).[11]

IX. Conclusion

Many countries have an economic structure dominated by resource wealth that is expected to be exhausted within a generation. These countries urgently need to design policies, especially maintaining appropriate fiscal frameworks, to share the benefits of the resource wealth equitably and sustainably across generations, and to mitigate the adverse economic and fiscal impacts of resource revenue volatility.

Resource-rich countries must overcome the challenge of poor governance and actively seek to diversify their economies with policies conducive to a friendly business climate. Only by doing so would they be able to leverage their resource wealth to positively transform lives, one generation at the time. This is particularly true for hydrocarbon producers for whom the quest for the decarbonization of the global economy to mitigate climate risks poses the threat of an economic collapse. To produce long-lasting results, efforts to diversify must be accompanied with an effective competition policy and the removal of bottlenecks to innovation and technology diffusion.

Exiting the trap of resource abundance and poverty requires significant and efficient investment in human capital. History has taught us that resource-rich developing countries which dedicate significant effort in fostering human capital accumulation are generally able to sustain high growth, reduce poverty significantly, and escape the state of fragility. To underpin such efforts, strengthening state capacity and transparency with the establishment of pro-growth institutions is undeniably the right place to start.

References

Acemoglu, D., Johnson, S., and Robinson, J.A. 2012. "Chapter 4. An African Success Story: Botswana." *In Search of Prosperity*, edited by Dani Rodrik. Princeton: Princeton University Press, pp. 80–120.

Adams Jr, R.H., and J. Page. 2003. "Poverty, Inequality and Growth in Selected Middle East and North Africa countries, 1980–2000." *World Development* 31(12): 2027–48.

---

[11] https://eiti.org/other-countries

Agosin, M.R., C. Larraín, and N. Grau. 2010. "Industrial Policy in Chile." IDB Working Paper Series No. IDB-WP-170.

Auty, R.M. 1994. "Industrial Policy Reform in Six Newly Industrializing Countries: The Resource Curse Thesis." *World Dev.* 22(1): 1165–71.

Backer, L.C. 2009. "Sovereign Wealth Funds as Regulatory Chameleons: The Norwegian Sovereign Wealth Funds and Public Global Governance through Private Global Investment." *Georgetown Journal of International Law* 40: 101–217.

Bhattacharyya, S., and R. Hodler. 2014. "Do Natural Resource Revenues Hinder Financial Development? The Role of Political Institutions." *World Development* 57: 101–13.

Cabezon, E., and C. Henn. 2020. "Norway's Public Sector Balance Sheet." *Applied Economics Letters* 27(11): 930–6.

Chami, R., P. Montiel, and R. Espinoza. 2021. "Macroeconomic Policy Issues in Fragile States: A Framework." In *Macroeconomic Policy in Fragile States*, edited by Ralph Chami, Raphael Espinoza, and Peter Montiel, Oxford University Press. © International Monetary Fund. DOI: 10.1093/oso/9780198853091.003.0001

Charnavoki, V., and Dolado, J.J. 2014. "The Effects of Global Shocks on Small Commodity-Exporting Economies: Lessons from Canada." *American Economic Journal: Macroeconomics* 6(2): 207–37.

Cherif, R., and F. Hasanov. 2015. "The Leap of the Tiger: How Malaysia Can Escape the Middle-Income Trap." IMF Working Paper No. 15–131.

Cockx, L., and N. Francken. 2014. "Extending the Concept of the Resource Curse: Natural Resources and Public Spending on Health." *Ecological Economics* 108: 136–49.

Cockx, L., and N. Francken. 2016. "Natural Resources: A Curse on Education Spending?" *Energy Policy* 92: 394–408.

Collier, P., and A. Hoeffler. 1998. "On Economic Causes of Civil War." *Oxf. Econ. Pap.* 56: 563–95.

Corden, W.M., and J.P. Neary. 1982. "Booming Sector and De-industrialisation in a Small Open Economy." *The Economic Journal* 92(368): 825–48.

Crivelli, Ernesto, and Sanjeev Gupta. 2014. "Resource Blessing, Revenue Curse? Domestic Revenue Effort in Resource-Rich Countries." *European Journal of Political Economy* 35: 88–101.

Deléchat, Corinne, Ejona Fuli, Dafina Mulaj, Gustavo Ramirez, and Rui Xu. 2018. "Exiting from Fragility in Sub-Saharan Africa: The Role of Fiscal Policies and Fiscal Institutions." *South African Journal of Economics* 86(3): 271–307.

Dungey, M., R. Fry-McKibbin, and V. Linehan. 2014. "Chinese Resource Demand and the Natural Resource Supplier." *Applied Economics* 46(2): 167–78.

Eicher, T.S., and S.J. Turnovsky. 2003. *Inequality and Growth: Theory and Policy Implications (Vol. 1).* Cambridge, MA: MIT Press.

Frankel, J.A. 2003. "Experience of and Lessons from Exchange Rate Regime in Emerging Economies." NBER Working Paper No. 10032.

Friska, P. 2013. "Sustaining Growth and Enhancing Economic Diversification in Botswana." Staff Report on Common Policies for Member Countries, IMF Country Report SM/13/246. Washington, DC: International Monetary Fund.

Goderis, B., and S.W. Malone. 2011. "Natural Resource Booms and Inequality: Theory and Evidence." *Scandinavian Journal of Economics* 113(2): 388–417.

Government of Norway. 2015. "Background: Norway's Fiscal Framework." Retrieved from https://www.regjeringen.no/en/whatsnew/Ministries/fin/press-releases/2015/expert-commission-reports-on-the-application-of-the-fiscal-rule/background-norways-fiscal-framework/id2423652/

Government of Norway. 2020a. "About the Fund." Retrieved from https://www.nbim.no/en/the-fund/about-the-fund/on November 25, 2020.

Government of Norway. 2020b. "Investment Mandate Global Pension Fund Global." Retrieved from https://www.nbim.no/en/organisation/governance-model/executive-board-documents/investment-mandate—government-pension-fund-global/on November 25, 2020

Government of Norway. 2020c. "Expert Commission reports on the application of the fiscal rule." Retrieved from https://www.regjeringen.no/en/aktuelt/expert-commission-reports-on-the-application-of-the-fiscal-rule/id2423498/on April 24, 2020.

Gylfason, T. 2001. "Natural Resources, Education and Economic Development." *Eur. Econ. Rev.* 45: 847–59.

Sinn, Hans-Werner. 2008. "Public Policies against Global Warming: A Supply Side Approach." *International Tax and Public Finance* 15(4): 360–94.

Hartwell, C.A., R. Horvath, E. Horvathova, and O. Popova. 2019. "Democratic Institutions, Natural Resources, and Income Inequality." *Comparative Economic Studies* 61(4): 531–50.

Herzer, D., D.F. Nowak-Lehmann, and B. Siliverstovs. 2006. "Export-led Growth in Chile: Assessing the Role of Export Composition in Productivity Growth." *The Developing Economies* 44(3): 306–28.

Hillbom, E., and J. Bolt. 2015. "Changing Income Inequality and Structural Transformation: The Case of Botswana 1921–2010." WIDER Working Paper No. 2015/028.

Humphreys, M., J.D. Sachs, J.E. Stiglitz, G. Soros, and M. Humphreys. 2007. *Escaping the Resource Curse.* New York: Columbia University Press.

Iimi, A. 2007. "Escaping from the Resource Curse: Evidence from Botswana and the Rest of the World." *IMF Staff Papers* 54(4): 663–99.

International Monetary Fund (IMF). 2008. "Norway's Oil Fund Shows the Way for Wealth Funds." IMF Survey. Retrieved from https://www.imf.org/en/News/Articles/2015/09/28/04/53/sopol070908a on April 20, 2020.

International Monetary Fund (IMF). 2012. "Macroeconomic Policy Frameworks for Resource-Rich Developing Countries," Background Paper 1.

International Monetary Fund (IMF). 2015. "The Commodities Roller Coaster. A Fiscal Framework for Uncertain Times." Fiscal Monitor, chapter 1, October 2015. Washington.

International Monetary Fund (IMF). 2018. "Public Wage Bills in the Middle East and Central Asia." Fiscal Affairs Departmental Paper Series, No 18/01.

International Monetary Fund (IMF). 2019. "How to Mitigate Climate Change." Fiscal Monitor, chapter 1, October 2019. Washington.

Ismail, K. 2010. "The Structural Manifestation of the 'Dutch Disease': The Case of Oil Exporting Countries." IMF Working Paper, WP/10/103.

James, A. 2015. "The Resource Curse: A Statistical Mirage?" *Journal of Development Economics* 114: 55–63.

James, A., and D. Aadland. 2011. "The Curse of Natural Resources: An Empirical Investigation of US Counties." *Resource and Energy Economics* 33(2): 440–53.

Keiko Takahashi. 2010. "Managing windfall revenues from LNG Projecys in Papua New Guinea," Papua New Guinea: Staff Report on Common Policies for Member Countries, IMF Country Report No. 10/163. Selected Issues Paper. Washington: International Monetary Fund.

Kim, I., R. Baqir, F. Vardy, and K. Ogata. 2005. "Democratic Republic of Timor Leste: Selected Issues and Statistical Appendix." International Monetary Fund Country Report, (03/228).

Lashitew, A.A., M.L. Ross, and E. Werker. 2020. "*What Drives Successful Economic Diversification in Resource-Rich Countries?*" *The World Bank Research Observer*, lkaa001. https://doi.org/10.1093/wbro/lkaa001

Leamer, E.E., H. Maul, S. Rodriguez, and P.K. Schott. 1999. "Does Natural Resource Abundance Increase Latin American Income Inequality?" *Journal of Development Economics* 59(1): 3–42.

Lebdioui, A. 2019. "Chile's Export Diversification since 1960: A Free Market Miracle or Mirage?" *Development and Change* 50(6): 1624–63.

Lessmann, C., and A. Steinkraus. 2019. "The Geography of Natural Resources, Ethnic Inequality and Civil Conflicts." *European Journal of Political Economy* 59: 33–51.

Lim, C.P. 1987. "Changes in the Malaysian Economy and Trade Trends and Prospects." In *Trade and Structural Change in Pacific Asia*, edited by C.I. Bradford and W.H. Branson. Chicago, IL: University of Chicago Press, pp. 435–66.

Lledó, V., S. Yoon, X. Fang, S. Mbaye, and Y. Kim. 2017. "Fiscal Rules at a Glance." International Monetary Fund, 2–77.

Lustig, N., C. Pessino, and J.R. Scott. 2013. "The Impact of Taxes and Social Spending on Inequality and Poverty in Argentina, Bolivia, Brazil, Mexico, Peru and Uruguay: An Overview," CEQ Working Paper No. 13, August.

Matsuyama, K. 1992. "Agricultural Productivity, Comparative Advantage, and Economic Growth." *J. Econ. Theory* 58: 317–34.

Norges Bank Investment Management. 2020. Retrieved from https://www.nbim.no/ on April 17, 2020.

Organisation for Economic Co-operation and Development (OECD). 2018. OECD Economic Surveys: Chile 2018, OECD Publishing, Paris, https://doi.org/10.1787/eco_surveys-chl-2018-en.

Organisation for Economic Co-operation and Development (OECD)/World Trade Organization (WTO). 2019. Aid for Trade at a Glance 2019: Economic Diversification and Empowerment, OECD Publishing, Paris, https://doi.org/10.1787/18ea27d8-en.

Official Norwegian Reports. 2015. NOU 2015: 9, Chapter 1, The Application of the Fiscal Rule: The Assessments and Main Conclusions of the Commission, 10.

Papyrakis, E., and R. Gerlagh. 2007. "Resource Abundance and Economic Growth in the US." Eur. Econ. Rev. 51(4): 1011–39.

Poplawski-Ribeiro, M., M.M. Villafuerte, M.T. Baunsgaard, and C.J. Richmond. 2012. "Fiscal Frameworks for Resource Rich Developing Countries." Staff Discussion Note. International Monetary Fund.

Pouokam, N. 2021. "Sharing Resource Wealth Inclusively Within and Across Generations." IMF Working Paper No. 2021/097.

Sachs, J.D., and A.M. Warner. 1995. "Natural Resource Abundance and Economic Growth." National Bureau of Economic Research (Working Paper No. 5398, December).

Sachs, J.D., and A.M. Warner. 1999. "The Big Push, Natural Resource Booms and Growth." J. Dev. Econ. 59: 43–76.

Sao Tome and Principe. 2004. "Oil Revenue Management Law, Law 8/2004," São Tomé, December. Available on the Web at: http://www.anp-stp.gov.st.

Satter, A., and G.M. Iqbal. 2016. "Elements of Conventional and Unconventional Petroleum Reservoirs. " In Reservoir Engineering: The Fundamentals, Simulation, and Management of Conventional and Unconventional Recoveries, edited by Satter, A., and G.M. Iqbaltte. Amsterdam, Netherlands: Gulf Professional Publishing, pp. 11–28.

Segura, A. 2006. "Management of Oil Wealth Under the Permanent Income Hypothesis: The Case of São Tomé and Príncipe (No. 6–183)." International Monetary Fund.

Tapsoba, S.A.-J. 2014. "Designing a Fiscal Framework for Algeria," Algeria: Staff Report on Common Policies for Member Countries, IMF Country Report 14/34. Washington: International Monetary Fund.

Torvik, Ragnar. 2002. "Natural Resources, Rent Seeking and Welfare." J. Dev. Econ. 67: 455–70.

United Nations (UN). 2006. "A Case Study of the Salmon Industry in Chile." In Conference of Trade and Development. Transfer of Technology for Successful Integration into the Global Economy. New York: United Nations Publications.

von Haldenwang, C., and M. Ivanyna. 2018. "Does the Political Resource Curse Affect Public Finance? The Vulnerability of Tax Revenue in Resource-Dependent Countries." Journal of International Development 30(2): 323–44.

Veisi, M. 2017. Essays on the Links Between Natural Resources, Corruption, Taxation and Economic Growth. Thesis submitted to the University of Manchester, UK.

Wei, Y., and X. Liu. 2006. "Productivity Spillovers from R&D, Exports and FDI in China's Manufacturing Sector." Journal of International Business Studies 37(4): 544–57.

World Bank. 2011. *The Changing Wealth of Nations: Measuring Sustainable Development in the New Millennium.* Washington, DC.

World Bank. 2014. *Fundacion Chile Incubator: Chile Case Study.* Washington, DC. Available at: https://openknowledge.worldbank.org/handle/10986/20109 License: CC BY 3.0 IGO."

World Bank. 2018. *The Changing Wealth of Nations: Building a Sustainable Future.* Washington, DC.

20
Climate Change

Amar Bhattacharya, Maksym Ivanyna, William Oman,
and Nicholas Stern

I. Introduction

Prosperity and well-being can only be sustained and increased over time if humanity safeguards the ecological basis of modern societies—critical global commons like fresh air, clean water, sustainable food supplies, biodiversity, and a stable climate.[1] If the natural wealth is not preserved, living standards will inevitably deteriorate, and ultimately the planet's habitability will be threatened. Prosperity will not be shared with future generations, and the poor will suffer disproportionately from the negative consequences. Inclusive growth requires sustainability.

The bad news is that the economic growth models of the twentieth century are not sustainable. These models—albeit diverse—have undeniably produced material progress: income per capita has increased multiple times, billions have been lifted out of poverty, and the average life span has increased by decades (World Bank 2020c; Stern and Bhattacharya 2019). At the same time, these growth models have had an unprecedented ecological footprint that threatens the viability of modern societies. Indeed, economic activity has for the past two centuries—and particularly the past 70 years—driven environmental change on a global, even geological scale (Crutzen 2002).[2] It has altered the chemical composition of the ocean and atmosphere, led to freshwater overuse and reduction of wildlife populations at an alarming rate, and brought the Earth close to an irreversible disruption in key planetary systems—those that are necessary for human development as we know it (Rockström et al. 2009).

[1] We thank Fatma Bahr Ibrahim and Jaime Sarmiento Monroy for research assistance. We also thank Sebastian Acevedo, Eddie Buckley, Valerie Cerra, Jean Chateau, Barry Eichengreen, Jean-Marc Fournier, Xuehui Han, Fuad Hasanov, Andy Jobst, Emanuele Masetti, Wayne Mitchell, Marco Pani, Augustus Panton, Ian Perry, Kateryna Rybachuk, James Rydge, Thomas Schinko, Gregor Schwerhoff, Tito da Silva Filho, Nikola Spatafora, Sebastian Weber, as well as participants in the Inclusive Growth book seminar series organized by the IMF Institute for Capacity Development for their comments.
[2] This acceleration in Earth System indicators since 1950 has come to be known as the Great Acceleration (Steffen et al. 2015).

Amar Bhattacharya, Maksym Ivanyna, William Oman, and Nicholas Stern, *Climate Change* In: *How to Achieve Inclusive Growth*. Edited by: Valerie Cerra, Barry Eichengreen, Asmaa El-Ganainy, and Martin Schindler, Oxford University Press. © Amar Bhattacharya, Maksym Ivanyna, William Oman, and Nicholas Stern 2022. DOI: 10.1093/oso/9780192846938.003.0020

One of the key disrupted systems is the changing climate. Every year, the world's economy releases several dozen gigatons of greenhouse gases (GHGs) into the atmosphere. As a result, the average global temperature has already risen by more than 1°C since the nineteenth century. Nine of the ten warmest years on record have occurred since 2005 (NOAA 2020). Global warming causes sea-level rise, increasing frequency and severity of natural disasters, and higher pressure on ecosystems—resulting in severe socio-economic damage across the globe. If GHG emissions continue unabated at the current pace, humanity has only about a decade before it risks triggering catastrophic climate scenarios that would threaten the livability of the planet for itself and other species (Stern 2015; Weitzman 2011; Westerhold et al. 2020).

Carbon-intensive growth—that is, growth fueled by greenhouse gas emissions—is strikingly non-inclusive through its impact on climate change. The costs and risks of climate change have been systematically underestimated (DeFries et al. 2019). Climate change disproportionately affects the poor, as they suffer higher impacts from the shocks and long-term impacts of climate change and have fewer means to adapt. If unchecked, climate change can lead to tens of millions of displaced people, mostly in the developing world. Carbon-intensive growth also puts at risk jobs that will become stranded in the future, when polluting sectors will have to be rapidly retired to avoid catastrophic climate change. The more decarbonization is delayed, the more disorderly future shocks to polluting sectors will be. Large numbers of jobs will become stranded, incomes will be lost, and wealth will be destroyed, driving millions into poverty.

Crucially, those who are set to suffer most from climate change have contributed—and continue to contribute—least to it. The consumption-based annual emissions of the wealthiest 1 percent of the global population account for more than twice the combined emissions of the poorest 50 percent (UNEP 2020).

In contrast, decisive climate action has become increasingly attractive. Low-carbon solutions are now less costly than fossil fuel-based investments because of rapid technological advances. Social norms are changing too, as hundreds of countries, regions, cities, and businesses are pledging carbon-neutrality by mid-century and there is growing public support for climate action.[3]

Crucially, the benefit of effective climate action is potentially enormous. It can help the world economy recover from the effects of the Covid-19 pandemic by providing an immediate impetus to economic demand, creating millions of jobs, training, and investment opportunities. Over the medium term, it can spur innovation and discovery and create new sources of economic growth. It would also lift millions out of poverty and reduce inequalities, while delivering multiple environmental co-benefits, notably clean air and water, and preserved natural

---

[3] Carbon-neutrality means balancing emissions of carbon dioxide with its removal.

wealth (Stern 2015; Meckling and Allan 2020). Over the longer term it is the only path to a sustainable future by stabilizing climate and making our economies more resilient. Indeed as the New Climate Economy has underscored, it can "unlock the inclusive growth story of the 21st century" (The Global Commission on the Economy and Climate 2018).

Governments should:

- Eliminate fossil fuel subsidies, and put a price on carbon, while mitigating the impact on the poor and affected workers, businesses, and regions;
- Reinforce carbon pricing with sector-specific policies: regulations, energy efficiency standards, feebates;
- Promote sustainable use of natural resources, using such policy measures as payments for ecosystem services, regulations, agricultural and water subsidies reform, incentives for circular economy;
- Boost public investment in sustainable and resilient infrastructure, including in nature-based solutions—restoration of degraded lands and conservation of existing ecosystems while mitigating the impact on the poor;
- Align the financial system with climate objectives: manage financial stability risks posed by climate change, align social and private returns to green investment, mobilize resources for investment, including a major boost to international climate finance;
- Deploy industrial and other policies to drive climate-friendly innovation, with a focus on the coordination of policy areas and on long-term policies and policy planning;
- Implement information campaigns to steer social norms and behaviors to lower energy demand and lower carbon intensity of consumption and business activity, and educate the public about climate change risks, including early warning systems and evacuation plans in case of natural disasters;
- Develop insurance instruments and social safety nets to mitigate the immediate impact of climate shocks;
- Promote active labor market policies, entrepreneurship, financial inclusion, regional investment strategies to facilitate structural transformation and the transition to a low-carbon economy for affected workers, businesses, and regions.
- More fundamentally: integrate sustainability considerations into public financial management and corporate governance; use better models and go beyond GDP when deciding on policy priorities and measuring well-being and sustainability.

Climate action involves global cooperation, changes to investment and consumption patterns, addressing multiple market failures, and ensuring social justice. It requires decoupling of economic output and reductions in emissions, known as "absolute decoupling."[4] The need for comprehensive climate action is made more urgent by the Covid-19 pandemic, which has claimed millions of lives, caused severe economic damage, and amplified inequalities. Building back better—creating sustainable, resilient, and inclusive economies—is a priority as countries are crafting recovery policy packages (The Coalition of Finance Ministers for Climate Actions 2020; IMF 2020).

This chapter provides an overview of the climate challenge that we face, and of the transformation that is required, with a focus on the critical importance of making our economies both sustainable and inclusive.

II. Science and Economics of Climate Change

A. What Is Climate Change?

Climate change results from a combination of two major factors. The first is the greenhouse effect. Discovered and thoroughly described already in the nineteenth century (Fourier 1824; Tyndall 1861; Arrhenius 1896), it is about the property of certain gases (so called greenhouse gases—GHGs) to trap solar heat in the atmosphere and reflect part of it back to the Earth's surface. The key GHGs in the atmosphere are water vapor, methane, nitrous oxide, and most importantly carbon dioxide—the product of our breathing and fossil-fuel burning, among other processes. Part of the carbon dioxide is absorbed by plants and phytoplankton, or dissolves into oceans, but the unabsorbed extra, once released, stays in the atmosphere for centuries. In the end, higher concentration of carbon dioxide and other GHGs means more solar heat is trapped, and hence the planet gets warmer—a robust relationship established using close to a million of years of data (Figure 20.1).

The second factor in climate change is increased GHG emissions due to economic activity. On average, global GDP has increased by almost 3.5 percent annually since 1960, and carbon dioxide emissions followed, albeit at a slightly slower pace—2.5 percent. Ever-increasing emissions combined with a limited absorptive capacity of the planet have resulted in an unprecedented concentration of carbon dioxide in the atmosphere—as much as 417 parts per million (ppm) in 2020 versus 278 ppm before the industrial revolution (in 1750) (WMO 2019)—a level last seen around 3.2 million years ago, when global temperatures were 2°C warmer and sea level was 20 meters higher than present (de la Vega et al. 2020).[5]

---

[4] A review of the evidence on decoupling finds that large, rapid absolute reductions of emissions requires sufficiency-oriented strategies and strict enforcement of absolute reduction targets (Haberl et al. 2020).

[5] "Parts per million" is a way to report small concentrations of gases or other substances. Essentially, carbon dioxide concentration of X ppm means X molecules of carbon dioxide in one million of molecules of air.

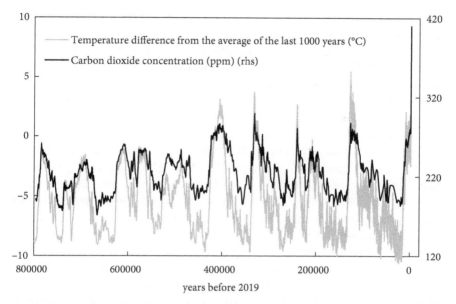

Figure 20.1 Carbon Dioxide Concentration in the Atmosphere Goes Hand in Hand with Higher Temperatures

Note: The data comes from the composition of air trapped in ice cores in Antarctica

Sources: NOAA, based on Lüthi et al. (2008) and Jouzel et al. (2007). The CO_2 concentration for 2019 is from WMO (2019).

The result of the combination of the greenhouse effect and increased atmospheric concentration of GHGs is that our planet is warming. The average global temperature has already increased by more than 1°C since the end of the nineteenth century (NOAA 2020). If GHG emissions continue their current trend—a so-called Representative Concentration Pathway 8.5 (RCP8.5) scenario—the projected temperature increase is 4–6°C by 2100 (IPCC 2014)—an unprecedented change likely unseen in millions of years (Hansen et al. 2013).

It is not only about global warming. Other climate conditions are changing too. Increased evaporation combined with other factors changes precipitation patterns, generally making dry areas even drier, and wet areas even wetter (IPCC 2014). The weather also gets more volatile: heat waves and cold spells, as well as torrential rains and dry spells, increase in frequency. This volatility then leads to a higher chance of natural extreme events: droughts, floods, tropical cyclones, forest fires.

With changing climate come large-scale changes in the planet's key ecosystems. The sea level is projected to rise by about one meter by 2100 under the RCP8.5 scenario, prompted by expanding warm water and melting polar glaciers (IPCC 2014). Mountain glaciers are also melting at an accelerating pace (Marshall 2014). Oceanic water gets not only warmer but also more acidic—a process of so-called ocean acidification—threatening many marine species. On land too, climate change is one of the key reasons for the rapid loss of biodiversity, as many species do not have time to adapt. Some species do, and even expand their area of habitat, but often with dire consequences: the spread of malaria in the case of mosquitos (Reiter 2001), Lyme disease in the case of ticks (Dumic and Severnini 2018), or the decline of forests due to bark beetle (Katz 2017).

The larger and faster climate change occurs, the more it affects the environment, and the effect is highly non-linear. For example, warming of 2°C instead of 1.5°C would essentially wipe out all coral reefs on this planet (instead of 70–90 percent), and expose 37 percent of the population to extreme heat at least once every five years (instead of 14 percent) (IPCC 2018). Going above 2°C significantly increases the probability of even larger, nearly unpredictable and likely irreversible environmental changes. Examples include methane runoff from Arctic permafrost or hydrate deposits in the Arctic Ocean, which would unleash runaway warming; the melting of Greenland or the West Antarctic ice sheets, which would raise sea levels by several meters; or an abrupt biodiversity loss. Large ecosystems could drastically change through what are known as "tipping points" or a global cascade of tipping points: the Amazon rainforest could suddenly turn into a savannah, the West African and Indian monsoon patterns could swiftly change; major oceanic currents could slow and change directions (Preuss 2008; Lenton et al. 2019; Trisos, Merow, and Pigot 2020; Staal et al. 2020; DeFries et al. 2019) Changes like these would not only drastically disrupt our normal way of living, but could make the planet uninhabitable.

B. Socio-Economic Damages from Climate Change

Even for small temperature increases, climate change brings about substantial socioeconomic damages and exacerbates poverty and inequalities. Key channels of impact are disruptions to agriculture, lower labor productivity, damage due to natural disasters, and sea-level rise.

Historical micro-level evidence suggests that agricultural output and labor productivity are significantly adversely affected by climate change. Even though no country is immune, the damages are larger in poorer countries, as these countries' socioeconomic systems are typically less able to cope with climate shocks: people there have less resources to adapt, and tend to reside in hotter areas, where the marginal impact of additional warming is larger (Burke, Hsiang, and Miguel 2015; IMF 2017; IPCC 2018). Climate change has already increased global between-country inequality by 25 percent over the past half-century (Diffenbaugh and Burke 2019). Without a meaningful mitigation effort, the situation will likely worsen in future: by 2070, some estimates project that, under business-as-usual scenarios, 3.5 billion people—overwhelmingly in developing countries—will reside in areas with mean annual temperature of over 29°C. Such annual averages

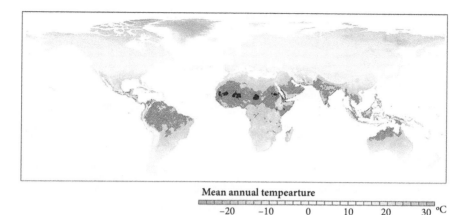

Mean annual tempearture

−20   −10   0   10   20   30 °C

Figure 20.2 Significant Expansion of Areas Hotter than 29°C on Average by 2070

Source: Reprinted from (Xu et al. 2020). Small dark areas are those with mean average temperature (MAT) of over 29°C at present climate. Shaded areas are those with expected MAT of over 29°C by 2070 under RCP8.5 scenario. Background colors represent current MATs.

are currently observed only in a few sparsely inhabited regions of the Sahara Desert (Figure 20.2). Within countries, climate change also disproportionately affects the poor (Hsiang, Oliva, and Walker 2019). By 2030, it could push over 100 million people into extreme poverty, primarily because of disrupted food production, lower labor productivity due to deteriorating health, and natural disasters (World Bank 2020b).

Natural disasters claim thousands of lives and billions of US dollars of losses every year (EM-DAT). No country is spared a disaster risk, but low income countries are suffering more damages relative to their economy, and more deaths relative to their population (Figure 20.3). Poorer people are not necessarily more exposed to natural disasters, but they are more vulnerable, as they live in lower-quality housing, rely more on fragile infrastructure (for example, unpaved roads) and on vulnerable sources of income, such as income from agriculture or ecosystems (World Bank 2020b). In addition, weaker organizational capacities and a lower supply of skilled workers—which are typical of poorer countries—are expected to exacerbate damages by making reconstruction following extremes more difficult, which increases total damages from natural disasters (Hallegatte et al. 2007).

Sea level rise is projected to displace 630 million people by 2100 under the RCP8.5 (high emissions) scenario (Kulp and Strauss 2019). The majority of the displaced are in developing South-East Asia, which will exacerbate global inequalities further.

The damage from climate change is not limited to the channels above, and there is considerable geographic variation in how it manifests itself. For example, in the United States, it is projected that extreme heat will impose large health,

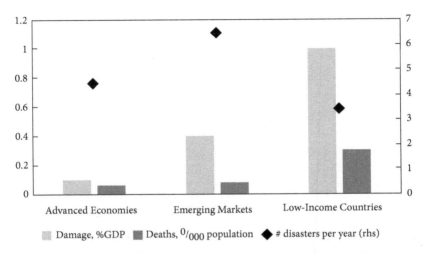

Figure 20.3 Frequency and Magnitude of Natural Disasters in 1980–2020
Source: EM-DAT, average 1980–2020. IMF country classification. Natural disasters significantly affect all country groups, but low income countries suffer relatively more.

energy, and labor costs on Southern states; sea-level rise and hurricanes are projected to impact coasts; humidity levels will require infrastructure restructuring in the North-East; lower crop productivity will impact land markets across the country; and more frequent wildfires and water shortages will impact Western states (Houser et al. 2015). In developing countries, gradual warming creates food security and water security risks (IPCC 2018).

More generally, a critical point is that climate change is likely to uncover previously hidden interdependencies between the economy and natural systems, revealing new and potentially enormous disruptions and social costs (DeFries et al. 2019). Indeed, large output losses and sharp increases in poverty and inequality several decades in the future are likely to occur through channels other than short-term temperature variations.[6] Such channels include the collapse of ecosystems, mass migrations, conflicts, and so forth. It is essential, therefore, to limit the extent of climate change in order to minimize the risk of unpredictable catastrophic outcomes.

C. Other Environmental Threats

Climate change is not the only phenomenon that threatens the sustainability of modern societies. Many other ecological conditions are under threat:

---

[6] See (Bhattacharya et al. 2021) for a detailed discussion of socioeconomic damages due to climate change and methods to assess them.

- *Release of chemically active nitrogen and phosphorus into lakes and oceans*— mostly due to excessive use of chemical fertilizers in agriculture—results in low content of oxygen in the water (so-called anoxic waters) and conditions where only certain bacteria and fungi can survive. Large areas of anoxic waters are already present around the globe, e.g. in the Baltic Sea (Conley et al. 2009), and if nitrogen and phosphorus release is left unchecked the whole ocean may be under threat.

- *Biodiversity loss* is orders of magnitude higher than what is normally observed in the fossil record, and much faster in the last 50 years than at any time in human history (Rockström et al. 2009; IPBES 2019). This is in part due to climate change, but also due to habitat loss, invasive species, and unsustainable harvesting. Biodiversity is key to adaptation and resilience, and it is a major source for innovation (Dasgupta 2021). Yet, not only do hundreds of species go extinct every year, but the abundance of surviving wildlife has critically decreased since 1970—for example, by as much as 83 percent for freshwater reptiles (WWF 2018). Over 90 percent of fisheries nowadays are either fully exploited or overexploited (FAO 2018).

- *Chemical pollution* is another area that challenges the global ecosystem. Globally, 100 million metric tons of plastic waste are dumped into nature every year—the pollution getting worse during the Covid-19 crisis. Traces of plastic are found even at the bottom of the Mariana Trench or in Arctic sea ice, and the average person ingests five grams of microplastic every week (WWF 2019; Reuters 2020).

- *Local air pollution*, in particular due to fossil-fuel burning, reduces the average person's lifespan by three years, and is responsible for an estimated 6.5 million deaths annually (Lelieveld et al. 2020).

- *Unsustainable freshwater use*, combined with ever less predictable rainfall patterns, causes more frequent water shortages and droughts, leading to harvest loss, malnutrition, and eventually social conflict.

- *Soil erosion* due to unsustainable farming practices threatens food production.

- *Deforestation* goes on in many regions around the globe, especially in the tropics—threatening not only global biodiversity and climate, but also local eco-services like clean air and water (IUCN 2017). From 2001 to 2019 386Mha of tree cover was lost globally—an area equivalent to six times France (Global Forest Watch 2020).

The environmental issues above are tightly linked to each other and to climate change, and they are often driven by the same factors or misguided policies. For example, fossil-fuel burning is a major cause of climate change and local air pollution. Unsustainable farming practices erode soil, deplete freshwater reservoirs, reduce forest area, and disrupt marine ecosystems due to nutrient run-off, which in turn reduces the planet's ability to absorb carbon dioxide and leads to loss of biodiversity—itself essential to our ability to adapt to climate change. Wildlife habitat loss, due to land use changes and unsustainable harvesting, not only fuels climate change but also increases the propensity of wildlife to transmit viruses— among animal species, and often to human beings, as in case of Lyme disease, Ebola, HIV/AIDS or Covid-19 (Vidal 2020; Allan, Keesing and Ostfeld 2003; IPBES 2020).[7] As with climate change, a degraded environment disproportion- ately hurts the poor, since they tend to live in more affected areas and have less resources to adapt. Tackling climate change can therefore generate many environ- mental and inclusion co-benefits, and can become self-reinforcing.

D. What Needs to Be Done?

Returning to a sustainable development path requires stabilizing our planet's cli- mate, and doing so at a level at which large-scale catastrophic outcomes have a very low chance of materializing. That is, under the current scientific consensus, the global temperature increase must be limited to no more than 2°C above pre- industrial levels, though even this upper boundary may turn out to be unsafe as scientists are still learning about the planet's response to a temperature shock of this size (Lenton et al. 2019). Environmental degradation must also be reversed, and adaptation measures must be put in place to tackle the climate changes that are bound to occur despite mitigation efforts. Importantly, the transition must be just and inclusive.

Limiting global warming to 2°C means a 25–30 percent reduction in CO_2 emissions by 2030, and eventually reaching net-zero by 2080 (Figure 20.4), and a similar mitigation path for other GHGs (Climate Action Tracker 2020).[8] A safer goal of 1.5°C warming requires carbon-neutrality by 2050–2060 (Climate Action Tracker 2020). The 2018 IPCC Special Report on Global Warming of 1.5°C played a key role in the shift in understanding and public opinion by highlighting the already evident impacts of climate change and the grave risks of global warming beyond 1.5°C (IPCC 2018). Waiting can hardly be justified. The transition to a low-carbon economy (e.g. net zero emissions) will have to happen anyway—non- zero GHG emissions in the long run means perpetual warming, which will even- tually make our planet uninhabitable. Waiting will only make the transition less

---

[7] More than half a million unknown viruses in nature could still infect people if contacts with wildlife and habitat loss are not dramatically reduced. Climate change aggravates the issue not least because it induces migration of both people and wildlife, and because of appearance of new viruses from melting glaciers (IPBES 2020; Zhong et al. 2020).

[8] Net-zero means GHG emissions net of those removed from the atmosphere, for example by restored forests or potentially by direct carbon capture and storage technologies, though these tech- nologies are still at the early stages of their development.

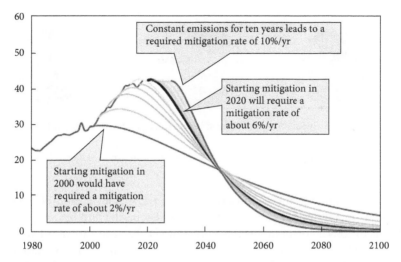

Figure 20.4 CO_2 Emissions Must Go Down to Limit the Global Warming

Note: The mitigation curves are estimated so that there is a 66 percent chance of staying below 2°C (IPCC 2018). The mitigation curves for staying below 1.5°C are steeper. The calculations are subject to significant uncertainties, including the emission paths of GHGs other than CO_2.

Source: Reprinted from (Andrew 2020), data from Global Carbon Project.

gradual—as the global carbon budget is being depleted—and increase the likelihood of irreversible catastrophic outcomes (Stern 2015). Rapid decarbonization—when entire carbon-intensive industries need to be abruptly retired in the face of runaway climate change—would also create stranded assets, regions, and jobs. The stranded jobs would have a large impact on poor countries, as many workers there would lose their incomes and pension rights—their only ticket out of poverty (Bhattacharya and Stern 2020).

Encouragingly, most major economies have committed to a target of net-zero emissions by mid-century and all G7 countries have set more ambitious targets for reduction in emissions by 2030 as a first step towards that goal.[9] Although these commitments mark an important shift, all countries will need to come on board and more ambitious cuts will be needed by 2030 from present emission levels to put the world on track to meet the 1.5°C target.

Where do current GHG emissions come from? Two thirds are the result of fossil-fuel burning—for electricity, heat, and transportation (Figure 20.5).

---

[9] In June 2019, the United Kingdom became the first major economy to commit to the net-zero target by 2050. This was followed by the European Union in December 2019. In October 2020, Japan and Korea committed to a net-zero target by 2050, as did China to net-zero by 2060 in December 2020 and the US to net-zero by 2050 with the incoming Biden administration. All of the G7 countries have followed this commitment by setting targets of emission reduction close to or in excess of 50 percent by 2030 compared to 2005 levels that were announced at the Major Economies Forum on Climate and Energy April 22–23, 2021.

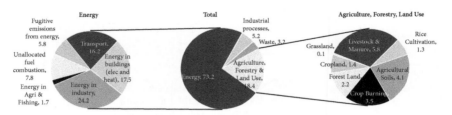

Figure 20.5 GHG Emissions Are Highest in the Energy Sector. Large Shift to Renewables is Needed

Source: Adapted from Our World in Data, data from Climate Watch, World Resources Institute, as of 2016.

A significant amount of carbon dioxide is also released as a result of industrial processes (mainly production of cement, but also plastic and others), land use (e.g. due to conversion of forests into agricultural land), and agriculture (e.g. crop burning). Oil and natural gas extraction (fugitive emissions), livestock and waste (landfills) are the main sources of methane emissions. The use of chemical fertilizer in agriculture is the main source of nitrous oxide emissions.

The transition to a low-carbon economy requires a comprehensive transformation of all emitting sectors. It also requires participation of all stakeholders. Innovation and investment must transform carbon-intensive industrial processes and infrastructure. This transformation should be complemented by sustainable food and energy choices by households—that is, by changes in consumption patterns, especially in advanced economies and among high-income households, which account for the majority of emissions due to their personal consumption patterns.

Infrastructure investment is central to inclusive growth and to the transition. The next 10–15 years are critical, as the global economy will likely grow by a half and a billion more people will come to live in cities—requiring investment in the world's urban, land use, and energy systems of more than US$90 trillion. Locking such a vast amount of new investment in high-carbon assets would delay decarbonization by decades and make it progressively more expensive. The additional cost of investing in low-carbon infrastructure has been estimated at US$3–4 trillion, or about four percent of the total (The Global Commission on the Economy and Climate 2018), but this is now likely to be negligible given falling costs and as savings on operating costs can more than offset upfront investment costs. Moreover, there would be large associated benefits such as cleaner air, better health, less congestion, and fruitful ecosystems.

The transformation of the energy sector is perhaps the biggest challenge. In order to stay well within 2°C, the composition of energy demand must change drastically—from a primary energy mix that is over 80 percent based on fossil fuels, as is the case now, to relying predominantly on renewables by 2050 (Bhattacharya et al. 2016). Shifting investment patterns from fossil fuels to renewables is key, and the world is now adding more renewable power capacity than from all fossil fuels combined. Still, as of 2020 about 40 percent of total global energy investment was concentrated in the fossil fuel sector (IEA 2021).

This transition is not going to be easy. Climate change is a negative externality: without appropriate policies, polluters do not bear the full cost they inflict on current and future societies. This externality is uniquely challenging: it is global in scope and impacts; it involves significant uncertainty and risk in the scientific chain of causation; it is long-term; and its effects are potentially enormous and irreversible.[10],[11] As a consequence, governments need to play an active role in mitigation, and they need to cooperate internationally.

As hard as it is to cooperate, countries have found ways to do so and make progress in dealing with climate change. The Paris Agreement of 2015 was signed by 197 parties (members of United Nations). Its aim is to "strengthen the global response to the threat of climate change by keeping a global temperature rise this century well below 2 degrees Celsius above pre-industrial levels and to pursue efforts to limit the temperature increase even further to 1.5 degrees Celsius" (UNFCCC 2020). Each country is supposed to submit its own plan of mitigation and adaptation efforts—so-called nationally determined contribution (NDCs), and a special UN agency (UNFCCC secretariat) is responsible for tracking the progress. A major problem at present is that the NDCs that have been submitted, even if implemented, are consistent with about 3°C warming (UNEP 2019). Countries need to step up their efforts to return to sustainability. All G7 countries have recently pledged to become carbon-neutral by mid-century. They were among hundreds of other countries, regions, and businesses.[12] These pledges are examples to follow, but they must be accompanied by coherent decarbonization strategies.

The good news is that, if properly designed, mitigation policies can be a powerful source of inclusive growth. What is more, these policies may yield important co-benefits in the form of better adaptation to climate change and reduced pressure on the environment. We explore the policy options in the next section.

III. Climate Change Mitigation

Successful mitigation requires comprehensive and coordinated government action using multiple tools and policies. An important tool is putting a price on

---

[10] More details in (Bhattacharya et al. 2021)

[11] The Stern Review described climate change as "the greatest market failure the world has ever seen." Naturally, dealing with such a uniquely multifaceted externality is extremely difficult (Stern 2007).

[12] The details of the pledges differ. The updated list of "Climate Ambition Alliance: Net Zero 2050" can be found at https://climateaction.unfccc.int/views/cooperative-initiative-details.html?id=94.

carbon to reflect its social cost, and to encourage low-carbon consumption, investment, and innovation. Pricing carbon should be part of a broader policy package, which includes public investment, industrial policy, regulations, policies to align financial markets with climate objectives and steer private investment toward low-carbon assets, as well as policies to steer social norms and behaviors to a lower carbon intensity of consumption and business activity (Stern and Stiglitz 2021). A key point is the need for a systemic approach to policymaking that ensures the alignment of all policies with climate objectives. We go through each policy area in more detail below.

A. Put a Price on Carbon

Pricing carbon is essential for mitigation.[13] If GHG emissions are free then there is no incentive to reduce them: the benefit accrues to the emitters—coal power plants, cement factories, drivers of gasoline cars, and many others—while the cost is born by everyone. By contrast, if GHG emissions are costly, this sends a signal throughout the economy. Carbon-intensive goods become more expensive—an incentive to consume less of them, for example by saving energy, and to rebalance consumption patterns toward low-carbon goods and services. Carbon-intensive inputs also become more expensive for businesses, which incentivizes them to innovate and make their production processes more climate-friendly. Moreover, as demand for low-carbon goods and services increases, so does investment to expand their production. In the end, the price of carbon is a gauge that drives millions of decisions by multiple economic actors towards cutting GHG emissions and reaching mitigation goals in the most cost-effective way given individual and local circumstances.

Likely the most efficient instrument to a put price on carbon is a carbon tax (IMF 2019). It is essentially a charge on the carbon content of fossil fuels. For example, to produce one million btu of energy one has to burn about 46kg of coal, which would emit about 95kg of carbon dioxide into the atmosphere.[14] Alternatively, one could burn about 27 cubic meters of natural gas, which would release about 53kg of carbon dioxide.[15] Or instead, one could entirely eliminate emissions by using, for example, solar panels or wind turbines. A carbon tax is also relatively simple to administer, as most governments can rely on the existing machinery of excise taxes. The carbon content of fossil fuels is stable, so there is no need to measure actual emissions.

---

[13] By "pricing carbon" we mean pricing all GHG emissions, not only those of carbon dioxide. Admittedly, as emissions of carbon dioxide constitute over three quarters of total GHG emissions, they attract most of the policy focus. Instruments to cut other emissions are less developed.

[14] Btu—British Therma Unit—a standard unit of measurement of energy.

[15] Source: US Energy Information Administration. These numbers are approximations.

An alternative to carbon taxes is an emission trading scheme (ETS), also known as cap-and-trade schemes. A typical ETS consists of the following sequence:

1) The government sets a medium-term goal for GHG emissions and draws a list of emitters who are obliged to participate in the scheme.
2) The government then allocates the corresponding amount of emission permits among the participating emitters.
3) Emitters are then required to hold enough permits to cover their emissions; and they can trade the permits with each other.

In a world with perfect information, an ETS with auctioned emission permits would be equivalent to a carbon tax, with the tax rate being equal to the permit's market price. In practice, there are differences. First, an ETS fixes the resulting amount of emissions but leaves the carbon price uncertain and volatile, which is bad for business planning. A carbon tax fixes the carbon price, but leaves the resulting emissions uncertain, so there is a risk that the mitigation target is not achieved. Second, an ETS is generally harder to administer than a carbon tax. The allocation of emission permits is less transparent than taxation. For example, a general feature of most ETSs is that some businesses get permits for free due to lobbying or competitiveness concerns. Besides, there are fixed costs to trading the permits and verifying the emissions, so ETSs usually cover only the largest emitters, and as a result their coverage of total emissions can be low.

The macroeconomic effects of a carbon tax or an ETS are similar. In the short term, a higher carbon price increases the price of carbon-intensive goods and services, most importantly energy. For a worldwide carbon tax of US$75 per ton of carbon dioxide, the electricity price would on average go up by 43 percent, and the gasoline would be up by 14 percent (IMF 2019). As energy becomes more expensive, households and firms use it more efficiently, and so energy demand goes down. Total energy spending by businesses and households increases, however—crowding out other spending by households, and reducing businesses' before-wage profits. Businesses may in turn reduce investment, labor demand, and wages.

The direct dampening effect of energy prices on businesses' and households' energy demand is not the whole story. In the medium term, the effect can be off-set by productivity gains driven by low-carbon innovation, which is induced by a carbon tax (IMF 2020a). The tax also yields revenues—up to five percent of GDP in some countries, in the case of a US$75/ton tax (IMF 2019)—so the overall effect, and the acceptability of the carbon tax itself—depend on how the government decides to recycle it (Klenert et al. 2018). One option is to make the reform revenue-neutral and to reduce other taxes.[16] For instance, if labor income taxes

---

[16] Revenue-neutral means no changes to total government revenue.

decline, wages go up, and so does the labor supply. After-wage profits of businesses go up too, which may eventually lead to higher investment (IMF 2020a). In this case, the overall effect of the carbon tax reform on economic activity may turn out to be positive—a so-called "double dividend" (supporting both climate change mitigation and the economy), as for example in Ireland (Conefrey et al. 2013). More generally, consumption taxes, carbon taxes being one of them, are considered to be less dampening for economic activity than income taxes (Acosta-Ormaechea, Sola, and Yoo 2019).

There are other options to spend the carbon tax revenue. A "double dividend" is also possible if governments boost public investment or invest in health and education, especially in countries that need to make substantial progress towards the Sustainable Development Goals (Gaspar et al. 2019). A "double dividend" may turn into a "triple" dividend if the public investment is also consistent with climate objectives. Likely less efficient but more politically feasible options to spend the revenue are distributing emission permits for free in an ETS, which would relieve the initial adverse impact on the emitters but may defeat the goal of emission reduction, or a universal dividend, which would essentially offset energy price increases for households. A more socially just and efficient policy is to introduce transfers that fall with income and take geographical disparities into account.

The effects of carbon taxes go beyond economic activity. Reducing the use of fossil fuels has important environmental and other co-benefits, which are not reflected in national accounts. Lower local air pollution is one. Coal burning and fossil fuel-based transportation are major air pollutants and health hazards, lowering the world's average life expectancy by over a year (Lelieveld et al. 2020). Moreover, production and transportation of fossil fuels is prone to environmental disasters with long-term negative consequences. Other co-benefits of carbon taxes stem from reduced use of cars, the overwhelming majority of which still run on fossil fuels: reduced congestion, fewer traffic accidents, and smaller road damages.[17] In most countries the local co-benefits alone—that is, leaving aside the contribution to climate change mitigation—are enough to offset the potential dampening effect of carbon taxes on economic activity for a wide range of carbon prices (IMF 2019).

Despite its co-benefits and relatively mild macroeconomic effects, carbon pricing has yet to take off in most countries. As of end-2019, 58 carbon tax or ETS initiatives were active or scheduled for implementation around the world (Figure 20.6). Together these initiatives covered only 20 percent of global GHG emissions, although this number increased from less than five percent in 2010, and there are important ETS initiatives—notably in China and Germany—being

---

[17]   As of 2018, despite significant growth, electric vehicles still constituted only about two percent of all newly sold passenger cars in the world (IEA 2019).

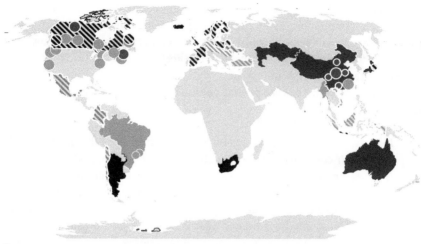

- ETS implemented or scheduled for implementation
- ETS or carbon tax under consideration
- ETS implemented or scheduled, ETS or Carbon Tax under ....
- Carbon tax implemented or scheduled for implemented...
- ETS and carbon tax implemented or scheduled
- Carbon tax implemented or scheduled, ETS under consid...

Figure 20.6 Carbon Pricing Policies Around the World
Source: World Bank Carbon Pricing Dashboard, as of November 1, 2019.

launched in 2021. The effective carbon price varied from a few US dollars/ton in two dozen jurisdictions to more than US$90/ton in Sweden and Switzerland, with 86 percent of global emissions not being covered by a carbon price, resulting in a global average of just US$3/ton (accounting for non-taxed emissions) (World Bank2020a; Cullenward and Victor 2020).[18] This is much lower than US$50-100/ton that is needed to be on track for a 2°C warming scenario (Stern and Stiglitz 2017; IMF 2019).

Aggravating the situation, many countries still subsidize fossil fuels-based energy, with total fossil fuel subsidies estimated at around $5 trillion, taking into account co-benefits of lower GHG emissions (Coady et al. 2019). In the first half of 2020, G20 countries allocated at least $170 billion in public support for fossil fuel-intensive sectors as a response to the Covid-19 crisis (IISD 2020).

In many countries carbon pricing and energy subsidy reforms were met with broad public opposition and eventually went off track. Households are worried about losing jobs and spending too much of their income on energy, which is especially important for the poor. Businesses are worried about competitiveness. Both are worried about inflation. All these concerns are valid and need to be

---

[18] The highest nominal carbon price also masks the fact that, across countries, many sectors are typically exempt from carbon taxes (Cullenward and Victor 2020).

addressed to make the reform more politically acceptable and inclusive. And success is not impossible: many countries and jurisdictions, starting with Finland in 1990, have been able to introduce and maintain carbon tax, and many others were able to implement a sustainable and effective energy subsidy reform (for example, Brazil, Turkey, Namibia).

Successful reforms feature several common strategies (Clemens et al. 2013; IMF 2019):

- *Inclusive decision-making.* Extensive consultations with all stakeholders about their concerns, the reform's objectives and its expected outcomes.
- *Gradual approach* with tax increases scheduled well in advance—starting with lower taxes for those more exposed to international competition and on products more consumed by poor (e.g. kerosene). Going gradual slows down inflation and buys time to affected stakeholders to adjust and to governments to demonstrate the benefits of the reform.
- *Efficient and equitable recycling of revenue.* Targeted measures for the most affected, especially the poor, are crucial. The poor typically spend more than the rich on energy products relative to their income (IMF 2019). Energy price increases can also spill over to prices of other essential goods. It is important to compensate the poor for the resulting reduction in their purchasing power. But the compensation does not have to cost much if it is well targeted, because in absolute terms the rich spend much more on energy products than the poor, so they benefit more from lower prices (IMF 2019; Clemens et al. 2013). The measures can come in the form of means-tested direct transfers, in-kind transfers (e.g. more pro-poor spending on health, education or infrastructure), or tax subsidies (e.g. earned-income tax credits). A universal dividend—though less efficient than targeted measures— might be a more feasible yet still equitable option if government capacity is low, and simplicity of the reform is a priority (Klenert et al. 2018). The revenue should also be used to smooth the transition for the most affected sectors and regions. The measures can come in form of retraining displaced workers or supporting their pensions, support for entrepreneurship, or region-specific targeted public investment.

Finally, carbon pricing strategy must take into account political economy factors. In some sectors, such as transport, consumers (and thus voters) may be very sensitive to price increases. In others, production may be concentrated in competitive, internationally-traded goods, and incumbent firms may be politically connected and able to block carbon pricing policies that increase firms' costs (Cullenward and Victor 2020). These political economy considerations may strengthen the case for sector-specific carbon pricing policies as well as non-price policies, to which we turn below.

B. Regulate and Set Standards

An important complement to carbon taxation is the direct regulation of GHG emissions or energy efficiency. For example, building energy codes, energy efficiency standards for appliances, and emission standards for cars are a commonplace in many countries (Evans, Roshchanka, and Graham 2017). Regulation plays in favor of low carbon products (e.g. people purchase more energy efficient goods), but it does not incentivize people to use the product less once it is purchased. However, the importance of regulation increases when the effect of taxation on emissions is uncertain, or the tax is simply too low for some industries for political reasons (Weitzman 1974; Mansur 2013). Also consumers of energy-intensive products often underestimate hard-to-assess future energy costs and give preference to easy-to-observe price discounts—a case of so-called "energy-cost myopia," which would cause producers to compete on prices at the expense of energy efficiency had there been no efficiency standards (Nordhaus 2013; Schleich et al. 2019). Similar to carbon pricing, regulations and standards should come with financial incentives or government programs for the poor to enable them to comply. At the same time, it is important to remove regulations that create barriers to investment in low-carbon technologies, such as regulations that require the use of specific fuels for buses in public transportation systems. International coordination can play an important role in setting expectations, for example by setting proximate dates for the phase-out of coal or internal combustion engines for road transport.[19]

C. Price Other Environmental "Goods" and "Bads"

Pricing and regulations are also the primary policy responses to other environmental issues. Some of them require corrective taxation (increasing price) of "bads," like in case with GHG emissions and climate change. Some could be better resolved by corrective subsidizing (decreasing price) of environmental "goods."

Forests, wetlands, and other ecosystems need to be protected and restored. Not only are they carbon sinks helping us with climate change, but they also shelter biodiversity, protect local climate, air, water, and soil, serve as a buffer against natural disasters, and provide recreational services. One way to protect them is to pay farmers and other landowners for their sustainable management and conservation. So-called payments for ecosystem services is an increasingly common practice in many countries at a national and local level (UNEP 2008; Bösch,

---

[19] The UK and Japan for example have set dates of 2035 for ending new sales of cars with internal combustion engines. All of the major economies could align behind this target.

Elsasser, and Wunder 2019). At a global level, UN's REDD+ program aims to compensate developing counties for the carbon emissions that are offset due to sustainable forest management (UN 2020). Success of these programs depends on the details of their design: it is important, for example, to make sure that protection of some areas does not crowd-in deforestation in others, or that the payments for ecosystem services accrue to those who de-facto manage the forests and wetlands, in particular indigenous communities. Where the payment schemes are less effective, regulation can be an important instrument to protect forests, especially given that over 70 percent of them are publicly owned (White and Martin 2002). Logging concessions must be regulated so that the harvesting rate is below the forest renewal rate, and some critical areas, like virgin forests or habitats of endangered species, must be closed to logging altogether.[20]

Another important area to reform is how modern societies produce and consume food. The global food system is full of inequalities and inefficiencies: over 800 million people in the world are still malnourished, and at the same time around two billion are obese or overweight, and over a third of total food production is lost or wasted (The Global Commission on the Economy and Climate 2018). Intensive agriculture and agricultural expansion disrupts interactions with wildlife and increases contact among people, wildlife, livestock and their pathogens, which has led to almost all pandemics to date (IPBES 2020).

- Agricultural subsidies in 2016–2018 were close to one percent of the world's GDP, contributing to inefficient use of water and chemical fertilizer, overgrazing, soil erosion, deforestation, and loss of biodiversity. These subsidies must be reformed to fully reflect the social cost of food production, and to promote climate-smart agricultural practices, such as agroforestry, crop diversification, conservation of soil and water, and others—a sustainable way to increase agricultural yields and support subsistence farmers (FAO 2020).
- Sustainable and equitable allocation of water permits is especially important as over four billion people around the world are currently living in areas where demand of water outstrips supply, thus depleting reservoirs and aquifers (The Global Commission on the Economy and Climate 2018). Water subsidies are as much as 0.6 percent of the world's GDP contributing to its unsustainable use (IMF 2015).
- Sustainable wildlife harvesting is also a priority. Overfishing may be tackled through the sale and effective enforcement of fishing quotas, combined with regulation on fishing boats size, restrictions on harmful fishing methods,

---

[20] Virgin forests are which have never been logged before.

and protecting endangered species (World Ocean Review 2020). Similar principles apply to other wildlife.

- On the consumption side, a higher excise/sales tax on meat could be an efficient way to address higher social cost of livestock production compared to the plant-based food (Godfray et al. 2018).[21]

Governments should also price chemical pollution and incentivize "circular economy"—an economic system aimed at eliminating waste and pollution, and keeping products and materials in use. Limiting air and water pollution can be done through corrective taxes, regulations, outright bans, or issuing emissions quotas, which can then be traded. Use of single-use plastic can be reduced if governments ban it or charge a disposal fee (UNEP 2018). Incentives for "circular economy" can make production and consumption less resource intensive. These incentives include: taxes and subsidies to foster repair, sharing, resale, and remanufacturing; regulations to harmonize collection and sorting; fees and regulations to disincentivize landfilling and incineration and promote reuse and recycling (Ellen MacArthur Foundation 2021).

Pricing and especially regulations would only be effective if the rules are adhered to. Trust is of utmost importance here. Regulations are more likely to be followed if their rationale is well-explained to the public and if the public is inclined to cooperate and trusts government—which itself depends on how inclusive growth is. Sustainability begets inclusion, and inclusion begets sustainability. Compliance can also improve if the rules are simple and based on indicators that are easier to observe. Government's capacity to enforce can be strengthened by utilizing information technologies. Satellite imaging and remote sensing are now widely used, for example to track deforestation, e.g. by (Global Forest Watch 2020), or illegal fishing (Imagesat International 2017).

D. Align Financial System with Climate Objectives

Reforming finance and ensuring that it enables—rather than hinders—deep decarbonization is critical for the transition to inclusive, resilient and sustainable growth, for several reasons:[22]

---

[21] Producing one calorie of beef, for example, requires about 25 times more land, ten times more water, and emits 25 more time GHGs than producing one calorie of pulses (Ranganathan et al. 2016). In the United States, carbon footprint of a typical vegan diet is 85 percent lower than that of an average diet (Clark et al. 2019).

[22] Finance's role in climate policy is emphasized in Article 2 of the Paris Agreement, which calls for "making finance flows consistent with a pathway towards low greenhouse gas emissions and climate-resilient development" (UNFCCC 2020).

- *Incomplete knowledge and risk, and capital market failures.* Without appropriate policies, there is a wide gap between the social and private return to green investments (Stern and Stiglitz 2021). Private investors have generally elevated perceptions of the risks of green investments because of uncertainties about future climate policies and carbon prices, ability of these projects to deliver carbon abatement, as well as these projects' high upfront capital costs and relative lack of technological maturity, not least due to lack of historical data on which to base investment decisions, and generally lower degree of liquidity (Nelson and Shrimali 2014). As a result, investors tend to view expected return on low-carbon projects as too low given perceived risks. Likewise, the expected private return to carbon-intensive projects could be too high if financial climate-related risks are not properly regulated.
- *Short-termism.* Climate risk stems from a "tragedy of the horizon": catastrophic effects of climate change will be felt beyond the traditional horizons of market participants and most decision-makers, which extends only a few years (Carney 2015). Without adequate policies, financial asset prices will not reflect the long-term benefits of climate change mitigation.
- *Lack of transparency about exposure to climate risks.* Even if desired, rebalancing of investment portfolio from polluting (carbon-intensive) to green investments would be inhibited in absence of clear information (taxonomy) about which assets are polluting or green.
- *Network and coordination externalities.* Addressing climate change involves major structural changes in core systems of the economy: energy, land, cities, transportation, industrial supply chains. These changes require complex coordination, which goes beyond carbon pricing, especially in the presence of multiple market failures (Hepburn, Stern, and Stiglitz 2020; Stern and Stiglitz 2021).
- *Knowledge spillovers.* These typically occur when investors are unable to capture the full return on their R&D investments into low-carbon technologies (Acemoglu et al. 2012).
- *Unpriced co-benefits of climate change mitigation and adaptation.* Actions that help society mitigate and adapt to climate change have many potential co-benefits that are not priced by markets. Co-benefits include lower pollution and congestion, the protection of ecosystems, access to energy, and faster technological progress.
- *Weak carbon price signal.* In a context of regulatory uncertainty, a large drop in the price of fossil fuels—which tend to be quite volatile—can more than offset the price signal sent by a carbon tax. In addition, most sectors are still at early stages of decarbonization, in which key technologies and low-carbon firms are nascent—in contrast to incumbent carbon-intensive firms (Energy Transitions Commission 2020; Aklin and Mildenberger 2020). At the same time, price signals work best by driving optimization of emission reduction

when technologies are commercially mature. For this reason, it is important to complement carbon pricing with financial sector and other policies to ensure early redirection of investment to low-carbon technologies and firms that are viewed as risky—for example because the carbon price signal is seen as volatile and unreliable for investment decisions (Cullenward and Victor 2020).

Political economy factors, such as lack of political acceptability of carbon taxes, also play an import role.

Taken together, these market failures and political economy factors lead to a lack of financing of green projects, and a socially undesirable level of financing of polluting activities. This is especially the case in developing and emerging economies, which are characterized by high transaction costs in unstable institutional contexts, meaning that fossil fuels—which benefit from lower upfront capital costs and are perceived as less risky than low-carbon projects—are favored in investment decisions (Hirth and Steckel 2016). The global financial system continues to be unaligned with climate objectives. In 2019, the largest 33 banks allocated about $650 billion to fossil fuel projects (WRI 2019). In addition, equity valuations across countries do not reflect projected incidence of climate physical and transition risks (IMF 2020).

The inadequacy of finance is also reflected in the misalignment of global capital flows between regions and sectors with abundant liquidity and regions and sectors that are relevant to climate-transition investments but cannot obtain capital. This leads to a paradox: trillions of dollars in savings in high-income economies earn a negative real interest rate, while $11–23 trillion in climate-smart investment opportunities in emerging-market and developing economies are not being financed (Green Climate Fund 2020).

Aligning the financial system with climate objectives is the primary goal of The Network of Central Banks and Supervisors for Greening the Financial System (NGFS), the Coalition of Finance Ministers on Climate Action, and COP26 Private Finance Agenda.[23] The next section outlines the policy options.

Financial and Monetary Policies for Climate Change Mitigation and Adaptation

The role of financial and monetary policies in the fight against climate change is threefold. First, managing the financial stability risks posed by climate change. Second, closing the gap between the social and private returns to green investment. Third, mobilizing resources for investment in resilience to climate change.

---

[23] https://www.ngfs.net/enandhttps://www.bankofengland.co.uk/events/2020/february/cop26-private-finance-agenda-launch

Managing the Financial Stability Risks Posed by Climate Change

There are three main types of climate risks: physical, transition, and legal risks (Carney 2015). Physical risks arise from climate hazards and longer-term shifts in climate patterns. Transition risks stem from the process of structural change in the transition to a low-carbon economy, for example when high-emission financial assets rapidly lose value and become "stranded" as more ambitious climate policies are implemented worldwide.[24] Legal risks relate to firms' fiduciary responsibilities. These risks are of a systemic nature, in that they can potentially affect the entire economy and financial system.

Three broad types of financial and monetary policy instruments should be used to manage climate-related financial risks (Krogsrup and Oman 2019). First, those that redress the underpricing and lack of transparency around climate-related financial risks. Second, those that reduce the short-term bias in the financial sector. Third, those that seek to reflect climate risks in macroprudential policies (policies aimed at safeguarding the financial system).

The first category involves gathering high-quality climate-related financial data, introducing mandatory climate-related financial risk disclosures (regarding both physical and transition risks) by firms and financial institutions, conducting climate-related stress tests of financial institutions and financial systems.[25] The Financial Stability Board's Task-Force on Climate-related Financial Disclosures is an important step in this direction.[26]

The second category includes prudential and corporate governance reforms to reduce the role of short-term shareholder value maximization in firms' behavior and strategies. An example is corporate accounting according to the CARE (Comprehensive Accounting in Respect of Ecology) model, which incorporates social and environmental issues into firms' balance sheets and income statements, extends financial solvency to environmental and social solvency, and extends the principles of protection of financial capital to the protection of natural and social capitals (Admati 2017; Rambaud and Feger 2020).

The third category is strengthening risk management by Central Banks and financial institutions, and includes liquidity and capital requirements and sectoral capital buffers targeting credit to climate-exposed sectors. Central banks must also ensure that their collateral frameworks fully reflect climate risks.

More generally, central banks should coordinate their actions with other actors, notably governments, the private sector, civil society and the international community, and consider green monetary-fiscal-prudential coordination (Bolton et al. 2020). In particular, policy frameworks should follow a "double

---

[24] According to the ECB, climate risks are firmly embedded in advanced economies' economic structures, with about 40 percent and 32 percent of jobs in the euro area and the United States, respectively, being in carbon-intensive sectors (Schnabel 2020).

[25] See (Bhattacharya et al. 2021) for more details.

[26] https://www.fsb-tcfd.org/

materiality" approach by assessing both the impact of climate change on financial institutions and financial institutions' impact on climate change (see Oman and Svartzman 2021).[27]

Closing the Gap Between the Social and Private Returns to Green Investment
The main policies are of two kinds. First, macroprudential regulations, including a surcharge on brown assets in banks' capital requirements. Second, de-risking and incentives for green private investment: loan guarantees and subsidies, feed-in tariffs with transparent phase-out horizon, risk guarantees (e.g. first-loss capital).[28,29] While de-risking measures can increase green private investment, frameworks must be developed to assess and monitor related fiscal risks and costs, notably ensuring the transparency of direct and contingent long-term public liabilities (IMF 2021; Gabor 2020). Monetary policy, notably central bank exclusion of carbon-intensive assets, would also increase the capital cost of polluting investments. Central banks could also purchase low-carbon project bonds. Such bonds should be issued, following corresponding mandate changes if necessary, by national or regional development banks.[30]

A further instrument is creating new low-carbon financial assets with embedded notional/shadow carbon prices—for example, carbon remediation assets. Value of such assets would depend on amount of GHG emissions they help avoid at a predetermined notional/shadow price (Aglietta et al. 2015; IPCC 2018).

Mobilizing the Resources for Investment
Central for developing countries' ability to make progress on mitigation and adaption is to develop domestic and international financial sources and capital flows from the geographies where the savings are, to the geographies and sectors where the investments for the climate transition are. Financing the large upfront resources that will be needed for climate and development transitions will be challenging for several reasons. First, all countries, but especially emerging markets and developing countries, are facing much more difficult debt and fiscal constraints as a result of the pandemic. Second, while investments in sustainable infrastructure yield strong economic benefits, these returns are typically realized over a long time period and often difficult to capture for private investors because of large spillovers. Third, while there are abundant pools of long-term savings,

---

[27] For instance, ECB Executive Board member Isabel Schnabel has noted that central banks' actions should not "reinforce market failures that threaten to slow down the decarbonization objectives of the global community" (Schnabel 2020).
[28] A feed-in tariff is a price for generated electricity that is fixed for producers at a lower than market price level, whereas the difference between the market price and the tariff is paid by government.
[29] First-loss capital refers to arrangement by which an investor or grant-maker agrees to bear first losses in an investment in order to crowd-in co-investors.
[30] There is evidence of significant carbon intensity in the portfolio of financial assets bought by the Bank of England and the European Central Bank (Matikainen, Campiglio, and Zenghelis 2017).

and interest rates in international markets are at exceptionally low levels, many emerging markets and most developing countries find it difficult to access long-term finance and the cost of capital is a major impediment for scaling up sustainable investments.

Some estimates project that the low-carbon infrastructure investment gap in developing countries could reach $15–30 trillion by 2040 (Green Climate Fund 2020). A key pillar of the Paris Agreement is the pledge by developed countries to jointly mobilize US$100 billion per year to address the needs of developing countries. Yet, this pledge is unlikely to be met in 2020 (Independent Experts Group on Climate Finance 2020). Boosting international climate finance is essential to coordinated and effective global climate action, especially in times when most developing countries are devastated by the Covid-19 pandemic (Stern 2020). Developed countries must deliver on the commitment to mobilize $100 billion in climate finance a year in 2021 and build on that to expand international public climate finance prior to 2025 when the next target will be set. Because of their mandates, instruments, and financial structures, multilateral development banks (MDBs) are the most effective international means to support enhanced climate action in developing countries and for mobilizing and leveraging climate finance at scale. There is also great scope and need for mobilizing private finance at scale through better public-private partnership to unlock investments, mitigate risks and create ne asset classes attractive to long-term institutional investors.

Mobilizing the resources for green investment in developing countries would contribute to both climate change mitigation and reducing global and local inequalities. For example, an $800 million private investment in the Lake Turkana wind power plant in Kenya was enabled by partial risk guarantees (capped at $24 million) and technical assistance by the African Development Bank. The plant produces seventeen percent of the country's total electricity supply, supports over three hundred local jobs, and is projected to yield $35 million of tax revenue annually (LTWP 2019).

At the global level, proposals have been made to reshape the international monetary system to mobilize considerable resources for climate resilience. One proposal is to use the IMF's Special Drawing Rights (SDRs) to fund the paid-in capital of the Green Climate Fund (Bredencamp and Pattillo 2010). Another proposal is to create a substitution account at the IMF in order for central banks and governments with excess international foreign exchange reserves to deposit them at the IMF in exchange for SDRs (Aglietta and Espagne 2018). These SDRs could be lent to developing countries when market conditions become adverse, so that these countries can continue to finance their development policies—notably their climate policies. The IMF would thus play its role of lender of last resort in the international monetary and financial system. Countries with excess SDRs could also lend them to multilateral development banks, which could in turn finance investments required to meet Paris Agreement emission reduction pledges.

E. Accelerate Public Investment in Sustainable Infrastructure

Public investment in sustainable infrastructure speeds up the transition and is often necessary to finance projects with low private returns but large environmental co-benefits. It is also needed to coordinate and crowd in private investment, even in the presence of a high carbon price. For example, renewable energy investment in remote areas requires high quality transmission grids. Discarding a gasoline car requires adequate substitutes for commuting. With large output and employment spillovers (or multipliers) to the rest of economy, low-carbon public investment is also an effective fiscal policy tool to boost economic activity (Hepburn et al. 2020; Batini et al. 2021).

Examples of public investment include:

- *Climate-friendly infrastructure:* energy-efficient public buildings, renewable energy including storage and transmission grids, electric vehicles chargers, railroads to provide a substitute for trucks, electric vehicles for public transit.
- *Investing in nature:* restoration of degraded lands, forests, wetlands, marine ecosystems (coral reefs, seagrass fields) and other natural areas, as well as expanding the area of parks, reserves, and other protected lands. This is often-overlooked area with large social return.[31] For example, restoring just twelve percent of degraded agricultural land can feed additional 200 million people by 2030—reducing malnutrition by 25 percent globally (The Global Commission on the Economy and Climate 2018). Expanding existing protected areas by a factor of two would provide adequate habitat and a space to adapt to mild climate changes for most animal species on the planet, thus putting a halt on the biodiversity loss (Hanson et al. 2020).[32] At the same time, investment in sustainable agriculture has a dramatic potential to increase cropland efficiency, and thus reduce its area to satisfy global food demand—by two times if crops were grown where they are most productive, and attainable crop yields were achieved globally (Folberth et al. 2020). Natural habitat and wildlife conservation as well as the transition to a sustainable use of resources may deteriorate the livelihoods of the poor, at least in the short run, and should thus be accompanied by mitigating measures. For example, Ol Pejeta Conservancy in Kenya runs multiple community projects around its borders, including conservation education, helping fund local schools, financial and technical assistance to local farmers, and managing human-wildlife conflicts.[33] Zambia's Community Markets for

---

[31] For example, the financing gap between what is needed to preserve biodiversity and ecosystems and what is actually spent on this purpose is over $700 billion a year (Deutz et al. 2020).

[32] To cover about 34 percent of the land's surface, as opposed to current 15 percent, and 17 percent that are targeted by the Convention on Biological Diversity (https://www.cbd.int/)

[33] https://www.olpejetaconservancy.org/community/

Conservation program teaches alternative livelihood skills to former wildlife poachers and supports local farmers, thus promoting conservation.[34] Many countries around the world compensate farmers for the damages caused by wildlife (Nyhus et al. 2008).

- *Investing in sustainable urban infrastructure.* By 2050 two thirds of the world's population is expected to live in cities, using the infrastructure that is largely planned and built today (The Global Commission on the Economy and Climate 2018). Examples include: climate-friendly public transport, walking and biking infrastructure to reduce car traffic; improving water and sanitation; retrofits of public buildings; slum upgrading; and expansion of green areas.

A successful climate-friendly public investment strategy requires effective public financial management (PFM). Besides following the best general practices, governments should incorporate climate change considerations focusing on the entire PFM cycle—from macroeconomic analysis and planning to revenue, investment and spending management and policy—i.e., climate-responsive PFM (PEFA 2020). PFM practices should be aligned with climate objectives, as advocated in "Helsinki Principles" (The Coalition of Ministers for Climate Action 2019), for example by introducing climate-related provisions in regulatory frameworks for public investment or procurement, or climate-related procedures to evaluate performance of expenditure and taxes. Fiscal rules may have to be aligned with climate objectives.

F. Support Climate-Friendly Innovation

Innovation is key to sustainable growth. Achieving socio-economic progress without depleting our natural wealth is only possible if societies learn to use this wealth sustainably. Innovation is even more important for the transition to sustainable growth, as the global economy needs a push to switch from traditional and well-established industrial processes and consumption patterns to new and unexplored ones. Energy and technological systems' inertia pose a significant challenge to this transition.

Public sector interventions have traditionally been key in enabling innovation and structural change. Ideas are free to share and use once they are out, but producing them is costly, and not all of them turn out useful. This creates a strong case to subsidize innovation, and many governments are doing it, especially for basic research. With climate change mitigation, the role of government is even

---

[34] https://itswild.org/

more important, as private returns to innovation in this area can be very low, especially if carbon is underpriced. There is a case to support not only basic research, but also turning this research into viable products and bringing them to the market, thus overcoming the so-called "innovation death valley" (Grubb, Hourcade, and Neuhoff 2014).

Policy instruments to support innovation include:

- *Incentives for private climate-friendly innovation:* de-risking (e.g., loan guarantees, feed-in tariffs with transparent phase-out horizon, public procurement to guarantee initial demand for new products and services); inward investment promotion; R&D tax deductions and credits.
- *Public funding of climate-friendly innovation:* funding centers of expertise; funding of universities and research institutes; grants for basic research, including sustainable innovation contests; spending on education and job training in climate-friendly industries.
- *Public wealth funds:* public equity investments can give direction and confidence for investments in industries of the future. State investment banks can likewise be critical by providing patient capital to support "mission-oriented" innovation and investment (Mazzucato and Penna 2016; Detter, Fölster, and Ryan-Collins 2020).

Applying these policy instruments must be accompanied by frameworks to monitor and assess fiscal risks, as well as by following the best governance practices for state-led innovation policy (Aiginger and Rodrik 2020; Cherif and Hasanov 2019; IMF 2021). More general policies, like aligning financial systems with climate objectives and pricing carbon, are essential too.

Despite lackluster progress and uncertainty with carbon pricing to date, climate-friendly innovation already shows remarkable progress. Each year since 2000 the world has been adding more solar power generation capacity than the year before—significantly outpacing the market forecasts (Figure 20.7). The prices of photovoltaic panels and storage per unit of energy went down by four times since 2010 (Figure 20.7). The initial demand for the storage and new installments likely came from subsidies and feed-in tariffs notably in Germany, China, the United States and UK, but the current dynamics is mainly driven by the rapid increase in efficiency of the energy production and corresponding decrease in prices.[35] This progress suggests that a carbon-free energy future is viable. The bad news, however, is that it shows that private actors and often policymakers underestimate potential returns to new climate-friendly technologies, so they underinvest in them in the absence of bold government action.

---

[35] As of 2020, low-carbon solutions are competitive in sectors representing a quarter of total GHG emissions—up from zero in 2015 (SYSTEMIQ 2020).

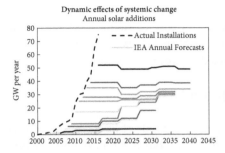

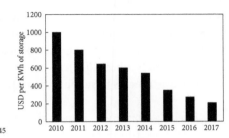

Figure 20.7 Solar Energy Deployment and Price: Far Better than Expected
Source: Bloomberg New Energy Finance.

G. Provide Nudges and Information to Change Social Values

Separately from policies that aim to change relative prices, policies should steer social values and norms toward sustainable consumption and investment choices. Low energy demand and low demand for land- and GHG-intensive goods are key to achieving the 1.5°C goal (IPCC 2018). In this vein, providing education and clear and accessible information on climate change, its risks, and ways to tackle it is an essential complement to carbon pricing and financial incentives. Examples include:

- Requiring labelling and certification that reflect the carbon and ecological footprint of goods or services being sold or advertised: regulations requiring labelling of appliances, cars, and buildings by energy efficiency; information on carbon footprint of goods and services (e.g., flights) in their sales and advertisement; standardized food labelling to reduce the consumer confusion about the food safety, and hence waste.
- Government support for independent certification of sustainable practices: for example, Forest Stewardship Council for forests, Marine Stewardship Council for fisheries, or Roundtable on Sustainable Palm Oil for palm oil.
- Mandatory disclosure of climate-related risks by businesses—to inform potential investors.
- Education and information campaigns are essential. Research by McKinsey & Company shows that many technologies existing today, especially in agriculture and energy efficiency, not only reduce GHG emissions, but also yield positive return on investment even if the carbon price is zero (McKinsey and Company 2009). Yet, they are not fully utilized. For many households and businesses adoption of these technologies, the "smart" choice, is a matter of education and awareness. Education can serve to promote both mitigation and inclusion. For example, the FairWild Standard initiative works with local communities around the world—mostly subsistence farmers—to

promote the sustainable harvesting of wild plants while developing viable business models.[36]

- Ensuring that executive leaders and managers in the public and private sectors have a strong understanding of climate change and the associated challenges is also essential.
- Mandatory work-at-home (WAH) policies during the Covid-19 pandemic, complemented by technological solutions that made the WAH feasible, could lead to a permanent shift in preference to work at home, which could reduce commuting and business travel, and hence decrease GHG emissions.

H. Cooperate Internationally

No single country can resolve the climate change crisis alone. Getting to net-zero GHG emissions by mid-century means everyone must participate, and acting together is larger than the sum of individual actions (Bhattacharya and Stern 2020). By acting together, the world will benefit from stronger demand expansion and investment recovery, economies of scale, learning by doing, lower costs for new technologies and the necessary collective actions on climate and biodiversity that are urgently needed. Global cooperation is crucial.

While global issues like climate change would be best resolved by a global government, at present cooperation among national governments is done via international agreements. Signing (and implementing) one is a voluntary action, but they do serve as a mechanism of moral suasion and accounting for progress and effort that each country puts in towards global good. Not every agreement turns out effective, but there are many examples of success. The Montreal Protocol of 1987 phased-out the use of ozone-depleting substances called chlorofluorocarbons (CFCs) and effectively stabilized the ozone levels in the stratosphere, even though the full recovery is yet to be observed (Solomon 2019). Effectiveness of the Paris Agreement on climate change is yet to be assessed, but it could serve as a useful international framework for cooperation.

Some countries freeride on international commitments to gain competitiveness against those who cooperate. As a result, global GHG emissions may not decline but rather "leak" to the freeriders. One way to reduce freeriding is to implement an international carbon price floor—world-wide, regional, or among large emitters. A relatively small carbon price would be a politically feasible complement to other mitigation policies, and at the same time it would not affect international competitiveness if implemented by all parties (IMF 2019).

---

[36] https://www.fairwild.org/

Freeriding in carbon-intensive trade-exposed sectors could also be deterred by border carbon adjustment—essentially a tax on the carbon content of imports if the carbon price is too low in the country of origin (Condon and Ignaciuk 2013). For climate-induced trade restrictions to work as intended, however, it is essential to establish clear rules and procedures, in particular on quantifying the carbon content of imported goods and on computing the effective carbon price in the country of origin. It is also important to support the transition to zero-carbon for low-income country producers and exporters through technology transfer and finance.

Free trade agreements and international treaties must also be aligned with countries' climate objectives. For example, the EU-Mercosur free trade agreement gives Brazil, Argentina, Paraguay and Uruguay access to the EU single market for sugar, ethanol, poultry and beef. This raises questions on the agreement's compatibility with EU emission reduction objectives, as livestock farming accounts for 80 percent of new deforestation in Brazil, implying significant imported emissions (Nepstad et al. 2006).

Another crucial area for cooperation is international climate finance, which is discussed above.

IV. Building Resilience and Adaptation

Some damage from climate change cannot be undone even with the strongest mitigation effort. The planet is warming, the sea level is rising, the frequency and magnitude of natural disasters are increasing. We need to learn to live with these changes, adapt to them, and minimize their adverse impact on our well-being.

In addition to physical risks stemming from climate change, we also need to adapt to risks stemming from the transition to a low-carbon economy. Carbon-intensive industries will shrink, which means workers and capital will need to be retired or reallocated, and some of them may become "stranded": once a coal power plant is built, it is hard to repurpose it for something else. Financial stability can be at risk too (Carney 2015). An additional risk for fossil-fuel exporters is that shrinking fossil fuel demand will mean a significant shortfall in government revenue and a deterioration in the trade balance (UNCTAD 2019). Dealing with these risks and making sure that the transition is socially just are key to the success of climate change mitigation.

It is important to understand that mitigation is necessary, despite the existence of transition risks. Our ability to adapt even to moderate temperature shocks is quite limited (Dell, Jones, and Olken 2012)—whether due to habit persistence, financial constraints or technological feasibility. Adaptation quickly becomes prohibitively expensive as we move up the ladder of projected average global temperatures—even half a degree makes a sizeable difference, and damages increase non-linearly (IPCC 2018). And if we go above 2°C and trigger the chain of cata-strophic risks, it would be virtually impossible to adapt without a drastic drop in our welfare or technological advances, which seem unfeasible at present. Ultimately, the cheapest and most effective way to adapt is climate change mitigation.

The good news is that many mitigation policies are helpful for adaptation too. In the financial sector, disclosure and prudential regulation of transition and physical climate change risks not only helps steer investors to green assets, but also induces them to accumulate sufficient capital buffers to withstand the risks that are already in their portfolio. Restored wetlands and forests not only serve as carbon sinks, but also absorb storm surges and smooth wind and temperature fluctuations. Decentralized wind and solar power production and storage (for example, in the form of an electric vehicle battery) not only emit zero GHGs into the atmosphere, but also provide uninterrupted electricity supply in times when electricity grids are damaged by a natural disaster. Agroforestry and crop diversi-fication not only make for a more climate-friendly land use, but also make food supply less sensitive to climatic shocks. A steady flow of public investment in infrastructure maintenance can reduce current and future emissions and generate large savings while building a country's resilience to climate shocks (Rozenberg and Fay 2019).

Many policy instruments used for mitigation are applicable, and in fact essential for, adaptation. Adaptation is less ridden with market failures than mitigation—reducing GHG emissions benefits the world, but the benefit of building a storm-resistant house is private. There is still a lot of space for active government involvement, however. Whether the issue at hand is an imminent natural disaster or longer-term gradual change, individuals and businesses are often uninformed about the climate risks they face. When these risks materialize, coordination and cooperation among different actors are essential. Insurance against risks is rid-dled with information externalities, and often needs to be mandated or subsi-dized. Investing in adaptation is in people's private interest, but those who underinvest may inflict damage on others: a storm-resistant house may withstand strong winds, but not another non-fortified house falling on it. Investment may also be lower because of financial constraints, land tenure issues and misaligned landlord-tenant incentives. It therefore makes sense to subsidize or regulate pri-vate investment for adaptation. The role of public investment is important too: building individual storm-resistant houses helps, but investing in, for example, coastal forests may provide a safety cushion for everybody.

To build resilience and adapt to climate change, governments should focus on two broad objectives (IMF 2017).

The first objective is to enhance society's ability to smooth the impact of climatic shocks and to transform structurally in case the shocks are longer-term or permanent. For example, if a hurricane destroys fisheries or tourism infrastructure on a coast, those involved in these industries need to be able to start all over again or move inland to find another activity. Structural transformations are never easy, especially for the poor, and the role of governments is to minimize the burden by properly regulating product markets, promoting financial inclusion, supporting entrepreneurship, and importantly, helping the displaced workers retrain and find new jobs. Equally important is to have policies and resources in place to minimize and smooth the initial impact of a shock.

The second objective is to reduce exposure and vulnerability to climatic shocks. Helping victims of a hurricane is paramount, but they may need less help if their houses are hurricane-proof, the hurricane warning comes well in advance, and there is a clearly communicated evacuation plan. Very often the damage from climatic shocks is irreversible—human lives are lost—and so it is important to prepare for these shocks in advance rather than deal with their aftermath. The key policies to increase resilience are providing information, e.g. early warning systems for natural disasters, encouraging and mandating private investment in resilience, and investing in resilient infrastructure.

Below we discuss the policies needed to progress on each of these two objectives.

A. Smooth Impact of Shocks and Ease Adjustment to the Permanent Ones

To adjust to climate shocks and to smooth their impact, countries need well-functioning macroeconomic and structural policies.

Maintaining macroeconomic stability is key. Climate shocks have immediate adverse effects on economic output and employment and may hurt the economy further through a deterioration in confidence, uncertainty, financial instability, inflation or deflation, and external imbalances. To reduce the damage and prop up internal and external demand, governments should employ a set of counter-cyclical macroeconomic policies: accommodative monetary policy and expansionary fiscal policy—through well-targeted social safety nets, unemployment benefits, a reduced tax burden, and discretionary actions, such as public investment.

For the economy to be able to smooth such shocks, it is important to maintain the buffers. Low and stable inflation gives space for accommodative monetary policy when needed. Sustainable public debt is key for the government to be able to deploy expansionary fiscal policy (Stern and Zenghelis 2021). Private savings by households and firms serve as a cushion beyond the government assistance, and financial institutions should provide possibilities to save that are suitable for everyone, even for the poorest. Financial institutions also need to maintain sufficient capital buffers against climatic shocks.

It is important to explicitly take changing climate into account when projecting the size of the needed buffers. Banks should be required to disclose climate-related risks, whether stemming from potential physical damage or transition to the low-carbon economy, and the banking stress-tests by financial authorities should explicitly gauge the effects of large but plausible climatic shocks on financial stability. Considerations about fiscal space and the appropriate level of public debt should also account for the potential government spending in case of a large but plausible natural disaster. Assessing the impact of climate shocks on public debt sustainability at a 20- or 30-year horizon is key. Exporters of hydrocarbons should create extra fiscal space to compensate for potential loss of government revenue during the transition to a low-carbon economy.

An alternative and often a complement to maintaining the buffers is buying insurance (Mills 2005). Examples are individual insurance policies against floods, forest fires, crop failure among others, and inter-governmental initiatives, such as the Caribbean Catastrophe Risk Insurance Facility (CCRIF), which offer the possibility for countries to insure against large natural disasters.[37] As opposed to maintaining buffers, insurance requires smaller upfront cost, and it can provide quicker and more efficient access to the funds when they are most needed.[38] However, the fast-evolving and uncertain nature of climate change leads to large precautionary insurance premia, which combined with financial constraints often results in low or no coverage for the poorest—those who need the insurance the most. In some cases it makes sense to subsidize the insurance for the most vulnerable, or for lower-income countries, for example through the World Bank's Disaster Risk Financing Insurance (Surminski, Bouwer, and Linnerooth-Bayer 2016). At the same time, improperly designed insurance schemes may reduce incentives to mitigate and physically adapt to the whims of nature. For example, subsidized flood insurance may increase housing construction in flood-prone areas. Details of the insurance design matter and many disincentives can be avoided. For example, index insurance for small farmers predicates the payments on easily observable indicators, like rainfall shortage, which are independent of a farmer's effort. CCRIF has similar arrangement at a country level (Miller and Swann 2016).

Structural transformation requires going beyond macroeconomic stability and buffers. If climate change makes traditional economic activity unviable then government policies should aim to facilitate discovery and expansion of more suitable activities. The policy options include: prudent but not excessive regulation of product markets allowing easy entry and exit of businesses, financial inclusion

---

[37] https://www.ccrif.org/
[38] Consider keeping a fund of 10 percent of GDP to cover for once-in-20-years natural disaster versus paying half percent of GDP each year for 20 years.

and financial markets development, as well as general support of entrepreneurship—like business training, business incubators, financial and logistical support.

Perhaps one of the most important areas to reform is the labor market. To help "stranded" workers to find new activity and sources of income, governments should engage active labor market policies (ALMPs), which include job training, assistance with the job search, well-targeted job and wage subsidies, and public works programs (ILO 2017). In areas where climate change impact is highly localized, governments should combine the scaled-up ALMPs with more general strategies like public investment and incentives for R&D, and all policies can be designed so that the structural transformation or transition contribute to the environmental sustainability. For example, the Philippines' Green Jobs Act subsidizes hiring and training of workers for jobs that help preserve the environment (ILO 2017; Stern et al. 2020).[39] Retraining coal workers to work in the solar energy industry is a feasible and efficient instrument for the just transition (Louie and Pearce 2016)—especially if combined with the renewable energy investment into former coal-mining regions, as has been done for example in North Macedonia (Bellini 2019).

B. Reduce Exposure and Vulnerability

The first step to reduce the damage of climatic shocks is providing information. Well-designed early warning systems (EWSs) alert public about an upcoming natural disaster and give time to prepare, evacuate, or plan a relief. Predicting disasters well in advance and with fair accuracy is extremely hard. The work to improve EWSs continues, including the use of machine learning, big data and remote sensing, as for example at Famine EWS Network (FEWS NET) (Voosen 2020). Early warning about a natural disaster should come with clearly communicated evacuation plan, with special attention paid to the poor, who often lack awareness about the upcoming events, do not have means to transport themselves out of a danger zone, or sustain themselves while the disaster unfolds. During hurricane Katrina in the United States in 2005 about 25 percent of New Orleans residents—disproportionately poor—did not evacuate despite the early warning well in advance, citing lack of shelter, lack of transportation, poor health, and unclear government communication as the main reasons (Eisenman et al. 2007). Going beyond the immediate danger of natural disasters, public information about current and expected climatic risks can be a key factor shaping construction and residency decisions, thus reducing aggregate exposure to these risks.

Governments should also encourage or mandate private investment in resilience. As is the case with mitigation, policy options include building codes and

---

[39] See (Bhattacharya et al. 2021) for more examples.

other regulations, as well as tax deductions or charges, subsidies, subsidized lending, and (partial) loan guarantees among others. Special attention should be paid to the poor, who often lack financial resources to invest or comply with regulations. For example, Thailand's Baan Mankong program provides infrastructure subsidies and subsidized housing loans for the urban poor if they decide to upgrade their communities (Norford and Virsilas 2016). The World Bank's Global Program for Resilient Housing consults governments on resilient housing and employs drones, cameras, and machine learning techniques to automatically identify the highest risk areas where policy intervention would be most needed (World Bank 2019).

An important complement of the private investment is the investment in resilient public infrastructure. Examples of "grey," human-engineered infrastructure include seawalls and levees in low-lying coastal areas, drainage and water reservoirs in flood-prone areas, hurricane-proofing of power lines, or irrigation systems where regular rainfall is in short supply. Importantly, investing in nature or "green" infrastructure in many cases can be the most efficient way to build resilience, along with providing co-benefits like climate change mitigation, local economy support, and better health (Browder et al. 2019; IUCN 2020). For example, without coral reef annual damage from coastal flooding around the world would double (Beck et al. 2018). A prerequisite for the "green" infrastructure to work is sustainable use of natural resources—water, forests, coastline ecosystems, soils, etc. Also important is to strengthen the resilience of the transport system (e.g., to floods), notably for roads that are essential for food security, and making supply chains more resilient to disruption through sourcing decisions and inventory management.

Just as with mitigation, investment in resilient public infrastructure requires effective public financial management.[40] Many countries are developing nationwide climate change strategies and incorporate adaptation into medium-term budget frameworks (Farid et al. 2016). The UN's Sendai Framework for Disaster Risk Reduction provides a roadmap for national strategies (UN 2015). A plan how to finance the current and future adaptation spending is crucial. In developing countries, for example, the financing needs for the nationally-determined adaptation goals up to 2030 are likely six to thirteen times larger than the current level of international adaptation finance (UNEP 2016).

When adaptation to local changing conditions is not feasible, the option of last resort is migration or resettlement. Papua New Guinea, China, and Vietnam have already relocated communities due to their increased vulnerability to flooding

---

[40] Some general principles for resilient infrastructure are to address deficient management and governance of infrastructure systems, identify critical infrastructure assets and systems so as to provide them with resources, include resilience into regulations and incentives; and use financial incentives to account for the social cost of infrastructure disruptions (Hallegatte, Rentschler, and Rozenberg 2019).

(López-Carr and Marter-Kenyon 2015). Climate-induced migration in Sub-Saharan Africa, South Asia and Latin America is expected to rise by over 170 million people by 2050—more than sixty percent of the current number of migrants (Rigaud et al. 2018).[41] Both legal and economic institutions must be strengthened to handle these increased, and often rapid and unpredictable migration flows. Sea level rises may lead to the unprecedented disappearance of some sovereign states— Small Island Developing States (SIDS)—for reasons unrelated to wars, with potentially significant geopolitical and financial consequences. The enormous adaptation needs of such countries, and possibly the need, ultimately, to relocate their populations, will pose a collective action problem, since such measures are unlikely to be financed by the private sector.

It is important to understand that on a planetary scale the option to relocate is not feasible. We need to mitigate climate change if we are to avoid global catastrophic scenarios.

V. Beyond GDP Growth: New Metrics and Policy Framework for Sustainability

As is the case with many other issues in this book, the success of the low-carbon transition crucially depends on the measurement of progress—that is, how we measure our well-being and its sustainability over time. Policies that seek to maximize GDP growth—the traditional and widely-reported indicator of economic performance—have a tendency to be biased against mitigation of environmental issues and to prioritize income over lives, towards dealing with the aftermath of natural disasters rather than preventing them, and towards investing in physical infrastructure rather than using natural resources sustainably. There is a clear need to go beyond GDP to guide policies (Stiglitz, Sen, and Fitoussi 2009; Stern and Stiglitz 2021).[42]

The key priority is to keep track of our wealth, and natural capital in particular.[43] The System of National Accounts must transition from a flow-centered focus on GDP to a stock-centered focus on a broad definition of capital. The United Nations Environment Programme's Inclusive Wealth Index (IWI) is a step forward along these lines (Managi and Kumar 2018; Dasgupta et al. 2015; Asheim and Weitzman 2001). A similar approach is used in the World Bank's Changing

---

[41] Current stock of international migrants is as of 2019, according to the United Nations.

[42] Nicholas Stern was a member of the Commission on the Measurement of Economic Performance and Social Progress (Stiglitz, Sen, and Fitoussi 2009).

[43] Natural capital is defined as the stock of natural ecosystems on Earth including air, land, soil, biodiversity and geological resources, which underpin our economy and society by producing value for people, both directly and indirectly. The stock of natural ecosystems provides a flow of services (ecosystem services).

Wealth of Nations project (Lange, Wodon, and Carey 2018), while the UN's System of Environmental-Economic Accounting delineates the main principles behind measuring natural capital/ecosystems in physical and monetary terms (Hein et al. 2020).

While the projects above constantly update their methodology to measure the sustainability better, significant challenges remain. It is hard to reliably assess stocks of natural assets like wildlife, biodiversity, freshwater, soil, and especially to account for all ecosystem services they provide and their quality.[44] It is even harder to estimate prices at which natural assets should be valued. Many natural assets are not traded on markets, and even when they are, market prices often do not fully reflect these assets' true social value because of externalities—some of which have yet to be discovered by science.

Dependence between prices and available stocks of natural assets can also be highly non-linear. The usefulness of many ecosystem services is not adequately perceived until their deterioration is advanced. It is therefore important to understand that price non-linearities and uncertainty may lead to an underestimation of the role of natural capital, and paint a rosy picture of sustainability.

Despite these difficulties, the policy dialogue and further research into the natural capital accounting should continue (Turner, Badure, and Ferrini 2019).

In addition, the wealth indexes can be complemented by a dashboard approach, e.g. reporting a broad set of social and environmental indicators along with GDP (Laurent 2019). An advantage of the dashboard approach is that it allows for different dimensions of well-being to be complementary and cumulative, and it does not require assessing prices/weights at which the dimensions are to be summed up in a single index.

Another proposed alternative to the policy focus on GDP growth is the introduction of a legally-binding climate constraint in the form of annual, national carbon budgets that are binding on all aspects of policy, including budget laws (High Council on Climate 2019).

VI. Dealing with Climate Change: How to Make the Great Transformation Inclusive?

The transition to a low-carbon economy is our only option, but it is a major undertaking. It involves the rise of new sectors and industries, but also the retirement of some old ones. It creates new jobs and offers new opportunities, but it requires altering our consumption habits and learning new skills. If the transition is inequitable or socially unjust, it will ultimately fail. But if done right, it could

---

[44] As a result, these assets are not being accounted for, e.g. their value is assumed zero.

unlock new sources of development—a growth story for the twenty-first century, which would not only be sustainable, but also inclusive. Inclusion is thus critical to addressing climate change.

Many policies discussed in this chapter bring about important inclusion co-benefits by design. Climate change and other environmental issues disproportionately affect the poor, especially those living in developing countries. Climate change mitigation would therefore be particularly beneficial for the poor.

How mitigation is achieved also matters. Poor subsistence farmers are often de facto owners and primary users of natural assets that are key to the mitigation and adaptation: forests, wetlands, agricultural land, coastal waters. Prompting sustainable use of these assets—investing in land restoration and sustainable agriculture, creating financial instruments to reflect the true social value of these assets, and paying for the provided ecosystem services—would not only help our planet but also provide sustainable livelihood for the owners. These policies would also help empower women as they make up more than 40 percent of agriculture labor force around the world and they are often responsible for the food production and collection of fuel and water in the poorest households (Doss 2011). Investment in sustainable urban infrastructure—water and sanitation, slum upgrading, green areas, public transport—is another example of a policy with widely shared benefits.

Mitigation and adaptation policies also create job and training opportunities, including for the youth, low-skilled, and long-term unemployed. Ethiopia's National Forest Sector Development Program aims to reforest 15 percent of the country, contribute 50 percent to the national emission reduction target by 2030, and at the same time create over six hundred thousand jobs—over a quarter of the country's unemployed (MEFCC 2018). Carbon taxes can reduce economic activity in the short run, but their effects on net creation of jobs are much less clear, as the renewable energy industry is more labor-intensive than coal. In the United States solar and wind already employ almost three times as many people as coal despite a smaller share in total energy production (Heutel 2018).

Unlike fossil fuel deposits, potential for solar and wind energy production is widely distributed across the globe and within countries (Deng et al. 2015). This creates opportunities to reduce disparities by investing and creating jobs in laggard regions, provide electricity supply even where the grids are down or non-existent, together with an additional co-benefit of energy self-sufficiency and security for more countries.

For some policies, inclusion must be deliberate:

- The effect of a carbon tax on the poor's purchasing power should be alleviated by well-targeted social transfers or other pro-poor public spending programs.
- The "stranded" workers and regions need to be helped via job training, help with reallocation, and regional investment programs.

- Regulations to promote energy efficiency or build up resilience should come with financial incentives or government programs for the poor to enable them to comply.
- Natural disaster evacuation plans should be designed in a way that even the most vulnerable have information and means to escape and weather the disaster.
- Natural habitat and wildlife conservation as well as transition to sustainable use of resources should be accompanied by mitigating measures for the poor.

Success of the transition also depends on other more general policies and factors. It is key to maintain an inclusive decision-making process: extensive communication about the reform's risks and benefits and consultations with all stakeholders. Going beyond GDP in measuring well-being and sustainability helps focus policy measures on the right priorities. Macroeconomic stability and secure property rights are necessary conditions for massive investment to take place. Effective decentralization frameworks are needed to spur investment by local governments. Structural reform and social safety nets, investment in health, education, and infrastructure are key to smooth structural transformation, abate policy effects for the poor and the most affected, and advance inclusive growth agenda in general. And at the basis of it all are inclusive political institutions and effective governance and anti-corruption frameworks.

The timing of reforms also matters. The costs generated by increased carbon taxation would be reduced if such increases are introduced at times of low commodity prices, when electricity and fuel for vehicles are relatively cheap. Changes in taxation in general as well as structural reform are better implemented during economic booms, when the cost of adjustment to the new rules is attenuated by faster economic growth. Recessions, by contrast, are the most appropriate time to expand financial incentives and boost investment in sustainable infrastructure—helping to both tackle climate change and expand the economy when it is most needed, while contributing little to inflation. The severe downturn caused by the Covid-19 pandemic is a prime example of a time when green recovery policies should be employed (Stern et al. 2020; Bhattacharya 2020; Bhattacharya and Stern 2020).

A. Making the Post-Covid-19 Economy Sustainable

The Covid-19 pandemic is a profound crisis that differs in fundamental ways from previous crises, as it combines health, economic, and financial aspects and has resulted in extraordinary policy action. To a significant extent, it is endogenous, as it is rooted in unsustainable modes of production and consumption. The pandemic likely originated in a pathogen that passed from wild animals to humans in the context of ecosystem degradation (IPBES 2020). The climate change challenge is similar to the pandemic in some ways: both revolve around questions of system resilience, political economy, and international cooperation. It is also different, because the geological changes triggered by carbon-intensive growth pose an existential threat to civilization, and will last for millennia, if not millions of years.

In addition to climate change, the twentieth century saw unprecedented ecological change and degradation of ecosystems and biodiversity, together with dramatic increases in human and domestic animal populations. This has led to unprecedented contact between humans and animals, providing ample opportunities for pathogens to transfer between species and generating a worldwide increase in emerging zoonotic diseases and outbreaks of epidemic zoonoses (IPBES 2020). Pandemic risks have been exacerbated by globalization, a key channel being air traffic, which doubled between 2006 and 2018 to over 4.3 billion passengers, thus generating the largest vector in history for the spread of emerging diseases.

Given the link between unsustainable economic activity and pandemics, Covid-19 is unlikely to be a one-off. It is likely just the first instance of a century of shocks related to environmental degradation. In the words of Tooze (2020), we are living through the "first economic crisis of the Anthropocene." Worryingly, unsustainable growth is being exacerbated by the crisis, with accelerating deforestation and wildlife poaching, reversals of environmental regulations, and the implementation of carbon-intensive economic recovery policies. All of this strongly underlines the importance of making the global economy sustainable and resilient.

Precisely, the Covid-19 crisis could prove to be a watershed moment in our collective ability to tackle climate change and ecological degradation. In 2020, GHG emissions are projected to have fallen by a record amount. The challenge is immense, as this decline needs to be maintained for three decades to achieve carbon neutrality by 2050. Instead, emissions have rebounded following the gradual reopening and recovery of economies. The broader context is encouraging, however, with public support for ambitious climate action having grown substantially in developed countries in the context of the Covid-19 crisis. Equally important, the crisis has shown governments' ability to intervene rapidly on a large scale, driving a decisive increase in the role of the state (Helm 2020).

The stakes of the transition to a sustainable global economy are clearly immense. To enable this "Great Transformation" in the required timeframe, governments must ensure that recovery plans are compatible with climate stability and national carbon budgets. Rapidly-implementable, labor-intensive public investment with high economic multipliers and large climate co-benefits are essential to underpin a sustainable recovery and avoid locking in emissions (Stern et al. 2020; Bhattacharya 2020). Specifically, a survey of policymakers suggests that five policies should be prioritized: clean physical infrastructure, building efficiency retrofits, investment in education and training, natural capital investment, and clean R&D (Hepburn et al. 2020). In lower- and middle-income countries, the focus should be on rural support spending.

VII. Conclusion

Business as usual cannot continue. A decade of current GHG emissions remains before global mean temperatures surpass 1.5°C and risk triggering catastrophic irreversible changes to the planet's ecosystems, thus putting our livelihoods in jeopardy and driving millions into extreme poverty. A just transition to a net-zero emissions, climate-resilient world is the only viable way forward. The transition represents not a cost or a burden but the greatest economic, business and commercial opportunities in modern times (Stern 2021). If it is achieved, not only will climate stability be safeguarded, but our societies will be more prosperous, healthier, and more inclusive over the long term. This chapter outlines the key policies and policy framework changes that are required for a successful transition: putting a price on carbon, promoting sustainable use of natural resources, aligning the financial system with climate objectives, boosting public spending on sustainable infrastructure and innovation, deploying low-carbon industrial and innovation policy, systematically integrating climate change into public financial management, building resilience and adapting to the climatic changes that are coming, better measurement of well-being and sustainability, and crucially, making the transition fair by ensuring socially just outcomes. There are still many open questions about both the specifics of such policies and the science of climate change, but the essence of what must be done and how to do it is clear. In the words of "A Letter to the Future," carved in memory of Okjökull—the first extinct glacier in Iceland: "This monument is to acknowledge that we know what is happening and what needs to be done. Only you know if we did it."

References

Acemoglu, Daron, Philippe Aghion, Leonardo Bursztyn, and David Hemous. 2012. "The Environment and Directed Technical Change." *American Economic Review* 102(1): 131–66.

Acosta-Ormaechea, Santiago, Sergio Sola, and Jiae Yoo. 2019. "Tax Composition and Growth: A Broad Cross-country Perspective." *German Economic Review* 20(4): e70–e106.

Admati, Anat R. 2017. "A Skeptical View of Financialized Corporate Governance." *Journal of Economic Perspectives* 31(3): 131–50.

Aglietta, Michel, Étienne Espagne, and Baptiste Perrissin Fabert. 2015. "A Proposal to Finance Low Carbon Investment in Europe." Department of the Commissioner-General for Sustainable Development Paper.

Aglietta, Michel, and Étienne Espagne. 2018. "Le système monétaire international face aux cycles biogéochimiques." Annales des Mines-Responsabilite et environnement 4: 64–8.

Aiginger, Karl, and Dani Rodrik. 2020. "Rebirth of Industrial Policy and an Agenda for the Twenty-First Century." Journal of Industry, Competition, and Trade 20: 189–207.

Aklin, Michaël, and Matto Mildenberger. 2020. "Prisoners of the Wrong Dilemma: Why Distributive Conflict, Not Collective Action, Characterizes the Politics of Climate Change." Global Environmental Politics 20(4): 4–27.

Allan, Brian, Felicia Keesing, and Richard Ostfeld. 2003. "Effect of Forest Fragmentation on Lyme Disease Risk." Conservation Biology 17(1): 267–72.

Andrew, Robbie. 2020. It's Getting Harder and Harder to Limit Ourselves to 2°C. January 15. https://folk.universitetetioslo.no/roberan/t/global_mitigation_curves.shtml.

Arrhenius, Svante. 1896. "On the Influence of Carbonic Acid in the Air upon the Temperature of the Ground." Philosophical Magazine and Journal of Science 41: 237–76.

Asheim, Geir B., and Martin L. Weitzman. 2001. "Does NNP Growth Indicate Welfare Improvement?" Economic Letters 73(2): 233–9.

Batini, Nicoletta, Mario di Serio, Matteo Fragetta, Giovanni Melina, and Anthony Waldron. 2021. Building Back Better: How Big Are Green Spending Multipliers? IMF Working Paper 2021/087.

Beck, Michael W., Iñigo J. Losada, Pelayo Menéndez, Borja G. Reguero, Pedro Díaz-Simal, and Felipe Fernández. 2018. "The Global Flood Protection Savings Provided by Coral Reefs." Nature Communications 9(2186).

Bellini, Emiliano. 2019. "North Macedonian Utility Plans Three More Tenders for 110 MW of Solar." PV Magazine. Accessed May 8, 2020. https://www.pv-magazine.com/2019/12/04/north-macedonian-utility-plans-three-more-tenders-for-110-mw-of-solar/.

Bhattacharya, Amar. 2020. Rebooting the Climate Agenda: What Should Priorities Be? Brookings Institution report.

Bhattacharya, Amar, and Nicholas Stern. 2020. "From Rescue to Recovery, to Transformation and Growth: Building a Better World after Covid-19." London School of Economics and Political Science. April 27. https://www.lse.ac.uk/granthaminstitute/news/from-rescue-to-recovery-to-transformation-and-growth-building-a-better-world-after-covid-19/.

Bhattacharya, Amar, Joshua P. Meltzer, Zia Qureshi, and Nicholas Stern. 2016. Delivering on Sustainable Infrastructure for Better Development and Better Climate. The New Climate Economy report, The Global Commission on the Economy and Climate.

Bhattacharya, Amar, Maksym Ivanyna, William Oman, and Nicholas Stern. 2021. "Climate Change." IMF working paper.

Bolton, Patrick, Morgan Després, Luiz Awazu Pereira da Silva, Frédéric Samama, and Romain Svartzman. 2020. The Green Swan, Central Banking and Financial Stability in the Age of Climate Change. Report by Bank for International Settlements and Banque de France.

Bösch, Matthias, Peter Elsasser, and Sven Wunder. 2019. "Why Do Payments for Watershed Services Emerge? A Cross-Country Analysis of Adoption Contexts." World Development 119: 111–19.

Bredencamp, Hugh, and Catherine A. Pattillo. 2010. Financing the Response to Climate Change. IMF Staff Position Note 2010/06.

Browder, Greg, Suzanne Ozment, Irene Rehberger Bescos, Todd Gartner, and Glenn-Marie Lange. 2019. Integrating Green and Gray: Creating Next Generation Infrastructure. Washington, DC: World Bank and World Resources Institute.

Burke, Marshall, Solomon M. Hsiang, and Edward Miguel. 2015. "Global Non-linear Effect of Temperature on Economic Production." Nature 527: 235–9.

Carney, Mark. 2015. "Breaking the Tragedy of the Horizon—Climate Change and Financial Stability." September 29.

Cherif, Reda, and Fuad Hasanov. 2019. "Principles of True Industrial Policy." Journal of Globalization and Development 10(1): 1–22.

Clark, Michael A., Marco Springmann, Jason Hill, and David Tilman. 2019. "Multiple Health and Environmental Impacts of Foods." PNAS 116(46): 23357–62.

Clemens, Benedict, David Coady, Stefania Fabrizio, Sanjeev Gupta, Trevor Alleyne, and Carlo Sdralevich. 2013. Energy Subsidy Reform: Lessons and Implications. Washington, DC: IMF.

Climate Action Tracker. 2020. "CAT Emissions Gaps." September. https://climateactiontracker.org/global/cat-emissions-gaps/.

Coady, David, Ian Parry, Nghia-Piotr Le, and Baoping Shang. 2019. "Global Fossil Fuel Subsidies Remain Large: An Update Based on Country-Level Estimates." IMF Working Paper No. 19/89.

Condon, Madison, and Ada Ignaciuk. 2013. Border Carbon Adjustment and International Trade: A Literature Review. Trade and Environmenal Working Paper 2013/06, OECD.

Conefrey, Thomas, John D. Fitz-Gerald, Laura Malaguzzi Valeri, and Richard S.J. Tol. 2013. "The Impact of a Carbon Tax on Economic Growth and Carbon Dioxide Emissions in Ireland." Journal of Environmental Planning and Management 56(7): 934–52.

Conley, Daniel J., Svante Björck, Erik Bonsdorff, Jacob Carstensen, Georgia Destouni, Bo G. Gustafsson, et al. 2009. "Hypoxia-Related Processes in the Baltic Sea." Environment Science & Technology 43(10): 3412–20.

Crutzen, Paul J. 2002. "Geology of Mankind." Nature 415: 23.

Cullenward, Danny, and David G. Victor. 2020. *Making Climate Policy Work.* Polity Press.

Dasgupta, P., A. Duraiappah, S. Managi, E. Barbier, R. Collins, B. Fraumeni, H. Gundimeda, G. Liu, and K. J. Mumford. 2015. "How to Measure Sustainable Progress." *Science* 350(6262): 748.

Dasgupta, Partha. 2021. "The Economics of Biodiversity: The Dasgupta Review." London: HM Treasury.

de la Vega, Elwyn, Thomas B. Chalk, Paul A. Wilson, Ratna Priya Bysani, and Gavin L. Foster. 2020. "Atmospheric CO2 During the Mid-Piacenzian Warm Period and the M2 Glaciation." *Nature Scientific Reports* 10.

DeFries, Ruth, Ottmar Edenhofer, Alex Halliday, Geoffrey Heal, Timothy Lenton, Michael Puma, et al. 2019. *The Missing Economic Risks in Assessments of Climate Change Impacts.* Grantham Research Institute on Climate Change and the Environment policy brief.

Dell, Melissa, Benjamin F. Jones, and Benjamin A. Olken. 2012. "Temperature Shocks and Economic Growth: Evidence from the Last Half Century." *American Economic Journal: Macroeconomics* 4(3): 66–95.

Deng, Yvonne Y., Martin Haigh, Willemijn Pouwels, Lou Ramaekers, Ruut Brandsma, Sven Schimschar, et al. 2015. "Quantifying a Realistic, Worldwide Wind and Solar Electricity Supply." *Global Environmental Change* 31: 239–52.

Detter, Dag, Stefan Fölster, and Josh Ryan-Collins. 2020. *Public Wealth funds: Supporting Economic Recovery and Sustainable Growth.* WP 2020–16, UCL Institute for Innovation and Public Purpose.

Deutz, Andrew, Geoffrey M. Heal, Rose Niu, Eric Swanson, Terry Townshend, Zhu Lic, et al. 2020. *Financing Nature: Closing the Global Biodiversity Gap.* The Paulson Institute, The Nature Conservancy; The Cornell Atkinson Center for Sustainability.

Diffenbaugh, Noah S., and Marshall Burke. 2019. "Global Warming Has Increased Global Economic Inequality." *PNAS* 116(20): 9808–13.

Doss, Cheryl. 2011. "The Role of Women in Agriculture." ESA Working Paper No. 11–02.

Dumic, Igor, and Edson Severnini. 2018. "'Ticking Bomb': The Impact of Climate Change on the Incidence of Lyme Disease." *Canadian Journal of Infectious Diseases and Medical Microbiology* 2018, Article ID 5719081.

Eisenman, David P., Kristina M. Cordasco, Steve Asch, Joya F. Golden, and Deborah Glik. 2007. "Disaster Planning and Risk Communication With Vulnerable Communities: Lessons From Hurricane Katrina." *American Journal of Public Health* 97(1): 109–15.

Ellen MacArthur Foundation. 2021. "Universal Circular Economy Policy Goals."

Energy Transitions Commission. 2020. "Making Mission Possible: Delivering a Net-Zero Economy."

Evans, Meredydd, Volha Roshchanka, and Peter Graham. 2017. "An International Survey of Building Energy Codes and Their Implementation." *Journal of Cleaner Production* 158: 382–9.

Food and Agriculture Organization of the United Nations (FAO). 2018. *The State of World Fisheries and Aquaculture*. Food and Agriculture Organization of the United Nations.

Food and Agriculture Organization of the United Nations (FAO). 2020. *Climate-Smart Agriculture*. Accessed April 10, 2020. http://www.fao.org/climate-smart-agriculture/en/.

Farid, Mai, Michael Keen, Michael Papaioannou, Ian Parry, Catherine Patillo, Ter-Martirosyan Anna, et al. 2016. "After Paris: Fiscal, Macroeconomic, and Financial Implications of Climate Change." IMF Staff Discussion Note 16/01.

Folberth, Christian, Nikolay Khabarov, Juray Balkovič, Rastislav Skalský, Piero Visconti, Philippe Ciais, et al. 2020. "The Global Cropland-Sparing Potential of High-Yield Farming." *Nature Sustainability* 3: 281–9.

Fourier, Par M. 1824. "Remarques Generales sur les Temperatures Du Globe Terrestre et des Espaces Planetaires." *Annales de Chimie et de Physique* 27: 136–67.

Gabor, Daniela. 2020. "The Wall Street Consensus." Center for Open Science Working Paper.

Gaspar, Vitor, David Amaglobeli, Mercedes Garcia-Escribano, Delphine Prady, and Mauricio Soto. 2019. "Fiscal Policy and Development : Human, Social, and Physical Investments for the SDGs." IMF Stuff Discussion Note No. 19/03.

Global Forest Watch. 2020. *Forest Monitoring Designed for Action*. Accessed April 10, 2020. https://www.globalforestwatch.org/.

Godfray, Charles J., Paul Aveyard, Tara Garnett, Jim W. Hall, Timothy J. Key, Jamie Lorimerand. 2018. "Meat Consumption, Health, and the Environment." *Science* 361 (6399).

Green Climate Fund. 2020. *Tipping or Turning Point: Scaling Up Climate Finance in the Era of Covid-19*. Green Climate Fund Working Paper No. 3.

Grubb, Michael, Jean-Charles Hourcade, and Karsten Neuhoff. 2014. *Planetary Economics: Energy, Climate Change and the Three Domains of Sustainable Development*. New York: Routledge.

Haberl, Helmut, Dominik Wiedenhofer, Doris Vir'ag, Gerald Kalt, Barbara Plank, Paul Brockway, et al. 2020. "A Systematic Review of the Evidence on Decoupling of GDP, Resource Use and GHG Emissions, Part II: Synthesizing the Insights." *Environmental Research Letters* 15(6).

Hallegatte, Stéphane, Jean-Charles Hourcade, and Patrice Dumas. 2007. "Why Economic Dynamics Matter in Assessing Climate Change Damages: Illustration on Extreme Events." *Ecological Economics* 62(2): 330–340

Hallegatte, Stephane, Jun Rentschler, and Julie Rozenberg. 2019. *Lifelines: The Resilient Infrastructure Opportunity*. Washington, DC: World Bank.

Hansen, James, Makiko Sato, Gary Russell, and Pushker Kharecha. 2013. "Climate Sensitivity, Sea Level and Atmospheric Carbon Dioxide." *Philosophical Transactions of the Royal Sociey A: Mathematical, Physical and Engineering Sciences* 371(2001).

Hanson, Jeffrey O., Jonathan R. Rhodes, Stuart H.M. Butchart, Graeme M. Buchanan, Carlo Rondinini, Gentile F. Ficetola, et al. 2020. "Global Conservation of Species' Niches." *Nature* 580: 232–4.

Hein, Lars, Kenneth J. Bagstadt, Karl Obst, Bram Edens, Sjoerd Schenau, Gem Castillo, et al. 2020. "Progress in Natural Capital Accounting for Ecosystems." *Science* 367(6477): 514–5.

Helm, Dieter. 2020. *September 2020 (and March 2021): The Temporary and the Permanent Impacts of Coronavirus*. mimeo.

Hepburn, Cameron, Brian O'Callaghan, Nicholas Stern, Joseph Stiglitz, and Dimitri Zenghelis. 2020. "Will Covid-19 Fiscal Recovery Packages Accelerate or Retard Progress on Climate Change?" *Oxford Review of Economic Policy* 36(IS1).

Hepburn, Cameron, Nicholas Stern, and Joseph Stiglitz. 2020. "Carbon Pricing" Special Issue in the European Economic Review." *European Economic Review* 127: 103440.

Heutel, Garth. 2018. "Do Climate Policies Have a Negative Effect on Jobs?" *High Country News*. December. Accessed May 28, 2020. https://www.hcn.org/articles/economy-do-climate-policies-have-a-negative-effect-on-jobs.

High Council on Climate. 2019. "First Annual Report."

Hirth, Lion, and Jan Christof Steckel. 2016. "The Role of Capital Costs in Decarbonizing the Electricity Sector." *Environmental Research Letters* 11(11).

Houser, Trevor, Solomon Hsiang, Robert Kopp, and Kate Larsen. 2015. *Economic Risks of Climate Change: An American Prospectus*. New York: Columbia University Press.

Hsiang, Solomon M., Paulina Oliva, and Reed Walker. 2019. "The Distribution of Environmental Damages." *Review of Environmental Economics and Policy* 13(1): 83–103.

International Energy Agency (IEA). 2019. *Global EV Outlook*. Paris.

International Energy Agency (IEA). 2021. *World Energy Investment*. Paris.

International Institute for Sustainable Development (IISD). 2020. *Doubling Back and Doubling Down: G20 Scorecard on Fossil Fuel Funding*. Winnipeg, Canada.

International Labour Organization (ILO). 2017. *Green Initiative Policy Brief: Active Labour Market Policies*. Geneva.

Imagesat International. 2017. "Maritime-Executive." *Using Satellite Imagery to Combat Illegal Fishing*. Accessed April 10, 2020. https://www.maritime-executive.com/blog/using-satellite-imagery-to-combat-illegal-fishing.

International Monetary Fund (IMF). 2015. "Is the Glas Half Empty of Half Full? Issue in Managing Water Challenges and Policy Instruments." IMF Staff Discussion Note.

International Monetary Fund (IMF). 2017. *The Effect of Weather Shocks on Economic Activity: How Can Low-Income Countries Cope?* World Economic Outlook, Chapter 3, IMF.

International Monetary Fund (IMF). 2019. "Fiscal Monitor: How to Mitigate Climate Change."

International Monetary Fund (IMF). 2020. "Global Financial Stability Report No. 2020/001."

International Monetary Fund (IMF). 2020. "Mitigating Climate Change." World Economic Outlook report, Chapter 3.

International Monetary Fund (IMF). 2020a. "Mitigating Climate Change." World Economic Outlook report, Chapter 3.

International Monetary Fund (IMF). 2021. "Private Finance for Development: Wishful Thinking or Thinking Out of the Box?" IMF Departmental paper series.

Independent Experts Group on Climate Finance. 2020. "Delivering on the $100 Billion Climate Finance Commitment and Transforming Climate Finance."

Intergovernmental Science-Policy Platform on Biodiversity and Ecosystem Services (IPBES). 2019. *Global Assessment Report on Biodiversity and Ecosystem Services.* Bonn, Germany.

Intergovernmental Science-Policy Platform on Biodiversity and Ecosystem Services (IPBES). 2020. *Biodiversity and Pandemics.* Workshop report.

Intergovernmental Panel on Climate Change (IPCC). 2014. *Climate Change 2014: Synthesis Report. Contribution of Working Groups I, II and III to the Fifth Assessment Report of the Intergovernmental Panel on Climate Change [Core Writing Team, R.K. Pachauri and L.A. Meyer (eds.)].* Geneva.

Intergovernmental Panel on Climate Change (IPCC). 2018. *Global Warming of 1.5°C.* Special Report.

International Union for Conservation of Nature (IUCN). 2017. *Deforestation and Forest Degradation.* Issues Brief.

International Union for Conservation of Nature (IUCN). 2020. *Nature-Based Solutions to Disasters.* Issues Brief.

Jouzel, Jean, Valérie Masson-Delmotte, O. Cattani, Gabrielle B. Dreyfus, S. Falourd, Georg Hoffmann, et al. 2007. "Orbital and Millennial Antarctic Climate Variability over the Past 800,000 Years." *Science* 317(5839): 793–6.

Katz, Cheryl. 2017. *Small Pests, Big Problems: The Global Spread of Bark Beetles.* Yale Environment 360. Accessed March 5, 2020. https://e360.yale.edu/features/small-pests-big-problems-the-global-spread-of-bark-beetles.

Klenert, David, Linus Mattauch, Emmanuel Combet, Ottmar Edenhofer, Cameron Hepburn, Ryan Rafaty, and Nicholas Stern. 2018. "Making Carbon Pricing Work for Citizens." *Nature Climate Change* 8: 669–77.

Krogsrup, Signe, and William Oman. 2019. *Macroeconomic and Financial Policies for Climate Change Mitigation: A Review of the Literature.* IMF Working Paper 19/185.

Kulp, Scott A., and Benjamin H. Strauss. 2019. "New Elevation Data Triple Estimates of Global Vulnerability to Sea-Level Rise and Coastal Flooding." *Nature Communications* 10(4844).

Kumari Rigaud, Kanta, Alex de Sherbinin, Bryan Jones, Jonas Bergmann, Viviane Clement, Kayly Ober, et al. 2018. *Groundswell: Preparing for Internal Climate Migration.* Washington, DC: World Bank.

Lange, Glenn-Marie, Quentin Wodon, and Kevin Carey. 2018. *The Changing Wealth of Nations: Building a Sustainable Future*. Washington, DC: World Bank.

Laurent, Éloi. 2019. *Sortir de la croissance*. Paris: Les Liens qui Libèrent.

Lelieveld, Jos, Andrea Pozzer, Ulrich Pöschl, Mohammed Fnais, Andy Haines, and Thomas Münzel. 2020. "Loss of Life Expectancy from Air Pollution Compared to Other Risk Factors: A Worldwide Perspective." *Cardiovascular Research* 116(11): 1910–7.

Lenton, Timothy M., Johan Rockström, Owen Gaffney, Stefan Rahmstorf, Katherine Richardson, Will Steffen, et al. 2019. "Climate Tipping Points—Too Risky to Bet Against." *Nature* 575: 592–5.

López-Carr, David, and Jessica Marter-Kenyon. 2015. "Human Adaptation: Manage Climate-Induced Resettlement." *Nature* 517(7534).

Louie, Edward P., and Joshua M. Pearce. 2016. "Retraining Investment for U.S. Transition from Coal to Solar Photovoltaic Employment." *Energy Economics* 57: 295–302.

LTWP. 2019. *Sustainability Performance Report: Powering the Nation*. Lake Turkana Wind Power.

Lüthi, Dieter, Martine Le Floch, Bernhard Bereiter, Thomas Blunier, Jean-Marc Barnola, Urs Siegenthaler, et al. 2008. "High-Resolution Carbon Dioxide Concentration Record 650,000–800,000 Years Before Present." *Nature* 453: 379–82.

Managi, Shunsuke, and Pushpam Kumar. 2018. *Inclusive Wealth Report 2018: Measuring Progress Towards Sustainability*. New York: Routledge.

Mansur, Erin T. 2013. "Prices Versus Quantities: Environmental Regulation and Imperfect Competition." *Journal of Regulatory Economics* 44: 80–102.

Marshall, Shawn. 2014. "Glacier Retreat Crosses a Line." *Science* 345 (6199): 872.

Matikainen, Sati, Emanuele Campiglio, and Dimitri Zenghelis. 2017. *The Climate Impact of Quantitative Easing*. Policy Paper, The Grantham Research Institute on Climate Change and the Environment.

Mazzucato, Mariana, and Caetano C.R. Penna. 2016. "Beyond Market Failures: The Market Creating and Shaping Roles of State Investment Banks." *Journal of Economic Policy Reform* 19(4): 1–22.

McKinsey & Company. 2009. "Pathways to a Low-Carbon Economy: Version 2 of the Global Greenhouse Gas Abatement Cost Curve."

Meckling, Jonas, and Bentley B. Allan. 2020. "The Evolution of Ideas in Global Climate Policy". *Nature Climate Change* 10, pp. 434–438.

Ministry of Environment, Forest and Climate Change (MEFCC). 2018. *National Forest Sector Development Program, Ethiopia: Volume III Synthesis Report*.

Miller, Alan, and Stacy Swann. 2016. *Innovative Insurance to Manage Climate Risks*. EMCompass Note 9, International Finance Corporation.

Mills, Evan. 2005. "Insurance in a Climate of Change." *Science* 309(5737): 1040–4.

Nelson, David, and Gireesh Shrimali. 2014. *Finance Mechanisms for Lowering the Cost of Renewable Energy in Rapidly Developing Countries.* Climate Policy Initiative.

Nepstad, Daniel C., Claudia M. Stickler, and Oriana T. Almeida. 2006. "Globalization of the Amazon Soy and Beef Industries: Opportunities for Conservation". *Conservation Biology* 20(6): 1595–1603

Newman, David J., and Gordon M. Cragg. 2007. "Natural Products as Sources of New Drugs over the Last 25 Years." *Journal of Natural Products* 70: 461–77.

National Oceanic and Atmospheric Administration (NOAA). 2020. *State of the Climate: Global Climate Report for Annual 2019.* National Oceanic and Atmospheric Administration National Centers for Environmental Information. https://www.ncdc.noaa.gov/sotc/global/201913.

Nordhaus, William. 2013. *The Climate Casino: Risk, Uncertainty, and Economics for a Warming World.* New Haven, CT: Yale University Press.

Norford, Emily, and Terra Virsilas. 2016. "What Can We Learn from Thailand's Inclusive Approach to Upgrading Informal Settlements?" *World Resources Institute: CityFix.* Accessed May 12, 2020. https://thecityfix.com/blog/thailands-inclusive-upgrading-informal-settlements-terra-virsilas-emily-norford/.

Nyhus, Philip, Hank Fischer, Francine Madden, and Steve Osofsky. 2008. "Taking the Bite Out of Wildlife Damage." *Conservation Journal* 4(2): 37–43.

Oman, William, and Romain Svartzman. 2021. "What Justifies Sustainable Finance Measures? Financial-Economic Interactions and Possible Implications for Policymakers." *CESifo Forum* 3/2021(22): 3–11.

Public Expenditure and Financial Accountability (PEFA). 2020. *Climate Responsive Public Financial Management Framework (PEFA Climate).* Public Expenditure and Financial Accountability. https://www.pefa.org/resources/climate-responsive-public-financial-management-framework-pefa-climate-piloting-phase.

Preuss, Paul. 2008. *IMPACTS: On the Threshold of Abrupt Climate Changes.* feature story, Berkeley Lab.

Rambaud, Alexandre, and Clément Feger. 2020. *Improving Nature's Visibility in Financial Accounting—CARE & Ecosystem-Centred Accounting.* Natural Capital Coalition.

Ranganathan, Janet, Daniel Vennard, Richard Waite, and et al. 2016. *Shifting Diets for a Sustainable Food Future.* World Resources Institute.

Reiter, Paul. 2001. "Climate Change and Mosquito-Borne Disease." *Environmental Health Perspectives* 109: 141–61.

Reuters. 2020. "The Plastic Pandemic: Covid-19 Trashed the Recycling Dream."

Rockström, Johan, Will Steffen, Kevin Noone, Asa Persson, F. Stuart Chapin III, Eric F. Lambin, et al. 2009. "A Safe Operating Space for Humanity." *Nature* 461: 472–5.

Rozenberg, Julie, and Marianne, Fay. 2019. *"Beyond the Gap: How Countries Can Afford the Infrastructure They Need while Protecting the Planet".* Washington, DC: World Bank.

Schleich, Joachim, Xavier Gassmann, Thomas Meissner, and Corinne Faure. 2019. "A Large-Scale Test of the Effects of Time Discounting, Risk Aversion, Loss Aversion, and Present Bias on Household Adoption of Energy-Efficient Technologies." *Energy Economics* 80: 377–93.

Schnabel, Isabel. 2020. *When Markets Fail—The Need for Collective Action in Tackling Climate Change*. Speech at the European Sustainable Finance Summit, Frankfurt am Main, September 28.

Solomon, Susan. 2019. "The Discovery of the Antarctic Ozone Hole." *Nature* 575: 46–7.

Staal, Arie, Ingo Fetzer, Lan Wang-Erlandsson, Joyce H.C. Bosmans, Stefan C. Dekker, Egbert H. van Nes, et al. 2020. "Hysteresis of Tropical Forests in the 21st Century." *Nature Communications* 11(4978).

Steffen, Will, Wendy Broadgate, Lisa Deutsch, Owen Gaffney, and Cornelia Ludwig. 2015. "The Trajectory of the Anthropocene: The Great Acceleration." *The Anthropocene Review* 2(1): 81–98.

Stern, Nicholas. 2007. *The Economics of Climate Change: The Stern Review*. Cambridge: Cambridge University Press.

Stern, Nicholas. 2015. *Why Are We Waiting?: The Logic, Urgency, and Promise of Tackling Climate Change*. Cambridge, MA: MIT Press.

Stern, Nicholas. 2020. *Financing Climate Ambition in the Context of Covid-19*. Grantham Research Institute on Climate Change and the Environment commentary.

Stern, Nicholas. 2021. *G7 Leadership for Sustainable, Resilient and Inclusive Economic Recovery and Growth—A Summary Report*. An independent report requested by the UK Prime Minister for the G7.

Stern, Nicholas, and Amar Bhattacharya. 2019. *The New Global Agenda:Scale, Urgency, and the Future of Multilateral Development Banks*. Revitalizing the Spirit of Bretton Woods, Bretton Woods Committee.

Stern, Nicholas, and Dimitri Zenghelis. 2021. *Fiscal Responsibility in Advanced Economies through Investment for Economic Recovery from the Covid-19 Pandemic*. Grantham Research Institute on Climate Change and the Environment and Centre for Climate Change Economics and Policy, London School of Economics and Political Science.

Stern, Nicholas, and Joseph Stiglitz. 2017. *Report of the High Level Commission on Carbon Pricing*. Paper of the Carbon Pricing Leadership Coalition, Washington, DC: World Bank.

Stern, Nicholas, and Joseph Stiglitz. 2021. *The Social Cost of Carbon, Risk, Distribution, Market Failures: An Alternative Approach*. NBER Working Paper 28472.

Stern, Nicholas, Sam Unsworth, Anna Valero, Dimitri Zenghelis, James Rydge, and Nick Robins. 2020. *Strategy, Investment, and Policy for a Strong and Sustainable Recovery: An Action Plan*. A CEP Covid-19 Analysis Paper No. 005.

Stiglitz, Joseph E., Amartya Sen, and Jean-Paul Fitoussi. 2009. *The Measurement of Economic Performance and Social Progress Revisited: Reflections and Overview*.

Paris: Commission on the Measurement of Economic Performance and Social Progress.

Surminski, Swenja, Laurence M. Bouwer, and Joanne Linnerooth-Bayer. 2016. "How Insurance Can Support Climate Resilience." *Nature Climate Change* 6: 333–4.

SYSTEMIQ. 2020. "The Paris Effect: How the Climate Agreement Is Reshaping the Global Economy."

The Coalition of Finance Ministers for Climate Actions. 2020. "Better Recovery, Better World: Resetting Climate Action in the Aftermath of the Covid-19 Pandemic."

The Coalition of Ministers for Climate Action. 2019. "Helsinki Principles."

The Global Commission on the Economy and Climate. 2018. "Unlocking the Inclusive Growth Story of the 21st Century: Accelerating Climate Action in Urgent Times." The New Climate Economy report.

Tooze, Adam. 2020. "We Are Living Through the First Economic Crisis of the Anthropocene." Article in *The Guardian*. May 7. https://www.theguardian.com/books/2020/may/07/we-are-living-through-the-first-economic-crisis-of-the-anthropocene.

Trisos, Christopher H., Cory Merow, and Alex L. Pigot. 2020. "The Projected Timing of Abrupt Ecological Disruption from Climate Change." *Nature* 580: 496–501.

Turner, Kerry, Thomas Badure, and Silvia Ferrini. 2019. "Natural Capital Accounting Perspectives: a Pragmatic Way Forward." *Ecosystem Health and Sustainability* 5(1): 237–41.

Tyndall, John. 1861. "On the Absorption and Radiation of Heat by Gases and Vapours, and on the Physical Connexion of Radiation, Absorption, and Conduction." *Philosophical Transactions of the Royal Society of London* 151: 1–36.

United Nations (UN). 2015. *Sendai Framework for Disaster Risk Reduction 2015–2030.* United Nations.

United Nations (UN). 2020. *UN-REDD Programme.* Accessed April 10, 2020. https://www.un-redd.org/.

United Nations Conference on Trade and Development (UNCTAD). 2019. *Commodity Dependence, Climate Change and Paris Agreement.* Commodities & Development Report. Geneva.

UNEP. 2008. *Payments for Ecosystem Services: Getting Started.* Forest Trends and The Katoomba Group, United Nations Environment Programme.

United Nations Environment Programme (UNEP). 2016. *The Adaptation Finance Gap.* United Nations Environment Programme. Nairobi, Kenya.

United Nations Environment Programme (UNEP). 2018. *Single-Use Plastic: Road to Sustainability.* United Nations Environment Programme. Nairobi, Kenya.

United Nations Environment Programme (UNEP). 2019. *Emissions Gap Report.* UN Environment Programme. Nairobi, Kenya.

United Nations Framework Convention on Climate Change (UNFCCC). 2020. "Paris Agreement." Accessed March 10, 2020. https://unfccc.int/process-and-meetings/the-paris-agreement/the-paris-agreement.

Vidal, John. 2020. "Destroyed Habitat Creates the Perfect Conditions for Coronavirus to Emerge." *ENSIE.* March 18. Accessed March 21, 2020. https://www.scientificamerican.com/article/destroyed-habitat-creates-the-perfect-conditions-for-coronavirus-to-emerge/?fbclid=IwAR3z0J2Z8gQTmld3zljwfENjmH1Y4aUm5mVOjXvZX-sfCM3ViGtsW50HlnhE.

Voosen, Paul. 2020. How a Team of Scientists Studying Drought Helped Build the World's Leading Famine Prediction Model. Published in *Science*: Climate, Earth. https://www.sciencemag.org/news/2020/04/how-team-scientists-studying-drought-helped-build-world-s-leading-famine-prediction

Weitzman, Martin. 2011. "Fat-Tailed Uncertainty in the Economics of Catastrophic Climate Change." *Review of Environmental Economics and Policy* 5 (2): 275–92.

Weitzman, Martin L. 1974. "Prices vs. Quantities." *Review of Economic Studies* 41(4): 477–91.

Westerhold, Thomas, Norbert Marwan, Anna Joy Drury, Diederik Liebrand, Claudia Agnini, Eleni Anagnostou, et al. 2020. "An Astronomically Dated Record of Earth's Climate and Its Predictability over the Last 66 Million Years." *Science* 369(6509): 1383–7.

White, Andy, and Alejandra Martin. 2002. *Who Owns the World's Forests? Forest Tenure and Public Forests in Transition.* Washington, DC: Forest Trends.

World Meteorological Organization (WMO). 2019. *Greenhouse Gas Bulletin.* No. 15, 25 November 2019, Geneva.

World Bank. 2019. "Global Program for Resilient Housing." World Bank Brief.

World Bank. 2020a. *Carbon Pricing Dashboard.* Web-portal. Accessed March 27, 2020. https://carbonpricingdashboard.worldbank.org/.

World Bank. 2020b. "Reversals of Fortune." Poverty and Shared Prosperity report, Washington, DC.

World Bank. 2020c. *World Development Indicators.* Accessed January 23, 2020. https://databank.worldbank.org/home.aspx.

World Ocean Review. 2020. *Fisheries.* Accessed April 10, 2020. https://worldoceanreview.com/en/wor-1/fisheries/fisheries-management/.

World Resources Institute (WRI). 2019. *GREEN TARGETS: A Tool To Compare Private Sector Banks' Sustainable Finance Commitments (as of July 2019).* Washington, DC.

Worldwide Fund for Nature (WWF). 2018. *Living Planet Report 2018: Aiming Higher.* Gland, Switzerland.

Worldwide Fund for Nature (WWF). 2019. *No Plastic in Nature: Assessing Plastic Ingestion from Nature to People.* Gland, Switzerland.

Xu, Chi, Timothy A. Kohler, Timothy M. Lenton, Jens-Christian Svenning, and Marten Scheffler. 2020. "Future of the Human Climate Niche." *PNAS* 117(21): 11350–5.

Zhang, Yi Ge, Mark Pagani, Zhonghui Liu, Steven M. Bohaty, and Robert DeConto. 2013. "A 40-Million-Year History of Atmospheric CO2." *Philosophical Transactions of the Royal Society A: Mathematical, Physical and Engineering Sciences* 371.

Zhong, Zhi-Ping, Natalie E. Solonenko, Yueh-Fen Li, Maria C. Gazitúa, Simon Roux, Mary E. Davis, et al. 2020. *Glacier Ice Archives Fifteen-Thousand-Year-Old Viruses.* preprint, bioRxiv.

21
Country Case Studies

Sriram Balasubramanian, Lahcen Bounader, Jana Bricco,
and Dmitry Vasilyev

I. Introduction

Countries' success in ensuring strong, sustainable, and inclusive growth has varied considerably.[1] In general, the share of the population that has access to basic services such as health, education, infrastructure, and finance is correlated with per capita income (Cerra 2021). The level of development is associated with a range of other policies and outcomes too, such as the ability to raise tax revenue and use it effectively for social safety nets and initiatives to strengthen the business environment. However, correlation is not determination, and at every development level, countries' performances differ. In addition, countries may do well on some dimensions but fall short on others.

Achieving inclusive growth requires policy actions across many fronts. How have countries fared along different dimensions of inclusive growth? What have been countries' experiences with implementing reforms to improve it? This chapter aims to take a holistic review of policies and actions that were effective in making growth inclusive. The chapter reviews some case studies in countries' experiences, with examples drawn from different regions and levels of development.

We begin these case studies with the example of the Nordic countries, which are typically among the top performers on nearly every dimension of well-being. For example, the Nordic countries regularly rank at or near the top of the World Happiness Report and score first in other cross-country rankings of quality of life (e.g., the OECD better lives index). We examine the key features of the policy framework that has driven these successes.

Emerging and developing economies face stiff challenges. At lower levels of development, countries have to make difficult choices in prioritizing the use of

[1] We thank Valerie Cerra, Martin Schindler, Barry Eichengreen, Craig Beaumont, Miguel Segoviano, Khaled Sakr, Yuanyan Sophia Zhang, Valentina Flamini, Prakash Loungani and other IMF collegues as well as participants in the Inclusive Growth book seminar series organized by the IMF Institute for Capacity Developments for their comments.

Sriram Balasubramanian, Lahcen Bounader, Jana Bricco, and Dmitry Vasilyev, *Country Case Studies* In: *How to Achieve Inclusive Growth*. Edited by: Valerie Cerra, Barry Eichengreen, Asmaa El-Ganainy, and Martin Schindler, Oxford University Press. © Sriram Balasubramanian, Lahcen Bounader, Jana Bricco, and Dmitry Vasilyev 2022. DOI: 10.1093/oso/9780192846938.003.0021

their limited resources. They face an array of hurdles such as poor infrastructure, a legacy of weak governance, less diversified economies, and a large share of the population in poverty or located in hard-to-reach rural areas. Even so, while it may be difficult to replicate the broad successes of the Nordic countries, EMDEs made progress along some dimensions.

Following the discussion of the Nordic model, we next present case studies of select EMDE countries. The countries of India, Brazil, and Egypt—representing three different regions—have faced different challenges and headwinds based on their circumstances. In many dimensions of inclusive growth, they still have scope for considerable improvements. Even so, they have undertaken successful reforms in some areas, providing hope that a commitment to reform can bear fruit. Their experiences can provide lessons for other countries, especially for other EMDEs with similar resource constraints and challenges.

II. The Nordic Model of Inclusive Growth

The Nordics are widely seen as being successful in achieving inclusive growth, although they still face challenges in some areas (Figure 21.1). For this chapter, the Nordics comprise Denmark, Finland, Norway, and Sweden. These countries share some common features in their policy frameworks, often referred to as the "Nordic model," but there are significant policy differences among this group, and their policy frameworks have evolved over time.

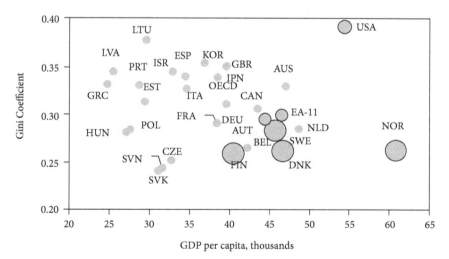

Figure 21.1 GDP per Capita and Gini Coefficient (x-axis, index; y axis, in thousands USD PPP-20210)

Source: OECD

A. Main Features of the Nordic Model

The foundation of the Nordic model is a strong economy, with high levels of employment and productivity, which generates the resources needed to support strong social services. A central theme of the model is maintaining the flexibility to adapt to developments in trade and technology. Key elements of the Nordic model include:

- *Cooperative labor markets*: enterprises and unions seek sustainable wages and conditions, providing an environment conducive for investment and training. Flexibility to adopt new technology or changes to improve efficiency is enabled, such as by employers and unions providing re-employment support for those losing jobs as seen in Sweden. Wage dispersion is low (Figure 21.2), reflecting the bargaining priorities of unions to protect low-income workers.
- *Competitive markets and innovation*: productivity is likely promoted by high openness to trade and sound regulation of goods, services, and network industries that limits entry/exit barriers which in turn promote competition and innovation. R&D spending and intangible investment are relatively high and digitalization amongst firms is one of the highest in the OECD. (See Figure 21.3.)
- *Strong social services and welfare are underpinned by sound fiscal policy*: Investment in public education and health services supports high-quality human capital, while universal social welfare limits poverty, together with promoting social inclusion. As a result, government spending is high relative to GDP (Figure 21.4), especially in Finland and Denmark (2nd and 3rd in the OECD at around 55 percent of GDP).[2]

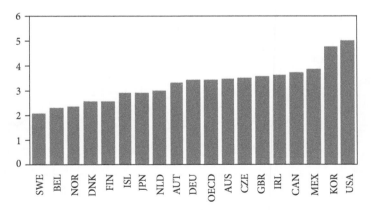

Figure 21.2 Wage Dispersion
(Income decile 9/decile 1)
Source: OECD

---

[2] OECD statistics: https://data.oecd.org/gga/general-government-spending.htm

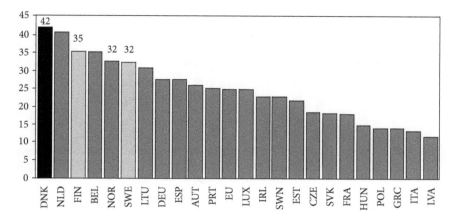

Figure 21.3 Firms with High Level of Digital Intensity
(Percent of firms)

Source: OECD.

Note: Data of Australia, New Zealand and Switzerland are from 2017, Austria and Colombia from 2019, and the others from 2018.

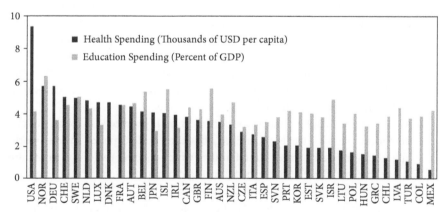

Figure 21.4 Social Services: Public Spending on Health and Education, 2019
(Thousands of US dollars per capita and percent of GDP)
Source: OECD

- *Tax burdens are relatively high*, but the tax system seeks to limit the impact on potential growth, by relying to a relatively large extent on income and consumption taxation. In particular, personal income taxes are among the highest in the OECD, yet the labor tax wedge (including social security and payroll taxes) is contained, helping to protect employment (Figure 21.5).[3,4] Corporate income tax revenue is modestly below OECD average, limiting

[3] OECD statistics on income revenues: https://data.oecd.org/tax/tax-revenue.htm#indicator-chart
[4] OECD statistics on labor tax wedge: https://data.oecd.org/tax/tax-wedge.htm#indicator-chart

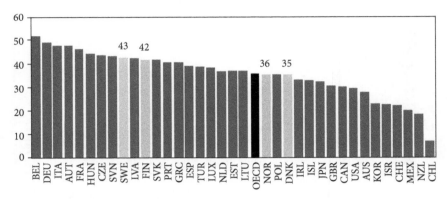

Figure 21.5 Tax Wedge, 2019
(Percent of labor cost)
Source: OECD

drag on investment and productivity. Taxes on goods and services are relatively high, yet these have less impact on growth. The prudent medium-term fiscal policy supports moderate public debt, providing fiscal space to cushion shocks, and underpinning public confidence in the ability of the government to sustain strong services and welfare support, which helps make high taxes more acceptable. Kleven (2014) finds that the high tax levels in the Nordic countries are supported by broad tax bases and substantial third-party reporting, which discourage tax evasion, while the subsidization and public provision of goods that are complementary to working (e.g. subsidized child care) encourages a high labor supply.[5]

- *Gender equity*: High female labor participation is promoted through policies including parental leave, subsidized childcare, and scope for shorter working hours for those with young families which made it easier for women to enter the workforce and return following childbirth. Gender wage gaps are among the smallest across OECD countries.
- *Climate change*: The Nordics also have some of the most ambitious climate targets in the world and invest a considerable amount into climate change mitigation making them leaders in this area as well. Most Nordic countries implemented their climate targets into domestic law binding future ruling parties to abide by these reduction goals in the next years to come. Sweden is currently topping the Climate Change Performance Index (CCPI) and Denmark has announced to end all oil and gas activities in the North Sea by 2050. However, challenges remain, while the Nordics are on track to meet their EU climate targets, current annual rates of reductions are below what is required to meet their own targets.

---

[5] Kleven (2014) also considers social and cultural influences and finds that correlations are quite striking and favor the notion that the Nordics are more socially motivated, but that the evidence is difficult to interpret.

B. Inclusive Growth Policies in Nordic Countries

The following sections highlight key aspects of the policy frameworks in Denmark and Sweden as an example.

Denmark

Denmark enjoys one of the world's highest standards of living. Strong institutions combined with sound economic and social policies have delivered robust economic performance and high social inclusion. The business climate ranks among the best in the world and education levels are high. Measures of well-being suggest Danes are among the happiest people in the world, as in other Nordic countries (IMF 2019a).

Inequality effects of new policies are usually analyzed, reflecting the importance attached to equality by Danish society. If policies are estimated to lead to sizable negative impacts on equality their political feasibility is questionable (IMF 2016). While this approach is not enshrined in law, it is a common practice when new policies are discussed in parliament.[6]

The "flexicurity" labor market model has fostered high employment and incomes with low-income inequality. Denmark's labor market model combines flexibility for businesses with security for its citizens through active labor market policies (ALPMs), high mobility, and a comprehensive income safety net (Figure 21.6). Despite high union and collective bargaining coverage, Danish employers can hire and fire employees without large costs, so they can quickly adapt to changing market conditions. In return, laid-off workers are supported for up to two years through an unemployment insurance fund with high replacement rates for low-income groups (up to 90 percent of previous earnings).

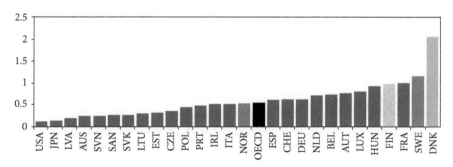

Figure 21.6 Public Spending on Active Labor Market Policies
(2016 or latest available year, percent of GDP)
Source: OECD Economic Survey Denmark 2019.

---

[6] According to Danish officials, before policies are enshrined in law, there are opportunities to discuss their impact on inequality during parliamentary debates. However, "inequality impact studies" are not mandatory.

In addition, they receive extensive job search services and educational training that is matched with current skill shortages, and employers that hire the unemployed or unskilled workers can receive subsidies.[7] Nonetheless, the very high ALMP spending does not translate in higher employment for the low-skilled when compared with countries that spend much less on ALMPs (OECD 2019).

Recent reforms have succeeded in boosting labor participation rates and reducing long-term unemployment, but challenges remain. Policies have been designed to keep people in employment longer, incentivize labor participation, avoid inactivity traps, upgrade skills, and improve migrant integration. For example, the 2011 pension reform raised the employment rate of older workers by linking the statutory retirement age to life expectancy. More recent initiatives include the 2018 tax reform that increased deductions for pension contributions. Nonetheless, youth inactivity has risen since the crisis due to the high skills needed to enter the Danish labor market. Moreover, skill shortages are increasing and access to skilled foreign labor remains cumbersome.

Sweden

Strong employment has contributed to enhanced well-being and reduced poverty in Sweden. Sweden is a knowledge-based economy, well-integrated in global value chains, which ensures high standards of living, well-being, income, and gender equality, as well as high environmental quality to its inhabitants.

The policy framework in Sweden, the so-called "Swedish model," puts inclusive growth at its core and is based on three pillars. In particular, it aims to "increase prosperity to the benefit of all, while safeguarding the autonomy and independence of citizens" and is based on three pillars: (i) a flexible labor market, (ii) a universal welfare system, and (iii) an economic framework that promotes openness and stability.[8] To ensure the effective functioning of these pillars, a number of prerequisites are present in Sweden: strong public finances, trust in the system, high employment, and strong social partners.

The first pillar is a flexible labor market that supports adaptation to new developments and technologies. The characteristics of the Swedish labor market are coordinated wage formation, an active labor market policy including employer-financed "job-security councils," and generous unemployment benefits. Wages in Sweden are set through collective agreements between the unions and employers rather than through state interventions and laws. For instance, there are no statutory minimum wages in Sweden. In the past, unions have been usually constructive and embraced transformation in return for income security and active labor support measures. This framework resulted in steady real wage growth that has

---

[7] Danish Agency for Labor Market and Recruitment, "Flexicurity" https://star.dk/en/about-the-danish-agency-for-labour-market-and-recruitment/flexicurity/

[8] Government Offices of Sweden (2017) "The Swedish Model."

been in line with productivity advancements. Three active labor market policies support mobility in the labor market by (i) providing training to laid-off workers, (ii) providing subsidies to employers that hire unemployed people, and (iii) matching unemployed people with jobs. A unique feature of the Swedish model is job-security councils. These are funded by employers and actively help laid-off workers to find a job as soon as possible through financial support and job counseling. By "not protecting the job but the worker" this active labor market policy is enabling Sweden to support structural economic change. Lastly, generous unemployment benefits provide income security but are made conditional upon active job search or participation in training to incentives work.

The second pillar is a generous welfare policy that aims to achieve high and equitably distributed prosperity while promoting high employment and competitiveness. Swedish welfare policy can be distinguished by a high degree of universality, i.e. public services and transfers are designed as social rights that cover the entire population and not only disadvantaged groups. This approach avoids costly needs-testing and enhances the efficiency of the system.[9] This covers welfare services such as childcare, schools, and healthcare, social transfer systems such as social insurance, parental leave insurance, and unemployment insurance. These services support a high employment rate among women and the highest employment rate in the EU (Figure 21.7).

The third pillar is the orientation of economic policies towards a stable economy while promoting openness and competition. The mandate of shielding the economy against major fluctuations is with the central bank. The Riksbank is tasked with attaining a 2 percent inflation target and supporting sustainable growth and a high level of employment. Fiscal policy aims to contribute to prosperity and equitable

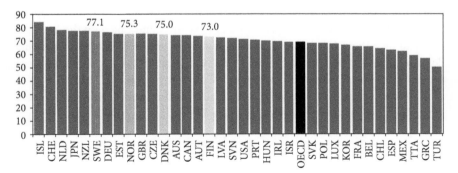

Figure 21.7 Employment Rates, 2019
(Total, annual % of working age population)
Source: OECD

---

[9] While need-tested services also exist in Sweden, there are intended to work as the last social safety net when the rights-based system is insufficient.

distribution of prosperity gains while stabilizing the economy through unemployment insurance and fiscal support in severe economic situations. An important prerequisite for this is Sweden's large fiscal buffers.

Sweden Has Adopted Labor Market Reforms in Recent Years, but Challenges Remain

Seeking to raise employment of the low-skilled and migrants, the budget for 2018 boosted resources for education and streamlined active labor market policies with the aim of increasing employer participation. Nonetheless, unemployment rates of the foreign-born and low-skilled much exceed that of natives, partly reflecting bargained high de facto minimum wages which do not allow for a wage adjustment for lower-skilled.[10,11] Further reforms, including employment protection and public employment services, should support the employment of the low-skilled and migrants, aided by enhanced education and training (IMF 2019b). Sweden also has a long history of highly concentrated wealth, high regional inequality and has experienced one of the fastest increases in inequality in recent years.[12]

The Nordic model may not be easily replicated in a wholesale manner, but it may provide inspiration for policies other countries may consider for improving inclusive growth. The sustainability of the Nordic model hinges on a high level of social trust and responsibility, including strong social norms to be working despite the availability of social supports. These social conditions including a more ethnically and culturally homogeneous population have facilitated high levels of trust and cooperation and high tax compliance. As a result, Nordic policies and institutions cannot be easily exported to other countries that are more heterogeneous or very large. Nonetheless, it is still important to learn from it and adapt parts of it that are transferable.[13] For instance, in 2008 the European Council adopted the common principles of flexicurity and called on the Member States to take them into account when drawing up and implementing "national flexicurity pathways."[14] To help assess progress made in the implementation of the flexicurity principles, the Employment Committee agreed in 2012 on a set of monitoring indicators. These indicators are used in the annual Joint Employment Report on employment developments in the EU.

---

[10] Legally there are no minimum wages in Sweden.

[11] Ljungqvist and Sargent (2008) show how unemployment dynamics depend upon a country's labor market policies through their effect on job separation and finding rates, which depend on the interaction of policies and shocks.

[12] https://nordregio.org/nordregio-magazine/issues/state-of-the-nordic-region-2020/sweden-inequality-in-sweden-grows-much-faster-than-in-the-nordics-overall/

[13] https://theconversation.com/what-the-world-can-learn-about-equality-from-the-nordic-model-99797

[14] http://ec.europa.eu/social/BlobServlet?docId=1515&langId=en

III. India: Economic Reforms for Inclusion, 1990–2020

A. Introduction

India has been one of the fastest-growing emerging market economies over the last few decades. The country's rapid growth combined with a large population, demographics, and abundant natural resources makes it an interesting case study to understand inclusive growth and its challenges (Figure 21.8).

B. Main Features of the Indian Model

The main features of the Indian growth model have been a combination of high growth driven by economic reforms, improved macro-economic stability, and welfare schemes for the poor. All of these have contributed to enormous growth and poverty reduction.

High Growth Through Economic Reforms
GDP has grown almost five-fold since the 1990s and the per capita income has increased by four times over the same time period (Figure 21.9). This increase in growth was kick-started by the liberalization reforms in the 1990s and subsequent structural reforms over the years (Ahluwalia 2019). These reforms include dismantling of the "license-raj" (industrial licensing), opening up of Foreign Direct Investment (FDI) in many sectors, and liberalization of trade policies. While some of these reforms have taken some time, they have been pursued by various administrations. Recently, the introduction of pro-poor agricultural marketing reforms announced by the National Democratic Alliance (NDA) government is

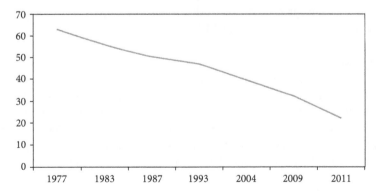

Figure 21.8 Poverty Headcount Ratio at $1.90 a day (2011 PPP) (% of population)
Source: World Bank

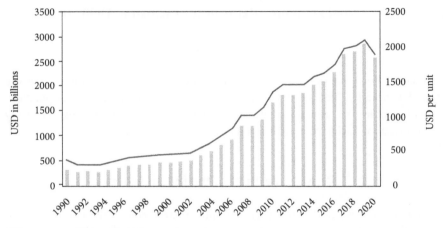

Figure 21.9 GDP and GDP per capita (1990–2020)
Source: IMF WEO October 2020

Table 21.1 Growth Rates for Country Classifications 1980–2023

		1992–2002	2003–2017	2018–2023
Advanced economies	3.0	2.7	1.7	1.9
All EMDEs	3.4	3.8	6.0	5.0
India	5.2	5.8	7.6	7.9
China	9.2	10.2	9.4	6.1
ASEAN-10	6.1	4.6	5.4	5.0
All EMDEs excl. India and China	2.6	2.6	4.3	3.7

Source: IMF and (Ahluwalia M. S. 2019)

expected to boost growth.[15] Many policymakers consider this rapid growth to be central to the poverty reduction story (Bhalla 2002).

The increase in growth is noteworthy when compared with other countries during similar time periods (Table 21.1).

Macro-economic Stability

India's focus on macro-economic stability in recent decades has been pivotal to its growth story. The continuity of economic policies aimed at fiscal prudence along with the Reserve Bank of India's (RBI) monetary policies has provided a good platform for sustained growth. In addition, much of this growth has been accomplished with a sustainable level of government debt. That is, even though the average ratio of public debt to GDP has been high, much of India's debt profile is

---

[15] https://www.ifpri.org/blog/covid-19-crisis-opportunity-long-delayed-agricultural-reforms-india

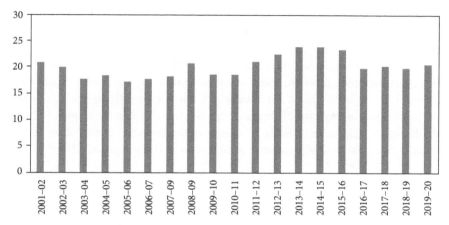

Figure 21.10 Ratio of External Debt to GDP (Percentage to GDP, 2001–2020)
Source: Reserve Bank of India Statistics

consistent with debt sustainability given that it has been largely held by residents, denominated in domestic currency, and with a relatively long maturity.[16] The ratio of external debt to GDP has been relatively low (Figure 21.10).

Recent policies such as the Goods and Services Tax (GST) and the Insolvency and Bankruptcy Code (IBC) have further provided a stable environment for investors. Furthermore, the introduction of inflation targeting in 2016 by the Reserve Bank of India (RBI) helped to reduce fiscal dominance in the economy and the influence of inflation in reducing real incomes of India's poor.[17]

Redistribution Through Welfare Policies

The welfare policies of successive administrations in the country were major drivers of poverty reduction besides economic growth. Overall, India has a very thin benefit system. Since there is no social security system, welfare benefits are focused on providing income support to the poorest of the poor and comprise mainly of food price subsidies and subsidies for heating oil and fuel. The previous administration (from 2004–2014) focused on food subsidies and cash transfers but this resulted in large leakages in the system (due to corruption) including food wastages. The Mahatma Gandhi Rural Employment Guarantee Scheme (MGNREGS) was one such initiative that was started in 2005. It was one of the world's largest employment guarantee schemes that provided direct cash to the poor. This accounted for an average of 2.3 percent of GDP in 2008 (Ahmad 2013). The employment scheme helped pioneer cash transfers in India until 2014.

---

[16] https://www.imf.org/en/News/Articles/2019/12/23/pr19488-india-imf-executive-board-concludes-2019-article-iv-consultation

[17] https://economictimes.indiatimes.com/news/economy/indicators/india-adopts-inflation-target-of-4-for-next-five-years-under-monetary-policy-framework/articleshow/53564923.cms

However, there were leakages in the system that led to the NDA government using digitization and the Direct Benefits Transfer (DBT) system (discussed below) to improve efficiency.

Since 2014, a variety of other schemes have also been introduced to reduce leakages through digitization, and also improve sanitation and health care among the poor. The Swachh Bharat initiative, which was started with the goal of universal sanitation coverage for all Indians, has improved the lives of poor Indians significantly.[18] The scheme helped to improve the coverage of sanitation in the country from less than 50 percent in 2014 to almost 100 percent in 2019.[19]

C. Inclusive Growth in India

Inequality in India has been increasing in recent years driven largely by urban inequality (Balasubramanian, Kumar, and Loungani 2021). As seen in Figure 21.11, the net Gini coefficient for consumption has been gradually increasing in the last few decades. Compared to other countries such as China and Indonesia, the increase in inequality is not as large.[20]

One can also measure inequality through the Growth Incidence Curves (GIC). The GIC could be represented in terms of growth rate in incomes for a percentile of the income distribution (Ravallion and Chen 2003) or by using the mean

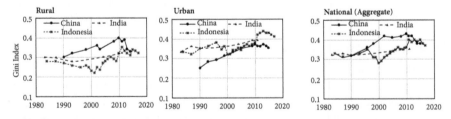

Figure 21.11 Comparative Consumption Gini Coefficients: China, India, and Indonesia

Source: Balasubramanian, Kumar, and Loungani 2021.

---

[18] The initiative "aimed at eliminating open defecation in rural areas during the period 2014 to 2019 through mass behavior change, construction of household-owned and community-owned toilets and establishing mechanisms for monitoring toilet construction and usage." https://swachhbharatmission.gov.in/SBMCMS/about-us.htm

[19] These and other key structural reforms, and their contribution to enhancing gender and income equality, are described in recent IMF India Article IV Staff Reports and India Selected Issues papers (see IMF, India: 2017 Article IV Consultation Staff Report. IMF Country Report No. 17/54, 2017a, (IMF, India: 2017 Selected Issues. IMF Country Report No. 17/55, 2017b)) and the references contained therein.

[20] It's important to use this as a benchmark but the Gini on its own has many shortcomings. An important caveat here is that all the countries have consumption survey data so the comparison is relevant.

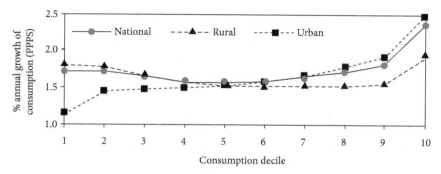

Figure 21.12 Growth Incidence Curve (1983–2011)
Source: WB Povcalnet database

income in the quantile group for a percentile of the income distribution as in (Lakner and Milanovic 2016). As shown in Figure 21.12, we use the mean income in the quantile group similar to (Lakner and Milanovic 2016).[21] For every decile of the population and subpopulation (rural, urban) we compute annual consumption growth rates in 2011 PPP dollars. An upward sloping GIC indicates higher growth among relatively richer groups (more unequal) while if all growth is equally shared by all quantiles of the population, then the GIC should be flat. As seen in Figure 21.12, for the national aggregate, the 1st decile bottom 10 percent grew by only 1.7 percent whereas the 10th decile (topmost decile) top 10 percent grew by almost 2.38 percent from 1983–2011.[22] Similarly, for the rural areas, the 1st decile bottom 10 percent grew by 1.75 percent whereas the 10th decile top 10 percent grew by almost 1.95 percent. Unsurprisingly, much of the inequality seems to be in the urban areas with the 1st decile bottom 10 percent growing by 1.25 percent (lesser than the rural bottom 10 percent, 1st decile) and the 10th decile top 10 percent growing by 2.5 percent (much higher than the rural top 10 percent, 10th decile) respectively. This further corroborates that much of the Indian inequality story is driven by urban inequality than anything else.

Poverty reduction in India has been achieved through a combination of rapid growth and redistributive welfare policies in the country. Even though many efforts have been done to eradicate poverty, approximately 270 million people are still considered to be poor.

Economic growth has played an important role in eradicating poverty. Besides improving the quality of life in the upper and middle classes, rapid growth has

[21] Note that this GIC is anonymous and that we are not accounting for movement of individuals between deciles over time.

[22] The decile levels arrange the data in order from lowest to highest and are done on a scale of one to ten where each successive number corresponds to an increase of 10 percentage points. In the case of GIC, the 1st decile represents the 10th percentile of the consumption distribution whereas the 10th decile value represents the 100th percentile of the consumption distribution.

Table 21.2 Annual GDP (%) and Population in Poverty for India 1993–2012

	Annual growth of GDP (%)		Population in poverty	
	Economy	Agriculture	% in poverty	Millions
1993–1994	0	0	45.3	403.7
2004–2005	6.2	2.9	37.2	407.1
2011–2012	8.5	3.5	21.9	269.8

Note: The annual averages are for the period preceding the year indicated. Thus, 6.2% is the annual average growth of GDP from 1993–1994 to 2004–2005.

Sources: Central Statistics Office (2014) and Rangarajan (2014).

also reduced poverty significantly. Table 21.2 below highlights the impact economic growth had on poverty in the last few decades:

As seen in the table, the percentage of the population in poverty fell from 403.7 million (45.3 percent) to 269.8 million (21.9 percent) people within the span of two decades. Much of this correlation can be attributed to the vast set of opportunities that opened up for the poor as a result of rapid growth during this time. It was also during this phase that education and health indicators for the poor improved significantly. Besides growth, redistribution policies mentioned earlier also helped achieve inclusive growth.

One of the main recent re-distribution initiatives has been the Direct Benefit Transfers (DBT) to the lowest income people in India. With the aim of improving the efficiency of welfare schemes to improve targeting of beneficiaries, deduplication, and reduction of fraud, the DBT was formally announced as a flagship initiative in 2013 (Narayanan 2013).[23] The JAM trinity (Economic Survey 2015/2016)—Jan Dhan, Aadhar, and Mobile—has further improved the efficiency of the DBT scheme.[24] The Aadhar initiative has ensured that over a billion Indians have a digital ID and there has been an equal number of mobile connections in the country. Both of these have been integrated with the Pradhan Mantri Jan Dhan Yogana scheme (Today 2019) which has created more than 410 million bank accounts for Indians who are poor. One of the biggest advantages of the DBT scheme is that the transfers are targeted to persons with incomes below the poverty line, i.e the 10th and 20th decile levels in the GIC shown earlier. While there are still data challenges in terms of micro-data, general trends seem to indicate substantive progress in uplifting the poor.

The evolution of DBT in recent years has improved the efficiency of direct transfers significantly. Figure 21.13 below shows the evolution of DBT transfers

---

[23] See IMF, India: 2017 Article IV Consultation Staff Report. IMF Country Report No. 17/54, 2017a.

[24] Pradhan Mantri Jandan Yogana (PMJY) is the flagship scheme to open bank accounts for the poor. Aadhar is the world's largest bio-metric exercise which has created more than a billion digital IDs for residents in India. Mobile refers to more than 700 million mobile phones in India. The JAM trinity integrates all these three features to enable DBT transfers.

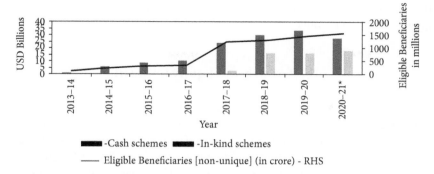

-Cash schemes ■■■ -In-kind schemes

—— Eligible Beneficiaries [non-unique] (in crore) - RHS

Figure 21.13 DBT Overall Progress vs Year 2013–2020/21

Note: *2020–21 as of 2/14/2021
Source: Government of India DBT data

from 2013 onwards until early 2021. The DBT transfers have increased from almost 1,034 million USD in 2013/14 to almost 33,660 million USD in 2018 (approximately 1.3 percent of India's GDP) followed by approximately further 27,757 million USD till early-2021. There has been a more than 50 percent increase in transfers since data was first shared in 2013. The integration of the JAM Trinity has accelerated significantly and the resulting improvements in efficiency have further improved the outcomes especially in the context of identification of fake accounts and reduction of corruption due to the elimination of middlemen in many of these transactions (Kumar 2019).

There are many plausible scenarios through which this could impact inequality in India. Since the DBT scheme is targeted at the lower decile levels, i.e. the transfers are directly transferred to the 10th and 20th decile of the population, if all of the efficiency gains are transferred back to the DBT schemes, it could result in strong income growth of the poor and could reduce inequality between the lower and top decile levels. If the efficiency gains were used elsewhere other than the DBT schemes, the reduction in inequality could be lower. Lastly, if the expansion of DBT continues for the next 5–10 years, there could be substantial growth in incomes for the 10th and 20th decile levels, further reducing inequality between the lower and the top decile levels.

There are also challenges within the DBT system that needs to be met to sustain outcomes. These include the need for greater penetration of the JAM trinity among the remaining population, more tracing and elimination of fake recipients, and improvements in the infrastructure to sustain these transfers at a larger scale. Data privacy concerns, and as a consequence, access to micro-data for researchers also need to be addressed as India ramps up these initiatives.

In retrospect, the Indian inclusive growth model provides an important perspective in addressing inequality. While it is still a work in progress, it provides a large enough case study for other countries to learn from, especially on the impact efficacy of the welfare schemes mentioned above. A combination of rapid growth, macro-economic stability, and targeted welfare schemes can promote inclusive growth as shown in India.

IV. Growth and Equity in Brazil

Brazil has been striving to strengthen its inclusive growth since the early 2000s. The commodity boom of 2000 to 2014 and social policies of the 2000s improved GDP growth and equity and reduced both informality and poverty. At the same time, growth in Brazil was still lower than that of its peers. The 2015–2016 crisis and subsequent slowdown once again reinforced the need for Brazil to improve its inclusive growth. The case of Brazil allows us to explore how long-standing growth constraints and successful macroeconomic and social reforms affect development.

A. Growth Dynamics

Since 2000, growth in Brazil, on average, underperformed average growth in EMDEs and emerging Asian economies (Figure 21.14, left chart). Albeit slower than in its peers, growth had been accelerating in the 1990–2000s, supported by the commodity boom and increasing external demand. However, in 2015–2016, large macroeconomic imbalances, a loss of investors' and consumers' confidence, lower commodity prices, and tight financing conditions triggered a deep recession.

Brazil grew slower than its peers with similar income per capita. Figure 21.14 (right chart) illustrates a standard growth theory idea that countries at a higher income level grow slower. Since per capita GDP in Brazil in 2000 was above that of Emerging Asian economies, the theory predicts that Brazil should have grown slower than them in the years that followed. Slower convergence with advanced economies and slower growth would, in this model, be explained by the smaller gap between Brazil and advanced economies. However, between 2000 and 2015, Brazil grew even slower than most economies with similar income per capita due to country-specific growth constraints (Figure 21.14, right chart accordingly shows that economies with income per capita broadly similar to Brazil grew faster, as indicated by their position above Brazil).

Hausmann et al. (2005) and Arnold (2011) found that low domestic savings and high cost of finance were binding constraints for growth. Hausmann et al. (2005) noted that both saving and investment rates were low.[25] At the same time, Brazil actively borrowed abroad and was limited by external borrowing

---

[25] Gross national saving and total investment averaged 18–19 percent of GDP in the 2010s and declined by 1–2 percent of GDP in the 2010s.

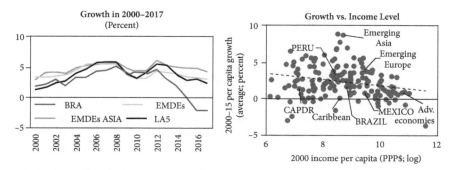

Figure 21.14 Growth Dynamics

Sources: World Bank, World Development Indicators; IMF staff estimates.

constraints. Brazil also had high real interest rates and loan-deposit interest spreads. These high interest rates and accumulating external debt indicated that Brazil's growth constraint stemmed from low domestic savings rather than low return on investment.[26] Entrepreneurs wanted to invest despite a weak business environment, high taxes, inadequate infrastructure, and insufficient human capital but were limited by Brazil's constrained financial resources.

Accumulated fiscal imbalances contributed to the 2015–2016 recession and became an important constraint on subsequent growth. Unsustainable public finances and a governance crisis caused large macroeconomic and policy uncertainty. As of 2018, Brazil had higher debt and taxes, and a weaker business environment relative to its peers (Balasubramanian et al. 2021). Given its relatively young population, public pension spending in Brazil is high, amounting to about 14 percent of GDP in 2018. Large pension expenditure stemmed from low retirement age (54 vs 64 years in the OECD economies), generous benefits relative to earnings (70 vs 53 percent in the OECD), and special regimes for civil servants and armed forces (IMF 2019). High-skilled workers and public employees benefited from the pension system more than the low-skilled and those in rural areas, as (the present discounted value of) the difference between lifetime pension benefits and contributions were higher (IMF 2019). Reducing pension and other current expenditures became a key near-term task.

Between 2016 and 2019, Brazil passed several important laws improving fiscal sustainability. It introduced a fiscal rule imposing a ceiling on current expenditure. The landmark pension law, approved in October 2019, was expected to reduce spending by 11 percent of GDP over ten years relative to the counterfactual

---

[26] Capital inflows could not compensate for low domestic savings and provide enough financing for investment. In emerging market economies, domestic saving is positively correlated with investment—the empirical puzzle named after Feldstein and Horioka (FH). Using panel data analysis, David et al. (2020) show that lower domestic saving causes lower investment, particularly in emerging market economies.

without this reform. The new pension law was also intended to improve domestic savings and address an important growth constraint.

B. Inclusive Policies

With growth in 2000 to 2014 being higher than in the 1990s, Brazil achieved significant progress in the reduction of poverty and informality before the recent recession of 2015–2016. Between 2000–2014, the poverty rate declined from 9.9 to 2.4 percent but somewhat increased during the 2015–2016 recession (Figure 21.15, left chart). The female labor force participation rate continued its rising trend in the early 2000s and stabilized around 55 percent after 2004. Available survey data shows a decline in informality from 34 to 28 percent of adults between 2005 and 2015.[27]

Brazil was able to reduce its poverty rate more than many other counties with similar GDP growth rates and initial poverty rates (Figure 21.15, right chart). The 2003–2013 commodity boom that drove GDP growth was particularly helpful in reducing poverty rates, as it created a demand for a low-skilled labor force. In addition, innovations in social assistance contributed to poverty reduction in Brazil.

The 2000–2014 commodity boom reduced poverty and informality rates by boosting demand for a low-skilled labor force and providing resources for fiscal expenditure (IMF 2018). Labor-intensive domestic mineral mines were especially helpful in reducing poverty, as they increased employment. Capital-intensive off-shore oil and gas producers contributed to the reduction of poverty mostly through the fiscal channel: the government had resources to increase public

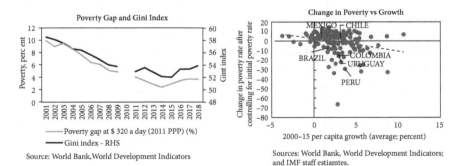

Figure 21.15 Inequality and Poverty

---

[27] An informal worker is a salaried worker in small firms, non-professional self-employed, and zero-income worker.

investment and employment. Higher-income due to the commodity boom also increased domestic demand and drew labor from agricultural and informal sectors into services and construction.

Brazil has been at the forefront of anti-poverty government policies. In 2003, Brazil launched the Bolsa Familia Program (BFP). In 2015, this program constituted 0.44 percent of GDP or one-third of the annual spending on the social safety net program (almost two-thirds belonged to social pensions) (World Bank 2018). This program provides conditional cash transfers (CCTs) to the extremely poor while supporting human capital accumulation by requiring better school attendance, vaccination, and pre-natal visits. About 60 percent of the poorest quintile receive CCTs and about 80 percent of CCTs go to the two poorest quantiles (World Bank 2018). In 2018, more than 20 percent of the population was enrolled in the BFP. The BFP helps increase women's share in the household income, as 90 percent of direct recipients are women.

While the BFP has clearly been instrumental in supporting the poor, its effects on (formal) employment have been the focus of many studies. Potentially, larger social assistance and higher tax rates on marginal earnings can reduce labor supply (Moffit 2002; Borjas 2005). In addition, the BFP eligibility criteria can potentially create incentives to stay in the informal economy: informal workers can underreport their incomes to become eligible for stable BFP transfers. However, Fruttero et al. (2020) found that the BFP has been instrumental in reducing informality and supporting formal labor market participation for both men and women, especially in younger cohorts. Fruttero et al. (2020) offer two explanations why CCTs improve formal labor market participation: (i) transfers cover the costs of job searching; (ii) they also improve psychological well-being that is necessary to break free from a cycle of poverty (Mullainathan and Shafir 2013).

Brazil has reduced the gender gap between 1990 and 2014. The female labor force participation rate increased from 42 percent in 1990 to about 55 percent in 2004 and plateaued afterward. Women's relative wages have also improved: women's wages were only 53 percent of men's wages in 1995; this share increased to 70 percent in 2014 (Pinheiro et al. 2016). According to the WEF's Global Gender Gap Index, the gender gap declined from 35 percent to 31 percent between 2006–2014.[28] A decline in the educational gap between men and women played a major role in these improvements: by 1991 women had more years of education than men and by 2000 this gap had increased further, while overall years of education continued to increase both for women and men (Beltrão and Alves 2013). Policies also contributed to this positive dynamic. For example, the

---

[28] The Global Gender Gap Index consists of four sub-categories: economic participation and opportunity, educational attainment, health and survival, and political empowerment.

administration of President Lula de Silva introduced the National Plan for Women's Policies in 2004 focusing on women's access to education, financial services, the labor market, health services, and protection against violence.

While Brazil has reduced inequality to an extent, it remains one of the most unequal economies in the world. Between 2000–2014, the Gini coefficient declined from 58.4 to 51.9 (Figure 21.15, left chart). Using state-level Gini coefficients, Goes and Karpowicz (2017) found that labor income growth, formalization, and schooling contributed to the decline in inequality during 2004–2014. However, the Gini coefficient is based on surveys and may not take into account the income of top earners. Tax data provided by the World Inequality Database shows that the top 10 percent of earners received around 55 percent of total income between 2001–2018 and that this share was stable. Assouad et al. (2018) explained persistently high inequality by large regional inequality stemming from the colonial and slave-owning period. In the twentieth century, meanwhile, industrialization favored a minority of formal workers, while a limited agrarian reform led to the high concentration of land ownership. Education is still unequally distributed, and most adults do not have secondary schooling (Medeiros 2016). Providing access to education and closing the quality gap between private and public schools is necessary to reduce inequality.

In summary, Brazil provides an important case for development economists and policymakers. Some long-term constraints, such as low domestic savings, limited Brazil's growth in the 2000s. Accumulated fiscal imbalances became an important growth constraint and contributed to a deep recession in 2015–2016. The public pension system that had required reforms for many years connected these two constraints: large spending on pensions reduced incentives to accumulate private savings, limiting public saving, and undermining public sustainability. At the same time, Brazil achieved progress in reducing poverty rates and informality. It did so by boosting employment during the commodity boom and creating an effective social assistance system.

V. The Middle East: The Case of Egypt

Egypt has averaged economic growth of about 4 percent over the past two decades, mainly driven by capital deepening. While Egypt is considered as a fast-growing economy in the Middle East (MEs) region (Figure 21.16, left side), economic growth has been insufficient to improve the living standards in a context marked by high population growth. Figure 21.16 shows the GDP per capita during the past decade, 2010–2019, which point to a wide gap between Egypt and MEs and EMDEs. This performance could be explained by the growth model relying mainly on capital deepening, while labor and productivity contributions were lagging (IMF 2018a).

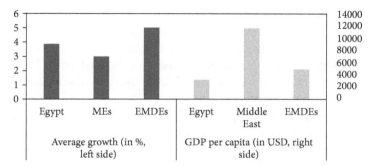

Figure 21.16 Average Growth and GDP per capita from 2010–2019
Source: World Economic Outlook (October 2020)

Like many other emerging market economies, Egypt is perceived as a country with high inequality. During the Arab Spring in 2011, inequality and poverty have been cited as the main cause of the uprisings. Since then, inequality and poverty have been an important concern for both policymakers and the general public (World Bank, 2015).

Looking at official measures of income inequality suggests low-income inequality, in stark contrast with the general perception. For instance, Enbaby and Galal (2015) confirm that the wide perceptions of income inequality are at odds with standard measurements, such as the Gini index, which shows only slightly declining levels of income inequality. The conflict between perceptions and evidence from available data has given rise to a "MENA inequality puzzle" (Verme et al. 2014), which is particularly relevant to Egypt. This section explores this puzzle, together with measurement issues, and provides some explanations from the literature.

On the macroeconomic front, Egypt implemented in the past inconsistent macroeconomic policies which, by 2016, had led to a build-up of significant imbalances. Large budget deficits, loose monetary policy, and a fixed exchange rate had resulted in a drastic reduction in foreign exchange reserves, high inflation, and unsustainably high levels of public debt. Growth had fallen and unemployment increased, especially among women and youth. As part of an IMF program concluded in late 2019, an Extended Fund Facility (EFF), Egypt paid special attention to policies and reforms to reduce inequality and alleviate poverty. These reforms consist of targeted cash transfers, reducing energy subsidies, and policies to increase female labor participation.

A. Inequality Between Perceptions and Official Data

The Gini coefficient is arguably the most commonly used measure of inequality. Since 1958, the Egyptian income distribution has been relatively egalitarian by the standards of developing countries, with the Gini index ranging from a high of 32.8 in 1999 to a low of about 31.5 in 2017. This narrow range points to the relative stability of income inequality in Egypt despite facing significant economic changes and shocks over this period. However, as highlighted in Verme et al. (2014), Gini estimates in Egypt are characterized by a large discrepancy between different studies in the literature.

Figure 21.17 shows that Egypt is more egalitarian than many emerging economies and several advanced countries. The most unequal countries are on the right with a high Gini index. Egypt's Gini is just over 0.3, which is low by international standards and even by the standards of the rest of the MENA countries.

However, there are significant perceptions of high inequality in Egypt. Measures of public perceptions come from the World Values Survey (WVS). The WVS is a global survey of views and opinions across a wide range of issues and is conducted every five years. The survey asks a question on people's attitudes toward inequality, measured on a scale from one to ten, where one indicates a desire for more equality and ten indicates a tolerance for higher inequality.

Figure 21.18 depicts the results from WVS surveys during 2001, 2008, and 2012 for the same question on inequality. The figure clearly shows that the group

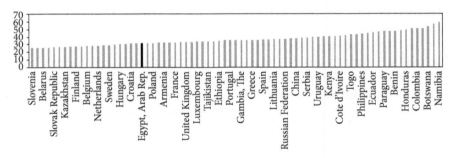

Figure 21.17 Gini Index for 75 Countries from Around the World in 2015
Source: World Bank

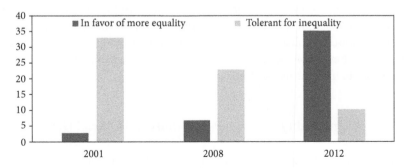

Figure 21.18 Public Perception of Inequality (as % of Respondents)
Source: World Values Survey (2001–2012).

in favor of income equality has been rising over time—comprised more than 35 percent of respondents in 2012 (up from 2.6 percent in 2001). At the same time, the group tolerant for inequality has become smaller, reaching 10 percent of respondents in 2012 (down from 32.8 percent in 2001). The increase in aversion to inequality in Egypt is comparable to MENA countries, while greater than elsewhere in the world (WVS 2001, 2008, 2012).

Overall, the change in people's perceptions observed over the period from 2000 to 2012 has been a result of two factors. First, economic aspects became more important as the country experienced various shocks. For instance, spillovers from the Global Financial Crisis (GFC) in 2008 and the economic crisis following the uprisings of 2011 had a major impact on people's lives and wellbeing. Second, regional factors have been also behind the changing perceptions on inequality, as rising globalization during 2000–2012 and the opening to GCC countries have made people more aware of income distribution in the region.[29]

The relatively low and stable measured inequality is at odds with the general perception of high inequality. This observation could hide a few data issues as raised in Alvaredo and Piketty (2014). Data sources relying on income surveys are insufficient to derive reliable estimates of income inequality in Middle East countries, and particularly in Egypt. Household income and expenditure surveys could underestimate the level of inequality possibly by a very large margin (e.g. Latin America). To check the reliability of Gini coefficient estimates, one would need reliable fiscal data on income tax in order to complement survey results, as household surveys often fail to account for top incomes.

B. Solving the Puzzle: Data vs Perceptions

Several studies investigate whether inequality is underestimated or misreported. Hlasny and Verme (2018) focus on understanding whether the low estimates for the Gini coefficient in Egypt are a result of top households systematically under-representing their incomes in surveys. Their main finding is that households' income survey data do not appear to suffer from this potential systematic bias. However, Van der Weide, Lakner, and Ianchovichina (2016), using data on house prices to estimate the top tail of the income distribution, find evidence that inequality is considerably underestimated in Egypt, where the Gini coefficient for urban Egypt was revised from 0.36 to 0.47. Johannesen (2015) provides evidence of high wealth inequality using data on financial assets held abroad by MENA individuals. The author uses a dataset from the Bank of International Settlements (BIS) on cross-border bank deposits to estimate the size of wealth hidden in tax

---

[29] People tend to approach inequality thinking about the region (MENA) as a single community. The middle class in Egypt compares themselves not only to rich people in Egypt but also to the middle class in GCC countries, which raises inequality perceptions (Verme et al. 2014).

haven bank deposits. The findings indicate that the size of haven deposits is not linked to expenditure inequality, suggesting that quantitative evidence does not support the perception of such wealth held abroad while.[30] Using different approaches and data sources, these papers show mixed results on the accuracy of Gini estimates.

Another stream of this literature, such as Assaad et al. (2018), has examined inequality of opportunity, which can better capture the notion of unfairness and social injustice that may lie at the root of popular perceptions. Assaad et al. (2018) use survey data between 1988 and 2012 to link individual wages to parental education as well as household consumption to parental education of the household head. While inequality of opportunity did not show any increase during the study period, the paper shows that the wealth of those born to middle-class families collapsed toward those born to lower-class families, and the gap between the latter and those with an upper-middle-class background narrowed. At the same time, those at the higher end of the income distribution have remained quite apart from the rest. This finding shed light on the growing discontent of the middle class, which is potentially behind rising inequality perceptions.

Moreover, one of the sharp observations on the inequality of opportunity is related to education. As shown by Assaad (2013), the probability of a boy from a poor family enrolling in university is estimated to be only 9 percent compared to 97 percent for a boy from a most advantaged family. In addition, estimates of inequality of opportunity in educational achievement (TIMSS scores for eighth-graders) also show considerable inequality in Egypt.

Attempts to solve the inequality puzzle for Egypt clearly indicate mixed results suggesting that there are several factors at play. Missing top incomes, data quality issues, and inequality of opportunity are all good candidates for an underestimated Gini coefficient, which is one piece of the puzzle. On the other hand, people's beliefs are also important to examine in order to explain the other piece of the puzzle. Indeed, perceptions about inequality and the unfairness of the distribution could be determined by regional or global inequality, and not only on a national level. Also, the middle-class growing discontent could be related to upward mobility rigidity. People judge inequality not only by the perceived gap between their own income and the income of others but also by the perceived gap between their actual income and their expected income. With high growth rates in the run-up to the GFC, people feel frustrated that benefits of growth are not shared, and their income did not grow as expected.

---

[30] Expenditure inequality stands for the measurement of inequality from households' expenditures as opposed to households' income.

C. Policies in Favor of More Inclusion

Inconsistent economic policy management, together with other structural factors and the economic hit of the 2011 revolution, led to large imbalances. Low economic growth and investment, rising inflation, high government debt, and high unemployment characterized this period. To counter these imbalances Egypt engaged in a home-grown economic reform program, supported by the IMF over three years, starting from November 2016. The program achieved its key objective of macroeconomic stability, which is a precondition to attract investment, raise growth, and create jobs. This sets the stage for broader reforms, such as improving the business climate and fostering inclusive growth.

Indeed, one component of the authorities' program was to address extensive fuel subsidies, which were a significant drain on the budget and benefited the rich. These subsidies made fuel in Egypt one of the cheapest in the world, encouraging excessive consumption and benefiting the well-off far more than the poor because those with means consumed more. Phasing out fuel subsidies created more room in the budget for better-targeted social spending, as well as more investment in health, education, and public infrastructure.

The authorities' reform program also entailed a modern social spending system of a couple of cash transfer programs targeted to those most in need. For example, Takaful and Karama, which were implemented in March 2015 and expanded during the program, are conditional and unconditional cash transfer programs. "Takaful" or "Solidarity" is a conditional (on school attendance among other criteria) cash transfer program aimed at supporting vulnerable families' consumption, reducing poverty while encouraging families to keep children in school and providing them with needed health care. The main goal of this program is to build the "human capital" of the next generation and give them an opportunity for upward mobility. On the other hand, "Karama" or "Dignity" is an unconditional cash transfer program aiming at supporting poor elderly citizens. These programs were the most cost-effective way to ensure that the poor did not bear the costs of these economic adjustments. Social policy centered around Takaful and Karama was critical to ensuring public support for the broader reforms Egypt needed to undertake to stabilize the economy and to lay the foundation for higher and more inclusive growth.

These cash transfer programs have enrolled about 2.25 million families with a significant social and economic impact. The International Food Policy Research Institute (IFPRI) has conducted an evaluation of these programs in late 2018 through a survey conducted across the country (IFPRI 2018). The findings of this assessment point to about 89 percent of the sample are either very satisfied or somewhat satisfied. About 93 percent of transfer recipients reported no difficulties in receiving this support. On the economic impact, these programs have helped households to increase their consumption by about 8.4 percent, compared to people who did not receive the transfers.

Policies were also implemented to foster job creation for women and the youth. Policies in favor of women inclusion in the labor market, implemented in 2017, were centered around allocating more public expenditure to improve the availability of public nurseries and other facilities to enhance the ability of women to actively seek jobs. Efforts in this area also included establishing a joint Ministerial committee as well as representatives of the Women's council, academia, and business community with the objective to improve women's participation rate in the labor force. The committee is working with UN women to introduce and effectively implement gender budgeting in the future. It is also responsible for simplifying rules and facilitating registration of home-based nurseries, to expand job opportunities for women and child-care for working mothers (IMF 2018b). The outcome of these policies was positive but somehow limited to the extent that female labor participation has increased only slightly from 21.8 percent in 2017 to 22.1 percent in 2020. Other programs included Forsa, a program that helps create job opportunities, launched in early 2018, and Mastoura, a program for micro-credit directed to women, which covered more than 6000 projects in its first phase of inception in 2017.

Further, Egypt's recent policies are focused on revamping the growth model allowing more room for the private sector to take the lead in job creation. The government has undertaken several structural reforms to promote inclusive growth. For instance, the authorities have initiated reforms in areas related to competition policy, the public procurement system, management and transparency of State-Owned Enterprises, industrial land allocation, and management of public finances. These reforms have the potential to significantly improve the investment climate and, therefore, boost job creation, which would absorb a large and growing young population.

More broadly, the path to inclusive growth and more equality in income is tied to the opportunities offered by the economy. Significant progress has been achieved with a positive impact on, both, social and economic levels. Looking forward, broadening and better targeting these programs together with sustainable economic growth are sine qua non conditions to make growth more inclusive.

VI. Lessons and Conclusions

The country cases demonstrate that achieving inclusive growth requires a multi-pronged approach to policies. In each country example, government policies address several facets of the economy and society that are key to inclusion. For example, these range from labor market policies to business regulation and policies for trade, migration, and capital flows to the use of tax policy and public spending. Programs also need to target different groups that fall behind, especially the extreme poor, who are also often women or youth.

The Nordic model represents some of the best practices in inclusive growth and exemplifies the wide span of policies that bear on success. The policy framework creates an extensive role for government, but not just in terms of redistribution. The government facilitates a strong business environment for stable and sustainable growth by ensuring macroeconomic stability. It fosters competition and innovation in domestic markets and promotes integration with international markets. Social partners cooperate in labor markets to reduce wage inequality while ensuring labor market flexibility and social cohesion. The government combines broad safety net programs to support incomes and assure access to public services, with policies such as retraining to help people find new jobs and adjust to changing economic conditions.

The efficacy of policy measures depends on their interaction with other measures and the country's economic conditions. For instance, Sweden does not have a minimum wage, yet protects worker wages through a strong collective bargaining system. With Sweden's high rate of employment and strong capacity in mobilizing fiscal revenue, it can afford a system of universal social services. In contrast, a system of universal income services is out of fiscal reach for most developing countries, as in the case of India.

The cases show that policies to promote high and stable economic growth are still relevant for achieving inclusion. High rates of growth were especially pivotal in reducing poverty in India and Brazil over much of the past two decades. Growth led to increases in jobs and incomes in the private sector. Growth also expanded public resources to raise social assistance programs. Conversely, bouts of economic instability or episodes of crises have set back progress in inclusion, especially in poverty reduction.

Growth is not a panacea though and well-designed public programs can go a long way in fostering inclusion. Brazil realized more poverty reduction than Chile, despite having lower growth per capita during 2000–2015. Its Bolsa Familia Program covered a large share of the extreme poor and coupled its income support with conditionality to improve education, health, and support to women. Unconditional and conditional cash transfers were successful features of social assistance in Brazil and Egypt and direct benefit transfers in India. Education has been important across the board for helping people escape from poverty and raising the labor force participation of women.

Likewise, poorly designed or targeted policies can impede inclusive growth. Although on the surface it may seem that a generous pension system could be a feature of inclusion, the case of Brazil demonstrated that an overly generous and poorly targeted system contributed to fiscal deficits and low domestic savings, which factored into high-interest rates and lower growth relative to peer countries. Prior to the reform introducing the direct benefit transfers, India's social assistance was plagued by leakages and corruption. Egypt's extensive energy subsidies mainly benefited higher-income households and were large drains on public finances that could have been used for programs more targeted to the poor. And even well-managed inclusive growth frameworks, such as in Denmark and Sweden, have room for improvement on some dimensions, such as enhancing work opportunities for the low-skilled and foreign-born workers.

Technology can drastically improve the scope for implementing effective policies, even in developing countries. This is illustrated best in the case of India, where the use of digital IDs has enabled the expansion and more efficient administration of public transfers, with less corruption, as well as spurred the creation of millions of bank accounts that increased financial inclusion.

Statistics on distribution are important for understanding the state of inclusiveness and for designing the policy response. The case of Egypt demonstrates that official data on inequality had not suitably reflected the perception of it. More work is required, for all countries, to fill in data gaps related to misreported income and wealth. The example also suggests that the public's tolerance for inequality may not be adequately represented by the Gini coefficient as an indicator. It may also depend on perceptions of the scope for social mobility over time and over generations, and whether improvements in economic and social match expectations of them.

References

Ahluwalia, M.S. 2019. "India's Economic Reforms: Achievements and Next Steps." *Asian Economic Policy Review* 14(1): 46–62.

Ahmad, E. 2013, April. Effects of Mahatma Gandhi National Rural Employment Guarantee Scheme on expenditure in rural households.

Alvaredo, F. and T. Piketty. 2014. *Measuring Top Incomes and Inequality in the Middle East: Data Limitations and Illustration with the Case of Egypt*. Economic Research Forum Working Paper 832.

Arnold, J. 2011. "Raising Investment in Brazil," OECD Economics Department Working Papers, No. 900, OECD Publishing, Paris.

Assaad, R. 2013. "Equality for All? Egypt's Free Public Higher Education Policy Breeds Inequality of Opportunity." In *Does Free Education in Egypt Lead to Equality of Opportunity?*, edited by A. Elbadawy and C. Krafft. Cairo: Population Council.

Assaad, R., C. Krafft, J. Roemer, and D. Salehi-Isfahani. 2018. "Inequality of Opportunity in Wages and Consumption in Egypt." *Review of Income and Wealth* 64: S26–S54.

Assouad L., L. Chancel, and M. Morgan. 2018. "Extreme Inequality: Evidence from Brazil, India, the Middle East, and South Africa", AEA Papers and Proceedings 2018, 108: 119–23.

Balasubramanian S., L. Bounader, J. Bricco, and D. Vasilyev. 2021. "Is There a One-Fits-All Approach to Inclusive Growth? A Case Study Approach," IMF Working Paper WP/21/111.

Balasubramanian, S., R. Kumar, and P. Loungani. 2021. "Inequality and Locational Determinants of the Distribution of Living Standards in India." IMF WP/21/50.

Beltrão, K.I., and J.E.D. Alves. 2013. "The Reversal of the Gender Gap in Brazilian Education in the Twentieth Century." *Cadernos de Pesquisa* 39(136): 125–56.

Bhalla, S.S. 2002. *Imagine There's No Country: Poverty, Inequality and Growth in the Era of Globalisation*. USA: Peterson Institute for International Economics.

Borjas, G.J. 2005. *Labor Economics*. New York: McGraw-Hill/Irwin.

Central Statistics Office. 2014. National Accounts Statistics (various years). Ministry of Statistics and Programme Implementation, Government of India. Accessed 23 March 2018: www.mospi.nic.in

Cerra, V. 2021. "An Inclusive Growth Framework." In *How to Achieve Inclusive Growth*, edited by V. Cerra, B. Eichengreen, A. El-Ganainy, and M. Schindler. London: Oxford University Press.

Danish Agency for Labor Market and Recruitment, "Flexicurity" https://star.dk/en/about-the-danish-agency-for-labour-market-and-recruitment/flexicurity/

David A., C.E. Gonçalves, and A.M. Werner. 2020. "Reexamining the National Savings-Investment Nexus Across Time and Countries," IMF Working Paper WP/20/124.

Economic Survey, G. 2015/2016. Spreading JAM across India's economy. Economic Survey, Government of India.

European Council. 2008. Implementation of the common principles of flexicurity within the framework of the 2008–2010 round of the Lisbon Strategy- Report by the "flexicurity" mission. 17047/1/08.

El Enbaby, H. and R. Galal. 2015. September. "Inequality of Opportunity in Individuals' Wages and Households' Assets in Egypt." In Economic Research Forum Working Paper Series No (Vol. 942).

Fruttero A., A.L. Leichsenring, and L.H. Paiva. 2020. "Social Programs and Formal Employment: Evidence from the Brazilian Bolsa Família Program," IMF Working Paper WP/20/99.

Goes Carlos, Izabela Karpowicz. 2017. "Inequality in Brazil: A Regional Perspective," IMF Working Paper WP/17/225.

Government Offices of Sweden. 2017. Ministry of Finance "The Swedish Model".

Hausmann, R., D. Rodrik, and A. Velasco. 2005. "Growth Diagnostics," John F. Kennedy School of Government, Harvard University (Cambridge, Massachusetts).

Hlasny, V., and P. Verme. 2018. "Top Incomes and the Measurement of Inequality in Egypt." *The World Bank Economic Review* 32(2): 428–55.

International Food Policy Research Institute. 2018. "Egypt's Takaful and Karama Cash Transfer Program Evaluation of Program Impacts and Recommendations". IFPRI Policy Brief.

International Monetary Fund (IMF). 2016. "Denmark 2016 Article IV Consultation—Staff Report," Box 1. Income Inequality in Denmark.

International Monetary Fund (IMF). 2017a. India: 2017 Article IV Consultation Staff Report. IMF Country Report No. 17/54. Washington DC: International Monetary Fund.

International Monetary Fund (IMF). 2017b. India: 2017 Selected Issues. IMF Country Report No. 17/55. Washington DC: International Monetary Fund.

International Monetary Fund (IMF). 2018. "Poverty and Inequality in Latin America: Gains during the Commodity Boom but an Uncertain Outlook," IMF Regional Economic Outlook (Western Hemisphere Region), Chapter 5, May 2018.

International Monetary Fund (IMF). 2018a. Egypt 2017 Article IV Consultation, Second Review Under The Extended Fund Facility.

International Monetary Fund (IMF). 2018b. Egypt Third Review under the Extended Fund Facility (EFF).

International Monetary Fund (IMF). 2019a. "Denmark 2019 Article IV Consultation—Staff Report," IMF Country Report No. 19/178.

International Monetary Fund (IMF). 2019b. "Sweden 2019 Article IV Consultation – Staff Report", IMF Country Report No. 19/88.

International Monetary Fund (IMF). 2019c. "Brazil 2019 Article IV Consultation – Staff Report," IMF Country Report No. 19/242.

Johannesen, N. 2015. Economic Inequality in the MENA Countries—Evidence from Cross-Border Deposits. mimeo.

Kleven, H.J. 2014. "How Can Scandinavians Tax So Much?" *Journal of Economic Perspectives* 28(4): 77–98.

Kumar, S.B. 2019. For Indian farmers, Direct Benefit Transfers can work better than fertilizer subsidies. International Food Policy Research Institute.

Lakner, C., and B. Milanovic. 2016. "Global Income Distribution: From the Fall of the Berlin Wall to the Great Recession." *World Bank Economic Review* 30: 203–32.

Ljungqvist, Lars, and Thomas Sargent. 2008. "Two Questions about European Unemployment." *Econometrica* 76(1): 1–29.

Medeiros, M. 2016. "Income Inequality in Brazil: New Evidence from Combined Tax and Survey Data," World Social Science Report 2016.

Moffitt, R. A. 2002. "Welfare Programs and Labor Supply." In *Handbook of Public Economics*, edited by A.J. Auerbach and M. Feldstein (org.)., Vol. 4. North-Holland: Elsevier.

Mullainathan, S., and E. Shafir. 2013. *Scarcity: Why Having Too Little Means Too Much.* New York: Henry Holt.

Narayanan, K. 2013. Press Information Bureau, Government of India. Retrieved from Press Information Bureau, Government of India: https://pib.gov.in/newsite/mbErel.aspx?relid=92113.

Organisation for Economic Co-operation and Development (OECD). 2019. "OECD Economic Surveys: Denmark 2019," OECD Publishing, Paris.

Pinheiro, L.J., A.T. Lima Junior, N. Fontoura, and R. Silva. 2016. Women and Labor: Brief Analysis of the 2004–2014 period. Technical Note, IPEA, Brasilia.

Rangarajan, C. 2014. Report of the Expert Group to Review the Methodology for Measurement of Poverty. Planning Commission, Government of India. Accessed 23 March 2018: www.planningcommission.nic.in

Ravallion, M., and S. Chen. 2003. "Measuring Pro-poor Growth." *Economics Letters* 78(1)93–9.

Today, I. 2019, April. Over Rs 1 lakh crore deposited in Pradhan Mantri Jan Dhan Yojana accounts, reveals RTI. India Today Magazine.

van der Weide, R., C. Lakner, and E. Ianchovichina. 2016. "Is Inequality Underestimated in Egypt? Evidence from House Prices," World Bank Policy Research Working Paper 7727.

Verme, P., B. Milanovic, S. Al-Shawarby, S. El Tawila, M. Gadallah, and A. El-Majeed. 2014. *Inside Inequality in the Arab Republic of Egypt: Facts and Perceptions Across People, Time, and Space.* Washington, DC: World Bank.

World Bank. 2015. *Inequality, Uprisings, and Conflict in the Arab World. MENA Economic Monitor.* Washington, DC.

World Bank. 2018. *The State of Social Safety Nets 2018.* Washington, DC.

22

Conclusions and Resources for Next Steps

Valerie Cerra

I. Recap of Main Takeaways

A. High and Rising Disparities: The State of Affairs

Over the past few decades there has been a sharp rise in income inequality across many advanced economies and some emerging economies.[1] The causes are varied, but have generally been attributed to skill-biased technological change, a rise in market power of firms (given the skewed concentration of capital ownership to the rich), as well as some types of global economic integration, especially that of financial flows. The poor have also suffered disproportionately from the effects of macroeconomic volatility, including the deep recessions associated with the global financial crisis and Covid-19 pandemic. In fact, the economic collapse associated with the Covid-19 pandemic dramatically increased poverty and inequality. Within countries, structural changes have had differential impacts, with some regions and individuals benefitting from change while others are left behind. Institutions and policies have played a role in shaping these outcomes, as large differences exist even between countries at the same level of development.

Although progress has been made in many dimensions of inclusive growth, disparities across and within countries remain high. For example, many countries in Latin America and Africa benefited from a declining trend in inequality from 2000–2019, but the level of inequality remains among the highest in the world. There was substantial improvement in financial inclusion during last decade, driven in part by financial innovation, particularly mobile money, but there are still persistent gaps for women, the lower educated, and the poor. As with poverty reduction, overall economic development helped improve many dimensions of inclusive growth, as have global campaigns launched in the context of the Millennium Development Goals and more recently the Sustainable Development Goals. But even so, there are still substantial inequalities across countries and within countries, especially among some vulnerable groups and lagging regions. Moreover, many of the world's poorest are trapped in fragile states, gripped by

---

[1] I thank all of the book authors for their inputs and comments.

Valerie Cerra, *Conclusions and Resources for Next Steps* In: *How to Achieve Inclusive Growth.* Edited by: Valerie Cerra, Barry Eichengreen, Asmaa El-Ganainy, and Martin Schindler, Oxford University Press. © Valerie Cerra 2022. DOI: 10.1093/oso/9780192846938.003.0022

conflict and violence, and with weak political governance characterized by extensive corruption.

Despite improvements during the last decades, gaps between men and women continue to exist across all parts of the world. Such gaps are especially large in developing countries and, geographically, in the MENA, Central Asia, and South East Asia regions. In nearly all countries, women experience worse outcomes than men in labor markets, including participation rates, wages, and employment. Women are under-represented in political positions, such as among parliamentary representatives, ministers, and local elected officials and in top corporate positions, especially as CEOs and as members of companies' board of directors. Women also face gaps in some health outcomes and in access to education, especially in STEM fields. Significant income gaps, including in advanced economies, point to unequal opportunities and persistent cultural norms that prevent gender equality.

Youth are another vulnerable group. They face more difficulties to join the labor market (high unemployment and inoccupation rates), are more likely to have less secure forms of employment ("gig" economy, informality) and are vulnerable to poverty (lower-paying jobs, fewer financial buffers, lack of social transfers targeted to working-age youth). These inadequate outcomes are disconnected with rising educational attainment, which gives rise to higher expectations for finding good jobs with potential for career advancement.

To make matters worse, intergenerational social mobility is low, especially in developing countries.[2] In many advanced countries, there is a growing concern that younger generations will have fewer opportunities for upward mobility than preceding generations. Such perceptions affect life satisfaction and well-being, views about inclusiveness of social and political institutions as well as people's policy preferences. Social mobility has been correlated with income inequality: countries with higher income inequality tend to have lower intergenerational mobility—the "Great Gatsby curve." These poor youth outcomes and lower social mobility are a major source of discontent among youth that can threaten social stability if left unaddressed (rise in protests, populism).

There is also considerable disparity in elderly poverty rates across countries, mostly driven by different levels of pension coverage, social protection benefits, and accessibility of health care. The risk of old age poverty is generally more pronounced in less developed countries, where social protection coverage is inadequate and many older persons rely only on family support. However, the pandemic highlighted risks for elderly across the globe, including in developed countries, where some groups of elderly still face inadequate support. Absent the "right" policies, elderly poverty could increase further because of demographic

[2] OECD, 2018. World Bank, 2018.

and economic trends (such as population ageing, climate change, fiscal challenges, and changes in family structure).

The Covid-19 pandemic has exposed and exacerbated many of these longstanding societal inequalities. Progress on reducing global poverty has stalled and reversed. The pandemic highlighted the fragility and inadequacy of many health systems and income support programs. A higher share of women and lowerincome workers have been affected by the crisis, given occupational specializations. Disruptions to schooling intensified the substantial shortfalls in human capital, as lower-income students have less access to the Internet than others. Youth labor market prospects are sensitive to economic downturns and the effects of joining the labor market in a recession can be persistent, with past studies showing lower expected earnings up to a decade after past recessions.

B. Headwinds Going Forward

Looking ahead, a number of current trends and global forces suggest continued challenges and risks for improving inclusive growth. These include the likely scarring effects of the Covid-19 pandemic that has been widening income gaps and other disparities. The future impact of technological progress and automation is more uncertain than ever. Continued technological advancements in communications, combined with differences in opportunities across countries, is likely to maintain incentives for further globalization, including in financial flows, trade, and migration. Over coming decades, climate change is expected to result in large weather shocks, alterations of agriculture, and further pressures for migration.

The Covid-19 pandemic has further raised income inequality and adversely impacted education and labor market outcomes of vulnerable groups. As the world emerges from its economic and social impacts, these gaps are expected to persist and new vulnerabilities to arise. The pandemic is expected to leave economic scars, such as persistent declines in labor force participation (especially of women), earnings, and school attainment.[3] The pandemic has also led to a rise in sovereign and corporate debt, which risks future bouts of macroeconomic crises for many countries. In the past, major crises have acted as a catalyst for equality in some areas (e.g. women entering the labor market during and after the Second World War), but they may also result in the widening of gaps. Thus, it is important to take advantage of the heightened recognition of the need to build a greener, fairer, and more resilient growth model to help steer changes in the right direction.[4]

---

[3] See Cerra, Fatas, and Saxena (2021) for an analysis of the likely scarring effects of the Covid-19 recession.

[4] See Georgieva (2020).

Rapid advances in technology, especially automation and artificial intelligence, represent another force that is likely to affect inclusive growth. There is a significant dispersion in experts' views on the direction and speed of these developments and their impact on societies and economies. While such technological progress has the potential to be beneficial at large, there are also important downside risks for inequality and inclusion, both within and across countries. Automation and AI are already replacing humans in a variety of routine and non-cognitive tasks, and may in some scenarios do so more broadly even for other tasks. As a consequence, technological progress of this type will have the potential to deprive many developing countries of their key comparative advantage (cheap labor), while excluding them from participating in some of the gains provided by new technologies and leading to premature deindustrialization. While the most adverse scenarios may not come to pass, they are sufficiently probable that policymakers should plan and prepare for them.

Global integration in terms of trade and cross-border capital and labor flows is likely to continue, although the growth may no longer exceed the rate of GDP growth as in past decades. In some cases, inequality creates the incentives for integration. For example, migration is driven by a very powerful market force— large wage differentials between countries. Likewise, offshoring of production stages to lower income countries, financed by capital flows, is attractive for companies due to lower labor costs in developing countries. Conversely, globalization impacts growth and inequality, although the impact varies by the type of integration and the characteristics of the countries involved. Many of these trends toward structural change are likely to continue creating winners and losers, not just between countries but also among different groups and regions within countries.

Climate change will adversely affect most countries, and across all income groups, but disproportionally affect developing countries and lower income people. Human economic activity associated with the economic growth models of the twentieth century leaves an ecologic footprint at a geological scale. In particular, anthropogenic greenhouse gas emissions into the atmosphere cause global warming and systemic changes in the planet's climate. Climate change is expected to generate significant socio-economic damages even if the global temperature is kept to a moderate rise. These include adverse health outcomes for many, reduced agricultural productivity, and increased magnitude and frequency of natural disasters. The damages depend on country circumstances, but they are generally larger for the poor, as they have fewer resources to adapt, are more dependent on agriculture, and tend to live in already more adverse climate conditions. For large temperature increases the socio-economic consequences can be catastrophic, for example, rendering large swathes of the planet uninhabitable (due to heat levels or inundation) and thus leading to mass migration and, potentially, conflict. Continued unsustainable growth leading to climate change coupled with adverse health conditions would also increase the probability of future pandemics.

C. The Policy Response

The policy response needs to take on these challenges and promote inclusive growth along three dimensions. It starts with the pre-market distribution of endowments, especially the stocks of human capital. The government has a clear role for providing public goods of education and health to ensure equality of opportunity for all and also because a healthy and educated workforce is the foundation for growth. Policy interventions also address the distribution of market incomes by influencing the development of private institutions and by direct regulatory measures. These are needed to create dynamic and competitive markets, with labor markets that can absorb the workforce and make efficient use of its talents. It also includes ensuring access to finance, as well as managing market forces for integration and structural change so as to smooth the processes and avoid disruptive macroeconomic crises. Government policies also affect the post-market distribution of net disposable incomes, mainly through the use of taxes and transfers—however, achieving equality of opportunities is the most effective path to achieving inclusive growth.

For the most part, promoting inclusion also promotes growth. There has been an evolution in thinking on the relationship between growth and inclusion. Much of the early literature considered inequality to be a function of development, first rising, then falling as in the Kuznets Curve. In terms of policy, the early literature focused on distortionary effects of redistribution and heavy regulation that imposed a tradeoff between growth and inclusion. It argued that inequality provides incentives in market economy to exert more labor effort and that the rich's higher propensity to save could help finance the accumulation of capital, a key input for economic growth.[5] But much of the more recent literature demonstrates that growth and inclusion can be complementary. In fact, inequality and poverty can be detrimental to growth. For instance, in the presence of credit constraints and poor public education and health systems, excessive income inequality in a society prevents the poor from accumulating assets and human capital, which results in a lower potential growth rate of output. In fact, high inequality and poverty rates may mean that significant potential in the global talent pool remains untapped. In addition, in countries with weak institutions, inequality could exacerbate conflicts and increase uncertainty, which can depress investment and long-term growth rates. Promoting broad-based growth can be a virtuous cycle, as the empirical evidence strongly suggests that economic growth is associated with poverty reduction by raising incomes in the poorest deciles of the income

[5] See, for example, Ravallion (2016) for a discussion of the history of literature and thought on poverty. Early thought emphasized the need for poverty as an incentive for work and as a component of a functioning economy, and anti-poverty programs were mainly palliative. The modern view is more optimistic, seeing elimination of poverty as feasible and as part of a vibrant growing economy, with policy focused on removing constraints on individual efforts and freedoms.

distribution. Government policies play a prominent role in shaping the relationship between growth and inclusiveness. Governments can prioritize policies that simultaneously enhance growth and inclusion, such as improving equality of opportunity by expanding access to high-quality education and health, elements that are crucial in the accumulation of human capital.

Education and Health

Education and health create endowments of human capital. For most people, and especially for the poor, labor income is the main component of income and life-time earnings, which are driven to a significant degree by skills and education. Governments have a vital role to play in promoting equality of opportunity: it matters intrinsically (e.g. on moral grounds), and it boosts overall growth. In education and health, there is no inherent trade-off between efficiency and equity.

Equally important would be adapting the education system to the needs of future labor markets. As the world increasingly uses technology to do repetitive tasks, educational reforms in many countries are ever more crucial to support an educated workforce that complements technology, engages in lifelong learning, facilitates structural change, and can support climate science.

Multisectoral approaches can be successful in improving health. Past advances in health outcomes, such as deworming and the eradication of polio have significantly improved consumption and incomes. Upgrading public health delivery, including for primary care, needs to be combined with enhancements in nutrition and improvements in infrastructure that assure sanitary conditions and clean water supplies to thwart disease.

To create stronger, more resilient, and more inclusive education and health systems, policy goals should include improving the quality, and not just the quantity, of education and health care. It should address lifelong outcomes, including for disadvantaged groups. To this end, policies should focus on results—learning and well-being—rather than inputs, such as spending. Country experience suggests moving from narrow, piecemeal interventions to systemic reform by adopting a "whole-of-government," multi-sectoral approach. Successful reforms have been achieved in some countries at different development levels. Reforms must be underpinned by a robust evidence base. This will both catalyze action and help design effective interventions.

Labor Market Policies

The labor market is at the heart of inclusive growth. It is at the center of where many non-labor market policies and institutions materialize, such as education policies. There is no uniquely optimal set of labor market policies. Some require trading off efficiency against equity, although many do not. There are opportunities to identify win-win situations. For example, racial, gender or other biases can lead to occupational misallocation and thus large losses in economic efficiency—reducing discrimination achieves moral and economic objectives. And while AI and automation may replace some tasks and jobs, the freed-up resources can support addressing climate change which will, at least in the medium term, require additional labor resources. Flexible labor markets are increasingly important to facilitate the needed structural change and support labor reallocation.

For advanced economies, policies can benefit inclusive growth by focusing on individuals rather than jobs, to facilitate a dynamic and efficient economy while protecting individuals. This requires viewing the set of labor market policies holistically, taking into account how different policies can complement or offset each other, rather than individual policies in isolation. It should focus on providing equal opportunities and, importantly, flexibility that allows different market participants to choose according to their individual needs and preferences (e.g., part-time vs full-time, labor-force participation or home production). Crucially, anti-discrimination policies should be clearly enshrined and enforced.

For emerging and developing countries, putting in place conditions for growth is the first priority for addressing inclusiveness more generally, to generate sufficient economic activity to provide meaningful employment opportunities for all and reduce the extent of informality. Providing incentives for formalizing markets (i.e., reducing informality) is key. To this end, enhancing administrative capacity is crucial, including to prepare for the implementation of IG-relevant labor market institutions prevalent in AEs, such as unemployment insurance systems.

Youth and Elderly Policies

Improving inclusive growth for youth requires complementary policy interventions. Building human capital through improved access to high-quality education and health is fundamental. Then, fostering the link between school, training (building skills, experience, and networks) and work would support youth integration into labor force. It is also important to ensure a dynamic and competitive business environment conducive to job creation and a flexible labor market that can absorb new entrants. In some cases, bloated public sector employment needs to be reduced if it creates disincentives for private sector development.

Maintaining adequate income support and healthcare provision is key to protecting the elderly against income and health shocks, especially for those not covered by private pensions or health insurance. In developing countries, this often may require increasing coverage, while for all countries there is also a need to preserve fiscal sustainability, such as by reducing regressive transfers (e.g., energy subsidies that unduly favor the rich).

Gender Policies

A multitude of policies can help close gaps at each point of an individual's life cycle. For example, in some places the ability to exercise basic rights such as accessing schools and commuting to work are threatened by violence. All societies should vigorously prosecute and condemn behavior that makes lives more insecure. This is a particular problem for girls and women in some countries. In developing countries, providing easy access to contraceptives allows women to improve their education, better plan their career, and increase their authority in the household. Similar effects are obtained in advanced countries by providing full day subsidized child and elder care opportunities, which allows women to fully participate in the formal labor market. Active labor market policies designed to retrain laid off workers also have a very positive effect on women returning to the labor market after childbearing and child rearing. Quotas can have positive effects both in shaping attitudes towards women in power and allowing women to obtain the necessary experience that glass ceilings prevent them from obtaining.

To achieve full gender equality, cultural norms about the role of women and men in society need to change and implicit biases need to be eliminated. Targeted policy measures are required to advance this process to address gender equality gaps across social, economic, and political dimensions. In fact, there can be large societal gains from desegregating occupations by gender. Men can be excellent nurses and women excellent mechanics and gender stereotypes affect both genders' choices of occupations. Programs such as "use-it-or-lose-it"-incentivized paternity leave has been shown to work in the Swedish context. This may also help with the household division of labor, as women will be less identified (by the child, school, and society as large) as the main caretaker and men as the main income earner.

Migration
To complement efforts to improve inclusion for vulnerable groups such as youth, women, and the less educated, governments need to contend with migrant workers. Trying to stop this force by administrative measures is not a promising approach, like trying to stop the ocean tides. Indeed, there are benefits, not just costs to migration for both receiving and sending countries. For receiving countries, the evidence does not support most myths about immigration, such as depressing wages, requiring large fiscal spending on welfare, or increasing crime. Receiving countries can benefit from the higher growth and in some cases complementary labor skills provided by migrants, provided they facilitate integration into the formal labor markets. For sending countries, brain drain can be a cost, especially for developing countries. But emigration also tends to generate an inflow of remittances, which on balance are found to be beneficial.

Markets, Innovation, Diversification
In addition to creating a healthy, educated, and flexible labor force, promoting inclusive growth requires a dynamic business environment. Two key features of the economy—innovation-led growth and competition—are key to supporting

sustained broad-based growth. Innovation-led growth creates productivity gains and broad-based growth. Although innovation increases inequality at the top as its benefits flow to innovators, it can support social mobility, provided that market entry and access to finance can be assured. In this regard, the relationship between innovation and competition is not straightforward. Some market power that generates rents from innovation may be needed, but at the same time, too much market power that limits competition entrenches the incumbents, stifles firm entry and innovation, and has in practice contributed to a decline in labor bargaining power and the labor income share. In fact, the market for innovation is riddled with many market failures and policy intervention is essential to support it. In addition, with a recent rise in market power in many sectors (e.g. Big Tech and Big Agriculture) as evidenced by firm markups and market concentration, it becomes important to design competition policies that address not only static consumer welfare but also dynamic effects such as firm entry, technology diffusion, innovation, and inclusive growth.

In their quest for inclusive growth, policymakers should strike a delicate balance between encouraging innovation and promoting competition while limiting harmful market power. Considering competition policies, innovation policies, and inequality in isolation, as it has been the case in the past, is not viable anymore. Instead, it is necessary to set up a consistent framework for these different policies. A first step could be to put forward institutional reforms expanding the mandates of the different agencies to take into account the other policy objectives. This would also require changing the priorities of competition agencies to focus on the markets that affect the poor as well as the spillovers and dynamic effects both on inequality and innovation.

Policymakers could take a much more proactive approach in foreseeing the formidable effects of a rapidly changing technological and market landscape on inclusive growth. They can encourage innovation and competition in industries that are adapting to these trends. For example, embracing climate change policies and investing in green industries could be a win-win future-oriented industrial policy. Moving ahead on climate technology could help transition old industries, such as those reliant on fossil fuels, and their workforces, while also combatting climate change.

Financial Inclusion

Access to finance is a key element to bringing new ideas to the market and expanding businesses. Indeed, viewed as a dimension of financial development, financial inclusion is crucial to inclusive growth; it contributes to fostering long-term growth and reducing income inequality and poverty. Access to financial services allows for efficient allocation of capital and better risk management. Financial development and inclusion is positively related to firm dynamism and entrepreneurship. Credit from microfinance institutions serves well household enterprises and micro-entrepreneurs, while larger enterprises and transformational entrepreneurship can benefit from different sources of finance, such as venture capital.

The level of a country's financial inclusion is affected by structural conditions, including income and demographics, though can be deepened by factors such as a high level of remittances. Financial exclusion can be voluntary if costs of access are high or benefits too low. Policies should not target a specific level of inclusion, but rather should aim at removing market frictions, including building a regulatory framework conducive to financial innovation and competition in the financial sector, easing access to credit by medium, small and micro enterprises, and promoting financial literacy and capability.

Financial Globalization

Integration with international financial markets can increase the availability of credit. However, while financial globalization has the potential to foster economic growth, the evidence shows that it tends to exacerbate inequities. As with financial inclusion, the distributional impacts of capital flows depend on countries' conditions such as the depth of financial markets and the strength of institutional and policy frameworks. Higher levels of educational attainment, stronger creditor rights, and more effective rule of law in countries on the receiving end of capital flows can help to reap the benefits in terms of growth while minimizing the costs in terms of distribution. Although it is primarily the government's role to establish the institutions and policies to reap the benefits of financial globalization, the private sector can also play a role, such as by designing training programs for workers and supporting knowledge spillovers into the domestic economy. In addition, undertaking effective macro- and micro-prudential measures can minimize the risk that financial globalization could undermine macroeconomic stability.

Regional Policies

Technological change, innovation, and globalization, among other structural economic changes, often lead to disparate gains and losses across different regions of a country. Regional disparities are to a significant extent the outcome of efficient market forces related to spatially concentrating economic activity to take advantage of knowledge spillovers and to reduce transportation costs. Thus, government intervention that forces dispersed economic activity could constrain growth. However, regional disparities also reflect market and policy failures which hamper the adjustment to shocks and structural change. These include coordination failures, barriers to mobility, congestion costs, a distorted allocation of public services, and labor-market rigidities. High regional inequality, regardless of its cause, can lead to political polarization, weaker social cohesion, populism, political instability, and conflict.

All this creates a strong case for government intervention to address regional disparities. There are three components to the policy strategy. Spatially blind, people-based policies[6] can mitigate regional disparities and foster overall growth. These include improved public education and health, progressive taxation, and strong institutions. Spatially connective policies, aimed at integrating lagging regions into the national economy, can enhance mobility and opportunity. These can include improving transportation and communication infrastructure, increasing the portability of social benefits, and reducing impediments to geographic mobility such as in housing markets. However, greater mobility may worsen outcomes for those still left behind, including the less skilled and elderly. Spatially targeted, place-based interventions may be justified, on second-best as well as risk-sharing and political-economy grounds, where other policies prove insufficient. These interventions could include regionally targeted public investment projects or location decisions of public institutions, tax and subsidy incentives, and regulatory relief.

Tax Policy
The government plays a direct role in supporting inclusive growth through its tax, transfer, and spending policies. The impact of these policies on inclusiveness are interdependent. The analysis of the effects of spending measures on inclusiveness needs to be analyzed jointly with those of revenue policy and tax collection measures. In advanced economies, tax-benefit systems achieve significant redistribution. In developing economies, the redistributive impact of fiscal policy is generally limited due to lower social transfers and lower tax bases. However, raising additional revenue through taxes that are not progressive (such as consumption taxes) can still be beneficial for inclusion if used for pro-poor spending. Likewise, environmental taxes can be regressive, but at the same time climate change disproportionately affects vulnerable groups and developing countries at large. In many countries, carbon taxes have the potential to yield more revenue while also improving environmental quality with no negative impact on economic growth and with an improvement in the welfare of everyone. Any regressive impact on poor households should be compensated by rebates or by pro-poor uses of the additional revenue.

There is widespread consensus that a minimum level of tax revenue is necessary for countries to ensure that the state can provide its essential functions that support redistribution and growth. Taxes affect growth through employment, investment, and productivity. They affect "inclusiveness" mainly through the progressivity of the tax system and by affecting other dimensions of equality, such as equal treatment by gender, equality of opportunity, intergenerational equity and by treating people in similar circumstances the same. Tax policy often involves a

---

[6] Refers to general policies for individuals everywhere; not targeted to a specific region.

trade-off between efficiency and equity. Good tax design can diminish this tradeoff while strong implementation and enforcement by the tax administration can minimize both tax avoidance and evasion. A well-managed tax policy and administration can also reduce mistrust in government, which affects attitudes about redistribution.

Some tax policy reforms can be progressive with a limited or positive impact on growth. For example, some income tax expenditures—specific provisions in the tax code that allow certain people or companies to pay less taxes—accrue disproportionately to people with high incomes. Eliminating tax expenditures could reduce income inequality while making additional revenue available for pro-inclusive tax and expenditure changes. Individual-based, rather than family-based, income taxation can raise women's labor-force participation rate.

Tax design to promote inclusive growth depends on country circumstances and level of development. For advanced and some emerging market economies promising options include a more progressive personal income tax system, a more neutral taxation of capital and corporate income, improvements in VAT design, and enhanced use of carbon taxes, property taxes and taxes on inheritances. For developing countries, enhancing tax administrative capacity is crucial. They should also improve and simplify their VAT and excise policies, better protect their income taxes against avoidance and evasion, reduce discretionary tax incentives, enhance their fiscal regimes for extractive industries, and better exploit taxes on property and pollution.

Tax policy may need to guide inclusion in the face of changing economic and labor market conditions. For instance, disruptive automation scenarios could require entirely new models of how to provide safety nets for workers, such as proposals of a universal basic income, and how to tax capital and labor. Global tax frameworks may become more important if new technologies deprive developing economies of their previous comparative advantage of cheap labor. Global tax and regulatory regimes may be needed to share the gains from technological progress globally, and to provide avenues for developing economies to develop.

Spending and Transfers

Public expenditure policy is the most effective tool available to governments to foster inclusive growth. Public expenditure policy can affect economic growth and the distribution of income both in the short- and the long-run. All countries rely on public investment in efficient infrastructure and other basic services such as health and education. The public sector also needs to provide social insurance. These need to be achieved while also maintaining debt sustainability. Advanced countries tend to have broad tax bases that facilitate their higher level of public spending; they can focus their efforts on better targeting through means testing.

In developing countries, a priority is to expand coverage of public goods and services (which requires widening their tax bases and improving tax administration to finance it, as described earlier). Beyond increasing the coverage of social spending, priorities could focus on better linking wage to performance in the public sector, replacing universal subsidies with well-targeted transfers, prioritizing inclusive and efficient infrastructure investment, and strengthening budget institutions and fiscal frameworks. Developing a national social registry and mastering incidence analysis tools would also help in the design of efficient and inclusive public spending measures. The package of spending measures should be cost-effective, consistent with fiscal sustainability and should take into account country-specific circumstances. Assessing the incidence of alternative public expenditures on different population groups and the complementarities or trades-offs with growth can help identify whether mitigating measures are needed.

Macro Stability

Macroeconomic stability plays a key role in inclusive growth. Thus, beyond the composition of tax and spending programs, fiscal sustainability is important to avoid debt crises. The evidence shows that crises and recessions leave scarring effects on employment, human capital formation and health conditions, across a diverse set of countries. Put differently, many seemingly short-run temporary fluctuations or cycles in fact have long-run effects. Recessions vary in their impact on different segments of the income distribution depending on whether they are driven by asset price cycles or other factors, but earnings of those in the bottom end of the income distribution are often among the most affected due to job losses. This implies that there is a stronger role for macroeconomic stabilization policies than thought previously. Conversely, inequality can magnify business cycle fluctuations and initial wealth disparities can have short-run and long-run effects.

Policymakers thus need to monitor and avoid the buildup of vulnerabilities that lead to costly economic crises with adverse consequences for inclusiveness. Specifically, buildup of vulnerabilities can happen in the financial sector as manifested through monetary or macroprudential policies that fuel credit booms or encourage excessive risk taking; it can happen in the fiscal sector as manifested through pursuing procyclical fiscal policies and adopting a deficit bias; it can happen in the currency market as manifested through active involvement of the public and private sector in external borrowing or encouraging capital flows in the face of possibly misaligned exchange rates; and it can happen in the real economy as manifested through following excessively accommodative monetary policy that generates high inflation or excessively tight monetary policy that triggers a recession. All of these vulnerabilities can lead to detrimental distributional impacts.

Fiscal Frameworks for Resources

Strong macroeconomic management is especially critical for resource-rich countries, many of which have struggled to generate growth and inclusion from their resource wealth. An inclusive use of resource wealth requires a resource wealth management framework that recognizes the exhaustibility of non-renewable natural resources, shelters the rest of the economy from the impact of fluctuations in global commodity prices, and is based on solid institutional rules that can help prevent corruption. Good governance is the bedrock that makes all these objectives possible. In addition, the experiences of Chile and Malaysia as resource-rich countries that implemented national economic diversification programs have proved that by joining forces, the government and the private sector can foster innovation and technology diffusion. Some countries need to couple policies for private sector growth with a reduction in bloated public sector employment and high public wage bills. In addition, in many cases, using resource wealth to finance investment in human capital has paid off well, both in terms of institutional and economic growth. Policies to promote education are critical in the case of developing resource-rich countries that have depleted most of their resource wealth, but lack the supply of skills needed to make innovation and technology diffusion possible. Heightened climate risks pose additional challenges for hydrocarbon producers that urgently need to turn to new economic models consistent with sustainable and green growth.

Governance and Politics

The government's ability to deliver inclusive growth also crucially depends on the quality of governance. The poor are typically more dependent on essential government services. In countries where the quality of governance is particularly low—capacity is weak and corruption is rampant and systemic—government intervention in the economy can create a vicious circle of increasing inequality, worsening institutions and non-inclusiveness. Improving governance is a complex task requiring political leadership, active civil engagement and extensive communication with the public. Some measures to improve governance include structural reform, automation, improving rules and procedures to limit the discretion and hence space for policy error; human resource policies, capacity building, effective anti-corruption frameworks to incentivize public officials to take decisions in the best public interest; and transparency, accountability, and inclusive political institutions to inform and monitor policymaking. The appropriate mix of policies depends on government's capacity and country's political, economic, and cultural circumstances. In countries where corruption is socially unacceptable, relying on trust and morale may be superior to strict anti-corruption frameworks. In countries where law enforcement is itself ridden by low capacity and corruption, prevention and automated processes that obviate the need for human discretion are often better than punishment.

Political regimes, institutions, and processes form the basis for the government response to inclusive growth. In particular, they play a key role in aggregating voters' preferences for redistribution and reform and matching these preferences with policies offered by different political candidates and parties. Empirical studies confirm that political economy forces shape national policy responses to inequality. The demand for redistribution depends on its net expected financial gains; economic conditions; habituation effects; beliefs about the determinants of success (good luck or effort); trust in government, and perceptions about inequality. Lower participation rates among poorer voters can reduce the implementation of redistributive policies as often those who would benefit most from redistribution vote the least. In supplying redistribution, governments use a wide array of policies and instruments, reflecting policy preferences, political systems, historical legacies, and capacity constraints.

There is a growing sense that countries' national politics and institutions have not been sufficiently responsive to the needs of all citizens over the last three decades, resulting in growth that left many behind and contributing to the rise of nationalist sentiment and a "new" populism. Lessons from history cast doubt on the ability of the "new" populism to provide lasting solutions to the lack of inclusive growth. Experience has shown that crises often catalyze overdue reforms, though long-lasting reforms tend to be mostly observed in good times. The pandemic could help build consensus about the role of the post-pandemic government and a new social contract to address inequality, in developed and developing economies alike. However, policy implementation will be constrained by low growth, high government debt, low trust in public institutions, and rising political cleavages. This could make the "new" populism self-sustaining as populist governments are able to harness popular discontent against the media, immigrants, or experts. Given this, three areas for policy interventions will be critical in any new social contract: investing in "local communities"; helping the creation of "good jobs"; and, improving processes of deliberations and communications to rebuild trust in public institutions.

Climate Policies

Tackling climate change is one of the most complex and far-reaching aspects of ensuring inclusive and sustainable growth. It requires addressing multiple market failures, both local and global, engineering substantial redistribution, and ensuring social justice. Governments need to play an active role, and they need to cooperate internationally. To minimize the chance of global catastrophic risks, the world will need to bring net greenhouse gas emissions to zero by around mid-century. The key mitigation policies involve putting price on carbon while helping the poor and affected sectors to cope with the transition, aligning financial sector policies with climate objectives, incentives for green investment and innovation, and promoting international cooperation including mobilizing financial resources for lower income countries. Even with strong global mitigation efforts, adaptation is necessary for many countries to cope with climate changes. The key policies are information and investment to reduce the exposure to climate shocks; and macroeconomic policies to smooth and facilitate the structural transformation. Inclusion should be a key consideration both for mitigation and adaptation policies. Some policies, like investment in renewable energy, are inclusive by design.

Others, like pricing carbon, should be complemented by compensating measures for the poor and "stranded" workers. A just transition to a low-carbon economy is the only viable way forward.

Global

The inclusive growth policy responses discussed above are strongly linked to the globally agreed Sustainable Development Goals, guided by the UN agenda. In addition, while most of the discussion has been focused at policy making at the national level, achieving inclusive growth at a global level will increasingly require global solutions. In addition to addressing climate change (such as through the Paris Agreement), there is a role for global policies such as fiscal transfers to developing economies, globally coordinated tax regimes, and regulations, including antitrust regulations, intellectual property regimes and data information policies, that open up opportunities for developing economies to participate in economic and technological progress.

II. Knowledge Gaps

This book synthesized the theory, empirical findings, and policy experiences on the many dimensions of inclusive growth. The previous section discussed some key takeaways. But despite the voluminous literature on most of the topics, there are still substantial gaps in our knowledge. Some of these are related to the impact of recent trends or conditions, such as technological advancements and the Covid-19 recession; others are functions of insufficient data especially in developing countries, and the difficulty of identifying the causal impact of policies and of understanding their interaction with other country conditions. This section summarizes some of the key areas in which additional research could be helpful in further expanding our knowledge to improve inclusive growth.

A. Technology: Impact, Uses, Policies

Technology, including the use of automation and artificial intelligence, has been advancing rapidly. Some uses, such as remote conferencing and teleworking, have accelerated further as a result of the Covid-19 crisis and are generally complementary to skilled workers. These technologies have the potential to increase overall productivity and incomes but also to disrupt labor markets and increase inequality. Important avenues of research are to further examine the evolving impact of these new technologies on labor markets, the extent and timeframe for which AI may replace labor, and to analyze what policies could help to disseminate more broadly the benefits of new technologies across society, with a particular emphasis on unskilled workers, and across countries.

There is also a need to understand the impact of new technologies on competition and patterns of globalization. Will technological progress lead to ever more "superstar" firms (such as Amazon, Google, etc.), and what (global) regulatory frameworks can be developed to channel these developments? For some jobs (IT, web design, advertising), there is now a possibility to work for a foreign employer without leaving the country. The impact of that on migration flows and wage dynamics could be further studied. If technology replaces low-skilled workers and low-skill tasks, it could substitute for trade from EMDEs and shift the pattern of comparative advantage. If so, what export path remains open for developing countries to pursue if low-skill jobs are filled by robots? Most of the literature on the distributional impact of FDI has focused on the offshoring of parts of the production chain. Given the recent advances in automation, however, more attention could be paid to the distributional impact of reshoring.

More work could be done on how to steer technological progress to make it more inclusive. This requires understanding better the risk of misuse of technology and beneficial uses of it, and how and whether policy can affect the extent to which AI replaces or complements labor. For example, recent studies have shown that artificial intelligence is biased against minorities and women because of the sample sets used to train the systems. What is the current cost suffered by women in terms of failed employment applications and denied credit access? And what would need to be done to address this problem? The rapid development of fintech represents an opportunity for better access and usage of financial services. However, not everyone has been benefitting at the same pace. The impact of fintech on financial inclusion gaps deserves more attention. New digital technologies will likely have major implications for taxation, but these effects are still to be fully understood. For instance, the emerging gig-economy revolutionizes certain sectors of the economy (transportation, tourism), which can make taxation harder (e.g. how to tax Uber drivers or Airbnb tenants?). Yet, it could also enable tax administrations to use more and better data to enforce taxes. This might ultimately also change tax policy design, e.g. to more effectively tax capital income or wealth, or even to personalize consumption taxes and make them more progressive in an efficient manner. On the spending side, technology could be leveraged to improve the delivery of education and health care for everyone.

Innovative policies will be required to deal with technological progress if it has disruptive effects as some fear. Taxing robots and introducing a UBI are frequently proposed, but are either difficult to implement and/or carry important downsides (such as how to finance a UBI scheme or how to phase it in). Social safety nets will need to be reformed and new models of taxation and ownership should be considered. These may include taxing the rents of digital superstars and/or redistributing capital ownership at least in part to governments or the broader population. These will require cross-cutting policy analysis to account for costs and benefits, country circumstances, and political economy issues.

B. Data

Data is a constraining factor for furthering our knowledge on the relationship between different policies and inclusive growth. To start with, more frequent and granular data is required on incomes of individuals. Developing distributional data needs to contend with the many measurement issues discussed in Chapter 1, including inaccurate or evasive reporting of income data.

Data on income needs to be complemented by sufficient disaggregation by individual characteristics, such as gender, age, ethnicity, citizenship status, and region in order to better understand poverty and inequality among different groups. Better data on disparities in all their dimensions can help to identify underlying drivers and to formulate effective policies. This will involve strengthening statistical systems, developing new sources of data, and creating new visualization tools.

Beyond data on individual incomes, there is scope to improve data on public sector policies and private sector conditions. A few examples include improving data on job quality (including contract types in AEs and informal jobs in EMDEs), digital trade and e-commerce, and indicators of de-jure and de-facto governance policies (e.g., strength of anti-corruption frameworks, strength of AML regulations, extent of transparency, automation, digitalization; human resource policies at public institutions).

Data and technology can be developed to monitor public or private conditions in real time and at higher frequencies. An important example would be use of big data and machine learning to provide early detection of corruption or poor governance. This might include detecting money laundering using cross-country bank transactions data; looking for suspicious patterns in procurement and public investment; and linking asset declarations with public policy decisions.

There are also evolving issues on the security and privacy of data. It is now widely argued that Big Tech's access to data creates a non-level playing field for new entrants and thus reduces competition. But there are also debates on the ownership and use of personal data of individuals, such as their financial transactions, medical records, locational information, and Internet access. Laws and regulations on data privacy and protection vary across countries and are constantly changing. For example, the EU has codified data privacy and protection into EU law as fundamental rights, whereas the United States has been less restrictive of cross-border data flows. The implications and impact of these approaches merit further analysis.

C. Political Economy and Governance

The book identifies many policies to improve inclusive growth, but it cannot always provide clear guidance on how policymakers can address multiple barriers to make policy reforms happen in areas such as tax policy, governance, regional policies, globalization, and climate change, among others. Which reforms are successful and why? What is the contribution of policy sequence, perception of fairness, communication, timing? What factors determine trust in government and does higher trust facilitate reform implementation? How can the society overcome lack of political will at the top, if at all? Are there features of feasible reforms (e.g. they are not perceived as encroaching on special interests at the top) that launch a virtuous cycle of gradual improvements? This could potentially include "islands of excellence" or decentralization reforms, which can improve governance locally and foster potential political leaders and civil society for macro-level reforms.

The literature on the political economy of inclusive growth in low-income countries is rather scant. It would be important to examine in greater depth what shapes demand and supply for redistribution in these countries. Similarly, there is more anecdotal evidence than a comprehensive theory on how political regimes are linked with redistributive outcomes, and how lasting reforms can be achieved that are beneficial for inclusive growth. Research in this area may facilitate the design of nuanced policy measures at the country level, by developing a typology by level of income or political systems.

Essential ingredients of a new social contract include "investment in local communities," "job creation," and rebuilding trust in government. Thus, it would be useful to look at empirical evidence on each of these elements to be able to understand which country-specific circumstance matter, and how, in order to better inform their design. In particular, how do local communities help build resilience to economic shocks and what is the role of fiscal decentralization in building these local communities?

Economic diversification takes time and unless it is supported by the political framework in place, it risks falling into the trap of vested interests for the polarization of resource wealth. Future research could investigate how the political economy and the form of the state affect the commitment to reduce resource dependence through economic diversification and use resource wealth to reduce inequality within and across generations.

There is also scope to understand the political economy of international cooperation. This is most relevant where there are considerable spillovers of country policies, such as those related to globalization issues or cross-border tax regimes. It is also relevant to areas in which international cooperation is required to solve global issues, most notably to tackle climate change, as well as to deal with technological change and its cross-country impact.

D. Covid-19 Impact

At the time of writing this book, the world is in the midst of the Covid-19 crisis. This has had large and differential impacts on different groups. For example, lower income and less educated people and women (and racial minorities in some countries such as the United States) have had a larger presence in the "essential sectors." The impact of the crisis on health and economic outcomes on different groups will likely endure and require ongoing study. This is most pertinent for the educational progress of students and the integration of youth into the labor market during the time of this major global recession and period of remote work.

The Covid-19 pandemic also created many social, professional, and behavioral changes, such as remote working. For example, men, in larger proportion could work from home or lost full-time jobs and ended up spending more time with their children. It could be interesting to quantify the long-term impact of these changes on social norms. As another example, Covid-19 led to a greater use of mobile money instead of cash. The impact on financial inclusion gaps would be a promising avenue for future research. It would also be interesting to analyze the changes in trust in experts and government officials and attitudes toward public services and redistribution that have arisen due to the occurrence of a health and economic crisis that was clearly exogenous in origin and required considerable response from both experts and the public sector.

E. Fiscal Sustainability/Crisis Response

Another legacy of the Covid-19 crisis for both advanced and emerging countries has been the increase in poverty rates and inequality as well as the rise in debt related to both automatic and discretionary fiscal measures. Government will need to continue to cushion the negative effects of the crisis among the poor and provide stimulus for a robust recovery. However, they face limited resources in the context of low tax revenues and high debt. A critical policy issue will be to analyze which policies are the most cost-effective way of reducing poverty and inequality while also containing fiscal deficits. Beyond addressing the impact of the Covid crisis, achieving SDGs will entail large costs that may jeopardize fiscal sustainability for some countries. What role can the private sector play in providing the key public services and help close the financing gap?

More generally, there is scope to build on existing research on the nexus between crises and inequality where disagreements on causes and effects are plentiful. Thus, research will need to use innovative methods and economic theory to more effectively establish causality between inclusiveness, crises, and macroeconomic policies. More research is especially needed to better understand the relationship between macroeconomic policies such as monetary policy, macro prudential policies and exchange rate policy on the one hand and measures of inclusiveness on the other. It will also be useful to study the design of governance policies to prevent corruption in times of crisis (e.g., corruption in FX black market, capital outflows and regulatory capture, subsidies, and business regulations).

F. Customizing Policies for Countries and Regions

There are several areas in which we need to better understand how to tailor policies to country-specific circumstances. This is particularly relevant for developing countries, where poor data impedes analysis. For example, empirical tax research is mostly focused on advanced economies where (micro) data are widely available to inform policymakers on the impact of sometimes detailed tax reform proposals. Results obtained for advanced economies might not always carry over to developing countries due to their large informal sectors, a much more skewed income distribution, weaker tax administration capacity and other structural differences. Likewise, advanced economies have achieved high levels of social and human development with a significant variation in terms of levels of overall and social spending. What is the adequate level of spending, including social spending, for a developing country? Which country model (e.g., Nordic countries versus Asian countries like Korea and Singapore) would better fit developing countries?

At the subnational level, we need better evidence on the impact of spatially blind, spatially connective, and spatially targeted policies aimed at reducing regional disparities. Why do similar interventions appear to work in some cases, but not in others? How do the pre-conditions for successful intervention depend on the context? Such analysis is challenging: controlled experiments are infeasible; there may be important complementarities across different policies; and there may be significant threshold effects, externalities, and spillovers. We also need better evidence on the cost-effectiveness of regional policies. Interventions should not generate an inefficient allocation of resources, but rather maximize the aggregate economy's future innovation and growth potential.

G. Labor Markets and Vulnerable Groups

The literature would benefit from expanding and deepening the analysis of labor market issues, especially in EMDEs. Labor market issues are at the heart of structural challenges in these countries as they grapple with high informality and continue to advance on the development path. Policymakers would benefit from the further development of a diagnostic framework for inclusive labor markets in developing countries to help policymakers structure their analysis of the labor market along various dimensions and to identify labor (and non-labor) market policy gaps. Many developing countries are unable to collect enough tax revenue to finance needed public services, infrastructure, and social protection due to the large size of the informal sector. Hence, a better understanding on how developing countries can reduce informality could be useful in the design of inclusive growth strategies. More research on adjustment costs and adjustment policies would also be useful, including labor market adjustment to trade, technology and other shocks, the impact of adjustment on inequality, and the role of traditional labor market policies and institutions, given countries' conditions and circumstances. In particular, very little is known about geographic and employment mobility within developing countries. And other than public sector employment, how can the government create the best business environment that creates good jobs? Again, there is an important distinction between advanced and developing countries, given demographic trends and the relative importance of the informal sector.

Policies that promote the accumulation of human capital such as expanding access to health and education have the potential to enhance both economic growth and reduce inequality of opportunities. So, it is vital to strengthen the evidence base on learning and health outcomes and inequities, as well as their drivers and to analyze how to increase in a cost-effective manner the access to, and utilization of, education and health care services by disadvantaged groups.

More understanding is required to design optimal policies to improve inclusion of disadvantaged and vulnerable groups in labor markets. Youth, and especially disadvantaged youth, are a key group that face such multidimensional challenges. It will be important to better understand how to address skills mismatches, such as those where educational attainment has improved but does not always equip youth with skills demanded by the labor market and evolving economic structure. At the other end of the age spectrum, research could expand on policies that could help keep people productive in the labor force for more years given increasing longevity and rapid technological progress. There is a dynamic component to labor markets too: countries differ in the extent of economic and social mobility across generations. What policies are most effective in improving opportunities for upward social mobility, while also safeguarding against absolute downward economic mobility?

Gender inequality in its various dimensions, including labor market and social norms, remains ripe for further analysis. For example, apart from some field studies, empirical analysis of the macroeconomic impact of policy measures to address gender inequality (e.g., legislated quotas in political and business higher echelons) is still poor. Numerous studies have pointed at the benefits of transparency to foster policy-makers' accountability; however, although several NGOs around the world promote and defend gender equality in the budgetary process, a rigorous analysis of the impact on the quality and results of the process in countries where such NGOs are operating is still missing. What are the pros and cons of mandatory labor income transparency? There is a growing proportion of single mothers. How do we need to rethink policies in order to align more with their needs? What measures other than incentivized paternity leave can help make the father an equal partner in the household? What kind of interventions help reduce intimate partner violence?

The gender aspect of migration requires a closer look. In some cases, most migrants are men (e.g., construction workers from Central Asia), in others most are women (e.g., nurses from the Philippines). The consequences for female labor force participation in the sending countries, as well as gender inequality in wages, deserve to be investigated. More generally, there is scope for additional work on the impact of migration on income inequality in receiving and sending countries and the impact of remittances on macroeconomic outcomes (especially investment, interest rates).

H. Finance, Markets, and Economic Structure

Regarding finance, the literature on examining the nexus between financial inclusion, financial stability, and capital flows is rather scarce. For example, the expansion of financial services coupled with complex technologies and limited financial capabilities could pose risks to financial stability. On the one hand, financial inclusion could deepen the ties of the real economy to the financial sector, creating more systemic risk. On the other hand, financial inclusion could diversify credit. This relationship between financial inclusion and financial stability could be explored, including the opportunities and risks stemming from fintech and mobile-phone-enabled peer-to-peer lending platforms. In addition, studying how capital flows foster or hinder financial inclusion would help understand an important channel through which capital flows affect inclusiveness. Research on the impact of macroprudential policies on financial inclusion as they mediate capital flows could be beneficial. Moreover, although most of the literature focuses on the impact of capital flows on inequality, more attention could be paid to understand the impact of inequality on capital flows. This could also help design policies that would not only reduce inequality but also mitigate global imbalances.

Turning to product markets, more empirical evidence on the rising market power of firms and its economic implications on inequality and inclusive growth is needed. This evidence would shed more light on the relationship between market power, competition, and inclusive growth. The discussion about whether big firms, especially Big Tech, are harmful to the economy is ongoing, and what to do about it—what kind of competition policy is needed—requires further research.

Additionally, innovation is important for productivity gains and broad-based growth, and the question of when and how the state should intervene to promote innovation (e.g. what kind of programs, incentives, and support needed) and how to share the fruits of innovation is yet to be answered. These policies may need to be differentiated between advanced and developing countries.

I. Natural Resources and Climate Policies

In the case of resource-rich countries, there are still considerable gaps in understanding how to effectively reduce resource dependence and diversify into dynamic industries. Prudent management of resource wealth could also benefit from better forecasts of the quantity and value of resources reserves, especially given price risks of hydrocarbon reserves that will be impacted by the global transition to non-fossil fuel sources of energy.

There is considerable importance for further research on the impact of climate change and policies to mitigate it and adapt to the changes. This includes analyzing the potential use and effectiveness of industrial and financial sector policies to stimulate green innovation and investment, as well as the potential misuse and dependence on the quality of governance. More work is also needed to develop financial asset classes that properly reflect climate change mitigation and ecosystem services and to design these assets in the most effective way. Climate change is expected to have vast but differential impacts on countries and populations. Further research could better evaluate the effect of climate change and natural disasters on poverty and inequality, and explore risk scenarios for economic and social upheavals, including shifts in agricultural viability and patterns of comparative advantage across countries, pressures for mass migration, among other issues. Proper valuation of damages from environmental pollution would be useful, as well as the other side of the coin: proper valuation and accounting for global ecosystem services would be helpful, including the role of nature-based solutions to tackle climate change.

III. Next Steps and Other Resources

This book has aimed at providing a high-level synthesis of the key issues for achieving inclusive growth. As elaborated in Chapter 1 in the context of an inclusive growth framework, there are many dimensions to inclusive growth involving interdependent inputs from the private and government sectors. Countries also face different circumstances based on their level of development, economic structure, existing institutions, and other factors and thus they will differ on the areas that they need to prioritize. As discussed in Chapter 2, there are many policies and channels in which growth and inclusion can be jointly improved, especially with regard to promoting equality of opportunity. The rest of the chapters have provided overviews of the state of knowledge and policy experience in each of the critical areas related to inclusive growth.

Once priority areas for improving inclusive growth are determined, there will naturally be a desire for more details on policies in a given topic area. Beyond the information provided in this book, what information and resources can country officials exploit to take next steps and to tailor solutions to their specific conditions and needs?

Many organizations provide a range of additional support on topics covered in this book. International organizations and multilateral development banks, such as the IMF, World Bank, EBRD, WTO, ILO, UN, OECD, as well as many multilateral and bilateral donors provide information, analysis, capacity development, and financial support for economic stability and development. For example, the IMF's Institute for Capacity Development develops free online training courses on topics related or complementary to inclusive growth. The IMF, World Bank and other multilateral institutions also provide detailed policy recommendations and hands-on expert advice tailored to specific countries. They also facilitate discussions of the potential cross-border distributional impact of policies, including through organizing conferences and high-level panel discussions and in some cases as part of official policy commitments. Table 22.1 lists a selected set of such resources that can be tapped as the next steps in implementing policies for inclusive growth.

References

Cerra, Valerie, Antonio Fatás, and Sweta C. Saxena. 2021. "Fighting the Scarring Effects of Covid-19." *Industrial and Corporate Change: Special Issue on Macroeconomics and Development*, 30(2): 459–66.

Georgieva, Kristalina. 2020. "The Next Phase of the Crisis: Further Action Needed for a Resilient Recovery," IMF blog.

Ravallion, Martin. 2016. *The Economics of Poverty History, Measurement, and Policy*. New York: Oxford University Press.

Table 22.1 Selected Resources for More Information and Policy Support

Resource	Topic(s)	Description
IMF Institute for Capacity Development		
Instructor led courses for country officials https://www.imf.org/en/Capacity-Development/training/icdtc	Macro, fiscal, finance, statistics, legal issues	Training courses and peer-to-peer learning for officials of member countries, led by IMF staff and staff at regional training centers.
A Peek into Training on Inclusive Growth https://www.youtube.com/watch?v=L9saOyZdLV8	Inclusive growth	Video event highlighting themes of the IMF inclusive growth course
IMFx Free Online Courses https://www.imf.org/external/np/ins/english/learning.htm https://www.edx.org/school/imfx	Macro, fiscal, finance, statistics, legal issues	Various free online courses in macroeconomics and finance, available for both country officials and the general public.
Online course on Inclusive Growth https://www.edx.org/course/inclusive-growth	Inclusive growth	Provides 6-module course on inclusive growth, comprised of: an IG framework; measurement; fiscal policy; labor markets; governance; and climate change.
Online course on Financial Development and Financial Inclusion https://www.edx.org/course/financial-development-and-financial-inclusion https://www.imf.org/en/Capacity-Development/training/icdtc	Financial inclusion	Provides 7-module course on financial development and financial inclusion, comprised of: framework and link to growth; measurement; financial intermediaries and capital markets; financial inclusion for households and micro-enterprises; SME access to finance; policies to manage risks of SME lending; uses of Fintech. *Example: building an online credit registry system to improve access of MSEMEs and individuals to credit in the West Bank and Gaza.*

Continued

Table 22.1 Continued

Resource	Topic(s)	Description
Online course on Energy Subsidy reform https://www.imf.org/en/Capacity-Development/training/icdtc	Energy subsidies	Defines and measures energy subsidies and reviews their economic, social, and environmental implications. It also presents toolkits to assess the distributional effects of alternative subsidy reform scenarios and to design a fuel pricing mechanism. Reviews what works best in energy subsidy reform and illustrates successes and failures in terms of particular countries.
Online course on Macroeconomic Management in Resource-Rich countries https://www.imf.org/en/Capacity-Development/training/icdtc	Macro, fiscal	Discusses macroeconomic policy issues and challenges faced by RRCs, providing an understanding of: the macroeconomics of growth and diversification; managing fiscal policy; macroeconomic policy coordination; and managing public-sector assets in RRCs.

International Monetary Fund (IMF)

Resource	Topic(s)	Description
High-level Panel on Promoting an Inclusive Recovery https://www.youtube.com/watch?v=N0ygERnKb2k	Inclusive growth	Seminar with IMF Managing Director and other high-level panelists discussing how to promote an inclusive recovery
IMF Technical Assistance https://www.imf.org/en/Capacity-Development/what-we-do	Macro, fiscal, finance, statistics, legal issues	The IMF serves as a global hub for knowledge on economic and financial issues and shares its knowledge with member countries through hands-on advice. Technical assistance areas include expenditure policy, including for education and health care, tax diagnostics, revenue forecasting, distributional analysis, macro frameworks and forecasting, governance issues such as public financial management, fiscal transparency, central bank safeguards, anti-money laundering, anti-corruption frameworks, rule of law.

Resource	Topic	Description
How-to-note series https://www.imf.org/en/Publications/SPROLLs/How-To-Notes	Fiscal policy and administration	Discusses global experiences in areas such as the organization of tax policy units, the design of tobacco excises, tax policy in fragile states, and management of VAT refunds.
Technical notes and manuals https://www.imf.org/en/Publications/SPROLLs/Technical-Notes-and-Manuals#sort=%40imfdate%20descending	Macro, fiscal, finance, statistics, legal issues	Offers hands-on guidance on issues from IMF experts to expand the dissemination of their technical assistance advice, drawn in part from unpublished technical assistance reports.
Special series on Covid-19 https://www.imf.org/en/Publications/SPROLLs/covid19-special-notes	Macro, fiscal, finance, statistics, legal issues	Notes produced by IMF experts to help members address the economic effects of Covid-19.
Medium-Term Revenue Strategies https://www.imf.org/en/News/Articles/2019/10/28/sp102919-mediumterm-revenue-strategy	Taxation	Together with partners in the Platform for Collaboration on Tax (IMF, OECD, World Bank, UN), the IMF helps countries develop Medium-Term Revenue Strategies—a high-level road map for tax system reform to support economic and social development. It includes an explicit link to the expenditure needs of a country as part of its development agenda; and contains a component that focuses on the management of the tax system reform process, i.e. how to make it happen.
African Training Institute, www.imfati.org Center for Economics and Finance, https://www.cef.imf.org/ China-IMF Capacity Development Center, www.imfcicdc.org/ Joint Vienna Institute, https://www.jvi.org/home.html Singapore Regional Training Center, https://www.imfsti.org South Asia Regional Training and TA Center, www.sarttac.org/	Various	Regional training centers associated with the IMF and other international organizations provide instructor led courses, webinars, and other capacity development opportunities.

Continued

Table 22.1 Continued

Resource	Topic(s)	Description
International Monetary Fund (IMF)		
IMF Governance Diagnostics https://www.imf.org/en/News/Articles/2018/04/21/ pr18142-imf-board-approves-new-framework-for- enhanced-engagement-on-governance https://www.imf.org/en/Publications/CR/ Issues/2019/08/23/Republic-of-Mozambique- Diagnostic-Report-on-Transparency-Governance- and-Corruption-48,613	Governance	Comprehensive diagnostic reports on governance prepared by member countries with assistance from IMF staff and in broad consultation with stakeholders. *Example: Mozambique 2019*
IMF-WB Climate Change Policy Assessment https://www.imf.org/en/Topics/climate-change/ resilience-building#CCPA	Climate change	IMF and WB staff provide an overarching assessment of countries' climate change strategies, including their Nationally Determined Contributions and gives policy recommendations for further actions
The Managing Natural Resource Wealth Thematic Fund (MNRW-TF) https://www.imf.org/en/Capacity-Development/ trust-fund/MNRW-TTF	Sharing resource wealth	Finances regional conferences, training, and capacity development in resource-rich countries to build capacity to manage their natural resource wealth in a socially responsible way.
World Bank		
The Growth Report: Strategies for Sustained Growth and Inclusive Development https://openknowledge.worldbank.org/ handle/10986/6507	Growth and poverty reduction	Provides information on policies that promote sustainable growth and poverty reduction; country case studies; identification of constraints and barriers for achieving inclusive growth

Informality Scenario Analysis https://www.worldbank.org/en/research/brief/a-toolkit-for-informality-scenario-analysis	Labor markets	A toolkit including a discussion of literature, alternative policies, and a theoretical model on informality, as well as a practical excel spreadsheet to project informality over the medium term under alternative scenarios.
Financial inclusion support framework https://www.worldbank.org/en/topic/financialinclusion/brief/financial-inclusion-support-framework	Financial inclusion	Provides technical assistance on national financial inclusion strategy, and monitoring and evaluation; financial infrastructures, such as payments and credit reporting system; diversified financial services for individuals and enterprise; financial consumer protection and financial capability. *Examples: (a) The development of a National Financial Inclusion Strategy and a financial education framework as part of the updated national curriculum in Vietnam; (b) In Indonesia, the adoption of regulations on agent banking, digital financial services (e-money), alternative dispute resolution, Financial Information Service System (SLIK) credit reporting and internal dispute resolution; (c) The design, testing and rollout of a financial education program for members of savings and credit cooperatives in Rwanda; (d) In Ethiopia, the development and implementation of the financial inclusion module in the National Living Standards Measurement Study (LSMS) survey, including the publication of the final report and data.*
The Financial Sector Reform and Strengthening Initiative https://www.firstinitiative.org/projects	Financial inclusion	Funding projects to strengthen financial sectors. *Examples:* *(a) Credit Guarantee Strengthening in Egypt; (b) Digital Finance and De-risking Agricultural Financing in Rwanda; (c) Strengthening Liquidity Framework and Financial Inclusion in El Salvador; (d) Insolvency and Secured Transactions Reform to Promote MSME Access to Credit and Financial Inclusion in Zambia; (e) Increasing Financial Inclusion in Swaziland* *Microfinance and Financial Consumer Protection in CEMAC region*

Continued

Table 22.1 Continued

Resource	Topic(s)	Description
World Bank		
Education practice https://www.worldbank.org/en/topic/education https://www.worldbank.org/en/about/contacts	Education	Research and projects to support access to quality education and lifelong learning. Works with countries to improve their education systems and identify the best ways to deliver learning for children, young adults, and those who need skills later in adulthood and for whom the future of work poses new challenges. *Examples: (a) in Ethopia, a general education quality improvement project; (b) in Lao PDR, an early childhood education project covering 32K 3–4 yr old children; (c) in Uzbekistan, an improving pre-primary and general secondary education project to provide 100K children with half-day kindergarten programs.*
Healthcare practice https://www.worldbank.org/en/topic/health https://www.worldbank.org/en/about/contacts	Health	Research and projects to support countries' efforts to achieve universal health coverage and to provide quality, affordable health services to everyone, regardless of ability to pay, by strengthening primary health-care systems and reducing the financial risks associated with ill health. *Examples: (a) in El Salvador, the Strengthening Public Health Care System Project improved health services for poor and rural citizens, particularly women and children; (b) in South Sudan, the Provision of Essential Health Services Project is helping reduce maternal and child mortality and child malnutrition; (c) in Yemen, the Emergency Health and Nutrition Project has vaccinated nearly 12 million children, and is delivering critical health and nutrition services and addressing cholera outbreaks through integrated health, nutrition, water, and sanitation interventions.*
Atlas of Social Protection Indicators of Resilience and Equity (ASPIRE) database https://www.worldbank.org/en/data/datatopics/aspire	Social protection, labor markets	Indicators for 125 countries on social assistance, social insurance and labor market programs based on both program-level administrative data and national household survey data.

Name / URL	Topic	Description
Urban, Disaster Risk Management, Resilience, and Land Global Practice https://www.worldbank.org/en/topic/urbandevelopment	Regional	Part of its mandate includes helping identify priorities of lagging regions, and connect urban and rural spaces.
Climate Change Knowledge Portal https://climateknowledgeportal.worldbank.org/	Climate change	Provides global data on historical and future climate, vulnerabilities, and impacts for countries and regions.

OECD

Name / URL	Topic	Description
Inclusive Growth Portal https://www.oecd.org/inclusive-growth/stories/	Various	Provides information on inclusive growth indicators for monitoring and evaluation; case studies on inclusive growth strategies; policy strategies for fostering inclusive growth; inclusive growth policies in response to the Covid-19 crisis.
Better Lives Index http://www.oecdbetterlifeindex.org/#/11,111,111,111	Various	Compares well-being across countries, based on topics related to material living conditions and quality of life.
Framework for measuring and assessing job quality https://www.oecd-ilibrary.org/social-issues-migration-health/measuring-and-assessing-job-quality_5jrp02kjw1mr-en	Labor markets	This study discusses the three dimensions of job quality (earnings quality, labor market security and quality of working environment), highlighting the main limitations and providing examples across countries and socio-economic groups.
Jobs Strategy https://www.oecd.org/employment/jobs-strategy/	Labor markets	This report provides detailed policy recommendations across a broad range of areas in order to help countries address challenges associated with high levels of inequality, slow growth in productivity and wages, and labor market adjustments on the back of the digital revolution, globalization and demographic changes. The strategy considers job quality and inclusiveness as central policy priorities.
Product market regulation indicators https://www.oecd.org/economy/reform/indicators-of-product-market-regulation/	Competition, innovation, product markets	Indicators of product market regulation, including an economy-wide indicator of pro-competition regulations and a group of indicators that measures regulation at the sector level.

Continued

Table 22.1 Continued

Resource	Topic(s)	Description
OECD		
Going for Growth https://www.oecd.org/economy/going-for-growth/	Various	Reports on country-specific reform priorities to prepare for the future and turn mega-trend challenges into opportunities, for all. Reports on progress toward achieving reform priorities.
Migration hub https://www.oecd.org/migration	Migration	Large sources of policy analysis on migration in OECD countries.
Social Expenditure Database (SOCX) http://www.oecd.org/social/expenditure.htm	Social protection	Provides comparable statistics on public and (mandatory and voluntary) private social expenditure at the program level as well as net social spending indicators for 37 OECD countries.
Regional Development Policy Committee, and Centre for Entrepreneurship, SMEs, Regions and Cities http://search.oecd.org/regional/regional-policy/regionaldevelopment.htm http://www.oecd.org/cfe/	Regional development	Helps local and national governments unleash the potential of entrepreneurs and small and medium-sized enterprises, promote inclusive and sustainable regions and cities, boost local job creation, and implement sound tourism policies.
World Trade Organization (WTO)		
World Trade Organization https://www.wto.org/index.htm	Trade	The WTO helps governments with the implementation of WTO agreements
Aid for Trade https://www.wto.org/english/tratop_e/devel_e/a4t_e/aid4trade_e.htm	Trade	Helps developing countries trade, and address infrastructure obstacles to international trade.
Enhanced Integrated Framework https://enhancedif.org/	Trade	Assists least developed countries in their use of trade as an engine for growth, sustainable development and poverty reduction.

United Nations

Name	Topic	Description
UNDP https://www.undp.org/	Various	Helps countries achieve the Sustainable Development Goals. Provides research. Publishes the Human Development Report.
UN Women https://www.unwomen.org/en	Gender	Provides technical and financial support for the empowerment and rights of women and girls. Supports policy formulation and leads UN's work on gender equality.
UN Climate Change and Environment https://www.un.org/ldcportal/climate-change-and-environment/	Climate change	Provides the UN convention on climate change and related information on countries' Paris Agreement commitments, mitigation and adaptation plans.

Other Institutions

Name	Topic	Description
Global Knowledge Partnership on Migration and Development (KNOMAD) https://www.knomad.org/about-us	Migration	KNOMAD is a global hub of knowledge and policy expertise on migration and development issues. KNOMAD aims to generate a menu of policy choices, based on analytical evidence, evaluation of policies, data collection, and quality control through peer-review. It provides technical assistance and undertakes pilot projects. The World Bank has established a multi-donor trust fund to implement KNOMAD. KNOMAD works in close coordination with the Global Forum on Migration and Development (GFMD) and the U.N. agencies working on migration.
The Global Migration Group (GMG) https://www.unhcr.org/global-migration-group.html	Migration	GMG is an inter-agency group that brings together heads of agencies. It seeks to promote the wider application of all relevant international and regional instruments and norms relating to migration, and to encourage the adoption of more coherent, comprehensive and better coordinated approaches to the issue of international migration. The GMG is particularly concerned to improve the overall effectiveness of its members and other stakeholders in capitalizing upon the opportunities and responding to the challenges presented by international migration.
The International Organization for Migration (IOM) https://www.iom.int/	Migration	IOM is the leading intergovernmental organization in the field of migration and is committed to the principle that humane and orderly migration benefits migrants and society. IOM is part of the United Nations system, as a related organization.

Continued

Table 22.1 Continued

Resource	Topic(s)	Description
European Commission, DG Migration and Home Affairs https://ec.europa.eu/home-affairs/what-we-do/policies/international-affairs/eastern-partnership/financial-assistance_en	Migration	Provides financial and technical assistance through an array of financial instruments for EU members states and partners countries.
African Development Bank, Initiative on Migration and Development https://www.afdb.org/e	Migration and remittances	Goal is to maximize the development impact of remittances, support the development of financial services for migrant workers, and create incentives to channel funds into productive uses in the country of origin.
InterAmerican Development Bank Migration Initiative https://www.iadb.org/en/social-investment/migration	Migration	Uses financial and non-financial instruments to tackle migration challenges in the Latin American region, contributing to the successful integration of migrants to their host.
Asian Development Bank, Human Mobility and Migration https://www.adb.org/themes/social-development/social-protection/human-mobility-migration	Migration	Supports its developing member countries to facilitate human mobility while maximizing its benefits.
Transparency International, National Integrity System Assessments https://www.transparency.org/en/national-integrity-system-assessments#	Governance	Comprehensive assessment of a country's anti-corruption efficacy sector by sector.
Commitment to Equity Institute (CEQ) https://commitmentoequity.org/	Tax and benefit incidence	Works to reduce inequality and poverty through comprehensive and rigorous tax and benefit incidence analysis, and active engagement with the policy community. The Institute has four main areas of work: methods and policy tools, a data center on fiscal redistribution, advisory and training services, and bridges to policy.

European Bank for Reconstruction and Development (EBRD) technical cooperation https://www.ebrd.com/ebrd-and-gender-equality-overview.html	Gender	The Strategy for the Promotion of Gender Equality 2016–2020 and Women in Business Programmes provide analysis, financing and technical cooperation. *Examples: (a) in Egypt and Morocco, capacity building to support Central Banks and regulators to establish sex-disaggregated data to inform policy choices for women entrepreneurship; (b) in Kyrgyz Republic, gender responsive SME Strategy following the completion of gender responsive investment climate assessment; (c) in Tajikistan, gender responsive regulatory impact assessment introduced to inform gender policy reforms, supported by capacity building of government officials jointly with the OSCE.*
Green Climate Fund https://www.greenclimate.fund/	Climate change	Catalyzes financing to help developing countries invest in low-emissions, climate-resilient development.
Climate Investment Funds https://www.climateinvestmentfunds.org/	Climate change	Provides long term financing for clean technology, energy access, climate resilience, and sustainable forests in developing and middle-income countries.
Our World in Data https://ourworldindata.org/	Various	Provides free, open access and open source data and charts on a long list of economic and social indicators on global living conditions and the earth's environment.
SDG Tracker https://sdg-tracker.org/	Various	Free, open-access resource where users can track and explore global and country-level progress towards each of the 17 Sustainable Development Goals through interactive data visualizations.

Continued

Table 22.1 Continued

Resource	Topic(s)	Description
World Economic Forum, Global Social Mobility Index https://www.weforum.org/reports/global-social-mobility-index-2020-why-economies-benefit-from-fixing-inequality	Social mobility	An index to assess the state of social mobility worldwide.
WEF Global Competitiveness Report https://www.weforum.org/reports/the-global-competitiveness-report-2020	Various	Reports on priorities for long-term prosperity. Assesses and ranks countries on indicators such as enabling environment, human capital, markets, innovation, and readiness for economic transformation.
Peterson Institute for International Economics https://www.piie.com/	Various	Provides expert analysis and practical policy solutions on a range of issues for strengthening prosperity and human welfare in the global economy.
European Union, Smart Specialization Platform https://ec.europa.eu/jrc/en/research-topic/smart-specialisation	Regional development	This supports innovation-led territorial development.
Brookings Institution, Cities & Regions program https://www.brookings.edu/topic/cities-regions/	Regional development	Provides research and organizes events on regional issues.
Brookings: The Hamilton Project https://www.brookings.edu/project/the-hamilton-project/	Regional development	Provides policy proposals on how to foster economic growth in the U.S.
Berlin Institute for Population and Development https://www.berlin-institut.org/en/	Regional development	Provides research on issues of regional and global demographic change.
Alliance for Financial Inclusion https://www.afi-global.org/	Financial inclusion	Provides capacity building and evidence-based solutions for financial inclusion policy and regulation.

Name / URL	Category	Description
Financial alliance for Women https://financialallianceforwomen.org/	Financial inclusion, gender	An international consortium of financial institutions that support women with access to capital, information, education and markets.
Women's World Banking https://www.womensworldbanking.org/	Financial inclusion, gender	Designs and invests in the financial solutions, institutions, and policy environments in emerging markets to create greater economic stability and prosperity for women, their families and their communities.
UK Social Mobility Barometer https://www.gov.uk/government/publications/social-mobility-barometer-poll-results-2019	Social mobility	Survey data on the experiences and perceptions of social mobility of the U.K. population.
Pew Research Center https://www.pewresearch.org/	Social attitudes	Provides research and survey data on attitudes, beliefs, and behaviors of people worldwide.
European Social Survey https://www.europeansocialsurvey.org/	Social attitudes	Provides research and survey data on attitudes, beliefs, and behaviors of people in European countries.
Partnership on AI: Shared Prosperity Initiative https://www.partnershiponai.org/shared-prosperity-initiative/	Technology & AI	A multistakeholder initiative encouraging private sector actors developing and deploying AI to commit to an inclusively-designed economic future for the benefit of all.
Oxford Handbook of AI Governance (forthcoming)	Technology & AI	Handbook summarizing current thinking on AI governance.
Economics for Inclusive Prosperity https://econfip.org/	Various	Useful website where top academics provide a wealth of reference materials on many disparate policy areas.
International Labour Organization https://www.ilo.org/global/lang--en/index.htm	Labor markets	Supports cooperation and policy development between governments and employers' and workers' organizations in fostering social and economic progress. Also provides data, analysis, and programs to promote decent work for all.

Index